PRODUCTION
AND
OPERATIONS
MANAGEMENT

Martin K. Starr
Rollins College

Crummer Graduate
School of Business

Cincinnati, Ohio
www.atomicdog.com

~To my family—for their positive outlook and creative path-finding

and

~To Michael Taylor Starr—whose planning horizon encompasses the twenty-second century.

When ordering this title, use ISBN 1-59260-093-X.
To order only the online version of this title, use ISBN 1-59260-094-8.

The cover photo collage is a visual breakdown of some of the most basic elements of Operations Management. It is about process and stages, as represented by the flowchart. In the gears, we see an icon of industry, but also a symbol of how all the pieces must precisely fit together. In the lower right of the image is analysis, in the upper left, logistics. From manufacturing, to warehousing, to global distribution, we are reminded that industry, its technology, and the goods that it produces, revolves around the human element.

Cover Designer: Joe Devine, Director of Interactive Media & Design

Cover photo: Copyright 2004 Atomic Dog Publishing and its licensors. All rights reserved.

ISBN:1-59260-092-1

Library of Congress Control Number: 2003112429

Printed in the United States of America by Atomic Dog Publishing, 1148 Main Street, Third Floor, Cincinnati, OH 45202.

10 9 8 7 6 5 4 3 2

Brief Contents

Contents

16   Production Scheduling   584

17   Cycle-Time Management   622

Part 5   Transition Management: Preparing for the Future   679

18   Product Development and Project Management   680

Preface

A LIVING TEXT FOR PRODUCTION AND OPERATIONS MANAGEMENT (P/OM)

Production and Operations Management is a multimedia publication of Atomic Dog Publishing. This company is well-known for simultaneously providing two forms of publication. These are (1) Internet publications and (2) paper books. The Internet publication format is known as digital media. An important point about digital media is that it can be revised on an as-needed basis. Paper books must often wait years for revision; three years is a typical revision period for paper book publishers in the production and operations (P/OM) field.

Even before 9–11, three years was too long to wait for revision of educational materials. The 3-year interval was determined by various factors often encountered by production and operations managers. These are optimal run size and economic inventory levels for given demand rates. The technology of the Internet does not have the same cost and demand characteristics. The problem with three years for paper book revisions is that major changes in subject matter are likely to occur over that period of time. Also, students are more comfortable with recent events than with old news, which is termed "ancient history."

After 9–11, the 3-year time span became even more unacceptable. The winds of change blew stronger than ever. Accelerated changes occurred in the technology of both products and processes. The names of companies seemed to change faster than they did before 9–11. Events swept across entire industries, altering assumptions about how to conduct business after 9–11. Terror altered travel plans worldwide. Disney, Universal Studios, and other firms in the hospitality industry, as well as restaurants, hotels, airlines, and retailers, were affected. The market became sensitized to troublesome events. The increase in volatility afflicts all goods and services. Planning and scheduling in a turbulent environment lead to new rules for P/OM.

Changes in policies and more visible bankruptcies altered entire industries over a short period of time. Similarly, the SARS (severe acute respiratory syndrome) epidemic hurt certain airlines more than others because of the geographic location of centers of the disease. Cathay Pacific Airways reported losing $3 million per day. Beijing and Toronto were listed as places to avoid by the World Health Organization. (*The New York Times*, April 23, 2003.) Other illnesses loom as business factors, including terrorist events such as anthrax contamination at U.S. post offices and government buildings.

Such news items can be added regularly to the Internet webpages of *Production and Operations Management*. News and ideas can be placed as marginal notes from the instructor at the appropriate locations of the text. The section on how operations management handles crises is a natural place to consider a note on SARS. Other sections that might gain from this type of update include reallocation of capacity and production scheduling (and rescheduling).

The section describing qualities of safety and security is a relevant location for discussions concerning the effect of health warnings (e.g., hepatitis and botulism) on carriers, hotels, restaurants, and retailers. A natural question is what to do about such dangers. How can customers be protected? What steps are required to inform the public that necessary measures have been taken to ensure safety? Use of the Internet allows "breaking news" that is relevant to P/OM (e.g., new regulations such as auto emissions and seat belts) to be quickly inserted. This ability to amend and append as desired is what is meant by a living text and immediate, evergreen content, for which the Internet is a natural host.

There are pros (as well as cons) for paper text publishing. Many people find it easier to read a book than a screen. Also, as is often said, "it is not necessary to boot up a book." Until recently, it was easier to put marginal notes on a paper page, and that was another advantage for paper. Now, however, students can readily insert their own marginal notes on the Internet page. Some say that it is easier to thumb the pages of a paper book than to do whatever the equivalent might be with a PC or laptop. On the other hand, the Internet ability to search through hundreds of pages in seconds (for a specific name or reference) is a real plus of the Internet. For the present, reading a laptop screen in the bright daylight of the park is not ideal. With the Atomic Dog Publishing (ADP) combination, students can read the paper book in the park with their sunglasses on (not applicable for digital media). They can take an interactive quiz with their laptop online (not applicable for paper media). Combination is what makes the ADP dual format of paper and pixels so ideal for twenty-first century students. Accordingly, the Internet format of the text will be updated as needed with webpage items to reveal interesting events. The paper text will be updated as needed but in line with editing and rerun costs. The combination of paper and pixels provides a balance of pros and cons.

CONVENTIONAL TEACHING SEQUENCES

The conventional teaching progression goes through the five parts of the text in numerical order. Part 1 provides the systems approach, and Part 2 explains strategic concepts of P/OM that are essential for planning what to do. Parts 3 and 4 are tactical factors for designing the process and running the system in an optimal fashion. Part 5 provides project methods required for the research and development (R & D) to launch a new product or service. In that sense, Part 5 is also strategy revisited to restrategize.

The parts and chapters of this text follow a conventional sequence that is best described as strategies of P/OM (Part 2) followed by tactics of P/OM (Parts 3 and 4). Part 5 closes the loop with feedback to change strategies.

Systems perspective (Part 1) ties the strategy-to-tactic-to-strategy cycle together. When tactics fail to deliver what the strategies proposed, then revision of strategy is required. In the figure shown here, follow the arrows—starting with Part 2 and ending with Part 2 (via Part 5).

Part 1   "Overview and Introduction to Production and Operations Management (P/OM)" (Planning for crucial decisions to meet objectives requires looking at all of the parts of the system that are relevant to achievement of the objectives. Being aware of the big picture is one of the first requirements for success. It takes time to become familiar with all the elements that may count.)

Part 2   "Strategic Perspectives for Operations Management" (Strategies are created with knowledge of what can be done, and what can be done well is particularly important. It is essential to play to one's strengths and avoid the weaknesses. There is a need to understand how everything changes and develops over time. That is why strategies are examined under the microscope of life cycle planning.)

Part 3   "Designing the Process, Analysis, and Improvement" (Part 3 has one foot in strategy creation and the other foot in tactical evaluation. It is essential to note that strategies have to be carried out by actions that are called tactics. If the tactics fail to deliver what the strategies envisioned, then it is necessary to go back to the drawing board.)

Part 1 provides the systems perspective. Being in the center, at the hub, is the symbolic location for tying all of the other parts together. Part 1 is the view with a wide-angle lens.

Part 4   "Operating the System and Making Product—P/OM Tactics" (Part 4 operates at the level of total detail that is 100 percent characteristic of tactics. The process for doing work has been created and developed in Part 3. Failure to perform is operating failure of the process. As noted, this leads to a return to Part 2 for reevaluation of strategies. New and improved strategies must be forthcoming.)

Part 5   "Transition Management: Preparing for the Future" (Part 5 provides the means for reevaluation and reformulation of strategies. This includes the project techniques that are required to lead to the next product line and the new and improved process configurations.)

Strategy and tactics are military terms used by production and operations managers because these terms accurately describe what must be done to plan for achievement of P/OM objectives. Military strategists plan the battles that need to be fought. Once the military strategies are in place, the strategists turn to their tacticians, who zoom into every corner of the system to prepare the tactical details of exactly where, specifically when, and precisely how these battles will be fought. As more than one armchair general has discovered, "the devil is in the details."

This means that "good" strategies for which "good" tactics cannot be found are misrepresented as being good. Although, at first, they appeared to be good strategies, it turned out that they are not satisfactory. They cannot be used so they can hardly be good strategies. Repair of flawed strategies is achieved by means of the feedback loop. This strategy correction loop is shown in the figure as Part 4 going to Part 5, and Part 5 returning to Part 2. Outcomes are measured on the plant floor where tactics are visible. Strategies are evaluated in the boardroom.

Connecting strategies and tactics is a systems problem for which there must be managerial responsibility. This translates into P/OM managers planning strategies with their colleagues in marketing, finance, HRM, accounting, etc., for the products and services that are to be brought to the customers. Once configured, production and operations managers zoom in for tactical details of work configurations, process design, materials management, production scheduling, quality attainment, productivity levels, and cost structures.

THE OM, PM, OR P/OM COURSE (GRADUATE OR UNDERGRADUATE)

This text is designed for students taking the production and operations management course required of most graduate and undergraduate business majors. The difference between graduate and undergraduate coverage is determined by what is by-passed for undergraduates or by what is added-on for graduate students. For example, end-of-chapter supplements have been designed for graduate students. However, there are instructors of undergraduate classes that choose to use some supplements. The chapters and their supplements have been designed to be self-contained so that instructors are free to mix and match in accord with their beliefs about what counts in a time-constrained environment.

The dynamics of the changing business environment have necessarily and profoundly altered the content of the OM course. A lot of the "old" methods and practices have been rendered obsolete by computers. Decision models exist now that could not be solved earlier, lacking massive computing capabilities. Use of intuition is augmented by quantitative analysis. Process capabilities are growing in scope and scale.

This text, *Production and Operations Management*, has been developed through extensive research to reflect both the new practices and traditional concepts and methods that instructors of production and operations management feel are important for students to know.

Systems Approach

The systems approach integrates OM decisions with the functional areas of business whose challenge is to make the firm perform as a team. The systems approach followed by this text is both systematic and constructive. It combines the methods of analysis and synthesis. This approach leads to better decisions and provides better problem-solving skills for complex situations.

Organization

The text is comprised of five parts that can be arranged in various ways because they are self-contained. The following figure shows a feedback loop between strategies and tactics. In this figure, Part 5 has been combined with Part 2 (to represent strategic planning), and Part 3 has been combined with Part 4 (to represent tactical decision making). This allows instructors to easily incorporate systems thinking and emerging practices into their P/OM courses.

Real-World Themes with Spotlights

Quality concepts such as continuous improvement, which pervades the cultures of all excellent companies, are woven into the fabric of each chapter. Two chapters are devoted specifically to quality. Chapter 4 develops the total quality management (TQM) environment with discussion about the Malcolm Baldrige National Quality Award and 1S0 9000 certification criteria. Chapter 7 covers quality control methods including statistical applications. Spotlights and cases highlight quality issues, implementations, and applications. There is much to be learned from showcasing companies that are striving to create and maintain quality in their operations. There is also much to be learned from failures.

Technological changes are forcing companies accustomed to the old methods to either adapt or disappear. A major focus of this text is the impact of information systems and their ability to create "smart" operating processes. The impacts of new technologies including some that are just being developed, are found throughout the text. Students are introduced to worldwide manufacturing and service implications of evolving technologies (such as expert systems, object-oriented programming, and digital data systems). Commercial software packages are referenced to familiarize students with the relevant applications to P/OM.

People and teamwork are a major component of P/OM. Strong teams are essential for quality achievement. Spotlights about people appear throughout the text to emphasize the creative contributions that managers can make. Students gain the understanding that participating in business today means team membership.

Globalization of business is a major emphasis of the AACSB International guidelines. The AACSB International (the Association to Advance Collegiate Schools of Business) is the accrediting organization for business schools all over the world. Understanding AACSB International is important for anyone seeking a business career. It is worth visiting the AACSB webpage at http://www.aacsb.edu. Globalization is addressed throughout the text in examples, spotlights, and cases to reflect the increasingly global nature of business. Among the many global topics explored in the text are the reach of global communications, the extent of global logistics systems, and global impact on the supply chain.

Service and manufacturing applications are balanced throughout the text in recognition of the service industry's increasing importance in the global economy. Also, it is crucial to appreciate manufacturing's growing awareness of the importance of providing exceptional

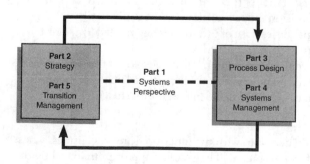

service to customers. There are similarities and differences between services and manufacturing in methods, decision models, processes, and work configurations, as well as in the management of projects. Technology is bringing about significant changes in the similarities and differences. For example, personal contact has been a hallmark of service organizations. With voice recognition, and with self-service systems such as banking ATMs (see the spotlight on automated teller machines), people increasingly interact with machines. The personality of the voice responding to requests for flight information has been carefully designed to make the customer feel good about services rendered by the airline or AMTRAK.

Ethics and environmental initiatives are stressed as major operational responsibilities. Chapter 20's coverage of environment (includes ISO 14000) as well as ethics (and they are both independent and related) is the culmination of Part 5, on preparing for the future. Chapter 20, which covers environmental, ethical, and technological forces, is preceded by Chapter 19, which discusses change management. It is followed by the Saturn case which focuses on the environmental initiatives taken by the auto manufacturer to ensure reuse of materials and parts. Recyclability of car components is a critical part of environmental preservation. So distinctly different from the Industrial Revolution, the evolution of environmental concern marks a new era in the P/OM field.

Problem-solving methods introduced in the text present the quantitative foundations of logic so that students know how and why they work. Most of the methods and problems presented can be performed by computer. The feat is to understand what these methods do rather than how to do them. The text is supported by spreadsheet models, solvers, and solutions. Tower of Brahma, the Planning Tree, and Six-Sigma epitomize problem-solving spotlights.

FROM THE STUDENT'S POINT OF VIEW

Strong search capability exists with the Internet text. It is a powerful organizing indexability that links outline and textual points. It can help in answering personal queries of students such as "Where was reference made to purposeful action?" or "What was the contribution of Dr. Deming?" Search engines (e.g., Google) are better understood and more skillfully used by some than others. Search skill improvement applies to text materials as well. Students can practice and improve their success rates with text searching.

Computerized search capability is more powerful than any manual system using static textbook indexes. Dynamic search capabilities exemplify the leverage that computers provide to operations in general. Consider the work assignment to be "find XYZ2." Assume that it is known that XYZ2 appears at least once, but it is not known where, in an un-indexed 1,000-page document. The production manager has sufficient budget for one person to do this job. That person has a relatively fast reading speed (say 1,200 words per minute or two text pages per minute).

The most likely assumption is that XYZ2 will be found on the 500th page. The pessimistic option is that it will be found on the last page. The optimistic estimate is that XYZ2 will be found on the first page. The manager decides to use the most likely estimate. This means that 250 minutes will be required to find one instance of XYZ2 and that is over four hours of work. P/OM opts to use the relatively free search engine, which will find one or more instances of XYZ2 in less than one minute. It will not always be true that finding information using search engines outstrips traditional manual labor. Generally, it saves time, costs less, and produces higher quality results. However, if the person knows the vicinity of the item, and the search engine cannot read superscripts, then the manual approach may be superior.

By using this example, it is hoped that the student, about to begin the P/OM journey, will appreciate the importance of understanding alternative methods of doing work. Production and operations managers know what options exist and how to evaluate these options. This was an example of a tactical evaluation where the strategic goal was to find XYZ2. Perhaps, finding XYZ2 was not the right strategy to have followed. If so, the example illustrates the importance of first, do the right thing (strategy) and, then, do it the right way (tactics).

The Systems Viewpoint is presented at the beginning of each chapter as it applies to the material in that chapter. The systems approach is likened to using a wide-angle lens. Much material gets into the picture. If properly done, all of it is relevant to understanding the situation. For example, the management of inventory is a direct report to production. From the systems point of view, however, marketing goals and objectives need to have major influence in reaching inventory decisions. In this way, factors that are organizational as well as external need to be included in the framework.

Strategic Thinking is part of the roadmap concept. The systems viewpoint includes the entire map of relevance. Strategic thinking is based on current positions and proposed destinations. In each chapter, the strategic thinking paragraphs identify the underlying goals of the subject matter of the chapter. Also, these statements connect the relationship of strategic thinking to the systems point of view. This means that in a chapter devoted to tactical issues, the strategic drivers are identified.

Dynamic graphics have been designed to clearly illustrate concepts and organize information. Atomic Dog Publishing has special skills for animating the graphics. Special attention has been given to the use of the mouse as an interactive learning device. Pointing, dragging, and clicking will derive responses from the graphics that can be repeated in a learning sequence unique to each student. The learning potential of graphics is carried to a level that illustrates again the power of operations properly coordinated by new technology. Every effort is made to design each figure so that it has maximum impact as a learning aid.

Illustrative photographs have been carefully selected to capture students' interest. The prime purpose of photos is to help students visualize structures and situations that their minds' eye could not produce unaided. A proper photo is worth a thousand words, designed to aid someone to visualize something that they have never seen before. Photos assist understanding of real-world applications of operations.

Key terms have been linked to appropriate text locations within each chapter. This allows students the opportunity to review their understanding of the key topics within each chapter. This reinforces student comprehension. Key terms are useful search subjects. They help students review assignments for their comprehension. It is smart to engage in these new study habits before taking a feedback quiz. These quizzes are described here. Note that key terms are likely to appear in the summary that ends every chapter. Authors would prefer to use good synonyms to avoid being repetitious and redundant. A useful exercise for students is to identify synonyms for key terms, and then use search capabilities to find them.

Summaries appear at the end of each chapter. A summary does not cover every point that was raised in the chapter, but it highlights the main points that were made. Good summaries tend to be repetitious without being boring. Reiteration aids learning. Advertising research documents the fact that repetition is annoying, but it increases memorability. Learning theory substantiates the claim. Summaries and key terms are usefully different forms of the same thing. Both are intended to crystallize essential elements for student self-evaluation.

Review questions at the end of each chapter are designed to cover important concepts. This starts the process of self-evaluation. Students will discover as a result of trying to answer these review questions whether or not they understand the P/OM materials that have been covered to date.

Problems at the end of each chapter tend to be quantitative. Especially designed for graduate students, there is a challenge to solving these problems. MBA students often want to skip quantitative exercises until they realize that industrial engineers and Wharton graduates are totally comfortable with the numbers.

End-of-chapter questions are constructed using multiple-choice questions. These are designed to provide feedback to students about their understanding of the field's concepts and models. The quizzes are interactive, which means that the students are told what is right and wrong. In addition, errors are explained and students are referred back to appropriate sections for reexamination. This interaction represents the best of new technology applied to operations management in the education and publications field.

Additional readings at the end of each chapter provide opportunity for further research and exploration into chapter topics. The reference list for the Internet is updated regularly and as needed. The reference list for paper book publication is updated as feasible. For customers of Atomic Dog Publishing, what could be better?

Notes appear at the end of each chapter. They reflect current research in P/OM and some historical foundations of the P/OM field.

Real-world examples appear often in each chapter. Spotlights focus on real companies (Chick-fil-A®, BluWorld, Inc., Boutwell-Owens, Enron, Ford Motor, Global Concepts, Inc., McIlhenney, Inc., Polaroid, Shouldice Hospital, Starbucks, World Source One, Inc.). Spotlights also interview real people who are important to the P/OM field (Robin Cohn, Tom Doran, Henry Ford, Eli Goldratt, Lars Kolind, Stephanie Kwolek, Curt Reimann, Bruce Richardson, Jonathan Shay, Don Stuart, E. Cathy Truett.). Significant developing technologies are reported in spotlights (ATMs and RFID, nanotechnology, paving in-place recycling, robotic vehicles, smart cards, web services). Spotlights hone in on pressing issues (job creation, software-based negotiations, benchmarking what is excellent performance, the Sarbanes-Oxley 2002 law, how much innovation is too much, and e-shopping operations).

There are four real world cases throughout the text. These are:

Tom's of Maine for industry perspective on quality. The case explores the quality culture pervading this manufacturer of natural personal care products with a special focus on the process of making toothpaste.

Rosenbluth International for industry perspective on service. The case provides an unprecedented look into the inner workings of a high-tech service operation with a focus on the complex automated airline reservation process.

Global Concepts, Inc., at Celestica's facility at Little Rock for industry perspective on advanced logistics and manufacturing support solutions. The case explores the management system developed by Global Concepts, Inc., for application at Celestica's repair, remanufacturing, and distribution center in Little Rock, Arkansas. Global Concepts is a high-tech, knowledge-based, business process analysis consulting company.

Saturn Corporation for industry perspective on protecting the environment with strong net benefit to the company. The case presents analysis of Saturn's environmental initiatives for the automobile building and dismantling process. It includes perspectives for team building, union relationships, and product/process design. The case presents the Saturn story from its inception to the new product line of 2003.

Supplements are included for 13 chapters to enrich topical coverage.

STATEMENT FROM THE AUTHOR

This preface was written to be read by both instructors and students. For students, the acquisition of knowledge about the P/OM field is the destination. For teachers, learning methods are the journey for the students to achieve the destination. How the trip is made (the learning experience with new Internet technology) is exciting. It elevates the importance of the destination for all of us.

ONLINE AND IN PRINT

As discussed earlier, *Production and Operations Management* is available online as well as in print. The online chapters demonstrate how the interactive media components of the text enhance presentation and understanding. For example,

- Animated illustrations help clarify concepts.
- Chapter quizzes test your knowledge of various topics and provide immediate feedback.
- Clickable glossary terms provide immediate definitions of key concepts.
- The search function allows you to quickly locate discussions of specific topics throughout the text.
- Highlighting capabilities allow you to emphasize main ideas. You can also add personal notes in the margin.

You may choose to use just the online version of the text, or both the online and the print versions together. This gives you the flexibility to choose which combination of resources works best for you. To assist those who use the online and print versions together, the primary heads and subheads in each chapter are numbered the same. For example, the first primary head in Chapter 1 is labeled 1-1, the second primary head in this chapter is labeled 1-2, and so on. The subheads build from the designation of their corresponding primary head: 1-1a, 1-1b, etc. This numbering system is designed to make moving between the online and print versions as seamless as possible.

Finally, next to a number of figures in the print version of the text, you will see an icon similar to the one on the left. This icon indicate that these figures in the online version of the text are interactive in a way that applies, illustrates, or reinforces the concept.

SUPPLEMENTAL MATERIALS

Production and Operations Management is supported by a set of teaching supplements that offer many option combinations to suit instructors' individual preferences and approaches:

- Instructor's Manual
- Solutions Manual with Test Item File
- PowerPoint Presentations

ACKNOWLEDGMENTS

I thank Polly Starr for her solid research contributions. This text could not have been successful without Polly, who contributed spotlight features that are best called gourmet fare. Her graphic designs capture the essence of why visual images are crucial. I appreciate the valuable hours of discussion about the cases, basic philosophical issues, and proper pedagogy. My colleague, Dr. Jim Gilbert (Rollins College), and Professor Tim Smunt (Wake Forest University) provided valuable feedback with their reports of both student and teacher needs. Connie Morris has been supportive for seven years and went through every aspect of the CEM-Rollins seminar series that led to many of the references and points made in this text. I also want to acknowledge the contributions of the Atomic Dog Publishing team. Tom Doran, Steve Scoble, Dan Jones, and Ed Laube are all renaissance editors offering the benefits of new technology in the twenty-first century. In the trenches where books are made, using great production skills, the team of Kathy Davis, Rebecca Roby, Vickie Putman, and Joe Devine resulted in the high-quality product that is the holy grail of P/OM perfectionists. Great production calls for open minds, strong support, wideranging vision, and creative mentalities. These were given in abundance from all of the above, who were the Dog's best friends. I acknowledge their contributions with thanks and appreciation.

Martin K. Starr

About the Author

Martin K. Starr is Distinguished Professor Emeritus of Operations Management and Management Science at the Crummer Graduate School of Business, Rollins College, in Winter Park, Florida. Starr is also Professor Emeritus of Management Science at Columbia University's Graduate School of Business. He established the Operations Management Department at Columbia's Business School. Professor Starr was director of the Center for Enterprise Management (CEM), which did research and consulting at both Columbia University and Rollins College.

CEM research at Columbia was known for comparing the performance of U.S. firms with Japanese firms in America. Later, the benchmarking was extended to European firms in America. CEM at Rollins benchmarked supply chain performance in the healthcare system. It developed cost/benefit simulation models to determine optimal mix of nursing services and technology. Other studies involved plant layout reengineering and computer training methods, including distance learning.

Professor Starr has published 25 books on a variety of subjects including texts on global alliances, inventory, operations management, systems management, and product design. He has published over 100 articles on various subjects that include project management, product design, systems engineering, intellectual property, knowledge management, innovations in education, marketing dynamics, and recently, on security operations.

Starr is past president of TIMS (The Institute of Management Sciences) and past president of POMS (Production and Operations Management Society). He is currently chair of the Council of Past Presidents (of POMS). He was editor-in-chief of the journal Management Science for 15 years.

He has been consultant to many companies including CNL, ABB, Bristol-Myers Squibb, Citibank, DuPont, GE Capital, IBM, Eastman Kodak (Rochester and Cape Town), Lehman Brothers, DaimlerChrysler, Fiat, Honda, Boston Consulting Group, Lever Brothers, Merrill Lynch, Exxon, Mobile, Hewlett-Packard, YPF, and Young & Rubicam, to name a few.

Overview and Introduction to Production and Operations Management (P/OM)

The overview is the starting point. Many parts interconnect. The overview identifies those elements that drive others. This is familiar territory, and it is said in many ways. Formally, x is a function of y where x might be cash and y is the admission paid to enter a theme park. Also, it is said that y leads to x much as a sunburn is caused by being on the beach on a cloudless day. Such interrelationships form the foundation of the production field where the product is x and the forces that make the product are y. Operations are the drivers for both goods and services. Part 1 starts the development of the means for understanding these relationships.

Chapter 1 is entitled "Production and Operations Management (P/OM) and the Systems Approach." Chapter 1 defines production and operations management and explains how the P/OM management field is applicable to both manufacturing and services. It also elaborates on the advantages of the systems perspective that links operations management to all other managerial functions in the organization. This chapter explains why operations management (OM) and production and operations management (P/OM) are often used as interchangeable terminology. It also explains when these terms are not interchangeable.

The text is written for students of all management functions who need to know why P/OM is an important organizational partner for the achievement of competitive success. Chapter 1 provides a description of typical operations management positions, so that managers of all functions can understand the various ways in which they can expect to interact with operations managers. For students who would like to know more about OM as a potential concentration, Chapter 1 provides career path information and career choice guidance. OM planning and decision making offer exciting competitive leverage for those organizations that know how to use it.

Chapter 2 is entitled "P/OM's Key Role in Productivity Attainment." It immediately illustrates the reliance on P/OM for competitive leverage. P/OM is the function responsible for creating and running highly productive systems. This chapter defines productivity and explains its importance. Various measures of productivity are developed. As part of the systems viewpoint, productivity is related to price–demand elasticity, which is shared with the marketing domain.

Also, economies of scale are explained and division of labor is tied to the management of operations. The history of operations management has been to continually invent and develop methods that improve productivity. This history is developed because there are various work configurations that are entirely relevant to career selection.

1

Production and Operations Management (P/OM) and the Systems Approach

Chapter Outline

This section defines production and operations management (P/OM) and explains how this management field is applicable to both manufacturing and services. It also elaborates on the advantages of the systems perspective, which links production and operations management to all other managerial functions in the organization.

After reading this chapter, you should be able to:

- Define and explain operations management and contrast it with production management.
- Explain the categories of the systems approach, what it means, and why it is important to P/OM.
- Detail the systems approach that is used by P/OM.
- Understand how P/OM—using the systems approach—increases the competitive effectiveness of the organization.
- Understand why this text is titled *Production and Operations Management*.
- Distinguish between the application of P/OM to manufacturing and services.

- Explain how special P/OM capabilities provide competitive advantages.
- Relate information systems to the distinction between production and operations.
- Explain how the input–output (I/O) model defines production and operations.
- Describe the stages of development of companies with respect to OM and P/OM.
- Discuss positions in P/OM that exist in the organization and career success in P/OM as a function of process types.
- Explain the effects of globalization on P/OM careers.

THE SYSTEMS VIEWPOINT

Chapter 1 explains production and operations management (P/OM). It is easy to say P/OM, but it takes a long time to say production and operations management. Differences and similarities will be explained as the text continues. However, if one term is more easily used than the other to stand for both production and operations management, that term is *operations management*. Most production managers will accept the appellation of operations manager but not vice versa. Therefore, *operations management* will sometimes be used instead of production and operations management. Also, OM will be used in place of P/OM; PM is not a good substitute for P/OM unless manufacturing is clearly involved.

If the part that operations managers play is to be effective, it should be systems-based. Compare the operations manager to the coach of a sports team. What is the coach's job for a baseball, football, basketball, or soccer team? It is to guide the team to achieve competitive excellence. The coach knows that to make the team win requires coordinating the contributions of the individual players. Winning takes teamwork, and the coach tries to develop that cooperative ability. Teamwork skills require a systems viewpoint. The systems viewpoint means that everything that is important to goal achievement is included in the analysis. If the goals cannot be achieved, then the strategies must be changed. (In this paragraph, P/OM applies, so production and operations managers are described as operations managers.)

STRATEGIC THINKING

The systems viewpoint requires strategic planning. Goals and strategies must be congruent and realistic. Assume that the game being coached is called business and that players' positions are known as marketing, finance, operations, etc. The successful coach emphasizes coordination of these functions to pursue a strategy aimed at achieving the objectives. Apply this same statement to football, baseball, basketball, soccer, etc., and it works as well. Managers of all functional areas need to understand P/OM, and P/OM managers need to understand areas that interact with their own. To understand global competitors requires understanding their strategies within the context of the international character of their operations management systems. That is why this text directs P/OM managers to focus on the use of the systems approach for strategic planning and tactical actions.

1-1 EXPLAINING PRODUCTION AND OPERATIONS MANAGEMENT (P/OM)

Production: Activities used to create (and deliver) goods or furnish (and deliver) services to customers.

Operations management: Managing activities used to produce (and deliver) goods or furnish (and deliver) services to customers.

Production and **operations management** is the work function that oversees making goods and providing services. Because it provides what others sell, finance, and account for, it is an indisputable partner in the business.

This book will familiarize students with the language and abbreviations used by production and operations managers—such as writing P/OM (or even faster, OM) for operations management. Important P/OM terms are explained in the text and their definitions are also presented.

The OM language describes methods, tools, procedures, goals, and concepts that relate to the management of people, materials, energy, information, and technology. Operations managers learn how to study a process by observing it and mapping its flow; from that platform, its performance can be improved. OM allows the state of a production process to be assessed.

1-1a Use of Models by P/OM (or OM)

The Greyhound bus driver is an operations manager assessing highway-driving conditions. The driver knows how rain slows velocity (v), which cuts down miles that can be driven per day (m). The manager in charge of operating the fleet of buses could describe this relationship as follows: $m = vt$ where m is the driver's output in miles driven per 8-hour day; v is the velocity, measured in miles per hour; and $t = 8$ hours.

This method of quantitative description is often used by OM to build a model—*a representation of the real situation.* The model permits OM to test the effect of different t's and v's. A general quantitative model that describes output is $O = pt$, where O is output per day. O changes as a function of the production rate per hour (p) and the length of time worked (t).

P/OM develops models to describe productivity (p) as a function of scheduling, training, technology, and capacity.

There are various OM models used to make equipment selection, workforce and production scheduling, quality control, inventory, distribution, plant location, capacity, maintenance, and transportation decisions, among others. Decision models organize the elements of a problem into actions that can be taken, forecasts of things that can happen that will affect the results, and thereby, the relative likelihood of the various outcomes occurring. Thus, decision models organize all of the vital elements in a systematic way.

1-1b   Working Definitions of Production and Operations

The generic or collective definition of operations emphasizes rational design, careful control, and the systematic approach that characterizes the methodology of P/OM. Production/operations is a big umbrella that always includes services and often includes **manufacturing.** Production almost always stands for manufacturing alone.

Defining Operations

Operations are purposeful actions (or activities) methodically done as part of a plan of work (a strategy) by a process that is designed to achieve practical ends (objectives). This definition is applicable for manufacturing without reservation. This definition further justifies the use of the term *operations* for manufacturing.

Defining Operations Management (OM)

Operations management is the systematic planning and control of operations. This definition implies that management is needed to ensure that actions are *purposeful*—designed to achieve practical ends so goals and targets are required. These statements apply equally well to P/OM.

Production and operations management (P/OM) makes sure the work is done *methodically*—that is, characterized by method and order. The fact that a *process* is used suggests the presence of management to install a procedure for working systematically.

Operations management is responsible for a *plan of work*—a thoughtful progression from one step to another. Plans require details for accomplishing work. These details are often called the *tactics of the plan. Practical ends* are not realized without operations management that is able to provide strategies and tactics for public service objectives, which can include the ability to gain market share on a bus route or participation in a recycling plan. Everyone wants to be able to gain market share. There is a need to review why some organizations consider it embarrassing to make a profit. That could include your local bus company.

Operations management uses *methodology* that consists of *procedures, rules of thumb,* and *algorithms* for analyzing situations and setting policies. They apply to many different kinds of service and manufacturing processes. In brief, operations management consists of tactics such as scheduling work, assigning resources including people and equipment, managing inventories, assuring quality standards, process-type decisions that include capacity decisions, maintenance policies, equipment selection, worker-training options, and the sequence for making individual items in a product-mix set.

The functions of P/OM overlap and interact. They are driven by demand from the market, where OM manages the supply to meet the demand.

Manufacturing Applications of P/OM

The operations used by manufacturing can be represented by many different verb and object phrases that describe doing things to various materials, such as pressing metal, cutting paper, sewing clothes, sawing wood, drilling metal, sandblasting glass, forming plastics, shaping clay, heat-treating materials, soldering contacts, weaving fabric, blending fuels, filling cans, and extruding wires. Similarly, there are a variety of assembly phrases, such as snapping parts, gluing sheets, fitting components, and joining pieces together. This kind of work is done in factories.

Manufacturing Examples   Autos, planes, refrigerators, and lightbulbs are made in factories. On the other hand, fast-food chains like McDonald's and Burger King view the assembly of sandwiches from meat, buns, and condiments as a manufacturing application that demands the highest levels of quality for cleanliness and consistency. Also, costs must be kept low enough so that a profit can be made at a price that attracts customers. The price

Manufacturing: The processes that constitute the transformation function of the I/O model; those processes that produce goods.

Operations: Activities that are used to produce (and deliver) goods or furnish (and deliver) services to customers.

Operations used by manufacturing include such diverse activities as rail cutting (shown here) as well as turning metal on a lathe, annealing for metallurgical properties, and assembling, which fits components together and joins them.

Spools of woolen thread are made in the woolen mills of Trefriw, Gwynedd, Wales, United Kingdom. Textile manufacturers use this thread to weave fabric.

Information systems: Good information systems capture all data relevant to P/OM planning and decision making.

of fast-food products, said to be highly elastic, strongly affects the demand volume. The concept of manufacturing sandwiches is a departure from traditional restaurant operations. It provides a P/OM basis for requiring methodical performance to achieve practical goals.

Service Applications of P/OM

Service operations in the office environment are quite familiar, i.e., filing documents, typing input for the word processor, and answering the phone. There are similar lists of verbs and objects that apply to jobs done in banks, hospitals, and schools; grant a loan, take an X-ray, and teach a class are a few examples. Movies are one of the biggest export products of the United States. Operations management for entertainment and sports provides great opportunities. In the United States, administration of the law is a major industry that requires operations management. In recent years, law firms have begun to understand the importance of productivity management and quality improvement.

Jobs in the service industries are not as well paid as jobs in manufacturing. This is because the rational design of service industry operations is well behind that of manufacturing. In the earliest years of manufacturing, many employees were paid small amounts of money. The kinds of operations that each person could do made only minor contributions to the profitability of the enterprise. Successful firms integrated the minor contributions of the many. As manufacturing operations and the technology behind them became better understood and the process was rationalized, fewer people were needed because each could make greater contributions.

The service industries are in the process of rationalizing operations so that individual contributions will become increasingly valuable in the same way that occurred in manufacturing. Consider the labor-intensive environment of check processing in a bank. It is reminiscent of the labor-intensive character of work that dominated manufacturing from the turn of the twentieth century through the mid-twentieth century and still exists in various places in the world.

Service Examples   Those who have worked for UPS, RPS, Federal Express, DHL, or the post office are able to list the various service operations related to delivering mail and packages. Those who have worked for the IRS will have another set of job descriptions to define specific operations that characterize tax collection activities of the federal government. Also, if one has worked for The Gap, Banana Republic, Eddie Bauer, The Limited, Wal-Mart, The Sharper Image, K-Mart, Sears, or other retail operators, he or she will be able to define processes that are pertinent to merchandise selection and pricing, outsourcing, distribution logistics, display, and store retailing. The experience will have similarities and differences with supermarkets that must also cope with dated products such as milk and greens that speak for themselves regarding freshness.

Successful mail-order (and Internet) companies like Lands' End, Amazon, L.L. Bean, Victoria's Secret, Norm Thompson, and Barnes & Noble are good examples of entrepreneurial firms that have struggled to master changes in technologies to gain the operational advantages of smart logistics. Distribution, in retail, mail order, and Internet B2C (business-to-consumer web customers), is a production process that lends itself to all of the benefits that excellent **information systems** and new technology can bestow.

The credit card business is another splendid example of a situation that combines many aspects of service functions. MasterCard, VISA, and American Express are totally dependent upon smart operations management to provide profit margin excellence. The IT component of the credit card business model is almost transparent, but it is still very difficult to do well with consistent performance.

1-2 PRODUCTION AND OPERATIONS MANAGEMENT: THE SYSTEMS APPROACH

There are two approaches that P/OM can use:

1. The functional field approach
2. The systems approach

FIGURE 1-1
Traditional Organization Chart Shows Self-Contained Functional Areas

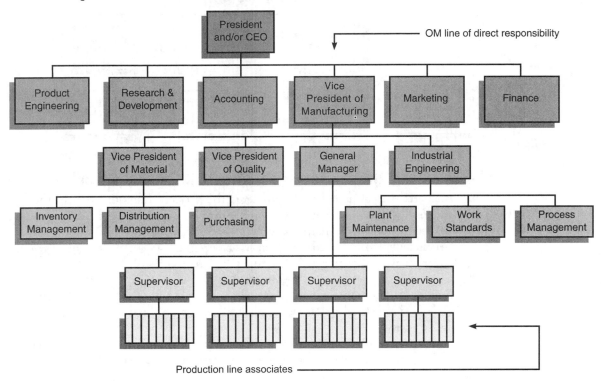

Production line associates

With the **functional field approach,** operations management is explained with minimum reference to other parts of the business—such as marketing and finance. The functional field approach concentrates on the specific tasks that must be done to make the product or deliver the service. It is tactical, not strategic.

A typical organization chart—but with details mainly for P/OM—is shown in Figure 1-1. The P/OM department is headed by a senior vice president of operations, who has the plant manager as well as staff heads reporting to him or her. The chart could also detail marketing, finance, human resources, R & D, and other functions.

There are no lines connecting people in the other functional areas to people in OM. The only connection is at the president's level. Within the P/OM area, there are a limited number of connections, and these are hierarchically structured. The traditional organization chart does not reflect the systems approach wherein anyone can talk to anyone else if they are part of the problem or the solution. Teamwork is difficult to achieve with self-contained functions.

The **systems approach** integrates P/OM decisions with those of all other business functions.

The challenge is to make the firm perform as a team. The systems approach entails having all participants cooperate in solving problems that require mutual involvement. It begins with strategic planning and moves to tactical accomplishments.

Heiner Müller-Merbach has provided a useful way of describing the systems approach as a combination of concepts.[1] Figure 1-2 depicts the various meanings that he has associated with the systems approach.

"The systems approach focuses the consideration of wholes and of their relations to their parts. The systems approach is necessarily comprehensive, holistic and interdisciplinary. However, there are several types of systems approaches around, quite different from each other and competing with one another,"[2] Müller-Merbach notes.

Functional field approach: The functional field approach is widely used; with this approach, operations management is strictly tactical.

Systems approach: The big view that includes everything that might account for what is happening; accents connections and interactions between all functions.

FIGURE 1-2
Taxonomy of the Systems
Approach

1-2a Using the Systematic–Constructive Approach

The systematic systems approach is considered the Western tradition whereas the systemic systems approach is characteristic of Eastern philosophies. The systems approach this book uses is systematic: analytic, synthetic, and constructive.

The systems approach called *introspection* is based on the analytic reduction of systems into their parts, which is characteristic of the sciences.

The systems approach called *extraspection* is characteristic of philosophy and the humanities. It strives to integrate objects and ideas into higher-order systems using synthesis. The field of general systems is closely associated with this effort to develop meta-systems of knowledge.

Say that a desktop computer stops working. Following introspection, it is opened up and taken apart. By means of analysis, components are tested to find the cause of the trouble.

Synthesis is required to reassemble the computer. Using extraspection, perhaps a better overall configuration can be found.

Combine analysis and synthesis to obtain the third systems approach, called *construction*. It is "characteristic of the engineering sciences and their creative design of systems for practical purposes."[3]

Creative design that uses both analysis and synthesis is the systems approach described in this book.

1-2b Why Is the Systems Approach Required?

The systems approach is needed because it produces better solutions than other approaches—including the functional field approach. It leads to better decisions and provides better problem-solving for complex situations, enabling those that use it to be more successful.

Think of the systems approach in terms of the sports team. If the players are coordinated by communication and training, they play a better game. Similarly, in business, those that use the systems approach are the leading competitors in every industry.

1-2c Defining the System

OM system: Alternative name for the P/OM system; OM is more service-oriented than P/OM.

Elements that qualify to be part of a system are those that have a direct or indirect impact on the problem, or its solution; on the plan, or the decision. Thus, an **OM system** is everything that affects process planning, capacity decisions, quality standards, inventory levels, and production schedules. An OM system incorporates all factors with an effect on the purposes and goals of the organization.

Figure 1-3 is a symbolic picture of a system. The shape encloses all factors that have an effect on the purposes and goals of the system. Anything outside of that system is treated as independent of the problems and opportunities inside of it.

Figure 1-4 shows an organization chart with the system's shape mapped across it to reflect the fact that the problems and opportunities include various people and functions. The problem map cuts across OM as well as other functions.

FIGURE 1-3
Representation of a System

- - -▶ Weak interactions are outside the system.
───▶ Strong interactions are inside the system.

This is a symbolic representation of the fact that people in departments falling inside the shaded area are involved with the problem being considered. Major responsibilities appear to fall within the domain of the general manager, plant maintenance, purchasing, and several supervisors.

The key to understanding the relevant system is to identify all of the main players and elements that interact to create the system in which the real problem resides. Even though the problem solution may be assigned to the operations management team, the resolution requires cooperation of all the organizational participants in the problem.

FIGURE 1-4
System's Mapping Across a Traditional Organization Chart

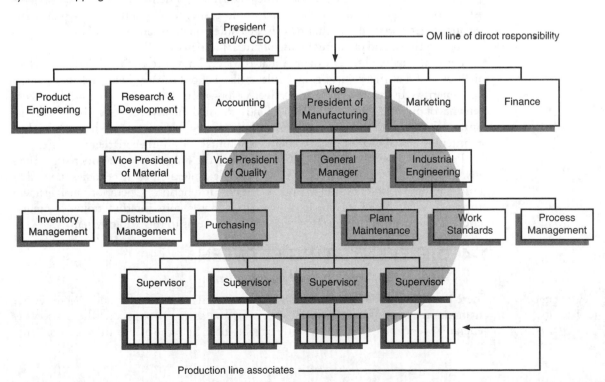

1-3 STRUCTURE OF THE SYSTEMS APPROACH

The systems approach requires identification of all the elements related to purposes and goals. The question to be answered: What accounts for the attainment of the goals?

1. The visual concept depicted in Figure 1-3 is one way to answer the question.
2. Another way is to use a math model that shows what accounts for the performance of the system and the attainment of its goals. The equation, shown here, is read "The goals y_i are a function of all relevant factors x_j and t_j." That is:

$$\{y_i\} = f\{x_1, x_2, \ldots, x_j; t_1, t_2, \ldots, t_j\}$$

3. The systems approach requires control of timing. It is to be noted that the previous equation includes measures of time (t_j) as an important systems parameter. By recording conditions over time, it is possible to measure rates of change—which are also important systems descriptors. Timing is critical to the performance of symphony orchestras, sports teams, and business organizations. To achieve *synchronization* of functions, and harmony, the systems approach is required.
4. The systems approach requires teamwork. Coordination of all participants is essential. Designing a productive process for making hamburgers, VCRs, delivering packages, or servicing cars requires the cooperation among all members of the system. To operate a process properly, it is necessary for all to have the systems perspective. In particular, the attainment of quality requires a dedicated team effort. A mistake by anyone involved in gaining the perception of quality is like the weak link of a chain, which causes the whole system to fail.

1-3a Examples of the Systems Approach

As previously pointed out, managing a sports team is an excellent example of a purposeful effort that is enhanced by using the systems approach. Another fine example is a symphony orchestra. The conductor of the orchestra makes certain that all participants are synchronized (on the same timeline). If the violins, woodwinds, and brass treat their participation as if they were separate functional fields, bedlam would result. Everyone looks to the conductor to keep the components of the system related and balanced.

For current purposes, the main example to explore is a generic business model whereby the operations managers make the product and/or deliver the services. Using the systems approach to coordinate the business-unit team is essential to balance supply and demand, meet schedules, minimize costs, guarantee quality-standards fulfillment, maximize productivity, and optimize the use of critical resources.

For fun, a more abstract example that is widely known to both children and adults might be useful at this point. Jigsaw puzzles strike a chord because being able to assemble them smartly requires a systems perspective. Vision is needed to relate the interdependent elements of pieces using clues of various kinds. Puzzle difficulty increases when pieces are cut to look alike and if little color differentiation is provided. Edges are important when the internal spatial characteristics send no real hints concerning congruent outlines.

Puzzles become geometrically more difficult as the number of pieces increases. Similarly, as a system becomes larger with more complex interactions, it becomes more difficult to fathom its structure and to understand how it functions. Operations management problems are composed of complex subsystems, which require interfunctional communications to uncover the *patterns* that relate the subsystems to the whole system.

1-4 DIFFERENTIATING BETWEEN GOODS AND SERVICES

Service: Includes every form of work except manufacturing of goods.

There is less difference than similarity between OM in manufacturing and OM in **service** organizations. Manufacturing is the fabrication and assembly of goods, whereas services generate revenues either independently of goods or to help the user of those goods. Banking, transportation, health care, and entertainment are all services. They change the customer's location, financial condition, and sense of well-being. Increasingly, manufacturers recognize the importance of servicing customers, and service systems recognize the value of using manufacturing capabilities.

The methodology of OM was first developed by and for manufacturing, but it has now been extended to services with great success.

Service industries involve an increasing percent of the workforce. Thus, more attention needs to be directed toward achieving coherent and efficient operations for services.

Similarities between services and manufacturing can be noted when service operations are based upon repetitive steps in information processing. Almost identical methods apply with respect to production scheduling, job design and design of the workplace, process configurations, and quality achievement. High volume repetitive operations on physical items (i.e., for fast foods or blood testing) is production whether they belong to manufacturing or services. Similar analogies can be made for lower volumes of production and services delivered.

The similarities stop and significant differences occur when the operations involve contact between people. Person-to-person activities that require transfer of information and/or treatments offered by one to another are difficult to schedule; activity times vary more than with machines. Human-to-human interactions involve many more intangibles than interactions between people and machines. The contact aspect of services requires different methods for analysis and synthesis than are needed for manufacturing systems.

At the same time, care should be taken to avoid stereotyping services as being all too human and, therefore, difficult to control for quality and productivity. It does a disservice to services to consider them quixotic or flawed by humanism, while manufacturing is admired for its elegant, efficient technological component. A most respected thinker has written, "Until we think of service in more positive and encompassing terms, until it is enthusiastically viewed as manufacturing in the field, receptive to the same kind of technological approaches that are used in the factory, the results are likely to be . . . costly and idiosyncratic."[4]

The point to make is that services that are currently rendered in an inherently inefficient way often can be transformed into rational repeatable activities that emulate the best of manufacturing environments. However, often is not always. Some services are not amenable to the concept of manufacturing in the field. One would be fearful if the services rendered by a doctor were based on a repetitive manufacturing model. At the same time, many aspects of open-heart surgery are the better for such systematization. The same can be said for blood testing, taking X-rays, and other repetitious aspects of the health-care business. Juxtaposed to this, some products, such as artwork, are epitomized by being custom-made.

Rush hour traffic on an 8-lane toll highway will be serviced by eight tollbooths, including some that are equipped for e-pass (electronic pay). A significant difference between toll service operations and manufacturing is that when the tollbooth operator is idle, there is no way to build up an inventory of time to be used when the waiting lines are long. However, toy manufacturers prepare inventory in September to satisfy Christmas demand.

Another significant difference between the provision of services and manufacturing occurs because of inventory. It is not considered possible, usually, to stock services. For example, when the machine repairperson is idle there is no way to build up an inventory of repair hours that can be used when two machines go down at the same time. In most service businesses, this is one of the great waste factors.

On the other hand, many companies use automated systems to provide custom-tailored information such as stock, bond, and mutual fund quotes for anyone knowing the symbols. Phone-call requests for product information are answered by a digitized voice that instructs the caller to use a Touch-Tone phone to input the product of interest and his or her fax number. The appropriate fax is automatically transmitted within a minute. This entire service transaction, without human intervention, is becoming increasingly common and epitomizes an automated manufacturing process.

1-5 CONTRASTING PRODUCTION MANAGEMENT AND OPERATIONS MANAGEMENT

What is the difference between *production* management and *operations* management? Production is an old and venerable term used by engineers, economists, entrepreneurs, and managers to describe physical work both in homes and in factories to produce a material product.

Traditionally, **production management** involves planning and decision making for the manufacture of goods such as airplanes, cars, tires, soup, paper, soap, cereal, shoes, shirts, skirts, sweaters, dentifrice, clothing, furniture, and the parts that go into many of these products. Parts and components manufacture is a large portion of finished goods manufacture. Production managers are responsible for food, clothing, and shelter, as well as luxuries.

Production management: Managing activities used to produce (and deliver) goods to customers.

Operations management is a more recent term associated with services performed by organizations such as banks, insurance companies, fast-food servers, and airlines. Government jobs are also in the services. Healthcare providers, including hospitals and schools, belong in the services category. It is not surprising that there has been a rapid growth of service jobs in the U.S. economy. The current ratio of service jobs to manufacturing jobs is nearly four to one, compared to an approximate one-to-one ratio in the 1950s. As a result, the number of people that are now engaged in operations is far larger (and still growing) than the number of people that work in the production departments of manufacturing firms.

Manufacturers have come to view service to the customer as part of the quality of their products (i.e., repairing defective product as well as providing regularly scheduled maintenance). Auto manufacturers learned a great deal from Acura when Honda launched that division with a service mission that eclipsed anything in auto service that preceded it. One of the best automotive service operations before Acura was Honda itself. Xerox established strict guidelines for the maximum allowable downtimes that would be tolerated for its copying machines. Until the 1990s, IBM provided no service to its small customers. After a serious fall from grace, IBM changed its policy and became a full-service company to all customers using HelpWare support run by its Personal System's HelpCenter.

In this transition era, preventive maintenance targets generating customer satisfaction instead of additional revenues. Many manufacturers have established toll-free 800 telephone numbers permitting their customers to call without charge for information about the products they make and to register complaints. Plant tours educate customers and convey information about quality efforts with the intention of attracting new customers and building loyalty.

1-5a Information Systems Are Essential for Manufacturing and Services

The growing recognition of the importance of the service function in manufacturing has broadened the situations to which the term *operations* is applied. Manufacturers have become more comfortable with the notion that they must cater to the customer's service requirements. Information systems provide the necessary data about customer needs so that operations management can supply the required services.

Both services and manufacturing are increasingly responsive to—and controlled by—information systems. Therefore, knowledge of computers, computer programming, networking, and telecommunications is essential in both the manufacturing and service environment.

Schools of business include both goods and services under the term *operations*, whereas industrial engineering departments are still inclined to teach "production" courses. Nevertheless, there is inevitable convergence of both to an information-dominated workplace. *Operations is the familiar management term for an information systems environment*, so the word "operations" fits nicely.

Programming and maintenance (both service functions) have become increasingly important to manufacturing. Further, the relevance of service to customers increasingly is viewed as a part of the total package that the manufacturer must deliver. Manufacturing joins such distinguished service industries as transportation, banking, entertainment, education, and health care. In that regard, note the following trends for manufacturing:

1. The labor component (the input of blue-collar workers) has been decreasing as a percent of the cost of goods at an accelerating rate for over 50 years.

2. The technological component as a percent of the cost of goods has been increasing for many years. In the past 20 years, this effect has become multiplicative, with computers controlling sophisticated and costly equipment across vast distances via satellites and networks.

3. As information systems play a larger part in manufacturing, highly-trained computer programmers (sometimes called *gold-collar workers*) and white-collar supervisors add to growing sales and administrative (overhead) costs, which have to be partitioned into the cost of goods. These costs are an increasing percent of the cost of goods. Traditional methods for assigning these costs can lead to detrimental OM decisions. New accounting methods, called *activity-based costing (ABC)*, should be used to improve overhead accounting. Operations managers need to discuss these issues with their colleagues from accounting.

4. The systems approach requires communication between functions and the sharing of what used to be (and still are, in many traditional firms) mutually exclusive databases. The databases of marketing and sales, OM, R & D, engineering, and finance are cross-linked when advantageous. That sharing is crucial to enabling the systems approach to work. There are many examples of both manufacturing and service industries where shared databases have been installed and utilized successfully.

5. The technology of the twentieth century is moving rapidly into retirement along with a lot of executives who grew up with its characteristics. It's a new ball game with new players who feel free to deal with the distinction between services and manufacturing as well as between operations and production in their own way.

Practitioners now have stepped into the twenty-first century, but they have yet to get accustomed to it. It is a good bet that the taxonomy of the twenty-first century will categorize production as a subheading under operations, and services will be an integral part of manufacturing.

When a discussion applies equally well to both manufacturing and services, it is often referred to as P/OM. As explained earlier, it is increasingly common to call it OM. In this text, OM will be used to describe both manufacturing and services. P/OM will be used only in situations where the manufacturing component is critical and conclusions are likely to be different from those applicable to service systems.

1-6 THE BASIC OM TRANSFORMATION MODEL: AN INPUT–OUTPUT SYSTEM

All operations management and production systems involve **transformation**. Alteration of materials and components adds value and changes them into goods that customers

Transformation: One of the most important parts of the P/OM system. It is the transformation process capability to cut metal, polish brass, take temperatures, build cars, and so forth.

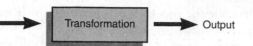

Input–output is the basic OM model.

want to own. The raw materials and components before transformation could not be used—and therefore had no utility—for the customer. Service conversions have customer utility even though no transfer of goods takes place. The conversion may be a change of location or related to the customer's state of well-being (e.g., visiting the doctor or the repairperson fixes the machine).

The manufacturing transformation of raw materials into finished goods is successful if customers are willing to pay more for the goods than it costs to make them. Consider what has to be done to make a product. The raw materials for glass, steel, food, and paper have no utility without technological transformations. New processes are constantly being invented for improving the transformations and the products that can be obtained from them.

The same transformation rules apply to services. The conversion is successful if customers are willing to pay more for the services than it costs to provide them. To illustrate a service transformation, consider an information system in a bank. A check that is issued results in the electronic transfer of funds (ETF) from the paying account to the paid account, clearly an input–output transformation.

Another information transformation is to take raw data and turn it into averages and standard deviations. The latter is characteristic of the operations aspect of market research. As another service example, consider the transformation that is at the heart of the airline business—moving people from one place (input) to another (output) for profit. Other inputs are fuel, food, and the attention of the flight attendants.

Figure 1-5 presents a picture of a generalized input–output transformation model. Generalized means that it is a standard or generic form that could be applied to any system where conversions are taking place. Inputs are fed into the transformation box, which represents the process. The "process" can include many subprocesses. If the process is to make a sandwich, then important subprocesses include cooking the hamburger and toasting the buns.

The inputs are combined by the process, resulting in the production of units of goods or the creation of types of services. The transformed units emerge from the facility (factory, office, etc.) at a given rate. Time needed to carry out the transformation determines the production rate. The transformed inputs emerge as outputs to be sold or used beneficially.

The transformation model depicts work being done. This work involves the use of resources made up of people, materials, energy, and machines to achieve transformations. Figure 1-6 illustrates the expanded version of the input–output transformation model. There are many boxes now within the transformation grid. Each box represents operations that generate the product line, which can be goods or services. Productive OM systems have well-designed transformations.

Transformations are being accomplished when people are served chili at Wendy's or when they give blood to the Red Cross, have their teeth cleaned by the dentist, or visit Disney World to be entertained. A travel agency will have secured the necessary reservations and tickets for the customer's flight to Orlando, Florida, and for the hotel. The travel agent designs the trip and fits it to the customer's specifications concerning dates and costs using reservation and other information systems to complete all necessary transactions. When the desired outputs are fully specified, the transformations can be planned, along with the inputs, and the plan can be carried through to completion. The culmination of the transformation process constitutes the desired output—a visit with Mickey Mouse.

Inputs   Transformations   Customers

FIGURE 1-6
Expanded Input–Output
OM Model

1-6a Costs and Revenues Associated with the Input–Output Model

Cost management is a key function associated with all aspects of OM. A major portion of the cost of goods or services originates with operations. Figure 1-7 is meant to illustrate how costs are related to the I/O model. Controlling costs is of prime concern to all managers.

For the most part, costs are readily categorized into variable costs and fixed costs. Generally, costs are considered to be easily measured, although the treatment of overhead costs is subject to debate. Also, a variety of accounting methodologies exist. The differences between them are not trivial because they can impact OM decisions in significantly disparate ways. OM and accounting coexist in the same system, and they are interdependent when the measurement of costs interacts with OM decision making. Quality, another key criteria associated with all aspects of OM, interacts with costs in a variety of ways, as do productivity, timeliness of delivery, and styles and sizes of products and services.

Inputs Associated with Variable (or Direct) Costs

The input components of the transformation model that apply to an airline transportation process include fuel, food, crew pay, and other costs. Variable operating costs increase as there are more flights flown and more people flying. Variable costs are also called *direct costs* because they can be applied directly, without ambiguity, to each unit that is processed.

The same reasoning applies to a manufacturing example. The variable costs for the inputs include labor, energy, and all of the materials purchased from suppliers and used to make the product. Materials include raw materials, subassemblies, semifinished materials, and components. The more finished the purchased materials, the less work that has to be done by the purchaser (i.e., less value can be added by the purchaser).

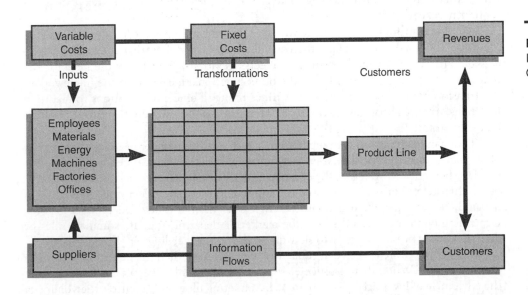

FIGURE 1-7
Input–Output OM Model:
Cost and Revenue Structure

Decisions about fixed costs (also called *indirect costs*) are not easily reversible. The measuring tape signifies how much overhead is incurred. How thick is the bundle of big bills that management must pay even if no revenue is coming into the company?

Transformations Associated with Fixed (or Indirect) Costs

When Delta or American Airlines buys aircraft from Airbus Industries or Boeing, the airline increases its already substantial fixed cost investment in planes. Fixed costs are also called *indirect costs* because they are part of overhead and must be allocated to units of output by some formula.

Often the charge per year—called *depreciation*—is calculated by dividing the cost of the investment by the number of years in the estimated lifetime of the investment. For example, a $30 million aircraft with a 15-year lifetime would generate $2 million of depreciation per year. This is called *straight-line depreciation* because the amount per year does not change. There still remains the question of how to allocate a portion of the $2 million as an applicable charge for a particular passenger flying from Milan to New York on that aircraft. Determining the appropriate fixed costs to be charged to each job, unit made, or passenger mile flown is a joint responsibility of OM and accounting.

An alternative approach for adding capacity without increasing investment is to lease instead of buy aircraft. This shifts the financial burden of buying capacity to the variable input cost mode. The same distinction applies when a manufacturer analyzes the net long-term economic value of renting a factory building instead of either building or buying a facility. Leasing a facility shifts the fixed costs of building acquisition to the variable costs associated with inputs.

Delta and American also have investments in maintenance facilities, airport terminals, training and education systems, as well as in their workers and management. The payments that airlines make to support the operations of airports generally are fixed and not variable costs. Airports—like factories—are major fixed-cost facilities; treat them as fixed costs because the same expenses must be met no matter how many flights depart or arrive there. However, if part of the airport charges is based on the number of flights an airline makes, then both fixed and variable (input) costs must be considered. As for investments in training and management, companies use consultants as a way to keep down their fixed costs. For similar reasons, they often lease transportation.

Outputs Associated with Revenues and Profits

Passengers pay the airline for transportation. The number of passengers (units) that are transported (processed) by the airline is the output (sometimes called *throughput* to emphasize the output rate) of the system. It usually is measured by passenger miles flown system wide (or between two points) in a period of time. Throughput is managed to balance supply (capacity) and demand. The demand level for transportation between any two points is related to marketing factors, not the least of which is the price for a roundtrip ticket.

All of the airlines do not charge the same amount for a roundtrip ticket. By adjusting price, airlines often can affect the percent occupancy of their flights. Such *marketing decisions* are part of the total system that affects operations. They typify the need for systems coordination to relate OM with the other functional areas within the framework of the transformation model. Southwest Airlines has used efficient operations to maintain low costs, which allow low prices to be charged. This has made Southwest Airlines uniquely profitable.

The manufacturer can measure output in terms of the number of units of each kind of product it produces. Because there may be many varieties such as sizes and flavors, it is usual OM practice to aggregate the output into some common unit, such as standard units of toothpaste produced. Both forms of information would reflect the variability of demand, but the aggregate measure much less so than the detailed product reports. Depending upon the demand levels, the marketing department could stimulate sales by dropping prices or raising prices to slow demand that is exceeding supply capabilities.

If lower prices are effective in generating new business, then the demand is said to be elastic to price. When there is price elasticity, operations must keep costs down so that the advantage of low prices can be obtained. Marketing ultimately controls the volume of business that production must process. Financial planning has determined the operating capacity for peak demand. This, in turn, translates back to the amount of inputs that need to be purchased to meet demand.

The systems perspective is required to make sure that all participants are connected directly to the revenue-generating capacity of the OM I/O system. The information system helps to foster the process of keeping connected. Many kinds of data are regularly transmitted between participants. For example, information about what is selling—and what is in stock—leads to production scheduling decisions. It also leads to initiatives by the sales department. The levels of inventory are perpetually examined to make sure that no stock outages occur, and care is taken to keep track of what is in the finished goods inventory.

1-7 OM INPUT–OUTPUT PROFIT MODEL

The purpose of this section is to link the equation for profit—which is familiar to people in the business field—to the input–output transformation model.

The **I/O profit model** is derived from the costs and revenues shown in Figure 1-7. The model assigns the costs and revenues of the traditional equation of profit to the inputs, the outputs, and the transformation process—all based on a specific period of time (t).

In Equation 1-1, total costs, TC, are subtracted from revenue, R, yielding profit, P.

$$P = R - TC \qquad \text{(Equation 1-1)}$$

In Equation 1-2, total costs, TC, equal the sum of total fixed costs, FC, and total variable costs, $vc(V)$. The latter is the variable costs per unit (vc) multiplied by (V), which is volume in production units for the time period (t).

$$TC = FC + vc(V) \qquad \text{(Equation 1-2)}$$

Equation 1-3 represents the calculation of revenue where price per unit, p, is multiplied by V, sold in (t). $p(V)$ equals revenue.

$$R = p(V) \qquad \text{(Equation 1-3)}$$

Equation 1-4 is the statement of how the factors of profit (P) come together. It is useful in other ways as well. Setting profit equal to zero and solving for demand volume provides the breakeven volume. Questions surface about how demand volume changes according to the prices charged. Another interesting issue is the relationship of FC on vc.

$$P = R - TC = p(V) - FC - vc(V) = (p - vc)V - FC \qquad \text{(Equation 1-4)}$$

> **I/O profit model:** The input–output model captures all costs and revenues so profit can be determined.

1-7a How Has the Profit Model Changed over Time?

Nothing in the structure of the profit model has changed over time; the equations are the same. What has changed is the technology that the fixed costs can buy, and in turn, that investment affects the variable costs. In addition, there have been major changes in the knowledge base about the productivity of processes and the quality they can deliver. Knowledge has been developed that affects the volume of output that the fixed costs can deliver.

It is the production system (or the system of operations) embedded in the profit model that has changed a great deal. The performance of the input–output transformation system has been altered, resulting in increased productivity of the system. The architecture of the operating system has been changing for many years, but recently at an accelerated rate.

1-8 THE STAGES OF P/OM DEVELOPMENT

The profit model operates differently according to the stage of development of the company's input–output operating system. Therefore, the issue of stage is the next point to address. The *stage* reflects the degree to which a company's activities are planned for in a coordinated way. Thus, stage determines company effectiveness (ability to do the right thing) and efficiency (ability to do the thing right). As a company improves its stage of operations, it is expected that its profitability will increase. However, it is necessary to relate the company's stage of development to that of its competitors.

Each company's input–output profit model indirectly and directly reflects the impact of the competitors' input–output models. The cost structures, prices, volumes, and profit margins reflect the influence and extent of the competition. If the competitors all are at the same stage and one of them starts to move to a higher stage, the expected result is that the advancing company will gain market share, while the remaining companies experience a decrease in volume. This then gets translated into higher variable costs and lower profit margins. The OMs should be on top of the competitive analysis, which means that all participants fully understand the stages of development of all competing companies.

How a company manages its profit model provides insight into the role that P/OM can play in a company. Decisions concerning capacity and the resulting economies of scale capture only a portion of the story; the extent to which new technology is utilized to offset high variable labor costs also plays a part. The development stage relates as well to the management of the throughput rate, quality attainment, and variety achievement.

Stage I companies operate on the premise that there is no competitive advantage to be gained by changing the production process. Therefore, the process usually is relatively unrefined and often out-of-date. Management, seeing no leverage in processes, pays minimal attention to production and operations. Stage I firms squeak by on quality. Because the competitors are not much better, everyone appears indifferent. In such firms, management and its resources are insufficient to do more than keep up with demand. Survival occurs only when and if the competition is in the same boat. Marginal firms do not survive long in a market that is dominated by higher-stage companies.

1-8a Special OM Capabilities

At the other end of the spectrum, there are companies that use operations to gain unique basic advantages through the development of special capabilities. The concept of competing on capabilities is clearly formulated by Stalk, Evans, and Shulman.[5] The advantages gained can vary from speeding up distribution, to tactical superiority in managing inventories, or product preeminence obtained from effective product development and total quality management (TQM).

Stage IV companies practice *continuous improvement (CI)*, which means that they persistently remove waste. They aggressively seek to innovate in their unswerving pursuit of quality. Stage IV companies have a high level of basic advantages that are unique to them, whereas Stage I companies have virtually none. Stages II and III fall in-between on various scales of performance.

This approach is based on work done by Wheelwright and Hayes (W&H) cited in their article in the *Harvard Business Review*.[6] They have created a framework applicable to manufacturing firms (P of P/OM). This approach also utilizes work by Chase and Hayes (C&H) detailed in their article in the *Sloan Management Review*.[7] Their framework is applicable to service firms (OM of P/OM). This article puts together the concept of stages of development for both manufacturing and service firms.

1. A Stage I company is centered on meeting shipment quotas and providing service when requested. C&H call it "available for service," and cite, as an example, a government agency. A Stage I company has no planning horizon and is predisposed to be indifferent to P/OM goals. It is reactive to orders and has no quality agenda. Worker control is stressed. The company is not conscious of special capabilities for itself or for its competitors. W&H describe such firms as being internally neutral, which means that top management does not consider P/OM as able to promote competitive advantage and, therefore, P/OM is kept in neutral gear.

2. A Stage II company manages traditional P/OM processes and has a relatively short-term planning horizon. It makes efforts to secure orders and to meet customers' service desires. The primary goal of Stage II companies is to control costs. Quality tends to be

Stage IV companies aggressively seek to innovate and pursue quality. Thomas Edison said that "Genius is 1 percent inspiration, 99 percent perspiration." Stage IV companies do not shirk the hard work.

defined as products or services that are not worse than some standard. These companies consider the most important advantages to be derived from economies of scale, which means that as output volume increases, costs go down. W&H describe such firms as being externally neutral; they strive to have parity in P/OM matters with the competition.

3. A Stage III company installs and manages manufacturing and service processes that are equivalent to those used by the leading companies. C&H describe this as "distinctive service competence." A Stage III company makes efforts to emulate the special capabilities of the best companies. Quality and productivity improvement programs are utilized in an effort to be as good as the best. Stage III firms have a relatively long-term planning horizon supported by a detailed P/OM strategy. W&H describe such firms as being internally supportive, meaning that P/OM activities support the Stage III company's competitive position.

4. A Stage IV company is a P/OM innovator. It has short- and long-term planning horizons that are integrated. Long-term P/OM planning requires excellence in **project management** to bring about changes needed to adapt to new environments. Short–term P/OM involves meeting standards by controlling the production process. Both short and long are crucial elements in the success of the firm. Both demand that P/OM be a part of the top management strategy team because the production processes are held to be a source of unique advantage gained through special capabilities, as are product and service design.

    Project management is a P/OM responsibility that offers significant advantage to those in OM who know how to use project management methods to innovate quickly and successfully for competitive advantage. W&H describe such firms as externally supportive, which means that competitive strategy "rests to a significant degree on the firm's manufacturing capability." C&H conclude that Stage IV firms offer services that "raise customer expectations." Stage IV firms use the systems approach to integrate service and manufacturing activities.

Figure 1-8 provides a useful way to represent the classification system for the manufacturing and/or service system stages of P/OM development.

It takes a lot of work to progress through successive stages. It is unlikely that an existing P/OM organization can skip a stage. Only with total reorganization is it possible for a Stage I company to become a Stage III or IV. **Reengineering,** which is defined as starting from scratch to redesign a system, is an appealing way to circumvent bureaucratic arthritis and jump stages. However, it is costly and, if not done right, has a high risk of failure. Mastery of this P/OM text can lower that risk.

Project management: Managing non-repetitive activities in a way that is both professional and effective.

Reengineering: Term used to signify that the current processes are to be completely redone.

1-9 ORGANIZATIONAL POSITIONS AND CAREER OPPORTUNITIES IN P/OM

To qualify for an operations management job, there are several reasons it helps to have an undergraduate degree in business or an MBA. First, the degree aside, P/OM has much real content. There are many concepts to learn and a special P/OM language to master. Being comfortable with technology also is helpful. Understanding detailed technology remains an engineering specialty. The specific course of study for operations is demanding; there are entirely new phenomena to learn.

	Internally	Externally
Neutral	Stage I	Stage II
Supportive	Stage III	Stage IV

FIGURE 1-8
Stages of P/OM Development

A single, introductory course in P/OM will not suffice. The system's perspective, instrumental for success, requires knowledge of various business functions including marketing, finance, accounting, and human resources management. The business school is becoming a proponent of the systems approach. The ideal academic situation for a P/OM career is a concentration or major in P/OM. However, many graduates from other concentrations, with some exposure to P/OM, find themselves attracted to P/OM jobs.

1-9a Career Success and Types of Processes

It is essential when talking about careers in P/OM to recognize that *one of the major differences in P/OM jobs relates to the kinds of processes* that are involved in the transformation of inputs into outputs. This means such things as the continuity of processing, the number of units processed at one time, the volume of throughput between setups, and the degree of repetition of the operations.

It can be seen from the historical development of P/OM that manufacturing started with custom work, which in many ways resembles an artist at work. Consider the shoemaker who fits and makes the entire shoe for each customer. Most often, the left shoe differs from the right shoe. However, for store-bought shoes, such attention to fitting the customer is not possible.

Services often are of the custom variety. The medical doctor sees one patient at a time and treats that patient as warranted. Service processes can prosper by making them more like manufacturing. In time, manufacturing learned how to process small batches efficiently. Some service systems, like elevators, lend themselves to batch processes.

Continuous flow processes were developed by a variety of industries, including chemical processors, refineries, and auto assembly manufacturers. Fast-food chains emulated this kind of process to handle a continuous flow of information and to assemble hamburgers. Until the late 1970s, there were basically three different ways to get work done. A fourth was added when computers began to change the way processes were achieved. The four categories are:

- *Project.* Each project is a unique process, done once, like launching a new product, building a plant, or writing a book. Both service providers and manufacturers need to know how to plan and complete projects that are associated with the evolving goals of "temporary" organizations. Projects appeal to people who prefer nonrepetitive, constantly evolving, creative challenges. Projects do not attract people who opt for a stable environment and the security of fixed goals—associated with the flow shop. There is a unique profile of people who prefer the project environment to other process types and who excel in that milieu.

- *Batch processing.* Facilities are set up, and *n* units are made or processed at a time. Then the facility is reset for another job. When $n = 1$, or a very few, it is called *custom work,* and it is done in a custom shop. When *n* is more than a few, and the work is done in batches, it is called a *job shop.* The average batch size in job shops is 50. The work arrangement ceases to be a job shop when the work is done in serial flow shop fashion. With the job shop, many different kinds of goods and/or services can be processed. As the batch size gets larger for manufacturing or services, more effort is warranted to make the process efficient and to convert it to a serialized production system. Job shops, with their batch production systems, appeal to people who prefer repetitive assignments within a relatively hectic environment. The job shop generally involves a lot of people interactions and negotiations. The tempo of batch production is related to the number of setups, cleanups, and changeovers.

- *Flow shop processing.* As the batch size increases so that production can be serialized, either continuously or intermittently, it is rational for both manufacturing and services to pre-engineer the system. This means that balanced flow is designed for the process before it is ever run. It is expected that variable costs will decrease as the fixed-cost investments increase. Continuous process systems require a great deal of planning and investment. Flow shops run the gamut from crude setups arranged to run for short periods of times (such as days or weeks) to continuous process systems that have been carefully designed and pre-engineered for automation. The more automated processes appeal to people who like a controlled, stable, and well-planned system.

- *Flexible (programmable) processing systems.* As far back as the 1980s, a new process category began to emerge that continues to grow faster than any other P/OM segment. Flexibility is derived from the combination of computers controlling machines, making this option the high-tech career choice. People who enjoy working with computers prefer these technologically-based environments. There are two aspects to this attraction. First is the application of the technology to do the work, and second is the programming of the computers to instruct and control the equipment that does the work. Associated with the adoption of the new technology is much experimentation. Openness to learning is essential because the systems are continuously changing and need high levels of adaptability.

An assessment has found that this category continues to grow, but the extent of its application has narrowed. Flexibility has been stymied by design constraints and higher costs than had been expected. Each product design decision removes degrees of freedom for further design opportunities. The second crankshaft is easier to make than the seventh one. While progress has been slowed, there is belief that *mastery* of flexible technology will continue to be improved. Investments in FMS are conditioned by the payoffs resulting from being able to increase variety without incurring large setup costs for each new product design being made on the same production line (called *economies of scope*).

There are specific categories of people who prefer working in different process surroundings. There are also people who prefer either manufacturing or services; these issues usually are more important than type of industry preferences. For example, airplanes and automobiles are both assembly-oriented industries. Real advantages often accrue to both industries from employee cross-hiring. However, industrial preferences do play a part in career choice.

The same should be said about preferences for different kinds of service industries. A person having expertise in the hotel business is likely to gravitate among resorts, hotels, and restaurants with a great deal of crossover between them. The Ritz Carlton Corporation has made some remarkable competitive strides with respect to the quality of hotel service that can be applied broadly to this class of service. Club Med, which represents one of the best of the resort industry, has a very strong—transferable—P/OM orientation.[8] Media and entertainment are two other service areas with a strong draw on career selection.

Certain industries and services have intense regionality, i.e., Florida, Hawaii, and the Caribbean for the resort business; Michigan and Tennessee for automotive activities; New York City for publishing and entertainment; Amsterdam for diamonds. Starbucks is growing in Japan, and tourists walk past Starbuck's Café in Beijing's Forbidden City in China. Other service industries like McDonald's and Wendy's have their ups and downs depending upon local economies, competitors, and so forth. A few other service organizations must include Mr. Goodwrench, The Gap, and Century Theaters. All of these are widely spread over the map. People have strong regional preferences. Operations must take these into account.

1-9b Operations Management Career Paths

There are many different kinds of P/OM careers. No one can describe all of them because the scenarios of opportunity are always changing. Consider the *actual* pattern of developments that started with Y2K (the year 2000). The Y2K fear was that computers would be unreliable when the calendar shifted from 1XXX to 2XXX. Computers, with fixes for changing two-digit dates into four-digit dates, worked well.

However, as the year 2000 took effect, it was people who became irrational. Technology hardly failed at all. In ways that are strikingly similar to scripts written by ratings-driven writers of TV shows and box office–driven movie writers, the main themes were *money greed on Wall Street, irrational politics in Washington, DC, and real-life fanatics copying the movies to create the World Trade Center disaster of 9/11/01.* These events underlie the changes that are occurring in operations management. For example, the management of security operations at airports has changed markedly in scope and importance. The importance of operations-oriented accounting to identify real costs, cash flow, and breakeven points is another example of new P/OM careers.

Line position means responsibility for producing product or service. The term comes from working on the production line. *Staff* positions by definition are not on the production line, but supportive of the line. Staff positions provide information, guidance, and advice on topics such as cost, qualities, suppliers, inventories, and work schedules. Titles for both line and staff positions vary in different companies, and specific details of responsibilities would differ for each position. However, the generalities regarding accountability remain the same.

Knowing about career paths provides a useful perspective for a person starting the study of P/OM. It should be noted, however, that the field is dynamic and changing. It is involved in organizational experimentation with teamwork and the systems approach. The use of multifunctional teams is increasing and likely to spawn new kinds of positions and career opportunities.

1-9c Global Aspects of Career Paths

Among the vast possibilities of exciting new careers are managers of global P/OM support networks, which need to connect and synchronize factories and service systems located all over the world. P/OM is an international endeavor. With the North American Free Trade Agreement (NAFTA) accepted and the General Agreement on Tariffs and Trade (GATT) being implemented, the European Union (EU) is a giant market for goods and services as well as a new environment for manufacturing and service operations. The Pacific Rim has come alive with manufacturing, and great new markets are opening up in Southeast Asia. The agreement to create a free trade zone for the Americas stretching from Alaska to Argentina (34 countries including the United States) is yet another indicator of the internationalization of operations management. Suppliers from everywhere will be competing in the global market. A career in P/OM will involve much travel and an equally large amount of global communication. All of the careers that are listed will require the ability to coordinate and synchronize systems on a global scale.

Manufacturing jobs are followed by a list of service professions. Both include line and staff positions. Titles can only approximate the progression from top management through middle management to first-level management. For services there is an even greater problem to get titles that fairly represent progression through the management hierarchy.

In the following list, twelve traditional career paths are provided that highlight differences between line and staff positions.

P/OM Careers in Manufacturing—Line
1. Corporate Vice President of Manufacturing
2. Divisional Manager of Production
3. Plant Manager
4. Vice President of Materials Management
5. Project Manager of Transitions
6. Department Foreman or Forelady, Department Supervisor

P/OM Careers in Manufacturing—Staff
7. Director of Quality
8. Inventory Manager, Materials Manager, or Purchasing Agent
9. Production Schedule Controller
10. Project Manager/Consultant (Internal or External)

11. Performance Improvement Manager
12. Methods Analyst

P/OM Careers in Services—Line
1. Corporate Vice President of Operations
2. Divisional Manager of Operations
3. Administrative Head
4. Department Manager or Supervisor
5. Facilities Manager
6. Branch Manager or Store Manager

P/OM Careers in Services—Staff
7. Quality Supervisor
8. Materials Manager or Purchasing Agent
9. Project Manager/Consultant (Internal or External)
10. Staff Schedule Controller
11. Performance Improvement Manager
12. Systems or Methods Analyst

By explaining some of the titles in more detail, it is possible to provide quick insight into various aspects of the P/OM field. Also, it further clarifies differences between manufacturing and service systems.

1-9d Manager of Production—Manufacturing or Service Operations

The manager of operations in services and the production manager in a manufacturing plant are in line positions, meaning that they are responsible for the inputs, the outputs, and the transformation process. They work with technology and a hierarchy of people to oversee the production of the product. As a rule, they report to the corporate vice president who, in turn, reports to the president of the company. Middle managers and selected staff functions report to them. This is a high-level position, but the character of the job depends upon the stage of the company. In Stage IV firms, this person will regularly be invited to lunch in the boardroom because of top management's keen interest in operations.

1-9e Department Supervisor

The supervisor's position is a line job. In manufacturing, the supervisor, who is often called the *foreman* (or *forelady* or *foreperson*), typically oversees some part of the production process. In service operations, the title of supervisor commonly describes the person responsible for some specific function such as reservations and ticket processing or insurance premium collection. The workers look to the foreman or supervisor for help with problems that arise. Fewer firms today consider the supervisor a police officer who makes sure that everyone is doing their job. To signal this change, many firms are calling both workers on the line and their supervisors "associates." Japanese companies in the United States started using the term *associate* to describe workers as well as supervisors with the idea of empowering employees. Similar practices can now be found among companies all over the world.

In many factories, supervisory jobs are held by people who are promoted from the shop floor. The same applies to service operations. At the same time, some companies like to place a new business graduate into a foreman's job so they can learn the ropes. It is not unusual for a foreman to become the operations manager, but in many companies an engineering degree for manufacturing and a business degree for services are considered desirable.

1-9f Inventory Manager or Materials Manager

The inventory or materials manager holds a staff position that is accountable for controlling the flow of input materials to the line. The function of this job is to determine when and how much to order, and how much stock to keep on hand. There are myriad titles associated with these jobs. Many manufacturing and some service firms have vice presidents of materials management because the cost of materials as a percent of the total cost of goods sold is high. In service firms like McDonald's and American Airlines, materials are similarly important.

1-9g Director of Quality

There are a great number of jobs in the quality assurance area and even more titles. Most of these jobs are staff positions that range from auditing quality levels to doing statistical analyses for control charts. The director of quality or quality manager (who could be a vice president) is in charge of the various quality activities that are going on in the firm. In some companies, line workers have been given quality responsibilities, so it is possible to find supervisors with quality team assignments. Quality adjustments to inputs, including vendors, and to the transformation process are common. Quality positions usually focus on improving the quality of outputs by inspecting for defects, preventing them from happening, and correcting their causes. Quality management is just as important in service firms as it is in firms manufacturing goods, but it is more elusive and, therefore, challenging to deal with it.

1-9h Project Manager/Consultant (Internal or External)

There are important P/OM jobs relating to projects, which can include the development of new products and services as well as the processes to make and deliver them. Constructing a refinery, putting the space station into orbit, writing this CD/book—all are projects. Consultants, both internal and external, are usually engaged in project management. External consultants are employees of a consulting firm. P/OM is an excellent entree for a consulting career. Internal consulting applies only to the company for which the employee works (e.g., GE and Bristol Meyers are two companies that have very successful records using their own internal consultants).

During these turbulent times, transition management is used with various scenarios such as downsizing, turnarounds, and business process redesign. Companies have created positions that indicate responsibility for some form of transition in the job title. For example, a project manager of transitions is in charge of downsizing or rightsizing the company, turnarounds—restoring a company that is in trouble to good financial health, and reengineering—starting from scratch to redesign the firm. Various new job titles have appeared to indicate that the management of change is in place.

1-9i Performance Improvement Manager

Continuous improvement (CI) is a new item on the agenda of many companies. There are a variety of jobs that signify a company's interest in pursuing CI goals. The titles of such positions are more varied than most others in the P/OM field. For example, PIPs are Productivity Improvement Programs, and some firms have appointed managers to head these initiatives. In general, performance improvement managers are hybrids. They work on improving processes by means of total quality management (TQM), which includes waste reduction and value-added augmentation. They are likely to be responsible for coordinating supplier activities to achieve just-in-time (JIT) deliveries. Fast-paced project development is another responsibility. Another new title is based on variants of the words for best-in-class benchmarking, which means comparing the system with the best one. In this category, as well as with the project manager/consultant mentioned earlier, there exist reengineering titles that represent new opportunities for P/OM.

SUMMARY

The chapter begins with an explanation of production and operations management (P/OM) and introduces the use of models by operations managers. Next, the systems approach is defined as systematic and constructive methodology using a systems taxonomy. The importance of the systems approach as employed by P/OM is detailed and explored with examples. The application of P/OM to manufacturing of goods has similarities and differences compared to its application to services. In that context, production management is compared to operations management. It is explained how information systems play a vital role in both manufacturing and services. The basic model of P/OM—the input–output transformation model—is developed, along with the costs and revenue that are associated with its use. This leads to a discussion of the input–output profit model and how it has changed over time. The stages of P/OM development are introduced with attention paid to special capabilities derived from P/OM that allow a company to reach highly competitive stages of development. This leads to deliberation about the kind of P/OM positions that might be encountered by another manager in the organization, as well as the type of careers that P/OM offers.

Two Spotlight feature boxes conclude this chapter. These boxes illustrate real applications of the materials in the chapter. See Spotlight 1-1: Atomic Dog Publishing and Spotlight 1-2: Alliance for Innovative Manufacturing (AIM).

KEY TERMS

Functional field approach

Information systems

I/O profit model

Manufacturing

OM system

Operations

Operations management

Production

Production management

Project management

Reengineering

Service

Systems approach

Transformation

REVIEW QUESTIONS

1. What is operations management? Define OM. Compare it to P/OM. Distinguish between production and operations management.

2. What are the differentiating characteristics of services as compared to those of manufacturing? Illustrate the distinctive aspects of each by naming industries and citing specific companies that represent each.

3. To what category of P/OM does hotel management belong? What fixed and variable costs are appropriate for this industry?

4. To what category of P/OM does agricultural management belong? What fixed and variable costs are appropriate for this industry?

5. How do information systems relate to operations management?

6. Why is the systems approach essential to assure real participation of OM in a firm? What does the systems approach have to do with company strategy?

7. What types of costs are usually associated with inputs? Give specific examples from the education field.

8. What costs are identified with the equipment that provides transformations? Give specific examples from the fields of manufacturing and transportation.

9. How do outputs convert into dollars of revenue? How are these dollars related to fixed and variable costs as described in Questions 7 and 8?

10. Explain the stages of P/OM development and try to identify some companies that might be representative of each stage.

11. What changes have occurred over time in the following profit model?

$$P = (p - vc)V - FC$$

12. Describe career paths of P/OM for both manufacturing and service systems.

PROBLEMS SECTION

1. Develop the transformation process to
   a. produce #2 lead pencils.
   b. bake bread.
   c. complete this homework assignment.

2. Draw the input–output model that could be used to run a hotel. Label the variable costs for labor and materials, and detail those costs. What are the fixed costs for this model?

3. What are the headings for the columns and the titles for the rows? The stages refer to the development level of the P/OM function.

	Stage I	Stage II
	Stage III	Stage IV

4. Draw an input–output model for a Burger King fast-food outlet. Label as many of the specific and detailed inputs and outputs as you can. (Use Figure 1-7 as a model of categories to include.) What transformations link the inputs with the outputs? (It may be helpful to visit a Burger King. Observe what is going on and if possible talk to the manager about how they cook and assemble their food.)

5. Repeat what you have done in Problem 4 for a McDonald's fast-food outlet. (You may want to visit a McDonald's. As mentioned earlier, observe what you can and talk to the manager if possible.) Then, make a detailed comparison between Burger King and McDonald's.

6. A manufacturing plant and equipment cost $120 million and are estimated to have a lifetime of 20 years. Straight-line depreciation is to be used. Additional fixed costs per year are $4 million. Variable costs are $1.50 and price is set at $2.50. What will annual profit be if the annual volume is
   a. 10 million units?
   b. 5 million units?
   c. 20 million units?
   d. 8 million units?

7. A manufacturing plant and equipment cost $120 million and are estimated to have a lifetime of 20 years. Straight-line depreciation is to be used. Additional fixed costs per year are $4 million. Variable costs are $2.50 and price is set at $3.50. What will annual profit be if the annual volume is 10 million units?

8. A manufacturing plant and equipment cost $180 million and are estimated to have a lifetime of 30 years. Straight-line depreciation is to be used. Additional fixed costs per year are $4 million. Variable costs are $1.50 and price is set at $2.50. What will annual profit be if the annual volume is 10 million units?

9. A service center has installed a new computer system with local area networking at a cost of $1.6 million. The system is expected to serve for 8 years, and straight-line depreciation is acceptable. There are additional fixed costs of $300,000 per year. This service repair center charges each customer a flat fee of $30. The variable costs are $20. What will profit be if the annual volume is
   a. 50,000 units?
   b. 25,000 units?
   c. 75,000 units?

10. Four companies are described as follows. Characterize each in terms of the stage of P/OM development that seems appropriate as described in Section 1-8. Classify each situation and explain the reason for the classification used.
    a. This manufacturer pays little attention to the quality of the product. The owner is convinced that customers are plentiful but not loyal. Hard sell is stressed.
    b. This service organization tries to keep up with its competitors by copying everything they do as soon as possible. The president believes that development costs are saved and that being a fast imitator results in a competitive advantage.
    c. This manufacturer is constantly working at being as good as the best of the competitors. They have improved quality repeatedly while holding costs constant. The production manager participates in strategy formulation.
    d. This service organization aims at global leadership based on the finest operations in the world. The service is constantly being improved, which gives the organization a proactive leadership role in its industry.

END-OF-CHAPTER QUESTIONS

1. Production and operations management is symbolized by P/OM because
   a. production management is more important than operations management.
   b. production and operations management are identical and of equal importance.
   c. production and operations management are similar in many important ways.
   d. production management is less important than operations management.
   e. the International Standards Association in Geneva chose that designation.

2. The distinction between production and operations is best described as
   a. production makes goods; operations delivers services.
   b. production is automobile manufacturing; operations is everything else.
   c. production is heavy manufacturing; operations are light manufacturing.
   d. operations are associated with banks, airlines, insurance companies, and restaurants only; production is everything else.
   e. Shakespeare in *A Midsummer Night's Dream* (while thou dost operate; yet not produce a single product).

3. The Greyhound Bus driver's productivity (miles driven per day) is measured by m where $m = vt$, where v is velocity and t is time driven per day (see Section 1-1a). If the company was to increase the length of a driver's shift from $t = 8$ to $t = 10$ hours, how would driver productivity change?
   a. The equation $m = 10v$ reflects a productivity increase of 50% over $m = 8v$.
   b. The equation $m = 10v$ reflects a productivity increase of 25% over $m = 8v$.
   c. The equation $m = 10v$ reflects a productivity increase of 15% over $m = 8v$.
   d. The equation is irrelevant because the driver's performance will be affected by traffic.
   e. The driver's performance is tracked by computer using GPS, and management will penalize drivers for unscheduled stops.

4. The distinction between strategies and tactics is best described by which of the following statements?
   a. Good strategies overpower poor tactics.
   b. Strategies are plans; tactics are objectives; they work together.
   c. The strategy is *make 1,000 SUVs per shift*; the tactic is *never on Sundays*.
   d. The strategy is *no work on Sundays*; the tactic is *make 982 SUVs per shift*.
   e. Good strategies are not "good" if the best tactics are not good enough.

5. The functional field approach to P/OM is
   a. primarily tactical in its perspective.
   b. essentially strategic in its point of view.
   c. not well-represented by a traditional organization chart.
   d. connected, coordinated, and interrelated with marketing.
   e. connected, coordinated, and interrelated with finance.

6. The systems approach to P/OM is
   a. primarily tactical in its perspective.
   b. essentially strategic in its point of view.
   c. not well-represented by a traditional organization chart.
   d. independent of marketing and finance goals.
   e. challenged to achieve teamwork.

7. The systems approach is based on a powerful philosophy. Which of the following statements is most accurate?
   a. There is one systems approach but two different schools of thought.
   b. The systemic approach is typical of the analytical Western-world approach.
   c. The systematic approach is typical of the holistic Eastern-world philosophy.
   d. The joint contributions of introspection and extraspection are not systematic.
   e. The constructive approach is neither systemic nor systematic.

8. The input–output model (I-T-O) defines production and operations. Managing the model is what P/OM does because
   a. engineering is required to manage transformations.
   b. economic theory is required to manage input rates.
   c. marketing management is required to manage output rates.
   d. the input–output model operates with random transformations (T).
   e. I-T-O captures all the costs and revenues of the system.

9. Stages of P/OM development are beneficial for benchmarking the status of a firm.
   a. Stage I characterizes SMB (SMB = small and medium-size businesses).
   b. Stage IV firms are large-size business organizations.
   c. Stages are useful to assess the firm's prospects for future development.
   d. Transitions from Stage I to Stage III are common because only internal issues are involved.
   e. Transitions from Stage III to Stage IV require changing a neutral stance to a supportive stance.

10. Career opportunities of many kinds exist in the P/OM field. Before seeking specific careers, it is important to sort out the truth from fiction. One of the following statements is false. Which one is it?
    a. Jobs requirements and expectations are different according to the type of P/OM process.
    b. Flow shop processing fits well with managers who enjoy stabilizing and controlling systems.
    c. Managers who like to work with many people in hectic environments do well in the batch production environments, which include many service systems.
    d. Global firms require that their managers speak many languages.
    e. The profile of managers who do well with projects is well-known and unique.

ADDITIONAL READINGS

Abernathy, William J., K. B. Clark, and A. M. Kantrow. *Industrial Renaissance*. New York: Basic Books, 1983.

Chase, Richard B., and Robert H. Hayes. "Beefing-Up Operations in Service Firms." *Sloan Management Review* (Fall 1991): 17–28.

Horovitz, Jacques. *Winning Ways: Achieving Zero-Defect Service*. Productivity Press, 1990.

Levitt, Theodore. "Production-Line Approach to Service." *Harvard Business Review* (September–October 1972).

Müller-Merbach, Heiner. "A System of Systems Approaches." *Interfaces*, vol. 24, no. 4 (July–August 1994): 16–25.

Parkinson, C. Northcote. *Parkinson's Law*. Boston: Houghton Mifflin Company, 1957.

Peters, Tom, and R. H. Waterman, Jr. *In Search of Excellence*. New York: Basic Books, 1983.

Stalk, George, Philip Evans, and Lawrence E. Shulman. "Competing on Capabilities: The New Rules of Corporate Strategy." *Harvard Business Review* (March–April 1992): 57–69.

Tihamér von Ghyczy, "The Fruitful Flaws of Strategy Metaphors," *Harvard Business Review* (September 2003): 86–94.

Wheelwright, Steven C., and Robert H. Hayes. "Competing Through Manufacturing." *Harvard Business Review* (January–February 1985): 99–109.

NOTES

1. Heiner Müller-Merbach. "A System of Systems Approaches." *Interfaces*, vol. 24, no. 4 (July–August 1994): 16–25.

2. Ibid, 16–17.

3. Ibid, 17.

4. Theodore Levitt. "Production-Line Approach to Service." *Harvard Business Review* (September–October 1972). Although this article is old, it is still totally relevant. It is considered a classic. Our interpretation of "idiosyncratic" is eccentric and erratic.

5. George Stalk, Philip Evans, and Lawrence E. Shulman. "Competing on Capabilities: The New Rules of Corporate Strategy." *Harvard Business Review* (March–April 1992): 57–69.

6. Steven C. Wheelwright and Robert H. Hayes. "Competing Through Manufacturing." *Harvard Business Review* (January–February 1985): 99–109.

7. Richard B. Chase and Robert H. Hayes. "Beefing-Up Operations in Service Firms." *Sloan Management Review* (Fall 1991): 17–28.

8. Jacques Horovitz. *Winning Ways: Achieving Zero-Defect Service*. Productivity Press, 1990.

SPOTLIGHT 1-1
Atomic Dog Publishing

Atomic Dog Publishing—A Better Way

Cincinnati, Ohio
www.atomicdog.com

Founded in March 2000, Atomic Dog Publishing (ADP) is a next generation publishing company that specializes in developing web-based print and interactive textbooks. ADP's textbooks blend online content delivery, interactive multimedia components, and print to form a completely unique learning and teaching environment.

From the outset, the company's publications are designed to be immediate (evergreen content), interactive, and affordable (25 to 40 percent less than competitive titles).

Traditional Publishing Model

The traditional textbook publishing process is linear—a textbook project begins at a certain point and proceeds systematically through a series of steps. It is one-way—the end-user of the textbook has very little input or influence on the process.

Traditional Process

For higher education publishers looking to move their textbooks online, breaking down decades' worth of content, in some cases, and managing those digital assets once completed compose just one part of the challenge. A second, even more daunting, part is developing a textbook delivery platform. The integration of traditional print content with multimedia technologies is yet another. Instead of addressing the problem in a holistic way, most publishers have chosen to tackle the content problem and find partners in order to cobble together a delivery solution.

However, if a publishing company is truly serious about building interactive, digital textbooks, then it must change the entire publishing model, from author acquisition to sales and marketing. The rich media capabilities, dynamic interaction, immediate delivery, and demand for timeliness that the web represents require a complete rethinking of *"What is a textbook?"* Most publishers are not in a position to undertake such a radical transformation and at the same time protect their existing business models.

Atomic Dog Publishing Model

ADP's publishing model is a continuous process, with feedback across all levels, and one where end-users (students and instructors) play an integral role. Atomic Dog has three functional groups that do not exist within a traditional publishing company—Interactive Media, Engineering, and Quality Assurance (QA)/Customer Support.

Interactive Media works with authors and editors to develop a storyboard calling for key animations and interactive learning objects. Static charts, figures, tables, and references to external material take on new meaning in a digital textbook. Authors have to break free from traditional thinking and embrace the pedagogical possibilities of a digital textbook.

In addition to technology development, Engineering is concerned with the conversion of content (manuscript) source files into XML and bringing the content into ADP's proprietary learning environment.

Quality Assurance has two key roles—(1) enforcing strict quality standards across all functional groups (as shown by the following box) and (2) interacting with and supporting the end-users, both students and instructors. During the production process, Interactive Media and Engineering work with the production team to produce equivalent online and print versions of the textbook.

When work is completed by Production and Engineering, the textbook is handed over to QA for final testing and sign-off before being "released." After adoption by an instructor, QA/Customer Support interacts with students and instructors to answer registration and usage questions, as well as collect feedback on problems and new feature requests. The process then feeds back into itself, resulting in a continuously evolving textbook—analogous to a software revision process.

New Breed Publishing Model

The power of the Atomic Dog Publishing Model is that it is continuous, nonlinear, highly interactive, and designed to get its products to market faster and at lower cost than traditional publishers.

Source: Atomic Dog Publishing.

SPOTLIGHT 1-2
Alliance for Innovative Manufacturing (AIM)

Take an Online Plant Tour at Home with AIM: How Everyday Things Are Made

Stanford University, through a cooperative venture with industry partners in the Alliance for Innovative Manufacturing (AIM), takes students on plant visits and guided tours of many kinds. The material is exceptionally well-designed and informative. Over 40 different products and processes with over 4 hours of video are available to build an understanding of how things are made. For example, there is a 13-minute video on how to make glass bottles. Knowledgeable guides talk the viewer through the stages and steps of processes as well as products. There are 12 minutes on casting, 20 minutes on molding plastics, 17 minutes on forming and shaping, about 5 minutes on machining, and 4 minutes of video on assembly operations. There are video controls for pause, slow down, etc. Exercises take the form of "what did you learn," "think about it," and FAQs. There is about an hour of video discussing careers in manufacturing. Dr. Mark Martin is the host of many other experts from industry. Finally, here are some of the "how they are made" products: airplanes, motorcycles (and engines), cars, jelly beans, chocolate, and clothes.

Don't miss this chance to find out what every P/OM student (manufacturing or service) needs to understand. It took a long time for many smart people to figure out how to make all the things we take for granted.

The AIM website references books that are of the same genre. A very significant series is available that describes *How Products Are Made*. These are published by Gale Publishing of Thomson-Gale. The seventh volume was published in March 2002. The first volume is dated December, 1993. About 250 firms are listed sponsors and supporters of these not inexpensive reference books, which explain in detail (but not for engineers) how silver, paper currency, pianos, and hundreds of other products are made. "The set includes everything from artificial turf to the artificial heart valve" [*American Reference Books Annual (ARBA)*, January 2003].

At the same website, AIM references *Watch It Made in the U.S.A.: A Visitor's Guide to the Companies That Make Your Favorite Products*, 3d ed., by Karen Axelrod and Bruce Brumberg. The publisher is Avalon Travel Publishing, and this edition was published in September 2002. This book describes more than 300 companies that are open for actual plant visits. There is information about hours and fees (90 percent are free) for factories, visitor centers, and company museums across the country. There is additional information at http://www.factorytour.com.

AIM deserves much credit for its efforts. It is referred to as a continuous learning community composed of industry practitioners and academics (both students and faculty) qualify.

Source: The New York Times, Circuits, September 11, 2003; http://manufacturing.stanford.edu; and http://www.stanford.edu/group/AIM.

Supplement 1 Decision Models

A Distribution Problem: How to Ship—Plane or Train?

A decision matrix arranges outcome data into rows and columns. The following matrix presents a decision problem where the rows are shipping "strategies" (plane or train) and the columns are "states of nature"—so called because they are events not under the decision-maker's control. In this case, the states of nature are weather conditions.

Outcomes are the entries in the cells of the matrix. They will reflect the fact that planes will be delayed if there is fog, while trains are not affected by the weather. The buyer has promised the shipper a bonus if the delivery can be early. Conversely, the buyer sets a penalty if the delivery is delayed. The decision problem is organized by the matrix as follows:

Probabilities	Low	High
States of Nature	Fog (F)	Clear (C)
Strategy 1: Plane	Delayed	Early
Strategy 2: Train	On time	On time

Before putting numbers in this matrix, look at the symbolic representation of the following decision matrix. It shows outcomes as $O(i,j)$ where i represents different strategies (rows), and j represents different states of nature (columns). Also, the probabilities of the states of nature—obtained by some forecasting method—are represented by $p(j)$'s, $j = $ either F or C.

Probabilities	p(F)	p(C)
States of Nature	Fog	Clear
Strategy 1: Plane	$O(P,F)$	$O(P, C)$
Strategy 2: Train	$O(T,F)$	$O(T,C)$

CALCULATING THE NUMERICAL OUTCOMES OR PAYOFFS

Assume the following set of values describes the profit that the shipper gets if the delivery is early, late, or on time. Weather permitting, the flight arrives on time and the company makes $4,500. If the flight is delayed, the firm can still earn $1,500. Train delivery will earn $3,000 either way because the train arrival time will not be subject to weather. In addition, shipment by plane costs $800 and by train $300. These costs will be subtracted from the profits. Often, the payoff portion of the matrix is calculated by formulas or observations. The payoff matrix for each outcome is shown with probabilities of 0.1 and 0.9 obtained from weather forecasts. (Note: The sum of the probabilities must always be equal to one.)

Probabilities		0.1	0.9
States of Nature		Fog	Clear
	Cost		
Strategy 1: Plane	–800	+$1,500	+$4,500
Strategy 2: Train	–300	+$3,000	+$3,000

After subtraction:

Probabilities	0.1	0.9
States of Nature	Fog (F)	Clear (C)
Strategy 1: Plane	+$700	+$3,700
Strategy 2: Train	+$2,700	+$2,700

Calculating the Expected Values (EV)

An expected value is a measure of the average outcome. There is an expected value for each strategy. It is obtained by multiplying the probabilities for each state of nature by the outcome in that column and adding the products across all of the columns. The computing formulas are shown here:

$$EV(Plane) = p(F) \times O(P,F) + p(C) \times O(P,C)$$
$$EV(Train) = p(F) \times O(T,F) + p(C) \times O(T,C)$$

Now using numbers:

$$EV(Plane) = 0.1 \times 700 + 0.9 \times 3700 = 3,400*$$
$$EV(Train) = 0.1 \times 2700 + 0.9 \times 2700 = 2,700$$

The decision—noted by an asterisk—is to ship by plane because that strategy has an expected value of $3,400 whereas the expected value for shipping by train is EV(Train)$2,700.

Problem for Supplement 1

1. The forecast of 0.1 and 0.9 is based on last year's weather. When the past five years of weather data is consulted, the following results are obtained.

Year	1	2	3	4	5
P(Fog)	0.1	0.2	0.3	0.2	0.5

Determine the best strategy for each year. Then decide how to use all of the weather data to reach the best possible decision.

P/OM's Key Role in Productivity Attainment

Chapter Outline

his section illustrates the existing competitive edge organizations gain by using P/OM planning and decision making. P/OM is the function responsible for creating and running highly productive systems. The history of operations management has been to continually invent and develop methods that improve productivity.

After reading this chapter, you should be able to:

- Understand the importance of productivity to an organization.
- Evaluate the applicability of various measures of productivity.
- Explain what contributes to good productivity.
- Discuss how to improve productivity.
- Explain why productivity is a systems issue.
- Relate productivity and price–demand elasticity as a systems link between P/OM and marketing.

- Describe the effects of quality on elasticity and explain why this type of elasticity is critical to P/OM.
- Apply the concepts of economies of scale and division of labor to the management of operations.
- Explain how the history of P/OM shows continual improvement in the P/OM input–output transformation model with resultant increases in productivity.

THE SYSTEMS VIEWPOINT

Productivity gets good grades when a high rate of output is obtained at low cost. This is the case even when the output is hard to measure, as in some service operations. Although P/OM is custodian of the production process and responsible for its productivity, everyone in the company is involved in attaining excellence in productivity. Everyone has the ability to increase or decrease the organization's productivity. Those managers who have cultivated the systems point of view recognize that good productivity is contagious; so is poor productivity. Employees sense whether the company culture promotes high or low productivity, and they respond in accordance with the cultural norm. This makes the productivity condition a contagion factor with systems-wide implications.

Another strong systems-type interaction relates to price–demand elasticity, which links the price charged and the volume that can be sold. Competitive pressures to reduce prices lead to demands that P/OM improve productivity to decrease costs. Also, business lost because of price competition decreases volume, which reduces capacity utilization, leading to larger overhead charges per unit. Reductions in discounts that are based on volume increase variable costs per unit.

From a broader point of view, P/OM history shows that the overall trend in global economies is to increase productivity. Productivity growth has reflected the impact of a continuous stream of developments in technology and operations management methodology.

STRATEGIC THINKING

A highly productive manufacturer of buggy whips in 1926 would be no better off today than an inefficient and lackadaisical one. The most productive maker of engineering slide rules during the 1950s was Keuffel & Esser. Although this company had the largest market share then, it is no longer in existence. K & E did not have a strategy to cope with the advent of electronic calculators and then computers. High productivity is necessary but not sufficient to assure competitiveness.

Adaptability is critical when product design technology (or style) changes. For example, the most efficient supplier of iceboxes had no advantage when refrigerators replaced the older technology. Additionally, some companies were really good at making vinyl records (collectors items now) but that did not help them survive rapid changes as the music industry moved from 8-track tapes to 8 mm audiocassettes to CDs and now to DVDs. Regarding videotape formats, the Betamax system by Sony was the first successful commercial product. Matsushita aggressively pursued the VHS format, which replaced Betamax but that is of little consequence now since DVDs are outmoding any tape system. Five-and-a-quarter floppy disks have disappeared, and 3.5 inch floppy disks are on the way to oblivion as well.

The lesson to learn from all of these cases is that productivity excellence is useless without market acceptance. P/OM strategic thinking is "find the best product configurations and then make them at the lowest cost, highest quality, and overall at max productivity levels." As Peter Drucker is quoted to have said, "Do the right thing, and then do the thing right." Strategy planning for operations is directly concerned with "Do the right thing."

Later on, there will be attention paid to the strategies of choosing the "right" processes. *Product design* and *product development* lead to *process design* and *process development*. Product and process are both components of the strategic imperatives for P/OM.

2-1 PRODUCTIVITY—A MAJOR P/OM ISSUE

Productivity is a critical business variable that directly impacts the "bottom line"; improved productivity raises net profits. P/OM is responsible for the productivity of the process. This is such a critical factor in a company's overall productivity that excellence in productivity achievement is a major P/OM issue.

Productivity is a system property that interacts with other system properties such as reliability and consistency, as well as customers' perceptions of quality. Productivity interacts with the variable costs of goods and services, as well as with the fixed costs of facilities, training, and technology. Productivity interacts with the availability of management as a resource (say) on the regular work shift as compared to the "graveyard" shift.

2-1a The Measurement of Productivity

Productivity measures the performance of the organization's processes for doing work. The American Production and Inventory Control Society (APICS) definition follows, but other definitions also will be given. Productivity is an important way of grading how well P/OM and the rest of the system are doing. Productivity is a score like RBIs (runs batted in) or ROI (return on investment).

Productivity is defined as "an overall measure of the ability to produce a good or a service. It is the actual output of production compared to the actual input of resources. Productivity is a relative measure across time or against common entities. In the production literature, attempts have been made to define **total productivity** where the effects of labor and capital are combined and divided into the output."[1]

Operations management views the measurement of productivity as essential for assessing the performance of the organization's productive capacity over time and in comparison to the competition. Operations management, from a production point of view,

Total productivity: See
Multifactor productivity.

views productivity as the ratio of output over input. When outputs are high and inputs are low, the system is said to be efficient and productive.

$$\text{productivity} = \frac{\text{outputs}}{\text{inputs}} = \text{measure of production efficiency}$$

The productivity measure compares the quantity of goods or services produced in a period of time (t) and the quantity of resources employed in turning out these goods or services in the same period of time (t).[2]

This measure is relatively easy to accomplish for physical goods. It is more difficult to find appropriate measures for some services. Measuring the outputs for education, health care, and creative knowledge work provide some instances of intangibles that are highly valued, but elusive to calculate. The effort has to be made to appraise the value of these outputs in a standardized way in order to provide a benchmark (or standard) for measurement.

Sales perceives productivity as high customer sales volume (called an *effective marketing system*) accompanied by low producer costs (called an *efficient producer system*). Thus:

$$\text{productivity} = \frac{\text{effectiveness}}{\text{efficiency}} = \frac{\text{high customer sales volume}}{\text{low producer expenses}}$$

From a systems point of view, the inclusion of sales provides a correct measure of productivity. It is hardly productive to make a lot of product that is not sold, even if the cost of making it is low.

At the same time, P/OM employs productivity measures to assess how well the production system is functioning. The kinds of questions that are being addressed are: how many resources are consumed to produce the output, and how many units of output can be made with a fixed amount of capacity?

Both ways of viewing productivity have benefits. They stem from different interests that need to be shared. The best interests of the company are served by merging what is learned about P/OM's efficiency and sales effectiveness.

Addressing the specifics of measuring productivity: Productivity is a ratio of output units produced to input resources expended per unit of time (t). For example, productivity could be measured as units of output per dollar of labor in a period of time. That would provide a measure of **labor productivity.** The dimensions for output and input are as follows:

$$\text{output} \frac{\text{units}}{\text{hour}}, \text{ and input} = \frac{\text{dollars}}{\text{hour}} = \text{hourly wages}$$

Then, productivity measured over a specific period of time, t

$$\text{productivity}(t) = \frac{\text{output}(t)}{\text{input}(t)} = \frac{\text{units of output}(t)}{\text{dollars of labor}(t)}$$

This relationship measures how many dollars of labor resources are required in period (t) to achieve the output rate (t), and indicates how much output is being obtained for each dollar spent.

Converting Output into Dollars for Labor and Multifactor Productivity

Another way of stating the measure of productivity is to put a dollar value on the output volume per unit of time. The input cost is already stated in dollars per hour. The advantage of this method is that it can deal with the productivity of the system across different kinds of units; for example, the productivity of a paint company that puts paints of many colors in cans of many sizes could be measured. This approach is used for national accounting of productivity where there are many different kinds of units to be included (i.e., furniture, clothing, and foods). Dollars can standardize the output measure across diverse categories.

Productivity measures can be common-sense ratios, like the number of metal gears produced per hour or the number of meals served from noon until 1 P.M. by a quick-service restaurant.

Labor productivity: Partial accounting for productivity that is due to the use of human labor to do the job.

Labor productivity, often measured as the ratio of sales dollars to labor cost dollars, is called a *partial measure of productivity*.

$$\text{labor productivity}(t) = \frac{\text{output}(t)}{\text{input}(t)} = \frac{\text{sales in dollars}(t)}{\text{dollars of labor}(t)}$$

> **Multifactor productivity:**
> Also called **total productivity;**
> reflects the joint effects of
> many factors including labor
> and capital.

Multifactor productivity is measured by the U.S. Labor Department. Total productivity is an alternate name. Multifactor productivity is measured on a regular basis to determine whether the U.S. industrial base is improving its competitive position in the world.

"A change in multifactor productivity reflects the difference between the change in output (production of goods and services) and the change in labor and capital inputs engaged in the production of the output. Multifactor productivity does not measure the specific contributions of labor, capital, or any other factor of production. Instead, it reflects the joint effects of many factors, including new technology, economies of scale, managerial skill, and change in the organization of production."[3]

Multifactor productivity is measured in dollars as the ratio obtained when the costs for all the resources used are divided into the total output of goods and services.

$$\text{multifactor productivity}(t) = \frac{\text{all outputs of goods and services}(t, \$)}{\text{total input resources expended}(t, \$)}$$

Trends in Multifactor Productivity

Table 2-1 shows the average annual percent changes in multifactor productivity for the United States over different periods of time.[4]

U.S. productivity averaged just slightly under 2 percent per year from 1948 through 1973. That was considered to be healthy, though not robust, growth. Then came "the shrinking era," which lasted for 20 years from 1973 through 1993. These were tough years for U.S. manufacturing firms. The U.S. auto industry observed that new Japanese plants in America (transplants in Tennessee, Ohio) in the 1970s were much more (twice on average) productive than traditional U.S. auto plants in Detroit.

There began a long learning process on the part of U.S. auto manufacturers to increase their productivity. It took 20 years, but it worked. U.S. auto making reflects more productive processes. The improvement applies to more than automobiles. After many years of declining growth rates, and even some years of negative growth (average annual shrinkage of 0.1 from 1979 to 1990), U.S. productivity has accelerated to levels above the post–World War II years.

The renewal of U.S. productivity growth is not surprising. Great efforts have been made in the manufacturing sectors to improve efficiency. Subjects such as total quality management (TQM), reengineering, and turnarounds, discussed in the general press, are not fads. They herald solid accomplishments. Adoption of new technology promises more developments yet to come.

However, it is important to separate the manufacturing component of the total productivity measure from the service component. Measures of service productivity are much

TABLE 2-1		Average Annual Percent Changes in Multifactor Productivity				
Years	1948–1973	1973–1979	1979–1990	1990–1993	1993–1996	1996–2003
Multifactor productivity	1.9	0.3	–0.1	0.4	1.4	2.0

Note: U.S. Department of Labor data is available through 2000.

lower than those of manufacturing and have not been posting notable improvements around the world. There have been substantial investments in computers and telecommunications within the service sectors, but only recently are there real signs of improvement. At last, broad-based changes in productivity can be reported. This will accelerate as OM managers learn how to apply the new technologies to service systems. This productivity comparison constitutes a significant difference that currently exists between services and manufacturing.

Capital Productivity

There are many ways to measure productivity in line with other purposes. The following equations measure **capital productivity** in two different ways. Capital productivity is a partial accounting for productivity due to invested capital. First, there is the number of units of output per dollar of invested capital.

Capital productivity: Partial accounting for productivity that is due to invested capital.

$$\text{capital productivity}(t) = \frac{\text{output}(t)}{\text{input}(t)} = \frac{\text{units of output}(t)}{\text{dollars of capital}(t)}$$

The second measure of capital productivity is a pure ratio based on dollars of output per dollar of invested capital.

$$\text{capital productivity}(t) = \frac{\text{dollar value of output units}(t, \$)}{\text{dollars for capital resources}(t, \$)}$$

Such measures of capital productivity might help organizations in the service sectors to address the value of returns on investments in computers and telecommunications. By extending this reasoning, it is possible to develop other partial measures of productivity with respect to areas such as energy expended, space utilized, and materials consumed.

Students and practitioners of business know that productivity improvements translate into more profits and greater profitability for organizations, and improve the state of the economy. In the same vein, economists believe that productivity improvements translate into higher standards of living and greater prosperity. Productivity measures get factored into inflation calculations as well as other economic scenarios. Increases in productivity are generally regarded as a means of checking inflationary trends.

This is because by working smarter—not harder—profit margins increase and there is more money available to invest in other business opportunities. The shortage of capital drives interest rates up. However, if there are more jobs available than people to fill them, labor becomes scarce, and rising salaries begin to fuel the expansion of inflation. **Relative productivity** compares the performance of competitive processes for which P/OM is accountable. The contribution of P/OM to the well-being of the national economy should be recognized.

Relative productivity: Measure of comparison between similar processes.

2-1b Operational Measures of the Organization's Productivity

Productivity measures can be common-sense ratios such as the value of pieces made in a factory divided by the cost of making them, or the number of documents produced by the typing pool divided by the number of people doing word processing. Such operational measures of productivity are valuable to companies that are focused on continuous improvement.

A productivity measure used by restaurants is the daily dollars generated per table. Many fast-food restaurants use dollars generated per square foot. Airlines measure plane occupancy per flight and average occupancy per route, as well as for all routes flown. Department stores use sales dollars per square foot of space. Mail-order companies measure sales dollars for categories (i.e., fashion, toys, and luggage) by type of illustration (i.e., color and size) on a percent of page basis. Trends in same-store sales can be followed as a benchmarking guide to retail productivity. Many companies measure the productivity of their complaint departments by the ratio of the number of complaints dealt with per day divided by the number of complaint handlers.

Formulating appropriate productivity measures to capture the effectiveness of operations is an OM challenge. It takes insight and creativity to measure what really matters in performance and what really can be controlled and corrected.

2-1c Productivity Is a Systems Measure

Every function in the company that has some measurable accomplishment can be evaluated with respect to productivity. The productivity of the company is the composite of the contributions of the individual functions.

Volume of output sold is a measure of the productivity of the sales department. Cost of goods sold is a measure of the productivity of the process designers, the R & D department, and the operations managers. It also is a measure of the purchasing department's ability to find the best materials obtained at the lowest possible costs and highest qualities.

Output delivered to the customer is a measure of the ability of the distribution system to be on time with undamaged delivery. Output delivered is subject to warranties. Does the company listen to the "voice of the customers" with respect to difficulties in repairing or returning defectives? If not, future sales productivity can be impaired. Further, warranties exercised represent productivity decreases.

Productivity issues are woven into all parts of the supplier-producer-customer chain and the input–output transformation process. This further explains why productivity is a systems issue. The supplier-producer-customer chain has a global reach. Therefore, the next section explores the impact of international factors on productivity.

Productivity Is a Global Systems Measure

Although much knowledge exists about production systems and operations management, there have been and continue to be serious productivity problems in the world. These problems have afflicted many developing countries where capital to invest in new technology is scarce, and technical knowledge and training are lacking. There also have been productivity problems in industrialized countries where early productivity growth was not sustainable, as in the United States.

Japan's phenomenal productivity growth rates of the 1980s could not be maintained. Nevertheless, Japanese productivity in a variety of industries continues to be formidable. Thus, with respect to auto parts, "On average, the plants in Japan were 18 percent more productive than ones in the United States, and 35 percent more productive than ones in Europe."[5] Further, "Japanese parts makers surveyed increased their productivity by almost 38 percent from 1992 to 1994; the American companies made gains only in the mid-20s."[6]

Such data needs to be questioned for accuracy. Although the basic trends are generally accepted, it is unsatisfactory to measure manufacturing sector productivity as output per person directly employed. Productivity improvements can be registered by companies that reduce the number of direct employees, increase the use of part-time help, rely more on subcontracting of parts, and employ outside maintenance companies, among other things. It is to be noted that Japanese firms typically rely heavily on their suppliers and part-time help. Other aspects of Japanese manufacturing methods logically account for world-class productivity accomplishments. Nevertheless, the phenomenal Japanese productivity records have diminished substantially in recent years.

Other leading industrial nations have experienced productivity declines. Many hypotheses have been offered to explain the inability to sustain stable productivity growth in a turbulent era of new technological development. One suggestion is that the productivity of industrial nations is converging to a global mean.[7] Another is that old technology gets used up, and it is difficult to switch to the new technologies and make them profitable.[8] It also takes smarter management. In spite of this, the U.S. economy shows many signs of increased productivity while reducing the manufacturing labor force and increasing the service sector labor force.

Competitors keep jockeying and leapfrogging each other with the adoption of new technologies that initially reduce productivity. There are various causes for the reduction. The new technology is imposed on old processes by employees who lack training and experience with the new technology. Product life is short. This allows little time to enjoy the advantages of new technology applied to evanescent and even obsolescent product lines. Furthermore, the global economies have been buffeted by economic conditions of deflation and recession, which penalize high-volume export industries such as those of Japan and the United States.

Increasingly, companies buy from suppliers located around the world and sell in markets that are equally dispersed. Production facilities, including fabrication, assembly, chemical and drug processes, and service facilities are located globally. Therefore, productivity performance becomes the result of international interactions. If productivity is being measured in dollars or local currencies, exchange rate problems can distort the picture. On the other hand, exchange rate imbalances cause gains and losses that relate to the productivity of investments. These are reflected in ROI (return on investment) measures.

2-1d Bureaucracy Inhibits Flexibility and Productivity

Another factor that accounts for poor productivity is bureaucracy—the great inhibitor of flexibility. Bureaucratic systems are rampant worldwide. North America and Europe have more than their share, and they are equally prevalent in Asia, Latin America, and Africa. The definition of the term that is being used here is bureaucracy as institutionalized officialism, which has layers of red tape to cut through in order to conclude activities and operations. Bureaucracy spreads its reach as it proliferates through an organization placing controls over controls in the quest for low risk.

It can be noted that bureaucracy plays an important stabilizing role in organizations that are undisciplined and prone to accidents. Routines known to be safe are insurance against risk of catastrophic damage. The down side of bureaucracy is that the pendulum swings too far. Once bureaucracy gains control it strives to remove corrective counterswings, and that impedes "give and take" in favor of rigidity.

Flexibility is related to productivity in a number of ways. Conditions change and the ability to adapt to new situations is measured by flexibility. New technology and the need to be global are among the most important changes in conditions that require flexibility. Product life is shorter and the need to modify product designs requires flexibility. The productivity advantages associated with producing large volumes of identical units is being replaced by methods that permit smaller volumes to be produced having greater variety. Design variations are being used for different countries and even for various regions of the same country.

Bureaucratic organizations are dedicated to resisting change. What every operations manager should know is that bureaucracy is, by intent, the protector and champion of the status quo. Bureaucracy is the opponent of operational change. When bureaucratic constraints are removed, often by decentralization, and more recently by reengineering, afflicted organizations regain some ability to rebound.

Japanese organizations that exhibited great resilience when they first started their major export drives also began to succumb to the problems of age and success. Age is correlated with circulatory insufficiencies in human beings and a lack of communication in organizations. This lack also is associated with zero empowerment of employees to do what makes sense instead of what the rule book dictates.

Success leads to complacency and arrogance—even though it does not have to do so. Bureaucratic organizations are very successful at inhibiting innovation and change. It remains to be seen how successful organizations worldwide will be in learning to counter these inhibitors.

Size of Firms and Flexibility

It is worth noting that small- and medium-sized firms, and new businesses as well, tend to exhibit greater flexibility and adaptability to change than large, centralized organizations.

That is why under stress, Dell, Ford, GM, IBM, Sears, and other giant corporations used different forms of decentralization to improve their chances of recovering market preeminence. Organizational awareness of the need for flexibility has surfaced, but solutions for big bureaucratic companies have been elusive. The Iacocca Institute at Lehigh University in the United States now supports its "global village" as well as research on "agile manufacturing," which is a pseudonym for flexibility.

Small- and medium-sized firms are organizations with about 300 people. That number has been suggested by various managers, and there also is a great deal of unanimity that the upper limit should be no more than 500.[9] Given the usual proportions of administrative personnel and those of other functions, this suggests that a sensible limit for the size of an efficient production system is in the neighborhood of 100 to 200 people. By using divisional structures, it is reasonable to assume that a number of relatively autonomous divisions of sensible size can be related within the firm.

Research and Development (R & D)

The characterization of age and size also applies to the productivity of R & D departments. Some of the largest expenditures for R & D amounting to billions of dollars have been highly unproductive. IBM and GM spent multiple billions of dollars over many years while their fortunes declined.

There is ample evidence that small research budgets produce the most impressive results. The employees of a small start-up company are in constant communication. Large research units have all of the problems that previously have been mentioned in connection with bureaucracy. Smaller dynamic organizations utilize the systems approach without having to consciously decide to do so. Everyone knows everyone else and they talk regularly. In many cases, the employees achieve a high degree of interfunctional coordination.

The productivity of R & D efforts is a legitimate concern of P/OM. Applied research and development fosters the next wave of new products and services. P/OM should be part of the team that carries the ball from start to finish for actual new product implementation. The way in which this is done is the concern of P/OM. Poor productivity in R & D translates into inferior processes, difficult operations, poor quality, high costs, and low profit margins. The rules for achieving high levels of productivity in research and development are similar to those that apply to good project management, which is an OM responsibility.

2-2 PRODUCTIVITY AND PRICE–DEMAND ELASTICITY

When a company is competing on price, it means that it will lose sales if a competitor offers a lower price that it cannot match. Everyone in the company looks to OM at this point. The CEO or the president asks for increased productivity that translates into greater output volume at the same or lower total costs. It is assumed that quality will remain unchanged.

To ask for increased productivity is a special way of asking for lower costs. Unions often take it to mean work faster for the same pay, which makes them reluctant to participate in productivity improvement. Speeding up production can compromise quality. Operations management should try to avoid supporting productivity increases gained in this way; the improvement is temporary, at best. Other ways of obtaining lower costs include the use of cheaper components and raw materials that lowers quality.

The CEO had something else in mind. When requesting increased productivity, the CEO meant using technology and good OM methods to improve the process, not lower the quality.

The CEO's call for increased productivity is in response to competitive bids. Decreasing quality to match lower prices is not a way to keep customers. Improved productivity, if it is to translate into greater customer satisfaction and loyalty, must come from working smarter, not harder. This means improving productivity by means other than asking people to work faster, which usually degrades quality.

This highlights a strong functional interaction between marketing and OM. The managers of these areas are associates working together to manage the effects of price-demand **elasticity** on production costs and on meeting quality standards.

2-2a Elasticity Relationship

Elasticity is a rate-of-change measure that expresses the degree to which demand grows or shrinks in response to a price change. In Equation 2-1, elasticity is expressed as a function that relates changes in price (p) with changes in demand volume (V_p). Thus, volume is a function (f) of price—in line with the degree of elasticity represented by beta (β).

$V_p = f(p, \beta)$

$1 \geq \beta \geq 0$ (Equation 2-1)

Spelling this out in more detail, V_p is the demand volume associated with price p, and the elasticity coefficient, β. The degree of elasticity increases as beta moves to one (1). Demand is described as being completely *inelastic* when beta equals zero (0).

A product with high elasticity experiences large decreases in demand when there are price increases, whereas, a product with low elasticity experiences small decreases in demand with the same degree of price increases. Low elasticity, called *inelasticity*, means that demand levels are relatively insensitive to price changes.

Marketing managers frequently ask market researchers about price elasticity of products or services to determine how fast demand falls off as price is increased. Figure 2-1 shows a highly elastic situation ($\beta = 1$) where the demand volume changes greatly with price changes. In the same figure, an inelastic case is shown ($\beta = 0$) where demand volume does not change at all with price changes. The midway case ($\beta = 0.5$) falls between the other two. The equation used for these lines is called Equation 2-2.

$V_p = kp^{-\beta}$ (Equation 2-2)

Note: k in Equation 2-2 is a constant that reflects the demand volume level when beta is zero.

Perfect inelasticity—when demand does not change, no matter what the price—is an accurate description of the situation when an industrial customer is dependent on one supplier for special materials. Most customers try to get out of such a constraining situation.

Elasticity is a complex relationship. The rate of change between price and demand is not always smooth and regular. There can be kinks in the line or curve. These occur, for example, when an increase in price causes demand to increase, which might happen when price becomes high enough to have "snob appeal," which opens a new market. Despite difficulties, it is important to measure elasticity, thereby relating price and volume.

> **Elasticity:** Degree to which demand grows or contracts in response to price decreases or increases.

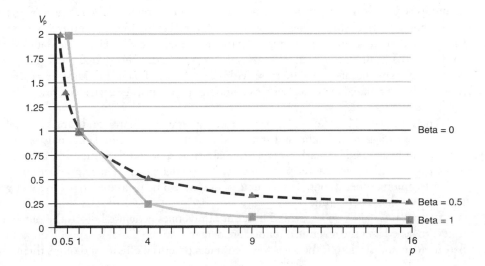

FIGURE 2-1
Price Elasticity for Beta = 0, 1.0, and 0.5, with $R = 1$

The elasticity–productivity tie between operations management and marketing is:

1. Demand volume falls as price rises, but this is relative to what prices competitors charge. When a competitor lowers prices, it is equivalent to a price increase for the customer who stays with a supplier who does not lower prices.

2. To be competitive, it is often necessary to find ways to match price decreases offered by competitors. This is a price–demand volume elasticity issue that assumes quality is unchanged.

3. If marketing lowers the price, then the profit margin will decrease in accordance with the formula $(p - vc)V$, where $(p)V$ is revenue and $(vc)V$ is total variable cost.

4. P/OM is asked to find a way to decrease total variable cost without degrading quality.

5. The only way to achieve number 4 is by means of technology-based or methodology-based productivity improvements.

6. Marketing tries to control demand volume through pricing.

7. OM tries to match supply to demand through production scheduling and capacity planning. Marketing and OM should work together, combining their interactions—the systems approach.

The Market Research Store Case

To understand these issues in a concrete way, consider the productivity problem of the Market Research Store (MRS). Service industries are especially concerned about productivity because so many are labor intensive and the cost of labor in the United States is relatively high. The Market Research Store is a market research firm that processes information.

There are many small- and medium-sized firms that perform the market research function for large companies and advertising agencies. Small- and medium-sized market research businesses have an advantage over large competitors because of their low overhead. Entry into the field does not require a large investment, and labor costs are the main operating expense. Consequently, low labor costs, but not unskilled labor, are sought. Often this means making use of part-time people or training people who are willing to work at lower rates because their skills are being improved. High productivity is not associated with part-time labor, except for special groups of people such as married women with children and the elderly. The source of the labor pool is crucial.

Creation of questionnaires and design of focus groups to collect data is knowledge work. Because it entails substantial skills that would be costly if bought outside, it is done by the owners. This ability is often the most valuable asset of the firm.

The input–output transformation model provides a basis for understanding the pressure to achieve high levels of labor productivity. The main input for market research activities is data. It has to be collected and put into the computer. The major input activity is labor intensive with people sitting at computers, keying information into a program that can calculate averages and prepare standard-format reports. The same data may be entered twice in order to check for consistency between data-entry operators. The input costs are variable because they increase with the amount of data that must be processed. In addition, purchased materials such as computer paper, printer cartridges, and electricity add to the variable costs.

The outputs of the Market Research Store are graphs, charts, and tables, as well as other forms of aggregated data, and statistical reports, such as regression analyses. These data would be studied by market research analysts to spot trends, determine conditions, and write reports about market performance. They might suggest new product comparison tests, among other things. The volume of output can be measured in a variety of ways that relate to processing time.

Output rates also can be treated in terms of revenues generated. Both the number of units processed and the revenue obtained are demand-driven variables. When output falls because demand slacks off, the sales force contacts potential clients and offers them market research studies at discounted prices. The lower prices are somewhat effective in bringing in new business because demand is at least partially elastic to price. Marketing has some control over the volume of business that production must process.

The Market Research Store has a minimum capital investment in computers and printers. Its owners have no intention of trying to attract additional investment capital. Its computers and printers are networked in a topsy-turvy fashion. When heavy loads occur, the MRS rents additional equipment. It owns the software to do statistical analyses, graphics, and desktop publishing—all of which are needed for their clients' reports. The owners of the MRS are so busy processing clients' reports and dealing with processing problems that they have little time to determine if other types of computers, different network configurations, and alternative software packages would be better for them.

The problem is that one of their long-term competitors has invested in developing networks to connect homes and offices with laptop computers. This allows part-time employees to sign out a laptop computer from the stockroom and work from home at labor rates that are more favorable than MRS can offer. The result is that the competitor is regularly underbidding MRS with many of its oldest clients. The volume of work is dropping off and the owners of MRS are perplexed. They do not have the money to support the technological expansion that is required to compete with their market research adversary. Somehow they need to increase the productivity of their operations because the market is sufficiently price elastic to put them in trouble.

The owners of MRS hope that there are better methods for doing work using essentially the same equipment they have used in the past and leasing some additional equipment if that would give them an advantage. At first, they competed fiercely, dropping prices to meet their competition. Unfortunately, they began losing money on jobs, which limited their aggressive stance. Are there operations management methods, which can return the MRS to a competitive position? Because the owners are excellent in market research questionnaire development, response analysis and interpretation, and report writing, it may be presumed that they are not familiar with the methodology of OM. If that is the case, they have a good chance of saving a substantial amount of money by hiring an operations manager.

The MRS can obtain great productivity improvements by using better production methods, available to those who have studied the field of OM. Further, certain kinds of market research jobs are more profitable than others. OM and marketing can work together to ascertain which jobs are best for profits and to make every effort to sell those jobs. In addition, some customers and types of jobs are less price elastic than others. For example, customers are willing to pay more for situations that require precision. This is equivalent to paying for higher quality.

By specializing in certain kinds of jobs and providing the highest quality reports, MRS can improve its competitive position over time. Also, by using teamwork, MRS has a good chance to pull out of its difficulties and start planning for a better tomorrow. This will include the use of up-to-date technology. The MRS should consider the advisability of following their competitor's lead with part-time employees working at home using laptop computers networked to the central office.

Summing up, an OM approach to improving productivity can be found for this company. It must address making shifts in the products that MRS sells and making changes in their processes. MRS will gradually learn to use new technology to their advantage through training its employees to perform with excellence in the new environment.

2-2b Elasticity of Quality

The volume of goods or services sold as a function of price is the traditional focus of elasticity analysis. Years ago that simple model may have sufficed, but it no longer is valid. This subject is of mutual concern to OM and marketing.

Customers in the marketplace take both price and quality into account. Customers' quality expectations usually override price considerations. This also applies to commercial and industrial customers.

Using new technology such as laptops connected to the Internet allows employees to work virtually anywhere, on many subjects, without geographical restriction. This raises productivity.

TABLE 2-2	Study	Quality	Beta Values	Elasticity
Comparing Elasticities and Betas with Higher or Lower Quality Levels	1	Lower	Closer to 1	More elastic
	2	Higher	Closer to 0	Less elastic

A product or service that has special qualities is said to have uniqueness, which means that other competitive products have a lower degree of substitutability. For example, a product with a special feature, or a service rendered by a well-liked person, has a competitive advantage. The competitive analysis would show that they are not competing head-on, as if they were identical, perfect substitutes for each other. Perceived high quality renders a product less vulnerable to substitution, which means that the product is less quality elastic.

How can the effects of quality on demand levels be determined? This is equivalent to asking how to determine the quality–demand volume elasticity. There are ways in which market research can approach this issue that are similar to the way price–demand volume elasticity is determined. Essentially, it is necessary to establish how much extra money customers would be willing to pay for superior quality or for an added quality feature.

By noting the distribution of the additional amounts of money that people would pay for superior quality or an added feature, it is possible to quantify the effects of quality and price on demand elasticity. In effect, two price elasticity studies are conducted. The first study is done without the added quality. The second study is done with it. Throughout this discussion, it should be kept in mind that *the achievement of quality standards is a direct responsibility of OM*.

Table 2-2 indicates that the demand elasticity in the second study should be less than in the first one. This is because the added quality in the second study makes alternative products or services less substitutable.

Although this is a book about OM and not market research, these functions are highly interdependent. Market research enables OM to determine the kind of connections that link quality, price and demand elasticity in the customer's mind.

These factors relate design and process decisions with the financial choices that are available to the firm. The system interaction includes the fact that quality varies with the kind of equipment that is used and the amount of training that the employees receive.

2-3 ECONOMIES OF SCALE AND THE DIVISION OF LABOR

There are three principles that OM must be schooled in to take advantage of productive opportunities. They are **economies of scale**, the division of labor, and economies of scope. The third point will be considered later.

Economies of scale: Reductions in variable costs directly related to increasing volumes of production output.

Economies of scale are reductions in variable costs directly related to increasing volumes of production output. Economies of scale are driven by volume (V). Scale, as used here, is another word for volume. The equation for total variable costs is both an OM and marketing responsibility.

Total variable costs = $vc(V)$

V is a function of the total market size that exists, the number of competitors and their shares, and the controllable variables of the organization's price and quality. Although marketing and OM work together on the consequences of V, OM is working on the reduction of vc—which is also a function of V—with no loss in quality.

Materials and labor are an important component of the variable per unit cost, vc. The design of the product or service determines what materials are needed. It is common knowledge that greater purchase volumes generally are rewarded with discounts. That is only one of the interactions of vc and V. The machines that can be used for high-volume

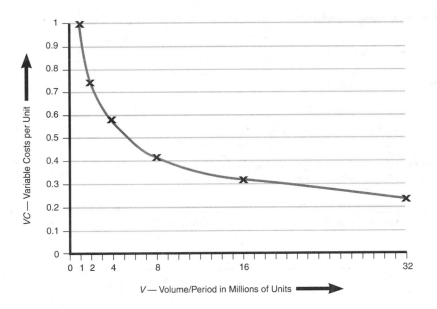

FIGURE 2-2
Economies of Scale
Per unit variable costs decrease
between 20 to 30 percent with
increasing volume.

outputs are significantly faster than the kind that are economic for low-volume outputs. High volumes can sustain pre-engineering and improvement studies of the interactions between the design of jobs and the processes used, while low volumes cannot. High volumes generate learning about how to do the job better; low volumes do not.

The design of jobs determines the amount of labor and the skill levels that are required. The responsibility for low unit variable costs leads OM to want high volumes so that it can take advantage of the resulting economies of scale.

For many reasons, including the material discounts previously discussed and a general learning effect, variable costs per unit decrease as volume increases. This result, called the *economies of scale*, is quite similar to the Boston Consulting Group's (BCG) "Experience Curve," which yields a 20 to 30 percent decrease in per unit costs with each doubling of the volume.[10] It is reasonable to consider the "doubling of volume" as a surrogate for the "doubling of experience," as in BCG terminology.

An approximation of this relationship is shown in Figure 2-2.

A coincident concept, proposed by Adam Smith (a Scottish economist) in the 1700s, was for the division of labor.[11] Labor was to be divided into specialized activities that could be honed to ever-greater skill levels. This notion follows from the theory that "practice makes perfect." To make division of labor worthwhile, the volume of production must be sufficient. Adam Smith said, "The division of labor depends on the extent of the market." With a large enough volume, activities could be segmented, and serialized process flows could be developed. Division of labor appears in the history section, which follows.

2-4 THE HISTORY OF THE IMPROVEMENT OF P/OM TRANSFORMATIONS

Literacy in OM requires an understanding of how the OM field has developed with respect to the transformation process and, thereby, productivity, quality, and variety. The stages of history have moved production and operations capabilities from custom work through high-speed continuous output systems.

Attention shifts from custom crafts, which are art-based, to the theory of production, which has evolved over time. This theory consists of six steps and a potential seventh one. There is an emphasis on manufacturing because the theory evolved from the production of goods, but it lends itself to service operations.

Figure 2-3 depicts OM history in a timeline chart. Dates mentioned are approximate because it is not possible to pinpoint exactly when each contribution was made.

The flexibility concept joins computers and equipment in the bank, plant, or plane. This revises the way that machines operate.

FIGURE 2-3
The Histo-Map: A Timeline of OM Developments

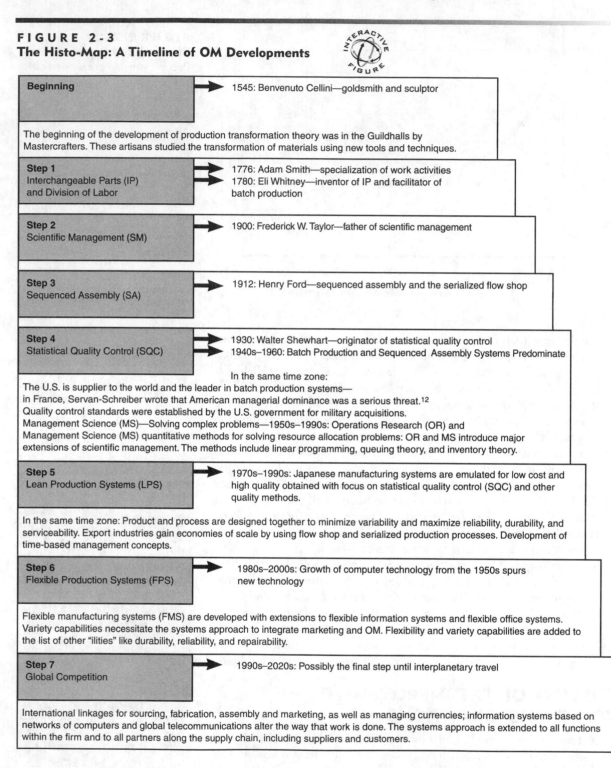

Beginning

1545: Benvenuto Cellini—goldsmith and sculptor

The beginning of the development of production transformation theory was in the Guildhalls by Mastercrafters. These artisans studied the transformation of materials using new tools and techniques.

Step 1
Interchangeable Parts (IP) and Division of Labor

1776: Adam Smith—specialization of work activities
1780: Eli Whitney—inventor of IP and facilitator of batch production

Step 2
Scientific Management (SM)

1900: Frederick W. Taylor—father of scientific management

Step 3
Sequenced Assembly (SA)

1912: Henry Ford—sequenced assembly and the serialized flow shop

Step 4
Statistical Quality Control (SQC)

1930: Walter Shewhart—originator of statistical quality control
1940s–1960: Batch Production and Sequenced Assembly Systems Predominate

In the same time zone:
The U.S. is supplier to the world and the leader in batch production systems—
in France, Servan-Schreiber wrote that American managerial dominance was a serious threat.[12]
Quality control standards were established by the U.S. government for military acquisitions.
Management Science (MS)—Solving complex problems—1950s–1990s: Operations Research (OR) and Management Science (MS) quantitative methods for solving resource allocation problems: OR and MS introduce major extensions of scientific management. The methods include linear programming, queuing theory, and inventory theory.

Step 5
Lean Production Systems (LPS)

1970s–1990s: Japanese manufacturing systems are emulated for low cost and high quality obtained with focus on statistical quality control (SQC) and other quality methods.

In the same time zone: Product and process are designed together to minimize variability and maximize reliability, durability, and serviceability. Export industries gain economies of scale by using flow shop and serialized production processes. Development of time-based management concepts.

Step 6
Flexible Production Systems (FPS)

1980s–2000s: Growth of computer technology from the 1950s spurs new technology

Flexible manufacturing systems (FMS) are developed with extensions to flexible information systems and flexible office systems. Variety capabilities necessitate the systems approach to integrate marketing and OM. Flexibility and variety capabilities are added to the list of other "ilities" like durability, reliability, and repairability.

Step 7
Global Competition

1990s–2020s: Possibly the final step until interplanetary travel

International linkages for sourcing, fabrication, assembly and marketing, as well as managing currencies; information systems based on networks of computers and global telecommunications alter the way that work is done. The systems approach is extended to all functions within the firm and to all partners along the supply chain, including suppliers and customers.

2-5 DISCUSSION OF THE HISTORY OF P/OM

The capability of P/OM processes to deliver goods and services has changed in steps or stages over time. The study of the history of OM production transformation processes allows us to determine which events triggered these stages of production theory. The ultimate goal is to learn the theory, understand it, and possess the advantages that accrue for being literate.

2-5a Artisans, Apprentices, and Trainees— The Beginning

The Renaissance period (1300s–1600s) signaled a surge of intellectual and productive vitality in Europe. That surge swept away the dark ages and fostered accomplishments in the arts and sciences centered around artisans, apprentices, and craft guilds. Production transformations were by hand, and output volumes were very small.

Before the Industrial Revolution began (around 1770), craft guilds emphasized pride of workmanship and training for basic manual operations with appropriate hand tools. The shoemakers' children learned from their fathers and mothers. Process techniques were handed down from generation to generation.

From a transformation point of view, this was good management of the labor inputs. The use of apprentices improved productivity in the artisans' shops because the less skilled (and lower paid) apprentices did much of the preliminary work. This freed the master craftsmen to devote their time to the activities requiring higher skills. On-the-job training produced a continuous stream of greater skills.

Apprenticeship still has significance for many service functions. Great chefs almost always are the pupils of great chefs. The formula would seem to reside in the balance of art and science. When the important knowledge resides in the minds and hands of skilled workers, then the percent of art is high and the percent of science is low. Over time, this percentage has shifted in manufacturing so that engineering, technology, and computer programming play an increasing role.

The art element is disappearing, which means that the valuable know-how now resides mostly in the minds, not in the hands, of the critical workers. It used to be that the tool and die department was crucial to the success of metal-working companies, and the best die makers were considered artists. (Tools and dies are the shape formers in the metal-working businesses.)

Now, **computer-aided design (CAD)** and **computer-aided manufacturing (CAM)** are primarily science, and the old industrial arts are giving way to the new programming arts. This also is happening in service industries and is an effect that can be expected to accelerate in the future.

2-5b Interchangeable Parts (IP)— Production Theory's First Step

Eli Whitney invented the concept of **interchangeable parts** for the fabrication of rifles around 1780, which coincides with the dates usually given for the beginning of the Industrial Revolution. The notion of interchangeable parts was the catalyst around which new methods for production transformation began to develop. These methods spawned and supported the Industrial Revolution.

Whitney was not the sole inventor of interchangeable parts. In France, Nicolas LeBlanc had invented the same OM concept. Neither Whitney nor LeBlanc knew about each other's ideas. Whitney obtained a U.S. government contract for "ten thousand stand of arms." The contract was awarded because of his newly developed production capabilities.

The concept of interchangeable parts is defined as follows: It allows batches of parts to be made, any one of which will fit into the assembled product. For example, headlights, fenders, tires, and windshield wiper blades are not specially made for each car. One 60-watt bulb is like another and does not have to be fitted to each socket. The reason that the parts are interchangeable is that each one falls within the **design tolerances.**

Machines that could produce parts to conform to the designer's tolerances were the keystone. Hand labor, better suited to custom work, began to be replaced by machinery. The effects of this change hastened the Industrial Revolution. Within a short time, IP was an accepted part of the production transformation process being applied to the manufacture of rifles, sewing machines, clocks, and other products.

Computer-aided design (CAD): Software that creates design drawings for any product.

Computer-aided manufacturing (CAM): Software that communicates design specifications to the CAM software, which translates the specs into instructions for the production machinery.

Interchangeable parts: Manufacturing concept that makes batches of parts, any one of which will fit into the assembled products.

Design tolerances: Minimum and maximum dimensions for parts that fit together for proper performance.

In 1776, Adam Smith saw that the use of the division of labor as a means of increasing productivity was market volume dependent. The pin factory that he studied had sufficient production volume to warrant specialization. The production transformation process was revolutionized—combining worker specialization with interchangeable parts changed all of the productivity standards. Expectations were raised to new levels.

2-5c Scientific Management (SM)— Production Theory's Second Step

Scientific management:
Systematic approach to doing work well.

Frederick Winslow Taylor (1865–1915) introduced **scientific management,** the numerical measurement and analysis of the way work should be done. One of his landmark studies dealt with the speed and feed rates of tools and materials for metal cutting. Other studies focused on how to lay bricks and how to move iron castings. Taylor's testimony at hearings concerning the setting of rational railroad fees for shipments in interstate commerce brought national prominence to his analytic methodology.

This step in production theory added the idea that the transformation processes could be improved by studying and simplifying operations. This view required rationalizing the job, the workplace, and the workers. Strangely, it had been overlooked until the turn of the twentieth century. Finding economies of motion and putting materials near at hand were the kinds of improvements that Taylor addressed. In this step, the workplace and the design of the job were enhanced to improve the productivity of the transformation process. These industrial engineering ideas, often called *methods engineering,* have proved to be as useful for service applications as for manufacturing.

Called the father of "scientific management," Taylor was one of the key progenitors of industrial engineering (IE). There were others as well. Associated with this era are Henry L. Gantt, Frank and Lillian Gilbreth, and other individuals who were attempting to develop a theory of managing workers and technology in the United States. Henri Fayol was developing similar management theories in France.

Taylor started the process of systematizing all of the elements that are part of the manufacturing system. The same industrial engineering techniques developed by Taylor are still used by banks, insurance companies, and investment houses as well as by truckers, airlines and manufacturers. They are well-suited for repetitive operations such as those that characterize fast-food chains and information processing systems. Industrial engineering methods are recognizable as the forerunners of techniques that are currently applied in the search for continuous improvement.

Taylor and his associates developed principles and practices that led to a present-day backlash. He and other contributors to scientific management have been accused of dehumanizing the worker in pursuit of efficiency. Today, the accusation might hold, but it did not when judged by the value system of the early 1900s.

The criticism does not damage the case for benefits that can be derived from using the industrial engineering approach, which grew out of scientific management. Work simplification and methods engineering are both IE techniques for making jobs better for workers.

2-5d Sequenced Assembly (SA)— Production Theory's Third Step

Sequenced assembly:
Continuous flow assembly line.

In 1912, Henry Ford developed **sequenced assembly,** which allows assembly to be a continuous flow shop process. Timing must be perfect so that what is needed for assembly arrives on time. Ford developed the sequenced assembly process as a continuous flow production line for automobiles, changing the pace from batch to continuous sequenced assembly.

The serialized flow shop was born. The key was learning to achieve synchronization and control of the process flows. The moving assembly line required a high level of component interchangeability. Ford succeeded in achieving complete synchronization of the process flows.

By means of the principles of interchangeability, division of labor, and flow synchronization, Ford altered the production transformation process. He changed the perception of productivity standards and goals in a conclusive way. In so doing, he built an industrial empire that helped the United States become the world leader in productivity. The United States continues to maintain its lead,[12] although other nations—especially those considered to be less developed countries—have been improving their productivity consistently.

Ford's contribution to production theory and to the revision of the transformation process had a major impact on the Japanese automobile industry. It also affected other industries of many kinds all over the world. There was a new rhythm to the transformation process.

Contrast U.S. and Japanese production processes in the 1980s. The major portion of production and operations activities in the United States utilized batch processes. Batch work with small lots does not lend itself to the kind of synchronization that applies to the automobile industry or the continuous flows of chemical processes.

When the Japanese export industry began to compete aggressively in global markets, they chose to shun batch-type production systems. Instead they elected to specialize in high-volume, serialized flow shops, which extended the concept and application of assembly synchronization to manufacturing and assembly systems.

2-5e Statistical Quality Control (SQC)— Production Theory's Fourth Step

Interchangeable parts required manufacturing methods that made batches of parts conforming to tolerance limits. Shewhart developed the theory of **statistical quality control (SQC)** that enabled manufacturing to design and control processes that could achieve these objectives. SQC was focused on the producer's ability to control the variability of the process that was making the parts that had to fit within the specified tolerance limits. For the first time, the output of the transformation process could be stabilized and controlled. This was a major contribution to production theory.

> **Statistical quality control (SQC):** Methodology to stabilize and control a system

Walter Shewhart's major work, which was published in 1930, described his concepts about why SQC works and how to apply it.[13] Deming and Juran also participated in the development of SQC theory and later on played a crucial role in its implementation and dissemination.[14]

The United States was the first country that consistently used SQC, which it did through the 1940s and the early 1950s, but by 1960 the majority of SQC users were in Japan. U.S. organizations reported that they had dropped SQC to make cost reductions. Quality was considered good enough to replace costly staff departments with inspectors at the end of the production line. By the 1980s, however, under great competitive pressure from quality-driven Japanese organizations, many U.S. companies restored SQC and enhanced it with broader concepts into total quality management (TQM) activities.

Organizations like Motorola and Xerox are considered to be pioneers leading the development of TQM within the framework of the systems approach. The total quality management approach applied to the production transformation system integrates the goals of productivity and quality. It represents a major step forward in the theory of production and an organizational feat to have gained broad acceptance at all levels.

The next three steps are in formative stages, and their impact on productivity cannot be fully evaluated at this time.

2-5f Lean Production Systems (LPS)— Production Theory's Fifth Step

During the 1970s–1990s, Japanese organizations spearheaded by Toyota, Mazda, Nissan, Honda, and Mitsubishi developed a new kind of production methodology called **lean production systems.** These systems combine a deep understanding of quality with a desire to be fastest and a fanatical distaste for all kinds of waste.

> **Lean production systems:** Processes that have been designed to minimize their inherent wastes—of time, materials, and money.

Time wasted was singled out. Every effort was made to use pre-engineering of products and process design to maximize quality achievements, minimize variability, and do it all as rapidly as possible. Part of being lean was being fast—in production. The Japanese were not fast in reaching decisions. For the most part, the export industries became lean producers with high-output volume targets, minimum cycle times, and rapid new product development.

By introducing time management and goals for short cycle times and rapid project development, other new factors were introduced into the production transformation system. The timing of transformations rose to a new level of importance, and, secondly, rapid project management began to mean that the transformation process could be changed from doing one thing to another very quickly.

The Japanese auto industry has been leading in the development of lean and fast production systems. Toyota's production planners, who were architects of the revised production system, stated that Toyota's ideas were a continuation of the concepts that Henry Ford had been developing.[15] In Europe, the notion of leanness was directly associated with speeding up cycle times and project development times. Half-time systems were advanced by Saab. The goal was to cut in half the time currently required to do any operation.

Most U.S. organizations are trying out some aspects of lean and rapid manufacturing methods. Focusing on TQM and JIT, Motorola's management set the goal of reducing defectives to less than four defects per million parts.[16] Having demonstrated that a near-zero defects objective is attainable, Motorola now has set another radical target, which is to reduce existing cycle times by 90 percent. This means that a part that currently takes ten minutes to produce eventually will be made in one minute instead of five minutes, as dictated by the half-time objective previously mentioned. Highlighting reduced cycle time objectives brings new features to the production transformation process.

2-5g Flexible Production Systems (FPS)— Production Theory's Sixth Step

Computer technology and production machinery technology are two distinct areas of technological development. When these technologies are combined, opportunities develop for computers to instruct and control machines instead of needing hands-on control by human operators.

These developments were quite primitive in the 1960s and 1970s. They became more sophisticated and reliable in the mid-1990s. Although, today, few factories in the world do not employ extensively some form of computer-controlled machinery, nevertheless, flexible manufacturing equipment still must be classed as being experimental. The sixth step is predicted by many; rejected by few. The real issue is how long it will take to come.

The initial thrust was in manufacturing. **Flexible manufacturing systems (FMS)** are designed to produce a high variety of outputs at low cost. Computer-controlled change-over is engineered into the system. Instead of human hands changing machine settings, electronics and mechanics provide the interface between the computer and machinery. They are flexible, allowing fast and inexpensive changeovers. The equipment can be programmed to move from one product setup to another product setup in an instant.

Another characteristic of FMS is design and machine software that talk to each other. Computer-aided design (CAD) software does the new design drawings and is able to test the characteristics, such as strength. CAD can communicate the design specifications to software that translates, instructs, and controls the production machinery; this software is called CAM, which stands for computer-aided manufacturing. CAD and CAM work together to determine the feasibility of manufacturing the new design and suggest improved design alternatives.

CAD/CAM technology is used to design and manufacture many different products such as semiconductors, automobile grills, and aircraft parts. John Deere has invested millions of dollars in the creation of CAD/CAM systems for the manufacture of tractors. Boe-

Flexible manufacturing systems (FMS): Designed to produce a variety of outputs at low cost.

ing used CAD/CAM to design all of the parts of its 777. Design has moved from the draftsman's table to the computer.

The flexibility concept joins computers and equipment of many other kinds, including assembly-line processes and office machines. It also is possible and often desirable to include human beings in the network. Flexibility can be applied to information systems—flexible information systems (FIS) and to flexible office systems (FOS) as well as to FMS.

The capability to produce small numbers of many varieties includes extensive application of systems thinking to integrate marketing needs and OM scheduling abilities. Using marketing forecasts, OM managers decide what to make, but the decisions are constrained by the FMS menu, which was predetermined at the planning stage.

The need to produce increased variety is market-driven. The transformation process has to be able to change over from making one thing to another, quickly and inexpensively. A great deal of effort is going into altering the transformation process so it can deal with the goal of increased variety. Technology and methodology must enable nearly instant setups and changeovers from one model to another to satisfy market demands. The payoff will be increased productivity of the joint production–marketing system, as exemplified by customized jeans.

Levi Strauss has put the customer directly in touch with the factory. "Sales clerks at an original Levi's store can use a personal computer and the customer's vital statistics to create what amounts to a digital blue jeans blueprint. When transmitted electronically to a Levi's factory in Tennessee, this computer file instructs a robotic tailor to cut a bolt of denim precisely to the customer's measurements."[17]

There is a dedicated strategic effort to achieve competitiveness through flexibility in America. It combines the goals of leanness (speed) and flexibility and is known as Agile Manufacturing Enterprises.[18] This name is meant to emphasize the ability to react quickly and with flexibility. The agile organization is supposed to be alert and nimble, keen and lithe. Bureaucratic organizations cannot qualify.

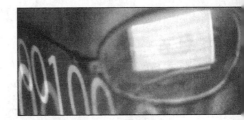

CAD (computer-aided design) terminals communicate design specifications for the construction of planes and ships to an integrated computer-aided manufacturing (CAM) network that reaches throughout the manufacturing system.

2-5h Global Competition: Year 2007 Plus—Production Theory's Seventh Step

It is conjectured that in the future the transformation process will continue increasing in complexity and productivity. On a worldwide scale, a broad range of goods should be within the spending capabilities of more people. More management will be needed to plan and control the systems. More operations managers will be required with far fewer workers on the production line. More people will be sharing services—such as education and health care—that are mutually rewarding. Onerous service tasks will be relegated to service robots. Hopefully, people will have more time to spend their money as they wish.

The input–output production transformation model will be internationalized. There will be global competition at every link in the supply chain. International sourcing, fabrication, assembly, distribution, and marketing will prevail. The costs of the inputs and the values of the outputs will be affected by dozens, if not hundreds, of different currencies. Managing currencies will be part of the transformation process. The euro is a good model for other regional currencies.

Information systems will be based on international networks of computers. Global telecommunication systems will transmit conversations that are spoken in 80 different languages. Translation will be accomplished by language-capable computers with voice-language recognition. Voice response in the appropriate language will be the norm.

The systems approach will extend to all functions within the organization and all partners along the supply chain, including suppliers and customers. Production transformation processes will require the best of management while decreasing burdensome labor components. Substantial productivity increases will be required. There have been many unexpected turns in the road, and there will be more as 2007 gets nearer.

SUMMARY

Productivity is a critical business variable because it strongly impacts the bottom line. Because it is so important, productivity is a major P/OM issue. There are many ways to measure productivity, including those used to describe the national economy. The measures can be made in terms of labor productivity, capital productivity, or both. For business units, the measures relate more directly to the kinds of activities the company does. These are the operational measures of productivity used by an organization. Productivity measures should be adjusted to capture the relevant system—so the systems approach applies.

Bureaucracy inhibits flexibility and, therefore, constrains productivity improvement. Small firms are less bureaucratic than large ones and, therefore, are more flexible and able to pursue initiatives

for greater productivity. Research and development (R & D) organizations are related to OM and should be studied in terms of their productivity, which is usually better for smaller organizations.

Productivity and price–demand elasticity are interdependent. The importance to OM of the elasticity relationship for both price and quality are explained. Then, economies of scale and the division of labor are linked to productivity. Finally, the history of the improvement of OM input–output transformations and resultant productivity increases is presented in seven steps.

Two Spotlight feature boxes conclude this chapter. These boxes illustrate real applications of the materials in the chapter. See Spotlight 2-1: Boutwell Owens and Co., Inc. and Spotlight 2-2: Chick fil-A®—A Successful Business Model.

KEY TERMS

Capital productivity
Computer-aided design (CAD)
Computer-aided manufacturing (CAM)
Design tolerances
Economies of scale
Elasticity

Flexible manufacturing systems (FMS)
Interchangeable parts
Labor productivity
Lean production systems
Multifactor productivity
Relative productivity

Scientific management
Sequenced assembly
Statistical quality control (SQC)
Total productivity

REVIEW QUESTIONS

1. Why is productivity measurement important to operations management?

2. What is the importance of productivity measurement to marketing management?

3. What role does the systems approach play with respect to productivity measurement?

4. What is good and bad about bureaucracy with respect to productivity? One hundred years ago, it was considered a major organizational advance over what preceded it. Why is it now considered an impediment?

5. Explain how the division of labor might help the Market Research Store put together a report for a client.

6. What are the six historical steps in the development of production theory? Is the suggested seventh step likely to have an impact on the future of operations management?

7. Explain the concept of interchangeable parts for
a. a vacuum cleaner.
b. a jigsaw puzzle.
c. a flashlight.

8. Describe what is meant by lean (or agile) production systems.

9. How does the global viewpoint create any new problems or opportunities for operations management?

10. What is the relationship between productivity and elasticity of price and demand volume?

11. What is the relationship between productivity and elasticity of quality and demand volume? Is price implicitly included?

12. Explain what economies of scale are and how they relate to productivity and to the systems approach.

PROBLEMS SECTION

Data for Problems 1-6: In a 1-year period, the Productive Components Corporation (known as PCCorp) has shipped units worth $1,200,000 to its customers. It produced units worth $250,000 for finished goods (FG) inventory. PCCorp has $50,000 of work-in-process (WIP) units. During the same 1-year period of time, PCCorp had a labor bill of $140,000. Its capital expenses for the year are calculated to be $430,000. Materials were purchased costing $530,000. Energy expenses were $225,000, and miscellaneous expenses were estimated to be $75,000.

1. Calculate the labor productivity for PCCorp with respect to units shipped.

2. Calculate the multifactor productivity composed of labor and capital for units shipped plus finished goods for PCCorp.

3. What is PCCorp's total productivity?

4. What is PCCorp's capital productivity?

5. The value of the units shipped must be reduced because $350,000 worth of them have been returned as defective. Of the finished goods units (FG), $150,000 worth have been found to be defective. All work-in-process (WIP) units are within tolerances. Rework on the defective units reduces their value by 70 percent. What is the cost of the quality problem that has surfaced? Discuss what this means in qualitative terms regarding productivity.

6. Calculate the multifactor productivity composed of capital, materials, and energy consumed for the total reworked output, which consists of units shipped plus FG plus WIP.

7. Productivity relates the value of outputs to the cost of inputs. Good productivity is shown by high values; improved productivity is shown by higher values over time.
   Does the following equation capture the meaning of productivity?
   $$Productivity = pV / (vc)V$$
   where pV = price per unit x volume per year
   and $vc(V)$ = the variable cost per unit x volume per year.

8. Because V is in both the numerator and the denominator of the productivity equation,
   $$Productivity = pV / (vc)V.$$
   Reduce the equation: $Productivity = p / (vc)$ and interpret the results.
   Is productivity well described by the ratio of price per unit to variable cost per unit?

9. Elasticity describes how V (sales volume) changes as a function of p.
   a. Does the following equation capture the meaning of elasticity?
   $$V_p = kp^{-\beta}$$
   As in the text, elasticity of demand volume V_p is a function of a price, p. The coefficient of elasticity is beta, which ranges from zero to one, and k is a constant.

b. Explain the following statement: If beta equals zero—indicating perfect and complete inelasticity—the constant, k, has a value equal to the demand volume for the product or service that is irrespective of price.

c. Why is it critical for OM to make every effort to continually raise the quality standards for the product described in Problem 9(b)?

d. Fill in the following table for the elasticity equation:
$$V_p = kp^{-\beta}$$
letting k = 5,000 and β = 0, 1, 0.5, and 0.25.

P	V_p ($\beta = 0$)	V_p ($\beta = 0.25$)	V_p ($\beta = 0.5$)	V_p ($\beta = 1.0$)
1.00				
1.50				
2.00				
2.50				

10. Link productivity, elasticity, and profit (P) using the typical profit equation:
    $$P = (p - vc)V - FC$$
    where p = $1.00, vc = $0.50, and fixed costs (FC) = $10,000. Also, k = 100,000 units per year when β = 1.0 and p = $1.00.
    a. Describe what occurs if the price is raised to $2.00.
    b. Assume that increasing investments in technology improve productivity, such that by increasing FC to $15,000, vc is reduced to $0.40. Does this investment make sense? Do the necessary calculations and explain the results.

11. For Problem 10, assume that the equation for the economies of scale is
    $$vc_v = KV^{-\alpha}$$
    letting α = 0.5 and K = 160.
    Also, vc_V is the per unit variable cost for volume V, K is a constant. and alpha (α) is the coefficient for economies of scale. As in Problem 10, solve for a. Why is Part b not applicable?

12. Explain how the application of the division of labor into specialized workstations might increase the size of the alpha coefficient in Problem 11. How might this affect the profit equation?

END-OF-CHAPTER QUESTIONS

1. The measurement, by a firm, of its productivity improvement is most analogous to which one of the following measures?
   a. tracking an auto's miles per gallon
   b. logging pounds of fertilizer applied
   c. daily measure of dieter's weight
   d. on-wall charting of Junior's height
   e. amount of frequent flier miles

2. The traditional measure of productivity is
   a. cost per calorie of work.
   b. output per unit of input.
   c. input per unit of cost.
   d. efficiency per dollar.
   e. efficiency of the sales force.

3. The productivity of a sales force is properly measured by
   a. the number of sales representatives working for the firm.
   b. the dollar sales of the best sales rep divided by the worst.
   c. the average sales per sales representative.
   d. the effectiveness multiplied by the efficiency.
   e. the measure of labor productivity.

4. Multifactor productivity measurement is used by the U.S. government because
   a. it combines in one overall cost all input factors that create the total output of goods and services. This is the best way to measure national productivity.
   b. it is the tradition of many governments to combine the labor and capital factors. This is the best way to measure GDP.
   c. correlations can be performed on the multiple factors to indicate the degree of independence of the factors from each other.
   d. the years 1973 through 1979 had an average multifactor productivity measure of 0.3. This was followed by even worse years, which provided strong evidence that government action would be needed to correct the situation.
   e. the American auto industry finds it useful to employ multifactor analyses when they lobby the U. S. Congress. It is not likely that measurable change can occur as a result.

5. Productivity issues are woven into all aspects of the supplier-producer-customer chain. It follows, then, that productivity is a systems measure. With this agreed upon, which of the following statements is false?
   a. Capital productivity is of some interest in the broad context of the systems measure.
   b. Japanese productivity in automobile manufacturing is still extremely high although Japan has suffered serious national deterioration of productivity over many years.
   c. Poor European productivity has affected U.S. productivity in some ways.
   d. Worldwide, old technologies have been used up and new technologies are difficult to assimilate, but that is taking place gradually.
   e. Bureaucracy is one of the organizational factors at the heart of the productivity slowdown in many industries. That situation is being solved by bankruptcies and closures of companies.

6. Measures of the elasticity of demand as a function of price have always been thought to be the exclusive domain of marketing managers. P/OM has shown that this is not the case and, in this regard, which of the following statements is false?
   a. Rational product prices (goods or services) reflect the cost of making and delivering the products.
   b. Product prices and quality are tightly tied together; quality is driven by P/OM costs.
   c. Marketing managers believe that the elasticity effect is derived from psychological factors, and P/OM dismisses these statements as being irrational.
   d. So-called demand–price elasticity overlooks the true relationship, which is demand–price and quality elasticity.
   e. The volume of production (V) affects production unit costs; the price of the product affects the demand volume (D); there is a need to align V and D.

7. What are the relationships among product quality, productivity, and price elasticity? Identify which one of the following choices is wrong.
   a. As productivity increases the price–elasticity relationship becomes more elastic, which means that a change in price drives a more significant change in demand (+ or –).
   b. Perceived product quality is related to consistency of performance, utility, reliability, durability, as well as intangible qualities, e.g., appearance. Consumers will pay more for better levels of tangible qualities. Price–elasticity curves reflect this relationship.
   c. As processes become more productive, greater amounts of cash flow (funds) can be directed to improving perceived product quality.
   d. Price elasticity can be affected by advertising, the expenditure for which is facilitated by productivity improvements that decrease waste and increase free cash flow.
   e. Economies of scale improve productivity, but the change in production volume could lead to new methods that decrease product qualities such as reliability of the product and consistency of performance between different products coming off the same line.

8. What do economies of scale and the divisions of labor do to the P/OM system? Which one of the following choices is incorrect?
   a. Breaking the job into parts and assigning individuals or teams to each part allows more repetitive practice, which provides learning to do the job better.
   b. Doing the job better frequently saves money and improves quality of outputs.
   c. Saved money can be used to lower prices, increase quality, and advertising budgets.
   d. Increased quality can decrease elasticity, which permits prices to be raised without decreasing demand, which generates more revenues.
   e. Better revenues mean higher profits, which allow redesigning jobs to have more team members using less technology and thereby further increase the division of labor.

9. The history of P/OM improvement of the transformation function of the input–output model is a clear set of steps in both theory and application. Which of the following statements is incorrect?

   a. Apprenticeship was one of the first stages of learning to do operations efficiently. Even so, it remains a major component of success, especially in service operations.

   b. Without interchangeable parts, manufacturing would be costly. For example, each Saturn would have to be handmade from start to finish.

   c. The service sector has found some similarities to interchangeable parts manufacture. For example, the Shouldice Hospital in Toronto, Canada, treats hernia operations as cars along an assembly line. This improves quality of operations and lowers the cost.

   d. Statistical quality control is used to monitor product dimensions at the process level. Since the development of SQC, firms have the ability to achieve near-zero defects from any production system.

   e. Scientific management produced better ways to cut metals and improved bricklaying. This translates into less costly stock transactions, better flight schedules, and quick-service restaurant efficiencies.

10. Lean production systems are also considered to be agile and fast-moving. Which of the following methods and attributes do "agile" systems not employ? (Note: if there are some unfamiliar terms, search for them on the Internet before choosing an answer.)

    a. design of parts to be interchangeable, modular, and group technology-based

    b. parts that can be assembled with efficiencies of sequenced assembly methods

    c. inspection procedures to weed out defectives in the pursuit of zero-defects

    d. flexible programming to allow fast setups and changeovers

    e. globally-connected systems that permit immediate communications between partners along the supply chain

ADDITIONAL READINGS

Anupindi, Ravi, Sunil Chopra, Sudhakar D. Deshmukh, Jan A. Van Meighem, and Eitan Zemel. *Managing Business Process Flows*. Upper Saddle River, NJ: Prentice Hall, 1999.

Baumol, William J., Sue Anne Blackman, and Edward N. Wolff. *Productivity and American Leadership: The Long View*. Cambridge: MIT Press, 1991.

Britton, Andrew. Economic Commission for Europe Discussion Papers. *Economic Growth in the Market Economies 1950–2000*, vol. 1, no. 1, 1991. New York: United Nations (GE.91-23315).

Deming, W. E. *Out of the Crisis*. MIT Center for Advanced Engineering Study, 1986.

Fabricant, Soloman. *A Primer on Productivity*. New York: Random House, 1969.

Forrester, Jay W. "Changing Economic Patterns." *Technology Review* (August/September 1978).

Juran, J. M., and F. M. Gryna, Jr. *Quality Planning and Analysis*, 2e. New York: McGraw-Hill, 1980.

Ohno, Taiichi. *Toyota Production System: Beyond Management of Large-Scale Production*. Japan: Diamond Publishing Co. Ltd., 1978.

Servan-Schreiber, Jean-Jacques. *The American Challenge*. New York: Atheneum, 1968.

Shewhart, W. A. *Statistical Method from the Viewpoint of Quality Control*. Washington, DC: The Department of Agriculture, 1939.

Smith, Adam. *An Enquiry into the Nature and Causes of the Wealth of Nations*, 1776.

NOTES

1. Jon F. Cox, John H. Blackstone, and Michael S. Spencer. *APICS Dictionary*, 7th ed. APICS Educational and Research Foundation, 1992.

2. Soloman Fabricant. *A Primer on Productivity*. New York: Random House, 1969, p. 3. This definition adds "in a period of time (*t*)" to Fabricant's definition. He is considered to be the "father of productivity measurement."

3. The U.S. Department of Labor, Bureau of Labor Statistics, *News*. USDL 94-327 (July 7, 1994). The Bureau of Labor Statistics public database, LABSTAT, is available on the Internet.

4. The U.S. Department of Labor, Bureau of Labor Statistics, Press release. (February 1995). Available at http://data.bls.gov/servlet/SurveyOutput-Servlet; June 2003.

5. *The New York Times* (November 5, 1994): D19.

6. Ibid., but this quote is attributed to Donald P. Wingard, managing partner for Andersen's Americas Automotive Practice.

7. William J. Baumol, Sue Anne Blackman, and Edward N. Wolff. *Productivity and American Leadership: The Long View*. Cambridge: MIT Press, 1991.

8. Jay W. Forrester. "Changing Economic Patterns." *Technology Review* (August/September, 1978).

9. Cited by the study, "Foreign-Affiliated Firms in America," conducted by the Center for the Study of Operations at Columbia University, 1991.

10. Boston Consulting Group. *On Experience* was published as part of the *Perspectives* series by the BCG company in 1968, with a third printing and preface by Bruce Henderson, then president of BCG, in 1972.

11. Adam Smith. *An Enquiry into the Nature and Causes of the Wealth of Nations*, 1776 (a five-volume treatise).

12. Jean-Jacques Servan-Schreiber. *The American Challenge*. New York: Atheneum, 1968.

13. W.A. Shewhart. *Statistical Method from the Viewpoint of Quality Control*. Washington, DC: The Department of Agriculture, 1939. This is a classic in the OM field.

14. W. E. Deming. *Out of the Crisis*. MIT Center for Advanced Engineering Study, 1986. Also, a valuable reference is J. M. Juran and F. M. Gryna, Jr. *Quality Planning and Analysis*, 2e. New York: McGraw-Hill, 1980.

15. T. Ohno. *Toyota Production System: Beyond Management of Large-Scale Production*. Japan: Diamond Publishing Co. Ltd., 1978.

16. Called the six-sigma program, the goal is to strive for 3.4 defects per million parts.

17. *The New York Times* (November 8, 1994): 1.

18. The agile manufacturing strategy and recommendations for future action were developed by an industry-led team, partially funded by the Office of the Secretary of Defense Manufacturing Technology (MANTECH) Program and facilitated by the Iacocca Institute at Lehigh University. The study resulted in the publication of two volumes entitled *21st Century Manufacturing Enterprise Strategy: An Industry Led View of Agile Manufacturing*, dated November 1991 and released by Agility Manufacturing Enterprise Forum at Lehigh University.

SPOTLIGHT 2-1
Boutwell Owens and Co., Inc.

Boutwell Owens and Co., Inc.

A "total package service" provider that takes packaging from the drawing board to the loading dock—An example of excellence in entrepreneuring.

Boutwell Owens and Co., Inc., is a small family-owned manufacturer of paperboard cartons, inserts, "skin" packaging, and retail display cards in Fitchburg, Massachusetts. The company succeeds in a somewhat stagnant market because of its emphasis on quality and service. Boutwell sees itself not as a printer of product packages, but as a "total package service" provider that takes packaging from the "drawing board to the loading dock."

Boutwell Owens provides different levels of service to companies depending on their size. For small companies, they "get them into the marketplace with a sharp-looking package," said Ward McLaughlin, Boutwell's president. For large companies, Boutwell not only designs their packaging, but manages their inventories as well. Customers include such familiar names as Radio Shack, GTE, Polaroid, Oral B, Milton Bradley, and Honeywell.

Today's market demands bring on a whole new dimension of salespeople. Successful salespeople are trained and educated to interact at all levels with the customer base (called *depth selling*). Selling a package that will sell the customer's product is the goal, rather than on the basis of the lowest price. A good understanding of a target cost point needs to be established. The salesperson needs to be well versed in art and structures to help direct the customer with the building of files as well as directing the customer to the proper stock on which to print art. Selling goes beyond just marketing and purchasing. A true professional will work with the customers' manufacturing, planning logistics, and equipment to ensure that the product flows through their plants quickly and smoothly.

Boutwell is successful because, according to vice president of operations Larry Kelley, "We're a job shop. We do whatever the customer needs done. We'll take on the jobs that no one else will do. Our consistency and commitment to improvements truly make our company stand out in front of the competition. We put a lot of emphasis toward training and educating our teams on procedures and policies. This type of commitment has made a big difference. We are a company that takes a big interest in our customers' needs and works toward filling those needs."

President Ward McLaughlin points out that "a company comes to us mainly because of our ability to . . . get them out of trouble, and when they find out that our quality and service stay equal to what we first initiated, they stay" with Boutwell.

The company runs three shifts to meet demand. Its workforce has grown from 60 to 170 employees since 1985. Boutwell is proud of its ability to set up machines fast and meet tight deadlines. Fast turnover of orders is critical when dealing with large retailers. "The Wal-Marts, the Kmarts, the big retailers are pretty relentless," said Brian Jansson, vice president of finance. "Orders will be canceled automatically if you're late."

Source: Communications with Brian Jansson; assistance from Ward McLaughlin, July 9, 2003. Original contact: Bruce Phillips. "Building Packages That Move the Product." Fitchburg-Leominster Sentinel and Enterprise (June 27, 1994).

SPOTLIGHT 2-2
Chick-fil-A®—A Successful Business Model

Chick-fil-A®, Inc., Independent Operators, and the Loyalty Effect

S. Truett Cathy, founder and chairman of Chick-fil-A, Inc., looks back to 1967 when the first Chick-fil-A® restaurant opened and says of himself at that time, "I did not expect . . . to be running a chain of 1,000 restaurants. I grew into it one day at a time with help from talented people around me. When you get this big, you grow through the talent of others." Truett Cathy learned to divide tasks and trust other people to do the job well.

Creating a "loyalty effect" through a lifetime commitment to the success and well-being of its operators, the Chick-fil-A company buys real estate, builds a restaurant, and turns over the responsibility of a million-dollar business to a franchisee; many Chick-fil-A franchisees are under 30 years of age. Truett explains to each applicant that a commitment to Chick-fil-A is like a marriage with no consideration given to divorce. Each new operator runs a single restaurant and holds no outside employment or other business interest. Unlike some franchisees who might think of themselves as investors with no direct contact with the store itself, Chick-fil-A expects operators to work full-time in the restaurant they've built, serving customers and team members who have become loyal to them. The Chick-fil-A operator is the CEO, operations manager, president, and treasurer of his or her own business.

The Cathy family's loyalty to their operators is evident. Operators are supported with training, technology, and anything else they need. Chick-fil-A is on the leading edge of information technology. Because each restaurant is a separate legal and tax entity, the company offers hundreds of separate tax filings as a service to operators. Its payroll system is web-based, allowing operators to write checks in their restaurant. Trust develops as it becomes clear that everyone is working together, depending on each other, and not just bound by a franchise agreement.

The Chick-fil-A franchise agreement has not changed since 1967. The only money required from an operator is a $5,000 refundable initial capital commitment. The company supplies the initial capital for the restaurant. The agreement calls for the operator to sub-lease the restaurant, paying Chick-fil-A 15 percent of gross sales plus 50 percent of net profits from the restaurant as a service charge. Operators own their own business even though they work closely with Chick-fil-A, Inc. In 2002, more than half earned more than $100,000; many earned more than $200,000; and a few topped $300,000.

Truett Cathy looks for several specific traits in seeking operators. Character is paramount. According to Cathy, everything else can be learned. Applicants must demonstrate that they really want the opportunity with an entrepreneurial attitude. They must set high standards of excellence for themselves. Their appearance must be neat and clean. They must demonstrate their ability to make long-term commitments and handle financial responsibility. Cathy encourages his operators to think and experiment under reasonable circumstances. Otherwise, he writes, "We will end up with a bunch of timid operators." Many of the operators have been Chick-fil-A team members who are eager to succeed and ready to pour their hearts and souls into their own restaurant.

One operator from Mesquite, Texas, says of his business, "The most important people are our employees. Some people will say customers are most important, but if we create the right atmosphere where our employees enjoy their jobs and have opportunities for growth, they will get a kick out of their work. They're part of a winning team. That feeling will spill right over to the customer." This Texas operator used his initiative to get involved with the entire school system in town. He sometimes surprises teachers by showing up with a party tray of Chick-fil-A Nuggets or a brownie tray to thank them for the work they do. Giving creates a level of loyalty that leads to long-term success.

The most important job an operator has is selecting his people, which is similar to organizing a baseball team. One operator in Dayton, Ohio, writes, "Sometimes during an interview I will 'accidentally' knock a stack of papers off my desk and see if the interviewee will pick them up. If the person is service-oriented, they'll immediately reach down for them." She continues, "We also learn whether potential employees can think for themselves and react appropriately to an irate customer through role-playing situations."

There is a saying at Chick-fil-A that an operator gets the people he or she deserves. Cathy visited a store where he saw a team member who obviously was not getting the job done. He asked the operator, "Why in the world did you hire that person?" The answer was, "He needed the job so badly." Cathy replied, "Well, put him on the payroll, but don't ask him to show up for work. You'll be better off if he stays home."

Thousands of teenagers work as part-time employees of Chick-fil-A restaurants at one time or another. Truett expects his operators to teach them good permanent work habits and attitudes. To make a positive impact on the people around us, he urges us to avoid complacency as we measure ourselves against the national average. "Look what it means to be average," he writes. "You're the worst of the best and the best of the worst."

Truett Cathy never gives up teaching people the Chick-fil-A way.

See the Spotlight feature box in Chapter 20, S. Truett Cathy: "Never Overextend Yourself."

Source: S. Truett Cathy. "Eat Mor Chikin: Inspire More People. Doing Business the Chick-fil-A Way." Decatur, GA: Looking Glass Books, 2002.

Supplement 2

Decision Trees

Decision trees (DTs) provide another method for representing decision problems. There are certain kinds of problems that DTs can organize that are very cumbersome in matrix form. It is a toss-up, however, as to which is preferred.

The decision problem presented in Supplement 1 (in Chapter 1) can be modeled with decision trees. Later on, a productivity decision example will be given where decision trees are much preferred to matrices, and by extension, where they must be used. First, the decision tree is drawn in Figure 2-4 to represent the shipper's situation.

Following are the rules for using DTs. It is helpful to observe how the problem is translated from decision-matrix form into a decision tree.

Start with the various strategies emanating from the first decision box. Some trees have many decision boxes, although this tree has only one. Also, there can be many lines that fan out from any decision box. This tree has only two.

Label the strategies with their costs. At the end of each strategy line, there is a chance-event circle. From that circle emanate the states of nature that can occur. There is a line for every state of nature, and each is labeled with the appropriate probability and revenue. By tracing out the costs and revenues encountered along each branch of the tree, a unique endpoint for profits is derived. Label the net value (N.V.) of each endpoint.

Work backwards through the tree. Wherever two or more states of nature merge at a chance-event circle, obtain the expected value for profit at that circle and mark it.

Continue working backwards through the tree. Whenever two or more strategies (such as by plane or by train) merge at a decision-point box, carry the largest expected value to that box. For this tree, the choice is between 3400 and 2700. Because the former is larger, and this tree is profit oriented, label the decision-point box with $EV = 3400$. If the decision problem is not in terms of profits, then use net costs and expected costs.

When the decision tree has a sequence of strategies (see the next example), then, working backwards, follow that sequence of strategies that accounts for the largest EV for profit. This is the EV that has been carried to the first decision-point box of the network. For the preceding tree, the strategy ship by plane, which is the top branch of the tree, is the winner.

DECISION SEQUENCES OF GREATER LENGTH— A GAME OF CHANCE

Decision problems that involve a sequence of alternative strategic choices are particularly well-suited to decision tree organization for solution. When there are many sequences of the type "if this, then that," the decision tree is the only sensible way to represent such complexity.

Start with a simple example. Assume the following game of chance:

If X chooses to play the first game, called A, and wins, then X can play the second game, called B. X does not have to play B or A.

To play A or B costs $50.

FIGURE 2-4
Decision Tree for the Shipping Decision

$EV = 0.1 (700) + 0.9 (3700) = 3400$

N.V.

Plane $800

$1,500   F (0.1) $700

$4,500   C (0.9) $3,700

$EV = 3400$ X

Train $300

$3,000   F (0.1) $2,700

$3,000   C (0.9) $2,700

N.V. = Net Value
F = Fog
C = Clear

$EV = 0.1 (2700) + 0.9 (2700) = 2700$

61

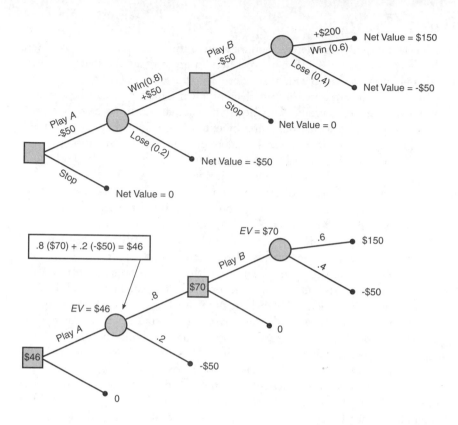

FIGURE 2-5
Decision Tree for Game

If X wins A, X receives $50. There is an 80 percent probability of winning A. If X wins the second game, B, X receives $200. There is a 60 percent probability of X winning B. What should X do?

Figure 2-5 shows that the expected value for trying to play both games is $46. There is a 20 percent chance that X will lose the first game and be out the $50. However, there is an 80 percent chance that X will win the first game, which means that X just breaks even. X must go on to play the second game.

DECISION-MATRIX EQUIVALENT

When the tree in Figure 2-5 is converted into its decision-matrix form (see Table 2-3), it is possible to appreciate the economy of representation of the tree approach for large, multistage decision problems.

In the following problems, a productivity decision problem is posed that is best resolved by the decision-tree method.

	Probabilities			
	0.48	0.32	0.20	EV
	Win A	Win A	Lose A	
	Win B	Lose B	Stop	
Play A	0	0	–$50	–$10
Play A and B	$150	–$50	–$50	$46
Do not play	0	0	0	0

TABLE 2-3

Decision Matrix for Two-Stage Problem

Problems for Supplement 2

1. The Pin Factory can buy a new machine—called M1—that costs $40,000. There is an 80 percent chance that sales will get an order for which this machine can be used with significant productivity advantages. If that order does not materialize, then the machine will not be used for the foreseeable future. Normally, one would wait to see if the order was received, but that cannot be done in this case because the M1 has a 3-month lead time. If M1 is purchased today, it will be online just in time.

   If the order is received and the machine is online, then the Pin Factory will earn $50,000. It also will be given the opportunity to bid on a much bigger job. The bigger job requires buying four more M1 machines, which will be delivered in time to be online for the new job, if the Pin Factory wins the bid. The management team estimates that the probability of winning the bid is 60 percent. The revenue from getting the new order will be $300,000. Should the Pin Factory decide to try for these orders?

2. American Auto Supply (AAS) has been given an opportunity to become a certified supplier by one of the major auto companies in Detroit. They have been offered the following proposition:

   Stage 1: Submit engine-mount parts from a sample mold. If they pass, there will be an order for 100,000 engine-mount parts, and a chance to:

   Stage 2: Submit samples for shock-absorber assemblies. If these pass lab tests, there will be an order for 100,000 shock-absorber assemblies, and a chance to:

   Stage 3: Submit samples for bumper assemblies. If these pass the tests, there will be an order for 100,000 bumper assemblies.

   The deadline is tight for accomplishment of each stage.

   The conditions are that AAS pays for the molds and all costs associated with making sample parts. There is no reimbursement for tooling-up for parts that fail to pass the test. Further, engineering has stated that these parts are difficult to make to meet the specifications. The chances of success by the deadline are estimated to be 50 percent for the engine-mount and bumper assemblies. There is a 40 percent chance of failure for the shock-absorbers assemblies.

   Total direct costs (TDC) for 100 samples are as follows:

Parts	TDC	Ppu
Engine mounts	$ 8,000	($0.20)
Bumpers	$16,000	($0.40)
Shock absorbers	$10,000	($0.20)

   The profits per unit (ppu) if awarded the contract for 100,000 units are listed next to the total direct costs within parentheses. Should AAS accept the challenge?

3. Because the deadline is so tight, American Auto Supply has asked for changes in the proposition to give them more latitude in preparing the samples. The changes being requested appear in rewritten Stages 2 and 3, as follows:

   Stage 2: Submit samples for either the shock-absorber assemblies or the bumper assemblies, not both. If the second part passes the lab tests, there will be an order for 100,000 units. Then AAS can go on to qualify for the third part. Therefore, Stage 3 would become:

   Stage 3: Submit samples for the third part, which is either the bumper assembly or the shock-absorber assembly. If these pass the tests, there will be an order for 100,000 units of that assembly.

Strategic Perspectives for Operations Management

In Part 2, strategy is defined. OM's participation with other functions in developing strategy is explained. OM's role in carrying out strategy through tactics is described. The focus moves from new products (goods and services) in Chapter 3 to quality attainment in Chapter 4. These two chapters, which comprise Part 2, provide the framework for understanding how operations management participates in strategic planning. It also prepares the way for understanding the important relationship of tactics to strategies.

Chapter 3 is entitled "P/OM Strategies: Forecasting Life Cycle Stages." Chapter 3 explores strategic planning for new and existing products. Referred to as "life cycle planning," this involves understanding the strategic interactions of P/OM with marketing. Life cycles include the introduction and growth of new products. The next stage of stable maturity has been getting shorter as technology and marketing communication have evolved. Decline of share may be followed by redesign or by withdrawal from the market. Methods to evaluate consumer acceptance are necessary. Forecasting models to estimate demand (in terms of sales and market share) are developed. Forecasting ability is enhanced when there is access to market research data. These ideas are basic to the formulation of operational strategies.

Chapter 4 is entitled "Quality Management: Strategic Issues." Chapter 4 examines the role quality plays in strategic planning. This involves answering such questions as: How should strategic planners set the right quality goals and what must production and operations managers do (strategically/tactically) to attain goals that have been set? It is necessary to understand total quality management (TQM) to answer these questions. TQM is the application of a systems concept of quality that cuts across functional areas. It will be shown that quality definitions are central to quality achievements. To rate idea and design acceptability, scoring models for quality measurement are introduced. Starting with the foundation of strong definitions, the fabric of quality is woven in Chapter 4.

Treatment of tactical factors must follow strategic perspectives. Discussion of tactical factors begins in Part 3 and continues in Part 4. Part 5 returns to strategic perspectives, tying the tactical and strategic together.

P/OM Strategies: Forecasting Life Cycle Stages

Chapter Outline

C hapter 3 explores strategic planning for new and existing products. Referred to as "life cycle planning," this involves understanding the strategic interactions of P/OM with marketing. Life cycles include the introduction and growth of new products. The next stage of stable maturity has been getting shorter as technology and marketing communication have evolved. Decline of share may

be followed by redesign or by withdrawal from the market. Methods to evaluate consumer acceptance are necessary. Forecasting models to estimate demand (in terms of sales and market share) are developed. Forecasting ability is enhanced when there is access to market research data. These ideas are basic to the formulation of operational strategies.

After reading this chapter, you should be able to:

- Clarify the distinction between strategy and tactics.
- Detail how P/OM can contribute to the strategy planning team.
- Explain what "Best Practice" means to P/OM.
- Define life cycle stages and why they are important.
- Forecast relevant information for production scheduling.

- Teach others about choosing forecasting techniques.
- Contrast various forecasting methods.
- Do a linear regression analysis.
- Show how to evaluate forecast errors.
- Explain why it is important to maintain forecasting history.

THE SYSTEMS VIEWPOINT

Organizations that base their plans on where they have been rather than on what appears to be happening in their future are like drivers who steer by looking through the rearview mirror. The systems viewpoint integrates the past, present, and future. Forecasts are necessary to describe the future. These forecasts must coordinate demands for products and services with supplies of resources that are required to meet the demands. Forecasts for market demands set the agenda for how the entire company will use its people, commit its resources, call on outside suppliers, and plan its work schedules. As such, the forecast is the platform for strategic planning. Good strategy is aimed at modifying the forecast to influence what the future might bring rather than just accepting the forecast as an inevitable truth. In this way, management earns its rewards by better fitting production capabilities (short- and long-term) to marketing possibilities. This systems point of view has the best chance of maximizing profits.

STRATEGIC THINKING

Strategic thinking (planning) to realize objectives involves teamwork. OM is part of that team. The hub and spoke diagram in Figure 3-1 puts strategy planning at the center of the system and all of the business functions at the end of the spokes. The coordinating function is management. The coordinating system's mechanism is strategy. After there is agreement about strategies to be followed, the OM function decides on the tactics to be used to pull together the various functions.

3-1 OPERATIONS MANAGEMENT STRATEGIES FOR SURVIVAL AND SUCCESS

Strategy: Comprehensive and overall planning for the organization's future.

Strategy is the comprehensive and overall planning for the organization's future. It has to be product-oriented and marketing-aware in order to take the customer and the competition into account, and process-oriented and P/OM-oriented to deliver the product that customers want. It needs to be systems-oriented to coordinate marketing and P/OM. This entails broad-based, cooperative goal setting followed by planning to achieve four goals:

1. Survival of the organization under the stress of technological change as well as economic and political factors.
2. Adaptation to a global business environment. This must include adjusting to the effect of different values—such as more importance placed on recycling than at the home base.
3. Conversion from a reactive mode to a proactive mode, which means not just waiting for things to happen.
4. Profit maximization must include sufficient cash flow to assure achieving point 1 shown here.

Successful strategies are required for the organization's effective pursuit of its clearly defined goals.

Strategic business units (SBUs): Independent subdivisions considered to be profit-making entities for the company.

Many companies are divided into **strategic business units (SBUs)** in order to help them define clear, strong, and effective strategies. Each strategic business unit develops plans centered on its own set of products, and each can be compared to similar business units with respect to process performance. Comparisons also can be made with OM and marketing effectiveness. The systems perspective is essential to the competitive advantage of successful SBUs.

Tactics: Detailed procedures required to carry out strategic plans.

Illustrating the distinction between strategies and **tactics** helps to further define strategy: Do the right "thing" (strategic choice) before doing the "thing" right (tactical choice)! As an example, consider the company that tried to make better buggy whips in order to fend off the competition of Henry Ford's Model T. That company would have been well advised to work on an electric starter because the Model T engine had to be hand-cranked to start it.

Another analogy that is used to help differentiate between strategies and tactics is: Know where you want to go (the strategic choice—a goal) before deciding on the best way to get there (the tactical choice—the means to an end). This is equivalent to stating that the goals set by strategies are like destinations. The decision to fly, drive, or take a train is a tactical decision that cannot be made until the origin and destination are known.

3-2 PARTICIPANTS IN PLANNING STRATEGIES

Because strategies are the future plans for the company, strategies must be created by those who know enough about the business to do such planning. Usually, therefore, strategies will be formulated by those at the top of the organization, aided by those with special knowledge who may be located anywhere inside or outside the company. The cast of characters involved in strategic planning usually is composed of a top management group, line

FIGURE 3-1
Hub and Spoke Diagram
Strategy planning is the hub and business functions are at the end of the spokes.

and staff managers, and various specialists in relevant fields. The participants change as conditions are altered.

Strategy development is a continuous and ongoing process, because strategies must be revised as conditions change. It is a matter of survival through adaptation. A new competitive product entry, an improvement in the competitor's delivery system, a change in the law or in economic conditions, or a new technological development that enhances the competitor's process often will call for modification of prior strategies. Therefore, the nature of the changes that are occurring will determine which specialists may be consulted. Those responsible for strategic planning must know enough to seek out the appropriate specialists as conditions warrant.

3-2a P/OM's Role in Developing Strategies

From the systems point of view, only in small companies can one person know enough about the business to do strategic planning by himself or herself. As firms get larger, no one person can handle all of the activities that need to be done.

In larger firms, the systems perspective dictates that representatives of all of the functional departments that define "knowing enough about the business" play a part in strategy development. Figure 3-1 illustrates that no one person holds all the cards.

There are some additional differences between organizations with respect to who participates in planning the strategies for products and processes. If the technology used for the process is recent and complex (new and high-tech), then operations managers are more likely to be part of the strategic planning team, or at least be consulted by them. Such proactive participation applies to both manufacturing and service industries.

Chembank's operations managers participated in strategy formulation for a variety of new products. They were the only part of the bank that was on top of the technology for new banking products using computerized voice-responding systems for account information inquiries and PCs for home-banking. Similarly, in General Electric's smart manufacturing plants, OM is coordinated with the other functions by means of a common understanding of strategic goals. In smart plants, P/OM is part of the strategic planning team.

If P/OM know-how is not properly represented, then strategic planning is operating at a limited or damaged level. The same is true if other functional areas are not represented. The benefits of the systems approach are missing, and the organization is operating at a disadvantage with respect to survival under technological stress, adaptation to a global environment, and conversion from reactive to proactive competitive positions.

Because of pollution concerns, factories in many countries have employed technology to monitor and control harmful emissions. Many auto companies are developing hydrogen cars after finding that electric cars were not providing satisfactory performance for their cost.

Cycles: Repetitive patterns of sequenced values, which generally return to the same starting point.

Synergy: Agents producing a greater effect when acting together than the sum of their separate effects.

Syzygy: Point when maximum tidal pull is exerted because the planets and the moon have lined up.

3-2b Who Carries Out the Strategies?

Operations managers are always involved in carrying out strategic plans, even when they are not part of the strategic planning team. Operations is where the work is done that creates the product that the customer buys. This applies to the operations room of banks and airlines and the production department of the manufacturer.

Independent of who formulates company strategy, decisions that stem from that strategy are carried into action by tactics. Tactics are the procedures used by the line managers of the organization to carry out the strategic plans. Tactical applications are the normal operating mode of line managers of the organization and include production scheduling, materials planning, and quality control.

The terms strategy and tactics have military origins. Strategy is directed at winning the "war" while tactics are designed to win the "battles." Generals and admirals decide what battles have to be fought, when, where, and with what. The line officers carry out the mission determining the "hows."

Use of the terms strategy and tactics is common in companies where line management is recognized as being an OM responsibility. Overseeing production workers who are on the line, making goods and delivering services, is only part of the job. Line managers must be aware of the company's goals and objectives to be an effective part of the strategy team.

Strategic planners determine the what, when, and where of new products. OM is then responsible for how to make and deliver these new products. New product decisions require planning future capabilities and capacities. Strategies also are concerned with the production and replacement of existing products at given costs and levels of investment. Regardless of whether P/OM participates in the development of such strategic plans, these plans are administered by operations managers.

In organizations that are strongly integrated, operations managers participate in planning the evolution of both new and existing products. That evolution over time is called the product life **cycles.** Plans for the life cycles—called life cycle strategies—set in motion the designing of the input-transformation-output systems that are the basis of production. Life cycle strategies will be further defined and discussed in this chapter.

Synergy is an action of separate agents that produces a greater effect than the sum of their individual actions. One plus one makes three. **Syzygy,** besides being the only word in the English language that has no vowels and three y's, comes from a Greek word for "conjunction." It is the point when maximum tidal pull is exerted because the planets and moon have lined up to support each other's gravitational forces.

Stage IV organizations capitalize on synergy and syzygy by encouraging broad communication about all matters relating to strategic planning. Stage IV organizations achieve the teamwork ideals of the systems approach, whereas Stage I organizations do not have what it takes.

Stage I companies are moving to Stage II and higher as most American organizations have come to realize that important strategic leverage is gained through the participation of P/OM. It is an exciting time for operations managers because in almost every organization P/OM is being integrated into the corporate planning fabric. Successful new competitors are not Stage I companies. Often from abroad, they have fully-coordinated strategic planning teams.

3-2c Adopting "Best Practice"

Being "in the know" prevents P/OMs from inadvertently working against the company's success. Yet, what is to be done if the stage of the organization, or the politics of the organization, or the chemistry of the managers causes policies to be followed that do not place the operations managers onto the strategy teams?

By working actively (as compared to working passively) in the realm of

1. new product development and
2. quality enhancement practices,

P/OM can get involved with the strategic domain, without ever having been appointed to a strategic planning committee.

Passive participation of P/OM is characterized by doing just what is asked and nothing more. Active participation involves learning about what is being done elsewhere and then trying to get Best Practice adopted whenever possible. P/OM must play an instrumental role at both the strategic and tactical levels to determine what Best Practice is regionally, especially with competitors and, ultimately, anywhere in the world.

Both new product development and quality enhancement practices are gateways to the strategic domain. Total quality management (TQM) is susceptible to either continuous improvement or to the marked departure from prior procedures (starting out with a clean piece of paper) that reengineering requires. New products, whether goods or services, provide opportunities for reinventing, or reengineering, process flows. The constant effort to improve products and process flows provides a transition between strategies and tactics for operating the system.

3-2d P/OM Is a Scarce Resource

Strategies for the introduction of new products and for replacement of existing products must be formulated with the fact in mind that operations managers' time and talents are limited resources. Managerial capabilities must be spread over both new product start-ups and ongoing output responsibilities.

Because OM is a scarce resource, its personnel should be used wisely. This means bringing P/OM knowledge to bear as early as possible—in the strategy formulation process. By doing so, it is possible to avoid squandering limited OM time and talent on remedial "fire fighting" and efforts to play "catch-up" later.

3-3 UNDERSTANDING LIFE CYCLE STAGES: CRUCIAL FOR P/OM ACTION

Throughout the company, the planning function marches to the drumbeat of life cycle stages. Operations managers need to be aware of the timing and stages that drive the project management schedules of new products, as well as the production and delivery schedules of the company's mature products.

Cycles are composed of four stages that appear in a regular way over time. All products and services go through the following stages:

1. Introduction to the market
2. Growth of volume and share
3. Maturation, because maturity is the phase of relative equilibrium
4. Decline, because the condition of deteriorating sales leads to restaging or withdrawal

These life cycle periods are discrete stages in each product's life that need to be understood in order to manage that product. Marketing is responsible for using different pricing, advertising, and promotion activities during appropriate stages. OM is responsible for intelligent management of the transformation system, which changes in various ways according to the life cycle stage. The changes or transitions between stages require knowing how to adjust the production system's capabilities.

3-3a Introduction and Growth of the New Product (Goods and Services)

There are two main phases of life cycle stages. The first consists of the introduction and growth of the product. The "idea" for the product and its development precedes the introduction. The entire team works on ascertaining the marketing feasibility of the idea, as well as the feasibility of making it and delivering it. R & D may have made sample product so that market research can test its customer acceptability. When it is approved, OM

and engineering swing into action to create the production system that can make and/or assemble it. During this process of bringing the idea to reality, there are many "make or buy" analyses.

None of this is easy. It takes a lot of effort and attention to detail. There is much time and talent needed to conceptualize the product, design its specifics, organize the process for making it, cost it out, pilot test it, and so forth. When the product is accepted, it is released for production and marketing. All of this takes place in the introductory stage.

3-3b Maturation and Decline of the New Product (Goods and Services)

When the new product or service stops growing, it is considered mature. This means that its volume is stabilized at the saturation level for that brand. The competitors have divided the market, and only extraordinary events, such as a strike at a competitor's plant, are able to shift shares and volumes.

Previously OM had to deal with producing larger and larger quantities of product. Now the input–output relationship reaches equilibrium. Marketing takes specific actions during this phase to maintain the product's share of the market. Prices often are lowered. Coordination between OM and sales is essential to meet delivery schedules on time. Finally, the product begins to lose share, volume drops, and, depending on the strategy, the product is either restaged or terminated.

It is expected that a new product will have been introduced previously that has grown to a reasonable extent. It is the replacement for the other product and has been assigned the capacity of the product that has been replaced. The cycle of the new product is similar to that of the one that is replaced in that it goes through introduction, growth, maturation, and decline. Figure 3-2 illustrates the trajectory that represents the evolution of new product or service life cycle stages.

Consider the revenue-generating lifetime of the new product. (This consideration is applicable to goods and/or services—so product should be read as either or both.) During the introduction, expenditures usually are high to bring the new product to the distributors, retailers, and customers. The cash flow is negative.

More is being spent on the introduction of the product and promotion of growth than the product revenue returns. Later, when the customer base has been established, net revenue increases, and expenditure decreases. During the stable period of product maturity, if the product enjoys a loyal following, promotions of any kind may be unnecessary. Eventually, competitive moves are likely to lead to price cuts and the withdrawal of the product from the market. The extent of the stable interval has been decreasing in many categories because of technological changes as well as aggressive competitive behaviors.

FIGURE 3-2
Evolution of Life Cycle Stages

Product life cycles have been speeding up, which means that growth has to occur faster. The product does not stay in the mature stage as long and has to be replaced more often. More new product introductions are required to replace waning products. The challenge for OM is the rapidity of adjustment to all of the life cycle stage changes and to go through them frequently.

OM thinking is crucial to each of the four stages. The new design that is about to enter production has been finalized. There still are many questions to be answered. How much product must be made for distribution at start-up? How much product will be needed to keep the supply lines filled to meet the demand during growth? How much capacity is to be used at each of the stages? How much training will the evolving work configurations require? Make or buy decisions can change. What should be bought at first, at the lower volumes, might be better made in the plant, at the higher volumes that are associated with maturity.

3-3c Protection of Established (Mature) Products (Goods and Services)

Organizations that have been successful with their new product introductions can bank on having established products or services that generate cash flow. The "bank" is not as good as it used to be though, because the competitive rate of new product introductions has increased markedly in recent years. OM requires the cash to pay labor and buy materials from suppliers. Generally, OM spends more cash than any other department in the company. These cash accounts for operating expenses may total 70 percent of all cash spent by the company.

Because of global organizations, there are more competitors in the game, and because there are more competitors, each organization competes harder. Increased competition has led to higher levels of market volatility. Nevertheless, for most product categories, there is still plenty of opportunity to benefit from the mature product life cycle stage. OM benefits from the security of established products because they have stable material and labor skill requirements. They also provide the opportunity to improve the productivity of these processes.

3-4 FORECASTING LIFE CYCLE STAGES FOR P/OM ACTION

Life cycle stages provide a classification for understanding the kinds of trends that can be expected in demand. During the introduction, the demand is led by the desire to "fill the pipeline." This means getting product into the stores or into warehouses or wherever it must be to supply the customers.

When growth starts to occur, there is a trend line of increasing sales. The trick is to estimate how fast demand will increase over time, and for how long a period growth will continue. There are good methods used by market research to find out what is happening. This information is fed back through sales to OM for purposes of production scheduling.

3-4a Perspectives on Forecasting

An umbrella manufacturer is preparing production and distribution schedules. There is a sign on the wall: "Where will it rain next week?" When it rains, umbrella sales pick up. Meteorological models have improved in recent years so that fairly good weather forecasts can be made. Many businesses, especially when scheduling outdoor events, hire weather forecasters who have a good track record.

Forecasting is not the term generally used to talk about the composition of a random draw of cards or how a roulette wheel performs. Those are statistical phenomena for which probabilities are known. Las Vegas and Atlantic City have built their gambling casino profits on the laws of probability—but customers still have to come and play. Customer attendance is not a known probability. The casinos try to forecast attendance.

To compete in the global market, companies must deal with different time zones around the world. For example, banks use state-of-the-art technologies to process transactions that occur when their front office is closed. The backroom is operating 24/7. Airlines and computer software firms operate around the clock with operations and support systems.

Forecasting: Describing future events and their probabilities of occurrence.

Forecasting is used to foretell sales demand volume even though the probabilities have never been formally studied. Businesspeople often use their sense of what is happening to reach decisions that might be better made if someone had kept a record of what had taken place already. There is often some empirical basis for estimating what is likely to happen in the future.

Marketing models for predicting sales (lacking a contract) deal with levels of uncertainty that make forecasts of demand volumes, market shares, and revenues difficult, but not irrational. One of the best sources of information about the future is the past. For new products, there is no past, and so other methods can be tried.

The focus is on using existing data to develop forecasts. The Rivet and Nail Factory has to forecast sales of products to develop departmental schedules for the next production period. The Mail Order Company has to forecast demand in order to have the right number of trained agents and operators in place. Ford Motor Company has to forecast car sales so that dealer stocks are of reasonable size for every model.

In every sales forecasting situation, the volatility of demand will determine how likely it is that a good forecast can be made. Stable patterns that persist for a long period of time make company forecasters confident that a credible job of forecasting can be done. Shaky estimates make company forecasters uneasy, so they search for new factors to correlate with the demand system.

Sales patterns are becoming less stable with increasing competition and information. Food sales that once were stable now are affected by medical reports about the food's effect on health. Auto and home sales are among many products that are strongly influenced by interest rates, which fluctuate more in a global environment. Exports and imports are sales that move around the globe in response to currency fluctuations that are increasingly unstable. Consequently, better forecasting methods need to be used by the companies that are affected by increased volatility.

How well can one forecast the future? The answer will depend on the stability of the pattern of the **time series** for the events being studied. The underlying pattern can be hard to find, but not impossible. Even if a pattern is found, the question remains, how long will it persist? When will it change? Those willing to forecast accept the challenge.

Time series: Stream of numbers that represents different values over time.

3-4b Extrapolation of Cycles, Trend Lines, and Step Functions

Extrapolation: Process of moving from observed data to the projected values of future points.

Extrapolation is the process of moving from observed data (past and present) to the unknown values of future points. The extrapolation of time series is one of the main functions of forecasting.

A time series is a stream of data that represents the past measurements. Each event is time-tagged so that it is known where it is located in the series of data. Figure 3-3 shows a linear trend extrapolated by extending a line drawn between the last two observations.

FIGURE 3-3
Extrapolation of Trend Line

FIGURE 3-4
Cyclical Pattern Extrapolation of Sales Pattern Forecasts

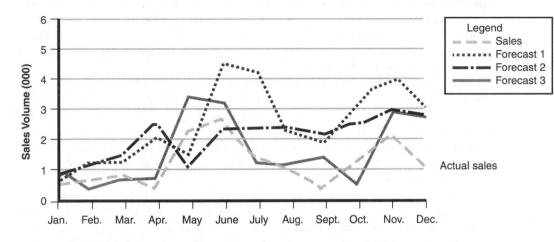

Figure 3-4 shows an erratic pattern of peaks and valleys, which represents an erratic cyclical pattern of monthly sales. Three forecasts had been made for those sales by extrapolating the cyclical patterns of prior months' sales.

Extrapolations of time series can be based on

1. Cyclical wave patterns
2. Trend lines
3. Step functions
4. Combinations of any or all of these patterns

Step functions look like stairs—going up or going down. It is hoped that the forecast can predict when the next step will occur and how far up or down it goes. Short-term cycles can be piggybacked on long-term cycles. All kinds of combinations are possible. The key point is that cycles, trends, and steps are the basic pallet for the development of forecasting models.

Time series data also can reflect erratic bursts called impulses. If these spikes appear from time to time and some pattern can be associated with them, they could be added to the list of what can be extrapolated or projected into the future.

3-4c Time Series Analysis

It is always useful to try to find causal links between well-known cycles—such as the seasons—and demand patterns that are being tracked. Thus, there are seasons for resort hotels and home heating oil. Cycles are one form of time series that is often used by business to forecast other events related to that time series. There are other categories of time series that are useful to know about. **Time series analysis** deals with using knowledge about cycles, trends, and averages to forecast future events.

The term time series analysis deserves explanation. Time series analysis is "analysis of any variable classified by time, in which the values of the variable are functions of the time periods."[1]

The time series consists of data recorded at different time periods such as weekly or daily for the variable, which could be units produced or demands received. Forecasters attempt to predict the next value or set of values that will occur at a future time. In time series analysis, external causes are not brought into the picture. The pattern of the series is considered to be time-dependent. That is why APICS' definition states "the values of the variables are functions of the time periods."

Time series analysis: Analysis of a stream of numbers in a time series.

Using symbols, a forecast is to be made from some series of numbers $x_1, x_2, \ldots x_n$. The numbers might be monthly sales figures for the past year. The question is: What use can be made of these numbers to indicate the monthly sales figures for next year? How will the forecasted time series be used? Production schedules will be drawn up to satisfy demand. Orders will be placed for inventory to be purchased. Workers will be hired and trained, or let go as the production crew is downsized. Rented space will be increased or decreased, or it will stay the same. Many decisions that are interrelated require believable forecasts before they can be made.

Time series analysis uses statistical methods, including trend and cycle analysis, to predict future values based on the history of sales or whatever the time series describes.

If the time series shows a linear trend, as in Figure 3-3, there is a constant rate of change for increasing the size of the numbers. Linear decreases also can occur. Nonlinear trend lines occur where the rate of change is geometric. In such cases, it is possible to extrapolate the curve by eye, but also, the rate of change can be calculated, and projections can be made mathematically.

Similar reasoning applies to step functions. If they occur regularly, a good estimate can be made of the period between steps and the timing of future steps. Step functions are characteristic of systems that can only change in given quantities. Thus, if sales must be made in lots of 100 units, then each change in demand will occur in hundred-unit steps. The sales for January could be 400, 500, or 600. It could step up or down, or stay the same as December sales, which were 500.

3-4d Correlation

When a series of x numbers (such as the monthly sales of 35mm cameras over a period of years) is causally connected with the series of y numbers (the monthly sales of 35mm film), then it is beneficial to collect the information about x in order to forecast y. In this case, the direction of causality is from x to y because cameras sold create the demand. Thus:

$$y = f(x)$$

To forecast the y series of numbers $y_1, y_2, \ldots y_n$, collect the x series of numbers and modify each element of x to produce the equivalent value of y. Thus:

$$y_i = f(x_i)$$

This relationship is not perfect. Therefore, y is said to be correlated with x. A correlation coefficient (r) can be calculated to measure the extent of correlation of x with y, where r can take on values from -1 to $+1$. At -1, x and y are perfectly correlated—going in opposite directions. As x gets large, y gets small, and vice versa. When $r = 0$, there is no correlation and when $r = +1$, x and y are perfectly correlated going in the same direction. Note that for the historical forecast, if each month of the time series is identical with the one 12 months before, then the autocorrelation coefficient would be equal to 1. The equation for correlation coefficients is given with the material on **linear regression.**

Linear regression: Statistical technique for determining the best straight line that can be fitted to a set of data.

3-4e Historical Forecasting with a Seasonal Cycle

The historical forecast is based on the assumption that what happened last year (or last month, etc.) will happen again. The pattern is expected to repeat itself within the time period. This method works if a stable pattern (which is often seasonal) exists. The hotel and resort business is typically involved with historical forecasts, as is the agriculture business. In each case, special circumstances can arise that lead to the desire to modify the historical forecast. In the case of hotels and resorts, the state of the economy can modify the ups-and-downs of occupancy rates. Agricultural pursuits are modified by rainfalls and temperature fluctuations (see modifications to the historical forecast in the sections that follow).

Month	Actual Sales Last Year	Forecast of Sales Next Year		TABLE 3-1
				Historical Forecast with Seasonal Data
January	1,500	1,500		
February	1,600	1,600		
March	1,800	1,800		
April	2,000	2,000		
May	2,300	2,300		
June	2,500	2,500		
July	2,350	2,350		
August	2,100	2,100		
September	1,850	1,850		
October	1,650	1,650		
November	1,550	1,550		
December	1,400*	1,400		

*Note: The December estimate of 1,400 units is based on the prior year's sales.

When last year's monthly sales values are used to predict the next year's monthly sales values, the method is based on using past history to forecast. The same concept applies to weekly or daily sales, which can be forecast on a semiannual, quarterly, or monthly basis. Table 3-1 shows the historical forecast technique applied to data that exhibit a seasonal cycle. No modification has been made for an overall change in annual sales, which is the basis of the historical forecast.

The method for making a modified historical forecast is also presented. It should be pointed out that in practice the greatest percent of all forecasts are made by using the nonmodified historical method.

When stable, cycles can provide insights that are very important for OM tactical planning. When they work, historical cycles allow OM to excel at capacity planning and production scheduling for mature manufactured products and services. The historical forecast is not appropriate for a new product introduction unless there is similarity to some other product that is already on the market.

3-5 FORECASTING METHODS

This text discusses the following eight forecasting methods:

1. Base series modification of historical forecasts
2. Moving averages for trends
3. Weighted moving averages
4. Regression analysis and correlation
5. Use of multiple forecasting methods
6. The Delphi method
7. Means of comparing forecasts using forecasting errors
8. Exponential smoothing

Mathematical equations are used for various kinds of forecasting. It is important to stress that equations do not make forecasts "the truth." Also, a great deal of good forecasting can be done without mathematics. Further, with or without mathematics, no forecast is ever guaranteed.

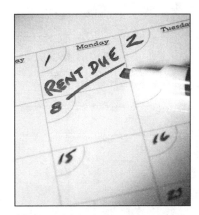

Historical cycles can become apparent by studying the calendar. In the case of P/OM, there are regularities and patterns that lend themselves to capacity planning, production scheduling, and purchasing decisions for both manufacturers and service systems.

3-5a Base Series Modification of Historical Forecasts

If the time series pattern remains fixed, but the demand level has increased overall, then a base series modification can be used. Assume that in 1999 the quarterly demands were 10, 30, 20, 40. This gives a yearly demand of 100 units. Further, assume that in 2000 the yearly demand is expected to increase to 120 units. Then the quarterly forecasts would be adjusted:

120 (10/100) = 12
120 (30/100) = 36
120 (20/100) = 24
120 (40/100) = 48

The adjusted quarterly demands total 120 units. The cyclical patterns are matched. The next year, assuming the pattern continues and the base level increases to 150, the time series would be 15, 45, 30, 60 with the sum of 150.

3-5b Moving Averages for Short-Term Trends

Moving averages might be used to extrapolate next events if the following occurs:

1. If there is no discernible cyclical pattern, and

2. If the system appears to be generating a series of values such that the last set of values provides the best estimate of what will be the next value,

3. Then, there is **forecasting momentum** in the time series' movements.

Forecasting momentum: Time series being forecast is observed to follow a course or direction that appears to be the result of an inherent force (momentum).

A decision must be made concerning how many readings should be included in the moving average set (N). Is it better to use two, three, four, or more periods? The quest is to find the optimal number of prior periods to include in the moving average series. How far back to go depends on the speed with which the series changes and the recency of events that tend to determine the future. "Very recent" means few values; "not so recent" means more values. That is a workable rule of thumb.

When the magnitude of the trend is great, and the pattern is very consistent, then the fewer the number of periods in the set the better. If the trend is gradual (up or down), and if fluctuations around the average are common, then having more periods of time in the set is better than having too few.

A moving average supplies a forecast of future values based on recent past history. The most appropriate (often the last, and latest) N consecutive values, which are observations of actual events such as daily demand, are recorded. These data must be updated to maintain the most recent N values. Then, using the last, and the latest, N values:

$\hat{x}_t$ = *the forecast value of x in period t*

(The hat sitting on top of x signifies it is the forecast.)

x_t = *the actual value of x observed in period t*

The computing equations are

$$\hat{x}_{t+1} = \frac{(x_t + x_{t-1} + \dots + x_{t-N+1})}{N}$$ (Equation 3-1)

and

$$\hat{x}_{t+2} = \frac{\hat{x}_{t+1} + (x_{t+1} - x_{t-N+1})}{N}$$ (Equation 3-2)

Each next period's forecast is updated from the last period's forecast by dropping the value of the oldest period of the series $x_{t-N=1}$ adding the latest observation, which is x_{t+1}.

This yields Equation 3-2 for the forecast of the second period ($\hat{x}_{t+2}$). In this way, new trends are taken into account, and old information is removed from the system. The moving average method applies to any time period: hours, days, weeks, months, or years.

Month (t)	Actual(x_t)	Forecast ($\hat{x}_t$)	Error ($x_t - \hat{x}_t$)
1	10		
2	30		
3	40		
4	40		
5	50	30	+20
6	60	40	+20
7		47.5	

416
-145
271

As an example, consider a 4-period monthly moving average in Table 3-2.

Four values of x_t are required before a forecast $\hat{x}_t$ can be made and before the error can be calculated.

The first forecasted value is 30. It is derived as follows:

$$(40 + 40 + 30 + 10) / 4 = 30$$

When the actual demand occurs, it turns out to be 50. The error of the forecast is +20. The forecast has fallen short by 20 units.

The sixth period forecast using Equation 3-2 is

$$30 + (50 - 10)/4 = 40$$

It also could be calculated using Equation 3-1:

$$(50 + 40 + 40 + 30)/4 = 40$$

If the forecast of 40 is incorrect, and the actual result is 60, then the following period forecast is

$$(60 + 50 + 40 + 40)/4 = 47.5$$

The moving average is slowly increasing with the trend in the actual values of x. Being slow is acceptable if there is a gradual trend with some variability in successive values. In this case, the OMs might wish for a faster response in order to schedule production closer to actual. Also, if there is a turn in the trend line, this method will follow the turn, but slowly. Some things can be done to speed things up.

The situation can be addressed in a number of ways. One approach is to decrease the number of observations N in the moving average. This will make the forecasts more responsive to recent events. Try it out with $N = 2$ and see for yourself that the seventh week forecast will be 55 instead of 47.5 as in the previous example. Another approach is to use weighted moving averages.

3-5c Weighted Moving Averages (WMA)

A way to make forecasts more responsive to the most recent actual occurrences is to use weighted moving averages. The new forecast equation is

$$\hat{x}_{t+1} = w_t x_t + w_{t-1} x_{t-1} + \ldots + w_{t-N+1} x_{t-N+1} \qquad \text{(Equation 3-3)}$$

w_t = weights for periods t

Let the sum of the weights w_t be 1; thus,

$$\sum_{t-N+1}^{t} w_t = 1$$

Note that when all weights are equal, the weighted moving average is the same as the moving average.

Thus:

$$w_t = w_{t-1} = \ldots = w_{t-N+1} = \frac{1}{N} \, \forall_t \, (\forall_t = \text{ for all } t)$$

and

$$\hat{x}_{t+1} = \frac{1}{N} x_t + \frac{1}{N} x_{t-1} + \ldots + \frac{1}{N} x_{t-N+1}$$

are equivalent to Equation 3-1.

Choosing weights that allow the latest period to have the greatest impact, and later periods decreasing importance, the equation is derived:

$$\hat{x}_{t+1} = 0.4x_t + 0.3x_{t-1} + 0.2x_{t-2} + 0.1x_{t-3}$$

where the weights 0.4, 0.3, 0.2, and 0.1, sum to one.

The biggest weights are assigned to the most recent events when there is a continuing trend. This would not be applicable where the values cycle. Thus, Thursday's sales are not the best predictors of Friday's sales—when sales on Fridays are more like sales on other Fridays than any other day.

In a rapidly changing system, w_t may be much greater (>>>) than w_{t-1} and $w_t >>> w_{t-1} >>> w_{t-2} \ldots$ etc. This is equivalent to reducing the size of N, which was discussed in the section on moving averages.

As has been noted, with the previous method of moving averages, all the w_t were treated as being equal. Then, using Table 3-2 for $t = 5$, which requires a forecast for $t + 1 = 6$:

$$\hat{x}_{t+1} = \hat{x}_6 = 0.25(50) + 0.25(40) + 0.25(40) + 0.25(30) = 40$$

Using the weights (.4, .3, .2, .1) and the numbers from the previous example of Table 3-2, the result is obtained:

$$\hat{x}_{t+1} = 0.4(50) + 0.3(40) + 0.2(40) + 0.1(30) = 20 + 12 + 8 + 3 = 43$$

The weighted system is responding more rapidly to the possible trend. It has raised the forecast to 43 as compared to the unweighted moving average of 40. The same effect is seen for the next period. Introducing the sixth period's actual value of 60, the new forecast for the seventh period has a better reaction rate, rising to 51 from 47.5.

$$\hat{x}_7 = 0.4(60) + 0.3(50) + 0.2(40) + 0.1(40) = 24 + 15 + 8 + 4 = 51$$

Thus, weighted moving averages can track strong trends more accurately than unweighted moving averages. It should be noted that the procedures can easily be programmed for computers.

3-5d Use of Linear Regression Analysis

Another valuable method that assists forecasting is regression analysis. This method is useful when trying to establish a relationship between two sets of numbers that are time series.

The first assumption that is generally made is that the relationship between the correlate pairs is linear. It is the easiest assumption to check. However, if nonlinear relations are hypothesized, there are strong, but more complex methods for doing nonlinear regression analyses.

The numbers can be simultaneous so that $x(t = 1)$ and $y(t = 1)$ are considered correlate pairs. In more general terms, these pairs would be $x(t = k)$ and $y(t = k)$. Or, alternatively, one time series can lead to another period that is later or earlier.

Thus, when $x(t = k)$ and $y(t = k + r)$ are paired, the time series y leads the time series x by r periods. It also is said that the time series x lags the time series y by r periods. Whichever way it is stated, it means that future values of y can be predicted on the basis of actual observations of the values of x—which are made r time units before the forecast date.

When outcomes are to be forecast, the knowledge that one time series leads another can be valuable information. The pairs of points x_t, y_{t+r} (t = now) can be plotted, and a regression line can be calculated as described as follows and as drawn in Figure 3-5. It is then possible to forecast a sequence of future outcomes by matching pairs of points that are offset in time by five years along the regression line. Then it is possible to make extrapolations to predict future points.

Consider the fact that sales of after-market tires—replacement tires, not tires that come with a brand new car—are related to new car sales as well as used cars that are on the road. To keep this illustration simple, assume that the sale of light truck replacement tires is well forecast by the sales of new light trucks five years earlier.

For real situations, used truck tires might have to be considered, and they would have different lead times depending upon their age. The number of trucks of different ages that are on the road would be part of the picture.

Regression analysis makes use of the least-squares method to estimate the value of future outcomes, y_{t+k}, if a leading factor x_t can be found. Causality between y_{t+k} and x_t is not assumed. A causal factor that is common to both x and y and which operates as an unknown link may be responsible for whatever relationship is found. Least-squares analysis is based on minimizing the sum of the squared deviations of each of the points that do not lie directly on the regression line.

In the example that is used, tire sales are to be forecast from a time series of light truck sales. These data are shown in Table 3-3.

It has been assumed that the strongest relationship between light truck sales and light truck tire sales in the aftermarket is when the two time series are five years apart.

It is appropriate to fit a least-squares line to these data. This line will be an estimate of the way in which truck sales affect tire sales five years later. For this example, a linear trend is assumed. More complex equations can be used for nonlinear trends. Once the line is determined, it can be used to extrapolate future tire sales.

The model uses what are called *normal equations*. Normal equations are based on assumptions of linear relationships between x_t and y_{t+5}. These linear relationships are used to derive the least-squares line. The least-squares line minimizes the total variance of the distances of the observed points from the theoretical line. The normal Equations 3-4 and 3-5 achieve this objective.

$$\sum_{t=1}^{t=N} y_{t+5} = aN + b\sum_{t=1}^{t=N} x_t \qquad \text{(Equation 3-4)}$$

$y = aN + bX$ (*simplified*— see the last row of Table 3-4)

$$\sum_{t=1}^{t=N} x_t y_{t+5} = a\sum_{t=1}^{t=N} x_t + b\sum_{t=1}^{t=N} x_t^2 \qquad \text{(Equation 3-5)}$$

$XY = aX + bX^2$ (simplified—see the last row of Table 3-4)

For our example, $N = 5$, which is the total number of pairs of x_t and y_{t+5}. Table 3-4 presents the data needed for this analysis.

Year t	Light Truck Sales x_t (in Year t) (in millions)	Year $t + 5$	Light Truck Tire Sales y_{t+5} (in Year $t + 5$) (in millions)	TABLE 3-3
				Forecasting Light Truck Tire Sales Five Years After the Light Truck Sales
1	6	6	4	
2	8	7	6	
3	12	8	10	
4	8	9	10	
5	16	10	12	

TABLE 3-4	T	x_t	y_{t+5}	$x_t y_{t+5}$	x_t^2	$y_{(t+5)}^2$
Data from Table 3-3 and Calculations to Parameterize the Normal Equations	1	6	4	24	36	16
	2	8	6	48	64	36
	3	12	10	120	144	100
	4	8	10	80	64	100
	5	16	12	192	256	144
	Sums	50	42	464	564	396
		$X = 50$	$Y = 42$	$XY = 464$	$X^2 = 564$	$Y^2 = 396$

The equations with numbers derived from Table 3-4 are

$$42 = a(5) + b(50) \quad \text{(using Equation 3-4)}$$

$$464 = a(50) + b(564) \quad \text{(using Equation 3-5)}$$

Solving for a and b, obtain: $a = 61/40$; $b = 11/16$.

These values are introduced in the least-squares line:

$$y_{t+5} = a + bx_t = \frac{61}{40} + \frac{11}{16} x_t \qquad \text{(Equation 3-6)}$$

which simplifies to

$$y_{t+5} = a + bx_t = 1.53 + 0.69 x_t \qquad \text{(Equation 3-7)}$$

This least-squares line and the actual scatter of values around it are shown in Figure 3-5.

To show how to use this line, assume that when $t = 6$, $x_t = 10$. The regression line indicates that in year 11, $y_{t+5} = 8.43$, which means that 8,430,000 tires would be the sales forecast.

Next, assume that when $t = 7$, $x_t = 20$. The regression line indicates that $y_{t+5} = 15.33$ million tires should be the sales forecast for year 12. This line would be used for forecasting only if the observed data appear to fit it well. These data do fit well. The following correlation coefficient supports the visual confirmation of a good fit.

FIGURE 3-5
Scatter Diagram Using Least-Squares Method for Regression Analysis

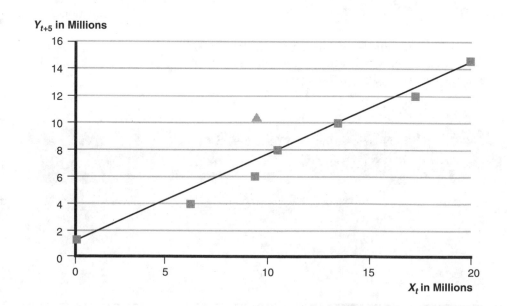

Correlation Coefficient

The correlation coefficient is

$$r = \frac{n\sum_{t=1}^{t=N} xy - \sum_{t=1}^{t=N} x \sum_{t=1}^{t=N} y}{\sqrt{\left[n\sum_{t=1}^{t=N} x^2 - (\sum_{t=1}^{t=N} x)^2\right]\left[n\sum_{t=1}^{t=N} y^2 - (\sum_{t=1}^{t=N} y)^2\right]}}$$

which equals:

$$\frac{(5)(464) - (50)(42)}{\sqrt{[5(564) - (50)^2][5(396) - (42)^2]}} = 0.84$$

There is a strong positive correlation.

Coefficient of Determination

The coefficient of determination (r^2) is a measure of the variability that is accounted for by the regression line for the dependent variable, in this case, y_{t+5}.

$$r^2 = \frac{a\sum y + b\sum xy - \frac{(\sum y)^2}{n}}{\sum y^2 - \frac{(\sum y)^2}{n}}$$

$$= \frac{1.53(42) + 0.69(464) - \frac{(42)^2}{5}}{396 - \frac{(42)^2}{5}} = \frac{32}{43} = 0.74$$

The coefficient of determination always falls between 0 and 1.

The x values account for a majority of the variability in the y values.

Pooling Information and Multiple Forecasts

Methods for pooling information to provide stronger forecasts should be explored. It is critical that all parties share their forecasts as much as possible and try to find ways to combine them. Usually, stronger forecasts can be obtained if both data and experience are pooled.

One of the keys to success in combining forecasts is trial and error. What seems to work is retained and what fails is discarded. As an example of pooling, the results of the regression analysis just completed could be augmented by a Delphi-type estimation of light truck tire sales for the next year. The Delphi participants might be the regional sales managers.

Formal methods can be used to evaluate how well different forecasting techniques are doing. At each period, the method that did best the last time is chosen for the forecast that will be followed. Forecasts are still derived from the alternative methods, but they are recorded and not followed. When the actual demand results are known, the various forecasting methods are evaluated again, and the one that is most successful is chosen to make the prediction for the next period.

Averaging of forecast results also is used. The results of taking forecasts from more than one method and averaging these results to predict demand has been successful in circumstances where choosing the best method (as described earlier) produces frequent alteration of the chosen method.

The Delphi Method

Delphi is a forecasting method that relies on expert estimation of future events. In one of its forms, the experts submit their opinions to a single individual who is the only one that knows who the participants are and what they have to say. The person who is the Delphi manager combines the opinions into a report, which, while protecting anonymity, is then disseminated to all participants. The participants are asked whether they wish to reevaluate and alter their previous opinions in the face of the body of opinion of their colleagues. Gradually, the group is supposed to move toward consensus. If it does not, at the least, a set of different possibilities can be presented to management.[2]

The regression results could be shown to the Delphi panel of experts with the questions: "Do you think sales will be higher, lower, or the same as the regression results? Why?" Consensus might lead to modification of the managers' targets that were based on the regression results. Why not let these "experts" talk to each other and discuss their opinions? If one of the experts is the CEO, or a Nobel prize winner, the dialogue might not be unbiased. People with greater debating capabilities are not necessarily people with more insight. The Delphi method is meant to put all participants on an equal footing with respect to getting their ideas heard.

3-6 COMPARATIVE FORECASTING ERRORS

All forecasting errors $x_t - \hat{x}_t = \epsilon_t$ are based on comparing, the actual demand for time period t, with $\hat{x}_t$, the forecast demand for that same period. Two kinds of forecasting errors can occur.

First, actual demand is greater than the forecast. This is a forecasting underestimate. By convention, when actual demand is greater than forecast demand, the error term ϵ_t is positive. Second, actual demand is less than the forecast. This is a forecasting overestimate, and in this case, ϵ_t is negative.

To choose a forecasting method, it is necessary to be able to compare the errors that each method generates for particular circumstances. There are five major measures of error that are used. The choice is dependent upon the situation and what kind of comparison is wanted. Thus, absolute measures are used to count all errors conservatively.

Absolute measures are signified by open brackets $|\epsilon_t|$, which mean that positive and negative errors are treated the same way. The reason for doing this is to prevent positive and negative errors from canceling each other out.

The most common measure of error is called mean absolute deviation (MAD). To calculate MAD, take the sum of the absolute measures of the errors and divide that sum by the number of observations.

$$\Sigma_t |\epsilon_t| \div n$$

Also, quite common is the mean squared error (MSE) measure. It is calculated by squaring all of the error terms and adding them together. Then, this sum is divided by the number of observations. Because squares of both positive and negative errors become positive numbers, MSE does not allow the two kinds of errors (+ and −) to cancel out each other. However, the squares of large errors become significantly larger than the squares of small errors. Therefore, MSE magnifies large errors. MAD treats all errors linearly and is a more conservative measure.

Cumulative forecast error (CFE) is simply the sum of all the error terms and is useful when overestimation errors do cancel out underestimation errors. As an example, if the error term represented inventory shortages when actual demand is greater than forecast demand, i.e., $x_t > \hat{x}_t$, and if it stood for stock on-hand when $x_t < \hat{x}_t$, assuming that stock on-hand could be used to fulfill shortages, the CFE would represent the net inventory situation.

Sometimes the standard deviation of the error distribution, σ_ϵ, is used. It is the square root of the MSE. Another method for comparing errors is called mean absolute percent error (MAPE). It is the result of dividing each absolute error term by its respective actual demand term. This gives a fraction that describes how large the error is as compared to the demand. Multiply the fraction by 100 to convert to percentages. Then, all of the terms are summed and divided by the number of observations, as shown in Table 3-5. This table examines one forecasting method with observations taken over $n = 4$ weeks. All are row sums—taken across columns.

					Sum	
Week number, t	1	2	3	4		
Actual demand, x_t	3	8	5	7		
Forecast, $\hat{x}_t$	6	4	9	6		
Error, $x_t - \hat{x}_t = \epsilon_t$	−3	+4	−4	+1	−2	CFE
Error squared, $|\epsilon_t^2|$	9	16	16	1	42	
Absolute error, $|\epsilon_t|$	3	4	4	1	12	
Absolute percent error, ($|\epsilon_t|/x_t$) 100	100	50	80	14.3	244.3	

TABLE 3-5

Table of Computations for Comparing Forecast Errors

Each of the forecast error measures is presented in the following equations:

MAPE:

$$\sum_{t=1}^{t=N} (|\epsilon_t|/x_t)100 \div n = 244.3/4 = 61.08$$

MAPE reveals poor forecasts. Note that for week one, the absolute percent error was 100, and the next two weeks are large percentages as well. Because the fourth week was reduced to 14.3, perhaps the system is stabilizing.

CFE:

$$\sum_{t=1}^{t=N} \epsilon_t = -2$$

as shown in the sum column of Table 3-5. This minus CFE measure may reveal a bias toward overestimation. The sample is too small to tell.

MAD:

$$\sum_{t=1}^{t=N} |\epsilon_t| \div n = 12/4 = 3.0$$

This is the most conservative estimate of error. Without knowing the size of demand, these 3 units of error might seem very small. They are not, and the MAD measure of 3 is significant because the average demand is $23/4 = 5.75$. MAD is more than 50 percent of the average demand.

MSE:

$$\sum_{t=1}^{t=N} \epsilon_t^2 \div n = 42/4 = 10.5$$

As expected, the MSE measure of 10.5 units is large. It is more than three times MAD and 1.8 times the average demand of 5.75.
MSE was magnified by the fact that the error values of 3, 4, and 4 became 9, 16, and 16.

Standard deviation:

$$\sigma_\epsilon = \sqrt{MSE} = \sqrt{\sum_{t=1}^{t=N} \frac{\epsilon_t^2}{n}} = \sqrt{10.5} = 3.24$$

The standard deviation of the error distribution is closely approximated by MAD. That is because the square root of the MSE removes the magnification of error that is inherent in MSE. It should be noted that MSE is a preferred measure when larger errors have disproportionate penalty as compared to small errors. This would be the case when the penalties are proportional to the square of the errors.

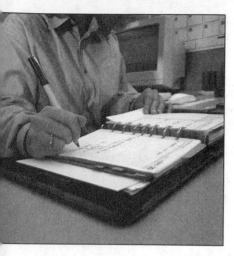

Mail-order companies need to forecast demand in order to have the right number of trained agents and operators in place.

New measures can be devised when special circumstances exist. Thus, if underestimation results in stock outages that lead to severe penalties whereas overstock carries a small charge, it is necessary to adjust the comparative measures that are used to evaluate forecasting systems.

3-6a Keep a Record of Past Errors

Managers change forecasts that are derived by numerical methods because they know about other factors that are not included in the calculations. This results in modifications of forecasts that can be called predictions and estimates.

It is, therefore, wise to maintain a *history of all forecasting errors*, i.e., a history of: $x_t - \hat{x}_t = \epsilon_t$. This should be done for all methods that are used and for all personnel that are making the forecasts, predictions, and estimates. Some people are good at forecasting and others are not. Also, some people are good at forecasting under certain circumstances and not good in others.

Companies gain major advantages by finding out who can make good estimates under what circumstances. Further, there are situations where people can learn to make better forecasts, predictions, and estimates as a result of feedback about how well they have done in the past. When a record is not kept, all such advantage potentials are lost.

SUMMARY

Strategic planning requires teamwork, and OM should be part of the team. The chapter discusses OM's role in helping to develop strategies and its assignment to carry them out. OM is responsible for seeking out and adopting "Best Practice." Life cycle stages are developed. This includes the introduction and growth of new products, followed by their maturation and decline. OM is expected to protect established products. Forecasting is critical for dealing to advantage with the life cycle stages. Time series analysis is treated with extrapolation and correlation. Important forecasting methods and measures are covered, including moving averages, weighted moving averages, regression analysis, correlation coefficients, coefficients of determination, multiple forecasts, and the Delphi method. Also, the means for evaluating the different forecasting methods by comparing the kinds of errors they generate is explained. A supplement on the exponential smoothing method is provided.

Two Spotlight feature boxes conclude this chapter. These boxes illustrate real applications of the materials in the chapter. See Spotlight 3-1: Bluworld Innovations and Spotlight 3-2: Transformation of Ideas into Sustainable Businesses.

KEY TERMS

Cycles
Extrapolation
Forecasting momentum
Linear regression

Strategic business units (SBUs)
Strategy
Synergy
Syzygy

Tactics
Time series
Time series analysis

REVIEW QUESTIONS

1. Contrast strategies and tactics from an OM perspective.

2. What is suboptimization and why is it a concern of OM?

3. What is meant by the statement "OM is a scarce resource"?

4. What is a time series? How would it be used to make predictions about emerging technological developments?

5. Is there a basis for predicting periods of prosperity and of economic slowdowns on the basis of cycles?

6. What are life cycle stages? Why does the concept of life cycle stages unite P/OM with other members of the organization in using the systems approach?

7. Detail the life cycle stages and explain them.

8. What is extrapolation and how is it used?

9. What is correlation? What is autocorrelation? Distinguish between them.

10. What is an historical forecast? When is it used?

11. Why are long life cycle stages considered desirable? Does this apply to start-up and growth as well as the mature stage?

12. How does the hub and spoke diagram for a large company differ from that of a small company? Draw the contrast with the classic organization chart. Relate both of these types of diagrams to organizational structure and infrastructure.

13. What is Best Practice when applied to a business system?

14. When are multiple forecasts desirable?

PROBLEMS SECTION

1. If a series of numbers is {14, 23, 28, 34} what is the best estimate for the next value? What method can be used?

2. A time series for actual sales figures is given in the following table.

Month	Actual x_t	Forecast $\hat{x}_t$	Error $x_t - \hat{x}_t = \in_t$
1	10		
2	30		
3	40		
4	40		
5	50		
6	60		
7	50		
8	40		
9			

a. Use the moving average method with $N = 3$ to develop forecasts for months four through nine. Calculate the error terms, $x_t - \hat{x}_t = \in_t$.

b. Employ weights of 0.5, 0.3, and 0.2 to obtain weighted moving average forecasts for the same time period. Calculate the error terms $x_t - \hat{x}_t = \in_t$. Compare the results in parts 2(a) and 2(b).

3. It has been stated that sales for next year will be 50 percent greater than this year, but the historical pattern will continue to hold. Complete next year's forecast.

Month	Actual Sales Last Year	Forecast of Sales Next Year
January	1,500	
February	1,600	
March	1,800	
April	2,000	
May	2,300	
June	2,500	
July	2,350	
August	2,100	
September	1,850	
October	1,650	
November	1,550	
December	1,400*	

*Note: This December estimate of 1,400 units is based on the prior year's sales.

4. The Highway Department is considering using a 6-month moving average to forecast crew hours needed to repair roads month by month for the coming year. To test whether this method is accurate, use last year's data (shown in the following table) to predict the last six months' crew hours to compare with the observed values. Start with the average of January through June to compare with the actual value of 200 for July and so on through December. Remember that the prediction for the next month is the average of the actual values of the previous six, not the predicted values!

Month	Crew Hours	Month	Crew Hours
January	110	July	200
February	120	August	220
March	140	September	280
April	180	October	120
May	250	November	100
June	200	December	80

5. In reference to Problem 4, prepare an analysis of the error in using the 6-month moving predictor.

6. Referring to Problems 4 and 5, use a 3-period moving average to forecast the last six months and compare directly to the 6-month forecast developed there. Here, the first forecast is the average of April, May, and June to compare with the actual value of 200 for July and so on through December.

7. Referring to Problems 4, 5, and 6, use a 6-period weighted moving average to forecast the last six months and compare directly to the 6-month and 3-month forecasts developed there. Use the weights 0.1, 0.1, 0.1, 0.2, .0.2, and 0.3 with the 0.3 weighting the most recent datum point.

8. The following table presents data concerning the sales of minivans for 10 years. It is believed that the demand for minivan replacement tires is highly correlated with the sales figures three years earlier.

Year t	Minivan Sales x_t in Year t (in millions)	Minivan Tire Sales y_t in Year t (in millions)
1	10	4
2	12	6
3	11	7
4	9	5
5	10	8
6	12	7
7	10	5
8	9	7
9	8	8
10	7	6

Do an analysis of x_t and y_{t+k}, where $k = 3$ years, using the least-squares method and linear regression. Note that seven years of data will be used to prepare the regression line. The forecast for tires will go from year 11 through year 13.

9. Using the information given in Problem 8, it is now stated that there is another person in the company who feels that $k = 4$ should be tried. Use it and compare the results. Note that six years of data will be available to prepare the regression line. The forecast for tires will go from year 11 through year 14.

10. What does autocorrelation have to do with the methodology used in Problem 8?

11. This table presents the results of forecasting using moving averages. Comparison is made of actual demand and the forecast for a period of seven days.

Day number, t	1	2	3	4	5	6	7
Actual demand, x_t	4	5	2	3	1	3	4
Forecast, $\hat{x}_t$	3	6	2	4	3	1	3
Error, $x_t - \hat{x}_t = \epsilon_t$							
Error squared, ϵ^2_t							
Absolute error, $|\epsilon_t|$							
Absolute percent error $(|\epsilon_t| / x_t) 100$							

Complete this table and then work out each of the following forecast error evaluation methods:

MAPE:

$$\sum_{t=1}^{t=N} (|\epsilon_t| / x_t)100 \div n$$

CFE:

$$\sum_{t=1}^{t=N} \epsilon_t$$

MAD:

$$\sum_{t=1}^{t=N} |\epsilon_t| \div n$$

MSE:

$$\sum_{t=1}^{t=N} \epsilon_t^2 \div n$$

Standard deviation:

$$\sigma_\epsilon = \sqrt{MSE} = \sqrt{\sum_{t=1}^{t=N} \epsilon_t^2}$$

Discuss the results comparing the various evaluation methods.

12. The time series for ϵ_t is as follows:

{+600, −300, +500, +100, −50, +60, −40, +30, −50, +20} Measure MAD, MSE, CFE, and σ_ϵ.

13. The time series for ϵ_t is as follows:

{+600, −300, +500, +100, −50, +60, −40, +30, −50, +20} Analyze this time series in such a way as to shed additional light on what seems to be happening.

14. It should be noted that MSE is preferred to MAD when larger errors have disproportionate penalties as compared to small errors. This would be the case when the penalties are proportional to the square of the errors.

Two forecasting methods are used. The first method gives the error time series for as follows:

{+600, −300, +500, +300, −500}

The second gives this time series:

{+100, −200, +800, +100, −100}

Compare the two time series using the various forecast error evaluation methods. Discuss the results in light of the statement concerning penalties.

END-OF-CHAPTER QUESTIONS

1. The difference between tactics and strategies is best described by which of the following statements?
   a. Strategies are what CEOs create; tactics bubble up from the plant floor.
   b. Strategies lead to forecasts; tactics are based on predictions.
   c. Strategies are long-range plans; tactics are short-range plans.
   d. Strategies require adaptation but not conversion to a proactive stance.
   e. Strategies are concerned with profit maximization, not with cash flow sufficiency.

2. P/OM's role in developing strategies is to
   a. bring technological knowledge to the table.
   b. serve as the hub of the system, pulling together the other functional inputs.
   c. be the coordinator between marketing and finance.
   d. keep a record of past errors in the forecasting capacity.
   e. establish production capacity to match supply with forecasted demand.

3. Life cycle stages are not properly described by one of the following multiple choices. Which is the incorrect choice?
   a. Forecasting is not related to life cycle stage analysis.
   b. Synergy can account for faster than expected growth of market share during start-up.
   c. New products of Stage IV organizations move up faster and stay put longer.
   d. Life cycles are getting shorter as technology developments accelerate.
   e. An efficient sales force can alter the time period of various life cycle stages.

4. Forecasting is one of the most powerful generic methodologies that can help P/OM planners. The best forecasts can be obtained by
   a. ignoring short-term cycles.
   b. concentrating only on long-term cycles.
   c. removing trend lines from the data.
   d. looking for patterns that can be extrapolated.
   e. using time series analysis software.

5. Correlation is a statistical measure of similarity or dissimilarity. Which of the following options is incorrect?
   a. With correlation of one, the two variables are tracking each other perfectly.
   b. If correlation is two, a calculation error has been made.
   c. If correlation is minus one, the two variables move in perfectly opposite directions.
   d. Life cycle growth of market share has a correlation of one with profitability.
   e. Life cycle market share and sales volume are well-correlated if market size is steady.

6. Historical forecasting is based on the assumption that
   a. moving averages are seldom useful for capturing trends.
   b. the past will repeat itself.
   c. base series modification will be necessary.
   d. weighted moving averages capture more information than unweighted moving averages.
   e. use of multiple forecasting methods will improve the prediction.

7. What does base series modification of historical forecasts of demand level accomplish?
   a. Base series modification treats demand level as a constant but changes the pattern of variation in line with expectations.
   b. Base series modification changes either the demand level or the pattern of variation as deemed necessary.
   c. Base series modification keeps the pattern of variation between time periods fixed but changes the demand level of the time series.
   d. Base series modification is equivalent to utilizing the moving average methodology.
   e. Base series modification requires regression analysis to provide the coefficients of correlation.

8. In forecasting, when are weighted moving averages preferred to (plain) moving averages?
   a. when the manager prefers to make the forecast equally responsive to the last three or four actual occurrences
   b. when the manager believes that successive values in the time series are random
   c. when there is enough computing power to go through the extra calculations involved
   d. when the manager prefers to make the forecast more responsive to the most recent actual occurrences
   e. when it is known that the competition is using WMA

9. What best describes the Delphi method for forecasting?
   a. Oracle software is used to organize information and provide a prediction.
   b. A poll is taken by a licensed pollster to determine, for example, who will win the next presidential election.
   c. Forecasts are chosen that produce the least forecasting error in a benchmark study.
   d. Forecasts are based on price elasticity and the average price charged per unit.
   e. Experts' estimations of future events are used to converge on a consensus forecast.

10. Which of the following statements about comparative forecasting errors is incorrect?
    a. The most common measure of forecast error is MAD (mean absolute deviation). It prevents positive and negative errors from canceling each other.
    b. Mean squared error (MSE) also prevents positive and negative errors from canceling each other, but the squares of large numbers overpower those of smaller numbers.
    c. Standard deviation is the square root of MSE. It does not prevent positive and negative errors from canceling each other. However, for sigma the squares of large numbers as compared to the squares of small numbers is not as overpowering.
    d. Cumulative forecast error (CFE) is useful when overestimation errors do cancel out the effects of underestimation errors.
    e. Mean absolute percent error (MAPE) provides a ratio that describes how large the error is as compared to the value of the variable (say, demand).

ADDITIONAL READINGS

Armstrong, J. Scott. *Principles of Forecasting.* Dordrecht, Netherlands: Kluwer Academic Publishing (paperback version— April 2001).

Box, G. E. P., and G. M. Jenkins. *Time Series Analysis: Forecasting and Control.* San Francisco: Holden-Day, 1970.

DeLurgio, S. A., and C. D. Bhame. *Forecasting Systems for Operations Management.* Burr Ridge, IL: Irwin, 1991.

Drucker, P. *Managing in Turbulent Times.* London: Pan Books, 1981.

Magaziner, I., and R. Reich. *Minding America's Business.* New York: Vintage Books, 1982.

Makridakis, S., S. C. Wheelwright, and V. E. McGee. *Forecasting: Methods and Applications.* New York: John Wiley & Sons, 1983.

NOTES

1. The definition of time series analysis is given by Jon F. Cox, John H. Blackstone, and Michael S. Spencer in the *APICS Dictionary*, 7th ed. APICS Educational and Research Foundation, 1992.

2. See Murray Turoff and Starr Roxanne Hiltz, http://eies.njit.edu/~turoff/Papers/delphi3.html. A version of this paper appeared as a chapter in *Gazing into the Oracle: The Delphi Method and Its Application to Social Policy and Public Health.* Michael Adler and Erio Ziglio (eds.). Kingsley Publishers, January 1996.

SPOTLIGHT 3-1
Bluworld Innovations

Using the Systems Approach to Create Stress-Free Environments

Bluworld Innovations utilizes operations management techniques to create profits from nature.

Bluworld Innovations creates stress-free environments through the use of indoor waterfalls. The Florida-based company was founded in 1998 by two brothers, Jimi Beach and Sean Drummond. Jimi, the chief designer, has always believed that as humans, we all have an instinctual attraction to water. According to Beach, "We are born of water, it sustains all life."

In 2002, demand quickly exceeded capacity when the two brothers found themselves in front of a national trend utilizing flowing water as a main feature in interior design. Jimi's vision combined with Sean's engineering talents enabled the two to win several national design awards for their custom indoor waterfall creations, point-of-purchase displays, and waterfall sculptures, all designed and built within a custom shop environment.

The company had just raised one million dollars and had to make critical decisions on how to allocate these funds. Sixteen individual sales channels were uncovered in a market analysis completed by Mark Hayes, the CEO. According to Hayes, "There is no way we can achieve our vision of being a market leader if we try to service every channel." Hayes chose a systems approach to better understand the variables and constraints associated with each sales channel. A decision model was created to forecast sales demand based on empirical price elasticity information derived from the furniture industry. Each sales channel was ranked according to two variables: the amount of resources required to obtain a market leadership position

and the profitability of each channel on a per unit basis. The primary goals of the model were to determine which sales channels would be most profitable and the amount of resources required to obtain a leadership position in each of these channels. This model proved instrumental to the development of Bluworld's marketing strategy. (1) Bluworld would reconfigure the shop from a custom shop design to a job shop design and take advantage of several economies of scale; (2) Bluworld would outsource all internal components to Asian factories; (3) Bluworld would create strategic alliances with distribution vendors and raw material suppliers to reduce capital needs and increase quality control; and (4) instead of opening company-owned galleries, Bluworld would license the name to established showroom/gallery operators. This strategy is helping Bluworld dominate three core sales channels: (1) the mass-produced consumer line waterfalls sold in retail stores; (2) custom waterfalls specified from showroom galleries; and (3) water art sold in fine art galleries. By setting up these decision models, Bluworld was able to increase the bottom line profitability from 10 percent to 19 percent. Additionally, Bluworld has adopted the process of using statistical control charts throughout the job shop to determine the causes and effects of costly errors. This process alone added 2 percent to the bottom line. According to Hayes, "The advantages to using a systems approach go far beyond increasing profits. It has helped us develop a much deeper understanding of our business, which increases the overall passion we all share for our corporate vision."

Source: Mark Hayes, CEO BluWorld Innovations, LLC. For more information on Bluworld waterfalls, contact Mark Hayes at 407-426-7674 or Mark@BluworldUSA.com.

SPOTLIGHT 3-2
Transformation of Ideas into Sustainable Businesses

A Discussion with Lars Kolind, Chairman, PreVenture A/S

Lars Kolind is famous for his major organizational changes at Oticon Holding S/A. He reorganized Oticon by cutting away hierarchies and fostering new patterns of communication, which catalyzed project creation in new product development. It was essential for Oticon to break with the past because the company had lost its leadership role to new technologies in the hearing-aid markets of the world. Kolind's plan was to go to a flat, project-oriented organization, (labeled "the spaghetti organization"). That plan successfully returned the company to technological and market preeminence.

When Lars Kolind left Oticon in 1998, he began working with an early-stage business development firm called PreVenture A/S. It is likely that this incubator for start-ups will be studied by academic researchers as a modification of similar principles applied to Oticon. Danish-based *Growth.dk a/s*, now PreVenture a/s, "aims at making transformation of ideas into sustainable businesses (that are) systematic, knowledge-based, efficient and fun." On its webpages, under the heading "How We Work" is the statement "Based on the Oticon experience we are creating a model for the design and development of small, knowledge based high growth companies in the 21st century. We work in five phases in the life of a start-up business:

1. Business Conception: From idea to business plan

2. Business Discovery: From business plan to market introduction

3. Business Launch: From market introduction to documented user acceptance

4. Business Expansion: From documented user acceptance to breakeven in first market

5. Business Transition: Introduction to mass market and adjustment of owner structure"

Companies that partner with PreVenture must agree to use (and, if possible) improve the growth model developed by Lars Kolind and his team. That model structures and disciplines the operations of the start-ups in accord with the five phases.

PreVenture partners include Isabella Smith A/S, a trading company with products related to TV host Isabella Smith. Retail Internet A/S runs a permission-based email marketing service called Jatak.com; YellowTel A/S provides access to information about products and services in both Poland and Sweden; KeepFocus A/S offers a system that helps reduce electricity, water, and heat usage. It provides visual alerts if resource consumption exceeds normal levels. 24-7 MusicShop AG has a system for legal and secure distribution of digital music on the Internet; Homelinc distributes digital media from Internet and PC to A/V equipment in the home. Webpages are listed at http://www.preventure.dk for all partners, and this provides a lot of interesting research opportunities for students and teachers alike.

In a fashion typical of Lars Kolinds' broad systems thinking, PreVenture A/S creates value for various constituencies. Entrepreneurs increase their probability of success using the growth model. Shareholders and investors do well because adherence to the model provides architecture and structure for learning to improve continually. PreVenture holds shares in its partner companies, which is a good formula for mutual success. Employees of the firms enjoy stability of employment and potential financial gains. A systematic process provides sustainability from which everyone gains.

When asked about his current business philosophy, Mr. Kolind said, "I realized that what I learned about large organizations during my 10 years as CEO of Oticon holds also for small and young businesses. There should be no such thing as an employee, only associates. Everyone should be given maximum freedom to choose what he or she wants to do, and everyone should be urged to utilize the broadest possible set of competencies in their work. I continue not to believe in hierarchies—let teams do the work.

"I am convinced that complete transparency is the only effective basis for communication and knowledge sharing. I have no intention of managing an organization through carefully thought out plans and budgets. Success is about vision and values. I am surprised how many companies still maintain hierarchical organizations and information systems. They remind me more about the 1920s than of the 21st century. We know today what it takes to create organizations, which are uniquely competitive and innovative, yet also sustainable."

Source: Lars Kolind, from the webpages of PreVenture S/A and from personal correspondence with Mr. Kolind (February 18th–28th, 2003).

Supplement 3

Forecasts Using Exponential Smoothing Methodology

Often, the use of the exponential smoothing method for forecasting is preferred to the weighted moving average method. Like the weighted moving average (WMA) method, exponential smoothing calculates an average demand—usually giving more weight to recent actual demand values than to the older ones.

Exponential smoothing is a simpler method, requiring fewer calculations than WMA, which needs N weights and N periods of data for each forecast estimate. Exponential smoothing needs only three pieces of data. Also, it can be more effective because only one weight, alpha (α)—called the smoothing constant—has to be chosen. This makes it easier to experiment with past data to see which value of alpha provides the least forecast error.

Exponential smoothing has been found to be more effective in a variety of situations. Many forecasting and control systems employ exponential smoothing because it works better than the older methods of moving averages and WMA. It has proved effective for diverse applications. Fighter aircraft use exponential smoothing to aim their guns at moving targets. In effect, they forecast the location of enemy jets during flying missions. This application shows how fast the exponential smoothing method can track a consistent, but dynamically changing pattern.

Manufacturers use exponential smoothing to forecast demand levels, which experience the same kind of nonrandom but volatile shifts from time to time. In such cases, the situation is dynamically changing, but the recent past has the most information about the near future. Exponential smoothing can catch these shifts and make rapid adjustments to inventory levels. Other manufacturers use it because it requires less computational work and is readily understood.

Exponential smoothing methodology remembers the last estimate of the average value of demand and combines it with the most recent observed, actual value to form a new estimated average. As in prior materials, hats over the x's stand for forecast values of demand; t is now; and $t + 1$ is the next period for which the forecast is to be made.

$\hat{x}_t$ is the last forecast made—it was for period t, which is today, meaning the present time. The new forecast of demand to be made for period $t + 1$ is $\hat{x}_{t+1}$. The actual result observed for the period t, which is the present time is x_t. All x_t values—no hats—are recorded values of actual demand.

Equation 3-8 forecasts demand in period $t + 1$ as an alpha-based average of the actual demand in the last period t, and the demand that had been forecasted for that period, t.

$$\hat{x}_{t+1} = \alpha x_t + (1 - \alpha)\hat{x}_t \qquad \text{(Equation 3-8)}$$

The preceding period's forecasting equation would then have been:

$$\hat{x}_t = \alpha x_{t-1} + (1 - \alpha)\hat{x}_{t-1} \qquad \text{(Equation 3-9)}$$

The period before t, i.e., $t - 1$, would be described by Equation 3-10.

$$\hat{x}_{t-1} = \alpha x_{t-2} + (1 - \alpha)\hat{x}_{t-2} \qquad \text{(Equation 3-10)}$$

Replacing $\hat{x}_t$ in Equation 3-8 with its right-hand side in Equation 3-9 yields Equation 3-11:

$$\hat{x}_{t+1} = \alpha x_t + (1 - \alpha)[\alpha x_{t-1} + (1 - \alpha)\hat{x}_{t-1}] \qquad \text{(Equation 3-11)}$$

Combining terms leads to the simplified version in Equation 3-12:

$$\hat{x}_{t+1} = \alpha x_t + \alpha(1 - \alpha)x_{t-1} + (1 - \alpha)^2 \hat{x}_{t-1} \qquad \text{(Equation 3-12)}$$

Substituting the right-hand side of Equation 3-10 into Equation 3-12, and continuing in this fashion, yields Equation 3-13—which is the generalized form for the forecast of demand for period $t + 1$:

$$\hat{x}_{t+1} = \alpha x_t + \alpha(1-\alpha)x_{t-1} + \alpha(1-\alpha)^2 x_{t-2} + \alpha(1-\alpha)^3 x_{t-3} \ldots + \qquad \text{(Equation 3-13)}$$

The response rate of the exponential smoothing model is a function of the alpha value that is used. When alpha is large, the actual demand in the prior period is given great weight in the forecast for the next period. If alpha is one, the forecast for the next period is the actual value of the prior period. The forecast results are markedly affected by the alpha that is used, as is shown in Table 3-6.

Table 3-6 employs the same numbers that were used for the moving average and weighted moving average calculations. The table shows the effect of α on the forecast for the next period, $t + 1$, namely, $\hat{x}_{t+1}$.

The exponential smoothing updating system requires only one operation. Thus, if $\alpha = 0.700$, and the sixth period actual result was found to be $x_6 = 60$, and the forecast for the sixth period was for 40, then the seventh period forecast is $\hat{x}_{t+1=7} = 54$ (read subscript as $t + 1 = 7$)

$$\hat{x}_{t+1=7} = 0.700(60) + 0.300(40) = 54 \text{ (read subscript as } t + 1 = 7)$$

Small values of alpha are used for stable systems where there is, at most, some small amount of random fluctuation. Large values of alpha are used for changing and evolving systems where much credence can only be placed on the last observation. New products, as they move through their life cycle stages, start with a large alpha value, which gradually diminishes as the product enters its mature stage. For most production scheduling systems in both the job shop and the flow shop, alpha is kept small, in the neighborhood of 0.050 to 0.150, to decrease the system's response to random fluctuations. In the previous example, the system was changing in a marked way.

TABLE 3-6		
Exponential Smoothing with a Range of Alphas	$\alpha x_t + (1-\alpha)\hat{x}_t = \hat{x}_{t+1}$	α
	$0.000(60) + 1.000(40) = 40$	0.000
	$0.100(60) + 0.900(40) = 42$	0.100
	$0.200(60) + 0.800(40) = 44$	0.200
	$0.300(60) + 0.700(40) = 46$	0.300
	$0.375(60) + 0.625(40) = 47.5$	0.375 moving average result
	$0.400(60) + 0.600(40) = 40$	0.400
	$0.500(60) + 0.500(40) = 50$	0.500
	$0.550(60) + 0.450(40) = 51$	0.550 weighted moving average result
	$0.600(60) + 0.400(40) = 52$	0.600
	$0.700(60) + 0.300(40) = 54$	0.700 <-- as discussed in text: forecast for period 7
	$0.800(60) + 0.200(40) = 56$	0.800
	$0.900(60) + 0.100(40) = 58$	0.900
	$1.000(60) + 0.000(40) = 60$	1.000

Problems for Supplement 3

1. Using the data in Problem 2 in the Problems Section, apply exponential smoothing to develop a forecast comparable to what is asked for in parts a and b. Note that exponential smoothing goes back to the first prediction, so assume that the forecast for t = 1 is 20 and sequentially calculate all forecasts through $t = 9$. However, only analyze the errors for $t = 4, \ldots, 8$ for direct comparison with the $N = 3$-period moving averages calculated in parts a and b of Problem 2 in the Problems Section. Run for alpha of 0.3 and 0.7 and discuss the benefits of each kind of approach.

2. Simulate the effect of using $\alpha = 0.05$ on the following set of very seasonal data:

Month	Sales	Month	Sales
1	500	7	10,000
2	800	8	7,000
3	1,200	9	6,000
4	2,000	10	1,000
5	4,000	11	500
6	8,000	12	300

Now, choose $\alpha = 0.85$ and compare the results.
To initiate the calculations, assume that the forecast for $t = 1$ is 600.

4

Quality Management: Strategic Issues

Chapter Outline

This section describes the conceptual foundation of quality management. That foundation must allow two viewpoints to coexist and prosper. There is a difference between the way a producer (manufacturer or service provider) views quality and the way that their customers view quality. Quality may be the most complex, multidimensional business variable that exists in the business world today.

Note the difference between producers who are the POM folks and their colleagues in marketing who focus on the customers. Finally, there are organizational issues that relate to global ISO standards and other standards as well. These include the Malcolm Baldrige National Quality Award system. Mastery of Chapter 4 provides a portal to Chapter 7, which is the quantitative (statistical) platform for tracking and correcting processes that drift from the specified quality levels.

After reading this chapter, you should be able to:

- Distinguish between producers' and consumers' quality concepts.
- Analyze quality in terms of its many dimensions.
- Explain how quality is measured for both tangible and intangible quality dimensions.
- Detail the things to consider when developing a rational warranty policy.
- Discuss ISO 9000 standards in an international context.
- Address and apply the costs of quality.
- Describe the control monitor feedback model.
- Relate quality mapping and the House of Quality (HOQ).
- Explain quality prizes being given worldwide.

THE SYSTEMS VIEWPOINT

Everyone in the company contributes to the quality of the product. In recognition of this fact, excellent companies train everyone in quality. It applies to every aspect of manufacturing and service. The manufacturer must include service (repair and maintenance) for the product. Service requires proper administrative support and office management. The systems viewpoint is inherent in the definition of good quality for both goods and services because it links what customers want to the production transformation process that makes and delivers the goods and services. Quality goals are determined by the voice of the customer, and P/OM tries to keep on target. The P/OM approach is to look into each activity where quality could be improved. The process may begin with analysis of the low-hanging fruit subject to highly developed quality standards. Then P/OM can orchestrate and synchronize the system to produce quality products (goods and services).

STRATEGIC THINKING

Marketing has the ears to hear the voice of the customer. The perception of quality is in the eyes of the customer. The communication between market researchers and P/OM is crucial to determine what the company will deliver to the customer. Sometimes what can be done for the budgeted costs is not what all of the customers want. The product has to satisfy a variety of customer types (called *market segments*). Before it is possible to measure how good a job is being done, a set of standards needs to be drawn up and agreed upon. There can be so many dimensions for product qualities that strategic thinking about quality will be a formidable task. For example, the qualities associated with automobiles by different market segments number in the hundreds. The costs associated with achieving the right quality level for each quality dimension must be factored into the selling price and what the competition provides. The decisions and compromises involved are what strategic thinking for this chapter is all about. Since 9/11 (2001), safety and security qualities have joined the list of things that cannot be taken for granted in the quality context.

The quality of life changed around the world in September 2001. The airlines understood the sea change immediately. Few of them knew what to do about it. Theme parks, hotels, and restaurants found that customers were reluctant to take vacations away from home. What are the systems connectives? They are many. It takes less than one month for the slowdown at the airlines and theme parks to be felt by the gas stations, department stores, supermarkets, and the stock market. There are so many issues to consider in the year 2004 that simplifying the organization may be crucially important.

4-1 WHY IS BETTER QUALITY IMPORTANT?

Quality is one of the most important variables in the business system. When it comes to gaining competitive advantage, quality has tremendous leverage with new and old customers alike.

Products having better quality have a marketplace advantage. Because customers prefer to buy products they perceive to be of better quality, they often are willing to pay more for the superior qualities. Products perceived to be of lower quality are less likely to be substituted for products of better quality. Therefore, lower quality is equivalent to higher elasticity. This means that price increases drop demand rates faster than with products having higher quality (and lower elasticity).

Better quality translates into greater protection against competitors that compete on price.

Better quality saves money for the company by decreasing defectives that must be scrapped or reworked. This can be a very big savings because much money and time have been used to add value to the product, which then fails inspection and has to be scrapped. With so much value added, rework is the only reasonable way to go. In turn, rework expenses often are considerable. Further, the company with a better product can afford to offer a superior warranty, which has marketing attraction for customers. Even with the superior warranty policy, the better product leads to less frequent rework and replacement.

Better quality increases customer loyalty. An investment in quality can be called a *customer holding expense*. The greatest part of marketing expenditures is to attract new customers, called the *switching expense*. Retaining current customers makes good sense. The trade-off between the cost of getting new customers and the additional price paid for better quality, which holds onto existing customers, favors the investment in quality.

Alienating existing customers with product weaknesses and failures has a host of other side effects, which are undesirable. Word spreads quickly about product failures. There are a growing number of consumer protection publications. Government agencies pursue other aspects of consumer protection using various means to remove defective products from stores. Large-scale auto callbacks are given prime-time coverage on TV.

Better product quality obtained at a reasonable price generally goes hand-in-glove with growth in market shares and increases in revenues. Sometimes quality improvements result in decreases in court costs for claims of harm caused by malfunctions and other types of liability. Another advantage of better quality is that people who work in companies that really have better quality enjoy an environment of higher morale.

4-2 WHY IS TOTAL QUALITY MANAGEMENT IMPORTANT?

Total quality management (TQM) is called *the prime directive* in this book. What is meant by this? The "prime directive" denotes a critically important and overriding rule that cannot be compromised. *If quality management is to achieve the best results, then TQM is the procedure of choice.*

> **Total quality management (TQM):** Applying systems vision to every aspect of quality in the organization.

Translating this into quality-specific terms, the prime directive for TQM is that the systems approach to quality must be used company-wide. Thus, as an unequivocal rule:

> TQM *is a management strategy that requires a company-wide systems approach to quality.*

The attainment of TQM is the critical precursor of excellence in quality. To begin with, it is an organizational matter. Everyone in the organization has one or more roles that are related to the attainment of quality. People must be able to communicate with each other in the common pursuit of quality for TQM to operate. The achievement of TQM requires that the entire system be seen in perspective (i.e., view of things in their true relationship or importance).

TQM enables the systems approach to operate effectively. This is because everyone in the company knows the goals. They also know they share the same objectives for attaining quality. Like the orchestra that needs to play in synchronization to achieve quality sounds, the company needs to synchronize its players to achieve company-wide quality. Ignore or discard any one of the elements and the quality chain is as weak as the weakest link. That, too, is the philosophy of TQM.

Some people do not like the name "TQM," and they think that it has been overblown or overused. However, everyone agrees that what TQM stands for is here to stay. There is so much business publication that the name for any concept is likely to get used, and misused too, in a very short time. It is, therefore, necessary to examine the concept of TQM carefully to see what makes it so important and successful that business and academia alike are proponents of the concepts.

Those who practice the systems approach know that this is a sound foundation for the attainment of superior quality. If the practice of TQM is done right, it can put a faltering company back on track. If done badly, TQM can alienate those who put themselves on the line to support it. The label "TQM" assures no one of anything. It is essential to read the ingredients on the label of this system of practice. All TQMs are not alike.

4-3 TWO DEFINITIONS OF QUALITY

Before the correct and sound approach to TQM can be developed, it is necessary to define quality. The word *quality* is used in two different ways.

1. *The producer's view*—Qualities are properties of things without distinction about being good or bad. Thus, the product conforms in all regards to the company's quality specifications.

2. *The consumer's view*—Qualities relate to the "degree of excellence" of things. Thus, consumers expect and deserve a quality product.

The two definitions of quality are held and exercised by different interests. One person can have both points of view, depending on what hat they are wearing at the time. Everyone has an intrinsic sense of what quality means to them as a consumer. They want the best that can be had, so they are always judging the "degree of excellence."

FIGURE 4-1
Cost of Quality and Dollar Volume of Sales—Yield Maximum Profit as a Function of the Quality Level

As a producer, it is often necessary to compromise and set quality standards that are not the best in their class. Inexpensive automobiles do not have the same set of qualities as the expensive ones. There are different markets for town cars and compacts. It is the producer's problem to choose appropriate quality standards so that the market judges them to be excellent for that price class.

Producers strive to balance the market forces for high quality with consumers' cost preferences and the company's production capabilities. Figure 4-1 illustrates a common economic concept of the optimal quality level.

There are valid exceptions to the relationships that Figure 4-1 depicts. The cost of quality does not necessarily rise as the quality level increases. The fact that many times quality can be improved without spending any money will be discussed at a later point. There also is the issue of how improved quality is obtained, allowing that money is spent. Is it on training, technology, or both?

According to Figure 4-1, there is a limit to how much quality can be improved. This concept can be faulted as not taking scientific possibilities and the ingenuity of creative people into account. There also is a question about the dollar volume of sales approaching saturation with respect to improvements in the quality level. Given all of those issues, it is difficult to know where the point of maximum profit with respect to quality level really will occur. Nevertheless, the quality level standards must be set, and that should be done with the notion of maximum profit in mind.

Some producers may be born with an innate sense of how to set quality standards so as to best balance the costs and benefits. Most producers have to learn how to deal with such issues. This is an essential part of what the study of OM is about. The lessons involve developing models about quality that increase awareness of the categories of quality and the means of improvement.

4-4   THE DIMENSIONS OF QUALITY

Dimensions of quality: No form of quality can be achieved until that form is defined.

The **dimensions of quality** are the descriptors that must be examined to determine the quality of a product. The wine business is an enormous industry on a global scale. How do the presidents of wine companies characterize the quality of their products? They measure their production output by bouquet, color, and taste plus chemical analyses. Cars are evaluated, within categories of cost, by their power, safety features, capacities, fuel efficiencies, and style, among other things. Appearance and style dimensions, so often important, are difficult to rate. Experts at ladies' fashion shows are at no loss for words, and yet this multimillion-dollar industry is only able to explain successes and failures after the fact.

When rating the quality of cities to live in, the authors of such research base their studies on dimensions that define the quality of life. The complex set of criteria includes amount of crime, cost of living, job availability, transportation, and other factors. Special needs emerge, such as the quality of schools for families with children.[1]

The starting point for managing quality is to define the set of quality dimensions, recognizing the special needs of market niches and segments. Not everyone will agree about what should be on the list or about the importance of the dimensions that are on the list. Individuality accounts for different perceptions about the quality of the product with respect to its various elements.

A small sample of customers was asked what qualities could be improved in the service they received from their bank. Their answers included length of time waiting for tellers should be decreased; availability of officers for special services should be increased; bank should be open longer hours; rates on interest-bearing accounts should be increased; and service charges should be dropped. Also, the turnover in personnel should be decreased.

An even smaller group of bank officers was asked to define the quality of the services their bank offered or should offer. Their answers show what a different perspective prevails between customers and producers, thus: the number of different products that the bank offers (CDs, checking accounts, passbooks, mortgages, loans, investment services) should be large; the average speed of tellers per transaction should be small; the variability of tellers' times should be decreased; the percentage of times that customers wait longer than five minutes should be small; and the average length of waiting lines for tellers should be about three people.

What could bring these two groups closer together? The customers describe quality in terms of excellence. The bankers describe quality in terms of how well they meet the standards that have been established by their banks. They also talk about changing the standards. The balance between these two positions is related to the costs and benefits of providing more of what the customer wants.

4-4a Models of Quality

This section presents models of quality in the form of lists. The lists are generic categories of quality. They will enable producers and consumers to check off and define all of the dimensions of quality that are applicable to their products.

These eight categories were derived by David Garvin, a Harvard professor who researched quality issues. His eight dimensions for categorizing quality are shown in Table 4-1.[2]

1. Performance
2. Features
3. Reliability
4. Conformance
5. Durability
6. Serviceability
7. Aesthetics
8. Perceived quality

TABLE 4-1

Eight Quality Dimensions Recommended by David Garvin

The quality dimensions shown in Table 4-1 are discussed here. The automobile is used as an example. The qualities of autos are widely known. Although this is a manufactured product, the eight quality dimensions are applicable to services as well. A good exercise for strictly service systems is to apply what happens when the eight dimensions are related to getting a mortgage at a local bank or setting up a vacation getaway at Club Med. Describing qualities provides excellent practice in taking the first steps that are essential to install a quality program.

The *performance dimension* relates to the quality of the fundamental purpose for which the product is purchased. How well does the car do what it is supposed to do?

The *features dimension* refers to product capabilities not considered to be part of normal performance expectations. These might be air-conditioning, stereo, an antilock brake system, and air bags.

The *reliability dimension* relates to performance that can be depended upon with a high level of assurance. The car starts and it drives. It does not break down, but the windshield wipers do not work. How that car measures up for reliability is an issue to be discussed.

The *conformance dimension* alludes to the degree to which the measured production qualities correspond to the design quality standards that have been specified. This is definitely the producer's concern and not the consumer's. P/OM is responsible for meeting the conformance dimensions of quality. They are the quality standards.

The *durability dimension* deals with how well the product endures in the face of use and stress. Some cars are still on the road after being driven well over 100,000 miles. Those cars deserve a quality medal for high durability. There is a relationship between reliability and durability for autos, but it needs to be analyzed.

The *serviceability dimension* is related to how often, how difficult, and how costly it is to service and repair the product. Serviceability for cars involves the combination of preventive and remedial maintenance. This quality dimension applies to services for manufacturing products and the products of service firms.

The *aesthetics dimension* refers to the appearance of the product. For autos, design styling counts. Industrial designers and operations managers form a powerful team that epitomizes the systems approach. Together, as a team they consider all of the linked factors that relate to manufacturability in addition to the eight quality dimensions.

The *perceived quality dimension* relates to the customers' perceptions of the product's quality. This dimension integrates the prior seven dimensions with the customers' values for them. Market research is one of the most important means for determining the customers' perceptions. The blue book, which is the used-car dealer's bible for determining the trade-in values of automobiles, reflects perceived quality.

Table 4-2 presents a different and more detailed categorization of quality dimensions. It emphasizes the difference between tangible and intangible attributes. Because it is more detailed, it shows the weakness of attributing quality to one or two dimensions. Quality resides in the totality—which is inherent for the systems approach.

For different individuals, certain dimensions are more important than others. Overall, it should be evident that quality definition is enhanced by requiring and enabling a systems perspective.

Quality Dimension—Purpose Utilities

Purpose utilities are related to the specific, functional classes of use, i.e., soap to wash the face, tires to keep the wheels rolling, and credit cards for purchases without cash. Often, purposes seem to be clear, but market research is needed to explore alternative uses for a product. When awareness of alternative uses develops, then quality standards may have to be developed to assess the product's performance in comparison with that of competitors.

Many customers consider shower soap to be different from face soap. Snow tires have a special market niche with their own quality dimensions. The point about "alternative uses" is that it is necessary to explore in-depth the way customers perceive quality in order to properly deal with the quality dimensions. Only then can P/OM make sure that conformance to the correct set of standards is taking place.

TABLE 4-2

**An Extended Taxonomy
of Quality Dimensions**

I. Functional Qualities (the "ilities")
  1. Utility of main purpose or performance
  2. Dependability of function
     a. Conformance to standards from day one, and on, over time
     b. Reliability: Does it function properly over time?
     c. Durability: How long does it function with heavy use?
        (i) How much wear (stress) can it take?
        (ii) Does functional deterioration occur with use or time?
     d. Failure characteristics and expected lifetime
     e. Maintainability—Serviceability I
        (i)   Cost of preventive maintenance (PM)
        (ii) Frequency and time required for PM
        (iii) Cost of predictive maintenance (PREDM)
     f. Repairability—Serviceability II
        (i) Quality—as good as new?
        (ii) Cost and time for remedial maintenance (RM)
     g. Guarantees and warranties
  3. Human factors using the product
     a. Safety and security—Can be tested partially
     b. Comfort—Market researchable
     c. Convenience—Market researchable
II. Conceptual (Nonfunctional) Qualities
  1. Aesthetics
  2. Style
  3. Appearance
  4. Image
     a. Self-image of user: Related to price
     b. Self-image of user: Related to prestige
  5. Timeliness of design
  6. Demography of ownership
  7. Variety
     a. Degree of choice
     b. Rapidity of new models and selection obsolescence

Frequently, there are regional differences in quality perceptions. Hard water areas have their own special quality dimensions for soap. Snow tires have little impact in the South. Such effects are amplified in the international marketplace. This issue of alternative uses (which can run counter to conventional marketing wisdom) creates a critical marketing–production situation. OM has one set of standards for region A and another for region B.

Quality definition is not simple. The measurement of how well a product or service performs its conforming functions is essential if standards are to be determined. There is no point in measuring the wrong things. When the standards are established to everyone's satisfaction, then OM can make the right products, test them, and improve the production process.

Assumptions must be made about the way in which the measurable, physical factors relate to the consumers' evaluations of the "ilities" of the product. The "ilities" include utility, dependability, reliability, durability, serviceability, maintainability, repairability, and warrantability. Manufacturability, which includes assembly, should be added to this list.

Quality Dimensions—Other "ilities"

There are different ways for describing dependability. Durability refers to the ability to resist wear, stress, and decay. Reliability refers to the ability to continue to provide the functional utility attributes—within conformance standards or limits—over a given period of time. The width of the limits represents an important aspect of the definition of quality for the design.

To understand these limits, consider the following transactions between designers and operations managers.

1. Telephone cords have 4-pin modular connectors at each end. One connector is plugged into the modular wall jack and the other is plugged into the telephone.

   The 4 pins of the connectors are gold plated to ensure adequate conductance. OM will have to oversee the plating and can cost it out in terms of both materials and labor. R & D and the designers decide how thick the plating should be for specifications furnished by marketing and market research concerning how many insertions and removals the connectors should be able to withstand.

   This durability specification used to be 10,000 insertions. That has been reduced significantly. It is not believed that this compromises the way the product is viewed by the customer. From a production point of view, productivity rises and costs are reduced. There is more time for OM as a scarce resource to do other things that need attention.

2. Some lightbulbs are made to have long lifetimes. The materials used in such bulbs are different from those in the regular lifetime bulbs, and manufacturing processes are different as well. The durability dimension of each kind of bulb is involved.

   With respect to durability, parts of a product will become worn with use, whereas other parts will deteriorate with age, independent of use. Most often, both kinds of forces are at work. Generally, the expected performance will increasingly deviate from the initial design standard over a period of time. That is what happens to lightbulbs; as they age, they become increasingly more dim.

   They would fail a test that measures durability of the output in lumens of light. The lightbulb output is decaying and slowly drifting to total failure, but it may be quite awhile before it gets there. OM has to develop standards and testing procedures to determine how many hours of acceptable output the lightbulbs it is producing have.

Drift-decay quality phenomena: Decay of product performance can occur as a result of usage or age.

This **drift-decay quality phenomena** in which performance of a product gradually diminishes are characteristic of a great many functional attributes of mechanical, chemical, and electrical products. An electric lightbulb, when it is first used, will generate some given number of lumens. A typical 75-watt bulb starts its life with about 1,170 lumens of light. It ages as a function of both hours of use and the number of times that it is turned on and off.

OM needs to work with R & D and engineering to test durability of outputs. Materials used and characteristics of the process play an important part in product performance. For many products such as food, time spent as work in process and in final storage can reduce the useful life of the product in the consumer's hands.

Table 4-3 presents a chart that describes how the measurements for all of the dimensions in the quality tables can be obtained. The distinction between manufacturing and services need not be drawn because the products of both types of producers have many tangible and intangible elements.

TABLE 4-3		Quality Dimensions	
How Quality Is Defined and Measured		Tangible	Intangible
	Conformance to specifications	SQC/TQC Zero defects	Arbitrary critiques by experts
	Consumer perceptions	Market research	Market research
	Management evaluations	Competitive comparisons	Competitive comparisons

Definition of Failure—Critical to Quality Evaluation

Failure occurs when a product ceases to perform in an acceptable fashion. Accordingly, sometimes failure can be judged objectively. Sometimes it is in the mind of the customer. With respect to the objective kind of failure, there are engineering as well as logical conventions that define physical failure. The car does not start. The lightbulb is burned out. However, if the light source is considered "failed" after its output falls below a certain threshold, then OM needs to include that fact in its quality standards.

A certain percent of lightbulbs fail at start-up. Failure probabilities follow a U-shaped curve, which is known as the Weibull distribution. Customers who buy a new bulb, insert it, and see it fail are unlikely to write a letter of complaint. The store where it was bought could question the authenticity of the claim. There is ample room for customer hard feelings about the quality of a simple product like a lightbulb.

OM needs to address the questions: Why do these early failures occur? Is there something in the production process that could be changed? Marketing needs to develop a policy for the early failures. OM and marketing working together might be able to remove the commodity stigma that is associated with lightbulbs—that all lightbulbs are alike. The same commodity stigma applies to gasoline, aspirin, vodka, detergents, and salt.

Operations managers should be fully aware of how they can influence the failure rates and characteristics of the products that they are producing. They also should be working closely with R & D and engineering design to develop new production capabilities that can increase the product's expected lifetime or **mean time between failures (MTBF).** The measure MTBF is often used to depict reliability. A competitive benchmark of expected lifetime is a useful guide. However customers' willingness to put up with failures is the ultimate standard for acceptability.

> **Mean time between failures (MTBF):** Product's expected lifetime of satisfactory utility in normal application.

In the case of lightbulbs, MTBF is often as low as 750 hours, which can require changing bulbs every month. *In a 31-day month, there are 744 hours.* Marketing managers should be fully aware of their products' MTBF rates and the failure characteristics of competitors' products. They should also know from their OM colleagues what it would cost to improve the MTBF by (even) 1 percent as well as how much could be saved on warranties, etc.

There are many reasons why failure and reliability, as definitions of quality, play an extremely important role. Some types of failure are life threatening while others are not. This consideration plays an important part in the costs of protection through insurance and litigation. Every effort must be made to ensure safety and to document that this effort has been honest. The courts of law expect it.

Some types of failure do not permit repair, whereas others do. The definition and specification of quality also should be concerned with the ease of maintenance and the cost of replacement parts. These factors affect the consumer's judgment of quality.

Warranty Policies

A product warranty is a guarantee by the producer to protect the customer from various forms of product failure. The specifics are spelled out in contractual fashion. Thus, it is typical to state for how long a time, and for how much use, the product is covered. The conditions of use are generally stated.

What is the basis for a sensible warranty policy? First, there are the competitive marketing requirements. If DaimlerChrysler guarantees 50,000 miles and 5 years, what should Ford offer? Does it make sense to offer a warranty policy that costs more than it gains? Warranties involve interactions between products and promises made by production and marketing. The systems approach is essential to make certain that costs and gains are, at least, balanced.

Second, the operational reliability of the product is critical. How many cars will fail, in what ways, after how much time? Given the schedule of failures by time and type, it is possible to figure out how much a blanket, or partial, warranty will cost the company. It is feasible to determine how many customers will be left without company support. These customers will not be repeat purchasers of that brand of auto in the future. Policies of partial warranties to cover different components under varying circumstances also can be formulated in terms of costs and ultimate customer dissatisfaction. OM will be instrumental in helping to determine a rational warranty policy.

Management must know the reliability of its products and services to come up with a rational specification of guarantees and warranty periods. An important systems dialogue must take place to set the terms of warranty coverage and period. The essence of this thinking should be founded on the knowledge of the product and the process. That is the responsibility of the OM and quality control functions within the organization.

The Service Function—Repairability

The Repairability (and/or maintainability) quality dimension requires that a service function be developed and operated. Speed of service is an attribute that usually is considered very important. A service policy is an agreement between the company and its customers concerning how fast service will be rendered, what service steps will be taken, and what charges will be borne by the customer (warranty contract).

Nikon has a service policy of repairing the entire camera and not just the parts that are responsible for the immediate cause of failure. Their service policy includes furnishing an estimate by mail or phone before beginning work. Service policies are taken very seriously by customers who require service. Organizations distinguish themselves from one another by the care that they show and the fairness of their service policy.

Another service issue is the use of preventive versus remedial service. In the 1960s, autos received preventive maintenance every 3,000 miles. Typically, the service interval is now 7,500 miles or more. The preventive maintenance advantage from an OM perspective is that it can be scheduled. It also reduces the severity, frequency, and cost of unexpected failures.

Setting up the service policy requires an understanding of the product to determine the preventive maintenance service interval and the charges for that service, as well as the cost of repair parts. In some instances, the service function is a profit center. On the other side of the coin, breakdowns result in calls for nonscheduled maintenance. They jeopardize customer loyalty and usually involve higher costs for the same procedures as preventive maintenance. A broken down car must be towed. From this point of view, the service function is a cost center with opportunities to reduce costs through careful planning.

How should the optimal maintenance function be designed? Should it be a profit center, a cost center, or can it be allowed to function on a reactive basis? OM is the only business function that can propose reasonable alternatives and cost each out in an approximate fashion. These alternatives are not likely to include the optimal service policy, but using iteration, successive service scenarios can be tested and then implemented to achieve gradual improvement over time.

4-4b Functional Human Factors—Quality Dimensions

Quality management also must focus on the importance of the qualities of the human factors such as safety, security, comfort, and convenience. The human factors area relates equally well to the office, the factory, and the process equipment, as well as products in use, including such services as plane trips and taxi rides. Ergonomics is another name for human factors.

Many human factors of quality are overlooked until they exceed reasonable limits and are then rejected. For example, the comfort of a car seat might be considered acceptable until it passes a threshold, and then it becomes a factor for evaluation of the product. Using market segmentation according to body types, only some customers may find the car seat uncomfortable.

Many safety factors cannot be seen. If tires get a reputation for coming apart and causing rollovers, word of mouth will have a negative effect on sales. Consumers have a hard time dealing with such issues. The safety of foods is often an invisible factor. For example, the customer relies on the food company to take proper measures to ensure that salmonella is not present. Contaminant control is an operations management responsibility.

The health quality of foods related to processing and ingredients such as trans-fatty acids and partially-hydrogenated oils is a difficult quality area. Nutritionists decry the use of too much fat, too many calories, too much sodium, etc. POM makes the product that uses these ingredients. However, the recipes are part of the product design, which relates to management strategy, marketing planning, and market research information. Because the underlying properties of food are invisible to the consumer, labeling has taken on importance that is proportional to the consumer's ability to use that kind of knowledge. Who is in charge of the consumer's education?

4-4c Nonfunctional Quality Factors— Aesthetics and Timing

Nonfunctional qualities play a major role in the consumer's judgment of quality. Appearance and style are intangibles, and customer satisfaction with aesthetics is difficult to measure. There can be high variability in what constitutes preferred designs, and there are ambiguous design criteria for what works. Because appearance, style, and other nonfunctional qualities are intangibles, expert opinion and market research are the only ways to measure satisfaction. Nevertheless, these dimensions and their roles are as important to the definition of quality as any that are found in the functional categories of quality.

Market research often attempts to determine the image that consumers conjure up of themselves to justify the purchase of items. Self-image is significant for high-ticket items such as Rolls Royces or Jaguars. Self-image applies to a broad range of acquisitions such as health club memberships, art purchases, top-of-the-line camcorders, maid service, and trips into space on Russian satellites.

How consumers interpret intangible qualities involves sociological and psychological dimensions of quality. Thinking along these lines is not easily associated with OM, which strives to meet the standards that are specified. That is why industrial designers play a major role in product design decisions. There is broad systems responsibility to achieve effective nonfunctional attributes for a product. Ultimately, OM is charged with making exactly what the designers fashion.

Timeliness is another elusive nonfunctional quality dimension. It is most evident in the fashions and styles of clothing, athletic footwear, records, and the acquisitions of the school-age market segments. The extent to which styles go in and out of fashion is often overlooked by those who are not in the seller's chair. Car colors change and so do the cases of laptops. Apple's e-Mac and then I-Mac have brought style and swift change to what had been drab computer appearances. The home furnishings product class also has dynamic style shifts. For example, the furniture suit business (like Thomasville) requires being on top of inventory shifts of types and colors of wood. Restaurants are no more immune to changing tastes than cell phones or children's toys.

The Variety Dimension

Marketing can assist strategic planners in their evaluation of the importance of **variety** of choice. Variety is defined as the number of product alternatives (in a given product class) that are made available to the customer. Variety can include different quality dimensions at different prices. The key to defining variety is that the customers see the various choices as substitutable alternatives. As an illustration of variety as a quality consider the number of flavors that Jello offers.

Variety: The number of product alternatives (in a given product class) that are made available to the customer.

Does the customer want to buy Jello dessert that is green or red at Publix? If it is green, will it be lime- or kiwi-flavored? In a Super Mercado in Brazil, it might be avocado-flavored. Having set down what the customer seems to want, what does OM have to do to switch the production line from green to red? How much does that cost? Will it be less expensive to switch from red to green? The answers to the questions are based on operational considerations.

Variety often increases a brand's market share because people like to switch flavors from time to time. They might switch away from their favored brand to get a different flavor occasionally. Variety of the product line and process capabilities to shift inexpensively from one color, flavor, or size to another are correlated through the mechanism of price elasticity. If it costs a lot to add another variant, customers must be willing to pay for the additional choice.

Customized product is the apex of variety. Suits made to fit the customer are one of a kind. Suits off-the-rack and then altered to fit are still customized but at a lower level. Industrial consumers often want altered or tailor-made equipment. The highest variety levels fall within that range of customization. OM produces the level of variety determined by marketing strategy. Because variety entails additional production costs, marketing has to factor these expenses into the equation. OM is the knowledge base in the business unit that can inform marketing about the costs of variety to raise everyone's awareness of the trade-offs and net benefits.

At the same time, variety develops loyal customers in different market niches by appealing to a wide spectrum of customer preferences. Different bank certificates of deposit appeal to different segments in the population. The various color choices of automobiles, the different styles of TVs, the variety of items on a menu, all attest to the fact that choice is a quality that is a competitive factor that must be understood by marketing and operations alike.

4-5 SETTING INTERNATIONAL PRODUCER STANDARDS

There are quality standards in the United States. There are similar but not identical quality standards in many countries around the world. Standards are going global because suppliers exist throughout the world. The International Organization for Standardization (ISO) is supported by 140 countries. ISO is constantly engaged in setting standards for products, processes, information systems, and the environment with respect to every type of organization and activity. The organization makes a point of declaring that ISO is not an acronym of its name but is derived from the Greek prefix meaning "equal" (as in *isobars*). The English acronym would be IOS, and in French it would be OIN (standing for Organisation Internationale de Normalisation). This information underscores the true international character of the ISO 9000 and ISO 14000 families of standards, which are known as "generic management system standards." ISO 9000 and ISO 14000 are discussed in this text.

An example of the breadth of interest of ISO is ISO 10303, STEP (STandards for the Exchange of Product Information). This is called a *data backbone* because it is used to transfer digital product information along a globally diverse supply chain. A typical application transfers CAD data. STEP permits suppliers and designers to communicate in spite of the many different languages that are spoken along the supply chain. Among industries that employ STEP are aerospace, automotive, shipbuilding, and construction.

STEP is a common language that permits technically competent translation of requirements into universal digital format. ISO 10303 is discussed and updated in ISO bulletins. At http://www.ISO.ch, enter ISO 10303, STEP in the search box. Then, click on *step02-04.pdf*, which will be one of several items found by the search.

4-5a U.S. Quality Standards

The U.S. military established standards in the 1940s, during World War II, which related inspection sample sizes and observed sample values of averages and variability to the probable true values of the entire production batch.[3]

Practically speaking, almost every purchase made by the military was subject to these standards. This introduced quality standards to a broad range of private businesses in the United States.

The American National Standards Institute (ANSI) and the American Society for Quality Control (ASQC) have jointly published a series of quality specifications—called the Q90 series—which reflect the standards of the International Standards Organization.

In fact, Q90 through Q94 are Americanized versions of the international standards ISO 9000 through ISO 9004.

4-5b Origin of International Organization for Standardization (ISO) and ISO 9000 Series

The organization, ISO, provides certification of conformance to quality standards that is known as ISO 9000. ISO officially began operation on February 23, 1947. Because "International Organization for Standardization" would have different abbreviations in different languages ("IOS" in English, "OIN" in French for Organisation internationale de normalisation), it was decided at the outset to use a word derived from the Greek isos, meaning "equal".

ISO non-governmental organizations form a network of the national standards institutes, currently numbering 147 countries, on the basis of one member per country. ISO is the worlds largest developer of standards. The United States representative is the American National Standards Institute (ANSI).

The importance of the **ISO 9000 series** is exemplified by the certification awarded to Mitsubishi Power Systems in 2003 which is shown in Figure 4-2.

ISO 9000 series: Generic management systems standards for quality.

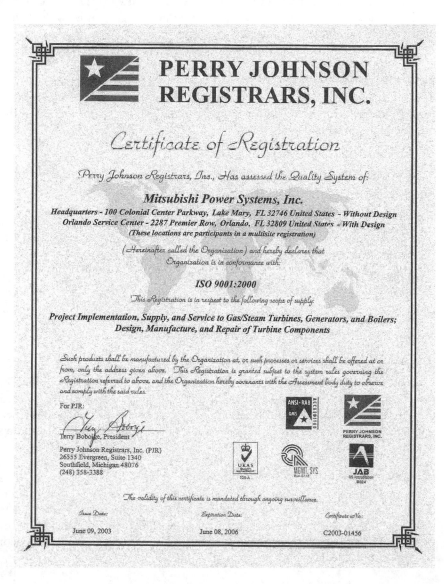

**FIGURE 4-2
ISO 9001 Quality Assurance Certificates**

The certificate names the specific group that "has established and is maintaining a quality system."

Source: Perry Johnson Registrars, Inc.

Mitsubishi Power Systems Background Information

Mitsubishi Power Systems (MPS) is a company solely owned by Mitsubishi Heavy Industries. MPS is divided into three sites: 1) Headquarters in Lake Mary, Florida, 2) Orlando Service Center in Orlando, Florida, and 3) Wind Turbine and Selective Catalytic Converter (SCR) in Los Angeles, California. MPS is therefore combining all locations into one multi-site registration.

Headquarters is primarily concerned with the sale and construction of new combustion turbine and combined cycle (combustion turbine and steam turbine) turbine-generator projects.

The Orlando Service Center is primarily concerned with products and services associated with maintenance of existing power plants.

The Los Angeles facility is primarily concerned with the new wind turbine and Selective Catalytic Converters (SCR) projects.

MPS ISO 9001 Registration

Currently, Headquarters and the Orlando Service Center have obtained ISO 9001 registration. The Los Angeles facility is currently in the process of obtaining certification and will be added to the certificate once complete.

Note that the Certificate of Registration includes any exceptions taken to the ISO 9001 standard. Headquarters has taken exception to design as it is not included in their scope of work while the Orlando Service Center has not taken exception to any of the ISO 9001 standard requirements. The certificate expires after three years.

Scope of ISO 9001 at MPS

The MPS quality management system (QMS) includes defining customer requirements through improving customer satisfaction. This includes but is not limited to the following disciplines and functions:

- Management Commitment and Responsibility
- Documentation Requirements
- Planning
- Resources
- Sales and Marketing
- Purchasing
- Product Realization
- Design and Development
- Monitoring, Measurement, and Analysis of Data
- Customer Satisfaction and Continuous Improvement

Why is ISO 9001 Important to Customers?

Customer satisfaction is the primary objective of the ISO 9001 quality system. There must be continual improvement as shown in the quality objectives that support the quality policy. This is accomplished by the adoption of a process approach which can be checked and improved. Minimizing defects leads to lower cost and meeting customer and applicable regulatory requirements.

Why do we need international standards?

Between 1947 and the present day, ISO published more than 13,700 International Standards. ISO's work program ranges from standards for traditional activities, such as agriculture and construction, through mechanical engineering, to medical devices, to the newest information technology developments, such as the digital coding of audio-visual signals for multimedia applications.

Standardization of screw threads helps to keep chairs, children's bicycles and aircraft together and solves the repair and maintenance problems caused by a lack of standardization that were once a major headache for manufacturerers and product users. Standards establishing an international consensus on terminology make technology transfer easier and can represent an important stage in the advancement of new technologies.

Without the standardized dimensions of freight containers, international trade would be slower and more expensive. Without the standardization of telephone and banking cards, life would be more complicated. A lack of standardization may even affect the quality of life itself: for the disabled, for example, when they are barred access to consumer products—public transportation and buildings—because the dimensions of wheel-chairs and entrances are not standardized.

Standardized symbols provide danger warnings and information across linguistic frontiers. Consensus on grades of various materials give a common reference for suppliers and clients in business dealings.

Agreement on a sufficient number of variations of a product to meet most current applications allows economies of scale with cost benefits for both producers and consumers. An example is the standardization of paper sizes.

Standardization of performance or safety requirements of diverse equipment makes sure that users' needs are met while allowing individual manufacturers the freedom to design their own solution on how to meet those needs.

Standardized protocols allow computers from different vendors to "talk" to each other. Standardized documents speed up the transit of goods, or identify sensitive or dangerous cargoes that may be handled by people speaking different languages. Standardization of connections and interfaces of all types ensures the compatibility of equipment of diverse origins and the interoperability of different technologies.

Agreement on test methods allows meaningful comparisons of products, or plays an important part in controlling pollution — whether by noise, vibration or emissions. Safety standards for machinery protect people at work, at play, at sea... and at the dentist. Without the international agreement contained in ISO standards on quantities and units, shopping and trade would be haphazard, science would be — unscientific — and technological development would be handicapped.

Standards contribute to making the development, manufacturing, and supply of products and services more efficient, safer, and cleaner. ISO generic management standards can deal with quality (ISO 9000) and the environment (ISO 14000) though the vast majority are highly specific to a particular product, material, or process.

Standards enhance global competitiveness of businesses and quality of life by promoting and facilitating voluntary consensus standards and conformity assessment systems. The existence of divergent national or regional standards can create barriers to trade. International standards are the technical means by which political trade agreements can be put into practice.

Initially these standards are voluntary but may become market requirements if adopted by regulatory or governments.

The original ISO materials were written in great detail with guideline books that contain policies, rules, and principles. They applied to both manufactured and service products. Being familiar with the statements of these standards in their original 9000 to 9004 form is helpful in understanding the transformation and growth of global-based quality requirements.

ISO 9000: Provides overall guidance for prospective users of the ISO standards. It explains the ISO system, in general, and gives directions for using the other components of the ISO 9000 series as described in the following standards.

ISO 9001: Applies to firms that are engaged in the pre-market stages including design and development, and also in the in-market stages including production, installation and servicing.

ISO 9002: Applies to firms that are only engaged in the in-market stages of production, installation, and servicing and not engaged in the pre-market stages of design and development.

ISO 9003: Applies to firms that deal with testing and inspection of products when they are acting as an inspection agent or as a distributor.

ISO 9004: Describes the accepted quality management system and serves as a guide to the application of that system to production systems for goods and services.

Many U.S. companies require their suppliers to adhere to ISO 9000 standards or the ANSI/ASQC equivalent standards Q90–Q94. In the same sense, U.S. companies wanting to do business in Europe and in Asia are committing resources to the considerable work that needs to be done for certification. Environmental standards ISO14000 are being globally adopted in growing numbers.

4-5c Japanese Quality Standards

Japanese companies adhere to ISO 9000 when it is useful to do so in order to participate in European and U.S. markets. At the same time, over a long period of time, the Japanese have published their own, often quite stringent, quality standards for products as diverse as fiber-optic cable, cellular telephones, high-definition television, and rice.

Japanese Industrial Standard Z8101: Set of Japanese standards equivalent to the EURO/U.S.A.–ISO standards.

For many years, they also have utilized systems of quality standards, such as the **Japanese Industrial Standard Z8101.** These specifications resemble those developed in the United States.

The Japanese government has been under pressure to open their markets, which are said to be blocked by excessively rigorous standards that tend to favor domestic producers. Because this will be happening, OM must be alert to follow continuous changes in Japanese standards over time. Some of these will permit the entry of American products into markets that are not currently available. This is another illustration of the degree to which OM must be in the network to receive the latest information about international standards and specifications.

4-5d Database of Quality Standards

Collecting and maintaining a worldwide database of prices and qualities for potential global-based suppliers—and of actual and possible customers as well—provide a real competitive advantage. In business environments where every factor has been carefully studied, it has become essential to know what quality standards can be realized for given prices. Even commodities (say, grains or oils) have different purities, cleanliness, and ingredients. Such a database can be made to reflect changes in prevailing suppliers' prices for various conditions of supply and demand. The demand for the best quality potatoes (say, McDonald's and Frito-Lay) will be chasing diminished supply in those parts of the world where growth is diminished by drought. A well-fashioned database can alert the purchasing agents to changing conditions that might significantly impact the company.

Costs of quality: Costs of preventing defects, of appraisal, and of failures.

Some companies offer a database with prices, qualities, and delivery dates. This allows buyers and suppliers to connect. Oracle's Internet Procurement and e-Business Suite can be tailored to fit the needs of the organization. DemandStar by Onvia asks "Are you a government agency?" and "Do you want to sell to government?" Then they say, "Reduce costs and save money . . . (this is) a better way to find suppliers online." In the United Kingdom, but globally by Internet, Digital Trading advises its supply chain customers that "mass customization is a reality" (http://www.digitaltrading.co.uk). Leaders in electronic databases that allow online collaboration are IBM, Microsoft, SAP, Oracle, and Clarus Corp. (http://www.claruscorp.com/products/procurement.asp). Business-to-business (B2B) e-commerce is growing at hundreds of trading sites. Quality and price are main factors in this growing arena. The **costs of quality** are crucial determinants of price.

FIGURE 4-3
Percent Defectives Versus Prevention Costs

4-6 THE COSTS OF QUALITY

A good approach to understanding quality is to analyze the costs associated with achieving, or failing to achieve, it. There are many shapes that cost curves can take. Therefore, nothing should be taken for granted in a specific case. However, it is useful to state some generalizations about the costs of quality. First, there are three basic costs of quality. These include the costs of prevention, appraisal, and failure.

4-6a The Cost of Prevention

Prevention involves the use of conscious strategies to reduce the production of defective product, which by definition does not conform to agreed-upon quality standards. The entire system must be designed, coordinated, and controlled to prevent defectives. This includes the materials and equipment used, appropriate skills, and the correct process to deliver product conforming to standards. Presumably by spending more, the percent of defectives can be reduced. Figure 4-3 shows this kind of relationship, although the real shape of the curve would have to be determined for a specific situation.

If something wrong is being done, causing defectives to occur, and the error is noticed and corrected, improving quality, then it is fair to say that quality is free. Defectives have been prevented from occurring by remedying a wrong. In service organizations as in manufacturing there are many examples of cost-free quality improvements. Philip Crosby wrote a book about quality being free[5] and established a quality school for executives that used this focus as part of its curriculum.

The cost of prevention goes up when quality standards are raised. *It is a reasonable policy to raise the quality standards whenever the prior standards are being consistently met.* The costs involved in achieving these ever more stringent specifications will increase, gradually at first, and then markedly as the technological limitations of the materials and the process are approached. This is shown in Figure 4-4.

In manufacturing, the **tolerance limits** define the range of acceptable product. As an example, the lead that fits into a mechanical pencil might be specified as 0.5mm. This describes the outside diameter of the lead. No one supposes that each piece of lead that comes in a container marked 0.5mm will be exactly 0.5mm. The tolerance limit sets the standard. Each piece of lead must fall within the range 0.5mm plus or minus one twentieth of a millimeter (0.5 ± 0.05). This means that the outside diameter could be as wide as 0.55mm and as thin as 0.45mm.

Figure 4-4 illustrates the exponential increase in costs as the tolerance range is tightened and approaches the technological limits of the process. When the tolerance range becomes tighter (i.e., 0.005 is tighter than 0.05), the cost of getting all of the units produced to fall within that range becomes greater. When the designer specifies a narrower acceptable range, the existing equipment's output range is usually too wide. More output

Tolerance limits: Plus and minus parts of tolerance limits (e.g., 6.00±0.05) are like goalposts.

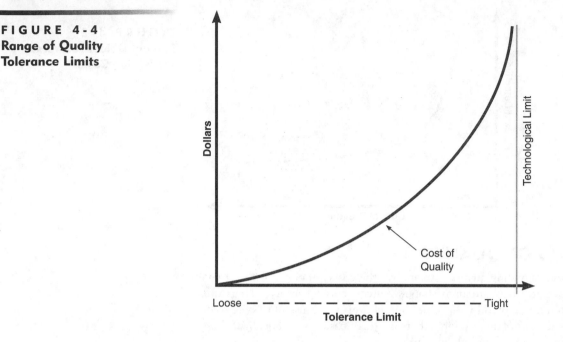

FIGURE 4-4
Range of Quality
Tolerance Limits

will not conform. Everything that falls outside the tolerance range limits is called defective. These defectives must either be scrapped or reworked, which is considered part of the cost of failure.

Another example of prevention is related to the methods of Taguchi. These are aimed at designing products that can be manufactured with minimum defectives. Statisticians often talk about the design of experiments that permit testing various alternatives to determine which produce the least variance. That thinking is applied by the **Taguchi methods** to design products that conform to specifications with the least variability.

It is said that the United States and Europe use goalpost standards for quality. When a product is accepted by a go, no-go gauge, that is equivalent to having the football go anywhere between the goalposts. It counts as one point after touchdown or as a three-point field goal. Quality control chart limits are just like goalposts, too. Taguchi proposes an optimal quality point and deviations from that as loss function measures.

Alternatively, move the goalposts close together so that most field goals would miss the mark and not qualify for points. That is what Motorola created with the Six-Sigma system. **Six-Sigma** is a very stringent quality standard allowing only 3.4 defectives per one million parts. Goal-seeking (such stringent or extreme quality requirements) is assisted by many techniques, among which are Taguchi methods. Six-Sigma is a powerful advocate of preventing quality failures. However, it also teaches defect detection and correction when prevention fails. It is akin to requiring near-zero defects, which is an **extreme quality achievement.**

4-6b The Cost of Appraisal (Inspection)

When product is examined to see if it conforms to the agreed-upon standards, it is undergoing inspection and appraisal. Both terms are used interchangeably and have to do with the evaluation of whether or not the product conforms to the standards. Product that is not judged to conform, because it fails to fall within the tolerance limits, is sorted out. There must be a policy regarding what to do with product that does not conform, for each way that it may not meet specifications. Some types of defectives have to be scrapped; others can be reworked and sold for scrap or at a discount.

The usual way to sort out the items that do not fall within the tolerance limits is to inspect all of the items. It is possible to use **acceptance sampling methods,** which, as the name indicates, consist of inspecting a sample of the production lot. If the sample fails to pass, then the entire lot is inspected and detailed. *Detailing* means removing the defectives

Taguchi methods: Optimal quality point and a loss function to describe deviations from that optimal.

Six-Sigma: Product design and production processes that deliver near-zero defects (6-sigma is 3.4 defects per million parts).

Extreme quality achievement: Conformance to standards must be as near to perfect as possible.

Acceptance sampling methods: Set the inspection parameters for drawing a sample from a production lot.

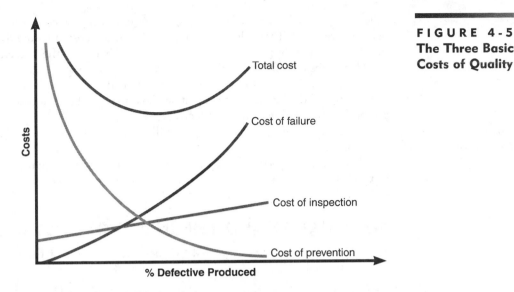

FIGURE 4-5
The Three Basic
Costs of Quality

so that every item in the lot conforms to the specifications. Therefore, when detailing, the inspector separates the bad from the good.

Figure 4-5 shows that the cost of inspection increases as the percent defective in the production lots increases. The reasons for the cost increase are that more inspectors are needed and an increased amount of detailing is necessary. If sampling is used, more samples of greater size will be taken. All other things being equal, the increase in inspection costs would be almost linear, and not too steep, as a function of increasing percent defectives.

Figure 4-5 puts together Figures 4-3 and 4-4, adds the cost of failure, and then adds the three kinds of costs.

4-6c The Cost of Failure

Figure 4-5 shows three costs curves. The newly added cost is the cost of failure, which rises linearly, at first, as the percentage of defectives increases. This might reflect a replacement cost for failed items that are under warranty. Then, as the percent of defectives continues to rise, product failure costs can be far more severe. The curve starts to move up geometrically. Severe costs of failures occur when customers begin to defect to competitors as a result of product failures. This lost revenue stream, often called the *lost* **lifetime value (LTV) of a customer,** has to be taken into account. An estimate of the average lifetime value of a customer is an important guide for deciding how much to spend to prevent failures that damage customer loyalty. LTV can be a significant amount of revenue. For example, it can be thousands of dollars lost if a regular pizza customer of a particular fast-food take-out service defects to another one because of dissatisfaction. The lost revenue stream is significantly greater when a business traveler permanently shifts hotel chains.

Further, serious failures could involve liability of very large sums of money. The expense of litigation in court trials, as well as the accompanying bad publicity, has costs that are difficult to estimate. Additional costs of failures are related to **product callbacks,** which require rework involving labor and material costs. Product callbacks often carry other penalties beyond the cost of repairing or replacing failed product. These include possible legal damage claims, bad publicity, and the loss of customers. Curves that chart the cost of failure are likely to have steeply ascending, exponential, or geometric shapes.

Figure 4-5 puts the cost of failure together with the cost of preventing defectives and the cost of inspection. The prevention curve should be read as follows: With greater expenses for equipment and training, the percent of defectives decreases. This is consistent with Figure 4-3.

The three kinds of costs are added together in Figure 4-5, resulting in a *total cost curve.* This curve has a U shape because total costs are minimized at some level of percent defectives. There can be major disagreement with this proposition. Many situations exist

Lifetime value (LTV) of a customer: Stream of revenue spent by each loyal customer over the lifetime of his/her relationship with a store (or brand).

Product callbacks: Costs that include labor and material rework, decreased customer loyalty, and litigation losses.

in which, for small increases in the prevention costs, the percent defectives will be dramatically reduced. There also are conditions when the cost of failure does not rise exponentially because inspection catches defectives. Therefore, the percent defectives produced are substantially higher than the percent defectives shipped.

Note that if the cost of failure rises very fast, then the indicated minimum point is pushed toward the zero level of percent defectives. Then the total cost of quality increases geometrically as the percentage defectives rises.

Zero defects was the goal set by Phillip Crosby of Crosby Associates and Crosby Associates II.

The curves for the costs of quality are logical in certain circumstances; they are conjectural and plain wrong in others. However, modeling quality costs remains a worthwhile endeavor.

> **Zero defects:** When zero defects is not the standard, then some level of defects is expected.

4-7 QUALITY AND THE INPUT–OUTPUT MODEL

To achieve specified output quality, two basic components of the input–output model must be treated.

First: The quality of input components—materials received from suppliers—must be maintained at designated levels. Also, work skills must be maintained. Often, because of employee turnover, new workers must be adequately trained. Other inputs, including energy and cash flow, also must be maintained at designated levels.

Second: The transformation process must be controlled to deliver the desired output quality. This often is related to internal transfers made between departments within the company.

4-7a Controlling Output Quality

The fundamental control model for quality is based on feedback and correction. This is the basic process by which OM adjusts the production system to conform to specifications for the product.

Figure 4-6 shows the information linkages of this system. The monitor (M) checks actual output measures against conformance standards. Deviations from standards are sent to the controller (C), which has been instructed to reduce the variation. After the controller has made its corrections, the monitor should pick up the fact that standards are being met again.

The monitor (M) measures $(q–s)$ where q is the output quality and s is the conformance standard. M sends information about deviations to the controller (C). A model of this kind should be developed for each quality dimension that counts. Many quality standards can be monitored by automated quality control equipment.

How should this job be organized? If it can be done automatically, then there is a lot of control equipment to maintain and monitor. Assume that 30 dimensions are being

FIGURE 4-6
Quality Control
Feedback Model

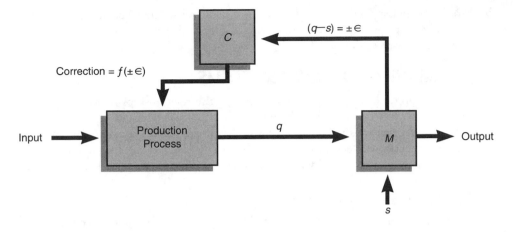

FIGURE 4-7
Quality Correction $= f(\pm\in)$

monitored and controlled. The cost of this control effort might be larger than the benefits. Perhaps less than 30 dimensions should be monitored.

Figure 4-7 shows the difference $(q - s) = (\pm\in)$. This measure of epsilon is the error term, which the controller (C) has been programmed to interpret and correct. The controller adjusts the production process in line with its instructions.

Say the product is paint and that color brightness is being monitored. The controller adds or subtracts white pigment to or from the mixture according to deviations from the standard.

4-8 TQM IS SYSTEMS MANAGEMENT OF QUALITY

TQM should have been called SMQ—standing for *systems management of quality*. Because it was not, every time that TQM appears, it is necessary to translate that name into systems terms. This means that partial quality concepts are not acceptable. Instead, it must be understood that TQM invokes complete organizational involvement, subsequently called *company-wide*, in the pursuit of quality. This total systems scope means that everything and everyone that has anything to do with quality achievement (directly and indirectly) must be included in planning, designing, and then in controlling the production processes.

Because total quality management requires using the systems approach to quality, all of the people, functions, factors, and elements that play a relevant part in determining quality must be included in setting standards, monitoring observations, and controlling for deviations of the process. The role of every component, ingredient, and person that participates in the process, and thereby in the quality of its product, must be understood and taken into account. This is done in planning and designing the standards for products, processes, and control systems. How else can the control system correct deviations from standards?

When the input–output process is connected to the control model, as in Figures 4-6 and 4-7, a major part of the systems structure required for total quality management is in place. The part that is missing is the organizational arrangement that allows for the interchange of information between the people who plan for quality and make decisions about it.

Summarizing five points that have been made:

1. There must be clear and unambiguous standards that are set and jointly held for all relevant quality dimensions.

2. Someone or something (people or machines) must serve as monitors, which entails their comparing the outputs of the process to the agreed-upon standards.

3. Process managers must strive constantly to meet the standards that have been set for the products. The achievement of process standards requires that all suppliers meet specified standards.

4. Process managers and controllers must be in communication to deal with any process exceptions and deviations from the standards that trigger the controller to take action.

5. Procedures to handle deviations from quality standards will have been predetermined. Controllers, programmed to correct unacceptable deviations, are empowered by process managers to do so.

4-9 MAPPING QUALITY SYSTEMS

The systems approach to quality requires mapping the relationships between customers and those that supply them. Although all functions of business should be thinking about customers, marketing is assigned the responsibility to represent them. In the same way, OM and engineering are accountable for supplying product to customers. This permits mapping the mutual concerns of sales and marketing with operations and engineering.

4-9a House of Quality (HOQ)

House of Quality (HOQ):
Mapping and tracking system for all relevant quality dimensions for a real product.

A well-known name for this mapping procedure is the **House of Quality (HOQ)**.[6] The "walls of the house" correspond to matrices of rows and columns. In their most basic form, the rows are lists of customer needs and the columns are lists of operations that are designed to satisfy those needs.

The "roof of the house" relates columns to columns. In one form of the House of Quality, this is equivalent to analyzing design and process interactions. Because this is difficult to explain in words, Figure 4-8 is presented. It shows a strong relationship between the energy required to close the door of a car and the energy required to open that door.

Although Figure 4-8 refers to a manufacturing example of an automobile door, the same kinds of interactions can be applied to services. Examples exist for academic institutions, retail stores, investment brokers, and fast-food outlets.

The House of Quality helps to identify who should be participating in the dialogue about quality. International TechneGroup Incorporated (ITI) adapted the House of Quality to include more complete marketing information (the WHYs).[7]

The WHATs, called *customer needs*, are represented by the marketing department. The WHYs sort out the WHATs for different demographic groups and other market segments. The HOWs are the *process capabilities* and the *design factors* that are supposed to satisfy customer needs. The HOW MUCHes make comparisons between this firm's HOWs and those of competitors. There is a lot of information about the market segments, design constraints, and the competitors' products. The structure is composed of interrelated matrices, as shown in Figure 4-9.

The matrix that results when the WHATs rows are crossed with the HOWs columns constitutes a grid of numbers. That matrix is one of four that constitute a TQM scoring model. The four are

WHATs versus HOWs—What customers want and what the product delivers

WHATs versus WHYs—Different market segments have different needs

HOWs versus HOWs—Physical constraints limit what a product delivers

HOW MUCHes versus HOWs—Comparisons between competing products

4-9b Quality Function Deployment (QFD)

As shown in Figure 4-10, it is possible to visualize a cascade of linked houses, which carry customer needs (often called the *voice of the customer*) from design specifications to production planning. This permits operations, on the floor of the plant or by telephone contact with the customer, to be linked with customer perceptions of quality.

Quality function deployment (QFD): Extending quality throughout the firm's activities.

This linked structure typifies the ideal realization of **quality function deployment (QFD)**. The figure conveys the idea of moving from strategies to tactics. The direct impact of tactics on the development of strategies also is revealed. If the postal sorting machine jams frequently in the house on the far right, then speedy delivery of the mail is not achievable. Customer needs and wants in the house on the far left will not be realized by this linkage. The voice of the customer has spoken, but is anyone listening?

FIGURE 4-8
House of Quality

The systems approach requires listening and hearing in both the feedforward and the feedbackward directions. Otherwise the linkage is strictly figurative and not operational.

The name specifically associated with mapping or charting the quality system throughout the organization is quality function deployment. QFD is a comprehensive program with a complete agenda for extending quality throughout the firm's activities.[8]

The QFD approach originated in Mitsubishi's Kobe shipyard in 1972. Toyota and its suppliers further developed the methods and their application. Many U.S. companies, both in services and manufacturing, have employed its use. The list of applications includes automakers, banks, electronic firms, retailers, schools, and stockbrokers. The Ford Motor Company played a leading role in the early application of QFD concepts in the United States.

It is necessary to assign responsibility for each of the quality dimensions within and throughout the entire organization, as well as outside it. Each organization must determine the best deployment system, including the extension to suppliers. It also is evident that when the customer is included in the deployment pattern, there is an even greater opportunity to achieve excellence in quality. Some questions to consider: Who are the players and what training have they received? What mechanisms exist for communicating? How does the computer tie in?

Competitive systems undergo incessant change. Quality dimensions have to be reevaluated. This results in the need to constantly alter the way in which the quality function is

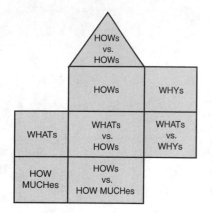

FIGURE 4-9
International TechneGroup
Incorporated (ITI)'s House
of Quality

Reprinted with permission of International TechneGroup Incorporated, Milford, OH.

> **Action learning:** Training technique that rotates employees through a variety of jobs.
>
> **Quality circles (QCs):** Groups with teamwork assignments for quality achievement.

deployed. Changes in the environment and in competitors' products necessitate upgrading the system's dynamics by constantly improving the quality function's deployment.

The procedures used in constructing the HOQ can help determine where accountability for quality resides. That is why the HOQ can affect organizational design as well as the quality of products. The basic idea is that cross-functional mapping of all elements that participate in the attainment of quality goals is a process in its own right.

Anything that affects quality must be included within the boundaries of the quality system. This is another way of saying that the map must include all factors that affect any of the quality dimensions. To be sure all relevant factors are included, it is necessary to name all of the participants that plan, design, and control quality. These participants can then identify additional contacts that they make on an informal basis. Many communications that are made in the pursuit of quality are hidden.

It is a good idea to develop an *organization chart* to reflect the deployment of the quality function. This then can be studied to determine whether there are bureaucratic forces within the organization that inhibit instead of encourage and foster quality. Even as a technique, it should be noted that the HOQ provides discipline and procedure, but its regimentation can inhibit discussion and creative thinking.

In this regard, it is important to make the House of Quality model as user-friendly as possible. This will encourage cross-functional communication. Different approaches exist for promoting interfunctional problem solving. **Action learning** is a technique for rotating people through a variety of jobs in pursuit of broader understanding. Whatever serves to enhance communication between engineers, designers, marketers, and operations is worth promoting.

Another aspect of QFD is the extent of the deployment. In Japan, there are tens of thousands of firms that are said to have total dissemination, called *company-wide total quality control* or *CWTQC*. A distinction should be drawn between CWTQC and QFD. QFD pinpoints those in the organization who have responsibility for quality. CWTQC postulates that everyone in the organization plays a part in quality attainment.

4-9c Teamwork for Quality

CWTQC is often identified with groups of workers who meet regularly in what are sometimes called **quality circles (QCs).** These groups are organized around products. Membership in a circle belongs to anyone that influences the quality of the specific products. The circle concept has been called by different names and has met with varying degrees of success.

Teamwork for productivity is enhanced when the quality perspective is brought to light. Absenteeism and turnover diminish because the team's morale is high when there is a concerted effort to produce quality products, which endear customers. Pride in the job done and in the quality of the product is not a convenient fiction of human resources managers. It is a real force to reckon with and a source of energy for continuing excellence.

The negatives also must be addressed. When the team is not well-designed, if the support of top-down management is not sincere, the quality circle effort will backfire. Backfire means that the situation after failure is worse than it was before the effort was made. Training is important, but it must be targeted with clear goals in mind to be successful. Without training, or with poor training, the backfire is also plainly heard.

FIGURE 4-10
Linked Houses Convey the
Customer's Voice Through
to Manufacturing

TABLE 4-4

1. Create constancy of purpose toward improvement of product and service, with the aim to become competitive, stay in business, and provide jobs.

2. Adopt the new philosophy. We are in a new economic age. Live no longer with defective materials and poor workmanship.

3. Cease dependence on inspection. Require statistical evidence of process control from suppliers.

4. End the practice of awarding business on the basis of price. Reduce the number of suppliers.

5. Improve constantly and forever. Use statistical methods to detect the sources of problems.

6. Institute modern aids for training on the job.

7. Institute leadership. Improve supervision.

8. Drive out the fear to express ideas and report problems.

9. Break down barriers between departments.

10. Eliminate production quotas, slogans, and exhortations.

11. Create work standards that account for quality.

12. Institute a training program in statistical methods.

13. Institute a program for retraining people in new skills.

14. Put everybody in the company to work to accomplish the transformation. The transformation is everybody's job. Emphasize the previous 13 points every day.

Deming's 14 Points for Quality Achievement[9]

Technology interacts with quality in a variety of ways. New processes are better able to control tolerances at reasonable cost. Materials with new properties are appearing regularly. Control systems based on new technologies are able to function with increasing precision. There are optical scanners and other kinds of auto-sensory systems that can serve as inspectors. They can collect information on many dimensions and in greater detail than human inspectors. Computers analyze and chart multiple quality dimensions, spotting problems faster than they did in the past. Such rapid results allow quick feedback and correction.

4-10 INDUSTRY RECOGNITION OF QUALITY

General MacArthur's effort to put Japanese industry back on its feet after World War II was incredibly successful. There are many people, both Japanese and American, who played a part in that effort. One whose name stands out is Dr. W. Edwards Deming.

Deming espoused the notion that firms with outstanding quality products could capture markets that otherwise would not be available to them. Such firms would be able to stay in business and create new jobs. He also believed that improvements in quality benefited consumers, workers, and producers alike.

Deming's 14 points, in Table 4-4, are representative of the broad systems view that he held, in which every aspect of business played a part in quality achievement.

The MacArthur Commission, which had been set up to deal with Japanese industry, called on Deming to help Japanese firms after World War II. The Japanese managers found Deming's ideas and his 14 points appealing. They listened to him, further developed many of his ideas, and consulted with him for years.

4-10a The Deming Prize

Since 1951, the Japanese Union of Scientists and Engineers (JUSE) has awarded the **Deming Prize** to companies (from any country) that have achieved outstanding quality performance. Deming, as an American statistician, advised Japanese manufacturers about

Deming Prize: Awarded since 1951 by JUSE (Japanese Union of Scientists and Engineers).

various principles of quality including his work with Dr. Shewhart on statistical process control (SPC). The Japanese felt that Deming's influence was so great that they named the prize for him.

The scope of this highly regarded prize is twofold. It emphasizes success with both SPC and QFD. This encompasses organizational efforts and participation of many employees in such activities as quality circles. In addition, the prize rewards companies with high standards and low defective rates.

Deming himself made a point of acknowledging the fact that service companies have won the award. "Service organizations have won the Deming Prize in Japan; for example, Takenaka Komuten, an architectural and construction firm, won the Deming Prize in 1979. They studied the needs of users (in offices, hospitals, factories, hotels, trains, subways)." He listed three other service firms that won the Deming Prize in successive years (1982, 1983, and 1984). Deming considered quality methodology essential for such diverse services as care of the aged and "perhaps even the U.S. mail."[10]

American companies that have won the Deming Prize are Florida Power and Light (FPL) and a Texas Instruments division located in Japan. Although FPL won the prize in 1989, the company's quality effort was restructured in 1990 because the initiative to win and the promotional celebration thereafter had created a bureaucracy, which was moving the company off the track of its real business.

Baldrige Award: Quality improvement act signed into law on August 20, 1987.

The 2002 Malcolm Baldrige National Quality Award recipients are Motorola Inc. Commercial, Government and Industrial Solutions Sector, Schaumburg, Illinois (manufacturing category); Branch-Smith Printing Division, Fort Worth, Texas (small business category); SSM Healthcare, St. Louis, Missouri (healthcare category).

Source:

http://www.nist.gov/public_affairs/releases/baldrige2002.htm.

4-10b The Malcolm Baldrige National Quality Award

During the 1980s, U.S. companies felt the power that Japanese competitors exercised because of their devotion to quality. A variety of government initiatives were undertaken in the United States to spur improvement of the quality of American products. The Malcolm Baldrige National Quality Award was conceived as a program to trigger competitiveness among U.S. companies with respect to their adherence to management principles that resulted in quality products.

One of these steps was the passage of Public Law 100-107. This was the Malcolm Baldrige[11] National Quality Improvement Act, and it was signed into law on August 20, 1987. Thereby, the U.S. Congress established the **Baldrige Award** for those companies that lead in quality accomplishments.

The funding for the Baldrige Award comes in part from the Foundation for the Malcolm Baldrige National Quality Award. Donor organizations from private enterprise have succeeded in raising funds to permanently endow the award program. The National Institute of Standards and Technology (NIST), which is part of the U.S. Department of Commerce, manages the award program. The American Society for Quality Control (ASQC) assists in that management under contract to NIST.

In the first seven years (1988–1994), there were 22 Baldrige Awards (for an average of 3.14 per year). Six awards (27 percent) were given to service organizations (and one distributor). The award winners range in size. These 22 companies are listed in Table 4-5. There is a special small business category; the other two categories are manufacturers and service companies. There is a maximum of two winners per category, and only companies located in the United States can win. Judging is done by the Board of Examiners, which consists of about 270 individuals, all volunteers. Most are from the private sector, with some from academia.

The criteria for the award can be characterized as being representative of TQM. This means that the criteria framework is systems-oriented. It is also characterized by dynamic relationships as shown in Figure 4-11 on page 124. There are seven core components that span all aspects of quality and performance and add up to the total score of 1,000 points, as shown in Figure 4-12 on page 125.

In the next eight years (1995–2002) there were 29 Baldrige Awards (for an average 3.6 per year). Ritz Carlton Hotels received a second Baldrige. Several school systems received awards as did a healthcare provider organization. All of these companies are listed in Table 4-6 on page 126.

The criteria for the award change slightly from year to year, but it still can be characterized as being representative of TQM. The criteria framework is increasingly systems-oriented.

TABLE 4-5

Malcolm Baldrige Award-Winning Companies (1988–1994)

Year	Company	Location	Product or Service*
1988	Globe Metallurgical, Inc.	Cleveland, OH	(M) iron-based metal products
1988	Motorola, Inc.	Schaumburg, IL	(M) electronic equipment
1988	Westinghouse Commercial Nuclear Fuel Division	Pittsburgh, PA	(M) nuclear fuel
1989	Milliken and Co.	Spartanburg, SC	(M) textiles
1989	Xerox Corp.	Stamford, CT	(M) business products and systems
1990	Cadillac Motor Car Co.	Detroit, MI	(M) luxury automobiles
1990	Federal Express Corp.	Memphis, TN	(S) express delivery service
1990	IBM-Rochester	Rochester, MN	(M) computer systems and hard disk storage devices
1990	Wallace Co., Inc.	Houston, TX	(D) industrial pipe, valves, and fittings
1991	Marlow Industries, Inc.	Dallas, TX	(M) thermoelectric cooling devices
1991	Solectron Corp.	San Jose, CA	(M) printed circuit boards, systems assembly, and testing
1991	Zytec Corp.	Eden Prairie, MN	(M) computer power supplies; repair facility
1992	AT&T Transmission Systems	Morristown, NJ	(M) telecommunication transmission equipment
1992	AT&T Universal Card Services	Jacksonville, FL	(S) credit and long-distance calling card services
1992	Granite Rock Co.	Watsonville, CA	(M) concrete and road treatments; also retails building materials
1992	Texas Instruments Defense Systems & Electronics Group	Dallas, TX	(M) defense electronics equipment
1992	The Ritz-Carlton Hotel Co.	Atlanta, GA	(S) hotel management
1993	Ames Rubber Corp.	Hamburg, NJ	(M) rubber rollers for copiers
1993	Eastman Chemical Co.	Kingsport, TN	(M) chemicals, fibers, plastics
1994	AT&T Consumer Communications (S) (domestic and international services) Basking	Ridge, NJ	(S) long-distance services
1994	GTE Directories Corp.	Dallas, TX	(S) publishing and selling advertising for telephone directories
1994	Wainwright Industries, Inc.	St. Peters, MO	(M) stamped and machined metal products

* M = manufacturer, S = service provider, D = distributor
Source: Malcolm Baldrige National Quality Award—Profiles of Winners, 1988–1994.

Even a relatively cursory analysis of the point allocations indicates the breadth of perspective of the Baldrige approach. Note that customer focus and satisfaction is 25 percent of the score. The emphasis is somewhat different from the Deming Prize.

Just as Florida Power and Light experienced difficulties after winning the Deming Prize, other companies that have won the Baldrige Award have found that being a winner presents new challenges. These include being on display, going on the lecture circuit, freezing the winning combination, and losing flexibility to respond to new competitive factors. There also is the winner's tendency to become bureaucratic and powerful with respect to quality, which is only successful when everyone is empowered and participating. Nevertheless, applications for the Baldrige Award continue to increase. There were 49 applications in 2002 and 68 applications in 2003, which is a 39 percent growth rate.

FIGURE 4-11
Baldrige Criteria for Performance Excellence Framework: A Systems Perspective

Source: Malcolm Baldrige National Quality Award—*2004* Award Criteria, United States
Department of Commerce, National Institute of Standards and Technology.

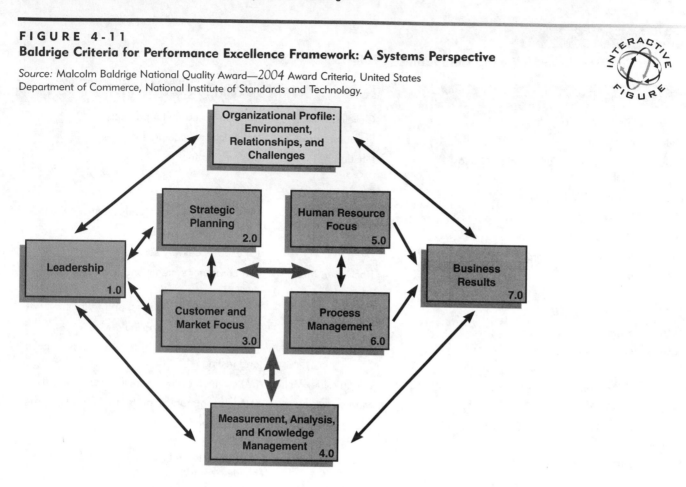

2004 Categories and Items	Point Values
1.0 Leadership	**(120 pts.)**
1.1 Organizational Leadership	(70 pts.)
1.2 Social Responsibility	(50 pts.)
2.0 Strategic Planning	**(85 pts.)**
2.1 Strategy Development	(40 pts.)
2.2 Strategy Deployment	(45 pts.)
3.0 Customer and Market Focus	**(85 pts.)**
3.1 Customer and Market Knowledge	(40 pts.)
3.2 Customer Relationships Satisfaction	(45 pts.)
4.0 Measurement, Analysis, and Knowledge Management	**(90 pts.)**
4.1 Measurement and Analysis of Organizational Performance	(45 pts.)
4.2 Information and Knowledge Management	(45 pts.)
5.0 Human Resource Focus	**(85 pts.)**
5.1 Work Systems	(35 pts.)
5.2 Employee Learning and Motivation	(25 pts.)
5.3 Employee Well-Being and Satisfaction	(25 pts.)
6.0 Process Management	**(85 pts.)**
6.1 Value Creation Processes	(50 pts.)
6.2 Support Processes	(35 pts.)
7.0 Business Results	**(450 pts.)**
7.1 Customer-Focused Results	(75 pts.)
7.2 Product and Service Results	(75 pts.)
7.3 Financial and Market Results	(75 pts.)
7.4 Human Resource Results	(75 pts.)
7.5 Organizational Effectiveness Results	(75 pts.)
7.6 Governance and Social Responsibility Results	(75 pts.)
Total Points	**(1,000 pts.)**

**FIGURE 4-12
Malcolm Baldrige 2004
Award Examination Criteria
Categories**

Source: Malcolm Baldrige National Quality Award—2004 Award Criteria, United States Department of Commerce, National Institute of Standards and Technology.

TABLE 4-6

Malcolm Baldrige Award-Winning Companies (1995—2002)

Year	Company	Location	Product or Service*
1995	Armstrong World Industries, Inc.	Lancaster, PA	(M) building products (home and commercial interiors)
1995	Corning, Inc.	Corning, NY	(M) telecommunications products (fiber optics)
1996	ADAC Laboratories	Milpitas, CA	(M) high-technology healthcare products
1996	Custom Research Inc.	Minneapolis, MN	(S) smart market research
1996	Dana Commercial Credit Corp.	Toledo, OH	(S) leasing and financial services
1996	Trident Precision Mfg. Inc.	Webster, NY	(M) sheet metal and electromechanical components (small business)
1997	3M Dental Products Div.	St. Paul, MN	(M) crown and bridge materials and adhesive
1997	Merrill Lynch Credit Corp.	Jacksonville, FL	(S) diverse line of credit products
1997	Solectron Corp., Inc.	Milpitas, CA	(M) electronics and supply chain consulting
1997	Xerox Business Services	Rochester, NY	(S) document outsourcing and consulting
1998	Boeing Airlift and Tanker Programs	St. Louis, MO	(M) C-17 Globemaster 111 airlifter
1998	Solar Turbines Inc.	San Diego, CA	(M) midrange industrial gas turbine systems
1998	Texas Nameplate Comp., Inc.	Dallas, TX	(SB) info labels affixed to refrigerators, trucks
1999	STMicroelectronics, Inc., Region Americas	Carrollton, TX	(M) integrated circuits for consumer electronics, etc.
1999	BI	Minneapolis, MN	(S) performance improvement programs (small business)
1999	The Ritz-Carlton Hotel Company, LLC	Atlanta, GA	(S) luxury hotels worldwide
1999	Sunny Fresh Foods	Monticello, MN	(SB, M) further-processed egg products
2000	Dana Corporation—Spicer Driveshaft Division (now Torque Traction Technologies, Inc.) HQ,	Toledo, OH	(M) largest independent supplier of automotive drive shafts in North America; Dana provides common products to a globally diverse customer base
2000	KARLEE Company, Inc.	Garland, TX	(M) precision sheet metal and machined components
2000	Operations Management, Inc. (OMI, Inc.)	Greenwood Village, CO	(S) operation and maintenance of small- to medium-size municipally-owned water and wastewater systems
2000	Los Alamos National Bank	Los Alamos, NM	(SB) independent, full-service community banking
2001	Clarke American Checks, Inc.	San Antonio, TX	(M) state-of-the-art digital printing; handle servicing phone calls at industry-leading service levels
2001	Pal's Sudden Service	Kingsport, TN	(SB) quick service restaurant (QSR) with leadership in key business drivers of quality, service, etc.
2001	Chugach School District	Anchorage, AL	(E) school district is 22,000 square miles with 214 students, accessible only by aircraft; smallest organization ever to win a Baldrige Award
2001	Pearl River School District	Pearl River, Rockland Co., NY	(E) excellence in k–12 grade public school educational program
2001	University of Wisconsin–Stout	Menomonie, WI	(E) 27 undergraduate and 16 graduate degree programs; unique approach with tech labs and industry partnerships
2002	SSM Health Care	St. Louis, MO	(HC) private, not-for-profit healthcare provider system with an innovative automated information system
2002	Branch-Smith Printing Division	Fort Worth, TX	(SB) designing, printing, binding, and mailing sheet-fed printed multipage bound materials
2002	Motorola Commercial, Government & Industrial Solutions Sector	Schaumburg, IL	(M) leading worldwide supplier of two-way radio communications; customers include fire, police, and public service organizations

* M = manufacturer, S = service provider, SB = small business, E = education, HC = health care, D = distributor

Source: http://www.quality.nist.gov.

SUMMARY

The reason that better quality matters is explained. TQM—the systems management approach to quality—is the way to obtain better quality, but first quality has to be defined. There is a difference in the way that consumers and producers think about quality. Various dimensions of quality are explored. One of these is the warranty policies that companies offer. Another is the kind of services that is given. How international standards are set is discussed, including U.S., international ISO 9000, Japanese, and other quality standards. The costs of quality are explored, including the costs of prevention, appraisal, and failure. Control of output quality is enhanced by the use of a feedback model, which is explained. The use of mapping to understand quality is demonstrated using the House of Quality (HOC) and quality function deployment (QFD). Quality circles are discussed, and prizes for best quality are detailed.

Two Spotlight feature boxes conclude this chapter. These boxes illustrate real applications of the material in the chapter. See Spotlight 4-1: Promoting Quality with a Body of Knowledge that Connects Process and Results and Spotlight 4-2: WorldSource One, Inc.

KEY TERMS

Acceptance sampling methods
Action learning
Baldrige Award
Costs of quality
Deming Prize
Dimensions of quality
Drift-decay quality phenomena
Extreme quality achievement

House of Quality (HOQ)
ISO 9000 series
Japanese Industrial Standard Z8101
Lifetime value (LTV) of a customer
Mean time between failures (MTBF)
Product callbacks
Quality circles (QCs)
Quality function deployment (QFD)

Six-Sigma
Taguchi methods
Tolerance limits
Total quality management (TQM)
Variety
Zero defects

REVIEW QUESTIONS

1. What is the competitive role of quality and why is it important?

2. What is TQM and why is it important?

3. What are the differences between consumer and producer definitions for quality?

4. How does the systems approach apply to the following statement

   "Quality—like a chain—is betrayed by its weakest link."

5. Discuss the statement "Although the name TQM may be viewed by some as faddish, the concept is not."

6. What quality dimensions apply to the software industry?

7. Set down appropriate quality dimensions for an automobile.

8. What problem exists because quality standards can age?

9. Explain OM's relationship with market research.

10. Explain how consistency of conformity translates into low reject rates.

11. Discuss the strengths and weaknesses of quality circles. Are they similar to student cohort work groups?

12. What are the ways to reduce the cost of detailing?

13. Explain what the House of Quality does and how it works.

14. Describe how QFD functions.

15. What prize competitions exist for quality and why are these prizes given?

PROBLEMS SECTION

1. The costs of quality are given by the following equations:
    $$C_a = 100D + 1000$$
    $$C_p = -50D + 6000$$
    $$C_f = De^{0.5D}$$
    where:
    C_a is the cost of appraisal,
    C_p is the cost of prevention, and
    C_f is the cost of failure.

    Note that D is the percent defectives and $0 \le D \le 100$.

    Determine the total cost of quality when there are no defectives. $D = 0$ and product quality is perfect.

2. Given the information in Problem 1, determine the total cost of quality when $D = 100$. No company could stay in business with $D = 100$, as will be apparent from the calculations.

3. Given the information in Problem 1, determine the total cost of quality when $D = 0$, 10, and 15. Plot all of the points.

4. Using the information in Problem 1, comment on the shape and position of these cost of quality curves.

5. Using the information in Problem 1, is there a minimum total cost? What is it?

6. Assume that the cost of appraisal is the same no matter what the value of D.

    Can this situation be explained in a rational way?

    Calculate the minimum total cost of quality with appraisal costs removed.

7. Make a list of the variables that should be included in a model for a rational warranty policy for each of these four products. Develop a specific warranty policy.
    a. Automobile (specify the type and cost)
    b. Four-pack of lightbulbs (specify the type and cost)
    c. Something that breaks easily
    d. Something that is highly unlikely to break down

8. How should responsibility for quality be positioned within and throughout the U.S. government? Should there be a Department of Quality? Relate this discussion to both products and services. Then, relate this discussion to the quality of safety and security.

9. Develop a House of Quality matrix for the Computer Laptop Company, which manufactures and markets laptops for the mid-price range market such as students in college. Label the rows with the customers' needs and label the columns with the properties of the product. Consider customer service to be an important requirement.

10. The tolerance limits for the lead in the mechanical pencil are (0.5 ± 0.05). What tolerance limits should be specified for the tube in the pencil into which the lead is inserted? Discuss the quality problems that are related to this issue. Does it make sense to go back to the operations managers of the company that makes the lead to ask them what it would take to get tighter tolerances?

11. The quality feedback system informs the controller about the error term: $(q - s) = \pm \epsilon$. The controller takes corrective action based on $(\pm \epsilon)$. When the system is in equilibrium, $(q - s) = 0$ and no corrective action is warranted. Assume that the standard is $s = 2$. The controller's correction of q is $f(\pm \epsilon_t) = \theta \epsilon_t = -(0.5)\epsilon_t$. In the following case, the value of q, which is regularly 2, has just jumped to 3. Show how the quality controller corrects the production process. Note: The table provides early guidance and suggests a way to organize calculations.

T	q	s	ϵ_t	$-(0.5)\epsilon_t$	$q - (0.5)\epsilon_t$
1	2.0	2.0	0	0	2
2	3.0	2.0	1	−0.5	3 − (0.5)
3	2.5				

    Note: Corrective action is taken on the last value of q in column 2. This produces changes to q as shown by $q - (0.5)\epsilon_t$ in column 6.

    Fill out the table to $t = 5$. Explain what is happening. How would a θ-value of −0.3 behave? How would a θ-value of −0.7 behave? Discuss.

12. Given the information in Problem 11, assume that the standard is $s = 2$. Also, the correction made by the controller is $-(1/2)(\pm \epsilon)$. The value of q, which is regularly 2, has just fallen to 1. Show how the quality controller corrects the production process.

T	q	S	ϵ_t	$-(0.5)\epsilon_t$	$q - (0.5)\epsilon_t$
1	2.0	2.0	0	0	2
2	1.0	2.0	−1	0.5	1 + (0.5)
3	1.5				

    Fill out the table to $t = 5$. Explain what is happening. How does this situation differ from that in Problem 11? How would $\theta = -0.3$ behave? What about $\theta = -0.7$? Discuss.

END-OF-CHAPTER QUESTIONS

1. The difference between producers' and consumers' quality concepts is best described by which of the following statements?
   a. Consumers like products that they conceive of as having high quality at low prices, which translates into good value. Producers like products with high margins, which may result from high prices and low costs.
   b. Producers believe that by conforming to blueprint specifications (which provide consistency of product qualities), consumers award top quality ratings to such products.
   c. Consumers define quality by choosing products that please them. Producers define quality in terms of consistently meeting their own product specifications.
   d. Consumers are not all alike, which means that quality is a variable that depends on the market segment. Producers select the quality of their products to appeal to the largest market segments.
   e. There is no difference between producers' and consumers' quality concepts.

2. P/OM's most important role in developing TQM (total quality management) is to
   a. bring process knowledge to the table.
   b. show everyone how each person in the company impacts quality and what each of them can do to improve quality.
   c. provide leadership company-wide for constant improvement.
   d. keep records of all defectives that occur and their causes.
   e. reengineer the system as soon as competitors bring out a new product.

3. Listed among the quality dimensions are the "ilities." These include
   a. possibilities.
   b. probabilities.
   c. facilities.
   d. reliabilities.
   e. impossibilities.

4. Human factors are important quality dimensions. These include consideration of
   a. safety and comfort.
   b. the ergonomics of variety.
   c. effects of irrationalities.
   d. nonfunctional quality factors.
   e. aesthetics and timing.

5. Which of the following statements is incorrect?
   a. ISO 9000 explains the ISO system.
   b. ISO 9001 applies to firms that are involved with production.
   c. ISO 9002 applies to firms that act as inspection agents.
   d. ISO 9004 serves as a guide to the Japanese Industrial Standard Z8101.
   e. ANSI/ASQC standards Q90 – Q94 are equivalent to the ISO 9000 standards.

6. The method of the costs of quality provided an economic business model that could permit a company to allocate its quality budget in an optimal way. Assume you own a seafood restaurant and want to apply the cost model to your business. Which allocation would you choose?
   a. prevention, 10%; inspection, 15%; failure, 75%
   b. prevention, 10%; inspection, 40%; failure, 50%
   c. prevention, 20%; inspection, 25%; failure, 55%
   d. prevention, 30%; inspection, 40%; failure, 30%
   e. prevention, 40%; inspection, 50%; failure, 10%

7. What does the quality control (input–output) feedback model signify? Which of the following statements is incorrect?
   a. The (input–output) electronic control system consists of a monitor and a control unit. The latter can adjust the production process to conform to specific standards.
   b. The quality control feedback system can operate on at least one dimension of production output. Control systems can be applied to more than one variable.
   c. The House of Quality model provides standards for many quality dimensions that can serve as benchmarks for the monitor-control feedback system.
   d. Feedback models provide powerful means for mapping quality systems. Therefore, it pays to create a feedback model before building appropriate House of Quality maps.
   e. Quality function deployment allows everyone (in the HOQ) to be consulted about where it pays to install a feedback control system.

8. Industry recognition of quality takes on many forms, including prizes and awards. Which of the following statements is incorrect?
   a. The Deming Prize has been given by JUSE (Japanese Union of Scientists and Engineers) since 1951 to companies from any country that has an outstanding record of quality performance.
   b. The Malcolm Baldrige National Quality Award was established in 1987 by the U.S. Congress for recognition of outstanding quality achievement. It is awarded to many categories of companies, but they must all be located in the United States.
   c. The Sterling Award (see http://www.floridasterling.com/newSite/about/index.htm) has been given to 34 organizations since 1992 by the governor of the state of Florida. It is awarded for significant improvement and achievement of performance excellence. The Sterling criteria are based on the Baldrige Award criteria.
   d. EFQM has been awarding the European Quality Awards (EQA) since 1992 to high-performing organizations in Europe. Award assessors come from a pool of senior managers and top academics in Europe. "The European Quality Award sits at the pinnacle of dozens of regional and national quality awards." In 2001, the committee wrote that they were shocked to find that no big company qualified for the prize. This was a wakeup call because their prize standards are based on the Baldrige Award and the Deming Prize in Japan. See http://www.efqm.org/model_awards/eqa/intro.htm.

e. In the United States, the National Institute of Standards and Technology (NIST) and the American Society for Quality Control (ASQC); in Europe, EFQM; and in Japan, the JUSE, provide prizes and awards to encourage companies from abroad to relocate in their region of the world. They have been very successful in doing this.

9. The scoring models used by the Baldrige Award Committees are
   a. first benchmarked against a House of Quality model.
   b. based on pure numbers derived from ratios where the quality dimensions such as innovation and leadership cancel out.
   c. regularly updated by the U.S. Department of Commerce to reflect new knowledge.
   d. combinations of numbers using the products of the powers.
   e. reflections of the personal opinions of the Baldrige Board of Examiners.

10. Dr. W. Edwards Deming was influential in helping Japanese industry reestablish itself after the destruction of World War II. Deming helped Japanese industry become the benchmark leader for quality practices. Deming's 14 points capture the essence of his principles for quality achievement. Which of the following principles is not part of the 14 points?
    a. Reduce the number of suppliers.
    b. Improve supervision and institute leadership.
    c. Start training in statistical methods.
    d. Use instinct to detect problems.
    e. Cease dependence on inspection.

ADDITIONAL READINGS

Bounds, G., L. Yorks, M. Adams, and G. Ranney. *Beyond Total Quality Management.* McGraw-Hill, Inc., 1994.

Crosby, Philip B. *Quality Is Free (The Art of Making Quality Certain).* McGraw-Hill, 1979. Also by Philip Crosby, *Zero Defects: Myth and Reality,* 2001. (available from the bookstore at http://www.philipcrosby.com).

Deming, W. Edwards. *Out of the Crisis.* MIT Center for Advanced Engineering Study, 1986.

Deming, W. Edwards. *The New Economics for Industry, Government, Education.* MIT Center for Advanced Engineering Study, 1993.

Dodge, Harold F., and Harry G. Romig. *Sampling Inspection Tables,* 2e. John Wiley & Sons, Inc., 1944.

Hauser, John R., and Don Clausing. "House of Quality," *Harvard Business Review* (May–June 1988): 63–67.

King, Bob. *Better Designs in Half the Time.* Methuen, MA: Goal/QPC, 1989.

Marsh, S., J. W. Moran, S. Nakui, and G. Hoffherr. *Facilitating and Training in QFD.* Methuen, MA: Goal/QPC, 1991.

Pande, Peter S., and Lawrence Holpp. *What Is Six Sigma?* McGraw-Hill, 2001.

Pande, Peter S., Robert P. Neuman, and Roland R. Cavanagh. *The Six Sigma Way: How GE, Motorola, and Other Top Companies Are Honing Their Performance.* McGraw-Hill, 2000.

NOTES

1. See, for example, D. Savageau. *Places Rated Almanac.* Prentice-Hall, Inc., 1993.

2. *Harvard Business Review* (November–December 1987).

3. Harold F. Dodge and Harry G. Romig. *Sampling Inspection Tables,* 2e. John Wiley & Sons, Inc., 1959. These tables specified the parameters for efficient sampling plans that could be used to accept or reject production lots.

4. DQS is the German Society for the Certification of Quality Systems. Deutsche Gesellschaft zur Zertifizierung von Qualitätssicherungssystemen mbH.

5. Philip B. Crosby. *Quality Is Free (The Art of Making Quality Certain).* McGraw-Hill, 1979.

6. A successful popularization of the HOQ method resulted from the article by John R. Hauser and Don Clausing, which appeared in the *Harvard Business Review* (May–June 1988): 63–73. Also, a book on the subject was written by Bob King. *Better Designs in Half the Time.* Methuen, MA: Goal/QPC, 1989.

7. International TechneGroup Incorporated of Milford, Ohio, has software called *QFD/Capture,* which permits participants from all contributing functions to use a DOS, Windows, or Macintosh environment to enter data and analyze its impact on quality.

8. QFD was developed in Japan in the late 1960s by Professors Shigeru Mizuno and Yoji Akao. With the help of Professor Akao, the QFD Institute was founded in 1993. It is located in Ann Arbor, MI. See http://www.qfdi.org.

9. Dr. Deming continuously fine-tuned his 14 points. As a result, there are many variations of them. Table 4-4 was one of his final versions. It had been prepared for Dr. Deming's Quality Seminars, which were given at Columbia University's Graduate School of Business in the mid-1990s.

10. W. Edwards Deming. *The New Economics for Industry, Government, Education.* MIT Center for Advanced Engineering Study, 1993.

11. See http://www.quality.nist.gov.

SPOTLIGHT 4-1
Promoting Quality with a Body of Knowledge That Connects Process and Results

An Interview and Discussion with Dr. Curt Reimann, Director (Emeritus) of the Malcolm Baldrige National Quality Award

To Curt W. Reimann, Director (Emeritus) of the Malcolm Baldrige National Quality Award, the major objective of the Baldrige Award is to "promote change at the national level, by way of a body of knowledge about quality that connects process and results." Reimann says the Baldrige Award serves to promote quality awareness, to recognize quality achievement of U.S. businesses, and to publicize successful quality strategies. Reimann was also director for quality programs at the National Institute of Standards and Technology (NIST)* and directed the Baldrige Award from its inception until (his retirement in) 1995. He continues to do supportive consulting work (with NIST's Manufacturing Extension Partnership program) that provides services to small manufacturing companies via state-based centers.

Reimann played an instrumental part in developing and annually revising the award examination, which operationalizes the basic concepts of total quality management and makes performance assessable. Reimann says that "Through the Baldrige Award criteria, we have created an integrated organizational management discipline, built around the factors that determine competitive success. Product and service quality are among these factors, but by no means are they the only factors. The discipline must integrate all aspects of performance—productivity, speed, innovation, market knowledge, workforce development, and many others."

The quality-improvement thrust of the Baldrige Award "goes well beyond the contest itself," according to Reimann. "To me, the contest 'pays the rent' for everything and gets most of the attention." But the real purpose of the Baldrige Award is information transfer and its affect on all U.S. institutions. In this regard, the award is now open to health and educa-

tion organizations. Also, many U.S. states, and other nations, including Japan, have established awards based on the Baldrige model.

Reimann supports the inclusion of the Baldrige Award concepts and criteria in business school curricula. "From the point of view of national competitiveness, the teaching of the Baldrige Award principles in business schools represents a very important development—one that could influence the next generation of business leaders."

A chemist by training, Curt W. Reimann has a Ph.D. from the University of Michigan and was a scientific researcher and science manager in chemistry at NIST before becoming involved with the Baldrige Award. He is currently a chaired professor at Tennessee Technological University, College of Business Administration.

Sources: Discussions and correspondence with Dr. Curt W. Reimann, July 3, 2003. Also, "Quality and Performance Management in the 21st Century," Dr. Curt W. Reimann, *Mayberry Newsletter,* Tennessee Technological University, 1999.

* About NIST
The National Institute of Standards and Technology was founded in 1901. It is a nonregulatory federal agency within the U.S. Department of Commerce, Technology Administration, located in both Gaithersburg, MD, and Boulder, CO. NIST's mission is to develop and promote measurement, standards, and technology to enhance productivity, facilitate trade, and improve the quality of life. NIST carries out its mission using four programs: (1) the Baldrige National Quality Program (promotes performance excellence); (2) the NIST Laboratories (conducting research that advances the U.S. technology infrastructure); (3) Manufacturing Extension Partnership (a nationwide network of local centers offering technical and business assistance to smaller manufacturers); and (4) the Advanced Technology Program (accelerates the development of innovative technologies by cofunding R&D partnerships with the private sector). See http://www.nist.gov/public_affairs/general2.htm

SPOTLIGHT 4-2
WorldSource One, Inc.

Five Barriers to Change—Perspectives from Dave Crowell, CEO, and Chalotte Bentley, President, WorldSource One, Inc.

"People engaged in multinational commerce tend to use two languages. The first is English, and the second is the language of performance improvement." Dave Crowell should know. He and business partner Charlotte Bentley have delivered ISO 9000, quality management, and Baldrige-based training to business people from dozens of countries.

When Dave and Charlotte started WorldSource One, Inc., their idea was to provide training and consulting services to multinational corporations and to the far-flung operations of Uncle Sam. Their clients include Goldman-Sachs, Johnson & Johnson, and federal government organizations like the Army, Navy, and the IRS.

Language was a huge training concern 20 years ago, but it has proved to be a minor issue today. Most of the management-level employees of multinational organizations speak, write, and understand English—at least well enough so that English is clearly the business language of choice around the world. "I was training managers for NCR Corporation in Belgium, and when it was coffee time, their coffee preferences ranged from *very strong coffee* to *tea with milk*, but their choice of language did not vary—it was English all the way!"

"We've had more trouble with the conceptual side than the language side," explains Dave. "While training Johnson & Johnson employees in Kuala Lumpur, Malaysia, we discovered that a few of the Baldrige Award concepts were not getting through to participants from Japan, Korea, China, and several other countries. For example, one difficult concept was the Baldrige concept of promoting diversity in the workplace. After a prolonged discussion, we realized that many Asian companies have a very homogeneous workforce, and becoming more diverse is a completely unfamiliar concept in their environment."

Charlotte reports similar conceptual problems working with U.S. Army employees in Germany and other European countries. "One Army client that manages real estate—housing, offices, ranges, and such—had employees from over 60 countries. This organization was well-versed in *diversity*, but had trouble with the concept of *empowerment*. In many parts of Europe, the boss is still the boss, and hierarchical structures are still firmly in place. Empowerment, which is alive and prospering in North America and Japan, is still an emerging concept in parts of Europe."

Dave, a former quality management executive with IBM, NCR, and EG&G, and Charlotte, a lifelong educator and curriculum expert, have completed dozens of workshops and seminars for people who use English as their second or business language. Charlotte points out that simultaneously covering a subject in several ways (with lectures, visuals, demonstrations, hands-on interactive workshops, and classroom projects, for example) pays huge dividends in terms of increasing understanding. Dave adds his observation that letting go of jargon and adopting standard English terminology also make a big difference in improved comprehension. "As experts in a subject like the Baldrige Criteria or ISO 9000, we often forget that we've slipped into a vocabulary of special meanings for dozens of otherwise normal English words." Business jargon is deadly to a foreign audience.

There are other quality management training issues, and most of these relate to factors other than language. Thanks to Dr. Deming, Dr. Juran, and countless others who promoted the principles of quality management for several decades, managers around the world have a reasonably good understanding of the basics. It's the barriers to change that slow their progress.

Based on their Baldrige and ISO 9000 training experience, Dave and Charlotte have identified five specific barriers to change that must be considered by all students of quality and performance improvement.

First, many people still think that *higher levels of quality cost more or take more time*. They are reluctant to listen to any arguments to the contrary, and persist on doing things the hard way—*do it, do it over again, eventually get it right most of the time*.

Second, there is a *silver bullet crowd*—those who firmly believe that a *single tool, method, or practice will solve all of the problems within an organization*. Unfortunately, they try something for awhile, discard it, and go on to another method. Soon, their organizations are scattered with the bones of all those programs that didn't work.

The third barrier is a *lack of systems thinking*. Many American managers, and their European and Asian cousins as well, are notoriously deficient in terms of *systems thinking—the big picture interaction of people, processes, technology, and feedback*. According to Charlotte, "You simply cannot benefit from the Baldrige Criteria or from ISO 9000 until you understand what systems are and how they work. It's fundamental knowledge!"

Speaking of knowledge, that's the fourth barrier. Dave is convinced that business and other organizations have a long way to go in terms of *knowledge management*. "I'm not talking about portals, servers, and complex technological concepts. Most organizations need better methods of keeping track of what works and what does not, and of finding and institutionalizing the best practices found in their own organizations. Companies are losing generations of knowledge and know-how when they downsize, resize, reorganize, or deliver golden parachutes."

The fifth barrier is actually a "set" of *industry-specific barriers* that have become deeply embedded over time. There are many cases that we could cite, but homebuilders are a familiar example. Many of them are so enamored with the *punch list* concept that they are largely incapable of even thinking about *preventing errors and defects*. Most claim that it's easier, more expedient, and even cheaper to do "it" over again, sometimes even twice, than to organize a preventive approach. That's not true, of course, but it is widely *believed* and that's all that counts.

Time goes on, however, and WorldSource One Baldrige training and consulting programs continue to impact clients around the world. They are conducted in English, free of jargon, and resolutely targeted at the five barriers.

Source: Communication with WorldSource One executives Dave Crowell (CEO) and Charlotte Bentley (President), October 2003.

Supplement 4

A Scoring Model for the House of Quality

A Scoring Application of the HOQ is shown in Figure 4-13, which rates the qualities of a gas service station.

	Importance of Need	Fast Pumping of Gas	Auto Credit Card Reader	Easy Access to Station	Limited Personnel	TOTAL
Service Speed	5	9	8	6	3	130
Payment Ease	1	4	3	2	1	10
Helpfulness	3	5	X	X	1	18
TOTAL		64	43	32	19	158

FIGURE 4-13
Rating the Qualities of a Gas Service Station

Customer needs (rows) are assigned a measure for their relative importance (5, 1, and 3) and the process steps (columns) are rated at each intersection with respect to how well that part of the process satisfies customer needs. This matrix provides the component process quality ratings for one service station. A separate matrix is created for each service station that is being considered.

For all numbers, the larger they are, the more important they are considered to be. Row values are multiplied by the weights. There is always concern about additive scoring models. If apples and oranges are being treated as if they were the same, it is because fruit is the measure of interest.

The first column of Figure 4-13 has a sum value of 64, which indicates that fast pumping is the leading quality of this station. Customers also like the automated credit card readers that let them make payments without waiting for station personnel. That column gets a 43. Easy station access is of relative importance with a sum value of 32. Limited personnel appears to handicap customer perceptions of quality. It gets only 19.

Service speed (weight of 5) is being satisfied (130), but helpfulness (weight of 3) and payment ease (weight of 1) are not being properly addressed by this service station. They are 18 and 10, respectively. Helpfulness probably should be addressed first because it is more important in the mind of the customer than payment ease. There could be an interaction if, by making payments easier, customers will consider the station as being more helpful.

Problem for Supplement 4

The Pin Company has a supplier rating system, which is based on mapping the company needs for quality, fast and reliable delivery, and low prices against the capability of the suppliers to satisfy these needs.

The two matrices in Figure 4-14 present the data that have been collected for Suppliers X and Y. Make a comparison of X and Y and choose the preferred supplier. Explain the choice.

Note: The process variables are

1. *Own delivery trucks*—Relates to how many trucks each supplier leases or owns.

2. *Inspected before delivery*—Relates to the procedures used by the supplier to check the quality of outgoing shipments.

3. *Factory stage*—Relates to the kind of equipment that the supplier uses to make the products where state-of-the-art or ahead of it gets the highest rating.

4. *Percent of the business*—Refers to how many other customers each supplier has and what percentage of the supplier's total business the Pin Company represents. The best percentage is considered to be about 10 percent.

Supplier X

	Importance of Need	Own Delivery Trucks	Inspected Before Delivery	Factory Stage	Percent of the Business	TOTAL
Quality	5	4	7	3	6	
Delivery	3	9	2	3	2	
Prices	4	3	5	5	7	
TOTAL						

Supplier Y

	Importance of Need	Own Delivery Trucks	Inspected Before Delivery	Factory Stage	Percent of the Business	TOTAL
Quality	5	2	6	7	1	
Delivery	3	1	3	6	1	
Prices	4	5	2	5	8	
TOTAL						193

F I G U R E   4 - 1 4
Comparing the Qualities of Gas Service Stations X and Y

CASES

Case 4-1
Industry Perspective on Quality: Tom's of Maine

Tom's of Maine, a manufacturer of "natural" personal care products, was founded in 1970 by Tom and Kate Chappell. The Chappells started their company after moving to Maine, seeking a simpler life and a deeper connection to the land. As part of this move, they began using natural foods and products, but were not able to find the natural personal care products they wanted for themselves and their children. So they decided to make and sell their own. (Tom's of Maine considers "natural products" to be those that are minimally processed, derived from natural resources, and free of artificial colors, sweeteners, preservatives, synthetic flavors, and fragrances.) From this simple beginning in the 1970s, the company has grown to become a significant player in the mass market for personal care products. With annual sales of approximately $40 million, and 160 employees, Tom's of Maine distributes natural, environmentally-friendly products to over 40,000 stores.

Nestled in the picturesque New England town of Kennebunk, Maine, the company is headquartered in a renovated red-brick factory building on the Mousam River. The office area, well lit and open, bespeaks Tom's of Maine's commitment to the environment with abundant, colorful, animal-related artwork. Recycled ingredient containers, transformed into freestanding art by local students, adorn the corridors. Framed copies of the company's mission statement and posters with handwritten excerpts from customer letters also are displayed. A mile from town, the manufacturing plant is housed in a rustic wooden structure next to a defunct railroad depot. A pleasant minty aroma pervades the inside of the facility in which all Tom's of Maine products are manufactured.

Common Good Capitalism

Tom's of Maine has remained true to the Chappell's original vision to manage their business for both profit and the common good of the community, the environment, and one another. Tom's of Maine strives to integrate the corporate values of commercial success with the belief that companies have a responsibility at all times to the common good of society. Tom Chappell explains that with "common good capitalism," private aspirations or aims (such as what a business owner does with the profits from the business) are accountable to a higher good, a common good. Tom Chappell wants the community in which his company operates to be able to recognize the business as a valuable, contributing presence.[1]

Product Variety

Tom's of Maine manufactures and sells a variety of natural personal care products including flossing ribbon, alcohol-free mouthwash, antiperspirant and deodorant, shampoo, shaving cream, and toothpaste—with and without fluoride. Sales of toothpaste account for the majority of Tom's of Maine's total revenue. We will now examine Tom's of Maine's manufacturing process for toothpaste.

Production Process for Toothpaste
Preproduction Activities

First the raw materials for the toothpaste must be received (#1). (Numbers in parentheses refer to the numbers on Figure 4-15—Production Process for Toothpaste at Tom's of Maine.) These materials include printed tubes with caps; natural ingredients (including calcium carbonate, fluoride, carrageenan, glycerin, sodium lauryl sulfate, flavors); toothpaste boxes; inner pack wrap; and shipping cartons.

Every incoming raw material is scrutinized against supplier specifications and United States Pharmacopoeia (USP) and Food and Drug Administration (FDA) requirements (#2). The FDA regulates ingredients that alter normal bodily functions, i.e., fluoride in toothpaste and antimicrobials in deodorant. Typical quality control (QC) tests at this stage include chemical assay, microbiology, organoleptic (appearance, smell, taste), and moisture content. OC tests normally are completed within 48 hours of receipt of a sample of the ingredient. If a problem with a one-half pound preshipment sample is detected, the sample is rejected, discarded, and the shipment is stopped. (To avoid production-scheduling problems if a shipment is rejected, Tom's of Maine generally has a 1-week supply of all materials on hand. Lead time to order ingredients is 2 to 12 weeks.) The tubes and boxes are tested against specifications provided by the marketing department to determine that printing and colors are correct.

One problem that may arise at this stage is that the density of the calcium carbonate sometimes doesn't meet requirements. Calcium carbonate is the ingredient that dictates how much water is absorbed in the toothpaste mix, so its density must be right. Testers also must be sure that the pH rate (a scale of acidity–alkalinity) is within a narrow range of specification. If higher than the specification range, the shelf life of the toothpaste will be reduced. Shelf life is 18 to 36 months, depending on storage conditions—the colder the better!

Tom's of Maine holds one week's worth of ingredients in a transition warehouse at the plant (#3a); an off-site warehouse about 10 miles away is for longer-term storage (#3b). Materials stored in the off-site warehouse stay an average 20 to 25 days. Liquid ingredients are stored in bulk tanks and 55-gallon drums; powdered ingredients are stored in 50-pound bags. No supplies are used without a completed "released for use" sticker, which tells the date the supply was

Tom's of Maine sells a variety of natural personal care products.

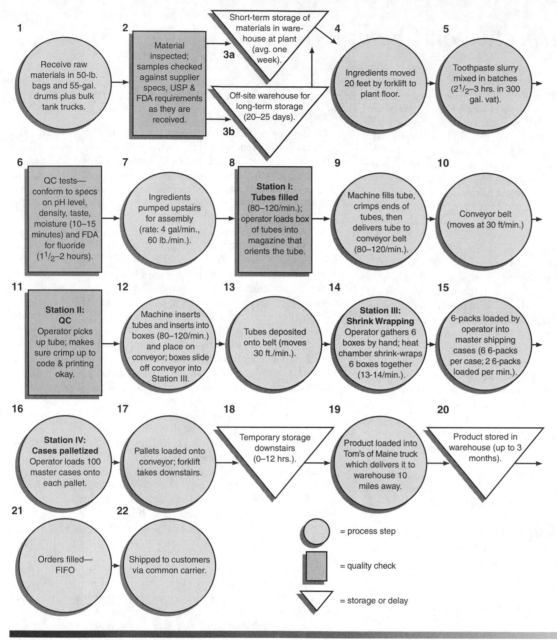

1 Receive raw materials in 50-lb. bags and 55-gal. drums plus bulk tank trucks.

2 Material inspected; samples checked against supplier specs, USP & FDA requirements as they are received.

3a Short-term storage of materials in warehouse at plant (avg. one week).

3b Off-site warehouse for long-term storage (20–25 days).

4 Ingredients moved 20 feet by forklift to plant floor.

5 Toothpaste slurry mixed in batches (2½–3 hrs. in 300 gal. vat).

6 QC tests—conform to specs on pH level, density, taste, moisture (10–15 minutes) and FDA for fluoride (1½–2 hours).

7 Ingredients pumped upstairs for assembly (rate: 4 gal./min., 60 lb./min.).

8 Station I: Tubes filled (80–120/min.); operator loads box of tubes into magazine that orients the tube.

9 Machine fills tube, crimps ends of tubes, then delivers tube to conveyor belt (80–120/min.).

10 Conveyor belt (moves at 30 ft/min.)

11 Station II: QC Operator picks up tube; makes sure crimp up to code & printing okay.

12 Machine inserts tubes and inserts into boxes (80–120/min.) and place on conveyor; boxes slide off conveyor into Station III.

13 Tubes deposited onto belt (moves 30 ft./min.).

14 Station III: Shrink Wrapping Operator gathers 6 boxes by hand; heat chamber shrink-wraps 6 boxes together (13-14/min.).

15 6-packs loaded by operator into master shipping cases (6 6-packs per case; 2 6-packs loaded per min.).

16 Station IV: Cases palletized Operator loads 100 master cases onto each pallet.

17 Pallets loaded onto conveyor; forklift takes downstairs.

18 Temporary storage downstairs (0–12 hrs.).

19 Product loaded into Tom's of Maine truck which delivers it to warehouse 10 miles away.

20 Product stored in warehouse (up to 3 months).

21 Orders filled—FIFO

22 Shipped to customers via common carrier.

◯ = process step

▢ = quality check

▽ = storage or delay

FIGURE 4-15
Production Process for Toothpaste at Tom's of Maine

tested and released, who analyzed it, and the quantity. This allows Tom's of Maine to trace every ingredient back to its original tester. Ingredients in the transition warehouse are moved 20 feet by forklift into the batch preparation area on an as-needed basis (#4).

Tom's of Maine has close relationships with a few suppliers. The company works closely with suppliers to understand their processes and improve them. Target supplier flaw rate (also called the *defective rate*) is 0.1 percent. Tom's of Maine shares flaw rate information with suppliers and works with them to improve the rates. When Tom's of Maine first started buying from its tube supplier, for example, the flaw rate was 0.5 percent. After working closely with them to increase

quality, the same supplier has achieved a 0.01 percent rate, and now supplies all of Tom's of Maine's toothpaste tubes.

Continuous Batch Preparation

Tom's of Maine makes one to three varieties of toothpaste per day, mixing the ingredients in a 300-gallon vat or "change can" weighing 3,600 pounds. The toothpaste ingredients (calcium carbonate, fluoride, carrageenan, glycerin, sodium lauryl sulfate, and natural flavors) are mixed at high speeds of up to 600 rpms for 2 1/2 to 3 hours (#5). This toothpaste mixture is called "slurry." After the mixing is complete, the operators scrape the mixing blades to remove as much of the mixture as possible from them; this also facilitates cleaning and preparation of the equipment for the next batch.

Tom's of Maine has 26 varieties of toothpaste in all. In a 20-day month, 20 days are spent on making toothpaste. When filling 4-ounce tubes, 8 batches of one flavor are made in one 16-hour day, which yields approximately 84,000 4-ounce tubes. When filling 6-ounce tubes, 8 kettles of the mixture are made, which results in 59,000 tubes in one 16-hour day. Tom's of Maine usually devotes two days per month to making spearmint toothpaste, which is its best selling flavor.

Tom's of Maine has an extensive preventive maintenance program, which regularly checks parts and machines. These preventive checks are done during production. While a liquid product (such as deodorant or mouthwash) is being produced, maintenance checks are performed on the equipment used to produce "nonliquid" products, such as toothpaste. When nonliquid products are being processed, checks are performed on the equipment used to make liquid products. A supply of replacement parts is maintained at the factory.

Twelve people are involved in making a batch of toothpaste, including a foreperson, a production supervisor, four mechanics (who work alternating shifts from 5 A.M. to 11 A.M., Monday through Friday), one quality assurance (QA) lab supervisor, one lab assistant, three batch mixers, and one batch supervisor.

QC Tests on Slurry

After mixing is complete, each vat of slurry is tested for conformity to specs on pH level, density, taste, moisture, and FDA requirements for fluoride level (#6). Two taste testers taste the slurry for acceptability. The reject rate on the slurry is below 0.01 percent. The rework rate on slurry is about 0.25 percent. QC tests on slurry generally take 10 to 15 minutes. Results of the chromatography tests for fluoride dispersion (samples of which are taken when the mixing is complete) are not available until after the toothpaste has been inserted into the tubes. This test takes about 1 1/2 to 2 hours. Tom's of Maine has only had to reject one batch in 14 years because fluoride was not dispersed evenly throughout the mixture. If a batch is rejected for any reason, the contents are discarded.

Pumping of Vat Contents to Production Line

After the QC tests on slurry are complete, the ingredients are pumped upstairs at a rate of 5 gallons or 60 pounds per minute for continuation of the production process (#7). When all the slurry in the vat has been emptied, the empty vat is moved out of the way and a new vat of slurry that has been prepared off-line is rolled into place. This changeover takes about 5 minutes.

Four-Station Assembly Process

Upstairs in the plant, the four assembly stations are set to receive the toothpaste slurry. The empty printed tubes, open at the bottom, have caps already screwed on. The aluminum tubes are lined with a plastic phenolic coating. Without this coating, the calcium carbonate would react with the aluminum. Tom's of Maine uses aluminum tubes because they are recyclable.

All hand operations in the production process serve a dual purpose: They perform a specific function (such as picking up a tube and placing it in the box) as well as serve as quality checks.

Thirteen people are involved in this serialized part of the production process including a foreperson, a production supervisor, three mechanics, one operator at Station I, two operators at Station II, two operators at Station III, one "floater" (who keeps the floor clean, moves boxes, and generally troubleshoots), and one operator and one forklift operator at Station IV.

Stations I through III are synchronized by a conveyor. Operators' idle time is taken up by moving material from station to station, i.e., moving pallets on finished goods to the conveyor, which takes them downstairs. The speed of the conveyors used is approximately 30 feet per minute.

Station I—At the first station, a machine operator loads a box of tubes into a magazine that orients the tube (#8). The empty boxes are collected and then sent back to the supplier for reuse. The machine fills each tube and passes each through a series of four crimping stations, which fold the end of the tube three times; the fourth station prints a batch code and expiration date on the tube (#9). The machine then delivers the tube to a conveyor, which moves at 30 feet per minute (#10). Tubes are filled at a rate of 80 to 120 per minute (6-ounce tubes at 80 to 81 tubes per minute; 4-ounce tubes at 83 to 120 per minute). These rates are referred to as the "quality sweet spots," the processing rates at which a less than 0.01 percent flaw rate is achieved.

Station II—Two operators pick up tubes off the conveyor and visually check that the crimp is up to code (it is not leaking; printed with correct lot and expiration date) and that the printing is acceptable (#11). Every tenth or twentieth tube is check weighed on a digital scale. One operator loads a magazine with toothpaste boxes and inserts stories (#12). These operators are rotated once every hour to minimize the adverse effects of repetition and "overuse" injuries. The filled boxes slide off the conveyor into Station III (#13). Air is blown toward the boxes as they slide so that if a box has not been filled, it is blown off the conveyor and into a bin.

Station III—One operator gathers six toothpaste boxes by hand, stacked in two groups of three boxes (#14). The operator puts the six boxes under a plastic sheet and loosely wraps the boxes with plastic. The six boxes are then shrinkwrapped together by a machine with a heat chamber. Six-packs are shrinkwrapped at the rate of 13 to 14 per minute.

Station IV—Another operator puts six 6-packs into a corrugated master case (#15), producing a little over two master cases per minute. The batch code is put on the case; then the case is loaded onto a pallet. An operator loads 100 master cases onto each pallet (#16). The master cases are "stretch-wrapped" onto the pallet. Pallets are then loaded onto a conveyor and taken downstairs (#17). From there, a forklift operator moves the pallets downstairs, where they are stored (#18) until the truck is loaded, either the evening of the day the tubes are filled or the next morning. The truck ships the pallets to the warehouse the next morning (#19).

Four operators work in the warehouse. The product is stored in racks in the warehouse for up to three months (#20). Orders are filled on a "first-in, first-out" basis (#21). The warehouse is arranged randomly; each product is marked with a product code. Shelf life for toothpaste is 18 to 36 months. Turnover at retail outlets typically is faster than this. The product is shipped to customers via common carrier (#22).

QC Charts and Checklists

Tom's of Maine uses a variety of QC charts and checklists during the toothpaste manufacturing process to meet GMPs (good manufacturing practices). These charts include a "Production Order" and "Toothpaste Manufacturing Checklist" used when the toothpaste ingredients are mixed; a "Toothpaste Checklist" used in preparing the 4-station assembly process; a "Fill Report," which is a quality control check used after the tubes are filled; and a record of "Tube Defects per Day," which records such problems as bad or loose caps, bumps in the tube lining, printing problems, defective liners, or metal shavings.

Forecasts and Production Scheduling

Forecasts for unit sales are generated by Sales & Marketing. Manufacturing uses MRP to convert the Sales & Marketing forecast into a production schedule and purchasing plan.

Quality Emphasis

Producing quality products is a major emphasis at Tom's of Maine. The company's Stewardship Model outlines the standards by which all products are produced:

- Tom's of Maine products must have environmentally safe, natural ingredients. The products are packaged in ways that respect nature as well. Consumers are encouraged to recycle the product packaging. Tom's of Maine recycles as much as possible of the packaging in which its supplies are delivered.
- All products must be proven safe and effective for consumers. But Tom's of Maine's product ingredients are never tested on animals. To avoid animal testing, alternative tests are used. For instance, as an alternative to the traditional rabbit eye test for mucus membrane sensitivity, a vegetable protein is used that reacts in the same way as the rabbit's eyes.
- Consideration of customer needs and keeping customers happy is another quality concern at Tom's of Maine. Like all health- and environmentally-conscious consumers, users of Tom's of Maine's products are very astute. They demand more information about the products they purchase than the average customer. For this reason, Tom's of Maine includes three panels of product information on its toothpaste packages compared to one panel of information on the average toothpaste carton. There is also a story insert describing the company's mission and consumer letters.
- Customer feedback is solicited on every package. Every letter, phone call, or e-mail Tom's of Maine receives—about 1,400 per month—is read (or received) and tabulated. Approximately 80 percent of the letters are positive. All letters are answered by a member of the Consumer Dialogue Team, which is comprised of 10 people from all departments in the company. The quality assurance and production departments receive copies of all complaints.
- Tom's of Maine also strives for a high quality of life for its employees. To this end, there are no weekend or overnight shifts at the plant, and there is frequent rotation on production lines. Employees are members of various teams including the Consumer Dialog Team, Engineering Team, Production Team, and Quality Assurance Team.
- Service to community is an important quality consideration for Tom's of Maine. In keeping with Tom Chappell's theory of "Common Good Capitalism," employees are encouraged to devote 5 percent of their work time to doing volunteer work in the community. They are given time off—with pay—to perform this volunteer service.

What Does the Future Hold?

Tom Chappell says Tom's of Maine plans to grow at a rate of 15 percent annually by entering new markets and offering new products every year, while "keeping an eye on the inward or spiritual aspect of how we do things." (Spiritual growth is, unfortunately, not quantifiable.) By 2003, Tom's of Maine was offering over 85 products in categories from oral care to body care, and self care.

For the near term, Tom's of Maine plans to manage growth through continuing to improve productivity efficiencies with faster equipment instead of expanding the production facility or increasing the number of employees and work shifts. Tom's has plans to build a new facility if growth meets projections. Tom's of Maine also hopes to continue expansion into foreign markets. Currently they export their products to England, Canada, and Japan.

You might say that Tom's of Maine was slightly ahead of its time in 1970 in targeting the market for healthier, more environmentally-friendly products. Consumers today are seeking products that are pure and natural, without chemical additives.[2] Mass marketers such as Johnson & Johnson and Del Laboratories all recently have identified the natural products market as a growth area and are producing such products.

Tom Chappell believes that an emphasis on the science of plants will grow the business. To this end he has brought aboard specialists in plant chemistry and the medicinal value of plants to ensure that Tom's of Maine's products remain not only natural but also provide the most efficacious use of natural ingredients for consumers.

Questions

1. Discuss how quality fits into Tom's of Maine's overall strategy and the relationship between strategy and success at Tom's of Maine.
2. Identify and discuss some of the tactics Tom's of Maine uses to fulfill its mission to provide natural and environmentally-safe products.
3. Discuss the eight dimensions of quality (performance, features, reliability, conformance, durability, serviceability, aesthetics, and perceived quality) with regard to Tom's of Maine toothpaste. Which dimensions do you think are most important to the success of this product and why?
4. What happens to toothpaste slurry? Detail its path step-by-step until the finished product is stored.
5. What happens to a 50-pound bag of powdered raw materials? Detail the process steps from receipt of the materials until the empty bag is returned to the supplier.
6. Identify the costs Tom's of Maine incurs with regard to appraisal, prevention, and failure.
7. Identify the various quality control measures Tom's of Maine employs as related to raw material inspection, work-in-process inspection, and finished goods inspection.

Notes

1. Tom Chappell. *The Soul of a Business: Managing for Profit and the Common Good.* Bantam, October 1993.
2. Tom Chappell. *Managing Upside Down.* William Morrow & Co., 1999.
3. *The Wall Street Journal,* Tuesday, May 11, 1993.

References

Tom's of Maine, "Natural Care Newsletter," Vol. I, Issue 2, 2002.
Tom's of Maine 1993 Annual Report. "The Private Good and The Common Good—Finding a Middle Way."
Mary Martin. "Toothpaste and Theology." *Boston Sunday Globe* (October 10,1993).
"Putting It Mildly, More Consumers Prefer Only Products That Are 'Pure,' 'Natural.'" *The Wall Street Journal* (May 11, 1993).
"Tom Chappell: Minister of Commerce." *Business Ethics,* vol. 8, no. 1, (January/February 1994).
Http://www.toms-of-maine.com.

Source: Tom's of Maine. Printed with permission.

part 3

Designing the Process, Analysis, and Improvement

In Part 3, process flows are designed, analyzed, and improved. Processes are classified and charted. Quality control systems are devised for processes. Managing the process technology takes teamwork. Multiple talents working together are crucial for P/OM success. Chapters are devoted to the component topics, which are integral parts of process design. For example, here are some highlights associated with each chapter in Part 3.

Chapter 5: Understanding the behavior of various process configurations

Chapter 6: Flow-charting methods to organize information

Chapter 7: Applying quality methods to get the best performance of the system

Chapter 8: Managing existing technology; understanding when it is economically sensible to upgrade and replace it

Chapter 9: Designing jobs and organizing systems to enhance teamwork

Chapter 10: Capacity decisions; management of supply chain and process bottlenecks

Chapter 11: Four main components of facilities planning

Chapter 5, "Process Configuration Strategies," describes the variety of process methods used for doing work. The custom shop, the job shop (batch work), the flow shop, intermittent flow shops, and flexible process systems are explained in detail so that a choice can be made. Processes also are differentiated with respect to assembly (synthetic), disassembly (analytic), and combinations. Knowing the type of process is necessary to manage it. Thus, work configurations and process types are classified in a useful way for operational purposes (design, analysis, and Improvement).

Chapter 6, "Process Analysis and Process Redesign," introduces flow-charting methods for process analysis and redesign. Process flowcharts and layout charts are crucial graphics for understanding the nature of the process. They organize the information to allow analysis and change. Three major areas for process improvement are reduction of setup times, switching to better materials, and improving maintenance procedures. Specific methods for process improvement are explained for all three areas.

Chapter 7, "Methods for Quality Control," starts with "finding and benchmarking the best." This mind-set is required for quality achievement. Quality control methods are explained using the seven classical tools for achieving better process qualities. These include data check sheets, bar charts, histograms, Pareto charts, cause and effect (Ishikawa) diagrams, statistical quality control charts (SQC), and statistical run analyses. Chapter 7 also examines acceptance sampling and treats negotiations between suppliers and buyers in terms of Type I and Type II errors, which are broadly applicable for P/OM.

In Chapter 8, "Management of Technology (MOT)," management of P/OM technology is related to responsibility for the transformation process. As technology changes, there is pressure to adopt the new technology while using old technology systems. This "technology trap" can be avoided. Examples of process technology at different stages of development for glass and automotive windshield glass are not widely known and interesting. Glass technology provides a unique model of constant change and adaptation by P/OM. Other technologies discussed include packaging and delivery, testing, control of quality, and design for manufacturing and assembly.

Chapter 9, "Planning Teamwork and Job Design," details how P/OM plans for achieving effective teamwork. Proper job designing recognizes the importance of people as part of the process. Effective training is dependent upon good job design. There is no point in training people to perform badly designed jobs. Setting time standards for productive jobs is detailed. The methods are called *job observation studies*. Work sampling is applied to improve the way teams function and job design. Managing work systems includes systems for job evaluation and improvement, work simplification, and job enrichment.

In Chapter 10, "Capacity Management," capacity management is explained in various ways and related to peak and off-peak demand. Modular part design and group technology production methods are presented as methods for augmenting capacity. Bottlenecks limit capacity. They need to be identified and can be altered. The effects of delay on the capacity of the supply chain are illustrated by means of a supply chain game. The breakeven model for choosing among alternative capacity configurations is developed. Linear programming is shown to be a preferred method for determining how best to use and design capacities. The relevance of the learning curve model for expanding capacity is a highlight.

In Chapter 11, "Facilities Planning," four main components of facilities planning are presented: first, where to locate regionally; second, how to select specific structures and sites; third, how to choose layouts; and fourth, equipment selection methods. Service and manufacturing location decisions are treated. Transportation modeling is used to minimize costs of shipping plus additional costs. For example, per unit costs of production differ by location. The same applies to marketing differentials. Scoring models are an important feature of Chapter 11. They permit tangible and intangible factors to be used for site selection. Design for manufacturing criteria are developed for equipment selection and related to layout interactions. Workplace layout is a part of job design. Layout modeling allows intangible factors to be considered as well as the tangible transport (flow) costs that characterize layout load models.

5

Process Configuration Strategies

This section describes process configuration strategies. The custom shop, the job shop, the flow shop, and flexible process systems are explained in detail so that a choice can be made. Processes also are differentiated with respect to assembly (synthetic), disassembly (analytic), and combinations. Knowing the type of process is necessary to manage it. Thus, work configurations and process types are classified in a useful way for operational purposes (design, analysis, and improvement).

After reading this chapter, you should be able to:

- Distinguish between processes and work configurations.
- Explain the three major kinds of work configuration.
- Discuss why maintenance of equipment is a process.
- Explain how simulation can be used to improve a process.
- Distinguish between synthetic and analytic processes.

- Reveal why it is essential to chart every process step.
- Compare the custom shop to the job shop.
- Define cycle time and use it to design a flow shop.
- Explain flexible process systems.
- Relate all of the work configurations with respect to volume and variety.

THE SYSTEMS VIEWPOINT

Strategies are more likely to be successful if they have been formulated using the systems approach. An equivalent statement is that strategies are more likely to be successful if they have been formulated using all of the factors that are relevant to their success. The systems approach allows the process choice to be based upon what the competition is doing, the state of technology, what the customer will like, the costs of production, the control of quality, and the ability to schedule delivery. Note the systems implications of sourcing, which are detailed in this chapter. First, however, focus on processes.

The process is composed of subprocesses. Each is like an input–output system that is connected to another input–output system. Each is a link of the means–end chain, and a process in its own right. The connected links form a chain of conversions. The chain is the total process.

Although the parts of the process can be studied individually, the systems approach ultimately always focuses on the whole. The systems approach often uncovers relationships in one part of the chain that affect relationships in other parts of the chain.

Before an appropriate process design can be fashioned, it is essential to have a common understanding of what a process is, and be able to define the term.

STRATEGIC THINKING

Interrelated systems components are driven by strategic issues that underlie the purpose of the process. The strategic drivers for the process are the rationales for the transformations. The sequences of linked, input–output systems form process chains to make the product and deliver services. Strategic decisions must translate cost, quality, and delivery requirements into specific methods used to realize the objectives. That is why process configurations link strategy with tactics.

5-1 WHAT IS A PROCESS?

> **Process:** Series of activities or steps required to transform materials and deliver services.
>
> **Process steps:** Stages of the *process*.

A **process** is a series of activities or steps that are goal-oriented. The *APICS Dictionary* defines **process steps** as: "The operations or stages within the manufacturing cycle required to transform components into intermediates or finished goods."[1]

There is no reason to limit this definition to manufacturing. It applies equally well to service functions. The steps of the process are specific and concrete. They tell how to make things like air conditioners, or cars; how to fill things like cans with beans or tubes with toothpaste; or how to provide medical or travel services.

Process steps often require the use of science and technology. Chemistry may be required to make the product. Instructions for what steps to take are varied; they may be recipes for making bread or blueprints for making the breadbox. Processes are named for what they make, like cheese, auto assembly, and research reports.

5-1a Work Configurations Defined

> **Work configuration:** Type of production process.

It is important to distinguish between processes, which are the steps and activities required to make the product, and work configurations that help accomplish production. There are many kinds of processes, but only a few basic types of **work configuration.** The work configuration is the physical setup used to make the product. It is the arrangement of people and equipment and the way materials and work in process flow from place to place in the plant, or in the office.

As noted, the type of activity flow used for the process is called the work configuration. There are six fundamental kinds of work configuration:

- Custom shops—for "one of a kind" items
- Job shops—for batch processing
- Flow shops—for serialized processing
- Flexible manufacturing systems—for rapid model changeovers
- Continuous flow processing—for nonstop systems
- Projects—for developing new structures and systems

> **Project:** Work configuration that is used for start-up purposes with major new undertakings.

Projects are a type of work configuration that is used for start-up purposes, such as for major new undertakings like building a bridge. The focus of this chapter is on processes for production systems that are up and running, so projects will not be treated here. Continuous flow processing will be discussed, but because it is very specialized and highly engineered, it will not receive the kind of attention the other five categories receive.

The kind of work configuration that is used is a function of volume and variety. Large volumes of identical items are not treated in the same way as small volumes of many different kinds of items. Work configurations constitute a main theme of this chapter.

The process steps must be fully specified. This means that the technology of the process is explicit and the work configuration for carrying out the process is explained in detail. This level of specification is absolutely essential for process design and control. No technicalities can be ignored.

The maintenance program for jet engines is a process. Inadvertently, an O-ring was left out of a jet engine on a 727 that plunged 20,000 feet before the pilot could shut down that engine and safely level out. Tragedy was averted and the same lesson was learned again: In a process, each part has a place and each step of the process must be taken correctly every time the process is used. In this case, the lives of many people depended upon rigorous adherence to process specifications.

Note that the concept of "inadvertent behavior" is totally unacceptable for proper process management. There can be no surprises. Accidents are inadmissible. Haphazard performance must be designed out of the process. Extensive use of checklists or other means of achieving conformance are mandatory. Further, the pilot's training included situations of this kind so that disaster could be averted. The maintenance process had failed, but the flying process was able to handle the contingency.

The concept of "normal accidents," as explained in Charles Perrow's 1984 book *Normal Accidents: Living with High-Risk Technologies* (reissued in 1999 by Princeton University Press) is not reasonable within the framework of the operations management mandate. The belief that technological complexity renders accidents inevitable overlooks the notion that "nothing is left to chance" and the quality objective (e.g., Phil Crosby) to achieve zero defects. This topic became popular in the press during the Y2K era of anxiety as the millennium year 2000 approached. ("Is Complexity Interlinked with Disaster? Ask on Jan.1," *The New York Times*, December 11, 1999.) The answer on January 1, 2002, was that Y2K had come and gone without problems. On the other hand, movies had anticipated September 11, 2001, but they were not believed to be a real possibility. In retrospect, operations management could have helped to prevent 9/11. P/OM has now been enlisted to prevent future incidents of similar destructive scope.

5-1b Process Simulations

Simulations are "pretend" runs of what might occur using models of processes. For example, pilot training uses simulations of contingencies to eliminate the serious repercussions of unintentional errors. Process simulations are imitation processes that mimic the real-world process. Contingency planning requires first identifying *things that might happen* before addressing *what might be done* to avoid damage and disaster.

The board game Monopoly® is a simulation of real estate transactions. People buy and sell real estate. Some make money while others lose it. Except for the latter fact, Monopoly is not a very accurate simulation of real estate dealings. Another example of a simulation is "rotisserie baseball," where the performance of real players is used to simulate the behavior of fictitious teams on which the betting is fierce.[2]

Simulations are successfully used for training, testing, and analyzing. Factory processes and production schedules can be created and improved. Under controlled conditions, contingencies artificially arise that allow individuals to practice remedial actions. This learning takes place without being involved in actual crises.

Computer simulations have been used to test the design of the Boeing 777. In this way, the plane has been flown before it is built. It is subjected to engine failures and turbulence beyond anything that will ever be experienced in actual flight. Simulation modeling also is used for production scheduling and inventory control. It is a powerful means of studying the performance of the system as a whole—which is in keeping with the systems approach. Simulation is one of the best methods available for designing good processes. It is a methodology that embodies the systems approach, and it is especially effective where nothing should be left to chance.

The process for flying an airplane is detailed. The manuals for procedures are filled with information. All of the controls have to be coordinated. Each procedure for taking off and landing must be precisely stated and checked. Maintenance processing is intricate. Every wire, chip, and instrument in the Boeing 777 must do its job correctly. Onboard instrumentation must call attention to problems and flaws. Designing the planes and then building them are two more processes. Four processes are mentioned in this paragraph, and all of them use simulation to improve the performance of that process.

The Three Mile Island reactors in Pennsylvania are famous for the fear they caused. (See Meltdown at Three Mile Island at http://www.pbs.org/wgbh/amex/three.) Running a nuclear power plant requires a precise process. Technicalities cannot be ignored. There is no room for error. Proper use of P/OM can meet the challenge.

Simulations: Pretend runs of various product and process design options.

5-2 CLASSIFYING THE PROCESS

The definition of a process must be able to encompass the great diversity of processes such as Disney theme parks, the Houston chain of restaurants, cable television services, power generation systems, automated teller machines (ATMs), newspapers produced and delivered every day, health-care centers, and academic centers that use pedagogical processes for educational purposes. With such enormous diversity, it is imperative that a strong classification system be developed for process types.

5-2a Charting the Process

1. It also is critical to be able to chart in total detail every step of the process. To get an idea of what is required, try to specify in detail the program that would enable a robot to dress itself. It is hard to separate the methods used from the technology required.

2. The program required to just tie shoelaces poses enough of a problem to make the point. There is difficulty in setting down the appropriate detail to enable machines to do things that people do by intuition.

5-2b Choosing the Process Technology

It is necessary to be able to deal with the question of how to choose a process technology. In choosing the process, the work configuration tends to be chosen by default. Should it be one that excels with high volumes of a few varieties or one that excels with low volumes of a high number of varieties? Excels means that the process has some winning combination of higher quality, lower costs, and shorter delivery times than the processes used by competitors.

Consider again, what is a process? It is a detailed description of the input–output transformation sequence. Different kinds of equipment can be used to make the same things. The choice will depend upon what work configurations are best-suited for the expected volumes and varieties of product outputs.

5-2c Means and Ends

The study of P/OM requires understanding what is needed to achieve the desired ends: Technology and training are essential at all levels within the organization, and in the suppliers' organizations, to achieve the strategic objectives of the company. From a systems point of view, it is important to note that the ends of one part of the process are often the means of the next part of the process.

Ends: Final part of the means–end chain, until another system is defined.

Supply chain: All of the elements that make up the products and services delivered to customers.

A means–end model connects strategies with tactics. **Ends** are objectives; *means* are the process components designed to achieve them. Raw material transformations are the means to making components. Components are converted into parts. Parts are assembled into products. Products are grouped together into boxes. Cartons of boxes are delivered to carriers. Carriers move cartons to distributors, and they in turn make deliveries to retailers who sell the products to customers. This **supply chain** is a specific example of a generic means–end chain.

The means–end supply chain does not stop with delivery. Customers use the products and begin the chain of payment. They return money to the retailer who pays the wholesaler who pays the producer or a distribution center if there are additional levels in the distribution hierarchy. The goal was to create the means for obtaining revenue. That objective started the entire systems process. Thus, when that customer's money enters the bank, there is a short-term conclusion to the process. In the long-term, other factors also must be considered to assure that customers remain loyal. The marketing process is a critical part of the means–end chain.

5-2d Strategic Aspects of Processes

Managers choose the components of a means–end chain to go from where they see the firm is to where they want the firm to go. That choice is driven by strategies to achieve the selected goals. The strategic drivers are designed to achieve the purpose of the process. Another way of viewing the strategic drivers for the means–end chain is by identifying the process as an interconnected set of transformations of linked, input–output systems. Strategic decisions about processes translate cost, quality, and delivery requirements into specific methods used to realize objectives. The choice of *process configurations link strategy with tactics*.

5-3 TYPES OF PROCESS FLOWS

There are many ways of categorizing process flows. One of the best ways is to note the difference between analytic and synthetic processes. Combinations of the two basic types of processes are common, but all processes tend to be more like one than the other.

It makes sense to broadly define analytic and synthetic processes at this time so that the comparison can be kept in mind. Synthetic processes combine things, usually putting many parts together to make one or a few products. Analytic processes take things apart, creating many products from a few.

5-3a Synthetic Processes

A **synthetic process** is a process in which a variety of components come together, ultimately to form a single product. Progressive assembly, which follows the instructions of how to build sequentially the subassemblies and final assemblies, is an example of the synthetic function. Instructions for construction emphasize the correct order for putting things together.

Any sequential process can be delineated by an assembly diagram such as the one drawn in Figure 5-1. This kind of schematic is used by process designers to make sure that all the nuts and bolts are assembled in the right order. The sequence of assembly goes from twigs to branches (which are subassemblies) to the trunk (which is the final assembly). If the trunk started to spread out again at the roots, the process would be starting to be analytic. Processes that combine assembly (synthetic) and disassembly (analytic) are more common than pure processes of either kind.

Synthetic processes employ synthesis that is defined as many inputs combining to form a whole. The purest example of synthesis is many to one, but in reality this is often tempered by a relatively synthetic process, which combines the many to form a few.

> **Synthetic process:** Combines the various materials, components, subassemblies, etc., into a single, basic product or into several similar products.

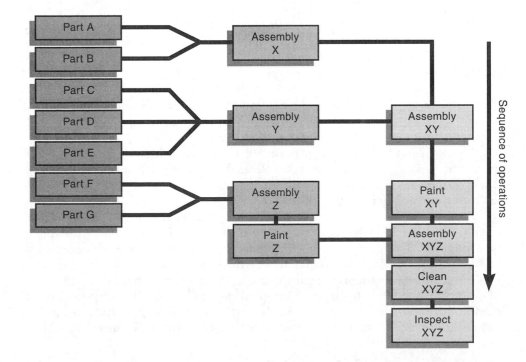

FIGURE 5-1
An Assembly Chart (Many Parts to One)

BOX 5-1

Synthetic Process— How an Automobile Is Assembled (Many Parts to One)

The following six steps are brief descriptions of the synthetic process that Mazda uses to assemble a vehicle.

Stamping (Step 1)

The Stamping Department produces major body panels such as roofs, side panels, and fenders. Employees unload and stack stamped panels for delivery to the Body Assembly Department.

Body Assembly (Step 2)

The Body Assembly Department is probably the best place to see how the automated operations free the production team to perform other tasks, which are less physically demanding. After assembly, a completed white body is sent to the Paint Department.

Paint (Step 3)

Before primer and topcoat applications, various coatings are applied to each vehicle for corrosion protection, prevention of water leaks, wind noise, and paint chipping. Robots apply topcoat and perform some sealer and undercoating operations.

Trim & Final (Step 4)

Vehicle personality becomes evident here—"our car" starts to look like "your car." The Trim & Final Department uses innovative technology such as the tilt line, which allows employees to work comfortably to install underbody components such as fuel tanks and wire harnesses. Installation of front and rear windshields is an automated operation, as is engine and transmission installation.

Quality Control (Step 5)

To ensure that all quality standards and engineering specifications are met, each employee inspects his/her own work and the Quality Control Department's employees give each vehicle a rigorous inspection. These activities occur throughout the manufacturing process and before shipping to customers.

Shipping (Step 6)

When a vehicle is ready for delivery, it is transferred to Mazda North America's (MANA) Shipping Yard where MANA coordinates delivery to both Ford and Mazda distributors. Mazda North American Operations, headquartered in Irvine, California, coordinates deliveries of vehicles and auto parts to 850 dealerships in North America.

Synthesis characterizes the automobile assembly plant, where many components are brought together to form a few car models. Box 5-1 illustrates an automobile assembly process, showing what goes into making an automobile and in what order these components are introduced to the assembly process.

Another typical synthetic process is that required to bring a number of different kinds of information together with the purpose of analyzing the data and then writing the final report. This is the main function of the Market Research Store, which should be as much a master of the synthetic process as the automobile assembly plant.

A prime objective for every kind of synthetic process is to have a smooth flow of the items being processed. As these items flow along, they become more and more complete. The stage of completion could be specified by the percent of the total processing time that has been consumed up to that point.

For the auto assembly process, a total processing time of 32 hours is not unusual; the engine might join the chassis at the point where more than 70 percent of total assembly time has passed. The first completion of data analysis for the market research report might occur when less than 30 percent of the total report writing process is completed.

To keep the process from being interrupted, it is necessary to have an ample supply of the right components (parts or information) on hand at the places where they are needed. They could be brought to where they are needed, as they are needed, which is called **just-in-time.** Alternatively, they could be brought to where they are to be used long

Just-in-time: Inventory delivery principle associated with a lean-and-mean company philosophy.

before they are needed to avoid any slip-ups in the timing of the deliveries. That kind of protection is called **just-in-case.**

This issue of storage of components and timing of their delivery is directly related to the rate at which the process is working. Three important questions need to be answered:

1. How many units come off the line every hour? Say that there are ten. This means that every six minutes a unit is complete

2. How long does it take to make a unit? The fact that a unit is complete every six minutes does not always mean that it took six minutes to complete it.

3. How many lines are operating and have to be fed with components or information?

Assume that the information assembly process to write a report is initially poorly balanced. This means that the process would be erratic, stopping and starting. Because it did not flow smoothly, there would be times when data was backed up waiting to be processed. At other times, idle people and idle computers would be sitting around waiting for data to process.

The operations manager can smooth the flow by creating workstations at which specific tasks would be done. The tasks would follow the logical progression of the assembly chart. Some things cannot be done before others. The time to complete tasks at each workstation would be made about equal, creating what is called a balanced line.

In this chapter, perfectly balanced lines are assumed. Later chapters treat the real-world complication of lines that are not perfectly balanced. This occurs when the amount of work at stations is unequal. Stations have different amounts of idle time. Perfect balance also assumes that there is no rest time at any station. Perfect balance assumptions are difficult and sometimes impossible to achieve when people dominate the activities at workstations. Perfect balance can be approached using machine assistance for people at workstations. One can most easily visualize perfect line balance as resulting from a totally mechanized and robotic assembly system where the entire synthetic process is synchronized.

For this case, assume that a paced conveyor belt is used. It is stopped at each station for C minutes. The *cycle time* of C minutes is the pace that is set for the conveyor belt. That means that a finished unit comes off the production line every C minutes.

5-3b Analytic Processes

An **analytic process** is characterized by progressive disassembly. It is the reverse of the synthetic process as it breaks up one thing into many things. Going backwards on the assembly chart, the treeing process is reversed. It starts with the trunk and moves out to the branches and then to the twigs. A variety of products can be obtained from the "source." This type of process is illustrated in Figure 5-2.

The name "analytic" process is derived from the fact that analysis is involved. Analysis is defined as breaking up a whole into its parts to find out their nature. An analytic process breaks up the whole in order to use the parts for various reasons. See Box 5-2 for an example of the analytic process as it pertains to chocolate products.

Just-in-case: Inventory delivery principle associated with a play-it-safe production philosophy.

Analytic process: Turns a single, basic ingredient into several or (even) many products.

**FIGURE 5-2
Analytic Process (One Source to Many Products)**

BOX 5-2

Analytic Process— Chocolate Products

- The basic process is composed of cleaning, grinding, conching, and mixing ingredients of various kinds in different amounts.
- Micronizing is a preroasting thermal (or heat) treatment needed to obtain a clean separation from the husks (shells).
- Winnowing is shelling the beans.
- Cleaning at various stages is essential before grinding (milling) because various kinds of impurities that damage quality must be removed.
- Grinding (milling) precedes liquification.
- To produce a powdery product from high-fat cocoa mass, it must be partially defatted so cocoa butter is extracted by pressing, which leaves a solid material known as cocoa press cake.
- Pulverizing cocoa press cake produces cocoa powder, which is used in many ways by food industries and by final consumers.
- Cocoa butter is refined in several stages before conching.
- Dutching is the alkalization (adding alkalies) of powder and liquor to modify the flavor and color of chocolate, called dutched cocoa and chocolate.
- Conching is a high-energy mixing to distribute cocoa butter and flavoring.
- Tempering is a heating and cooling process to set up the correct crystal structure in the fat.
- Differences in the quality of chocolate are due not only to beans and recipes used; they are dependent on the production process used.
- End products include cocoa powder, chocolate flavored syrups, chocolate chips, dark chocolate, milk chocolate candy bars, and cocoa butter.

Source: **Courtesy of Chocolate Manufacturers Association.**

The purest example of an analytic process would be where one thing is converted into many derivatives without having to add anything else. Most analytic processes have one main, basic ingredient that is converted into a number of derivative products often with the help of additional materials.

Chocolate requires an analytic process to convert the main raw material—cacao beans cut from (9-inch) pods that grow year round on the cacao trees—into many different products such as cocoa powder, unsweetened, bittersweet, semisweet, sweet, milk, and white chocolate, in various forms such as chocolate bars, chips and syrup. Other derivatives are chocolate chips, bakers' chocolate, and cocoa butter. Sugar is an additive for many of the products. Milk chocolate requires the addition of milk solids and sugar. Less expensive chocolates substitute fats and emulsifiers for cocoa butter.

The analytic process also applies to information systems. Previously, it was used to describe a synthetic process where data from a variety of sources were combined to create a report. The analysis of data, used by laboratories, functions in the opposite way. A blood sample is drawn and tested, yielding data on blood sugar, cholesterol, and red cell count, among other things. The final report decomposes the blood sample into many end categories. These are used by doctors to evaluate health and to diagnose symptoms of health problems.

5-4 SOURCING FOR SYNTHETIC PROCESSES

The flowcharts for synthetic processes show how various materials, components, and parts are fed into the main stream, where they are joined together to form the product that marketing will sell. Purchasing the materials, components, and parts (or data) from different sources requires dealing with many different suppliers.

Typically, the operations manager is not responsible for the sourcing decisions. Because these decisions impact strongly on the performance of operations, there is a need for coordination. The systems approach is essential to make certain that purchasing and OM are playing on the same team.

There are prices, qualities, and delivery reliabilities to compare. These include on-time delivery of the correct amount with the agreed-upon quality and cost. Acquisition strategies for synthetic processes are significantly different from those needed for analytic processes, though both require comprehension of the mechanisms that apply to their particular kind of supply chain.

Synthetic processes usually involve many parts and one or more suppliers for each of them. All of these parts cost the company consequential amounts of money. The cost of materials for synthetic processes has been a large percent of the cost of goods sold (COGS). It can be as high as 80 percent. It is, on average, around 40 to 50 percent, and it is increasing for many firms.

Being the low-cost producer is a major goal of most firms. Even Rolls Royce, with its very high price tags, has redesigned its operations to reduce costs significantly. Because of the impact of purchase prices on total costs, most synthetic process industries are very strict with their suppliers.

Increasingly, a rational cost structure for purchased products from all suppliers has become the objective of companies with synthetic processes. To achieve this, it is necessary to have suppliers that are the low-cost producers for all of the parts and components the company purchases. This creates the potential for cost advantages from savings that are made on all of the parts and components that are purchased. If the savings that can be made are not taken, they are called *opportunity losses*. Those firms that are on top of the situation, thereby avoiding opportunity losses and realizing the potential savings, achieve significant competitive advantages. Companies using synthetic processes are particularly vulnerable if they are ignorant of this fact.

The cost of materials component of the COGS is normally understated for synthetic processes. This means that the COGS is also understated. The costs are understated because the costs of purchased materials do not include all of the costs of quality.

In particular the costs of failures, as measured by losses of customer loyalty, are totally missed. Also the cost of rework due to suppliers' defectives is not usually associated with the cost of purchases. Missing these factors understates the costs. Further, the cost of designing and installing supplier certification programs has been growing as competitors pay increasing attention to the triad of critical dimensions: price, quality, and speed of delivery. The cost of materials should reflect the cost of the supplier certification program.

Suppliers that do not deliver on time delay production and that, in turn, holds up deliveries to customers. Delivery on time is a critical quality dimension in its own right. Delivery delays can have a substantial impact on customer loyalty. With this in mind, the choice and management of suppliers to ensure that the highest delivery standards are set and met is becoming another competitive requirement for synthetic processes.

5-5 SOURCING FOR ANALYTIC PROCESSES

Typically, analytic processes begin with the purchase of the single commodity, which the process transforms into many derivative products—such as cacao beans into chocolates, sweet crudes into various fuels, corn into breads, sugars, fuel additives, and grapes into wine and vinegar. For analytical processes, purchasing agents choose worldwide sources for the basic input component. The price, quality, and delivery of the core purchasing ingredient are subject to the kinds of fluctuations that characterize that particular commodity market.

Commodities are considered materials that are generic. Within any one commodity class, the materials are treated as being relatively indistinguishable from each other. "Relatively" is used because operations managers of analytic processes know that qualities of commodities vary, which greatly affects the quality of their finished products.

The sourcing decisions have a major impact on how well the process functions. Because it is seldom OM that reaches these sourcing decisions, a systems approach is essential to coordinate the operations and procurement of materials. It also is important to note that the systems approach focuses on many different issues according to whether the materials will be subject to synthetic or analytic processing.

Analytic processes, by their definition, have a totally different supplier situation than that which applies to synthetic processes. There are many suppliers of the same few commodities. Frequently, price is the main factor that drives the acquisition of the input materials. Yet, as was stated earlier, it is always subject to quality considerations, which OM and the agency doing the sourcing coordinate within the framework of the systems approach.

Prices are established by the specific commodity exchange that trades in that commodity. The Chicago Board of Trade and the New York Mercantile Exchange are well-known commodity trading exchanges in the United States for many of the raw material ingredients that require analytic processes. Most countries have equivalent exchanges.

Sourcing in the commodity markets requires a variety of special skills. Purchasing strategies play a major role in determining the average price paid for a commodity. The average is taken of the price paid across many transactions. This can include both buying and selling the commodity. Some contracts are made at present prices; others involve commodity prices at future dates. The operation of futures markets is discussed in courses and books on financial trading. There are different traditions and techniques required to successfully buy corn, coffee, salt, rice, gold, platinum, copper and other metals, cattle, hogs and other livestock, as well as fuels and oils from plants and flowers such as sunflowers and peanuts. There are different ways of bidding for commodities and establishing contracts in the futures markets.

Factors such as weather can affect crop prices for commodities such as oranges and grains. The prices of metals, including gold, copper and platinum, will vary according to local and world events. The average prices that are affected by such extraneous factors get translated into the eventual prices of the derivative products. A freeze in Florida drives the price of oranges up, and a crisis in Russia causes the price of gold to jump. When many farmers have abundant crops that they bring to the market, the excess of bumper crops drops the prices.

Money is made and lost by managers of analytic processes who trade in their commodities as another necessary side to their business. The advantage that can be realized by astute maneuvering in the commodity markets is one of the features of dealing in analytic processes. It is hard to overlook the fact that some very large coffee companies have made more money trading in green coffee bean futures than in selling bags and cans of their brand of coffee. The same kind of parallel exists for other commodities where the trading required for purchasing provides a business opportunity in its own right.

5-6 MARKETING DIFFERENCES

The marketing approach for analytic products is different from that of synthetic products. When a company is making and selling both, there is a decision required as to how to specialize or generalize the selling function as well as the producing function.

5-6a Marketing Products of Synthetic Processes

For synthetic processes, it is important to be very focused and sharp about marketing and selling the basically one product to be sold. At the same time, one product permits concentration on the marketing plan. There is only one sales force, and it does not have to divide marketing resources among several different product lines. At the end of the supply chain, marketing is specialized. Upstream, at the beginning of the chain, purchasing deals with an array of suppliers. It is production dealing with suppliers and processes that has an array of differences to master.

5-6b Marketing Products of Analytic Processes

For analytic processes, there are often quite disparate end products. Each addresses a different market constituency. Each requires different marketing techniques. Gasoline for autos is an entirely different market from industrial fuels, and both contrast with kerosene for jets. A variety of marketing plans are needed, and separate sales forces are required. The marketing budget must be allocated to diverse end products. Downstream, at the end of the supply chain, marketing is diversified. Upstream, where the supply chain begins, purchasing is focused.

A commodity is often defined as a group of items that are indistinguishable from each other. There is reason to take exception to this characterization. The qualities of commodities are not homogeneous within any category. Differences are often *overlooked or dismissed* by the commodity purchasing process. The end-user, however, recognizes the difference.

First, consider the statement (often heard) that the computer has become a commodity. To begin with, that means that the brand is irrelevant. It also means that one does not care who is the manufacturer of the components. *Intel Inside* is an attempt to counter this trend by means of advertising. The question "Does that work?" is still not answered definitively as of mid-year 2002. However, the production process to make a computer is increasingly a combination of synthetic processes (all leading to essentially the same thing) and analytic processes (being customized and leading to many variations of significance).

A major strategic advantage is available to those who capitalize on the differentiation of commodity qualities. They can buy on terms of quality as well as by price. The quality advantage can be utilized to advantage at the downstream end of the analytic process in each of the markets of the derivative products.

There are many types of wheat grains. Varieties of corn are so numerous that only experts can catalog them. Some soy-bean products are cleaner than others. Some crops just barely qualify with respect to nutritional standards for cattle feeds; others are considered to be superior. The standards apply to quality requirements that range from minerals to vitamins.

Cranberries are graded by the cooperatives that sort and package them. Wet harvesting is less expensive and inferior to dry harvesting. Wet cranberries need to be dried and then sorted according to their color and bounciness, a surrogate for firmness. Within the grading categories for cranberries there exists a great deal of product quality variability.

Many commodities are shipped in bulk using railroad boxcars, large trucks, and the cargo holds of ships. The method of transportation and the care with which the shipment is arranged will affect the quality of the merchandise when it is received. The logistics of transport are very important in this regard for quality as well as with respect to the timeliness of delivery.

Educating the consumer about quality differentials for various commodities is not usual. Utilizing the differences for creating consumer preferences and price differentials has been done successfully for wine grapes. There is a complex mystique about vintages. Prices can range from under $5 to $500. To a somewhat lesser degree, the same marketing approach using quality differentiation has been applied effectively to coffee beans.

The choice of quality grades for commodity inputs to the analytic processes will have major impact on the quality of the derivative products. Instead of talking about *GIGO* (garbage-in, garbage-out), the time has come to talk about *QUIQUO*, which emphasizes the more positive aspect of process management (quality-in, quality-out).

It is better to see the glass as being half filled than to see it as being half empty. Those who say that quality should play a larger part in determining purchasing decisions for analytic processes are on-target. Price alone cannot continue to be the key to sourcing and purchasing for analytic processes.

Chocolate fanciers know that all cacao beans are not alike. Most chocolate comes from forastero trees, which grow in West Africa and Brazil. Scarcer and more flavorful beans come from criollo and trinitario trees, which are found in Central America. Having the best beans is essential for preparing the best chocolates.

5-7 BEST (PROCESS) PRACTICE

Best practice: Process standard based on identifying those who perform the process in the best way.

Benchmarking: Method for comparing processes with one that is considered to be the best.

Best practice is a process standard that has strong roots in the systems approach. The idea is to identify those who perform the process in the best ways yet known. Striving to make one's own process the best in the "class" is like aiming to win the gold at Olympic events; the prior year's records of gold medal winners are the standards for best practice in that event. The procedure of comparing one's own process against the best is called **benchmarking**. It is used to compare various activities in OM, such as quality attainment, sales effectiveness, and purchasing performance, and also to compare production processes and determine product excellence.

Best ingredients are a necessary but not sufficient condition for product excellence. Best process (*BP*) must be combined with best ingredients (*BI*) to bring out the best product (*BPR*). The factors in the equation are multiplicative:

$$(BP)(BI) = (BPR)$$

If either (*BP*) or (*BI*) = 0, meaning low quality, then (*BPR*) = 0. Thus, for example, in Box 5-2, for the highest quality chocolate product, the conching step must knead the mixture until it is totally smooth. This process step can continue for as long as three or four days to achieve best process (*BP*) results. If this is combined with the best cacao beans (*BI*), then best product (*BPR*) can be attained.

There must be a three-way understanding of the system, calling for a meeting of the minds between marketing, purchasing, and operations. The payoff for coordination of the functions is great. Purchasing and OM working together combine (*BI*) and (*BP*), while marketing exploits the advantage of superior quality (*BPR*).

The resulting differentiation raises commodity products above the customary concept of being indistinguishable and homogeneous and places them into special niches—like Godiva chocolates. This increases profit margins of the derivative products of analytic processes. It also provides an opportunity for developing competitive advantage in terms of the quality of commodities.

5-8 MIXED ANALYTIC AND SYNTHETIC PROCESSES

Most processes are combinations of synthetic and analytic processes. For example, maple syrup from the maple tree is a commodity that gets converted into maple sugar, pancake syrup, candies, and cakes. To produce each end product requires that other commodities be added to the mixture.

Generally, one type of process predominates, that is, the process is primarily either synthetic or analytic. In the case of maple syrup, the process is predominately analytic even though additives are needed to produce the final set of products.

The assembly of computers is a synthetic process. Also, the computer chips inside the computers are constructed and assembled by a synthetic process. Yet, many of the computer chips—sourced from all over the world—are treated as if they are commodities. To counter the concept that all chips are alike, Intel spends freely to advertise its chips as being unique and special. Nevertheless, a computer is a mixture of A and V processes. So too are cars, VCRs, published books, clothing, and cans of food.

5-8a The OPT System and the Theory of Constraints

OPT is a production process scheduling system. It will be encountered whenever serious production scheduling efforts are being used. OPT stands for "optimized production technology." This system is highly sensitive to the existence of bottlenecks. It is often referred to as a production **theory of constraints** for finite scheduling—which means lot-by-lot scheduling.[3] The methods of OPT belong in the context of tactical scheduling activities.

The concepts of OPT were initiated by a professional consulting company set up by Eliyahu Goldratt, who developed the OPT principles concerning *synchronized production scheduling*. The term OPT was, at first, taken into common P/OM usage to represent finite scheduling principles. However, over time, there was a shift to "theory of constraints," which came to be the preferred usage.

5-8b OPT and V-A-T

OPT classifies processes by means of the acronym *VAT*. A V-process is analytic, starting with a single commodity at the bottom and branching out into refined products at the top. An A-process is synthetic, starting at the bottom with several inputs, which are combined to yield a single marketable product. The combination is named by OPT as a T-process. The charts in this text have been guided by these conventions.

OPT focuses attention on the fact that each type of process (V and A and T) has unique production scheduling aspects. Also, each type of process has characteristics that work best with specific types of work process configurations. Proper matching of work process configurations with the synthetic components and the analytic components of process flows can provide significant advantages.

5-9 WORK PROCESS CONFIGURATION TYPES

There are fundamental differences in the way that both synthetic and analytic processes can be designed or configured. A primary factor for classification is the number of units produced at one time. That number is often referred to as the lot size, N. Lot size applies to discrete production runs as compared to continuous production output systems, which include flow shops (assembly lines) and continuous (liquid) flow systems.

Another classification factor is the variety level. It is customary to find that, as the lot size goes up, the variety level diminishes. In part, this is a statement that reflects old technology where set-up time was inversely related to time and cost per part. New *flexible process systems (FPS)* technology has altered this formula to a degree.

5-9a The Custom Shop

The **custom shop** is the work configuration in which products or services are "made-to-order." Custom work is like tailoring a suit of clothes to fit one specific individual. This kind of work process is usually associated with a lot size of one, i.e., $N = 1$.

OPT: Also known as the *theory of constraints*.

Constraints, theory of: Production scheduling system that optimizes overall performance (throughput) by recognizing constraints.

Custom shop: Work configuration used for products or services that are made-to-order, and actually one of a kind.

The OR (operating room) is a crucial part of the healthcare P/OM (production and operations management) system. Most operating rooms are job shops in which the variety of work that can be accomplished is quite substantial. However, there are brilliant flow shop operating rooms. For example, Shouldice Hospital in Toronto has an incredible performance record for successful hernia operations. At the Texas Heart Institute in Houston, Dr. Denton Cooley and his associates have performed over 100,000 open-heart operations with flow shop methods.

General-purpose equipment (GPE): Flexible machinery that can do many different kinds of jobs.

Job shop (JS): Used when there are many varieties of products to process in small quantities.

Special-purpose equipment (SPE): Efficient in repetitive production of the same kind of unit.

Many custom shops, like machine shops and cabinetmakers, use synthetic processes, doing one custom job after another. As for analytic processes, laboratories might be viewed as custom shops where a specific ingredient (such as blood) is broken down into its components for detailed analysis.

What does the custom shop look like? Not too much space is required to house the limited materials needed for the jobs at hand. There is **general-purpose equipment (GPE),** needed by relatively few people with craft skills who turn out the product. Often, the workers are owners and entrepreneurs operating in a small workshop housed in a store or garage.

The information equivalent is a small office just large enough to allow for word processing equipment, some files, and telephones. If a service is offered, such as a travel agency, there must be desks for clients and agents to sit at together. Behind the scenes, and occupying little space are the telecommunications capabilities and computer reservation systems of the travel agency.

5-9b The Job Shop

The job shop is not a custom shop or a flow shop that operates a serialized production line. The **job shop (JS)** is a work configuration for processing work in batches or lots. N, the lot size, can vary within these guidelines. The job shop produces N units at a time for shipment, for stock, or a combination.

There are over 100,000 job shops in the United States and a larger number in Europe. Job shops account for over 70 percent of all manufactured parts in the Western world. Both in the United States and in Europe, the typical lot size is 50 units. Because these numbers remain about right through the dot.com failures of 2002, there is continued need for purchasing agents that are set up to order inventory in small quantities

The work configuration of the job shop has equipment at various locations, and batches of work queue up waiting for processing at each location in accordance with what needs to be done. The equipment is of the general-purpose type so it can be used to do many different jobs.

For most job shops, the variety of the work that can be accomplished is quite substantial. This is in keeping with the large array of process equipment, the broad range of skills of the machinists, and the kind of demands that are the basis of the job shop business. The demands received by job shops arise from industrial firms that place orders for the great variety of parts, often in substantial numbers, but not enough to warrant using the serialized production configuration of the flow shop.

The job shop is able to produce the entire line of products, which any combination of general purpose machine tools can create. The capabilities of the job shop are extensive, and it can turn out a lot of different items. For example, a drill press will make holes of different sizes in various materials. A lathe is used to turn the outside diameters of cylindrical parts.

Job shops have some **special-purpose equipment (SPE)** for larger batch sizes. Instead of using a turret lathe, an automatic screw machine can turn out many more cylindrical parts once it is set up. In general, for higher volumes of output, the job shop has intermediate-level equipment that falls between GPE and SPE.

Figure 5-3 illustrates an operations or routing sheet for a part manufactured in a job shop. The sequential steps for die-casting and machining are listed on the operations sheet. It furnishes information about where the equipment to be used is located.

The bill of materials, which often is found on blueprints, spells out instructions about materials and tools. Thus, together, the routing sheet, the bill of materials, and the blueprints provide all the information needed to do the job.

Information processing equipment is general purpose most of the time. Computers are wonderful general-purpose machines, which when loaded with software can become highly specialized. In banks, dedicated, special-purpose equipment (SPE) is required to handle checks. The high volumes of transactions in check handling are treated with both

Bill of Materials

Item Motor switch MS60

Drawings 95.6—95.8

Sheet No. _1_ of _1_

Assembly 3 HP motor X22

Part No.	Part Name	No./Item	Material	Quantity/Item	Cost/Item	Operations
P14	Casing	1	Zn	0.2 lbs	$5.15	Cast, trim
P21	Spring	2	Sprg. St.	—	1.64	Buy
•	•	•	•	•	•	•
•	•	•	•	•	•	•
•	•	•	•	•	•	•
P7	Clips	4	AL15	—	0.25	Buy

Operations Sheet

Part No. ___P14___

Part Name ___Casing___

Blueprint No. ___95.7___

Economic Lot Size _750_

Process Time/Lot _6hrs_

Setup Time ___See below___

Use for Motor Switch MS60

Motor Switch MS61

Subcontract Hamilton

Quantity per ___1___

___1___

500/order

Material ___Zn___

% Scrap ___10___

Supplier Vaun

Weight 0.2lb/

Cost $1.65/

Operation No.	Operation	Location/Machine	Std. Time in Minutes Operations	Setup
1	Change die	F5	—	30
2	Injection molding	F5	3	—
3	Remove	F5	5	—
4	Deflash	F4	7	—
5	Tumble	F7	20	10
6	Plate	G3	10	12

F I G U R E   5 - 3
The Bill of Materials and the Operations Sheet Used by a Job Shop

In typical flow shop configurations, conveyors are used to transfer work from station to station. Bottle factories transfer empty bottles to filling equipment, and then to labeling, capping, packaging, and shipping operations. Procedures are highly automated at rates that yield a minimum number of defectives while maintaining high productivity.

Flow shops (FS): Serialized work configurations.

job shop and flow shop configurations, according to the processing transactions. Over time, banking equipment is moving towards total flow shop configurations. Many word processing applications are job shops.

What does the job shop look like? The space is much larger than for the custom shop. It has to be big enough to contain the materials, general-purpose equipment (GPE), and people with skills. Most job shops are running many jobs at the same time, but there are considerable variations in size.

5-9c The Flow Shop

Flow shops (FS) are serialized work configurations where one unit of work is at various stages of completion at sequential workstations located along the production line. They are dedicated production facilities, which, like auto assembly lines, can be kept running day-after-day. Demand is sufficient to warrant a sequential production process that moves work from one station to the next. Usually, a paced conveyor carries the work from station to station, stopping for a carefully chosen period of time at each station. The length of time that it is stopped is called the *cycle time*. A great deal of effort goes into balancing the line. The cycle time includes some time for rest, which reduces the output rate.

FIGURE 5-4
Comparing Job Shops and Flow Shops

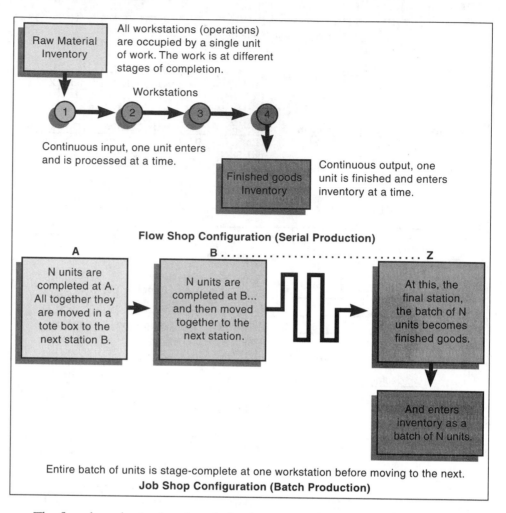

Raw Material Inventory

All workstations (operations) are occupied by a single unit of work. The work is at different stages of completion.

Workstations

Continuous input, one unit enters and is processed at a time.

Finished goods Inventory

Continuous output, one unit is finished and enters inventory at a time.

Flow Shop Configuration (Serial Production)

A

N units are completed at A. All together they are moved in a tote box to the next station B.

B . . . . Z

N units are completed at B... and then moved together to the next station.

At this, the final station, the batch of N units becomes finished goods.

And enters inventory as a batch of N units.

Entire batch of units is stage-complete at one workstation before moving to the next.
Job Shop Configuration (Batch Production)

The flow shop also is often described as being a serialized production process, which means sequentially in order, regular and continuous. To contrast the operating characteristics of the job shop with those of the flow shop see Figure 5-4.

Usually, the supply capabilities of the flow shop are equal to or greater than the average demand. For those intervals when demand exceeds supply, the flow shop might be replicated in parallel. This often is the case when the labor component of the flow shop is high and the capital investment component is low. Sometimes the rate of throughput can be increased by using more powerful technology.

As an alternative method of increasing the supply, the flow shop can be changed from a one-shift basis to a multishift basis. This can include overtime operations or a temporary shift to a two- or three-shift basis. When demand is seasonal, flow shops are configured to provide multishift operations to match peak load demands with a single-shift basis for off-peak times.

Flow shops are dedicated processes where materials and components from suppliers merge and join the production line in an uninterrupted sequence. It is more difficult to configure analytic processes, from start to finish, as a flow shop. Once the ingredients for the derivatives have been obtained, it is possible to run with the flow shop configuration.

A flow shop for chocolate-making can be initiated after the conching of the blended mixture of liquor and cocoa butter (see Box 5-2). At that point, a synthetic process can be used to make chocolate bars, chocolate kisses, and so forth. To feed the flow shop there always must be a supply of chocolate blend.

Some analytic processes can be designed to permit the fanning out of the derivative products as part of a continuous flow process stream. These are called **continuous processes,** the work configuration where the product flows through pipes continuously as

Continuous processes: Produce one product continuously or fan out derivative products as part of a continuous stream.

it is being treated and processed. Good examples of such continuous processes come from the chemical and petrochemical industries. They may be used for making plastics and synthetics such as nylon thread. Also, petroleum-refining and beer-making typify continuous process flow shops, designed to be high-volume, cost-effective systems.

An excellent example of efforts to approximate a continuous flow for analytic processes is found in the area of distribution. Related to rationalization of the distribution process is the field called **logistics.** Logistics concerns the use of methods for obtaining effective procurement, storage, and movement of materials. Logistics processes operate the distribution systems, which move finished goods downstream in the supply chain.

Distribution of product is a fanning-out process. Shipments of goods go from the producers' sources to warehouses, and from there to regional distribution centers that move the goods to retailers. The retailers distribute the product to the ultimate consumers. Meanwhile, cash flow moves up the chain from the customers to the producer.

The *supply chain* epitomizes analytic processes. Great efforts are being made to keep product moving throughout the supply chain in quantities that are related to actual needs at various nodes in the network. Thus, value adding is maximized by the proper procurement schedule that minimizes storage at every stage. When material arrives as needed, the process is characterized as being *just-in-time*.

Henry Ford's sequenced assembly line received so much publicity that flow shops came to be identified with synthetic processes by terms such as "mass production." Analytic processes deserve as much attention. When there is sufficient demand, job shop assignments for batches of work that relate to analytical processes can be converted into the much more economic flow shops that disassemble the basic commodities into a set of final products. These often entail the transfer of liquids. They are continuous flow-through processes such as encountered in refining petroleum, but they are also used for milk and its by-products.

Combinations of analytical and synthetic flow shops abound in extracting and blending by vintners and beer makers. Telephone switching centers are able to continuously connect and disconnect lines with each other, using process techniques that bring things together and disassemble them in great numbers and with incredible speed. The operations within computers that allow them to perform in this way follow the same mixture of analytics and synthetics.

> **Logistics:** Science and operations of procurement and supply.

The Benefits and Constraints of Flow Shops

The advantages of converting both analytic and synthetic processes into flow shop form are three-fold:

1. Cost per unit can be significantly reduced.
2. Qualities of the product can be raised to higher standards.
3. Consistency of the qualities can be improved.

Flow shops must be justified by volume. The fixed costs required to design and equip the process are high. The increased fixed costs needed to equip the system must be traded off against the decrease in variable costs associated with a less labor-intensive process. The marketing department and the sales force must be able to generate enough demand to allow capital expenditures to be amortized over a reasonable period of time.

5-10 ECONOMIES OF SCALE—DECREASING COST/UNIT BY INCREASING VOLUME

Economies of scale are reductions in costs per unit that are achieved as a result of producing larger volumes of work. The flow shop epitomizes this concept of being able to work more efficiently when there is large enough volume of work to support process studies and investments in process equipment.

The theory can be dated back to Adam Smith. The flow shop in practice was first applied by Henry Ford, who made it work for an entire production line (the model T

> **Economies of scale:** Reductions in cost per unit that can be obtained by producing greater quantities of goods and services.

Ford). Henry Ford recognized that repetitive tasks could be done more efficiently if people specialized in particular aspects of the sequential work process, and he applied the theory to sequenced assembly of automobiles.

There had to be enough call for doing each of the repetitive jobs on a regular basis to allow for the development of specialized workstations where people did the same thing over and over again. Thus, person D is assigned the exclusive use of the hammer, and person J is assigned to the exclusive use of the screwdriver. D becomes the hammer specialist and J, the screw-driving expert. Adam Smith called this method of organizing people working on the process "the division of labor."

In present-day terms, added efficiencies are gained from being able to train people to increase their competence as specialists. If there is no body of knowledge about how to use a hammer so that everyone is equally good whether they are trained or not, then specialization in the use of hammers is pointless. The same can be said if training would improve the way the job is done, but training is not used.

In many companies, there is a lack of understanding that training can improve any and every activity. In part, this is because there is a lack of know-how and, worse yet, no one even knows that the know-how exists. For whatever reason, if the body of knowledge for training is not available, then one of the main reasons for specialization is missing. Yet, there are additional reasons for flow shop type specialization.

Economies of scale can be gained from the use of special-purpose equipment. SPE often requires different work routines and leads to training by the supplier of the equipment. Even if that training is not offered, the worker learns to use the new equipment and a form of self-training occurs. The hammer specialist is given a pneumatic hammer and gradually develops new skills in hammering. Repetitive tasks can become boring, but alternatively, even without SPE, learning and self-training can reward the repetitive job assignment.

Further economies of scale become possible because of volume production. These include expanded levels of coordinated promotional, advertising, and marketing activities. High-volume purchasing should earn well-deserved discounts. Work in process can be minimized in a well-designed flow shop process. In a related advantage, value adding can be maximized. There is focus of purpose because of concentration on doing the same things over and over. This can be turned to advantage.

When sufficient demand exists, the flow shop is the preferred process. It is the simplest and most efficient production configuration. Economies of scale make it worthwhile to try to aggregate enough volume to justify using it.

When sufficient demand does not exist, the use of the flow shop provides one of the best strategies for getting the demand level to be sufficient. The flow shop tends to support itself by lowering costs. This allows for decreases in price and/or increases in marketing support. The superior quality of flow shop product (if the flow process is properly designed) enhances customer preference and supports increased demand volume.

The negative press that the flow shop gets because repetitious work is boring and mind-numbing can be overcome with proper job design and the rotation of jobs. These subjects are addressed in discussions about human resources management.

The contrast between job shop and flow shop production is worth examining. Lacking specialization, working with batches is a less efficient production configuration. Being a greater producer of product variety is the direct cause of increased complexity. The traffic of batches of work moving around in tote boxes generates patterns of interference. Controlling traffic requires extra planning to avoid tie-ups and blockages. Job shop batches interact with each other, waiting for their turn, competing for facilities and floor space. The mix of jobs is seldom the same. The pattern is always changing. Repeated planning is required and costly. The correctness of each plan will vary. Sometimes the plan will be perfect and more often somewhat off-the-mark. Consequently, the precision, scope, and timing of each day's job shop plan will be less on-target than for the flow shop.

5-10a   Economies of Scope

Interesting alternatives are coming into being with the technological development of flexible systems. Their downside is expense and the need to pioneer in their use and development. Flexible manufacturing systems (FMS) and flexible process systems (FPS) are discussed under the generic terminology of FMS. It should be noted that flexibility is associated with the **economies of scope,** a uniquely different rule of economics than the economies of scale.

Economies of scope are realized when setup cost reductions allow more frequent setups and, thereby, smaller lot sizes can be run. If it costs nothing to change production from green socks to red socks, then greater variety can be achieved without losing time or money. The value of variety will then determine how much a firm might be willing to invest in equipment and training that would allow the green to red and back to green shift.

The technologies required to allow economies of scope are computer systems connected to mechanical devices that turn out the product. In the beginning, there must be product designs that take into account what the manufacturing devices can do and how the computers can control them. For example, it might be possible to go from white to tan to light green to black without expenditures for cleaning up between colors. At going back to white, the equipment would be cleaned up and started again on the cycle. In this case, the costs of adding color in this way have to be balanced against the benefits.

> **Economies of scope:** Realized when set-up cost reductions allow more frequent changeovers without increasing the cost per unit of output.

5-11   THE INTERMITTENT FLOW SHOP

An alternative work configuration that has many flow shop benefits is called the *intermittent flow shop.* It can be used when demand volume is not sufficient to justify a full-scale flow shop. The design of an **intermittent flow shop (IFS)** allows it to be set up and run for an interval of time, then shut off.

IFSs are not as efficient as permanent flow shops because they need to be turned on and off as required. This means that the same complete engineering of the process will not pay. Also, to have a large flow shop investment not running for long periods of time is counterproductive. Nevertheless, the IFS can be viewed as a step in the transition of a company process as it moves from being a job shop to a flow shop.

IFSs are turned on when high output volumes are needed in short periods of time. They can be used to build up stock when the savings of flow shop speed counterbalance the cost of carrying stock. Sometimes a special order is received that requires larger volumes of product than are normally made. The intermittent flow shop is a possible solution.

The ability to use serialized production for work that formerly or also had been done in batches requires planning and investment. Once it is planned and the facilities are available, it gets called into being by need, but requires both set-up times and learning times to get the line running. As with pure flow shops, the intermittent form can be used for both synthetic and analytic processes. The criteria for establishing optimal runs apply.

A flow shop that can be shut down and dismantled does not have the same high level of special-purpose equipment as a full-time dedicated flow shop. It will not be as cost efficient, but it still makes use of the principles of flow shops.

These principles relate the total time required to make a complete unit of product, requiring i operations (say $i = 10$ for the following equation)

> **Intermittent flow shop (IFS):** Run for an interval of time and then shut down until required again.

$$\sum_{i=1}^{i=10} t_i$$

to n, which is the number of workstations (Figure 5-4), and C (the cycle time).

The relationship *with no idle time* at any station is specified by:

$$nC = \sum_{i=1}^{i=10} t_i$$

Product	1	2	3	4
Station 1	a	b	c	d
Station 2	e	f	g	h
Station 3	i	j	k	l

TABLE 5-1

Flexible Process System with Three Workstations and Four Products

It is assumed that the job consists of ten steps. The sum of the times to do them is 30 minutes. The whole job, all ten steps, could be done at one station. Then $n = 1$ and $C = 30$. The cycle time is 30 minutes and, therefore, the production rate is 60/30 = two units per hour.

Assume that the same job will be done with two stations. Then, $n = 2$, and $C = 15$. The cycle time has been cut in half. The production rate is doubled since 60/15 = 4. On the ledger, the balance of costs must be tested. The cost of the extra station is to be weighed against the doubling of the output rate.

Determination of when to use the IFS form of flow shop is guided by the principle that flow shop production is more costly to set up than batch production, but thereafter per unit costs are lower. It is necessary to calculate the demand level at which the total costs are about the same for batch production or the intermittent flow shop. This is the *point of indifference* as to which work configuration is used. It also is referred to as the point where the two kinds of processes break even with respect to total costs.

5-12 FLEXIBLE PROCESS SYSTEMS

There is another alternative to the classic flow shop that is of relatively recent technological origin. It is the **flexible process system (FPS)**. For manufacturing it is called the flexible manufacturing system **(FMS)**. Applied to services it is called **FPS** or **FOS** for flexible office system.

Flexible process system (FPS): Encompasses flexible manufacturing systems (FMS) as well as flexible information systems.

Flexible systems may be used as if they were flow shops even though they produce variety. The reason is that computer programming and computer-driven equipment operate together to change set-ups in seconds. The economics of these systems facilitate increasing physical variety (called *diversity* to distinguish it from marketing variety). The effect (principle) has been referenced as economies of scope.

Each station is capable of doing a set of different things and switching from one member of the set to another in an instant. Table 5-1 is a simple illustration of the principle. Station 1 can shift instantly between the operations a, b, c, and d. Station 2 shifts between e, f, g, and h. Station 3 shifts between i, j, k, and l.

One product that this FMS can make is aei. Other products are bfj, cgk and dhl. *If only the columns are products*, then four different products could be made with flow shop speeds and costs. *If all possible combinations* (using all three stations) were products, then there would be $4 \times 4 \times 4 = 64$ different products that could be made with the workstation advantages of flow shop processes.

If the three stations are connected and coordinated to work together, they constitute a cellular manufacturing system. This requires programming so that each station can do its work, and methods of conveyance can move the work from one station to another. The components of the cell are programmed to coordinate activities on a number of items having somewhat different designs.

Although they are different, as a general rule, jobs of similar family characteristics will be assigned to particular manufacturing cells. In that way, variants of the programming can be economically developed. The efficient production of families of parts is a concept that is known as *group technology*. Consequently, this application of FMS is classified as **group technology cellular manufacturing systems.**

Group technology cellular manufacturing systems: Workstations linked together on common sets of projects and families of parts.

High-technology systems are coming into use to convert paper trails into digital form. The processes that will foster and expedite paperless offices and check-free banking will be characterized by a great amount of flexibility. Freedom from paper requires radically new forms of processes. Slow adoption of what seems so logical and economical stems in some part from the effort to shoehorn old-tech methods into new-tech systems.

FIGURE 5-5
Home Shopping Online Processing

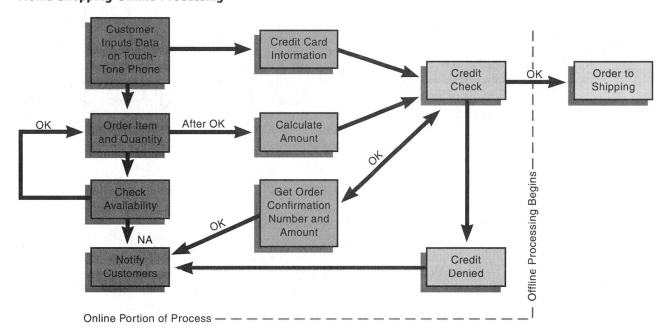

Online Portion of Process — — — — — — — — — — — — — — — — — —

There is ample evidence that the use of optical scanning methods and voice-activated request systems has decreased reliance on old-style record keeping. Credit card companies and many banks are employing new technologies to revamp the accustomed information systems approach for recording, storing and informing transactions.

Home shopping networks on TV are breaking new ground in information processing. Figure 5-5 depicts a home shopping process system where the customer communicates with the computer using a Touch-Tone phone to input the item wanted, quantity, and credit card information. While the customer remains online, the computer completes the credit card check and determines item availability. If all checks out, the customer is given a confirmation number and told the amount that is being deducted from their account.

It is expected that with interactive cable, customers will be able to browse through catalogs and interact even more directly with the computer system. These are representative of the truly flexible service systems currently being developed.

5-13 SHIFTING WORK CONFIGURATION TYPES

Hayes and Wheelwright[4] developed the matrix shown in Table 5-2. It captures an important aspect of the relationship between product life cycle stages and process life cycle stages.

The product life cycle stages are labeled product structure by the authors. This terminology is translatable to categories of volume and variety.

Process life cycle stages are labeled process structure by the authors. This terminology is equivalent to type of work configuration.

The relationship depicted by the matrix indicates that as products move from low volume and high variety (left) to high volume and commodity products with no variety (right), the process type moves from the job shop (top) to the continuous flow system (bottom). The diagonal, moving downward and from left to right, delineates the progression. Also, the authors distinguish between smaller job shops and larger ones by calling the latter batch work.

This matrix takes an operations-oriented approach to defining product life cycles instead of the focus that marketing uses. It defines product life cycles in terms of increasing volume and decreasing variety. The power of this matrix is in the connection that it

TABLE 5-2

Matrix of: Product Life Cycle Stages (Columns) Versus Process Life Cycle Stages (Rows)

Process Structure / Process Life Cycle Stage	Product structure—Product Life Cycle Stage			
	I Low volume—Low Standardization, One of a Kind	II Multiple Products Low Volume	III Few Major Products Higher Volume	IV High Volume—High Standardization, Commodity Products
JS	Commercial printer			
Batch		Heavy equipment		
FS			Automobile assembly	
CONT				Sugar refinery

Economies of Scale ⟶ Lower-Unit Costs ⟶

Legend: JS = job shop; Batch = larger lots than JS; FS = flow shop; CONT = continuous flow.
Reprinted with permission of the *Harvard Business Review*; An exhibit from "Link Manufacturing Process and Product Life Cycles: Focusing on the Process Gives a New Dimension to Strategy," by Robert H. Hayes & Steven C. Wheelwright, Jan.–Feb. 1979, pp. 133–140. Copyright © 1978 by the President and Fellows of Harvard College; all rights reserved.

makes between the growth in demand volume and the nature of the process that can deliver enough product to balance supply and demand.

It is possible to use a flow shop for lower-volume and higher-variety products. This would be like moving heavy equipment in Table 5-2 down one box and off the diagonal. Auto-assembly could be raised one row and made a batch process. Such off-the-diagonal positions are permissible and special. However, the following admonitions should be kept in mind:

1. If the actual company process falls above the diagonal, it is not well suited to handling the larger volume that the market demands, and it can provide more flexibility for variety than the market requires. Both of these deviations have costs that exert pressure on the company to move back to the diagonal to be on a par with its competitors.

2. If the actual company process falls below the diagonal, it is geared to handling higher volumes than the market demands, and is less able to cope with the flexibility needed for the variety levels that the market requires. Once again, both directions for the deviations have costs that exert pressure on the company to move back to the diagonal.

As the authors of the matrix state, "A company that allows itself to drift from the diagonal without understanding the likely implications of such a shift is asking for trouble."[5]

5-13a Expanded Matrix of Process Types

Six classes for work configurations were mentioned at the start of this chapter. Project work configurations were dropped from that list because they apply to start-ups and not online production systems. That leaves five to consider. Because the matrix in Table 5-2 illustrates only four process types, a new matrix has been constructed to reflect the positioning of the five process types. Table 5-3 presents the classification in list form.

In addition to Table 5-3, Table 5-4 illustrates the expanded matrix. The directions for economies of scale are the same as in Table 5-2. Flexible process systems have been added. Therefore, *economies of scope* are represented by the bottom (FMS) row of the matrix.

This makes clear how the FMS process category can act like a custom shop or a job shop. It has the economic advantages of the flow shop. It can emulate all of the different work configurations, except continuous process flow systems.

Process Type	Variety	Volume
Customized	Highest level	One at a time
Job shop	Medium level	Medium volume
Flow shop (assembly)	Low level	High level
Continuous flow	Lowest level	Highest level
Flexible system	High level	Few at a time

Expanded Matrix of Process Types

The FMS-type process is used most effectively when it acts like a custom shop or a job shop, yet having the economic advantages of the flow shop. It also can emulate the job shop or the flow shop, but the economic advantages of being a flow shop in disguise are lessened as the lot size increases.

Because of the ability to handle the entire range of volumes and variety levels, the Xs in Table 5-4 are entered into three stages of the product life cycle. The fourth stage, which represents continuous production of commodity products, is possible for FMS but not economical.

5-14 THE EXTENDED DIAGONAL

Expanding the matrix is equivalent to extending the diagonal of that matrix. The most upper-left box is now related to producing units one at a time. If the custom shop manager decides to make two units on a customized basis, then, that would move the X one box to the right of the diagonal. To do this, perhaps some process steps would need to be modified to facilitate making two units more efficiently than first one and then another one. Off-diagonal positions can be viewed as requiring special process descriptions. Whether on or off the diagonal, there is an opportunity to describe how process configurations can be interpreted creatively to satisfy variations in demand volume that would benefit the bottom line even though they are off-diagonal activities.

5-14a Adding the Custom Shop

The smooth progression along the diagonal is not disrupted by the addition of the customized shop. Customized process abilities are associated with the highest level of variety and the most unique products. Hence, the custom shop creates a new northwest corner for the matrix because it can produce higher variety at lower volumes more economically than the job shop.

This places the job shop second in position on the matrix where it fulfills the mission of producing lot sizes in batches of 50 units on average. As discussed previously, assembly line flow shops turn out only a few major product types. They produce a low variety of goods or services in quite high volumes on serialized production lines. Continuous flow systems are better served by dedicated equipment than by flexible systems.

	One	Med	High	Cont
CS	X			
JS		X		
FS			X	
CONT				X
FMS	X	X	X	

Matrix of Product Life Cycle Stages Versus Process Life Cycle Stages

Legend: CS = custom shop; JS = job shop; FS = flow shop; CONT = continuous flow; FMS = flexible manufacturing system.

5-14b   The Role of FMS

The addition of flexible systems stops the diagonal progression and bends the variety level back to the highest level that can be obtained. The volume also circles back to one or a few at a time, like the custom shop. Because of the ability to achieve instantaneous changeovers from one job to another, the process acts as if it were a flow shop.

Flexible systems make a distinct break with the past. This is the first time that production technology permits hybrid results. The hybrid in this case combines the variety of the job shop with the economies of scale advantages of the flow shop. This new technology opens processing vistas not conceived of until recently. Flexible systems continue to gain in power as the underlying computer-driven technology evolves. Nevertheless, in spite of their promise and actual use in various factories, the overall developments remain tentative and experimental.

5-14c   Applied to Services

It is also convenient to extend the basic matrix shown in Table 5-2 (which applied to manufacturing) so that it can reflect the same set of considerations when applied to services. This results in Table 5-5.

The systems view of relationships between service products and processes is similar to the relationships for manufacturing. The fact is that processes tend to develop from higher variety to lower variety as market success moves demand volume from low to high. Supply, in order to match demand, requires alterations of the process type.

5-15   AGGREGATING DEMAND

Demand is affected by variety, price, and the quality of the product. Using these controls, it is possible to aggregate demand. The accumulation of volume is done in order to move toward process configurations for higher-volume levels. One of the most used controls is lowering the price. This usually (but not always) increases demand in line with price-elasticity relationships. Increasing the variety of an item (say 2 colors instead of 1) is another means of increasing aggregate demand that is often used.

The elasticity relationship of product quality and price with demand volume is not the classic model where only price elasticity is taken into account. When customers cannot find substitutes for unique qualities of products, they will pay more to get what they like. This makes those product qualities into forces for less elasticity. Figure 5-6 relates supply capabilities, product variety, product quality, and price to demand.

They are all interrelated. Boxes 3 and 4 drive Box 1, each according to its own relative elasticity. Not to be overlooked is the effect of work process configurations on Box 2. Supply feeds demand, and how they match determines the economic feasibility of the system. A fifth box representing the product design is always present. A change in product design can alter the parameters for demand aggregation.

TABLE 5-5		

Matrix (For Services): Product Life Cycle Stages (Columns) Versus Process Life Cycle Stages (Rows)

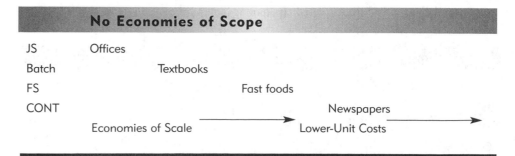

Legend: JS = job shop; Batch = larger lots than JS; FS = flow shop; CONT = continuous flow
Reprinted with permission of the *Harvard Business Review*; an exhibit from "Link Manufacturing Process and Product Life Cycles: Focusing on the Process Gives a New Dimension to Strategy," by Robert H. Hayes & Steven C. Wheelwright, Jan.–Feb. 1979, pp. 133–140. Copyright © 1978 by the President and Fellows of Harvard College; all rights reserved.

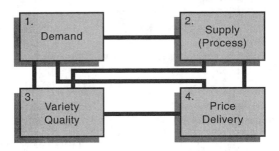

FIGURE 5-6
Factors That Affect Aggregation of Demand (All Lines Flow Two Ways)

Flexible manufacturing systems are outstanding potential sources of control over the factors shown in the Figure 5-6. If the FMS process costs are at a minimum—paralleling flow shop economies of scale—it is possible to gain market share and aggregate volume by lowering prices. The same kind of reasoning applies to the advantages of high variety which FMS permit. Superior quality of FMS products is derived from programming the system, which calls upon the enhanced control features and excellent tolerances that are characteristic of FMS systems.

Using an FMS permits a company to aggregate volume of new products that can then be assigned to conventional flow shop processes. In other words, flexible manufacturing systems can help facilitate the transformation of batch-type processes to dedicated flow shop facilities. In essence it is the process that facilitates the growth in demand that can then sustain flow shop configurations.

SUMMARY

One major differentiating characteristic of processes is whether they are synthetic or analytic. Synthetic processes assemble; analytic processes disassemble. It is noted that the theory of production constraints (also referred to as the OPT system) makes this structural distinction before attempting to synchronize production schedules.

Process configuration strategies are explained. There are basically six different ways to do work, and five of these are appropriate for online production systems. The five types of work systems are customized one-of-a-kind output, job shop batches, serialized output of the flow shop, small lots with high variety from flexible process systems, and continuous output flows from refinery-type systems. These work configurations are explained, including the cycle time of the flow shop.

Two Spotlight feature boxes conclude this chapter. These boxes illustrate real applications of the materials in the chapter. See Spotlight 5-1: Ford Motor Company and Spotlight 5-2: Where Will All the New Jobs Go?

KEY TERMS

Analytic process
Benchmarking
Best practice
Continuous processes
Constraints, theory of
Custom shop
Economies of scale
Economies of scope
Ends
Flexible process system (FPS)

Flow shops (FS)
General-purpose equipment (GPE)
Group technology cellular manufacturing
   systems
Intermittent flow shop (IFS)
Job shop (JS)
Just-in-case
Just-in-time
Logistics
OPT

Process
Process steps
Project
Simulations
Special-purpose equipment (SPE)
Supply chain
Synthetic process
Work configuration

REVIEW QUESTIONS

1. What does the statement mean that the management of supply is related to the management of demand?

2. It is said that the existence of the demand for a product leads to the creation of the industry that can supply products to satisfy that (need) demand. If need drives supply, then what accounts for the sales of DVDs, CDs, VCRs, air conditioners, and laptop computers? Consumers did not ask for these products until long after they were developed. Producers took the risk of tooling up for high volumes of production in order to obtain low enough prices so that consumers would buy these items.

3. Is it true that the drivers of demand are price, quality, and variety? Are there other drivers?

4. What is a process?

   a. Does a process differ from a procedure? How?

   b. Does a process differ from a method? How?

   Hint: Use the dictionary to look up "procedure" and "method." Then, relate process to technology and note the relationship between process and product technology.

5. What is a custom shop and why is the custom shop a natural start for an entrepreneur?

6. What rules apply for managing a successful custom shop?

7. Au Bon Pain is a fast-food franchise that has been described as stressing high quality coffee, buns, sandwiches, and soups. Which are more applicable for ABP: the rules for running a good custom shop or those for a good job shop?

8. Describe a job shop. What rules apply for managing a successful job shop?

9. Would an entrepreneur prefer a job shop to a custom shop?

10. Contrast analytic processes with synthetic processes and give examples of both kinds of systems. Can simulation be used to study these processes?

11. Discuss the advantages and disadvantages of moving from one work configuration stage to another. Refer to Tables 5-2, 5-4, and 5-5. Consider moving down the diagonal to higher volumes as well as up the diagonal to higher variety. Discuss the use of simulation to evaluate the benefits of employing each work configuration.

12. What are economies of scope? Do they eliminate economies of scale or can these two kinds of process economies work together?

13. What kind of a business process is exemplified by a supermarket? Deal with the entire process of ordering, stocking the shelves, customers shopping, checkout counters, etc.

14. What kind of business process and work configuration is used by the post office? Discuss the process. Try to estimate how many transactions are handled per minute by the local post office.

PROBLEMS SECTION

1. Much used by the automobile industry for the assembly process is a paced conveyor to move the chassis from station to station. This is usually cited as an example of a pure synthetic process.
   a. Is this true?
   b. If the assembly process of an older auto assembly plant in New Jersey takes 32 hours, and there are 1,000 workstations along the conveyor path, what is the length of time that the conveyor is stopped at each station?

2. A new auto assembly plant has been built in Kentucky. It has an assembly process that takes 22 hours, and there are 800 workstations along the conveyor path. What is the length of time that the conveyor is stopped at each station?

3. With reference to Problems 1 and 2, what is the cycle time for each auto assembly plant? Comment on the comparison of the New Jersey plant with the Kentucky plant.

4. With reference to Problems 1, 2 and 3, what is the hourly production output rate at each plant? Assuming two 8-hour shifts, six days a week, compare the weekly output of the New Jersey plant and the Kentucky plant.

5. The average annual investment cost of a workstation in New Jersey has been calculated to be $100,000. It has been calculated to be $150,000 in Kentucky. The hourly cost at a workstation is $60 in New Jersey and $40 in Kentucky. How do the two plants compare with respect to the cost of labor for making a car?

6. An interesting comparison can be drawn between the Volvo method of building autos in Sweden and that of U.S. auto companies. Specifically, the Volvo Company has pioneered a team approach for assembling an auto. The Volvo team builds the car on a platform. Even the engine is put together by the same team and mounted on the chassis. This means that the workers come to the work instead of the work coming to the workers.
   a. If it takes Volvo workers 40 hours to assemble a car in this way, what is the cycle time?
   b. How many stations are there?
   c. Analyze the pros and cons of the Volvo assembly system.
   d. Does the Volvo system constitute a synthetic flow shop?
   e. Volvo does not use this team assembly method for its U.S. plant. Why is that so?

7. The highest volume item in a job shop is made in lots of 1,000 units once every week. As an alternative, it has been suggested that an intermittent flow shop (IFS) should be set up twice a year to satisfy the same demand. Use the following data to compare the costs of each production strategy.
   IFS setup costs = $50,000 per setup
   Cost per unit with IFS = $5.00
   Time per unit with IFS = 0.1 minute per unit

Regular batch setup costs = $1,000 per setup
Cost per unit with regular batch production = $8.00
Time per unit with regular batch production = 1.0 minutes
Carrying cost is 1 percent per month

8. Applying the information given in Problem 7, consider the following:

Since an IFS has been suggested, why not analyze, at the same time, the use of a programmable FMS. This particular product lends itself to membership in a family of parts that could be made with a group technology cellular manufacturing system. The investment for the manufacturing cell would be shared with other members of the family. An estimate has been made that its share of the annual investment would be $200,000 per year. The cost per unit would be $2.00 and the time per unit is 0.50 minute.

Do you recommend this option? Explain and discuss.

9. Define and compare the six basically different ways of doing work in terms of the seven factors listed here. Each kind of process system (i.e., one of the six types of work configurations) is best suited to a particular set of conditions. These conditions arise from factors such as the following:
   a. How complex is the character of the product line
   b. Equipment associated with the process
   c. Nature of the market
   d. Financial situation of the firm
   e. How many units are to be made or serviced
   f. How profitable is the venture
   g. What is the competition like

10. The approach to evaluating alternative work configurations can be modeled to provide more structure. To exemplify, a model is constructed to evaluate under what conditions the intermittent flow shop (IFS) will be selected in preference to the batch production of a job shop (JS).

For the IFS, setup, takedown and changeover costs have to be amortized over the lot size that is run. The IFS produces N units at a cost of c dollars per unit with a fixed set-up cost of S dollars.

Compare that cost with the cost of setup for the job shop production process, S'. The lot size is the same but the cost per unit, $c' > c$. The cost comparison is shown here with some hypothetical numbers for costs and a lot size of $N = 100$.

IFS: $(cN + S)/N = (3 \times 100 + 500)/100 = 8.00 per unit made
JS: $(c'N + S')/N = (4 \times 100 + 300)/100 = 7.00 per unit made

So, choose to use the job shop to make the 100 units. Next, assume that the lot size is 500 units.

IFS: $(cN + S)/N = (3 \times 500 + 500)/500 = 4.00 per unit made
JS: $(c'N + S')/N = (4 \times 500 + 300)/500 = 4.60 per unit made

So, choose the IFS.
Now, assume that both set-up costs are double.
a. What is the choice when the lot size is $N = 100$?
b. What is the choice when the lot size is $N = 500$?

11. If the total time to make a computer mouse is 24 minutes and it is made at four stations, how long is the cycle time? Hint: Use the following equation to determine the production output rate (productivity rate).

$$nC = \sum_{i=1}^{i=4} t_i$$

12. Create a board game to simulate the workflow through the four stations in Problem 11. Describe and discuss the procedures.

END-OF-CHAPTER QUESTIONS

1. The difference between processes and work configurations is best summed up by which answer?
   a. Maintenance programs for jet engines are examples of work configurations. Building the jet engine is a process.
   b. Simulations are processes. Board games are used to structure work configurations.
   c. Work configurations can be charted and improved. Process improvement is specified by technology with few degrees of freedom.
   d. Work configurations apply to manufacturing. Delivery of services is a process.
   e. Processes are composed of activities required to make a product or deliver a service, e.g., how to make cheese. Work configurations are physical arrangements used to make the product, e.g., flow shop or in batches.

2. What are the differences between synthetic and analytic processes?
   a. Analytic processes make synthetic materials that are close imitations of the real thing. Synthetic leather is used for autos and attaché cases.
   b. Synthetic processes combine components to make unique end products. Analytic processes are reversals of the synthetic process.
   c. Synthetic processes separate the whole into its parts, which are then used to make various end-products. Analytic processes are reversals of the synthetic process.
   d. Synthesis is a chemical process. Analysis is scientific method.
   e. Analytic process is progressive assembly. Synthetic process is the reverse.

3. Process timing includes the rate at which supplies are delivered to the workstations. Which one of the supply options listed here is not sensible?
   a. Delivery of *just enough* is a method that suggests efficiency. There is no need for extra storage space to contain the "more than enough" inventory; also, the carrying costs are kept to a minimum.
   b. Using the *just in case* method provides enough safety stock to take care of those situations where a problem arises such as when the delivery truck has a flat tire.
   c. *Just in time* is very efficient. It minimizes storage space and makes the supplier a partner to the process.
   d. *Play it safe* is a method that provides backup for risky factors in the supply chain. For example, if demand is volatile and the process might have to make more items to fill orders generated by the sale force, it pays to carry more materials and supplies.
   e. *Patience is a virtue* stresses going with the flow. If materials are short, slow the line, and if orders are greater than expected, fill them on backorder.

4. Which of the following statements about processes is incorrect?
   a. For synthetic processes, it is important to use very focused marketing because there is little room for error. The old saying *you win some, you lose some* does not apply.
   b. Analytic processes tend to produce commodities.
   c. Marketing of commodities derived from analytic processes is based on lowest price because unique qualities are not associated with commodities.
   d. Inputs to analytic processes are themselves commodities, which if carefully chosen for quality can play a role in the quality of the output commodities.
   e. Purchasing for synthetic processes is upstream, and quality requirements are stringent at that point because they strongly impact the product quality downstream.

5. Which of the following statements is incorrect?
   a. Use of special purpose equipment (SPE) is crucial to economic well-being for batch work in the job shop.
   b. Custom shop work is not only "made-to-order" but also only small quantities are made with one-of-a-kind being the essence of customization.
   c. Job shops process work in batches or lots. The average lot size of 50 units has been fairly constant over a long period of time for the United States and Europe.
   d. If supply is less than demand in a company using flow shop process design, a possible solution is to employ two or three shifts.
   e. Economies of scale are not as substantial with intermittent flow shops as they are with full-fledged flow shops.

6. Economies of scale are related to changes that occur in costs per unit made as the volume of production goes up or down. Economies of scope are related to the costs of changing over from one item to another on the same production line. Scope refers to variety of types of outputs and scale refers to volume of units produced. Which of the following statements is likely to be wrong?
   a. Three corn-growing farms merge in the belief that economies of scale will help their bottom line.
   b. Three firms merge combining egg and milk production, cheese manufacture, and farming corn, in the belief that product variety will operate as economies of scope and help their bottom line.
   c. Product life cycle stages and process life cycle stages are related by the cost and benefits of economies of scale (volumes of production) and economies of scope (variety of the product line). The variety of output of a commercial printer would be suitable for a job shop configuration.
   d. The demand for earth-moving equipment is segmented into heavy, medium, and light capacities. This multiple line of low-volume products is suitable for a batch work in job shops of substantial size. This industry has cycles, and during an expansion period, the batch configuration could be transformed into an intermittent flow shop.

e. The diagonal of the matrix of process types matches volumes of production required and variety of products demanded. If conditions shift, it is possible to move vertically or horizontally, leaving the diagonal. For example, a quick service restaurant utilizes a flow shop for certain items (burgers) and batch processes for others (salads).

7. Flexible manufacturing systems (FMS) are a subcategory of flexible processing systems (FPS). This is a work configuration category that developed after 1950. Which of the following statements is incorrect?
   a. Flexible work systems (FWS) permit a modicum of variety levels in the product line. With FWS, lot sizes can be as small as one.
   b. FMS are based on the marriage of computer controls and robotic tools. Also required are programmable means of moving work between stations.
   c. Flexible processing is the foundation for economies of scale. These apply to both the manufacture of goods and service deliveries.
   d. Computer software for word processing, spreadsheets, presentations, etc., represent some of the capabilities required for flexible office systems (FOS). The ability to move from one task to another with very little job-changeover time is the key.
   e. Group technology is a scheme for designing a quick-shift ability to produce members of a family of products, such as gears with different diameters and number of teeth.

8. Which one of the following statements is incorrect?
   a. Without computer-driven flexibility, there can be no economies of scope.
   b. For the most part, office environments are job shops.
   c. Publishers of paper textbooks can use home publishing software to complete one-at-a-time customized books. However, in general, publishers run batches of thousands of books through the print shop.
   d. Continuous production flow systems differ from discrete flow shop systems because the product is actually flowing on a continuous basis, as with chemical manufacturing, electrical production, and newspaper printing.
   e. Quick service restaurants are usually categorized as flow shops even though some are more efficient flow shops than others. To make the flow effective, the customer is made part of the workforce.

9. The owner of a job shop for printing pamphlets and catalogs wants to aggregate the volume of certain products to be able to install a flow shop factory within the job shop factory. This is akin to establishing a cellular manufacturing capability. Which of the following statements is incorrect?
   a. Lowering price aggregates demand—in most cases. However, there are situations where the price-elasticity curve is "kinked." That means it moves in the reverse direction. For example, prestige gifts lose credibility if price is dropped in such a way that the recipient of the gift will be aware that it was purchased by the gift-giver at a discount.
   b. Increasing variety without having to stop production for more than a few minutes is a way to aggregate volume without incurring large costs. For example, changing the flavor of toothpaste can be done quickly.
   c. Better quality is a guarantee that demand will increase, especially if there is no price increase. More demand is the same as aggregating volume.
   d. Speeding deliveries to customers is known to be an effective way to aggregate demand. However, there are no certainties so some market research might be in order.
   e. Dropping price, increasing variety, and cutting delivery times can be effective means of increasing demand for goods or services. However, the introduction of interesting new technology can have a dramatic effect. The size of computer memory and the speed of the system have been two examples of drivers for aggregating volume. New technology is classified as a quality improvement.

10. The assembly process of a remodeled automobile plant in New Jersey requires 32 hours to build a car at 1,000 workstations. A greenfield plant in Tennessee builds a comparable car in 24 hours at 1,200 workstations. How many cars are completed in an 8-hour shift for each plant? What is the cycle time for each plant? Which row in the table below contains the correct answers?

Row Option	Cars Completed New Jersey (in 8-hr. shift)	Cars Completed Tennessee (in 8-hr. shift)	Cycle Time New Jersey	Cycle Time Tennessee
a.	250	320	1.92 min.	1.50 min.
b.	240	400	2.00 min.	1.20 min.
c.	400	250	1.20 min.	1.92 min.
d.	250	400	1.92 min.	1.20 min.
e.	240	320	2.00 min.	1.50 min.

ADDITIONAL READINGS

Abernathy, William J., K.B. Clark, and A.M. Kantrow. *Industrial Renaissance*. NY: Basic Books, 1983.

Arnold, Horace Lucien, and Fay Leone Faurote. *Ford Methods and the Ford Shops*. NY: The Engineering Magazine Company, 1915.

Goldratt, Eliyahu M., and J. Cox. *The Goal*, 2e rev. ed. North River Press, 1992.

Goldratt, Eliyahu M., and R. Fox. *The Race*. North River Press, 1986.

Hayes, Robert H., and Steven C. Wheelwright. "Link Manufacturing Process and Product Life Cycles: Focusing on the Process Gives a New Dimension to Strategy." *Harvard Business Review* (January–February 1979): 133–140.

Hill, Terry. *Manufacturing Strategy: Text and Cases*, 2e. Homewood, IL: Irwin, 1994.

Normann, R. *Service Management: Strategy and Leadership in Service Business*, 2e. Wiley, 1991.

Sharp, Alec and Patrick McDermott, *Workflow Modeling: Tools for Process Improvement and Application Development*, Artech House, February 2001.

Smith, Howard and Peter Fingar, *Business Process Management (BPM): The Third Wave*, Meghan-Kiffer Press, December 2002.

Vollmann, Thomas E., William L. Berry, and D. Clay Whybark. *Manufacturing, Planning and Control Systems*, 3e. Homewood, IL: Irwin, 1992.

NOTES

1. Jon F. Cox, John H. Blackstone, and Michael S. Spencer. APICS Dictionary, 7th Ed., APICS Educational and Research Foundation, 1992.

2. "In Virtual Mudville, the Outlook Is Joyless as Rotisseries Halt," *The Wall Street Journal* (August 11, 1994): 1. This was the day before professional baseball went on strike.

3. Eliyahu M. Goldratt created OPT. His company, Creative Output in Milford, Connecticut, was the original consulting group. The theory is explained in novel form: *The Goal*, 2e rev. ed., by E.M. Goldratt and J. Cox. North River Press, 1992. Also, see *The Race*, E. M. Goldratt and R.E. Fox, North River Press, 1986.

4. Robert H. Hayes and Steven C. Wheelwright. "Link Manufacturing Process and Product Life Cycles: Focusing on the Process Gives a New Dimension to Strategy." *Harvard Business Review* (January–February 1979): 133–140. Specific reference is to Exhibit 1 on p. 135.

5. Ibid., 135.

SPOTLIGHT 5-1
Ford Motor Company

Understanding the History of Great Leaders in the P/OM Field Is Part of the Systems Approach—Henry Ford, Part 1

Henry Ford changed America a century ago, a time when auto manufacturers were rushing into business and usually disappearing nearly as quickly. What made Henry Ford's company a success was his idea of designing a car the average man could afford. His idea was to keep lowering manufacturing costs in order to continually reduce the price and enlarge the market. This business plan, which focused on the highly efficient sequenced assembly process, earned Henry Ford a major fortune.

Before Ford's Model T was introduced on October 1, 1908, most Americans had no choice but to watch and yearn as automobiles grew bigger, faster, and so expensive that only the rich could afford them. In 1906, *The North American Review* printed an article titled "An Appeal to Our Millionaires." It warned, "Unfortunately, our millionaires, and especially their idle and degenerate children, have been flaunting their money in the faces of the poor as if actually wishing to provoke them." This anti-auto feeling in the United States prior to the Model T's debut was summed up by no other than Woodrow Wilson, then president of Princeton University. In 1906, he described drivers of horseless carriages as "a picture of arrogance and wealth, with all its independence and carelessness." At the time, it was estimated that more Americans had died in car accidents in the first six months of 1906 than had been killed in the Spanish-American War.

In 1918, Woodrow Wilson was a U.S. president and owner of his own Model T. Wilson urged Henry Ford to run for elective office. A farmer's wife summed up the feelings of the country in a letter to Ford in 1918. She wrote, "You brought joy into our lives." By that time, the car had opened the American landscape, altered the outlook of consumers everywhere, and changed the way automobiles would be manufactured and sold.

How did Ford change America? First of all, he was a great mechanic and manufacturing innovator. Of all the automotive pioneers in Detroit at the time, none knew more about cars than Henry Ford. After several situations turned into disastrous failures, Ford was quoted as maintaining that, "failure is the opportunity to begin again, more intelligently." With all his talents and uncanny understanding of auto mechanics, his genius did not lie in working with his hands or reading blueprints. He was called a cut-and-try mechanic, unable to visualize things and put them on paper. His genius seemed to work by adding a sense of the whole to his machines. He knew his customers were mechanically illiterate and therefore the whole machine had to be simple to operate or they would not buy it in the numbers he envisioned. His success in accomplishing this goal depended on how much he could get other people to work for his interests, from financial backing to choosing his engineers and associates.

By 1923, Henry Ford's fortune was calculated at $750 million. When a prospective buyer offered $1 billion for the company, his son, Edsel, sent a message, "We are having too much fun to sell out."

With the belief that the Model T could not be improved but the process of making it could, Ford opened his new River Rouge plant in Dearborn, Michigan, where he was able to control the entire process of automobile manufacturing. Raw materials were brought in on the company's own fleet of ships and were methodically transformed into vehicles. The plant was dedicated to saving time and money. New tools and ideas were introduced each day. For instance, a new tool allowed a drill press operator to drill 10 holes at once (instead of one at a time). Ford developed one of the leading time-study departments in the United States. It was comprised of about 80 men who canvassed the factories, recording the number of minutes required to complete each new process. In only seven years, from 1919 to 1926, River Rouge grew to include 93 buildings, 75,000 employees, and output of 4,000 cars per day.

As Henry Ford grew older, he failed to accept that cars should be styled and have more than one color. He had created one of the world's major fortunes with his business plan, and he flatly refused to change it. Because the Ford family owned 100 percent of the stock, no one could tell him what to do, including his only son, Edsel, who had been made president of the company in 1919.

Even after the market forced him to abandon the Model T in 1927, Ford clung to the past and constantly interfered with his son's attempts to make Ford into a modern corporation like General Motors. By the 1930s, the Ford Motor Company was in chaos. Long-term planning was impossible because of the dispute between father and son. Edsel died of stomach cancer in 1943, and Henry promptly fired Edsel's supporters and told one employee, "We've got to build only one car."

There is another Spotlight feature box in chapter 11 dealing with history titled "The Ford Motor Company After Henry Ford, Part 2." There is also a third Spotlight feature box that discusses recycling at the Ford Motor Company, this box is in chapter 12. It is titled "The Ford Motor Company to the Present, Part 3."

Sources: Douglas, Brinkley. *Wheels for the World: Henry Ford, His Company, and a Century of Progress.* Viking 2003; Gordon, John Steele. *The Greatest Comeback.* American Heritage, July 2003; Hakim, Danny. "A Family's 100-Year Car Trip." *The New York Times* (June 15, 2003).

SPOTLIGHT 5-2
Where Will All the New Jobs Go?

The Shift from Labor-Intensive to Capital-Intensive

Agriculture is an operations-intensive series of processes that tend to be overlooked by traditional POM studies although agribusiness accounts for billions of global trade dollars. Farm products require inputs of labor, technology, and a great deal of energy, which are POM responsibilities. Managing the transformation process (growing, harvesting, processing, etc.) and handling the outputs (distribution) are crucial POM roles.

The percent of the total workforce engaged in farming in the United States changed dramatically from 1790 (more than 90 percent) to 2003 (less than 2 percent). These numbers relate to farming and not to food processing, which has grown to keep pace with the population increase. Agricultural output in the United States has grown dramatically, although there are fewer farms (of larger size) and the total farm workforce has declined precipitously.

Manufacturing has a different pattern both in timing and numbers. Nevertheless, the reduction in percent of workforce continues in a striking manner. The manufacturing percent of the total workforce in the United States reached a peak during the 1920s when it was about 55 percent (agriculture had declined to 29 percent). By 2003, the manufacturing workforce was less than 10 percent of the total workforce. As was the case with farming, manufacturing output increased in spite of the workforce percent reduction because of various factors. First, the total population had increased so that a diminishing workforce percent did not signify an absolute reduction of the same magnitude. Also, automation and "off-shore" manufacturing accounted for replacements of U.S. workers.

The Mexican off-shore effect is better called the cross-border effect. Factories on the Mexican side of the border shared with the United States are called maquiladores. In colonial Mexico, millers charged a "maquila" to process customers' grains. According to information found at http://www.madeinmexicoinc.com, manufacturers can expect to save up to 75 percent on labor costs. Hundreds of factories and their suppliers (from the United States, Canada, Europe, Japan, Taiwan, etc.) operate with lower labor prices than in the United States. Since the North American Free Trade Agreement (NAFTA) in January 1994, forces have emerged to reduce these labor cost imbalances.

Really off-shore are the outsourced factories in China. Low wage rates have made China the main contributor to the labor costs of products sold in the United States. As of September 2003, China's share of the U.S. import market "had grown to 16.3 percent, surpassing Mexico as the largest exporter to the US." This quote is from the World of Garment-Textile-Fashion website, found at http://www.fibre2fashion.com/news/NewsDetails.asp?News_id=4503.

The agricultural shift in process management and work configurations provides insights about what is currently happening in manufacturing as well as in service industries and IT occupations. Agriculture has been moving from laborious custom-type farm jobs to high-speed technology employed for land preparation, crop planting, watering, fertilizing, pest control, and harvesting. Although the shift is enormous, there remain enough itinerant laborers such as grape pickers coming from South America and Mexico to generate disputes about their status. Still, the change is inevitable. The advantage is shifting from direct labor costs to indirect technology investments as the process of farming continuously improves because of new technology.

In manufacturing, the shift-point is being reached where, in spite of cheap labor, technology has the economic edge. The total cost of using automation at home is becoming significantly lower than using trained labor abroad. Breakeven points for preferring automation are approaching in one industry after another. However, it is difficult to establish that large, up front investments in technology are preferable to low-cost, well-trained labor. The two ways to alleviate fear of market shifts are: first, to invest in flexible technologies, and second, to provide assurance of demand continuity permitting highly repetitive production volumes. Then, the cost advantages of increased productivity, and superior quality become apparent. Net Present Value calculations do not readily reflect such cost rewards and thereby penalize technology investments in comparison with direct, low-labor costs.

Further, off-shore manufacturing adds transportation costs that are usually considered to be so small in comparison to labor cost savings that they are overshadowed. Transport became efficient when it gained the technological benefits of large container ships and advanced materials handling. Nevertheless, transportation and other logistics costs will become relevant again in the equation as automation costs drop. The entire system of factors will again play a role in reaching sensible location decisions for manufacturing.

Joseph Carson, director of global economic research at Alliance Capital Management LP, says that factory unemployment is declining globally because new technology has made factories more efficient, permitting higher output with "far fewer workers." In spite of declining manufacturing employment, says Mr. Carson, "global industrial output rose more than 30 percent." (John Hilsenrath and Rebecca Buckman. "Factory Employment Is Falling WorldWide." The Wall Street Journal (October 20, 2003): A2, A8.)

Similar limitations will apply to entrepreneurs in manufacturing who will forgo profit to start up a business. For larger companies, when the tipping point in manufacturing is recognized, capital spending budgets will rise, but this will not restore former employment levels in manufacturing. With lower percentages of the total workforce in both agriculture and manufacturing, where will all the new jobs go?

Supplement 5

How Purchasing Agents Use Hedging

Process design should take into account purchasing strategies. When the costs of materials are volatile and fluctuate a great deal as a result of such things as weather (oranges) and gold (world tension), it is important to protect the production process from sudden exorbitant price increases in the basic materials that are used. That is where hedging comes into play.

Hedging is a purchasing strategy that often is utilized to protect against price fluctuations. Money is neither made nor lost because the buyer is locked into a fixed price, as follows:

1. A purchase is made for delivery of the commodity in a future month—cost is x dollars.

2. When production needs material, a cash purchase is made for immediate delivery—cost is y dollars.

3. Simultaneously a sale is made for delivery in the same future month—revenue is y dollars.

If $x < y$, the price has risen just when OM needs to buy the materials. However, the buyer is protected with a net cost of x for materials. This is because of the profit $(y - x)$ made from buying and selling futures in Steps 1 and 3.

If $x > y$, the price has fallen. The OM buyer will not gain that advantage having net costs of x because of the loss $(x - y)$ from buying and selling futures in Steps 1 and 3.

With hedging, the buyer always nets out paying x. The company will neither make nor lose money.

The advantage of hedging is stability. It insulates the production system from wild fluctuations. However, some companies prefer to speculate in the commodity prices of the raw materials that are used. Often this is because these companies are major buyers in those markets and can influence the selling prices of the commodities.

Problems for Supplement 5

1. In July, the price of the material used by the process was $0.58 per pound. The purchasing agent expected the price to rise by December and therefore bought a futures contract for 1,000 pounds to be delivered in December. In September, the company needed this material because demand had exceeded forecasts. The price of the material had risen to $0.68 per pound.

   What course of action should the purchasing agent take? What amounts of money will be involved? Show the financial transactions that take place, including the sums of money for costs and any revenues, if there are any.

2. Now, treat an alternative scenario: In July, the price of the material used by the process was $0.58 per pound. The purchasing agent expected the price to rise by December and therefore bought a futures contract for 1,000 pounds to be delivered in December. In September, the company needed this material because demand had exceeded forecasts. The price of the material had fallen to $0.48 per pound.

   What course of action should the purchasing agent take? What amount of money will be involved? Show the financial transactions that take place, including the sums of money for costs and any revenues, if there are any.

Process Analysis and Process Redesign

Chapter Outline

his section describes process analysis, which leads to process changes aimed at improving performance. Charting the process is the key element in the methodology. Each chart shows the various activities that are necessary to make the good or deliver the service. In addition to the sequence of activities are the times required to do the work under the configuration that has been used in the past

or that has been proposed for the future. In this introductory summary, it should also be noted that improvements can be made continuously by fine-tuning various parts of the stream of activities. On the other hand, the entire process can be redesigned, which allows many constraints in the form of equipment and training to be bypassed in favor of radical shifts.

After reading this chapter, you should be able to:

- Explain why process analysis and redesign are valued OM capabilities.
- Chart any process that needs to be studied using conventional symbols or those of your own choosing.
- Explain what activities should be captured for process charts.
- Delineate when more detailed symbols should be used on a process chart as compared to less detailed symbols.
- Explain the use of process flow layout charts.
- Discuss the choice of continual improvement of processes as compared to their redesign.
- Apply process improvement concepts to information systems.

- Describe the impact of setup times and costs on processes.
- Explain SMED and utilize SMED methods for reducing setup times and costs.
- Differentiate between internal and external setup costs.
- Discuss the benefits of a total productive maintenance (TPM) program.
- Explain the steps TPM advocates, and under what circumstances.
- Distinguish between preventive and remedial maintenance strategies.
- Explain why new developments like computer-aided process planning are of growing importance.
- Describe the use of machine-operator charts.

THE SYSTEMS VIEWPOINT

The systems approach is being used when process analysis for the job shop is focused on the total flow. This entails spanning the process from the first operation—including all the purchased supplies—to the last operation, which includes shipping, and contacting the customer to find out if the product was satisfactory and the delivery made on time. Because it is encompassing, the systems approach to improvement often entails altering the process technology internally and externally, at the suppliers' plants and at all points of distribution. Charting operations for process analysis and redesign should include all of the process transformations that affect customer satisfaction. Systems analysis and redesign always involve "the big picture," which is another name for the systems level of process change. Thus, total productive maintenance (TPM) is a systems approach to prevent failure and single-minute exchange of dies (SMED) is a systems approach to reduce setup times. TPM includes preventive, remedial, and predictive maintenance. The last of these three requires a systems understanding of the evolution of properties over time.

STRATEGIC THINKING

Strategic thinking for POM is related to altering the competitive situation by means of operating plans and decisions. Assume that the strategic decision has been made to increase the variety of the product line. The process for doing this starts with the designers and engineers of the product line working in conjunction with the marketing department's evaluation of sales with and without the enhanced variety levels from production. A factor that often enables greater variety of output from production without increasing total costs and thereby decreasing profit margins is the use of equipment that can rapidly change from making one item to another. In manufacturing these are changes of the dies and fixtures, which can be very time-consuming and costly. However, using the SMED approach that is mentioned in "The Systems Viewpoint" section, it is possible to find equipment that can run one job while workers are changing the setup to run a different job. Such equipment allows shifting between jobs with minor penalties (single-minute stoppage). Then, increased variety is obtained with small production penalties. Marketing power is increased when production flexibility is enhanced by a one-time fixed cost increase in the facility expenses.

Goals must be unambiguous. Target achievements must be consistent. Continuous improvement stems from understanding the job and importing new technology, or constant practice. Often, both are needed in conjunction with ingenuity. For example, in automobile assembly, the "doors off" system opens the work space so that technical assemblers can proceed unimpeded.

6-1 PROCESS IMPROVEMENT AND ADAPTATION

Continuous improvement of processes is an excellent goal for, and a valued function of, OM. An existing process represents an investment in equipment and training, which can be analyzed and redesigned to be as efficient as possible. Costs can be reduced without impairing (and perhaps increasing) reliability, which means only scheduled preventive maintenance. Output is often raised by productivity improvement studies (PIPS) without lowering quality, and sometimes raising it.

Citibank recognized the potential opportunities for continuously analyzing their customers' needs. Every branch bank is evaluated and adapted to the needs of its local customer markets. Changes in customer contact processes include tellers and platform officers and services. Paul Revere Insurance Company analyzed internal processes with emphasis on the fact that employees who work together are each other's customers. If every employee listens to the voice of their internal customers, the service experiences of external customers can be greatly enhanced. Airlines that empower their attendants to solve customers' problems and train them to do so are noticeably superior in customer ratings. This is hardly a surprise to those airlines that do it. In each case, it took conviction, analysis, and forthright action to improve the process.

The methods for analyzing processes are worthy of study. They are effective and capable of making substantial savings and other improvements that permit the firm to experience greater profit margins, market share, and cash flow. The methods are aimed at achieving best practice in processes.

Continuous process improvement includes streamlining operations, introducing new equipment, and improving the way the job is done and the training for it. Process innovations can occur through the work of R & D, or by means of copying the best.

The method of finding the best, called *benchmarking*, is based on comparative measures that identify leaders in specific kinds of processes. Benchmarking must identify external candidates for best processes, and then, by measuring, comparing, and analyzing, select those processes that will be used as a standard to be achieved. McNair and Leibfried stress continuous improvement using benchmarks as a guide, with the ultimate goal of being "better than the best."[1] They credit Xerox as having developed benchmarking in its current form, starting in the 1970s, and as a result of competitive pressure from Japanese copy manufacturers.

Benchmarked companies do not have to be in the same industry, at least for certain processes. Thus, Lands' End has been benchmarked by computer companies that are trying to become effective with mail order. Disney has been benchmarked by manufacturers that provide service to their customers. The Paul Revere Insurance Company has been benchmarked by banks for their team quality programs—modeled on the Olympics—which award bronze, silver, and gold pins.

Good process innovations also can occur because of external forces that impose safety restrictions, pollution regulations, and other governmental controls for the first time. Process adaptation also becomes essential when competitive process advantages occur that leave the others at a disadvantage.

6-2 PROCESS FLOWCHARTS

The use of process charts or process flowcharts is critical to understanding what is going on in the system, how the product is being made, or delivered as a service. **Process charts** are maps of the specific operations, transports, quality checks, storages, and delays that are used by either the present or the proposed system. There is a solid benefit for every organization to chart the processes that it uses to obtain revenues. Wasteful steps that can be removed or remodeled can significantly decrease costs and cut time.

Figure 6-1 shows a process chart for manufacturing an electrical panel box. The process chart uses triangles for storage, circles for operations, and squares for inspections. These are some of the conventional symbols. Other symbols will be introduced later. The person doing the process charting has discretion concerning what amount of detail is best for a particular purpose.

The chart shows that sheet metal is taken from storage for blanking operations on two different machines, which cut out the correct shapes. Two other machines do cold forming on the blanks for the boxes and covers in batches. Boxes and covers are painted and dried separately in batches. The chart does not point out that a label with the

Process charts: Graphics for doing process analysis.

FIGURE 6-1
Process Chart for Making Electrical Panel Box

company's name, logo, and the model number of the panel box assembly is applied to the cover. Then, covers and boxes are inspected and assembled with purchased hinges and rivets. The assembled unit is inspected for appearance and cover operation. Satisfactory product is stored in the warehouse.

It is to be noted that much information is not included in this process chart. Times required for operations, lot sizes, and distances that batches have to be transported are all missing. Some process charts have all this information. Also, operations can be broken down into smaller segments. For example, cold forming takes place in three steps that are bundled together for the purposes of this chart. There are many options in drawing up process charts. Simple charts, such as the one in Figure 6-1, are meant to provide an overview of the process at a glance.

6-3 BACKGROUND FOR USING PROCESS ANALYSIS

Charting an existing process is a starting point for analysis of that process to see if it can be done in a better way. Process analysis also should be used for a process that has never been done before. **Process analysis** examines the purposes of the process and tries to find the best possible way to achieve those goals.

> **Process analysis:** Detailed study of activities required to make the product or deliver the service.
>
> **Setup(s):** Start of the changeover cycle.

Process analysis is an important ongoing activity for job shops. When a job that has never been done before enters the shop, OM is responsible for setting up the process, often basing **setup** on similar jobs that have been completed. Therefore, OM's experience with prior processes is valuable. Old process charts can be used as guides for planning new processes. Frequently, similar product blueprints have similar process characteristics.

The new job offers an opportunity for modification and improvement of the old process. Using process analysis to adapt one system to fit another is a way of achieving improvement through redesign. Questions to be answered include which machines are to be run, when and where, by which operators, having what training? When orders are repeated, analysis and redesign of these processes makes sense.

For the flow shop, much time and attention needs to be paid to the design of the process sequence. It is more suitable to treat the flow shop as an engineering and capacity planning problem. Complete analysis is critical because the job runs continuously and even pennies that can be saved add up to big amounts. Most job shop processes do not have the volume to justify major pre-engineering with the use of simulation. The process charting described in this chapter applies to job shops.

Process charts for job shops trace the patterns of movement of all materials that come into and go out of the shop. From the receiving docks or the mail-in box to the shipping docks or the mail-out box, tracking by process charts should be done. Typically, the mix of orders in the job shop is so dynamic that it is necessary to improve old processes and invent new ones.

6-3a Process Management Is a Line Function

Process managers are responsible for the production line. That is why they are called line managers. They are getting out the product. Filling orders is their prime job, but they must take the time to plan the processes for the production line; proper planning saves time in the long run. With good systems in place, they can make routine the function of developing and improving process charts.

There are competitive advantages, including enhanced profitability, for those in OM who consistently avoid waste and disruption by improving process flows. A remarkable example of this is the hub and spoke process flow designed by the FedEx Company, which picks up packages at all locations and transports them by air to Memphis, where they are sorted and transported by air to their final destinations. Using bar codes, the location of any package is quickly determined. The process flows are fast and secure. FedEx is a splendid model of what excellence in process design can achieve.

Even so, *The Wall Street Journal* (December 17, 1999) reported "FDX Corp. reporting lackluster earnings and acknowledging that it has lost market share in a key sector to

United Parcel Service Inc. is revamping sales operations . . . ." It has been clear that since the initial public offering of UPS on November 10, 1999, FedEx has been improving its systems at a fast pace. FDX remains a leader in **time-based management (TBM).** For package delivery operations, this means continuous reduction of delivery times. In the logistics area, time is a key performance measure of competitive advantage.

> **Time-based management (TBM):** Attention paid to reducing time requirements.

In the broadest sense, there are great opportunities to gain increased profit margins from proper planning for job shop work. As the job shop and batch work take on characteristics of flow shops and continuous flow industries, profit margins increase as do returns on investments. To achieve the gains entails allocating planning time for process management. This means assigning the task of creating new process charts to operations managers who have the appropriate training and skills.

6-3b Demand Is Greater Than Supply

Successful job shops are generally backlogged. In other words, demand is greater than supply. Work must wait before it can be done, and there is pressure to make deliveries on time. This fact needs to be considered in reaching good process management decisions.

In a good job shop, there is concentrated effort on minimizing waste and disruption from machine breakdowns, worker errors, bad materials, and process distortions that cause defectives. Process managers jump to right the wrongs, which is called "putting out fires." The single, most important goal is keeping the orders moving out the door to customers. Therefore, it is an exciting challenge to prevent problems instead of correcting problems after they occur.

With a systems perspective at work, OM and marketing can determine which kinds of job orders fit existing capabilities of the shop better than others. Process charts provide the kind of information that enables such determinations to be made.

Marketing can work at selling the optimal mix of orders for the existing machine capacities, worker skills, and management competencies. Specific classes of new orders are complementary to the existing system while others do not fit as well. If the sales force is coordinated with OM, better focus for sales and marketing results in total systems improvement.

In a similar sense, some customers are prized for their steady, repeat business while others are occasional buyers who provide less profit for the company. OM and marketing need to be coordinated with respect to priorities for customers. Capacity changes can be made to fit the profile for profitable customers and eliminate resource drains for unprofitable customers.

Further coordination is required to recognize that certain new customers may have great potential for growing into the class of "most important" customers. This fact should be taken into account because when drawing up process charts, more attention is likely to be paid to streamlining the production process for prized customers. The effect of putting priorities on customers' orders is always encountered in materials dealing with scheduling.

6-3c Seven Points to Consider for Process Flow Design

1. Alternative process flow designs are always possible. It is useful, therefore, to understand what reasons account for the process flow designs that are being used.

2. Scheduling decisions interact with the designs for process flows that have been developed. Customers are usually very sensitive to delivery lead times, ergo to process features.

3. Product quality is a direct function of process flow design.

4. Product cost and productivity are direct functions of the process flow design.

5. Customers prefer to choose products that maximize value, where:

Value = f {Quality Worthiness / Total Price Paid}

6. Because process charting increases quality and decreases costs, it is a means of raising customer satisfaction.

7. Achieving the **best in class** value includes satisfactory delivery dates and service excellence, both of which are components of quality worthiness. These are OM process management responsibilities that relate to process charts.

Best in class: Top choice for setting the benchmarking standard.

6-3d The Purpose of Process Charts

Process charts make visible and accountable the appointment of people to machines, spaces, and places. The charts make assignments of product orders to people, and of materials to machines and stock rooms. Only when charts exist can processing plans be evaluated and improved. Charts can assist intelligence and creativity but they are not a substitute for either of them.

Without the assistance of charts, assignments tend to be made in terms of managerial perceptions of existing situations and not in terms of planned-for conditions. The process flow designs are reactive to circumstances and not proactive to opportunities. Updating plans for processes grants a degree of control over circumstances that are dynamically changing. The charts are information support systems that provide a concrete means for analysis and improvement.

Orders that produce learning about a new process (routing, equipment, skills, and training) can help the company develop competitive advantages. Embodying new technology in a process chart is equivalent to gaining competitive leverage.

Less dramatic, but of great importance to individual firms, are discoveries that lead to the conversion of a batch-type process into an intermittent flow shop. Discoveries that permit a firm to set up jobs in minutes that used to take hours, and ways to bring new products to market in months instead of years, are exciting opportunities for OM. All such major improvements stem from having a deep insight into the present processes, which enable the invention of a much better process.

If it turns out that several managers have differing views as to which orders, customers, and processes are important, the discrepancies should be addressed. There are methods for resolving the differences between multiple decision makers. One of the most used is a policy statement from the CEO or the president.

Distinguishing between orders, knowing which orders are more important than others, and why they are more important, is vital to achieving optimal process management. If, as is generally believed, important orders should go before less important orders, then agreement must exist as to what is important to the process managers and to other managers of the firm. Because they have different objectives, sales and process managers often do not see eye-to-eye on what is important. The systems viewpoint can help resolve this quandary.

A particular customer's order might be given top priority and assigned a preferred sequence by marketing. Process managers bristle at the notion that an order already in progress should be stopped and bumped. Major dislocations can arise that require two setups for one order. Difficult cleanups can occur when a new order is pushed in front of other orders that are waiting. The sequence of setups can increase costs greatly.

There usually will be agreement that orders that have large revenues are important. Often such orders will involve large unit volumes. Big orders are likely to be more important than orders that have small volumes. On the other hand, products that have high price tags and ample margins are likely to be more important than products that have low-profit value.

Life-time value of customers: The sum of expenditures by the average customer over the total period of time that the customer will purchase.

Total profit per order will not suffice as a measure of either order or customer importance. Major customers can place occasional orders for low-profit items. Most job shops associate the value of the customer with the importance of the order. The expected **life-time value of customers** would be a better measure of order importance, if it can be estimated. The investment in process analysis and improvement is justified when it lowers costs and improves quality for valuable customers.

6-3e The Use of Process Charts for Improvements

Process charts can be used to achieve an optimal layout for the factory floor, warehouse, or office. They permit measures of the effects of switching machines and people to alternative locations. A common objective is to minimize total transport—the sum of the number of units moved between adjacent workstations, multiplied by the transport distances—for frequently run jobs. If the weight or size is important, that can be factored in as total pounds or cubic feet moved. The right measure can determine when it would be sensible to alter the process by relocating workstations.

Shigeo Shingo, one of the most important founders of Japanese manufacturing methods, stated, "The prosperity of a resource-poor country like Japan rests solely on the high quality of its labor. Therefore, wasting labor on non-value-added work like transportation must be rejected. In fact, transportation should be seen as a grievous sin."[2]

In addition to transportation, there is a need to consider other important process functions and characteristics. These include the work configuration and the technology of the process being used, the inspection methodology, quality procedures, and delays that occur as a result of the interaction between supply (process) and demand (orders).

Process charts bring up the possibility of replacing older, larger, and slower machines with newer, smaller ones having faster processing rates. If the proper machines are chosen to be replaced, this could decrease the size of the waiting lines, also called *queues* or *work in process* (WIP). The WIP that forms between any two processing locations can be a profit drain. Decreasing queue length results in space saving, which can be important for reasons other than just the freed-up space.

6-3f New Orders

Process flowcharts for job shops should be drawn up for new orders, parts that have not been made in the shop before. Job shops vary with respect to the percent of orders regularly repeated. Most experience a high level of new orders. For small new jobs, the process charting is informal, even casual, whereas for large jobs greater care is taken in determining the routing and other particulars.

The custom shop does not experience the conflict of orders waiting for facilities and skills. There are only a few orders in the shop at any one time. Work is one-of-a-kind, so process repetitions are minimal. Therefore, process planning does not provide economic benefits. Further, reorders are nearly zero. This does not mean that it would not be helpful for a custom shop to develop process flowcharts. Such charts can help if the entrepreneurs of the custom shop wish to move toward a job shop, eventually processing large batches of work.

Many process flowcharts will be found on file in the job shop. This is a reflection of the fact that repeat orders are common, and the mainstay of the business consists of a catalog of parts that can be reordered. Most new work eventually joins the catalog of existing products.

New batch work interacts with the process flows of existing products. Scheduling conflicts between the newly received orders and older orders that already are on the shop floor must be avoided. Learning curves for new products include start-up problems with fixtures, jigs, software, and other tools that are used for the first time. Start-up problems are time drains. Pre-planning by use of process charts can help avoid blocking the use of equipment for which other jobs are waiting.

Overall, the use of process charts can improve operations in the job shop. They provide economic benefits by helping prioritize orders, eliminate conflicts, decrease waiting times, reduce traffic blockages, avoid bottlenecks, and minimize waste for repetitive activities.

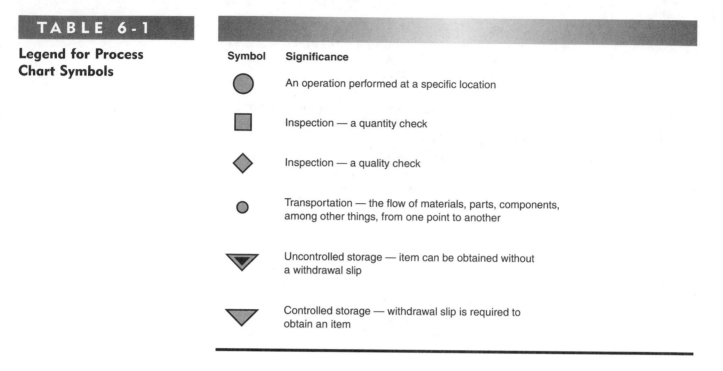

TABLE 6-1		
Legend for Process Chart Symbols	**Symbol**	**Significance**
	●	An operation performed at a specific location
	■	Inspection — a quantity check
	◆	Inspection — a quality check
	○	Transportation — the flow of materials, parts, components, among other things, from one point to another
	▽	Uncontrolled storage — item can be obtained without a withdrawal slip
	▼	Controlled storage — withdrawal slip is required to obtain an item

6-4 PROCESS CHARTS WITH SEQUENCED ACTIVITY SYMBOLS

The six symbols explained in Table 6-1 are the American National Standard symbols for Process Charts (ANSI Y15.3M-1979) published by the American Society of Mechanical Engineers (ASME). They were reaffirmed in 1986 and withdrawn in 1994 by the ASME. Although first set over 50 years ago, these symbols are no longer regulated because of the growth in types of processes, the need to encourage flexibility, and the impact of computerization of process analysis and redesign.

Figure 6-2 shows the "original" process chart for air conditioner chassis that move through a series of uncontrolled storages and transports until assembly. All of the symbols from Table 6-1 are displayed on each line of the chart. Only one symbol can be chosen for each line.

As shown by the process chart in Figure 6-2, the path used to transport air conditioner chassis from the press shop storage to the assembly area is long and circuitous. The distance that must be traveled between the press shop and the assembly building is about one football field in length. The chassis are moved to weekly storage, then to daily storage. From the daily storage they are moved to assembly every hour. This closely approximates just-in-time arrivals at assembly, but there are a lot of stops in between.

The process starts with uncontrolled storage and by means of transport moves to another storage, and so forth. A line connects the correct activity symbol for each row of the "original" process where "original" means that it is the existing process.

Various measures in the summary box describe the sequential list of activities along the connected pathway. There is the sum of the number of activities (eight). The total transport distance is 300 feet. In a manufacturing example, the length of time required for each unit of the order to go from the start of the process to its finish would be calculated and shown. This is the cycle time, C, which is an important process parameter.

The existing (original) process is analyzed and then redesigned as an improved process. Figure 6-3 represents the "improved" process. Steps 2 through 6 are removed by eliminating both the weekly and the daily storage bank. Instead, a new step 2 is added, as shown in Figure 6-3.

Process Chart

Process Chart	Original	Analysis
Job Name	Air Conditioner	
Part Name	Chassis	
Charted by	PS	

Date Charted 1/24/04
Part Number CH20

FIGURE 6-2
"Original" Process Chart

	○	◇	■	○	▽	▽	Total	Distance
Original	1	1	0	3	3	0	8	300'
Improved								
Difference								

Quantity	Distance	Process Symbols	Explanation
		○ ◇ ■ ○ ▽ ▽	Press shop storage
		○ ◇ ■ ○ ▽ ▽	Truck moves chassis*
		○ ◇ ■ ○ ▽ ▽	Weekly buffer
		○ ◇ ■ ○ ▽ ▽	Truck moves chassis**
		○ ◇ ■ ○ ▽ ▽	Daily bin
		○ ◇ ■ ○ ▽ ▽	Forklift truck***
		○ ◇ ■ ○ ▽ ▽	Assembled every hour
		○ ◇ ■ ○ ▽ ▽	Inspected every hour
		○ ◇ ■ ○ ▽ ▽	
		○ ◇ ■ ○ ▽ ▽	
		○ ◇ ■ ○ ▽ ▽	
		○ ◇ ■ ○ ▽ ▽	
		○ ◇ ■ ○ ▽ ▽	
		○ ◇ ■ ○ ▽ ▽	

*	4 times per week to the weekly buffer
**	Once a day from weekly buffer to daily bin
***	Hourly to assembly from the daily bin

This "proposed" process chart eliminates interim storage and moves the chassis directly to assembly. A heavy-duty, all-weather, covered conveyor is built between the two buildings to do this. A new opening is needed in the solid wall of the assembly building.

Press shop operations now can be synchronized to match assembly timing. The new distance that the conveyor will travel is about 80 feet. Transport distance is decreased by about 73 percent. The small trucks and forklift trucks are eliminated. Instead of eight activities, there are only four. Space is freed up. With continuous improvement, there may be even better numbers to report in the future.

FIGURE 6-3
"Proposed" Process Chart

Process Chart ___Proposed___ Analysis
Job Name ___Air Conditioner___   Date Charted ___1/30/04___
Part Name ___Chassis___   Part Number ___CH20___
Charted by ___PS___

	◯	◇	▢	○	▼	▽	Total	Distance
Original	1	1	0	3	3	0	8	300'
Improved	1	1	0	1	1	0	4	80'
Difference	0	0	0	-2	-2	0	-4	-220'

Quantity	Distance	Process Symbols	Explanation
		◯ ◇ ▢ ○ ▼ ▽	Press shop storage
	80 feet	◯ ◇ ▢ ○ ▼ ▽	Conveyor moves chassis*
		◯ ◇ ▢ ○ ▼ ▽	Assembled every hour
		◯ ◇ ▢ ○ ▼ ▽	Inspected every hour
		◯ ◇ ▢ ○ ▼ ▽	
		◯ ◇ ▢ ○ ▼ ▽	
		◯ ◇ ▢ ○ ▼ ▽	
		◯ ◇ ▢ ○ ▼ ▽	
		◯ ◇ ▢ ○ ▼ ▽	
		◯ ◇ ▢ ○ ▼ ▽	

* Transfer rate to assembly is 1 chassis every 2 minutes

6-4a Computer-Aided Process Planning (CAPP)

The ASME no longer sets the standard for the symbols. Process charting has become less regulated and more computerized. Many companies prefer to select symbols that suit their own purposes. There is increased use of process charts to get an overview, which can be accomplished better by using fewer symbols. In Figure 6-1, the chart form is simpler, and only three of the six symbols in Table 6-1 are used to provide the kind of useful information that can be captured in computer form for **computer-aided process planning.**

Computer-aided process planning: Application of computer software to evaluate the performance of a process.

For medium- and large-sized job shops, found in such industries as auto parts and paints, software is available to assist in process planning.[3] There also are factory simulations available from various software companies that examine the effects of using various process plans. These kinds of software will create process charts that permit analysis and redesign that take into account many processes moving simultaneously through the plant. Queues, bottlenecks and other interference can be altered by changing the timing of processes as well as by redesigning equipment assignments.

CAPP and factory floor simulations allow alternatives to be tested in pursuit of continual improvement, a goal of process planning. Benchmarking better processes, in other companies or divisions of the same company, should be brought into play if possible. Anheuser-Busch compares the process performance of all of its breweries on a regular basis. This is part of an ongoing process of continual improvement (CI).

6-4b Creating Process Charts

The various process charts should explicitly reflect everything that the process has to do with the cost of goods sold, cash flow, profit margins, productivity, and value-adding transformations. This requires:[4]

1. Stating the exact materials to be used and in the precise amounts that will be consumed. Inventory records indicate purchasing sources. This step provides supply chain information, which links the producer's process with its suppliers. New materials provide an opportunity to improve the process.

2. Noting the times required at every process step including storage and delays, transit, operations, quality control, and inspections. Productivity measures are available from this step; bottlenecks can be identified and methods improved.

3. Indicating the explicit spatial movement patterns of each part as it is transported from place to place within the plant or the office. Plant layout determines the flow patterns. Traffic problems are related to layout. Transport time and cost are to be minimized subject to plant design constraints.

4. Specifying technological transformations that are the fundamental steps of the process. Materials are transformed; information is converted; people and cargo are transported. New technology offers an opportunity to improve the process.

5. Defining the conformance standards for acceptance or rejection of work in process and finished goods is part of process management. Inspection and quality control protocols are indicated on the process charts.

6. Being able to access process charts for each of the various part numbers and products that have been made in the shop. Frequently run products should be kept up-to-date and receive continuous improvement efforts. Less frequently run products are worth cataloging. A new order can be received that uses a process similar to one that was previously charted. This step advocates creating an encyclopedia of all the processes that have ever been done and that might need to be repeated. It reflects the extent of the product line. Process charts can be drawn up for products, parts, and services that constitute potentials for future work. This can be an important systems link between operations and marketing.

7. Knowing how to assign or ship finished product that conforms to quality standards. This step provides supply chain data that links the producer's process with those of its customers.

8. Understanding that process flow-charting is equally applicable for manufacturing and service applications. In the latter case, it can be used to systematize service processes. The symbols need to be changed to conform to the service. For example, computer programmers use their own special set of symbols to characterize information processes.

6-4c Reengineering (REE): Starting from Scratch to Redesign Work Processes

Process redesign can take place in two ways. There is the method of continuous incremental improvements, which the Japanese call "kaizen" and apply to quality enhancement.[5] An alternative is **reengineering**—starting with a clean sheet of paper to redesign the process.[6]

Starting from scratch (zero-based planning) is not necessarily a requirement when new orders are received. Many organizations look for similarities with past orders for which process charts, tools and software, quality conformance standards, and experience with the process flows already exist.

There is a trade-off between zero-based planning and incremental improvement planning. Starting from scratch delays new order processing. It demands the use of the scarce time of process managers for planning instead of for turning out the product and shipping it to the customer. On the other hand, trying to adapt an old process for a new product usually creates suboptimal processes.

This is not always the case. If the degree of similarity between the old order and the new one is high, then there is an opportunity to use the existing process and improve upon it for the adaptation. Some analysis is needed before making that decision.

Although these are two different methods—continual improvement versus starting from scratch—when properly done, they both result in a new process flowchart. The decision about which way is best depends upon management's willingness to use short-term instead of long-term goals.

In some shops, there is a knee-jerk reaction where orders for new products automatically raise the question, "What is most like this?" If there are strong similarities with prior work, the process charts from the close parallel are used to create the new process charts. Often, exact copies are made.

Why reinvent the wheel? This is a misleading rationale. The wheel is constantly being reinvented. Hard rubber tires replaced wooden wheels. R.W. Thomson invented the pneumatic tire. J. B. Dunlop developed the tire industry. Vulcanization (heating rubber with sulfur in a mold) gave rubber the required physical properties, but synthetic rubber tires were a later development. Radial-ply tires replaced the older bias-ply design with better wear and reduced blowouts. Invention of the wheel has not stopped; the design of new wheels is continuous. What did not need to be reinvented was the idea of a circular wheel used for cars, airplanes, and trucks; what needed to be reinvented was how that wheel was to be made.

The idea of starting with a clean sheet of paper is appealing because it allows process managers to create improvements based on changes in technology. New people may have come on board with ideas for innovations that had occurred to no one previously. Different suppliers might contribute insights that had not been previously sought.

Changes in materials can significantly alter processes. Some interesting substitutions have taken place in different industries. A quick sampling includes steel in radial tires, vinyl in windshields, plastics in auto parts, aluminum for cans, paper for milk cartons. and computer diskettes for paper.

Companies that are doing well have the time and money to take the longer view and go for major redesign. Companies under the gun do not feel that they have the necessary resources. Even if a firm must opt for the short-term approach, awareness of its options is better. After all, decisions based on instinct are better than decisions by default.

6-5 PROCESS LAYOUT CHARTS

The office or factory floor plan is often used to decide where to locate the computer, various machines, conveyors, and storage. The floor plan shows the size and configuration of the work space and additional details such as the locations of doors, windows, elevators, and closets. Three-dimensional drawings are used when the height of ceilings is important.

Reengineering (REE): Starting from scratch to redesign the process.

Process Chart ___Original___ Analysis
Job Name ___Air Conditioner___
Part Name ___Chassis___
Charted by ___PS___

Date Charted ___1/24/04___
Part Number ___CH20___

Assembly Building

30 units/hr.

Assembly Operations

Press Shop

Press Shop Storage

2,100 units

240 units

Daily bin — 8 hrs.

Weekly Buffer

1,200

$$\begin{array}{r} 1,920 \\ 180 \\ \hline 2,100 \end{array}$$

FIGURE 6-4
"Original" Process Flow Layout

Among the reasons for detailing spatial dimensions are to:

1. Calculate the distances that parts will be transported.

2. Choose the best means for transporting parts—by hand, truck, or conveyor.

3. Be certain that there is clearance for large parts.

4. Understand the kind of space the process requires, including space for machines and people as well as tools and work-in-process storage space.

5. Understand the spatial aspects of what can be done to improve the process.

Especially with regard to the largest repetitive batch jobs, it is usual to trace out the paths on the floor plan. It then is possible to improve the process layout. This ties the use of *process flow layout diagrams* together with the process charts for analysis already introduced in Figures 6-2 and 6-3.

Figure 6-4 is the physical description and layout of the "original" method for moving air conditioner chassis from press shop storage to the assembly building.

Figure 6-5 illustrates the new arrangement in the "proposed" process flow layout chart.

Compare Figures 6-4 and 6-5. The reduction in physical distance is immediately evident by comparing the process flow layout charts. This comparison illustrates how the layout diagrams can assist in making flow process improvements. The cost of the structural modifications to allow the conveyor's entry into the assembly building must be taken into account.

FIGURE 6-5
"Proposed" Process
Flow Layout

A wall has been broken through that yields direct conveyor access to the assembly function. The altered process flow is shown in Figure 6-5. As was known from the process chart analyses, transport distance is decreased markedly, and space is freed up at the cost of structural change. The revised process is much closer to deliveries as needed or just-in-time systems.

6-6 ANALYSIS OF OPERATIONS

The process can be viewed as a total flow system. The activities that make up the flow are called the *operations*. Step by step, from start to finish, the term *operations* is generically employed to describe all operations on materials with machines in the factory, the office, the bank, etc.

The term *operations* often is applied to every kind of activity done in a process, but it is always applied to production transformations, which are the circles in Figure 6-1. People who provide services to other people often are called *operators*. Inspections for both quality and quantity are referred to as *operations*. So is the action of storing raw materials and work-in-process in a warehouse or bin. Similarly, the term is used to describe the transportation of batches between workstations, or cargo between marine terminals, and people between airports.

Operations can be decomposed into detailed elements such as searching for a part, reaching for it, grasping and turning it. This level of detail is generally reserved for discussion about time studies and human resources management. When changes are made to one or a few operations, then continuous improvement is the method being used. This is the operations level of process change as compared to the systems level.

Most process analyses start by looking at the operations level and noting that certain operations embedded in the processes are more likely than others to provide a basis for improvement. There also are typical transports and inspections that can be eliminated without losing delivery advantages and quality.

Improvements that are made to the individual operations of the flow process chart usually start with physical operations (the circles in Figure 6-1). Each of these operations can be analyzed separately for improvement. A new fixture might be designed that decreases cycle time or improves quality. A new cutting tool might be used to decrease machining time.

6-6a Value Analysis for Purchased Parts or Services

Value analysis (VA) is a systematic approach to investigating the functions served by purchased parts, their value to the final product, and whether they are being sourced at the best possible price and quality. It makes sense that high-dollar volume purchased parts receive attention, but often relatively unimportant parts shed light on great potentials for improvement. For value analysis, parts and services are equally applicable.

The function of a part was identified as fastening two parts together. A rivet was being used. VA asks its primary questions: Is this rivet necessary? and What value does it add? After discussion, the answers were clear: The two parts being joined could be cast as one part; it would be stronger and less expensive to make. Thus, questioning the need for the inexpensive rivet led to an improved product at a lower cost.

Value analysis also queries if there are other sources for parts. It encourages reexamining make versus buy options. It examines the use of alternative materials that could provide equal or better properties at equal or lower costs. Too tight tolerances can be relaxed, and process steps, such as an inspection, can be eliminated by making it right the first time. As part of the VA procedure, employees and suppliers are asked for their suggestions for improvement.

Value analysis has been used by many companies and governmental agencies to lower costs without impairing quality. A number of organizations stress the aspect of a methodical search for alternative materials to be used in place of the present materials. This is because technological change has been producing new materials in different industries. Awareness of applicability requires searching in places not normally accessed by designers and purchasing agents.

In the late 1940s, a large number of new materials began to appear, such as special plastics, composites, ceramics, and metal alloys. Value analysis was perfectly suited to the determination of whether the substitution of these new materials could lower costs and/or improve the performance of specific products.

There are many examples of the successful use of value analysis procedures. Performed under various names, VA is readily identified by the persistent use of a set of questions:

- What functions are served that justify the use of the present materials and what value do they have?
- What alternative materials might be used?
- What are the disadvantages of the alternative materials?
- What advantages (values) accrue by switching to an alternative?
- After reevaluation, are the present materials still the best ones to use?

When questions cannot be answered, appropriate assignments are made within the value analysis group or team. After researching the unanswered questions, the group meets again and goes through the same set of questions, making comparisons between present and proposed materials. All qualities and costs are compared.

Value analysis is part of the systems approach, enabling cross-boundary queries in quest of superior materials and services. It is apparent that many factors play a part in material choices. To illustrate, the marketing advantages of dent-free plastic door panels played an important part in the design of materials for the Saturn. Crash tests for safety are an integral part of material choices for autos, so the testing laboratories must be represented.

Value analysis (VA):
Systematic investigation of purchased parts decisions.

Major savings in headlight design were made by Ford and in the front grille design by Buick. The U.S. Navy recorded many success stories in its earliest support for the use of VA on all kinds of Navy equipment.

Value analysis comparisons between present and proposed materials are facilitated by using process chart analyses. The analysis of materials often has side benefits of improving specific operations. A furniture manufacturer replaced some wood parts with plastic. This produced major cost savings and quality improvement in the woodworking process, which traditionally does not consider plastic alternatives. Value analysis provided a nontraditional approach. In the same way, the elimination of paper trails in factories and offices, and the replacement with bar codes, optical scanners, and computers, has changed fundamental process procedures resulting in great improvements in quality, inventory, and production scheduling.

6-6b Other Process Activities

A process chart can be used to compare the present method for a quantity check (a square in Figure 6-1) with a revised method of inspection. Inspection operations for quantity checks are often related to withdrawing materials from the storeroom, assuring that an order is properly filled, and paying on a piecework basis. The proposal might be to replace a person with a scanner. Alternatively, the proposal might be to postpone the quantity check until a later stage in the process.

An inspection that provides a quality check (a diamond in Figure 6-1) can be postponed or eliminated. The process chart provides both visual and quantitative data that summarizes the pros and cons of making the change. Recent best practice assigns responsibility for inspections to the worker making the part or providing the service. Quantity and quality checks can often be made together.

Improvements can be made to transport operations (a little circle in Figure 6-1). The recorded savings in Figure 6-3 were due to a creative idea about cutting unnecessary transportation. It is noteworthy that, in this case, the transport function was singled out of the overall process flow for attention.

Improvements can be made to storage operations. The air conditioner press shop to assembly example works well here, too. Storage was eliminated in the proposed process flow layout charts (Figures 6-4 and 6-5). These were uncontrolled storages (a little dark triangle inside a bigger triangle—both with apex down—in Figure 6-1). This example also illustrates a case in which storage functions have been plucked out of the overall flow process to receive special attention.

With controlled storage (a triangle with apex down as shown in Figure 6-1), a withdrawal slip is required to obtain an item. The control feature is used to protect against pilferage and to ensure that a known level of inventory exists. However, controlled storage is more expensive to administer than uncontrolled storage, where an item can be obtained without a stock request form. The loss of inventory control in the uncontrolled case can increase the out-of-stock, order, and carrying costs. These additional costs must be compared with the savings obtained by removing administration of the storage.

6-7 INFORMATION PROCESSING

Figure 6-6 presents another application of a process flow layout diagram. It is the present floor plan schematic used for the information processing backroom of the Market Research Store. The pattern of movement that is shown is for the three most frequent kinds of market research reports the company sells. These are known as R_1, R_2, and R_3.

There is much movement back and forth, and there is crisscrossing of lines as sections of the research reports move out of initial process planning where work assignments are made. These are followed by data entry at dispersed terminals (T). Analysts are all grouped together. Sometimes additional data analysis is done at computer workstations (W). Approval must be obtained from various supervisors (S), who also are dispersed. Printers and copy machines (C) are scattered about the room. The assembly of final reports includes collating and binding. The manager oversees the entire process.

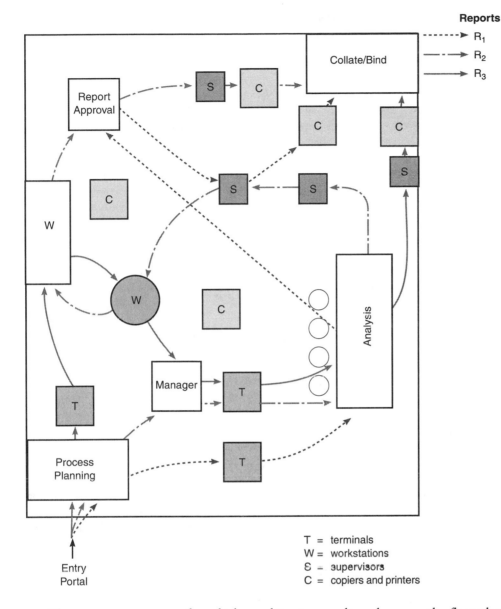

FIGURE 6-6
"Original" Information Processing

T = terminals
W = workstations
S = supervisors
C = copiers and printers

There are too many transfers of jobs resulting in more lines drawn on the floor plan than necessary. The present data transfer process appears to be chaotic and confused. *Information should be handled once and not repeatedly.* That is a standard axiom for information systems.

Figure 6-6 can have other jobs overlaid. Because the various orders will have different flow patterns, the number of lines will further increase. Simplification of the information transfer process for the Market Research Store can be achieved by standardizing some of the functions on the flow process layout diagram. Process improvement calls for reducing the complexity of the transaction paths; Figure 6-7 presents an abstract schematic diagram for a plan, which appears to reduce the confusion.

The amount of floor space is the same as in Figure 6-6, but the layout is different. In the proposed version, data entry, common to all reports, is done on a flow shop line as the first function in the shop. The data entry function will be engineered to be as efficient and cost effective as possible with data checking being computerized and automated. Analysis of each report is unique and done separately (as indicated in Figure 6-7 by the vertical lines marked R_1, R_2, R_3). At the final stages, all reports join a flow shop for printing, copying, collating, and binding.

The frenetic process flow pattern has been simplified by removing the supervisors' desks and by making each individual responsible for checking their own work at each

FIGURE 6-7
Proposed Process Flow Layout for the Market Research Store Information Processing

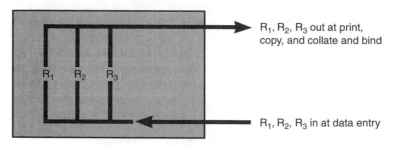

R_1, R_2, R_3 out at print, copy, and collate and bind

R_1, R_2, R_3 in at data entry

stage of the process. This organizational procedure increasingly is being used with success for improving the output quality of processes.

Companies everywhere have begun to employ this approach, disseminating responsibility and accountability to the people who are doing the work. Such empowerment removes bosses, chiefs, supervisors, and inspectors from the approval process. This smooths process flows by removing interruptions. It allows problems to be spotted before they would otherwise be found and puts the responsibility for correction in the hands of those who can make the corrections.

The information processing backroom of the Market Research Store has installed flow shop procedures for functions that are identical, no matter what the specific nature of the report. By using universal bar codes and optical scanners, data entry might eventually be fed automatically into the correct data bank for analysts' use. Assembling reports, which takes place at the end of the process, also is controlled by bar codes. This is similar to auto assembly, which uses bar codes to route parts so that all of the right components come together for a specific order.

Other ideas that could be tried for the modified process include the development of networking ability so that each person can transmit screens of data to every other person's screen in the room. This technology facilitates rapid sharing of information and decisions. Data entry can be accomplished by part-time employees working at home. Analysts also can work at home. Materials completed for the reports can be transferred from laptop and desktop PCs located anywhere to the "information factory" in the operations backroom of the Market Research Store. The backroom prints, assembles, and distributes the reports. Major process and technology improvements of these sorts can give the MRS a succession of competitive advantages.

6-8 PROCESS CHANGEOVERS (SETUPS)

Changeovers: Steps that need to be taken to prepare equipment and people to do a new job.

Put-away: End step before the next setup, make ready cycle.

Changeovers are the steps that need to be taken to prepare equipment and people to do a new job. The term *setup* is usually applied to the start-up of a new job, which means the cleanup from the old one. For process analysis, it is best to separate these two steps and deal with setup and **put-away** (cleanup) as two activities.

Of critical importance to job shop processes are the changeover costs and times. These are often treated as being synonymous so that mention of cost implies time and vice versa. Thus, the generic term *setup* is often used to include time and cost and everything that has to be done to change the process from one product to another.

Setup costs are often proportional to setup times. However, the relationship breaks down when a lot of technology is devoted to allowing very rapid setups. Then there is a cost of not using this technology for the purposes for which it was intended, namely, short runs of many designs that fit within the family of parts (technology group) that can be made on this equipment. Further, when the setup can take place off-line, it can take longer and still cost much less than when it must interrupt the production process.

Machines have to undergo cleanup from prior jobs and then be reset. People have to shift jobs, often moving from one location to another. The learning curve comes into play every time operators bring a new order online, which also is part of the changeover process.

Changeovers are a special form of operations. They occur because shifting gears to convert the process to deal with new orders requires taking the gearbox apart. Imagine the impact on driving if this were required to shift the gears of a car. Further, the analogy requires that many different cars be involved. Thus, a manual for changing over the gearboxes is needed for hundreds or even thousands of different car models. Each changeover is equivalent to a new order in the shop.

Leaving the analogy and returning to the job shop environment, envision this script: a "good" customer orders a few units of an item, which takes a couple of minutes to make, but the setup time is half a day. Here are numbers to consider:

Cost per unit	=	$0.80
Setup cost	=	$800
Order size	=	4 units
Lot size	=	number of units to be determined

To be realistic, assume that the setup cost includes the cost of labor of two people working four hours each and the cost of lost production related to four hours of downtime of two machines.

This item costs less than a dollar if the setup cost is ignored, but if the setup cost is amortized over the four items, they each cost $200.80. One additional assumption is that this item is reordered, from time to time, by various customers. What options are open to the process manager as he or she goes about preparing the production schedule?

The most apparent option is to run a larger number of items than four. If 40 items are produced, then the cost per item is reduced to $20.80, which is still far from providing a reason to celebrate. Running a lot size of 400 provides a cost per unit of $2.80, which might be reasonable from the customer's point of view.

6-8a Single-Minute Exchange of Dies (SMED)

Another option is the one that Taiichi Ohno of Toyota Motor Manufacturing U.S.A. Inc. took. He asked for, and got, a revolutionary reduction of setup times.

Before describing the character of that revolution, it is interesting to note the historical events that triggered the modification. Taiichi Ohno asked Shigeo Shingo, who was at that time with the JMA,[7] to cut setup times for a particular operation from four hours to three minutes. Shingo, who was an advocate of cutting all setup times to less than ten minutes, was shocked by Ohno's "utterly unreasonable directive"[8] into totally rethinking the anatomy of changeovers.

"In developing the idea of the **single-minute exchange of die (SMED)** setup, I blasted a tunnel through the mountain, so to speak, dramatically shortening the time it took to move between processes or operations. Cutting 4-hour setup changeovers to three minutes simply blasted out of existence the band-aid approach of economic lot sizes," Shingo wrote.[9]

The SMED system for cutting changeover times is based on the recognition that there are setup steps that can be done without shutting the machine down. Examples of SMED setups can be found in the activities of the pit crew, which changes the racing car's tires without shutting the car off. Changeover time in the pit is part of the racing team's performance.

Watching setup teams do their work, it will be seen that some steps could have been done before turning off the machine and starting the setup. Also, by redesigning setup procedures, it is possible to increase the number of such steps.

With this in mind, here are four steps that lead to cost (and time) reductions for setups:

1. Recognize those setup tasks that can be done when the machine is running. These tasks, which can be done before the machine is shut down, are called external setup elements. External setup elements can be done while the machine is working on another order, or while it is running the new order.
2. Study those setup tasks that can only be done when the machine is shut down. These are called internal setup elements.

Single-minute exchange of dies (SMED): Setups that take less than a minute.

For racing cars, the activities of the pit crew must be perfectly meshed. Every step is clockwork. What may seem to be minor errors often turn out to lose races. An example of SMED setups and changeovers is the functioning of the pit crew, which changes a racing car's tires without shutting down the engine. See http://www.davehawk.com/nascar/july01/nascarjuly01a.html.

3. Redesign and convert as many internal setup tasks as possible into external category tasks.

4. Each and every setup element for an operation should be scrupulously analyzed and examined in search of continuous improvement.

It used to be that setup times were larger for machines that worked faster. The trade-off for paying more for setting up was the lower per unit costs of the outputs. Although this relationship still generally holds, the application of SMED concepts reduces the downtime of high-volume equipment by doing much of the setup while the machine is working on another order or the new order.

Was Shingo's insight a special moment in history or inevitable? The same question can be asked about Henry Ford's development of sequenced assembly and Eli Whitney's invention of interchangeable parts. These are all major manufacturing inventions with lots of consequences for operations in general.

Perhaps the "time was right." Alternatively, maybe eventually the inevitable would have occurred. Such speculation does not diminish the contribution or the credit that these inventors deserve.

Further, flexible manufacturing systems can provide rapid built-in changeovers for a specific menu of production items. The SMED concept is substantially assisted by the development of programmable setups, which are enabled by computer-driven mechanical equipment. Robots are a type of programmable setup system that is gaining use globally.

Robots are ideal for rapid-changeover systems. The sound engineering concepts of SMED combine with the programmable capabilities of robotics to bring about a revolution in the engineering mind-set. The old engineering truism that changeover times and costs must increase with the use of volume-efficient equipment is disappearing.

The fact that SMED is having such a major impact on manufacturing makes it easy to overlook the fact that SMED concepts are not limited to manufacturing. The ability to move from one order to another with minimum changeover delay is applicable to many service systems. The restaurant business is filled with changeover costs. Cooking is setup intensive, and dishwashing exemplifies the takedowns and cleanups.

In education, consider the setup times required for each class. Every exam requires someone to write it. Many students must take it, at least enough to pay for the setup costs. Ask a professor about the agony of writing a make-up exam for one or two students who failed to take the scheduled exam. Someone must grade that exam. In travel, think about the setup times to get a cruise ship underway. Finally, consider the question: Are there setup times required to operate a computer? Because the setup times can be substantial, every business that relies on computers can gain advantages by decreasing setup times.

In summary, setup times are vital process parameters. The reduction of changeover times can dramatically improve the competitive advantages of a company. Consequently, this is one of the most promising methods for process improvement in the present operations environment. As setup times are reduced to minutes and then seconds, the economies of scope come into being. This means that variety can be achieved without a penalty. With increased variety, marketing, operations, and distribution have to coordinate their activities. A real systems effort is called for because increased variety adds more opportunity and complexity to challenge management.

6-8b Machine-Operator Charts: Process Synchronization

Another process chart that deserves attention is the **machine-operator chart (MOC)**. The MOC provides a means for visualizing the way in which workers can tend machines over time. It encourages visual analysis of the interaction of operators with the machines they operate. It permits evaluation of the efficiency of the relationship. The MOC permits intelligent assignments of operators to machines and allows for synchronization of operations (and operators) because time-matching is inherent in the charting.

The time that operators spend tending machines often includes setup times, which interrupt production. Product output is stopped while tool alignments are made and fix-

Machine-operator chart (MOC): Means for visualizing the way in which workers (can) tend machines over time.

FIGURE 6-8
Machine-Operator Chart—Original Process

tures and jigs are adjusted. Replacing the paper for the fax or the inkjet cartridge for the printer are other illustrations of machine-operator interactions that stop production. The cleanup activity is such a major fact of life for many processes that there is irony in the fact that setup has come to mean the whole changeover process including cleanup.

Figure 6-8 shows a machine-operator chart in which all of the *make readys* and *put-aways* are designed to be internal setup elements. The machine and the operator are both idle 50 percent of the time. In 16 time units, the operator is idle 4 + 4 = 8, and the machine is idle 2 + 4 + 2 = 8. Operator and machine are badly coordinated.

As an example, a part to be painted is mounted in the painting cabinet while the paint nozzles are shut off. The spray-paint nozzles are activated and then shut off so the part can be removed and a new one mounted.

In Figure 6-9, process designers have found a way to mount the next part while the prior one is being removed. The operator makes ready the next part to be painted while the prior part is being painted. The one exception is the first unit, which is loaded before the start-up of the paint cabinet.

The operator has externalized the make-ready element but is still constrained by the internal setup characteristics of the put-aways, which means that the machine must be turned off to remove the part. This partial SMED-like improvement has decreased the

Time	Operator	Machine	Time
0	Make ready 1st unit	Idle	0
2	Idle	Working 1st unit	2
4	Make ready 2nd unit		4
6	Put away 1st unit	Idle	6
8	Idle	Working 2nd unit	8
10	Make ready 3rd unit		10
12	Put away 2nd unit	Idle	12
14	Idle	Working 3rd unit	14
16	Make ready 4th unit		16
18	Put away 3rd unit	Idle	18
20			20

FIGURE 6-9
Machine-Operator Chart—Improved Process

FIGURE 6-10
Machine-Operator
Chart—Ideal Process

Time	Operator	Machine	
0	Make ready 1st unit	Idle	0
2	Make ready 2nd unit		2
4		Working 1st unit	4
	Idle		
6	Put away 1st unit		6
8		Working 2nd unit	8
	Make ready 3rd unit		
10	Put away 2nd unit		10
12		Working 3rd unit	12
	Make ready 4th unit		
14			14
16	Put away 3rd unit	Working 4th unit	16
	Make ready 5th unit		
18	Put away 4th unit		18
20		Working 5th unit	20
	Make ready 6th unit		
22			22

Total productive maintenance (TPM) can head off troubles by using proper diagnostic systems. The illustration shows seismic testing at a gas plant. Severe earth tremors can disrupt service, but steps can be taken to minimize damage. As another example, air traffic control equipment must be serviced with a zero breakdown policy to ensure safe landings.

Total productive maintenance (TPM): Rational blend of maintenance alternatives.

Remedial maintenance (RM): Maintenance after failure.

Preventive maintenance (PM): Maintenance performed before failure.

Predictive maintenance (PDM): Maintenance based on knowledge of signs and symptoms that something is likely to go awry in the future.

operator's idle time from 50 percent to 33.33 percent. The same decrease (50 percent to 33.33 percent) applies to the machine's idle time. This ignores the two periods of idle time that are required for the first part to be painted. Continuing with the spray paint example, the part to be painted is loaded onto a fixture while another part is being painted. When the spray unit is shut off to remove the part, the fixture with the next part drops into place in the paint cabinet.

Figure 6-10 depicts the successful application of SMED. Both *make ready* and *put-away* have been converted into external setup capabilities. Once the system is up-and-running, both the operator and the machine are 100 percent utilized.

A continuous circular conveyor enters the painting booth at the front. The part is spray painted as it moves along, leaving the spray booth from the rear. The conveyor circles back to the station outside the paint booth where the operator loads parts onto the conveyor and removes painted parts from it.

6-9   TOTAL PRODUCTIVE MAINTENANCE (TPM)

Total productive maintenance (TPM) is a systematic program to prevent process breakdowns, failures, and stoppages. Process disruptions can be caused by many factors such as poor materials, tool breakage, power failures, and absenteeism.

One important cause of disruption is machine breakdowns, including computer failures. Machine breakdowns can stop a process with large penalties to be paid. TPM is a systems approach to preventing such failures. TPM encompasses preventive maintenance strategies, which service equipment at regularly scheduled intervals. **Remedial maintenance (RM)** is required to repair equipment when failure occurs. **Preventive maintenance (PM)** is repair and replacement at scheduled intervals. The intervals are chosen to make it unlikely that a failure will occur before PM takes place. Partial preventive maintenance (PPM) is incomplete servicing scheduled at regular intervals to decrease the probability of failure and the need for remedial maintenance.

Predictive maintenance (PDM) is based on knowledge of signs and symptoms that something is likely to go awry in the future. A monitor is used for all of the variables that are apt to be tell-tales. For example, if a machine is vibrating more than usual, that may signal that a worn gear needs replacement. For service applications, if a customer has not returned to the supermarket within his or her accustomed buying interval, that might signify that an unregistered complaint has led the person to shop elsewhere. Predictive maintenance can be costly and should be justified by the cost/benefit analysis that indicates repair is possible to avoid high penalties. A variety of POM systems are well-suited to this application. Control charts provide management by exception for important quality variables that could readily include maintenance dimensions. *Poka-yoke* is a Japanese term for a method aimed at preventing production line failures. Control systems that monitor status are broadly applied in both early-stage and aging equipment failures associated with the Weibull (bathtub-type) failure distributions.

Total productive maintenance is a program that addresses all factors that slow down or stop a productive process. If the computer goes down as the bank is about to transfer substantial funds overseas at the end of the day, the interest that would not be earned might well be in the millions. Because of the risk exposure, backup systems would be part of the failure prevention system. This is because computer failures can be costly. TPM programs are absolutely essential when process stoppage is life threatening. Backing up equipment and using redundant systems do not constitute preventive maintenance, but they are TPM strategies.

There are two questions that can help determine how large an expenditure for TPM is reasonable:

1. How vulnerable is the specific process to a breakdown that will slow or stop production output?

2. How costly is the production disruption that will occur?

Job shop machine breakdowns are serious, but they can be finessed in several ways. First, the equipment is general purpose and, therefore, similar machines are available on the same plant floor. Second, the order being processed at the time of breakdown is one of many orders that are being worked on in the shop, so the extent of the disruption is limited.

Nevertheless, a worst-case scenario can occur where the order is already delayed, the customer is important and annoyed, and the breakdown occurs on the only machine that is well-suited for the particular order. An even worse case, discussed next, is stoppage of the flow shop.

When the costs of disruption are extreme, including life threatening, the vulnerability is often addressed by redundancy. That is, two pieces of equipment are used, one for the process and the other as backup. This is a TPM strategy calling for the redesign of the system. The cost of redundancy can be assessed as an alternative to the cost of failure. Used widely by banks, the design of "nonstop computers" (such as those of Tandem, which is now part of Compaq and is serviced by Tandem resellers such as Marshall) is based on duplication of functions, backup of components, and redundancy of circuits. Stratus was another computer designed for high-level carryon. Commercial jets can fly on one engine, but two are provided.

It is useful to note that redesign can mean changing the process methods, that is, the systems being used. It can mean changing the process technology, including substituting other equipment, and/or by using redundant equipment for fail-safe performance.

Consider a ceramic fixture used to hold a unit of work in a heat-treating chamber. Suppose that this fixture shatters every now and then. Because the fixture cannot be replaced with something more durable, and because it is not too costly, the redundancy level that the process manager suggests is six fixtures.

Why did the process manager select six instead of two or three? The answer lies with other factors that determine redundancy levels, including the **lead time (LT)** or amount of time needed to secure a replacement. Lead time starts with recognizing the need for the placement of an order and ends with the receipt of that order. The minimum order size might be six. In this case, assume that the LT is three to four weeks and the supplier is reluctant to produce only one fixture at a time because the setup costs are too high to run one at a time.

Lead time (LT): Interval that elapses between seeing the need for placing an order and receiving the goods or services.

For many machines, redesign is costly, redundancy is affordable, and lead time is short. In these cases, the goals of TPM are achievable by keeping one or more backups in stock and keeping contact with the supplier to make certain that lead times and availability have not changed.

Redesign is used when the cost of failure is high, the probability of a breakdown is too great, and it cannot be lowered by preventive maintenance or better practice. That is another example of total productive maintenance having a broader agenda than even the most dedicated preventive maintenance program.

It is useful to note that the cost of failure (c_f) and the probability of it occurring (p_f) lead to an expected cost of failure:

$$\bar{c}_f = (p_f)(c_f)$$

Redesign is essential when this number is large. It can be a large number, even though p_f is small, if c_f is large. In this regard, it is often stated that $c_f = \infty$ when the cost of life is involved. The expected cost of failure is infinite in this case, and redesign is warranted. Similar concepts and terminology are used to determine optimal levels of preventive maintenance when the expected costs of failure are not excessive.

Total productive maintenance (TPM) is a complete plan to prevent failures of various kinds. It is an across-the-board attack on machine breakdowns. It includes shifting to new technology, which is more reliable. It employs statistical quality control methodology and, based on results, leads to the redesign of systems with planned redundancy.

When these are not required, remedial and preventive maintenance are the remaining options. There are many different levels of preventive precautions that can be taken. The alternative is to wait for a failure and then use remedial maintenance (RM) to repair the problem. The zero-level of preventive maintenance is RM.

TPM addresses two kinds of failures:

1. The first and worst kind of failure stops the process. Remedial maintenance (which is repair) is called for immediately. It is considered a critical failure.

2. The second kind of failure leads to degradation of the system's performance. Repairs are made, but this kind of problem is not critical and tends to reoccur. The total cost of remedial maintenance becomes a large enough figure to command attention.

The cost-effective scenario for each kind of failure is different. In both cases, however, it often turns out that some level of preventive maintenance is warranted.

There is willingness to spend a great deal to prevent a failure if the cost of that particular kind of failure is high. Analysis of alternative strategies for failure prevention include the degree to which failure probabilities can be reduced and the cost of achieving that reduction versus the penalty cost of that failure. The conditions for a relevant trade-off analysis exist.

Figure 6-11 illustrates the relationship between the probability of failure (p_f) and the cost of prevention (c_p). It is seen that as partial preventive maintenance (PPM) moves from remedial maintenance (no preventive maintenance) toward maximum TPM, the probability of failure decreases quickly at first, and then slows down, even though proportionately greater amounts of money are being spent. When warranted, predictive maintenance (PDM) could be factored into the partial preventive maintenance plan. It would provide early-diagnostic remedial steps based on symptoms of failure in place of actual failure.

A power failure in a plant or office constitutes a breakdown of the first kind. Without the backup of a redundant power supply, the ongoing systems will be forced to shut down. To avoid power failure, the processes of the power plant are examined in detail. The intent is to pinpoint the causes and the preconditions of power failures. The techniques that apply are identical to those used for prevention of defective products with TQM and when applying statistical methods of process analysis.

Every potential cause is studied. A maintenance agenda is set up to remedy problems and reduce the probability of failure. Aircraft maintenance programs have been worked out with care and provide an excellent model to copy.

The second type of failure is epitomized by lightbulbs burning out. This kind of failure is seldom critical. There are usually several bulbs to light the space, and as soon as one burnout occurs, remedial maintenance can be employed.

FIGURE 6-11
Probability of Failure as a Function of Cost of Prevention

A plan can be developed for decreasing the number of lightbulbs that need to be replaced at one time, which costs a great deal because each replacement requires a new setup for correction of the fault. The use of one setup to replace all bulbs at the same time, whether or not they have burned out, is worthy of consideration. Families of bulbs belonging to different age groups can be used if markings differentiate to which family each bulb belongs.

One setup to replace all bulbs, burnt out or not, is a good example of the importance of setup theory for process management. The example also underscores the fact that TPM is part of process analysis. Should lightbulbs be replaced as they burn out, or in family groups, or should all bulbs be replaced at a proper interval?

It is generally less expensive to use preventive maintenance than corrective maintenance. A trade-off model should be employed as discussed in the following sections.

6-9a The Preventive Maintenance Strategy

There are 1,000 lightbulbs at risk for failure with rates described as follows. The TPM policy is to replace, all at once, the 1,000 light bulbs 6.5 times a year (every eight weeks). Each replacement entails a cost of $5.00 per bulb and a setup cost of $1,000. For this TPM policy, the total annual cost would be 6.5 (1,000 × $5 + $1,000) = $39,000.

Burned out bulbs are only replaced during the TPM sweep. This could mean that workplace light is not always sufficient. To avoid having insufficient light, there might be a basis for having some extra bulbs installed. The cost of such redundancy is not included in this sample analysis, but it readily could be added.

6-9b The Remedial Maintenance Strategy

The alternative strategy is to replace each bulb as it burns out. That costs $10 per lightbulb. The bulbs are rated as having an expected lifetime of 900 hours. The plant operates two 8-hour shifts seven days per week for a total of 112 hours per week (900 ÷ 112 = 8.0).

This means that on average, every eight weeks all of the lightbulbs will be replaced. Thus, each light bulb must be replaced 6.5 times per year (8 × 6.5 = 52 weeks). On average, 6,500 bulbs burn out each year, and that means the total cost of replacement on a one-by-one basis is $65,000. For this situation, since $65,000 − $39,000 = $26,000, the preventive maintenance strategy has a distinct advantage over remedial maintenance.

If a special (and costly) bulb could be designed to beep two hours before it burned out, a policy of PDM could be used. This knowledge would not save money, so who would buy the costly bulb? Management would buy it if safety factors applied.

6-9c Zero Breakdowns

Just like quality programs designed to achieve zero defectives, TPM can set down goals for zero machine and equipment breakdowns. A breakdown, by definition, is a malfunction. The failure was supposed to be headed off by the preventive maintenance program. A policy of **zero breakdowns** specifies that everything possible will be done to eliminate malfunctions and failures. Air Force One, the President's plane, is serviced with a zero breakdown policy. Most people balance their checkbook with a zero defects goal. On the other hand, baseball scoring assumes that defects will occur. A strikeout is a hitter's defect. On the other hand, a ground ball missed by the shortstop is a defensive error. Runs, hits, and errors are not about to be rewritten by a zero defect policy.

When a failure occurs, it compromises the process, and further analysis is warranted. This includes the possibility that shorter intervals between servicing could head off unscheduled repairs. The extra cost of replacing parts more frequently also can be examined. Preplanning is essential to achieve zero breakdowns as is the case with zero defects.

Cost trade-off models are easy to construct if the cost of an unscheduled repair can be calculated. One factor that needs to be included is the cost of process disruption. Usually this is a large cost, which explains why aggressive total productive maintenance (TPM) programs are viewed with favor by companies that try them out.

6-9d TPM for the Flow Shop

For the flow shop process, the worst-case scenario is when the breakdown stops the line. This occurs when a station along the path of the conveyor ceases being able to function. Unless the prior stations on the line are immediately notified to stop producing, WIP begins to accumulate, forming queues in front of the nonfunctioning machine. To avoid severe congestion and eliminate safety hazards, it usually is necessary to shut down the prior workstations.

This scenario has many costs associated with it. There is the cost of repairing the equipment (remedial maintenance) at the station. The cost of lost production can be considerable. Another cost that often is overlooked is the cost of line start-up, which might require relearning and the production of defectives.

Another kind of flow shop breakdown is when all the equipment stops because of a power failure. The same kind of effect is produced by a failure of the paced conveyor unless the work is suitable for hand carrying or moving by forklift between stations. In addition, some automobile companies empower workers to stop the line when serious problems develop with systems-wide implications. The kind of problems that are systems wide include passing defectives to downstream stations, which wastes their work, complicates repair, and hides the defect.

The severe costs of flow shop stoppages generally guide the choice of an effective complete program of preventive maintenance. This is done after the shift ends or on a weekend when there will be no interference with the maintenance team. These maintenance procedures require similar considerations regarding what is done online and off-line as those that applied to SMED changeover and setup situations. Predictive maintenance is worth consideration if PDM can be installed with a beneficial trade-off of costs and benefits.

The production line is gone over thoroughly, cleaned up, and prepared to run without further maintenance until the next scheduled overhaul. Aircraft receive major preventive maintenance at longer intervals than the more frequently scheduled minor preventive maintenance. The same applies to automobile servicing.

Equipment failure always is an important consideration for process designers. Interdependent serialized production systems that are prone to breakdowns cannot be tolerated. A breakdown anywhere in the chain halts the entire system. If redundant systems with immediate switchovers are not feasible for protection, then it is essential to use TPM, including PDM, to bring the process as near to zero-breakdown levels as possible.

Zero breakdowns: Requires eliminating any and all malfunctions and failures.

SUMMARY

How to analyze and redesign existing processes is the subject of this chapter. It provides information about how to create process charts and process flow layout charts. Process charts trace the present sequence of activity symbols. Process flow layout charts trace the paths of parts on the floor plan. Each can be analyzed leading to process improvements. Then each can show the proposed process side-by-side with the present one. The growing impact of computer-aided process planning is discussed. The use of reengineering (REE), process planning with a clean sheet of paper, is contrasted with continuous improvement. An example of information process analysis is given.

The chapter also includes discussion of SMED (single-minute exchange of dies) methods for decreasing the costs and times required to change over from one process to another. This has become increasingly important as companies strive to offer their customers greater product variety. Machine-operator charts allow synchronization of operator setups with machines. When setup constraints are reduced, major improvements can be made in productivity. Total productive maintenance (TPM) is explained with respect to preventive, predictive, and remedial maintenance strategies. All of these topics add up to a strong competitive ability with respect to the analysis and redesign of processes.

Two Spotlight feature boxes conclude this chapter. These boxes illustrate real applications of the materials in the chatper. See Spotlight 6-1: A Planning Tree of Management Options and Spotlight 6-2: Programming the Web.

KEY TERMS

Best in class
Changeovers
Computer-aided process planning
Lead time (LT)
Lifetime value of customers
Machine-operator chart (MOC)
Predictive maintenance (PDM)

Preventive maintenance (PM)
Process analysis
Process charts
Put-away
Reengineering (REE)
Remedial maintenance (RM)
Setups(s)

Single-minute exchange of dies (SMED)
Time-based management (TBM)
Total productive maintenance (TPM)
Value analysis (VA)
Zero breakdowns

REVIEW QUESTIONS

1. What are the conventional symbols used for process charting? Are there any other activities that make up processes that are not covered by the conventional symbols?

2. What are the distinctions between process charts and process flow layout charts? When should one or the other be chosen?

3. How does process charting apply to job shops? How does it apply to intermittent (short-run) flow shops? How does it apply to long-term, continuous flow shops?

4. What is CAPP and why is it important?

5. How do process charts show the receipt of materials from suppliers as part of the process? How do they show shipments of finished goods to distributors?

6. Why should process charts be drawn up by process managers who are responsible for everything that happens on the production line?

7. Explain the following statement:
   It is unfortunate if process managers are so busy taking care of existing customers that they do not feel they have time to plan for new jobs. Time should be allocated to setting up the systems to routinize the function of developing and improving process charts.

8. Is it sensible and justified that "prized customers" get more time and attention for process charting than others?

9. What are the purposes served by machine-operator charts?

10. How does process analysis aid in the discovery of new ideas?

11. What setup times are required to operate a computer? Describe them. Address the issue of reducing them.

12. TPM programs are absolutely essential when process stoppage is life threatening. Give examples and explain.

PROBLEMS SECTION

Problems Concerned with Process Analysis and Charting

The idea is to create process flowcharts that are serious attempts to capture the actual process that is taking place. Some environments in which this can be done include service-oriented, fast-food chains. Note: If possible, visit a fast-food restaurant at off-peak hours and talk to the manager about this assignment. Explain that it requires your understanding the process and how it is managed.

1. Analyze the way burgers are cooked and served at McDonald's. Then draw a process chart for the steps that are required. Draw a process flow layout chart for the McDonald's being studied.

2. Analyze the way french fries are made and served at Burger King. Then draw a process chart for the steps that are required. Draw a process flow layout chart for the Burger King being studied.

3. Analyze the way chili is made and served at Wendy's. Then, draw a process chart for the steps required to make and serve it. Draw a process flow layout chart for the Wendy's restaurant being studied.

   There are many processes with which most people have some experience, such as changing a tire (a service) or baking a cake (a product). These are presented here along with some other processes that can be charted.

4. Analyze the servicing process that takes place at a gasoline station. Then draw a process chart that compares self-service at the gasoline station with full-service for a fill-up and oil check. Draw the process flow layout chart for the station.

5. Analyze the service process of making travel arrangements. Then draw a process chart for a travel agent setting up the itineraries and reservations for a business trip to be taken by two company executives who are traveling by air from Chicago to Los Angeles. Draw a process flow layout chart for the agent and the agency.

6. Analyze the service process for putting a spare tire onto a car after having a flat. Then draw a process chart appropriate for changing the tire. Draw a process flow layout chart that shows where all the materials are kept and how they are moved around.

7. Analyze the process for baking a cake. Then, draw a process chart for baking a cake. Draw a process flow layout chart as well.

Problems Concerned with Creating a Production Process

Before it is possible to create a production process, it is necessary to know how the product, such as cheese or concrete, is made. Similarly, for services, it is necessary to know what steps are required to deliver the service, such as servicing copy machines or writing a research report. There are many sources of information about how to make and do things.[10]

8. Research the process for making cheese. Create a process chart for producing wheels of cheese in volume as a business venture. What work configuration (job shop or flow shop) do you recommend?

9. Research the process for making concrete. Create a process chart for mixing cement to make concrete in volume as a business venture. What work configuration (job shop or flow shop) do you recommend?

10. Research how to make a jar of jam. Create a process chart for producing jars of jam in volume as a business venture. What work configuration (job shop or flow shop) do you recommend?

11. Research the process for making vinegar. Create a process chart for producing 16- and 32-oz. bottles of vinegar to be sold in supermarkets. What work configuration (job shop or flow shop) do you recommend?

12. Research how to service copy machines. Create a process chart for providing this service on a business-like basis. What work configuration do you recommend?

13. Analyze how to write a research report. Create a process chart for providing this service on a business-like basis.

14. With respect to Problem 13 above, the Market Research Store has considered using virtual offices, meaning that some percent of their report writers work at home on personal computers. How might this concept change the process chart? How might it change the process flow layout chart?

15. Draw the machine-operator chart for the following situation:
    - There are two operators and one machine.
    - Make ready takes two time periods.
    - Machine processing time requires four periods.
    - Put-away takes two time periods.

    There has been no attempt to employ SMED concepts so both make ready and put-away have to be done as internal activities with the machine turned off.

    Figure 6-8, entitled "Machine-Operator Chart—Original Process," showed what occurs when this situation exists with one operator.
    a. What can be done with two operators?
    b. How does this compare with the 50 percent idle times associated with one operator in the original process?

16. Using the information in Problem 15, what can be done if SMED methods permit make ready for unit (n) while unit ($n-1$) is working on the machine?

The Preventive Maintenance Strategy Problem

In the subway system of Metropolis, there are 100,000 lightbulbs that are at risk for failure with rates described as follows. The complete preventive maintenance policy is to replace all of the bulbs at once, four times per year. These lightbulbs are long-life lightbulbs, which cost more than regular ones.

Each of these bulbs has an expected average life of 3,000 hours and cost $7.00. The setup cost for each subway station is $5,000 and there are 50 stations.

In the subway, each lightbulb remains lit, day and night, all year long, which is a total of 8,760 hours. Burned out and broken bulbs are only replaced during the TPM sweep. This could mean that station platform light is not always sufficient. At an extra cost, remedial replacement could be used. The total sweep would still take place, replacing all lightbulbs, whether or not they were newly replaced.

17. For this problem, ignore remedial replacement and its extra cost.
   a. Is a total replacement sweep four times per year likely to be sufficient? *Note:* The distribution is such that many lightbulbs burn out long before the expected lifetime is reached, and many last considerably longer than 3,000 hours.
   b. What is the total cost for following this TPM policy?

The Remedial Maintenance Strategy Problem

The alternative strategy (using the information in Problem 17) is to replace each bulb as it burns out. Replacement costs $5 per lightbulb in addition to the $7 purchase cost per bulb. As noted in the previous problem, the bulbs have an expected lifetime of 3,000 hours. Each lightbulb in the subway remains lit, day and night, all year long, a total of 8,760 hours. The expected number of times each bulb will burn out per year is 2.9. For ease of calculation, round this off to 3 times per year that each lightbulb must be changed.

18. For this problem:
   a. What is the total cost of following the remedial maintenance policy?
   b. Which is preferred, TPM or RM?
   c. If the purchasing agent is able to buy the bulbs for $6.00, will it make a difference?

19. How does the service (setup and changeover) procedure used for racing cars differ from that of regular auto servicing? Is there anything that can be learned from the difference? What does this query have to do with SMED?

20. Paint stores avoid having to carry thousands of different cans of paint for each of the colors customers want. The customer picks out the color that is wanted from color-coded chips or strips of paper. The code number is entered into the computer, which then generates the formula for that particular color. The machine that has the basic color ingredients is set to input six drops of this and four drops of that into a basic flat or semi-glossy or glossy white. For example, to make a lemon white the recipe is two drops of y, one drop of gy and two drops of oy. Note that the colors are added to only three basic types of white paint.

Draw the process diagram for this method of producing variety needed by the customer. Compare it to the situation where the paint company is obliged to make all of the different colors in the factory and ship them to each retailer.

21. The cost of controlled storage (CST), where a withdrawal slip is required to obtain an item, is $70 per item so controlled per month. The cost of uncontrolled storage (UCST), where an item can be obtained without a stock request form, is $10 per item so stored per month. An uncontrolled item that costs $30 is known to suffer pilferage losses of three items a month. There are 100 of these items in storage. Which is preferred, CST or UCST?

END-OF-CHAPTER QUESTIONS

1. Benchmarking is an important P/OM method intended to accomplish specific goals. Which of the following choices is incorrect?
   a. Benchmarking can be used to compare "best" performance against "existing" performance where "best" is identified as the performance of the leader in a specific activity.
   b. Benchmarking can be used to compare "today's" performance against "yesterday's" performance. The time interval can be adjusted to the circumstances. For example, a useful measure might be "this month (or year)" against "last month (or year)."
   c. Benchmarking can be used to compare various suppliers. For example, delivery time consistency might be of measured.
   d. Benchmarking cannot be used for process improvement because charting methods have been developed that are standard procedures.
   e. "Personal Best" is a benchmark used by sporting enthusiasts.

2. Lead time (LT) is a generic term for a production phenomenon. Which of the following statements is incorrect?
   a. Lead time occurs only in production and operations management systems (P/OM). *Note:* Logistics costs are generally part of P/OM accounting.
   b. Excessive lead time is the reason that synthetic materials are used instead of nonimitation materials. For example, faux leather is often used for autos and attaché cases because lead time to obtain real leather is excessive.
   c. Because long lead time is costly, every effort should be made to shorten lead time.
   d. The costs of lead time include the costs of the delivery system and the costs of waiting for deliveries to be made or having too much stock on hand.
   e. Lead time is a production phenomenon because production scheduling must account for any delays in supplies from outside sourcing as well as from bottlenecks within the system.

3. How do process flowcharts differ for custom work, job shops with batch production, flow shops as well as intermittent flow shops, and projects? Which of the following choices is wrong? *Note:* Answer e. is correct. This material is not discussed in this chapter, but because the comparison is relevant and useful it is offered at this time.
   a. An order for a new job of substantial batch size has been obtained. The item has not been made by this job shop before. Check to see if the product is similar to any other products that have been made previously. If feasible modify existing process charts. If not, draw up a new process flowchart to include the sequence and timing of all activities required.
   b. Intermittent flow shops do not require process flow-charting because they are temporary systems. Intermittent flow shop workers are much like artists whose procedures are discovered as they work. Because intermittent flow shops are never more than single shift, the investment in time and money is not significant.
   c. For the shop doing custom work, draw generic process flowcharts to capture the majority of the kind of work that is done. Usually, it does not pay to detail a new process chart for each custom job that is accepted. Also, custom workers are often much like artists whose procedures are discovered as they work.
   d. Flow shops are commitments to dedicated technology (special-purpose equipment) and well-trained employees at assigned workstations. The engineering required to assure smooth flows with good balance requires process flow charts that are detailed and worked over until costs of unnecessary idle time and bottlenecks are minimized.
   e. Projects have specialized flowcharts that are detailed with respect to the sequence and timing of all activities. Projects are similar to custom work in the sense that they are not repeated in batches (job shop) or made continuously (flow shop). What differentiates the two is that projects involve major commitments with big investments and large penalties for delays.

4. Which two of the following statements about process changeovers are incorrect?
   a. Single-minute exchange of dies (SMED) is a theory of production that explains when to switch from batch production to a flow shop system.
   b. Changeovers are an aspect of operations management where it has always been taken for granted that the greater the existing volume of production—the more costly it is to shift from one job to another. For example, a basic lathe (least expensive form) is used to make a wood post. When design of that post changes, it will take time to set up for the new version of the post. However, when the posts are made in batches of 10, the basic lathe is not recommended. Instead, a turret lathe is chosen because it is faster to shift tooling from one design to another.
   c. The learning curve comes into play every time operators bring a new order on line.
   d. Changeover costs are often proportional to changeover times. If computers can decrease changeover times, then product variety can be increased without penalties.
   e. Setup costs are proportional to take down and cleanup times.

5. Quick-changeover ability is a major P/OM objective. Which of the following choices is incorrect?
   a. Setup (and take-down) tasks that can be done while the system is doing another job are called external setup elements. Another way of saying this is setup tasks that Setup (and take-down) tasks that can only be done with the system shut down are called internal setup elements.
   c. Determine which setup tasks can be done with the machine running and which cannot be done with the machine running. Minimize total setup time with preference shown for reducing internal setup times.
   d. Hire creative operations-oriented people who can find ways to convert internal setup elements into external setup elements.
   e. The concepts of internal and external setup times do not apply to servicing (repair and maintain) aircraft in flight.

6. Total productive maintenance (TPM) is an important P/OM objective. Breakdowns are costly and disruptive. Inoperability and slowdowns can severely damage the bottom line. On a more personal note, consider what is the best choice given the options of taking the car in for regular servicing or breaking down on the expressway. But, there are no guarantees that servicing will prevent a breakdown. There are, however, changes in the probabilities of unanticipated failures. With these thoughts in mind, two of the following statements about smart maintenance are wrong. Which two of the following options are incorrect?

   a. Remedial maintenance (RM) must be justified by an analysis that shows that fixing something before it breaks is warranted economically.

   b. Slowdowns (meaning the equipment works at less than the customary rated speeds) cannot be avoided by using preventive maintenance (PM) methods. PM is designed limit failures and not degradation of performance.

   c. Fail-safe designs are applied to systems where failure can be at least damaging and possibly catastrophic. In the catastrophic case, the need for preventive maintenance of fail-safe backups is essential.

   d. Redundant components are a design method used to provide failure prevention. However, failure prevention through redundancy adds to the cost of quality. Savings can be made in TPM because remedial maintenance can be used for an equipment failure; a duplicate (or backup) system is still functioning.

   e. Predictive maintenance (PDM) is based on science and not art. It is associated with predicting the need for remedial maintenance rather than preventive maintenance.

7. Which of the following statements is incorrect?

   a. Reengineering (called *REE*, which means *starting from scratch*) is a sound concept for revamping a system that is in need of thorough change. Downsizing firms has been called reengineering by those who wanted to participate in the REE fad. This is an unfortunate mislabeling of REE. Cost reduction does not start with a clean piece of paper.

   b. Determining the optimal size for a work force to achieve clearly stated objectives is neither the method nor the language associated with reengineering.

   c. An alternative method for improving the performance of a system is continuous improvement (CI). The Japanese call this "kaizen" and have demonstrated that it works best when everyone in the company plays a part.

   d. Continuous improvement (CI) is practiced in the United States and Western Europe with great success. However, organizational issues arise when management changes because old habits tend to reappear when the champions of the new (CI) approaches are no longer present to oversee their accomplishments.

   e. Reengineering went through a period of being lauded as a cure for most business problems. REE was oversold when it became a journalistic sensation with the advent of the trade book, *Reengineering the Corporation* by Hammer and Champy in 1993. The book has been revised (June 2001). Business process reengineering (BPR) is another name for the same concept, which remains a viable approach to achieving major business improvement.

8. Which of the following statements is incorrect?

   a. Process charts are simple to use and powerful in application because the graphics provide an alternative mind-set that promotes another way of thinking.

   b. Sorting through details in rows and columns of numbers can be difficult. An equivalent process chart with flow-through rates allows insights concerning problems such as bottlenecks.

   c. A recommended use of process charts is to determine where in the process time studies should be located for setting company-wide standards and piece rates.

   d. Process charts are effective means of achieving an optimal layout for the factory floor, office, or warehouse.

   e. Traditionally, an isosceles triangle with vertex down appearing on process chart with sequenced activity symbols stands for a controlled storage, i.e., a withdrawal slip is required to obtain an item from this storage.

9. There are many ways to design symbols for process charts. The IT (information technology) industry has adopted symbols that are unique to computer programming. For the job shop, the ASME (American Society of Mechanical Engineers) no longer regulates the symbols to be used. Nevertheless, the old traditional symbols are well-known. The following statements adhere to the original ASME symbols. However, two of the statements are incorrect. Which answers are wrong?

   a. A small isosceles triangle within a larger isosceles triangle where both are drawn with their vertex down, appearing on a process chart with sequenced activity symbols, stands for an uncontrolled storage, i.e., no withdrawal slip is required to obtain an item from this storage.

   b. Eighth-of-an-inch circles stand for operations performed at specific locations on the job shop floor.

   c. Diamonds are inspections for qualities. For example, an empty toothpaste box is blown off the conveyor leading to shrinkwrap. That is an automatic quality inspection check and it would be so listed on the process chart.

   d. Quarter-inch circles stand for transports of materials, components, and other parts, from one location to another. Conveyors move toothpaste boxes to shrinkwrap.

   e. Quarter-inch square boxes stand for inspections of quantities. For example, six packs of shrinkwrapped toothpaste boxes are loaded by the operator into the master shipping case. Inspecting for 36 units in each box could be done by weight.

10. The office building has 2,500 lightbulbs. Compare PM and RM maintenance policies.

The preventive maintenance (PM) policy is to replace all bulbs at once 6.5 times a year. Each replacement costs $5 for the bulb and the work. There is a setup cost of $1,000. The remedial maintenance policy is to replace each bulb as it burns out. Each replacement costs $10 for the bulb and the work. There is no setup cost. Bulbs have an expected lifetime of 900 hours. The plant operates two 8-hour shifts, 7 days per week.

Which row in the following table contains the correct answers for the comparison?

Row Option	Preventive Maintenance	Remedial Maintenance
a.	$93,000	$56,000
b.	$78,000	$130,000
c.	$97,500	$162,500
d.	$117,500	$195,000
e.	$39,000	$65,000

ADDITIONAL READINGS

Brumberg, B., and K. Axelrod, *Watch It Made in the USA: A Visitor's Guide to the Companies That Make Your Favorite Products*, Avalon Travel Publishing, 3rd ed., October 2002.

Hammer, Michael, and James Champy. *Reengineering the Corporation*. New York: Harper Collins, 1993.

Hammer, Michael. *Beyond Reengineering*. New York: Harper Collins, 1995.

Imai, M. *Kaizen: The Key to Japan's Competitive Success*. New York: Random House Business Division, 1986.

Ishiwata, Junichi. *IE for the Shop Floor: Productivity Through Process Analysis*. Connecticut: Productivity Press, 1991.

McNair, C. J., and Kathleen H. J. Leibfried, *Benchmarking: A Tool for Continuous Improvement*. Harper Business, 1992.

Nakajima, Seiichi. *TPM Development Program: Total Productive Maintenance*. Connecticut: Productivity Press, 1989.

Ohno, Taiichi. *Workplace Management*. Connecticut: Productivity Press, 1988.

Robinson, Alan. *Continuous Improvement in Operations: A Systematic Approach to Waste Reduction*. Connecticut: Productivity Press, 1991.

Shingo, Shigeo. *A Revolution in Manufacturing: The SMED System*. Connecticut: Productivity Press, 1985.

Shingo, Shigeo. *The Shingo Production Management System, Improving Process Functions*. Connecticut: Productivity Press, 1992.

NOTES

1. C. J. McNair and Kathleen H. J. Leibfried. *Benchmarking: A Tool for Continuous Improvement*. Harper Business, 1992.
2. Shigeo Shingo. The Shingo Production Management System, Improving Process Functions. Connecticut: Productivity Press, 1992.
3. *CAPP Report*, Waltham, MA: HMS Software Inc., June 1994.
4. Shingo lists four process functions that should be under constant surveillance for improvement. These are processing, inspection, transportation, and delays.
5. M. Imai. Kaizen: *The Key to Japan's Competitive Success*. New York: Random House Business Division, 1986.
6. Michael Hammer and James Champy. *Reengineering the Corporation*. New York: Harper Collins, 1993; Michael Hammer. *Beyond Reengineering*. New York: Harper Collins, 1995.
7. JMA is the Japan Management Association.
8. Ibid. footnote 1, 150.
9. Ibid. 147, 149.
10. For learning about processes that are actually used for making things, see the 27 volumes of *The Science and Invention Encyclopedia*. Westport, CT: H.S. Stuttman, Inc. Another good book to consult about real processes is the Science Encyclopedia. New York: Dorling Kindersley, Inc., 1993.

SPOTLIGHT 6-1
A Planning Tree of Management Options

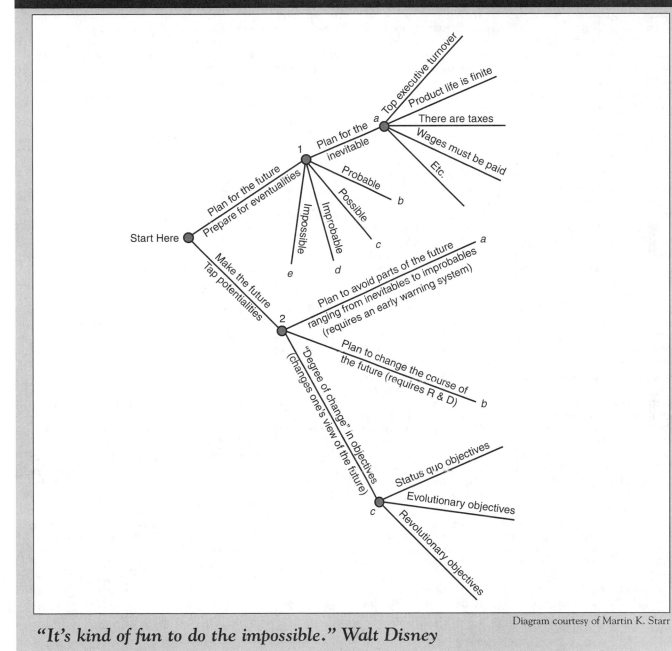

Start Here

Plan for the future
Prepare for eventualities

1 Plan for the inevitable

a — Top executive turnover
Product life is finite
There are taxes
Wages must be paid
Etc.

Probable   b
Possible   c
Improbable   d
Impossible   e

Make the future
Tap potentialities

2

Plan to avoid parts of the future ranging from inevitables to improbables (requires an early warning system)   a

Plan to change the course of the future (requires R & D)   b

"Degree of change" in objectives (changes one's view of the future)   c

Status quo objectives
Evolutionary objectives
Revolutionary objectives

Diagram courtesy of Martin K. Starr

"It's kind of fun to do the impossible." Walt Disney

SPOTLIGHT 6-2
Programming the Web

Improving business processes has a long and remarkable history. In Babylonia, 2285–2242 B.C., compliance with the Code of Hammurabi required clay records for all commercial transactions. Use of papyrus instead of clay tablets improved recordkeeping in ancient Egypt. A system for evaluating government programs and administrators was developed in China by 256 B.C. In ancient Rome, household expenses had to be documented in a codebook called a codex accepti et expensi and used as a basis of taxation and civil rights. Using an annual budget was a business innovation to control fiscal operations as well as financing Roman wars of conquest.

In England, an ingenious system of marking wood sticks was devised to update records. William the Conqueror (1027–1087) had taken possession of all property in 1066 and needed an inventory system. Twice a year, wood tally sticks were placed on a counting table covered by a checkered tablecloth, each check representing a county. We inherit the word "exchequer" from King William. (*Webster's Encyclopedic Unabridged Dictionary* defines "exchequer" as "a treasury, as of a state or nation" or more informally, as "one's financial resources.")

In 1494, two years after Columbus discovered America, Luca Bartolomes Pacioli (born in 1445 in Tuscany) invented and disseminated his method of double entry bookkeeping, ushering in a new era of accounting. The Italians were the first to use Arabic numerals regularly in business—an important improvement over Roman numerals. Luca Pacioli, knowledgeable in literature, art, business, and sciences, and believing in the interrelatedness of all subjects, was a Renaissance man. Pacioli's friend, Leonardo da Vinci, helped him with illustrations in one of his writings and, in turn, Pacioli helped da Vinci by calculating the amount of bronze needed for one of da Vinci's huge statues.

Dissemination of printed information was expensive. Gutenberg had invented the metal type printing press only 25 years before Pacioli wrote his famous "Summa de Arithmetica, Geometria, Proportioni et Proportionalita." In one chapter of this book, Pacioli provides complete instructions for the conduct of business, giving traders his improved and timely method of accessing information about their assets and liabilities. Translation of the "Summa" into five languages over the next century spread the "Italian method" throughout Europe.

Charles Babbage (1791–1871) is the "Father of Computing." Born in Teignmouth, Devonshire, United Kingdom, he designed calculating engines. In 1991, 200 years after his birth, the Science Museum in Kensington, England, constructed a calculating machine called the Difference Engine from drawings left behind by Babbage. Babbage's plan to build an improved device he called the Analytical Engine, capable of any mathematical operation, could not be funded by a government short of cash in the 1840s. Babbage believed in standardization. He standardized railroad gauge, postal rates, and screw threads, among other achievements.

Pacioli and Babbage would be interested in the list of 10 top technologies of 2003, published by the American Institute of Certified Public Accountants (AICPA). Both would appreciate the list's second technology—business information systems. The remaining technologies might puzzle them: information security, application integration, web services, disaster recovery planning, wireless technologies, intrusion detection, remote connectivity, customer relationship management, and privacy.

Web services were ranked eighth on the AIPCA list in 2002 and climbed to fourth place in just one year. Web services technology can connect companies, vendors, and customers instantly and interactively from anywhere in the world. Often, it is not even necessary to go to the web to get useful information. For example, to obtain a car's location from the GPS satellite network, an in-car computer can get information from a web services mapping site. The site knows the auto's location and can send a message back to the vehicle's dashboard display. Web services use computers to talk to computers as well as different applications or devices such as mobile phones.

In a few years, business will depend on web services. For the most part, these services will be invisible. Dr. Robert Sutor, program director of IBM's XML Technology, calls it a kind of stealth technology and compares web services to the plumbing in a house. The only problem is that developers must agree on common standards to make web services work. Charles Babbage would surely applaud Amazon, IBM, Microsoft, Oracle, Sun Microsystems, and all other web service providers in this standardization effort. An intelligent, interactive, central repository of business information is the goal of every company. Standardization will promote a single global electronic market.

More examples of web services are beginning to surface. Bekins, a moving company founded in 1891, now has a state-of-the-art information system. Incorporating web services is saving the company about $75 million annually. Web-based tools provide real-time tracking of shipments from the time of order to delivery. Bekins uses the latest standards in the industry for a complete business solution within their own intranet as well as the Internet. Their web services-based company includes everything from satellite tracking to a complete wall-to-wall asset and data management system. Trucking agents no longer compete for jobs. Jobs are posted via web services simultaneously to all agents who sign up for the system. Any agent can accept the job, and once accepted, it becomes unavailable to others. Because the system is so efficient, Bekins can accept lower-margin moving jobs that it would have refused in the past.

The last word goes to Charles Babbage. Although he lived 200 years ago, he left a message for future builders [and users] of calculating machines: "[You] alone will be fully able to appreciate the nature of my efforts and the value of their results."

Sources:

Http://www.acaus.org/acc_his.html; historical information.
Http://ei.cs.vt.edu/~history/Babbage .html; Charles Babbage, Part I.
Http://ei.cs.vt.edu/~history/Babbage.2.html; Charles Babbage, Part II.
Http://www.aicpa.org/news/2002/p030102.asp; AICPA 2003 Top10
Http://www.guardian.co.uk/online/story; "The third era starts here."
Http://www.bekins.com/tool/tools.html; Bekins Company.

Supplement 6

A Total Productive Maintenance Model to Determine the Appropriate Level of Preventive Maintenance to Be Used

The policies of TPM are employed to choose the optimal level of preventive maintenance to use, including the option of zero preventive maintenance.

A simple equation is written for the expected total cost of following three alternative strategies, called $x = 1, 2, 3$:

($x = 1$) No preventive maintenance, called *remedial maintenance (RM)*
($x = 2$) Partial preventive maintenance, called *PPM*
($x = 3$) Complete preventive maintenance, called *CPM*

Using numbers based on the type of curve shown in Figure 6-11 allows a comparison between the expected total costs of the three maintenance strategies, $x = 1, 2, 3$.

$$p_f c_f + (1 - p_f)c_{nf} + c_p = \overline{TC}(x) \qquad \text{(Equation 6-1)}$$

p_f = the probability of failure associated with the cost of prevention, c_p, and time period t

c_p = the cost of prevention

c_f = the cost of failure

c_{nf} = the cost of no failure, which is equal to zero (i.e., $c_{nf} = 0$)

$\overline{TC}(x)$ = the expected total cost of maintenance strategy x

Table 6-2 provides relevant data and the expected total cost for each maintenance strategy.

x	Strategy	p_f	c_f	c_p	$\overline{TC}(x)$
1	RM	0.50	$10,000	—	$5,000
2	PPM	0.30	$10,000	1,000	$4,000
3	TPM	0.10	$10,000	$2,000	$3,000

TABLE 6-2

Data Needed to Compare Maintenance Strategies

The TPM strategy is indicated because it has the lowest expected cost. Once again, it is useful to note that a superior TPM strategy (call it TPM +) might be developed that reduces the probability of failure to less than 0.1.

Problems for Supplement 6

1. Would a TPM + strategy be warranted if by spending $2,500 for the cost of prevention, the probability of failure could be reduced to 0.08?
2. What level of probability reduction would make the TPM and TPM + strategies equivalent? This value of p is called a breakeven point because, at least as far as the numbers are concerned, there is indifference between the choices of these two strategies.

7

Methods for Quality Control

Chapter Outline

This chapter presents methods for achieving and controlling quality. It starts with a zero-error mind-set and the ideals of the Olympic perspective—an attitude required for quality achievement. Quality control methods are explained using the seven classical tools for producing better quality. Suppliers' goods are checked for adherence to quality standards using acceptance sampling (AS). AS involves trade-offs that balance the cost of sampling against the risk of accepting more defectives than permissible. This leads to negotiations between suppliers and buyers based on the size of Type I and Type II errors. Type I errors occur when an innocent person is found guilty by a jury of peers (or when a medical test falsely proclaims cancer in a healthy patient). Type II errors occur when a guilty person is found innocent by a jury of peers (or when a medical test erroneously declares an ill person to be healthy).

After reading this chapter, you should be able to:

- Explain why quality is important to company success.
- Determine how many pieces to make to fill an order when the probabilities of defectives are known.
- Describe the seven classical process quality control methods.
- Show how to use data check sheets to create bar charts, histograms, and Pareto charts.
- Discuss the use of cause and effect (Ishikawa/fishbone) diagrams.
- Construct control charts for variables and attributes.
- Explain how to interpret control chart signals for $\bar{x}$-charts, R-charts, p-charts, and c-charts, including upper and lower control limits (*UCL* and *LCL*).
- Understand the meaning of "runs" on a control chart and know how to use them as early warning systems.
- Discuss the use of inspection with and without control charts.
- Describe acceptance sampling and explain when it is used.
- Detail the basis of the negotiation between suppliers and buyers with respect to risks of accepting and/or rejecting lots.
- Explain the use of the average outgoing quality limits.

THE SYSTEMS VIEWPOINT

In achieving effective team effort for gold medal quality, not all competitors strive to be the best in the world. Some are happy to be silver or bronze. Others consider being at the Olympics a sufficient reward. Companies have similar goal differences. It is important to realize that not all companies strive to be the best. Nevertheless, because quality failures are widely recognized to have negative impact on long-term performance, all companies consider quality improvement to be a common goal. Striving for quality unites all of the components and constituencies of the system. That does not mean that everyone strives with equal vigor and equivalent knowledge.

All of the parts that go into an assembly are multiplicatively interrelated so that the probability of failure gets increasingly worse and the number of extra parts that must be made increases geometrically. This is an example of the effect of systems interdependencies. When dependencies exist, the appropriate mind-set for achieving quality is to analyze and understand the entire system.

It is typical of dependent systems that suppliers and buyers are sharing risks. Without 100 percent inspection of the shipment, and using a test sample from the shipment, the buyer risks accepting more defects than an agreed-upon percentage (*p*). The seller (supplier) risks having the buyer reject the shipment based on a test, although with 100 percent inspection it would be found that the shipment conforms to an agreed-upon limit of no more than a specific *p*. Statisticians call seller's risk a Type I error and buyer's risk a Type II error.

These two types of errors are interdependent. Generally, as one gets larger the other gets smaller. At the cost of larger sample sizes, both error types are reduced. It is useful to be conscious of these errors as they affect general management decision making—as well as when negotiating quality sampling plans between buyers and sellers.

STRATEGIC THINKING

Type I and Type II errors are significant measures of the strategic decision performance of production and operations management. To view this situation in more general terms, Type I errors occur when a truly innocent person is found guilty by a judge or a jury. Type I errors also occur when a medical test falsely proclaims cancer in a healthy patient. When a supplier's shipment has been rejected by a test sample, that supplier may call for a 100 percent inspection. Defectives can be removed from the shipment by a procedure called detailing. Type I errors are called errors of commission because an action follows the test result. The innocent person goes to jail or even worse things can happen. The cancer prognosis will lead to further testing and treatment. The shipment can be detailed.

Type II errors occur when a guilty person is found innocent by a judge or jury of peers. The person goes free. The medical test erroneously declares an ill person to be healthy. There is no treatment and the true state of affairs may be learned at a later point. The shipment is accepted and the buyer may or may not discover that the percent defectives (*p*) were above the contract specification. These Type II errors are called errors of omission. How does one discover that he or she did not marry the person best suited to be a lifelong companion? The effects of Type I and Type II errors can be tactical or immensely significant strategies for competitive success. In this regard, balancing errors of commission and omission requires strategic thinking that unites all of the components and constituencies of the system. All of the parts that go into an assembly are multiplicatively interrelated. Information about supply and demand is seldom based on complete knowledge and is therefore sample data. Tests leading to strategic decisions may not be formal but they remain tests. It is not wise to set goals based on thinking about only one type of error.

Quality control charts are central to the methods for controlling quality that are discussed in this chapter. When a sample point falls outside of the chart's upper-control limit or the lower-control limit, that signals a possible change in the process. The outlier could be a real signal of trouble or it could be a Type I error that commissions a search for unwarranted causes. The other side of the coin is often overlooked. If the control limits are set wide apart (say, three-sigma) instead of closer (say, two-sigma), then signals of problems that are developing may not be given soon enough. This Type II error overlooks the opportunity to remedy a situation before it develops a more serious character. Setting control limits brings the production manager face-to-face with interacting error systems.

7-1 THE ATTITUDE AND MIND-SET FOR QUALITY ACHIEVEMENT

The most important goals for process analysis are higher quality, improved productivity, and lower costs. Quality is so important to the well-being of the firm that it is the key focus of this chapter. For quality methods to be successful, all participants in the organization must have their collective minds set on quality achievement. This is done by reducing the probability of failure (p_f) to meet a variety of standards for all components. If at the same time that (p_f) is being reduced, the standards are being raised, then the mind-set for being the best in quality achievement and competitive capability is functioning.

7-1a The Zero-Error Mind-Set

The appropriate **zero-error mind-set** is to abhor defectives and do as much as feasible to prevent them from occurring. When they occur, learn what caused them and correct the situation. Meanwhile, raise the goals and improve the standards. Tougher hurdles are part of the quality framework, which seeks continuous improvement. Do it right the first time is the motto of the approach that champions zero errors.

This is often termed, in an almost military manner, **zed defects.** The last letter of the English alphabet is called "zee" or "zed." The name has been used for parallel purposes, e.g., zero error driving and zero emotional defects. Quality guru Philip Crosby popularized the zed term, which he used as a cornerstone of his quality goals.

Those who say that no defects are permissible are at odds with those who say that a few defects are to be expected. The latter group goes on to say that one should learn from mistakes and take the necessary measures to prevent them from recurring. The safest position is to be flexible.

Good advice is to go for a "no defects" policy. If and when it fails to work, switch to a "learn from mistakes" policy. After corrective action has been taken to correct the mistakes, switch back to the zero-errors goal.

> **Zero-error mind-set:** Abhorrence of defectives and determination to prevent them from occurring.
>
> **Zed defects (ZD):** Policy that requires eliminating any and all causes of defects.

7-1b The Olympic Perspective

The **Olympic perspective** calls for team play with everyone striving to achieve the company's personal best. To the managers of the firm, "going for the gold" is no less a meaningful objective than for Olympic teams. The plan calls for breaking process quality records with continued improvements.

> **Olympic perspective:** The Olympic credo of striving to be better is readily translated into dynamic goals of continuous improvement for management.

7-1c Compensating for Defectives

In the job shop, the first items made, during and right after setup, are likely to be defectives. If the order size calls for 70 units and the expected percent defective to get the job right is p = percent, then prepare to make 73.7 or, rounding up, 74 pieces. This is called "**compensating for defectives**" and the methodology and concepts apply to batch production.

> **Compensating for defectives:** Because of start-up defectives, to ship the ordered quantity, produce more than the order size.

$$\text{Batch size} = \frac{\text{Order Quantity}}{(1 - p)} = \frac{70}{(1 - 0.05)} = 73.7$$

Expand this concept to an assembled unit (like a computer) that consists of n electronic components, each of which has a known probability p_i of being defective ($i = 1, 2, 3, ..., n$). Assuming that component failures are independent of each other, and that the components cannot be tested separately but only after assembly, then the number of electronic assemblies to make would be

$$\text{Batch size} = \frac{\text{Order Quantity}}{\prod_{i=1}^{x} (1 - p_i)}$$

Say the order quantity is 100 units and there are five components to be assembled, each of which has a 10 percent probability of being defective. How many units should be made in the batch?

$$\text{Batch size} = \frac{100}{(1 - 0.1)^5} = \frac{100}{0.59} = 169.5$$

With rounding, the decision is to make 170 units. The interesting effect of the multiplicative probabilities of five units is to increase the number of units that must be made to fill the order by 70 percent.

If there had been only one component (with $p = 0.10$) that could lead to defective performance, then the correct number to make to fill the order would be $100/0.9 = 111$.

With such examples of systems interdependencies, the correct attitude for quality achievement requires wanting to understand the entire system. It is unrealistic to set goals for only one cause of failure. The effort must be made to perceive all of the causes of defectives in order to measure the interactive probability of failure (p_j) or the probability of proper performance, which is $(1 - p_j)$.

7-2 QUALITY CONTROL (QC) METHODOLOGY

The body of knowledge that relates to quality attainment starts with the detection of problems. This is followed by diagnosis based on the analysis of the causes of the problems. Next comes prescription of corrective actions to treat the diagnosed causes. This is followed up through observations and evaluations to see how well the treatment works. The entire set of steps is called **quality control (QC).**

Figure 7-1 presents one version of the quality control model, which is related to the fundamental cycle of scientific method.

Deming applied the model of the scientific method to quality control. He used four steps (Plan-Do-Study-Act)[1], as shown in Figure 7-2. Shingo[2] felt that control of quality was missing from the Deming cycle—by interpretation, not Deming's intent. To avoid any confusion on this matter, the quality control function is shown in the Act box of Figure 7-2.

Often, the person doing the work does the checking and exercises the control. Sometimes, checking and controlling are done by a member of the quality control department. There are many instances where both are used. There are some instances where neither is used.

Quality originates with a thorough understanding of the process. If management does not have a complete understanding of all processes used by their businesses, the models for quality attainment in Figures 7-1 and 7-2 will not work. OM is involved in getting everyone in the company motivated to know all about the processes being used and changes under consideration.

Quality control (QC): The process of quality attainment that starts with detection of problems, followed by diagnosis of cause of problem, prescription of corrective actions to treat, and finally followed up through observation and evaluation.

Deming: Dr. W. Edwards Deming became a leader in the American quality revolution after 1980.

FIGURE 7-1
Cycle of Scientific Method

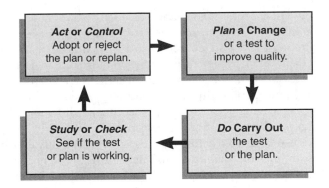

FIGURE 7-2
The Deming Quality Cycle

7-3 SEVEN CLASSIC PROCESS QUALITY CONTROL METHODS

Process quality control methods are used to analyze and improve process quality. There are seven time-honored and well-established methods, as shown in Table 7-1. These are data check sheets, bar charts, histograms, Pareto analysis, cause and effect charts, statistical quality control charts, and run charts.

Method 6 covers the preparation and employment of statistical quality control charts. It is the most elaborate and powerful approach of all the methods. Although Method 7 is commonly listed as a separate procedure, it is based on the use of the statistical control charts developed in Method 6.

The time period from which these methods are derived goes back to Shewhart.[3] Few modifications have been made, but all methods have been affected by computers and technology that can capture, analyze, and chart necessary data.

TABLE 7-1

Seven QC Methods

1. **Data check sheets (DCSs)** organize the data. They are ledgers to count defectives by types. They can be spreadsheets, which arrange data in matrix form when pairs of variables are being tracked. Sometimes, like spreadsheets they are called check sheets.

2. **Bar charts** represent data graphically. For example, the number of pieces in five lots can be graphically differentiated by bars of appropriate lengths. Often data is converted from check sheets to bar charts and histograms.

3. **Histograms** are frequency distributions. When data can be put into useful categories, the relative frequencies of occurrence of these categories can be informative.

4. **Pareto analysis** seeks to identify the most frequently occurring categories; for example, what defect is the most frequent cause of product rejections, next to most, etc. This facilitates identification of the major problems associated with process qualities. It rank orders the problems so that the most important causes can be addressed. It is a simple but powerful method that is the outgrowth of Methods 1, 2, and 3.

5. **Cause and effect charts** organize and depict the results of analyses concerning the determination of the causes of quality problems. The fishbone (or Ishikawa) chart is based on listing variables that are known to effect quality. **Scatter diagrams** help determine causality.

6. **Statistical quality control (SQC) charts**—of which there are several main types—are used for detecting quality problems, much as early warning detection systems (EWDS). SQC charts also can help discern the causes of process quality problems.

7. **Run charts** can help spot the occurrence of an impending problem. Thus, run analysis is another EWDS. It can be a great help in diagnosing the causes of problems.

The amount of computing required to track multiple measures of quality used to be prohibitive. Consequently, simple methods were developed during the period from 1930 through 1950. Data collection was straightforward. Uncomplicated charts were used to present results. These graphical techniques are so powerful that they are being used with increasing frequency born of great success. They can be understood by workers who are only briefly trained in quality control methodology, yet another advantage.

Computer power has been used intelligently by OM to extend the reach of quality analysis to a wide range of measures, without complicating the analysis. The seven methods can be utilized across a great spectrum of quality dimensions without creating unnecessary analytic complications. There is every good reason to avoid unnecessarily complex analyses in favor of simple methods that are easy to use and straightforward to understand.

7-3a Method 1—Data Check Sheets (DCSs)

Data check sheets (DCSs):
Spreadsheets can be used to count and record defectives by types and times of occurrence.

The first method to consider is the use of **data check sheets.** These are used for recording and keeping track of data regarding the frequency of events that are considered to be essential for some critical aspect of quality.

For a particular product, there may be several data points required to keep track of different qualities that are being measured. It is useful to keep these in the same time frame and general format so that correlations might be developed between simultaneous events for the different qualities.

A data check sheet, such as shown in Figure 7-3, could record the frequency of power failures in a town on Long Island in New York State. The data check sheet shows when

FIGURE 7-3
Data Check Sheet—
Type of Power Failures

Date	A	B	C	D	E	F	Comments	Location
12/6/03	X						Crew delay	P21
1/2/04			X				6 hr. service	P3
2/15/04				X			3 hr. service	P22
3/7/04				X			Snowstorm	P21
4/29/04			X				3 hr. service	P3
5/15/04						X	Flooding	R40
6/7/04				X			Crew delay	P5
7/29/04		X					R40/no service	P21–R40
8/21/04			X				Road delays	B2
9/30/04			X				Crew delay	R40
11/2/04				X			Partial crew	P3
12/14/04		X					Flat tire	P5
Total	1	2	4	3	1	1		

and how often the power failures occur. The DCS is a collection of information that has been organized in various ways, one of which is usually chronologically.

The information about when power failures have occurred can be used in various ways. First, it provides a record of how frequently power failures arise. Second, it shows where the failures occur. Third, it can reveal how quickly power is restored. Fourth, it can show how long each failure has to wait before receiving attention, usually because work crews are busy on other power failures. None of these measures explain the causes, however.

After the data check sheet is completed, problem identification follows. Then causal analysis can begin. The data check sheet can now be called the data spreadsheet to conform to the computer era. Data capture is more efficient now that it is operating with software on the computer. Organized collection of data is essential for good process management.

7-3b Method 2—Bar Charts

An often-used graphical method for presenting statistics captured by data check sheets is a **bar chart.** It is simple to construct and understand. People who are turned off by tables of numerical data often are willing to study a bar chart. Figure 7-4 shows a bar chart for the recorded number of power failures that were listed on the data check sheet.

The six types of failures listed as A through F on the data check sheets are represented with separate bars in Figure 7-4. The number of incidents is shown by the y-axis. Bar graphs compare the number of single-event types (e.g., types of complaints). A separate bar is used for each data set.

7-3c Method 3—Histograms

Histograms are bar charts that measure the frequencies (f_i) of a set of k outcomes ($i = 1,2, ..., k$). The purpose of the histogram is to reflect the distribution of the set of data. Therefore, histograms are drawn to show the frequency with which each outcome (of all possible outcomes) occurs divided by the total number events. The result is a bar chart representation of the distribution of relative frequencies. This is equivalent to a discrete probability distribution. When the sample size is n:

$$\sum_{i=1}^{n} f_i = n(i = 1,...,k)$$

Frequencies are converted to probabilities (or relative frequencies) when (f_i) is divided by n:

$$p_1 = \frac{f_1}{n}, p_2 = \frac{f_2}{n}, ..., p_k = \frac{f_k}{n}$$

and these p_i sum to one:

$$\sum_{i=1}^{k} p_i = 1$$

Note that in Figure 7-5, the x-axis describes the number of paint defects ($i = 0, 1, 2, ...,.8$) that have been found per hour during an inspection of autos coming off the production line. The y-axis records the observed frequency f_i for each number of paint defects. The sample size is normalized so that $\Sigma f_i = 100$ and f_i goes from zero to greater than eight.

Auto Finishes—Quality on the Line

In this sample of $\Sigma f_i = 100$, the relative frequency for the number of times that no paint defects are found is 15 out of 100. This is quite low and needs an explanation. In many auto companies, the standards for paint and finish are so high that few cars are found faultless. The definition of a defect is often set by anything that is less than the best that is available, and conformance to this standard is stringent.

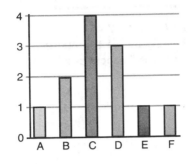

FIGURE 7-4
Bar Chart for the Type of Power Failure

Bar chart: Graphical method that uses bars of different lengths to present numerical and/or statistical data.

Histograms: Bar charts that illustrate the relative frequencies of a set of outcomes as a discrete probability distribution.

Highway driving takes a toll on automotive finishes. New car buyers are not willing to accept a product with any imperfections of the finish. Perfect finishes in automobile painting take a great amount of technology and manufacturing care.

FIGURE 7-5
Histogram of the Number of Paint Defects per Hour

Figure 7-5 shows that one defect is found 20 percent of the time. More than one defect occurs 65 percent of the time. There is a notable decrease in the number of paint defects.

Customers are very demanding about their car's finish. The paint standards are set high by automobile manufacturers to reflect this demanding attitude on the part of new car buyers. The Big 3 automakers of Detroit and the major automakers in Europe benchmark against the paint jobs on Japanese cars, which have set a new standard for best practice.

Automobile painting is regarded as a particularly difficult production process. Perfect finishes take a great amount of technology and manufacturing care. Defects arise in ways that are hard to eliminate. The systems perspective, in this example, links OM, marketing and governmental concerns.

Quality control of paint finishes is a critical responsibility of OM. Marketing views auto finishes as a crucial sales dimension. The government is concerned about the pollution associated with the painting process and wants to reduce it through regulation.

As a result, U.S. automakers have been trying to develop new processes that decrease the pollution associated with conventional petroleum solvents used for the clearcoat, top-layer finishes. A new powder-paint process that DaimlerChrysler, Ford, and GM are developing jointly promises more durable finishes with fewer defects and less pollution. "...The challenge is to efficiently produce paint finishes that rival those of Japanese carmakers."[4]

7-3d Method 4—Pareto Analysis

Pareto analysis: Determines the most frequent types of defects and puts them in rank order.

One goal of **Pareto analysis** is to determine which problems occur the most frequently. The problems can then be arranged in the rank order of their relative frequency of occurrence. Figure 7-6 shows how a Pareto chart can be used to analyze a restaurant's most frequent quality problems.

"Bad service" is the number one complaint. Among all five complaints, it occurs 54 percent of the time. "Cold food" is the second most frequent criticism with 22 percent of the objections. The third grievance is about ambiance—"Noisy" (12 percent). The fourth criticism is that the restaurant is "too expensive" (8 percent). Excessively salty food is the fifth complaint (4 percent).

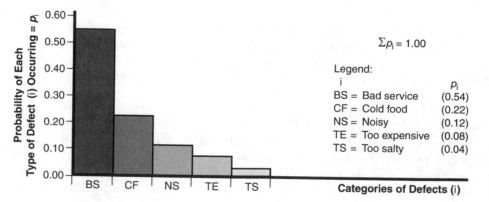

The rank order of the hierarchy of defect causes is evident in Figure 7-6. The probabilities reflect a high degree of skew (exaggeration) for the top two sources of complaints. This kind of skew is typical of Pareto frequencies that are found in actual situations. The first two causes of defects account for 76 percent of the complaints.

The 20:80 Rule

Pareto analysis is designed to separate the most frequent quality problems and complaints from less frequent ones. Often, 20 percent of the total number of problems and complaints occur 80 percent of the time. This is called the **20:80 rule.** Some things occur far more frequently than others. In the restaurant case, 2 out of 5 quality problems account for 76 percent of the complaints. What is important about these numbers is the need to be sensitive to the real issues of "what counts." Pareto attempts to separate the critical minority from the inconsequential majority.

Pareto Procedures

The procedure to get Pareto-type information can take many forms. First, it helps to develop a comprehensive list of all the problems that can be expected to occur. To do this, many people should be consulted both inside and outside the company. Surveys, telephone interviews, and focus groups can be used to find out what problems people say they have experienced.

Complaints are a valuable source of information. Accurate records can be maintained using data checklists—all the better if they are computerized. Organized efforts to secure serious complaint feedback is a marketing responsibility. Complaints are so vital to OMs that they should encourage marketing to keep Pareto data on complaints. They should monitor changes in complaints both by type and frequency. Clusters of complaints at certain times provide important diagnostic information for process managers.

Gathered in whatever way, the data are there to reflect the frequency with which all of the problems on the list have been experienced. Problems mentioned in the text range from power failures to scratches on an auto's finish and complaints about restaurant service.

Some of the problems arise during **inspection** of the product while it is on or leaving the production line. These are internally measurable problems. Other problems must wait for customer experiences. They are learned about through complaints from customers who write or call toll-free numbers set up by the company to provide information and receive complaints. Surveys also pick up complaints or they become apparent when customers seek redress within the warranty period. Retailers, wholesalers, and distributors know a lot and can communicate what they hear from their customers.

7-3e Method 5—Cause and Effect Charts (Ishikawa aka the Fishbone)

To determine the cause of a quality problem, start by listing everything in the process that might be responsible for the problem. A reasonable approach is to determine the factors that cause good (or bad) quality. These potential causes are grouped into categories and subcategories, as is done for the following example, which lists many of the factors responsible for the quality of a cup of coffee.

After the list a chart will be drawn. **Cause and effect charts** show at a glance what factors affect quality and thereby what may be the causes of quality problems. These charts are organized with the quality goal at the right.

The processes used to grow coffee beans, harvest, roast, store, and ship the coffee would be included in this cause and effect diagram if there was control over these factors. This coffee-making process begins with making a cup of coffee. All participating processes are part of the causal system.

Process charts play a crucial role in causal analysis. They map everything that is happening in the process and are often listed as an eighth process quality control method.

20:80 rule: Twenty percent of the total number of problems (complaints) that have been checked off (on the data check sheet) are likely to occur 80 percent of the time.

Inspection: Inspectors can reduce defectives shipped but not defectives made.

Cause and effect charts: All factors that impinge on quality are listed in a hierarchy of categories and subcategories. These are illustrated by the fishbone diagram.

TABLE 7-2	Variables for the Quality of a Cup of Coffee

Coffee Beans—Type Purchased

Source location (Sumatra, Colombia, Jamaica, etc.)
Grade of beans
Size and age
How stored and packed (how long stored before grinding)

Roasting Process

Kind of roaster
Temperatures used
Length of roasting

Grinding Process

Type of grinder
Condition of grinder
Speed and feed used
Fineness of grind setting
Length of grinding
Quantity of beans ground
Stored for how long before use

Coffee Maker

Drip type or other; exact specs for coffee maker
Size and condition of machine (how many prior uses)
Method of cleaning (vinegar, hot water, detergents)
How often cleaned
Number of pounds of coffee used

Water

Amount of water used

Type of water used (chemical composition)
Storage history before use
Temperature water is heated to

Filter

Type of filter used
(material: paper (and type), gold mesh, other metals)
Size of filter
How often used
How often replaced

Coffee Server

Type of container
Size of container
How often cleaned
How long is coffee stored

Coffee Cup

Type of cup
Size of cup
Cleaned how (temperature of water, detergent)
Cleaned how often

Spoon in Cup—Sweetener—Milk or Cream

Type of spoon (material/how often cleaned and how)
Type of sweetener used
Type of milk: 1 percent, 2 percent, half and half, skim, light cream, heavy cream, etc.

Causal Analysis

The quality of a cup of coffee is a growing business opportunity, challenge, and concern. Chains of coffee shops have opened thousands of stores all over the United States, Europe, and Asia. For example, see Starbuck's website (http://www.starbucks.com). A variety of business processes are involved in determining how consumers perceive quality.

Table 7-2 captures many of the multidimensional factors that determine the quality of coffee. Specifically, Table 7-2 presents a list of causal factors that should be considered by all participants in the system that affects coffee quality. After making the list, these variables can be charted using the fishbone construction method developed by Ishikawa.[5]

There are nine main variables and different numbers of subcategory variables. The latter are shown in Figure 7-7 as fins radiating from the nine lines of the main variables, connected to what looks like the spine of a fish. The subcategories are listed in Table 7-2 under the nine main variables.

The diagram is conducive to systems-wide discussion, involving everyone, concerning the completeness of the diagram. Have all the important factors been listed? When the fishbone diagram is considered complete, then follows the determination of what variations should be tested. Market research is used to connect the process variations tested to consumer reactions.

Returning to the power failure situation, consider some of the many causes of power failures that exist. The household consumer of electricity is unlikely to know which cause is responsible for any failure.

The electric utility, on the other hand, can do the necessary detective work to determine what has caused each failure. Method 4 (using Pareto charts) can provide a useful approach to identify the most frequent types of power failures, probably by region and

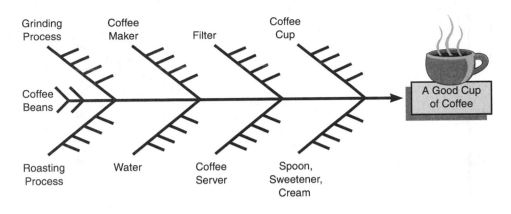

FIGURE 7-7
Ishikawa Diagram aka a Fishbone Diagram

extent. Method 5 (using Ishikawa diagrams) now helps with the search for causes of these problems. To sum up, Ishikawa diagrams enumerate and organize the potential causes of various kinds of quality failures.

Scatter Diagrams

Scatter diagrams are composed of data points that are associated with each other, such as height and weight. The pairs of data are plotted as points on the chart. The idea is that if data are related—that is, if x is related to y—this fact will show up in the graph. The graph for height and weight could be expected to indicate that as height increases so does weight.

> **Scatter diagrams:** Figures composed of data points that are thought to be associated with each other, as calories consumed (x) and weight (y).

Because even strong relationships are far from exact, the plots of points will be scattered around an imaginary line that could be drawn to capture the relationship. If a relationship exists, it might be seen. It also can be measured by statistical means. Spurious relationships can show up. There are no guarantees with scatter diagram methods; they are, at best, a way to probe for relationships.

Let x be one of many factors that the fishbone diagram indicates as a possible cause of the quality problem, y. If that is true, then y is a function of x.

$$y = f(x)$$

A scatter diagram is created for various values of x and y that have been obtained by experimentation, observation, or survey. Two results are shown in Figures 7-8 and 7-9. First, consider Figure 7-8.

The various (x,y) points are tightly grouped around the line: Although a relationship appears to exist, there is not sufficient information to assume that x and y are causally

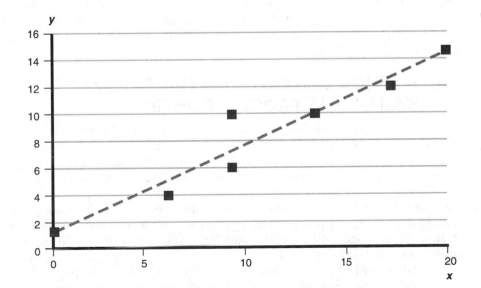

FIGURE 7-8
Scatter Diagram Implying Strong Correlation

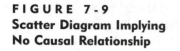

FIGURE 7-9
Scatter Diagram Implying No Causal Relationship

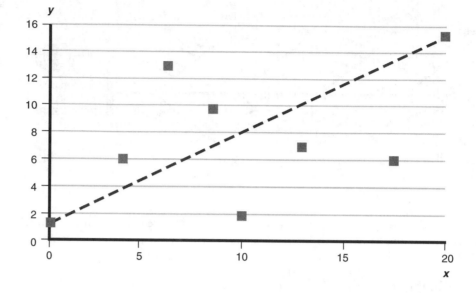

related. Further testing is in order and a logical framework for causality must be built. Still x and y appear to have something to do with each other instead of appearing to have no relationship.

In Figure 7-9 the various (x,y) points are far more widely scattered. This indicates that no strong relationship exists between x and y. The pattern is best described as a random assortment of points.

Although the scatter diagram does not give a statistical measure of the correlation between x and y, it graphically suggests that such does exist. It is reasonable to use statistical methodology to confirm strong correlations so that prescriptions can be made to reduce and/or remove quality problems.

Revisiting the power failure case, for diagnostic and prescriptive purposes, the cause of each power failure should be tracked down and noted: Lines are knocked down by cars and trucks as well as by wind storms; transformers fail more often under peak demands; and fires result from overloaded power generation equipment correlated with summer heat spells. Time of day, day of the week, date of the year may all be useful data for patterns to be found. The computer makes it easy to enter a lot of information and analyze the data for patterns.

Knowing the most frequently occurring types of failures might lead to solutions that could reduce their frequency. Overhead wires in certain locations could be buried at a cost that might be much lower than the expensive remedial actions taken after storm-caused failures. Power-grid sharing could be initiated before overloads occur. Strong correlations provide information that connects types of failures with the times and places that they occur, which may facilitate problem solving.

7-4 METHOD 6—CONTROL CHARTS FOR STATISTICAL PROCESS CONTROL

The prior five methods are significant as means to understand the nature of the process. Method 6, on the other hand, is a powerhouse for monitoring conditions of the process and for stabilizing processes. Method 6 includes a variety of control charting systems. Each variety is so significant a category that it deserves a new section in its own right.

Output from a process is measured with respect to qualities that are considered to be important. For quality to be consistent, it must come from a process that is stable, i.e., one with fixed parameters. This means that its average m and its standard deviation s are not shifting. To understand the concept of stability, it is necessary to develop the statistical theory of stable distributions.

A stable distribution is described as being stationary. This means that its parameters are not moving. **Statistical process control (SPC)** can provide methods for determining

Statistical process control (SPC): The control charting aspect of statistical quality control (SQC).

if a process is stable. **Statistical quality control (SQC)** encompasses SPC as well as other statistical methods, including **acceptance sampling,** covered later in this chapter. In common usage, SPC and SQC both describe the application of control charts as a means to warn about unstable systems.

It is important to note that in real production situations, a lot of data are collected. First, enough data are obtained to create reliable control charts. Then, more data are collected to examine whether the process is stable. Evidence of temporary instability often is thrown out as being associated with start-up conditions. The process is reexamined to see if it has stabilized after the start-up. The initial sample size is often 25 to 30 sets of data, followed by another 25 to 30 sets of data. Once the process is considered stable, then regular observations are made at scheduled intervals. If the process is not stable, and that often occurs when starting up a new system, then Steps 1, 2, 3, and 4 apply:

Control Chart Steps
1. Diagnose the causes of process instability.
2. Remove the causes of process instability.
3. Check results.
4. Go back through Steps 1–3 until stability is achieved.

7-4a Chance Causes Are Inherent Systems Causes

Variability exists in all systems. Two seemingly identical manufactured parts have their own signatures, like fingerprints, when measured to whatever degree of fineness is required. Systems with less variability may differ with respect to measurements in thousandths of an inch whereas systems with more variability may be noticeably different in terms of hundredths of an inch. The degree of fineness has to do with the kind of fit that is needed between parts, and this requirement is reflected by the tolerance limits the designers have set.

There are two basically different kinds of variability. The first kind is an inherent (intrinsic and innate) property of the system. It is the variability of a stable system that is functioning properly. That variability is said to be caused by **chance causes** (also called simple causes). These causes cannot be removed from the system, which is why they are called inherent systems causes. They are also called chance causes because they are predictable and stable in statistical terms, as are the number of heads from an honest coin throw.

A process that experiences only chance causes, no matter what its level of variability, is called a stable process. The variability that it experiences is called random variation.

7-4b Assignable Causes Are Identifiable Systems Causes

The second kind of variability has traceable and removable causes, which are called assignable or special causes. Unlike chance causes, these causes are not background noise. They produce a distinct trademark, which can be identified and traced to its origins. They are called assignable because these causes can be designated as to type and source, and removed.

The process manager identifies the sources of quality disturbances—a tool that has shifted, a gear tooth that is chipped, an operator who is missing the mark, an ingredient that is too acidic—and does what is required to correct the situation. Thus, tool, die, and gear wear is correctable. Broken conveyor drives can be replaced. Vibrating loose parts can be tightened. Human errors in machine setups can be remedied. These are examples of **assignable causes** that can be detected by the methods of statistical process control (SPC).

An alternative name that might be preferred to assignable causes is identifiable systems causes. Quality control charts are the means for spotting identifiable systems causes. Once identified, knowledge of the process leads to the cause, which is then removed so that the process can return to its basic, inherent causes of variability. The ability to do this enhances quality attainment to such a degree that Method 6 is widely acknowledged as powerful and necessary.

Statistical quality control (SQC): Encompasses statistical process control (SPC) as well as other statistical methods, including acceptance sampling.

Acceptance sampling: Inspecting acceptability of suppliers' shipments by using sampling of required qualities instead of 100 percent inspection.

Chance causes: See **Assignable causes.**

Assignable causes: Identifiable causes of process problems that create variability. They are traceable and can be removed.

A process that is operating without any assignable causes of variation is stable by definition, although can be large. Stability does not refer to the degree of variability of a process. Instability reflects the invasion of assignable causes of variation, which create quality problems.

There are different kinds of control charts. First, there is **classification by variables** where numbered measurements are continuous, as with a ruler for measuring inches or with a scale for measuring pounds. The variables can have dimensions of weight, temperature, area, strength, variability, electrical resistance, loyalty, satisfaction, defects, typing errors, complaints, accidents, readership, and TV viewer ratings. The fineness of the units of measure is related to the quality specifications for the outputs.

Second, there is **classification by attributes.** Output units are classified as accepted or rejected, usually, by some form of inspection device that only distinguishes between a "go" or a "no go" situation. Rejects result from measurements falling out of the range of acceptable values that are pre-set by design. Rejects are defective product units. Under the attribute system of classification, process quality is judged by the number of defective units discovered by the pass-fail test. It is charted as the percentage of defects discovered in each sample, and is called a **p-chart.** Also under the attribute system of measurement is the **c-chart,** which counts the number of nonconformities of a part. For example, in the eye of the specialist, a particular diamond can be categorized as having various imperfections, which are counted. Distributions of the number (c) of imperfections is the basis of the c-chart.

7-5 METHOD 6—CONTROL CHARTS FOR VARIABLES: x-BAR CHARTS

The $\bar{x}$-chart uses classification by variables. A sample of product is taken at intervals. Each unit in the sample is measured along the appropriate scale for the qualities being analyzed. The **control chart** is a graphic means of plotting points, which should fall within specific upper- and lower-bound limits if the process is stable.

Table 7-3 illustrates a sequence of quality measures, called x_i (i = output number) where x_i can be measured on a continuous scale that permits classification by variables. The sample subgroup size, n, is 3 in Table 7-3, and the sample subgroups are labeled with Roman numerals I, II, III, and so on.

There are two subgroup samples of 3. The output interval between them is 4. Subgroup sample sizes between 2 and 10 are common. The interval between subgroups varies widely, depending on the output rate and the stability of quality for the product. Relatively stable processes and those that do not carry severe penalties for undetected assignable causes can support larger intervals between samples than unstable or high penalty systems.

The sample mean for each subgroup $\bar{x}_j$ is obtained.

$$\bar{x}_I = \frac{x_1 + x_2 + x_3}{3}, \ x_{II} = \frac{x_1 + x_2 + x_3}{3}, \text{ etc.}$$

In general

$$\bar{x}_j = \frac{\sum x_i}{n}$$

Sidebar definitions:

Classification by variables: Variables like weight can be measured on a continuous scale.

Classification by attributes: Units are classified as accepted or rejected, e.g., it is too heavy for the delivery system.

p-chart: Plots successive sample measures of the percent defective for specific quality attributes.

c-chart: Control chart for variable numbers of defectives in a single unit.

x̄-chart: Basic quality control chart designed for variables measured on a continuous scale such as tire pressure and particle emissions.

Control chart: Chart is based on the process average for percent defectives, with upper- and lower-control limits and plotted points of successive sample means.

TABLE 7-3   Subgroup Sample Size Is 3; Interval Between Samples Is 4

Subgroup Sample I	Interval Between Samples I and II	Subgroup Sample II	Interval Between Samples II and III
x_1 x_2 x_3	x_4 x_5 x_6 x_7	x_8 x_9 x_{10}	x_{11} x_{12} x_{13} x_{14}

The grand mean, $\bar{\bar{x}}$, is the average of the sample means, that is:

$$\bar{\bar{x}} = \frac{\bar{x}_I + \bar{x}_{II} + \dots + \bar{x}_N}{N}$$

where N is the number of sample subgroups being used.

7-5a The Chocolate Truffle Factory (CTF)

Data have been collected by the OM department for the famous truffle bonbons made by the Chocolate Truffle Factory. They are marketed all over the world as being hand-dipped. Even though the company claims customization as an advantage, complaints are regularly received that the candies are uneven in size and weight.

This is an ideal opportunity to use an $\bar{x}$-chart to find out if the chocolate-making process is stable or erratic. Hand-dipping chocolates may lead to high variability in size and weight of product without creating an unstable production process.

The standard weight set by CTF is 30 grams of the finest chocolate. A perfect pound box would contain 16 chocolates, each weighing 28 grams. Company policy, based on principles of ethical practice, is to err on the side of giving more, rather than less, by targeting 2 extra grams per piece. However, extra chocolate is expensive. Worse yet, if weight and size are inconsistent, the larger pieces create dissatisfaction with the truffles that meet the standard. Also, consistency of size is used by customers to judge the quality of the product. Weight is easier to measure than size and is considered to be a good surrogate for it.

The company wants to test for consistency of product over a production day. Samples were taken over the course of one day of production at 10:00 A.M. and 11:00 A.M., and at 1:00 P.M., 3:00 P.M., and 4:00 P.M. The hours chosen are just before the line is stopped for tea break and/or for cleanup. A sample subgroup size of four consecutive observations was chosen for each of the five samples. This yielded 20 measures and five sample subgroup means.

For instructive purposes, this sample is about the right size. For real results, all five days of production for a typical week should be examined. Except as an example, a 1-day sample is too small. There is a rule of thumb widely used: *Practitioners consider 20 to 25 subgroup means as appropriate for a start-up or diagnostic study.*

Table 7-4 offers 5 sample subgroup sets of data as the columns (j) with one for each time period. Measurements are in grams. There is a range measure R_j in this chart that will be used later. It is the difference between the largest and the smallest number in the column.

Subgroup $j =$	I	II	III	IV	V	
Time:	10 A.M.	11 A.M.	1 P.M.	3 P.M.	4 P.M.	Sum
$x_i = 1$	30.50	30.30	30.15	30.60	30.15	
$x_i = 2$	29.75	31.00	29.50	32.00	30.25	
$x_i = 3$	29.90	30.20	29.75	31.00	30.50	
$x_i = 4$	30.25	30.50	30.00	30.00	29.70	
Sum	120.40	122.00	119.40	123.60	120.60	
$\bar{x}$	30.10	30.50	29.85	30.90	30.15	151.50
R_j	0.75	0.80	0.65	2.00	0.80	5.00

where $\bar{x}_j = \dfrac{\sum x_i}{n} ; i = 1, 2, \dots 4$

TABLE 7-4

Weight of Chocolate Truffles (in Grams)

FIGURE 7-10
x̄-Chart for Chocolate Truffles with Three-Sigma Limits

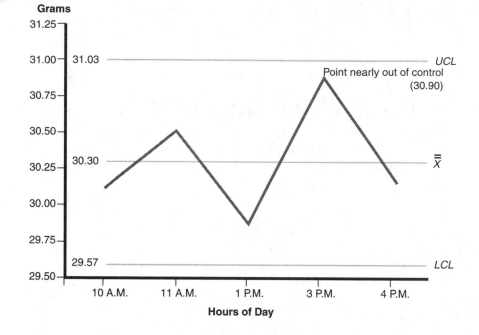

The grand mean value is (151.50)/5 = 30.30, which indicates that, on average, chocolate truffles are 1 percent heavier than the standard. This average value seems well suited to the ethical considerations of the firm because it is above, but not too far above, the target value of 30.00 grams. CTF's policy is ethical but expensive. Customers get more than a pound of chocolates on a regular basis.

In Table 7-4, individual sampled values fall below the 30-gram target five times, even though in all cases they are well above 28. The lowest value sampled was 29.50. The highest value is 32. The three highest values all appear at 3:00 P.M.

7-5b Upper- and Lower-Control Limits (*UCL* and *LCL*)

> **Control limits:** Upper-control limits (*UCL*) and lower-control limits (*LCL*) are developed in different ways depending upon the type of chart being used.

Control limits are thresholds designed statistically to signal that a process is not stable. Control limits will now be derived for the x̄-chart. Before doing that, study Figure 7-10 to identify what these control limits look like. Note that the 3:00 P.M. sample is identified on the chart as being nearly out of control.

This x̄-chart with *UCL* and *LCL* has no points outside the limits, and therefore no points are specifically out of control. Nevertheless, the 3:00 P.M. sample, when it is backed up by a lot more data, is the kind of visual warning that usually warrants attention.

Perhaps, the 3:00 P.M. sample is taken during the afternoon tea break, during which the chocolate mixture becomes thicker and the molding machine tends to make heavier pieces. The cleanup comes after 3:00 P.M. Tracking and discovering such causes will lead to the elimination of the problems. Although the process is stable, it appears to have too much variability (32.00-29.50). It may need to be redesigned. The chocolate mold-filling machines might need replacement or rebuilding. Workers using the filling machines might need additional training. From the previous comment on variability, it becomes apparent that there is a need to study the range measure. That will be done shortly.

The control chart drawn in Figure 7-10 is based on plotting the sample means ($\bar{x}_j$) from Table 7-4. It is important to note that the underlying distribution is that of the sample means. It is necessary to estimate the variability of this distribution of the sample means in order to construct control limits around the grand mean of a process. The upper-control limit (*UCL*) and the lower-control limit (*LCL*), shown in Figure 7-10, could have been determined by calculating the standard deviation for the sample means ($\bar{x}_j$) given in Table 7-4.

An easier calculation of variability uses the range, R. It is well suited for repetitive computations that control charts entail. Column values of R for CTF are given in Table 7-4. The range within each subgroup, is defined as:

$$R = x_{MAX} - x_{MIN}$$

The largest x value in the 10:00 A.M. sample subgroup is 30.50 and the smallest is 29.75, so $R = 0.75$.

UCL and LCL will be computed shortly using the average value of R for the subgroup samples.

Statistical quality control works because the variation observed within each subgroup (R_I, R_{II}, ... etc.) can be statistically related to the variation between the subgroup means. Only if the process is stable will the two different measures of variability be commensurable.

The between-group variability is related to the differences between the grand mean and successive sample means. Thus:

$$(\bar{x}_I - \bar{\bar{x}}),(\bar{x}_{II} - \bar{\bar{x}}),...,(\bar{x}_N - \bar{\bar{x}})$$

whereas, the within-group variability is related to the values (R_I, R_{II}, ... etc.). If the process is stable, the plotted points of the sample means—reflecting between-group variability—will fall within control limits that are based on within-group variability. If the process is unstable, some of the plotted points are likely to fall outside the control limits.

This reasoning applies to various kinds of control charts. Present discussion concerns the $\bar{x}$-chart. This is followed by application of control limits to the chart for ranges, called the R-chart, and, then, the p-chart for attributes and the c-chart for defects per part.

When the process is not stable because of the existence of assignable causes, between-group variability exceeds within-group variability. Note that the observations taken within the subgroup are always taken as close together as possible, whereas in the interval between subgroups, allow sufficient time for an assignable cause to enter the system. The subgroup size is kept small. That way, a high degree of homogeneity should exist for the observations within each subgroup. In a stable system, the same homogeneous condition will apply to all the samples, no matter when they were taken.

To construct the control chart:

1. Individual samples are taken from the parent population in groups of size n.

2. $\bar{x}$ and R measures are calculated for each sample subgroup.

3. The control limits UCL and LCL are computed.

The sample means $\bar{x}_I$, $\bar{x}_{II}$, $\bar{x}_{III}$, etc., are distributed in accordance with the size of n. Figure 7-11 is meant to illustrate how the distribution of the sample means is narrower than the distribution of the parent population. The distribution of the sample means is used for the control chart construction because it has less variability.

The relationship between the variability of a stable parent distribution and that of the distribution of the sample means is known as the central limit theorem. This is described by Equation 7-1.

$$\sigma_{\bar{x}}^2 = \sigma_x^2 \div n \qquad \text{(Equation 7-1)}$$

The left-hand side ($\sigma_{\bar{x}}^2$) is the variance of the distribution of sample means ($\bar{x}$ values).

The right-hand side of Equation 7-1 is the variance of the parent population distribution divided by n.

Translating the equation into words, sigma square of the sample means (x-bar) on the left side equals sigma square of the population values (x) divided by n on the right side.

Equation 7-2 is the equivalent relationship for the standard deviation parameter, which is the square root of the variance. This is called the standard error of the mean.

$$\sigma_{\bar{x}} = \sigma_x \div \sqrt{n} \qquad \text{(Equation 7-2)}$$

FIGURE 7-11
**Distribution of the Sample
Means Is Narrower Than
the Distribution of the
Parent Population**

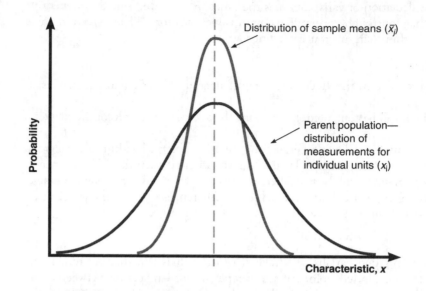

Translating into words again, sigma of the sample means (*x*-bar) on the left side equals sigma of the population values (*x*) divided by the square root of *n* on the right side.

If the subgroup size is equal to one, *n* = 1, then $\sqrt{1} = 1$, and the two standard deviations (sigmas) of the distributions are identical. A subgroup size of one defeats the purpose of measuring within and between subgroup variability. It would not be used, but it proves the logic of the equation.

A subgroup size of *n* = 2 is the smallest feasible size for SPC (statistical process control).

If *n* is a large number, then the $\sqrt{n}$ is also a large number and the standard deviation of the sample means ($\sigma_{\bar{x}}$) gets small, eventually approaching zero. The distribution of sample means takes on the appearance of a vertical line. This, too, is an extreme case, mainly useful to test the sense of the equation.

Continuing with the fundamental equations that underlie control chart theory, it should be noted that

$\sigma_{\bar{x}}$, which is the standard deviation of the distribution of the sample means, is calculated as follows:

$$\sigma_{\bar{x}} = \sqrt{\frac{\sum_{j=1}^{N} (\bar{x}_j - \bar{\bar{x}})^2}{N}}$$

(Equation 7-3)

(*j* = 1, 2,... *N*) where *N* = the number of subgroup sample means that are calculated. For small samples, the denominator of Equation 7-3 is often *N* – 1.

Meanwhile, to make certain that the relationship between the sample means parameter and that of the parent population is clear, review:

σ_x = the standard deviation of the parent population, calculated by Equation 7-4:

$$\sigma_x = \sqrt{\frac{\sum_{i=1}^{nN} (x_j - \bar{\bar{x}})^2}{nN}}$$

(Equation 7-4)

(*i* = 1, 2, ..., *nN*) where (*nN*) = the total number of observations. *nN* is the total sample size. (*n*) is the sample subgroup size. It is multiplied by the number of sample subgroups taken (*N*). For small values of *nN*, the denominator is often *nN* – 1.

Rather than going through the laborious calculations for sigma, the range R is the preferred measure. R will be employed for the control charts used in this chapter.

The grand mean used for the control chart can be measured in different ways, thus:

$$\bar{\bar{x}} = \frac{\sum_{j=1}^{nN} x_i}{nN} = \frac{\sum_{j=1}^{N} \bar{x}_j}{N} = \frac{606}{4(5)} = \frac{151.50}{5} = 30.30,$$

and the average range is

$$\bar{R} = \sum \frac{R_j}{N} = \frac{5}{5} = 1.00$$

The data used for $\bar{\bar{x}}$ and $\bar{R}$ come from Table 7-4.

The R measure must now be converted to represent the sample standard deviation. The conversion factors relating the range to the sample standard deviation have been tabled and are widely available. The conversion factor for upper and lower three-sigma limits is A_2. It is given in Table 7-5.

A_2 is used for UCL and LCL for the $\bar{x}$-chart.

D_3 is used for the LCL for the R-chart.

D_4 is used for the UCL for the R-chart.

The meaning of A_2 multiplied by $\bar{R}$ is shown in Equation 7-5:

$$A_2\bar{R} = k\sigma_{\bar{x}} = 3\sigma_{\bar{x}} = 3\frac{\sigma_x}{\sqrt{n}} \qquad \text{(Equation 7-5)}$$

The calculations for the upper-control limit $UCL_{\bar{x}}$ and $LCL_{\bar{x}}$ for the lower using three standard deviations ($\pm 3\sigma$) are as follows:

$$UCL_{\bar{x}} = \bar{\bar{x}} + A_2\bar{R} \text{ and } LCL_{\bar{x}} = \bar{\bar{x}} - A_2\bar{R}$$

The calculations for the Chocolate Truffle Factory are given by Equations 7-6 and 7-7:

$$UCL_{\bar{x}} = 30.30 + (0.73)(1.00) = 31.03 \qquad \text{(Equation 7-6)}$$
$$LCL_{\bar{x}} = 30.30 - (0.73)(1.00) = 29.57 \qquad \text{(Equation 7-7)}$$

Subgroup Size (n)	A_2	D_3	D_4
2	1.88	0	3.27
3	1.02	0	2.57
4	0.73	0	2.28
5	0.58	0	2.11
6	0.48	0	2.00
7	0.42	0.08	1.92
8	0.37	0.14	1.86
9	0.34	0.18	1.82
10	0.31	0.22	1.78
12	0.27	0.28	1.72
15	0.22	0.35	1.65
20	0.18	0.41	1.59

TABLE 7-5

Conversion Factors for x̄- and R-Charts

7-5c How to Interpret Control Limits

The limits used in Figure 7-10 resulted from the previous calculations. The 3:00 P.M. point would have been outside the control limits if two standard deviations had been used instead of three. The 3:00 P.M. point was 30.90, and the $UCL_{\bar{x}}$ for two-sigma would have been 30.79.

Using Equation 7-5: $\sigma(x\text{-bar}) = \sigma_{\bar{x}} = 0.243,\qquad 2\sigma\,(x\text{-bar}) = 2\sigma_{\bar{x}} = 0.487 = 0.49$

Then, from Equation 7-6:

$$UCL_{\bar{x}} = 30.30 + 0.49 = 30.79$$

The number of standard deviations used will control the sensitivity of the warning system. Three-sigma charts remain silent when two-sigma charts sound alarms. Alarms can signal out-of-control as well as false alarms.

Understanding how to set the control limits is related to balancing the costs of false alarms against the dangers of missing real ones. One-sigma limits will sound more alarms than two-sigma ones. The judicious choice of k for $\pm k\sigma$ is an operations management responsibility in conjunction with other participants to assess the two costs stated earlier. There must be an evaluation of what happens if the detection of a real problem is delayed. The systems-wide solution is the best one to use.

The probability of a subgroup mean falling above or below three-sigma limits by chance rather than by cause is 0.0028, which is pretty small, but still real. For two-sigma, it would be 0.0456, which is not small. Also, k can be chosen between two- and three-sigma. In some systems, two successive points must go out of control for action to be taken. There are fire departments that require two fire alarms before responding because of the high frequency of false alarms. When a response is made to out-of-control signals, knowledge of the process is the crucial ingredient for remedying the problem.

7-6 METHOD 6—CONTROL CHARTS FOR RANGES (VARIABLES)—*R*-CHARTS

R-chart: Control Limits are applied to the range (R) chart, which usually is a companion to the x̄-chart. Together the two charts supply powerful diagnostics for process behavior.

The $\bar{x}$-chart is accompanied by another kind of control chart for variables. Called an **R-chart,** it monitors the stability of the range. In comparison, the $\bar{x}$-chart checks for the stationarity of the process mean, i.e., checks that the mean of the distribution does not shift about—while the R-chart checks that the spread of the distribution around the mean stays constant. In other words, R-charts control for shifts in the process standard deviation.

The $\bar{x}$ and R-charts are best used together because sometimes an assignable cause creates no shift in the process average, or in the average value of the standard deviation (or $\bar{R}$), but a change occurs in the distribution of R values. For example, if the variability measured for each subgroup is either very large or very small, the average variability would be the same as if all subgroup R values were constant. Remembering that the sampling procedure is aimed at discovering the true condition of the parent population, the use of $\bar{x}$ and R-charts provides a powerful combination of analytic tools.

The equations for the control limits for the R-chart are

$$UCL_R = D_4\bar{R} \text{ and } LCL_R = D_3\bar{R}$$

The Chocolate Truffle Factory data from Table 7-4 can be used to illustrate the control chart procedures. Continuing to use k = three-sigma limits and the conversion factors given in Table 7-5, the R-chart control parameters are obtained.

$$D_4 (\text{for } n = 4) = 2.28, D_3 \text{ (for } n = 4) = 0, \text{ and } \bar{R} = \frac{5.00}{5} = 1.00$$

These are used to derive the control limits.

$$UCLR = (2.28)\,(1.00) = 2.28 \text{ and } LCLR = (0.00)(1.00) = 0.00$$

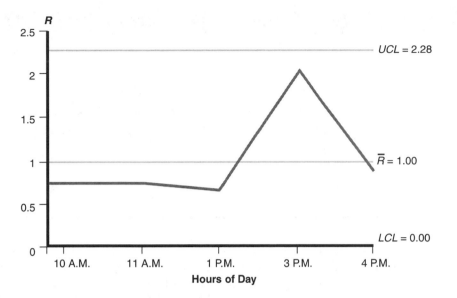

FIGURE 7-12
The *R*-Chart:
Three-Sigma Limits

Figure 7-12 shows that the *R*-chart has no points outside the control limits. The same pattern prevails as with the $\bar{x}$-chart. The 3:00 P.M. point is close to the upper limit. This further confirms the fact that the process is stable and is unlikely to do much better. However, the sample is small, and good chart use would throw out the 3:00 P.M. sample and take about 25 more samples before making any decision.

7-7 METHOD 6—CONTROL CHARTS FOR ATTRIBUTES—*p*-CHARTS

The *p*-chart shows the percent defective in successive samples. It has upper- and lower-control limits similar to those found in the $\bar{x}$- and *R*-charts. Compare what is measured for the *p*-chart to what is measured for the $\bar{x}$-chart. The attribute used is good (accepted) or bad (rejected).

Monitoring by variables is more expensive than by attributes. The inspection by variables requires reading a scale and recording many numbers correctly (for example, successive measurements of the weight of cans of peanuts that must be at least 16 ounces). Measurement error must be avoided. A reading of 15.99 is unacceptable whereas 16.01 is acceptable. Numbers have to be read arithmetically. Their significance must be understood to allow proper actions to be taken.

In comparison, with attributes and the *p*-chart, a go/no-go gauge is simpler. It is an unequivocal pass-fail exam. Many times it can be performed by a visual check—good or bad? Attribute measurement methods build in the acceptable and unacceptable ranges. Monitoring by attributes can often be automated. The engineering of the inspection process is an investment in simplifying the task. When error prevention is critical, assessment by attributes often is safer.

Only one chart is needed for the attribute, *p*, which is the percent defective. The *p*-chart replaces the two charts $\bar{x}$ and *R*. Also, only the upper-control limit really matters. The lower-control limit is always better as it gets closer to zero.

The value of *p* is defined as follows:

$$p = \frac{\text{number rejected}}{\text{number inspected}}$$

Assume that the Chocolate Truffle Factory can buy a new molding machine that has less variability than the current one. CTF's operations managers in cooperation with the marketing managers and others have agreed to redefine acceptable standards so that profits can be raised while increasing customer satisfaction. Also, it was decided to use a *p*-chart as the simplest way to demonstrate the importance of the acquisition of the new molding machine.

TABLE 7-6	Subgroup j	I	II	III	IV	V	
Weight of Chocolate Truffles (in Grams) (R = Rejects Due to Excessive Weight)	Time:	10 A.M.	11 A.M.	1 P.M.	3 P.M.	4 P.M.	Sum
	x_i						
	1	30.50R	30.30	30.15	30.60R	30.15	
	2	29.75	31.00R	29.50R	32.00R	30.25	
	3	29.90	30.20	29.75	31.00R	30.50R	
	4	30.25	30.50R	30.00	30.00	29.70	
	NR	1	2	1	3	1	8
	P	0.25	0.50	0.25	0.75	0.25	

Previously, a defective product was defined as a box of truffles that weighed less than a pound. What was in the box was allowed to vary, as long as the pound constraint was met. Now the idea is to control defectives on each piece's weight.

The new definition of a reject is as follows: A defective occurs when $x_i < 29.60$ grams or $x_i > 30.40$ grams. This standard set on pieces is far more stringent than the earlier one set on box weight. The new standards will always satisfy CTF's criteria to deliver nothing less than a pound box of chocolate.

It has been suggested that the data of Table 7-4 be tested against the p-chart criteria. Rejects are marked with an R on the table. The number of rejects (NR) is counted, and p is calculated for each subgroup in Table 7-6.

Table 7-7, which summarizes the results found in Table 7-6, shows that the p values are extraordinarily high. CTF either has to go back to the old standard or get the new machine. This analysis will provide the motivation for changing machines. The p-chart parameters are calculated as follows: first, compute

$\bar{p}$ = average percent defective, which is defined by:

$$\bar{p} = \Sigma \frac{\text{number rejected}}{\text{number inspected}} = \frac{8}{20} = 0.40$$

Companies that subscribe to the concepts of TQM are committed to obtaining defective rates that are less than 1 percent, and this is 40 percent. It is evident that the new criteria and the present process are incompatible. Constructing the p-chart confirms this evaluation.

The control chart for single attributes, known as the p-chart (there is a c-chart for multiple defects), requires the calculation of the standard deviation (s_p). For the p-chart computations, the binomial description of variability is used:

$$s_p = \sqrt{\frac{\bar{p}(1 - \bar{p})}{n}} = \sqrt{\frac{(0.40)(0.60)}{4}} = \sqrt{0.06} = 0.245$$

TABLE 7-7	Subgroup No.	NR	n	p
Summary of the Findings (NR = Number of Rejects)	I	1	4	0.25
	II	2	4	0.50
	III	1	4	0.25
	IV	3	4	0.75
	V	1	4	0.25
	Sum	8	20	

Shifting to more conservative 1.96 sigma limits means that 95 percent of all subgroups will have a p value that falls within the control limits,[6] which are determined as follows:

$$UCL_p = \bar{p} + 1.96s_p = 0.40 + 1.96(0.245) = 0.40 + 0.48 = 0.88$$

and

$$LCL_p = \bar{p} - 1.96s_p = 0.40 - 0.48 = -0.08 < 0.000 = 0.00$$

The LCL_p cannot be less than zero, so it is set at zero.

Note that UCL_p and LCL_p are functions of s_p that can vary with the sample size n. Thus, if the 11:00 A.M. sample had nine measured values, instead of four, then

$$s_p = \sqrt{\frac{\bar{p}(1-\bar{p})}{n}} = \sqrt{\frac{(0.40)(0.60)}{9}} = \sqrt{0.027} = 0.163$$

s_p has decreased, and this would reduce the spread between the limits, just for the 11:00 A.M. portion of the chart. The control limits can step up and down according to the sample size, which is another degree of flexibility associated with the p-chart.

The appropriate control chart for percent defectives for the data given in Table 7-6 for the Chocolate Truffle Factory is shown in Figure 7-13.

There are no points outside the UCL, although the 3:00 P.M. value of 0.75 is close to the upper limit's value of 0.88. The same reasoning applies, namely the process is stable, but the 3:00 P.M. sample should be eliminated from the calculations and 25 more samples of four should be taken.

7-7a c-Charts for Attributes: The Number of Defects per Part

The c-chart shows the number of defectives in successive samples. It has upper- and lower-control limits similar to those found in the $\bar{x}$, R, and p-charts.

The finish of an automobile or the glass for the windshield is typical of products that can have multiple defects. It is common to count the number of imperfections for paint finish and for glass bubbles and marks. The expected number of defects per part is $\bar{c}$. The statistical count c of the number of defects per part lends itself to control by attributes, which is similar to p, the number of defectives in a sample.

It is reasonable to assume that c is Poisson distributed because the Poisson distribution describes relatively rare events. (It was originally developed from observations of the

FIGURE 7-13
The p-Chart

FIGURE 7-14
c-Chart for Number of Defects per Part

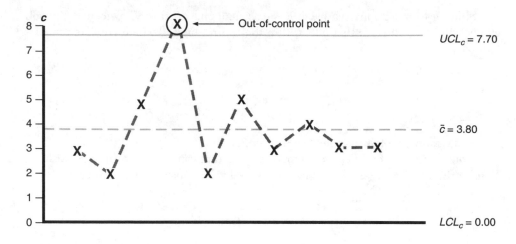

number of Prussian soldiers kicked by horses.) There is an insignificant likelihood that a defect will occur in any one place on the product unless there is an assignable cause. That is what the *c*-chart is intended to find out.

The standard deviation of the Poisson distribution is the square root of $\bar{c}$. Thus:

$$UCL_c = \bar{c} + k\sigma_c = \bar{c} + k\sqrt{\bar{c}}$$

and

$$LCL_c = \bar{c} - k\sigma_c = \bar{c} + k\sqrt{\bar{c}}$$

The best explanation is achieved by means of an example with tabled data charted in Figure 7-14.

The number of defects are counted per unit sample and put into Table 7-8.

Two-sigma control limits are calculated for $\bar{c} = 3.8$ and $\sqrt{\bar{c}} = \sqrt{3.8} = 1.95$:

$$ULC_c = 3.8 + 2\sigma_c = 3.8 + 2(1.95) = 7.70 \text{ and}$$

$$LCL_c = 3.8 - 2\sigma_c = 3.8 - 2(1.95) = -0.10$$

A negative *LCL* is interpreted as zero and the *UCL* is breached by the fourth sample. This violation seems to indicate that all is not well with this process. The control chart is shown in Figure 7-14.

It is possible to throw out the fourth sample and recalculate the charts. In reality, larger samples would be taken to draw up the initial charts, and then further samples would determine the stability of the process.

7-8 METHOD 7—ANALYSIS OF STATISTICAL RUNS

A run of numbers on a control chart is successive values that all fall either above or below the mean line.

TABLE 7-8

Database for a c-Chart

Sample No.	Number of Defects	Sample No.	Number of Defects
1	3	6	5
2	2	7	3
3	5	8	4
4	8	9	3
5	2	10	3

Legend: Total number of defects = 38; Total number of samples = 10; Average number of defects per sample = 3.8

Consider this scenario. For months, the control chart has indicated a stable system. However, the latest sample mean falls outside the control limits. The following conjectures should be made:

Has the process changed or is this a statistical fluke?

Was the out-of-control event preceded by a run of sample subgroup mean values?

A run is a group of consecutive sample means that all occur on one side of the grand mean.

If there was a run of six or more, assume that something is changing in the process. Look for the problem. Sample the process again, as soon as possible. Make the interval between samples smaller than usual until the quandary is resolved.

Sometimes a separate run chart is kept to call attention to points that are falling on only one side of the mean value of the chart. Separate charts are not required if the regular control charts are watched for **runs.** The charting decision is dependent upon the likelihood that runs will play a major role in controlling quality.

> **Runs:** A run of numbers on any control chart is a succession of values that fall either above or below the mean line.

The $\bar{x}$-chart in Figure 7-10 shows no runs. The R-chart in Figure 7-12 shows a run of three consecutive points below the grand mean. The p-chart in Figure 7-13 shows no runs. Charts often show short runs of two, three or four, because short runs are statistically very likely to occur.

Runs can appear on either side of the grand mean, $\bar{\bar{x}}$.

The probability of two consecutive $\bar{x}$'s falling above $\bar{\bar{x}}$ is $1/2 \times 1/2 = 1/4$.

The probability of two consecutive $\bar{x}$'s falling below $\bar{\bar{x}}$ is $1/2 \times 1/2 = 1/4$.

The probability that there is a run of two, either above or below $\bar{\bar{x}}$, is $1/4 + 1/4 = 2/4 = 1/2$.

The probability of a run of three above is $(1/2)^3 = 1/8$, and a run of three below is the same.

The probability of a run of three being either above or below is $(1/8 + 1/8) = 2/8 = 1/4$.

To generalize, the probability of a run of r above the grand mean is $(1/2)^r$, and the same below, so above and below is

$$p(r) = (2)(1/2)^r = (1/2)^{r-1} = \frac{1}{2^{(r-1)}}$$

Then, the probability of a run of six $(r = 6)$ is

$$p(r = 6) = \frac{1}{2^{(6-1)}} = \frac{1}{2^5} = \frac{1}{32} = 0.03125$$

Note that a run of 6 having a probability of $1/32 = 0.03125$ has about the same probability that a sample mean has of being above the UCL with 1.86σ limits. Thus, a run of six adds serious weight to the proposition that something has gone awry.

The run chart also shows whether the sample means keep moving monotonically, either up or down. Monotonically means always moving closer to the limit without reversing direction.

The run of three in Figure 7-12 is not monotonic. A monotonic run signals even greater urgency to consider the likelihood that an assignable cause has changed the process's behavior. Statistical run measures do not take monotonicity into account. Further, they do not factor in the slope of the run. Steep slopes send more urgent signals of change.

7-8a Start-Ups in General

Many, if not most, processes, when they are first implemented, moving from design to practice, are found to be out of control by SPC models. Process managers working with the SPC charts and 25 initial samples can remove assignable causes and stabilize the process. The continuity of the process that is required is characteristic of flow shop type configurations. Nevertheless, the p-chart has been used with orders that are regularly repeated in the job shop.

7-9 THE INSPECTION ALTERNATIVE

Some firms have practiced inspecting out defectives instead of going through the laborious process of classifying problems, identifying causes, and prescribing solutions. This approach to process management is considered bad practice. Inspection, in conjunction with SPC, plays an important role by providing sample means, allowing workers to check their own output quality, and inspecting the acceptability of the suppliers' shipments (called *acceptance sampling*).

> *Inspections and inspectors reduce defectives shipped. They do not reduce defectives made.*

7-9a 100 Percent Inspection or Sampling?

An option for monitoring a process is using 100 percent (100%) inspection of the output. There are times when 100% inspection is the best procedure. When human checking is involved, it may be neither cost-efficient nor operationally effective. Automated inspection capabilities are changing this.

The use of 100% inspection makes sense for parachutists and for products where failure is life-threatening. Inspections that are related to life-and-death dependencies deserve at least 100% and, perhaps, even 1,000% inspection. For parachute inspections and surgical cases, a second opinion is a good idea. It is human nature that it is easier to spot defects in the works of others than in one's own work.

NASA continuously monitors many quality factors at space launchings. Aircraft take-off rules are a series of checks that constitute 100% inspection of certain features of the plane. There are no serious suggestions about doing away with these forms of 100% inspection. There have been occasions when pilots forgot to do a checking procedure with dire consequences.

An economic reason to shun 100% inspection is that it is often labor intensive. This means it is likely to be more expensive than sampling the output. Sampling inspection is the other alternative. The few are held to represent the many. The body of statistical knowledge about sample sizes and conditions is sound and is treated shortly.

A common criticism of 100% inspection is that it is not fail-safe because it is human to err. Inspectors' boredom makes them very human in this regard. Sampling puts less of a burden on inspectors.

Inspection procedures performed by people are less reliable and have lower accuracy when the volume of throughput is high. Imagine the burden of trying to inspect every pill that goes into a pharmaceutical bottle. If the throughput rate is one unit per second and it takes two seconds to inspect a unit, then two inspectors are going to be needed and neither of them will have any time to go to the bathroom. With present scanner technology, the dimensions of the problem are changed.

In such a situation, sampling inspection is a logical alternative. If destructive testing is required (as with firecrackers), sampling is the only alternative. Otherwise, the firecracker manufacturer will have no product to sell. Destructive testing is used in a variety of applications such as for protective packaging and for flammability. The sampling alternative is a boon to those manufacturers.

7-9b Technological and Organizational Alternatives

The situation for inspection is changing in several ways, with important consequences for process management and quality control.

As automated inspection becomes more technologically feasible, less expensive, and/or more reliable than sampling, the balance shifts to 100% technology-based inspection. This is a definite new trend that promises consumers a step function improvement in the quality of the products they buy.

Robot inspectors have vision capabilities that transcend that of humans, including infrared and ultraviolet sight. They have optical-scanning capabilities with speeds and

Robotic welding has improved the quality of product while removing difficult and hazardous work from human welders. Robot programming allows many different tasks to be performed in sequence; robots move from one weld point to another. However, care must be taken to prevent robots from getting into each other's way.

memories that surpass humans. Additionally, they have the ability to handle and move both heavy and delicate items as well as dangerous chemicals and toxic substances.

There are other changes occurring with respect to who does inspections. In many firms, each worker is responsible for the quality control of what he or she has done. This is proving effective, but the job must be such that the operator is in a position to judge the quality, which is not always the case. For those situations, alternative quality controls are developed and supported by teamwork.

Teamwork originated with Japanese manufacturing practice, but it has spread so widely that it cannot be associated with any one country's style. Rather, it should be identified with the type of organization that accepts empowerment of all employees. The employees are often called associates.

Many organizations now champion the practice of having associates inspect their own work. No other inspectors are used. Quality auditors are gone. There may be a quality department, but it is there to back up the associates with consulting advice. This variant of traditional 100% inspection has been winning adherents in high places in big companies all over the world.

7-10 ACCEPTANCE SAMPLING (AS)

Acceptance sampling is the process of using samples at both the inputs and the outputs of the traditional input–output model. Acceptance sampling uses statistical sampling theory to determine if the supplier's outputs shipped to the producer meet standards. Then, in turn, AS is used to determine if the producer's outputs meet the producer's standards for the customers. Acceptance sampling checks conformance to agreed-upon standards. It should be noted that SPC is used during the production process. Also, AS operates with the assumption that the production process is stable.

In the 1920s at Western Electric Company, the manufacturing division of AT&T, statistical theory was used to develop sampling plans that could be employed as substitutes for 100% inspection. Usually, the purchased materials are shipped in lot sizes, at intervals over time. The buyer has set standards for the materials and inspects a sample to make certain that the shipment conforms. Sometimes the supplier delivers the sample for approval before sending the complete shipment.

Military purchasing agencies were some of the first organizations to require the use of acceptance sampling plans for purchasing. There were published military standards such as U.S. MIL STDS-105 D, and more recently ANSI/ASQC Z1.4-1981.

Similar standards applied in Canada and other countries as well. Sampling plans are often part of the buyer–supplier contract.

Acceptance sampling is particularly well suited to exported items. Before the products are shipped to the buyer, they are inspected at the exporting plant. Only if they pass are they shipped. The same reasoning makes sense for shipments that move large distances, even within the same country.

There are companies that specialize in acting as an inspection agent for the buyer. The inspectors sample the items in the suppliers' plants with their full cooperation. Suppliers that have a trust relationship with their customers sample their own output for acceptability to ship.

When done properly, acceptance sampling is always used in conjunction with statistical quality control (SQC). It is assumed that when the lot was made the process was stable with a known average for defectives ($\bar{p}$), which is used for either the average percent or average decimal fraction of defective parts. The sample is expected to have that same percent defectives.

Variability is expected in the sample. This means that there are more or less defectives in the sample than exactly the process average ($\bar{p}$). A sampling plan sets limits for the amount of variability that is acceptable. The reasons that the limits might be exceeded include:

1. The number of defectives found in the sample exceeded the limits even though the process was stable with a process average of ($\bar{p}$). There is a limit as to how much variability will be allowed before this assumption (1) and the lot are rejected.

2. With three-sigma limits, there is the expectation that 27 out of 10,000 sample mean points will fall outside of the control limits and 13.5 out of 10,000 will be above the upper-control limit.

3. The statistical variability exceeded the limits because the process was out of control (not stable) during the time that the lot was being made. For example, 35 out of 10,000 sample mean points fall outside of the three-sigma limits.

If the sample has too many defectives, then the lot can be rejected and returned to the manufacturer or it can be detailed. This means using 100% inspection to remove defectives. If the inspection was done at the supplier's plant, then there is no need to pay to transport the defectives in order to return them. Also, there is advanced warning that the defective lot has been rejected. This can alter the production schedule and lead to expediting the next lot.

7-10a Acceptance Sampling Terminology

The basic elements of sampling plans are

1. N = the lot size. This is the total number of items produced within a homogeneous-production run. Homogeneity means that the system remained unchanged. Often, conditions for a homogeneous run are satisfied only for the specific shipment. Large shipments can entail several days of production. Each time the process is shut down, or a new shift takes over, there is the potential for changes impacting the process. SQC can be used to check if the process remains stable.

   Every time there is a change of conditions, such as a new start-up (new learning for the learning curve), the stability of the process has to be checked. Each time one worker relieves another, it should be assumed that a new lot has begun. There may be a new start-up after a coffee break or the lunch hour.

   It is assumed that the sample is representative of the lot. It also is assumed that the average percent defectives ($\bar{p}$) produced by the process does not change from the beginning to the end of the run. If $\bar{p}$ does change, the sample should pick up that fact because there will be too many or too few defectives in the sample. The "too few" is not a cause for concern.

2. n = the sample size. The items to be inspected should be a representative sample drawn at random from the lot. Inspectors know better than to let suppliers choose the sample.

3. c = the acceptance number.

4. The sampling criterion is defined as follows: n items are drawn from a lot of size N, k items are found to be defective,
   if $k > c$, reject the entire lot,
   if $k = c$, accept the lot,
   if $k < c$, accept the lot.

   Example: Five items ($n = 5$) are drawn from a lot size of 20 ($N = 20$). The acceptance number is set at $c = 2$. Then if three items are found to be defective ($k = 3$), reject the entire lot because $k > c$. If two or fewer items are found to be defective, k is either equal to or less than c; therefore, accept the lot. It makes sense to remove the defectives from the lot. This means that ($n - 2$) units are returned to the lot. The defectives may be able to be repaired or require scrapping.

   When the acceptance number is $c = 0$, one defective rejects the lot.

7-11 O.C. CURVES AND PROPORTIONAL SAMPLING

Operating characteristic curves (O.C. curves) show what happens to the probability of accepting a lot (P_A) as the actual percent defective in the lot (p) goes from zero to one. Each O.C. curve is a unique sampling plan. The construction of O.C. curves is the subject of the material that follows. However, becoming familiar with reading O.C. curves is the first requisite.

A good way to start is to examine why the use of proportional sampling does not result in the same O.C. curve for any lot size. Proportional sampling is equivalent to taking a fixed percent (PRC) of any size lot (N) for the sample (n). Thus:

$$PRC = 100(\frac{n}{N})$$

and

$$n = \frac{PRC(N)}{100}$$

Set PRC at (say) 20 percent. Then if the lot size is $N = 100$, the sample size $n = 20$. If $N = 50$, $n = 10$; if $N = 20$, $n = 4$. Figure 7-15 shows three O.C. curves that apply where $c = 0$.

The three O.C. curves show that proportional sampling plans will not deliver equal risk. The $n = 4$ plan is least discriminating. Its probability of accepting lots with 10 percent defectives is about 60 percent.

The $n = 10$ plan has a P_A around 35 percent and the $N = 20$ plan has a P_A about 10 percent. Each plan produces significantly different P_A's.

It has been established that O.C. curves with the same sampling proportion (n/N ratio) do not provide the same probability of acceptance. They are not even similar O.C. curves.

Also, the acceptance number c has a big effect on the probability of acceptance. This can be seen by studying the O.C. curves in Figure 7-16.

When c is increased from 0 to 1 for $n = 10$ and $N = 50$, there is a marked decrease in the discriminating ability of the sampling plan. This is because the probability of accepting a lot with a given value of p rises significantly when the acceptance number (c) increases from zero to one. Consequently, c provides control over the robustness of the sampling test. $c = 0$ is always a tougher plan than $c > 0$.

Operating characteristic curves (O.C. curves): Graphics that show what happens to the probability of accepting a lot as the actual percent defective in the lot goes from zero to 100.

FIGURE 7-15
O.C. Curves for Three Proportional Sampling Plans

The other controlling parameter is *n*. Return to Figure 7-15 and notice that as *n* goes from 20 to 10 to 4, the probability of acceptance increases. The larger the value of *n*, the more discriminating is the sampling plan. The sample size *n* drives the value of P_A, whereas the effect of *N* is not great, except when it is quite small. The curves in Figure 7-15 would not differ much from those that would apply there if all of the sampling plans had the same *N* = 50.

Designing a sampling plan requires determining what the values of P_A should be for different levels of *p*. This is to provide the kind of protection that both the supplier and the buyer agree upon. Then, the O.C. curve can be constructed by choosing appropriate values for *n* and *c*. Note that an agreement is required. The design is not the unilateral decision of the buyer alone. The situation calls for compromise and negotiation between the supplier and the buyer. Figure 7-17 shows what is involved.

7-11a Negotiation Between Supplier and Buyer

Two shaded areas are marked alpha and beta (α and β) in Figure 7-17. The α area is called the supplier's risk. Alpha gives the probability that acceptable lots will be rejected by the sampling plan, which the O.C. curve represents. Acceptable lots are those that have a fraction defective $\bar{p}$ that is equal to or less than the process average $\bar{p}$, which operates as the limit for α.

The $\bar{p}$ threshold for alpha is also called the *average quality limit (AQL)*. It makes sense that the supplier does not want lots rejected that are right on the mark or better (with a lower value) than the process average. A sensible buyer–supplier relationship must be based on the buyer's knowledge of the process average $\bar{p}$.

The beta area represents the probability that undesirable levels of defectives will be accepted by the O.C. curve of the sampling plan. Beta is called the *buyer's risk*. The limiting value for beta, defined by the buyer, is called the lot tolerance percent defective, *LTPD*, or p_t. If decimal fraction defective is used instead of percent defective, the limit is called *lot tolerance fraction defective (LTFD)*. It is also known as the *reject quality limit (RQL)*.

LTPD (or *LTFD* or *RQL*) sets the limit that describes the poorest quality the buyer is willing to tolerate in a sampled lot. The buyer wants to reject lots with values of p that fall to the right of this limit on the x-axis of Figure 7-17. The use of sampling methods makes it impossible to be certain. There is a probability that the sample will falsely indicate that the percent defective is less than the limiting percent defective p_t. This is the probability of accepting quality that is inferior to the *LTPD*. Therefore, the buyer compromises by saying that no more than beta percent of the time should the quality level p_t be accepted by the sampling procedure.

7-11b Type I and Type II Errors

Decision theory has contrasted the two kinds of errors with which the alpha and beta risks of error correspond. These are Type I and Type II decision errors. The error falsely rejects good lots. It typifies the product that would have become a great success had it been launched, but it was bypassed because the test rejected it.

Alpha is known as a Type I error and identified as an error of omission.

The β error is the probability of incorrectly accepting bad lots, equivalent to making the mistake of launching a new product failure because the test incorrectly accepted it as a winner.

Beta is known as a Type II error and identified as an error of commission.

You have to know the costs of making each kind of error in specific circumstances to decide which is preferable. It is important to note that these two errors are related. As you get less of one you get more of the other.

7-11c The Cost of Inspection

Given the process average, $\bar{p}$, the α-level, the consumer's specification of p_t, and β, then a sampling plan can be found that minimizes the cost of inspection. This cost includes the charge for detailing, which entails inspecting 100 percent of the items in all rejected lots to remove defective pieces.

Such a sampling plan imputes a dollar value to the probability (α) of falsely rejecting lots of acceptable quality. The supplier can decrease the α-type risk by improving quality and thereby reducing the process average. Real improvement to $\bar{p}$ might be costly. It is hoped that the buyer would be willing to accept part of this increased cost in the form of higher prices. In one way or another, the supplier and the buyer will share the cost of inspection. Therefore, it is logical to agree that the rational procedure to be followed is to minimize inspection costs as they negotiate about the values for *LTPD* and β.

The sampling plan will deliver the specified α and β risks for given levels of $\bar{p}$ and p_t. If the process average $\bar{p}$ is the true state of affairs, then α percent of the time, $N - n$ pieces will be detailed. This means that the average number of pieces inspected per lot will be $n + (N - n)(\alpha)$. This number is called the *average sample number (ASN)*.

7-12 AVERAGE OUTGOING QUALITY LIMITS (AOQL)

An important acceptance sampling criterion is average outgoing quality (AOQ). AOQ measures the average percentage of defective items the supplier will ship to the buyer, under different conditions of actual percent defectives in the lot.

In each lot, the sample of n units will be inspected. The remaining $(N - n)$ units will only be inspected if the lot is rejected. The expected number of defectives in the unsampled portion of the lot is $\bar{p}(N - n)$. Out of every 100 samples, P_A will be the percent of samples passed without further inspection. The defective units in the samples passed will not be replaced (detailed).

On the other hand, $1 - P_A$ of the 100 samples will be rejected and fully detailed identifying all defectives. Thus:

$$(P_A)(\bar{p})(N - n)$$

is the average or expected number of defectives that will be passed without having been identified for every N units in a lot.

The average outgoing quality (AOQ) changes value as p goes from zero to one. See Equation 7-8.

$$AOQ = P_A p\left(\frac{N - n}{N}\right)$$

(Equation 7-8)

Note that P_A changes with p in accordance with the specifics of the sampling plan, which is based on the values of n and c that are chosen. Thus, AOQ is a function of all the elements of a sampling plan. It is, therefore, a useful means of evaluating a sampling plan. Specifically, for each value of p, an AOQ measure is derived. It is the expected value of the fraction defectives that would be passed without detection if the process was operating at value p. The AOQ measure reaches a maximum level—called the *average outgoing quality limit (AOQL)*—for some particular value of p. This is shown in Figure 7-18.

Table 7-9 presents the AOQ computations which are based on Equation 7-8.

AOQL value occurs when $p = 0.5$. This particular sampling plan ($P_A = f(p)$) is developed by the hypergeometric method described in Supplement 7.

The maximum value of AOQ, the AOQL, has been calculated as 12/64. This average outgoing quality limit (AOQL) describes the worst case of fraction defectives that can be shipped, if it is assumed that the defectives of rejected lots are replaced with acceptable product and that all lots are thoroughly mixed so that shipments have homogeneous quality.

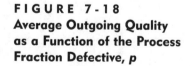

FIGURE 7-18
Average Outgoing Quality as a Function of the Process Fraction Defective, *p*

P	P_A	(N − n)/N	AOQ
0	1	3/4	0
1/4	3/4	3/4	9/64
1/2	1/2	3/4	12/64 (AOQL)
3/4	1/4	3/4	9/64
1	0	3/4	0

TABLE 7-9

Computing Average Outgoing Quality Limit (N = 4, n = 1, c = 0)

7-13 MULTIPLE-SAMPLING PLANS

Multiple-sampling plans are utilized when the cost of inspection required by the single-sampling plan is too great. Single-sampling plans require that the decision to accept or reject the lot must be made on the basis of the first sample drawn. With double sampling, a second sample is drawn if needed. Double sampling is used when it can lower inspection costs.

The double-sampling plan requires two acceptance numbers c_1 and c_2 such that $c_2 > c_1$. Then, if the observed number of defectives in the first sample of size n_1 is k_1:

Accept the lot if $k_1 \leq c_1$.
Reject the lot if $k_1 > c_2$.

If $c_1 < k_1 \leq c_2$, then draw an additional sample of size n_2.
The total sample is now of size $n_1 + n_2$.

The total number of defectives from the double sample is now $k_1 + k_2$. Then:

Accept the lot if $(k_1 + k_2) \leq c_2$.
Reject the lot if $(k_1 + k_2) > c_2$.

Double sampling saves money by hedging. The first sample, which is small, is tested by a strict criterion of acceptability. Only if it fails are the additional samples taken. Double-sampling costs have to be balanced against the costs of the single large sample.

Multiple sampling follows the same procedures as double sampling where more than two samples can be taken, if indicated by the rule: $c_j < k_j \leq c_{(j+1)}$. As with double sampling, the sample sizes are specified with upper and lower acceptance numbers, which get larger for additional samples. When the cumulative number of defects exceeds the highest acceptance number c_n the lot is rejected. Thus, reject the lot if:

$$(k_1 + k_2 + \ldots + k_j + \ldots + k_n) > c_n$$

In the same sense, the costs of multiple-sampling plans can be compared to single or double sampling. Sequential sampling may be cost-effective where many samples of large size have to be taken regularly. The sequential sampling procedure is to take successive samples with rules concerning when to continue and when to stop. In effect, it determines the spacing shown in Table 7-3.

Tables exist for single- and double-sampling plans that make the choice of a plan and the design of that plan much simpler.[7]

7-14 BINOMIAL DISTRIBUTION

For the binomial distribution to apply, the sample size should be small as compared to the lot size. The criterion is given after Equation 7-9, which is the binomial distribution.

$$P_A = Prob(j, n, p) = \frac{n!}{j!\,(n-j)!}\,(p^j)(q^{n-j}) \qquad \text{(Equation 7-9)}$$

n = sample size; p = the decimal fraction defective and $q = 1 - p$.

TABLE 7-10	Fraction Defective (p)	1 – p	$P_A = (1 - p)^{100}$
Binomial Derivation of O.C. Curve with $j = 0$	0.00	1.00	1.000
	0.01	0.99	0.366
	0.02	0.98	0.133
	0.04	0.96	0.017
	0.05	0.95	0.006
	.	.	.
	.	.	.
	1.00	0.00	0.000

P_A is the probability of acceptance as previously used in the chapter. The lot size N is assumed to be infinite so it does not appear in Equation 7-9. The assumption of large enough N is considered to be met when $n/N \leq 0.05$.

When $j = 0$, the probabilities are calculated for the sampling plan with $c = 0$. Just to be sure that the factorial is known, it is $n! = n(n-1)(n-2)...(1)$ and $0! = 1! = 1$.

The O.C. curve for $n = 100$, $c = 0$, is calculated from computing Equation 7-10 for sample size $n = 100$, and the acceptance number $c = 0$. With this sample size, it is expected that the lot is 2,000 or larger. Also, this sample size has been chosen to enable a later comparison with the use of the Poisson distribution for creating O.C. curves and because most tables for the binomial distribution[8] do not go up to $n = 100$.

$$Prob(0; 100, p) = \frac{100!}{0! (100 - 0)!} (p^0)(q^{100}) = q^{100} = (1 - q)^{100} \quad \text{(Equation 7-10)}$$

Note that 100! is divided by 100! and that equals one. Hence $p^0 = 1$. Table 7-10 is derived by using this binomial computing formula with the beginning of the entire range of possible values of fraction defectives. Figure 7-19 shows the plot of this O.C. curve.

For the acceptance number $c = 1$, it is necessary to derive the binomial for $j = 0$ and $j = 1$. Add these results together. Thus: $Prob(0; 100, p) + Prob(1; 100, p)$ will be used to derive the O.C. curve for $n = 100$ and $c = 1$. The computations follow in Equation 7-11.

$$Prob(1; 100, p) = \frac{100!}{1! (100 - 1)!} (p^1)(p^{99}) = 100p(1 - p)^{99} \quad \text{(Equation 7-11)}$$

In this case 100! is divided by 99!, which leaves 100 as a remainder. The result can be used for computing Table 7-11 with the beginning of the entire range of possible values of fraction defectives, p.

FIGURE 7-19
Binomial O.C. Curve—$c = 0$

Fraction Defective (p)	q = 1 − p	$P_A = 100p(1-p)^{99}$
0.00	1.00	0.000
0.01	0.99	0.370
0.02	0.98	0.271
0.04	0.96	0.070
0.05	0.95	0.031
.	.	.
.	.	.
1.00	0.00	0.000

TABLE 7-11

Binomial Derivation of O.C. Curve with $j = 1$

Calculation of $P_0 = 100p(1-p)^{99}$ when $q = 0.99, 0.98$, and so on, is done readily with a math calculator or the computer. However, for those who want a computing method without electronic aids, use logarithms and antilogs, remembering that decimals have negative characteristics.

To calculate the $c = 1$ plan, add the P_A values for each row of Tables 7-10 and 7-11, deriving Table 7-12.

Figure 7-20 combines the plot of this O.C. curve with $c = 1$ and that of Figure 7-19 with $c = 0$ so that a comparison can be made.

As expected, the O.C. curve for $c = 0$ is far more stringent than for $c = 1$.

7-15 POISSON DISTRIBUTION

An even easier method for creating O.C. curves uses the Poisson distribution[9] to approximate the binomial distribution when p is small (viz., when $p < 0.05$). The mean of this distribution is $m = np$ with n the sample size and p the fraction defective. A sample size of $n \geq 20$ is customary. Like the binomial, sampling with replacement is assumed. That means that N is large enough to be treated as not being statistically affected (diminished) by sampling.

The fundamental equation for the Poisson distribution is Equation 7-12:

$$P_A = Prob(j; m) = \frac{m^j e^{-m}}{j!} \qquad \text{(Equation 7-12)}$$

Let $j = 0$, which is equivalent to $c = 0$, and let $n = 100$. Then, because $m = np$, the mean $m = 100p$. Thus,

$Prob(0; m) = e^{-100p}$. It is simplest, however, to use the mean value in the center column of Table 7-13 to calculate the values of the probability of acceptance (P_A) in Table 7-13.

Fraction Defective (p)	P_A (c = 0) P_A (j = 0)	P_A (j = 1)	P_A (c = 1) Sum P_A (j = 0 and j = 1)
0.00	1.000	0.000	1.000
0.01	0.366	0.370	0.736
0.02	0.133	0.271	0.404
0.04	0.017	0.070	0.087
0.05	0.006	0.031	0.037
.	.	.	.
.	.	.	.
1.00	0.000	0.000	0.000

TABLE 7-12

Binomial Derivation of O.C. Curve with $c = 1$

FIGURE 7-20
**Binomial O.C. Curve
with c = 1**

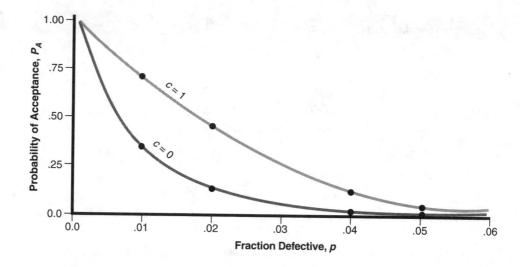

Observe that this result is essentially the same as that obtained by using the binomial distribution. As with the binomial, a sampling plan where $c = 1$ requires computations of P_A for $j = 0$, and $j = 1$.

The computing equation is

$$P_A = Prob(1; m) = \frac{m^1 e^{-m}}{1!} = me^{-m} \qquad \text{(Equation 7-13)}$$

Again, it is easier to use m in the middle column of Table 7-14 to calculate the amount that $j = 1$ increases the probability of acceptance, P_A.

Summing the third column contributions to P_A, row by row, from Tables 7-13 and 7-14 derives Table 7-15.

The Poisson approximation of the binomial is good for small values of p. Compare the binomial tables with the Poisson tables through the range of $p = 0.00$ to 0.05. These O.C. curves are sufficiently similar that either approach can be used. However, at 0.05 the error rises above 10 percent. Previously, it was stated that the Poisson should be used with $p < 0.05$, or 5 percent. Because the binomial is always more accurate, if there is doubt about using the Poisson, the binomial is not a difficult alternative.

It will be instructive to compare one larger value (for $c = 0$ and $p = 0.10$). The binomial result is

$$P_A = (1 - 0.10)^{100} = 0.000027$$

The Poisson result is

$$P_A = e^{-100(0.10)} = 0.000045$$

The Poisson approximation yields an error of 2/3 or 67 percent when $p = 0.10$, which is substantial. That is $(45 - 27)/27 = 2/3 = 0.67$.

Fraction Defective (p)	100p = m	$P_A = e^{-m}$
0.00	0	1.000
0.01	1	0.368
0.02	2	0.135
0.04	4	0.018
0.05	5	0.007
.	.	.
1.00	100	0.000

TABLE 7-13

Poisson Derivation of O.C. Curve with $j = 0$

Fraction Defective (p)	100p = m	$P_A = me^{-m}$
0.00	0	1.000
0.01	1	0.368
0.02	2	0.271
0.04	4	0.073
0.05	5	0.034
.	.	.
.	.	.
1.00	100	0.000

TABLE 7-14

Poisson Calculations for O.C. Curve with $j = 1$

Fraction Defective (p)	P_A (c = 0) P_A (j = 0)	P_A (j = 1)	P_A (c = 1) Sum P_A (j = 0 and j = 1)
0.00	1.000	0.000	1.000
0.01	0.368	0.368	0.736
0.02	0.135	0.271	0.406
0.04	0.018	0.073	0.091
0.05	0.007	0.034	0.041
.	.	.	.
.	.	.	.
1.00	0.000	0.000	0.000

TABLE 7-15

Poisson Distribution for O.C. Curve with $c = 1$

SUMMARY

The methodology of quality management is extensive. This chapter presents the major approaches used, including data check sheets, histograms, scatter diagrams, Pareto charts, and Ishikawa/fishbone diagrams. Then the most important of all, statistical control charts ($\bar{x}$-, R-, p- and c-charts) are explained—how they work and why they work. Average outgoing quality limits and multiple sampling are part of the treatment of acceptance sampling methods used for buyer–supplier quality relations.

Two Spotlight boxes conclude this chapter. These boxes illustrate real applications of the material in the chapters. See Spotlight 7-1: McIlhenny Company and Spotlight 7-2: Six-Sigma.

KEY TERMS

Acceptance sampling
Assignable causes
Bar chart
c-chart
Cause and effect charts
Chance causes
Classification by attributes
Classification by variables
Compensating for defectives
Control chart

Control limits
Data check sheets (DCSs)
Deming
Histograms
Inspection
Olympic perspective
Operating characteristic curves
   (O.C. curves)
p-chart
Pareto analysis

Quality control (QC)
R-chart
Runs
Scatter diagrams
Statistical process control (SPC)
Statistical quality control (SQC)
20:80 rule
$\bar{x}$-chart
Zed defects (ZD)
Zero-error mind-set

REVIEW QUESTIONS

1. Develop a data check sheet for:
   a. Basketball scores
   b. Top-ten players for runs batted in (RBIs)
   c. Some football statistics (provide some options)

2. Develop a data check sheet for setup times for:
   a. Service time in a sit-down restaurant
   b. Service time in a fast-food restaurant
   Note: First define service time explicitly.

3. Draw a fishbone diagram for the causes of poor reports.

4. An airline has requested a consultant to analyze its telephone reservation system. As the consultant, draw a fishbone diagram for the causes of poor telephone service.

5. Prepare a cause and effect analysis for the qualities of a fine cup of tea.

6. How do run charts give early warning signals that a stable system may be going out of control?

7. What are the purposes of control charts?

8. What would the blueprint look like for 2.54 centimeter (cm) nails to be tested by a go/no-go gauge that has (acceptable) tolerances of ±0.04 cm? Draw that blueprint.

9. Explain why service systems are said to have higher levels of variability from chance causes than manufacturing systems.

10. A job shop that never produces lot sizes greater than 20 units cannot employ the x-bar and R-charts of SQC. Why is this so? What kind of quality management can be used?

11. Stylish Packaging is a flow shop with a high-volume, serial-production line making cardboard boxes. An important quality is impact resistance, which requires destructive testing. Can SQC methods be used with destructive testing? What quality control method(s) are recommended? Discuss.

12. Can the consumer tell when an organization employs SQC? Can the consumer tell when it does not employ SQC?

13. Differentiate between assignable and chance causes of variation. What other names are used for each type of cause? Give some examples of each kind of variation. How can one tell when an assignable cause of variation has arisen in a system?

14. What is a stable system? Why is the condition of stability relevant to the activities of P/OM?

15. Why is the use of statistical quality control by drug and food manufacturers imperative? Would you recommend two-sigma or three-sigma control limits for food and drug applications of SQC? Explain.

16. One of the major reasons statistical quality control is such a powerful method is its use of sequenced inspection. Explain why this is so.

17. How should the subgroup size and the interval between samples be chosen? Is the answer applicable to both high-volume, short-cycle time products (interval between start and finish) and low-volume, long-cycle time products?

18. Differentiate between the construction of the $\bar{x}$-, R-, p- and c-charts. Also distinguish between the applications of these charts. Are the charts applicable to both high-volume, short-cycle time products (interval between start and finish) and low-volume, long-cycle time products?

19. What is meant by "between-group" and "within-group" variability? Explain how these two types of variability constitute the fundamental basis of SQC.

20. Use the concepts of "within-group" variability and "between-group" variability to answer the following questions:

a. Are the designer's specifications realistic?
b. Is the production process stable?
c. Is the process able to deliver the required conformance specifications?

PROBLEMS SECTION

1. Draw a scatter diagram for the following data where it is suggested that df (defective fraction) is a function of temperature T. Note the following definition of T.

Sample No.	T	Df
1	120	80
2	110	75
3	105	65
4	112	73
5	118	78

T is the temperature of the plating tank and df is the measure of defective parts per thousand, after plating. Does there seem to be a special relationship (correlation) between T and df?

2. After setup in the job shop, the first items made are likely to be defectives. If the order size calls for 125 units, and the expected percent defective for start-up is 7 percent, how many units should be made?

3. A subassembly of electronic components, called M1, consists of 5 parts that can fail. Three parts have failure probabilities of 0.03. The other two parts have failure probabilities of 0.02. Each M1 can only be tested after assembly into the parent VCR. It takes a week to get M1 units (the lead time is one week), and the company has orders for the next five days of 32, 44, 36, 54, and 41. How many M1 units should be on hand right now so that all orders can be filled?

4. Use SPC with the following table of data to advise this airline about its on-time arrival and departure performance. These are service qualities highly valued by their customers. The average total number of flights flown by this airline is 660 per day. This represents three weeks of data. It is suggested that a late flight be considered as a defective. Draw up a p-chart and analyze the results. Discuss the approach.

The Number of Late Flights (NLF) Each Day

Day	NLF	Day	NLF	Day	NLF
1	31	8	43	15	22
2	56	9	39	16	34
3	65	10	41	17	29
4	49	11	37	18	31
5	52	12	48	19	35
6	38	13	45	20	44
7	47	14	33	21	37

5. New data have been collected for the CTF. It is given in the following table. Start your analysis by creating an $\bar{x}$-chart and then create the R-chart. Provide interpretation of the results.

Weight of Chocolate Truffles (in Grams)

Subgroup j	I	II	III	IV	V	
Time:	10 A.M.	11 A.M.	1 P.M.	3 P.M.	4 P.M.	Sum
x_j						
1	30.00	30.25	29.75	29.90	30.05	
2	30.50	31.05	29.80	29.00	29.60	
3	29.95	30.00	30.05	29.95	29.90	
4	30.60	29.70	29.80	29.65	29.85	

6. For the data in Table 7-4, throw out the 3:00 P.M. data and substitute instead the following four values of x_j: (30.15), (29.95), (29.80), and (30.05).

Recalculate the parameters for the $\bar{x}$-chart and draw the revised chart. Discuss the results.

7. Recalculate the R-chart parameters without 3:00 P.M. data and using the new data supplied in Problem 6 for Table 7-4. Discuss the results.

8. What is the probability of a run of eight points all above the mean? What is the probability of a run of 10 points above or below the mean?

9. For the following tabulated data, draw the p-chart. Compare these results with those based on Table 7-7.

Subgroup No.	NR	N	P
1	1	9	–
2	2	9	–
3	1	9	–
4	3	16	–
5	1	9	–
	SUM	SUM	

10. A food processor specified that the contents of a jar of salsa should weigh 14 ± 0.10 ounces net. A statistical quality control operation is set up, and the following data are obtained for one week:

Sample No.				
1	14.10	14.06	14.25	14.06
2	13.90	13.85	13.80	14.00
3	14.40	14.30	14.10	14.20
4	13.95	14.10	14.00	14.15
5	14.05	13.90	13.95	14.60

a. Construct an $\bar{x}$-chart based on these 5 samples.
b. Construct an R-chart based on these 5 samples.
c. What points, if any, have gone out of control?
d. Discuss the results.

11. Use a data check sheet to track the Dow Jones average, regularly reported on the financial pages of most newspapers. Record the Dow Jones closing index value on a data check sheet every day for one week. Do an Ishikawa analysis, trying to develop hypotheses concerning what causes the Dow Jones index to move the way it does. Draw scatter diagrams to see if the hypothesized causal factors are related to the Dow Jones.

12. A method for determining the number of subgroups that will be sampled each day will be developed. Apply it to the situation where the total number of units produced each day is 1,000. The subgroup sample size is 30 units, and the interval between subgroups is 200 units.
a. How many subgroups will be sampled each day?
b. How many units will be sampled each day?
c. What should be done if the sampling method damages one out of three units?

Method: Dividing the production rate per day by the subgroup sample size plus the interval between samples (given in units) determines the number of samples to be taken per day. If the subgroup sample size is $n = 3$ units, and the interval between sample subgroups is $t = 4$ units, and the total number of units produced each day is $P = 210$, then the calculation to determine the number of subgroups sampled each day, called *NS*, is as follows:

$$NS = P/(n + t) = 210/(3 + 4) = 30$$

The total number of units that are sampled and tested for quality is $n(NS) = 90$. This means that 90 units would be withdrawn from the production line and tested. If the quality-testing procedure damages the product in any way, the sample interval would be increased and the sample size might be reduced to two.

END-OF-CHAPTER QUESTIONS

1. Embarking on a quest for better quality is an important P/OM objective. Which of the following answers is incorrect?
a. Use Pareto analysis to create a chart of customer complaint frequencies. Starting with the most frequent complaint, analyze what can be done to rectify the situation. Proceed to the next most frequent complaint. Continue in this way to address all complaints.
b. The use of a control chart to determine if price-marking errors are stable could be beneficial in evaluating the price-marking process.
c. A fishbone analysis and chart might help management understand the causes of damaged packaging on the shelves. This work could even reduce the number of damaged packages.
d. Draw an Ishikawa diagram to note all classes and subclasses of the causes of broken eggs inside of egg cartons. Take action as possible to remove the causes.
e. Employ scatter diagrams to study sales levels on different days of the week. This will help with scheduling check-out personnel and could lead to incentives for shoppers on days that have low turnout.

2. Which one of the following statements is incorrect about compensating for defectives?
a. Job shops are vulnerable to producing defectives at start-up. However, if the batch sizes are large (say in the hundreds of units) this problem is not as serious.
b. Flow shops may require some compensation for defectives produced when coffee breaks occur for workers on the line.
c. Flow shops may require some compensation for defectives produced when plant visits occur in which visitors speak to workers on the line.

d. Custom shops are not afflicted by defectives, so compensating for defectives is a non-problem.
e. Workers with small batches (say 50 units) are more likely to require compensation for defectives when no instrumentation is used to calibrate the settings.

3. A data check sheet has been created in spreadsheet form to reflect the output rate of a small direct mail agency. The number of envelopes completed in 10-minute intervals is observed five times a day for two weeks (10 days). The acceptable production rate runs from 33 to 39. Under 33 is not considered to be economic use of fixed cost resources. Above 39 creates bottlenecks in the mailroom and entails overtime pay, both of which are undesirable. Mailing rates that are less than 33 and more than 39 are labeled defectives. The analysis has been completed and reported in points a. through e., but there is one mistake. Locate the one answer that is incorrect.

Day/Sample #	1	2	3	4	5
1	31	36	43	41	26
2	36	38	42	40	35
3	36	35	37	38	34
4	32	33	35	37	38
5	30	32	33	34	36
6	31	38	37	37	36
7	36	36	32	30	32
8	43	42	37	35	33
9	26	38	35	32	34
10	32	33	35	34	36

a. In the 10 samples of $n = 5$ there are 18 "defective" production rates. That translates into an average percent defective of 36.0 percent, which is a larger number than most business managers will tolerate. Perhaps the specifications of 33–39 are too tight for the kind of work variability that is encountered.

b. There are 12 instances of processing rates that are too low and six instances of rates that are too high. The average output rate (including too highs and too lows) is 35.16 pieces ready for mailing per 10-minute interval. This is 0.84 lower than 36.00, which is in the middle of the tolerance range of 33 through 39. Perhaps this indicates that the problem of lows is more severe than the problem of highs.

c. Thirty-nine percent (of all "defective" production output rates) occurs in the first sample that is taken each day of the 2-week period. This is too high a percentage to occur by chance. Perhaps there is a setup (daily start-up) problem for the people working in the shop that could be corrected.

d. Weekly demand for the product is 12,000 pieces sealed and mailed. That is easily achieved with one shift working 8 hours per day for five days per week (8/5).

e. The patterns of underproducing and overproducing are accentuated during the first two days of sampling. Six of the 18 defectives (33.3 percent) occur within the first two days of sampling. Perhaps a setup problem arose for the people taking the samples as they began to measure output. Alternatively, there may have been an interaction between the observers and the observed.

4. Based on the sampled information collected by the small, direct mail agency in Problem 3, the company president raised some questions, which her operations manager answered. Which answers do you fault?

a. Q. Why does the structure of this study use the assumptions of a p-chart? Was it necessary to work with attributes based on pass or fail conclusions instead of measured variables?
A. It is true that the x-bar and R-charts provide more powerful analysis. However, they require more work. As an example, the length of time to complete each package for mailing could have been used as the variable under study. Such measurement is premature at this stage when the problem is that production output often falls outside of the 33–39 range.

b. Q. Would the company benefit from using Pareto analysis? Can that type of charting be applied to this production output rate situation?
A. Pareto analysis fits the bill. This Pareto chart has two bars. The first is 67 percent in height. It represents 12 undersupply situations that occur more often than the oversupply situation. The second bar representing oversupply is 33 percent in height. If the error of undersupply costs more than the error of oversupply, there is every reason to focus first on reducing the problems creating undersupply.

c. Q. What is the upper-control limit (UCL) for the p-chart? For these data, does the chart show a process that is satisfactory, stable, and in control?

A. The $UCL_p = 0.773$. This is obtained as follows: $UCL_p = .352 + 1.96(.215) = 0.773$. The choice of $k = 1.96$ is related to a 95 percent probability that all subgroups will have a p value that falls within these control limits. All values of p fall below this limit.

d. Q. What is the lower-control limit (LCL) for the p-chart? For these data, does the chart show a process that is satisfactory, stable, and in control?
A. The $LCL_p = .352 - 1.96(.215) < 0.00$, so zero is the best lower limit. The choice of $k = 1.96$ is related to a 95 percent probability that all subgroups will have a p value that falls within these control limits. All values of p fall above the zero lower limit.

e. Q. What role does the standard deviation play in the structure of the fishbone (Ishikawa) analysis? Can the company profit from the use of this charting method?
A. Fishbone diagrams identify causes of variability. They do not assess the amount of variability that is assignable to each cause. It would be possible and even beneficial to color code the vertebrae of the fish bones. For example strong positive causal effects would appear in red with a plus sign. Strong negative causal effects would be red with a minus sign. Medium effects would be in blue, etc.

5. The operations manager has retabulated the sampled information collected by the small, direct mail agency in Problem 3. He has increased the acceptable production rate range from 31 to 41. He explains that fixed costs of mailing can be decreased by substituting labor expense at the lower end of the range. At the upper end, he proposed removing some mailroom bottlenecks by automating certain functions. Now, mailing rates that are less than 31 and more than 41 are labeled defectives. His staff has completed the analysis and prepared a report, but there is one mistake. Locate the one answer that is incorrect.

a. In the 10 samples of $n = 5$ there are 8 "defective" production rates. That translates into an average percent defective of 16.0 percent, which is much better than the prior value of 36 percent. However, it is still too large. This shows that the range is not the culprit. The problem is the variability of how long it takes to do the job. That aspect of the situation should be studied.

b. There are four instances of processing rates that are too low and four instances of rates that are too high. Changing the acceptable range has not altered the average output rate, which is 35.16 pieces ready to mail per 10-minute interval. Underproduction remains more of a problem than overproduction.

c. The percent of all defectives that occurs in the first sample is 37.5, which is not much better than the 38.9 associated with the previous tolerance range. This is still too high a percentage to occur by chance. It is necessary to consider that a setup (daily start-up) problem exists for the people working in the shop and it should be corrected.

d. From the first sampled value on every one of the 10 days, observe that there is a run of numbers that are at or below the center point target of the tolerance range (36). There is only one instance of a number being greater (43) than the target value in the 10 observations.

e. The patterns of underproducing and overproducing are no longer accentuated during the first two days of sampling. Previously, there may have been an interaction between the observers and the observed, but that is no longer the case.

6. Statements about the achievement of quality are often technical, but their implications are so important that they need to be understood by managers who are neither engineers nor technically trained experts in SQC. Five such statements are now made, and two of them are considered to be "iffy." Can the reader spot the observations that need further discussion?

a. Spelling errors in letters answering complaints are considered grievous quality failures. Every hour a sample of four letters is taken and scrutinized for typos. On the wall is a *p*-chart that shows that defective letters are 2 percent of the total sample (average value). The manager explains that the company wants to catch a situation where error production jumps. This can happen because one of the letter writers is tired or not feeling well. The manager thinks that the control system keeps everyone on their toes and is well worth the expense.

b. Continuing with the system for answering complaints, the control limits are set at a one-sigma distance from the mean line ($\bar{p}$= 0.02). Because the standard deviation is 0.07, this means that the upper-control limit is set at 0.09 and the lower-control limit is zero. The manager feels a sense of comfort with this conservative one-sigma warning of impending trouble. Two-sigma would warn less frequently. The cost of investigating false alarms must be weighed against the cost of missing real problems.

c. A three-sigma upper limit for the complaint response system would be set at 0.23. Because one defective letter out of four represents a *p*-value of 0.25, that would signal a warning. Because of the sample size (*n* = 4), three-sigma and one-sigma are going to be warning at the same time. Perhaps, it would pay to change the sample size to 10. Then, one defective letter would have *p* = 0.10, and this would make the one-sigma upper limit more sensitive than the three-sigma limit.

d. Applying quality control charts to pool maintenance, a run occurs starting on Monday and going through Friday. (A run is a group of successive sample means all occurring on one side of the process grand mean.) The run of seven sample means above the grand mean are measures of the pH level of the water in the pool. The probability of this run occurring by chance is 1.5 in a hundred. The pool manager decides to wait for the readings from the next two days, stating that if both are above the mean, then corrective action will be taken.

e. The pool manager is delaying action until two more samples are taken. If Saturday's pH measure adds another sample mean to the run, then the odds of a run of seven occurring by chance is about 8 in a thousand. If Sunday's pH measure adds an eighth number to the run, then the odds will be about 4 in a thousand.

7. Four of the five statements that follow are correct. Which of the following statements is incorrect?

a. There are now inspection alternatives that have important consequences for process management and quality control. For a long time, 100% inspection was considered a trap. It sounded good but in reality was fraught with problems such as inspector weariness, lack of consistency and accuracy, and inability to match fast production rates. Automated and robotic inspection overcomes many of these problems. It can surpass human inspectors by being able to inspect things in hostile environments (such as searching for water on Mars). Robotic devices can be more accurate in chemistry, physics, and memory. However, 100% inspection will still fail when destructive testing is required.

b. Acceptance sampling is beneficial in many applications. For example, when the purchaser is across the ocean from the seller, it is possible to use AS before the shipments are loaded in the cargo holds. If the lots do not pass the test, they can be detailed (100 percent inspected) to remove all of the defectives before shipping.

c. The elements of acceptance sampling include lot size (*N*), sample size (*n*), the acceptance number (*c*), the number of defectives found (*k*), and the rule if $k > c$, reject the entire lot. These elements are fundamental parts of operating characteristic curves (O.C.curves). A weakness of ordinary O.C. curves is that they do not reflect buyer's and supplier's risks.

d. Nonstatisticians tend to believe that a sampling plan should maintain proportionality of the sample size to the lot size, i.e., (n/N) = constant. For example, let the sample size be 10 percent of the lot size. This approach will produce different acceptance plans, which means that proportionality is not an acceptable criterion for choosing sample sizes.

e. Each acceptance sampling plan can be examined to determine the imputed buyer's risk (beta error known as Type II) and the imputed supplier's risk (alpha error known as Type I). It is desirable that the creator of the sampling plan build in the alpha and beta that are in line with management's objectives and the negotiations between the buyer and the supplier. Otherwise, alpha and beta are default values determined after the fact.

8. Which of the following statements is incorrect?

a. Average outgoing quality (*AOQ*) is the average percentage of defective items the supplier will ship to the buyer—under different conditions of actual percent defectives (*p*) in the lot (*N*).

b. The average outgoing quality changes value as *p* goes from zero to one in this equation $AOQ = P_A p(N - n)/N$. It should be noted that P_A changes with *p* in accordance with the specifics of the sampling plan.

c. The *AOQ* curve resembles an upside-down catenary curve (or half of an ellipse) that reaches a maximum level called the average outgoing quality limit (*AOQL*) at some particular value of *p*. The *AOQL* describes the worst case of fraction defectives that can be shipped subject to two conditions. First, all defectives of rejected lots are replaced with acceptable product. Second, all lots have homogeneous quality.

d. Multiple-sampling plans are recommended when they cost less than single-sampling plans. Double sampling is only used when it can lower inspection costs by hedging. First, a sample size that is smaller than would be required for single sampling is taken. If it fails to accept the lot, then a second sample is drawn. It is useful to obtain the costs for both procedures when single sampling seems expensive. This notion extends to multiple sampling, which consists of more than two successive samples.

e. O.C. curves can be derived by using either the binomial or the Poisson distributions. The Poisson approximation of the binomial saves computational time, but it is only good for large values of p.

9. The foundation of statistical quality control (SQC) is based on several fundamental factors. Which one of the following is not correct?

a. The statistical structure of control charts compares "within-group" variability with "between-group" variability. They do not match when a change has occurred over time between groups; within-group variability remains the same. The mismatch signals that the system has gone out of control.

b. For starting up a control chart on a new process, it is desirable to have 20 successive samples. It is not unusual for initial sample means to be outside the control limits. Throw the outliers away and collect additional sample means. Also, analyze causes of other outages and remove the source of these assignable causes.

c. SQC charts are equally applicable to batch production in the job shop and continuous production in the flow shop. The p-chart might be more easily used with the job shop. The $\bar{x}$- and R-charts might apply more readily to the flow shop.

d. The best subgroup size and interval between samples is determined by the stability of the production process, the cycle time for a completed product, the cost of tracking problems, and the cost of ignoring problems. There are a lot of factors to take into account, but in general, intervals between samples should be small if process change can occur at any time, cycle time is short, cost of missing a process change is high, and sampling cost is reasonable. Similarly, use large samples if setup costs are high for each new sample, product cycle time is long, or "within-group" data is homogeneous. Use small samples when the process is likely to shift values during the sampling interval and when the cost of each observation within a sample is high.

10. Six-sigma as practiced by Motorola, General Electric, and Lockheed-Martin is TQM (total quality management). In business literature, the TQM emphasis is on the ample list of appetizers. However, TQM is a full-service menu, which includes the hardcore, statistical entrees that are not the subject of popular trade books. A good P/OM text must be fair and balanced in this regard. Statements a. through e. are intended to set an educational agenda for organizations that seek to achieve mastery of quality. One of the items is not feasible. Which is the incorrect answer?

a. Everyone in the firm should be familiar with the seven fundamental methods that must be exercised to achieve highest levels of quality. In particular, all employees should be able to create data check sheets and spreadsheets that allow tabulation and calculation of patterns and parameters applying to their own work. See the Table of Seven Methods for Quality Achievement.

b. Only those people involved with the production process can apply root cause analysis (RCA). The application of RCA (another name for fishbone and Ishikawa diagrams) must be performed by those who understand what makes the process tick.

c. A group of people within the organization should be trained in the statistical aspects of control chart construction and six-sigma derivations. If someone really understands six-sigma they should also be able to discuss the pros and cons of using five-sigma or seven-sigma as alternatives. To do this requires understanding fundamentals that underlie the cost structure of generic k-sigma plans (k is to be chosen as the optimal protection plan for each particular application).

d. Six-sigma is explained by GE at http://www.ge.com. Click on "To Quality"; then, "What is Six Sigma"; then, "Six Sigma Glossary"; and note the definitions of "Black Belt," "Green Belt," and "Master Black Belt." Big companies may find it useful to train some of their engineers in this fashion. "Master Black Belt" teachers are able to train the trainers. Small and medium-size companies (SMEs) may not be able to justify spending to train "Green Belts."

e. On an individual note, golfers and tennis players have a good chance of improving the game that they play and advancing their game to a higher plateau by using the seven methods for quality achievement shown in the table. Individual dedication may not be sufficient to include control chart methods (6.), but the other methods will go a long way to increasing "personal bests." The same applies to devoted chefs.

Table of Seven Methods for Quality Achievement

1. Data check sheets and spreadsheets with analysis
2. Bar charts
3. Histograms
4. Pareto analysis and charts
5. Root cause analysis and fishbone diagrams
6. Control charts for variables and attributes
7. Analysis of statistical runs

ADDITIONAL READINGS

Bounds, G., L. Yorks, M. Adams, and G. Ranney. *Beyond Total Quality Management*. New York: McGraw-Hill Book Co., Inc., 1994.

Crosby, P. E. *Quality Is Free*. New York: McGraw-Hill Book Co., Inc., 1979.

Crosby, P. E. *Quality Is Still Free*. New York: McGraw-Hill Book Co., Inc., 1995.

Crowden, D. J. *Statistical Methods in Quality Control*. Englewood Cliffs, NJ: Prentice-Hall, Inc., 1957.

Deming, W. E. *Out of the Crisis*. Boston: MIT—Center for Advanced Engineering Studies, 1986.

Dodge, Harold F., and Harry G. Romig. *Sampling Inspection Tables, Single and Double Sampling*, 2e. New York: Wiley, 1959.

Feigenbaum, A.V. *Total Quality Control*, 3e. New York: McGraw-Hill Book Co., Inc., 1991.

George, Michael. *Lean Six-Sigma for Service: How to Use Lean Speed and Six-Sigma Quality to Improve Services and Transactions*. McGraw-Hill Trade, Spiral Edition, June 2003.

Grant, Eugene L., and Richard S. Leavenworth. *Statistical Quality Control*, 6e. New York: McGraw-Hill Book Co., Inc., 1988.

Greene, Richard Tabor. *Global Quality: A Synthesis of the World's Best Management Methods*. Burr Ridge, IL: Irwin, 1993.

Ishikawa, K. *What Is Total Quality Control? The Japanese Way*. Englewood Cliffs, NJ: Prentice-Hall, Inc., 1985.

Juran, J. M. *Quality Control Handbook*, 4e. New York: McGraw-Hill Book Co., Inc., 1988.

Littauer, S. B. "Technological Stability in Industrial Operations." *Transactions of the New York Academy of Sciences*, Series II, vol. 13, no. 2 (December 1950), 67–72.

Main, Jeremy. *Quality Wars: The Triumphs and Defeats of American Business*. A Juran Institute Report. New York: The Free Press, 1994.

Pande, Peter and Lawrence Holpp. *What Is Six-Sigma,?* McGraw-Hill Trade, 1e., October 2001, (also an e-book).

Rath and Strong. *Rath and Strong's Six-sigma Pocket Guide*. McGraw-Hill Trade, Spiral Edition, March 2003.

Scholtes, P. R., et. al. *The Team Handbook*. Joiner Associates (608-238-8134). Madison, WI, 1989.

Shewhart, W. A. *Economic Control of Quality of Manufactured Product*. Princeton: D. Van Nostrand Co., Inc., 1931.

Shingo, Shigeo. *Zero Quality Control*. Connecticut: Productivity Press, 1986.

Wadsworth, H., K. Stephens, and A. Godfrey. *Modern Methods for Quality Control and Improvement*. New York: Wiley, 1986.

NOTES

1. W. E. Deming. *The New Economics for Industry, Government, Education*. Cambridge: MIT Center for Advanced Engineering Studies, 1993, 135. (Deming used study; not check for his Quality Cycles; see Figure 7-2)
2. Shigeo Shingo. *Zero Quality Control*. Connecticut: Productivity Press, 1986, 32.
3. Walter A. Shewhart. *Economic Control of Quality of Manufactured Product*. Princeton: D. Van Nostrand, 1931. Walter Shewhart's seminal work dates back to the research time he spent with the U.S. Department of Agriculture in the late 1920s.
4. "They use a less environmentally friendly system," Tom Meschievitz, director of Paint Engineering, General Motors—North American Operations. "Big 3 in low-pollution paint venture." *The Boston Globe* (May 26, 1994).
5. K. Ishikawa. *What Is Total Quality Control? The Japanese Way*. Englewood Cliffs, NJ: Prentice-Hall, 1987.
6. It is useful to note the effect of the value of k on the probability $(p_{\bar{x}})$ that a sample mean falls within the control limits $\pm k\sigma$. The following table shows the effect of k.

k	$(p_{\bar{x}})$	k	$(p_{\bar{x}})$
1.00	68.26%	2.00	95.44%
1.64+	90.00%	3.00	99.73%
1.96	95.00%	4.00	99.99%

7. Harold F. Dodge and Harry G. Romig. *Sampling Inspection Tables, Single and Double Sampling*, 2e. New York: Wiley, 1959.
8. A classic collection of mathematical tables is in *The Handbook of Mathematical Functions with Formulas, Graphs, and Mathematical Tables*. U.S. Department of Commerce, National Bureau of Standards, Applied Mathematics, Series 55. June 1964.
9. Poisson tables can be used to determine the probabilities of c or less defects where c and j are equivalent.

SPOTLIGHT 7-1
McIlhenny Company

McIlhenny Company—Manufacturing Tabasco® to the Highest Quality Standards

On Avery Island, about 100 miles west of New Orleans, McIlhenny Company makes a line of products whose brand name is known around the world. The diamond logo of Tabasco brand pepper sauce is one of the most recognized symbols of dependable quality by its customers. One of the reasons for its familiarity is the consistently high quality of the unique taste of the Tabasco sauce. Process masters are essential to achieve such constancy of high-quality production.

Product quality begins with planting and growing the ideal kind of peppers. Avery Island provides just the right kind of environment, as do Central and South American countries such as Brazil, Ecuador, Venezuela, Nicaragua, and Panama, where tabasco peppers are also grown. It is interesting to note that in 1870, Edmund McIlhenny received *letters patent* for his unique formula for processing peppers into a fiery red sauce. The same process is in use today. Avery Island remains headquarters for the worldwide company, which is still owned and operated by direct descendents of the founder.

Tabasco peppers must be picked at exactly the right time, which is when they are the perfect shade of red. Pickers use the *petit bâton rouge* (little red stick) as their color guide. The process for turning the peppers into the famous sauce is long and exact. To counter natural variations in the heat level of peppers due to weather conditions, steps are taken during the manufacturing process to minimize variation in the heat level of the final product. The peppers are mashed and mixed with a touch of salt and aged for three years.

The production sweetspot—where productivity is highest and (logically) quality problems are minimized—occurs at the fill rate of 300 2-ounce bottles per minute. In a 10-hour day, 170,000 2-ounce bottles are produced on each line. In a 250-day year, McIlhenny can fill and pack over 40,000,000 2-ounce bottles of its high-quality pepper product. These are packed with 12 or 24 2-ounce bottles per package and shipped all over the world. The warehouses at the Avery Island plant are gigantic adjacent spaces sepa-

The finished product: Hundreds of bottles of Tabasco pepper sauce sit on a conveyor belt in the Avery Island factory.

rated into domestic and international destinations. They are filled with products of all sizes (2-, 5-, and 12-ounce bottles plus the 1/8-ounce miniatures).

McIlhenny Company, a master of quality control, is also a supplier of country store products and lots of interesting information. Visit the company's webpage at http://www.TABASCO.com.

Sources: Visit with Mr. Stephen C. Romero, vice president of international sales, McIlhenny Company, April 2000; conversations with McIlhenny personnel, April 2001; Shane K. Bernard, Ph.D., historian and curator, McIlhenny Company, August 2001; Troy Romero, director of manufacturing, email correspondence (Lotus Notes), August 2001.

The Tabasco® marks, bottle, and label designs are registered trademarks and servicemarks exclusively of McIlhenny Company, Avery Island, LA 70513.

SPOTLIGHT 7-2
Six-Sigma

Can We Afford Six-Sigma Quality?

To answer this question requires analysis of the situation. How bad is current quality? What would an incremental improvement cost? What benefit can be gained from an incremental quality improvement? What would a dramatic six-sigma improvement cost? Is six-sigma improvement warranted? Alternatively, would benefits derived from improvement be greater than the cost?

First, define "how bad is current quality?" in terms of the level of defects experienced. A group of quality control practitioners and academics tried to estimate how many defects occur in a variety of circumstances. This resulted in the information shown in the table. Six-sigma (next to the bottom row) is normally measured in terms of a chain of failure probabilities that would apply to an electronic system with many interdependent components. This procedure results in slightly different values than derived by the usual three-sigma control limit calculations of statistical quality control charts. The benefits of the six-sigma *stretch* are not measurably altered by the alternative methods of calculation.

Before six-sigma efforts are accepted, management must define what it is calling "defective." For example, when is the coffee not hot enough, the delivery too slow, the finish too blemished, the movie too long, etc.? Often, product falls into what management calls an acceptable range. Then, by definition there are zero defects and no call for six-sigma quality goals. If, however, variability, which is inherent in the production of every physical "good" and service, causes products to fall outside acceptable limits, then some reduction in defective level will be warranted—if the cost does not exceed the benefits.

Motorola started the six-sigma crusade. Perhaps the reason stems from the fact that old attitudes about acceptable levels of defectives were no longer feasible in the era of integrated circuit boards. Motorola's Communications Sector operations manager summed it up. "We were using all the other popular quality-control ideas that everyone else uses. We had so many defects we couldn't even measure them. We have some large data-communications systems with tens of thousands of parts, so you can see how reckless it is to operate at three-sigma."

The questions that we began with have been answered. Current quality was bad at that time at Motorola. Incremental gains in defect reduction could be obtained by studying the systems and improving procedures. These steps were warranted by the benefits obtained. Extreme measures could be justified to improve the reliability of Motorola's systems because they were composed of tens of thousands of parts. The six-sigma was readily justified and became the new culture at Motorola.

As Motorola set out to rewire its quality attitudes, their process had a major contagious effect on other companies like GE, Allied Signal, Hewlett-Packard, Xerox, Ford, Bank of America, Sears, Home Depot, and Lockheed Martin Corporation. That does not mean that everyone caught the wave. It is doubtful that government tax advisors are going to embark on a six-sigma crusade. It might help the callers, but would taxpayers and the government want to pay for added qualities of advice?

What are the six-sigma methods? The best answer is that they are the correct methods to bring about both continuous, incremental improvement and, where necessary, reengineering the systems by changing the product design and/or the process being used to transform the inputs into the desired outputs. Six-sigma can best be viewed as an attack on variability. That is a war that can always be fought but it must be worth winning to embark on a six-sigma campaign. All of the statistical tools and the human motivation methods that are available can be used to reduce variability. Sometimes, there is the so-called "low-hanging fruit," which means that with little time and effort, significant reductions in defectives can be achieved. However, it should be kept in mind that relaxing quality standards will lower the percent defectives that are reported, but it will not dent variability.

Many of the companies have their own teaching units. Motorola University (MU) is well known for training people from a variety of companies. MU and many other organizations have open enrollment for black belt and green belt certifications. For differentiation, yellow belts are starters (about 20 hours of class training); green belts are intermediate (about 80 hours); black belts are near the top (about 125 hours of training); master black belts can train the trainers.

Sources: Stuart Gill, Mark. "Stalking Six-Sigma," *Business Month*, (January 1990).
See http://mu.Motorola.com (2004 schedule);
http://www.ge.com/sixsigma/geevolution.html; and
http://lean.mit.edu/Events/workshops/files_public/break2_lockheed_110601.pdf. (2001)

Application	Level of Defectives	Span of Standard Deviations
Government tax advice by phone	More than 10 in 100	$1.27\sigma = 10.2$ in 100
Doctors' prescription clarity	About 1 in 100	$2.30\sigma = 1.07$ in 100
Restaurant bill accuracy	Less than 1 in 100	$2.50\sigma = 0.62$ in 100
Payroll processing	About 1 in a 1,000	$3.05\sigma = 1.15$ in 1,000
Japanese auto defect goal	Less than 1 in a 1,000	$3.10\sigma = 0.97$ in 1,000
Good airline baggage handling	Less than 1 in 10,000	$4.00\sigma = 0.40$ in 10,000
Computer manufacturers	Less than 1 in 100,000	$5.00\sigma = 0.30$ in 1,000,000
Six-sigma—Motorola's goal	3.4 in one million	$6.00\sigma = 3.4$ in one million
Airline fatalities	Less than 3.4 in one million	More than 6.00σ

Supplement 7

Hypergeometric O.C. Curves

With this supplement, three methods of designing O.C. curves for single sampling will have been developed. Why bother with this third method when the binomial and the Poisson have been shown to be close enough under the demonstrated conditions? The reason for choosing one method instead of another is based on the relationship of the sample size n to the lot size N. In the case of the hypergeometric, the small size of N makes it necessary to do sampling without replacement.

This means that if there is a lot size of $N = 4$, and it is known that there is one defective in that lot, then for the first sample there is a one in four chance of drawing the defective part. If the defective is not found in this first sample, then the second sample has a one out of three chance of being the defective. The probability goes from 25 to 33.3 to 50 percent. The hypergeometric distribution takes this effect into account, whereas the binomial and the Poisson do not.

Stating this in yet another way, the hypergeometric distribution is used when the lot size N is small and successive sampling affects the results. Each next sample reduces the number of unsampled units remaining in the lot. Thus, the sample is first drawn from N units, then from $N - 1$, $N - 2$, ... units, etc.

If items are replaced to keep N of constant size, there is a significant chance that the same item would be sampled more than once. Also, with destructive testing, sampled items cannot be replaced because they have to be destroyed to be tested.

The hypergeometric distribution given in Equation S7-1 applies to a sampling plan with acceptance number, $c = 0$. [Repeated note: The factorial of any number is written $m!$ and is calculated by $(m)(m - 1)(m - 2)...(1)$.]

$$P_A = \frac{(N-x)!(N-n)!}{(N-x-n)!N!} \qquad \text{(Equation S7-1)}$$

x = the possible number of defectives in the lot and
$x/N = p$ is the possible fraction defective of the lot.

As x is varied from 0 to N, the appropriate values of P_A are determined. This allows a plot of P_A versus p (or $100\,p$, the percent defective). Thus, in the case where $N = 4$, $n = 1$, and $c = 0$, Equation S7-2 for P_A is

$$P_A = \frac{(4 - x)!\,(3)!}{(3 - x)!\,4!} = \frac{(4 - x)!}{4(3 - x)!} = \frac{4 - x}{4} = 1 - p \qquad \text{(Equation S7-2)}$$

where p is the symbol for fraction defective. The right-most term of Equation S7-2 is $(1 - p)$. It is obtained by substituting $x = Np = 4p$ into the next to the last term of the equation.

Varying p to derive P_A results in Table 7-16. This is the same distribution that was used to derive the values of AOQ and AOQL in this chapter.

The hypergeometric formula when $c > 0$ has the same additive requirements for the probability of acceptance with $j = 0$ and $j = 1$ that were shown for the binomial and Poisson distributions. Equation S7-3 gives the general hypergeometric equation.

x	$x/N = p$	P_A
0	0.00	1.00
1	0.25	0.75
2	0.50	0.50
3	0.75	0.25
4	1.00	0.00

TABLE 7-16

Hypergeometric Distribution

TABLE 7-17	x	$p = x/N$	P_A
Hypergeometric for O.C. Curves with j = 0 and c = 0	0	0.00	$\dfrac{50!\,10!\,40!}{10!\,40!\,50!} = 1.000$
	2	0.04	$\dfrac{48!\,2!\,10!\,40!}{10!\,38!\,2!\,50!} = 0.637$
	5	0.10	$\dfrac{45!\,5!\,10!\,40!}{10!\,35!\,5!\,50!} = 0.311$
	10	0.20	$\dfrac{40!\,10!\,10!\,40!}{10!\,30!\,10!\,50!} = 0.083$

$$P_j = \frac{C_{n-j}^{N-x} C_j^x}{C_n^N} = \frac{(N-x)!\,x!\,n!\,(N-n)!}{(n-j)!\,(N-x-n+j)!\,j!\,(x-j)!\,N!} \qquad \text{(Equation S7-3)}$$

The numerical example first derives the hypergeometric O.C. curve for c = 0 with j = 0, and then, using addition, for j = 1 and finally for c = 1. Also, for this example, the lot size is N = 50 and the sample size is n = 10. All calculations for Table 7-17 are based on Equation S7-3.

The next step is to determine the additions to the probability of acceptance when j = 1. Calculations for Table 7-18 are based on Equation S7-3.

Table 7-19 adds the respective rows of Tables 7-17 and 7-18.

TABLE 7-18	x	$p = x/N$	P_A+
Hypergeometric for O.C. Curves with j = 1	0	0.0	There are no defectives in the lot; therefore, the additional probability of acceptance with the relaxed acceptance criterion of j = 1 is zero. P_A + signifies that this is measuring the additional probability of acceptance.
	2	0.04	$\dfrac{48!\,2!\,10!\,40!}{9!\,39!\,50!} = 0.326$
	5	0.10	$\dfrac{45!\,5!\,10!\,40!}{9!\,36!\,4!\,50!} = 0.432$
	10	0.20	$\dfrac{40!\,10!\,10!\,40!}{9!\,31!\,9!\,50!} = 0.268$

x	P	c = 0 j = 0	j = 1	P_A c = 1
0	0.00	1.000	0.000	1.000
2	0.04	0.637	0.326	0.963
5	0.10	0.311	0.432	0.743
10	0.20	0.083	0.268	0.351

TABLE 7-19

The c = 1
Hypergeometric
Distribution

This c = 1 plan is a nonrigorous acceptance plan because it has such high probabilities of accepting 10 percent and even 20 percent defectives.

Problems for Supplement 7

1. Develop the hypergeometric for $N = 5$, $n = 2$, and $c = 0$.
   a. Write out the table for P_A.
   b. Draw the O.C. curve.

2. Develop the hypergeometric for $N = 5$, $n = 2$, and $c = 1$.
   a. Write out the table for P_A.
   b. Draw the O.C. curve.

3. Develop the hypergeometric for $N = 50$, $n = 2$, and $c = 0$.
   a. Construct the table for P_A.
   b. Draw the O.C. curve.
   c. Compare this result to the hypergeometric distribution that was developed in the supplement for $N = 50$, $n = 10$, and $c = 0$.

4. Develop the hypergeometric for $N = 50$, $n = 2$, and $c = 1$.
   a. Write out the table for P_A.
   b. Draw the O.C. curve.
   c. Compare this to the hypergeometric distribution that was developed in the supplement for $N = 50$, $n = 10$, and $c = 1$.

5. The situations in Problems 3 and 4 meet the binomial requirement that $n/N < 0.05$.
   a. Use the binomial distribution to create the table for P_A.
   b. Draw the O.C. curve.
   c. Compare the results of the hypergeometric in this case with those of the binomial distribution.

6. Comment on the use of the Poisson distribution for the situations given in Problems 3 and 4.

8

Management of Technology (MOT)

Chapter Outline

This section relates the management of technology to OM responsibility for the transformation process. As technology changes, there is pressure to adopt the new technology while using the systems and methods that characterize the old technology. This is a case of outside driving inside. The new-tech was not sought. It arose and the response was adopt it and see whether it could improve productivity, quality, etc. The other case is inside driving outside. There is a need for a process or IT improvement. R & D and engineering invent what is needed to do the job. Inside–outside may cost more, but necessity is the mother of invention. For outside–inside, invention mothers necessity. This case, called a *technology trap*, is discussed so that its wasteful aspects can be avoided.

After reading this chapter, you should be able to:

- Explain the role of technological transformation as it relates to OM.
- Discuss the specifics of technology management, relating it to the management of skills.
- Specify a ratio percent that reflects the mixture of skills and technology used over time.
- Explain the problem of applying new technology to old systems—why is this a technology trap?
- Explain technology timing.
- Discuss the evolution of the technology of an industry such as automotive windshield glass.
- Explain advanced technology for a complex industrial product, e.g., automotive windshield glass.
- Explain the interaction of process technology with the supply chain to deliver the product.
- Differentiate between the management of technology (MOT) for the original product market and the replacement product market.
- Explain OM's role in the management of the technology of packaging and delivery systems.
- Discuss the reason for including the technology of testing all aspects of product qualities as part of OM's responsibility.
- Explain how the management of testing technology relates to OM's awareness of legal statutes and governmental rules.
- Reveal why design for manufacturing (DFM) and design for assembly (DFA) are vitally important concepts.
- Explain why design for manufacturing and design for assembly are treated as a management of technology challenge.
- Discuss procedures for evaluating and selecting designs based on DFM and DFA criteria.
- Illustrate OM's technology management responsibilities for changeover capabilities.
- Describe the new technologies that OM will be managing in the future, including flexible systems, expert systems, cyborgs and robots, and miniaturization.

THE SYSTEMS VIEWPOINT

The management of technology is a shared (*systems*) responsibility with powerful leverage for company success and failure. Correct timing for the acquisition of new technology is more successful when it is a team effort because these decisions are best made with the involvement of all relevant forms of expertise. Timing issues increase the dimensional scope of the system that must be considered. Including relevant participants enlarges the playing field. Who can best provide estimates of when competitors will change technology? Competitive technology timetables are significant decision drivers. Who should lead and who should follow? OM evaluations of the effects of technology changes on productivity, unit costs, and quality will underlie proper OM strategies. The text explains why the management of technology for such basic operations as packaging, testing, and the delivery of products and services underscores the need for the systems approach.

STRATEGIC THINKING

At the technology interface, systems viewpoints and strategic thinking blend into each other. Judgments about the costs of adopting new technologies and their effects on customers' satisfaction (in both short- and long-term cases) will be crucial. Strategic planning is dependent upon forecasts of technology shifts and their rates of change. Financial advice concerning the best timing of major expenditures involves the market's sensitivity to the dynamics of how work is done at present and how that could change if the new technologies are adopted. Also involved is executive consideration of the availability of management as a resource that can deal with the changing technology. Measuring concepts that go along with the strategic systems approach to managing technology timing include computation of the payback period, breakeven point, breakeven time, and the length of the cost recovery period. For example, if replacing old equipment with new equipment in the office, or on the plant floor, has a payback period, or cost recovery period, of 3 months, that would be attractive and hard to ignore, whereas a period of 3 years might not be acceptable.

8-1 TECHNOLOGY COMPONENT OF TRANSFORMATION

Technology: Equipment employed to accomplish the transformation that is basic to the fundamental P/OM input–output model.

Technology plays a commanding role in accomplishing the input–output transformation that is OM's main concern. From the OM perspective, **technology** consists of equipment employed in a manner—defined by scientific knowledge about the conditions necessary—to bring about specific transformations. The equipment includes computers, machinery, tools, and communication systems. Combined with people's skills, materials are transformed and services are provided. Technology components of transformation also can be categorized by types of processes, such as physically transforming glass, rubber, or steel; assembling parts to make toasters, airplanes, or computer chips; transferring information; and providing services.

8-1a Management of the Technology Component

Management of technology (MOT): Requires knowing what technologies exist, their state of development, and when to shift from one format to another.

Management of the technology component of input–output systems transformations is often called **management of technology (MOT)** when it is taught as a subject in business schools. The management of technology functions at three distinct levels.

1. At the societal level, management of technology (MOT) for products and processes includes governmental regulations controlling technology for health and safety purposes. Also governmental, patent jurisprudence operates to stimulate invention of new technological transformation systems by protecting inventors against competi-

tion for lengthy periods of time. Illegal copying of an invention and profiting thereby is called *infringement*. The legal definition of *infringement* and the courts' punishment for this crime are continually undergoing revision, with resulting stricter laws and harsher punishments for infringement.

2. At the company level, management of technology is focused on satisfying customers and gaining competitive advantage. Some firms invest in the development of new technology to gain an advantage, which could be patent protection. Another option is to copy the new technology of competitors. This is not acceptable when it leads to successful charges of infringement. To avoid litigation, many firms pay competitors for the use of their new technology by licensing the rights.

3. Management of technology at the international level involves all of the areas of Levels 1 and 2. Each country has different rules and policies. There are many international agreements, which are constantly being altered by new trade agreements. A challenge to those managing technology is to keep up with the international scope of changes regarding the safety of the workplace and the protection of customers. Applicability of patents, the courts' rulings on infringement, and the regulation of license agreements are international subjects that require systems cooperation between the legal and operations management participants in the firm. To have international P/OM capability requires extensive knowledge and constant updating. Companies cannot do business on a global scale without this expertise.

8-2 THE TECHNOLOGY TRAP

Technological changes occur in clusters or droves. The *discontinuity* of major waves of new technology *can create a trap*, called the **technology trap.** Consider this headline: "Companies have spent vast sums on technology. Now they have to figure out what to do with it all."[1] This *Wall Street Journal* feature refers to information technology (IT). The problem applies to other kinds of new technology, but almost everything new about technology in the period 1990–2020 will be related to IT in one form or another.

> **Technology trap:** To avoid this trap, systems studies should upgrade the way that work is done in keeping with the capabilities of new technology.

The trap is wanting to be current, but not knowing how to use the new technology to reshape old systems. The key to the problem is recognizing that information systems have been in place for decades. Traditional ways of doing things are hard to change, thus new technology has been made subservient to the old systems. In other words, old systems are frozen into place, and the new technology has not been able to thaw out the old procedures in order to establish new ones.

The tendency to use new technology to mimic old systems is likely to be detrimental. Companies that have started out with a reengineering point of view and a reinvent business processes mind-set have succeeded in gaining technological advantages. Dr. Zuboff of the Harvard Business School has shown that those companies that have rethought the systems they use for doing work have profited from introducing computer technology. Those that computerized without altering the existing systems did not do well.[2] To be successful, companies must not only continually change their equipment, but also their processes, and most importantly, the mind-set of their management and employees.

8-3 TECHNOLOGY TIMING

Management of technology involves knowing when to shift from one form of technology to another. Should the old computer technology be replaced by the latest available, or should the organization wait for future developments? What does waiting cost? It entails continuing use of an older technology that might be slower or more expensive. Newer technology might produce a higher quality product. On the other hand, new technology often entails costs of learning and *shakedown risks* of unexpected bugs and glitches. Shakedown and break-in are both concerned with start-up problems.

The timing of shifts in technology involves assessment of the costs and savings made by changing now as compared to the costs and savings from deferring the acquisition.

These should include the advantage, particularly with industrial customers, of having the reputation of being a technology leader instead of a follower.

If the benefits of being a leader in technological development are not significant, then copying technology without infringing across the global boundaries that apply can prove advantageous. Being second can be a successful management of technology strategy. Postponement and deferral of new technology development may be a sound MOT strategy when:

1. Development costs are high.
2. Shakedown problems can alienate customers.
3. Infringement cannot be substantiated.
4. The benefits of new technology are likely to require more years of development.

Usually, investments are made in developing new technology when the payback period is relatively short compared to the expected lifetime that the development will be generating profits and savings. **Payback period** is the estimated number of years that will be required to produce enough profits or savings to offset the expenditures completely. Some companies prefer to talk about *breakeven time*, essentially the same concept at work. *Cost recovery period* also is used. It is the time required to accumulate profits that fully offset the expenses entailed in replacing old technology with new technology. All of these measure the time required to pay off alternative investments. It is a favored way to evaluate choices in technologies.

> **Payback period:** Defined as the period of time required for an investment to produce revenues that pay back the debt.

Different criteria will apply according to the specifics of the situation. However, as a rule of thumb, in stable markets that are estimated to last about 10 years, a 3-year payback period was often considered to be the allowable upper limit. In the days of rapidly evolving technology, much shorter time periods have to be set.

An alternative for evaluating technology changes is **net present value (NPV),** which discounts future earnings according to the expected interest rates that will prevail. With a 6 percent interest rate, earnings at the end of one year would be divided by 1.06. Earnings that apply only to the second year would be divided by $(1.06)^2 = 1.12$. Earnings that apply only to the nth year would be divided by $(1.06)^n$. NPV calculations are explained in many texts including the Supplement to Chapter 19.

> **Net present value (NPV):** Method for discounting the cost of future expenditures and the value of future savings.

NPV is a financial management tool. The fact that OM and finance must use it together to manage technological decision making is illustrative of the need for using the systems approach for MOT.

The OM decision to "make" or "buy" components is often related to technological expertise and to the cost of leading or following in technology. "Buy" avoids having to invest in and learn the new technology that "make" entails. The decision to buy uses someone else's expertise, which makes sense during current times of great technological volatility. It made less sense during past periods of technological stability, which have been called "the quiet times" by a creative colleague.

To keep abreast of technological developments, it may be essential to make certain components. Making also can provide opportunities to achieve best quality and gain competitive advantages. Evaluation of the make or buy decision is a constant challenge to OM.

Many companies have appointed people to the job of technology assessment and management. This job requires being able to evaluate the current status of technology and future state probabilities. It is part of the job to coordinate OM, finance, and marketing to determine as a team how to manage technological timing. Among the technology timing issues to be considered are

1. Assessing technology plans of competitors and the importance of matching them. Can customers tell the difference?
2. Knowing the cost and/or benefits of the current technological level of the firm.
3. Understanding the costs of transition and the payback period.
4. Knowing when to move up the technological ladder. Periods of volatility are to be avoided, whereas periods of relative stability are preferred.

5. Involving technological forecasting, which requires knowing that part of technology development is in the laboratory and the other part is on the factory floor or out in the field with the service crews.

8-4 THE ART AND SCIENCE OF TECHNOLOGY

The nature of work blends people and machinery together to form the technology of processes. What often is missed is the interplay of equipment capabilities (industrial science) and human skills (industrial arts). Both play a role in determining how specific forms of technology create processes for making and doing things. Technology is a synthesis of these two factors. Managing technology requires managing the combination of people skills with computers, robotics, and other equipment.

Before 1950, definitions of technology placed more stress on the "arts" part of the interactions that occur between people's skills using tools and machines than on the materials and machines themselves. This makes sense because skills with machines used to constitute a larger part of the technologies responsible for all kinds of products. Such skills included the ability to measure and test using calipers, micrometers, and all kinds of laboratory equipment, including microscopes, to assess the chemistry of products. At one time, rulers and scales were high-powered technological developments.

In their early interactions, machines did less and people did more. Go back to the seventeenth century, before the torrent of inventions associated with the Industrial Revolution. Look at how the percent contribution made by skills (as compared to the percent contribution made by machines) goes down over time. The equation for the percent contribution of skills over time $P(S)_t$ might be written:

$$P(S)_t = \frac{skills}{skills + technology}(100)$$ (Equation 8-1)

Alternatively, an equation for the percent contribution of technology $P(T)_t$ can be written:

$$P(T)_t = \frac{technology}{skills + technology}(100)$$ (Equation 8-2)

Figure 8-1, using Equation 8-1, shows the decline in the percent participation of human skills—as a generalized shape for an average process—over a period of 400 years.

As time goes on, engineering and science have made people increasingly peripheral to operations. The art skills are built into the equipment. The further back one goes in time, the more reliance on people's skillful contributions, the smaller the contributions of machine technology, and the more that materials used were closer to basic commodities and less specialized. Now, there is more value added by advanced technology and less by people's skills.

A water, wind and animal power 1600–1800
B steam power 1800–1900
C mechanical systems and electrical power 1900–???
D electronic digital control of power 1980–???

FIGURE 8-1
Participation of Skills as a Percent of Total Labor Plus Machine Inputs—Estimates from 1600 to 2000

The decrease is very slow for many years and then speeds up. Recent usage accelerates the decrease of the arts and skills portion relative to technology and science. The mixture within technology has shifted. In the first half of the twentieth century, machines developed capabilities for moving and lifting power. They were acclaimed for their sheer strength and endurance, not for their smartness and adeptness, which had to be derived from the human operator.

Starting in the 1950s, machine intelligence began to be developed. At first, the speed of doing simple calculations and the size and persistence of memory seemed to spell out the basic advantages of machine calculations. It was firmly believed that machine intelligence had serious limitations that would never approach human capabilities. These restrictions are falling by the wayside. Computers working together with machines now can perform an array of functions that surpass what humans alone can do in all forms of arts and skills.

Geometrically increasing numbers of applications can be cited where industry now places greater reliance on machines than people for physical skills, performance learning abilities, and fast decision making with large databases. The technological replacements apply to making things and providing services. They apply to the skills and equipment required to inspect and test results. Here too, human efforts are being replaced by technology.

On the other hand, the expanding role of technology has increased the amount of knowledge work required by industry. Such creative knowledge work, essential for planning, designing, and programming, is predominantly done by people with special training who are aided by computers. It has been said that the OM workforce has been replacing blue collars with scholars.

Thus, the increasing role of technology has changed the way operations must be managed in a number of ways. OM people must understand more about the technology of the process and the computers that are used to control the process. Skilled machinists, tool and die makers, and artisans with tools are being replaced by CAD-CAE-CAM (computer-aided design, computer-aided engineering, and computer-aided manufacturing) experts using electronic data interchange (EDI) via satellites and the Internet. Knowledge work has grown with greater technology, and managing such creative efforts has become part of the OM responsibility.

It is useful to assess the management of technology in terms of the degree of participation and the coordination of the components, which are the

1. arts and skills of people in making things and providing services.
2. industrial science capabilities of machines in making things and providing services.
3. applied science properties of materials.
4. increasing intelligence of machines.
5. important role of art in managing technology at the strategic level.
6. increasing role of science as a support for art in managing technology at the strategic level.

With respect to Points 5 and 6, it should be noted that the ratio of art to science in managing technology at the strategic level is very high. Planning and programming are essentially arts reminiscent of the skills of artisans in the 1500s. Science is gradually bringing greater support to strategic levels much as it did to tactical skill levels in the late 1800s.

8-5 THE DEVELOPMENT OF GLASS PROCESSING TECHNOLOGIES

With respect to Points 3 and 4, there are many different materials that could be used to illustrate the shift from art-based skills to technology-based processes; steel, rubber, paper, and glass are among them. Each provides wonderful examples of processes that increasingly make use of intelligent machines and a wealth of scientific knowledge about the properties of materials.

The woman in this illustration could be playing solitaire, but the odds are that she is a professional who is reviewing inventory levels, setting up today's menus, or designing a high-fashion gown. She might even be doing tool and die design work. Computer abilities have brought many women into the P/OM domain.

OM manages technology of products that are so taken for granted that few stop to wonder how this is done in a factory. What skills and technologies must be managed to make windshields? Everyone is familiar with windshields, having spent enough time sitting behind them. The manufacture of windshields will be addressed in this section with perspectives about glass in general, the history of change in technology, and amazing challenges that OM has faced up to in this multibillion-dollar industry.

It is simple to illustrate the shift from art to advanced technology using various glass-making categories. Glass processes run the gamut in the degree to which they require art and science in varying amounts. Masterful human skills are required for glass blowing, the art of shaping a mass of molten glass into various shapes by blowing a controlled stream of air through a tube into the mass. Glass containers have been found that date to the second millennium B.C.

Glass blowing is an example of one of the oldest industrial arts. The same low-technology equipment in the hands of a skilled artisan produces artwork, whereas in the hands of a novice it produces poor work. Glass blowing for valuable vases and other glass art is done in custom shops all over the world. Glass blowers can do things with glass that no machines can even approximate; various works of art in glass, such as produced by Steuben of Corning Incorporated, command prices that attest to this.

Having looked at the highest percent participation of art–skill level (near 100 percent) for glass blowing, next move to flat glass, which has occupied a range of positions over time. Prior to 1959, flat glass had to be cast, rolled, and polished through a labor-intensive process with serious quality problems.

Then the British firm of Pilkington introduced an entirely new technology called the *float process*. It had taken them seven years of experimentation to make the continuous ribbon of glass (melted sand) floating on a bath of molten tin acceptably flat. Float glass does not have the imperfections that rolling glass produces. Not only does it have higher quality, but it is also easier and less expensive to make.

When the method was perfected, Pilkington started to license it, which it still does today. The result was that OM in the glass industry experienced a sudden revolution in technology. There was an abrupt and severe decline in the skill to technology ratio for the new process. Conversely, the technology component of the new process was much higher than in any other glass-making operation. Replacing casting with the float-glass process had to be carefully managed as the float method became the primary method worldwide for making flat glass. At this time, it is used in first, second, and third world countries.

Flat-glass sales generate more revenue than any other glass product. This product is demanded worldwide for windowpanes in houses. The revolution in flat-glass production fell on OM's shoulders because the conversion had to be made from outmoded technology to the new technology without disrupting the supply of product to customers. An entirely new process had to be learned and brought online. The success of the industry to adapt is a tribute to the operations managers of the flat-glass industry.

8-5a Technological Innovations—Product and Process

The glass business has been an innovative industry. Improved products and processes have continually appeared. One reason for this success is that the customers of glass companies are the auto, construction, and telecommunication industries (fiber optics). Taken together, this constitutes a multibillion-dollar market, which aside from economic business cycles is growing on a global scale.

New product adaptations flourish when raw materials are readily available and inexpensive. Global companies aggressively compete for market share by utilizing new technologies. In many instances, the new products require increasing the technological composition of the system to be managed by OM.

The story about managing technology in the glass industry continues with the recognition that float glass is the starting component for automotive glass. Automotive glass requires the use of much higher levels of technology than household glass. Safety glass is mandated for automobile windshields in the United States and many other countries because it will not shatter under impact.

FIGURE 8-2
Process Flowchart for Making Windshields

Safety glass is a sandwich of two pieces of float glass (called *lites*) that are annealed by heating and cooling for strength. Placed between the inboard and outboard lites is a polyvinyl butyral laminate. The polyvinyl butyral bonds to the glass using temperature and pressure to form a sandwich.

The process for making windshield glass requires a mixture of high levels of labor skills with corresponding levels of technology or very advanced automated systems of technology working without human operators. The number of steps that must be taken and the need for skills and technology are evident from the process flowchart for making windshields, shown in Figure 8-2, which presents an illustration of the generic windshield-making process.

Many scientific breakthroughs in glass-manufacturing processes allow companies like Guardian Industries, Libbey-Owens-Ford (LOF) Co., and PPG Industries to equip cars with the large curved automotive glass windshields that distinguish modern-day autos from older ones. It should be noted that windshields can include special edge markings around the entire perimeter. These borders or frits protect ultraviolet degradation of the urethane used to install the windshield into the vehicle. Radio antennas and heating grids are embedded (respectively) in front and rear window car glass.

As the amount of glass increases, the heating and cooling of the car demands more energy. To counteract that costly effect, solar glass is installed, which controls all three parts of the solar spectrum—visible, ultraviolet (UV), and infrared (IR) light. Solar glass uses a multilayer metal/metal oxide coating on the inboard surface of the outboard glass in the laminated safety glass windshield structure. Silver coating and other layers reflect solar energy and control glare. Reflecting the sun's energy is a more effective way to manage the energy than adding materials to the glass substrate to absorb the energy.

Windshield production necessitates a highly-mechanized, mass-production flow shop process when the demand volume is sufficiently great. This kind of volume characterizes windshield production by the supplier for the original use by the auto manufacturer. Less highly-mechanized shops that permit smaller batches with quick model changeovers are used for the replacement market. Even so, replacement volumes are large enough to warrant relatively continuous production processes.

A typical production process is divided into bulleted segments.

- Rectangular flat glass brackets, purchased from an outside supplier, are automatically loaded onto two parallel preprocessing lines.

- The glass brackets are cut into lites on these two lines using CNC (computer numerical control) machines; these will become the inner and outer lites of the finished windshield.

- After cutting, the lites are transferred to CNC grinders where a Type 1 ground edge (SAE J 673 b Standard) is applied around the entire periphery.

- After applying a separating medium (usually diatomaceous earth), the cut and ground lites are booked together and automatically indexed into a print room, where a black enamel frit is silk screened onto the glass, obscuring the border. This black border protects ultraviolet degradation of the urethane used to install the windshield into the vehicle. The trademark also is silk screened onto the glass at this time.

- There also may be an additional silk screen of the inner lite with a grid of lines of silver enamel frit at the lower area of the windshield. This feature, know as EWD (electric wiper defrost), heats the area of the windshield where the windshield wipers would park, helping prevent ice buildup. The electric grid on the windshields is visible from the outside of the vehicle and works on a principle similar to that of heated back lites.

- The silk-screened lites are automatically loaded onto an automotive in-line windshield forming and annealing system. This furnace simultaneously forms the lites to the required design surface shape at a cycle time of 15 to 20 seconds.

- Glass lites are positioned automatically onto a supporting/forming frame. The lites are indexed through heating zones of the furnace until they reach the desired forming temperatures.

- Simple shapes are produced by controlling the heat and allowing the lites to sag into the support/forming frame by gravity. More complex and deep contours require sophisticated heat control and/or pressing to achieve the desired shape.

- The formed lites then proceed through the annealing zones of the furnace where they are cooled to develop acceptable stresses.

- The unload conveyor's mechanical set of fingers gently lifts the glass from the support/forming frame to the cooling conveyor.

- The formed lites are unloaded onto racks where they are washed and separated. A plastic interlayer is placed between the inner- and outer-formed glass.

- The glass-plastic-glass "sandwich" is put into an autoclave where heat and pressure bond the separate components into a single, strong, transparent windshield.

- Electric leads are soldered onto the windshield to complete construction of the EWD feature. The electric leads connect the EWD to the wiring harness to allow energizing of the silver grid area of the windshield.

- The production capacity is 150 to 240 windshields per hour, depending on the size and complexity of the windshield.

- Distribution is handled just-in-time from the glass to the assembly plants.

It should be apparent that production of automotive glass is not a static process. There is a lot of change going on as a result of research and development (R & D) that is invested in automotive windshield processes. Solar glass is a good example, but there are many others as well. In most companies, R & D is a separate department that works closely with OM to convert research ideas from theory to practice. The systems approach helps to blend the needs and interests of P/OM and R & D in pursuit of company objectives.

In the previous description, the percent of art skills required for running the process approaches zero. It is almost all technology. People do participate in controlling the process, and they are more critical than ever for designing the windshield, planning its production, setting up the process, and programming the "automotive in-line windshield forming and annealing system." People are essential for deriving creative solutions for problems associated with ever larger and more-curved windshields.

For all kinds of materials, including metals, plastics, ceramics, glass, paper, and wood, there are advances in technology that require new processes to take advantage of the enhanced properties of the materials. For the most part, these processes utilize computers to design the product and often to run the process. People are needed to plan the process, program the machines, and deal with inevitable contingencies.

The connection between the design of the product and the process is increasingly of major technological consequence. In Section 8-9, that connection is explored with respect to designing for manufacturing (DFM) and designing for assembly (DFA). It is worth noting how large a role assembly plays in the production of automobile windshields.

The linking of design with manufacture, assembly, and distribution depends upon the most advanced forms of new computer technology, such as CAD-CAE-CAM. Yet, at the same time, design is not an automated function. Designers are knowledge workers whose art is dependent upon innate skills.

All of this applies to the installation of *original* automotive glass (as contrasted with *replacement* glass). Some discussion follows for P/OM replacement problems.

8-5b Supply Chain Technology

Supply chains epitomize technological linkages that are managed by operations personnel. The design, production, and distribution of windshields is a supply chain system that is sensitive to technology at every one of its stages. Suppliers' technologies must be congruent with the producer's technologies, which, in turn, must be complementary to the customers' technological needs. OM is either responsible for coordination of this system or an integral part of the team.

Every time a new car model is launched, windshields, rear windows, and side glass must be designed to fit the model and to meet designers' specifications. That glass product must be fabricated in volume that is commensurate with the production schedules of the auto assembly plant. The glass must be on hand to be assembled with the rest of the car. Simultaneously, the same glass parts need to be stocked as replacement products. The following three "ifs" are relevant:

1. *If* the windshield fabricating process is a flow shop, then continuous delivery of flat glass from suppliers must be achieved and maintained. This condition is dependent on the suppliers using appropriate technology to achieve the needed volumes.

2. *If* the customer is an auto assembly plant, then the technology of the windshield producer must be capable of achieving a production schedule that matches the requirements of the assembly plant. Shipments will be made regularly in large quantities.

3. *If* the customer is a distributor for replacement glass, then the technology upon which production scheduling is based must be able to produce a variety of models quickly to meet retail demand.

In fact, Points 2 and 3 are often both true at the same time. The technology of the windshield producer must be able to combine the requirements of both kinds of customers. In general, technologies along the entire supply chain must be compatible and coordinated with respect to both quality and quantity to ensure smooth running of the system. Flows need to be balanced, matching supply and demand.

Auto factories (the customers) require enough inventory of windshields for all models scheduled to be made within the next production lead-time period. Lead time, in this case, is the elapsed time between ordering and receiving the windshields that are needed.

Although just-in-time deliveries are usually the goal, just-in-case stocks are kept on hand to provide buffer protection against the contingencies of the real world. As the key to success or failure, the technologies of the producers of windshields and their suppliers of float glass must interact properly with the technologies of their customers, who manufacture automobiles.

P/OM accountability starts by coordinating the design phase with fabrication and assembly (manufacture). Supply chain responsibility continues with setting up the inventory, delivery, and stocking policies. The entire system is technology driven.

It is not surprising that technology for the supply chain that deals with automotive replacement glass is different from the technology that is the foundation for the original glass market. Replacement glass is often produced as an added amount of product with the original production run. It is then sent in small batches to the distributors dealing with the service outlets that include glass retailers, collision and body shops, and dealer service stations, a unique supply chain system.

The demand for replacement auto glass in the United States is large. Windshield replacement alone is in excess of 8 million units per year. This demand is generated by thousands of different kinds of vehicles on the road. "There are over 15 thousand automotive glass SKUs . . . in North America, and this number is growing exponentially." [3]

Any one of them can experience glass breakage, which means that OM must adjust production scheduling to handle smaller batches of many more varieties. This necessitates other kinds of OM rules for fabrication, inventory scheduling, and warehousing based on alternative technologies.

An important part of the technology of supply chains is the means by which the various players (suppliers, producers, and customers) are able to know where things are located. This includes the trucks, trains, and planes used to carry the goods. Customers want to know when they can expect delivery of the various products they have ordered from suppliers.

The Association of American Railroads (AAR) has an information system that keeps track of where all railroad boxcars, tank cars, and hopper cars are in the country. Using this information, individual companies monitor their rolling stock. Security issues have dictated restricted access to railcar location data. An operations center links the railroads with national intelligence organizations (24/7). Security systems are enhanced by real time monitoring and capability for surveillance of designated trains.

UPS and FedEx use the combination of optical scanners, network telecommunications, and computer-database management to track package movements for their customers. Bar-code readers continuously send information to the tracking computer to trace package movements for their customers. Bar-code readers continuously send information to the tracking computer. Similar bar-coded information technology is used within factories to track the status of products and components.

Everyone that is part of the supply chain has something they are shipping or something they are receiving, or both. That model applies to adjacent stations within factories, banks, investment brokers, hotels, and restaurants. It is worth noting that the supply chain concept applies equally well to external and internal suppliers, producers, and customers; the systems point of view always encompasses the trio.

8-5c Replacement Versus Original Market Technology

The automotive replacement glass market is a system that entails dealing with greater variety than the automotive original glass market. Systems with greater variety generally

Reflection of the sky in the glass windows of an airline terminal is a part of the story. Is that glass darkening as the sun gets brighter? Does that glass cut the glare? How does it compare to windshield glass? Greenhouse glass has improved markedly. It used to fail on average every five years. Now, it may be good for more than 30 years.

also must cope with more variability, risk, and uncertainty than systems with lower levels of variety. The technology with which OM must deal is large batch and intermittent flow shop configurations.

To make the analogy more broadly applicable, consider the similarity that exists with replacement glass and the replacement tire market. There are so many tire sizes, grades, and styles for cars, trucks, and vans that the variety of models is the greatest source of problems. Like auto replacement glass, replacement tires have to be distributed through many different dealerships.

One company that has won acclaim for its success in the difficult tire replacement market is Kelly-Springfield. Their success has been based on their ability to:

1. Forecast well the need for each variety of product in the different market locations.

2. Produce the right amounts of each kind of tire to meet demand when it arises instead of by excessive stock levels.

3. Distribute tires so that the right models are in the correct places to fill customer demands on an as-needed basis. It should be noted that "fill or kill" tends to characterize this market where other brands are available as substitutes.

Good forecasting models and understanding of the markets are both critical ingredients of success. Next, strong quantitative scheduling models are used that take into account the fact that tire replacement producers have to cope with a great diversity of molds and many changeovers. No matter how continuous the engineers and process managers have been able to make the flow of materials, they still are dealing with the management of dissimilarity.

The management of technology for the production of variety must be able to deal with dissimilarity. Product multiplicity has more code numbers for stocking and inventory. It has more settings for machinery, and greater control must be exercised over the paths and storage of batches. It is common terminology to say that the entropy is higher for systems with product multiplicity and dissimilarity. The term *entropy* is a measure of disorder from physics that has been absorbed as a systems term to describe complexity. Entropy increases with greater uncertainty and increased disorder.

This results in higher unit costs for replacement products, even though replacement technology is more likely to use general-purpose equipment (GPE) than special-purpose equipment (SPE). The classic trade-off applies. General-purpose technology is less expensive than special-purpose technology, and it can be used to produce greater variety. The unit cost differentials can be considerable.

8-6 THE TECHNOLOGY OF PACKAGING AND DELIVERY

Glass windshields can shatter and chip if not properly handled. Transport, handling, and packaging technologies differ according to whether the market that is being served is for original transparencies (high-volume shipments) or for individual windshields that are shipped from the distribution center when requested by the auto service for specific customers.

Most products need some kind of protection during shipping. The production process can have near-zero defectives as a result of excellent quality management. Unfortunately, the damage done during delivery of the product can zoom the real defective rate—as seen by the customer—to outrageous levels. The manufacturer may not know about this situation for a long time. Complaints are not made on products not purchased. Feedback from warehouses, truckers, and retailers can take a long time. Awareness of such problems dawns slowly.

A consumer package goods company experienced a downturn in sales of its bar soap in a specific sales region. As part of the investigation for the causes of the problem, it was found that the product on the shelves of the supermarkets had damaged boxes. This condition was attributed to a change in handling procedures in the distribution center, which had started using a forklift truck to move the product. The forklift truck operator had previously worked in a scrap metal business. The problem was remedied by training.

A firm that manufactures dinnerware of medium-grade porcelain china discovered that full sets of dishes and cups were being delivered with three out of every ten pieces broken. They also found the company was infrequently called by customers to ask for replacements. More often, customers accepted the loss because it was not fine china, but they never ordered from this company again. Further, when the company was called to ask for replacements, the person representing the company had no interest at all in tracing the shipment to learn what caused the damage.

OM was on top of the issue of production defectives. The production process was stable and in control. Production had low-defective rates for this china product. The shipment-defective rates completely altered the "delivered rate of defectives." Package design, actual packing, and handling methods were the sources of trouble. From the systems point of view, the defective rate was unacceptable and more than one system had to be changed to remedy this situation.

The quality of the delivered product is part of TQM accountability. The packaging technology and handling methods are part of that accountability. The chinaware company must question every aspect of the systems that caused the breakage, and then it must determine what should be done to correct the problems to prevent any breakage from happening.

8-6a Systems Analysis

P/OM is responsible for delivering a quality product under all circumstances. P/OM must undertake a systems analysis of the delivery process where packaging is the technology. The systems analysis entails getting answers to three lines of inquiry.

1. What product-protection parameters have been specified for the packaging? What has the designer done to achieve these specifications? Typical questions would be:
    *   From what height can the package be dropped without breakage?
    *   Has the package been designed to withstand travel-specific stresses and strains (air, boxcar, truck, etc.)?
    *   How much vibration can the packaged product tolerate?
    *   What compression force will the package support?
    *   What happens if liquids are spilled on the packaging?
    *   Does humidity affect the performance of the package in terms of any of these quality dimensions?
    *   What are the temperature extremes the package can withstand?
    *   Finally, has the package design been adequately tested?

2. Did the actual handling of the package that resulted in broken product fall outside of the designer's specifications?
    *   If it did, in what ways did the actual treatment exceed the limits for which this product was protected?
    *   If it did not, can the packaging system be redesigned?

3. Has something permanently changed in the delivery system's way of handling the package?
    *   If so, can the packaging technology be upgraded, or can a new delivery system be found?
    *   If a new delivery system is feasible, will the current packaging technology suffice?
    *   If nothing has permanently changed in the delivery system, is the current package design satisfactory?

The systems approach focuses on getting to the root of the problem. Was the package designed correctly? Was the package tested correctly? If it was designed correctly, then what caused the breakage? If it was not designed correctly, how should the package be designed and tested?

The china had been packed in a fiberboard box, which was placed inside a corrugated box. There were no styrofoam inserts, which strengthen the box and protect its contents (called *unitized packaging*). Plastic "popcorn" was used.

Packages can be made of cardboard, plastics, wood, and combinations of materials. Inserts and fill offer even more options. There are too many kinds of packaging materials and systems of packaging to try to do more than present the basic scope of this subject.

8-7 THE TECHNOLOGY OF TESTING

Each kind of packing material has its own unique characteristics. Various tests have been developed to determine strengths and weaknesses. Corrugated boxes are marked with a figure to indicate the number of impact pounds the box can withstand before bursting. For example, "100 test" indicates less strength than "200 test" or "300 test."

Packaging experts have expressed concern that too few and too simple tests should not be interpreted as more than vaguely indicative of package integrity. The bursting-strength test reflects just one type of resistance on which a package must be rated. Even this one rating for impact is suspect for a variety of reasons. Humidity can affect the strength of cardboard and will not be reflected by the test measure. What passes a bursting-strength test in Maine may fall short in Florida. In short, correct measurement of package strength is dependent on a thorough understanding of packaging technology.

In general, testing technology is conditional upon a complete comprehension of the process being tested. The ramifications of testing technology apply to a great range of applications, which include designing products to have minimum variability in manufacturing.

8-7a Testing by Simulation

Empirical testing: Well-known as a check against poor design performance that might be hidden otherwise.

Simulation: The imitative representation of the functioning of a system or process by means of the functioning of a surrogate system or process.

An important testing alternative is **empirical testing,** simulating the worst cases of the kind of handling the package design can be expected to undergo. With this kind of experimental testing it also is possible to examine alternative package designs.

It is best to combine structural knowledge of packing materials—package engineering—with testing by **simulation,** which is a pragmatic procedure. Simulation for package testing means dropping, kicking, gouging, vibrating, pouring liquids onto, heating up, and cooling down, among other things. It is not easy to simulate all of these conditions. Still, it may be easier to use simulation methodology than engineering knowledge of the complex processes.

Simulation testing technology plays a most important part in designing windows for homes and office buildings. High floors of the latter do experience severe winds. The testing method should consider both broken panes and blown-in window frames. In addition, it must consider leakage. How high a wind should these windows protect against? Hurricanes are classified as winds above 75 miles per hour, and window designers need to provide protection for occasions above that level in hurricane zones.

OM working together with product designers and R & D can test the output of the process and reconfigure the way the product is designed and made. Testing technology is part of the OM kit of tools. Excessive auto recalls can be avoided by pretesting for contingencies. The silent interior of the car is a function of the way car doors are sealed. Models can be tested before the production system is finalized. Wind tunnels, which are used for testing airplane performance, also are used for testing the performance of windows.

Legal statutes and governmental rules are the concern of OM. Building to specifications requires knowing what the changing specifications are and what must be done to meet expectations. Knowing the law is part of the system's knowledge. Fulfilling the law is a matter of process. Testing is needed to determine if the requirements are being met.

Thus, after Hurricane Andrew the building codes for southern Florida, devastated by that storm, were changed so that roofs would not blow off and windows would not implode. The California highway system adopted more stringent building codes following the collapse of sections of highway during the 1994 earthquake.

8-8 QUALITY CONTROL TECHNOLOGY

One of the most important aspects of total quality management (TQM) is inspection and testing technology. Such quality testing technology is at the heart of quality control. The technology of testing has been advancing at a rapid rate. As in other aspects of technological development, increasing amounts of the art of quality achievement and control are being built into the machines by using science.

Inspection is epitomized by visual abilities, although there are many other senses for gathering information. Using vision, inspectors can check quality (is the finish on the car acceptable?) or quantity (how many parts were finished, or what is the number of air bubbles in a piece of glass?). The quantity of product is readily determined by optical scanners, which can count bar codes with more reliability than human inspectors.

Optical scanners at checkout counters reading the universal product codes (UPC) that are printed on all packages reflect applications of bar code technology. Now commonplace in supermarkets, they are being used in factories and banks to determine the status of transactions. They are used increasingly because their capabilities are improving. They have a great deal of information redundancy, which means that even damaged packages can be read as well as bar codes on round and odd-shaped surfaces.

The multiple functions of adding up the bill and deducting the item from inventory are readily programmed into the supermarket's computer system, with which the optical scanner communicates. The same technology working with a filling machine can determine how many pills to put into a bottle or when the fill level is reached for a bottle of juice.

For quality control applications, scanners must be able to perceive and differentiate along each of the critical quality dimensions. The criteria for product acceptability can be programmed precisely by computer software and translated into the language of the scanner so the inspection process can distinguish between acceptable and defective products. Inspection technology continues to develop along both quantitative and qualitative lines.

For perfumes, a good nose is a requirement. Are there machines that have a better analytic smelling capability? To judge wines, taste, vision and smell are essential. Are machines in the wings to take over these tasks? For now, these sensory skills are best supported by machines, not replaced by them. At the same time, there has been continuous development of machine inspection abilities. These include sensing systems for temperature, pressure, and weight. Visual sensors deal well with shape and size.

Sensory capabilities used to be only people skills; now technology has been developed to replace people in some areas. The complete replacement of human inspectors by machine inspectors is still far from being accomplished. Nevertheless, OM is experiencing a major "change" in inspection technology that is targeted right at the heart of operations.

New technology permits automation of the statistical quality control process. SQC monitoring equipment inputs data directly into a database. The statistical characteristics of the processes being monitored are continuously calculated. Appropriate quality control charts can be drawn automatically and submitted on a regular basis to QC inspectors for their interpretation. Symptoms and signs of systems being out of control can be incorporated in the programs.

Computer software is programmed to increase the frequency with which samples are taken as well as their sizes when the defective rate increases. When runs are detected and/or out of control, points are noted and the size and frequency of samples are adjusted. Under specific circumstances, the appropriate employee is notified about the situation so that interventions by workers can occur. The application of these methods to employee drug testing is an interesting extension of the same kinds of methodology and technology.

Testing procedures are the technology that quality control relies upon. Optical scanning is among machine sensory systems that are more sensitive than human ones, and are preferred. Computer programming of the SQC function is one of the most important technological developments at this time.

8-9 TECHNOLOGY OF DESIGN FOR MANUFACTURING (DFM); DESIGN FOR ASSEMBLY (DFA)

It used to be that designers only considered the needs of end users when designing the product. OM was not consulted about how best to fabricate and assemble the product. Later, designs that were not feasible to manufacture would have to be redesigned, which compromised other aspects of the product. The manufacturing process was jerry-rigged as a measure of last resort to make the product.

> **Design for manufacturing (DFM):** Changes are made in both design specifications and fabrication procedures to simplify operations.
>
> **Design for assembly (DFA):** Changes are made in both design specifications and assembly procedures to simplify assembly.

Design for manufacturing (DFM) and **design for assembly (DFA)** start with the goal of feasible fabrication and assembly. They then move on to higher-order quality objectives. It is now acknowledged to be good practice to have the design team include OM consultation from the start of the project to achieve feasibility and sensibility.

Because fabrication is distinctly different from assembly, it is useful to maintain separate agendas for DFM and DFA. On the other hand, often, but not always, the manufacture of parts leads to their assembly, so that both functions are complimentary. They should be dovetailed and designed to work well together. When a producer combines components from different suppliers, DFA must be coordinated by the assembler. Windshield glass epitomizes DFM and DFA combinations.

Even when it may not seem as if assembly is part of the product manufacturing cycle, it should be considered relevant. Pouring vinegar into a bottle is a kind of assembly of the product with its package. Packaging engineers and process managers for soft drink and beer companies view their technologies as an advanced form of serialized flow shop production. Packaging is often the ultimate stage of the manufacturing process, as in canning foods and boxing toothpaste. Consequently, the product and packaging should be designed and planned together.

The second order objective of DFM and DFA is to design parts that can be made with minimum variability. This may require testing the design by running pilot studies to produce sample product using the kind of equipment that will be employed in manufacture. Pilot studies are reduced-scale simulations of the full-scale production process; they make it possible to approximate the variability of dimensions during manufacturing. This is an example of the use of simulation to achieve design modification.

The objective is to pursue an aggressive strategy for designing a product that can be made by a process such that the manufactured product has minimal variation.

Figure 8-3 depicts this idea as a design feedback system:

This process is continued until the criteria for nearly optimal (rather than simply satisfactory) manufacturing and assembly conditions have been met. Nearly optimal means:

- The best design that could be found is adopted.
- The number of design–redesign feedback cycles is large enough so that the rate of improvement from continuing to cycle is considered negligible.

Table 8-1 shows how the variances (σ_i^2) of three designs can differ with respect to component assemblies. Each component is associated with a quality dimension (called Q_i). The third column, labeled:

$$TM(\sigma_1^2 + \sigma_2^2)$$

> **Tolerance matching:** Quality products must have parts that fit together properly.

is a measure of how well the two component parts fit together; this is called **tolerance matching.** It is often the case that this number is the sum of the variances of the two parts that fit together.

The fabrication variances of Design 2 are uniformly lower than those of Design 1 and Design 3 for both quality dimensions.

The column headed by

$$TM(\sigma_1^2 + \sigma_2^2)$$

for tolerance matching is taken as the sum of the variances of the two parts, which are assembled into each other like a key fitting into a lock cylinder.

FIGURE 8-3
Design-Test-Redesign
Tolerance Matching
Note: Test σ^2 is testing
dimensional variation. Redesign
starts the cycle all over again.
Thus, redesign and readjust
are followed by reconstruct,
retest, and redesign until they
get it right.

It is fundamental to statistical theory that the variance of two well-behaved distributions that are taken together is the sum of the individual variances of each distribution. Poisson and normal distributions are considered well-behaved. Both are unimodal and have stable statistical characteristics.

From the manufacturing point of view (DFM), the goal is to minimize the variability of each important dimension. From the assembly point of view, the goal is minimizing the assembled system's variability,

$$TM(\sigma_1^2 + \sigma_2^2)$$

In searching for the optimal, product design and process design technology are being modified by using a feedback system similar to that of quality control. The comparable cycle of improvement is the one used in quality control, which is plan-do-study-act or plan-do-check-act.

The difference from the quality control application in this case is that design of the product has not yet been completed and accepted. Further, the process for making the product has not yet been finalized, and the product has not been released for manufacture. There is time to experiment with pilot plant-type production.

The idea is similar to the package-testing example previously discussed in this chapter. The design is pilot tested in a manufacturing setting or assembly environment that comes as close as possible to the real-world, full-scale situation. Simulation of manufacture and/or assembly is the appropriate way to describe these experiments.

It may be best to start with two designs, both of which are considered feasible alternatives. The two variants are fabricated with a process that captures as much of the actual production system process as possible, with as large a sample size as possible.

The guiding principle of diminishing returns has been discussed earlier, but for those who are more comfortable with a number, 50 is used as an acceptable minimum and several hundred is a good target, if it can be achieved economically. The realities of the situation will determine what can and cannot be done in assembling a sample of sufficient size to use for DFM and DFA comparisons. Further, if it is feasible to produce a large sample, and if it is reasonable to employ statistical design methods, such as the analysis of variance, the power of the DFM/DFA study is enhanced.

The system must be stable by the criteria of SQC. The best quick check on this is to plot the values of the sample in a histogram to see if a unimodal distribution emerges. Bimodality is a clear indication that the system has to be stabilized. Other techniques should be used if possible to assure stability or to help stabilize the system.

Given a stable system, the comparison between the variances of the two designs can be made. The design alternative with the lowest variance may give direction to the search for another design alternative. It is best that a group consisting of designers, process managers, marketing managers, R & D scientists, and development engineers interpret the data and plan for the next set of designs to be produced.

	$Q_1 (\sigma_1^2)$	$Q_2 (\sigma_2^2)$	$TM(\sigma_1^2 + \sigma_2^2)$
Design 1	6	8	14
Design 2	5	3	8
Design 3	7	5	12

TABLE 8-1

Values of σ_i^2

8-9a Changeover Technologies

The technology used for setups and model changeovers is a major process driver. That technology determines the flexibility of the line. If the technology permits, a great number of models can be run in small batches with the cost efficiency of the flow shop, but the variety output of a job shop. DFM can play a crucial role. It allows the choice of a design with excellent setup characteristics instead of accepting a changeover situation by default.

Changeover technologies have been substantially decreasing the time it takes to shift what is being produced from one model to another. The engineering of changeovers, almost always dependent on the creation of new technology, has undergone a major revolution as envisioned by Shingo when he introduced his single-minute exchange of dies (SMED) philosophy. The new setup methods often increase productivity and improve quality at the same time.

8-10 THE NEW TECHNOLOGIES—CYBERNETICS

For OM to effectively manage technology, it is necessary to distinguish between old technologies and new ones that promise to alter the landscape significantly. Some of the new technologies have been the subject of study for a long time, but recent developments indicate they needed 20 or 30 years to reach the point of practical application. Some new technologies have not yet reached that point.

Cybernetics[4] is the study of similarities between human brains and electronic systems, including sensory devices, computers, and robotic analogs for doing work. It compares the way electronic signals are generated by information in the computer system with the human use of light and sound, among other things. In the human, signals are transmitted between adjacent nerve cells called *neurons*, across a boundary called a *synapse*. The state of the synapse determines whether or not a signal can pass across the boundary. This description has many similarities to electronic systems.

The resemblance between human systems and those of computers provides opportunities to learn by making comparisons. The outgrowths are impacting technology, including the development of:

1. New machines that permit flexible manufacturing and flexible processes

2. *Adaptive systems* that can emulate and surpass many human abilities

3. *Neural networks* for creating *artificial intelligence* as well as learning organizations and *expert systems*. (**Neural networks** are computer programs modeled like synaptic neuron networks in human beings.)

8-10a Flexibility—FMS, FOS, FSS, and FPS

Flexible manufacturing systems (FMS) are individual machines and/or groups of machines (called *cells*) that can be programmed to produce a menu of different products. The one thing the products on the menu have in common is the fact that the machine or cell can make all of them when supplied with appropriate tooling.

The changeover times for these computer-controlled systems are negligible, meaning that very small batches (typical of the job shop) can be produced with the economic advantages of serialized flow shops. Theoretically, the batch size can be one. **Flexible office systems (FOS)** and **flexible service systems (FSS)** are also an outgrowth of the new technological capabilities. **Flexible process systems (FPS)** is a generic name for the same technological capability when it is applied to any work situation that utilizes the flexibility concept in a manufacturing or nonmanufacturing environment.

Flexible warehouses are a good example. Areas of the warehouse are not dedicated to particular classes of items. Instead, products can be stored wherever space allows. The computer remembers where the items are by storing the product SKU code, the space code, and the number of units at that location.

Cybernetics: Study of similarities between human brains and electronic systems.

Neural networks: Models (artificial intelligence) of interconnected decision nodes paralleling the human brain and nervous system.

Flexible manufacturing systems (FMS): Programmed to produce a menu of different products. Changeover time to move from one menu item to another is negligible because of the computer.

Flexible office systems (FOS): Office processes are in many ways similar to manufacturing with both job shop batch production and flow shop (or intermittent flow shop) work configurations. When computer controlled, FOS can be designed to change over from one job to another with negligible setup times.

Flexible service systems (FSS): In quick-service restaurants, theme parks, the U.S. Post Office, FedEx, and UPS, there are ample examples of flexible service systems.

Flexible process systems (FPS): Generic name for all kinds of computer-controlled robotic and machine systems that can change over to offer a menu of products.

Germany	Japan	United States
80	50	7

TABLE 8-2

Comparison by Countries: Number of Varieties Produced by the FMS

With technological flexibility, questions arise concerning how many different products can be produced on the same flexible system. How big is the menu? That seems to depend on the culture of the FPS users. For FMS, American companies use fewer menu options than Japanese firms, which use fewer options than German companies. The numbers are not precise, but they are sufficiently different to override statistical differences. Table 8-2 provides some approximate numbers.[5]

Adaptive capabilities bring flexibility to automated systems. The latter are often called *fixed-automation* to indicate that they are economic to use if the demand exists for high-output volumes. They can deliver high quality, but have no capability to produce anything other than the single product that they were designed to produce. They are in trouble when demand falls off for the high-volume product they produce.

Fixed-automation does not even permit changeovers at high cost because they have been dedicated to one thing, such as a V8 engine. Ford Motor Company had built such a plant, but could not use it when the petroleum crisis in the 1970s killed the possibility of selling V8 engines. On the other hand, the windshield system of glasstech, INC., represents adaptive automation at its best.

8-10b Expert Systems

Expert systems are *computerized sequences* or strings of intelligent inquiries and answers that are copies of what the "experts" do to solve problems or to accomplish specific kinds of tasks. These smart procedures are developed by copying the way the experts go about solving the problems. The problems are complex so it is necessary to have a means of catching all the details. It is not always clear why experts do what they do. The simplest procedure is to ask.

Ultimately, all of the expert responses will have been obtained and emulated. For complex problems, it can take a long time to piece together the necessary conditions to be able to emulate the expert. The expert system may be dedicated to few or many variants. Different external factors can be encountered. Once completed, this expert program must be tested and debugged.

Consider an insurance expert in marine underwriting. This is a specialized insurance policy writer for ships who knows what questions to ask in order to determine the appropriate premium to charge. The expert system is built to conform to the questions and decisions made by this expert, incorporating experiences with many kinds of ships of different ages and other relevant data.

Figure 8-4 illustrates decision-tree representation of the marine underwriting expert system. Figure 8-4 is a simplified version of the questions that must be asked. After these questions have been answered, the policy situation is identified as one out of 15,552 different possibilities. Real marine underwriters have written policies for each of these situations and determine the appropriate premium in each case. The expert system is therefore able to identify the type of policy and premium that applies.

A list of questions associated with the decision-tree nodes, stages, and phases follows:

0. ∝—Start when?

1. What type of policy is wanted—*a*, *b*, *c*, or *d*?

2. Inboard or outboard engine—1 or 2?

3. What type of ship is it—3, 4, or 5?

4. Where is the ship berthed—6, 7, 8, or 9?

5. What kind of maintenance policy—10, 11, or 12?

> **Expert systems:** Computerized sequences or strings of intelligent inquiries with answers that are modeled on what "experts" would do to solve specific problems or to accomplish given tasks.

FIGURE 8-4
Expert System Decision Tree for a Marine Underwriter

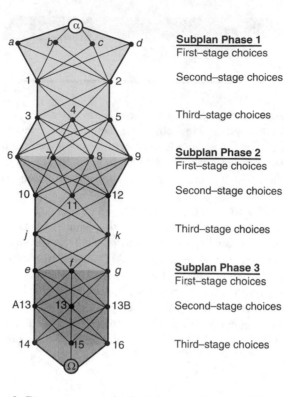

Subplan Phase 1
First–stage choices

Second–stage choices

Third–stage choices

Subplan Phase 2
First–stage choices

Second–stage choices

Third–stage choices

Subplan Phase 3
First–stage choices

Second–stage choices

Third–stage choices

6. Fire protection, built-in or portable—*j* or *k*?

7. Type of policy allowed—*e*, *f*, or *g*?

8. Optionals: radar, loran, etc.—A13, 13, or 13B?

9. Crew training—14, 15, or 16?

10. Are you ready to choose the policy Ω and determine premium?

11. Select Ω and reset system!

This requires obtaining all the necessary information an expert marine underwriter should have to draw up an appropriate maritime insurance policy for vessels of given sizes and characteristics. The variety (in details) of ships to be insured is enormous. Classes of situations must therefore be created to establish coverage and rates to be charged.

Questions are followed by appropriate answers. Once the expert program is written, all of the vessel's specifications can be input to the computer. The program will follow the inquiry to response strings. If successful, it will fill out the policy form and determine the coverage options and premiums to be charged.

These decision trees branch over and over, with many conditional paths leading to highly complex networks. If two more 3-part questions were added to the simple tree shown in Figure 8-4, it would be comprised of 139,968 unique policy situations.

Adding to the complexity are the various paths of best practice for the many kinds of situations that can arise. The networks are converted into computer programs that copy the best practice of experts. They have the advantage of being able to copy more than one expert and then combine all the best results. Expert systems can combine experts of one kind with experts of another kind. Also, an expert system's capabilities can learn and improve with experience.

It is noted that when an expert is confronted with a choice previously made, say A, sometimes the expert opinion has changed, or there can be recognition that this time A is accompanied by M whereas the previous time there was no M to consider. The expert now chooses B. The database must be amended, and M may have to be added as another consideration.

Why are expert systems used? There are many reasons, including the fact that experts are in short supply. Also, expert systems can combine the expertise of more than one person, which results in a meta-expert system. Expert systems can be used to reduce bottlenecks when demand is greater than the supply. Applications to complex manufacturing processes are warranted where there is a shortage of experts. Expert systems augment the selection process.

The fallibility of humans, even experts, can be alleviated. Expert systems can help to eliminate mistakes. Also, an expert system can provide a solution that can be reviewed by a human expert in much shorter time than that expert would need to derive the solution in the first place.

Imagine an expert system that provides an airline pilot with a recommendation about whether or not to land in bad weather. It could save lives. Expert systems can be used to monitor, in moments, complex multidimensional quality control; it could save lives. Expert systems can be used to monitor, in moments, complex multidimensional quality control systems readings that would take many hours and/or days for a human judge to evaluate.

Expert systems can guide ships through channels that are difficult to navigate; monitor and shut down NASA space launches when everything does not check out; provide safety checks (and shutdowns) for nuclear power plants. Expert systems can replace outmoded and archaic organizations that rely on too many people dealing with too much information that needs to be rapidly integrated.

Air traffic control (ATC) is an excellent candidate for expert systems. ATC is a network of people responsible for the position of planes in their sectors, which then get handed over to people in adjacent sectors. Expert systems provide instantaneous and seamless communications, just what is needed to assist the human controllers who at present are too fragmented.

Expert systems can read many controls at the same time and integrate the systems data. The applications of these ideas promise changes in the management of technology that are going to alter substantially the way things are done.

Discussion about expert systems should draw the distinction between them and **artificial intelligence (AI).** Expert systems are based on copying the procedures of the experts. AI is based on copying the nervous system of humans to develop mechanisms that have the capability of sensing and learning; there are strong analogies to the structure of the brain and the way the brain works.

Mechanisms that are analogous to human nervous systems are called *neural networks*. Neural networks are being designed to enable computers to read handwriting and to emulate the kinds of functions associated with intelligence in human beings. A machine with artificial intelligence should seem intelligent to an intelligent human being.

Part of the mystique of AI is defining a test that will conclusively indicate an intelligent machine. The search for the test is philosophical, and the field has attracted many who are more interested in the means to the end than the end. Still, though there are claims of success, artificial intelligence remains a research area. There will be increasing applications of intelligent machines in the smart factory and office.

> **Artificial intelligence (AI):** Based on copying the nervous system of human beings to develop mechanisms that have the capability of sensing and learning.

8-10c Cyborgs and Robots

Cyborg is a coined word that combines the *cyb* of *cybernetics* with *org* from *organisms*. Cybernetic organisms are a form of technology that pairs people and machines to achieve results neither could otherwise obtain. Someone wearing a pair of reading glasses is a cyborg. If the glasses adapted to the amount of light or changed depending on whether the person was looking at something near or far, the more supportive would be the interaction between the mechanism and the brain of the person. Strong cyborg interactions are reflected by highly adaptive behavior on the part of both the person and the machine.

Heroic measures to keep a person alive combine machine technology with the human body as a cybernetic organism. Anyone with a pacemaker is a grateful cyborg. The same principles apply to scuba diving. Air tanks strapped to the diver's back and a breathing device with a regulator that adjusts to depths are crucial to life in an underwater environment.

> **Cyborg:** A coined word combining "cyb" from *cybernetics* with "org" from *organism*.

Jacques Cousteau advanced the technology that permits people to stay underwater for long periods of time. "Cousteau was engaged in an extended stay program in Conshelf III, an 18-foot diameter sphere in which his team of six aquanauts spent 27 days at 328 feet (100m), followed by a 3-day decompression." [6] Although the predecessors of humanity were likely to have been water breathers, it is not a matter of skill to stay underwater for any length of time. Technology alone makes it possible.

Cousteau and others have pursued the idea that people could be given breathing implants similar to the gills of a fish (tissue capable of absorbing oxygen from water and releasing carbon dioxide from the blood stream). If that ever is done, a better example of a cyborg will be hard to find. Some practical reasons for wanting to be able to live underwater include the ability to mine for minerals and extract oil on the sea floor. Such cyborgs would provide a technological breakthrough.

It is easy to extrapolate to sustaining life in the space lab, on space trips, and in communities on the moon and Mars. Some practical reasons for wanting to be able to live in outer space include the ability to use gravity-free factories to produce products to much finer tolerances (i.e., ball bearings). Certain chemicals are dangerous to handle in the Earth's atmosphere, which would be stable on the moon. Various medical conditions would be advantaged by low-gravity treatment centers. Process management will never be the same, given the significant technological changes that will occur.

> **Robots:** Evolving from mechanical devices that perform complex, repetitive tasks into computer-controlled systems with broad sensory abilities, discernment, and forms of intelligence.

At the other end of the spectrum are the **robots** that do many jobs in the factory. The painting robots and the welding robots take careful programming to enable them to do the job right for each of the various car models that come down the line. They can change over from the positions required for one model to that of another in nanoseconds. Robots are excellent changeover devices. Consequently, when model flexibility is desired, the use of robots is generally warranted.

Yet to come are the home-cleaning robots and gardener robots who would combine the motor skills of a human with the strength of a machine and the intelligence that a programmer can instill. Already in existence is an egg-moving robot that can handle the egg with such daintiness of movement that the shell remains intact.

8-10d The Technology of Computer–User Interfaces

Programming is another illustration of the way technology necessitates bringing together machines interacting with operator skills. Instead of using their hands to set the machines and make them do their work, people program the machines or the computers that interface with the machines. Because programming is done by people to tell machines what to do, somehow they must both speak the same language.

Thus, the technology of computers is hidden from users. Programmers instruct machines by using special languages. When a user clicks a mouse, hundreds or even thousands of lines of code can be the internal response of the system, which is translated into the configuration on the screen.

Even computer-literate users do not understand "machine language." Instead, their literacy is bounded by understanding the software they use. There are enough problems dealing with relatively user-friendly software such as Word, Excel, PowerPoint, WordPerfect, and Lotus. The use of operating systems other than Windows, particularly Unix and Linux, are growing rapidly. There will be continual challenges to the fundamentals of computer literacy.

Machines that are run by programmed instructions can, in turn, respond with instructions for the people that run them. For both inputs and outputs, the form communication can take varies. It can be typed, handwritten, or vocal communication.

Programming technology is required for the regulation of factories and offices. It also is critical to make correct machine settings, for control over setups and changeovers, to schedule production, to maintain inventory control, and to schedule maintenance activities. The programming languages needed for many of these activities are not user friendly.

Individuals have begun to take for granted this entry of programming technology to communicate with their systems. They have become accustomed to user-friendly desktop publishing, graphics, word processing, spreadsheet calculations, database management, indexing, outlining, and spell checking. Scientists can work at home on simulations, scientific model building and analysis, and myriad other applications of methods so advanced they were once considered feasible only on mainframes.

This form of technology, if it is to be effectively used, requires higher levels of training than the kinds of technology that preceded it. Going and gone are the skills of tool and die masters who worked the materials by hand. They are replaced by the considerable knowledge required of those who must write machine instructions for CAD/CAM software for designers. The programs for computer-aided design must be congruent with the programs for computer-aided manufacture because CAM programs convert CAD instructions into directions for factory machinery.

There is every reason to encourage the development of new arts and skills of people in the use of powerful office network systems. This includes the need for knowing how to use hardware and software for telecommunications, office networks (LAN and WAN), and sharing of laser printers and other equipment. LAN is *local area networks* and WAN is *wide area networks*. These acronyms describe the scope of interconnected computers that share databases and equipment.

8-10e Other New Technology Developments— Materials and Miniaturization

When reference is made to new technology, this usually is taken to mean that an industrial science improvement has occurred in equipment and machinery. For example, Intel and Motorola have continuously increased the power of their computer chips. Usually, new technology replaces existing technology, which results in old technology. Gone are the ancient bulky and weighty calculating machines that were slow and costly.

The new technology also relates to stronger and better materials that have been developed. The weight of a typical VCR has been cut by more than 80 percent since the first unit was introduced by Sony. Automotive designers have had to reduce the weight of a car in order to satisfy government emission requirements. To do this, glass, plastics, aluminum, and laminates have been used extensively. The sweeping windshields of cars have saved much weight, added beauty, and provided this chapter with an industrial focus that reflects OM challenges and excitement.

Miniaturization has been pioneered by Sony for its own product line. To make small products requires processes that can fabricate and assemble miniaturized parts. This has led the company to manufacture its own equipment. As a result, Sony has developed entire manufacturing systems that are required for fabrication and assembly of products with very small components.

Improvements in management technology qualify as new industrial arts.[7] Advances in management that improve quality and productivity are legitimate candidates. Accordingly, TQM is replete with technological inventions. MRP, JIT, and SMED are other aspects of new and improved technologies. Another facet of new technology is rapid project development, which permits new products to be brought to market in half the conventional time. Flexible manufacturing equipment has been discussed in a prior section. It constitutes new technology that creates a unique class of work configuration, which, if properly used, can combine the economies of scale of the flow shop with batch shop economies of scope.

SUMMARY

This chapter begins with an explanation of why OM must understand how to manage technology. The reason is that technology is one of two crucial components of the input–output transformation model. The two components are people with production skills and technology with engineering capabilities to improve upon what people can do. Managing the combination is an OM responsibility.

There is a technology trap. By default, new technology is often applied to the management of the old system with unfavorable results. Technological upgrading requires excellence in timing. This is illustrated by using the automotive glass industry and, in particular, windshield manufacturing. Levels of technological sophistication are explored for the replacement versus the original market requirements and the supply chain technology appropriate to each. The technology of packaging and delivery is included, as is the tech-

nology of testing and quality control technology. The technologies of design for manufacturing (DFM) and design for assembly (DFA) are explored, including an example of how to evaluate and select the preferred design.

Discussion of managing technology could not be complete without mention of changeover technologies and description of the technologies including cybernetics, flexible processing systems, expert systems, cyborgs, and robots. The supplement treats Poka-yoke, the Japanese name for technology, to prevent defectives.

A Spotlight feature box concludes this chapter. The box illustrates real applications of the material in the chapter. See Spotlight 8-1: Who's Afraid of Nanotechnology?

KEY TERMS

Artificial intelligence (AI)
Cybernetics
Cyborg
Design for assembly (DFA)
Design for manufacturing (DFM)
Empirical testing
Expert systems

Flexible manufacturing systems (FMS)
Flexible office systems (FOS)
Flexible process systems (FPS)
Flexible service systems (FSS)
Management of technology (MOT)
Net present value (NPV)
Neural networks

Payback period
Robots
Simulation
Technology
Technology trap
Tolerance matching

REVIEW QUESTIONS

1. What are the effects of rapid technological change?

2. How is technology a component of the I/O transformation?

3. Explain the management of technology in three ways: societal, company, and international levels.

4. What is the technology trap?

5. What are the basic elements of good packaging and how do they relate to the management of technology?

6. What are shakedown risks?

7. How does packaging relate to the supply chain and what is supply chain technology?

8. What is the technology status of a glass blower?

9. When is the advantage of having a reputation for being a technology leader likely to pay off?

10. What is good technology timing?

11. Why is OM concerned about the licensing of technology? Relate the answer to an example.

12. How was flat glass made before the float-glass process was developed?

13. Explain the process for making windshields by referring to the process flowchart.

14. Relate OM's management of technology to R & D.

15. Compare the effects of replacement and original market demands on OM and MOT.

16. What is entropy and how is it relevant to MOT?

17. What should be done about delivery processes that increase the defective rate substantially?

18. Discuss OM's responsibilities with respect to testing technology.

19. What steps need to be taken to achieve DFM and DFA?

20. What are pilot studies?

21. Describe some new technologies.

22. How do expert systems work? Does OM have any use for them?

23. What methods are available for assessing the technology plans of competitors?

24. How can it be determined if customers are aware of and sensitive to the use of different technologies by competitors?

25. What is meant by knowing the cost and/or benefits of the present technological level of the firm?

26. How can the costs of transition from one technology level to another be estimated and used to determine the payback period?

27. What is the difference between payback period, breakeven time, and the cost recovery period?

28. Explain why it is considered better to change technologies when the development cycles enter a period of relative stability instead of during periods of volatility.

PROBLEMS SECTION

1. Bursting strength and product support (within the container) are listed for two different package designs. The container will be used to ship printers:

	Bursting Strength	Product Support
Box A	100 test	8
Box B	200 test	6

Assume that the computed value of the package design V is modeled as follows: $V=(BS)(PS)^2$ and the biggest number is the best. What does the scoring model value of each package indicate?

2. Compare technologies as follows: Turn on various computers and note the time it takes each to boot up. The distribution of times will represent a range of setup times for the computer. How variable are these setup times? Explain the meaning of this exercise to the management of technology by OM.

3. Is it reasonable to compare word processors (as technology) by the following method? Test how long it takes each word processor—on the same computer—to do the same task, such as repositioning from the first page to the fiftieth page of a 100-page document.

4. Use a multiplicative scoring model ($V_{D_i} = Q_1{}^2 Q_2{}^3 TM$) to evaluate alternative designs with respect to excellence for DFM and DFA. Table 8-3 presents the variances for two components and their tolerance match. In addition, an

importance weight is given to each component's quality–fit dimension and to the tolerance match between the components. The smaller the weight, the more important it is, which is in keeping with the preference for small variances. Note: V_{D_i} is the value of design i.

How does this situation differ from that in Table 8-1 shown earlier?

5. Calculate the payback period for a technology expense of $1 million if the new technology immediately starts to earn revenues of $100,000 per month. Operating costs plus depreciated fixed costs are estimated to be $30,000 per month. How does this payback period differ from the cost recovery period?

6. Create an expert system for determining an optimal diet for anyone interested. Build a decision tree such as the one shown in Figure 8-4.

7. Show how Figure 8-4, which designs an expert system for marine underwriting, leads to 15,552 uniquely different situations.

8. With respect to the material in Problem 7, explain the statement that two more 3-part questions would lead to 139,968 uniquely different situations.

9. With respect to the material in Problem 8, how many uniquely different situations would three more 3-part questions yield?

10. Why is air traffic control (ATC) an excellent candidate for expert system support?

	$w_1 = 2$ $Q_1(\sigma_1{}^2)$	$w_2 = 3$ $Q_2(\sigma_2{}^2)$	$w_{TM} = 1$ $TM(\sigma_1{}^2 + \sigma_2{}^2)$
Design 1	6	8	14
Design 2	5	6	11
Design 3	7	5	12

TABLE 8-3

Values of $\sigma_i{}^2$ for Each Design

END-OF-CHAPTER QUESTIONS

1. The management of technology (MOT) is an important P/OM responsibility. What forms does this responsibility take? All but one of the answers below is correct. Which answer is incorrect?
   a. Skills and technology blend together. Management must determine the right balance to use for job accomplishment, and this changes over time.
   b. Society depends on management knowledge about the employment of technology for health, safety, and security. Services include transportation, health care, and education. Management of intellectual capital (in the form of patents) is another instance of social requirements.
   c. Management of technology within the firm is often the crucial factor in determining competitive advantage or disadvantage. When to adopt the next generation machine is paramount in every manager's mind.
   d. Management of technology for P/OM at the firm level does not involve patents. There are lawyers to take care of the legal questions and accountants to determine the value of intellectual capital.
   e. Management of technology at the international level is broadened by the fact that countries outside the United States provide patent protection to their own nationals, and the laws of these countries may not align perfectly with those of the United States. In addition, appropriate technology for manufacturing may differ according to the blend of skills and technology that exists in different parts of the world. Manufacturing plants in China have quite different technology levels than those in the United States.

2. Technology management is challenging. Some of the problems associated with the management of technology are listed in a. through e. Which one statement is incorrect?
   a. Technology changes tend to occur in clusters. This is because opportunities to get into a new field bring many entrepreneurs to the marketplace where they innovate. This leads to improvements upon improvements. The market decides what it likes.
   b. Tomorrow's technology can make obsolete what was brand new today. This discontinuity can be a pitfall for those who invest in everything that is new. Picking correctly is a P/OM responsibility.
   c. Professor Clayton Christensen's hypothesis about disruptive technologies is based on the fact that customers may not embrace the fruits of new technology. This sends a signal to "good" companies that they should maintain course with what their customers like. A company that listens to the voice of the customer may be out of the running when the tune that voice is singing changes.
   d. The technology trap is a common phenomenon in which new equipment is put to work running old systems and procedures without studying the opportunities to change the systems and procedures in line with capabilities of the new technology.
   e. Postponement of new technology investments is often reasonable when learning can be achieved with minimum costs and disruption, and it is clear that infringement is not a possible competitor's complaint.

3. When is being second in the application of new technology on behalf of the company's customers a reasonable management of technology strategy? Which answer below is wrong?
   a. Development costs are high and patent protection is not likely to shelter the first to market with a new product design or product derived from a new process.
   b. Shakedown is testing a system being used for the first time (as a shakedown cruise for a new aircraft carrier). It is also testing an existing system to which new features have been added. The test is intended to uncover faults and defects. Shakedown is also used for training in new technology. All aspects of shakedown are hard on the first customers. The penalties can be reduced significantly by being second in line.
   c. If the expected lifetime of use is much longer than the payback period, it is often reasonable to avoid the burden of being first.
   d. If company A is first and companies B, C, etc., can easily imitate what company A has done without paying consequences such as infringement penalties, then there is reason for company A to question being the first to develop the new technology. Other factors must be present to make any one company decide to be first. That reason could be related to indirect benefits. The support for the Concorde by Britain and France established the company that makes the Airbus. There is no doubt that the reputation of Airbus was enhanced in a major way by the Concorde because Boeing never developed a supersonic plane. The Concorde, which first flew in 1976, was built by a European consortium led by the British Aircraft Corporation and the French Sud Aviation.
   e. If many years are required for the development of new technology, there must be government support (as was the case for Concorde). When Bell Labs developed the transistor, it was recognized that decades would be required for one firm to develop that technology. As a result, AT&T invited interested companies to a conference at which this new technology was given to all companies that wanted to participate in developing transistors.

4. A comparison between two alternative technologies is being made. Which one statement about such comparisons is incorrect?
   a. Comparing savings using net present value (NPV), the investment cost would be in present dollars, and the savings stream would be the sum of continually decreasing amounts of money as savings are realized month after month in the future. Also, it is necessary to subtract maintenance (and other) costs. They should be discounted to the same degree as the savings in each specific future time period. The technology to select is the alternative that has greater savings.
   b. Payback periods can be compared. Using this method, the amount to be paid back would be in present dollars. The savings stream is summed without discounting for the expected lifetime of the new technology and its savings.

Also, it is necessary to subtract maintenance (and other) costs from the savings that are being summed. The technology selected will have the shortest period of time to pay back the investment.

c. Total cost recovery periods can be compared. The same computations that were used with payback periods apply because savings minus maintenance (and other) costs are identical to the payback amounts. Choose the alternative that promises the shortest time interval to achieve total cost recovery of the investment in technology.

d. Comparisons of savings (whether they are discounted or not) are suspect because a variety of factors like the costs of materials, energy, and labor are not locked in over time. This warning is especially noteworthy if the savings are estimated to continue over a long time period (say, more than 20 years). The only way to make these calculations believable is to pinpoint the sources of savings and to estimate how they will change over the savings horizon.

e. Interest rates play a major part in net present value calculations, so it is necessary to estimate how interest rates will change over time. Forecasting interest rates is so challenging that some analysts prefer to use sensitivity analysis to bracket the most probable range of interest rates. Then, upper- and lower-bound NPVs can be used to compare alternative technologies.

5. There are many different materials that illustrate the shift from art-based skills to technology-based processes. Among these are steel, rubber, paper, and glass. The developments in glass making are as dramatic as can be found because at the skill level, glass work is highly regarded as artistry. On the other hand, advanced technology for automotive windshield glass illustrates a mastery over materials for commercial use. With respect to these issues, only one of the following statements about materials technology is wrong. Which option is incorrect?

a. Dale Chihuly is a world-renowned glass artist with custom-made creations that are magnificent. His Seattle studio is famous for apprenticeship training and its output, which demonstrates total mastery of glass skills. See http://www.chihuly.com.

b. In 1959, the British firm of Pilkington introduced entirely new glass technology called the float process for making flat glass. The continuous ribbon of glass (melted sand) floated on a bath of melted tin. The new process became the primary method for making flat glass worldwide, replacing casting, rolling, and polishing glass, a process with many imperfections. A major decline in the skill to technology ratio occurred.

c. To fabricate large glass windshields requires a mixture of high levels of labor skills with corresponding levels of technology. Production for original use and replacement markets use highly mechanized, mass-production flow shops.

d. Using advanced technology, some windshields are made without human labor in entirely automated systems. These applications have the further advantage of not requiring car and windshield designers to consult with manufacturers, which saves the expense of designing for manufacturing (DFM).

e. Float glass (house windows) is the starting component for automotive glass, which requires higher levels of technology than household glass. Safety glass is required in the United States. It is a sandwich of two pieces of float glass (called lites) that are annealed and then cooled for strength. Placed between the inboard and outboard lites is a polyvinyl butyryl laminate. The sandwich is bonded by heat and pressure.

6. OEM (original equipment manufacturer) describes a company that produces hardware to be installed and sold under a different company name. Computers like Dell, IBM, HP, and Compaq are filled with such parts. Sometimes the part is marketed under the name of the purchaser from the OEM. See, for example,

http://www.cnet.com/Resources/Info/Glossary/Terms/oem.html.

Windshields are bought from many large glass manufacturers and installed by GM, Ford, Toyota, etc. On the other hand, the replacement market for glass windshields is high volume with many models. Similarities exist with the tire market. For both windshields and tires, distribution requires many different dealerships. The characteristics of the replacement market are described in the following choices, but one of the statements is inaccurate. Which statement is faulty?

a. It is essential to be able to forecast with some accuracy the demand for each year and model of car. Windshields are not standardized items. Further, demands will differ by region of the country because brands and their models have varying appeal in different locations. For example, convertibles have larger market shares where the average temperatures are higher. Therefore, it really pays a replacement goods firm to study forecasting and test various methods to adopt the strongest protocol.

b. Stock levels should be ample to cover (uncertain) demands. The loss of many sales because the right stock was not available is a serious drain. Because dealers may not want to carry large stocks, it is a good idea for the glass companies to have their own warehouses as filled as possible with every variety of windshield.

c. Distribute the windshields so that the right models are in the correct places to fill customer requirements. Tie distribution policy tightly to the forecasting information.

d. Keeping track of forecasting success and failures by region is important. Constant tracking permits learning that enables the forecasting system to react more quickly to changing conditions. For example, there has been more rain than usual, or a shift in shopping patterns is emerging since the large, new mall opened.

e. Set up the production system so that fast changeovers can be accomplished. Smart investment in changeover technology permits the production system to quickly react to changing demands of the marketplace. Every year brings many new models, and the process must be able to start producing these models although, at first, demand will be low. As the car models age, the demand for new windshield models will grow. At the same time, old cars stop rolling and must be de-listed when demand ceases to be profitable.

7. Four of the following five statements are correct. Which statement is incorrect?

   a. Consumer package goods are not appetizing to customers when their shelf display packaging seems old or damaged. Thus, part of the P/OM assignment is to work with designers to achieve durable and attractive packaging. Packaging processes are production lines with elaborate technology. Sometimes, it is necessary to stop the packaging line to change labels even though the same containers are being used. Understanding the technology for raising and moving items is necessary to ensure that distributors handle merchandise without harming overall product quality.

   b. The technology of testing is related to every aspect of quality control: ingredients, packaging, delivery time, and delivery condition. A significant change has occurred in testing technology that permits accurate inspection of 100 percent of the items using automated sensing systems with computers. This alters the cost of quality in favor of inspecting out defectives instead of prohibiting failures under all circumstances.

   c. Products have various qualities that can change as a function of time. Freshness dating is an example of the dynamics of product qualities. After the date, cheese, milk, and bread can be expected to deteriorate in an obvious fashion. Reading freshness dates is not uniformly simple. Chemical methods of maintaining freshness and increasing shelf life include partial hydrogenation, which is likely to become a subject of discussion in the future. Radiation technology is used to maintain the freshness of military food packs. Package damage is a function of shipping methods and amount of handling. Technology of shipping by containers in palletized form has changed the scenario of distribution and had a significant impact.

   d. Optical scanners at checkout counters reading the universal product codes (UPC) have transformed the checkout operation at supermarkets. The same bar code use in plants and warehouses provides immediate registration of item locations and the quantities stored. Algorithms are programmed at smart warehouses to optimize the placement of input to and output from the warehouse.

   e. Design for assembly (DFA) is dependent upon tolerance matching so that parts can be put together easily. At the same time, tolerance matching can be programmed in the computer to provide just the right amount of clearance and play when parts are being assembled. The technology can be related to CAD (computer-aided design) software.

8. Which one of the following statements is incorrect?

   a. Cybernetics is the study of similarities between human brains and electronic systems. The parallels include sensory systems (for seeing, hearing, etc.), motor systems, memory, and computational abilities.

   b. The outgrowth of cybernetic studies has been development of new machines that permit flexible manufacturing and neural networks for creating artificial intelligence.

   c. Automated systems are dedicated to making a specific item (e.g., 4-door red Ford Mustangs) whereas flexible systems are capable of making a number of items (e.g., 2-door and 4-door red, blue, and white Ford Mustangs).

   d. Expert systems could be designed to optimize the level of variety that an FMS can produce. Expert systems capture the methods of those with experience in planning for flexibility. Expert systems in conjunction with the human experts can lead to more creative solutions than either of the players can produce alone.

   e. Miniaturization is another major factor in the development of new technology. The advantage of smaller chips that are faster and more powerful is apparent to any student of the history of computers. In the 1950s, large rooms were filled with systems that were significantly less powerful than many children's toys today. The effects on military operations and health care are remarkable. Education with Internet access, the Library of Congress on a chip, and nanosecond search engines may be the next industrial revolution.

9. Which one of the following statements is incorrect?

   a. Expert systems lend themselves to applications such as marine underwriting.

   b. Air traffic control is an excellent candidate for expert systems.

   c. The value of stock market portfolios could be enhanced by expert systems.

   d. Amazon uses expert systems to offer its customers additional book choices.

   e. Zagat's uses survey data to provide information about restaurant choices.

10. Which of the following statements is incorrect?

   a. Within a firm, the proper timing of technological change is not a matter of luck.

   b. During the dot.com bubble, high-level investments were made without the kind of analysis that management of technology considers essential. This resulted in enormous loses that might have been avoided by using MOT.

   c. Disruptive technologies are of major concern to top management. However, only those versed in P/OM and management of technologies are able to use the compass that tells which way to turn. See http://www.disruptivetechnologies.com.

   d. Technology assessment involves learning the plans of competitors. If this is done with tact, there will be no ethical questions to answer.

   e. Whoever needs role models for judging technology contests should take a look at glasstech, INC. This company epitomizes great technological creativity. It states on its webpage (http://www.glasstech.com/about_us.htm) that it is the world's leading manufacturer of glass bending and tempering equipment for the automotive and architectural markets.

11. Defect prevention technologies and techniques (DPTT) are called the Poka-yoke system (PYS) by Japanese P/OM process innovators. DPTT is distinct from defect detection through inspection. Which of the following statements is incorrect?

   a. The three costs of quality are (1) defect detection, removal, and repair, (2) defect prevention during production, and (3) defect occurrence in use.

   b. Automated detection technology now permits 100 percent inspection without the limitations that formerly existed when people were used for complete appraisal. However, inspection in place of prevention must be justified by the difficulties of building zero-defect, fail-safe products. "Build it right the first time" remains a sound rule for production.

c. Mechanical systems can prevent mistakes from being made. Analog and electronic sensors can detect conditions for producing a defective unit and stop work until those conditions are rectified. A mental set is required for engineering appropriate preventative steps. That mental set should start with design for prevention of faults.

d. To determine how much expenditure is warranted for preventing faults during production, it is necessary to know what the probability is of the fault occurring and how many defectives will be experienced over a period of time. Ultimately, the cost of prevention must be compared to the total cost of defectives to decide on an appropriate course of action.

e. Managers cannot deal with DPTT or PYS unless they are engineers. Technology components of such systems are too technical. In large organizations, it is advisable to have staff engineers (from process engineering) who can take responsibility for prevention technology.

ADDITIONAL READINGS

Ashby, W. Ross. *An Introduction to Cybernetics*. New York: Wiley, 1956.

Beer, Stafford. *Decision and Control: The Meaning of Operational Research and Management Cybernetics*. New York: Wiley, 1994.

Hessel, M. P., M. Mooney, and M. Zeleny. "Integrated Process Management: A Management Technology for the New Competitive Era." *Global Competitiveness: Getting the U.S. Back on Track*. (ed.). M. K. Starr. Norton for the American Assembly, 1988.

Hofstadter, Douglas, and the Fluid Analogies Research Group. *Computer Models of the Fundamental Mechanisms of Thought*. New York: Basic Books, 1995.

Jones, Billy Mac. *Magic with Sand: A History of AFG Industries, Inc.* Wichita State University Business Heritage Series, Center for Entrepreneurship, College of Business Administration, WSU, Wichita, KS, 1984.

Laube, David R. *Business Driven Information Technology*. Palo Alto, CA, Stanford University Press, September 2003.

Keen, Jack M., and Bonnie Digrius. *Making Technology Investments Profitable*. New York, John Wiley & Sons, November 2002.

McGrath, Michael E. *Product Strategy for High-Technology Companies*. McGraw-Hill Trade, 2e. October 2002.

McGrath, Michael E. *Product Strategy for High-Technology Companies: How to Achieve Growth, Competitive Advantage, and Increased Profits*. Burr Ridge, IL: Irwin, 1995.

Pollack, Michael G. "The AGR Channel-to-Market." *US Glass* (February 1994): 59. (AGR is auto replacement glass.)

Roberts, Edward B. (ed.). *Generating Technological Innovation*. Sloan Management Review, Executive Bookshelf. New York: Oxford University Press, 1987.

Shingo, Shigeo. *Zero Quality Control: Source Inspection and the Poka-Yoke System*. Norwalk, CT: Productivity Press, 1986.

Tooley, F. V. (ed.). *Handbook of Glass Manufacture* (2 volumes). New York: Ashlee Publishing Co., Inc., 1985.

U.S. Congress Joint Economic Committee, "The U.S. Trade Position in High Technology: 1980–1986." 1987.

Zuboff, Shoshana. *In the Age of the Smart Machine, the Future of Work and Power*. New York: Basic Books, 1988.

NOTES

1. From the "Technology Report" section of *The Wall Street Journal*, June 24, 1994.

2. Shoshana Zuboff. *In the Age of the Smart Machine, the Future of Work and Power*. New York: Basic Books, 1988.

3. Michael G. Pollack. "The AGR Channel-to-Market." *US Glass* (February 1994): 59. (AGR is auto glass replacement.)

4. Stafford Beer. *Decision and Control: The Meaning of Operational Research and Management Cybernetics*. New York: Wiley, 1994.

5. Studies from the Columbia Business School Center for the Study of Operations found results similar to those reported by Jay Jakumar of the Harvard Business School in *Technology Review* (July 1985): 78–79.

6. *The New Illustrated Science and Invention Encyclopedia*. Westport, CT: H.S. Stuttman, Inc., 1987, p. 2972.

7. M. P. Hessel, M. Mooney, and M. Zeleny. "Integrated Process Management: A Management Technology for the New Competitive Era." *Global Competitiveness: Getting the U. S. Back on Track.* (ed.). M. K. Starr. Norton for the American Assembly, 1988, pp. 121–158.

SPOTLIGHT 8-1
Who's Afraid of Nanotechnology?

The Ability to Construct Objects as Small as a Molecule Holds Both Promise and Peril

By Glennda Chui—Mercury News

The next big fight over the promise and perils of technology is shaking the world of the very small.

Nanotechnology — the construction of objects as tiny as molecules, a few millionths of an inch in size at most — is poised to transform our world, much as the harnessing of electricity did.

Within 15 years, experts predict, it will drive progress in virtually every field, from computing to medicine, manufacturing, energy and the environment. They envision factories that build things atom by atom, materials with properties we can't imagine today, sensors that can be scattered like dust and microscopic robots that cruise the bloodstream to deliver drugs or root out cancer.

But some worry the technology will backfire, threatening human health and unleashing new forms of pollution. It's happened before: The pesticide DDT, asbestos fire-proofing and ozone-destroying chemicals in spray cans and refrigeration were all considered benign until their harmful effects came to light.

Nanotechnology is haunted by an even more alarming idea.

In his 1986 book "Engines of Creation," Palo Alto theorist K. Eric Drexler popularized the notion of building things atom by atom, using tiny, self-replicating machines. At the same time, he warned that these ``molecular assemblers'' could multiply out of control, forming a gray goo that destroys life on the planet.

Three years ago, Sun Microsystems co-founder Bill Joy breathed new life into that notion with an essay in Wired magazine. He suggested that the world faces an unprecedented threat from a trio of technologies—nanotechnology, biotechnology and robotics—that have one thing in common: They are capable of producing things that make copies of themselves, and thus could evolve to become more powerful than humans.

That's also the premise of "Prey," a Michael Crichton novel being made into a movie. In it, rogue scientists create swarms of self-replicating nanomachines and release them into the desert, where they evolve into wily predators with all the attributes of living things.

Futuristic Visions

Most scientists believe things like molecular assemblers and nanorobots are decades away—if indeed, they can be built at all. The gray goo scenario, they assert, is pure science fiction and physically impossible.

But they worry that these futuristic visions will overshadow more practical concerns, such as the potential for new forms of pollution and the safety of workers in labs that handle nanomaterials.

"The basic concept that little nanothings will organize themselves and take over the world is highly unlikely," said Alexandra Navrotsky, a materials scientist at the University of California-Davis. "Which isn't to say that there aren't concerns. There ought to be any time you have a new technology and new materials."

Some nanotech scientists and business people fear a backlash such as the one that has stalled acceptance of genetically modified foods. A moratorium on sales of most GMO crops in Europe has been costing American corn growers $100 million to $300 million a year in sales. Although the moratorium is scheduled to be lifted this fall, European consumers are still reluctant to buy foods with genetically modified ingredients.

An advocacy group in Canada has already called for a moratorium on creating nanomaterials, whether for sale or in the lab, until their safety can be assured.

The British government, while supportive of nanotech research, has launched an independent investigation of the technology's risks and benefits.

In July, the environmental group Greenpeace called for the creation of a "citizens' jury" to help set priorities for nanotech research. While there is no reason to consider nanotechnology intrinsically good or harmful, the group said, researchers need to start a "meaningful public dialogue" to help shape the way the technology develops.

Education Efforts

In response to these worries the NanoBusiness Alliance, which is based in New York City and represents more than 250 companies, has formed a task force to examine the technology's potential effects on health and the environment.

Efforts are also under way to start a dialogue between nanotechnology enthusiasts, researchers and skeptics. The first such meeting was held in June in Washington, D.C. The goal is to educate the public and identify any problems before they get out of hand.

"If enough misinformation spreads, I think there's a tremendous potential to generate a social backlash," said Bo Varga, executive director of NanoSIG, a group based at NASA's Ames Research Center in Mountain View that promotes commercial development of the technology.

"I think there are some real issues that need to be discussed, and there is mounting concern," he said. "But in my personal opinion, the fear is overblown, and a lot of the practical issues have not been addressed."

Scientists are just starting to examine how nanomaterials travel through the environment and behave in the body.

It's been known for a long time that as particles get smaller, they become more reactive and potentially more toxic. That's because they have large surface areas relative to their weight; the bigger the surface, the more chance it has to react with anything in the vicinity.

Inhaled, small particles can lodge in the lungs and cause inflammation. Nanosized particles can even work their way from the lungs into other organs, including the central nervous system.

Some nanoparticles contain toxic elements such as cadmium, iron or nickel, either as deliberate additions or as contaminants left over from the manufacturing process.

"There's a huge regulatory vacuum looking at the potential toxicity of materials at the nanoscale," said Hope Shand, research director of the ETC Group, an advocacy group based in Canada. "If there are studies that have been done, we haven't seen them. We feel at this point there needs to be a mandatory moratorium on synthetic nanomaterials until we can see laboratory protocols to protect workers and protect the environment."

Nanotech advocates counter that there are already plenty of nanoparticles in the environment, released by smokestacks, tail pipes and natural processes such as wildfires and storms.

They say procedures are in place to protect workers and the public. Further, they argue that a moratorium on nanomaterials would only drive research underground, ensuring that most of it is done in countries where regulations may be more lax.

"Nanotechnology is nothing different from all the technologies we have gone through in terms of safeguarding the public's interest," said Meyya Meyyappan, director of the Center for Nanotechnology at NASA/Ames. "The important thing is to make use of what is on the books. That is the right thing to do, rather than creating some kind of chaos and fear."

A new center at Rice University in Houston has $15 million in federal funding to study the biomedical and environmental aspects of nanotechnology.

Among other things, it will examine how nanomaterials move around in the environment, whether they can accumulate in organisms and how their small size affects how they interact with living things, as well as how quickly they break down in the environment.

"You can make the best technology in the world, but if the public for some reason doesn't buy it, or has misinformed opinions about its consequences, it can tank your technology," said Vicki Colvin, director of the Center for Biological and Environmental Nanotechnology at Rice. "We

want to make sure nanotechnology develops responsibly."

Later this year, the Environmental Protection Agency will invite researchers to apply for $5 million in grants to study the effects of nanotechnology on human health and the environment.

And in May, the House approved spending $2.4 billion over the next three years to foster research into nanotechnology and encourage its commercialization.

Some, including Colvin of the Rice University center, have urged Congress to set aside some of that money—perhaps 3 to 5 percent—for studies of the ethical, social and environmental impacts. That's the approach that was taken in funding the Human Genome Project.

Although the House did not follow that recommendation, it did say such studies should be integrated into other research programs, and the results widely disseminated to the public. The nanotechnology research and development act is now awaiting action in the Senate.

Implications for Society

A few weeks ago, the National Science Foundation announced that it's spending more than $1 million for research on the societal implications of nanotechnology. The studies will be done at UCLA and the University of South Carolina.

What is needed, some scientists say, is substantial public discussion as nanotechnology forges ahead; otherwise activists will exploit peoples' fears, and the technology will flounder.

"I don't mean a PR exercise to explain to people why nanotechnology is a good thing," said Peter A. Singer, director of the University of Toronto's Joint Center for Bioethics.

"I mean a real, two-way, balanced discussion, so scientists can share what they're up to and and why they think it's good—and the public can share its concerns," he said. "A really good dialogue that can shape the way the technology folds out."

For more information, see: The National Nanotechnology Initiative, www.nano.gov; the Rice University Web site on environmental and health effects of nanomaterials, www.ruf.rice.edu/~cben/NanoEnviHealth.shtml; and ETC Group, http://etcgroup.org/

Contact Glennda Chui at gchui@mercurynews.com or (408) 920-5453.

Supplement 8

The Poka-Yoke System

Poka-yoke is the Japanese name for technology specifically designed to prevent defectives from occurring. It is proactive technology used to speed up quality control. This is in contrast to SPC, which is reactive, allowing the control charts to indicate that something has gone awry. Poka-yoke aims at prohibiting the possibility of certain specific kinds of problems.

Shigeo Shingo developed the Poka-yoke system for problem-prevention. These Japanese words mean "mistake-proofing," which can be considered in the same vein as weatherproofing. In the case of weatherproofing, steps are taken to prevent wind, rain, cold and/or heat from entering the building.

A Poka-yoke system mechanically or electronically carries out 100 percent early-warning inspection. When and if abnormalities arise with the process, this information is immediately fed back to people and/or machines that are trained and/or programmed to take immediate corrective action. The instantaneous feedback function is crucial because it allows corrections to be made on the spot.

Mistake-proofing technology follows mistake-eliminating methodology. This means that steps are taken to prevent problems from arising in the first place. Then, if problems do occur, the system is designed to catch them on the spot. This rapid feedback eliminates defectives and prevents them from corrupting other dependent parts of the system. Using SPC, it is possible to generate large amounts of defective product before correcting the situation and eliminating the problem.

Timing is of the essence. Poka-yoke systems are designed to prevent defectives, so this approach supports the goal of zero-defect programs.

One option is for machines to be designed to shut down automatically in the presence of a problem. Sensors can often determine machine abnormalities faster than product variability. Technology allows machines that are acting erratically to shut themselves down. Many kinds of operations can be brought to a halt before defect product is produced in quantity. A sensor determines that temperature is too high. NASA space launches are replete with Poka-yoke technology to prevent liftoff from occurring by reading equipment rather than product performance.

Put in terms of SQC, the goal of Poka-yoke is to take action before assignable causes are detected by a control chart. This requires inventiveness to configure a "mistake-proofing" system. In a case where the defectives could not be prevented, technology was used to mark the location of defects so they could be repaired quickly. This prevented having to shut down the machine until regular maintenance time.

Poka-yoke includes various warning systems like lights that flash and buzzers that sound when abnormalities or imbalances are detected. Figure 8-5 illustrates a Poka-yoke system application used in a Japanese company.[8]

Mechanical and electronic devices are not the only source of sensors. People are often able to sense process abnormalities. Training and technology combined with a sixth sense can provide early warnings that something is not right.

Noting the condition of machines is not part of normal quality control practice. Technology awareness makes mistake prevention an area of opportunity for OM and process managers. Sensing devices, switches, and motion detectors are among the arsenal of mechanisms that are mentioned by Shingo in his book, which cites scores of examples of Poka-yoke.[9]

To determine how much to spend on technology to prevent defects, answer the following questions and then combine them in a cost evaluation model.

---

8. This example is taken from the book cited in the next footnote.
9. Shigeo Shingo. *Zero Quality Control: Source Inspection and the Poka-Yoke System*. Norwalk CT: Productivity Press, 1986. See, in particular, Chapters 6 and 7, pp. 99–261.

Before Improvement	After Improvement
The operation depended on the worker's vigilance.	

Labeler

Label

Blank tape

Photoelectric tube

The tape fed out by the labeler turns sharply so that the labels detach and project out from the tape. This is detected by a photoelectric tube and, if the label is not removed and applied to the product within the tact time of 20 seconds, a buzzer sounds, and the conveyor stops.

Effect: Label application failures were eliminated.
Cost: ¥ 15,000 ($75)

FIGURE 8-5
A Poka-Yoke Device to Ensure the Attachment of Labels

Source: From *Zero Quality Control: Source Inspection in the Poka-Yoke System* by Shigeo Shingo. English translation © 1986 by Productivity Press, Inc., P.O. Box 13390, Portland, OR 97213-0390, (800) 394-6868. Reprinted by permission.

1. What is the probability of fault x occurring? Say that $p_x = 0.01$, which means there is one defective unit per 100 units produced.
2. How many units are produced per day? Say that $V = 4,000$ units per day.
3. How much does it cost when x occurs? This cost should include the cost of repair and the effect of the fault on other units as well as process equipment. Say that $c_x = \$100$ per occurrence of x.
4. How much will it cost to use technology to prevent the fault from occurring? Say that the technology costs $50,000 and it is company policy to amortize the expense of such technology within one year or 250 working days. Therefore, this cost is

$C(T_x) = \$50,000/250 = \$200.00$ per day

Then, the cost of prevention and the cost of defectives can be contrasted.

The cost of defectives is $C(D_x) = (p_x)(c_x)V$, and this is to be compared to the cost of technology, $C(T_x)$.

Thus, $C(D_x) = (p_x)(c_x)V = (0.01)(100)\ 4,000 = \$4,000$ per day.

Because the cost of defectives is twenty (20) times larger than the cost of technology to prevent those defectives, the investment for Poka-yoke type technology is a clear winner.

Problems for Supplement 8

A curved piece is inserted into a fixture, which holds the piece while it is being stamped. Defectives are made whenever the piece is inserted upside down. When correctly inserted, the piece curves to the left, as in Figure 8-6. When incorrectly inserted, it curves to the right. Training is ineffective because the people who do this job are from a constantly shifting group of part-time workers.

1. What technology can be used to prevent this defective from occurring?
2. How much can be spent on this technology, given the following information:
   $p_x = 0.10$
   $V = 5,000$ units per day; $c_x = \$1.00$ per occurrence of x
   Company policy amortizes the costs of preventive technology over one year or 250 working days.
3. Is it likely that the company will invest in the Poka-yoke?

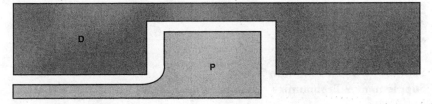

FIGURE 8-6
Piece P must be inserted into the die D with the curve to the left as shown. A defective is produced if the curve is to the right.

Planning Teamwork and Job Design

This section explores the importance of including people as part of the job design process. The same need for inclusion applies to planning teamwork. How long it will take to do a job is a detail that has major implications for production rates, costs of doing work, quality of outputs, and continuity. In this sense, it is necessary to explain how to set time standards for production jobs. Such standards are based on *job observation studies*. *Work sampling* provides another method for making useful observations about job characteristics. It is also a way to improve the way teams function and job design. Managing the work system also includes job evaluation, job improvement, work simplification, and job enrichment. Underlying the effectiveness of process is the commitment to training, which interacts with job design and team achievements.

After reading this chapter, you should be able to:

- Explain why, in times of technological volatility, training people in teamwork is increasingly important for successful OM.
- Describe the older training methods.
- Describe the newer training methods.
- Discuss the teamwork problems of performance evaluation.
- Explain why activity-based costing systems are increasingly vital for proper job design and for effective OM planning and decision making.
- Describe how to do a job observation (or time study) to determine standard output rates and costs.
- Explain leveling and normal time.

- Describe the method for determining adequate sample size for the time study.
- Explain how work sampling is used to improve job design.
- Describe the method for determining adequate sample size for the work-sampling study.
- Explain how job observation can improve job design.
- Detail the nature and applicability of synthetic time standards.
- Describe job design, improvement, and enrichment.
- Discuss the issue of wage determination.

THE SYSTEMS VIEWPOINT

P/OM, with its process orientation, manages technology and human resources (HR). The latter is greatly facilitated by strong systems identification with the department of human resource management (HRM). P/OM depends on the assistance of HRM for hiring and training that enhances teamwork for the mutual benefit of all personnel in pursuit of company goals. One difficulty of making the systems approach work is that people from different departments have various perspectives and unique orientations. The systems approach requires a dedicated effort to get finance, marketing, OM, and other functions to work as a team.

STRATEGIC THINKING

The common thread for all to follow is a comprehensive strategy that is clearly understood by all of the participants in the organization. Where is this vision and mission statement best developed, stored, and explained? It is at the interface of operations and human resource management. Given a bond of shared commonality, people recognize the strengths that come from their individual differences. Teamwork becomes more effective. Staying within the bounds of each department is equivalent to asking the same person who packed your parachute to inspect it. It is safer to have people with different points of view than the packer inspect the packing of the parachute.

Creative insights have a higher probability of occurring when there are more independent minds cooperating. However, there has to be shared strategic commitment. HRM and P/OM work well together when they share knowledge of the company strategy and commitment to the systems approach, which fosters coordination between the functional departments. Training for teamwork is a systems-wide concern where success is based on having a focused common strategy. Common focus is the foundation for quality of products as well as internal processes. For the systems approach to work, job design must encourage and facilitate teamwork based on focused commonality of strategy. Generalists sharing their knowledge about each other's areas of expertise should be rewarded for enriching the common focus.

9-1 TRAINING AND TEAMWORK

These are times of technological volatility. The result is that personnel are dealing with rapid shifts in what they are doing and how they are doing it. Operations managers must teach themselves first, and then others, how to adapt to extreme and sudden changes. Training in new process technologies is enhanced by teamwork that starts with a cooperative relationship between the operations management department and the human resource management (HRM) department.

In many companies, most of the people hired are interviewed by HRM. In general, the staffing of jobs in the company is influenced by the HRM department. HRM personnel play a major role in matching people and jobs. Many companies now screen for team players. These are people who enjoy cooperating with fellow workers instead of competing with them. Japanese companies in the United States regularly use this approach to hire workers. They have endeavored to steer clear of unions. However, when this has not been possible, efforts have been made for management to team up with the unions, as is the case with Toyota and GM's joint venture New United Manufacturing Motors Inc. (NUMMI).

GM had closed the NUMMI plant in the early 1980s because it was the worst GM assembly plant in North America. This Fremont, California, plant was reopened as an experimental joint venture of GM and Toyota in 1985. The first Corollas came off the NUMMI line in September 1986. In 2002, NUMMI was rated as one of the best auto assembly plants in North America. The 10 millionth car was produced during 2002 by 5,100 team members and hundreds of suppliers. NUMMI went on to produce the new Pontiac Vibe and the redesigned Toyota Corolla on a single production line in the year 2003.

HRM, in addition to playing a key role in hiring, is also the department that organizes training programs throughout the company. Training can foster the teamwork that P/OM's success requires. In addition, P/OM works closely with HRM to inform those who train and hire about requirements as operational needs are modified by competitive and technological changes. Training and teamwork are foundations for quality products and processes. Teamwork is a function of morale, which HRM influences through administration of payment and pension plans and in a variety of other ways as well. Close coordination of OM with HRM helps OM keep in touch with the state of employee morale.

9-2   TRAINING AND TECHNOLOGY

All OM systems are dependent upon the participation of people. The human factor always plays a part and teamwork counts. Even for entirely automated systems, people make plans, build plants, and maintain and change them. Generally, semiautomated combinations of people and machines provide greatest flexibility. Managers and engineers use adaptive systems to guide the achievement of flexible automation.

The basic equation relating people and equipment shown here has been used for many years:

Workers + Machines = Process Capabilities

What is lacking in this equation is the fact that people need training and teamwork to use technology effectively. Training provides skills, and skills with machines translate into quality and productivity. The systems approach provides recognition of the fact that a machine focus is too narrow. Equipment is confined and isolated in the picture of what makes a process work. Technology is a better word because it includes product design, materials used, process methods, and flows of information that reflect underlying systems and software. Therefore, the preferred equation is

Teamwork + Training + Technology = Process Capabilities

For each dollar spent on technology, companies can spend two or three dollars training people to use that technology in a skilled and efficient manner. The goal is to determine the correct blend of technology and training. The best guidelines for deciding this are as follows:

- Keep it simple.
- Count on people for quality outputs, strong productivity, and good ideas.
- Provide sufficient training to make *both* old and new technology work.
- Avoid going beyond the limits of technological expertise.

It has been widely written that GM expected Toyota to employ robotics and complex equipment at NUMMI, a joint venture between GM and Toyota. Instead, intense training was used with simple technology to produce a high-quality car in the old GM Fremont, California, plant that had been rated substandard.

This is a real example of choosing workers skillful with general-purpose equipment over automated operations using robotics and other special-purpose equipment. Thus, the decision to invest in elaborate machines has to be regarded with suspicion and carefully compared with the decision to train workers.

Technology and training can be traded off, but not completely. A glass blower's job description is heavy on training and light on technology. The auto windshield maker tips the scales in the other direction. The chef of a great Italian restaurant eschews a microwave. At the same time, Burger King revels in its continuous-chain infrared broiler, which cooks the burger just the right amount of time for the carefully controlled thickness of the patties.

9-3   OPERATIONS MANAGERS AND WORKERS

The daunting problem that P/OM has faced since it began to be studied by organizational theorists and industrial engineers has been how managers and workers should relate to each other. How employees best work together is a continuous topic of concern. Production and operations managers need to know how to foster competence, how to obtain commitment, how to develop and maintain motivation, and how to secure the loyalty of people who work in the system. All of this can be summed up as OM seeking to develop successful teamwork.

The past decade has seen such turbulence in downsizing of companies that the concept of loyalty to the firm by both workers on the floor and management is stretched thin.

Good relationships between managers and workers characterize globally successful competitors. In most prosperous firms, managers and workers are a team. Increasingly, multimedia, interactive shop-floor training programs are being employed as part of the teamwork.

There also are numerous examples of adversarial relationships between management and workers, especially when unions are involved.

The manufacturing workforce in the United States is shrinking in size. But, at the same time, manufacturing employees play a more important part than ever in achieving competitive performance. The service workforce continues to expand, but low productivity is distressing. Good relationships between managers and workers characterize globally successful competitors. In most prosperous domestic firms, management and workers are a team. Some firms use participative management, where workers help management reach decisions and share decision-making responsibilities.

Closer harmony with unions is evident in such plants as NUMMI and Saturn. On the floor, workers are making important creative contributions. The HRM component is increasingly recognized as a part of successful competitive strategies, with emphasis on selection, training, motivation, and commitment to excellence. HRM also must forge new relationships with unions that bring out the best of P/OM practice.

The U.S. steel industry has returned to profitability after years of serious "hard times."[1] Two factors that are usually cited are

1. The change of technology to continuous casting, processing the metal while red hot into final products, constituting a flow shop. Traditional methods can be categorized as labor-intensive, job shop operations. First the metal was poured into molds; then it was cooled; next the mold was stripped; then the metal was reheated for processing into the final product. The change saved energy and labor costs.

2. The changing relationships of the companies and their unions, which were traditionally highly adversarial, as they learned to become cooperative. Since the "hard times," the United Steel Workers and the companies they have organized have agreed on flexibility in assignments and cooperation, allowing for job rotation and job **cross-training.** Unions have been given more say. Often, the unions are given one or more seats on the board of directors.

In the steel industry, unions and management have learned to work together, using technology and training to survive and prosper. Similar accommodations have been made in aerospace, machine tools, and the chemical industries. The new connections between technology and human resources management are still being forged and tested in the automotive industries.

9-4 PRESENT TRAINING METHODS

Traditional training methods that are widely in use include on-the-job training, classroom instruction, audiovisual methods, workshops and seminars, case methods, games and simulations, role-playing, and self-instruction.

There are no mysteries about any of these traditional training methods. They have long been in place, and everyone who has held a job and gone to school has been exposed to some if not all of them. However, the technology that delivers training programs is undergoing constant upgrading.

Training program effectiveness is determined by four basic elements:

1. Objectives of training (what is needed)
2. Methods and design of the training programs
3. Delivery of the training program
4. Measurement of training program effectiveness

Figure 9-1 shows present methods for achieving traditional objectives.

For any of the methods, support and reinforcement of training in the actual work environment are critical if behavioral change objectives are to be met. Unfortunately, reinforcement is often bypassed for practical reasons like lack of time and money.

Current training trends show utilization of both traditional and innovative methods for a variety of applications, including organizational development, management and supervisory development, and technical skill development.

Cross-training: Permits workers to enjoy job rotation between stations of the flow shop and also between areas of specialization in the job shop.

Classroom instruction and discussion are widely used traditional training methods. The classroom can be augmented with new technology capable of asynchronous (off-line) participation. Classroom exercises require synchronous (online, real-time) participation.

Objectives	Methods
Information	Lectures
Skills	Demonstration, practice group exercises
Attitude	Experiential learning
Individual behavior	Practice, feedback, and experience
Organizational behavior	Team-building, management reinforcement

FIGURE 9-1
Relating Training Objectives and Methods

9-5 NEW TRAINING METHODS

The repertoire of training techniques has been expanding to include more experimentation and new technology. They now include cross-training, called *action learning;* team learning; computer-based training (CBT); and distance learning. All of these use various levels of interactive video and multimedia systems. Leading companies worldwide expect OM involvement in the development of advanced training methods. The list of companies to which this applies includes AT&T, Citicorp, Dell, Eastman Kodak, FedEx, GM, HPQ, Honda, IBM, Intel, Motorola, Texas Instruments, and Toyota.

9-5a Action Learning

Action learning, trading jobs for a period of time, has been very effective. It encourages systems thinking by allowing people to stand in each other's shoes and play each other's roles. Action learning encourages team building and leads to the cooperative environment needed for team learning.

9-5b Team Learning

Team learning adds to personal learning by emphasizing the interdependencies that exist between people working toward a common goal. It also is called *cooperative learning.* An example is teaching the baseball team to play together as a coordinated group instead of teaching each player how to be individually better at their assigned positions.

Team learning follows **team building,** which involves training groups of people to have a common focus. Often referred to as obtaining a personal commitment to the company "family," this approach is intended to do away with adversarial relations. The belief is that when internal competition is replaced with cooperation, then learning can begin.[2]

Although team-building methods remain experimental, they are being widely used. "Determined to achieve a 'cultural revolution,' Oldsmobile is putting—forcing, really—its independent-minded dealers through the team- and trust-building training used by another General Motors division, Saturn...."[3]

Team learning requires applying the systems approach. In every organization, there are people who, like a pitcher, catcher, or batter, can make greater contributions to winnings by being team players than by being individual stars. For business, team learning targets cooperation instead of what has come to be known as "personal best."

Honda of America has utilized team learning for its P/OM managers to enable them to shift easily across a broad spectrum of jobs. At Honda, the job description at any moment in time is related to what needs to be done. The Honda P/OM "associates" are not interchangeable, but they can play all the positions as needed. Hewlett-Packard employs team learning to achieve a higher level of performance than otherwise could be realized.

9-5c Computer-Based Training (CBT)

Scenarios and simulations that imitate real life can be run on the computer. The advantages of such instruction are that time can be compressed. Many things can be made to happen that would take years to occur in the real world. Extremes in demand and

Action learning: Trading jobs for a period of time allows one to stand in the other's shoes and encourages systems-wide thinking.

Team learning: Also called *cooperative learning;* applies to group effort to achieve excellence with a specific process.

Team building: Trust-building training is enhanced by a common set of goals.

Computer-based training has proven highly effective when the programmed instruction has been carefully worked out in detail and tested with actual trainees. Interactive video and computer-based training can be used at the student's discretion and time availability.

breakdowns in supply can be experienced by the student, enabling him or her to see how well a course of action works.

CBT is like training with a flight simulator. Horrible events—such as losing an engine while encountering hurricane-force winds—can be dealt with over and over again using a simulator *before* they are actually experienced while flying a real plane. Computer-based training offers the advantages of repeating a situation as needed and avoiding the risks of real losses if the wrong things are done. Such failures are simply part of the computer record.

There are several disadvantages. One is the cost of creating computer programs that capture all of the necessary elements of reality. Another disadvantage is that it may not be possible to make a computer behave like the real world. The full system of interconnected factors may not be known (or knowable) *a priori* to the simulation-model builder and the simulation programmer. Therefore, CBT is best used to deal with situations where training on the computer can be said to parallel reality. A reality check is always necessary. It must be explicit and convincing to the trainers and trainees.

9-5d Distance Learning (DL)

Distance-learning training can be delivered through the use of all-known media including online video, videotapes, computer screens, and printed manuals, as well as teleconferencing or videoconferencing, DL can travel (and often does) via satellites, to reach trainees in multiple physical locations individually and sometimes simultaneously. Networked computer-based training simulation methods are widely employed, and there are many other forms that it takes.

One of these is interactive video, which represents a range of options using TV and two-way communication. At its simplest, the camera is located in only one location, but the ability to communicate is two-way. Often, the camera follows the teacher, charts, and diagrams. Students can be located miles away, as is the case with the British Open University, which has successfully educated many thousands of students, every year, from all over the United Kingdom.

Within companies, there can be cameras at two locations so that the operations managers can converse and see each other. This also is called videoconferencing. It can be used in two ways: teams can train each other in respective skills, and they can transfer knowledge in a far more effective way than by telephone alone.

Distance learning is like a three-legged stool where the three legs are labeled "anywhere," "anytime," and "anyone." Self-paced learning has an enormous appeal to very busy people having different schedules. The quality of the education is always at issue, and the way to do it right is not yet clearly defined.

"Anytime" is often referred to as *asynchronous learning* where the classroom epitomizes synchronous education. Distance learning and in-class instruction are not opposites although DL allows the learning to take place "anywhere." As far as "anyone," some students prefer one or the other method of learning. Most students prefer each as being better in specific circumstances. The future of education and training in the year 2004 (and more) will find both approaches live and well.

There will continue to be improvements in both modalities of delivering education and their balanced use.

9-6 PERFORMANCE EVALUATION (PE)

Performance evaluation: Lauded for feedback it provides allowing employees *at all levels* to improve their performance. Criticized for being inaccurate and subjective, there is mistrust on the part of those who are below average.

Evaluation of individual performance (PE) is commonly used but can be counterproductive because the people who are measured distrust it. There is resentment based on the feeling that PE is not accurate, yet workers are permanently categorized by it. It should be noted that management performance evaluation may be less tangible than worker **performance evaluation.** In many organizations, both tangible and intangible factors are used.

As a counterpoint to negative reactions about PE, many companies claim that its use is essential to remove poor performers as quickly as possible, to provide incentives for excellent performance, and to provide feedback to people so they can improve their performance. Also, PE is a part of management practice all over the world.

Therefore, it is necessary to understand that a person's real contribution to the group may not be captured by the PE measures that are used. Most performance comparisons are made by determining **average performance.** Then, measures are grouped as being above and below the average. By definition, half of the people measured will be below the average. This immediately punishes part of the group, as always happens when the average is used, even if everyone in the below average group outperforms everyone else in the world.

Because the dimensions of the measures may miss some important contributions that individuals make to the system's performance, one must conclude that there are dangers in this approach. The measurement of team or group performance is not subject to most of these criticisms. Because performance measures are widely used for reasons that are logical, it may be possible to temper them with group performance measures.

Evaluation of worker performance begins with the measurement of output. Then, a standard is required to compare with the actual output. Process managers can define expected outputs for machines, but find definition elusive for people.[4]

Why is the question of performance evaluation so important? The reason is that the human resources component of the total cost of goods and service is sizable. It is larger in the service sector than in manufacturing, and it has been growing at a fast rate. The supply chain, of which manufacturing is just a part, has a great deal of direct labor in it. Warehousing, delivery, and retailing tend to be labor-intensive services in the supply chain that the producer cannot do without.

It reaches into the suppliers' organizations as well. Suppliers have varying levels of labor in their products and then these too must be delivered to the manufacturers. Human resources plays a significant role in management and staff functions. Many of these costs show up as overhead costs instead of labor. In short, there are many places where people play a part and the human resources costs are hidden.

Some industries are more labor intensive than others. The level of direct impact on factory costs is usually related to the efforts made to measure and control labor costs. In the banking industry, check processing remains labor intensive and performance evaluation is an ongoing activity. Major efforts are made to measure and control labor costs.

The problem of measuring on-the-line labor costs will continue to interest many companies. Measuring workers' performance remains critical wherever management wants to understand the company's costs and people play more than a trivial part in the cost structure of the system. The service sector can expect continuous growth in the performance evaluation area and in cost control of its labor component.

> **Average performance:** Many observations are taken to obtain average performance (or average time), which is then adjusted to obtain productivity standards.

9-7 USING PRODUCTION AND COST STANDARDS

Production standards are criteria specifying the amount of work to be accomplished in a given period of time. Standards are statements of expected output from which costs can be estimated. Production standards are widely used by manufacturing and service industries in this way.

Standards are needed to enable management to compute the real costs of production. Measurement of costs provides estimates of the cost of goods and services.

How standards are set will be discussed later. How standards are used will be examined now. Winning companies use standards as *targets to beat and not as goals to meet.* Just meeting goals can put a lid on accomplishments, whereas beating goals can motivate continuous improvement.

Here are a few P/OM situations that require good production standards:

How much to charge for a new product or service is dependent on what the real costs are. These costs are to be recovered, and then a profit is added on top of them.

Fixed and variable costs are used for breakeven analysis. This provides a capacity goal for the company. It cannot make money until it generates the breakeven volume. Direct labor is part of the variable cost component. Indirect labor, administration, and R & D are part of the fixed cost component.

> **Production standards:** Statements of the expected output rates from which the costs of the product can be estimated.

This gas plant worker is redirecting pipe flows. His job has been carefully studied for safety and efficiency. Job design is an implicit part of the training program. During training, workers may come up with suggestions for improvements. These should be fed back to the job designers and trainers.

Plant selection needs estimates of labor costs for different areas of the country.

Production scheduling allocates jobs, thereby assigning labor costs. Inventories of work-in-process and finished goods are storing labor costs on the shelves and in storage bins.

Determining an optimal product mix is dependent on being able to estimate profit per piece—based on cost per piece—for each product that could be in the mix.

The selection of technology in trade-off for labor requires knowing what the labor costs are now and what they are likely to be in the future. If labor costs are rising and the costs of technology are decreasing, when will it be reasonable to shift from labor to technology?

Companies that bid for jobs with municipalities, or bid as suppliers to companies, must know their labor costs. Otherwise they could lose money by winning contracts.

Capacity planning requires estimates of variable costs for different work configurations.

Especially with respect to services, the variability of labor expenses adds more uncertainty than most other costs to the organization's competitiveness. It is simple to predetermine the costs of materials, energy, space, insurance, and equipment. The quandary of estimating how much labor will be used to set up a job, and then produce a batch of given size, is complicated by behavioral factors. In this regard, the service estimate is more uncertain than the manufacturing estimate.

Labor estimation for the flow shop is easier than for the job and batch shop. This is another reason the flow shop is a preferred work configuration. Reduction of variability is a favorite reason P/OM tends to choose machines in place of people.

Even with the flow shop in place, there has been growth in the wage rates of indirect labor such as administrative, sales, promotional, clerical, and research personnel. It was anticipated that the growing number of computers would decrease such overhead charges. The reverse is true as, on average, they have continued to increase. It is, therefore, important to examine the basis for assigning indirect and overhead costs.

9-7a Activity-Based Costing (ABC) Systems and Job Design

> **Activity-based costing (ABC) systems:** Replaces traditional, volume-driven cost accounting methods with expenses only for resources actually used by the production system.

The method of assigning overhead costs to products based on direct labor dollars associated with specific job designs has been traditional. Many times the mix of resources required to make a product is badly reflected by volume-driven measures such as direct labor. In such cases, **activity-based costing (ABC) systems** should replace the traditional cost-accounting methods. Under such circumstances, actual expenses (*AE*) for resources including charges for materials, energy, and direct, short-term labor and overtime are subtracted from revenues (*R*) to yield the short-term contribution margin (*STCM*). Thus

$$STCM = R - AE$$

The other portion of operating expenses are assigned to resources that were acquired prior to actual use. These general expenses (*GE*) cover resources committed for purchasing, machine time, engineering, and administration. Permanent direct labor is a part of these expenses, which are divided into used and unused portions (*UGE* and *UNGE*). How much of purchasing's cost should be added to this particular job? How much inventory remained unused? These costs are subtracted separately from the short-term contribution margin to yield operating profit (*OP*). Thus

$$STCM - UGE - UNGE = OP$$

To illustrate, assume that all costs are multiplied by 10^4 and apply to one job and one week:

Materials of \$5 + Energy of \$3 + Direct Labor of \$4 = *AE* of \$12

STCM = Revenue of \$18 − *AE* of \$12 = \$6

The overhead to be allocated is measured by the company for one week and applied in normal fashion to this job. However, it will be broken into two parts as follows:

Assume that:

$GE = \$3$ with $UGE = \$1$ and $UNGE = \$2$

Then,

$STCM$ of $\$6 - UGE$ of $\$1 - UNGE$ of $\$2 = OP$ of $\$3$

The approach makes evident that overhead charges of $2 are labor costs that would have occurred whether the job was done or not.

It should be emphasized that ABC systems make clear the labor costs that would not have been incurred if the job had not been done. ABC also makes evident the labor costs that would have occurred anyway, and divides these into used and unused portions. This facilitates evaluation of job and process design.

Traditional costing systems lump and therefore hide the charges for resources that have been paid for whether or not they are utilized. The equation used by the leading proponents and creators of ABC to explain the subject[5] is (in units or dollars):

Activity Available = Activity Usage + Unused Capacity

$GE = UGE + UNGE$

It may be easier to understand what is being suggested by converting the previous equation into a cost equation as follows:

[Costs Assignable for Products Made (Activity Usage, UGE)
= (equals) Costs of Resources Available (Activity Available, GE)
− (minus) Costs of Resources Unused (Unused Capacity, $UNGE$)]

The costs of resources that are used are considered to be real costs that can and should be assigned to costs of goods sold. The costs of unused resources are cause for concern. Too much capacity may have been put into place. If that is the case, and there is repeated evidence of unused capacity, it should be reduced or alternative uses for that capacity should be found in the longer term. Unused capacity of all kinds, including labor, materials, energy, and technology, should be tracked.

ABC is the accounting system that accomplishes that goal. P/OM needs that information to reach intelligent decisions.

The subject of activity-based costing (ABC) is usually explored in accounting texts. More recently, P/OM has included ABC accounting methods when discussing the increasing irrelevance of using labor charges as the guide for allocation of overhead charges, or when discussing capacity planning. These are the two places where a discussion of activity-based costing (ABC) seems most appropriate.

Without ABC, the decision to buy new technology can be negatively impacted. Traditional net present value (NPV) accounting penalizes long-term planning where large income streams will not begin until far in the future. Meanwhile, labor-intensive situations that could be relieved by technology are penalized with large overhead charges. Job design is negatively impacted. As a result, the company tends to avoid these kinds of activities and loses out on potential opportunities to be a leader in the area.

An illustration of how the problem of assigning overhead costs to output has relevance for P/OM follows. In a lock manufacturing company, incorrect allocation of overhead caused the spring-making department to be closed. Thereafter, springs were purchased, which led to an increase in real costs and a loss of control over quality. The traditional accounting system had done a real disservice to P/OM. This was not a surprise to the process managers who had resisted the decision to shut down springs. The process design was flawed.

ABC can be credited with raising awareness of misleading information that traditional accounting methods can provide. The approach ties in with results that were obtained employing linear programming to optimize the use of limited resources years before ABC was developed.

When linear programming (LP) is used to determine an optimal product mix, it is frequently the case that full capacity utilization results in lower profits than properly configured partial capacity utilization. LP depends on good measures of labor productivity, availability of capacity, utilized capacity, and unused capacity. The labor productivity is a function of the design of jobs.

9-8 HOW TIME STANDARDS ARE SET— JOB OBSERVATION

Get a group of people together and compare their golf or tennis scores. Big differences exist. Check how many push-ups they can do and how fast they can input data on the computer terminal. Variability in the time it takes different people to do the same job description can be reduced by training, but it can never be eliminated. In many cases, companies use so little training that the distribution of times is larger than one might reasonably expect to be the case.

Some people might be good golfers, but poor typists. Variances in "time to accomplish" exist among people within jobs and different jobs require different skills. To find a common ground for setting standards and evaluating the efforts and outputs of workers, it is necessary to build a sound structure and begin the analysis on a simple level.

Diagnostic production studies, where the worker is observed constantly over a long period, go back in time to the early 1900s. The approach can be compared to 100 percent inspection. Both the job and the worker are examined in great detail. This method has shortcomings so it is seldom used. Its primary weaknesses are high costs, unreliable results, worker confusion, and hostility. However, when diagnostic studies lead to improvement of job design they are focusing on the right target.

One hundred percent observations gave way to sampling procedures, which were identified by the name *time and motion studies*. Time study and work-sampling methods also were derived from statistical developments that date back to the 1920s. It is now politically correct for P/OM to eliminate references to time and motion studies, stopwatches, and time studies. That does not mean that the functions are eliminated, just the references. The functions are being done, often in other ways as described ahead. However, the distinction should be made at this point between the study of how long it takes to do specific operations, which is a **time study,** and the study of the motions of which the job is comprised, a **time and motion study.**

Instead of tracking the worker continuously, time and motion studies were based on obtaining a sample of observations sufficient to answer such questions as how long it takes to do each of the component tasks. The main or core process steps are called *basic elements* that compose the job. Support steps are called *extraneous elements*. From this information, the expected daily output of workers on the line can be determined.

Time study: The study of how long it takes to do specific operations.

Time and motion study: Sampling and recording what workers do to make, finish, or pack a product. Can be used for service operations.

9-8a Cycle-Time Reduction

The job observation analyst studies the overall job with the purpose of breaking the job down into basic and extraneous elements. These basic elements, when added together, form the *job cycle*. This job cycle will be the shortest cycle of basic elements required to make the product. It is the repetitive core of the job. Short cycles constitute the main portion of the job. Having a short-cycle time is equivalent to gaining high output rates. Essentially the same considerations apply to process studies leading to *cycle-time analysis* and reduction.

In many instances, the spotlight shifts from the individual to groups of individuals or to the combination of people and technology. The fundamental idea is to time all elements that make up the cycle. This is another aspect of process analysis with emphasis on the basic elements and on the times required to perform them. These are often referred to as *diagnostic observations* instead of *time studies*, a term that carries some negative connotations.

Diagnostic observational methods are not well suited for long-cycle jobs, which do not have short-cycle repetitive basic elements following each other in sequence. Work sampling, used for long-cycle studies, is discussed ahead. The strength of job observational methods lies in their ability to deal with repetitive basic elements.

Job observational methods can be used to set standards or to study how work is done with the purpose of improving the job. The use of time studies for analyzing the performance of individuals has declined as technology has come to play a larger role and labor a smaller one. The decrease in piecework pay, or hourly pay, in favor of pay by the day, or salaried pay, also has lessened the need for standards that state the expected number of pieces per hour.

It also has decreased as emphasis is placed on the contribution of group performance to the reduction of cycle time. It has been said, if there is only so much time and money to be spent on organizing and improving the process, then process cycle-time reduction and benchmarking are areas of study that are likely to have greater leverage than classical kinds of time or job studies.

9-8b Computers Substitute for Stopwatches: Digital Versus Mechanical Clocks

The reasons for job observation include

1. Improving the job
2. Simplifying work
3. Determining expected output rates
4. Calculating each individual's real output rate

All four are applicable to service and manufacturing. The fourth reason is often prompted by need to determine if individuals are performing well, and for payment purposes. Check processing in the bank has a room filled with people doing the same things. Job performance evaluation is ongoing for each one of them. These same labor-intensive conditions that applied to most manufacturing operations circa 1940 still are used in many banks, insurance companies, and travel agencies in various places worldwide.

Although the names "time studies" and "time and motion studies" are out, old-fashioned, and unloved, similar procedures are still widely used. They are called by other names including *process analysis* and *cycle-reduction studies*. They are done in other ways. The difference may be that *cycle-time analysis places more stress on the group*. Some say there is less focus on minutia and unnecessary detail; they say that detail has been replaced by the bigger picture.

Although there is truth to this statement, nevertheless, standards continue to be set and used everywhere. They are still based on logic, measurement, and analysis. The new methods relying on computers and programming may be even more detailed than the old-fashioned time study.

Figure 9-2 is the job observation study sheet that is used by the High Compression DVD Corporation (called HCDVD). The job observation sheet is being used to study the packaging of 10 blank DVDs.

Two basic and four extraneous elements comprise the packing process. The two basic elements set the tempo for the complete short-cycle job. The four extraneous elements support the two main components of the packing process.

Stopwatches, once the mark of a time study observer, now are rarely seen in the United States. This is because technology has developed machines that can be set to pace the worker; computers (PCs and notebooks, as well as computers adapted to timing) are used to time workers with more accuracy than stopwatches offered. Computer databases have been developed that are timing workers, and computer databases contain synthetic time standards.

In a real sense, stopwatches with external observers changed. They underwent a metamorphosis becoming internalized computer timers that were part of the process

FIGURE 9-2
HCDVD's Job Observation Sheet

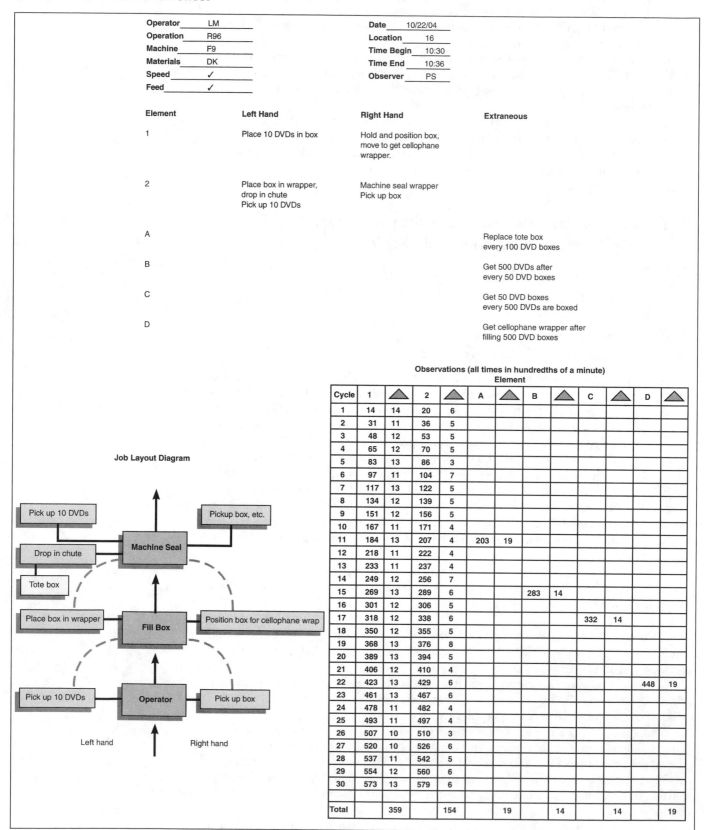

Operator	LM
Operation	R96
Machine	F9
Materials	DK
Speed	✓
Feed	✓

Date	10/22/04
Location	16
Time Begin	10:30
Time End	10:36
Observer	PS

Element	Left Hand	Right Hand	Extraneous
1	Place 10 DVDs in box	Hold and position box, move to get cellophane wrapper.	
2	Place box in wrapper, drop in chute Pick up 10 DVDs	Machine seal wrapper Pick up box	
A			Replace tote box every 100 DVD boxes
B			Get 500 DVDs after every 50 DVD boxes
C			Get 50 DVD boxes every 500 DVDs are boxed
D			Get cellophane wrapper after filling 500 DVD boxes

Job Layout Diagram

Observations (all times in hundredths of a minute)
Element

Cycle	1	△	2	△	A	△	B	△	C	△	D	△
1	14	14	20	6								
2	31	11	36	5								
3	48	12	53	5								
4	65	12	70	5								
5	83	13	86	3								
6	97	11	104	7								
7	117	13	122	5								
8	134	12	139	5								
9	151	12	156	5								
10	167	11	171	4								
11	184	13	207	4	203	19						
12	218	11	222	4								
13	233	11	237	4								
14	249	12	256	7								
15	269	13	289	6			283	14				
16	301	12	306	5								
17	318	12	338	6					332	14		
18	350	12	355	5								
19	368	13	376	8								
20	389	13	394	5								
21	406	12	410	4								
22	423	13	429	6							448	19
23	461	13	467	6								
24	478	11	482	4								
25	493	11	497	4								
26	507	10	510	3								
27	520	10	526	6								
28	537	11	542	5								
29	554	12	560	6								
30	573	13	579	6								
Total		359		154		19		14		14		19

equipment. As such, they could observe a great deal more without being as intrusive. When computers time workers, they are capturing the moments when the worker feeds the next unit (say a check to the optical reader). They can record every time a worker types the letter "q" or stops feeding data to the machine for any interval that is greater than 5 seconds. Computers using satellite hookups determine when truck drivers stop and how many miles they log between stops. Customer relation (call) centers have total monitor feedback for every one of the answering personnel reporting number of calls, length of calls, number of orders obtained, etc.

Computers determine and calculate the intervals between successive steps in the process just as if a stopwatch were at work in the hands of the old-fashioned time study observer. Surveillance has not disappeared. It has become more obscure and hidden. Labor, and especially unions, did not like the stopwatch. The surveyor is now an unseen machine and, in many organizations, employees do not know what about their performance is being scanned and tabulated.

Company computers count the number of entry data errors made as a check on clerical quality. Computers observe how long mail-order or airline reservation people spend on the phone. These are just a few more examples of a growing use of time studies without human observers, often done under the name of diagnostic observations.

Because of the parallel between computer and stopwatch as simple timers, it remains useful to consider how stopwatch methods are applied to time both the basic and extraneous elements of the cycle. Various kinds of stopwatches and stopwatch methods were available for different applications as well as to satisfy personal preferences. The major distinction was between *continuous and snap-back use of stopwatches.*

The snap-back approach was used to time each work element. When an element was completed, the watch hand returned to zero to begin timing the next element. Continuous readings are cumulative and require subtraction to determine element times. The computer notebook can be programmed to record in either mode. Subsequent calculations follow the same routines as with the stopwatch, but faster.

"Continuous" is the method shown in Figure 9-2. That can be verified by studying the columns headed 1, 2, A, B, C, and D. The snap-back system saved having to do repeated subtractions, but it was more demanding on the job observation analyst and needed a larger sample for the same precision that could be obtained from the continuous method. The computer as an observation tool can do a 100 percent study without error or intrusion.

The stopwatch is attached to a time study clipboard, which holds the job observation or time study sheet. HCDVD's completed time sheet for 30 cycles is shown in Figure 9-2. There is partial information about each basic element and how long it takes. More complete information is available on the left-hand, right-hand operation charts. In addition, there is information about the operation, the operator, the observer, the date, the equipment being used, the setup, materials used, and the speed and feed rates of the equipment.

Figure 9-2 also provides a left-hand, right-hand activity analysis sheet that gives the basic elements and their sequence. It explains the extraneous elements and gives the point at which they enter the work sequence. Job observation by computer can pick up the tasks done by each hand, if that seems useful. HCDVD's job layout diagram for packing DVDs is shown.

Enough data must be taken to capture all conditions under which the particular job might be done. This could include (for example) different plant settings where the domestic plant is older than the one abroad. Standards may be different in each location. Special methods, materials, locations, and other factors can produce different results. The effects of special factors must be taken into account when costing, pricing, and measuring productivity for delivery schedules.

Job observation studies should not be conducted for poorly designed jobs. They should be made only when it is agreed that the best design has been developed. Design the job before setting any standards. Because of variability, it makes sense to check on a study by replicating the results a sufficient number of times. When job observation results are contested, the variability of study conditions and/or their variance with actual conditions are frequently introduced to win the argument.

The job design (tasks, activities, operations) in Figure 9-2 has been broken down into six elements, but only two elements dominate the process. In this simple case, activities of an operator's left and right hands are described for each basic element. The other elements are long cycle ones used to support the short-element cycles.

The short-cycle job is putting 10 DVD blanks in a box, wrapping and sealing the box with clear plastic, and then dropping the box into the shipping chute. The long-cycle jobs are to refill the bins with DVD boxes that hold 10 DVDs, clear plastic wrapping material, and sealers.

Basic element 1 dictates that the left hand should be placing 10 DVD blanks, which are loose but grouped in tens, into a box while the right hand holds and positions the box so that the DVD blanks can be put into the box. The left- and right-hand operations are coordinated through job design and training.

Basic element 2 consists of the left hand holding the box for the right hand, which seals the box with a clear plastic wrapper. Then the left hand releases the box over a conveyor, which carries it away to a tote box at the end of the conveyor. Each box gently slides into the tote box, which can hold up to 105 of the boxes containing 10 DVD blanks.

Enter in the first column the time it takes to complete element 1 in the first cycle. The time it takes to complete element 2 in the first cycle is recorded next. The stopwatch is continuous, so the first value is 14 and the second is 20, meaning that element 2 required 20 − 14 = 6 hundredths of a minute.

Next, cycle 2 is observed with values of 31 and 36, which entails 31 − 20 = 11 and 36 − 31 = 5, all in hundredths of a minute. The time unit is chosen because it fits the job and can be read on the stopwatch. The stopwatch is a decimal-minute type, which reads directly in hundredths of a minute. The translation of these terms into computer capabilities is straightforward. Specific actions trigger the computer to note the time just as if a stopwatch had been built into the system.

The sample size is 30 cycles. These are all listed on the sheet. Thirty is chosen as a convenient start-up number that fits the size of the single sheet on the clipboard. Later, it will be determined if a larger sample is needed. The computer has no such restraints or limitations.

When the observations have been completed, the computations start. The sum of the times of the two core elements constitutes the job-cycle time. Cycle 1 required 0.20 min. Element 1 needed 0.14 min. and element 2 consumed the remaining 0.06 min. The second cycle ends at 0.36 min. This means that the second cycle consumed 0.36 − 0.20 = 0.16 min. In this second cycle, element 1 needed 0.11 min. and element 2 used the remaining 0.05 min. Cycles 3 to 30 are obtained in the same way.

The extraneous elements listed on the time sheet are operations that must be done once for every *n* times that the core cycle is repeated. They support the basic elements of the core process. The right- and left-hand activity chart lists the extraneous element A as the requirement that after 100 DVD blank boxes have been packed and shunted along the conveyor, the tote box they fall into at the end of the conveyor must be taken away and replaced with another one. This occurs once for every 1,000 DVDs that are boxed and removed.

Extraneous element B requires the worker to interrupt the basic work cycle once for every 50 DVD boxes completed. This means stopping after 500 DVD blanks have been packed to get a new supply of the DVD blanks. *Better job design* would allow A and B to occur at the same time, i.e., resupply DVD disks in lots of 1,000. Apply the same thinking to extraneous element C, which resupplies the DVD boxes in 50-unit lots. This could be increased to 100. Combining A, B, and C might be feasible. Extraneous element D obtains clear plastic or cellophane wrappers for 500 boxes.

Extraneous elements break into the short-cycle system regularly. Therefore, when they are included, the total job-cycle time is of much longer duration than the basic elements-cycle time. They disrupt the process and set back the learning curve. It is not unusual for a worker to slow down for awhile on the basic elements after an extraneous element occurs. Also, the worker might meet a friend while going to the storeroom and decide to chat a bit. That would not occur during the job observation study, but would occur in reality. The company would realize less production than the job observation study indicated.

9-8c Shortest Common-Cycle Time

For extraneous element D, the worker replaces the used-up role of plastic (cellophane) with a new one in the plastic wrapping machine. This takes place every 500 DVD boxes, or once every 5,000 DVDs. Because D has the longest extraneous cycle it constitutes *the shortest common-cycle time* necessary to encompass all element cycles that are part of the process.

This is something like finding the lowest common denominator to determine the value of a series of fractions. In this case, it means that 500 cycles of the basic elements are required to include one cycle of the longest extraneous element. A totally proper job observation study would include at least two occurrences of the longest extraneous cycle (D).

To observe 500 cycles imposes such a great observational burden that it may be decided to ignore perfection and include only one of these longest-term cycles. If the time to perform element D is variable, then it could be simulated several times to get a reasonable average value. The same applies to other extraneous elements that have low frequencies of occurrence in the sample. The effects of extraneous elements on the basic element times is another matter that can be simulated if the standard times (the ultimate goal of the study) appear to be sensitive to such effects.

Almost always, even the shortest-cycle, repetitive jobs include long-cycle, extraneous elements. The job observer must be on top of all of the longer-cycle elements that are to be included in the study. The same requirement concerning extraneous cycles applies to computers programmed to make job observations.

The layout chart could have added distances traveled to the picture on the time sheet. How far does the operator have to go to get DVDs, boxes, and clear plastic sheets? The more information the better when trying to reproduce the job observation study results at a later date. It may not be possible to recover finer points about the extraneous elements unless the necessary documentation exists somewhere. The computer (as observer) must be programmed to capture the way in which the basic and extraneous elements interact with the layout.

9-8d Productivity Standards

Productivity or production standards are measures of the expected output rate. They can be developed for short-cycle jobs using time study data. How much effort should be spent on developing standards depends to a great extent on the kind of work configuration being used. Enough product must be run in the job shop to warrant developing **productivity standards.** The flow shop qualifies, but in many cases the standards will have been predetermined by engineering design.

Productivity standards: Average performance adjusted by an allowance for rest and delay.

The 10-DVD box packer is part of a flow shop assembly operation for the company known as HCDVD. Several workers do the same operations at the same time. HCDVD workers are cross-trained, which means they are able to shift operations. Some make DVDs, others format them, label them, and still others pack them. This example takes focus on packing one kind of DVD. The company will have to consider the pack time characteristics of other kinds of DVDs. Each variant has its own individuality, output standards, and costs.

The productivity standard is used to calculate expected output. It is adjusted average performance with an allowance for *rest* and *delay*. The productivity standard enables the process manager to determine how many workers are required to meet expected demand. Labor costs can be estimated for the total job.

TABLE 9-1								
Element	**1**	**2**	**A**	**B**	**C**	**D**	**Total**	
TTO	359	154	19	14	14	19		
NO	30	30	1	1	1	1		
ECPO	1	1	1/100	1/50	1/50	1/500		
AT or ST	11.97	5.13	0.19	0.28	0.28	0.04		
LF or AL	0.95	1.00	1.00	1.00	1.00	1.00		
NT or AT	11.37	5.13	0.19	0.28	0.28	0.04		
CF(r&d)	110%	110%	110%	110%	110%	110%		
ST	12.51	5.64	0.21	0.31	0.31	0.04	19.02	

HCDVD's Job Observation Summary: Pack 10 DVDs in a Plastic Wrapped Box

TTO = Total time observed
NO = Number of observations
ECPO = Expected cycles per observation
AT or ST = Average time or selected time (in 0.01 minutes)
LF or AL = Leveling factors or allowances
NT or AT = Normal time or adjusted time
CF(r&d) = Correction for rest and delay (r&d)
ST = Standard time (in 0.01 minutes)

Table 9-1 summarizes and operates on the information collected for HCDVD. Basic and extraneous elements 1, 2, A, B, C, and D are listed. Total times, as summed on the time study sheet of Figure 9-2, are carried into the first row of Table 9-1. The total time for element 1 is 359; for element 2 it is 154. Then, for the extraneous elements A, B, C, and D, total times are 19, 14, 14, and 19, respectively.

The third row of the summary sheet lists the number of occurrences that can be expected for each observation of the basic elements. This is 1 for the basic elements of the core cycle and the appropriate fraction for the extraneous elements.

The first row is divided by the second row, yielding the average time for each element. This quotient is multiplied by the third row, yielding an average time per core cycle for each element. The results are shown in the fourth row as average time (also called *selected time*) per core cycle. To illustrate, average time for element 1: 359/30 = 11.96666; 11.97 x 1 = 11.97

This is in hundredths of a minute or 0.1197 minutes. The average time for element 2 = 0.0513 minutes, and so forth.

9-8e Training for Job Observation

Leveling factors: Used in time studies of work to convert average time of the person being observed (average performance) to normal time.

What if the observed worker is believed to be faster than average? It is necessary to adjust such performance to what is considered normal. **Leveling factors** are used to convert average time to adjusted or normal time. When the computer is used to record times, it captures all workers and the leveling problem is eliminated.

Process managers used to say that the toughest job in the time study procedure was picking an allowance or leveling factor. It is historically interesting that training for leveling was widely practiced. One of the most popular training methods used "movies" made by motion picture cameras. A movie was made of a normal worker doing the job. The picture was shown using projectors with variable speed controls. By adjusting the speed controls, it was possible to make a normal worker seem to work faster or slower. This illustrates another interaction between time studies and time and motion studies.

The important point to emphasize is that all of the time study raters within the company had to agree with each other on what constitutes normal performance speeds. This high degree of conformity meant there would be consistency of ratings for all employees in the same company.

9-8f Setting Wages Based on Normal Time

Normal time is adjusted average time. Pay scales can be set so that normal time workers are being paid wages similar to those being paid by other companies in the region for the same kind of jobs. This removes pay scale inequities between employees in the same company and among workers in other companies. Such parity is particularly desirable for workers within the same industry. Synthetic time standards provide benchmarks for stabilizing what is normal time in similar jobs across companies and industries. Jobs are broken down into components that are common to all work. Each standard component takes an expected (or average) amount of time to perform. Jobs can be constructed of synthetic components just as they can be broken down.

Normal time: The output rate of an average worker is the expected production rate of the process.

9-8g What Is Normal Time?

Before making a job observation study, workers should be told the full story. The purpose of the study is to develop standards that permit the company to anticipate costs and meet demand requirements. These standards are not meant to exceed what is reasonable. They are intended to prevent overworking operators. Good time standards remove unreasonable expectations, which entrap both management and employees.

An average worker should be selected for the study. The observer tries to make sure that the subject is operating under standard conditions, using routinized methods. When the subject of the study seems to work at a normal rate, the leveling factor is determined. For each element, the average time (row 4) and the leveling factor (row 5) are multiplied, which yields the normal time (row 6).

Assume that the observed worker is faster than normal. The observer estimates that this worker is producing 10 percent more output than an average worker. The observer assigns the worker a leveling factor of 110 percent. The normal time will be greater than the average time, meaning that the normal (slower) worker can be expected to take longer than the observed study time.

Examine element 1 in Table 9-1. The operator is working at 95 percent of normal in the judgment of the observer. Multiplication produces a normal time of 0.1137 minutes, which is less than the average time of 0.1197 minutes. Less time to complete an element means that the normal operator works faster and will be able to produce more units than the observed worker.

When the leveling factor is 100 percent, as it is for the remaining five elements in Table 9-1, average time and normal time are equal. This leaves the remaining numbers equal in rows 4 and 6. Many studies require a leveling factor that is not equal to 1. This is because operator skills differ in a variety of ways that are dependent on their motor skills, body size, and experiences.

9-9 LEARNING CURVE EFFECTS

The observer must allow time for learning to take place so that work time stabilizes. Repetition improves performance. Start-up (even for the nth time) requires getting back in practice. Learning always takes place, which increases capacity to produce. This raises productivity and lowers the number of defectives produced. Learning is a subject that belongs in discussions of capacity management.

Even with the most familiar, repetitive work, start-up is slower. With repetition, as the job is being relearned, the operator is said to start moving up the **learning curve.** The effect is substantial when the job is done for the first time. Nevertheless, learning takes place every time that the operator comes on to start a new shift.

Computer monitoring picks up the learning curve phenomenon. It provides a great deal of useful information about the learning curves of workers. It is valuable to study these records to determine how to help people move up their respective learning curves faster.

Learning curve: Repetition improves performance with eventual stabilization of output rates.

9-9a Job Observation Corrections

Leveling estimates introduce one kind of measurement correction. Time study errors also can occur when the stopwatch is misread or the reading is entered incorrectly. Statistical quality control (SQC) concepts apply. Look at the distribution of element time readings. Extreme numbers that do not seem to belong to the distribution are outlying values that can be thrown out of the sample. If however, outliers are taken seriously, then increased sampling may be warranted.

Subtraction errors can occur when the stopwatch provides continuous readings. They can best be corrected by using several analysts. It is more difficult for one person to redo the calculations. Snap-back readings are more demanding mechanically than continuous readings. Errors can be made in hesitating to snap back or forgetting to do so. Two observers, working together, can be used when breaking in a new observer.

There is yet another correction to be made. Called the *rest and delay correction factor* (*r&d*), it is shown in row 7 of Table 9-1. Some say that (r&d) is the "mother" of all corrections. The estimation of appropriate (r&d) factors is required for computerized observation systems.

Generally, the number chosen for (r&d) results from negotiations with unions or with workers and their representative groups. The agreed-upon numerical factor is often affected by who is the best negotiator, union or management. After all the finessing with exact observational methods and leveling, it comes as a shock that assigned values for (r&d) commonly range from 5 to 15 percent, depending upon the character of the job, the degree of personal needs, union–management negotiations, and so on.

The point to keep in mind is that without the (r&d) factor, workers might never have a moment to stop. In this case, the left and right hands would constantly be moving packing the DVDs. There would be no time to rest and no time to use the rest room. The best way to set the (r&d) factor is to enlarge the extraneous elements to include a given amount of time to use the rest facilities. A proper scenario should be developed and examined with an appropriate simulation.

Normal time is multiplied by the rest and delay factor, which is always more than 100 percent, yielding standard time. Thus, an (r&d) correction of 110 percent is to be applied to all of the elements as shown in Table 9-1. If some elements are particularly onerous, they might be given a larger (r&d) buffer. Also, it is reasonable, and simpler to calculate (r&d) assigned only to the basic elements.

Total standard time is the basis for calculating production output standards. The sum of the standard times for all the elements is the total standard time of the operation. For the HCDVD example, total standard time is 0.1902 minutes.

9-9b Expected Productivity and Cost of the Well-Designed Job

Before measuring productivity and getting a cost for the job, it is essential to evaluate the job design and improve it as much as possible. One method that is used is called *work simplification*. It removes unnecessary steps and streamlines work flows based on common sense considerations.

Assuming that this has been done, how many boxes of 10 DVDs will the normal HCDVD worker produce per hour?

$$POS = 60 \frac{min.}{hour} \div 0.1902 \frac{min.}{box} = 315.46 \frac{boxes}{hour}$$

where,

POS = Productivity output standard

(It is to be noted how the dimensions result in minutes canceling minutes and yielding boxes per hour.)

If 60 minutes per hour had not been used, then 1 divided by 0.1902 = 5.2576 boxes per minute. Multiplying 5.2576 by 60 yields 315.46 boxes per hour. For simplicity, round this output rate to 315 boxes per hour and call it the *expected output rate* for the job.

Assume that the wage rate for this job classification is $6 per hour. Then the labor cost for packing each box of 10 DVDs would be $6/315 = $0.01905. The expected cost of the operation is a little less than 2 cents apiece.

The major weaknesses of this form of study are defining a normal worker, applying the leveling factor, choosing values for the rest and delay correction, and overlooking influential extraneous elements. Defenders of time study methods claim that satisfactory solutions have been found for all of these problems.

Job observation is a skill, not a science. The use of the stopwatch and leveling both require training and practice. Time study practitioners seldom break down elements into less than 0.04 minutes because smaller intervals are difficult to observe. Another fact worth considering is that the worker's performance may not be stable in the sense of the equilibrium defined by Walter Shewhart for stable control charts. Equilibrium can be especially elusive because of "learning." Time studies should not begin until workers' learning ceases and performance has stabilized.

There remains the issue of determining an adequate sample size for the job observation or time study. How many cycles should be observed? Using automated (100 percent) computer observation eliminates this issue.

9-10 JOB OBSERVATION SAMPLE SIZE

Especially for service operations where no 100 percent computer monitoring system is feasible, observations of performance may need to be made on a sampling basis. This is done to understand the nature of the job, to improve it, to establish pay scales, and to set productivity expectation levels. When this is the case, the need is to set appropriate sample sizes.

Job observation studies are based on sampling n basic cycles of a job. Accordingly, a statistical issue arises about how large a sample (n_j) should be taken for each element, called j. Various formulations can be used depending upon the assumptions made.

Equation 9-1 controls statistical measurement error in terms of sample size for each element j.

Equation 9-1 answers the question: How large a sample (n_j) is needed (how many cycles should be observed) to obtain 95 percent confidence that the true element time (t_j) lies within the range?

$$\bar{t}_j \pm 0.05\bar{t}_j \qquad\qquad \text{(Equation 9-1)}$$

The right-hand side of Equation 9-1 states that the range is ± 5 percent of the observed average time.

This is the value 0.05 that appears in the denominator of Equation 9-2.

$$n_j = \left(\frac{1.96 \cdot s_j}{0.05 \cdot \bar{t}_j} \right) \qquad\qquad \text{(Equation 9-2)}$$

As for the 1.96 that appears in the numerator of the equation, note that 1.96 sigma defines two tails of a normal distribution each of which has an area of 0.025. This provides the confidence interval within which the true element lies 95 percent of the time.

Assume that $i = 5$ cycles have been observed and that these are the first five cycles in Table 9-1.

The average times

$$\bar{t}_j = \sum_{i=1}^{i=n} t_{ij} \div n = \bar{t}_j = \sum_{i=1}^{i=5} t_{ij} \div 5$$

of the first and second elements will be found to be

$\bar{t}_1 = 12.4$ and $\bar{t}_2 = 4.8$ from the tabled data in Figure 9-2.

These are now used to compute the sample standard deviation as shown in Equation 9-3.

$$s_j = \sqrt{\frac{\sum_{i=1}^{i=n} (t_{ij} - \bar{t}_j)^2}{(n-1)}}$$

(Equation 9-3)

Obtain s_j for the first five cycles of elements 1 and 2, as follows:

$$s_1 = \sqrt{\frac{5.20}{(n-1)}} = \sqrt{\frac{5.20}{4}} = \sqrt{1.3} = 1.140$$

$$s_2 = \sqrt{\frac{4.80}{(n-1)}} = \sqrt{\frac{4.80}{4}} = \sqrt{1.2} = 1.095$$

Now, put these values of $\bar{t}_j$ and s_j into Equation 9-2. This creates Equations 9-4 and 9-5. For element 1:

$$n_1' = \left(\frac{1.96 \cdot 1.140}{0.05 \cdot 12.4}\right)^2 = (3.60)^2 = 12.96 \approx 13$$

(Equation 9-4)

For element 2:

$$n_2' = \left(\frac{1.96 \cdot 1.095}{0.05 \cdot 4.8}\right)^2 = (8.94)^2 = 79.9 \approx 80$$

(Equation 9-5)

Whereas $n = 5$ is the number of cycles observed up to this point, n' (used in Equations 9-4 and 9-5) is the number of cycles that should be observed. Specifically n' is the required number of cycles to be observed so that there can be 95 percent confidence that the true element time lies within the range $\bar{t}_j \pm 0.05\bar{t}_j$. As previously described, this is ± 5 percent of the observed average time.

The required sample sizes are observations of 13 basic cycles for element 1 and 80 basic cycles for element 2. One element dominates the sample size decision. It is the element that requires the largest value of n'. The largest n', derived in Equation 9-5, is 80. Element 1, with an indicated study sample size of 13, is dominated by element 2 with $n' = 80$. The present sample size is 5. Therefore, 75 additional observations should be made to satisfy the statistical criterion just developed.

Extraneous elements should have no effect on the sample size for core elements. In this case, $s_j = 0$ for all of them because only one value was observed. If a larger sample indicated high variability, then it would be fitting to study extraneous elements apart from the overall core study. It would be unusual to base the study sample size on extraneous elements.

Because the largest value for n', which was 80, is much larger than the actual n, which is 5, additional observations should be taken. The procedure for sample size evaluation is repeated until the largest value of n'_j is equal to or less than the actual number of observations made, that is, max $n'_j \leq n$.

Good procedure, given the sample of 5 and the indicated need for 75 more observations to get to 80, is to take another 5 or 10 readings and then test again. Problem 2 in the "Problems Section" requests computations for the first 10 cycles.

These job observation procedures are suitable for short-cycle operations. They provide reasonable cost and output information. For long-cycle, nonrepetitive operations, work sampling is used. Synthetic time standards are used to make estimates for jobs that are being designed and do not yet exist. Both of these methods will be explained ahead.

9-11 WORK SAMPLING AND JOB DESIGN

Work sampling is applicable to both manufacturing and services. It is singularly well suited to services that do not lend themselves to time studies of the type previously discussed for manufacturers.

Service operations tend to be less repetitive than manufacturing operations. They have longer cycles and they are less routinized. They can be categorized in broad terms, as in the following illustrative case.

Workers often cannot account for the way in which they spend their time. This applies, in particular, to creative and knowledge workers, office and research personnel, and middle and top managers. Their work does not tend to be repetitive like manufacturing and assembly, where time studies can define jobs and rates of output.

Recognition of the opportunity to design jobs that foster teamwork has led P/OM to employ **work sampling,** also called *operations sampling*. This method can determine with reasonable accuracy the percentage of time workers are engaged in different tasks before and after job design.

In the 1930s, the English statistician, L.H.C. Tippett, reported on his experiments with work sampling in Great Britain's textile factories.[6] Unlike most procedures for sampling the quality of materials, observations of workers' activities are best made randomly over time. As with any sampling system, observations should be of sufficient number to paint an accurate picture of what the workers are doing.

Work sampling methods have to take into account the fact that employees who know they are going to be observed may act differently than if they do not think they are being observed. This means that the best sample is one that has not been anticipated by either the observer or the worker.

Work sampling often is used to determine what fraction of the time workers are idle and how they spend their time when engaged. For office workers, a general classification might include phoning, filing, keying at the computer terminal, and talking with others. It may be difficult to use the computer to track these kinds of jobs. An observer randomly sampled what was happening in the office to develop the data shown in Table 9-2.

When a sufficient sample has been taken, ratios can be formed as descriptive measures of what goes on in the system. In Table 9-2, there are 500 observations of what four people are doing at randomly chosen moments over 5 days. This captures 125 observations of each person. There are 25 observations per day, about three per hour in an 8-hour day. Assume that each observation captures what is going on in a given minute; this is about a 5 percent sample per day because $3/60 = 1/20 = 0.05$.

From Table 9-2, computer use (0.61) is six times as likely as talking (0.09) and filing (0.10) and three times as likely as phoning (0.20). Perhaps it seems to the manager that there is too much phoning. Greater controls over personal calls may be in order. For effective job design, it might be wise to expand the study to do a content analysis of transactions that are taking place over the phone.

P/OM's use of work sampling is not designed to catch workers off-guard. It is intended to map out the way they spend their time leading to teamwork improvements. Most peo-

Work sampling: Provides information about the percentage of time that various activities are being done during the day.

	Number of Observations	Fraction of Total
Phoning	100	0.20
Filing	50	0.10
Computer	305	0.61
Talking	45	0.09
Total	500	1.00

TABLE 9-2

Work Sampling Study in Office

ple are not aware of their allocation of time to activities. This can help employees utilize their time more fully. Therefore, instead of just observing whether workers are idle or busy, the expanded analysis notes specific allocations of time to functions. This type of study is more appropriately called *operations sampling* than work sampling.

9-11a Work Sample Size

How large a sample is needed? This is the same question asked previously with respect to time studies. The method employed is similar. The equation for *n* is

$$n_i = \left(\frac{1.96}{0.30}\right)^2 \left(\frac{1 - p_i}{p_i}\right) \qquad \text{(Equation 9-6)}$$

n_i = The number of observations to be taken to provide a sufficient sample for the *i*th activity.

p_i = The *i*th operation's activity level observed as a fraction of total observations that an operation occurs. When using this formula, the dominating activity for determining *n* will be the one with the smallest *p*.

k = The number of normal standard deviations required to give a specified probability for the confidence interval. In Equation 9-6, *k* has been selected to be 1.96 ($k = 1.96$) so that the probability is 95 percent that the true value of p_i falls in the range $p_i \pm (0.30)p_i$.

0.30 = The accuracy range specified by management such that the true value of p_i falls within the range $p_i \pm (0.30)p_i$.

The values of 1.96 and 0.30 were chosen to make the illustration easy to follow. They can be altered to suit particular situations. The smallest $p_i = 0.09$. This means that $p_i \pm (0.30)p_i$ spans the range from 0.063 to 0.117. That seems a reasonable range for the fraction associated with talking to people in the office.

Using Equation 9-6:

$$n = \left(\frac{1.96}{0.30}\right)^2 \left(\frac{1 - 0.09}{0.09}\right) = (42.6844)(10.1111) = 431.59 \qquad \text{(Equation 9-7)}$$

The sample size *n* can be rounded to 432. Because the actual sample taken was 500 observations, no more sampling is required.

9-12 THE STUDY OF TIME AND MOTION— SYNTHETIC TIME STANDARDS

Synthetic or predetermined time standards: Used to make estimates for jobs that do not yet exist from a subset of common elements.

A solution to problems associated with setting standards for new products, or where people are opposed to being studied on the job, was provided by **synthetic** or **predetermined time standards.** These standards are created from a subset of elements common to all jobs. The nature of any job can be described by the way in which the common alphabet of work elements is arranged.

Frank Gilbreth was the management pioneer who created the first such alphabet of job elements or modules more than 85 years ago. He called these modules *therbligs* and named 17 of them.[7] It takes too much detail to enumerate all of the symbols, but a representative group of four tells the story.

Grasp begins when a hand touches an object. It consists of gaining control of an object, and ends when control is gained.

Position begins when a hand causes the part to line up or locate, and ends when the part changes position.

Assemble begins when the hand causes parts to begin to go together; it consists of actual assembly of parts, and ends when the parts go together.

Hold begins when movement of the part or object, which the hand has under control, ceases; it consists of holding an object in a fixed position and location, and ends with any movement.

Once the standard work elements were identified, it became feasible to study all kinds of jobs, real and imagined. The predetermined times were based on the study of thousands of different operations in which each of these elements appeared. Motion pictures were made of many different kinds of jobs. These were analyzed to determine the appropriate statistical distribution of element times. Expected standard times were obtained from these distributions.

Tables of standard times for a representative set of work elements ("reach," "move," "grasp," and "position") are shown in Table 9-3. They are part of the total system of synthetic standards known as MtM-1, the methods-time-measurement system. In addition to the four work elements previously listed, the total set of predetermined standards includes move, turn, apply pressure, release, disengage, eye travel and eye focus, body, leg and foot motions, and simultaneous coordination of all of these. Using these, (as with Table 9-3) a standard time for any usual job can be derived.

The time measurement units (TMU) are given in terms of 0.00001 hour. This means that 1 hour is composed of 10^5 time measurement units. Equivalently, 1 hour = 100,000 TMU.

The procedure for using the synthetic time standards is

1. Describe the job design in detail and identify the work elements.

2. Determine the appropriate times for each work element.

3. Add the element times together. This requires that individual work elements be independent of each other. If not, interactions need to be taken into account. The sum must reflect the true total time for the job.

The MtM Association for Standards and Research has developed computer systems for combining the synthetic elements and deriving work standards. Two of these systems are called 2M and 4M, representing increasing levels of computer application. "4M can function as a stand-alone system, or be integrated with CAPP, CAD/CAM or MRP systems."[8] MtM-UAS (Universal Analyzing System) is a collaborative effort with German, Swiss, and Austrian MtM Association groups specifically designed to create standards for batch production.

Table 9-4 on page 321 illustrates a 2M application that can be run on PCs or mainframe computers. The specific operations to "form grooves" is shown as a computer printout. Time is in fractions of minutes, a software option, but the basic time unit remains the standard TMU.

9-12a Evaluation of Applicability

Some advantages of synthetic time standards, as compared to those derived from conventional study methods, are as follows:

1. The leveling factor problem is eliminated. Synthetic time standards average out rating differences across many operators.

2. Synthetic production standards are founded upon element times derived from very large samples of observations. This provides increased reliability of the derived standard time.

3. The speed of preparing cost estimates, as well as their reliability, for new jobs is improved. Production schedules can be quickly determined and modified.

Synthetic time standards are in a state of flux. Their technology is changing as they convert from tables and charts toward total computerization. Using an international perspective, they provide a common base for work being done at multiple global locations.

They are likely to be adopted by companies in parts of the world where labor costs are low.

Transnational and multinational corporations will continue to shift labor-intensive work to areas of the world where there are low costs. Companies will outsource those parts

TABLE 9-3   Time Values for Various Classifications of Motions

TABLE I – REACH – R

Distance Moved Inches	Time TMU A	B	C or D	E	Hand In Motion A	B	CASE AND DESCRIPTION
3/4 or less	2.0	2.0	2.0	2.0	1.6	1.6	**A** Reach to object in fixed location, or to object in other hand or on which other hand rests.
1	2.5	2.5	3.6	2.4	2.3	2.3	
2	4.0	4.0	5.9	3.8	3.5	2.7	
3	5.3	5.3	7.3	5.3	4.5	3.6	**B** Reach to single object in location which may vary slightly from cycle to cycle.
4	6.1	6.4	8.4	6.8	4.9	4.3	
5	6.5	7.8	9.4	7.4	5.3	5.0	
6	7.0	8.6	10.1	8.0	5.7	5.7	
7	7.4	9.3	10.8	8.7	6.1	6.5	**C** Reach to object jumbled with other objects in a group so that search and select occur.
8	7.9	10.1	11.5	9.3	6.5	7.2	
9	8.3	10.8	12.2	9.9	6.9	7.9	
10	8.7	11.5	12.9	10.5	7.3	8.6	
12	9.6	12.9	14.2	11.8	8.1	10.1	
14	10.5	14.4	15.6	13.0	8.9	11.5	**D** Reach to a very small object or where accurate grasp is required.
16	11.4	15.8	17.0	14.2	9.7	12.9	
18	12.3	17.2	18.4	15.5	10.5	14.4	
20	13.1	18.6	19.8	16.7	11.3	15.8	
22	14.0	20.1	21.2	18.0	12.1	17.3	**E** Reach to indefinite location to get hand in position for body balance or next motion or out of way.
24	14.9	21.5	22.5	19.2	12.9	18.8	
26	15.8	22.9	23.9	20.4	13.7	20.2	
28	16.7	24.4	25.3	21.7	14.5	21.7	
30	17.5	25.8	26.7	22.9	15.3	23.2	
Additional	0.4	0.7	0.7	0.6			TMU per inch over 30 inches

TABLE II – MOVE – M

Distance Moved Inches	Time TMU A	B	C	Hand In Motion B	Wt. Allowance Wt. (lb.) Up to	Dynamic Factor	Static Constant TMU	CASE AND DESCRIPTION
3/4 or less	2.0	2.0	2.0	1.7				
1	2.5	2.9	3.4	2.3	2.5	1.00	0	
2	3.6	4.6	5.2	2.9				
3	4.9	5.7	6.7	3.6	7.5	1.06	2.2	**A** Move object to other hand or against stop.
4	6.1	6.9	8.0	4.3				
5	7.3	8.0	9.2	5.0	12.5	1.11	3.9	
6	8.1	8.9	10.3	5.7				
7	8.9	9.7	11.1	6.5	17.5	1.17	5.6	
8	9.7	10.6	11.8	7.2				
9	10.5	11.5	12.7	7.9	22.5	1.22	7.4	**B** Move object to approximate or indefinite location.
10	11.3	12.2	13.5	8.6				
12	12.9	13.4	15.2	10.0	27.5	1.28	9.1	
14	14.4	14.6	16.9	11.4				
16	16.0	15.8	18.7	12.8	32.5	1.33	10.8	
18	17.6	17.0	20.4	14.2				
20	19.2	18.2	22.1	15.6	37.5	1.39	12.5	
22	20.8	19.4	23.8	17.0				
24	22.4	20.6	25.5	18.4	42.5	1.44	14.3	**C** Move object to exact location.
26	24.0	21.8	27.3	19.8				
28	25.5	23.1	29.0	21.2	47.5	1.50	16.0	
30	27.1	24.3	30.7	22.7				
Additional	0.8	0.6	0.85					TMU per inch over 30 inches

1 TMU	=	.00001	hour		1 hour	=	100,000.0 TMU
	=	.0006	minute		1 minute	=	1,666.7 TMU
	=	.036	seconds		1 second	=	27.8 TMU

TABLE III A – TURN – T

Weight	Time TMU for Degrees Turned 30°	45°	60°	75°	90°	105°	120°	135°	150°	165°	180°
Small – 0 to 2 Pounds	2.8	3.5	4.1	4.8	5.4	6.1	6.8	7.4	8.1	8.7	9.4
Medium – 2.1 to 10 Pounds	4.4	5.5	6.5	7.5	8.5	9.6	10.6	11.6	12.7	13.7	14.8
Large – 10.1 to 35 Pounds	8.4	10.5	12.3	14.4	16.2	18.3	20.4	22.2	24.3	26.1	28.2

TABLE III B – APPLY PRESSURE – AP

SYMBOL	FULL CYCLE TMU	DESCRIPTION	SYMBOL	COMPONENTS TMU	DESCRIPTION
APA	10.6	AF + DM + RLF	AF	3.4	Apply Force
			DM	4.2	Dwell, Minimum
APB	16.2	APA + G2	RLF	3.0	Release Force

TABLE IV – GRASP – G

TYPE OF GRASP	Case	Time TMU	DESCRIPTION	
PICK-UP	1A	2.0	Any size object by itself, easily grasped	
	1B	3.5	Object very small or lying close against a flat surface	
	1C1	7.3	Diameter larger than 1/2"	Interference with Grasp on bottom and one side of nearly cylindrical object.
	1C2	8.7	Diameter 1/4" to 1/2"	
	1C3	10.8	Diameter less than 1/4"	
REGRASP	2	5.6	Change grasp without relinquishing control	
TRANSFER	3	5.6	Control transferred from one hand to the other.	
SELECT	4A	7.3	Larger than 1" x 1" x 1"	Object jumbled with other objects so that search and select occur.
	4B	9.1	1/4" x 1/4" x 1/8" to 1" x 1" x 1"	
	4C	12.9	Smaller than 1/4" x 1/4" x 1/8"	
CONTACT	5	0	Contact, Sliding, or Hook Grasp.	

EFFECTIVE NET WEIGHT			
Effective Net Weight (ENW)	No. of Hands	Spatial	Sliding
	1	W	W x F_c
	2	W/2	W/2 x F_c

W = Weight in pounds
F_c = Coefficient of Friction

> Do not attempt to use this chart or apply Methods-Time Measurement in any way unless you understand the proper application of the data. This statement is included as a word of caution to prevent difficulties resulting from misapplication of the data.

Source: MtM Association for Standards and Research.

that require labor-intensive inputs. Control over costs requires standards; synthetic time standards will find increasing use in this regard.

The approach used by synthetic time standards is, in modified form, applicable to the standardization of programming work. Thus, in the United States, systems for developing standards that apply to the cost of writing lines of code have been studied for many years by a variety of companies. The synthetic time standards also have applicability to information processing and other services that conform to the manufacturing orientation.

Services continue to be labor intensive. Service operations in airports, hospitals, banks, and schools might be studied and systematized by the application of the synthetic

TABLE 9-4	Computer Printout for 2M Element Analysis

2M Data System for R5715B　　2M Element Analysis　　　　　　　　Requested by MMM
Element: MARK-T3　　　　　　Date 04/22/00　　　Time 13.46.46　　Learning Level:100
Manual Process: 0.3360
　　　　　Operation: Mark Roll by Forming Grooves with Marking Template

Scope	Starts:	Reach to marking template.
	Includes:	Position template, inspect roll, aside template, straighten roll, position template, inspect, place template on roll, straighten template, mark roll, and aside template.
	Ends:	Aside template and release.

				Manual Process: .3360
Line	Subelement	Description	Freq. Process Mins.	Manual Mins.
010	HB3	Get template, position to roll, and aside after inspection.	1.0000	.0450
020	VA	Inspect roll.	1.0000	.0090
030	AA1	Get roll and straighten.	10.0000	.1200
040	HB2	Get template, place to roll, and aside after use.	1.0000	.0360
050	VA	Inspect.	1.0000	.0090
060	PB2	Position template on roll.	1.0000	.0180
070	AA3	Get ends of template and straighten.	2.0000	.0600
080	AA1	Move hands to center and press.	1.0000	.0120
090	AB2	Position template and press.	1.0000	.0270
		Total Mins.:		.3360

Source: MtM Association for Standards and Research.

approach. Service operations have many characteristics that lend themselves to better organization and control using predetermined time standards. The potential application for service operations is significant. Thus, 2M with "MtM-UAS to provide time standards for tasks in a health care environment."[9]

9-13 MANAGING THE WORK SYSTEM

What is the status of the people part of OM systems? Are people working smarter, not harder? Is there a common goal to produce a quality product? Are managers viewed as consultants helping workers instead of as judges grading students?

9-13a Job Design, Evaluation, and Improvement

The answer seems to depend on where and when one looks. Many companies have adopted new approaches in dealing with employees. When times get rough, some of them revert to the old ways. Other firms seem to have permanently embraced the integrated empowering approach to employee relations. There is evidence that work system improvements can pay off handsomely. Companies worldwide that follow job design improvement principles that enhance teamwork and workers' sense of security outperform competitors.

There is benefit to be gained by viewing the entire set of jobs in a company as a system involving all employees, workers, and managers. Striving together as a team, their outputs are the revenue carners. Job improvement will result in a blend of effects, including lower costs, increased output rates, better deliveries, greater variety, and above all else, better quality.

Job evaluation: Evaluation of existing jobs permits job enrichment and improvement, and work simplification.

Job evaluation is a term often used to describe the analysis of a job and its improvement. It is more valuable to consider *job evaluation as system evaluation*, in which sets of interrelated jobs are analyzed and improved as an entire network of *linked efforts*. Traditional job evaluation looked upon each job as a separate and independent part of the workplace. This view is not as powerful as the system view.

9-13b Wage Determination

Wage determination: Based on normal time, a reasonable piecework wage can be determined by management.

Wage determination for OM employees is based upon the following:

1. Difficulty of jobs performed

2. Amount of training required

3. Amount of skill required

4. Value of these jobs to the company

There are problems defining an unambiguous basis for establishing wages. For example, the difficulty of a job and its value to the company may not be correlated. Skill required and value to the company may even be inversely related. There is a logical flaw in the old approach to wage determination that cannot be remedied by reasoning. This is apparent in reading about legal efforts to prove wage discrimination—say, between women and men.

The traditional approaches to wage determination are still practiced by many organizations, but they are changing. There is no redeeming benefit to studying the old ways. The newer approaches are to set acceptable costs for labor and target those costs as goals. In addition to such target costing and the use of activity-based costing (ABC), the wage levels are set by market forces for certain skills and experience.

Note that ABC-type thinking results in the attempt to determine what each job contributes to the profitability of the firm. Efforts to define the value of jobs to the company pay off not only in helping develop rational pay scales, but also by putting emphasis on the design of jobs to maximize contribution.

At the experimental end of the spectrum, groups of workers participate in deciding who gets raises and who does not get them. This is *wage self-determination* done by the group for themselves and the people with whom they work. There are many other kinds of arrangements for self-participation in setting wage rates and making joint decisions that improve **conflict resolution** and employee morale.

Conflict resolution: Before wage determination by teams is used, conflict resolution skills must be developed by management.

Old ways of determining wages are being replaced by a systems approach in world-class organizations. The systems approach is based on a common pay rate for team members working together. To the extent that the group is successful in generating profit for the company, they are rewarded as a group by bonuses.

In many companies now there is cross-training, so that many people do different jobs at different times. The old system would have trouble sorting out what each person should be getting paid. Accounting is far easier with the new approach. Everyone in the group receives the same pay, and all work for the same system. Some companies call the bonus system *gain-sharing*. An increasing number of unions are allowing cross-training. There is more emphasis on training, including the use of quality circles, quality of work life groups, and participation groups.

9-13c Work Simplification and Job Design

Work simplification should be used first to develop as good a job as possible. This takes into account the systems view of each job as a service to the next worker in the sequence. When this thinking has been applied, the application of time studies and job observations, including realistic productivity measures, can lead to significant improvements.

Suggestion system: Employee contributions are a great source of ideas for improvement. If no one reads the suggestions, the system is a sham.

The success of **suggestion systems** in companies, where employees are not driven by work standards and where there is little fear of losing one's job, indicates the extent to which improvement can be continuous. Good suggestions are rare in companies where the suggestion might result in someone being fired because a job no longer is necessary. Continuous job design improvement programs work when there is worker security; they work best when there is worker empowerment in a teamwork environment.

In recent years, there has been deemphasis on work simplification in many industries. This is because job shop lots are decreasing in size. Line changeovers to new and modified outputs are becoming more frequent. Computer-integrated flexible manufacturing systems and adaptive automation require intense preplanning that obviates the need for ongoing improvement of operations. Also, strong methodologies of operations research and management science, such as simulation, are increasingly being used to improve the performance of systems. When these methods compete for investment study dollars with the older methods, the new methods win. Individual job design improvement is disappearing as systems design improvement redefines the nature of all jobs as doing whatever it takes to foster teamwork and achieve objectives.

9-13d Job Design and Enrichment

As technology changes, operators tend to communicate with the computers that run the machines rather than with the machines themselves. This changes the pattern of communication in the factory and in the office. There is more time and opportunity for people to speak to each other. L- and U-shaped workstations have become commonplace in systems of interrelated jobs designed to facilitate communication between workers. Groups of people get together more often to discuss the system of work and how it can be improved. When the ideas of people are taken seriously, and when people know what happens to their work down the line, each job is enriched.

There is ample research evidence that whether the work is in Mexico, China, or the United States, some workers prefer simple, highly repetitive tasks, and others do not. Some like to switch roles. Others prefer to stay at the same tasks. When groups of employees are offered job enrichment opportunities, the group splits into those that want them and those that reject them. Consequently, there is an opportunity for management to explore preferences with each worker. Work assignments can be made according to worker preference in many work systems, because both types of work exist.

The flow shop can be particularly tedious for workers who like variety. As more stations are added, productivity rises. However, cycle time gets shorter, placing an increasing burden on station workers, who have shorter jobs to do with greater frequency. The quality of work can deteriorate under such circumstances. Worker dissatisfaction can increase. In the 1970s, the Vega plant of General Motors at Lordstown, Ohio, suffered a long and difficult strike shortly after it was built because of worker dissatisfaction with the flow shop pace. Job dissatisfaction, in the Vega case, was very costly to GM.

During the 1970s, organizations started to redesign their production lines so workers would be required to do many different jobs. Volvo of Sweden began experimenting with teams that built an entire car. Other organizations decreased the level of specialization in their line-balanced systems. This increased the size of each workstation and the work content per employee.

A group of GM employees sponsored by the United Auto Workers was sent to Volvo in Sweden for six months. Less than half preferred the Volvo system. GM has tried to make its flow shop design less tedious. By the late 1980s, General Motors set up lines where teams worked at different stations and the car was transferred by conveyor from one station to another. Again, the work content per employee is larger.

Overall, with cross-training and employee involvement in quality, the work content per employee continues to increase. Most of the complaints center around the paced-conveyor flow shop as well as its intermittent forms instead of the job shop, but there are tedious aspects of the job shop as well. The project is usually immune to such complaints. If there is any criticism on the part of project workers, it is the continual crises that afflict their nonroutinized workdays. There may be complaints for FPS, because human support teams can perform dull tasks to service their computer masters.

Cross-training for job rotation (where workers exchange jobs) has become increasingly acceptable. Job enlargement (with its larger work content) also has taken hold. Greater worker participation in decision making has been endorsed by both public and private organizations. The ultimate criterion is where the objectives of the organization can be met with less specialization and with less authority over workers.

9-13e The Motivation Factor

A remarkable case history was documented in the 1930s by a study group from Harvard at the Hawthorne Works of the Western Electric Company in Chicago. The study concerned levels of illumination and their affect on productivity. It was discovered that whether the illumination was raised or lowered, productivity was improved. The key finding (known as the *Hawthorne effect*)[10] was that employees responded positively to management's interest and attention. This response level overrode the functional affects of the illumination level. Such complex behavior differentiates people and machines.

Critics of the Hawthorne study claim that the result was a self-fulfilling prophecy. The workers gave the researchers what they wanted. Even if this is true, it still appears reasonable to expect positive reactions from workers to care and attention.

Motivation can be both positive and negative. The latter is associated with poor employee morale. When discussing incentives and motivation, the major difficulty is the measurement problem. Nevertheless, accepting the lack of precision involved, incentives are a real causal factor that can affect worker behavior. Incentives include wages, job title, office size and floor, organizational importance, ability to participate in decisions, vacations, leisure time, and variety of tasks assigned. For the most part, these categories represent intangible qualities that escape definition and measurement.

In summary, P/OM is a people-oriented function. P/OM deals with workers and suppliers. To make the process work, P/OM must be able to understand the changing role of people in the process. This has become even more true as OM moves onto an international stage. People throughout the global network are indispensable.

SUMMARY

This chapter begins by making clear that planning teamwork is the mutual goal of OM and HRM. What constitutes the traditional and then newer methods of training is discussed. The reason that performance evaluation is a controversial topic is succinctly stated. The chapter develops the ideas behind designing jobs for production and cost standards. This is followed by the study of time standards comparing traditional time study methods with a parallel discussion of how computers are used to determine how many pieces (or service steps) to expect per hour, the production standard. Next comes the study of time and motion for operations. This includes job design

improvement and the use of synthetic time standards to set production standards. Work sampling is covered. The chapter concludes with discussion of how to manage the design of larger work systems, including job improvement, evaluation, enrichment, and wage determination.

Two Spotlight feature boxes conclude this chapter. These boxes illustrate real applications of the material in the chapter. See Spotlight 9-1: Stephanie Louise Kwolek and Spotlight 9-2: Dr. Jonathan Shay.

KEY TERMS

Action learning
Activity-based costing (ABC) systems
Average performance
Conflict resolution
Cross-training
Ergonomics
Job evaluation

Learning curve
Leveling factors
Normal time
Performance evaluation
Production standards
Productivity standards
Suggestion system

Synthetic or predetermined time standards
Team building
Team learning
Time and motion study
Time study
Wage determination
Work sampling

REVIEW QUESTIONS

1. Why is training for teamwork a concern of P/OM?

2. What is action-learning training?

3. What is computer-based training?

4. Explain why good estimates of labor costs are needed to determine how much to charge for a new product or service.

5. Explain why good estimates of labor costs are needed to determine fixed and variable costs to be used for breakeven analysis.

6. Explain why good estimates of labor costs are needed to determine plant location and selection.

7. Explain why good estimates of labor costs are needed to develop excellent production schedules.

8. Explain why good estimates of labor costs are needed to determine an optimal product mix.

9. Explain why good estimates of labor costs are needed to determine when a technology upgrade should be made.

10. Explain why good estimates of labor costs are needed to make intelligent bids for jobs with federal or local municipalities, or with companies.

11. Frederick W. Taylor thought the relationship between the well-designed job, the best worker, and the reasonable wage

scale could be determined by logical analysis and intelligent experimentation. The concept of the well-designed (specialized and efficient) job has been attacked. The same is true of the notion of best workers and worst workers. A guaranteed wage and pay not related to individual productivity have been suggested as the only reasonable wage scale. Discuss from the systems point of view.

12. What is meant by the statement "Observations of productivity can be used for purposes of estimation and bidding, but they are unacceptable as a means of setting work standards for the amount of output each employee is expected to produce"?

13. Why is leveling no longer a major concern for job observation?

14. For the work sampling study in the text, what should be done about the manager's belief that there is too much phoning?

15. For the work sampling study in the text, the manager believes too much time is spent filing. What can be done about that?

16. What is meant by the statement "The design of industrial jobs is being replaced by systems design of interrelated jobs"?

PROBLEMS SECTION

1. Show all computations in tabled form needed to determine the largest value of n′ for the first 5 cycles of elements 1 and 2 in the table of Figure 9-2.

2. Show all computations in tabled form needed to determine the largest value of n′ for the first 10 cycles of elements 1 and 2 in the table of Figure 9-2.

3. Package Design International (PDI) is a medium-sized company. Typically, because of overload, its executives work 10- to 12-hour days. The president calls for reduction of the average period from order-entry date to delivery date.

   The OM department suggests building a supply chain simulator. The simulation would capture all factors that affect order to delivery times. This would be a training and problem-solving device costing an estimated $25,000. The operations manager estimates it will take 40 hours for each executive to learn how to use this simulator. There are five executives that would be expected to work with the simulator.

   The OM has told the president that the simulator would result in $250,000 of additional profit for PDI in the next year. Should the contract for the simulator be given?

4. Finding the shortest common-cycle time for time studies is like finding the lowest-common denominator for describing a series of fractions.

Cycle Number	Core Element	Core Element	Extraneous Elements			
	1	2	A	B	C	D
1	5	4	-	-	-	-
2	3	2	-	-	-	-
3	4	3	-	-	-	-
*	*	*	*	*	*	*
*	*	*	*	*	*	*
100	3	4	20	20	25	30

What is the shortest common-cycle time for the time sheet shown here?

5. As output volume (OV) rises, so do wages (W). This is shown by a plus sign at the end of the arrow connecting OV and W. As W increases, so does worker motivation (M). This is shown by a plus sign at the end of the arrow connecting W and M. Continuing in this way, increasing motivation conditions worker performance to raise output volume. Figure 9-3 illustrates this feedback relationship.

However, other factors might be considered in this systems dynamics diagram.[11] Thus, additional inputs (arrows) can be added to the figure to indicate that other factors also affect output volume, wages, and worker motivation, such as quality (Q). Create the diagram and do the analysis for quality (Q).

6. It has been decided to study the activities of the Market Research Store using work sampling. First, however, it has been concluded that any office can be used as a pilot operation where the methods can be developed and tested. Using Table 9-2 as a guide, choose any office and drop in 5 to 10 times, noting each time what every person who works in that office is doing. Then, develop the kind of information that is shown in Table 9-2. Even though the sample is small, analyze this data. How big a sample will be needed?

7. For the MRS study described in Problem 6, what categories of activities might apply? How often should observations be made? Would you recommend using random sampling or taking observations at set times that are known to the employees of the MRS?

8. A Spanish company packs green olives that have been soaked in brine into 1-pound jars. The olives are first divided into 1-pound-plus batches using a digital scale. On average, there are 32 olives to the pound.

   The olives are inserted in a jar and brine is added. Then the jar is sealed with a twist cap and put on a conveyor. The left-hand, right-hand chart is shown here:

	Left Hand	Right Hand
Element 1	Get olives. Put on scale. Measure 1 lb+.	Get jar.
Element 2	Put olives in jar.	Clamp jar. Get brine.
Element 3	Get screw cap.	Add brine.
Element 4	Screw on cap.	Unclamp jar.
Element 5	Move toward olives.	Put jar on conveyor.

   a. Sketch the process flow and layout.
   b. The time estimates are given in Table 9-5.
   c. Develop a sequence of work elements.
   d. Prepare a job observation or time sheet.

9. Use the information in Problem 8 to determine the standard time for the job.

10. Can predetermined time standards be used for the Spanish olive packing company? Develop the appropriate report.

11. A new set of data have been collected by HCDVD using operations sampling instead of time study–job observation.

FIGURE 9-3
Systems Dynamics Diagram for Output Volume (OV), Wages (W), and Motivation (M)

Activity	Description	Number of Times Observed
1	Place 10 DVDs in box.	212
2	Seal box, etc.	90
A	Put away 100 boxes.	10
B	Get 500 DVDs.	8
C	Get 50 boxes.	7
D	Get cellophane every 500 boxes.	12

How do these results compare with those derived by the time study in Figure 9-2?

12. With respect to job observation sample size and Equations 9-4 and 9-5, do the calculations for the following data and determine whether it is OK to stop taking additional sample observations.

Cycle Number	t_1	t_2
1	13	5.0
2	13	5.0
3	13	5.0
4	13	5.0
5	13	5.0
6	13	5.0
7	13	5.0
8	13	5.0
9	13	5.0
10	13	5.0
Totals	130	50.0

$\bar{t}_1 = 130/10 = 13.0$

$\bar{t}_2 = 50/10 = 5.00$

Data and Computations for $\bar{t}_j = \sum_{j=1}^{10} \dfrac{t_j}{n}$

How could this result have occurred?

13. Use activity-based costing to show how much overhead is not applicable to Job X. Assume that all costs are multiplied by 10^4 and apply only to Job X for a 1-week period.

> Materials costs = $7
> Energy costs = $3
> Direct labor costs = $5
> Revenue = $22

What is the short-term contribution margin?

14. Using the information in Problem 13, continue with the following additional data: The overhead to be allocated is measured for one week.

> GE = $4, with UGE = $2, and UNGE = $2.

What is the operating profit?

15. Using the information in Problems 13 and 14, what is the unused portion of overhead that should not be associated with the profitability of the job?

16. Using the information in Problems 13, 14, and 15, what is the used portion of overhead expenses that should be associated with the profitability of the job?

Element		1	2	3	4	5
Cycle	1	15	8	7	10	10
	2	13	8	8	11	10
	3	15	7	8	12	10
	4	17	9	9	11	11
	5	12	9	6	10	10
	6	14	7	7	10	9
	7	14	8	6	9	9
	8	13	8	6	9	10
	9	15	7	8	9	11
	10	16	9	7	10	9
Total time		144	80	72	101	99
Number of observations		10	10	10	10	10
Expected cycles		1	1	1	1	1
Average time		14.4	8.0	7.2	10.1	9.9
Allowance		1	1	1	1	1
Normal time		14.4	8.0	7.2	10.1	9.9
R & D correction		1	1	1	1	1
Standard time		14.4	8.0	7.2	10.1	9.9

TABLE 9-5

Olive Packing Times (in Hundredths of a Minute)

END-OF-CHAPTER QUESTIONS

1. Training and technology are competitors for budgetary allotments. There have been swings in allocations as computers, robots, and telecommunications have appeared to provide competitive advantage. At the same time, there have been numerous examples of where investments in training have provided more competitive advantage than the latest model of software or hardware. All but one of the following answers is correct. Which answer is incorrect?

   a. For each dollar expended on technology, there are companies that have spent three dollars on training to employ the new technology with effectiveness and efficiency.

   b. Expenditure on technology should push the envelope beyond the limits of current expertise to gain a competitive advantage.

   c. Team evaluations of training required to use new equipment are better guidelines than manufacturer's recommendations.

   d. For production workers, the use of general-purpose equipment requires greater investment in training than special purpose equipment.

   e. Unions are generally opposed to investments in technology that replace workers, but they are in favor of technology that requires skills and training to be used correctly.

2. Having dealt with issues of training competing with technology for budget allocations, there is now the need to allocate the training budget. Choices must be made between traditional training methods and advanced training methods. Selection will be based on evaluations of training program effectiveness. A variety of statements about training programs are listed here. Which statement do you think is incorrect?

   a. Training program effectiveness is determined by aligning training objectives with company needs and justifying the methods and delivery adopted for training.

   b. A training objective might be to instruct accountants in the use of spreadsheets, and an effective delivery method would be computer-based training.

   c. Measurement of training program effectiveness should be accomplished after the program is completed so as to avoid disturbing the instructors and biasing the data.

   d. Action learning is a training program that is high on the risk-return scale. This means that high uncertainty is accepted about events that may occur for each participant who is trading places. At the same time, the breadth and depth of experience for each participant will exceed anything that the classroom can deliver. Finance classes justify high risk–high return under certain circumstances. It is a good idea for human resource managers to learn about this kind of investment.

   e. Team learning as a training option is organizationally challenging. If team learning is greatly rewarding that might alter the options previously determined regarding how much new technology should be used with appropriate training.

3. The repertoire of new training methods does not include one of the following techniques. Which one does not qualify?

   a. Team building involves training groups of people to have a common focus.

   b. Team learning emphasizes the interdependence between people working toward a common goal.

   c. Team performance evaluation requires each team member to rate all the others.

   d. Distance learning occurs when training is delivered (usually to multiple locations) through networked computers, teleconferencing, videoconferencing, etc.

   e. Computer-based training is like training with a flight simulator.

4. Good production standards are required for a variety of applications. Listed are some of the ways in which the production standards are utilized. Which of the following answers is incorrect?

   a. Determining how many workers are needed requires determination of the production standard (expected output in pieces per worker per hour).

   b. Supply is calculated by multiplying the production standard by the number of workers per hour. If supply is less than demand, more workers need to be added.

   c. Assume that the time to make a unit does not change with production volume but the cost of making a unit does change. Then, the production standard changes as a function of cost. Production standards are used to compute the real costs of product output.

   d. Capacity planning requires understanding the complex relationship between variable costs and the volume of production. The production standard has already been factored into this relationship.

   e. If the time to make a unit decreases with increasing production volume (learning curve effect) then the production standard must be studied as a dynamic factor.

5. Revenue from a batch of 5,500 machine shop parts made to order and sold to an established customer is $22,000. The actual costs that apply to this job have been calculated from the point of view of activity-based cost analysis (ABC). Which statement is incorrect?

1	Revenue	$22,000
2	Actual materials cost	$ 6, 000
3	Actual energy cost	$ 2,000
4	Actual direct short-term labor	$ 4,000
5	Short-term contribution margin	$22,000 – $12,000 = $8,000
6	Permanent direct labor—Used	$ 1,000
7	Permanent direct labor—Unused	$ 3,000
8	General expenses	$ 1,000 + $3,000 = $4,000
9	Operating profit	$ 8,000 – $1,000 – $3,000 = $4,000

a. Operating profit shown in line 9 of the table is calculated as the short-term contribution margin (5) minus the permanent direct labor *used* for the batch and minus the *unused* portion of that expense. In this way, necessary and unnecessary overhead can be revealed. Steps can be taken to decrease unused expenses.

b. Revenue minus actual expenses to create the product equals the short-term margin contribution. Accounting for the actual expenses requires monitoring the job and all of its components. For example, how much time was expended by labor on the job and at what labor rates? Determining work in the back room by permanent labor on this job leads to general expense statements.

c. Activity-based cost systems raises awareness of how overhead is calculated and applied to specific jobs. Traditionally, overhead allocation is proportional to labor hours, which is inaccurate and misleading.

d. The price per part is $4.50 and the unused portion of the permanent direct labor is about 45 cents.

e. The used (assigned) portion of the permanent direct labor is 18 cents. This means that general expenses are 73 cents.

6. Industrial engineers pioneered in the development of methods to determine how long a job should take if it is done properly. Frederick W. Taylor was the father of scientific management, which was crucial to methods engineering and time and motion studies at the end of the nineteenth century and the beginning of the twentieth century. Although efficiency experts were the subject of jokes, business took them seriously. Nothing fundamental has changed. What has been altered is how the tasks of efficiency experts are now done without Charlie Chaplin's white-frocked doctors of mass production. When a stopwatch and clipboard are not in evidence, there is fair likelihood that the computer is capturing information and calculating expectations *under the table* (i.e., out of sight). Listed are some issues concerning time standards, job observation, time and motion studies, cycle time reduction, and productivity standards. Which answer is incorrect?

a. Job observation is a systematic approach to auditing what is being done in the production system. The audit includes time required to complete the job. From audit information, it is possible to determine how many workers are needed to meet demand and how much it will cost to fill the orders. Prices can then be set.

b. In line with price-elasticity theory, demand volume could increase or decrease. This leads to consideration of alternative work configurations. Time studies need to be done to determine output rates and costs for the various process options that are being considered. To consider strategic alternatives, it is essential to have time study information available. Using synthetic (predetermined) time standards can help to resolve problems and hasten decision making to optimize company strategy.

c. Any job being studied can be broken down into basic and extraneous elements. The basic elements, when added together, form the (basic) job cycle time. This job cycle will be the shortest period of time required to make the product. This is where effort to increase productivity should be focused.

d. Reasons for job observation include improving and simplifying the way the job is done; calculating expected output rates; and evaluating every individual's real output rate. All are applicable to both service systems and manufacturing.

e. The *shortest common cycle time* includes the longest extraneous cycle time. The *total standard time* spans the entire shortest common cycle time so that all extraneous cycle times are taken into account. Total standard time is the key to productive output, and it must include both the basic elements required to make the product and the extraneous elements. For example, Boston Market provides sides of mashed potatoes, cream of spinach, cranberries, etc., with requests for chicken, meatloaf, or turkey. Assume that the small containers in the hot table run out of stock every 20 orders. This triggers a request for replenishment while the customer may be waiting to be served. Eventually, from the back of the store, new containers are brought out to replenish whichever side dishes are required. In this example, the basic elements are the cycle times required for the servers to fill the customers' orders from the hot table. The extraneous elements are the time to refill the hot table inventories.

7. The job observation summary table for Becky's QSR (quick-service restaurant) is shown here with all calculations completed. Management has furnished comments and interpretations of these data. Which comment shows a lack of understanding about the purpose of this information?

Element	1	2	3	A	B	C	Total
TTO	620	360	200	10	50	30	
NO	40	40	40	1	1	1	
ECPO	1	1	1	1/20	1/50	1/15	
AVT/SLT	15.50	9.00	5.00	0.50	1.00	2.00	
LF/AL	0.92	1.00	1.10	1.00	1.00	1.00	
NT/ADT	14.26	9.00	5.50	0.50	1.00	2.00	
C(r&d)	100%	100%	110%	110%	110%	110%	
SDT	14.26	9.00	6.05	0.55	1.10	2.20	
							33.16

Legend: TTO = Total time observed; NO = Number of observations; ECPO = Expected cycles per observation; AVT/SLT = Average time or selected time (in 0.01 minutes); LF or AL = Leveling factors or allowances; NT or ADT = Normal time or adjusted time; C(r&d) = Correction for rest & delay; SDT = Standard time (in 0.01 minutes)

a. The basic job cycle time is 0.2931 minutes per person, paid and meal served. This is equivalent to 204.71 people served at the counter per hour or 3.41 people served per minute. However, these calculations just reflect the core elements of the work. The numbers to look at need to include the extraneous elements. That is, unless someone can be clever about not having extraneous elements interrupt the core work.

b. The total cycle time is 0.3316 minutes per person, paid and meal served. This is equivalent to 180.9 or 181 people served at the counter per hour or 3.02 people served per minute. If the process people can come up with a clever idea about not having extraneous elements interrupt the core work, it would be possible to serve 24 more people per hour.

c. The shortest common cycle time, which is like the lowest common denominator for a series of fractions, is 50 units. Upon completing 50 units, the QSR must restock certain items (extraneous element called B). It takes 0.5 minutes to do this. That has the effect of adding only 0.011 minutes to the total standard time.

d. The worst offender is extraneous element C. It adds 0.022 minutes to the total standard time of 0.3316. The percent increase is $(0.3316 - 0.3096)/0.3096 = 7$ percent. That is not insignificant.

e. No correction has been made for r&d for the core elements whereas there is a correction of 10 percent for the extraneous elements. This may be because leveling factors were used for the core elements but not for the extraneous elements.

8. Points a. through e. reflect on various considerations about what is being done in relatively undisciplined work situations. For example, in the office, people are free to move about and choose what activities they consider timely. Work sampling (also called *operations sampling*) is designed to ascertain work patterns in such nonrepetitive environments. All but one statement is acceptable. Which of the following statements is incorrect?

a. Observations of workers' activities are best made randomly over time. The reason for this is that when people know that they are going to be observed at a specific time, they will be ready. Some will have gone to the mirror to adjust their hair. Others will be filing because they think that filing is what the boss expects them to be doing.

b. Work sampling is often aimed at determining how much idle time workers have. The problem of identifying people engaged in "being idle" is difficult because thinking about the best way to do something may be indistinguishable from not thinking about a thing.

c. Talking is another activity that is difficult to assess. Idle chatter is entirely different from teamwork members problem-solving. The simple request for information, such as "what were you talking about?" may not be the solution. Personal phone conversations are difficult to sort out from business calls. Again, asking for details may not be rewarding.

d. P/OM's sampling of workers is not designed to catch workers off-guard. It is best, therefore, to ask workers, beforehand, if they can account for the way that they spend their time. When they cannot, it seems sensible to offer work sampling as a method to help in this regard.

e. There are formulas for sample size that are related to establishing confidence intervals. Such intervals reflect the variability of the data. If it turns out that all employees are on the telephone 96 percent of the time, then there is low variability in activity profiles, and the sample size does not have to be large to believe that the data are accurate.

9. Synthetic time standards can be used to estimate output rates and costs for jobs that have not yet been created or run as a pilot plant. (Pilot plants are less than full-scale production run simulations.) There is a long history in the use of basic work modules for predetermined time standards. The statements in a. through e. examine some aspects of this methodology. One statement is not acceptable. Which statement is incorrect?

a. Frank B. Gilbreth (author of *Cheaper by the Dozen*, and he did have 12 children) was the management pioneer who created the first set of job elements about 100 years ago. He called the modules *therbligs*, which was almost an inversion (palindrome) of his name. The 17 therbligs are also called an *alphabet* because they can be strung together like letters in a word.

b. *Grasp, position,* and *assemble* are three basic work modules. Many jobs are combinations of these elements. *Hold,* on the other hand, is not a fundamental part of any job.

c. A well-known set of work standards is called the MtM – 1. Later derivatives were known as MtM – 2. From these basic elements, even higher-order systems have emerged, e.g., master standard data (MSD) systems. For historical insight, see http://www.tlward.com/history.html.

d. Transnational and multinational corporations continue to shift labor-intensive work to areas of the world where direct labor is relatively inexpensive. Also, firms will outsource parts that require labor-intensive inputs. Control over costs requires standards. Synthetic standards will be increasingly important until automation replaces the labor-intensive component of both manufacturing and services.

e. Predetermined time systems do not require leveling because workers are not performing jobs that have to be corrected as being done at faster, slower, or average rates. This is an advantage of the predetermined systems.

10. Some general statements about managing the work system are given in parts a. through e. Which statement is not acceptable?

a. System-wide evaluations (of a set of interdependent jobs) is less valuable to the organization than individual job evaluations (done one job at a time).

b. Wage determination is a comparative matter. If the company across the street has similar jobs, it is important to note the wages being paid by that company. For comparison purposes, jobs can be classified by difficulty, training, skills required, and the value of the job to the company.

c. *Target costing* is a philosophy that some Japanese companies have pioneered. The idea is to set an amount that can be spent for a component. For example, given the wage rate, the specification states that the amount of labor that can be used to make the part is constrained to be no more than x. The designers are asked to produce practical specifications that meet the labor constraints. It may be decided to make the part in China at a lower wage rate so that the amount of labor allowed can be raised.

d. *Job enrichment* has as its foundation the motivation of workers to do a good job. It is theorized that in some cultures, but not all cases, pride in workmanship can be elevated by increasing the work content per employee. Volvo, the Swedish automaker, was known for small teams building an entire car. The concept was extreme. A group of workers from GM (Detroit) visited Volvo and worked in the Uddevalla plant. Most of this group, when the experiment ended, rejected the Volvo enrichment plan for themselves in the United States.

e. A well-known set of work standards began as MtM. Later versions were called MtM – 1 and, then, MtM – 2. From these evolving systems of elements, higher-order systems continued to emerge, e.g., master standard data (MSD) systems. For historical insight, see http://www.tlward.com/history.html.

ADDITIONAL READINGS

Barnes, Ralph M. *Motion and Time Study: Design and Measurement of Work*. Hoboken, NJ: John Wiley & Sons, July 1980, 7th ed.

Briscoe, Dennis R. *International Human Resource Management*. Englewood Cliffs, NJ: Prentice-Hall, 1995.

Certo, Sam. *Human Relations Today: Concepts and Skills*. Burr Ridge, IL: Irwin, 1995.

Cooper, Robin, and Robert S. Kaplan. "Activity-Based Systems: Measuring the Costs of Resource Usage." *Accounting Horizons* (September 1992).

Forrester, J. W. *Industrial Dynamics*. New York: Wiley, 1961.

Gilbreth, F. B. *Primer of Scientific Management*. New York: D. Van Nostrand, 1914.

Joy, Louis W., III, and Jo A. Joy. *Frontline Teamwork*. Burr Ridge, IL: Irwin, 1993.

Kaplan, Robert S., and David P. Norton. *The Balanced Scorecard: Translating Strategy into Action*. Cambridge, MA: Harvard Business School Press, September 1996.

Katzenbach, Jon R., and Douglas K. Smith. *The Wisdom of Teams: Creating the High-Performance Organization*. Harper Business, 1994.

Maskell, Brian H. *Performance Measurement for World Class Manufacturing*. Cambridge, MA: Productivity Press, 1991.

Neal, James E., Jr. *Effective Phrases for Performance Analysis: A Guide to Successful Evaluations*. Neal Publications, Prentice-Hall, Inc., January 2003, 10th ed.

Niven, Paul R. *Balanced Scorecard Step-by-Step: Maximizing Performance and Maintaining Results*. Hoboken, NY: John Wiley & Sons, March 2002.

Roethlisberger, F. J., and W. J. Dickson. *Management and the Worker*. Cambridge, MA: Harvard University Press, 1939.

Scholtes, P. R., et al. *The Team Handbook*. Joiner Associates (608-238-8134), Madison, WI, 1989.

Shenkar, Oded. (ed) *Global Perspectives of Human Resource Management*. Englewood Cliffs, NJ: Prentice-Hall, 1995.

Tilley, A. R. *The Measure of Man and Woman: Human Factors in Design*. New York: Henry Dreyfuss Associates. From The Whitney Library of Design, imprint of Watson-Guptill Publications, 1993.

Tippett, L. H. C. "Statistical Methods in Textile Research." *Journal of the Textile Institute Transactions*, vol. 26 (February, 1935).

NOTES

1. "Why American Steel Is Big Again." *The New York Times* (July 21, 1994): D6.

2. Jon R. Katzenbach and Douglas K. Smith. *The Wisdom of Teams: Creating the High-Performance Organization*. Harper Business, 1994.

3. "Team Spirit Is New Message at Olds." *The New York Times* (June 23, 1994): D1 (by-line James Bennet).

4. Brian H. Maskell. *Performance Measurement for World Class Manufacturing*. Cambridge, MA: Productivity Press, 1991.

5. Robin Cooper and Robert S. Kaplan. "Activity-Based Systems: Measuring the Costs of Resource Usage." *Accounting Horizons* (September, 1992).

6. L. H. C. Tippett. "Statistical Methods in Textile Research." *Journal of the Textile Institute Transactions*, vol. 26 (February, 1935): 51–55.

7. F. B. Gilbreth. *Primer of Scientific Management*. New York: D. Van Nostrand, 1914.

8. *The 4M System*. Publication of the MtM Association for Standards and Research, 1991, p. 3.

9. *2M—The Macro Matic Data Handler*. Published by the MtM Association for Standards and Research, 1990, p. 6.

10. F. J. Roethlisberger and W. J. Dickson. *Management and the Worker*. Cambridge, MA: Harvard University Press, 1939.

11. J.W. Forrester. *Industrial Dynamics*. New York: Wiley, 1961. This book develops the methods of systems dynamics.

SPOTLIGHT 9-1
Stephanie Louise Kwolek

Breakthrough Discovery—Inventing Kevlar

Photo courtesy of DuPont.

When Stephanie Louise Kwolek received her B.S. from Carnegie Mellon, she decided to accept a research job with DuPont until she could pursue her dream of medical school. She soon discovered that she liked the work so much, with its constant challenges and university-like atmosphere, that she decided to stay. In 1946, she was one of a small number of women in America working in chemical research. DuPont had already commercialized nylon with great success and was on its way to doing the same with Dacron polyester, Lycra Spandex, and eventually Nomex. The search continued for next-generation high-performance fibers.

In 1964, Ms. Kwolek provided the breakthrough, discovering that under certain conditions, the molecules of extended-chain aromatic polyamides would form liquid-crystalline solutions, and these in turn could be spun into highly orientated, very strong, and very stiff fibers. The result was Kevlar—a material best known for its use in bulletproof vests. It is also employed in more than 200 other end-use applications, including hot surface handlers such as the "Ove" Glove™.

Kwolek has earned 17 patents and the highest honors in her field. She was inducted into the National Inventors Hall of Fame in 1995 and received the National Medal of Technology in 1996. She has publicly supported and encouraged young people to believe in themselves and not to fear thinking differently. She believes that the creative process can be taught to a certain extent by exposing young people to books about creative people and by meeting and talking with creative people.

Today Stephanie Kwolek sees many people entering into research with the objective of quickly getting into management after acquiring some experience. This leaves little opportunity to make discoveries, particularly ones that open a new field. Such discoveries generally take more fundamental thinking and work than just making a modification to an existing product. New foundations have to be constructed.

Kwolek would like to see corporations place greater emphasis on long-term research. She does not see how people can be creative if they are constantly distracted. There must be time to read, think, and keep up with the literature. In her complex field of fiber research, she was given the freedom to amass a tremendous amount of knowledge that she used in making her discoveries. Without such a knowledge base, Kwolek thinks that it would be difficult for people to make breakthrough discoveries.

Even with a deep knowledge of fiber technology, Stephanie Kwolek had to use all her intuition, perseverance, and hard work to achieve her breakthrough. The moment of discovery was exciting because it was so unexpected. She had been assigned to look for the next-generation high-performance fiber. Kwolek started working with the more intractable para-orientated aromatic polyamides, which are made up of rod-like molecules, unlike the very flexible molecules in nylon. Not only did she have to make the polymers but she also had to find a solvent for them. She finally succeeded in finding a solvent, but the solutions turned out to be unlike anything she had previously seen in the laboratory. They were cloudy, opalescent upon being stirred, and of low viscosity, making them seem like poor candidates for successful new fibers.

To get a fiber, a polymer solution must be forced through the very tiny holes of a spinneret. The person in charge of the spinning unit refused to spin Kwolek's cloudy, low-viscosity liquid-crystalline solution. He said it would plug up the holes of his spinneret and, furthermore, it had the viscosity of water, unlike regular polymer solutions. He assumed the cloudiness was due to the presence of particulate. After much discussion, he did spin it, and it spun with no problems. The first sign that she really had something unusual occurred as she stood by the spinning equipment and tried to break some of the newly spun fibers. Unlike nylon, this fiber was very difficult to break by hand. At that moment, Stephanie Kwolek knew she had found an extraordinary fiber. Her discovery opened up a whole new field of polymer chemistry.

This story of successful breakthrough discovery highlights why serious research scientists contend that it is a management responsibility to find ways to provide incentives for people to stay in research long enough to build a body of knowledge and experience for long-term research results.

Edited with author's permission from "Hall of Fame Interview: Stephanie Kwolek," by Jim Quinn, *American Heritage of Invention & Technology*, Winter 2003, Volume 18, Number 3.

SPOTLIGHT 9-2
The Structure of Leadership

Perspective from Dr. Jonathan Shay, M.D.,, Ph.D., Author of Achilles in Vietnam and Odysseus in America

Photo by Jason Threlfal. Copyright Jonathan Shay.

Dr. Jonathan Shay, M.D., Ph.D., is the author of two books, *Achilles in Vietnam: Combat Trauma and the Undoing of Character*, 1995, and *Odysseus in America: Combat Trauma and the Trials of Homecoming*, Scribner, 2002. With his ability to span millennia and cultures, Dr. Shay has presented us with a gift of insight on leadership from his studies of Homer's *Iliad* and *Odyssey*, as well as from his work with the Veterans Administration in Boston. His research provides ways to prevent psychological injury in and after combat operations. These two books, numerous papers, and his lectures on the subject show how cohesion, leadership, and training of combat forces are vital to success of their units and can be accomplished only under competent and ethical leadership. Morale is high in units that enjoy working together as a team. In the Vietnam War, teams were divided. Individuals found themselves fighting next to strangers. Leadership did not inspire trust and morale plummeted.

Trust that results from cohesion, leadership, and training is shown to be an essential combat strength multiplier. It can affect everything, from the number of casualties to the outcome of war. Dr. Shay has emerged as an impressive voice for improving our military system. He has become an advocate for veterans. He believes that veterans whose social trust has been destroyed are injured just as surely as physical loss. He hopes for policies that produce skilled, cohesive units and competent, ethical leaders. Dr. Jonathan Shay's mission and message is prevention of psychological and moral injury in military service. He would like to see our policy makers work for a military ethic that creates and maintains well-founded trust.

From Dr. Shay's description of leadership principles used by Agamemnon, Achilles, and Odysseus (Ulysses in Latin), we recognize Homer's characters in our own lives today. The battle of Troy and the long return home by Odysseus is an allegory of our own combat troops returning to civilian society. In Agamemnon, the commander of the Greek army, we encounter a leader whose main motivational tools were shame and humiliation. He pitted subordinates against each other. Achilles was an outstanding leader, destroyed by Agamemnon's betrayal. Odysseus was a brilliant solo fighter, strategist, and staff officer, but failed as an independent leader of men.

We recognize profound truths of leadership because we have experienced them in our own lives as children, parents, employees, owners, and managers. The truth is that we all watch the trustworthiness of those who wield power above us. Agamemnon's betrayal of "what's right" causes his troops' motivation, loyalty, and perseverance to evaporate. They desert psychologically as well as physically because the trust is gone that held them together.

This Homeric episode is a reminder of what happens when a leader causes moral injury. It is a message for management of any organization, whether military, business, government, factory, home, or office. We watch for trustworthiness in our leaders. When a leader violates "what's right" in the use of power, the injury afflicts everyone. In leadership of organizations, there are no private wrongs.

Sources: Conversation with Dr. Shay and *Odysseus in America*. Scribner: New York, 2002; Berreby, David. "Exploring Combat and the Psyche, Beginning with Homer." *The New York Times* (March 11, 2003). There is also a listing of some of Dr. Shay's writings at http://www.belisarius.com. This website carries a banner titled "War, Chaos, and Business." At that URL, clicking on authors brings up Dr. Shay as well as other important contributors to the theories and best practices of military and business parallels. *War, Chaos, and Business* is the webpage created by the Kettle Creek Corporation of Nevada.

Supplement 9

Ergonomics or Human Factors

The traditional part of managing human resources from the point of view of OM is taking care of production employees. What is learned about doing that well can be extended to taking care of customers, a very valuable human resource to be managed. OM can help care for people making deliveries and those who work in the suppliers' organizations. OM may even be in a position to help the company provide for the well-being of anyone coming in contact with the company. OM knowledge about ergonomics could spare the company a lawsuit brought by someone walking on the sidewalk and who trips and breaks a leg.

Ergonomics, originally a British term, is the systematic study of how people physically interact with the working environment, as well as their equipment, facilities, and products. Ergonomic design of the system is the goal. Equivalent terms include *human factors, human engineering, or biomechanics.*

The prime rule of ergonomics is safety first for workers at their jobs and consumers using products produced by the company. In the United States, workplace safety is monitored by OSHA, the Occupational Safety and Health Administration created in 1970. There also is a Consumer Product Safety Commission to deal with the safety of products as diverse as children's toys and automobiles.

Acceptable levels of safety are difficult to specify. The ideal situation is "perfect" safety, but like zero defects, perfect safety is an unobtainable state. So-called *"safety factors"* are designed into bridges, ships, and planes. This is done to raise safety to as near-perfect levels as possible. Such safety levels are called *fail-safe systems.* This is supposed to mean that the system is immune to failure. Interpret this as follows: The probabilities of such occurrences are so small they can be ignored. According to Borel, these might be events associated with probabilities in the neighborhood of one in one in a million (0.000001).[12]

The design of facilities and the working environment is a form of industrial architecture. In many ways, it represents the same kinds of approaches and the same set of human factors objectives as those of industrial designers. Industrial design is the profession that assumes responsibility for the architecture of products, machines, and living spaces, among other things.[13] Industrial designers are responsible for achieving safety, comfort, and aesthetically pleasing design results.

The human factors area treats both the physiological and psychological characteristics of people. It attempts to provide high levels of safety and comfort. It is concerned with the appearances of things, and the way they affect efficiency. All the senses and interrelationships of the senses to both motor and mental responses are part of the fabric of these factors, which describe the interactions of the worker and the workplace, the plant, and the office as well as the customer and the product. The systems point of view is essential to capture the interactions between the workforce and the workplace.

Not just sight, illumination, and color concern the designer; hearing, noise, taste, smells, temperature changes, and body orientation are other factors that condition the attitudes, performance, safety, and comfort of the system's workforce.

What is not immediately apparent is the flaw in logic of an individual using himself or herself as a physical model of what other people need or want. Self is not a sufficient design guide for the consumer product design or for employee workplace considerations. The requirements of a representative distribution of people can be determined. A design based on statistical knowledge regarding these dimensions would satisfy the minimum requirements for a majority of potential users.

12. Emile Borel. "Valeur Pratique et Philosophie des Probabilités." *Traite du Cacul des Probabilités et de ses Applications,* tome IV, fascicule 3. (Ed.) Emile Borel (Paris: Gautier-Villars, 1950).
13. A. R. Tilley. *The Measure of Man and Woman: Human Factors in Design.* New York: Henry Dreyfuss Associates. From The Whitney Library of Design, imprint of Watson-Guptill Publications, 1993, p. 66.

Ergonomics: The systematic study of how people physically interact with their environment, equipment, facilities, machines, and products.

Individual preferences vary with respect to the amount of light that is both comfortable and satisfactory for accomplishing a given job. Many studies have been conducted to determine superior designs for controls such as dials, gauges, and tracking devices on airplanes, cars, and industrial machines.

The sense of hearing has been studied with equal fervor. Many production operations are quiet, but others produce extremely high noise levels with effects on workers and potential damage to hearing.

Problems for Supplement 9

1. What is the derivation of the word "ergonomics"?

2. It has been said that OSHA has more claims for repetitive stress or overuse syndrome (such as carpal tunnel) than any other occupational illness or injury. How can the design of the environment be put to work to alleviate this serious situation?

3. Because repetitive stress syndrome is the result of continuous repetition of certain motions, what sort of statistical studies might be undertaken to improve the design of the job?

4. What is meant by a fail-safe system?

5. Certain workers have a history of numerous accidents, whereas most workers have few accidents. What can be done for those who are accident prone?

6. Industrial designers have an orientation to the systems approach, which is critical for their success. Why is this so?

Capacity Management

This section defines capacity management in various ways and relates decisions about capacity to peak and off-peak demand. Modular design of parts (and service activities can be viewed in the same way) is a means for increasing capacity. Group technology production methods (applicable to service activities, too) are presented as another method for augmenting capacity. Breakeven models

are at the crux of capacity decisions. For this reason, breakeven analysis is developed as a means of choosing the best among a set of alternative capacity configurations. Also, linear programming is shown to be a preferred method for determination of how best to design and use production systems capacities. The relevance of the learning curve model (and thereby, investments in training) to increase capacity utilization is explained.

After reading this chapter, you should be able to:

- Define capacity and explain how it is measured.
- Discuss how efficiency and utilization relate to actual measured capacity.
- Explain why the goal of 100 percent utilization is an outdated objective that can be counterproductive.
- Discuss the problem of planning capacity to deal with peak and off-peak demand.
- Explain how bottlenecks affect capacity and discuss what to do about them.
- Describe the effects of delay on the capacity to make and deliver products and services throughout the supply chain.
- Set up the beer game to help team members visualize the effects of delay on out-of-stocks and overstocks.

- Explain the application of breakeven as a percent of maximum capacity to determine work configuration preferences.
- Describe why breakeven analysis is called a quintessential systems model.
- Explain how linear programming relates capacity and optimal product mix determination.
- Describe how linear programming depends upon systems-wide inputs.
- Explain how modular production and group technology are approaches that increase realizable capacity.
- Describe what the learning curve reflects and explain how learning increases actual capacity.

THE SYSTEMS VIEWPOINT

Capacity management relates to how the existing system is used. The systems viewpoint broadens the scope of inquiry to include questions about the existing arrangement and whether alternative configurations might not provide superior alternatives. The discussion of options cannot be pursued without consultations between marketing, finance, R & D, and OM. Capacity is always limited by the supply chain bottleneck. The viewpoint must be systems-wide to scan across facilities with excess capacity in order to spot the overloaded resources that are struggling to keep up with the rest of the system. Delays are another source of capacity problems that are often caused by factors that are outside the organization's boundaries. Thus, suppliers must be viewed as part of the system to understand swings in demand caused by delays that create above peak and below normal requirements throughout the entire supply chain.

STRATEGIC THINKING

Anyone who has ever played the beer model game is permanently converted to strategic systems thinking. As another option, the breakeven model (BEM) deserves an award for being the quintessential strategic systems model of the organization. In spite of the fact that a breakeven model relates every function, it has been taught for years as a capital budgeting function and nothing more. Next, consider linear programming. It is another model that demands systems thinking even though it can be taught as a means of modeling resource management, or simply as "the blending problem." LP is a way of looking at capacity management through the eyes of all participants in the big system. Modularity of parts (design) and group technology (for production of families of parts) are powerful strategic concepts that increase an organization's capacity to competitive proportions. The learning curve is another example of a systems concept that relates the learning individual and the learning organization to higher capacity achievement without spending. In this case, "capacity is free."

10-1 DEFINITIONS OF CAPACITY

Actual capacity: Realistic maximum amount of storage space or output rate that can be achieved with the existing configuration of resources and the accepted product or service mix plans.

Capacity: There are two basic types of capacity. One is storage space and the other is throughput flow rates.

Actual capacity is the greatest output rate that can be achieved with the existing configuration of resources and the accepted product or service mix plans. Altering the product or service mix can (and usually will) change actual realizable capacity. Modifying the existing configuration of resources, equipment, and people in the work force alters real capacity. The systems point of view includes cash as part of the resources because cash can be converted into new machines, which alter real capacity. The systems viewpoint also includes good ideas, which can increase **capacity** with minimum expenditures.

The classical formula for actual measured capacity is

$$C = T \times E \times U$$

where C = actual measured capacity (in standard hours)

T = real time available
E = efficiency
U = utilization

10-1a Standard Hours

T is determined by calculating the amount of *time* that is available when fully utilizing the resources that are already in place to make the product. Doubling the number of machines doubles the amount of available time, T.

E is the *efficiency* with which time T can be utilized to make different kinds of product. Then, $T \times E$ is equivalent to standard hours available to make the products.

U is how much of the available capacity can be (or is) *utilized*. Lack of orders or breakdowns of machines diminish U. When T and E and U are multiplied, the product is C, the actual capacity that is being (or has been) utilized.

Table 10-1 is used to illustrate the calculations.

Assume that this plant is rated with a *maximum capacity* of 150 standard hours of output. It never achieves the maximum, but comes closest to doing so on Wednesday. There are a variety of reasons why the plant does not achieve the maximum. Two factors are

| Standard Hours of Output | | | | | | TABLE 10-1 |
Product	Monday	Tuesday	Wednesday	Thursday	Friday	Capacity Utilized (C)
T101	25	20	65	18	30	
T102	65	10	25	40	0	
MW11	40	90	50	70	80	
TOTAL	130	120	140	128	110	

embodied in E and U, explained later. Another reason could be that the product mix has caused bottlenecks and flow disruptions.

E, the efficiency, is a proportional factor needed to convert to standard time. Machines or people that work slower have lower efficiency than those that have a higher productive output. Often, the best in the class is given an efficiency of one. It is to be expected that variations in efficiency will occur. Sometimes the source of the variation can be traced. If it is significant variation, then it should be studied and corrected. Unexplained fluctuations in capacity are unpleasant and unprofitable.

If a job is being done at 90 percent of the standard time because the supplier delivered defective product, remedial action must be taken with supplies on hand and the problem must be corrected with future deliveries.

For example, if toothpaste tube caps have a burr on the thread, then a tentative solution for the toothpaste producer is to assign a worker to file off the burrs. The supplier of caps is notified, and it is expected that the problem will be rectified in future shipments. Meanwhile, actual toothpaste line capacity is reduced by 10 percent.

U, the utilization, is applied as a proportional correction to standard time when there are machine breakdowns and/or people are absent. Even when everything is running as planned, the value of U is usually less than 100 percent. If the system is being run faster by turning up the speed of the machine, the value of U can exceed 100 percent. There are pros and cons related to running above maximum rated capacity. How long the maximum capacity is exceeded also counts.

U is a measure to be wary of when it becomes an objective of management to keep it as close to 100 percent as possible. There are sound economic reasons not to produce when the production quota has been met and the safety stock is sufficient. Shutting down the machine for 2 hours of an 8-hour day means that the U measure goes to 75 percent. Actual measured capacity is going to be reduced by a fourth.

Management must establish the fact that getting the job done early can be a good thing worthy of reward. Normal inclination is to avoid criticism for not fully utilizing the resource. A special effort is required to break through this illusion. The costs of making goods that are not yet sold must be analyzed. How long will they remain as inventory? Are there fluctuations in demand that they will buffer or is the buffer in place already? The costs of arbitrary utilization of capacity should be recognized for what they are—likely to be wasteful. An appropriate **decision model** can be constructed to answer these questions.

In the following example, U is assumed to be 0.963, which is likely to be viewed as a more reasonable utilization factor than 0.750. P/OM might not want a permanent situation where the utilization factor was much below 0.900. The desired numbers will be dependent on the situation. For example, in service organizations, a much lower number might be considered desirable in order to keep queues short. Cyclical industries expect to cycle between utilization factors in the 0.700 range and then up to more than 100 percent capacity. Overall, many companies prefer to have capacity in reserve and expect to operate effectively below the misleading ideal of 100 percent utilization.

For the data in Table 10-1:

$C = T \times E \times U$ for Monday might be
$C = 150 \times 0.9 \times 0.963 = 130$ actual standard hours

Decision model: Strategies, states of nature, probabilities of states of nature (forecast for these probabilities), expected values for outcomes, and strategies chosen for delivering outcomes in time with goals and objectives.

The ratio of actual standard hours to maximum standard hours would be

$R = 130/150 = 0.87$ or 87 percent

10-1b Maximum Rated Capacities

Capacity can be defined as maximum containment. Containment capacity takes many forms (i.e., the auditorium has a seating capacity of 360, or the gas tank will hold 16 gallons).

It also can be defined as maximum sustained output of goods or services. Both meanings are regularly used by P/OM. The capacity to contain or store inventory is the first of the two definitions of capacity.

The capacity to make inventory or provide service is the second definition of capacity. Production and/or operations capacity describes how many units can be served or made per unit of time. For services, a bank might compare the maximum number of people the bank teller can process per hour with the maximum number of people the ATM can process per hour. This is a service capacity comparison.

For manufacturing, compare the maximum number of hot dogs Oscar Meyer can make per hour with the maximum number of hot dogs Hebrew National can make per hour. This comparison is one that both companies would like to make in order to compare their PMCs (productivities at maximum capacity). PMC makes an excellent measure for benchmarking. Benchmarking is a systematic comparison of fundamental measures with those of competitors and the best departments of the company itself.

Consider using maximum containment as a benchmarking measure. Generally, the larger the storage facility, the more material sitting around without having value added, and the poorer the performance measure. However, if a company built substantial petroleum storage facilities early in 1973, it would have been in the catbird seat when the oil embargo in the fall of 1973 created severe petroleum shortages. The harsh effects of the oil crisis lasted through the end of March 1974.

The utilization of containment capacity is another important factor for P/OM to consider. Having extra capacity would not have been a boon to Mobil Oil unless the tanks were filled with crudes and fuels. On the other hand, high utilization of containment capacity runs counter to the desire for low inventory levels, just-in-time deliveries, and constant value adding.

> **Demand:** Units of product (goods and/or services) requested for delivery within a period of time constitute demand.

The two kinds of capacity situations have a trade-off relationship. Extracapacity and undercapacity are shown in Figure 10-1. When market **demand** falls below maximum supply capacity (MD < MSC), the production system can feed storage and build up inventories. When market demand exceeds maximum supply capacity (MD > MSC), the inventory can be used to help meet that demand.

In Figure 10-1, the diagonal line is the maximum capacity to supply product. It is a rate of output that at the end of period T has the capability of producing S units. Realistically, the curved line is sometimes below the diagonal and sometimes above it. For convenience, the market demand rate over the entire period T accumulates total demand of S.

Difficult to Store Service Capacity

The concept developed here and shown in Figure 10-1 does not apply to services as readily as to manufacturing. This is because most services cannot be stored. The extracapacity on the left side of Figure 10-1 is wasted idle time for service personnel. For goods it can represent building stock on-hand that can be drawn down when the undercapacity, right side of Figure 10-1 occurs.

Backordering Augments Service Capacity

If the customer is willing, backorders can be used to satisfy demand when there is no inventory available. This applies to services that cannot be stored. It applies as well to the manufacturer who is out of stock. The overloaded system does not have to turn away orders if the customer agrees to wait until other customers' jobs are finished.

10-2 PEAK AND OFF-PEAK DEMAND

There is another question about planning capacity. Should the maximum output capacity be great enough to handle peak load? This would be equivalent to providing enough electrical generating power to supply all needs for air-conditioning demand on extremely hot business days. Alternatively, should the telephone companies have enough capacity to take care of all phone calls without any delays for Valentine's Day and Mother's Day? These holidays are known as the heaviest traffic days for phone companies.

The rule for putting peak versus nonpeak capacity into place is

Buy peak capacity when: $C_p < C_{np}$

C_p is the extra investment required to assure peak capacity. In other words, it is the investment for peak capacity less that required to meet average demand, depreciated over the life of the system. Say it takes an extra $5,000,000 to increase capacity from average to peak. This amount is spread out over 10 years, or $500,000 per year.

C_{np} is the cost of not having capacity to meet demands that are greater than the average demand. It is determined by the costs of such events as brownouts, power failures, and loss of goodwill in the community. There are some lost revenues as well. Say that the total cost averages $30,000 per incident.

Figure 10-2 provides an illustration of the difference between peak and off-peak average demand, as well as the level of normal supply, which is above off-peak average in this case.

To illustrate with a case, assume that the probability that actual demand exceeds average demand is estimated to be 5 percent of the year or roughly 18 summer days. Total cost associated with C_{np} is

$$365 \times 0.05 \times \$30,000 = \$547,500$$

This is more than the investment to prevent any brownouts, so the best advice, based on these figures, is to buy the equipment to generate sufficient power to meet peak demands.

10-2a Qualitative Aspects of Capacity

"As is our confidence, so is our capacity."—William Hazlitt[1]

If our confidence is high, so is our capacity. But this is a different definition of the word. Usually, when capacity is treated in a P/OM context, the quantitative point of view prevails. There are, however, qualitative aspects that are important to cite.

It is not unusual to hear "he or she has the capacity to be a fine ballplayer, chef, manager, . . . etc." This invokes mental ability or physical skills. Organizations have capacities to deal with problems and opportunities. It is like an inventory of capabilities. Oftentimes, only when tested does the capacity to outperform the normal emerge.

In that sense, Motorola has the capacity to meet quality standards that are far superior to most other companies. Robert Galvin, former chairman of Motorola, challenged the company to develop peak capacity for quality production.

The company had been embarrassed by the Japanese company Quasar's purchase of the TV division, which had a history of severe defectives reported between 150 and 180 defects per 100 sets. Within three years, traditional Japanese quality had asserted itself. The defect rate had dropped to 3 or 4 per 100 sets. Service calls dropped from $22 million to less than $4 million. In-plant repair staff went from 120 to 15. Quality people liked to tell the story. Galvin did not like to hear the story being told, and threw down the gauntlet.

Motorola has since become a world leader in the production of quality products. Motorola set for itself an incredible quality goal of 3.4 defects per million parts. This is associated with six-sigma limits as compared to three-sigma limits in quality control. The company has reported being very close to achieving the goal. Motorola was the first company to win the Baldrige Award for quality ability. The turnaround is impressive.

Skillful management can increase the level of capacity that is achieved. Managing installed physical capacity properly means obtaining the maximum available capacity. This goal is particularly relevant when dealing with management of peak demand. If the maximum capacity of the process is less than the peak demand, knowing how to assign priorities will influence real capacity levels achieved.

10-2b Maximum Capacity—100 Percent Rating

Capacity as measured by maximum output volume per unit time, or throughput rate, comes closest to capturing the P/OM concept. That does not make it easy to measure. It is possible to produce at more than 100 percent of capacity for a period of time. Maximum capacity depends on who is doing the work and what is being made or serviced. Although 100 percent and maximum capacity are illusive concepts, they are useful standards to go by as long as the users are aware of their arbitrary nature.

When people are part of the process, some of the qualitative aspects of capacity cannot be ignored. Some people work faster than others. Most people fluctuate in their rates of output. There is a **learning curve** at work. People learn from practice how to do a better job. Some people can learn faster than others. Individuality allows some people to do certain jobs better than others. In this regard, all people are not alike. Ambiguity, opportunity, and challenge abound in this arena.

Machines can work at different speeds. Driving an automobile illustrates that. Different velocities are best for optimal fuel consumption, minimum tire wear, and life of the car. Machines can be set for certain speeds that engineers would say are equivalent to 100

Learning curve: Describes how repeated practice decreases the time required to do a job.

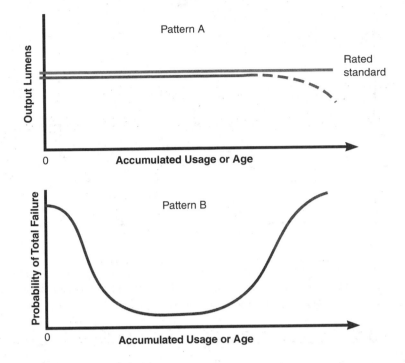

FIGURE 10-3
Wearout and Failure
Patterns as a Function
of Accumulated Usage
and Age—The Failure
Distribution (Pattern B)
Is the Weibull Distribution

percent of their capacities. Ask the engineer what will happen if the machine is set to work faster. A typical answer will be that the machine will wear out sooner.

Figure 10-3 shows two patterns that are typical of wear-out life and failure as a function of accumulated usage and age. Pattern A illustrates the output lumens of a lightbulb that is diminishing before final failure. Pattern B shows a Weibull-type distribution, which reflects the high initial mortality of certain products (such as lightbulbs). Then there is a period of low product mortality until it reaches the expected time of failure. Time-of-failure distributions must be understood if capacity is to be managed properly.

Setting the standard for the maximum capacity creates an interesting comparison between what people and machines can do. For highly repetitive jobs, most machines can be set to work faster than people. For heavy and difficult work, especially in environments that are very hot, noisy, and even life threatening, machines win without question. Thus, robots are the best choice for nuclear experimentation. Also affecting the determination of capacity is the fact that machines can break down and people can be absent. Maximum capacity is usually determined with all the systems on go.

On the other hand, automated voice mail systems, such as those operated by financial service companies and phone companies, are tedious. They can require listening to endless options. It is not unusual to have to listen to seven or eight alternatives before getting to the one that applies. It is so much faster for the customer to speak to an operator that many people who have Touch-Tone phones prefer to act as though they have a rotary phone in order to get a human operator.

The capacity of such systems may be difficult to evaluate because people manipulate the system to their own advantage. In the same regard, the bank teller can move certain requests faster than the ATM and vice versa. Further, especially with services, capacity measures are a function of the demand on the systems. Excess demand tends to deteriorate the performance of service systems. Requirements for special services that are common in many systems such as health care and education also make it difficult to establish maximum capacity figures.

Capricious Demand

Capacity planning is one of the most important business activities. It is filled with opportunity to manage to advantage and fraught with difficulties. This is especially true if demand is capricious and tough to forecast correctly. Capacity planning is done to reach

FIGURE 10-4
Dynamic Adjustment of Maximum Capacity

optimal supply decisions that, it is hoped, will match future demand patterns. This means that capacity planning does not have to be a single frozen value but can be a dynamic trajectory with fluctuations and oscillations.

10-2c Capacity Requirements Planning (CRP)

> **Capacity requirements planning (CRP):** Strategic issues of CRP relate to long-term planning for capacity including breakeven points and optimal allocation of resources.
>
> **Breakeven:** Breakeven connotes the fact that enough units of product were sold to offset the costs and begin to make a profit.

There are two aspects to **capacity requirements planning (CRP).** The strategic issues related to long-term planning including **breakeven** concepts and breakeven points and optimal allocation of resources are being treated in this chapter. The shorter-term, tactical issues are operating issues that properly belong to a discussion of material requirements planning.

The ability to alter capacity in steps or stages, as shown in Figure 10-4, is valuable for strategic planning.

It takes planning to keep as flexible as possible with respect to capacity. Combinations of negotiations (as in a power grid) and technology can be brought to bear on a temporary basis. Consider the discussion of rentals:

Part-time employees are a familiar means for making capacity adjustments, up or down. They do not require either severance pay or fringe benefits. Part-time employees relieve the firm of many other obligations associated with full-time employees. Rentals are an equivalent method for making capacity adjustments with equipment and space without taking on long-term commitments that lock the company into higher capacity than it is likely to need over the long term.

Coproducers and *copackers* are firms used to increase supply by subcontracting with them on a short-, medium-, or long-term basis. For example, a company that sells margarine might make enough to supply 60 percent of its market. The rest of its market demand is supplied by the output of a coproducer that has excess capacity. The product of the coproducer is packed in the subcontracting company's familiar package.

10-3 UPSCALING AND DOWNSIZING

Capacity planning is often constrained to an optimal size by the engineering requirements of the process. Many chemical processes must be designed and built to a specific size in order to operate properly. Glass windshields require a given number of steps that take exact amounts of time.

Serialized flow shop processes also are constrained by engineering factors, although to a lesser extent than continuous chemical flow process. Job shop and batch processes are far more flexible with regard to optimal production volume sizes.

To increase maximum capacities, processes can sometimes be operated above their rated capacities by using overtime and faster conveyor speeds. There are quality repercussions and the equipment is seldom designed for sustained overloads.

To meet greater demand, it is usually advisable to subcontract with coproducers until such time that additional demand warrants building another plant. Such processes do not have the flexibility of batch shops, which can be expanded and contracted within reasonable limits.

As the labor component of the process changes, the capacity adjustment reflects this fact, allowing an increase or decrease in the workforce. Because many services are notable for their labor percentage of the cost of goods sold, the capacity adjustment in services often involves people. The increase in service jobs continues to dominate the growth of jobs for the workforce in the United States.

Capacity planning involves not only machinery and labor, but also management. When demand slackens, the notion of reducing managerial capacity (downsizing) emerges. This is particularly the case where management size has grown because of the bureaucratic tendency to hire assistants for assistants. Parkinson's rule that "work expands to fill the time available for its completion"[2] is seen repeatedly during periods of strong markets. Parkinson's rule is carried one step further in the next paragraph.

In many organizations, "work expands until there is no time available for its completion." This means that new information is requested, new tasks are assigned, there are never enough people; everyone is busy. Capacity is increased until there are so many levels in the organizational hierarchy that communications almost never make it all the way up. The management at each level becomes self-protective and an outside consulting firm is often hired to downsize the company. This usually means slicing out the bulge of middle management. After considerable corporate malfeasance at the highest levels during the 2002 recession, compensation of CEOs, CFOs, and other top managers were reassessed and the Sarbanes-Oxley act put new constraints on their capacity to act.

For growth operations, excluding continuous processes such as the chemical plants described earlier, there is a need to adjust capacity to match increases in demand. Typically adjustments lead or lag, depending on the industry. Figure 10-5 shows an industry capacity-adding pattern that tries to stay ahead of the curve. This is the situation for electric utilities.

Ideally, the adjustments can be accomplished in an ascending staircase of steps. The timing and the size of the increments need to be carefully considered. The issue of whether there are natural increments of added capacity needs to be addressed. These natural increments are like buckets of supply that have minimum cost per unit of added capacity. If not, it may be necessary to reengineer the system by scrapping the current one and introducing a new one.

10-4 BOTTLENECKS AND CAPACITY

Another major issue in determining maximum capacity is the effect of bottlenecks, which limit throughput rates. Real capacity can be much lower than the apparent capacity of

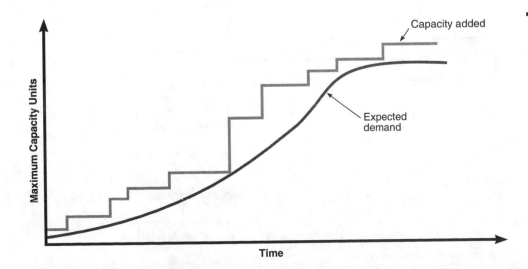

FIGURE 10-5
Growth Adjustments for Maximum Capacity

rapidly performing machines. The system's point of view requires that the subject of bottlenecks be thoroughly addressed when dealing with the design and measurement of capacity.

Toward this end, the effects of finite scheduling and synchronized manufacturing should be considered when dealing with capacity. A review of the **V-A-T** categorization (first developed by Eli Goldratt's organization and marketed as **OPT**) for classifying processes is applicable. V-processes are analytical. They start with a single commodity at the bottom and then branch out into refined by-products at the top. A-processes are synthetic, starting at the bottom with several inputs. These are then combined to yield a single marketable product. The classification would also apply to a few products instead of a single one.

OPT called combinations of A and V processes, a T-process. Although bottlenecks can and do appear in A and V processes, they are most likely to occur in the T-process. This is because conflicting patterns occur when synthesis and analysis are simultaneously present. It may help to point out that synthesis is also known as *aggregation* (or *assembly*) and analysis is known as *disaggregation* (or *disassembly*). Synthesis is also the act of combining, and analysis is the act of partitioning. Line balancing the flow shop, an OM topic discussed in material on serialized production systems, is primarily synthetic. When the flow shop is changed over to make different models, there are analytic characteristics

When determining capacity, it is essential to consider at least two kinds of bottlenecks. The first is a fixed bottleneck in an unbalanced line of a flow shop. Recall that the flow shop is an A-type system. Figure 10-6 illustrates a fixed bottleneck in such a system.

Note that Station C has a maximum throughput rate of 20 per minute. All the other stations are rated 30 per minute. Station C will continue to dominate the throughput rate until it is replaced with a new facility that has a matched production rate of 30 per minute.

The line is unbalanced by Station C. A queue, also called a *waiting line*, will develop upstream from Station C. Flow starts upstream and moves downstream as shown. As the queue grows, upstream stations will cut their output rate to 20 per minute.

They will do so because they see that the queue is growing and may even be impinging on their own workspace. It is also possible that Station C will refuse to accept any more deliveries. The stations downstream from C have no options. They receive 20 units per minute. Maximum capacity is determined by the bottleneck. OPT principles call for feeding the bottleneck for the reason that C sets the production pace. If it fails to have work, the production rate falls below 20 per minute.

V-A-T: Categorization for classifying processes. V-processes are analytic. A-processes are synthetic. T-processes are combinations of V and A.

OPT: Original name for a finite production scheduling technique. The lots are of finite size. Now called *Theory of Constraints* (TOC).

FIGURE 10-6
How a Fixed Bottleneck Decreases Capacity (Upstream Starts at A and Downstream Concludes at E)

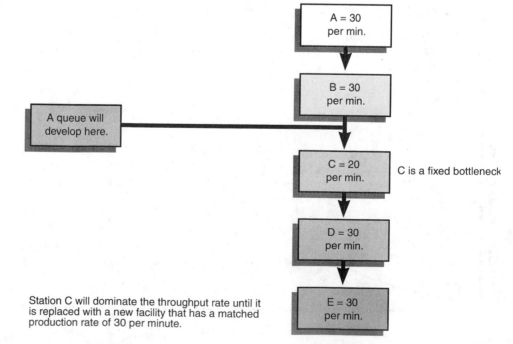

Station C will dominate the throughput rate until it is replaced with a new facility that has a matched production rate of 30 per minute.

The second type of bottleneck can float from station to station in a job or batch shop identified with V-type systems. These temporary bottlenecks are associated with orders that have large lot sizes. The large lot ties up each of the machines on the order's routing schedule. Floating bottlenecks can make the determination of maximum capacity extremely difficult.

One approach is to select some typical order schedules from past records. By simulating the performance of the batch shop under the condition of efficient scheduling, it is possible to determine the maximum capacity of the system.

It also is possible to note where the bottlenecks are most commonly found. By altering the number and types of general-purpose equipment (GPEs), bottlenecks can be shifted and capacity can be increased.

A few additional points:

1. In some batch shops, the degree of repetition is sufficiently high to allow the scheduling for an average or typical day of orders (called an *average order-schedule day*) to be used as the basis for maximum capacity determination. Better scheduling practices might push the upper limit higher.

2. The V-A-T classification associated with OPT reflects different possible definitions of maximum capacity. The V and T classes are producing mixed models, and some standard such as standard hours is required. In addition to A and V there is the T-type classification, a combination of A and V.

3. Finite scheduling is what it sounds like. Specific lot sizes are finite, bounded, and restricted. They are not unbounded, as is the potential output from a continuous production system or a flow shop. The lots are scheduled on a finite set of machines in such a way as to maximize throughput and speed deliveries.

4. Synchronized manufacturing occurs when finite scheduling succeeds in fitting jobs to machines so that flows are continuous, stations are balanced, and bottlenecks are fed without queues forming. This is another definition of maximum capacity for a given configuration of equipment.

5. Because equipment and jobs interact to create multiple bottlenecks as well as temporary and floating bottlenecks, the achievement of maximum capacity is a function of the jobs the sales department obtains as well as the facilities P/OM has selected. The mix is dynamic and can change rapidly. Measures of maximum capacity may have to be estimates of averages.

6. Permanent bottlenecks, when they can be identified, are true determinants of capacity. They are easiest to spot and deal with in the flow shop, but can exist in the batch system. A good illustration of this is when the tool crib has a long queue in front of it. Every worker must go to the tool crib to requisition tools for the next job. The bottleneck at the tool crib lengthens the setup and changeover times.

7. Ingenuity is required to deal with measuring actual capacity utilization and defining a meaningful rating of real maximum capacity. Further resourcefulness is needed to spot and remove bottlenecks to increase both measures of capacity.

Queues are the result of bottlenecks caused by unbalanced capacities. Discussion of queues is appropriate in a chapter on capacity, but the equations are a bit tangential to the essence of strategic planning for capacity.

10-5 DELAY DETERIORATES PERFORMANCE IN THE SUPPLY CHAIN

Any one of the components in the **supply chain** can be a bottleneck. The capacity of a supplier can be a bottleneck, for instance. Such a bottleneck will cause the producer to cut production runs. Simultaneously, the producer will notify all other suppliers to ship only a proportion of the regular order. Meanwhile, the manufacturer's warehouse will receive reduced shipments of the finished goods.

Supply chain: The linkage between raw materials and finished products (goods and services) delivered into the hands of the customers.

The distributor also will be shortchanged. Because the distributor does not have a sufficient inventory to meet all of the demands, retailers' orders will be cut. Finally, customers in the stores will be informed that they have to wait until more goods arrive. This situation, if not quickly remedied, can get progressively worse. Competitors, if they can, will surely take advantage of the failure to "hear the customer's voice."

In the previous scenario, every supply chain player is suffering because of the problems of one supplier. The systems approach deals with such interconnectedness of the supply chain. It focuses on finding ways to reveal what kinds of problems each participant can visit on the others, and on how to remedy failures to meet demand with quality products.

10-5a Contingency Planning for Capacity Crises

The producer may look around for a new supplier, or at least one that can make up the shortfall. A potential backup, even though more costly while the emergency exists, should have been known on a contingency basis. Before the supplier failed to deliver, were there any prewarnings? Did the supplier provide all necessary information about the pending problem? Could the supplier and the producer have worked together to eliminate or reduce the severity of the problem? After-the-fact is too late. Such contingency planning for capacity crises deserves to be done beforehand.

At the same time, the other suppliers will be looking for new customers. Their contingency planning should have taken into account the fact that, through no fault of their own, this crisis has arisen for each of them. When these suppliers find other customers, they may have reduced ability to supply the producer. The distributor may start stocking a competing brand, with serious long-term consequences for the producer's market share.

The retailers may find that the new competing brand is a hit with their customers. The loss of loyal customers is a serious blow stemming from this supply problem. One supplier's failure can destabilize an entire system, causing reduction in profit and losses in competitive leverage that will be hard to regain. Parts of the process linkages are shown in the systems dynamics chart of Figure 10-7.

10-5b A Supply Chain Game—The Better Beer Company

Why Use a Game?

A game is a powerful teaching method. The game simulates the situation in such a way that the players recognize the factors that are important. If the game is done well, it may even lead to players improving their performance if the players understand the drivers of outcomes.

FIGURE 10-7
The Supply Chain Game

Lead time delays and poor forecasting cause oscillations leading to shortages and overstocking.

What Can Be Learned from Playing this Game?

Retailers, distributors, and manufacturers can order too much beer or too little beer when information about actual demand for the brand is delayed along the links of a supply chain. The effects of ordering too much or too little as a result of information delays can be costly. The resulting imbalance of demand with existing capacity is important to understand. The game shows how the performance of a linked system is tied to the adequacy of forecasts about future demand. There are measures that can be taken to improve communications and reduce information delays. There are methods for improving forecasts as well. For example, it may not be possible to improve the national estimates of demand unless they are looked at as the sum of regional demands. Once improvement has been made in timeliness of information and better forecasts, the game players can achieve decreased costs.

Jay Forrester used simulation to demonstrate many of these effects in 1961 with his seminal work on systems dynamics.[3] This was at the Sloan School at M.I.T., where the "beer game" was developed in the 1960s. It is a supply chain simulation game[4] that seems to be more than ever entirely applicable and used for instructive purposes.

The "beer game" is quite involved and takes a long time to play. Figures 10-8 and 10-9 replace the game with some charts of simulations that reflect the effects of delays on decisions made by producers, wholesalers, retailers, suppliers, and customers. The simulations are called the *Better Beer Company*. The product that is at the heart of the simulation is called *Woodstock*.

In Figure 10-9, the next link in the supply chain connects the producer (manufacturer) and the distributor.

These charts show how the retailer, spotting what seems like a major increase in demand, orders substantially more stock to avoid outages. The retailer's order for more product takes three weeks lead time between placing the order and receiving the shipment. If the increase was just a random pulse in demand, then other retailers might counterbalance the effect by ordering less, because, by chance, they had less than normal demand. The distributor would hardly notice such effects, which tend to cancel each other. The retailer would gradually correct for the extra stock on-hand that resulted.

On the other hand, if there is a common cause for many retailers to experience increased demand, they would all increase their order sizes, perhaps even overreacting with an extra large order to avoid going out of stock. The escalation in order sizes from many retailers would be a red flag to the distributor, who would greatly increase orders placed with the producer.

The 4-week lead time that the producer takes to fill the distributor's orders adds to the delay and increases the chances of large oscillations occurring for all supply chain participants. The producer experiencing such a surge in demand would be best advised to try to meet it with overtime.

Figures 10-10 and 10-11 show the stock on-hand (SOH) and orders placed by the retailer and distributor. It is evident that large oscillations are costing all participants a great deal. This is in spite of the fact that a review of the orders made by both the retailer and the distributor leads to the conclusion that the ordering policies followed were sensible.

Figure 10-12 compares the end stock on-hand (SOH) results for the retailer and the distributor. The effect had seemed enormous to the retailer. However, when the comparison is made with the distributor, the retailer's swings were gentle. The effect is going to be even worse at the producer's level.

If the increased demand seems to be sustained over a reasonable period of time, the producer might invest in more capacity (equipment and people) for what seems like a reasonable change in demand levels. Patient evaluation of the permanency of common causes is easy to counsel, but hard to realize in the face of possible stock outages and unhappy customers, retailers, and distributors. The producer could not resist and invested in more capacity.

FIGURE 10-8
**Supply Chain Simulation
of the Distributor
to the Retailer Link**

Begin week 1 with 12 cases of stock on-hand (SOH). Supply at the start of the week is 4 cases so net SOH is 16 cases. As expected, the demand is for 4 cases so end of week 1 SOH is 12 cases. The retailer orders 4 cases and since lead time is 3 weeks, the 4 cases will be delivered at the beginning of week 5. Continue to read Figure 10-8 in this fashion. Note that in weeks 10, 11, and 12, the end SOH rose to 24 cases, double the normal amount.

Week	Begin SOH	Supply	Net SOH	Demand	End SOH	Order Quantity	Delivery Week
1	12	4	16	-4	12	4	5
2	12	4	16	-8	8	8	6
3	8	4	12	-8	4	16	7
4	4	4	8	-8	0	12	8
5	0	4	4	-7	-3	12	9
6	-3	8	5	-6	-1	8	10
7	-1	16	15	-5	10	4	11
8	10	12	22	-8	14	4	12
9	14	12	26	-6	20	0	13
10	20	8	28	-4	24	0	14
11	24	4	28	-4	24	0	15
12	24	4	28	-4	24	0	16
13	24	0	24	-4	20	0	17
14	20	0	20	-6	14	4	18
15	14	0	14	-8	6	8	19
16	6	0	6	-8	-2	10	20
17	-2	0	-2	-4	-6	4	21
18	-6	4	-2	-4	-6	4	22
19	-6	8	2	-4	-2	4	23
20	-2	10	8	-4	4	4	24

The final episode in this scenario is that the cause of the increased demand at the retail level was temporary. It was a common cause, such as might be created by a sensational TV program or a published newspaper article about the product. In reality, the glamour and appeal were gradually forgotten, and the special selling effects eventually disappeared. Remember, this is a game, and the scenario plus what follows are part of role-playing. They are not reality.

The producer now has more capacity than is likely to be used for a long time, if ever. The producer drops the price to be able to sell everything that its new capacity enables it to make. The distributor orders more to take advantage of the probable increase in demand that follows a drop in price. The retailer also is working on lower margins and prefers to push the competitive products.

The product can be beer or soft drinks, cosmetics or food. Supply chains can be extended to industrial products for original equipment manufacturers (OEM). The basic idea of linked supply and demand is valid as long as the relevant supply chain has been identified.

10-5c Cost Drivers for Capacity Planning

Activity-based costing (ABC) systems can always help in capacity decisions because they separate costs into those that are associated with resource capacities used and those that are unused. The producer, by monitoring production performance in terms of what is really contributing to the costs of output, would have identified the cost drivers, the costs

Week	Begin SOH	Supply	Net SOH	Demand	End SOH	Order Quantity	Delivery Week
1	64	16	80	-16	64	16	6
2	64	16	80	-32	48	32	7
3	48	16	64	-32	32	64	8
4	32	16	48	-32	16	64	9
5	16	16	32	-28	4	48	10
6	4	16	20	-24	-4	32	11
7	-4	32	28	-20	8	16	12
8	8	64	72	-16	56	16	13
9	56	64	120	-16	104	0	14
10	104	48	152	-16	136	0	15
11	136	32	168	-16	152	0	16
12	152	16	168	-16	152	0	17
13	152	16	168	-16	152	0	18
14	152	0	152	-24	128	16	19
15	128	0	128	-32	96	32	20
16	96	0	96	-32	64	48	21
17	64	0	64	-64	0	80	18*
18	0	80	80	-94	-16	128	23
19	-16	16	0	-64	-64	80	24
20	-64	32	-32	-32	-64	16	25

* FedEx delivery

FIGURE 10-9
Supply Chain Simulation of the Producer (Manufacturer) to the Distributor Link
To read the chart, follow the same procedure as with Figure 10-8. Thus, week 1 begins with 64 cases of beer at the distributor and end SOH is 64. Lead time is 4 weeks, so the order placed at the end of week 1 is received at the beginning of week 6.
*Note that the order for 80 cases made in week 17 is expedited via FedEx at extra cost to be delivered at the beginning of week 18.

FIGURE 10-10
Supply Chain Simulation Shows How the Retailer's Stock On-Hand Oscillates

of the main resource capacities being used. They literally drive costs and profitability. Traditional accounting systems lump many of these costs together and call them *overhead* or *burden*. ABC assigns overhead as correctly as possible, true to the spirit of the purpose. The purpose is to make each product or service reflect its true cost to the company so that it is possible to determine its true contribution to company profits.

FIGURE 10-11
Supply Chain Simulation
Shows How the Distributor's
Stock On-Hand Oscillates

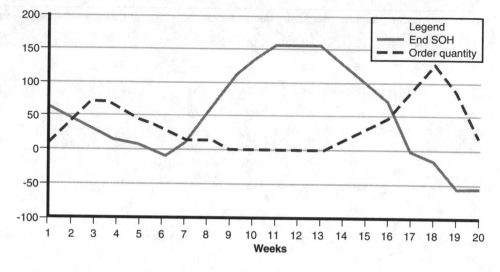

In this way, specific costs are obtained for all equipment and facilities being used to make the products of the product line. Each product can be differentiated by the amount of resources that it actually uses. This leads to knowing the real profitability of each product in the line.

Before the TV event that caused sales to jump, Woodstock beer was being charged with the same percent of overhead costs for sales as all other beers made by the company. This charge under conventional accounting hid the fact that Woodstock did not use sales force time to the same extent as the other beers. In fact, sales did almost nothing to sell it.

Sales force and selling expenses are important to this product category. The activity-based cost driver might well be sales force hours required. Various products in this line could be differentiated by the sales force cost driver. Knowing the real costs and profitability of Woodstock might make a big difference in the decision to add new capacity.

Woodstock literally sold itself to a special market segment that found the name appealing. It was unlikely that segment could continue to grow. Even permanent growth was not likely. It was believed that the brand franchise would continue to get smaller as the Woodstock generation disappeared. This logic should drive the capacity decisions for Woodstock. The advantage of ABC when making capacity decisions is that it reveals fundamental information about costs and profit margins.

ABC is used in other ways for capacity-related decisions. It provides process cost information to product designers. This helps them control manufacturing costs. Such cost information is related to volume and capacity. If cost drivers are related to capacity, as well

FIGURE 10-12
Supply Chain Simulation
Compares the SOH
Curves of the Distributor
and Retailer

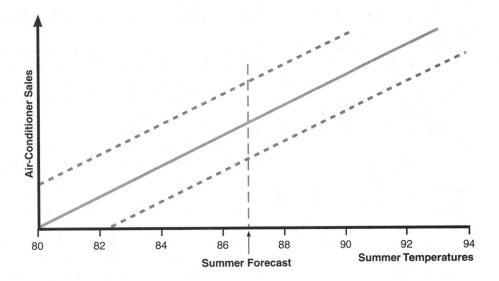

FIGURE 10-13
Air-Conditioner Sales
Versus Average Weekly
Summer Temperatures
Note that the summer 2005
forecast is for an average
temperature of 87 degrees.

they might be, with respect to particular machines, and often to the cost of setups, then designers for DFM and capacity decision makers need ABC.

10-6 FORECASTING AND CAPACITY PLANNING

When forecasting can be done with a reasonable degree of accuracy, reactive capacity decisions can be made. If the summer that is about to start is expected to average 10 degrees hotter than usual, and the air-conditioner manufacturer has a chart like the one shown in Figure 10-13, then production schedules can be set with some degree of confidence.

Figure 10-13 plots AC (air-conditioner) sales versus average weekly summer temperatures. A band is drawn above and below the line. Within that band, 90 percent of sales results have occurred. The band defines a confidence range. The forecast of weather has been correct within ±3 degrees. Putting it all together, there is a reliable forecast and a strong correlation between that forecast and sales.

Does the process possess the capacity to supply the demand? If it has more capacity than needed, the ABC issue arises of adjusting downward the resource availability by selling it off or by finding alternative products to utilize the capacity. If the process has insufficient capacity to supply the demand, then either sales will be lost or more capacity will be developed by using extra shifts and overtime, new equipment, and coproducers.

10-7 CAPACITY AND BREAKEVEN COSTS AND REVENUES

The breakeven model may be the most significant basis for making intelligent capacity decisions. To use breakeven, it is important to review direct and indirect costs.

The breakeven model uses the same costs and revenues as the input–output model that has been developed. This is not a review of costs, however, because the breakeven discussion of costs requires points be made in addition to those that applied to the efficiency of the input–output transformation process.

Variable costs per unit = vc are the inputs that tend to be fully chargeable and directly attributable to the product in the ABC accounting sense. They also are called *direct costs* because they are paid out on a per-unit of output basis. Direct costs for labor and materials are typical. Variable costs can often be decreased by learning to do the job better.

Material costs can sometimes be reduced using value analysis to improve material usage or find better materials at lower costs. Changing order sizes can increase discounts, and grouping purchases can result in lower transportation costs for full carloads. Lower cost suppliers directly decrease the variable cost of inventory being held and stored. OM

> **Variable costs per unit = vc:**
> Variable costs are charges attributable to each unit of product that is made and/or delivered.

has many avenues to pursue as it strives to continuously improve quality while reducing variable costs.

There are some classification problems for variable costs. Differentiating between direct and indirect labor costs provides an example. Office work is indirect because such costs usually cannot be attributed to a particular unit of output on a cost per piece basis. If a direct link can be made so that overhead costs can be assigned directly, then such costs should not be equally shared in the overhead pool with other products.

Total variable costs = TVC = (vc)V are the result of multiplying the variable costs per unit (vc) by the number of units or volume (V). These are also total direct costs.

Fixed costs = FC have to be paid, whether one unit is made or thousands. For this reason, administrative and supervisory costs are usually treated as fixed charges. Together with purchasing and sales, they are all bundled together as overhead costs. Salaries and bonuses paid to the CEO and to every other manager are overhead because they cannot be assigned to specific products and services.

It is possible, with activity-based costing, to more carefully assign fixed charges to each specific product. This is important because breakeven analysis is done for each product and not for a product mix. Incorrect assignment of overhead to the fixed costs will affect the breakeven value. It is generally believed that the basic proportions are evident and that roughly the right numbers are used. ABC can help confirm this and/or correct deviations from the fundamental rule that states, if they do not vary with volume, then they are fixed.

ABC may also help move some charges from the fixed to the variable category. This is possible when the cost per unit made or serviced can be identified by the accounting system and moved to the variable category.

Total costs = TC = FC + TVC are the sum of the fixed and the total variable costs.

Total revenue = TR = (p)V is the volume V multiplied by the price per unit p. When goods and services are sold in the marketplace, they generate revenue. This breakeven model treats revenue as a linear function similar to variable costs. Each unit sold generates the same amount of revenue equal to the price (p). Cumulative or total revenue (TR) is equal to the number of units sold to date (V) times the price (p), i.e., TR = (p)V. Total revenue equals zero when V = 0 because no units are sold. An assumption of breakeven analysis is that all units made are sold.

The breakeven analysis question is: How many units need to be made and sold in order to recover costs and breakeven? The results change over time as factors vary. Fixed costs often grow, prices change, and variable costs per unit decrease with proper OM attention.

Marketing is responsible for setting prices to create the required demand volume while still generating a fair profit. The way the demand volume changes as a function of the price set is described by the "price elasticity" of the product or service. Price elasticity is affected by customer quality expectations and the degree to which competitive products are substitutable. Advertising and promotion strategies are costs usually assigned to overhead. All these market drivers are crucial to the P/OM domain because they determine output volumes, and thereby affect capacity plans.

Total variable costs = TVC = (vc)V: The result of multiplying the variable cost per unit (vc) by the number of units or volume (V) produced.

Fixed costs (FC): Like rent, they have to be paid whether or not any units are sold. Like an insurance policy, they apply to a specific period of time. FCs are greater for flow shops than for job shops, and greatest for flexible manufacturing systems.

Total costs = TC = FC + TVC: TC are the sum of fixed costs and total variable costs.

Total revenue = TR = (p)V: Total revenue is price per unit (p) multiplied by the volume (V) sold (not just made) in a period of time, T. TR applies to the same period of time, T.

10-7a Interfunctional Breakeven Capacity Planning

As was the case with input–output process analysis, for breakeven, too, every functional manager should be involved. There is something for everyone to be concerned about with the breakeven model. Without interfunctional planning, all relevant information cannot be secured. Successful coordination of process activities is not likely to be achieved without the systems approach.

How much capacity as well as what kind of capacity needs to be addressed. What work configuration is to be used? Where should the capacity be located? Price will play a part in the revenue line. Technology used affects fixed and variable costs. Method of depreciation is another accounting issue that interacts with the finance-P/OM decision concerning technological investments to be made. The P/OM tie-in with marketing and finance is inescapable.

The domains of cost concerns are

1. P/OM is accountable for variable cost per unit, a function of the technology employed. Production volume and technology used are strongly correlated. P/OM should participate in decisions about both. These responsibilities determine $TVC = (vc)V$.

2. P/OM and finance are mutually involved in major determinants of fixed cost, FC. At the root of this relationship are the technology options and their affect on work configurations that can be used. Work configurations affect the variable costs and quality that can be achieved.

3. P/OM and marketing have to work out the price per unit (p) that customers are to be charged and the demand volume (V) that should result. These decisions lead to estimates of total revenue (TR), total profit (PR), and margin contribution, which is $(p - vc)V$.

10-8 BREAKEVEN CHART CONSTRUCTION

Breakeven charts were developed in the 1930s by Walter Rautenstrauch, an industrial engineer and professor at Columbia University.[5] Breakeven analysis (BEA) has become one of the most fundamental models of P/OM, providing important information for capacity decisions. Figure 10-14 illustrates the basic chart for one product and a given period of time.

Breakeven analysis can be done in either mathematical terms or in graphical form. To understand the breakeven approach to capacity planning, it may be easier to start with the graphical approach. Then the equivalent mathematical formulation will be developed.

10-8a Three Breakeven Lines

Line 1's fixed costs (*FC*) are derived in terms of a specific period of time such as a week, month, or year, which is consistent with the amount of capacity expressed by the *x*-axis. Fixed charges do not change as a function of increased volume or increased capacity utilization. They do change as a function of the time period. Depreciation is greater for three months than for one month, but it may not be three times as great because it depends on the method of depreciation that is used. Straight-line depreciation would be three times greater. Choice among depreciation methods often reflects tax regulations. It should also reflect the amount of resource that is "used up" and, in that regard, capacity decision makers need to consider applying activity-based costing (ABC).

Line 2 in Figure 10-14 is the total cost line where total cost ($TC = FC + TVC$) is the sum of fixed and total variable costs. *TC* is a function that increases linearly as produc-

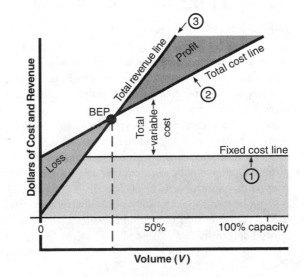

FIGURE 10-14
Linear Breakeven Chart

The ordinate (*y*-axis) is dimensioned in dollars of fixed cost for line (1), total costs for line (2), and dollars of revenue for line (3). The abscissa (*x*-axis) of the chart represents supply volume in units or the percent of capacity utilized for a given period of time. The *x*-axis terminates at 100 percent of capacity. This can be translated into whatever volume of units is equivalent at 100 percent for the given period of time.

tion volume gets larger. Total variable costs do not begin at the zero level. They are added to fixed costs, which are usually assumed to be the same at all volumes, even at zero production level. Vertical distances in the triangular area lying between the fixed cost line and the total cost line measure the variable costs (*vc*'s).

If overtime is needed, then the total cost line starts to curve up faster. This is illustrated in Figure 10-15, which serves to show that breakeven models can be designed for nonlinear systems.

Depreciation (normally treated as a fixed cost) should be added to the total variable cost, $TVC = (vc)V$, if it can be calculated as a function of machine utilization and wear. Reduction in the machine's life is directly attributable to having made the part. Taxes that are levied on the basis of units produced or revenue obtained also would be appropriate to add to the variable cost.

Line 3 in Figure 10-14 is the total revenue line, $TR = (p)V$. It is a linear function that increases with greater production volume when operating at a low enough share of the total market that free competition can adequately describe the situation. Companies with large market shares often experience diminishing effectiveness with advertising and promotions.

The saturation effect may lead to price discounts and decelerating revenues with increasing volume. This effect is illustrated in Figure 10-15, which demonstrates that breakeven models can be designed for nonlinear systems.

10-8b Profit, Loss, and Breakeven

In Figure 10-14, both profit and loss are shown. The lower-shaded area between the total cost line (2) and the total revenue line (3) represents loss to the company. Loss occurs to the left of the **breakeven point (BEP).** The upper-shaded area between the same lines represents profit to the company. Profit occurs to the right of the breakeven point. Because it is a linear system, maximum loss begins at the left side of the diagram. With growth of output volume, the loss decreases until it reaches zero at the *BEP*. Then profit starts and it increases linearly throughout the range of positive profits until maximum profit is achieved at 100 percent of capacity.

Figure 10-15 shows a nonlinear breakeven chart where there are two breakeven points. Operating at capacities that fall between the two *BEPs* is profitable. Using capacities to the right or left of the two *BEPs* results in losses. It also is noteworthy that there is an indicated capacity that will produce the maximum profit. The graphic model can be used to determine this optimal capacity if the real shapes of the cost and revenue curves can be determined.

Breakeven point (BEP): The sales volume point at which total costs exactly equal revenues. Profit is zero. Then, as sales volume increases, profit > 0.

FIGURE 10-16
The Profit and Loss
Breakeven Chart

The definition of the *BEP* is that volume (or percent of capacity) at which there is no profit and no loss. Literally, it is the point at which the total costs of doing business exactly balance the revenues, leading to the name "breakeven." This is

$$TR - TC = 0 = \text{profit}$$

The amount of loss is decreasing and cost recovery is improving as volume increases up to the breakeven point. At breakeven, cost recovery is completed. The *BEP* occurs at a specific volume of production (in units) or a given percent utilization of plant capacity. The values of *BEP* are critical for the diagnosis of healthy production systems. The concept is equally applicable to manufacturing and services, and it always applies to a specific period of time.

10-9 ANALYSIS OF THE LINEAR BREAKEVEN MODEL

Figure 10-14 has been redrawn in Figure 10-16 so that the y-axis becomes profit and loss. This is accomplished by rotating the total cost line to be parallel with the x-axis.

The **slope** of the line in Figure 10-16 reflects the rate at which profit increases as additional units of capacity are sold. Above breakeven, it means making profit faster but below breakeven it means creating losses faster. Because companies expect to operate above breakeven, the larger slope is preferred. However, during the years 2001 and 2002 there were a great number of dot.com failures because these companies could not get above the breakeven point and their *burn rate* of investors' money was too fast to support over a long planning horizon.

Next, consider the position of the *BEP*. If it moves to the right because of changes in the costs and revenues, then the organization must operate at a higher level of capacity before it starts to make a profit. Conversely, by reducing the breakeven point, profit can be made at lower volumes. Because companies want to operate above breakeven, lower *BEPs* are preferred.

Figure 10-17 shows two profit-loss lines marked A and B where A and B are labels associated with a specific (and unique) process alternative.

Alternative A has a lower *BEP* than alternative B. This makes A more desirable than B with respect to the position of the *BEP*. On the other hand, B generates more profit once the point V* has been reached.

At the demand volume represented by point V*, both alternatives yield equal profit. V* is the point of equivalent profit for alternatives A and B. If greater demand than V* can be generated, alternative B is preferred. If V* cannot be achieved, then choose alternative A. Figure 10-18 represents the four different situations that can arise in a two-by-two matrix.

Slope: Slope of the profit line before and after breakeven determines how fast loss and gain occur when demand falls below or rises above the BEP.

FIGURE 10-17
Profit and Loss as a Function of Volume of Production (*or Percent of Capacity*); the Profit and Loss Are Applied to Alternative Work Configurations, A and B.

Two of the cells lead to clear-cut decisions. An alternative that has a lower *BEP* and higher profit-rate slope is the winner. An alternative that has a higher *BEP* and a lower profit-rate slope is rejected. An alternative that has a lower *BEP* and a higher profit-rate slope is accepted. The two other cells are ambiguous situations requiring a forecast of the expected demand volume.

If the volume forecast is above the breakeven point (*BEP*) of the two alternatives (see V* in Figure 10-17), then choose alternative B, which has the highest slope-profit rate. If the volume forecast is below *BEP* = V* (in Figure 10-17), then choose alternative A. Below *BEP* = V* alternative A returns the greatest profit and also, as the volume drops further, A produces the least loss because it has the smallest slope.

Other combinations can occur. The forecast can span the volumes that fall above and below *BEP* = V*. Then, the procedure is to determine the expected profit by combining the profit and loss function with the probability distribution of demand using a decision matrix. The decision matrix approach is shown in the supplement to Chapter 10.

10-9a Linear Breakeven Equations

The math equivalent for the graphic breakeven chart is useful. The symbols of the equations have been presented previously and they are repeated here. The equations can be written in terms of the output volume (V), or percent of capacity used. This percentage is measured by

$$\% \ Capacity = (100) * \frac{V_{actual}}{V_{maximum}}$$

The percent of capacity measure is used with the flow shop because it is designed with a known maximum capacity rating. Capital-intensive industries also relate their performance to the percent of capacity used. On the other hand, labor-intensive industries (such as check processing) are more likely to use measures of production volume than percent of capacity.

FIGURE 10-18
Four Options for Choosing Among Alternatives Considering the *BEP* and the Profit Rate

		Breakeven Point	
		High	**Low**
Profit Rate (slope)	**High**	Use forecast	Accept alternative
	Low	Reject alternative	Use forecast

TR = total revenue per time period T
p = price per unit
V = number of units made and sold in time period T
FC = fixed costs per period T
vc = variable costs per unit of production
TVC = total variable costs = $(vc)V$
TC = total costs per period T = $FC + TVC$
TPR = total profit per period T

Total revenue for period T is

$$TR = (p)V$$

Total cost for period T is

$$TC = FC + (vc)V$$

Total profit for the interval T is (in terms of volume):

$$TPR = TR - TC = (p)V - FC - (vc)V = (p - vc)V - FC \qquad \text{(Equation 10-1)}$$

Breakeven point (V_{BEP}) is calculated by setting profit equal to zero, thus: $TPR = 0$. Then, Equation 10-1 becomes

$$(p - vc)V_{BEP} = FC$$

and

$$V_{BEP} = \frac{FC}{(p - vc)} \qquad \text{(Equation 10-2)}$$

10-9b Breakeven Capacity Related to Work Configurations

The fixed costs and capacities of flow shops are much higher than the fixed costs and capacities of job shops. General-purpose equipment (GPE) used in job shops is designed for high variety in low-capacity volumes. Special-purpose equipment (SPE) characteristic of the flow shop is designed for low variety in high-capacity volumes. Even the movement of materials between equipment is mechanized for the flow shop, whereas it is done mostly by hand in job shops.

In trade for the higher fixed costs of the flow shop, P/OM expects to obtain lower variable costs. On the other hand, the manager of the job shop does whatever is possible to keep high-variable costs under control. If there is sufficient stable demand to warrant investment in flow shop capacity, and if technology exists to deliver low-variable costs at the required quality levels, production and operations managers will select parts of the process for flow shop design.

Dialogue should be initiated by P/OM with marketing to investigate the possibility of accumulating sufficient stable demand if it does not currently exist. Modular production abilities allow P/OM to assist in achieving the demand levels that are appropriate for flow shop capacities.

Flexible-purpose equipment (FPE) is the third category of process capacity to consider. The fixed costs of flexible manufacturing systems (FMS), flexible processing systems (FPS), and flexible office systems (FOS) are even higher than those of the flow shop. Because flexible, or adaptive, automation can be operated remotely 24/7 (24 hours a day, 7 days a week), with time out for maintenance, the high fixed costs can be amortized across a broad product line.

It is necessary to have planned well ahead for the proper use of *FPSs*. The high fixed costs require that multishift production be used to increase the volumetric capacity of the system. This allows the *BEP* as a percent of capacity to occur at a reasonably low point, whereas single-shift production will underutilize the FPS equipment, and that can prove costly and ineffective.

With limited use of flexible technology, meaning that it plays a small role in plant processes, then the problem of underutilization is minimal. However, when the overall technology of the process is FPE, what is required is careful predesign of the use of the potential capacity to produce a broad mix of products that have strong market appeal. Large investments in flexibility demand great capacity planning.

10-9c Capacity and Margin Contribution

Breakeven analysis provides important parameters for evaluating capacity decisions. The critical rate of return on capacity is based on the slope of the profit line. The equally critical *BEP* is determined by the ratio of fixed costs to the per unit margin contribution which is equal to $(p - vc)$.

That is

$$(p - vc)V_{BEP} = FC$$

which means that total margin contribution at breakeven completely recovers the fixed costs and no more. In general, total margin contribution is equal to $(p - vc)V_{actual}$.

Japanese industry specialized in flow shop capacity following the MacArthur initiative to rebuild the Japanese economy after World War II. This concentration on flow shops challenged the Japanese export industries to amass the necessary demand levels to support the cost advantages gained from great production capacities. They met the challenge, at first by specializing in products with low prices and high reliability. Later, having penetrated the markets, they went upscale, still mastering new approaches to high-capacity production.

10-10 CAPACITY AND LINEAR PROGRAMMING

Linear programming (LP): Mathematical modeling technique employed by P/OM to achieve optimal use of resources.

Job shop capacity can be mismanaged. The mixture of jobs on different machines can block access by other jobs that would enhance margin contribution. **Linear programming (LP)** is a modeling technique used by OM to achieve optimal use of resources. LP shows that it is often not optimal to allow low margin products to block capacity that could be used by higher margin products. Sometimes, the optimal product mix does not fully utilize capacity because of this effect.

It is useful to demonstrate the point LP makes about unused capacity. Table 10-2 gives the production capacities of two departments (D1 and D2), which can make different amounts of two products, V and W. Also shown is the profit per unit for each product.

Table 10-3 shows various combinations of products V and W that can be made under the constraints of Table 10-2. It also shows the total profit for the day based on the computing formula $2V + 3W$. Unused departmental capacity is called **slack.** The computation of slack is given in Table 10-3.

Slack: Unused department capacity.

Slack is calculated—for each department—as follows:

$$Capacity\ used = V/V_{capacity} + W/W_{capacity}$$

(Note that $V_{capacity}$ and $W_{capacity}$ are given in Table 10-2 for each department.)

TABLE 10-2	**Product**	$V_{capacity}$	$W_{capacity}$
Production Capacities of Two Departments	Department 1—Forge	10.0 units per day	20.0 units per day
	Department 2—Heat treat	12.0 units per day	12.5 units per day
	Profit	$2 per unit	$3 per unit

Plan	V	W	D1 Slack	D2 Slack	Profit
1	5	5	25.00%	18.33%	$25.00
2	6	5	15.00%	10.00%	$27.00
3	7	5	5.00%	1.67%	$29.00
4	7.83	4.35	0.00%	0.00%	$32.20
5	5	7	15.00%	0.58%	$31.00
6	0	12.5	37.50%	0.00%	$37.50
7	8	4	0.00%	1.33%	$28.00

TABLE 10-3

Trial and Error Computation for Seven LP Solutions

$Slack = capacity\ unused = 1 - V/V_{capacity} - W/W_{capacity}$ for each department

To illustrate: For Plan 1

Department 1 capacity used: $5/10 + 5/20 = 3/4$
Department 1 slack: $1 - 3/4 = 1/4$
Department 2 capacity used: $5/12 + 5/12.5 = 0.81667$
Department 2 slack: $1 - 0.81667 = 0.18333$

Linear programming finds the optimal solution without employing trial and error, the method used to create Table 10-3. The trial and error method was not aimless or random, however; it was based on learning in which way improvement lies and then moving in that direction.

The important conclusion is that the maximum profit in Table 10-3 is achieved with some unused capacity for Department 1. This is Plan 6, which makes zero units of V and puts all of its capacity into the higher margin product, W. All of D2's capacity is used up, which means that nothing else can be made.

It is possible to prove graphically that this is the maximum profit solution; however, the LP method finds the optimal result automatically by efficiently finding the point of maximum profit.

Plan 4 has used up all of the capacities of both D1 and D2, but its profit is $32.20, which is $5.30 less than Plan 6 profit. This is 16 percent less profit and all capacity has been depleted. Using Plan 6 means that 3.75 percent of D1's capacity is still available to be employed by the V and W company in other ways or sold off if it cannot be used. Thus, LP ties in with ABC accounting, and with capacity planning overall.

10-11 MODULAR PRODUCTION (MP) AND GROUP TECHNOLOGY (GT)

Goods and services with large markets lend themselves to flow shop production. Those with small markets are not good candidates. Flow shop capacities are too large for jobs that should be run or done in finite lots. With creativity, there are times when a conversion can be made from job shop operations to intermittent and even permanent flow shop status. The transition can take place gradually. Both **modular production (MP)** and **group technology (GT)** provide opportunities to design for capacity (DFC).

It is easier to design high-capacity processes when starting from scratch than when attempting to change the system. Reengineering is the approach to use when wanting to bring about dramatic, instead of continuous, gradual change of an existing system. On the other hand, when starting up a new system, without the clear goal of achieving a flow shop, it is more likely that a job shop will result. There are at least three good reasons for this:

Modular production (MP): The principle of modularity is to design and produce the minimum number of parts that can be combined in the maximum number of ways to offer the greatest number of different products or services.

Group technology (GT): Processes that specialize in *families* of similar parts and/or activities.

1. There is a strong job shop tradition in the United States and Europe. It is based upon technology that preceded computer-controlled equipment and upon entrepreneurial endeavors of small- and medium-sized businesses. It also is based upon the kind of markets that characterized the 1950s and 1960s. They were smaller than national and international markets are today, and not sufficient to support high-volume processes.

2. It is easier to settle for a job shop that offers good profits than to persevere for a flow shop that has potential for even more profits, but with much more setup work and risk.

3. Some goods and many services cannot be produced by a flow shop. Artists' work is created in the freedom of the custom shop. Personal services require attention to details that, at least on the face of it, defy flow shop capacities.

In spite of these beliefs, opportunities often exist that permit aggregation of demand to flow shop proportions even though the markets of the products are relatively small. Modular product and process design presents one such opportunity.

This means specialization in the production of particular parts or in specific sequences of activities for services and programming strings of code, which can then be included as components of more than one product or service. The roots of such efforts exist in the well-developed concept of standard parts. Consider the chaos if screw threads were arbitrary and lightbulbs could have hundreds of different sockets. As it is, there are more than enough varieties of both.

10-11a Modular Production (MP)

The reason for wanting to achieve such commonality is that one part, operation, or activity, if used in several products or services, can accumulate sufficient demand volume to warrant investing in flow shop capacities.

The **principle of modularity** is to design, develop, and produce the minimum number of parts (or operations) that can be combined in the maximum number of ways to offer the greatest number of products or services.

Table 10-4 illustrates the modularity of N parts named (PA_i), $i = 1, 2, ..., N$.

These N parts are used in M products named (PR_j), $j = 1, 2, ..., M$.

Principle of modularity: See Modular production (MP).

TABLE 10-4

Specification of Parts Used in Products

Variety of Parts (PA_i)								
	PR_1	PR_2	PR_3	PR_4	...	PR_j	...	PR_M
PA_1	1	0	1	1	...	0	...	0
PA_2	0	1	1	2	...	0	...	0
PA_3	0	0	0	0	...	1	...	0
PA_4	0	1	1	0	...	0	...	0
.	.	.	.	.	...	.	...	.
.	.	.	.	.	...	.	...	.
PA_i	0	0	1	0	...	2	...	0
.	.	.	.	.	...	.	...	.
.	.	.	.	.	...	.	...	.
PA_N	0	0	0	1	...	1	...	1

Legend: PA_i denotes the part identified by the stock number i.
PR_j denotes the name or stock keeping number of the product.
All $_j$ varieties are listed in the finished goods catalog.

As shown in the *j*-column of the matrix, the product *j* assembly requires one unit of part 3, two units of part *i*, and one unit of part *N*. The sequence of assembly is not indicated.

PA_N denotes the last part listed in Table 10-4.

PR_M denotes the last product name listed in Table 10-4. It is a product using one unit of part PA_N.

With *N* different kinds of parts, a total of *M* different product configurations can be offered to customers. Some of these products require several units of a single part. For instance, PR_4 requires two units of PA_2, and PR_j requires two units of PA_i.

The maximum possible variety, which is the maximum value of *M* that can be obtained with *N* different parts, may be very large. This is especially so when there are different possible combinations of the parts and varying numbers of them in combination. The general objective is to have *M* as large as possible and *N* as small as possible.

This is equivalent to saying that the general objective is to have as many products as possible made with the smallest possible number of parts. A useful measure of the effective degree of modular design might be the ratio of the number of products (columns) that can be generated from a given number of parts (rows); that is, the objective: *MAX (M/N)*.

Many of the possible combinations cannot exist and would have no appeal as a product choice for customers. It is up to the team to find the right parts for modular specialization. Computers epitomize the modular concept. Customers can specify many different computers that are made of components that mix and match with ease. Companies specialize in a relatively few computer parts that make a relatively large number of computer products. The parts are made by flow shops with enormous capacities. This accounts for the ever lower price of computers.

Modularity applies to services and projects. When certain activities are used repeatedly in some service function, the steps can be standardized and the process to deal with them can be serialized for the flow shop or even automation. The ATMs used by banks provide a fine illustration of a service that has been designed to provide high-capacity, lower-cost equivalents of teller service.

Long ago it was recognized that parts of computer programs appear over and over. They were standardized and are regularly inserted as modules into computer programs by information systems programmers. Rewriting lines of code is like reinventing the wheel. Modular constructed housing can produce many versions of homes using the same basic parts. Furniture designers are masters of modular sections. Project managers have developed modular techniques to cut the costs of portions of what otherwise is a unique venture. Building developers thrive on separating what is unique about each structure from what is a repetitive activity.

Successful modular design increases demand, promoting increased capacity, allowing flow shop economies to be utilized. The kind of matrix shown in Table 10-4 must have been in the minds of the inventors of Lego and the earlier Erector sets. Modularity helps to assemble the flow shop by creating production systems that specialize in parts instead of products. Process planning that assists in the part orientation calls upon group technology.

10-11b Group Technology (GT Families)

Group technology deals with processes that specialize in families of similar parts and/or activities. It is technologically feasible to develop efficient flow shops that can make gears of similar design, but different size. The same applies to cams, springs, and so on. The changeover routines to go from one size gear to another are fast and inexpensive.

GT parts have similar design, and essentially the same production operations can be used to make them. There is a functional similarity to FMS but the variety level is far more simple. The technology required assures minimum transition costs as the production line shifts from one variant to another.

A company using group technology to improve the profit margin of its line of products or services might become so efficient in this specialized family of operations that it

FIGURE 10-19
Average Unit Costs Decrease with Increasing Experience

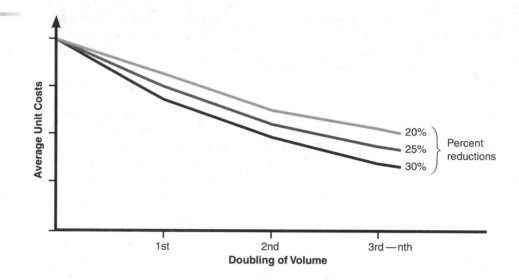

could gradually shift its emphasis from products to parts. Eventually, it would become a parts subcontractor to industry and supply institutions with the output of its most efficient operations. In Best Practice cases, divisions of companies achieve this status.

10-12 LEARNING INCREASES CAPACITY

Economic theory indicates that product can be delivered at lower unit costs when the output volume increases. This is well-known as "economies of scale." The Boston Consulting Group (BCG) confirmed this effect with many empirical studies of a wide variety of industries.[6]

Figure 10-19 shows some general shapes for this function where the decrease varies between 20 and 30 percent with each doubling of volume.

BCG calls this the **experience curve.** Generally, the rate of decrease in per unit costs is between 20 percent and 30 percent for each doubling of volume. Volume is a surrogate for experience and consequent learning. After doubling of volume has occurred several times, most of the payoff from learning will have been obtained. Reductions in average unit costs have to get smaller and smaller. Thus, price reduction potentials disappear as the market matures.

As the output volume gets larger, many factors operate to make the process more efficient. Workers learn their jobs better. It takes less time to do the jobs. More work gets turned out in a period of time, one of the main factors for the decrease in costs. This is equivalent to increasing C, the actual measured capacity. As a reminder:

$$C = T \times E \times U$$

where T = time available, E = efficiency, and U = utilization. There are two ways of accounting for the increase in C.

T becomes a larger number of available hours; because the same amount of work takes less time, more work can be done. Another way is that E becomes greater, even greater than 100 percent. It is just a formula that can be treated in either way as long as the effect is to increase actual capacity.

10-12a The Learning Curve

The learning curve is a model for individuals or groups. It describes how repeated practice decreases the time required to do the job. Thus, the learning curve captures the benefit of repetition and experience in quantitative terms for an employee or groups doing the same job routinely.

> **Experience curve:** Rate of decrease in per unit costs is between 20 and 30 percent for each doubling of production output volume.

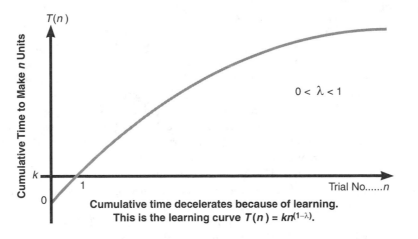

FIGURE 10-20
Learning Curve
Cumulative Time

Cumulative Time to Make *n* Units

$T(n)$

$0 < \lambda < 1$

k

1

Trial No......*n*

0

Cumulative time decelerates because of learning.
This is the learning curve $T(n) = kn^{(1-\lambda)}$.

Two related learning curves are shown in Figures 10-20 and 10-21. They are explained here with their respective quantitative models.

The equation $T(n) = kn^{(1-\lambda)}$ is read as follows:

$T(n)$ = cumulative time to make n consecutive units
k = time required to make the first unit (called $n = 1$); k is a constant characteristic of the product
n = the number of units to be made
λ = the learning coefficient, $0 < \lambda < 1$

When $\lambda = 0$, the cumulative time $T(n) = kn^1 = kn$. Thus, $T(n)$ increases linearly at the rate (kn), and there is no learning effect because each unit requires the same amount of production time, which is k.

When $\lambda = 1$, $T(n) = kn^0 = k$, which means that the job has been learned so well that after the first time, the rest of the units are made (literally) in no time at all. $\lambda = 1$, is unrealistic and a goal never to be achieved.

As $\lambda \rightarrow 1$, successive units take less time. The curve of Figure 10-20 shows decelerating improvement in learning. The cumulative time to make a unit never approaches a limit (as an asymptote). The value of λ reflects the learning coefficient. The larger that lambda is, the greater the learning rate.

Another useful form of the learning model is shown in Figure 10-21 where the average time to make a unit is calculated by dividing the cumulative time $T(n)$ by n.

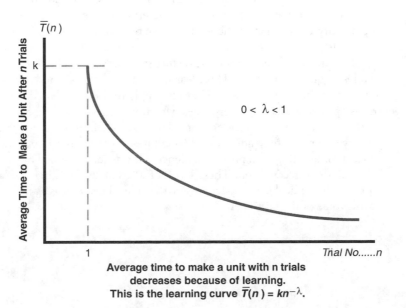

FIGURE 10-21
Learning Curve
Average Time

Average Time to Make a Unit After *n* Trials

$\overline{T}(n)$

k

$0 < \lambda < 1$

1

Trial No......*n*

Average time to make a unit with n trials
decreases because of learning.
This is the learning curve $\overline{T}(n) = kn^{-\lambda}$.

$$\overline{T}(n) = \frac{T(n)}{n} = kn^{-\lambda}$$

k, n, and λ are the same as before.

When $\lambda = 0$, $\overline{T}(n) = k$, which is the condition where no learning takes place. Every time the job is done, it takes the same k time units. When $\lambda = 1$, an unrealistic limit is reached whereby the average time (k/n) is reduced geometrically with each trial. Values of λ between 0 and 1 can yield reasonable decreases in the average time to do a job.

With continued practice, learning reaches a plateau where the output rate is relatively constant. When the employee takes a break, there may be some relearning needed. Often it is minimal. The effect becomes greater when the time between stopping and starting is longer. Therefore, for lunch breaks it might not be noticeable. After returning from a lengthy vacation, it is apt to be strongest.

The learning curve has been around a long time.[7] It has not proved directly useful, but it has provided conceptual insight into the problems associated with people doing small lots of different kinds of work. More time is spent learning and getting up to speed than producing effectively. Learning time can diminish productive capacity in the job shop, but good process management can alleviate the damage.

The learning effect for workers in flow shops is pronounced because of the high degree of repetition. There is a reverse effect with productive output declining because of monotony. The learning curve effect on production line start-up times, and the reverse effect, should be considered when designs for manufacturing (DFM) are prepared. New flexible technology provides opportunity for better productivity and quality for small lots.

Costing new products should take learning into account by pricing jobs at the average productivity rate for a reasonably large number n. Time observations for work standards do not begin until after workers' times stabilize at some plateau level.

10-12b Service Learning

In labor-intensive situations, learning curve concepts can be put to good use. How many repetitions does it take to learn a job? How do people differ in catching on? Does a master teacher help? How do the trainees of different trainers perform? What aspects of training make a difference in how quickly and how well experience is converted into improved performance? Who says there is only one plateau? There are better learning theories that allow for multiple plateaus or a succession of plateaus,[8] where learning starts again after a stable interval of continued practice on a lower plateau.

The learning curve's relationship to providing quality services efficiently should be highlighted. Productivity of service jobs has been a recognized problem that is often associated with the lower salaries that characterize services. In the same sense, there is an opportunity to systematize the learning function for the attainment of excellence in service quality.

The idea would be to raise the quality standards after a job has successfully plateaued at a lesser quality standard. Thus, learning curve plateaus could relate productivity with levels of quality improvement. They also apply to the time-based management system of stair-step reductions in process times, which was effectively employed by Japanese automotive manufacturers to lower costs. These kinds of efforts must be fully supported by employees or else they are doomed to failure. On the other hand, there would be great support for learning to improve excellence if it was accompanied by financial bonuses and other kinds of recognition. These kinds of ideas about learning and work standards are particularly applicable to services where they have been consistently underutilized in spite of the voice of the customer.

10-13 CAPACITY AND THE SYSTEMS APPROACH

Capacity decisions are among the most crucial P/OM responsibilities. They set in motion scenarios for start-up and growth that are difficult to alter, unless they have been planned to be dynamic. Following the curve means forecasting diligently and always playing catch-up. This is characteristic of the way some companies invest with the introduction of new products. The policy to lead the curve requires that OM work with marketing to create specific demand levels. The capacity to satisfy that demand has been designed and built ahead of time. This is characteristic of companies that prefer to accept risk in order to be the market share leader.

Unused capacity is to be avoided, but some of it may be inevitable. It is not possible to forecast perfectly, or feasible to plan perfectly. Teamwork is no guarantee of being able to create exactly the demand for which capacity has been prepared. The idea is to perform as well as possible while continuously improving.

Capacity can be installed all at once, or it can be gradually increased. The incremental approach entails low risk, but it can foul up meeting market demands, produce higher unit costs, and worst of all, lead to poor and inconsistent quality of product. The capacity decision must have financial support, market rationalization, and OM knowledge of how to convert the strategic plan into production-transformation capacity to be installed.

The resulting too much or too little of this or that leads to downsizing, which is demoralizing and costly. Alternatively, the last minute realization of the need for greater capacity is fraught with difficulties and buys the additional volume at a higher price than would have been incurred from original planning stages. Strategic plans shared by finance, marketing, and OM are the foundation for better capacity decisions, which with team learning can get better all the time.

Safety and security are crucial P/OM responsibilities. Signage requiring "hard hats and safety boots" may not provide sufficient protection. The fence must be secure (especially from climbing children) and alarms to signal forced entry may be necessary. In general, where there is danger in the environment, machines are better exposed to it than people.

SUMMARY

This chapter begins with the definition of capacity. The determination of capacity is one of the most important OM responsibilities. Capacity to meet peak and off-peak loads is discussed. The storage of capacity is an important topic. Services are especially affected by the difficulties of storing service capacity. It is shown how backordering augments service and manufacturing capacity.

Capacity requirements planning (CRP) is introduced. Adding and subtracting capacity through upscaling and downsizing are treated. Bottlenecks are the constraints on supply capacity. Understanding how to manage bottlenecks is an OM necessity. In the same way, delay creates oscillations of supply, which deteriorate productive performance in the supply chain. This leads to discussion of contingency planning for capacity crises and a supply chain game or simulation called the Better Beer Company.

In turn, cost drivers and forecasting for capacity planning are introduced, leading to the use of the breakeven model for capacity planning. It is shown to be a powerful planning tool that epitomizes the systems viewpoint by requiring interfunctional cooperation. Breakeven capacity is related to work configurations, margin contribution, and/or profitability.

Another significant interfunctional capacity planning model that is introduced is linear programming. It is usually called by its acronym (LP). Modular production (MP) and group technology (GT) both represent a focus on commonality of parts within product groups. Both approaches must be backed up by datasets that describe the variables of commonality. This permits the firm to add capacity creatively through design concepts. This proactive effort for design coherence and the efficient use of facilities can be called design for capacity (DFC).

The chapter concludes with a discussion of how learning increases capacity. The learning curve is introduced and applied to service learning. The relationship of capacity planning to systems thinking is reiterated. The chapter supplement combines forecasting, decision making, and breakeven analysis.

Two Spotlight feature boxes conclude this chapter. These boxes illustrate real applications of the material in the chapter. See Spotlight 10-1: Starbuck's and Spotlight 10-2: O.O.D.A.

KEY TERMS

Actual capacity
Breakeven
Breakeven point (BEP)
Capacity
Capacity requirements planning (CRP)
Decision model
Demand
Experience curve

Fixed costs (FC)
Group technology (GT)
Learning curve
Linear programming (LP)
Modular production (MP)
OPT
Principle of modularity
Slack

Slope
Supply chain
Total costs = TC = FC + TVC
Total revenue = TR = (p)V
Total variable costs = TVC = (vc)V
Variable costs per unit = vc
V-A-T

REVIEW QUESTIONS

1. Define capacity. Explain how capacity is measured. Why is it important?

2. Explain what is meant by the statement that maximum containment is a type of capacity measure that can have special meaning for services.

3. What motivated a company to build excessive petroleum storage facilities early in 1973? If events had worked out differently, would the storage facilities have been excessive?

4. Explain why maximum output is only one measure of capacity.

5. What is the relationship of maximum output to peak demand?

6. Give an example of a situation where what some might call excessive inventories turned out to be a blessing in disguise.

7. Give an example of constraints in capacity proving to be a blessing in disguise.

8. Should an airline have enough operators and trunk lines to prevent any calling customers from having to wait when they are responding to a 1-day offer of half-fare travel rates?

9. List six types of variable costs.

10. List six types of fixed costs.

11. To what extent are accounting data likely to be available in manufacturing organizations with respect to fixed and variable costs that are used in breakeven analysis?

12. To what extent are accounting data likely to be available in service organizations with respect to fixed and variable costs that are used in breakeven analysis?

13. To what extent are accounting data likely to be available in government organizations with respect to fixed and variable costs that are used in breakeven analysis?

14. What do FC and TVC = vc(V) and TC = FC + TVC have to do with the employment of breakeven analysis?

15. What is overhead cost or burden?

16. How should overhead be treated as an important component of breakeven analysis (BEA)?

17. Relate activity-based cost (ABC) systems to BEA.

18. Regarding airline capacity, air shuttles provide continuous, as-filled capacity, instead of scheduled flights. How does this concept increase capacity by innovative use of equipment?

19. What is capacity requirements planning (CRP)?

20. How do bottlenecks affect capacity and what can be done about them?

21. What is modular production (MP) and how is it a form of design for capacity (DFC)?

22. What is group technology (GT) and how is it a form of design for capacity (DFC)?

23. What method is appropriate for determining the optimal product mix? What data are needed to accomplish this goal?

24. The capacity planning problem requires good estimates of the variable costs for different work configurations and different volumes of supply. Explain.

25. What form of capacity control is downsizing? What are its goals and disadvantages?

26. Delay in the supply chain wreaks havoc. Why is this true?

27. Discuss the following observation: The breakeven chart can represent only one product at a time, whereas most companies produce a product mix consisting of a number of different items or services that must share resources, including capital and management time.

28. Describe situations in which nonlinear analysis might be required for the breakeven chart.

PROBLEMS SECTION

1. The peak load for Swimsuits Inc. (SWIM), a manufacturer of bathing suits, occurs in March and April when the cutters and sewers occupy every square foot in the plant. This determines the maximum output capacity of the company, which is 250 suits per hour. SWIM works a 10-hour day, six days a week. Adding shift time is considered impossible. Therefore, it has been suggested that floor space be expanded by renting an adjoining loft for $1,200 per week. This would increase maximum output capacity by 12 percent. The sales manager believes that SWIM could sell 18,000 bathing suits per week during the 10-week season, at a profit of $1.00 per suit based on existing costs of materials and labor. During the summer, the SWIM plant is less than 50 percent utilized.

   Explain why the loft should or should not be rented. Are there any other capacity-based observations to be considered?

2. The new manager of the electric utility notes that recent summers have been warmer than average. Consequently, for next year she revises upward the probability that actual demand will exceed average demand; this is estimated to occur 8 percent of the year or roughly 29 summer days. She estimates that each power incident can cost far less than her predecessor had spent. Using different management techniques to deal with brownouts, she hopes to reduce the cost per incident to $10,000. Because the previous manager had not invested in additional capacity to cover maximum peak-load requirements, that option is still available. She faces the prospect that it will cost an extra $3,000,000 to increase capacity from average to peak. This amount is spread out over 10 years, or $300,000 per year.

   Should peak-load capacity be installed?

3. The classical formula for actual measured capacity is

   $$C = T \times E \times U$$

   where

   C = actual measured capacity (standard hours)
   T = time available (actual hours)
   E = efficiency
   U = utilization

   If $T = 240$ standard hours, how can the actual capacity be more than that, say 280 standard hours?

4. In Alba, Italy, many famous restaurants rely on having enough truffles for the culinary delights, which customers travel miles to enjoy. Although customers pay a hefty price for the truffle dishes, the export market for truffles has much larger margins. Truffles are found by using pigs that can smell the strong aroma, then digging under the ground to get them. Weather conditions have caused the truffle hunters to stay at home, so a truffle shortage is arising at the distributors' level. There are several regional distributors to whom the truffle hunters sell their findings. What are the constraints on capacity?

   Hint: It would help to draw the supply chain that characterizes this product. Make certain to indicate that the supply chain starts with a scarce resource that has to be found in the woods. It cannot be farmed. Also, at the end of the supply chain there are two competing sources of demand, one domestic and the other international.

   Note how currency fluctuations might affect the shipments of truffles at home and abroad.

5. Company capacity is 1 million units per year for a new food product. The sales force can sell 5 million units over a 5-year period, but only 100,000 in the first year. The breakeven volume is

   $$V_{BEP} = 50,000 \text{ units}$$

   with $p = 3$, $vc = 2$, and $FC = 50,000$. What is the situation? What recommendations do you support?

6. The Global Company has engaged a management consultant to analyze and improve its operations. His major recommendation is to "conveyorize" the production floor. This would represent a sizable investment for Global.

   In order to determine whether or not the idea is feasible, a breakeven analysis will be utilized.

   The situation is as follows: The cost of the conveyor will be $200,000 to be depreciated on a straight-line basis over 10 years. The conveyor will reduce operating costs by $0.25 per unit. Each unit sells for $2.00. The sales manager estimates that, on the basis of previous years, Global can expect a sales volume of 100,000 units. This represents 100 percent utilization of capacity. Current yearly contribution to fixed costs is $100,000. Current vc rate is $0.50 per unit.

   Should Global install this conveyor?

7. Zeta Corporation is considering the advantages of automating a part of its production line. The company's financial statement follows:

Zeta Corporation		
Total sales	$40,000,000	
Direct labor		$12,000,000
Indirect labor		$ 2,000,000
Direct materials		$ 8,000,000
Depreciation		$ 1,000,000
Taxes		$ 500,000
Insurance		$ 400,000
Sales costs		$ 1,500,000
Total expenses	$25,400,000	
Net profit	$14,600,000	

The report is based on the production and sale of 100,000 units. The operations manager believes that an additional investment of $5 million can reduce the variable costs by 30 percent. The same output quantity and qualities would be maintained. Using 5-year straight-line depreciation of $1,000,000 per year, construct a breakeven chart. Based on the breakeven analysis, should Zeta introduce the automation?

8. Referring to the linear programming problem discussed in the text of this chapter, show the calculations required to determine D1 and D2 slack for Plans 2 through 7, which appear in Table 10-3.

9. A product is currently moved on pallets by a forklift truck. Should a conveyor belt be installed to replace the forklifts? The capacity would remain the same, but the cost structure differs. The Zeta Corporation uses a 1-year time period for comparison.

	Option 1 Forklift Truck	Option 2 Install Conveyor
V_{max}	18,000 units per year	18,000 units per year
FC	$10,000 per year	$12,000 per year
vc	$0.50 per unit	$0.45 per unit
p	$2.00 per unit	$2.00 per unit

10. Machine 1 is being challenged by Machine 2, which has greater capacity, lower variable costs, and higher fixed costs but Machine 2 requires a much larger investment. Should the organization buy Machine 1 or Machine 2? The sales department states that demand is larger than supply and that, if they matched demand, they could deliver 6,000 units per quarter. The organization uses a 3-month time period ($T = 3$) for its breakeven analysis.

It could also be $T = 1$ quarter.

	Option 1 Machine 1	Option 2 Machine 2
V_{max}	5,000 units per quarter	10,000 units per quarter
FC	$2,500.00 per quarter	$6,500.00 per quarter
vc	$0.50 per unit	$0.10 per unit
p	$2.00 per unit	$2.00 per unit

11. The learning equation

$$T(n) = kn^{(1-\lambda)}$$

is said to apply to a particular job with the following values:
$k = 3$ minutes to make the first unit, $n = 1$
$n = 25$ units, which is the number of units to be made
$\lambda = 0.5 =$ the learning coefficient
Plot $T(n)$, which equals the cumulative time to make n consecutive units, from 1 to 25.

12. Using the information in Problem 11, plot

$$\overline{T}(n) = \frac{T(n)}{n} = kn^{-\lambda}$$

from $n = 1$ to $n = 25$. k and λ are the same as in Problem 11.

END-OF-CHAPTER QUESTIONS

1. Capacity planning and utilization of existing capacity are PO/M responsibilities. To save page flipping, "the classical formula for actual measured capacity is $C = T \times E \times U$," where C is actual measured capacity in standard hours and T is real-time theoretical capacity available in standard hours. $E =$ efficiency and $U =$ utilization. All but one statement in a. through e. provide appropriate and useful insights about capacity. Which answer is out of line?
   a. Realistic measures of capacity equal theoretical measures of *maximum* capacity, (i.e., $C = T$) when efficiency, E, is equal to 100 percent and utilization, U, is equal to 100 percent.
   b. Utilization, U, is less than 100 percent when demand falls below the theoretical supply capacity, T.
   c. Utilization, U, is less than 100 percent when equipment breakdowns diminish the theoretical supply capacity, T.
   d. Efficiency, E, is less than 100 percent when process components are slowed down by lack of training, defective materials, setups, and changeovers.
   e. For actual measured capacity (i.e., $C = T \times E \times U$) to be greater than T, utilization, U, must be greater than 100 percent, which is not possible.

2. Capacity to produce units of product (throughput) and capacity to store units of product (containment) are related in many important ways for P/OM decision makers. The discussion in parts a. through e. provides many insights. Which of these statements is incorrect?
   a. Market demand can be highly variable, reaching extreme levels at certain times. For example, production processes cannot make enough toys starting in September for Christmas. One solution is to manufacture the toys year round, storing the inventory in warehouses until needed. The capacity of the warehouses must be large enough to hold inventory from January through August.
   b. Warehouses that store the toys will be empty after Christmas. Then, they will begin to fill up again. There will be significant carrying charges for storing inventories of toys.
   c. The inventory carrying costs include the cost of storage space. These costs can be compared with the costs of developing and running a process that can make enough toys starting in September. The output would be shipped to customers starting in September, which could be in line with normal delivery practice.
   d. Service organizations deliver products that are difficult (sometimes impossible) to store. For example, secretarial, educational, and healthcare services cannot be put into inventory. The capacity for throughput in these services must be utilized when they are created. Therefore, overcapacity in service operations is discouraged by the cost factors.
   e. Undercapacity in manufacturing results in lost sales or backorders unless inventory exists to ship to demand. Undercapacity in service systems results in lost orders because services cannot be backordered.

3. There are numerous issues related to capacity planning. These include familiar references to corporate downsizing that followed the implosion of dot.com business, the stock market's decline, and recession. Capacity reduction took on many forms with the most apparent being workforce reduction. With the resurgence of business, and the stock market upturn, another capacity issue emerges which is upsizing (or upscaling) capacity. Return to higher production capacities will not necessarily be accompanied by a growth in workforce size that is symmetrical to the earlier reduction. *Dynamic resizing* (downturn–upturn cycles) can be taken as opportunities to replace worker skills with new technology. The discussion found in a. through e. continues this dialogue. Which one point of discussion is inappropriate?

   a. *The Wall Street Journal* headline states that Alpha Company plans downsizing. It intends to eliminate N people over the next 6 months. The accompanying article does not state that the firm's processes will be downscaled to lower capacity. It is assumed that existing equipment will be maintained but run at lower volumes. After downsizing the workforce, it is not unusual for management to raise capacity by replacing personnel (as possible) with high-productivity equipment.

   b. All resources are part of capacity. That means that people, space, inventory, equipment, parking lots, cafeterias, computer memory, etc., are part of the capacity to produce different things. Capacity changes affect supply to meet demand for products, meals to feed workers, paperwork to support accounts receivable, etc.

   c. There is need to balance capacity across all product lines and staff supportive functions when changes in demand require alteration of supply. The balancing problem exists whether the move is upscale from downsizing or vice versa.

   d. An issue that arises with dynamic resizing is the fact that flow-through capacity may not be evenly distributed. There can be too much capacity in one part of the system and too little capacity in another.

   e. There are two types of bottlenecks associated with production processes. These are fixed and floating bottlenecks. Fixed types constrain capacity and must be removed to increase capacity. The floating type is temporary and not relevant to capacity issues of process resizing.

4. Supply chains are the lifeblood of the organization. Supply chains connect the downstream (raw material sources) with the upstream (fabrication or service facility). Further upstream are consumers fed by retailers who are supplied by distributors. Along the entire chain, every element can become a bottleneck. A truck gets a flat tire and suddenly becomes the system's bottleneck. Four out of five of the answers below are correct. Which is the incorrect assertion?

   a. Bottlenecks cause delays that can substantially deteriorate the performance of the supply chain. Delays throw off the timing of supply chain ordering which results in overstocking and understocking. Both can severely penalize the firm, its suppliers, and its customers.

   b. The beer game is a simulation of "purchasing difficulties" that can arise when a company experiences a temporary, capricious (erratic, unpredictable, whimsical) demand.

That can happen as a result of a competitor's workforce going on strike, a hurricane closing a plant, the decision of the food channel to feature the brand, or a TV personality saying that brand is his or her favorite. Retailers nationally or regionally experience a sudden demand shift. Purchasing decisions try to cope with the question of how temporary is the change in demand levels. The beer game illustrates how hard it is to deal with such effects.

   c. Simulations of supply chain behaviors can only be done with fast computers that have substantial memories. Simulation players develop strategies and input their numbers for order sizes based on computer selection of prior period demands. The scale effect is significant. Small-scale models do not operate in the same way that real-scale systems operate. That is why realistic databases are required to understand the behavior of these delay-sensitive systems.

   d. Lead-time effects are nontrivial in creating large swings in stock on-hand. As the lead time decreases, it is possible to rectify problems faster by placing an order for quick delivery. That accounts for the growth in services of FedEx, UPS, and the U.S. Postal Service's Priority and Express mail.

   e. If retailers can communicate quickly with their distributors, and the distributors with their manufacturers, about increases and decreases in demand that they are experiencing, then rapid adjustments all along the supply chain can be made to compensate for changes. The large-scale fluctuations can be reduced.

5. For linear breakeven analysis, use the data in the table. It has all been verified to be correct. However, one of the conclusions in points a. through e. is incorrect. Which one is wrong?

1	Maximum total volume for the year (V_{max})		1,000 units
2	Fixed costs per year	(FC)	$ 6,000
3	Variable costs per unit	(vc)	$ 6.00
4	Selling price per unit	(p)	$ 22.00
5	Expected operating volume (supply = demand)		650 units
6	Total costs at expected demand		
7	Margin contribution	(p – vc)	
8	Breakeven point volume	(V_{BEP})	
9	Profit at maximum total volume		

   a. Maximum total annual revenue is $22,000. The total variable costs at the expected annual demand of 650 units are $3,900.

   b. The total costs at the expected demand of 650 units are $9,900.

   c. The total profit at the expected demand of 650 units is $4,000.

   d. The breakeven volume is 375 units, which is below the expected demand of 650 units, and this supports the fact that profit will be made.

   e. If the company could operate at 100 percent capacity, the total annual profit would be $10,000.

6. A correction has been made by the forecasting team based on product design revisions. Quality has been changed. This includes the item and its service warranties. The price has been raised to $24 per unit. There is an increase in the variable costs to $14 per unit and a decrease in the fixed costs to $5,000. Expected demand is 500 units. Conclusions based on linear breakeven analysis about the product design revision are listed in points a. through e. One conclusion is incorrect. Which one is wrong?

1	Maximum total volume for the year (V_{max})		1,000 units
2	Fixed costs per year	(FC)	$ 5, 000
3	Variable costs per unit	(vc)	$ 14.00
4	Selling price per unit	(p)	$ 24.00
5	Expected operating volume (supply = demand)		500 units
6	Total costs at expected demand		
7	Margin contribution	(p – vc)	
8	Breakeven point volume	(V_{BEP})	
9	Profit at maximum total volume		

a. Maximum total annual revenue is $24,000. The total variable costs at the expected annual demand of 500 units are $7,000.

b. The total costs at the expected demand of 500 units are $12,000.

c. The total profit at the expected demand of 500 units is zero.

d. The breakeven volume is 500 units, which is at the expected demand of 500 units. No profit will be made.

e. If the company could operate at 100 percent capacity, the total annual profit would be zero.

7. The table summarizes data presented in Problems 5 and 6 for the original design and the revised design. The third column presents data for the new design (Problem 7). Examine the commentaries to these three problems in statements a. through e. One of them is off base. Which one is not acceptable?

Variable	Original Design	Revised Design	New Design
	Problem 5	Problem 6	Problem 7
Price (p)	$22/unit	$24/unit	$22/unit
Fixed costs (FC)	$6,000	$5,000	$4,000
Variable costs (vc)	$6/unit	$14/unit	$10/unit
Margin contribution (p – vc)	$16/unit	$10/unit	$12/unit
Max total variable costs	$6,000	$14,000	$10,000
Total annual costs	$12,000	$19,000	$14,000
(V_{BEP})	375 units	500 units	333 units
Maximum annual profit	$10,000	$5,000	$8,000
Slope	$16/unit	$10/unit	$12/unit

a. Compare the original design and the revised design (Problems 5 and 6) with respect to breakeven points (BEP) and slopes. The original design (Problem 5) possesses revenue and cost attributes that produce a lower BEP (375 versus 500 units) and a better profitability slope ($16 versus $10 per unit of profit per each additional unit sold). Therefore, keep the original design.

b. Compare the original design and the new design (Problems 5 and 7) with respect to breakeven points (BEP) and slopes. The new design (Problem 7) possesses revenue and cost attributes that produce a lower BEP (333 versus 375 units) but the original design has a better profitability slope ($16 versus $12 per unit of profit per each additional unit sold). There is a quandary. To solve this dilemma, it is necessary to determine whether the probabilities of operating above the BEP are greater than the probabilities of operating below the BEP.

c. The application of a decision model is essential when there is a quandary because one alternative has a better breakeven point and the other alternative has a greater profit-loss slope.

d. Compare the revised design and the new design (Problems 6 and 7) with respect to breakeven points (BEP) and slopes. The new design (Problem 7) possesses revenue and cost attributes that produce a lower BEP (333 versus 500 units) and the new design has a better profitability slope ($12 versus $10 per unit of profit per each additional unit sold). There is no quandary. Choose the new design if faced with this choice.

e. To solve the dilemma of choosing between the original design and the new design (Problems 5 and 7), the market manager is asked for the demand forecast for the next year. The results reported by the market forecasters show a strong likelihood that the annual demand will be 400 units. Therefore, it is decided to stay with the original design.

	Demand Volume	Demand Volume	Demand Volume
Original Design	**400 units**	**500 units**	**600 unit**
Total revenue	$8,800	$11,000	$13,200
Total costs	$8,400	$9,000	$9,600
Total profit	$ 400	$ 2,000	$ 3,600
New Design			
Total revenue	$8,800	$11,000	$13,200
Total costs	$8,000	$ 9,000	$10,000
Total profit	$ 800	$ 2,000	$ 3,200

It is useful to note that margin contribution (p – vc) measures the slope of the profit-loss line. Slope and margin contribution are one and the same. The power of the decision model lies in how it combines the breakeven point, the margin contribution rate, and the probability of operating at each level of volume that the company's capacity permits. See Section 10-9 and Supplement 10.

8. Gamma Company has applied linear programming to resolve a production capacity problem. The company has two departments: paint and polish. The option exists to use this capacity on different production combinations of the original design (OD) and the new design (ND). Management has furnished comments and interpretations of these data in a. to e. Which one comment is inappropriate?

Table A

Department Capacities	Original Design (OD)	New Design (ND)
Paint Department	400 units per day	200 units per day
Polish Department	250 units per day	400 units per day
Profit	$10.00 per unit	$12.50 per unit

Table B

Plan	Original Design	New Design	Paint Slack	Polish Slack	Total Profit
1	400 units	0 units	0	NF	NF
2	250 units	0 units	37.5%	0	$2,500
3	0 units	200 units	0	50%	$2,500
4	100 units	100 units	25%	35%	$2,250
5	150 units	100 units	12.5%	15%	$2,750
6	160 units	105 units	92.5%	90.25%	$2,912.50
7	175 units	107 units	97.25%	96.75%	$3,087.50
8	181.8	109.1	0	0	$3,181.75

a. Linear programming is a mathematical method that can find the optimal product mix. Computer programs are able to do this for very large databases. The basic input data for a small problem is shown in Table A. It consists of the capacity of the paint department and the polish department to produce finished product.

b. The profit per unit for each product alternative design is given in Table A. It is essential to know the profit per unit because the product mix will be determined by the production schedule that maximizes profit. Row 1 of Table B states that 400 units of the original design use up all available capacity in the paint department, i.e., slack is zero. Row 1 also states that 400 units of the original design are not feasible (slack = NF) because there is insufficient capacity to turn out 400 units in the polish department.

c. Table B is based on cut-and-try efforts. It can be shown that row 8 is the product mix that will maximize profit at $3181.75. Row 8 indicates that with 181.8 units per day of the original design and 109.1 units per day of the new design, that the slack (available capacity) is zero in both the paint department and the polish department. This means that all available capacity is used up for the max profit solution.

e. The maximum profit solution will always use up all available capacity. There is no waste and all resources are directed toward making money.

f. Rows 4, 5, 6, and 7 in Table B show how the optimal solution is being gradually approached. The number of units to be made is increasing as the slack in both departments is decreasing and the total daily profit is increasing.

9. Gamma Company's competitor, Omicron, is introducing modular production (MP) as a means of improving the company's use of production capacities. Points a. through e. are management's reflections on how modular production can improve performance. One of these reflections is not correct. Which one of the statements is not correct?

a. Modular production and group technology (GT) are both examples of designing for capacity (DFC). Group technology should be included in Omicron's initiative to expand capacity by creative product and process design.

b. One of the advantages of modular production is that the same module (or a GT family member) can be used in two or more products. This is equivalent to raising the demand level for that part. Higher demand moves production toward flow shop work configurations with cost reductions and quality improvements.

c. In a shop where many different products are made, if each uses different sizes of screws, nuts, and bolts, the inventory problem is more complicated than if these types of fasteners are standardized as much as possible. This illustrates in a simple form the principle behind MP.

d. The principle of modularity is design, develop, and produce the minimum number of parts (or operations) that can be combined in the maximum number of ways to offer the greatest number of products or services. The principle embodies market wisdom, process ingenuity, and design specialization advantages.

e. Methods of group technology are not related to part names or part numbering systems. The same observation applies to modular production parts. Principles of modularity and group technology are based on theories of production that transcend naming and numbering schemes used for identification.

10. Learning how to do a better job can include improvements in productivity. This could mean more units in a period of time and at a lower per unit cost. Learning can provide greater quality without a cost increase. Learning has resulted in innovations so that new types of units become available. Marketing relishes the opportunity to expand product variety without increasing costs or decreasing productivity. Learning theory does not directly address this breadth of opportunities. Instead, it concentrates on productivity. The management discussion from a. to e. runs through some of the applications of learning theory to operational efficiency. All but one of the observed points is appropriate. Identify the inappropriate commentary.

a. Pilot plants are used for learning how to produce a new physical product. Focus groups in market research are also learning environments. The point is to know as much as possible about the system so simulations are used for discovery.

b. Classical learning curve theory indicates that the average time to do a job can decrease exponentially with job repetitions. The acceleration rate is embodied in the learning coefficient, l. When l = 0, there is no learning. Each unit requires the same amount of time.

c. The Boston Consulting Group postulated the "experience curve" that describes economies of scale. As the volume (scale) of output increases, the costs per unit decrease. Change is a reduction in per unit cost of between 20 and 30 percent with each doubling of volume. There are many logical factors for the reduction such as sourcing discounts and improvements, technology thresholds that need volume for justification, and the benefits of repetition on human cognitive power.

d. Sports performance requires practice. Success with a musical instrument is also based on practice. Service mastery is different because it is based on personality and cannot be learned. Learning to play well in golf, tennis, chess, etc., is known to make step functions of capability known as plateaus of accomplishment. The trainee can remain for some time at a plateau before making another step function of improvement. Such plateaus do not apply to service capabilities.

e. Learning to improve at any job is handicapped by assignments to remedy problems. "Putting out fires" does not provide the environment or motivation for continuous improvement (kaizen).

ADDITIONAL READINGS

Almeida, Virgilio A. F., and Daniel A. Menasce. *Capacity Planning for Web Services*, 2e. Englewood Cliffs, NJ: Prentice-Hall PTR, September 2001.

Anderson, David M. *Design for Manufacturability & Concurrent Engineering: How to Design for Low Cost, Design in High Quality, Design for Lean Manufacture, and Design Quickly for Fast Production*. Cambria, CA: CIM Press, 2003.

Baloff, N. "Estimating the Parameters of the Startup Model—An Empirical Approach." *The Journal of Industrial Engineering*, 18, 4 (April 1967): 248–253.

Blackstone, J. H. *Capacity Management*. APICS South-Western Series in Production and Operations Management, 1989.

Boston Consulting Group, Inc. *Perspectives on Experience*. BCG, 1972.

Christopher, Martin. *Logistics and Supply Chain Management*. Burr Ridge, IL: Irwin, 1994.

Cockcroft, Adrian, and Bill Walker. *Capacity Planning for Web Services*, 2e. Englewood Cliffs, NJ: Prentice-Hall PTR, September 2001.

Forrester, J. W. *Industrial Dynamics*. Wiley, 1961.

Gopal Christopher, and Gerry Cahill. *Logistics in Manufacturing*. Burr Ridge, IL: Irwin, 1992.

Leonard, George. *Mastery*. New York: Plume, Penguin Group, 1992.

Parkinson, C. Northcote. *Parkinson's Law*. London: John Murray, 1958.

Rautenstrauch, W., and R. Villers. *The Economics of Industrial Management*. New York: Funk & Wagnalls Co., 1949.

Senge, Peter M. *The Fifth Discipline*. Doubleday/Currency, 1990.

Susman, Gerald I. (Editor). *Integrating Design and Manufacturing for Competitive Advantage*. Oxford, UK: Oxford University Press, April, 1992.

Visit http://www.ambcbenchmarking.org for the Agile Manufacturing Benchmarking Consortium™ whose objective is to conduct benchmarking studies of business processes.

Vogel, Harold L. *Entertainment Industry Economics: A Guide for Financial Analysis* 5e. (breakeven point volumes in the entertainment industry). Cambridge, UK: Cambridge University Press, May 2001.

Vogel Harold L. *Travel Industry Economics: A Guide for Financial Analysis*, (breakeven point volumes in the travel industry).Cambridge, UK: Cambridge University Press, January 2001.

Yu-Lee, Reginald Tomas. *Essentials of Capacity Management*, Chichester, UK: Wiley Europe, Ltd., April 2002.

NOTES

1. This 1823 quotation can be found in *Characteristics*, page 89. William Hazlitt. *Characteristics*. Publisher unknown. London, England, 1823.

2. C. Northcote Parkinson. *Parkinson's Law*. London: John Murray, 1958.

3. The Sprague Electric Company played an important role in this research, which was published as follows: J.W. Forrester. *Industrial Dynamics*. Wiley, 1961.

4. Peter M. Senge. *The Fifth Discipline*. Doubleday/Currency, 1990, 27–54.

5. W. Rautenstrauch and R. Villers. *The Economics of Industrial Management*. New York: Funk & Wagnalls Co., 1949.

6. Boston Consulting Group, Inc. *Perspectives on Experience*. A collection of articles published by BCG, 1972. An article by Bruce D. Hendersen describes the experience curve.

7. There was real interest during the 1960s and a belief that productivity could be improved substantially by observing the learning curve phenomenon. See, for example, Nicholas Baloff. "Estimating the Parameters of the Startup Model—An Empirical Approach." *The Journal of Industrial Engineering*, 18, 4 (April 1967): 248–253.

8. The text reference is *Mastery of Self*, a book about multiple plateaus for learning tennis and other sports. George Leonard. *Mastery*. New York: Plume, Penguin Group, 1992.

SPOTLIGHT 10-1
Starbucks

Blending Quality Coffee and Best Practice Ideas at Starbucks

Blending coffee, people, and brilliant business ideas, Starbucks has endeared itself to customers all over the world. Starting in 1971, Starbucks opened its first location in Seattle's Pike Place Market. Howard Schultz joined the company in 1982 as director of retail operations and marketing. Starbucks began to provide coffee to fine restaurants. After a trip to Italy where he was impressed with the espresso bars in Milan, Howard convinced the founders of Starbucks to test the coffee bar concept in a new location in Seattle. The experiment succeeded, spreading to nearly every state, to Canada, and then to many countries around the world.

The number of Starbucks sites, including licensed stores in locations such as airports and grocery stores, reached 6,294 in 2003 and continues to grow. Hoovers OnLine reports that 2002 sales were $3,288.9 million, and 2002 net income was $215.1 million. One-year sales growth was 24.2 percent. As of September 2002, Starbucks had 62,000 employees with a 1-year employee growth rate of 14.8 percent. The company has expanded into coffee ice cream (with Dryer's) and Frappuccino bottled coffee drinks with Pepsi-Cola.

Today, Howard Shultz is chairman and chief global strategist. Orin C. Smith is president and CEO. There are three other regional presidents, five executive vice presidents, and 24 senior vice presidents. In 2001, Starbucks announced its fourth 2-for-1 stock split. The company values open and honest communication and wants its stakeholders to know about its business practices as well as its social and environmental initiatives. (See Investor Relations online at http://www.starbucks.com.)

Thousands of Starbucks stores have become T-Mobile HotSpots, providing high-speed wireless Internet service. Customers can check their e-mail, surf the web, download files, and get work done in coffeehouse comfort.

What has caused this growth? The answer is quality—of people, relationships, and products. Starbucks is committed to sourcing and serving the highest quality coffee, tea, beverages, food, and merchandise. Its guidelines for decision making include environmental and social responsibility. This is not lip service. In Nicaragua, Starbucks helped in building lavatory facilities and improved water quality at the Modesto Armijo School, which is attended by 1,200 elementary school children from San Juan de Rio Coco. Partnering with five Guatemalan coffee farms, Starbucks built and continues to maintain health clinics, day-care centers, and schools that serve 5,000 people in local farming communities. Relationships with people in Starbucks' farming communities are long-term and aimed at encouraging social development and sustainability. The company does not expect to change cultural norms, but it is committed to purchasing coffee and cocoa from suppliers at fairly-traded prices (well above prices paid by the normal commodity-coffee buyers) in order to meet the company's environmental, social, economic, and quality standards.

A world away from coffee's origins, in the small town of Winter Park, Florida, the dean of a prestigious business school had a problem. In his busy schedule, there was no time during the day to have uninterrupted conversations with faculty members or to mentor students who needed his undivided attention. The dean told his secretary to start making appointments for him at the local Starbucks. Over caramel Frappuccinos©, problems were quickly solved and relationships improved. Starbucks' mission is to make money by improving the quality of life of its customers, workers, and suppliers. So far, its efforts are succeeding.

Printed with permission of Starbucks Corporation on July 11, 2003

SPOTLIGHT 10-2
O.O.D.A.

How Fast Do You React? (Ask Fighter Pilots and Business Managers)

The late Colonel John R. Boyd of the U.S. Air Force is credited with developing time-based theories about achieving successful military operations. His strategies have engaged many military strategists in discussions about implementing his ideas. At the same time, many business school academics and industry executives have been impressed with the applicability of Colonel Boyd's ideas when transferred to a competitive business context.

Part of Boyd's core thinking relates to the O.O.D.A. loop. This is a repetitive cycle of activities that starts with *observation* of the situation. The second O. in the loop stands for *orientation*. This consists of assessing our (fighter plane's) position relative to the orientation of the adversary. The D. stands for using the information obtained in O.O. to make a *decision* about which maneuvers will provide an advantage in a dogfight. The A. in the O.O.D.A. loop is the *action* of carrying out the decision.

Before the O.O.D.A. loop was identified and named, the dogfight used to be a matter of honed instinct and fast reactions for fighter pilots. In 1986, Colonel John Boyd defined the concept of the O.O.D.A. loop. He advocated a conscious effort to accelerate the time to complete the loop using new training and technology.

Quoting from Boyd's military briefing (titled "Patterns of Conflict" and posted on the website at http://www.d-n-i.net/boyd/pdf/poc.pdf), "to win, we should operate at a faster tempo or rhythm than our adversaries, or better yet, get inside adversary's Observation-Orientation-Decision-Action time cycle or loop." His explanation is that being faster unnerves the adversary. Whoever has the fastest O.O.D.A. loop appears to the adversary to be unpredictable, which generates confusion and disorder.

Military aircraft are now designed to provide pilots with superior O.O.D.A. loop performance. Pilot training leverages that advantage. Other applications of the O.O.D.A. loop are in sports and business. For example, the quarterback of a winning football team goes through the O.O.D.A. loop in completing passes that lead to touchdowns. In horse racing, jockeys are faced with little time to plan their alternative strategies depending upon the orientation of the competing horses on the track. Jockeys describe their racing experiences as requiring immediate assessment and instant decisions. Many Western movies show the advantage of being the fastest gun in the West, which is a classic example of the O.O.D.A. loop winner.

In business, competitive decisions must be made rapidly and correctly. Once made, they are hard to reverse. Recognition of the importance to business of Colonel Boyd's O.O.D.A. loop thesis appeared quickly after its publication in December 1986. *The New York Times* (November 15, 1987) published an article written by Thomas Hout and Mark Blaxill (VP and consultant with the Boston Consulting Group, respectively) titled "Managing for Increased Competitiveness: Make Decisions Like a Fighter Pilot." In this article they stated, "Build an organization with fast response time in serving customers and preempting competitors, and you will grow profitably."

The O.O.D.A. loop is preemptive when new products are developed faster and better than those of the competitors. Competitors cannot get a fix on the intentions of fast-movers. The initiative is seized when your orders can be delivered to customers ahead of those of your competitors. Firms that deal with fast-delivery system vendors have a competitive advantage. The speed of just-in-time is just-right. It reduces waste and increases margins. Timing can be the suppliers' contribution to the firm's O.O.D.A. loop. There is a clear advantage when production and operations managers work closely with product and process designers. Logically, these two activities should be congruent so that quality can be maximized; redesign and retooling can be minimized.

Hout and Blaxill recommend a tight-knit operations architecture, "rooted in systems thinking. If each working part of the company is closely linked with others and work is done right the first time, the company will do everything faster than its competitors."

It is evident from studying dogfights that winners have the faster O.O.D.A. loop, even if they do not call it that. (See: Norman Franks. *Dog-Fight: Aerial Tactics of the Aces of World War I*. Greenhill Books, London, July 2003.) The same can now be said for competitive advantage in companies that break out of the traditional bureaucratic mode. Operational decisions that are made on the plant floor without requiring upward review provide significant competitive advantage and, it is noteworthy, the employees that are so empowered are happier with their jobs.

Value-adding is going on at a much higher rate in firms that can reach decisions at the right time. That means that jobs waiting around for sign-offs are reduced in number. Projects proceed to completion at a faster rate. The implications of marketing decisions (such as pricing) can be discussed without having to find ways to justify crossing boundaries. Three important questions need to be answered. What is the organizational structure of a fast-moving company? How slow or fast is our company? How slow or fast is our competitor's loop?

Sources: Hout, Thomas, and Mark Blaxill. "Managing for Increased Competitiveness: Make Decisions Like a Fighter Pilot." *The New York Times* (November 15, 1987); http://www.belisarius.com. Click on "Patterns of Conflict."

Supplement 10

The Breakeven Decision Model

In this supplement, breakeven analysis and decision making are interrelated. When demand is uncertain, it must be forecast for the purpose of using breakeven analysis to do capacity planning. Capacity planning, given uncertain demand, will require a forecast. The issue being treated in this supplement is how to put BEA and capacity planning together.

It is easier to describe this combined model using an example that could be from either a manufacturing or a service industry. The choice was made to use an unspecified generic industry called ANY *Industry*.

The company is comparing present technology with advanced technology. The problem involves capacity planning, cost analysis, and demand analysis. The latter is based on prices charged and qualities perceived by the company's customers. The problem is that there is no clear-cut answer about what to do. One choice has a better *BEP*; the other choice has a better rate of return slope and demand is uncertain. This is a challenging P/OM problem.

The P/OM department at ANY has drawn up breakeven charts for the alternatives. (These are requested in the problem section for this supplement.) They have calculated the breakeven point and the rate of return of profit for both the present technology and the advanced technology.

Table 10-5 presents the data to calculate the *BEP* and the profit rate. Assume the time period is one year.

The breakeven point is 6,667 units or 66.7 percent of total capacity for the present technology. The breakeven point for the advanced technology is 6,857 units or 68.6 percent of full-capacity utilization.

These may seem to be relatively high breakeven points, but they are not unusual for many industries. Although it would be nice to have breakeven percentages ranging from 30 to 45 percent, capital intensive industries, such as farm equipment and auto production, have high breakeven points. In this case, the advanced technology option is worse than the present technology option. At such a high breakeven point, there is an immediate preference for the lower *BEP*. ANY Industry prefers a lower *BEP*, but this preference gets stronger when the choice is between already high values.

However, before any decision can be made, it is necessary to examine the relative profits of the two plans at greater than breakeven percentages of capacity. The easiest comparison is at 100 percent of capacity.

Profit at 100 percent of capacity:

Present Technology	Advanced Technology
+$500,000	+$550,000

There is a 10 percent advantage for the advanced technology.

	Present Technology	Advanced Technology
Fixed costs*	$1,000,000.00	$1,200,000.00
Per unit variable costs ($)	50.00	25.00
Per unit revenue ($)	200.00	200.00
Annual capacity	10,000 units	10,000 units

TABLE 10-5

Breakeven Data for ANY

*Fixed costs are depreciated on an annual basis.

It also will be useful to examine the relative losses of the two plans at less than breakeven percentages of capacity. An easy comparison is at 50 percent of capacity, well below breakeven.

Profit at 50 percent of capacity:

Present Technology	Advanced Technology
– $250,000	– $325,000

There is a 30 percent advantage for the present technology.

In summary, the present technology has a small *BEP* advantage (66.7 percent versus 68.6 percent). It also has an advantage when demand falls below the *BEP*. Advanced technology has the advantage above the *BEP*.

Which should be chosen, the lower *BEP* with its lower rate of profit and lower rate of loss, or the higher *BEP* with its higher rate of return and higher rate of loss? This question can only be answered by ANY if it has a believable forecast to use with the appropriate decision model.

ANY's forecast of annual customer demand is given in Table 10-6. The derivation of Table 10-6 should be stated in an actual situation. That permits evaluation of its believability.

A specific amount of profit is associated with each level of demand. The total amount of profit (*TPR*) can be read from the breakeven charts or calculated directly using the following equations. $TPR = (p - vc)V - FC$ which becomes

For present technology: $TPR = 150V - 1,000,000$

For advanced technology: $TPR = 175V - 1,200,000$

For present technology, at 0 percent demand, there is a loss of $1 million. At 100 percent capacity (equivalent to 10,000 units) there is profit of $500,000.

Relate the probability distribution to the profit at each demand level D. Multiply profit at D by the *probability of D*. Add up these products for all demand levels to obtain the average (or expected) profit for the given strategy.

As derived in Table 10-7, ANY's expected profit for present technology is

$$\text{Expected Profit} = \sum_{V=0}^{V=100\%} (P_V)(TPR_V) = \$95,000$$

The *BEP* for present technology is 66.7 percent. Multiplying columns (3) and (1) of Table 10-7 determines the expected demand, which is 73 percent:

TABLE 10-6	Demand Level *D*	Probability of Demand Level
Forecast of Demand for ANY	40% of capacity	0.05
	50% of capacity	0.10
	60% of capacity	0.15
	70% of capacity	0.20
	80% of capacity	0.25
	90% of capacity	0.20
	100% of capacity	0.05
		1.00

(1) Demand (D) as a % of Max Capacity	(2) TPR_V Profit @ D	(3) P_V Probability of D	Columns (3)(2) $(P_V)(TPR_V)$
0%	−1,000	0	0
10	−850	0	0
20	−700	0	0
30	−550	0	0
40	−400	0.05	−20
50	−250	0.10	−25
60	−100	0.15	−15
70	+50	0.20	+10
80	+200	0.25	+50
90	+350	0.20	+70
100	+500	0.05	+25
		1.00	+95

Expected Profit = $95,000 (Profits in Table 10-7 in 000s)

TABLE 10-7

ANY's Expected Profit for Present Technology

$0.05(40\%) + 0.10(50\%) + 0.15(60\%) + 0.20(70\%) + 0.25(80\%) + 0.20(90\%) + 0.05(100\%) = 73$ percent

The same kinds of calculations are now done for advanced technology. The expected demand is unchanged because the same demand distribution applies. Determine the profit at 73 percent capacity utilization. It is $77,500. That is the benefit of knowing the expected demand. Expected profit is calculated the long way in Table 10-8, where profits are expressed in 000s.

Expected Profit $= \sum_{V=0}^{V=100\%} (P_V)(TPR_V) = \$77,500$

(1) Demand (D) as a % of Max Capacity	(2) TPR_V Profit @ D	(3) P_V Probability of D	Columns (3)(2) $(P_V)(TPR_V)$
0%	−1,200	0	0
10	−1.025	0	0
20	−850	0	0
30	−675	0	0
40	−500	0.05	−25
50	−325	0.10	−32.5
60	−150	0.15	−22.5
70	+25	0.20	+5
80	+200	0.25	+50
90	+375	0.20	+75
100	+550	0.05	+27.5
		1.00	+77.5

Expected Profit = $77,500 (Profits in Table 10-8 in 000s)

TABLE 10-8

ANY's Expected Profit for Advanced Technology

Following this analysis, it is recommended that ANY Industry retain its present technology. The advanced technology will lower expected profits.

Management should note a few cautions. First, the competition may be shifting in the direction of the new technology, which could be evolving. It might be advisable for the company to invest minimally at this time in order to learn the new technology and be better able to assess it as time passes. Later, both the fixed costs and variable operating costs of the advanced technology may decrease. Further, ANY may be able to increase capacity, currently limited to 10,000 units per year. Quality issues and long-term application of TQM perspectives also should be considered.

If the advanced technology in any way affects the probability distribution, that must be taken into account. Perhaps the new equipment will permit faster delivery and/or more reliable tolerances or delivery schedules. The decision regarding technological choices might be sensitive to shifts in the distribution of the probability of demand.

With the addition of forecasting, the breakeven model has become a unifying systems-wide decision model. All of the functions should be playing a part in preparing the forecast and estimating the costs and revenues.

The decision model with forecasting overrides the problem of what to do when one strategy has a better BEP, but a poorer marginal rate of return, than another strategy. The forecast changes the approach from what is traditional breakeven analysis, where the BEP number is derived and all decision makers have in mind an estimate of the likelihood that the company will operate above or below that point. Without this estimate, the breakeven point is meaningless. The decision model has merged the BEP and the marginal rate of return into a single problem.

Problems for Supplement 10

1. Draw the breakeven chart for ANY's present technology situation. Indicate the breakeven point and the rate of return of profit.

2. Draw the breakeven chart for ANY's advanced technology alternative. Indicate the breakeven point and the rate of return of profit.

3. Table 10-9 presents a shift in the forecast.

What is the effect of the change in the forecast? Will it alter the recommendations?

TABLE 10-9	(1) Demand (D)	(2) Profit @ D	(3) Probability of D	(3)(2)	(3)(1)
ANY's Expected Profit for Advanced Technology with Revised Demand Forecast (Profit in 000s)	0%	−1,200	0		
	10	−1,025	0		
	20	−850	0		
	30	−675	0		
	40	−500	0		
	50	−325	0.10		
	60	−150	0.15		
	70	+25	0.20		
	80	+200	0.25		
	90	+375	0.20		
	100	+550	0.10		
			1.00		

11

Facilities Planning

Chapter Outline

This section discusses the four major components of facilities planning. The first question is where to locate the plant, or the branch, or the warehouse. This is a regional determination. The second issue is to find the specific structure and site to use. The third factor comes before moving in and it is to design the layout. The fourth is to select furniture, lighting, decorative features, and equipment for doing the job. In fact, these four components interact, and no one of them can be considered exclusive of the others.

After reading this chapter, you should be able to:

- Explain the four distinct parts of facilities planning.
- Discuss who is responsible for doing facilities planning.
- Describe the nature of facilities planning models.
- Explain why facilities planning requires the systems approach.
- Describe the application of the transportation model.
- Apply the transportation model to solve one aspect of the location decision problem.
- Determine the relative advantages of rent, buy, or build.
- Describe the use of scoring models for facility selection.

- Deal with the effect of multiple decision makers on the location, site, and building decisions.
- Describe the factors that should be taken into account when equipment is being selected.
- Explain why facilities planning is said to be interactive, meaning that consideration goes back and forth between facility selection, equipment selection, and facility layout.
- Describe what facility layout entails.
- Explain how job design and workplace layout interact.
- Evaluate the use of quantitative layout rules (algorithms).
- Discuss the use of heuristics to improve layouts of plants and offices.

THE SYSTEMS VIEWPOINT

Regional facilities planning calls upon a wealth of knowledge and great skills. Facilities planning on a nationwide level requires expertise from so many areas that it is folly to think that one person alone can do it successfully. International facilities planning takes global team efforts with country specialists. In all cases, a better job is done by broad-based visionaries and generalists who know how to work together as a team. When generalists and specialists combine their efforts, pooling their viewpoints and knowledge, it is certain that a systems approach is required. When locations and specific structures must be considered together, these are joint decisions that are best approached using the systems approach.

STRATEGIC THINKING

Strategic thinking is essential to avoid suboptimization. The easiest way to define suboptimization is that it is less good than optimization. It is a result, or series of results, that strays from achieving the objectives that drive strategies. For example, say that a theme park assigns the manager of each of its attractions to minimize waiting time of customers. That objective for each ride will produce different effects than a single strategic objective to minimize the total waiting time of customers over the course of many rides and an entire day of being in the park. The sum of the suboptimizations will not add up to an optimal solution. The sequence of rides taken, the timing of starts and completions, the encouragement of choosing certain intervals to eat and use the restrooms reflect the larger strategic framework.

When the real problem is too big to grasp because there are too many options, the systems approach is indicated. However, dividing the (facilities) problem into regional subproblems to make it workable can jeopardize the quality of the solution. It is likely to yield a suboptimal (less than best) solution. Location, site, and building decisions are major components of the larger facilities planning problem. Strategies that yield suboptimal results can damage competitive capabilities. Thus, layout and job design are partners in the achievement of a good flow shop. They need to be considered together. In the job shop, production scheduling, shop-floor layout, and job design are interdependent and best approached as a system. The same kind of reasoning applies to the optimal facility design for a project. In all such situations, facilities planning is a multidimensional systems problem. The appropriate strategy must encompass all relevant elements of the minimum coherent system.

11-1   FACILITIES PLANNING

> **Facilities planning:** Four main components are geographic location, structure and specific site, equipment choice, and layout.

Facilities are the plant and the office within which OM does its work. In addition to the buildings and the spaces that are built, bought, or rented, facilities also include equipment used in the plant and the office. There are four main components of **facilities planning** and they strongly interact with each other. These four are

1. *Location of facilities.* Where, in the geographic sense, should the various operations be located? Location can apply to only one facility but more generally includes a number of locations for doing different things. Thus, "where is it best to . . ." fabricate and assemble each product, locate the service center, situate the sales offices, and position the administration?

    Many location factors have to be dealt with in a qualitative fashion. Common sense prevails. Qualitative factors such as being near supplies of raw materials and/or sources of skilled labor vie with being close to customers. Seldom can all desires be satisfied. The options may be to choose one over the other or to compromise with an in-between location. There are similar problems for distributors who want to be located close by all kinds of transportation facilities (road, rail, airports, and marine docks).

    Other location factors are better dealt with in a quantitative fashion because common sense does not work. The reason is that some real problems are too big to grasp all of the possible options. Because of this, optimal location assignments are often counterintuitive. For example, if a transportation analysis is made manageable by dividing the problem into regional subproblems, the solution may be seriously suboptimal (far from being the best that is possible). The systems approach, which endeavors to include all relevant factors, is needed in this case.

    At the same time, there are strategic issues concerning centralization or decentralization of facilities. Should there be a factory in each country? Would a central warehouse be more desirable than regional warehouses or can they both be used to an advantage? Such decisions might be best reached with a combination of qualitative and quantitative considerations.

2. *Structure and specific site selection.* In what kind of facility should the process be located? How should the building or space be chosen? Is it best for the company to build the facility, buy, or rent it? Choice of a specific building is often decided after the location is chosen. However, there are circumstances where the location, site, and structure should be considered together. This makes structure and site decisions complex problems best resolved by using the systems approach.

3. *Equipment choice.* What kind of process technology is to be used? This decision often dominates structure and site options. In turn, there may be environmental factors that limit the choice of locations. Equipment choice can include transport systems and available routes. Interesting systems problems arise that combine all three aspects of facilities planning.

4. *Layout of the facility.* Where should machines and people be placed in the plant or office? There is interaction of equipment choice with layout, structure, site, and location. The size of the facility is determined by both current needs and future projections to allow for growth. Thus, facilities planning is systems planning. Once the location, site, and structure are determined, layout details can be decided.

Thus, what path do conveyors, AGVs, and other transport systems take? AGVs are automatic guidance vehicles, which are computer controlled along prescribed transport paths. Other transport systems include manual systems (like wheelbarrows) and forklift trucks, among others. **Layout** is an interior design problem that strongly interacts with structure and specific site selection and equipment choice.

Usually, location is addressed first because its consequences may dominate other decisions. This is particularly true when transportation costs are a large part of the cost of goods sold. Location also may be crucial because of labor being available only in certain places. Closeness to market can affect demand. Closeness to suppliers can affect prices and the ability to deliver just in time. Tax considerations might play a part.

Once the location is known, a search for appropriate building structures can be done. However, when several locations are considered suitable and when buildings have been identified that qualify, then the various packages of locations and structures have to be considered together.

Circuit board layout is detailed and precise. The same level of consideration should be carried to the design of the office and the plant. The layout of a customer service center facility should address seating arrangements, computer and telecommunication locations, and enhancements for information retrieval that will speed up the service to customers.

Layout: Plan for the arrangement of the working environment of the company's facilities.

11-1a Who Does Facilities Planning?

The treatment of all four of the facilities planning issues is classic P/OM. Their importance is not in question, but the way that these four issues are done and the role of P/OM in the planning process have been changing. In the global world of international production systems, international markets, and rapid technological transfers, facilities planning requires a team effort. It is no longer the sole responsibility of P/OM.

Team effort is required to deal with the issues properly. They deserve consideration by the entire strategic planning team of which P/OM is one important member. Beside the fact that all functional areas should be participants in location decisions, there are additional considerations.

Governmental regulations—from international to national to municipalities—have to be addressed. Legal issues need to be resolved. Lawyers from many countries often are consulted. There are negotiations with communities regarding such matters as financial incentives and tax breaks.

To **rent, buy,** or **build** requires specialists who know domestic and international real-estate markets. Trade rules and tariffs are special for trading blocks and their partners. They are constantly changing for GATT, NAFTA, EU, and other trade groups.

Currency conditions and banking restrictions must be interpreted by specialists. The list of special complications to consider is long and particular to each situation.

Rent: Payments made regularly by a tenant to a landlord.

Buy: Do a rent or buy analysis.

Build: Alternatives to "build a new facility" would be either "rent" or "buy."

11-2 MODELS FOR FACILITY DECISIONS

P/OM's role and its contributions to facilities management are primarily of two kinds. First, P/OM's experience, with what succeeds and what fails for facilities planning, adds valuable

Models: Attempts to image the real thing can be physical, like a plant layout model.

Transportation models: Minimize shipping costs or maximize profits where production facility location and market (shipped to) differentials exist.

Best location: Specially tailored to the particulars of the situation, e.g., close to the market, near suppliers, able to draw on highly-skilled work pools, facilitates joining about 12,000 other maquiladoras (U.S. (and others)-owned and -operated assembly factories located along the 2,100 mile border that separates Mexico and the United States, employing over 1 million workers).

Location factors play a major role in the economics of timber shipments. The source of the wood and its nearness to timber mills is the first link. Then, mill to shipping port is link two. The third link is from receiving port to lumberyard. Wood is heavy and the transport is costly so it may pay to do as much work as possible within the first link. Location factors play a major role in the hotel and resort business. What are the analogies and/or differences to transporting timber?

insights to the planning team. Second, P/OM knows how to use facilities planning **models** developed by operations researchers, management scientists, and location analysts.

Location decision models can use measures of costs and preferences to reach location decisions. **Transportation models** use costs, and scoring models use preferences. Other models—such as breakeven analysis—can help to select a facility and to choose equipment. Plant, equipment, and tooling decisions need close consultation between engineering, P/OM, and finance. These issues need to be guided and coordinated with top management.

Supermarket and department store locations are often chosen to be at the center of dense population zones. A center of gravity model can be used to find the population center, or the sales volume center—instead of the center of mass—which an engineer finds for structures or ships. Columbus, Ohio, is a popular distribution center because a circle around it within a 500-mile radius encloses a large percentage of U.S. retail sales.

Plant layout models for flow shops require detailed engineering in cooperation with P/OM process requirements. The technical aspects of the process are vitally important in determining layout for a flow shop. Layout for the job shop may be one of the few areas where P/OM is expected to do the job on its own. In actuality, good layout decisions may be based more on models that assist visualization than on models that measure layout-flow parameters.

Nevertheless, there is a need to know that there are layout models for minimizing material transport distances. This is the measured path that work in process must travel in the plant. These models are interesting for special applications, as well as for their quantitative properties. Although their use tends to be limited, they are discussed in this chapter.

How models are used is what counts. Some applications can be criticized as overriding complex issues with simple metrics. The study of P/OM provides the basis for exercising good judgment about choosing models and methods. Layout goals now encourage communication and teamwork instead of imitation of machine performance, which lends itself to precise measurement.

11-3 LOCATION DECISIONS— QUALITATIVE FACTORS

Best location is related to the function of the facility and the characteristics of its products and services. Also, location decisions always are made relative to what other alternatives exist—just as building decisions are made relative to what else is available. When the building location decision is taken jointly, it is possible to decide to wait for another alternative to appear. This enlarges the scope of the problem and provides another example of the need for a systems-oriented perspective to resolve some location issues.

11-3a Location to Enhance Service Contact

Service industries locate close to their customers to achieve the kind of contact that characterizes good service. Bank tellers and ATMs (automated teller machines) are such contact points. No one wants to travel many miles to make deposits or withdrawals. The closer bank will get the business.

Branch banks, gas stations, fast-food outlets, and public phones are scattered all around town, because distance traveled is one of the main choice criteria used by customers. Shopping malls are located so that many people find it convenient to drive to them. For retail business, best location is decided by the ability to generate high customer contact frequency.

An interesting exception to the advantage of proximity for contact are the services rendered to vacationers. Traveling many miles for sun and surf, or for snow and skiing, the service starts with the airline providing transportation. Then the hotel or resort offers food, shelter, sports, and entertainment.

Facilities planning and management are crucial to success in the hotel and resort business. Location may be at the top of the list. Services, in general, are strongly affected by location, structure, site, equipment, and layout because they all participate in making contact with customers successful.

Government institutions locate services close to the citizens who need them. Municipal governments provide police and fire protection to those who live within the municipality and pay the taxes. Effective federal service requires regional offices.

11-3b Just-in-Time Orientation

Extractors like to be close to their raw materials. On average, gold mining reduces a ton of ore to 4.5 grams of gold. The reduction process has to be near to the mines. Fabricators like to be close to their raw materials and customers. A balanced choice has to be made, which will depend on the specific product. Assembly plants like their component suppliers to be close. They encourage suppliers to deliver on a just-in-time basis. The advantage to the supplier is that enough volume of business must be given by the producer to justify the location. Services usually profit by being close to the customer. Creative solutions are a goal.

The decision to be a nearby just-in-time supplier requires a mutual interchange of trust and loyalty. Just-in-time suppliers benefit from the proximity by being a single source (or one of very few sources) to their customer. Communication can be face-to-face and frequent. Customers benefit from reduction of inventory. Suppliers benefit from stability and continuity.

11-4 LOCATION FACTORS

Six factors that can affect location decisions are

1. *Process inputs.* Closeness to sources is often important. The transportation costs of bringing materials and components to the process from distant locations can harm profit margins.

2. *Process outputs.* Being close to customers can provide competitive advantages. Among these are lower transport costs for shipping finished goods and the ability to satisfy customers' needs and respond rapidly to competitive pricing—which can provide market advantages.

3. *Process requirements.* There can be needs for special resources that are not available in all locations (i.e., water, energy, and labor skills).

4. *Personal preferences.* Location decision makers, including top management, have biases for being in certain locations that can override economic advantages of other alternatives.

5. Tax, tariff, trade, and legal factors. Trade agreements and country laws are increasingly important in reaching global location decisions.

6. *Site and plant availabilities.* The interaction between the location and the available facilities makes location and structure-site decisions interdependent.

Shipping costs are the primary concern for the first factor; however, there also can be price advantages for raw materials in certain regions and countries among others. For the second factor, being close to the customer has delivery and design advantages. For the third factor, alternatives exist such as processing bulk materials at the mining site to reduce their mass, and then further refining at a location close to the customer. Thus, process and transportation costs interact.

The fourth factor is individual, intangible, and often encountered. For the fifth factor, taxes and tariffs can add costs to either the production or the marketing elements. Legal factors are difficult to estimate and can be substantial. The sixth factor can require the decision to defer making a decision.

Blackpool Grand Theatre in Lancashire, England, U.K. (box office telephone: 01253 290190) is an historical Victorian theatre. It is the location for production of theatrical events that take enormous P/OM skills to produce. The raw materials (including audience) must be brought to the theatre in batches for transformation. What is that transformation? The cost of the product is in euros. If you want to book seats, the program can be found at http://www.blackpoolgrand.co.uk.

11-5 LOCATION DECISIONS USING THE TRANSPORTATION MODEL (TM)

Transportation costs are a primary concern for a new start-up company or division. This also applies to an existing company that intends to relocate. Finally, it should be common practice to reevaluate the current location of an ongoing business so that the impact of changing conditions and new opportunities is not overlooked. Relocating and moving costs can be added to the transportation model (TM).

When shipping costs are critical for the location decision, the TM can determine minimum cost or maximum profit solutions that specify optimal shipping patterns between many locations. Transportation costs include the combined costs of moving raw materials to the plant and of transporting finished goods from the plant to one or more warehouses.

It is easier to explain the TM with the following numerical example than with abstract math equations. A doll manufacturer has decided to build a factory in the center of the United States. Two cities have been chosen as candidates. These are St. Louis, Missouri, and Columbus, Ohio. Several sites in the two regions have been identified. Real-estate costs are about equal in both.

11-5a Suppliers to Factory—Shipping Costs

The average cost of shipping the components that the company uses to the Columbus, Ohio, location is $6 per production unit. Shipping costs average only $3 per unit to St. Louis, Missouri. In TM terminology, shippers (suppliers, in this case) are called sources or origins. Those receiving shipments (producers, in this case) are called sinks or destinations.

11-5b Factory to Customers—Shipping Costs

The average cost of shipping from the Columbus, Ohio, location to the distributor's warehouse is $2 per unit. The average cost of shipping from St. Louis, Missouri, to the distributor's warehouse is $4 per unit. The same terminology applies. The shipper is the producer (source or origin) and the receivers are the distributors or customers (destinations or sinks). The origins and destinations are shown in Figure 11-1.

Total transportation costs to and from the Columbus, Ohio, plant are $6 + $2 = $8 per unit; for St. Louis, Missouri, they are $3 + $4 = $7. Other things being equal, the company should choose St. Louis, Missouri. However, the real world is not as simple as this.

The complication appears as soon as there are a number of origins competing for shipments to a number of destinations. Another complication is when the supply chain involves what is called transshipment, where destinations become origins. The Columbus

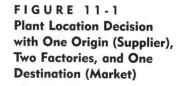

FIGURE 11-1
Plant Location Decision with One Origin (Supplier), Two Factories, and One Destination (Market)

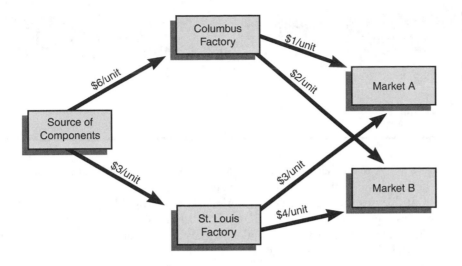

FIGURE 11-2
Plant Location Decision with One Origin (Supplier), Two Factories, and Two Destinations (Markets)

factory was a destination for and an origin for shipments of finished goods to the market. Where the supply chain has many linkages, the transportation model is structured to reflect the transshipment alternatives. Two plants and two markets are shown with one source of components in Figure 11-2.

With these multiple facilities, the TM comes closer to capturing the character of real distribution problems. The issue is: Which plants should ship how much product to which distributors? If it turns out that the solution indicates that one plant should ship no units at all, that is equivalent to eliminating that plant and selecting the other one.

The data for the problem are only partially represented by the costs of transportation that are shown on the arrows in Figure 11-2. In addition, supply and demand figures are needed. The supply is what the plants can produce at maximum capacity. The demand is what the markets want to buy and consume. The minimum cost allocation can be determined by the transportation model, which can be solved by using linear programming or various network methods. The method shown here is trial and error, but there are other systematic ways (rules called algorithms) for solving the transportation problem. Table 11-1 presents the data.

The matrix entries are the costs of transporting finished goods from factory plant i to market j. Factories are distinguished by rows, $i = 1, 2$. Markets are represented by columns, $j = A, B$. In this case, $i = 1$ stands for the Columbus, Ohio, plant location and $i = 2$ represents St. Louis, Missouri.

As for supply and demand, each market requires 40 units per day to be shipped from either P_1 or P_2, or a combination. Each plant can be designed to have a maximum productive capacity of 90 units per day—which in total is larger than the sum of the demands of both markets. This means that one plant could supply all demands. What is best—Columbus, St. Louis, or both?

Total daily supply potential of 180 units per day exceeds total daily demand of 80 units per day by 100 units. To correct the imbalance between supply and demand, a slack, or dummy, market (M_D) is created to absorb 100 units per day. The dummy market does

Plant i	Supplier to Plant Transport Costs	Plant to Market j Transport Costs		Max Supply Quantities
		$j = A$	$j = B$	
$i = P_1$	$6/unit	$1/unit	$2/unit	90 units/day
$i = P_2$	$3/unit	$3/unit	$4/unit	90 units/day
Market demand (units/day)		40	40	

TABLE 11-1

Data for Transportation Analysis

TABLE 11-2

Trial and Error Pattern of Shipments

Plants P_i	Markets M_j			Supply
	M_A	M_B	M_D	
P_1			90	90
P_2	40	40	10	90
Demand	40	40	100	180

not exist. A plant that is assigned the job of supplying only the dummy market would be eliminated. A possible pattern of shipments is shown in Table 11-2.

If this was the minimum cost solution, then P_2 would be the best plant location. It supplies the real markets M_A and M_B. It still has slack of 10, which is assigned to the dummy market (M_D) so P_2 will work at 8/9 of capacity, supplying only real demand. Further, the plant P_1 will be eliminated because it has been assigned the task of supplying only the dummy market.

Is this shipping pattern the best solution—resulting in minimum total transportation costs? It is now necessary to test this pattern to find out if there is any better arrangement.

The matrix of total per unit transportation costs is shown in Table 11-3. See Table 11-1 for the basic data.

Supplier per unit transportation costs have been added to the finished goods per unit transportation costs. Shipments to the dummy market cost $0 because it does not exist.

11-5c Obtaining Total Transport Costs

Combine the data in Tables 11-2 and 11-3 by multiplying costs by quantities to derive Table 11-4. This shows a total cost of $520 for the specific shipping pattern of Table 11-2 that uses only plant 2.

Next, it is appropriate to develop the method for finding the optimal (minimum cost) solution.

11-5d Obtaining Minimum Total Transport Costs

To obtain minimum total transport costs, there is a 3-step procedure:

1. Start with a feasible solution. It should balance supply and demand. It also should leave some cells unassigned, as was done in Table 11-2. A method will be given shortly for getting started in a systematic way. It is called the **Northwest Corner (NWC) method.**

Northwest Corner (NWC) method: Put the largest possible shipment in the upper-left corner and move downward and toward the right as further assignments are made.

2. Select the lowest-cost, nonassigned cell. It is $7 at P_1M_A. Determine the change in cost if one unit is moved to that cell. Make sure that the supply and demand totals are unchanged. This requires subtracting one unit and adding one unit at appropriate places in the matrix. If no saving is obtained (costs increase or stay the same) go to the next lower cost cell and repeat step 2. Ultimately, every nonassigned cell will be tested.

3. If a decrease in total cost is obtained, then ship as many units as possible to the location where one unit produced a decrease.

TABLE 11-3

Total per Unit Transportation Costs

Plants P_i	Markets M_j		
	M_A	M_B	M_D
P_1	6 + 1 = $7	6 + 2 = $8	0
P_2	3 + 3 = $6	3 + 4 = $7	0

Plants P_i	Markets M_j			Row Total Costs
	M_A	M_B	M_D	
P_1			$90 \times 0 = 0$	0
P_2	$40 \times 6 = 240$	$40 \times 7 = 280$	$10 \times 0 = 0$	$520
Column total	240	280	0	$520

Total Cost Transport Pattern Using Only Plant 2

11-5e Testing Unit Changes

What happens to the total cost of $520 if one unit is shipped from P_1 to M_A? Rearrange the total shipping schedule, as shown in Table 11-5. The total cost of this shipping arrangement is $521 per day. Because one unit shipped from P_1 to M_A produces a greater total cost, more than one unit shipped in this way will be even worse. Can the total cost be lowered by shipping one unit from P_1 to M_B? Refer to Table 11-6.

The total cost result is again $521 per day. No way to decrease total cost has been found. There are no other possibilities to study for alternate shipping routes. It can be concluded that the first solution shown in Table 11-2 is optimal. It provides a minimum total cost solution.

The location chosen is St. Louis, Missouri. The exact location of the plant has not been decided. Also, it has not been determined whether the plant will be rented or built. These issues are not addressed by this model. The plant selection was made on the basis of minimum transport costs. The strategic objectives can be criticized as being too restricted.

Another factory is now added to demonstrate some other points. The supply and demand quantities, and the per unit costs are given in Table 11-7.

11-6 NORTHWEST CORNER (NWC) METHOD

As before, the assumption is that transportation costs dominate the plant location decision. The initial assignment pattern shown in Table 11-8 is derived by the Northwest Corner method explained here. Supply and demand are balanced with a dummy market, called M_D.

To use the Northwest Corner (NWC) method, begin in the upper (northern) left-hand (western) corner of the matrix.

Allocate as many units as possible to P_1M_A—this is 40 units. More than 40 units exceeds demand. Assign as many units as possible without violating whichever constraint dominates—because it is smaller. The row constraint is 50 units; the column constraint dominates with 40 units.

P_1 still has 10 units of unassigned supply. Move east to allocate those 10 units at P_1M_B. All of P_1's supply is now allocated. M_B still requires 30 units to sum to the demand row value of 40. Moving south, these units are assigned from plant 2. Movement from the NWC is always either to the right or down.

Plants P_i	Markets M_j			Total Costs
	M_A	M_B	M_D	
P_1	$1 \times 7 = 7$		$89 \times 0 = 0$	$ 7
P_2	$39 \times 6 = 234$	$40 \times 7 = 280$	$11 \times 0 = 0$	$514
Totals	$241	$280	$0	$521

Total Transportation Cost—One Unit at P_1–M_A

TABLE 11-6

Total Transportation Cost—One Unit at P_1–M_B

Plants P_i	Markets M_j			Total Costs
	M_A	M_B	M_D	
P_1		$1 \times 8 = 8$	$89 \times 0 = 0$	$ 8
P_2	$40 \times 6 = 240$	$39 \times 7 = 273$	$11 \times 0 = 0$	$513
Totals	$240	$281	$0	$521

P_2 still has 60 unallocated units remaining. These are assigned to the dummy market, M_D. They will not be made or shipped. To complete the matrix, P_3's supply of 90 units must be allocated. Place them in the P_3M_D cell. Supply and demand quantities tally now.

The NWC method always can be made to satisfy the requirement for an initial feasible solution. The procedure could start at any corner, but the NWC method is conventionally accepted as the way to start. Whatever method is used to obtain an initial feasible solution, it must produce $(M + N - 1)$ assignments for a matrix with N rows and M columns. The condition that there will be $(M + N - 1)$ assignments applies to the initial feasible solution, all intermediate solutions, and the final and optimal solution.

If upon testing the shipment of one unit into an empty cell, the result is an improvement, then all the units that can be moved are moved into the new cell. No change is made if there is no improvement. The NWC provides just enough shipments so that every shipment has at least one other shipment in its row or column. That is necessary for being able to move units to empty cells without changing the row and column totals.

11-6a Allocation Rule: M + N – 1

The total number of different paths assigned to shipments should never exceed $(M + N - 1)$. To remove any ambiguity, another way of saying this is that the number of shipment cells cannot exceed $(M + N - 1)$ where M = the number of destinations or markets and N = the number of origins or plants.

In Table 11-8, there are $3 + 3 - 1 = 5$ shipments. This is the number of shipments derived by means of the Northwest Corner (NWC) rules. A better solution can *never* be obtained *with more than five* shipments. In general, a solution with more than $(M + N - 1)$ active cells (assigned) would be worse.

There are $M \times N$ cells $(3 \times 3 = 9)$ in total, with $M + N - 1 = 5$ assignments and $(M \times N) - M - N + 1 = 4$ boxes that are empty with no assignments.

The logic of the $M + N - 1$ assignments also is related to the mathematical nature of the system of equations that can be used to solve this problem. Thus, the problem is solvable using linear programming where each row and column is expressed as a separate inequation called a *constraint*. (An equation has an = sign. An inequation has either $\leq$ or $\geq$ sign.)

There are supply and demand constraints. Because total supply and total demand sum to the same amount (using the dummy markets or, if needed, dummy plants), the number of independent constraints is one less than the sum of the number of rows and columns.

The exception to the rule that results in less than $(M + N - 1)$ assignments is known as *mathematical degeneracy*. The condition is purely mathematical and always can be

TABLE 11-7

Supply, Demand, and per Unit Costs for Three Plants and Three Markets

Plants P_i	Markets M_j			Supply
	M_A	M_B	M_D	
P_1	$7	$8	$0	50 units/day
P_2	$6	$7	$0	90 units/day
P_3	$8	$10	$0	90 units/day
Demand	40	40	150	230 units/day

Plants P_i	Markets M_j			Supply
	M_A	M_B	M_D	
P_1	40	10		50 units/day
P_2		30	60	90 units/day
P_3			90	90 units/day
Demand	40	40	150	230 units/day

TABLE 11-8

Northwest Corner (NWC)—Initial Feasible Assignment

resolved by adding a small extra amount to the appropriate row or column total. There should not be more than $(M + N - 1)$ assignments.

11-6b Plant Cost Differentials

The plants (being in different regions of the country or different countries in the world) might produce units at different costs. Some explanations for the differences might be:

1. Different type processes and cultural factors
2. Tax, tariff, and government regulation differentials
3. Different labor and material costs

Also, for the global setting, transportation costs between plants and markets might play a role in location decisions.

The per unit production cost differentials reflect any factors that relate to the source. They are simple to factor into the matrix of transport costs. To every element in a row, the cost is added that characterizes the source of that row.

Table 11-9 reflects the addition of the special production costs (shown in parentheses next to the plant) to the transportation costs of Table 11-7. Plant 2 has a per unit cost disadvantage of $16 as compared to plant 3, and $8 as compared to plant 1.

11-6c Maximizing Profit Including Market Differentials

Instead of using a cost matrix and minimizing total costs, the procedures can be reversed to permit maximization of a profit matrix. The power of including market-by-market revenues is shown here. For each cell, calculate the per unit revenue less the per unit shipping costs and other special per unit costs. This provides cell-by-cell data on per unit profit. Table 11-10 shows how this information is derived where per unit revenues are $50 for market A, $60 for market B, and the dummy market M_D has zero profit.

The 4-step procedure for profit maximization is

1. Start with a feasible solution that balances supply and demand and follows the $(M + N - 1)$ rule. The NWC method yields the same result as Table 11-8. Using the per unit profit data from Table 11-10, calculate the total profit (TPR_1) for the first feasible (NWC) solution:

$$TPR_1 = 40 \times 23 + 10 \times 32 + 30 \times 25 = 920 + 320 + 750 = \$1,990$$

Plants P_i	Markets M_j			Supply
	M_A	M_B	M_D	
P_1 ($20)	$27	$28	$0	50 units/day
P_2 ($28)	$34	$35	$0	90 units/day
P_3 ($12)	$20	$22	$0	90 units/day
Demand	40	40	150	230 units/day

TABLE 11-9

Per Unit Transportation and Special Production Costs

TABLE 11-10					
	Markets M_j				
Supply, Demand, and per Unit Costs for Three Plants and Three Markets	**Plants P_i**	M_A	M_B	M_D	**Supply**
	P_1 ($20)	$50 – 27 = $23	$60 – 28 = $32	$0	50 units/day
	P_2 ($28)	$50 – 34 = $16	$60 – 35 = $25	$0	90 units/day
	P_3 ($12)	$50 – 20 = $30	$60 – 22 = $38	$0	90 units/day
	Demand	40	40	150	230 units/day

2. Select the highest-profit, nonassigned cell. It is $38 at P_3M_B. Determine the change in profit if one unit is moved to that cell. Make sure that the supply and demand total constraints are satisfied. This requires subtracting one unit and adding one unit at appropriate places in the matrix. If no profit increase is obtained, go to the next high-est per unit profit cell and repeat step 2. Ultimately, every nonassigned cell will be tested.

    Table 11-11 shows the unit shift to P_3M_B. The profit change based on shifting one unit (indicated by Δ) is calculated:

    $$PR_\Delta = -(1 \times 25) + (1 \times 38) = +\$13$$

    As a reuslt, all 30 units are shifted to P_3M_B and the next calculation of total profit is called TPR_2.

    The change in total profit (TRP_Δ) is calculated and shown to be positive.

    Total profit change based on shifting one unit (indicated by Δ) is calculated:

    $$TPR_\Delta = (40 \times 23) + (10 \times 32) + (29 \times 25) + (1 \times 38) = 920 + 320 + 725 + 38 = \$2,003$$

    Profit has increased by $13 for the single unit change, so move as many units as possible to P_3M_B, as explained in step 3, which follows.

3. When an increase in total profit is obtained, ship as many units as possible to the location where a single unit produced a profit increase. The maximum amount that can be shifted for this example is 30 units, as shown in Table 11-12.

    $$TPR_2 = (40 \times 23) + (10 \times 32) + (30 \times 38) = 920 + 320 + 1,140 = \$2,380$$

    The increase in profit over TPR_1 is 13×30 units = $390.

4. Continue in this way, evaluating changes until profit cannot be increased any further. No further changes should be made because all evaluations of unit changes are neg-ative and would decrease profits if used. The evaluation of unit changes that produces no further profit increase is shown in Table 11-13.

    The final solution is called TPR_4 because it is the fourth iteration result. The basis for this result is shown in Table 11-13.

    $$TPR_4 = 40 \times 30 + 40 \times 38 = 1,200 + 1,520 = \$2,720.$$

    The increase in profit of TPR_4 over TPR_1 is $730, which is a 37 percent improve-ment in profit.

TABLE 11-11	**Right-Hand Matrix Shows Unit Shifts from the Original Matrix**				**Basis for Total Profit TPR$_\Delta$**		
Unit Shift for the Profit-Based Transportation Model	**Plants P_i**	M_A	M_B	M_D	M_A	M_B	M_D
	P_1	40	10	0	$\rightarrow$	40	10	0
	P_2	0	30	60	0	29	61
	P_3	0	0	90	0	1	89

	Unit Shift				Basis for Total Profit TPR$_2$		
Plants$_i$	M$_A$	M$_B$	M$_D$		M$_A$	M$_B$	M$_D$
P$_1$	40	10	0	→	40	10	0
P$_2$	0	29	61		0	0	90
P$_3$	0	1	89		0	30	60

TABLE 11-12

**Unit Change
to Total Change**

11-6d Flexibility of the Transportation Model (TM)

The TM can include much more than just transportation costs. It can reflect price differences in markets (regional, domestic, and international). Production efficiency differentials can be shown, as well as special location-based costs such as taxes, tariffs, and wage scales. The costs of governmental rules concerning pollution control, employee health and safety, and waste disposal vary widely around the world.

Imbalance in supply (S) and demand (D) can be handled by creating dummies to absorb whichever is greater. If S is greater than D (S > D, as was the case for all of the previous examples), create market dummies that can absorb part of the oversupply. In symbolic terms, create M$_D$.

If S < D (which is the case when peak demands are not being met), then create dummy plants to pretend to produce all of the demand. Markets that are shown to be supplied by dummy plants (P$_D$) are not being supplied because the dummy plants do not exist. This raises a question of increasing capacity in optimal locations in order to satisfy demand most effectively. Trial and error may pay off in these investigations.

The TM is a systems organizer for more than just the distribution cost data. Market and process differentials can be represented, so their spokespeople also should be represented when the model is used. The TM as a profit maximizer is a good systems tool, whereas, as a cost minimizer it reflects the more tactical interests of P/OM.

11-6e Limitations of the Transportation Model

The limitations of the transportation method also should be understood by management. The cost equations and constraints on supply and demand are all linear. This means that the model does not allow discounts. It does not permit cost savings that learning curves and the experience horizon promise when larger volumes are handled. Basic discounts such as a car lot savings permit might be factored into the TM analysis by programmers familiar with methods for dealing with discontinuities in the cost functions.

The TM model does not shed light on other factors that influence location decisions such as the kind of community, weather, crime, and quality of schools, among others. Intangible factors are bypassed by this quantitative method. When intangibles are critical, then transportation cost differentials of the various alternatives can be combined with other relevant costs and combined with the intangible factors in a dimensional scoring model analysis.

	Basis for Total Profit TPR$_4$				Evaluation of Unit Changes for the Fourth Matrix		
Plants$_i$	M$_A$	M$_B$	M$_D$	→	M$_A$	M$_B$	M$_D$
P$_1$	0	0	50		−7	−6	*
P$_2$	0	0	90		−14	−13	*
P$_3$	40	40	10		*	*	*

TABLE 11-13

**Per Unit Profit Changes
for All Nonassigned Cells
of the Fourth Matrix**

Legend: Asterisks (*) are assigned shipments.

11-7 STRUCTURE AND SITE SELECTION

It would be highly unusual to choose a structure without having carefully considered location preferences. It is quite usual to choose a location and then search for a specific structure and site. Often, the list consists of combinations. Various locations, each with attractive sites and/or structures, are cataloged. Location and structure-site decisions eventually are considered simultaneously.

Thus, North Carolina and Tennessee could be chosen as tax-advantage states in the United States. If market differentials exist, they also could play a part in the selection among regions of the country. After choosing location, the search for sites and structures becomes more specific. In comparing alternatives, all relevant elements of location, site, and structure should be included. If relocation is involved, the decision may be to select a new site or stay with the current one, and redesign and rebuild the facility.

11-7a Work Configuration Decisions Determine Structure Selection

Flow shop structures permit serialized, sequential assembly with materials being received and introduced to the line as close as possible to the point of use. Access by suppliers at many points along the walls of the building is needed. Gravity-feed conveyors can be used instead of mechanized conveyors when the structure is multistoried. There are many similar issues that arise that relate the building type with the work configuration. Part of the design of a good flow shop is the design of the structure.

Job shops do not entail large investments in the design of the process. In general, good flow shops do require large capital investment. The same large investment applies to extensive FPS systems. It follows that the kind of structure that will be adequate to house job shop processes is less restricted than for flow shops. More real-estate choices are suitable for job shops than for flow shops. Rentals are more likely to be feasible for job shops than for flow shops or for FMS systems.

Service industries are often associated with particular kinds and shapes of structures. Airports, hospitals, theaters, and educational institutions typify the site-structure demands for service specifics. Technological information and knowledge of real-process details are required to reach good decisions.

11-7b Facility Factors

Companies that build their own facilities to match work configuration requirements make fewer concessions. Continuous-process industries—like petrochemicals—have to build to process specifications. Even for the job shop, special requirements for space and strong floor supports—say for a large mixing vat—can influence the choice of structure. When renting, building, or buying, expert help from real-estate specialists, architects, and building engineers should be obtained to ensure proper evaluation of an existing facility or to plan a new structure.

Among the facility elements to be considered are

- Is there enough floor space?
- Are the aisles wide enough?
- How many stories are desirable?
- Is the ceiling high enough?
- Are skylights in the roof useful?
- Roof shapes permit a degree of control over illumination, temperature, and ventilation. What are the maintenance requirements for roofs?

For new construction, in addition to costs, speed counts. Building codes may not be acceptable. Industrial parks may be appealing. Special-purpose facilities usually have lower resale value than general-purpose facilities. Good resale value can be critical, allowing a company flexibility to relocate when conditions change.

Technical information and knowledge of real process details are needed to design service structures like airport terminals. What arrival and departure demands characterize the system? Airports must be designed for airline and flyer's utilities as plants are designed for manufacturing necessities.

Company services should be listed. Capacities of parking lots, cafeterias, medical emergency facilities, male and female restrooms—in the right proportions—must be supplied. Adequate fire and police protection must be defined. Rail sidings, road access, and ship-docking facilities should be specified in the detailed facility-factor analysis.

External appearance and internal appearance are factors. An increasing number of companies are using the factory as a showroom. Some service industries use elegant offices to impress their clients. Others use simplicity to emphasize frugality and utilitarian policies. Some consider appearance to be a frill. Others take appearance seriously and illuminate their building at night. Japanese management stresses cleanliness as a requirement for maintaining employees' pride in their company. When Sanyo acquired dilapidated facilities, they painted the walls and polished the floors.

11-7c Rent, Buy, or Build—Cost Determinants

The costs of land, construction, rental rates, and existing structures are all numbers that can be obtained and compared with a suitable model. That model must be able to reflect the net present value of different payment schedules over time. An appropriate discount rate must be determined in conjunction with the financial officers of the firm.

Cost-benefit analysis is a model analogous to a ledger with dollar costs listed on one side and dollar equivalents for the benefits on the other side. The lists are summed. Net benefit is the difference. With intangibles such as community support, workers' loyalty and skill, union-management relations, and flexibility to relocate, it is difficult to get dollar figures. Thus, estimates of qualities need to be made and used in a scoring model.

Location, structure, and site come as a package of tangible and intangible conditions that have costs—some of which are difficult to determine but which are worth listing:

1. The opportunity cost of not relocating.
2. The cost of location and relocation studies. The collection of relevant data is facilitated through the cooperation of regional chambers of commerce.
3. The cost of moving may have to include temporary production stoppage costs. Inventory buildups may be able to help manufacturers offset the effects of stopping production. Inventory cannot help service stoppage.
4. The cost of land—often an investment. Renting, buying, or building has different tax consequences, which can play a part in reaching decisions.
5. The costs of changing lead times for incoming materials and outgoing products as a result of different locations.
6. Power and water costs differ markedly according to location.
7. Value-added taxes are used in many European countries. VAT is proportional to the value of manufactured goods.
8. Insurance rules and costs are location sensitive.
9. Labor scarcities can develop that carry intangible costs.
10. Union-management cooperation is an intangible cost factor.
11. The intangible cost of community discord can be significant.
12. Legal fees and other costs of specialists and consultants are location sensitive, especially for small- and medium-sized organizations.
13. Workmen's compensation payments and unemployment insurance costs differ by location.
14. The costs of waste disposal, pollution and smoke control, noise abatement, and other nuisance-prevention regulations differ by locations.
15. Compliance with environmental protection rules differ by location.
16. The costs of damage caused by natural phenomena are affected by location, which determines the probabilities of hurricanes and earthquakes, as well as floods and lightning. Insurance damage rates have risen markedly and do not cover production stoppages.

This oil rig in the Persian Gulf is like a company town. Employee team members must work together on a variety of functions. There are always new problems such as those stemming from maintenance under the corrosive conditions of being at sea. Team members are part of production and operations as well as engineering and almost every service system that a small city requires.

17. Costs of reducing disaster probabilities—such as using raised construction to reduce flood damage risk.

18. Normal weather conditions produce costs associated with location: heating, air conditioning, snow removal, frozen pipes, and more absentee days because of the common cold.

19. Extreme weather conditions, such as cold and heat, cause facilities to deteriorate faster than normal weather conditions. Exteme wind conditions, such as tornadoes and hurricanes, require special building protections.

How can the many tangible and intangible costs be brought together in a unified way? Scoring models provide a satisfying means for organizing and combining estimates and hard numbers. This topic is covered in the next section.

11-8 FACILITY SELECTION USING SCORING MODELS

If all of the facility costs were readily measurable, then an equation could be written for total costs—of the general form:

Total Costs = Σx_i (i = A through Z)

where A through Z includes costs associated with the location, structure, and site. Unfortunately, many factors cannot be reduced to dollars and cents. Part of the equation can be in dollars and the rest has to be cast as an estimation of costs. The total cost equation only can be symbolic:

Total costs = f (Tangible costs + Intangible costs)

The objective is to choose the location/structure/site option or alternative that minimizes total costs.

The **scoring model** permits the simultaneous evaluation of tangible and intangible costs. The method allows intangibles to be dealt with in a quantitative fashion with as many factors considered as seems necessary. However, the most practical idea is to concentrate on the important factors.

The comparison among strategic location alternatives is equivalent to measuring the ratios of the cost estimates for the different intangible and tangible cost factors. This is a way of measuring relative advantage. Each ratio portrays opportunities to improve. The numerators and denominators are equivalent to the utilities of different options.

> **Scoring model:** Compares quantitatively alternative options for a broad variety of situations; ratios produce *pure numbers*. See http://www.myfico.com.

11-8a Intangible Factor Costs

The ratios measure the degree to which one option is better than, or preferred to, another. The dimension of *community attitude* (CA) is a good instance of an intangible factor. CA cannot be measured in a precise and nonambiguous way—as for example, dollars of rent. Therefore, an estimate is made by someone who knows the community attitude aspect of the location decision. In effect, the estimate states a preference for one community's attitude as compared to the other.

Assume that Orlando, Florida, has been given the top rating for CA. Because this problem is being stated in terms of costs, the best rating is "one," which is the smallest positive integer. Scoring models can be created with the goal of cost minimization or (alternatively) profit maximization. Terms must be consistent with whichever goal is used. For profits, the preference is large numbers. This will not apply to weighting factors that are used in the scoring model. Large weights are always more important than small weights. To sum up, the model presented now is a cost minimization formulation. The most important factors have large weights, and the most preferred situations have the smallest numbers.

It is possible to set the scoring model for any number of comparisons. However, to keep things simple for the current explanation, just two cities will be used. This model can be extended to three, four, five, or more without any changes in method. The value of the community attitude ratio for two cities will be called V_{CA}.

Orlando, Florida, is being compared with Edison, New Jersey, by a high-tech manufacturer currently located in Buffalo, New York. The old Buffalo facility is to be closed. There is general agreement to move south, but healthy debate about how far south to move. Edison, New Jersey, has been rated a 2 for supportive community attitude.

There are a number of ways to interpret the ratio:

$$V_{CA} = \frac{Orlando}{Edison} = \frac{1}{2}$$

First, the rater's preference for Orlando, with respect to community attitude, is two times greater than for Edison. The other side of the coin is that the rater's preference for Edison is half that of Orlando. Getting something that is less preferred is construed as a cost. The ratio of the cost estimate for the best alternative with respect to community attitude is obtained by dividing 1 by 2. Because costs are best when they are small, 1 is better than 2.

Second, the cost of choosing Edison instead of Orlando with respect to CA is 2/1 = 2. This could be interpreted as any amount of money. The weighting factors will introduce a means of scaling the relative utilities. Ultimately, tangibles (such as dollars) and intangibles (such as community attitude) can be related in this way. See the next point.

Third, the scoring model deals with the importance (V_{CA}) of CA relative to all the other factors by weighting (W_{CA}) the value of the ratio, thus:

$$(V_{CA})^{W_{CA}}$$

This enables the model to consider simultaneously the costs of both tangible and intangible factors. The preference measures and actual cost dimensions are weighted to express their importance to the total evaluation of the location alternative. To mix tangible costs with intangible costs, weights are used to express the relative importance of each. Then, all of the costs are combined. This treats measured values as though they also are preferences.

In fact, because apples and oranges are being compared, the scoring model can only work by combining the dimensionless ratios into a dimensionless value, V. This is a multiobjective model. Some of the objectives are in conflict. There is the objective to move to a location that has the best CA. This location might not be the one with the lowest taxes. A list of six objectives follows. They apply—three tangible and three intangible factors—to the two sample locations, sites, and structure problems.

Tangible Costs—Measured in Dollars:

1. Building costs—based on annual (straight line) depreciation—fully equipped with general-purpose equipment
2. Taxes per year
3. Energy costs per year

Another tangible factor is labor. Companies choose locations based on cheaper labor markets (including low-cost labor countries). Material costs also can differ according to location. To keep this scoring model manageable, labor and material costs have been treated as equivalent at both locations.

Intangible Costs—Measured in Preferences:

4. Ease of relocating if and when such becomes necessary
5. Product quality as a function of skills and morale
6. Community attitude

If one location is best for all six objectives, and the location planners agree that the list of objectives is correct and complete, then there is no need for the scoring model. The choice is obvious. If, however, as is more usual, one location is best for some of the six objectives, and the other location is best for the remaining objectives, then the use of the

	Objectives (a)	Orlando	Edison	Weight (d)
TABLE 11-14	**Tangible costs ($)**			
	Building costs (b)	$500,000	$300,000	4
Factors for Comparison of Alternative Locations	Taxes	$ 50,000	$ 20,000	4
	Energy Costs	$ 20,000	$ 30,000	4
	Labor costs	equivalent	equivalent	0
	Material costs	equivalent	equivalent	0
	Total tangible costs	$570,000	$350,000	4
	Intangible costs (c)			
	Relocation flexibility	1	6	3
	Workforce quality	2	3	5
	Community attitude	1	2	1
	Pollution regulations	equivalent	equivalent	0
	Room for expansion	equivalent	equivalent	0

Notes:
(a) Cost minimization objectives for all factors; 1 is best.
(b) Buildings and facilities use annual (straight line) depreciation. General-purpose equipment costs are also depreciated.
(c) Intangibles are measured by preferences with the scale of 1 to 10, where the most preferred has the lowest cost. Had the table been constructed for profits, value 10 would be optimal.
(d) The larger the weight, the more important the factor is considered to be relative to the other factors. This applies for both cost minimization and profit maximization. These weights have been chosen to go from 1 to 5. Other ranges could be selected. The weight of zero removes the factor from consideration because any factor to the zero power is equal to one.

scoring model is not only warranted but needed. Six different dimensions, representing conflicting objectives, must be combined to provide a reasonable basis for evaluation.

11-8b Developing the Scoring Model

The tangible objectives are directly measurable. The other three objectives are intangible and require an estimate of preference. To systematize the scoring model, each objective can be assigned a scale position between 1 (best) and 10 (worst). Assume that the proposals for the Orlando and Edison locations have been evaluated as shown in Table 11-14.

The first three tangible factors are dollars that can be added together because all costs are based on a 1-year period. This yields $570,000 and $350,000 for the Orlando and Edison locations, respectively. Two additional dollar costs are not included because they are equivalent and cancel each other out. They are given zero weight.

Discounting methods can be used to compare net present values for time streams of money. Total tangible costs can be used as a single factor to represent all of the cost factors. It has the same weight of 4 as the other dollar factors. Companies will have different measures for the relative importance or utility of dollars. Organizations with large asset bases will consider small amounts of money to have low weights. Conversely, small- and even medium-sized companies usually treat cash-flow expenses as having large weights. In this case, management has evaluated dollars with an importance weight of 4, which is high.

This makes sense because to this company the purchase of a new building is a substantial investment. Edison has a cash outlay advantage over Orlando that is noteworthy at the outset.

Dollar expenditures are more important than any other factor—except workforce quality, which carries a weight of 5. The factor called *workforce quality* is considered to be a surrogate for product quality that results from a skilled workforce with high morale and pride of workmanship.

Consider the intangibles. Orlando leads in all cases. For workforce quality and community attitude, both Orlando and Edison have fine ratings although Orlando has the edge. When it comes to relocation flexibility, Edison does not seem to satisfy the company's expectations. As for pollution regulations and room for expansion, the two locations are equivalent and need not be considered (given zero weight) because they cancel out in ratio.

11-8c Weighting Scores

The fourth column of Table 11-14, captioned "Weight," presents weighting factors, or index numbers that have been scaled from 1 to 5. Choosing the weights is a subjective task that may not be easy to accomplish. The weights need to be chosen to capture the relative importance of each objective.

According to the weights assigned in Table 11-14, workforce quality (at 5) is the highest value that can be selected. Community attitude (at 1) is least important. Relocation flexibility (at 3) is somewhat less important than costs (all of which are at 4). It is expected that all costs are going to have an equal weight. However, very large costs that could bankrupt a firm may be given more weight with good reason. Also, it is implicit that costs to be paid tomorrow have higher weight than costs to be paid five years from now. The net present value model does the weighting for us in a sensible fashion.

The arrangement of weighting values could change if the company's capitalization were altered or if the location objectives were modified. It is useful to keep in mind that the numbers used for the scoring model were derived by a team of company managers after discussion and analysis of the situation.

The weighting is arbitrary, but not random. The same can be said about the preferences for the intangible factors. Say that the management team—composed of five executives including the CEO—agreed to accept the numbers in Table 11-14. Hopefully, such agreement means that there is consensus about both preferences and importance of those preferences. It could be that four out of five want to please the CEO.

If factors such as community attitude, product quality, and flexibility could be associated with dollar values, there would not be a dimensional problem to resolve. Everything would be measured in dollars, and there would be no need for weights.

11-8d Multiple Decision Makers

Each manager on the site-selection team will provide individual ratings (numbers) for all of the factors. If averages are used to combine the preference scores and the weights, the effect would be to decrease the differentials between locations. Averaging the scores of **multiple decision makers** reduces variability. This is because individual extremes tend to cancel each other. If the P/OM rated relocation flexibility for Edison as nil and gave it a 10 while the CFO considering it to be fair, rated it 4, then the average would be 7. If averaging is used, the results can be compared with the results for the individuals. The managers can identify problems and areas to be further studied by comparing their preference scores and weights.

Multiple decision makers: Quantitative scoring models can work with more than one person's evaluations of locations, suppliers, products, processes, etc.

This is similar to the Delphi method, which identifies differences in opinions and encourages convergence of informed opinion. Managers with dissimilar preferences and weights can discuss why they selected the ratings they did. It is assumed that such transfers of information result in a leveling of opinion, i.e., more agreement.

Scoring models organize a lot of information that is relevant for location decisions. Managers can study what is known and what is not; what is agreed upon, and what is not; what is important and what is not; whether consensus exists about what is important; what appears to require additional research, etc. Ultimately, the decision has to be made about accepting or rejecting the solution indicated by the scoring model.

Pooling and polling opinions of many people in the company about location decisions increases involvement and builds pride in the company. It leads to interfunctional communication about the facility decision. If the company has agreed to move people who want to be relocated, the approach tends to motivate more people to participate in the move.

Information about the choices should be made available throughout the company. If feasible, cost factors should be shared. When the factor lists are made up, broad participation leads to better idea generation. Notions appear that otherwise might be overlooked and the process moves faster. The decision to relocate is better shared than sprung as a surprise.

11-8e Solving the Scoring Model

The scoring model takes ratios like the one previously developed for community attitude:

$$V_{CA} = \frac{\text{Orlando}}{\text{Edison}} = \frac{1}{2}$$

and raises them to a power W_{CA}, which is the importance weight of the CA factor. These are called the *powers* of the factors. Thus:

$$(V_{CA})^{W_{CA}} = (0.5)^1$$

(See Table 11-14, row 3 of intangibles, c, and column d—for these data.)

The powers of the factors are multiplied to derive the system's ratio, V, which is the combined score that is being sought.

$$V = (V_\$)^{W_\$}(V_{RF})^{W_{RF}}(V_{WQ})^{W_{WQ}}(V_{CA})^{W_{CA}}$$

where $\$$ = building costs and other dollar expenditures

RF = relocation flexibility
WQ = workforce quality
CA = community attitude

Each ratio $V_j^{W_j}$ has Orlando in the numerator and Edison in the denominator. Therefore, if V = 1, then both locations have the same cost score. If V < 1, choose Orlando because it has a lower cost score than Edison. If V > 1, choose Edison because Orlando has a higher cost score than Edison.

This is the symbolic representation of the scoring model. In words, it is a multiplicative model that derives the products of the preference (and cost) ratios raised to powers that represent the importance of each factor. In essence,

$$V = \frac{\text{preference for location } a}{\text{preference for location } b}$$

Pure number: See **Scoring model.** Quantitative comparison of two options poses problems of combining multiple dimensions; ratios of the products of the powers yield a pure number because all dimensions are canceled.

V is a **pure number,** meaning that it has no dimensions. For example, if low cost, little weight, and small size are the desirable components of a product design, then a and b can be compared, as follows:

$$V = \frac{\text{preference for product design } a}{\text{preference for product design } b} = \frac{\text{dollars } a}{\text{dollars } b} \times \frac{\text{pounds } a}{\text{pounds } b} \times \frac{\text{centimeters } a}{\text{centimeters } b}$$

V = a pure number (dimensionless), which means that dollars, pounds, and centimeters cross out in each ratio. For conceptual understanding, note how price-earnings ratios are dimensionless ratios widely used to evaluate how pricey a stock is in the market. Another widely employed ratio measures actual capacity used as a percentage of the maximum capacity available.

Turning to the numbers given in Table 11-14:

$$V = \frac{\text{preference for location } a}{\text{preference for location } b} = \left(\frac{\$570,000}{\$350,000}\right)^4 \left(\frac{1}{6}\right)^3 \left(\frac{2}{3}\right)^5 \left(\frac{1}{2}\right)^1 = 0.002 = \frac{1}{500}$$

With this result, Orlando will be chosen because the ratio is less than 1. The combined weighted costs of Edison (in the denominator) are greater than the combined weighted costs of Orlando (in the numerator).

The scoring model is useful for a wide range of applications in addition to the location problem. It is appropriate for product-, process- and service-design decisions, equipment selection, warehouse-location plans, etc. The scoring model's multiplication method of evaluating alternatives by means of weighting factors is reasonable to handle multidimensional problems. It has a strong scientific foundation and is frequently used by those who are familiar with dimensional analysis.[1]

11-9 EQUIPMENT SELECTION

The building blocks for resolving the equipment selection problem have already been put into place. The first issue that has to be decided is: What work configuration is going to be used? This starts as a capacity planning problem. The capacity required must be resolved before any equipment decisions can be made.

General-purpose equipment for the job shop and batch production come in many varieties and can be purchased new or used. There are more equipment selection constraints with continuous production processes and with flow shop systems. Equipment selection in the latter two cases requires careful and detailed engineering analysis. As a suggestion, the analysis along the lines of points 1 through 4 follows:

1. For choosing between specific machines, conveyors, forklift trucks, and other pieces of equipment, the net present value of the investments and operating costs should be determined. The reason that traditional financially discounted cash-flow analyses should be used is that it permits purchase price to be combined with the time stream of operating costs.

2. The classical breakeven model can provide critical data about equipment selection. This provides a benchmark regarding the volume of work that must be done on the alternatives before they start making a contribution to profit.

3. The scoring model, described for site selection, also is useful for evaluating some of the intangible factors that new equipment decisions involve. These include: difficulty learning to use new equipment, assessing the competitive benefits of new equipment, improvements in quality and productivity that could be expected, and the variety of jobs that can be done on the new equipment.

4. Setup times of equipment alternatives must be compared. Using activity-based costing, it is possible to estimate downtime expenses as well as to determine the effect of setup costs and time on optimal lot sizes.

New equipment decisions are a P/OM responsibility. Still, the financial involvements require teamwork with financial control and accounting managers. Cooperation with engineers and R & D is warranted to make certain that all technical issues are properly addressed.

11-9a Design for Manufacturing—Variance and Volume

Without proper tools and equipment, even a skilled and motivated worker is hard pressed to do more than a mediocre job. Poor tools compromise quality. TQM requires that all the homework should be done concerning equipment performance, costs, and quality before reaching equipment selection decisions. The estimates of performance should not be naive. They must be used to explain expected variation in the qualities of the product.

Part of the work entailed in **design for manufacturing (DFM)** is equipment performance evaluation. First, the productivity of equipment must be related to the volume of work that has to be done. This means comparing the production rates of each alternative. Second, different degrees of variability are associated with the equipment alternatives. This relates quality of product to equipment selection.

Design for manufacturing: Equipment performance evaluation is part of the DFM procedure. The inherent variability of the technology must be compatible with designers' tolerances.

Like fingerprints, each piece of equipment produces unique variations. Original equipment manufacturers (OEM) can categorize the tolerance capabilities of the machines that they sell. This helps to select equipment but tests must be conducted to determine the output variability of specific products made on the machines. The observed level of variability must be compatible with the designer's tolerances. It also must meet the DFM expectations of the process managers. There often is a great deal of difference between various manufacturers' equipment that otherwise appears to be of the same class. Equipment choice that ignores this information is selling process management short.

11-9b Equipment Selection and Layout Interactions

Equipment selection precedes facility layout. The two interact so strongly that it is logical to have an idea about layout requirements before facility choice. Size, weight, height, and number of pieces of equipment are critical layout parameters. Planning requires knowledge of equipments' footprints (space needed) and signatures (vibration, noise among others).

Movement of materials is another equipment factor. Elevated conveyors can carry materials near the ceiling whereas sufficient aisle clearance must be available for AGV and trucks. Equipment dictates facility layout design. It may influence facility location—when the ideal building exists somewhere.

P/OMs have a good idea of the equipment that will be required at the chosen facility and, therefore, of the general adequacy of a particular structure. The process of deciding what to do is interactive, going back and forth between facility selection, equipment selection, and facility layout. It is not unusual to find that equipment selection must accommodate an existing facility.

11-9c Life Cycle Stages

Life cycle stages: Facility decisions are a function of the life cycle stages of the items in the product line.

The effect of **life cycle stages** (start-up, growth, maturity, and withdrawal) on equipment selection is significant. Equipment selection is dominated by volume considerations. Volume increases are what life cycle stages are all about. Therefore, it is to be expected that equipment changes will be made over time in keeping with the life cycle stages.

The dynamics are hard to manage unless they have been consciously planned. It might seem reasonable to start off with machines that are economic to use at low volumes. Then, as growth in demand occurs, growth in supply would follow. However, if the risk is low that such growth will occur, then there is reason to start with equipment that has greater capacity than will be needed at first. The period of underutilization can be a short time in the life of a machine. As the equipment approaches full utilization, the costs per unit tend to decrease. With machines that are economic at low volumes, success brings volume increases. This leads to overtime, which inflates per unit costs.

Planning equipment selection should include timing of transitions in supply capability. Planning also must address the work configuration that will be attained eventually. The flow shop remains a worthy goal. When and if that state of affairs is achieved, low-volume general-purpose equipment will not be called upon unless the planning process includes the launching of new products at the proper points in time.

Replacement for wear is part of the planning. There is gradual deterioration in the performance of equipment that should be factored into the life cycle considerations. Maintenance can change the rate of deterioration and must be factored into the plan. Although some equipment is nearly maintenance-free, other equipment requires costly programs with skilled labor and downtime expenses. Appropriate equipment for start-up may not be able to be fully depreciated at replacement time. There is a market for used general-purpose equipment, which may be a consideration that can add flexibility in the early stages of product life. Planning is required to have used-up, and phased-out, low-volume equipment, or to have found new uses for it.

11-10 LAYOUT OF THE WORKPLACE AND JOB DESIGN

It is hard to believe that until the 1980s, workers in American and European auto-assembly plants had to bend down to install the new tires on the wheels, and then tighten the tire bolts. The auto-assembly conveyors ran flat out near the ground. The layout made the job not much different from changing a flat tire on the road. Visitors to Japanese auto plants saw that the conveyor lifted the car up at the point of tire attachment. This carried the car above the worker and allowed putting the tire on at shoulder level. Workers could stand tall and attach the tires to the wheels without bending. Thereafter, conveyors that lifted the car were installed in world-class auto-assembly plants.

This simple anecdote illustrates how good layout interacts with good job design. It also shows how layout of the workplace is a 3-dimensional situation that lends itself to creative solutions for alleviating back problems. It is noted that job design in the flow shop is partnered with layout.

Productivity increases and quality improves when the layout and job are properly designed in the job shop. Travel time and distance traveled are reduced. Paths are kept clear. Queues at workstations are reduced. Production scheduling, shop-floor layout, and job design are connected in a systems sense. The benefits of improved quality derived from better layout must be continuously monitored because process changes are constantly occurring.

11-10a Opportunity Costs for Layout Improvement

It has been substantiated that proper workplace layout design can provide product and process quality improvements (QI), throughput and **cost benefit** productivity improvements (PI), and health benefits (HB) for employees. All of these are welcome because they do result in higher profits. The evaluation of jobs and workplaces within the process and along the supply chain can lead to layout improvements.

> **Cost benefit:** Comparison of costs and benefits that applies to alternative facility configuration decisions.

The paradigm that is used for such evaluations is like a balance scale or a seesaw. All of the costs of doing the job with the new layout X are put on one side of the ledger. All of the costs of not using layout X are put on the other side of the ledger. The lowest cost–highest benefit side (based on QI, PI, and HB) wins the contest. This describes the way that a trade-off model works.

Improving layout and job design involves **opportunity costs** trade-off analysis. Opportunity costs are the costs of doing less than best. By doing something that is not the best, the cost to be paid is the difference in net benefits. This follows the same kind of reasoning that underlies the improvement method of the transportation model.

> **Opportunity costs:** Costs of choosing options that are less than the best.

In this case, there are opportunity costs for not having the best possible layout design. The equation for this trade-off model states that layout design improvement should be made if:

$CPI < OC(QI + PI + HB)$, where

CPI = Cost of layout plan improvement

OC = Opportunity costs incurred for not having used the best possible layout with respect to QI, PI, and HB

$OC(QI)$ = Opportunity costs for quality improvements

$OC(QI)$ could have been obtained if layout design improvement had been made. They also are the opportunity costs incurred by not rectifying quality deficiencies.

For example, improved conveyor layout would yield a better car, which is then translated into:

- Larger market share
- Greater revenues
- Fewer warranty claims

- Less service calls at company expense
- Higher prices that could be charged
- Smaller company discounts on ticket prices
- Better worker attitudes and morale
- Less dealer discontent
- More effective advertising campaigns
- $OC(PI)$ = Opportunity costs for improved productivity

$OC(PI)$ could have been obtained if layout design improvement had been made. They also are the opportunity costs incurred by not rectifying factors that deteriorate productivity. Not having to bend down and work in a crouched position would enable workers to work faster as well as better. The cost of installing four tires to each car could be reduced. It is possible that one or more workers could be freed up to do other jobs in the time now allotted for the repetitive job at the production rate. Job observations and time studies can be used to get good estimates for the opportunity costs for productivity.

Unlike $OC(QI)$, the costs $OC(PI)$ and $OC(HB)$, discussed next, are often measurable.

$OC(HB)$ = Opportunity costs for health benefit savings

Not to be overlooked, $OC(HB)$ might have been obtained if layout design improvement had been made. For example, auto conveyors raise the cars so that tire assembly can be done without bending down. Many back pains are thus avoided. There are also many similar opportunity costs incurred by not rectifying layout factors. For example, a badly designed layout for repetitive work on the computer can negatively impact health—e.g., carpal tunnel syndrome.

The costs associated with bending and crouching include back problems for workers that result in medical claims, higher health insurance, absenteeism, and lost time on the job. Computer operators have been experiencing a problem with their hands and wrists that is called *carpal tunnel syndrome*. Redesign of the computer keyboard, pads for the wrists to rest on, and other redesigns of the wrist support system have improved the situation. However, the strain of such repetitive work has led to the conclusion that keying jobs on the computer are best redesigned to include a regular rest period every hour. Job design, work schedules, and job layout must be treated together as an integrated system to deal with this issue.

11-10b Sensitivity Analysis

It is noteworthy that many of these opportunity costs are not easy to measure. Nevertheless, the costs are real and can be important. They do not disappear because they are considered difficult to measure with accuracy.

Estimates can be made more easily for a range running from a high to a low figure. By using high and low estimates, it is possible to test the sensitivity of the following equation to the range of estimation. Also, it is possible to find out what values of $OC(QI)$, $OC(PI)$, and $OC(HB)$ can lead to equality, thus:

$$CPI = OC(QI + PI + HB)$$

is a systems breakeven value for layout improvement that takes into account quality, productivity, and employees' health.

These next steps are associated with the procedure called **sensitivity analysis**, noting the balance between the right- and left-hand sides of the equation. Say that the following inequation holds:

$$CPI < OC(QI + PI + HB)$$

Then, the current design can be improved and should be altered. This is because the cost of layout improvement (*CPI*) is less than the total opportunity cost for improvements of the three kinds.

Sensitivity analysis: By using high and low estimates, it is possible to test the sensitivity of a business model (e.g., linear programming, scoring, and transportation models) to a range of conditions.

If the cost of layout improvement (*CPI*) is more than the total opportunity cost for improvement of three kinds, as in the equation,

$$CPI > OC(QI + PI + HB)$$

then, cost justification is lacking to improve the current design.

However, there can be circumstances where the inequation lies in the direction, indicating that no change should be made, but a change could be made anyway. The reason could be that there is agreement that the opportunity costs, say for health benefits, cannot be properly estimated. Safety comes under health benefits, and when threats to safety exist, the opportunity costs of *HB* can be regarded as infinite. This means that *CPI* is always less than the sum of the opportunity costs. Then, continuous layout design and workplace improvement are warranted.

In the same sense, if managerial intuition rejects the model's solution, then deeper analysis of the quality and productivity opportunity costs is likely to show that one or both of these costs have been seriously underestimated. The job and workplace design may be creating a situation that has not yet surfaced in traceable costs. Deterioration of worker morale is often detectable before it impacts quality/productivity on a measurable level. P/OM's hunches about negative interactions between layout and process design are worthy of respect.

11-11 LAYOUT TYPES

There are at least five basic types of layouts that will be found in plants and offices. These are

1. *Job shop process layouts*. Similar types of equipment or jobs are grouped together. The lathes are in one place and the presses in another. For services, filing is in one room and copy machines are in another. Inspectors are in one place; designers are in another. Job shop process layouts should facilitate processing many different types of work in relatively small lots. Mobility of equipment enables OM to set up intermittent flow shops when that configuration is attainable. Space must be allocated for work completed at one station and waiting for access to another station. Equipment mobility and layout flexibility allow this configuration to be rearranged to suit the high variety of order mixtures that can occur.

2. *Product-oriented layout*. This layout is typical of the flow shop. Equipment and transport systems are arranged to make the product as efficiently as possible. The layout is designed to prohibit disruptions to the flow. The product-oriented layout is most often associated with assembly lines.

3. *Cellular layout*. This layout is used with a group of machines that work with each other to produce a dedicated family of parts, as in group technology. The layout is engineered to facilitate efficient transfer of parts between machines in the cell. Tooling and transfer are part of the computer programming system, which is capable of nearly instantaneous changeovers enabling small runs of a limited number of parts.

4. *Group technology layout*. This layout is used to efficiently produce a family of parts but there is no emphasis on computer controls and machine cells as in type 3 (listed here). The layout is focused on taking advantage of the similarity of design of the parts.

5. *Combinations of product and process orientation are very common*. Some of the products in the job shop achieve demand volumes that allow them to be run for long periods of time as intermittent flow shops. Modular product-designed parts often have the high volumes that allow cellular manufacture or group technology layouts with, in some cases, serialized flow shop advantages. At the same time, other jobs in the shop remain at low volumes that are only suited to the process layout of job shops. The combination produces a mixed-layout orientation, which also is called a *hybrid layout*.

The complaint department of a large organization with a number of different products has the job shop process layout. Within that group, there are certain subgroups that handle high frequency requests with flow shop dedication. Sixty percent of the complaints can be treated in the highly repetitive fashion. The remaining 40 percent require special treatment for customer satisfaction. The analogy can be extended to families of complaint types and the use of group technology process layout.

Volvos are manufactured in Sweden on fixed platforms. The work does not move. Workers move to it and around it. Shipbuilders and home builders move around the work. Modular housing exemplifies hybrid layout where the parts are made in a factory and then brought to the site where they are assembled, similar to Volvos.

With fixed platforms, workers carry or drive their tools to where they are needed. Commercial airplanes are moved along a production line, albeit slowly. Commercial airline layout is a different form of hybrid, one that combines fixed and moving positions. The fixed-position layout is necessary for power plants, refineries, and locomotives. It is much more controversial (i.e., Volvo), so that deserves an extra word.

Volvo uses the fixed platform because Swedish workers find it more interesting to participate in building the whole car than doing a repetitive step along an assembly line. Worker motivation is improved. In Sweden, worker motivation is important because unemployment benefits are a large percentage of earned wages and readily available. Bored workers are likely to prefer the government benefits to the company wages.

The United Auto Workers (UAW) arranged an interesting experiment in which a group of GM workers were given the opportunity to work with Volvo for six months. Most of these workers said they preferred to work on the GM flow shop assembly layout in spite of, and because of, its repetitive nature. The Volvo layout required knowing and doing too many things. Some preferred the Volvo system and remained with Volvo.

Group technology (GT) for families of parts is a layout that many companies, such as Caterpillar, John Deere, and Cummins Engine, have found rewarding. GT cells are usually part of hybrid layouts. The group technology concept uses a product layout with the capability of producing an entire family of parts.

Special equipment is required that has rapid changeover capabilities to make parts that are identical except for size and/or other dimensional characteristics. Crankshafts, motors, and pumps are typical parts for GT. The production cells use flexible machine-tool organization. Group technology layout is usually a self-contained part of a process layout job shop.

11-12 LAYOUT MODELS

The plant layout problem can be tackled with different kinds of models. There is good engineering knowledge for laying out flow shop processes. There is also a basis for spending the money to do the job well. There is less solid knowledge about achieving excellence for job process layouts and less monetary justification.

Four points to bear in mind:

1. Job shops and the batch production environment are subject to major changes in the product mix. What is optimal for one set of orders may be downright poor for the jobs in the shop one month later. Therefore, layouts that are likely to be good for the expected range of order types are better than those that are excellent for one type and not good for others.

2. The degree to which a few order types dominate the job shop will modify the statement in point 1 and allow some product layout to be mixed in with the process layout. It will be found that the per unit costs of operating product layouts will be significantly less than the costs associated with process layouts. The comparison is even more extreme if GT cells can be set up.

3. Flexibility is desirable, but on the other hand, it is expensive and disruptive to keep moving equipment around the plant. A balance has to be found between these two objectives. If the character of the batch work changes a great deal over time, it is best to go for the most general form of process layout. If layout is to be changed from time to time, it is essential to set up the layout system with this purpose in mind. Modular

office layouts that are well-planned have remarkable flexibility for making quick changes without paralyzing the workforce.

4. Use quantitative models with caution. Creative thinking and common sense pay off in achieving good layouts. Precise measurements count when trying to squeeze a machine into a tight spot. More questionable is the use of elaborate mathematical models to minimize total distance traveled or handling costs.

11-12a Layout Criteria

What criteria determine a satisfactory layout? Seven measures of layout effectiveness are

1. *Capacity*—Output and throughput rate. Goal: Maximize total volumes and rates.
2. *Balance*—The degree to which the throughput rates of consecutive operations are balanced. This is particularly applicable for flow shops and projects. It is more difficult to evaluate job shops on the same basis. Nevertheless, balancing work rates for job shops is always desirable. Goal: Perfect balance.
3. Amount of *investment and operating costs*. Goal: Minimum.
4. *Flexibility* to change layouts. Goal: Maximize ease of change.
5. Amount of *work in process* (WIP). Goal: Minimize units of inventory.
6. *Distance* that parts travel; one foot instead of two inches traveled thousands of times per day adds up to sizeable waste. Goal: Minimize total travel time and distance.
7. *Storage for WIP and handling equipment* to move parts from one place in the facility to another. Goal: Minimize space set aside for storage and equipment required to move the parts.

11-12b Floor Plan Models

All seven of these criteria can be evaluated crudely yet with reasonably correct perceptions by using **floor plan models.** The floor plan drawings are graphic methods of trial and error that are used by interior decorators. They use little paper cutouts that represent the furniture. A dollhouse is the 3-dimensional deluxe version.

Plant layout models can be 2- or 3-dimensional. Often 2-dimensional floor plans, with cutouts made from templates, are used to represent the various pieces of equipment. When conveyors are employed, overhead space requirements may be important, and 3-dimensional "dollhouse" models are preferred.

These techniques are useful for an incremental approach to a satisfactory layout. They do not bring any quantitative power to bear. Although an optimal layout based on the numbers may be far from satisfactory, the quantitative information might assist creativity.

> **Floor plan model:** Drawings of the plant floor to achieve capacity goals, obtain balanced workloads and minimum operating costs, low levels of work in process and least storage space, and minimum travel distance for people and parts.

11-12c Layout Load Models

A relatively simple quantitative approach examines alternative layout plans in terms of the frequency with which certain paths are used. Usually, the highest frequency paths are assigned the shortest plant floor path distances to travel. The objective is to minimize the total unit distances traveled.

The physical space is divided into areas that conform to floor layouts including stairs, elevators, rest rooms, etc. The locations are designated as A, B, C, D, and E in Figure 11-3.

The average distance that must be traveled between areas A, B, C, D, and E are shown in Table 11-15. These distances (in feet) are designated as d_{IJ}. They are physical measurements related to the floor plan shown in Figure 11-3. The matrix is read from row I to column J (both are capitalized letters).

This matrix is symmetric so the distance from A to D is 32. That is the same as the distance from D to A. However, symmetry does not always hold because of one-way passages, escalators, conveyor belts, and gravity feed delivery systems.

FIGURE 11-3
Layout of Plant or Office Floor (with Areas *A, B, C, D,* and *E,* and Work Centers 1 Through 5)

TABLE 11-15

Distances (d_{IJ}) Measured Between Locations *A*, *B*, *C*, *D*, and *E*

Columns are from Locations J = A, etc.	Rows are to Locations I = A, etc,	A	B	C	D	E
	A	0	10	20	32	40
	B	10	0	16	18	20
	C	20	16	0	12	15
	D	32	18	12	0	10
	E	40	20	15	10	0

Note: Read from row *I* to column *J*.

Work centers: Assignment of work centers to specific space locations on the plant or office floor should minimize costs (or times) of transport of materials, work in process, and finished goods.

Layout planning involves locating equipment and people to do certain kinds of jobs that are designated as **work centers** at specific locations on the plant floor. Work centers are equipped to do specific kinds of jobs—like the press shop, copy room, hamburger grill, and darkroom. Processing orders on-hand causes materials to move between the work centers and, therefore, between the physical locations. The materials are at different stages of work in process. Further, they represent various orders and job types. Also, order-batch sizes vary.

What is needed next is a measure of the amount of materials or the number of trips between the various work centers that different jobs entail. If order-process batches are of about the same size, then a random sample of jobs could be taken to estimate how many trips occur between each center.

If batches are not similar, then the idea is to capture those jobs that are most important either because they are the most frequent, involve the largest number of units, are the most difficult and costly to transport, or are the most profitable. Matrices appropriate to these special jobs should be created and studied. Perhaps no more that 20 percent of the jobs that are done in this batch production environment consume 80 percent of the transport resources. For the jobs that are most important, the objective is to minimize the total distance traveled.

Table 11-16 presents the information relating the number of units that move between work centers on an average day in a stable work-flow environment. These data are called wc_{ij}. The matrix is read from row i to column j (both are lowercase letters).

Table 11-17 shows the assignment of work centers (labeled 1 through 5) to the floor plan areas (with letter designations) given in Figure 11-3. This pairs up the floor plan locations A through E with the work centers 1 through 5. The assignments are: A1, B2, C3, D4, E5. Work centers are movable to different floor plan locations.

Multiplying the two matrices in Tables 11-15 and 11-16 is equivalent to multiplying $(d_{IJ})(wc_{ij})$, which yields unit-distances traveled. The equation for this volume of unit-distances of flow is written:

$$f_{IJ,ij} = (d_{IJ})(wc_{ij}).$$

TABLE 11-16

Number of Units Flowing Between Work Centers 1, 2, 3, 4, and 5 (wc_{ij})

Columns j and Row i	1	2	3	4	5
1	X	100	60	80	20
2	40	X	50	10	90
3	80	90	X	60	30
4	120	10	40	X	70
5	110	5	5	30	X

Note: Read from row *i* to column *j*.

TABLE 11-17

Layout Assignments

Row *i* to Column *j*	A	B	C	D	E
1	X				
2		X			
3			X		
4				X	
5					X

The assignments are A1, B2, C3, D4, E5 with work centers 1, 2, 3, 4, and 5 to letter floor areas. There are 5 x 4 x 3 x 2 x 1 = 120 different assignments of work centers to floor areas that are possible.

Table 11-18 shows the results for daily work flows on the shop floor.

The column totals in Table 11-18 are summed to give the grand total of the total daily work flows. The summing equation is

$$F_{I,J}{}^{i,j} = \sum_{I,J}^{i,j} f_{IJ,ij} = \sum_{I,J}\sum_{i,j}(d_{IJ})(wc_{ij})$$

The grand total of unit-feet traveled is the double sum of the multiplicative products as shown in the previous equation.

The total number of unit-feet traveled *in this layout* is 23,025. *There are better layouts;* a reassignment is suggested. Calculations show that an improvement results when the new assignments of A1, B4, C5, D3, and E2 are used. These numbers are the basis of Table 11-19, where the new assignments of work centers to plant floor locations is reflected by the column headings and row names.

TABLE 11-18

Total Daily Work Flows

	A1	B2	C3	D4	E5
A1	0	1,000	1,200	2,560	800
B2	400	0	800	180	1,800
C3	1,600	1,440	0	720	450
D4	3,840	180	480	0	700
E5	4,400	100	75	300	0
Totals	10,240	2,720	2,555	3,760	3,750

Number of Units Moving Between Work Centers Multiplied by the Distance Traveled From Rows designated by *Ii* to Columns designated by *Jj*

TABLE 11-19

Total Daily Work Flows: A Reassignment Matrix

	A1	B4	C5	D3	E2
A1	0	800	400	1,920	4,000
B4	1,200	0	1,120	720	200
C5	2,200	480	0	60	75
D3	2,560	1,080	360	0	900
E2	1,600	200	1,350	500	0
Totals	7,560	2,560	3,230	3,200	5,175

Number of Units Moving Between Work Centers Multiplied by the Distance Traveled Between Work Centers.

Improvement results when A1, B4, C5, D3, and E2 are the new assignments.

The total number of unit-feet traveled per day in this layout is 21,725. Unit-feet traveled has been decreased by 1,300. That is an improvement of almost 6 percent. It is likely that additional decreases can be achieved by studying the matrices and trying to eliminate incorrect assignments of heavy-unit volumes to large distance movements.

This analysis has tested only two configurations out of 120 possibilities. How good was the original assignment? There is no way of telling. It could have been selected randomly. A starting point strategy and evaluation of that strategy are needed to achieve improvements. The starting point concept bears similarities to the NWC method for the TM.

In fact, the original was chosen because it could be improved with a sensible heuristic (rule of thumb). This explains the reassignment. There remain 118 other possible assignments of work centers to locations.

This is because there are 5! (factorial) ways ($5 \times 4 \times 3 \times 2 \times 1 = 120$) to assign five work centers to five locations.

The improved version is based on a reasonable heuristic. This means that it should be better than an alternative picked at random. Still other layouts exist that conform with the general idea of the heuristic. Because better is not best, more calculations are warranted.

How was Table 11-19 constructed? First, Table 11-20 is derived by literally rearranging the rows and the columns from the order 1, 2, 3, 4, and 5 in Table 11-16 to the new order of 1, 4, 5, 3, and 2, as shown in Table 11-20. A practical approach is to read off each entry in Table 11-16 and enter it in the appropriate cell in Table 11-20. For example, 80 should appear at the intersection of $i = 1$, $j = 4$ in both tables. It may be useful to do a few of these transformations before continuing.

Second, multiply Table 11-20 by the numbers in Table 11-15 to derive Table 11-19. Again, it may be useful to do a few of these multiplications to get the understanding derived from doing operations rather than just reading about them.

11-12d Flow Costs

Say that the cost of a unit moving one foot is the same between all locations and work centers. Then, the costs of transporting units will not lead to a new matrix for total daily work-flow costs. However, if the costs of transport are different between either work centers, or floor locations, or both, then the following equation is needed to describe how these different transport costs arise for each cell in the matrix.

$$cf_{IJ,ij} = (d_{IJ})(wc_{ij})(c_{IJ,ij})$$

The total costs would then be obtained by summing across all of the cells.

$$CF_{I,J}^{i,j} = \Sigma_{I,J}^{i,j}\, cf_{IJ,ij} = \sum_{I,J} \sum_{i,j} (d_{IJ})(wc_{ij})(c_{IJ,ij})$$

Another way of stating this is to refer to matrix multiplication. Thus, if the costs of transporting units are different, then it is necessary to multiply the matrix of total daily work flows so that the appropriate costs per unit and per foot are expressed. Note that

---

TABLE 11-20

Number of Units Flowing Between Work Centers 1, 2, 3, 4, and 5 (wc_{ij})

Columns are *j* and Rows are *i*	1	4	5	3	2
1	X	80	20	60	100
4	120	X	70	40	10
5	110	30	X	5	5
3	80	60	30	X	90
2	40	10	90	50	X

Note: Read from row *i* to column *j*.

these transport costs need not be symmetric. The cost of down-moving gravity-flows is usually much less than the cost of carrying units up to higher floors.

If the cost is $1 per unit per foot traveled, then the matrices in Tables 11-18 and 11-19 also represent the total daily work-flow costs. These costs would be $23,025 for the first assignment tested and $21,725 for the second and improved assignment.

11-12e Heuristics to Improve Layout

Two **heuristics (rules of thumb** for improving the system's performance) come to mind when searching for policies that might help to improve plant or office layout.

1. Assign work centers with large unit flow rates between them to locations as close as possible.
2. Assign work centers with small unit flow rates between them to locations as distant as possible.

In Table 11-16, look at those pairs of work centers that have the largest work-flow rates between them. These are in descending order:

Work center 4 to work center 1 has a wc_{ij} of 120 units.
Work center 5 to work center 1 has a wc_{ij} of 110 units.
Work center 1 to work center 2 has a wc_{ij} of 100 units.

Assign these work centers to locations that are as close as possible. Note (in Table 11-15) that the distance between A and B is 10 feet and between C and D is 12 feet.

Using the D_{IJ} data in Table 11-15, the biggest distances are between locations A and D (32), and between A and E (40).

This means that the original layout of A1, B2, **C**3, **D**4, and E5 assigned 120 units to the second biggest distance (viz., 32 between A and D) in the matrix of Table 11-16. Further, the original layout assigned work center 1 to location A and work center 5 to location E. That means that 110 units were assigned to move the largest distance between locations—viz., 40 between A and E.

To follow the heuristic "assign the largest number of units to the shortest distance" would mean assigning work center 1 to A and work center 4 to B. That was done in the second matrix, which reassigned work center 4 to location B. Because work center 1 was already assigned to A, the next best distance from A is 20 at C. Therefore, work center 5 was assigned to C in the second matrix.

The second part of the heuristic calls for assigning the centers with the smallest work-flow rates between them to the locations that are as distant as possible.

The two smallest flow rates between centers (in the matrix of Table 11-16) are both 5, as follows:

Work center 5 to work center 2 has a wc_{ij} of 5 units.
Work center 5 to work center 3 has a wc_{ij} of 5 units.

Work center 1 has been assigned to location A. Work center 4 has been assigned to location B and work center 5 has been assigned to location C. The shortest distances from C are to D and E. These are 12 and 15, respectively. Assign work center 3 to location D and work center 2 to E. This is the second matrix iteration (called the *reassignment matrix*) shown by Table 11-19.

The heuristic did its job, but it is not clear whether further improvement is still possible. Trial and error with the improved matrix can be used to test further shifts.

Heuristics (rules of thumb): Methods for discovery, guides for problem-solving, and procedures for experimental learning. One of the most popular is the trial and error technique with feedback to reward steps in the right direction.

SUMMARY

The subject of facility management comprises choosing the location, determining the structure and the site, selecting equipment, and preparing the plant or office layout. There are numerous qualitative factors to take into account. Then, the quantitative modeling can begin.

The transportation model is used to minimize shipping costs or maximize profits where production location and market differentials exist. Scoring models are discussed, which can be applied for site or equipment selection. The layout of the workplace and job design interact strongly, which is analyzed. Floor models that minimize distance traveled are explained.

After quantitative modeling, it is necessary to return to the qualitative factors to evaluate the relevance and quality of the solutions offered by the models. Throughout this facilities planning chapter, the systems approach is explained because teamwork is desired in making location, site, and equipment decisions.

Two Spotlight feature boxes conclude this chapter. These boxes illustrate real applications of the material in the chapter. See Spotlight 11-1: How Good Is Your Production Scheduling? and Spotlight 11-2: Ford Motor Company.

KEY TERMS

Best location
Build
Buy
Cost benefit
Design for manufacturing
Facilities planning
Floor plan model

Heuristics (rules of thumb)
Layout
Life cycle stages
Models
Multiple decision makers
Northwest Corner (NWC) method
Opportunity costs

Pure number
Rent
Scoring model
Sensitivity analysis
Transportation models
Work centers

REVIEW QUESTIONS

1. What is meant by "The basis for location decisions differs according to which parts of the supply chain are involved"?

2. How many assignments of four work centers to floor locations can be made with a 4-story building? (No splitting of work centers is allowed.)

3. With four work centers, there are how many possible layouts?

4. Finding the best locations for police and fire stations is a pressing urban problem. Discuss the nature of this problem and what variables are likely to be important. How does this compare to the facility layout problem?

5. Is it true that plant selection should in part be based on estimates of labor costs for different areas of the country?

6. For the scoring model, what happens when a weight of zero is chosen for one of the factors?

7. What enables the horizontal and vertical "stepping-stone" pattern to work for shifting assignments when using the transportation model?

8. Some of the following industries tend to form high-density clusters in specific geographic areas. Identify those industries that have strong clusters and try to find the rational explanation for these specific clusters. In the same sense, identify those industries that do not have strong clusters and try to find the rational explanation for the lack of clustering.

   a. Financial services
   b. U.S. automobiles
   c. Stockyards
   d. Steel
   e. Textiles
   f. Semiconductors
   g. Aerospace
   h. Resort hotels
   i. Motion pictures
   j. Publishing
   k. Cigarettes
   l. Petroleum
   m. Credit card processing
   n. Non-U.S. automobiles
   o. Theme parks
   p. Advertising agencies
   q. Soy products
   r. Pharmaceuticals

9. Gasoline station location often is based on traffic density studies. What would be the criteria for a good location in terms of traffic density and patterns?

10. Recent emphasis on variety has led to flexible product layouts that can be quickly converted to produce mixed models. How can this be done using a product layout rather than the more typical process layout?

PROBLEMS SECTION

1. Use the trial and error heuristic to determine the best layout for the following data:

Locations			
	A	B	C
A	0	4,000	2,000
B	4,000	0	3,000
C	2,000	3,000	0

Daily flow costs per unit distances from and to work centers:

	1	2	3
1	X	$50	$70
2	$20	X	$40
3	$30	$80	X

2. Use the scoring model to resolve the following equipment selection problem. A choice is to be made between two alternative information technology (IT) systems. The following data apply:

	System 1	System 2	Weights
Investment cost	$5,050,000	$5,060,000	3
Operating costs (annual)	$400,000	$500,000	3
Downtime	3	2	7
Ease of repair	2	3	5
Ease of learning	4	5	2
Flexibility	4	2	4

Characteristics are scaled so that large numbers are less desirable than small numbers. Large weights are more important than small ones, and the scale runs from 1 to 7.

3. A matrix of supply and demand is shown here:

						Supply
						20
						30
						50
Demand	10	10	10	20	50	100

Use the Northwest Corner method to assign shipments for the first feasible solution. You will note that a twofold problem is encountered.
a. What are these conditions called?
b. What can be done about them?

4. The American Company has two factories, A and B, located in Wilmington, Delaware, and San Francisco, California. Each has a production capacity of 550 units per week. American's markets are centered in Los Angeles, Chicago, and New York City. The demands of these markets are for 150, 350, and 400 units, respectively, in the coming week. A matrix of shipping distances is prepared. Determine the shipping schedule that minimizes total shipping distance.

Estimates of shipping distances (in miles) are shown in the following matrix, along with supply and demand.

	Los Angeles	Chicago	New York City	Supply
Wilmington	3,000	1,000	300	550
San Francisco	400	2,000	3,000	550
Demand	150	350	400	

5. The Northwest Corner (NWC) solution is shown here for a new plan that has been proposed for the 3-plant, 2-market problem.

Northwest Corner—Initial Feasible Assignment

	Markets M_j			Supply
Plants P_i	M_A	M_B	M_D	
P_1	40	20		60 units / day
P_2		40	30	70 units / day
P_3			60	60 units / day
Demand	40	60	90	

The profits per unit shipped are

	Markets M_j		
Plants P_i	M_A	M_B	M_D
P_1	$23	$32	$0
P_2	$16	$25	$0
P_3	$30	$38	$0

What is the total profit associated with the NWC assignment?

6. Using the information in Problem 5, ship as many units as possible into P_3M_B. How many units will that be? Draw the revised TM. Compare the profit of this shipping plan with that of the NWC assignment.

7. Using the information in Problem 5, ship as many units as possible into P_1M_D. How many units will that be? Draw the revised TM. What is the profit of that shipping plan? Compare the profit of this shipping plan with that of the NWC assignment.

8. Using the information in Problem 5, ship as many units as possible into P_2M_A. How many units will that be? Draw the revised TM. What is the profit of that shipping plan? Compare the profit of this shipping plan with that of the NWC assignment.

9. Using the information in Problem 5, ship as many units as possible into P_3M_A. The stepping pattern is more difficult but still uses horizontal and vertical moves from one shipping assignment to another. How many units will be shipped to $P_3 M_A$? Draw the revised TM. What is the profit of that shipping plan? Compare the profit of this shipping plan with that of the NWC assignment.

10. The cost of improving plant layout is $100,000 to be depreciated over a 5-year period. The estimated annual improvements in profit are $6,000 from better quality, $4,000 from higher productivity, and $11,000 from health benefits. Is the layout improvement recommended?

11. The cost of improving office layout is $27,000 to be treated as a one-time expense. The office manager does not have any way of estimating improved profits resulting from quality changes but says that the new layout will save time and miles of walking for the 40 office employees. She estimates that the new layout will cut the amount of walking for the average employee by 100 miles per year. How much will the layout improvement be worth?

12. Using the layout load model, determine a good arrangement for work centers at locations for the numbers given in the following matrices.

Distances measured between locations A, B, C, D, and E (d_{IJ}) from row I to column J

I\J	A	B	C	D	E
A	0	10	20	32	40
B	10	0	16	18	20
C	20	16	0	12	15
D	32	18	12	0	10
E	40	20	15	10	0

Number of units flowing between work centers 1, 2, 3, 4, and 5 (w_{ij}) from row i to column j

i\j	1	2	3	4	5
1	X	50	60	80	20
2	40	X	50	10	90
3	80	90	X	60	30
4	50	10	40	X	70
5	60	5	5	30	X

If the cost of a unit moving one foot is one dollar ($1 per unit per foot traveled), what is the total daily work-flow cost of the solution obtained?

END-OF-CHAPTER QUESTIONS

1. Facilities planning applies to plants, offices, customer service call centers, hospitals, and classrooms. Applications are as diverse as work systems. For all such planning, there are four fundamental components. Five are listed below. Which one of these is not applicable?

  a. The geographic location selection of the facility could be as broad as Europe or North America. It could be by country within Europe or state within the United States. Part of the facility (say, fabrication) could be located in one place and another part (say, final assembly) could be located in another.

  b. Structure desired raises issues of build, buy, or rent. Interactions of existing structures with specific sites make it necessary to consider structure and site together. Build helps to disconnect structure and site.

  c. When structure and site decisions precede geographic location, the facilities planning effort is more effective. Time and money can be saved because lengthy analyses of geographic factors are essentially by-passed.

  d. Equipment choice is driven by process technology decisions. This consideration can become crucial in determining structure and site. Process technology may be a function of facility location. For example, if the market in Brazil is large enough to justify a flow shop being located there, then special-purpose equipment may require a new building close to a railroad siding.

  e. Planning moves up and down the hierarchy, and this includes feasible layouts of equipment and people. Layouts frequently involve decisions about materials moving via conveyors, forklift trucks, gravity chutes, AGVs (automatic guidance vehicles), etc., and people moving up and down stairs, or by elevators.

2. Six factors are well-known as critical determinants of location decisions. Several of these are discussed in choices a. to e. Which one statement is not logical for the location decision?

  a. Process inputs dominate location decisions when the cost of transporting raw materials and components to the production transformation process from distant locations is prohibitively high. Indonesian hardwood is an example, where trees are brought to lumber mills that are close to where they are harvested.

  b. Steps can be taken to reduce the large costs of transporting materials that will be discarded during production. For example, mine mouth processing plants grind ore to very fine particles. These "iron-rich fines" are separated from the rock using flotation methods or magnetically. They are then palletized for shipping to iron and steel plants, some at great distances. The production process for making steel and iron has been divided into two parts to reduce the shipment of unused materials.

c. Process outputs become important to location decisions when companies want to inspect products before they are shipped to them. For example, it is difficult for New Orleans' customers to determine the quality of product being made in Nagoya.

d. Many non-U.S. auto assembly plants have been located in states such as Alabama and Tennessee. This is partly because, by relocating their plants, they gain shipping cost advantages over manufacturing the cars abroad and sending them to the United States by sea. Although other factors are operating as well, this is an example of location decisions that are influenced by process outputs.

e. The transplants are auto companies from abroad that moved their auto assembly to the southeastern United States. One of the reasons that have been given for so many firms making this move is that there are tax, tariff, trade, and legal advantages. There are also marketing factors when a company can say "made by American workers."

3. Discussion continues about the six well-known factors that are critical determinants of location decisions. Found in choices a. to e., which one statement is not logical for the location decision?

   a. In the automobile business, service is crucial. Acura and Lexus set up separate service facilities so as to differentiate themselves from Honda and Toyota. These companies view their process outputs as services (include parts and maintenance) that require locating very close to their customers.

   b. Special process requirements lead to location selection near energy supplies, water for hydro-power, cooling and runoffs, skilled labor force, ample labor supplies, lots of space, and for warehouse distribution centers, a location that is as close as possible to all major markets. That location can differ because markets vary by product types.

   c. Locations selected by grouping of like-industries have always turned out to have economic advantages. Tires stay in Akron; the diamond district in New York City is all within a few square miles; silicon valley was the place to be for semiconductors and their users; Detroit-Dearborn and environs have workers who know how to make cars, and their loyalty to the Big 3 is so great that the auto-assembly transplants had to go to Kentucky, Tennessee, and Alabama.

   d. Top executives may have personal preferences for locations that override the logic of business location analysis. Studies have shown that managers (like other people) can put down deep roots that are difficult to dislocate. Location decision makers do not recognize that they are rationalizing reasons for location selection that overlook other places that should be considered. This applies as much to offices and plants as to hospitals, schools, restaurants, and gas stations.

   e. The full-scale systems problem is addressed by including costs due to location with respect to both suppliers and customers. Such a business analysis method exists and it is called the transportation model.

4. The transportation model resolves location problems, quantitatively, on a large scale (i.e., with many alternatives, using computer programs). Smaller problems can be solved with paper and pencil, or a spreadsheet. A small problem is presented here with all necessary data based on per unit output of the product. Two plants, called P_1 and P_2, have equal supply capabilities of 90 units per day. Two markets, called M_A and M_B, have equal demand requirements of 40 units per day. Plant to market (distributor) shipping costs are given as well as the supplier to plant transport costs for raw materials and components for one unit. Which one statement a. to e. is incorrect?

Plant	Supplier to Plant Transport Costs	Shipping Costs from Plant to M_B	Shipping Costs from Plant to M_A	Supply (Units per Day)
P_1	$6 per unit	$1 per unit	$2 per unit	90 units per day
P_2	$3 per unit	$3 per unit	$4 per unit	90 units per day
Market demand (units per day)		40 units per day	40 units per day	

   a. A total of 80 units per day is demanded by the two markets. That demand level can be satisfied because each plant has a supply capability of 90 units per day. The total supply capability is 180 units per day.

   b. The shipping costs to both markets are better for P_1 than for P_2. However, the supplier transport costs favor P_2. These costs have to be added together to make a comparison. That yields the following costs where M_D is a dummy market added to make total units demanded per day equal to total daily supply capability.

	M_A	M_B	M_D	Supply
P_1	6 + 1 = $7 per unit	6 + 2 = $8 per unit	$0 per unit	90 units
P_2	3 + 3 = $6 per unit	3 + 4 = $7 per unit	$0 per unit	90 units
Demand	40 units	40 units	100 units	180 units

   c. If the decision is made to have P_1 ship 40 units to M_A and P_2 ship 40 units to M_B, then the total shipping cost will be $600 per day, which has the advantage of keeping both plants busy.

   d. The dummy market M_D will not receive any units, which is how a dummy functions. It allows supply to equal demand, which the transportation model requires. A dummy production facility is required when demand is greater than supply. A dummy plant will make zero units. The market to which the dummy plant ships has a demand shortfall.

   e. There is no direct information about the location of the two plants or where the markets are situated. There is no information about the location of the supplier. However, because shipping costs are given, it should be possible to make an informed guess about the respective locations. Note that specific locations are interesting for the storytelling, but they are not relevant to the analysis.

5. The shipping plan has not yet been decided for P_1 and P_2. The decision could be momentous because one of the plants might be shut down. The analysis continues with data

unchanged. Results are stated in points a. through e. One report is wrong. Identify that report.

	M_A	M_B	M_D	Supply
P_1	6 + 1 = $7 per unit	6 + 2 = $8 per unit	$0 per unit	90 units
P_2	3 + 3 = $6 per unit	3 + 4 = $7 per unit	$0 per unit	90 units
Demand	40 units	40 units	100 units	180 units

a. There is an allocation rule that states with M markets and N plants there cannot be more than M + N − 1 shipments. The dummy satisfies the requirement that total supply equals total demand. Shipments ≤ (3 + 2 − 1 = 4).

b. Report 1 recommended the shipping pattern ($P_1 - M_A$, $P_1 - M_D$, $P_2 - M_B$, $P_2 - M_D$). It has a total cost of $560. Management rejected this report as too costly.

	M_A	M_B	M_D	Supply
P_1	40 units	0 units	50 units	90 units
P_2	0 units	40 units	50 units	90 units
Demand	40 units	40 units	100 units	180 units

c. Report 2 recommended the shipping pattern ($P_1 - M_B$, $P_1 - M_D$, $P_2 - M_A$, $P_2 - M_D$). It has a total cost of $560. Management rejected this report as too costly.

	M_A	M_B	M_D	Supply
P_1	0 units	0 units	90 units	90 units
P_2	40 units	40 units	10 units	90 units
Demand	40 units	40 units	100 units	180 units

d. Report 3 recommended the shipping pattern ($P_2 - M_A$, $P_1 - M_D$, $P_2 - M_B$, $P_2 - M_D$). It has a total cost of $520. Management rejected this report as too costly.

	M_A	M_B	M_D	Supply
P_1	0 units	0 units	90 units	90 units
P_2	40 units	40 units	10 units	90 units
Demand	40 units	40 units	100 units	180 units

e. The shipping costs to both markets are better for P_1 than for P_2. However, the supplier transport costs favor P_2. These costs have to be added together to make a comparison. That yields the following costs where M_D is a dummy market added to make total units demanded equal to total supply capability.

6. Structure and site selection generally follow the location decision. Some basic statements about structure and site are presented in points a. through e. Which one of these statements is unreasonable?

a. The fast-food industry searches for sites in all major cities, and most structures follow a prescribed architectural and interior plan. Thus, McDonald's, Wendy's, Chick-fil-A, Koo Koo Roo, IHOP, and Fazoli's can be identified instantly from their characteristic features and the fact that one is exactly like another.

b. Structure and site decisions should be analyzed by a cost-benefit analysis that includes the costs of building and operating at a specific location, and the revenues that can be generated from the traffic pattern. In addition, the effects of competitors at present and likely to move into the neighborhood in the future should be included.

c. Location, structure, and site come as a package of tangible and intangible conditions that have costs. Some of these costs are difficult to determine but must be discussed. For example, neighborhood stores have been known to oppose attracting fast-food customers with 24/7 hours, loud music from cars at all hours, and complaints along similar lines.

d. Insurance rules and costs are structure and site sensitive.

e. Weather conditions have to be considered in determining operating costs in a geographic location. Site has its own issues related to specific conditions such as snow removal and drainage. In addition, fire and police protection can vary in accord with the site chosen.

7. Which location (structure and site) should be chosen? A scoring model has been created to capture the tangible and intangible factors that characterize these two locations, called Q and R. The choice will become the new call center for this large book and record retailer. Annual numeric costs are used. Intangible factors are scaled 1 to 10 with 1 being best. Decision objective is minimization so the best ratio will be as small as possible. Largest weights are most important. Findings are reported in points a. through e. Which one of the findings is incorrect?

	Location Q	Location R	Weight
Tangible Costs			
Buildings and land	$10 million	$ 15 million	3
Salaries	$500,000	$300,000	3
Other operations	$100,000	$100,000	3
Intangible Costs			
Telecommunication system	2	1	4
Workforce availability	3	2	2
Workforce skills	2	4	3
Community attitude	2	1	1

a. Total tangible costs for Q are $10.6 and for R are $15.4. Numbers have been rounded because the ratio of Q to R is 0.688 no matter how many millions of dollars is involved. Location Q is preferred to R. The ratio of 0.688 when raised to the power of 3 (importance weight) is 0.326. This gives Q about three times more advantage than R based on costs alone.

b. Telecommunication system's capability is important to this choice because it has the highest weight of 4. R has a two-to-one advantage with respect to this factor. When raised to the power of 4, that gives R 16 times more advantage than location Q. Combining the cost factor with that of telecommunication gives R more than five times the advantage of Q.

c. A discrepancy has arisen. One analyst states that the final ratio is 2.935, which means that location R is the winner, being almost 3 times more favored than Q.

d. A second analyst disagrees and states that the final ratio is 0.935, which means that location Q is the winner, but only by a hair's breadth.

e. It has been pointed out that workforce skills are not favorable for R. Location Q is preferred two to one and that is before using the weighting factor. After raising the ratio of ½ to the third power, R is at an eight-to-one advantage.

8. There are some basic rules for equipment selection. The first step is to agree on the work configuration to be used. Once the issues of special-purpose equipment versus general-purpose equipment are resolved, the points cited in a. to e. are guidelines. However, one of these is not correct. Which answer is wrong?

a. For choosing between specific machines, conveyors, forklift trucks, and computers as well, the net present value of the investments and operating costs should be determined. Discounted cash-flow analysis permits purchase price to be combined with a time stream of operating costs including maintenance costs.

b. Life cycle stages do not influence equipment selection because the tolerances required for products have nothing to do with stages in the marketplace.

c. The breakeven model provides a benchmark regarding the volume of work that must be done before profit can be made with the new equipment. Relationships between supply and demand should be examined when selecting equipment.

d. Scoring models are useful for equipment selection. They can help to organize the relevant data in much the same way that they were used for site choice. For example, scoring models can help with intangible factors such as how long will it take to train employees to use the equipment productively? How safe are the systems?

e. Setup times on alternative equipments should be compared. What variety of jobs are likely to be done on the new equipment?

9. There are at least five basic types of layouts that can be found in plants and offices around the world. Their identification and discussions about them are covered in points a. through e. One of these treatments is incorrect. Identify which of the different layout discussions is flawed.

a. Job shop process layouts are characterized by clusters of similar types of equipment such as lathes and drill presses. In offices, desks with phones are grouped in standard fashion. Computers, file cabinets, and copy machines are usually situated nearby. Kitchens of restaurants are filled with the general-purpose equipment that allows restaurants to produce to the menu.

b. The product-oriented layout is typical of the flow shop where special-purpose equipment and transport systems move the product efficiently from workstation to workstation. This is the sequenced assembly that started with Henry Ford and which characterizes auto-assembly operations today.

c. Cellular layouts are increasingly used as factories within a factory. They produce a quota of parts in an intermittent flow shop arrangement. Teamwork of cell members is

particularly important. Because of cross-training, members can spell each other and shift between positions.

d. Project layout charts are used to monitor and control the degree of completion of project steps and stages. They reflect status and project future accomplishments. These layout charts send signals about likely troubles that are developing. They have been around for years and are considered to help report what is going on in complex project management situations.

e. Group technology layouts can efficiently produce a family of parts. The computer may play a role in achieving changeovers but there is no emphasis on the tightly knit team-play found in cellular layouts. GT layout is focused on process abilities to produce similar parts using changes in fixtures, jigs, and equipment settings.

10. Every company must get down to the details of layout load models. It is the stage where interior decorating of the home, plant, office, or restaurant kitchen takes place. The difference in layout between McDonald's and Burger King is not coincidental. Layout criteria include capacity, balance, flexibility, volume flows, distance traveled, costs, and time. Gamma Company's matrix of distances measured between locations (A, B, C, D, and E) on the plant floor is shown next to the matrix of units flowing between work centers (1, 2, 3, 4, and 5). Number of units is on an average day with a stable work-flow environment. Where on the plant floor ($A - E$) should the work centers ($1 - 5$) be located so as to minimize the total unit-distances traveled?

	A	B	C	D	E		1	2	3	4	5
A	00	10	20	32	40	1	X	100	60	80	20
B	10	00	16	18	20	2	40	X	50	10	90
C	20	16	00	12	15	3	80	90	X	60	30
D	32	18	12	00	10	4	120	10	40	X	70
E	40	20	15	10	00	5	110	5	5	30	X

The discussion in points a. through e. makes pertinent observations that help to clarify what the layout load floor plan procedure is all about. However, one observation is wrong. Which is that?

a. Equipment 1 is located on the floor plan at A. Equipment 2 is located at B. The matrix for A_1 and B_2 indicates that 1,400 unit-feet moved in a day.

	A_1	B_2
A_1	00	1,000
B_2	400	00

b. For the assignment A_1, B_2, C_3, D_4, and E_5, the total number of unit-feet traveled in one day is 23,025.

c. Controversy exists between the reports of two analysts who disagree on the best solution found yet. One states that the assignment A_1, B_4, C_5, D_3, and E_5 is the best yet with unit-feet traveled per day equal to 21,725.

d. The second analyst states that the assignment A_1, B_5, C_4, D_2, and E_3 is best yet with unit-feet traveled per day equal to 21,530.

e. A heuristic approach pays heed to the fact that 120 units are shipped from work center 4 to work center 1 and assigns them to locations B and A because they are close to each other. The heuristic proceeds in the same way.

ADDITIONAL READINGS

Allen, Robinson, and Stewart (eds). *A Plant Floor Guide*, Dearborn, MI: Society of Manufacturing Engineers, 2001.

Bridgman, P. W. *Dimensional Analysis*. New Haven, CT: Yale University Press, 1922; paperback edition, 1963.

Burnham, John M. *Integrative Facilities Management*. Burr Ridge, IL: Irwin, 1994.

Cedarleaf, Jay. *Plant Layout and Plant Improvement*. Colville, WA: Bluecreek Publishing Co., 1997.

Davies, R. L., and D. Rogers. *Store Location and Assessment Research*. New York: Wiley, 1984.

Gopal, Christopher, and Harold Cypress. *Integrated Distribution Management*. Burr Ridge, IL: Irwin, 1993.

Hauser, John R. *Applying Marketing Management: Four PC Simulations*. Danvers, MA: The Scientific Press, boyd & fraser publishing co (text with diskette for various kinds of scoring models), 1986.

Howard, Kevin. "Postponement of Packaging and Product Differentiation for Lower Logistics Costs." *Journal of Electronics Manufacturing*, vol. 4 (1994): 65–69.

Johansson, Henry J., Patrick McHugh, A. John Pendlebury, and William A. Wheeler III. *Business Process Reengineering*. New York: John Wiley, 1993, 180, 186.

Karaska, G. J., and D. F. Bramhall. *Location Analysis for Manufacturing: A Selection of Readings*. Cambridge, MA: M.I.T. Press, 1969.

Koelsch, James R. "Work Smart." *Manufacturing Engineering* (November 1994): 65–67.

Lilien, Gary L. *Marketing Management: Analytic Exercises for Spreadsheets*. Danvers, MA: The Scientific Press, boyd & fraser publishing co (text with diskette for various kinds of scoring models), 1993.

Moore, James M. *Plant Layout and Design*. New York: McGraw-Hill, 1962.

Munton, A. G., N. Forster, Y. Altman, and L. Greenbury. *Job Relocation*. New York: Wiley, 1993.

Owen, Jean V. "Making Virtual Manufacturing Real." *Manufacturing Engineering* (November 1994): 33–37.

Reed, Ruddell, Jr. *Plant Layout*. Homewood, IL: Irwin, 1961.

Vincke, P. *Multicriteria Decision-Aid*. New York: Wiley, 1992.

NOTE

1. These references are presented for historical information. The "Additional Readings" section provides relatively current sources. L. Ivan Epstein. "A Proposed Measure for Determining the Value of a Design." *Operations Research*, vol. 5, no. 2 (April 1957) 297–299. The scoring method is used to evaluate alternative aircraft designs by a major aircraft manufacturer. Other applications are described by C. Radhakrishna Rao in the text. *Advanced Statistical Methods in Biometric Research*. New York: Wiley, 1952, 103. Also, relevant to multidimensional modeling, see Walter R. Stahl. "Similarity and Dimensional Methods in Biology." *Science*, vol. 137, no. 20 (July 1962): 205–212. The basic explanation was stated by Paul W. Bridgman. *Dimensional Analysis*. New Haven, CT: Yale University Press, 1922; paperback edition, 1963.

SPOTLIGHT 11-1
How Good Is Your Production Scheduling?

Discussion Based on The Tower of Brahma

"In the great temple at Benares beneath the dome which marks the center of the world, rests a brass plate in which are fixed three diamond needles, each a cubit high and as thick as the body of a bee. On one of these needles, at the creation, God placed sixty-four discs of pure gold, the largest disc resting on the brass plate and the others getting smaller and smaller up to the top one. This is the Tower of Brahma. Day and night unceasingly, the priests transfer the discs from one diamond needle to another, according to the fixed and immutable laws of Brahma, which require that the priest on duty must not move more than one disc at a time and that he must place this disc on a needle so that there is no smaller disc below it. When the sixty-four discs shall have been thus transferred from the needle on which, at the creation, God placed them, to one of the other needles, tower, temple, and Brahmans alike will crumble into dust, and with a thunderclap, the world will vanish."*

Operational Conclusions

The process is clearly detailed, i.e., move the disks subject to the placement rules. The objective is to take all of the disks from one needle and move them to another needle following the rules. The complexity of this seemingly simple set of tasks is underscored by the following conclusions:

"The number of transfers required to fulfill the prophecy is $2^{64} - 1$, that is 18,446,744,073,709,551,615. If the priests were to effect one transfer every second, and work 24 hours a day for each of the 365 days in a year, it would take them 58,454,204,609 centuries plus slightly more than 6 years to perform the feat, assuming they never made a mistake—for one small slip would undo all their work."

This explanation is quoted from the *World of Mathematics*, op. cit.

Production scheduling is reflected in various aspects of this game. There are repetitive rules that apply, although the identical production steps do not reoccur as the stack of disks is reduced on one needle and increased on another. In that regard, there are also rules that apply with respect to which empty needle is to become the fully-loaded needle. The first move made will determine where the final stack resides and that depends upon whether the number of disks is odd or even.

A typical factory system involves so many options that it is not possible to determine an optimal production schedule. Instead of optimization, heuristic methods are used to "satisfice." Heuristics are rules of thumb that are intended to produce the most satisfactory solution that can be found in a reasonable time. There is no heuristic for the tower of Brahma because there is only one solution algorithm. However, the number of steps to achieve the objective corresponds to the levels of complexity that arise when trying to make a number of different items using general-purpose equipment.

There is yet another analogy to be drawn. Computer programmers can recognize that the Tower of Hanoi uses recursive functions to build a stack. This is common to programming methods. It is also apparent that recurrence relations dominate the methodology for carrying out the assigned tasks.

How likely is it to make a mistake in managing the activities required by this project? This is a simple routine for a computer. However, humans tend to get preoccupied, and if you have a momentary lapse one mistake sets the entire program back to the beginning.

Try a simple example using three poles (in place of diamond needles) and three disks of cardboard (large, medium, and small) in place of golden disks. There are various Towers on the web. Try http://thinks.com/java/hanoi/hanoi.htm.

Author's Note Concerning Names and Systems for Large Numbers

The number of transfers in the U.S. and French numbering system is 18.4 quintillion (18.4×10^{18}).

In the English and German numbering system, it is 18.4 trillion.

Name	U.S. and French Systems	English and German Systems
quintillion	10^{18}	10^{30}
quadrillion	10^{15}	10^{24}
trillion	10^{12}	10^{18}
billion	10^{9}	10^{12}
million	10^{6}	10^{6}

A gigabyte is 1,000 megabytes (mb = 10^6), which is 1 billion bytes in the U.S. and French systems. A terabyte is one thousand billion bytes in the U.S. and French systems.

*Tower of Hanoi (also known as the *Tower of Brahma*) from Volume 4 of the *World of Mathematics*. "Pastimes of Past and Present Times," by Edward Kasner and James R. Newman," published by Simon & Schuster, 1956, page 2425. The quoted material is sourced by Kasner and Newman from W.W.R. Ball, *Mathematical Recreations and Essays*, 11th ed. New York: Macmillan, 1939.

SPOTLIGHT 11-2
Ford Motor Company

The Ford Motor Company after Henry Ford, Part 2

The first traffic light in the United States went up in Cleveland, Ohio, in 1914. Henry Ford's Model T had brought a new freedom to America. The Model T's price just before World War I was $360. Billboards advertised "Even You Can Afford a Ford." Farmers, who were the last segment of the population to accept automobiles, loved the Model T. By attaching a belt to the crankshaft or rear axle, a farmer gained a power source and labor-saving device for hundreds of uses on the farm. Custom Model Ts became taxis, buses, trucks, fire engines, delivery vans, and police cars. Model Ts accounted for two-thirds of all automobiles in America.

In the late 1930s, the Ford Motor Company was failing. Edsel Ford, Henry's only son, was appointed president of the company and tried to modernize it against his father's wishes. He produced the Continental and its sister, the Lincoln Zephyr, with the only V-12 engine in the American auto industry. After a long family dispute over the goals and leadership of the company, Edsel died. Henry Ford continued his preoccupation with the past. Labor problems were rampant. By 1945, Ford Motor executives had lost track of the company's operations. Concern from the War Production Board led the Secretary of the Navy to release Henry Ford's grandson from service so that he could take over the company. The elder Henry reluctantly agreed to make his grandson, Henry Ford II, president. Two years later, in 1947, Henry Ford died.

Henry Ford II turned out to be a gifted executive who made considerable progress in saving the Ford Motor Company. He was 28 years old and not experienced when he took control of the company. He recruited Ernest Breech from GM to reorganize the company. An immediate change was the accounting system. That was followed by decentralization of management. Henry Ford II had read Peter Drucker's book *Concept of the Corporation*. Its tenet: No institution can exist under one-man rule. Employees willing to change could find job security at the Dearborn plant. Those attached to the old system retired or were fired.

Ford Motor Company was no longer dominated by an individual. Six divisions were created by 1948 (expanding later to 16 divisions). Each division, responsible for its own production, was required to become a profit center based on quarterly accounting estimates. The newly combined Lincoln-Mercury Division, headed by general manager Benson Ford (Henry II's younger brother), proved profitable. Loss operations were sold. Capital was plowed back into new plants and the first automated machines and computers. From a $2,000 profit in 1946, Ford Motor Company's profit jumped to 64 million dollars a year later. The new management style was successful.

Henry II faced a myriad of challenges including the overseas development of operations in 78 countries. The new International Division netted $48 million in 1949. The

Thunderbird (1955) gave Ford a 2-seater of its own. Ford's F-Series truck line came to maturity in the 1960s. The Mustang, introduced in 1964, was a great success. Automotive safety efforts intensified in the late 1960s. By 1970, these efforts helped to reduce the death toll on U.S. highways for the first time since 1958, even though Americans drove 5 percent more miles. Ford ranked fifth in size among U.S. corporations. Disappointment followed as a new line called the "Edsel" flopped. It was discontinued in 1960, remaining a prize collectors' item today. In 1972, Ford had high hopes for its lineup of five small cars: Mustang II; Pinto; the twins, Maverick and Mercury Comet; and Capri (imported from Ford of Europe). Unfortunately, developments did not go as smoothly as planned.

From 1970 to 1978, Lee Iacocca was president of Ford Motor Company under chairman Henry Ford II. The two men were profoundly different in outlook. High on Iacocca's priority list was styling, to the extent that a car's design was "frozen" before the engineers could package all the components. Whether this may have accounted for the Pinto disasters, litigation over the Pinto's fuel tank resulted in the recall of 1.5 million cars. The company culture became fixated on cost, profit, money, and short-term results. Henry II quietly began taking power away from Lee Iacocca, firing him in 1978 and retiring in 1980. Henry Ford II left behind a 35-year legacy of hard work when he died in September 1987.

Philip Caldwell was made CEO in 1980. He had come up through the ranks at Ford with no shortcuts. He and his executive vice presidents were hailed in *The Wall Street Journal* as a new breed of manager, the kind of men who ran the company "before it was overrun by flamboyant marketing managers." The company certainly needed new leadership. If competition from Japan and increasing public perceptions of inferior quality of Ford products were not bad enough, the country was experiencing a deep recession. The government had issued a mass of safety, emissions, and fuel economy regulations. There was an urgent need to retool all factories and reduce the weight of all cars to make them more fuel efficient. Between 1979 and 1981, Ford's share of the car market dwindled as did owner loyalty. (Ford's critics' acronym was "Fix Or Repair Daily.")

See Spotlight 5-1, Understanding the History of Great Leaders in the P/OM Field Is Part of the Systems Approach—Henry Ford, Part 1," for the beginning of the story. See Spotlight 12-1 for the conclusion.

Sources: Banham, Russ. *The Ford Century: Ford Motor Company and the Innovations That Shaped the World.* New York: Artisan (a division of Workman Publishing Company), 2002; Brinkley, Douglas. *Wheels for the World: Henry Ford, His Company, and a Century of Progress.* Viking, 2003.

CASES

Case 11-1
Industry Perspective on Service at Rosenbluth International

Until recently, Rosenbluth International, headquartered in Philadelphia, Pennsylvania, was one of the largest privately held companies in the world. It provided comprehensive corporate travel management services worldwide. With an annual travel volume in excess of $3 billion and with over 4,300 associates, Rosenbluth International owned operations in 15 countries. Founded in 1892 and recognized as a leader in integrated information management, Rosenbluth International developed innovative business applications and integrated service systems that enabled it to provide highly personalized service to its clients.

In July 2003, American Express signed a definitive agreement to acquire Rosenbluth International and completed the acquisition in October 2003. Hal Rosenbluth (chairman and CEO of Rosenbluth International) took an active role as senior advisor in the integration process. He will continue to focus on customer and employee needs. Some assets of Rosenbluth International were not included in the acquisition. See the American Express announcement at http://home3.americanexpress.com/ corp/latestnews/rosenbluth.asp.

Treating this as an ongoing case, every effort is being made to continue to record the details of this major organizational change and its impact on production and operations management issues—over time. In that way, the story can be updated on a regular basis, as new events of significance occur. Knowing where Rosenbluth International has been is valuable, particularly as more information becomes available concerning where Rosenbluth International is heading. Reporting on the company's history provides operational benchmarks and major insights.

Rosenbluth International has played a major role in the corporate travel industry. This company revolutionized corporate travel management through the creation of its patented DACODA product, which mathematically reverses airlines' yield management formulas to find corporations the lowest possible fares at all times. More recently, Rosenbluth has been praised globally for the creation of its comprehensive Global Security Suite, which includes a real-time traveler locator to help companies find their people in the event of a crisis.

The company was established in Philadelphia in 1892 by Marcus Rosenbluth as a steamship ticket office. Rosenbluth built his business by providing exceptional service to customers and exploiting an historic change—the European immigration to America. Rosenbluth's first clients were immigrants who wanted to bring their relatives to America from Europe. They entrusted Marcus Rosenbluth with their savings until $50 could be sent overseas for the transatlantic passage to New York and a train seat to Philadelphia.

Over 100 years later, president and chief executive officer Hal Rosenbluth continued to provide superior service to customers and to exploit opportunities for change in his growing company. Hal Rosenbluth began working in the family business the day after he graduated from the University of Miami in 1974. In the late 1970s, when the company had sales of $20 to $30 million annually, Rosenbluth identified airline deregulation as another monumental change to be exploited in the travel industry. Prior to deregulation, the processing of airline reservations was fairly simple. A travel agent's tasks consisted of asking clients if they wished to fly first class, coach, or economy; finding the most convenient arrival and departure times; and securing seats on those flights. With deregulation, new airlines, new routes, myriad new fares, and constant changes in all of these became a huge source of frustration for travelers and posed an enormous challenge to the travel industry.

Rosenbluth capitalized on the confusion created by deregulation by providing guaranteed lowest priced air fares to corporate customers. This is a much needed, distinctive service. The company purchased computers and leased access to the airlines' new computerized reservation systems (CRSs) for direct access to flight information. Because the airlines' information technology had certain biases (their flights were listed first and so were easier to book), Rosenbluth set out to develop its own independent reservation software with a "bias" toward lowest possible airfares.

Corporate Culture

Employees: Hal Rosenbluth believes that employees serve customers better in a caring, nurturing atmosphere where coworkers are encouraged to work as a team. The latest book (2002) by Hal Rosenbluth (and Diane Peters) is titled *The Customer Comes Second: Put Your People First and Watch 'Em Kick Butt.* That title succinctly summarizes the corporate culture with respect to employees.

All Rosenbluth employees, who are referred to as "associates" and "leaders," receive a company orientation for two days. Reservation agents, who are referred to as *Customer Care Associates (CCAs),* additionally receive formal reservations training for two to eight weeks. This training consists of role-playing, computerized tutorials, and mentoring. CCAs are taught to extend "elegant service" to clients, which begins with the consistent greeting, "Welcome to Rosenbluth International; this is Crystal Larson, how may I help you?"

Elegant service continues throughout the client contact with CCAs, using language such as "Certainly" (rather than "Sure") and "May I place you on hold?" (rather than "Can you hold?").

Once on the job, training continues. All CCAs are cross-trained in at least three areas. This helps them understand the entire reservation process better and provides the opportunity to spread tasks among a larger group of associates, if necessary. Rosenbluth associates are guided by a formal total quality management program to constantly review the company's processes and identify areas of possible improvement. Ad hoc teams are formed to implement continual improvement actions.

Client relationships: Rosenbluth opened its corporate travel division in 1964. In 1984, the DuPont Company was the first company to consolidate its travel program with one travel agency.

DuPont selected Rosenbluth and remains one of its largest clients. Every corporate client's relationship with Rosenbluth is different. Sales associates nationwide work to bring in new business for the company. Clients work with the sales associates before signing on to achieve mutual business plans that ensure that all client requests are addressed. Some client offices have on-site reservation centers.

Supplier relationships: Rosenbluth sees developing close relationships with suppliers to be a win–win situation. For example, Marriott trains and empowers Rosenbluth associates to solve problems in the same way as Marriott employees.

Linton—Centralized Support Facility

Many of Rosenbluth's centralized support operations are conducted at its Linton, North Dakota, facility. In 1988, Hal Rosenbluth set up a temporary data processing office at a vacant John Deere warehouse in Linton as a philanthropic gesture to help the farmers whose crops were being destroyed by drought. Because the Linton associates learned so quickly and so well and possessed the cooperative spirit that Rosenbluth looks for, Rosenbluth made the office permanent. Linton is a branch office and "business unit" for reservations. (Rosenbluth is organized into approximately 45 business units domestically; most of the business units are comprised of more than one branch location.) Today the Linton facility employs over 150 associates and has annual sales of approximately $15 million. Employee turnover at the Linton facility is roughly 2 percent.

The following discussion focuses on the operations in Linton in examining the systems involved in Rosenbluth's computerized reservation process, customer service, and accounting operations for processing airline tickets. In addition to reservation operations, Linton also provides 75 percent of customer service for all postreservation operations for Rosenbluth and operations for processing all airline tickets issued by the company. (Reservation operations and customer service are referred to as *front-room operations* in a travel agency. Processing of airline tickets and client reporting activities are referred to as *backroom operations*.)

The description of operations that follows is based on processes that have been in place before the new arrangement with the American Express Company was finalized, that is, pre–August and September 2003. If and when these systems are redefined, process steps will be altered to reflect the synergies of amalgamation.

Computerized Reservation Process

Approximately 38 Customer Care Associates (CCAs) work in reservation operations at Linton. CCAs handle 30 to 40 calls per day. Reservation operations at the Linton facility include the following areas:

1. *Corporate reservations:* Approximately 20 CCAs) handle corporate clients for Linton business unit reservations (60 percent of the time) and overflow from other business units (40 percent).

2. *International reservations:* Branch offices take international reservations and email them to Linton for processing by one of four CCAs.

3. *Internal reservations:* Three CCAs handle travel for Rosenbluth employees who are traveling on business.

4. *Hotel desk:* Four CCAs handle high-volume hotel reservations; requests for these are taken by the branch offices and then sent to Linton for processing. The hotel desk is usually used for smaller hotels and clients who request that reservations be made directly with the hotel rather than through the airline reservation systems.

5. *Data entry:* The data entry team of four CCAs builds customer profiles based on the profiles submitted by the client on paper.

6. *Satellite ticket printing (STP ticketing):* 380 clients have satellite ticket printers in their own offices; processing these tickets is handled at Linton.

7. *Leisure travel:* Three CCAs in Linton provide vacation planning services to employees of corporate clients. Reservations for leisure travel involving airline tickets are handled at the National Leisure Center in Pittsburgh. Land-only reservations are made at Linton.

Because gross margins in the travel industry are less than 3 to 4 percent, success depends on the efficiency of the reservation process. This process converts a client's request for travel services into the tickets, itineraries, and other travel documents sent to clients. Altogether Rosenbluth's business units issue between 50,000 to 60,000 tickets a week; in the event of fare wars or carrier bankruptcies, this could go up to 100,000 to 120,000 per week. Rosenbluth has approximately 2,100 CCAs working at all business units on a typical day. CCAs handle 2 1/2 to 3 phone calls for every transaction completed. An average reservation takes approximately 13 to 15 minutes from the time the call is answered to finalizing the "after-call work" in the documentation of the record. Average monthly total phone time for all of Rosenbluth's reservation centers was nearly 2 million minutes.

About 95 percent of corporate reservations are taken by telephone. In addition to telephone reservations, Rosenbluth also accepts reservations in person at a branch location, by email, by voice mail, and by fax. All reservations pass through the same automated quality control checks as traditional phone reservations. (Rosenbluth Vacations, the business unit that offers vacations to consumers, accepts reservations through online services such as Prodigy® and CompuServe®, and is testing interactive TV and Travel Channel applications.)

The computerized reservation process for reservations received by phone, email, or fax is shown in the reservation flowchart in Figure 1. This process is used by CCAs at all locations, which are networked with the computer hardware housed in Philadelphia. This OM process will be discussed using the steps that are listed in the order of the script on the CCA's computer screen. (Numbers in parentheses refer to the numbered items in Figure 11-4.) The following discussion assumes that an airline reservation is received via telephone call.

Upon answering the call (# 1), the CCA follows a script displayed in a Windows format on the terminal that prompts him or her through the reservation. The CCA accesses the caller's profile (# 2) and reconfirms the traveler's delivery address (# 3); if it has changed, the profile needs to be updated. The CCA makes changes as necessary (# 4). The CCA then asks the client for information about desired travel destinations and times. The CCA then accesses airline availability using the airline-owned CRS (computer reserva-

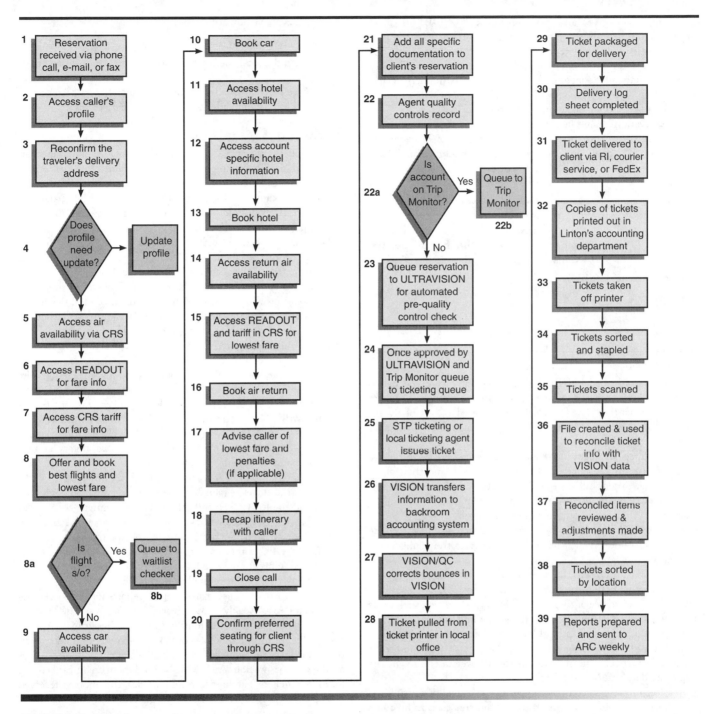

FIGURE 11-4
Reservation Flowchart

tion system) (# 5) and calls up Rosenbluth's proprietary READ-OUT® database, which lists airfares in ascending order of price in one quadrant of the work screen (# 6).

The CCA accesses tariff (fare plus tax) information through the computerized reservation system (# 7). The CCA scans all the information on the screen and tells the client the best times and lowest fares available for the desired outgoing flights (# 8). If a

desired flight is sold out (# 8a), the associate will send the information to an automated waitlist checker (# 8b), so if a seat on the flight opens up, the information is relayed to a queue in the associate's computer terminal. If needed, car and hotel availabilities are accessed and bookings completed (# 9– # 13).

Next, READOUT and tariff information are examined for return flights (# 14 and # 15). The associate books the return flight (# 16), advises the caller of the lowest fares (# 17), recaps the itinerary for the caller (# 18), and then closes the call (# 19). "Talk time" on the call, from answer to close, is typically 2 1/2 to 3 1/2 minutes.

Post-call, the associate confirms the client's preferred seating through the CRS or the telephone when necessary (# 20). The software automatically appends the reservation with client-related information such as corporate ID numbers, frequent flyer numbers, meal requests, and seat assignment information (# 21).

Reservation teams maintain daily service statistics that are updated on a real-time basis. The goal is to answer 90 percent of calls within 10 seconds and the remaining 10 percent within 20 seconds. For example, the following statistics might be gathered on a typical day:

	Number of Calls	Average Speed of Answer (seconds)	Number of Abandons	Total Service Factor
Corporate/domestic	357	6	12	94%
International/VIP departments	69	5	1	96%
Group department	20	2	0	100%

"Abandons" occur if the caller hangs up before the call is answered. Average abandon time is less than one minute. A promise to clients regarding how fast calls are answered is part of Rosenbluth's "Total Service Factor." The total service factor is the total percentage of calls answered within a specified number of seconds. This percentage averages the number of calls answered, the average speed of answer, the number of calls abandoned, and their abandoned time. Rosenbluth International contracts for a specific service level with many clients. Both staffing and network design/monitoring are often dependent on this service level.

If the CCA has noted any errors on the screen (e.g., the phone number for a hotel is incorrect), he or she gives the changes to a data entry associate.

The CCA then runs the reservation record through one or two automated quality control systems (# 22 and # 23). The ULTRA-VISION® system seeks to eliminate errors in the reservation; its fare checking module ensures that the lowest fare was identified and booked. In addition, Rosenbluth's patented Trip Monitor™ system is a value-added service available to customers. Trip Monitor™ repeatedly rechecks the reservation for a lower fare through the departure date (# 22a and # 22b).

After the reservation record goes through quality control, the ticket, itinerary, and any other travel documents such as boarding passes are printed out at the local business unit or at a satellite ticket printer (# 24, # 25, and # 28). If printed at the business unit, an associate packages the ticket for delivery (# 29) and then completes a delivery log sheet (# 30). Tickets are delivered to the client via Rosenbluth International couriers, an independent courier service, or FedEx (# 31).

If CCAs have downtime, they

1. work on records in the queue,
2. work in the total client satisfaction center if cross-trained to do so, or
3. update their knowledge of the travel industry with computer-based learning modules or articles from periodicals.

Backroom Operations

As the tickets are printed, the reservation record is simultaneously transferred to the backroom system Rosenbluth calls VISION® (# 26). The quality control editor program within the VISION system automatically checks the reservation template to make sure that information in fields such as customer name, ticket numbers, form of payment, credit card numbers, agent numbers, and customer numbers are correct. VISION flags errors such as missing data or incorrectly formatted data. VISION also checks the "dollar savings comparison fields," the accuracy of the internal Rosenbluth number, and different fare remarks and reason codes. The system "bounces" the reservations with errors (less than 1 percent of total ticket volume) to a QC associate's computer screen (# 27); the QC associate fixes problems 100 percent of the time. Reports of errors go back to business units requesting them. Eight associates work in the VISION quality control area.

Two copies of all airline tickets issued by Rosenbluth are printed out in the backroom operations area at Linton (# 32). The first copy is for the agency's records; the second copy is for the Airline Reporting Corporation (ARC) in Louisville, Kentucky. If the ticket was charged to a credit card, there is a charge form as well. The agency copy is stored for two years in the "ticket library" in Linton; international tickets are stored at overseas business units. Currently 5 to 6 million ticket copies are stored in Linton.

After the ticket is taken off the printer (# 33), all copies are sorted and stapled (# 34); then the ticket is scanned (# 35). (For Worldspan and SABRE, the tickets are compared to a written report rather than scanned.) A file is created and used to automatically reconcile the ticket information with the data in VISION (# 35). Reconciled items are reviewed and adjustments made (# 37). Tickets are then sorted by ticketing location (# 38).

Linton backroom associates prepare reports for each ticketing location for ARC weekly (# 39). Every Thursday over 1,000 reports are sent via FedEx to ARC. Jointly owned by the airlines, ARC is responsible for reconciling sales of tickets each week for all participating airlines. Accredited travel agencies must report ticket sales for the previous week to ARC and also send them credit card charge forms for tickets purchased. ARC divides the money received among the airlines and pays the travel agencies their commission on ticket sales, which is typically 10 percent.

If the agency's reported information does not reconcile with the airlines' information, the airline notifies the agency (in the form of a debit or credit memo) and differences are examined. Less than 1 percent of the tickets need to be reconciled for differences. Situations that would cause these differences include the agency charging too much or too little for a ticket, taking an incorrect commission on a ticket, or using an expired or invalid fare.

If a customer is due a refund, the ticket is sent back to the business unit that booked the reservation; the business unit calculates the amount due to the client and then sends the information to Linton. Linton verifies the information and includes it with the weekly report to ARC.

In the case of a lost or missing ticket, the traveler who lost the ticket contacts the CCA or business unit that took the reservation. This information is relayed to the Linton backroom operations area. Rosenbluth notifies the airline in writing of the lost ticket. If the ticket is not used in 60 to 90 days, the airline will reimburse the travel agency (less a $25 to $50 administrative fee).

Another function handled by Linton backroom associates is commission tracking, which ensures that Rosenbluth is paid the proper commissions from its nonairline suppliers. Associates follow up on commissions due to make sure they are collected. They send the suppliers notices that enumerate the amount due when commissions have not been paid. Large suppliers, including Marriott, Holiday Inn and Choice Hotels, send a magnetic tape of all transactions, so the process in these cases is automated.

Total Client Satisfaction Center (TCSC)

If problems arise after the trip or additional information is needed, the client calls the reservation center where he or she made the reservation. If the issue requires additional research, it is forwarded to the Total Client Satisfaction Center (TCSC) for resolution via an electronically filed Detailed Information Request (DIR) script. In Linton, 28 TCSC associates take DIRs from CCAs who submit them on behalf of clients with problems, complaints, or questions. Linton TCSC associates typically handle 150 to 175 DIRs per day and may receive 180 to 200 calls per day from CCAs who handle clients' inquiries. TCSC associates respond to all inquiries within 24 hours. Front-line empowerment of associates provides immediate resolution to many problems. TCSC associates not only address and resolve issues involving clients, but also provide customer service assistance for other associates and suppliers. If a client has changes

or problems during a trip, the client can call the business unit or Rosenbluth International's En Route Service.

Total client satisfaction is measured by a complaint ratio (reported complaints to transactions), which is typically .05 percent; periodic client surveys; and other measurements.

The top two requests are for copies of tickets or invoices that the client misplaced or lost. Many client calls deal with fare inquiries; this is not surprising because the airlines issue 50,000 to 60,000 fare changes per day. Other common inquiries deal with requests to check on frequent flyer mile accounts and hotel no-shows.

Bottlenecks

Bottlenecks in the computerized reservation process are caused by volume fluctuations and failure of the technical systems. One common potential bottleneck is overflow of incoming calls. This problem was solved in 1994 with the installation of a state-of-the-art telecommunications network, the only one of its kind in the travel industry. With Rosenbluth's network operations, overflow can be handled by any office on the network. Call volumes at all reservation centers are monitored by the Network Operations Center (NOC), Rosenbluth's telecommunications control facility located in Philadelphia. If the NOC detects high call volumes at a facility, it can automatically reroute the overflow to where the available associates are. Routing for a particular client is worked out when the account is set up. During the winter of 1994, the NOC moved over 80,000 calls in January and February.

In the summer of 1994, Rosenbluth opened a new facility in Fargo, North Dakota, largely devoted to handling excess capacity during peak travel seasons. Known as an "IntelliCenter," this 200+ agent office is electronically networked with every Rosenbluth location around the world. IntelliCenter CCAs, like those in all Rosenbluth offices, have instant access to each caller's travel data, including company policy, reservation records, and personal preferences through Precision and VISION. Future opportunities for the IntelliCenter include multiple shifts and around-the-clock service.

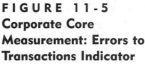

FIGURE 11-5
Corporate Core Measurement: Errors to Transactions Indicator

Core Measurements

Rosenbluth collects data for various core measurements or "business unit quality indicators" in the areas of staffing (e.g., associate satisfaction and client retention), telephone statistics (e.g., average speed of answer), and service levels (e.g., air dollar savings). One of the most important of these measures to Rosenbluth is *errors to transactions*, an example of which is shown in Figure 11-5. The average ratio of errors to transactions for this period is 0.18 percent. Some of the other most important measures include associate satisfaction, service issues, transaction levels, and productivity.

Future of Rosenbluth and the Travel Industry

Rosenbluth International faces a series of trends that will affect the way it operates in the future. These trends include economic and societal realities, technology developments, globalization of business and competition, security issues, and the constant need for reengineering.

The top trends are related to economic issues, societal climate, and security problems. Since the World Trade Center attacks, the entire travel industry is changing. Possibilities of further terrorism continue to haunt business and leisure travel decisions. Travel patterns continue to change, and they show no sign of stabilizing in the near future. Uncertainty abounds given ongoing U.S. military involvements, terrorist threats, and serious incidents in a variety of travel destinations. On its webpage, Rosenbluth predicts a price increase of about 4 percent for business air travel in 2003. Leisure travel, on the other hand, is down and prices have been declining. Overall, the pricing of airline tickets has been volatile.

The cruise business has increased. Travel by train and auto has been a beneficiary of air travel insecurities. These are trends that every travel agency has to take into account. Success will be related to the ability of an agency to decrease costs and to increase revenues for its products.

That is a struggle. Major airlines such as US Airways and United Airlines have encountered serious financial problems. US Airways has emerged from bankruptcy and has undergone the court-controlled reorganization. Airlines (both U.S.–based and international) have downsized and continue to search for ways to decrease costs while increasing revenues.

If a travel agency can assist in these goals, it can prosper. Rosenbluth has made innovative moves to change its value to its customers as well as its suppliers. To assist in these volatile times requires great organizational adaptability. A visit to http://www.rosenbluth.com will bring to light the creativity of the Rosenbluth organization. Note the TrackPoint system, which is part of the Global Security Suite of Products. Also, see Rosenbluth's Program Manager, which assists its clients to achieve cost-effective corporate travel. The Rivery is a gracious meeting site developed by the Rosenbluth organization with Ritz-Carlton trained staff. Meanwhile, Meetings@Rosenbluth does provide meeting consulting help to all size companies.

Travel agency commissions are undergoing change. The booking of tickets by customers directly online has increased significantly. In 1995, travel agents sold about 80 percent of all airline tickets, and agent commissions accounted for 12 percent of airlines' operating expenses. In direct response to the airline commission caps, Rosenbluth introduced 1-800-903-1616 phone service (Travelution) so that business travelers could access CCAs directly to book international and domestic plane and hotel reservations. This service was launched because of Rosenbluth's belief that, as a result of commission caps, airline reservation centers would be inundated with phone calls. The new Rosenbluth phone service targets business travelers who do not have time to wait when trying to book travel arrangements.

Hal Rosenbluth believes that events provide new opportunities even though they may outmode the accustomed ways of doing business. The company tries to improve its position in the travel market by furnishing potential clients with value-adding services such as expense management and credit card reconciliation. Rosenbluth is always striving to decrease their suppliers' costs of doing business and to increase the revenue flows of their suppliers.

The trick is to gain leverage with both clients and suppliers. To do this, Rosenbluth focuses on the display of new technology partnerships. At the webpage, click on the virtual tour of the *Continuum North America*. It is a collaborative sales exposition sponsored by Rosenbluth and its partners in the travel business. The Arrival Area is where customers sample British Airway's Terrace Lounge and information furnished by various rental car companies. The Departure Area demonstrates the features of eticketing. Hotel Area shows Holiday Inn's Model Room, and the laptop on the king-sized bed has Rosenbluth's FlashPoint installed. That product notifies travelers when information arises that could impact their travel plans. Not to be discounted is Telesuite right outside the hotel; it has the best video-conferencing capabilities. Rosenbluth describes the Continuum as the only working travel laboratory in existence. Also, this is an impressive way to gain leverage with clients and suppliers.

The new technology allows customers to purchase an airline reservation at an automated teller machine or on the Internet. It encourages using electronic tickets. As the airlines have come to prefer this, the "ticketless environment" has prospered. Hal Rosenbluth accurately predicted that at first travelers would still want documents to prove they have reservations; but he said in 1994 that in 10 years documents will exist only 5 percent of the time. This prediction seems on-target in 2003. Colleen McGuffin, general manager at Linton, had also forecast that dealing with ARC will become "paperless." Hal Rosenbluth had foreseen that the travel environment won't be "agentless," but he expected less agent involvement. These predictions seem to be coming true.

The globalization of business is another major trend affecting the travel market. With its roots in international travel, more than 58 international locations, and volatility growing in the supply chain, Rosenbluth International is well positioned to deal with the vast "global distribution network" in the current environment of high uncertainties.

For a long time, Rosenbluth International has been reengineering its operations. Years before the advent of electronic tickets, Rosenbluth and DuPont had begun to study and map out an "ideal state" for business travelers, where there are no tickets or boarding passes, no check-ins, no car rental forms, no cash advances, and no expense reports (see *Business Travel News*, September 12, 1994). Their stated goal was then to use smart-card technology on which all travel information is stored. "With one swipe—flash—you're on the plane, in your hotel room."

Questions

1. Every Rosenbluth ticket jacket says "We promise to apply the lowest applicable airfare for routing flown based upon time parameters requested by the traveler or traveler's corporate travel policy." Describe the systems Rosenbluth has in place to fulfill this promise to customers.

2. Describe the way in which Rosenbluth uses technology to solve potential bottleneck problems with incoming calls.

3. Explain the differences between ULTRAVISION and Trip Monitor. Why does Rosenbluth International charge an additional fee to clients who use Trip Monitor?

4. How does Rosenbluth measure productivity?

5. Discuss the potential for the use of EDI in this system. What advantages would it offer over voice or fax communications?

6. Discuss ways to continue reducing errors in ticketing.

7. Using Figure 11-4 as a guide, discuss ways to reduce the steps in the reservation process and thus increase customer service. How and when can errors be reduced in the process?

8. Discuss ways in which Rosenbluth can reduce the internal paperwork and the copies that its systems generate.

9. Given Hal Rosenbluth's vision for revolution, brainstorm ways to reengineer operations in light of future changes projected in the travel industry.

10. Based on predictions for future trends, what actions should Rosenbluth take?

References

American Express News Release dated July 15, 2003. *American Express to Acquire Rosenbluth International, A Leading Global Travel Management Company: Two Corporate Travel Leaders Join Forces to Deliver Higher Level of Agency Service, Technology Innovation, and Global Reach*; http://home3.americanexpress.com/corp/latest-news/rosenbluth.asp.

Felicity Barringer. "From Milking Cows to Manning Computers." *The New York Times* (August 11, 1989).

Charles Boisseau (*Houston Chronicle*). "Airlines Experimenting with Ticketless Systems." *The Cincinnati Enquirer* (September 18, 1994).

Mary Brisson. "Rosenbluth Starts In on Res Reengineering." *Business Travel News* (November 22, 1993).

Donna J. Israel. "Technology Today: The Future Is Now." *Business Travel Management*, vol. 6, no. 6 (June 1994).

"Many Happy Returns." *Inc. Magazine* (October 1990).

Jennifer McNamara. "Starting from Square One: Times Call for Reengineering, Megas Discover." *Business Travel News* (September 12, 1994).

"Rosenbluth International Honored for Excellence in Customer Service." *CIO: The Magazine for Information Executives*, special issue (August 1993).

Hal F. Rosenbluth. "Tales of a Nonconformist Company." *Harvard Business Review* (July–August 1991).

Hal F. Rosenbluth. "What's Ahead in Back-Office Automation." *Business Travel News* (June 3, 1991).

Hal F. Rosenbluth and Diane M. Peters. *The Customer Comes Second: Put Your People First and Watch 'Em Kick Butt*. HarperCollins Publishers, August 2002. This is a major revision of a 1992 book.

Julie Schmit. "Delta Trims Travel Agent Commissions." *USA Today* (October 29, 1994).

Thomas G. Watts. "New Visions on the Old Frontier." *Dallas Morning News* (April 28, 1991).

Http://www.Rosenbluth.com.

Operating the System and Making Product— P/OM Tactics

Military tactics are related to the movement of troops and material. Maneuvering and logistics are often included as the descriptive part of the *details* concerning the use of resources. Military tactics are concerned with *specific details* as contrasted with the *big strategic picture* that was the basis for planning and deciding *whom* to battle, *when* to fight, and *how and where* to engage the enemy (competitor). Tactics for P/OM are much the same as in the military situation.

P/OM recognizes as strategic the issues of *who* are the competitors, *what* markets are engaged, and *how, when,* and *where* are the products brought to the marketplace? The tactical issues are the specific details that Chapters 12 through 17 now address.

Specific details about making products and delivering services must be decided after planning strategies are set. Doing the right thing must come before doing the thing right. Doing *the right thing* is the strategic part of the equation and doing it *the right way* is the tactical part of the story.

Part 4 provides specifics, details, and the particulars required to make the system run. Running in the P/OM context is a tactical plan for producing goods and services that customers want. The tactical methods of Part 4 are concerned with *how* to get the job done in the right way. That means obtaining specific output qualities, being on time, and having great efficiencies so that costs are competitive. The costs must be competitive so that the firm can charge the right price. Selection of price was a strategic decision at the outset of the planning process. It is constantly reviewed as tactical information refines both the objectives and the consequences.

Tactics, not strategies, are at issue. Strategies already have been developed and implemented. They are responsible for setting the stage. This means the scenarios are drawn up that materials management and production scheduling must now carry out in the most productive way possible. Tactics are the elements that are not included in strategic planning that fulfill the objectives of the strategies.

Chapter 12, "Materials Management (MM)," explores materials management. One of the responsibilities of materials management is purchasing from external suppliers. Some materials are more critical than others because of the role they play in the final product. That will have an effect on how they are treated. Materials also need to be differentiated with respect to the dollar volume that is used to make the product. When dollar volume is greater, there is more opportunity to save money by carefully managing ordering policy. The information system supporting purchasing, receiving, inspection, and storage is part of materials management. Correct selection of suppliers is necessary. Certification of suppliers may be required. A systems perspective is essential for successful materials management in job shop, batch work, flow shop, intermittent flow shop, and project environments.

Chapter 13, "Aggregate Planning," moves the focus inside the plant or service facility. There it deals with workforce planning and the control of inventories based on forecasts of demand. The policy of a constant workforce for *level* production is contrasted with a *chasing* policy using hiring, layoffs, overtime, and subcontracting in an effort to meet demand forecasts with adequate supply. Combined policies (level and chasing) are explored using models of aggregate scheduling. Specific aggregate schedules can apply to batch production and mixed-model flow shop environments.

Chapter 14, "Inventory Management," explains how to manage inventories of materials that are continuously under demand such as toothpaste, gasoline, machine lubricants, lightbulbs, and automobiles. Satisfying demands for the same product over long periods of time is typical of flow shop production capability. The economic order quantity (EOQ) model is used with continuous demand patterns to decide how much material to order and how often to order. Often, the production line can run several different items (sequentially, over time) and still meet all demands. This entails using the economic lot size (ELS) model, which is able to provide optimal schedules for such intermittent flow shop production. Extending these concepts to perpetual and periodic inventory systems is relevant to materials management. It is relevant to know when each approach is preferred. The quantity discount model provides further insight for inventory management.

Chapter 15, "Material Requirements Planning (MRP)," explains how to manage inventories of materials that have sporadic demands. These materials are typically associated with the job shop and include service functions such as the office. Often their use is dependent on one or more job shop end-items. What goes into a parent item is detailed by a bill of material, which characterizes the reliance of these inventory systems on good organization of information. Information systems that are appropriate for components and supplies with uneven demands are known as material requirements planning systems (MRP). The strengths and weaknesses of MRP methods are evaluated. Chapter 15 also examines capacity requirements planning known as CRP and distribution requirements planning known as DRP. Although tactical in immediate use, what is learned from MRP, CRP, and DRP can bring about changes in strategic plans.

Chapter 16, "Production Scheduling," explains how production scheduling permits loading and sequencing for the job shop. Loading consists of assigning jobs that are on hand to departments (or work centers). Loading applies to both services and manufacturing. Load charting is explained and three loading methods are detailed. These are based on the assignment method, the transportation method, and one heuristic method. Sequencing following loading is the next logical procedure. It completes the assignment by specifying the order in which jobs are to be done. A variety of sequencing policies are described.

Chapter 17, "Cycle-Time Management," explains why cycle-time management has become vitally important to manufacturing and service organizations. Line-balancing for cycle-time control is applied to intermittent and continuous flow shops. Differences are drawn between deterministic, stochastic, and heuristic line-balancing situations. Cycle-time management is shown to be one aspect of time-based management (TBM). Queuing models are introduced in this context of balanced work flows when arrivals and servicing times are random variables. Chapter 17's supplement demonstrates how simulation of queuing situations can be used when the queuing models are too complex to be solved mathematically.

Materials Management (MM)

This section starts the exploration of materials management. Materials are used in making goods and providing services. They are also used to support the administrative infrastructure. Materials flow through the supply chains, which must always begin with raw materials. P/OM transforms the raw materials into materials that are work in process and finally into finished goods. There are also many supplies needed for administrative purposes and to keep the offices and the bathrooms going. Materials can be made at home in the plant or outsourced. There is a lot of outsourcing going on. The terminology is responsible for a new name for purchasing from external suppliers. Systems perspective is essential for successful materials management in the job shop and flow shop environments.

After reading this chapter, you should be able to:

- Explain what materials management (MM) is and how it connects many functions.
- Discuss the systems perspective applied to materials management.
- Explain the "big picture" of materials as part of the cost of goods sold (COGS).
- Discuss differences in materials management that apply to each kind of work configuration.
- Explain the materials management information system.
- Lower the risks that buyers take.
- Describe "turnover" and "days of inventory" and explain why they are critical measures of systems performance.

- Explain what is needed for successful centralization of the purchasing function.
- Discuss the receiving, inspection, and storage functions.
- Discuss why bids are often required before purchasing is allowed.
- Explain the management of spare parts.
- Describe the use of value analysis for materials management.
- Explain the management of critical parts.
- Describe why parts with high-dollar volume deserve special attention.
- Explain how to treat parts that have lower-dollar volume.
- Describe why certification of suppliers is important to MM.

THE SYSTEMS VIEWPOINT

Materials management is a system of broad-based planning and control over one of the most important factors in the cost of goods sold (COGS). Two trends have been pervasive. The first is the marked decline of the direct labor component of the COGS. The second is the marked rise in the direct and indirect (overhead) cost of materials. Because materials costs are now critical to profitability, most organizations have created positions of high responsibility to oversee the many parts of the system that have

The tractor is digging in a gravel pit. This firm, which supplies gravel and stone to the construction industry, in turn must buy parts for its tractor as well as other supplies. The key is that firms that supply raw materials are themselves dependent on purchasing materials.

Materials management (MM): Organizing and coordinating all management functions that are responsible for every aspect of materials movements, storage, and transformation.

Materials management system (MMS): Triggered by marketplace demands (via forecasts), which deplete stocks that cause inventory managers to place replenishment orders through purchasing agents with suppliers and vendors.

Internal MM system: Controls production materials flowing to and through the process.

Work in process (WIP): Exists in the form of incomplete jobs that cannot be shipped or put into finished goods storage.

to be integrated for materials management. The *integrator* that keeps the materials management system together is the information system. It coordinates functions and permits purchasing to lower the buyer's risks.

STRATEGIC THINKING

Materials management is a tactical system of planning and control. The strategic component came into play during start-up, when deciding what goods were to be made and what services were to be offered. However, strategies must always be reevaluated. If the system is not performing as it was intended, then changes in strategies may need to be made. In this regard, two systems measures—"turnover" and "days of inventory"—are very helpful for monitoring how well purchasing and inventory managers do their job. They are also helpful in assessing how well the strategic plans are faring. Strategies can be tweaked or changed significantly if they are not delivering according to plans.

These two measures can be valuable in evaluating a system's performance under stressful conditions. In hard times, keeping inventories low is critical to cash-flow control. Insufficient cash flow can jeopardize the survival of the firm. Airline strategies (number of aircraft, number of gates, routes flown, etc.) needed to be reevaluated before the hard times occurred that led to bankruptcy for several major carriers.

12-1   WHAT IS MATERIALS MANAGEMENT (MM)?

Materials management (MM) involves organizing and coordinating all management functions that are responsible for every aspect of materials movements and transformations—called the **materials management system (MMS).** This system is triggered by demands (including those forecasted) that deplete stocks, causing inventory management to request replenishment through purchasing agents or direct contact with suppliers or vendors.

The distinction between vendors and suppliers is a matter of local usage. One, the other, or often both are used by various companies and/or industries in different regions of the United States and the world. Before it was absorbed by Compaq Corporation, which then merged with Hewlett-Packard Corporation (HPQ-2002), the Digital Equipment Corporation used "vendors" to sell its products. The publication *VarBusiness* honors "Top Vendors" in an annual award event. Ford Motor Company employs "certification" of suppliers to assure quality and reliability. For selling, reselling, and servicing, many companies have channel partners (see http://www.varbusiness.com).

12-1a   The Systems Perspective for Materials Management

Materials management as defined earlier is an interlinked system, as shown in Figure 12-1. Note that the demand for stock is based on production needs and forecasts.

MM connects the external sourcing of supplies to the internal scheduling of product to be delivered to the customer. Mismanage any part of the interlinked system and the adage that "a chain is as strong as its weakest link" applies.

The **internal MM system** requires control of production materials, which are process flows. Further, there is control of **work in process (WIP)** on the plant floor and finished goods in the warehouse. Some companies have external control over shipments of finished goods to distributors and customers as part of MM. Other companies limit MM to the regulation and use of incoming stock.

The materials management system must be synchronized and coordinated to be effective. The key to synchronization is knowing "when" materials are needed "where." Coor-

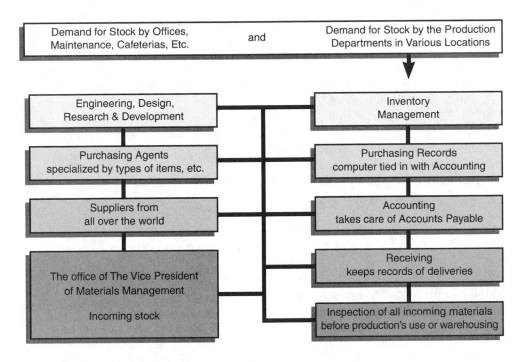

| Demand for Stock by Offices, Maintenance, Cafeterias, Etc. | and | Demand for Stock by the Production Departments in Various Locations |

Engineering, Design, Research & Development

Purchasing Agents specialized by types of items, etc.

Suppliers from all over the world

The office of The Vice President of Materials Management

Incoming stock

Inventory Management

Purchasing Records computer tied in with Accounting

Accounting takes care of Accounts Payable

Receiving keeps records of deliveries

Inspection of all incoming materials before production's use or warehousing

FIGURE 12-1
Systems Perspective of Materials Management for Incoming Stock Requirements

dination results in meeting the deadlines. It is worth noting in Figure 12-1 how many functions must be coordinated. Each deals with different aspects of materials management as part of the internal supply chain of the company. The incoming logistics system of the company is the outgoing logistics system of the supplier. **Logistics,** which are the tactics of materials management and product distribution, should always be in harmony with the company's strategies.

12-1b Taxonomy of Materials

Every business needs to acquire materials to function. The process of acquisition is known as *buying* or *purchasing*. There are three main classes of materials that have to be purchased and managed.

First, there are raw materials (RM). These are generally extracted from the ground and then refined, but they are still the basic ingredients. Examples include mined metals such as copper, gold, and platinum, chemicals such as sodium and potassium salts, manganese and phosphates, grains such as wheat and rye, beans such as coffee, natural gas, and petroleum.

Raw materials have **value added** by operations. Value adding occurs when purchased components are further transformed by the company's production process. Thus, refining, processing, packaging, and shipping when done by the organization are value-adding and profit-making processes.

All buyers of raw materials specify their required quality standards. Grains can be too dirty. All soy is not alike. Coffee prices vary with the perceived quality of the taste of the beans. Raw materials are often bulky and require special spacious storage bins. Companies prefer to locate their refining operations near the source of raw materials so they do not have to transport tons of materials from which pounds or even ounces are eventually derived for use.

Logistics: Tactics of materials management for buying, storing, and transporting materials of all kinds as required by the company's supply chain.

Value added: Raw materials have value added by the transformation process of P/OM, which makes them into parts or processed materials.

The farmer is working a field in Le Bic, Quebec, Canada. The farmer sends food along the supply chain but requires many materials, including seeds, fertilizer, fuel, and spare parts to do the job.

Organizations that are in the business of supplying raw materials at the very start of the upstream acquisition process are themselves dependent on purchasing. A quick summary includes the equipment to dig in the mines or harvest the crop. The deposits in which the mines are located must be acquired. The land to be planted and farmed must be procured. Mining requires tools and lubricants, and farming demands seeds and fertilizer. This leads to the somewhat trite statement that "every organization has a supplier." Both miners and farmers have offices to run to keep the records for themselves, their owners, and the tax office. Everyone needs to buy paper and clips. Few are without computers. Miners, refiners, farm workers, and office personnel all need the basic necessities for proper hygiene in the office or plant.

Second, components (C) and subassemblies (SA) are purchased materials that have greater value added than the raw materials. They are, in fact, composed of raw materials that already have experienced value adding. C and SA are characterized by some degree of fabrication, assembly, and manufacture. They are assembled into higher-order products by combining them with each other and with other parts made by the producer.

This results in the third class of materials that needs to be managed. Work in process (WIP) can be stored and eventually shipped as finished goods (FG). WIP has more value added than the purchased subassemblies. There is a progression of value adding that starts at raw materials and moves up the supply chain to finished goods that are sold and shipped.

Clearly defined quality standards for the components and subassemblies must be set by the materials managers for the producer. As some materials are transformed from raw materials to finished goods, they become less bulky. This characterizes the analytic processes, which start with tons of raw materials and reduce them to smaller amounts of work in process based on the thought that less bulky goods still require storage space.

The opposite effect occurs for many manufactured products, which employ synthetic processes. These assemble components into bigger and heavier subassemblies and eventually finished products like farm tractors, diesel locomotives, automobiles, and commercial airliners. There is clearly an advantage in having such large and heavy finished goods near to their marketplace so they do not have to be transported great distances to the customers.

Materials managers choose suppliers based on their locations. There has to be a balance between where to buy bulky raw materials and where to assemble big products. Decisions about where to buy materials and where to locate assembly for shipment to the marketplace are based on analyzing the costs of transport, handling, and storage. Being well-informed always represents an advantage because the alternatives being considered are better ones.

To illustrate, some organizations purchase all, or part, of the finished goods that they sell without acknowledging their use of outsourcing. The customer believes that the corporate brand name identifies the maker. This ploy may be because the organization does not have the capacity to meet demand and, therefore, employs the services of coproducers to augment their own output. The finished goods are either shipped directly to customers or put into finished goods inventory. There have to be tight quality controls on the standards and the meeting of those standards.

Coproduced (often called copacked) products have much of their value added by the supplier. The purchaser's profits are related to marketing, selling, and shipping the product. There are instances of where firms buy finished goods for sale in certain countries while making them in others. Analysis is based on running the numbers for alternative taxes and tariffs in the countries where finished goods are purchased and sold.

12-1c Cost Leverage of Savings in Materials

Purchases from suppliers represent a large percentage of costs that must be recovered before the organization can start to make a profit. Looking at this issue in another way, if either direct labor or materials costs could be reduced by the same percentage, the average organization would save two or three times as much by choosing the materials costs reduction. The numbers differ by industry, ranging as shown in Table 12-1.

	Percent Range	Average %
Direct labor costs	05–15%	10
Direct materials costs	60–80%	70
Indirect costs	35–05%	20
Totals	100%–100%	100%

TABLE 12-1

Comparison of Labor and Materials Costs as an Average Percent of the Cost of Goods Sold for a "Normal" Manufacturing Organization

Say that the expenditure of $5,000 on an operations improvement study could reduce labor costs by 10 percent from $150,000 to $135,000. There is a *net saving* of $10,000. Making use of the percentages in Table 12-1, which apply to a "normal" organization, materials costs would be seven times larger than the direct labor costs. "Normal" or not, this seems extreme for our purposes. To find a middle ground that might apply to service industries, let us choose a multiple of materials costs being three times larger than labor costs. This would be $450,000.

If the $5,000 study could reduce materials costs by 10 percent, that would produce a saving of $45,000, or a *net saving* of $40,000. Spending to reduce materials costs provides savings four times greater than the study expense to reduce labor costs. Thus, investments in improving materials costs instead of labor costs are preferred because they have better leverage.

When only manufacturing industries are considered, direct materials costs in Table 12-1 range between 60 and 80 percent. The average percent for direct materials would be 70 percent of the cost of goods sold. An expense of $5,000 on an improvement study to reduce material costs by 10 percent would produce savings 7 times greater than the $15,000 savings associated with reduction of direct labor costs by 10 percent. The net saving would be $105,000 – $5,000 = $100,000. Spending to reduce materials costs provides savings that are 10 times greater than spending to reduce labor costs. For the most part, manufacturers should prefer investments that reduce materials costs rather than labor costs.

The examples lead to conjecture about the persisting pressures for downsizing labor. Are these efforts on track in the year 2003? Do continued adversarial relationships between unions and management make sense? How can unions help to reduce materials costs? The 2002 Los Angeles longshoremen's port strike epitomized the problem of management not knowing how to convince unions that the use of technology for very labor-intensive work could be in everyone's best interest.

Even before 1960, manufacturing was becoming less labor intensive as a result of technology. This same situation occurred in agriculture over the decades before 1960. The cost of labor for farming is far less than the cost of energy in the agricultural equation. It is estimated that less than 3 percent of the workforce is currently engaged in farming.

Still, manufacturers pursue inexpensive labor. Outsourcing the labor component, plants have moved to Mexico, Thailand, Indonesia, Pakistan, and the Republic of China. There has been rotation from one location to another as problems have surfaced in locations that are far from corporate headquarters. At the current time, China has become one of the largest sources for labor-intensive production.

Many services are labor intensive and although technology has had an impact, it has not alleviated the need for human contact. In some service industries, Table 12-1 is essentially reversed, with materials being the smaller percentage of the cost of services rendered. Efforts are being made to control service labor costs. There also are numerous examples of the unionization of service industries.

Perhaps the key is to make services so valuable to people that they are willing to spend an extra amount for clearly better investment advice, education, health care, hotel treatment (Ritz-Carlton), and even car service (Lexus). Marketing six-sigma, very special service products, may be essential to success continuity in the twenty-first century. P/OM will be called upon to fashion appropriate production systems to deliver especially valuable service products.

Information is one of the "materials" used by services. When properly managed, information can reduce the labor costs of services. A well-run travel agency uses the computer to provide quality service at low labor costs. Mail-order companies can trade off manual labor costs for computer input–output costs. The latter wins handily.

It should be noted that when purchasing pursues a high-quality, low-cost buying program, the pressure to control prices is passed to suppliers' firms, which are upstream from the producer in the supply chain. The expected pass-along reaction of suppliers will be to put their own suppliers, who are further upstream, under pressure to reduce prices. Thus, at each level suppliers may first try to reduce costs by downsizing to control labor costs. Ultimately, they will turn to their own suppliers, searching for additional cost advantages.

It is to be expected that analysis will continue to indicate that for all suppliers, their materials costs have greater leverage than their labor costs. This may not always hold true, but it is worth noting that replacement of labor with technology continues unabated throughout most of industry.

It is not certain that these relationships will be found throughout every supply chain. Still, it is noteworthy that at the raw materials level, increasingly technology and energy pay a much larger part of the bill than labor. It also is likely that when averaging across the whole supply chain, the major leverage factor is materials.

12-1d The Penalties of Errors in Ordering Materials

Order errors include wrong specifications, incorrect quantities, and overpriced materials. Orders placed for materials should be as correct in every aspect as possible. Mistakes are more costly in some situations than in others, but in all cases, errors are to be avoided.

Worst cases are likely to be for start-ups and for the mature flow shop. In both of these cases, the process may have to be stopped until the materials problems are corrected. The least worst case is likely to be for the job shop where other jobs can be done while the materials errors are corrected.

Flexible and programmable systems also have some built-in advantages of being able to shift from one product to another, with minimum penalty, when materials problems are encountered. Projects, such as bringing out a new product (start-ups) or building an office tower, can be flexible or vulnerable depending upon the stage of the system.

Specifications of materials must be defined exactly. They must be priced right, delivered on time, and inspected for faults. Information about materials must be managed with skill. Stock outages can delay or halt production of goods and services. The need for on-time quality materials is as crucial for services as for manufacturing. Consider the factory that runs out of boxes to package products, the printer without paper, or the fast-food restaurant that runs out of french fries.

The costs of mistakes can be exorbitant. In an actual case, an Exxon refinery needed a replacement gasket costing $85. Several gaskets were listed as being in stock, but when examined, they turned out to be the wrong size. The cost to the refinery was substantial because it had to cut production and send a chartered plane 700 miles to get a proper gasket. The actual cost of this inspection error was not announced but it was costly. The penalty for mistakes depends on the kind of product, the life cycle stage of the product, and the process configuration that is being used.

12-2 DIFFERENCES IN MATERIALS MANAGEMENT = f (WORK CONFIGURATIONS)

This section's title should be read "Differences that occur in materials management as a function of the work configuration that is used." Materials management requires unique rules and decision models for different markets, life cycle stages, and production configurations. That is, certain kinds of problems are posed by the materials requirements of flow shops that are not the same as for job shop and batch work systems. Differences also apply to projects and flexible processing systems.

12-2a Flow Shops

Flow shops require a continuous supply of a specific set of unchanging materials. The line must be shut down when stock outages occur. Alternatively, carrying large amounts of inventory can be unnecessarily costly, requiring more storage space than is justified. Obsolescence, deterioration, and pilferage (usually in that order) are the curse of carrying large amounts of inventories.

Trade-off models are needed to evaluate and balance the disadvantages of having large amounts of stock on-hand (SOH) against the benefits of large order quantities placed long in advance of delivery so that substantial quantity discounts can be obtained. The trade-off model also must consider the possibility that too little inventory on-hand followed by supplier strikes, delivery slowdowns, and acts of nature can lead to production shutdowns caused by a lack of supplies.

Knowing when to order and how much to order is the management imperative of the supply chain. Therefore, an order policy that specifies "when" and "how much" to order for each item, independent of what is happening to other items, is a sensible approach to use for items that have smooth and continuous demands. The flow shop is the work configuration that satisfies this demand pattern.

The flow shop consumes supplies constantly. Its demand for supplies can be considered to be smooth and regular. This kind of a pattern applies also to the intermittent flow shop and to stable, big-batch order environments. Suppliers actively compete to supply the materials requirements of high-volume demand systems.

> **Trade-off models:** Generic models in which raising the size of (x) brings increasing advantages of one kind (benefit) while creating larger penalties of another kind (costs).

12-2b Job Shops

Job shops have a varied and changing set of materials requirements. These may include certain materials, the uses of which are repeated with some degree of regularity, and others that are unique or infrequent orders. Frequency of usage is reflected in the dollar demand, which is a good measure of item importance.

Generally, job shops involve smaller order quantities of far more kinds of materials than flow shops. When discounts can be obtained, they are lower. Being able to track stock levels for many items is important. It requires an information management capability. One widely-used information planning system— for job shops—is called *material requirements planning (MRP)*. The job shop work configuration can be viewed as having a continuing stream of minor projects with short start-ups, which lack the serious consideration given to major projects with complex start-ups.

The job shop needs to have planning done for materials requirements. Such planning involves having a good information system to track the components used for each job in the shop. The time when those components are required must be specified and acted upon with sufficient lead time, which is the replenishment time for an order. Lead-time data is part of the information system that materials management must track. Lead-time management is required to make certain that expected lead times are met and when possible to find ways to decrease the replenishment period.

Many suppliers are involved in job shop management. Changes from one to another are not unusual. A single decision that deviates from optimal materials planning cannot do too much harm. The cumulative effects of repeated instances of bad quality and/or late deliveries can impose significant penalties such as the loss of good customers.

12-2c Flexible Manufacturing Systems

Small penalties accrue to flexible manufacturing systems (FMS), especially if a large variety of products on the menu permit flexible shifting to other work orders while errors in materials are corrected. Minor penalties also characterize service-oriented job shops, where flexible processing routines enable switching to alternative tasks while corrective procedures are undertaken with suppliers.

Although there are special material requirements for flexible manufacturing systems, they reflect a blend of the flow shop and the job shop. If there are many different products produced on the same FMS, then the materials requirements are more like the job shop than the flow shop. On the other hand, if there are only a few items produced in large volumes, the flow shop character will prevail.

12-2d Projects

Project undertakings, such as building ships or theme parks, have stages when certain materials are used that will not be used again. Because the activity stages are nonrepetitive, the majority of orders are preplanned and placed once. Nevertheless, materials requirements can be planned and information systems can be used to track the timing of materials needed for specific project activities.

Order policies concerning when to order and how much apply only to those project materials that are used consistently and uniformly throughout the project. Such ordering policies are appropriate when demands are independent of the specific project activities. This is the case for lubricants for machines, food for workers, paper for the office, and lightbulbs. In contrast, if materials requirements are properly tracked, the right amount of cement can be ordered to be delivered on time for a specific construction job of known dimensions.

Often, much work on project materials is subcontracted to suppliers who as specialists are familiar with particular stages of materials requirements for the particular project. Cost of materials is often less crucial than on-time delivery. Sometimes, as with start-ups for new products, the materials required are unique. There is little experience in producing them. Discounts for quantity purchases are rare, whereas special set-up charges are not unusual. Careful follow-up with suppliers is essential when experience with their practices is limited.

When suppliers have minimum familiarity with the products they are supplying, this can lead to production difficulties. To illustrate, the supplier of the stage sets for a Broadway play may have never before dealt with some of the special effects that are to be used. Without follow-up, the director and cast may be in for some surprises when the dress rehearsals begin. On another tack, the unseasoned entrepreneur discovers a succession of bugs that prevent smooth start-up and constancy of output. Professional training in OM would have led to checklists and other procedures aimed at avoiding problems.

There are many tales or "war stories" that can be told about mistakes in materials management. The requirements are all the more difficult because of the fact that although purchasing and process management are part of the P/OM team, they are concentrating on different aspects of the system. Purchasing as a centralized or decentralized buying function is serving different product masters, various departments, diverse divisions, and even plants, not all in the same country.

When there is antagonism between the buyers and those for whom they buy, many problems can surface. To prevent this from happening, close communication should be established. Working with purchasing, a good relationship should be established with suppliers. There is increasing belief in a materials system with fewer suppliers and a greater trust relationship between all parties.

Expectations of buyers for the performance of their suppliers change when there is continuity of their supply-and-demand relationship. Buyers expect that improvements will occur in quality, price, and speed of delivery. Some buyers may expect that shipping patterns will move closer to *just in time* (meaning delivered as needed and often abbreviated *JIT*). The suppliers look for continuity and loyalty from their buyers. A good relationship is derived from mutual benefits perceived by both parties.

12-3 THE MATERIALS MANAGEMENT INFORMATION SYSTEM

Materials management information system (MMIS): Provides online information about stock levels for all materials and parts.

The **materials management information system (MMIS)** provides online information about stock levels for all materials and parts (RM, C, SA, WIP, and FG). Stock on order, lead times, supplier information, costs of materials, and discount schedules also are part of the MMIS. (RM = raw materials, FG = finished goods, C = components, WIP = work in process, SA = subassemblies)

An **intelligent information system** is desired rather than a system that acts like a ledger providing only the information that is specifically requested. An intelligent MMIS can provide unsolicited data that is timely for decision making. It can request action (i.e., noting that a withdrawal from stock should trigger a buy decision). That order may be automatically created and sent to the supplier's computer. The idea of a smart information system is not just user friendly. It is a system that can prompt decisions, detect errors, and provide a rapid-access, multifunctional systems database.

An intelligent information system is designed with parameters that capture the management issues of *what to buy, when to buy, from whom to buy, how much to buy*, and *how much to pay*. This MMIS is constantly working overtime. The same material management system may have to be able to consider when to make the parts instead of buying them and when to employ coproducers and copackers.

12-3a Global Information System— Centralized or Decentralized

Companies that can compete globally have been moving toward an organizational integration of the information required for materials control. They have been doing this on a global basis. In the past, a variety of materials management activities existed as individual operations, each attended by managers who seldom communicated with each other. Eventually, in the search for greater effectiveness, a single, central materials control department has appeared in numerous organizations.

Centralization in purchasing may not be best for every organization, but it is more likely to be the best approach when the information systems infrastructure supports a global network. If the worldwide database is not properly organized, then decentralization is the only organizational format that can cope with the numerous tasks that procurement entails.

Most organizations have a vice president in charge of materials control. This senior position may be essential to permit the centralization of the global materials management tasks. The responsibilities vested in a materials control department include at least four subfunctions, each of which has major international implications.

1. Purchasing from suppliers all over the world and having close relations with them. Regulating shipments as to carriers and delivery dates.

2. Maintaining stocks of inventory at various places worldwide, while knowing how much inventory is in place at each location (i.e., inventory stock control, on a global basis). Status in the warehouse includes control over the withdrawal procedures such as "first-in, first-out" or "last-in, first-out." **Expediting** means following up on orders and doing whatever can be done to move materials faster.

3. Inspecting incoming materials using various statistical methods of quality control for acceptance sampling. These inspections are taking place worldwide and must be coordinated by an information system that tracks location and status.

4. Running an international accounts payable department that can take advantage of terms for paying, such as 30 days before interest begins to be charged. Especially, in inflationary economies, such as those of Brazil (2000–2002) and Argentina (1960s–1990s), the interest rate terms can turn out to be as important as the buying price. The Brazilian annual inflation rate had been officially put at 6,000 percent— unofficially at 12,000 percent. Ford Motor Company's decision to build an auto plant in Sao Paulo might have been reversed if the extreme inflation rate had been forecast. Currency ratios also must be considered in purchasing decisions. The Argentine oil company YPF overpurchased during the high-inflation period items such as rubber tires. Rubber does not store well for too many years.

> **Intelligent information system:** Captures the management issues of *what to buy, when to buy, from whom to buy, how much to buy, how much to pay*, etc.

> **Expediting:** Actively following up on orders to make sure that deliveries will be on time. Expediters initiate remedial actions.

Each materials management activity interfaces with the others. They are the mutual responsibility of many departments within the organization. Coordination of activities is needed, and that is why good information management is stressed.

12-3b The Systems Communication Flows

Many forms of communication unite the various materials management groups within the larger organization. Some companies use paperless systems—at least in parts of the organization. Tandem non-Stop computer systems (part of Compaq and then Hewlett-Packard) developed a paperless factory in Texas as a role model. IBM in Santa Palomba, Italy, used electronic data interchange (EDI) in the 1970s. The system linked other European installations through an online, real-time information system aimed at providing assembly instructions for order fulfillment. Hewlett-Packard in California pioneered the use of bar-code control of assemblies. Chrysler connects Detroit with its suppliers everywhere using EDI.

By 1990, the Internet was being employed by every major company to facilitate purchasing. There were exchanges and auction sites set up during the dot.com boom of the late 1990s. Many of these failed because of inadequate business plans. However, the function of the Internet remains widely used by internal purchasing departments all over the globe.

Even so, most companies have paper-rich trails that are coordinated with computer records. The objectives for paperless organizations remain worthy goals that are gradually being approached. Satellites enable e-mail transmissions to abound, raising communication levels by exponential amounts. EDI using computer-aided design permits The Limited to transmit clothing manufacturing patterns and materials requirements to suppliers in Hong Kong and Indonesia moments after finalizing patterns in Columbus, Ohio, and Waltham, Massachusetts.

Electronic information mixes with paper for invoicing accounts payable and for tracking stock withdrawals and stock on-hand. Verbal communications and TV pictures augment the multimedia system. The communications are especially helpful when problems arise due to contingencies, which in the course of otherwise normal materials management can be counted on to occur. Many times, contingencies lead the materials control department to seek help with problems from its own research and development (R & D) department as well as the supplier's R & D department. Such interchanges can take place on a global basis.

12-4 THE PURCHASING FUNCTION

Purchasing agents (PAs):
Buy supplies the company requires.

Purchasing agents (PAs) and their buying organizations have the traditional role of bringing into the organization the needed supplies. Although this is very important, the role is changing, becoming more integrated within the organization and bringing in more important information, as well. Sourcing (which is the generic name for purchasing every kind of supply needed by the organization) has become a global system.

12-4a The Twenty-First Century Learning Organization

The purchasing department in the twenty-first century is an information-gathering agency. Totally on the up-and-up, by being everywhere and able to listen, it is able to learn about new technologies being used by suppliers and the organizations they supply worldwide. It is on top of new materials, new suppliers, new distribution channels, new prices, and new processes that produce quality levels previously not attainable. It has a global reach via satellites and telecommunications capabilities that constantly expand horizons.

This purchasing department is responsive to the marketing strategies of the various suppliers from whom it obtains the required materials. The old and waning role of purchasing is to push suppliers on price. Shopping around for the best prices is no longer done. It is far from "best practice." The price-tag approach has been thrown out in favor of a long-term relationship with a few trusted suppliers.

The importance of the buying function depends upon the extent to which the company requires outside suppliers. The determination of what to make and what to buy is an OM decision; however, purchasing department information can be crucial. It is evident that the decision often depends on the terms to buy, including price, quality, delivery, and innovations, among others, which purchasing learns about and communicates to the OM team.

Certainly, if the production department cannot make the product, then the importance of the buying function increases. Few mail-order companies and/or department stores produce any of the materials that they offer for sale. Supermarkets use the capacity of copackers to offer products with their name. Purchasing provides the leverage for such products.

Best practice retailers strive to achieve large, double-digit inventory turns. For example, if the items in this warehouse are replaced 20 times a year, management could not be faulted if it asked for turnover of 30 times. Lowering prices might be one strategy to try.

12-4b Buyers' Risks

Mail-order and department store purchasing agents (PAs) generate such large volumes that they are of equally great importance to the superstores (e.g., Wal-Mart) or the mail-order companies for which they work—and to the producers from whom they buy. Purchasing agents for flow shops also deal in such large volumes that making them happy is considered part of the supplier's business strategy. In many circumstances, purchasing managers are responsible for the success of their companies. In keeping with this responsibility is the salary levels that such buyers receive, in return for the risks they accept.

Purchasing for mail order and retail eventually drives the logistics of the supply chain. This OM sales-service area is involved in a situation where the ability to shift rapidly to new product designs and suppliers may be essential for success.

Fashion is fickle. Women's clothing styles change in complex ways. Manufacturers have been caught with large unsold inventories as a result of committing to a style that did not gain acceptance. When turnover is poor for retail or mail order, the goods are marked down and sold quickly at large discounts that provide no profit, and often at a loss. Books and toys that do not sell are marked down and remaindered.

12-4c Turnover and Days of Inventory— Crucial Measures of Performance

The performance of the purchasing agent in the supply chain is related to the speed (or velocity) with which goods sell and the amount of inventory that is on hand to be drawn down. There is also the replenishment rate. A small stock that is frequently replenished can satisfy large demand rates without entailing carrying charges for a stuffed warehouse.

Various ways exist for measuring these rates. Demand velocity (units per period like miles per hour) is measured as units sold—moved to the customer—per period of time. Average daily demand velocity is often called *average demand per day*.

Days of Inventory (DOI)

This measure is regularly reported by many firms. DOI is equivalent to dividing total stock on-hand by the average demand per day. It is the expected length of time before running out of stock if no further stock is added. DOI changes when new stock is added (DOI goes up) and when daily demand speeds up (DOI goes down) or slows down (DOI goes up).

Automobile companies, furniture manufacturers, and makers of baby strollers reflect the broad spectrum of companies that customarily report DOI. There is a comfortable level in each case, such that one month's supply of autos would usually be considered too little—six or more months of supply would be considered excessive. Ten months might be interpreted as a signal of dangerous inventory accumulation.

The computation of **days of inventory** is shown here, with a numerical example, where *Avg. inv.* stands for average inventory. This is the same as average dollar inventory

Days of inventory (DOI): Total stock on-hand divided by the average demand per day gives a measure of how long it will be before the stockroom and warehouse are empty.

(*Avg. $ inv.*). In the example that follows, *Avg. Inv.* is $5 million. Also, the daily cost of goods sold (i.e., *Daily COGS*) is the annual cost of goods sold divided by (say) 365. *Annual COGS* is $50 million. If there are 250 selling days, then change 365 to 250. Thus

Daily COGS = 50 ÷ 365 = $136,986.30

Days of inventory (*DOI*) = (*Avg. inv.*) ÷ (*Daily COGS*) = $5,000,000 ÷ $136,986.30 = 36.5 days

An alternative way to compute this number would be

DOI = 365 × (*Avg. inv.*) ÷ (*Annual COGS*) = 365 × (5) ÷ (50) = 36.5 days of inventory

Inventory Turns

Turnover: Turns are measured by annual net sales divided by total average stock on-hand.

Inventory turns: See Turnover.

Another measure that is used that captures the essence of supply chain objectives regarding throughput and value added is turnover. **Turnover** or **inventory turns** is measured as the number of times that the warehouse is emptied and refilled per year. Inventory turnovers can be measured with different time periods than a year, such as turns per month. If the summer months have low demand, then the inventory turns may decrease during that period speeding up in the fall.

The concept of turnover can be applied to retail stores, department stores, mail-order firms, and the family medicine chest. It is a very helpful performance measure to manufacturers and distributors moving goods off the factory floor to the customer.

The computation of inventory turnover is shown here, with a numerical example. The numbers used for this example are related to sales dollars rather than cost dollars. The latter were used to calculate days of inventory (DOI). Numbers for turnover are based on a sales price of $1.20 per dollar of the cost of goods sold. Also, average inventory is estimated in terms of sales dollars rather than cost dollars.

Annual net sales = $50,000,000(1.2) = $60,000,000

Avg. Inv. (*in sales dollars*) = $5,000,000(1.2) = $6,000,000

Inventory turns = (*Annual net sales*) ÷ (*Avg. inv.*) = 60 million ÷ 6 million

Inventory turns = (*Annual net sales*) ÷ (*Avg. inv.*) = 10 *turns per year*

Note the relationship between 10 inventory turns and 36.5 days of inventory. Thirty-six and one-half days is the interval between turns. Both measures tell different but related stories about the same system. Inventory turns give a sense of the velocity with which inventory moves out of the warehouse. Days of inventory states the inventory backlog to be worked off in terms of how long that will take.

Using these measures, companies can determine how well they are doing in moving materials throughout the supply chain. If a soft drink company fails to make as many units of beverage as had been forecast, then days of inventory of sugar may grow too large and new orders will not be placed. For toys, books, VCR tapes, and autos, excessive days of inventory are costly.

12-4d Turnover Examples

The Limited management said that it aims to achieve better than 100 turns per year in its warehouses. Wal-Mart targets turns as great or even greater. Thomasville, a furniture company, has taken the traditional two to four inventory turns for suites of furniture into ten or better per year.

SKU: Stock-keeping units where the SKU catalog numbers represent every different part carried, sold, or purchased by the company.

Price can be a crucial factor. When an item does not move at The Limited, its price is dropped and it is put onto a bargain table. The Limited does not have **SKUs,** so turnover is hard to measure for a specific item. Rather, the DOI of an item is the measure of performance.

Good turnover brings large rewards and a reputation for purchasing success. On the other hand, there are great risks of failure. Poor measures mark the marginal competitor. Buyers and purchasing agents have to accept the risk of making errors such as overestimating demand or paying too high a price. Penalties of being wrong are high.

12-4e Purchasing Agents (PAs)

Purchasing records provide a history of what has been done in the past. Documenting history is useful, including what the costs were, who the major suppliers were, what discounts were obtained, what quality levels achieved, and delivery periods for specific items. Without documentation, the supplier history of a company can be lost.

The skills and experience of purchasing agents are not readily transferable between different industries. They may vary between companies even in the same industry. Differentiation exists by types of materials, buying and shipping terms, and supplier purchasing traditions.

It is not possible to discuss all of the intricate relationships that have been developed by buyers and suppliers in order to achieve maximum satisfaction for both parties. A number of important procedures are covered, but new ones are being developed all of the time that take advantage of changes in the information, storage, and transportation technologies.

The purchasing function is responsible for bringing the exact materials that production needs before they are needed, or just in time. Purchasing interfaces P/OM and its suppliers. P/OM may have some decisive requirements and some exceptional information for suppliers. It is not surprising, then, that this part of the supply chain is tightly coordinated with P/OM. Whatever the organization's structure, purchasing must be part of the OM team.

When the purchasing process is technical, the purchasing agent may be an engineer or a person who has worked with the production department. Purchasing is usually responsible for the following functions, which might be called the *purchasing mission*:

1. Ordering what is needed in the right quantities and then meeting all quality standards at the best possible prices—always achieving delivery reliability. This mission must be coordinated with P/OM and marketing with respect to what is going to be needed when. Purchasing must be assisted by OM in predicting the amount of scrap. By increasing order sizes to compensate, costly reorders can be avoided for a small number of units needed to complete orders.

2. Receiving inventories is part of the materials management function. Often, but not always, "receiving" is the responsibility of purchasing. Some organization must determine that deliveries are on time and that P/OM will have what it needs as it schedules production runs. Will it be just in time, or will extra stock be carried just in case? These decisions require communication and coordination between POM and the PAs.

3. Inspecting the incoming goods to make sure that their qualities meet specifications and that the right quantities have been delivered.

4. Purchasing is the specialist in knowing which suppliers to use. Sometimes, the PAs are in charge of certification of suppliers. Keeping in touch with change is necessary.

5. Purchasing also is the materials management function to turn to when engineering design changes (EDCs) occur that demand changes in the specifications of purchased materials. What happens to the stock on-hand that is outmoded? How fast can the new specifications be made and shipped? If the company is constantly changing designs (which many are doing) then knowing which suppliers can cope with shifting demands is important.

6. Stability of supply relationships has value.

7. Purchasing must be adept at coordinating the materials that are needed for start-ups. The management dynamics that are associated with start-ups are entirely different from those that operate successfully for mature products.

Coordinating the goals of materials management with those of process management is one of P/OM's greatest responsibilities. Scenarios applicable to Functions 1 and 4 are common where a variety of suppliers are dealt with, and about one out of ten has serious failures. Consequently, there is regular shifting of suppliers over time, requiring P/OM adjustments.

There is a cultural *difference* in the importance of legal contracts in the United States as compared to many other countries. For example, Japan has far fewer lawyers than the United States, and the Japanese do not value legal contracts in the same way that the United States does. This *difference* has significant impact on the way P/OM proceeds in other countries.

A scenario applicable to Function 2 has the receiving dock forgetting to log in a shipment, which results in a "false" crisis when that item seems to have run out of stock. In some instances, the mistake is not traced and even though there is the necessary stock on-hand, it is lost in the warehouse.

The following story for Function 3 occurs repeatedly. Inspectors fail to check all of the quality standards and put defective received goods into inventory. The production line may be forced to shut down.

The situation that is involved with Function 5 is extremely serious in companies where technological change is moving at a rapid rate. Product malfunctions in the field lead to parts being redesigned and EDCs being issued, sometimes in bunches, in the hope that the problems will be corrected. Even with mature aircraft such as the Boeing 737, design changes in the reverse thruster were called for after it had been flying for many years.

12-4f The Ethics of Purchasing

Purchasing agents make buying decisions that involve enormous amounts of money. As labor costs have contracted and materials costs have increased, the power to buy is vested in few hands. All over the world, there are cases of supplier companies attempting to influence purchasing decisions. In some places in the world, this is not considered illegal or unethical.

In the United States, it is not ethical or legal. The following section on bidding mentions the way in which companies use bids to provide the appearance of purchasing decisions that are not influenced by gifts of any kind. The only sure way to avoid problems is to make certain that purchasing agents are trustworthy and moral.

It is understandable that purchasing agents achieve special arrangements with suppliers that they trust. After years of dealing with a supplier, a friendly relationship can develop that is an entirely ethical alliance. Both buyer and supplier value the long-term stability and goodwill of their relationship.

In the business environment of the United States, personal relationships are not considered to be a reasonable basis for enterprise decisions. They exist nevertheless in less blatant form than in other cultures. For example, in Latin America and the Middle East, personal friendships are held to be business assets that reduce risk and have monetary value.

Part of this cultural difference can be traced to the importance placed upon legal contracts in the United States that does not exist elsewhere. Japan has far fewer lawyers than the United States. The Japanese do not value legal contracts in the same way as in the United States. With the growth of global business, such factors play a major role in determining management's success in handling the affairs of subsidiaries outside the United States.[1] This emphasizes another international aspect of materials management and OM.

12-5 RECEIVING, INSPECTION, AND STORAGE

An important part of the materials management job is receiving shipments from suppliers. There is a need for a (receiving) unloading facility designed to take the supplies out of the shippers' conveyance. After unloading the supplies, there is usually a storage area to put them. The design of this facility differs depending upon what is to be unloaded (type of supplies), what the supplies are unloaded from (trucks, freight cars, hopper cars, ships, planes, etc.), and where they are to be unloaded.

The receiving facility is often called the *receiving dock*, and there is another location for shipping called a *shipping dock*. In many instances, these are the same place. In some instances, in the morning they are receiving docks and in the afternoon they are shipping docks.

In most situations, they are completely separate facilities. Wal-Mart uses **cross-docking** to transfer goods from incoming trucks at the receiving dock to outgoing trucks at the shipping docks. This means that a large percentage of goods never enters the warehouse but crosses from one dock to the other. Such cross-docking has been credited with

Cross-docking: Transfer goods from incoming trucks at receiving docks to outgoing trucks at shipping docks. The docks are adjacent.

saving substantial amounts of money and time. It is often cited as an example of how P/OM's creativity improved the logistics of distribution operations.

It is not unusual for the freight cars or hopper cars to be used as storage facilities with materials being unloaded as needed. Instead of moving chemicals and plastics from the hopper car to the warehouse, the factory draws directly on the reserves in the hopper cars. The DuPont Corporation has successfully cut down on the number of hopper cars with inventory that are sitting around on sidings by coordinating customers' needs with shipping schedules.

Supplies must be inspected to control the quality and quantity of what was ordered. Is the shipment exactly correct and has it been received undamaged? Specific quality checks are made using acceptance sampling methods. Acceptable materials are moved to the storage facility—often the company warehouse.

12-6 REQUIRING BIDS BEFORE PURCHASE

Bidding is a process by which the buyer requests competing companies to specify how much they will charge for their product. Competitive bids can involve more than price. Sometimes, purchasing requests suppliers to submit competitive bids for both cost and delivery time.

In some industries and government systems, purchasing is required to use the bidding process. It should be noted that there are always two points of view with respect to bidding—the buyer's and the seller's. Materials management is interested in the buyer's point of view of bidding, which is lowest costs, best quality, and fastest delivery, among others.

With discretionary bidding, purchasing agents might decide to use it to prevent charges of favoritism. It controls expenditures when there can be significant variation in supplier charges. Bid requests state specifically all of the conditions that must be met and ask for details of what the supplier intends, including prices, delivery dates, and quality specifications and assurances.

Bidding can be a costly process for the materials management buyer. This is especially the case when there are many criteria upon which competing suppliers will be rated. Cost also rises when there are many firms that are bidders. On the other hand, for bidding to work, there must be at least two suppliers willing to bid for the job.

Bidding is commonly required of government agencies. The IRS reviewed bids before choosing laptop computers. The armed services utilize bids for military acquisitions. Bids are familiar in situations where industrial firms have no prior supplier arrangements and in which costly purchases (including engineering and construction jobs) are to be made. The federal government almost always awards contracts to the lowest bidder. Other concerns that are taken into account by private industry are seldom allowable with government awards.

Bids can be requested where the price is fixed and the creativity and quality of the solution is at stake. Advertising agencies bid for accounts that have a set budget. Alternative bids are based on campaign creativity. The same applies to a P/OM request for proposals from a consulting organization where the budget allocation is fixed. Competing bids for a computerized materials management system are common.

With so much bidding action, it is not surprising that bidding models have been developed. The models can assist both the buyer who makes the requests for proposals (RFPs) and the sellers who offer the bids. Bidding models indicate that as the number of bidders competing increases, the size of the winning bid decreases. With more bidders, there is more variability.

Perhaps this is a good reason for the buyer to include many bidders. On the other hand, each extra bid adds to the ordering costs. There also is the fear that a low bid will be made by an organization that is less likely to produce quality work. Steps must be taken to ensure that quality is not compromised by price. Also, too many bidders may drive the expected profit so low that qualified suppliers refuse to join the bidding, leaving the field open to the less qualified.

Bidding: Buyer requests competitors to specify price and terms for their product.

A company may not choose to buy from the organization presenting the lowest bid. Price is almost never the only factor that needs to be taken into consideration when awarding a contract. Among other things, it is essential to consider quality and guarantees of quality, the experience of the supplier, the uncertainties of delivery, and the kind of long-term, supplier–producer relationship that is likely to develop.

Bidding is applicable for project procurement policies and for start-up purchase arrangements for the flow shop. It is less relevant for the job shop, although it may make sense when costly components are involved. Bidding is a useful protection when there is suspicion that special purchasing deals are being made between suppliers and company personnel.

12-7 MATERIALS MANAGEMENT OF CRITICAL PARTS

For projects and the flow shop, certain parts can fail that will shut down the line or seriously delay project completion. These are called *critical parts*. An entire refinery can be shut down. The cost of lost production may well run into millions of dollars.

How many spares of the various parts that are judged to be critical parts should be kept in stock? How likely is it that a spare part kept in stock for an emergency will ever be used? Often, severe technical problems are involved in purchasing critical parts for the maintenance function of complex technological systems.

This is a problem for the materials management–OM team that is familiar with the specific production equipment. It is able to evaluate the failure characteristics of the technology. Policies for stocking spare critical parts also are a function of the type of maintenance that is used. If preventive maintenance calls for replacing critical parts once every year, then that decision establishes the base requirements for stocking the part. When reliability is important, a technical basis must be used for purchasing spare parts.

For an important class of maintenance inventories, spare critical parts can be obtained inexpensively only at the start-up of the facility that will be needing the spare critical parts. If it turns out, later on, that an insufficient supply of these critical parts was acquired, the cost of obtaining additional spares is much higher.

A *failure model* can be constructed to determine how many spare parts should be kept in stock. This is best done for a specific case. It is then possible to generalize from that example. Start with engineering data or an accurate estimate. Assume that the failure data indicate that a particular critical part has a probability of i failures (p_i) over the lifetime of a flexible manufacturing machine, called the *complex machine*.

There is a cost c for each spare part purchased at the time that the complex machine is acquired. When a spare part must be purchased at a later time, due to an insufficient supply purchased at the start-up, the cost is estimated to be c'.

c' can be much larger than c because it includes the cost of doing whatever has to be done to fill the production void caused by failure of the part. Thus, c' might reflect the cost of buying finished parts from a coproducer. There also is a large cost per replacement part charged by the OEM (original equipment manufacturer). OEMs charge high prices for spare parts not acquired originally, especially when they are not carried in stock. Then, a special setup is required.

Replacement part manufacturers may use different work configurations than the original equipment manufacturers. The latter are seldom set up to make replacement parts economically. This characterizes the aftermarket for tires, auto parts, and windshield glass. In this example, it is assumed that the spare part cannot be obtained from an aftermarket replacement source.

12-7a The Complex Machine—How Many Parts to Carry

For the complex machine, the probability of i failures is (p_i).

Let $p_i \geq 0$ for i = 0, 1, 2, 3. If p_0 = 0, then there must be at least 1 failure and no more than 3 failures over the lifetime of the machine. Also, assume that the probability of failure is distributed as follows:

Number of Failures *i* Occurring During Machine's Lifetime (column)	0	1	2	3	
p_i	0+	1/2	1/3	1/6	Expected Cost
k					
k = 0	0	400	800	1,200	$666.67
k = 1	5	5	5 + 400	5 + 800	$271.67
k = 2	10	10	10	10 + 400	$ 76.67
k = 3	15	15	15	15	$ 15.00 MIN

TABLE 12-2

Failure Cost Matrix for the Complex Machine

Notes: The initial number of spares = k; c is the cost/unit as originally purchased; c' is cost of replacement.

Let c = \$5 and c' = \$400. The question is: How many spare parts (k) should be ordered at the time of the original purchase? The spare part is inexpensive if purchased initially. However, later replacement of the failed part costs 80 times the original price because of large setup costs and lost production time. The decision matrix for spare-part strategies is given in Table 12-2.

$i = 0$ failure; $p_0 = 0+$

$i = 1$ failure; $p_1 = 1/2$

$i = 2$ failures; $p_2 = 1/3$

$i = 3$ failures; $p_3 = 1/6$

The steps required to obtain the expected values in Table 12-2 are as follows. The outcome entries in the matrix are computed by two different relationships. First, when the number of failures is equal to or is less than the number of parts originally ordered with the machine, then the cost is simply kc.

Second, when the number of failures is greater than the number of parts originally ordered, the cost is

$kc + (i - k)c'$

The first line $i = 0$ failure; $p_0 - 0+$ needs interpretation. The value 0+ is meant to imply that although the probability of zero failures is rated as 0.00 over the life of the complex machine, nevertheless, there is a small possibility (+) that it might occur. For the basic calculation, this minimal probability can be ignored. The data are included in the decision matrix shown in Table 12-2.

The sum of these probabilities equals 1:

$$\sum_{i=0}^{i=3} p_i = 1$$

The minimum expected cost is obtained by ordering 3 spares—a result that could have been anticipated by the size of the numbers for c and c'. At least 1 failure will occur in line with the probability distribution given in the table. As is shown in the Problem Section at the end of this chapter, the result could be quite different if there was a substantial probability for zero failures.

For example, if 3 failures occur ($i = 3$) and only two parts were originally ordered ($k = 2$), then the cost is \$410, calculated as follows: $(2 \times 5) + (3 - 2) 400 = 410$.

After the matrix of total costs is completed, the expected values are obtained in the usual fashion:

Expected cost for k = 0: $400(1/2) + 800(1/3) + 1,200(1/6) = 666.67$

Expected cost for k = 1: $5(1/2) + 405(1/3) + 805(1/6) = 271.67$

Expected cost for k = 2: $10(1/2) + 10(1/3) + 410(1/6) = 76.67$

Expected cost for k = 3: $15(1/2) + 15(1/3) + 15(1/6) = 15.00$

For realism, assume that all numbers are in thousands. Having the lowest expected cost of $15,000, three spares should be ordered with the complex machine. This is $61,670 cheaper than ordering two, and more than a quarter of a million dollars cheaper than ordering only one spare part with the complex machine.

When the three parts arrive with the machine, they should be inspected carefully to make certain that they are properly made according to specifications. They must be able to do the job, if and when they are called upon.

The problem could be complicated and made more realistic by adding a charge for carrying a part in stock, changing the probabilities of failure after a failure occurs, allowing more than one spare to be reordered after failure, etc. All such issues, and others as well, can be treated in a more realistic albeit complicated model.

The key, however, is to note the high cost of having 3 failures and not being prepared for that eventuality. This mistake pits a $10,000 expenditure for two extra spares as insurance against having to pay more than a quarter of a million dollars to correct the problem. Different numbers would have other conclusions.

12-7b The Static Inventory Problem

The decision-matrix model effectively represents the **static inventory problem.** In materials management terms, this is deciding how much to buy *when there is only a one-time purchase*. The model is not representative of flow shop problems but it is fully applicable to the job shop and project manager. Variability of demand (in this case, the spare parts failure distribution) is only one way in which uncertainty about the order size can arise. Other causes are defectives (requiring additional parts to be made to fill the order), spoilage, and pilferage. All such factors can be accounted for with probability estimates and the decision-matrix methodology. A, B, and C are identical.

12-8 VALUE ANALYSIS (ALTERNATIVE MATERIALS ANALYSIS)

Value analysis has been a part of materials management since the 1940s. The idea behind **value analysis (VA)** is that

1. Materials are always being *improved* because of constant technological developments.

2. Unless a watch is kept on the relevance of materials, *opportunities to shift to new materials* that will improve the company's products will be missed.

3. Efforts should be made continuously to improve the material qualities of the product and to decrease product costs through *materials innovations*.

Value analysis is applied to all materials used by the process and for the product. VA works for materials in all domains including hospitals, hotels, restaurants, offices, manufacturers, and airlines. Airlines are beginning to save money by substituting electronic vouchers for paper tickets.

12-8a Methods Analysis

Value analysis and **methods analysis** are often seen as close relatives. Methods analysis is the systematic examination of all operations in any process in search of a better way of doing things. It encourages alternative processing by combining operations, eliminating unnecessary steps, and making work easier. Method analysts are widely employed to help OM work smarter and not harder.

To distinguish value analysis from methods analysis, the latter is primarily concerned with process improvement and secondarily with materials. Specifically, value analysis is the "analysis of the value of alternative materials." Inevitably, value and methods analyses must share common ground. Starting with different perspectives, they converge on the same kind of problems, providing similar kinds of problem resolution.

To reiterate, growth of interest in value analysis increases whenever materials technology seems to start a new wave of rapid and dramatic changes for particular industries.

Static inventory problem: Classical inventory problem with some special characteristics, namely, how much to buy when there is only one purchase occasion allowed.

Value analysis (VA): Search for alternative materials as replacements for the current ones with quality gains and cost advantages.

Methods analysis: Systematic examination of all operations in every process. The objective is to search for better ways to do the jobs that the company requires.

Such waves occur from time to time in metals, plastics, ceramics, and most recently in glass (i.e., expansive solar glass windshields).

On a related front, materials shortages raise interest in value analysis aspects of materials management. The petroleum shortage of the 1970s led to major P/OM distortions. Companies were faced with the need to make swift alterations in the composition of their products. Goods and services were affected. Other temporary shortages that occurred during the last 20 years include yellow fats, paper products, lumber, copper, and water.

Material shortages hit particularly hard at the flow shop, which is least flexible in adapting to changes in materials. Increasing numbers of organizations try to prepare for shortage situations by doing contingency planning. Sometimes, this even includes R & D efforts to prepare alternative formulations.

In addition to shortages, government agencies increasingly prohibit the use of well-established materials. The food industry has experienced bans on saccharine, cyclamates, food dyes, preservatives, and many other items. The detergent industry has been forced to reformulate its products several times because of ecological effects of phosphorous and enzyme additives. Government regulation of fuels to control auto emissions is another instance. Government regulations call for a small percent of all vehicles sold in 1998 to have zero emissions (as with electric cars). Thereafter, the percentage is expected to increase over time. Government restrictions can be expected to continue to grow in number and severity.

If proper value analysis of alternative materials has been done, then materials alternatives do not have to be hastily sought when either shortages occur or government edicts forbid the use of specific materials and/or change the way that they can be used. The procedures for value analysis should be applied to established products during their mature life cycle stages, as well as to new products during their start-up and growth life cycle stages.

Successful value analysis requires a well-structured approach. This is reflected by the consistent application of a set of relevant questions. For example:

1. How do materials affect what this product or service is intended to do?
2. How do materials affect the cost of this product or service?
3. Have there been prior changes in the materials used?
4. What other materials could be used?
5. How do alternative materials affect Questions 1 and 2?

The value analysis approach has been designed to increase insights by providing a structural framework to encourage the development of alternative materials management strategies. The starting point is the methods analysis of existing outputs and processes.

Often, the most important materials in the product and process are labeled *primary classes*; others are called *secondary classes*. Major efforts are placed on the primary classes, which are then related by analogy to other products, processes, and materials that are thought to provide similar properties.

Sometimes, by means of analogies, materials alternatives can be derived. Comparisons are developed between different joining methods—adhesion, cohesion, welding, brazing, and mechanical fastenings such as nuts and bolts, cotter pins, nails, etc. When things are to be held together, it is wise to know all of the ways that fastening can be achieved.

Both methods analysis and value analysis are used to discover new tactical, efficient alternatives. But P/OM must be on guard against investments in efficiency studies before effectiveness issues have been thoroughly considered.

12-9 ABC CLASSIFICATION—THE SYSTEMS CONTEXT

Materials management—from the inception of the purchasing process all the way through production and the shipping of finished goods—can be improved by utilizing an important systems concept called the **ABC classification.** The concept is that some materials are more important than others—further, that it is prudent to do what is important before doing what is less important.

ABC classification: Inventory items in rank order by dollar volume. Generally, 25 percent of *all* items (SKUs) contribute 75 percent of *total* dollar volume.

This concept can be applied in a number of different ways, two of which are discussed here.

12-9a Material Criticality

It is necessary for materials management to categorize the critical nature of parts, components, and other materials. There are various definitions of "critical" that fit different situations. When a part failure causes product or process failure, that is a critical part. For an airline engine, most of the parts may be critical, in this sense.

The following scenario might be relevant. This airline considers most critical any part that has greater than a 10 percent probability of failing within one year. Membership in the top-ranking group is called *A-critical*. Perhaps the top 25 percent of all critical parts can be considered to be A-critical.

A second set, called *B-critical*, is identified by the airline as any part that has greater than a 10 percent probability of failing within five years. A-critical items are excluded. Perhaps the next 25 percent of all critical parts can be considered to be B-critical.

The third set, called *C-critical*, might be associated with greater than 10 percent probabilities of failing after five years. Because 50 percent of the parts are in the A and B groups, the remaining 50 percent of the parts are in the C group.

As an alternative definition, part failure can have a probability (not a certainty) of stopping the process or product. Thus, a possible description of critical parts relates to the probability of process or product failure when the part fails.

The parts are rank ordered by the probability of causing process or product failure. Say that if the first part fails there is a 30 percent probability of product failure. The next part might have a 20 percent probability.

Perhaps the top 25 percent of critical parts has an 80 percent probability of causing (each independently) product failure. This kind of situation is pictured in Figure 12-2.

Some processes do not fail as a result of part failure but instead the production output is reduced by a significant amount. A curve similar to Figure 12-2 could be created for this kind of situation.

Criticality is a coined term that can mean *crucial to performance* or *dangerous to use*. Thus, an alternative definition of criticality could apply to the danger involved in using materials. Flammability, explosiveness, and toxicity of fumes could be crucial safety factors for materials management.

Whichever definition of criticality is used, the procedure is to list the most critical parts first. Then, systematically rank-order parts according to their criticality. Criticality should reflect the costs of failures, including safety dangers, loss of life, and losses in production output.

Criticality: When part behavior causes process or product failure or a marked degradation in performance.

FIGURE 12-2
ABC Curve for the Criticality of Materials

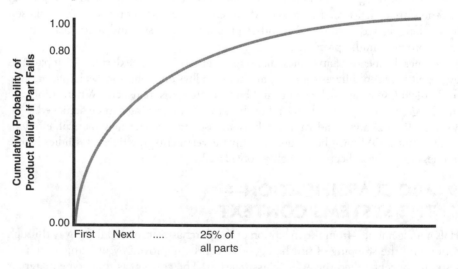

Parts Rank Ordered by Probability of Product Failure if Part Fails (Highest Probability Is First)

Spare parts and other backup materials should be provided to conform to remedial failure strategies. Also to be considered are replacement parts for preventive failure strategies. Further, spare parts must be inspected to ensure their continued integrity over time.

A large South American refinery decided to double its rubber spare parts inventory. Within two years, many of the parts had begun to deteriorate and could not be called upon to replace critical failed parts. The high penalty resulted in a return to the original policy. Organizations have found that poor spare parts policies can be the "Achilles' heel" for business.

12-9b Material Dollar Volume

The second set of ABC categories is based on sorting materials by their annual dollar volume. Dollar volume is the surrogate for potential savings that can be made by improving the inventory management of specific materials. Accordingly, all parts, components, and other materials used by a company should be listed and then rank ordered by their annual dollar volume. Thus:

$$DV_i (t = 1 \text{ year}) = c_i \sum_{t=0}^{t=1} q_i(t)$$

where: DV_i = the annual dollar volume of the ith item for $t = 1$ year

c_i = the dollar cost per unit

$\sum_{t=0}^{t=1} q_i(t)$ = the number of units of the ith item ordered per year

Start with those items that have the highest levels of dollar volume DV_i and rank order them from the highest to the lowest levels. The top 25 percent of these materials are called *A-type items*. The next 25 percent are called *B-type items*. The bottom 50 percent are called *C-type items*.

The ABC method requires studying each A-item separately to improve its performance. Details include how much to order at one time, which determines how often to order; who to order from; what quality standards to set; lead times for deliveries; the consistency of lead times; as well as all special agreements with suppliers. B-type items are studied in groups and with less attention to detail. Policies for C-type items are set to be as simple as possible to administer.

C-type items have low-dollar volume, which means that they have low price per unit. They may have low volume, too, but most are driven by the low price. Small penalties are paid for overstocking such items so they do not have to be ordered as often. Still and all, it may turn out that a C-type item can lead to a critical situation if the CEO's bathroom runs out of toilet paper—which is a typical C-type item.

If materials managers do not use this ABC systems approach, which sorts all materials into those that have more potential savings than others, then a major strategic capability for systematic and continuous improvement is being overlooked.

Companies differ with respect to what percent of all their items account for 75 percent of their total annual dollar volume. Generally, a small percentage of all items accounts for a large percentage of annual dollar volume as shown in Figure 12-3.

Figure 12-3 portrays a typical case where 20 to 30 percent of all items carried account for as much as 70 to 80 percent of the company's total dollar volume. Consider the hotel chain that stocks 1,000 different items for which the hotel spends $1 million annually. Twenty-five percent of these items, costing $750,000, constitutes the A-class of inventory items.

That is, 250 items control 75 percent of the annual dollar volume and, conversely, 750 items control only 25 percent of the annual dollar volume. It is highly unusual for the ABC curve to look like the one drawn in Figure 12-4. There, the percent of items always equals the percent of dollar volume. Rank order means nothing because all items are the same. Why is such a situation unlikely? It is because preference is not equally distributed

FIGURE 12-3
ABC Curve for Annual
Dollar Volume of Items

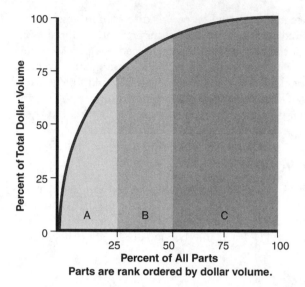

among choices. Many people choose to live in a few cities so the population is not randomly distributed to all square miles.

Consider the likely inventory of name tags at an airport kiosk. Some names are very popular and others are rare. Those favored one year are not found the next year. The following information is from the Social Security study of first names. In 2001, Emily was the most popular girl's name, and it was almost twice as popular as the third choice, which was Jessica. In 1990, Jessica was the most popular girl's name, and Michael was the first choice for a boy's name. In 2001, Jacob was the first choice for a boy, and Michael was second choice. Emily was not even on the list of the first 10 girls' names for 1990. The ABC curves of popular names for both boys and girls are highly skewed like Figure 12-3 and not like Figure 12-4. The items forming the A, B, and C classes are constantly changing. For further information, see the Actuarial Note # 139 of the Social Security Administration at http://www.ssa.gov/OACT/babynames.

Because the costs of inventory studies tend to be proportional to the number of items under consideration, MM always chooses to study and update A-class items. What is to be included in A-type classes will depend on β in the following equation:

$y = x^{\beta} \ (1 \geq x \geq 0),(1 \geq \beta \geq)$
y = percent of dollar demand
x = rank-ordered percent of all items

FIGURE 12-4
Straight Line ABC Curve
with Equal Increments

Beta is 1 in Figure 12-4. Beta is less than one-half in Figure 12-3. The Problem Section at the end of this chapter suggests that a curve be drawn for β = 0.5.

There is no fixed convention that A, B, and C-class breaks must occur at 25 and 50 percent. Some companies use only A and B classes. It is historically interesting that Del Harder of the Ford Motor Company is said to have developed the ABC concept in the 1940s and the curve that reflects the disproportionately large effect derived from a small number of items in the population.

12-10 CERTIFICATION OF SUPPLIERS

Certification of suppliers is a process for grading suppliers to ensure that suppliers' organizations conform to standards that are essential for meeting the buyer's needs. It is expensive and time-consuming. The certification process should be reserved for suppliers of A-type items with respect to both criticality and dollar volume.

In addition to establishing minimum standards that every supplier must meet, certification is like a bidding process for long-term relationships. Companies use the certification process to choose the best in the class—just like they use various criteria to hire students based on grades, dean's list, and personal evaluations. Most often, the requirements for suppliers are equivalent to the company's internal standards for itself with respect to excellence in quality and reliability.

The number of suppliers chosen can vary from one to several. Often, supplier organizations that do not make the grade are encouraged to improve. Many companies help potential suppliers upgrade those capabilities on which they are rated as deficient. Accepted suppliers are regularly reviewed to make certain that they maintain their "winning" status. Thus, although certification aims at long-term relationships, it is subject to reassessment. In numerous instances, the buyer raises the acceptance standards while assisting certified suppliers to meet the new and more stringent standards.

The rating procedures are formal evaluations of price, quality, delivery time, and the ability to improve all three. Suppliers' productivity improvement programs are expected to result in lower prices. Suppliers' total quality management (TQM) programs are monitored for expected improvements. ISO 9000 standards and the Baldrige Award criteria are used to provide the foundation. Lead-time management programs track delivery time reduction. Time-based management concepts form the basis for evaluation.

The buyer's materials management information system (MMIS) has to be able to handle many suppliers and potential suppliers for hundreds and even thousands of A-type items. Who can do this successfully? The list is impressive. Chrysler, Ford Motor Company, General Motors, Hewlett-Packard, Honda Motor Company, IBM, Motorola, Texas Instruments, and Toshiba are only a few of the companies that have made public their use of certification programs. Certification procedures demand the use of the systems approach.

Certification of suppliers: Process of grading (pass–fail) suppliers to assure conformance to standards set as necessary by P/OM. Grading can also be by ranked order.

SUMMARY

Chapter 12 starts with the query "What is materials management (MM)?" First, materials are used for the input–output transformation that produces goods and services. Second, materials managers design and operate optimal transformations using connected systems functions, which are parts of the organization's internal and external supply chain. These many interlinked components must be coordinated to minimize all materials costs (including out-of-stock costs). A classification system for materials (RM, SA, WIP, etc.) is presented to cover the different kinds of materials that need to be managed. Then, the cost leverage of savings in materials and the penalties of errors in ordering materials are explored.

Materials management is unique for each of the various kinds of work configurations (flow shop, job shop, and project environment), as well as for flexible processing systems. All configurations require intelligent information systems, which is based on designing systems parameters that provide timely decision making for the right variables—often in a global information systems context.

Purchasing is a crucial player on the MM team. It can take advantage of the global reach provided by telecommunications capabilities. The learning organization uses purchasing to gain twenty-first century opportunities for improving competitiveness. "Turnover" and "days of inventory" are important measures of the competitive performance of material managers. From another point of view, quality assurances and trusted suppliers can be essential. Turnover and DOI capture a part of the firm's success with customer satisfaction with quality. Nevertheless, supplier certification procedures are valuable. To achieve these goals, the use of the systems approach is valuable.

Also covered are the MM functions of receiving, inspection, and storage. MM's use of bidding is discussed as well as the categorization of parts in terms of their criticality. A failure model for critical spare parts is presented. Then, it is shown how MM's capabilities are enhanced by the application of value analysis. To conclude, materials are categorized into ABC classes that rank order their criticality and then their importance in terms of the potential savings that can be made by improving the way they are managed.

Two Spotlight feature boxes conclude this chapter. These boxes illustrate real applications of the material in the chapter. See Spotlight 12-1: Ford Motor Company and Spotlight 12-2: Paving in Place.

KEY TERMS

ABC classification	Internal MM system	Purchasing agents (PAs)
Bidding	Inventory turns	SKU
Certification of suppliers	Logistics	Static inventory problem
Criticality	Materials management (MM)	Trade-off models
Cross-docking	Materials management information system	Turnover
Days of inventory (DOI)	(MMIS)	Value added
Expediting	Materials management system (MMS)	Value analysis (VA)
Intelligent information system	Methods analysis	Work in process (WIP)

REVIEW QUESTIONS

1. What is materials management (MM) and who does it?

2. Why is the systems approach important for MM?

3. Present the taxonomy of materials.

4. Why is it said that materials have the greatest leverage for making cost savings?

5. What kinds of errors can be made in ordering materials and what are the penalties?

6. Explain differences in MM according to work configurations.

7. Describe the materials management information system (MMIS) and explain why it plays such an important role for P/OM.

8. Explain the difference between centralized and decentralized materials management.

9. Discuss how the information system participates in determining the degree of centralization of MM.

10. From the MM point of view, what is a global information system? Is it centralized or decentralized?

11. Discuss the effect of the systems communication flows.

12. Describe the purchasing function and the role of purchasing agents (PAs).

13. Why are PAs said to be part of the twenty-first century learning organization?

14. Define turnover.

15. Define days of inventory (DOI).

16. What ethical problems must be resolved by purchasing?

17. Describe the international issues that may create ethical quandaries for purchasing agents.

18. Detail the functions for receiving, inspection, and storage. How are they a part of MM?

19. Explain why bids may be sought by P/OM.

20. Explain why materials costs often are a large percentage of both factory costs and operating costs of services.

21. Why does the low bid tend to decrease with more bidders?

22. Discuss the materials management of critical parts.

23. What is a static inventory problem? How often does it arise in the real world?

24. Explain the role played by value analysis for materials management. Why is value analysis part of the OM-team effort?

25. Explain the role played by methods analysis. Why is methods analysis part of the OM-team effort?

26. Describe ABC classification as applied to material criticality.

27. Describe ABC classification as applied to material dollar volume.

28. Explain why supplier certification requires the systems approach to include all aspects of materials management. (*Note:* Do not overlook the use of bidding models, ABC concepts, and benchmarking, which permit comparison with the best in the class.)

PROBLEMS SECTION

1. Assume that downsizing could save the Market Research Store $5,000 in annual labor costs. The downsizing study costs $1,000. If, instead, the study focused on materials savings, what would be the net payoff for the first year—assuming average firm ratios for labor and materials costs?

2. If the ratio of labor costs to materials costs is 1/2 and labor costs are decreasing by 10 percent per year while material costs are increasing by 10 percent per year, what is the ratio at the end of the second year? (Note: This means that at the present time labor costs are 50 percent of materials costs.) Does the result seem reasonable?

3. If labor is 20 percent and materials 80 percent of COGS—say $20 and $80, then a 10 percent reduction in labor costs yields $18 added to $80 totals $98. This produces a 2 percent reduction in total costs [i.e., $(100 - 98)/100 = 0.02$]. Make the same comparison for a 10 percent reduction in materials costs.

4. Assume that the probability distribution has been changed for the decision matrix previously constructed for the complex machine spare parts failure problem. Thus, Table 12-2 should be altered to conform to the following data:

For the complex machine, let $p_i \geq 0$ for $i = 0, 1, 2, 3$. Note that now $p_0 = 1/6$, and that there can be no more than 3 failures over the lifetime of the machine. The probability of failure is distributed as follows:

$i = 0$ failure; $p_0 = 1/6$
$i = 1$ failure; $p_1 = 1/3$
$i = 2$ failures; $p_2 = 1/3$
$i = 3$ failures; $p_3 = 1/6$

How many spare parts should be ordered initially?

5. Assume that the probability distribution has been changed again for the decision matrix previously constructed for the complex machine spare parts failure problem. Table 12-2 should be altered to conform to the following data:

For the complex machine, let $p_i \geq 0$ for $i = 0, 1, 2$. Note that $p_0 = 3/4$, and that now there can be no more than 2 failures over the lifetime of the machine.

The probability of failure is distributed as follows:

$i = 0$ failure; $p_0 = 3/4$
$i - 1$ failure; $p_1 = 1/8$
$i = 2$ failures; $p_2 = 1/8$
$i = 3$ failures; $p_3 = 0.0$

How many spare parts should be ordered initially?

6. Referring again to Table 12-2, what would the decision be if zero failures are expected with 0.97 probability and the other failure rates for $i = 1, 2,$ and 3 are all 0.01?

7. Again turning to the problem shown in Table 12-2, if $c = 5$, $c' = 20$, and

$i = 0$ failure; $p_0 = 0.0$
$i = 1$ failure; $p_1 = 1/2$
$i = 2$ failures; $p_2 = 1/3$
$i = 3$ failures; $p_3 = 1/6$

how many spares should be ordered? Note that the initial acquisition cost remains the same but is now only 1/4 the failure replacement cost.

8. It has been stated that 16 percent of the beer drinkers drink 40 percent of all the beer that is consumed. Is this likely to be the case?

Would the curve that passes through these points be described by ß equal to 0.5?
Draw the curve for the equation

where $y = x^{\beta}$ $(1 \geq x \geq 0), (1 \geq \beta \geq)$

y = percent of dollar demand, x = rank-ordered percent of all items, and $\beta = 0.5$
This is equivalent to $y = \sqrt{x}$

9. For the ß in Problem 8, determine the percent of total dollar demand that occurs when the A category is set at 25 percent of all items.

10. Calculate the inventory turnover rate when monthly net sales are $120 million and average inventory evaluated at the selling price is $240 million. What might this product be and comment on this level of turnover for such a product.

11. Continuing with Problem 10, calculate the days of inventory (DOI) if average inventory is $120 million (calculated in terms of costs) and the monthly cost of goods sold (COGS) is $60 million. Use 30 days per month. What product might be described by these data? Comment on what might be an adequate level of DOI (days of inventory) for such a product.

12. Compare the answers obtained in Problems 10 and 11. Explain how these answers might relate to each other.

END-OF-CHAPTER QUESTIONS

1. Materials management is an important function in companies that have a large percent of their costs allocated to buying raw materials, components, and subassemblies. These are production companies that transform materials into finished products. At the extreme, there are companies that just assemble products from subassemblies made by another company. The discussion that follows in points a. through e. is transcribed observations of company executives in a meeting with the vice president in charge of materials management. The vice president of materials management agreed with all but one statement. Which one is that?

   a. When the cost of materials is a large percent of the cost of goods sold, then purchasing needs strong management support. A materials management function reporting at the top level of the company is vital because materials policies are strategic.

   b. Inventory management is not the purchasing agent's job. The materials manager should have an inventory department in addition to a purchasing department. The activities of these two departments should be coordinated because purchasing should be given guidelines about how many units to buy at a time.

   c. Accounts payable are important when materials constitute a major part of the cost of goods sold. Invoices need to be paid before suppliers will ship. Because production is dependent on bills being paid in a timely fashion, it is necessary for P/OM to establish an office for accounts payable.

   d. Coproduced and/or copacked products have much of their value added by the supplier. Because profit goes to those who do the value adding, copacking should only be used when the production system is unable to satisfy market demand.

   e. On average, direct material costs for job shop manufacturers has risen to 70 percent of the cost of goods sold. That is a high percentage and a big change, given that in 1950 labor costs were about 70 percent of the cost of goods sold. This information is important to both the company and union managers.

2. Turnover and days of inventory have been called crucial measures of performance. The table presents a number of factors that are useful for calculating these important benchmarks. There is also commentary about the interpretation of the measures under different circumstances. With which statements in parts a. to e. do you disagree?

1	Average total dollar inventory	$ 60,000,000
2	Annual total cost of goods sold (COGS)	$400,000,000
3	Sales price per dollar of cost of goods sold	$1.80
4	Annual net sales	$720,000,000
5	Average inventory in sales dollars	$108,000,000
6	Annual net profit	$220,000,000
7	Annual general administration and overhead costs	$100,000,000

   a. Days of inventory are calculated in two steps. First, divide line 2 by 365. That equals $1.0959, which is the daily total cost of goods sold (in millions). Second, divide line 1 by 1.0959. That equals 54.75 days of inventory. Using a 30-day month, 54.75 days is equivalent to 1.825 months. A good way to calculate inventory turns is to divide 365 days by 54.75 days, and that equals 6 and 2/3 turnovers per year.

   b. Inventory turns are calculated by dividing line 4 by line 6, and that equals 3 and 3/11. The difference occurs because the cost dollars have been converted into sales dollars.

   c. Days of inventory are calculated by dividing line 4 by line 3, which equals line 2. Then, divide line 5 by line 3, and that equals line 1. Next divide line 1 by line 2, and that equals 0.15. Multiply that result by 365 to obtain 54.75 days.

   d. Inventory turns are calculated dividing line 2 by line 1, equaling 6 and 2/3 turns per year.

   e. Six and 2/3 inventory turns per year is not a lot for a retail business like Wal-Mart or Kmart. It might be considered a threshold of acceptability for a furniture retail outlet like Thomasville. *The Wall Street Journal* in the local vending machine is always sold out by 10 A.M., which indicates that on 260 weekdays, a 100 percent turnover occurs. The WSJ, at this box, gets 260 turns per year. That is what the stocking policy for the vending machine aims to get. If more papers were filled each day, there might be days when turnover is not complete.

3. Materials management of critical parts is a significant responsibility of P/OM. There is likely to be no greater cost to a production system than the need to slow down or (worse

yet) shut down the process. To drive home this point, the production manager has listed a number of issues for management to discuss at a roundtable retreat that is being held in a few weeks. The list has circulated with a surprising result. Three managers have objected to one of the points listed in a. through e. What would likely be the point in contention?

a. Criticality needs to be defined. The definition of "critical" should be as follows: When a part (component, subassembly) failure causes the product or process to fail, that part is critical. In addition, if a part malfunctions in such a way as to partially impair or disable the associated product or process, then that part is critical.

b. Critical parts need to be identified by all the players. In addition to the obvious list of maintenance personnel, process engineers, and production managers, there is a need to interview customers, suppliers, workers (related to product or process), and product designers.

c. Failure records that allow review of all product and process incidents should be examined in detail. There may be cover-ups that are reported as aberrations rather than failures. Also, procedures need to be tightened for recording complaints of every kind with respect to the product and the process. Incidents for service products are particularly vulnerable to subjective errors.

d. Spare parts policies need to be reformulated in terms of the probabilities of failure and the distribution of times to failure. Regular inspections of critical spare parts inventories should be scheduled. Two problems occur often. First, the wrong part is received as if it were the critical spare part. It is given the SKU number of the critical spare. That unfortunate fact is not discovered until that critical spare is required. Second, the correct part is logged in but deteriorates in storage, or it is pilfered.

e. Spare part policies need to be reexamined when only one purchase order occasion exists. As a variant, spare parts can only be ordered at a reasonable price at the time the unit requiring spares is placed.

4. The custom-made steering engine for a large tanker ship has a high cost. Bidding specifications for building and installing the engine are not yet completed. (A ship's steering engine is akin to the power steering system for a car. The hydraulic system that moves the ship's giant rudder is similar in principle but not in scale.) At the same time that the steering engine is being built, spares can be made for parts that wear out and have to be replaced. The cost of spares at the time of initial ordering is relatively low, viz., $500. Spares cost a great deal more after installation of the steering engine, viz., $40,000. Data have been compiled by the maritime engineers before the bidding begins so that the shipping company can include a specific number of spare parts in the request for proposal (RFP). Spare part strategies are order none, one, two, or three. The probabilities of part failure are good estimates based on engineering pragmatics. There is zero probability of no failures; 1/2 for one failure; 1/3 for two failures; 1/6 for three failures. As they must, these sum to one.

Failure Cost Matrix

	0 Failures	1 Failure	2 Failures	3 Failures
0 spares	0	$40,000	$80,000	$120,000
1 spare	$500	$500	$40,500	$80,500
2 spares	$1,000	$1,000	$1,000	$41,000
3 spares	$1,500	$1,500	$1,500	$1,500

At the meeting to decide on how many spare parts to request with the RFP, a number of good points were made. These are listed as a. through e. There is agreement that one of the five points is heading in the wrong direction. Before proceeding further, identify the statement that needs to be dismissed.

a. The strategy to order three spares is the safest course of action. For the lifetime of the steering engine there has never been a case reported of more than three failures. However, three failures have been reported more than 16 percent of the time. This is causing concern for some of the managers who have suggested that the data are not showing a fourth failure, but the probabilities suggest that four failures could occur.

b. Management fears that it will be called to account for wasting money if three (or four) spare parts are ordered. The purchasing agent has found out that two is the average number of spare parts ordered with this steering engine. This information disturbs some of the project managers who are leaning toward three spares.

c. Using the decision-matrix approach, the optimal number of spare parts to request in the RFP is three. That strategy has the lowest expected cost of $1,500.

d. It is not reasonable to order zero spare parts. Data indicate that there has always been at least one failure. The average number ordered is two. If the company orders two spare parts, no one can get upset. They will say that management has been cautious and not wasteful.

e. If more than one spare is ordered, that would permit one to be kept on board the ship. Only one spare part is needed at a time. The extra spare(s) will be stored at the home dock. It seems logical that the probability of two failures within a short time is low. The reason for failures occurring needs to be studied. The purchasing agent has stated that use is the primary cause of failure. Age plays a part as well.

5. Another company has proposed bidding on the steering engine using new technology. The costs are the same but the probabilities of failure have shifted significantly. With the new design, there is an 80 percent probability of no failure; 10 percent of one failure; 10 percent of two failures; and zero percent of more than two failures. These probabilities sum to one. Another meeting was called to decide on how many spare parts to request with the RFP. A number of good points were made at the meeting. These are listed as a. through e. The same manager who went on the record with an incorrect evaluation of the first RPF has again opted for a strategy that the other managers reject. Identify the point of contention and the statement that needs to be dismissed.

a. Using the decision-matrix approach, the optimal number of spare parts to request in the RFP is two. That strategy has the lowest expected cost of $1,000.

b. The strategy to order three spares remains the safest course of action. This is in spite of the fact that new company has estimated that for the lifetime of the steering engine, there is zero probability of more than two failures.

c. Management will be called to account for wasting money if three spare parts are ordered. The purchasing agent points out no data exists for the average number of spare parts ordered with the new steering engine. This fact underscores the uneasiness of some of the project managers about going with relatively untried new technology. At the meeting, a manager asked, "What if the company is wrong about these probabilities?"

d. It is not reasonable to order less than two spare parts. The expected cost of one spare is $4,500. The expected cost of three spares is only $500 more than the minimum expected cost of two spares. Because the probabilities are uncertain, and the cost of an extra spare part is only $500, the best course of action is to go with three spares and temper the decision-matrix result with caution.

e. Because the design is based on new technology and the probabilities of part failure are not certain, the old steering engine should be purchased and the new one should wait for others to try out.

6. An ABC database of annual dollar volume per SKU (stock keeping unit) in the company's inventory can be drawn as curves to reflect graphically the cumulative ranked order contribution of each item's dollar volume to the total dollar volume of the firm. Knowledge of this information can be helpful in many ways to production and operations managers. The kinds of insights that are available from this information are given in statements a. through e. Which one of these is not proper for ABC?

a. C-class items are called the *trivial many*. They constitute about 50 percent of all item SKUs carried in stock, but they account for less than 10 percent of total dollar volume. Ordering policy for C-types can be as needed or on a regular periodic basis, e.g., on the third Monday of every week. Stock on-hand level is noted. Orders are placed to cover demand for the next interval of time.

b. Most of the time, if there is a stock-out, replenishments can be obtained for C-type items with minimal lead time. Customers will wait a short time without complaining. However, in some cases, it can be inconvenient to run out of stock (e.g., rest room supplies). The reason that items are classed as C-type is that optimal order policies will not save enough money to pay the bill for creating them.

c. B-type items are in the middle 25 percent of all items carried, and they account for about 15 percent of total dollar volume. That makes B-type items a little more worthy of analysis. It pays to watch them because some B-type items are increasing in dollar volume and could become A-types in the future. Also, at the top of B-type items in their rank order are almost A-types. It may pay to regroup the A- and B-types from time to time. There is no hard and fast rule as to where A's end and B's begin.

d. Neither growth in demand volume for a company's products nor price alterations can change the rank order of an item's dollar volume. This removes pressure on the part of the inventory managers to constantly update their records, which could become an ongoing clerical and analytic requirement.

e. A-type SKU are the cash users and cash generators for the company. They are called the *significant few*. The top 25 percent of all the company's SKUs account for about 75 percent of the total dollar volume. For these items with large cash flow, bad order policies penalize the company. Good ordering policies reward the company.

7. As a training exercise for its materials managers, AutoParts Retailers, Inc., has designed a table of eight items with their daily sales volume and price per unit. The manager-students are asked to arrange this table so as to create a standard (25%A–25%B–50%C) ABC curve. The answers in parts a. through e. are given to the manager-students for them to mark true or false. There is only one false answer. Which one is it?

AutoPart Item (SKU)	Daily Volume (SKU)	Price per Unit
AP303	200 units	$2.49
AP664	3 units	$39.50
AO829	5 units	$9.89
AP155	16 units	$149.99
AO447	7 units	$30.50
AP721	20 units	$4.12
AP267	1,003 units	$0.99
AO595	61 units	$3.25

a. The average daily volume of the A-type SKUs is 509.50 units, and the average price per unit of the A-type SKUs is $75.49.

b. The average daily volume of the B-type SKUs is 103.50 units, and the average price per unit of the B-type SKUs is $16.50.

c. The average daily volume of the C-type SKUs is 22.25 units, and the average price per unit of the C-type SKUs is $14.19.

d. The average daily dollar volume of the A-type SKUs is $1,696.41, as compared to the average daily dollar volume of the B-type SKUs, which is $355.75.

e. The average daily dollar volume of the A-type SKUs is $1,696.41, as compared to the average daily dollar volume of the C-type SKUs, which is $49.45.

8. The ABC data from AutoParts Retailers, Inc., given in Problem 7, have yet to be classified in the traditional way. Manager-students have been asked to do this. They have been instructed to draw the ABC curve before answering the company's true or false quiz (statements a. through e). There is only one false answer. Which one is it?

a. The top 25 percent of items (A-type, ranked by largest daily dollar volume) contributes 74.52 percent of total dollar volume in AutoParts Retailers, Inc., database.

b. B-type items are the next 25 percent of items (ranked by daily dollar volume). These B-types must be listed after the A-types because they occupy the range from 25 percent to 50 percent of all items in the rank-order hierarchy. This B-type group contributes 15.63 percent of total dollar volume. The cumulative percent of total daily dollar volume has reached 74.52 + 15.63 = 90.15 percent.

c. These numbers confirm the fact that C-type items (which are the next 50 percent of items ranked by daily dollar volume) account for 9.85 percent of total dollar volume. Note that the cumulative percent of total daily dollar volume has reached 100 percent, i.e., 74.52 + 15.63 + 9.85 = 100.00 percent.

d. The A-type items are AP155 and AP267. AP155, which is a starter motor, is first in rank order with daily dollar volume of $2,399.84. That is 52.71 percent of total daily dollar volume. Because 16 starter motors are sold per day at a price of $150 each, it is crucial for AutoParts Retailers to find out if there are always enough parts on hand. Does the customer ever walk away because there are none on hand? The order policy for AP155 and AP267 must result from detailed study of how much to order at one time, which determines how often to order, who to order from (are there backup suppliers), what quality standards are set by the buyer, how long and how variable are the lead times, etc. There is no room for error in this A-type category.

e. AP267 is second in rank order and contributes 21.81 percent to the total dollar volume. It too is important and deserves detailed study. AP303, which is third in rank and at the top of the rank-ordered B-type items, accounts for only 10.94 percent of total daily dollar volume. It does not require detailed study.

9. ABC is a powerful concept that applies to many different kinds of inventories. Regarding the inventory of land and people, a small percent of the total land area of the United States (less than 25 percent of the total resource) supports a large percent of Americans. As an estimate, that number is 75 percent. From an alternative viewpoint, a small percent of all dogs (rank ordered by weight) eats most of dog food consumed in the world. Beer drinkers and dessert gourmands closely fit the canine ABC curve. At a symposium on the inventory aspects of materials management, a number of points were stated (a. through e.) about disproportionality of resource utilization and its impact on materials management. Which one of these statements is flawed?

a. A mathematical model for the ABC effect is $y = x^\beta$, where y is percent of dollar demand ($0 \le y \le 1$), x is percent of all rank-ordered items ($0 \le x \le 1$), and β is the coefficient of disproportionality ($0 \le \beta \le 1$). When $\beta = 1$, the disproportionality effect is minimized. The result is a straight line where $y = x$.

b. Designers of mail-order catalogs strive to have β as close to 1 as possible.

c. Using Excel, the curve in point a. can be derived by clicking on "paste function," which has the icon f_n; go to *Math and Trig* in the left-hand window that opens. In the right-hand window, scoll down to *POWER* and click OK. A new window opens asking for *Number* (x) and *Power* (β). Let x change as it goes from zero to 100 percent. For the sake of illustration, let $x = 0.70$ and $\beta = 0.3$. Click on OK, and the result shown in the window gets placed in the cell. The value is 89.85 percent.

d. Data drive the curve and not vice versa. In other words, actual dollar demand data are collected. Then, the appropriate ABC curve can be drawn to match the data by the method described in c.

e. A company with 100,000 SKUs would use a random sampling of SKU data to get a picture of its ABC curve.

10. Certification is a process for grading suppliers. It is aimed at discovering which ones are most likely to match the company's culture and fit into its family of partners. Certification often is a necessary but not sufficient condition to assure a long-term supplier relationship. It is a growing requirement of a number of larger firms. A major chemical products company has invited a group of potential buyers to a symposium dedicated to explaining how this company will help the buyer certify its qualifications. The following list highlights some of the points that were covered. There is a consensus that one of the points is not acceptable. Which statement is not acceptable?

a. Because it is a costly process, certification should be used only for suppliers of A-type items. The A-types should cover both criticality and dollar volume.

b. Certification should set minimum standards for factors such as percent defectives and lead time.

c. Certification should permit comparisons between suppliers so that the "best in class" can be identified and selected. Scoring models can assist in the comparison and can provide tracking over time. That which passes today may slip, falter, and fail by the same criteria over time. Further, what is best today can be bested tomorrow.

d. Most companies have internal standards for the individual departments. The level of the internal standards can be used for external assessment.

e. Scoring for certification should not include the supplier's ISO 9000 certification. The fact that the supplier has achieved ISO certification can cause bad judgment and bias the company's own certification process.

ADDITIONAL READINGS

Arnold, J. R. Tony, and Stephen N. Chapman. *Introduction to Materials Management,* 4e., Prentice-Hall, May 2000.

Burt, D. N. *Proactive Purchasing.* Englewood Cliffs, NJ: Prentice-Hall, 1984.

Dobler, D. W., L. Lee, Jr., and D.N. Burt. *Purchasing and Materials Management.* New York: McGraw-Hill, 1984.

Ellram, Lisa M., and Laura M. Birou. *Purchasing for Bottom Line Impact,* vol. 4. National Association of Purchasing Management (NAPM), Homewood, IL: Irwin, 1995.

Hazardous Materials Management Magazine (as of November 2003): www.hazmatmag.com

Heinritz, S. F., P. V. Farrell, L. Giunipero, and M. Kolchin. *Purchasing: Principles and Applications,* 8e. Englewood Cliffs, NJ: Prentice-Hall, 1991.

Hickman, Thomas K., and William M. Hickman. *Global Purchasing: How to Buy Goods and Services in Foreign Markets.* Homewood, IL: Business One Irwin/APICS Series in Production Management, 1992.

International Federation of Purchasing and Materials Management (as of November 2003): www.ifpmm.org

Killen, Kenneth H., and John W. Kamauff. *Managing Purchasing,* vol. 2. National Association of Purchasing Management (NAPM), Homewood: IL, Irwin, 1994.

Leenders, Michiel R., and H. Fearon. *Purchasing and Materials Management,* 10e. Homewood, IL: Irwin, 1993.

Leenders, Michiel R., and Anna E. Flynn. *Value-Driven Purchasing,* vol. 1. National Association of Purchasing Management (NAPM), Homewood, IL: Irwin, 1994.

Materials Management in Health Care Magazine (as of November 2003): www.matmanmag.com

Miles, L. D. *Techniques of Value Analysis.* New York: McGraw-Hill, 1961.

Raedels, Alan R. *Value-Focused Supply Management,* vol. 3. National Association of Purchasing Management (NAPM), Homewood, IL: Irwin, 1994.

Schonberger, R., and J. Gilbert, "Just-In-Time Purchasing: A Challenge for U.S. Industry." *California Management Review,* vol. 26, no. 1 (Fall 1983): 54–68.

Tersine, R. J. *Materials Management and Inventory Systems,* 3e. New York: Elsevier North-Holland Publishing, 1987.

NOTE

1. An insight is available from Edward T. Hall. "The Silent Language in Overseas Business." *Harvard Business Review,* vol. 38, no. 3 (May–June 1960): 87–96.

SPOTLIGHT 12-1

Ford Motor Company

Recycling 85 Percent of a Ford, Part 3

"Red" Poling, one of Caldwell's executives and former chairman of Ford of Europe, was put in charge of cost management. He made a great effort to ameliorate the downsizing of 60,000 employees by communicating to UAW officials that quality had to improve. Plants that achieved this objective would remain open. He confided that the difference between Ford and its Japanese competitors was not the quality of workers but Ford's inferior management policy which did not emphasize continuous improvement in product quality. This admission eased tensions and enabled a satisfactory agreement in 1982 between the company and its union. Philip Caldwell conveyed the mission statement to all Ford workers: "Quality is Job 1." This was the cornerstone of Japanese manufacturing as preached by the guru of quality, W. Edwards Deming, who was a consultant to Ford Motor.

Ford spent $14 billion dollars on plant improvement and another $9 billion on R&D, earmarking $5.4 billion for overseas facilities. *The Wall Street Journal* (1984) wrote, "Ford has everything in motion." Modular assembly was introduced in 1985 (subassemblies produced on automated ancillary lines then feed the main assembly line). The Aerostar was the first vehicle produced with this method. Don Petersen, chairman and CEO following Caldwell's retirement, approved a $3.5 billion budget for the Taurus/Sable. Within that billion dollar budget, Ford engineers tore apart hundreds of cars sold by competitors, a process called *reverse engineering*, to learn Best Practices of other companies. The irony was that Taurus and Sable were not the top sellers in 1986; that honor went to the Ford Escort.

Starting in 1987, Ford bought several car companies. Aston Martin of England was the first, followed by Jaguar. Some said that Ford's executives could then drive Jaguars without guilt. In 1992, Ford bought 33 percent of Mazda. In 1999 Ford acquired majority interest in TH!NK, a Norwegian company with a zero-emission electric car. Land Rover and Volvo were added. As the market moved from sedans to sport utility vehicles, Explorers replaced the Bronco and Bronco II.

William Clay Ford, Jr. (Bill Jr.), as Chairman, and Jacques Nasser, as CEO and President, became the new leaders of Ford. The two men did not agree on how to run the company. However, under their leadership, the company entered a new marketplace, the virtual world of the Internet. Several web sites were linked and a new company, formed with Ford dealers, brought direct online sales to customers at FordDirect.com. The Big Three joined forces in the B2B revolution, creating the world's largest virtual marketplace, Covisint. Billions of dollars in transactions routinely travel on this global exchange, connecting Ford with suppliers that feed parts and components to its assembly plants.

2000 and 2001 brought recalls and replacements of all Ford Explorers' Firestone Wilderness AT tires, almost 20 million tires in all. With 100 Firestone-related lawsuits, it was clear that Ford Motor was going in the wrong direction. Ford's Board of Directors replaced Nasser with Bill Jr. (Oct. 2001) and the slogan was "Back to Basics." This put operating responsibility in the hands of a Ford for the first time in 22 years.

Bill Ford Jr., now Chairman and CEO of Ford Motor Company, calls himself an environmentalist/industrialist. His company has 300,000 employees and has produced 300 million vehicles. Bill Jr. wants to transform Ford Motor Company into a new model of clean, eco-efficient manufacturing. At the center of his efforts is the Rouge Complex in Dearborn, Michigan. It is the largest industrial redevelopment project in the world. In remaking the Ford facility into a flagship of sustainable flexible manufacturing, Ford uses more recycled material in cars and trucks than any other carmaker. For example, the 2000 Ford Focus contained an array of recycled materials, from old denim jeans to deaden sound to recycled plastic bottles and carpeting in the heater body and fan module. The car was 85percent recyclable by weight. Ford was the first auto company to certify its plants around the world under ISO 14001 (a series of environmental standards). To answer criticism that he is a hypocrite in some of his actions, Bill Ford has defended his position, stating that he sees no conflict between making money and doing the right thing. If Bill Ford Jr. maintains his standards to fit the needs of a new century, he will be fulfilling the legacy of Henry Ford's Model T.

See the Spotlight feature box in chapter 5, "Henry Ford, Part 1" and the Spotlight feature box in Chapter 11, "The Ford Motor Company after Henry Ford, Part 2," for the entire story.

Sources: *The Ford Century: Ford Motor Company and the Innovations that Shaped the World*, by Russ Banham, Artisan, a Division of Workman Publishing Company, Inc. New York 2002; *Wheels for the World: Henry Ford, His Company, and a Century of Progress*, by Douglas Brinkley, Viking 2003.

SPOTLIGHT 12-2
Paving in Place

"Together, the united forces of our communication and transportation systems are dynamic elements in the very name we bear—United States. Without them, we would be a mere alliance of many separate parts."
—President Dwight D. Eisenhower, February 22, 1955

In 1950, there were about 70 million cars, buses, and trucks on the world's roads. The number has continued to grow at about 16 million vehicles per year. In 2004, there are almost a billion cars, buses, and trucks worldwide. More than 200 million of these vehicles are in the United States, driving on 4 million miles of roads (90 percent of them surfaced) in the 50 states.

The National Highway System (NHS) is approximately 160,000 miles of roadway that include the interstate highway system. For a report on performance and ongoing efforts to maintain and improve this system, read the FY2002 performance report (FHWA-RD-02-101) at the Turner–Fairbank Highway Research Center website at http://www.tfhrc.gov/about/02101/index.htm.

Rehabilitation of roads, from weather and wear, can be done in a variety of ways. The repaving function provides a major recycling opportunity for both asphalt and concrete. Recycling concrete requires chopping and grinding. Pulverizing concrete in-place continues to be experimental because equipment is expensive and needs high maintenance.

Recycling asphalt in-place is relatively common. Visit http://www.arra.org/faq.htm for the Asphalt Recycling & Reclaiming Association's (ARRA) discussion of cold in-place and hot in-place recycling. In its outlook statement, ARRA proclaims, "Environmentalists, taxpayers and legislators will be pleased to know that ARRA member contractors are responsible for keeping literally millions of tons of asphalt out of North American landfills."

Repaving constitutes a production function that differs according to the system of construction (e.g., overlays of concrete on asphalt). Repaving of any kind creates disruption because roads are closed or traffic flow is constricted. Construction is noisy. Other costs are unpleasant odors from paving materials such as hot asphalt. Depending on how fast motorists are given access to repaved roads, there can be damage to car surfaces and tires. The paving process is expensive and creates traffic disturbances that cost untold amounts. The costs of pollution resulting from cars caught in construction traffic jams are also evident but difficult to measure.

Road building is an OM project activity in which the goal is to find and use the best production systems for doing the work. Various alternative work configurations can include doing as much work as possible on a flow shop basis at the site. For example, remove concrete and/or asphalt and recondition the paving materials at a portable plant that can be moved as the job progresses.

This would be entirely acceptable to environmentalists who have a cradle-to-grave approach in their evaluation of allowable processes. The five evaluation phases for repaving roads might be:

- Raw materials extraction—recycle the largest percent possible of the existing road.
- Manufacture and processing—perform recycling as close as possible to the source of the materials.
- Distribution and placement—repave as soon as possible using the recycled materials.
- Use and maintenance—patch and repair before repaving and maximize repaving intervals.
- Disposal—find alternative uses for all materials not consumed during recycling.

Concrete and asphalt are both excellent candidates for all five levels of the cradle-to-grave approach. Sources of aggregate from which cement is made are dwindling and thereby becoming more costly. Asphalt, derived from bitumens that are primarily hydrocarbons, are not welcome ingredients in landfills. There is every reason to applaud recycling such materials.

The Federal Highway Administration (FHWA) has been dedicated to investigating means for recycling "without impacting pavement performance and not costing an arm and a leg to do it." See http://www.fhwa.dot.gov/pavement/recycle.htm.

One of four areas of research that was agreed upon was to develop a performance-based mix design for cold in-place recycling (CIR) of asphalt pavements. The FHWA states, "Our new policy on pavements recycling is: Recycling and reuse can offer engineering, economic and environmental benefits. Recycled materials should get first consideration in materials selection."

Whether to recycle concrete and asphalt is not an issue. Recycling should be done if economic disadvantage cannot be shown. There is growing evidence that recycling can produce significant net benefits for all systems participants under many circumstances. Recycled concrete provides a balanced supply of raw materials for future use as aggregate. The problem is pressing because the U.S. highway system is deteriorating and the cost of a diminishing supply of aggregate from which cement is made is increasing.

There are multiple benefits derived from the development of fast-track concrete and asphalt paving machines. *Fast track* means that a series of techniques is used to decrease concrete pavement construction time. Recycling in place is a fast-track technology. Within the FHWA, experiments continue. Success may lie in new production techniques that emphasize the flow shop in place of customized job shop methods for paving the roads of America.

Aggregate Planning

Chapter Outline

This chapter moves the focus inside the plant or service facility. Operations managers must deal with workforce planning. The number of employees is strongly related to the outputs required from the input–output transformation process. Workforce planning is directly related to the control of inventories based on forecasts of demand. Although this discussion epitomizes tactical planning, nevertheless, there is an apparent interaction with strategic planning. When should plant managers pursue the idea of having a hiring policy consistent with a constant workforce with the goal of level production? Similarly, when should the goal be to adopt the notion of a chasing policy with workforce adjustments? Flexible workforce size is better fitted to the configuration of job shops and batch production than it is to flow shop production. The constant workforce is better suited to continuous, high-volume outputs that characterize flow shop output. In contrast, a chasing policy using hiring, layoffs, overtime, and subcontracting is an effort to be flexible in order to match variable and even volatile demand forecasts. Combination policies (hybrids of constant and chasing workforce size) are alternatives worth exploring. The methodology to find optimal resource allocations is known as *aggregate scheduling*. Aggregate scheduling with a flexible workforce size applies to batch production and mixed-model flow shop environments. Line-balancing methodology for planning to run an optimal continuous production system with a constant workforce is discussed in a later chapter.

After reading this chapter, you should be able to:

- Explain the function of aggregate planning (AP).
- Discuss the systems nature of AP in terms of classes of resources and product-mix families.
- Explain standard units of work.
- Relate the importance of forecasting to AP.
- Compare constant (or level) production with a chasing policy—supply chases demand.

- Detail the cost structure for aggregate planning.
- Describe how to use linear programming for AP.
- Describe how to use the transportation matrix for AP.
- Explain why a nonlinear cost model can be used as a benchmark for other AP models.

THE SYSTEMS VIEWPOINT

Aggregate planning matches classes of job outputs with the supportive resources needed to produce each of them. The concepts of "what does it take to make this class of items" or "what skills, know-how, and technologies are used to provide this class of services" are successful if based on broad systems thinking. Aggregate planning takes the expected demand for the job shop product mix and assigns available resources in an optimal *tactical* way (say minimum total costs). From the systems point of view, it is also sensible to extend the investigation to include alternatives to the product mix and the available resources. That is the linkage between tactics and strategic thinking.

STRATEGIC THINKING

Strategic thinking is engaged when the tactical performance of the system is not considered to be worthy of the investment of resources. Perhaps the company should rethink its product lines because the costs of doing business do not provide a satisfactory cash flow and/or return on the investments. Alternatively, the current product line might be acceptable if the system's capacity is altered with additional investments or by outsourcing some part of the production function. Good tactics are only as good as their performance measures indicate. When that is not good enough, P/OM must return to the beginning and reevaluate the strategic plan that is being utilized.

13-1 WHAT IS AGGREGATE PLANNING (AP)?

> **Aggregate planning (AP):**
> The specific purpose of AP is to schedule production for the job shop with a set of common denominators (e.g., standard hours).

Aggregate planning (AP) is required to design a generalized production schedule. The generalized schedule is intended to meet demand, which is expressed in standard units instead of specific units of A, B, and C. The reason that the term *aggregation* is used is because the specific identities of all units are merged into a *common pool of standard units* or standard hours.

Supply is stated in these aggregated units, and demand also is estimated in the same aggregated units. Demand is generated by a variety of customers for the different kinds of products made by the job shop or the different kinds of services offered by job shops such as the Market Research Store.

It is important to note that aggregate planning is an internal production management function that leads to detailed internal production scheduling in later stages. The specific purpose of AP is to decide when to schedule work and under what conditions to schedule it. The conditions can vary such as second shift, overtime work, and subcontracting.

In Figure 13-1, aggregate planning (the middle box) is shown as following strategic business planning (the first box—called the *Company Plan*). Aggregate planning is the producer's general plan for getting work done. It is not detailed scheduling (the bottom box) which follows aggregate planning.

Aggregate planning starts a chain reaction in the supply chain of suppliers-producers-customers. Once the internal assignments that relate to the factory and the office are scheduled, then the external flows begin to function. These are flows of materials from the factory to the warehouses by trucks and other transport systems, which must be coor-

FIGURE 13-1
Aggregate Planning Follows Strategic Planning

dinated. Transport from the warehouses to the customers must be organized. External flows from suppliers to the production transformation system must be activated. Equipment may have to be rented or bought and people hired and trained, or workforce reductions may be initiated.

The driver of AP is forecasted customer demand. This can take the form of customer orders and/or inventory plans. The forecasts are translated into production plans. The goal is to be prepared to make the product and deliver it when the actual demands are on hand. The same applies to delivering services to the customer at the optimum time.

Material flows inside the company can be scheduled in detail for specific items, or in categories of specific items that have been aggregated. Before trying to do detailed, tactical scheduling, aggregate planning (which is generic) should be used to avoid costly mistakes arising from not being prepared with the proper resources at the right time.

13-1a Aggregation of Units

When the specific classes of production items to be made are called apples, oranges, and pears, there is too much detail required for planning n-periods ahead for each category. It is much simpler to schedule the production of one aggregated item, called "fruit." Later on, the decision can be made about what kind of fruit to plant. This method is not without weaknesses. Some fruits will not grow on the same land with other fruits. Different fertilizers may be required. Irrigation requirements may differ. Harvesting can be a conflict between crops competing for attention or a lucky sequence of resource availabilities.

Service (1) products and manufactured (2) products are similar enough to farm (3) products to draw this analogy. These three categories share some characteristics and they differ in others. Aggregation methods take advantage of the similarities. Differences can be accounted for at a later time.

Standard units are used as the common denominator for aggregated units in the production-scheduling problem. Forecasts of specific items such as sweaters of different colors, cotton, wool, and mixtures are converted into the standard machine hours required to make each type of sweater. This is referred to as aggregation of the mixed-model product line of the job shop. It is the aggregation of finished goods used as the basis for planning what will be made in the period starting n-months ahead.

If the planning period is for *one quarter*, then it starts at the beginning of t_1 and it finishes at the end of t_3. Assume that planning period starts one month ahead (lead time $n = 1$), and it is now January 1; then the planning period starts February 1 and ends April 30.

Aggregate planning is achieved by collecting and lumping all items to be produced together. The idea is to strip away the specifics while retaining the aggregate properties of the product. The purpose is to match aggregate capacity against aggregate demand. This results in generalized determination of workforce requirements, including the possible use of multiple shifts, overtime, and part-time work to satisfy demand across a great variety of stock-keeping units.

Consider the paint manufacturer with a product line that includes water-based, oil-based, and acrylic paints. They come in many colors and can sizes. For aggregate planning, the standard product unit might be gallons of paint; the time period could be monthly; the **planning horizon** could be one year ahead. Alternatively, it might have been decided to separate aggregate planning for each type of paint—water-based, oil-based, and acrylic—on a week-by-week basis, for half a year.

The idea is to aggregate demands that use essentially the same resources. This allows effective utilization of resources across competing demands. By the same resources, it is meant that essentially the same equipment, materials, people, space, and experience are transferable between the different items to satisfy demand as capacity allows in an optimal manner.

Aggregate-planning methods can derive better solutions when P/OM can find:

1. Ways to expand the number of products that can be made by a specific class of resources

2. Ways to expand the number of resources that can make a class of products

Standard units: Jobs are converted from pieces of work (order size) into standard hours on a designated machine called the standard machine.

Planning horizon: Determine the appropriate planning horizon for forecasting demand.

FIGURE 13-2
Aggregate Planning with Planning Horizon and Updating Interval

Points 1 and 2 provide increased resources and flexibility to satisfy demand. Also, planning results can be improved by investing in more capacity of the right kind (scarce). Changing the product line and the order mix can result in other benefits. These are systems-oriented concepts for improvements using aggregate planning.

Also, to be effective, the forecast interval has to provide sufficient lead time to allow the resource mix to be changed in accordance with the plan. The paint company might decide to do aggregate planning using monthly time buckets with a planning horizon of six months and updating the conclusions once every three months. Figure 13-2 illustrates these time-planning concepts with the numbers just given.

13-1b Standard Units of Work

It was said that "aggregate planning is achieved by collecting and lumping all items to be produced together." This should be amended to " . . . lumping all items together that share the use of common resources." This point, which was previously made, is emphasized by the process of creating standard units.

This process requires that different parts, activities, products, and services all be described and accounted for in terms of an arbitrarily chosen, but agreed upon standard unit of work. Thus, a pint of deluxe external white paint might require two standard units of work. These two standard units will be added to the five standard units required to make a gallon of special green latex paint. These seven standard units will be added to the standard units of work required for other products or services.

The aggregated total will be used for workforce planning. Seven standard units of workforce time is required to make the pint of white, and the gallon of green, paint. Workforce planning is of great importance to all service industries. It applies to crew scheduling for airlines, hospitals, and banks. Because many job shops provide services and not goods, it pays to emphasize the fact that AP is useful to all kinds of job shops. It also can apply to intermittent flow shops, which have lumpy demands over time.

The Blackfeet Indian Pencil Company in Browning, Montana, is a small company that sells a variety of writing instruments such as markers and pencils. Demands are sporadic and aggregate planning is essential. Book publishers (like Atomic Dog) have to plan for erratic demand patterns, which sometimes tax their production capacities. Theme parks, hotels, and resorts have shifting demands as a function of seasons that lend themselves to aggregate planning. They cannot inventory low-season, unused capacities to accommodate peak demands. Nevertheless, they can use AP for workforce scheduling.

In addition to workforce planning, AP treats inventory and equipment availability. The AP model cannot always satisfy demand. Sometimes capacity is insufficient. At other times, some part of the system's resources will be idle because supply is greater than demand. As the AP models are developed, note in particular how certain kinds of supply (like overtime) provide protection against not being able to deliver the goods. However, P/OM may be happy to see that overtime supply is seldom utilized.

The direct approach for understanding standard hour computations is to work through an example of how planners aggregate demands for different products or services. This means changing actual hours of work into standard units of required production capacity. For the example that follows, the standard unit is selected as a standard machine hour (SMH) based on using a standard machine (SM) for the standard of comparison.

The total production capacity consists of four machines (people, departments, etc., also can be used when appropriate). The four machines called M1, M2, M3 and M4, work at different rates. It should be noted that the rate differentials apply across all of the jobs that these machines are assigned.

That is: M2 is fastest—for all of the jobs, and by the same amount in comparison with the other machines. For this reason, it is convenient to choose M2 as the standard machine (SM). It will be assigned an SM index of 1.0. Then, all of the other machines will have fractional SM indexes. Thus:

Machine Number	SM Index	Description
1	0.5	Half as fast as M2
2	1.0	Standard Machine
3	0.8	80% as fast as M2
4	0.6	60% as fast as M2

Each machine, department, or person is ranked by an index number that when multiplied by the actual machine hours available per week yields the standard machine hours (SMH) available per week. Thus, Table 13-1 provides the actual machine hours that are available per week converted by means of the SMH index into standard machine hours available per week.

There is a total of 156 standard machine hours (SMH) available per week. How many standard hours are in demand? The fact that there are 203.3 actual machine hours available per week has no significance for the resolution of the problem. Actual hours must first be converted to standard hours for application to the jobs that need to be done. This will be understood by examining the job requirements in Table 13-2, which represents a forecast of demand for next week.

Table 13-3 provides the *productivity rate* (e.g., the production output rate) of the standard machine for each of the jobs listed in Table 13-2.

The computations are guided by the following equation where unit dimensions are shown in parentheses. The dimension of *units* is in the numerator and denominator and cancels out. The remaining dimension is *SMH* (standard machine hours). Thus, demand in units has been transformed to demand in standard machine hours.

$$D(units) \div PR \left(\frac{units}{SMH} \right) = D(SMH)$$

where $D(units)$ = demand in units for each kind of job

PR = the production rate in units per SMH

$D(SMH)$ = demand in aggregated standard hours

Machine	SMH Index	SMH per Week	Actual Hours
M1	0.5	18 SM hours	36
M2*	1.0	54 SM hours	54
M3	0.8	64 SM hours	80
M4	0.6	20 SM hours	33.3
Total SMH		**156 SM hours**	

TABLE 13-1

Supply of Actual and SMH Hours Available per Week

M2* was chosen as the standard machine (SM). Note the asterisk (*). If M1 had been chosen as SM, the indexes would have been (1.0, 2.0, 1.6, 1.2), which is the result of multiplying the SMH index by 2. This kind of relationship is not unusual between machines. It often applies to skills. Some variation from perfect index relations can be tolerated as providing a reasonable approximation.

Job	A	B	C	D	E
Units demanded	300	210	240	1,800	400

TABLE 13-2

A Forecast of Demand for Next Week

Table 13-4 converts actual units of demand for jobs A through E into standard machine hours (SMH) of demand, as follows:

To satisfy demand—196 standard machine hours (SMH) are needed!

The transformation of the dimension *units* to *SMH* should be noted. It makes the generalized nature of standard machine hours understandable.

Both supply and demand have been converted to the common terms of SMH. As shown in Table 13-1, there are only 156 standard machine hours available. So, 196 – 156 = 40 SMH of demand will *not* be met.

The same reasoning applies to standard workforce hours (people hours) and to combinations of people and machines working together. Various weighting schemes can be used to bring different kinds of estimates of supply and demand into a *common framework*.

13-2   THE IMPORTANCE OF FORECASTS

Figure 13-3 shows the connection between the three activity levels of **production planning.** Note that the top box—call it the first level—aggregate planning—is the *only one* that requires a forecast. This will be used in addition to orders that are on hand. Activity level two is **loading,** and activity level three is **sequencing,** all to be explained shortly.

If all three levels of production scheduling are well managed, job shop profitability is significantly enhanced. Doing this complex job well requires total attention to detail and knowing the score.

> **Production planning:** First level is aggregate planning; it is the only level that requires a forecast. The second level is loading; level three is sequencing.
>
> **Loading:** Assign jobs to departments before sequencing jobs within departments.
>
> **Sequencing:** Primary basis for establishing optimal sequence is to minimize the time jobs spend waiting. There are other bases too.

13-2a   Planning Horizon for Aggregate Scheduling

First level. Set the planning horizon for forecasting, as required by AP, equal to or greater than the longest lead time. If it takes eight months to have an order filled or to hire five computer programmers, no plan can be carried out until five months have elapsed. The lead times include the interval required to train the appropriate workforce, obtain the needed facilities, and be able to do the jobs that are forecast.

13-2b   Loading Is Assigning Jobs to Departments

Second level. Assign jobs to departments (called *loading*) that have been equipped and staffed according to the aggregate plan. The jobs are bound to deviate in number and kind from the AP forecast. The estimate of total standard hours required might be fairly good, but how they get allocated to specific jobs will have greater variability. As usual in these situations, the errors tend to cancel out. The second level of production scheduling permits a comparison to be made of forecast versus actual demand. Feedback concerning accuracy may be helpful in improving future forecasts. Further, at the second level, the real resources that were collected and prepared, based on the aggregate plan, must now be used to deal with the actual demand on hand.

TABLE 13-3

Productivity Rates of Standard Machine

Job	A	B	C	D	E
Production rate of the standard machine in units per standard machine hour (SMH)	6	7	6	30	25

SMH of Demand—by Jobs

A	300/6	= 50 SM hours
B	210/7	= 30 SM hours
C	240/6	= 40 SM hours
D	1800/30	= 60 SM hours
E	400/25	= 16 SM hours
	Sum	**= 196 SM hours**

TABLE 13-4

Demand in Units Converted into Standard Hours

13-2c Sequencing Sets the Order for Doing Jobs at the Department

Third level. Sequence the work according to a good shop-floor control policy. This determines the order in which jobs will be done by each department. The interval between loading and sequencing is short (days or hours) whereas the interval between AP and loading is long (months). Sequencing decisions have an important effect on customer satisfaction. They are determinants of delivery schedules and affect costs as well. The quality of sequencing decisions is always a consequence of AP and loading decisions, and sequencing skills and knowledge.

13-2d Integration of the Three Levels

If the three levels of the job shop are not recognized, a number of problems and possible crises can result. Job shop "old timers" call it "organized chaos." Lack of careful attention to the three levels leads to random management of the system. Job shop management involves so many details (different jobs, machines, workers) that strong information management capabilities are essential.

At the aggregate planning level, forecasting plays a crucial role. It is not possible to do aggregate planning without a forecast. Therefore, if the company lacks the means to get a method-based forecast, all that remains is to guess. Some of the best forecasts (in retrospect) were based on common sense.

If management is not in control of the situation, losses occur because of neglect at all three levels. The costs are cumulative. They impair an organization's competitiveness. Errors made at the first level create unnecessary costs at the second and third levels. Errors

FIGURE 13-3
Three Levels of Production Scheduling
Level 1 is aggregate planning, which requires a forecast.

made at the second level create unnecessary costs at the third level. That is what is meant by cumulative costs.

Information is essential for forecasting and planning at level one and for decision making at levels two and three where the aggregate units have become specific jobs. Most companies maintain the necessary information about processing in the form of blueprints, bills of materials, operations sheets, and routing sheets. Some of these are on paper and others are available as computerized databases.

Methods for ordering materials required for the job shop follow aggregate planning. These include developing master production schedules, which are precise commitments of what is to be made in the shop or done by the service organization.

Aggregate planning gains utility from a statistical advantage of forecasting for aggregate phenomena as compared to forecasting values for specific components of the aggregation. Aggregate forecasts are always better than the set of component forecasts because the standard deviation of the total (T) of (n) components is equal to the square root of n multiplied by the standard deviation of the individual components. The equations are shown here. Consider as an example the sales estimates for the spring quarter. First, the variance of the estimate for the quarter is equal to the sum of the variances of the three months of April, May, and June.

$$\sigma^2{}_{Spring} = \sigma^2{}_{April} + \sigma^2{}_{May} + \sigma^2{}_{June} \text{ or more generally, } \sigma^2{}_{Total} = \sigma^2{}_1 + \sigma^2{}_2 + \ldots + \sigma^2{}_n$$

For illustrative purposes, it is reasonable to assume the variances of the components ($i = 1, 2, 3, \ldots, n$) are all about equal. Then,

$$\sigma^2{}_T = n\sigma^2{}_i$$

and

$$\sigma_T = \sigma_i \sqrt{n}$$

The square root effect makes the standard deviation of the total significantly smaller than the linear sum of n standard deviations. The standard deviation of the quarter is 1.73, which is 0.58 of the sum of three months taken separately, e.g., $\sqrt{3} = 1.73$ and $(1.73)/(3.00) = 0.58$.

13-3   BASIC AGGREGATE PLANNING MODEL

Job shops require a strong methodological approach for planning ahead. There is so much detail to capture the variety. Aggregate planning provides just the approach that the job shop requires. Demand and production output are treated in aggregation across a variety of different work facilities and output jobs. The aggregate is treated as one job made by one facility operating under several different modes, e.g., regular and overtime production, with and without subcontractors.

The organization's facilities are used to satisfy varying demand levels over time and in whatever way promises to minimize total costs. These total costs vary according to the production schedule used. Demands for different outputs are aggregated by considering them all to be a unified demand for the output capacity of the facility.

Figure 13-4 shows the demand side of the system. Varying demands for different items (1, 2, and 3) have been aggregated into a single demand called S_t. Previously, the components were months of the quarter. This time the components are different items. The sum of item demands in period t results in total sales called S_t.

Figure 13-5 shows the production factors of the system. The production factors of aggregate planning are

1. Demand over time (e.g., sales = S_t).

2. Supply (or production = P_t).

3. Overtime production occurs when the normal time production capacity level (ntc) is exceeded, ($P_t \geq ntc$).

4. Workforce level = W_t, and it is the measure of human resources required to meet demand.

FIGURE 13-4
Aggregate Demand as the Sum of the Demand of Three Items in Standard Units over Time *t*

5. Inventory level = positive I_t is the result of supply being greater than demand—stock accumulates; negative I_t results when demand exceeds supply and out-of-stock or backorder conditions occur.

6. All factors can be measured against planned normal capacity stated in standard units.

The aggregate supply resulting from production during period t is P_t. In other words, the amount produced during time period t is called P_t. Both the facilities used and the organization's workforce are likely to vary over time. The workforce level during time t is called W_t. For the prior period, called $t-1$, the workforce level is called $W_t - 1$. The same kind of time considerations applies to supply, demand, and inventory levels. An additional variable that the production manager wants to control over time is the inventory level

$I_t, I_{t-1}, I_{t-2}, \ldots I_{t-n} \ldots$ which is also shown in Figure 13-5.

Using the forecast for aggregate demand S_t over time, the aggregate planning problem to solve is

How should P_t, W_t, and I_t be controlled so as to optimize the systems performance?

More specifically, the aggregate planning problem requires period-by-period solutions that will optimize the total system's performance. There are interperiod dependencies, which mean that one period might not be as good as it could be in order that the total result for the entire planning horizon is best. This is classic systems thinking in which component performance may have to be suboptimized to obtain the system's optimal. (Note Tables 13-5, 13-6, and 13-7 as good examples of aggregate systems planning. Also note Figures 13-6a, 13-6b, and 13-6c. These tables and figures provide a great deal of information.)

FIGURE 13-5
Aggregate Planning for the Production Factors of the System

Chapter 13 Aggregate Planning 477

13-4 THREE AGGREGATE PLANNING POLICIES

Three policies are considered here:

1. *Do not vary the workforce.* This means keeping P_t constant over time. By formula: $P_t = k$ for the entire period, $t = T$. Keeping a constant workforce is called a *level policy*. In Figure 13-6a, P_t is constant. This is the condition for a **constant production strategy.**

   Both overproduction and underproduction occur when production is constant and demand varies. For most circumstances, keeping the workforce constant makes it easier to keep output constant. Then, the variability of demand determines whether overproduction (being overstocked) or underproduction (being understocked) is the problem to be faced at any point in time. Call this *Pattern A*.

   The policy that creates Pattern A is a constant, fixed, and level volume of production. Routine production sequences can be followed every day. This saves money because process alterations are avoided. Setups, takedowns, and changeovers, which can be costly, are minimized. However, there are likely to be costs associated with the fact that the "level policy" does not match demand.

2. *Vary the workforce, W_t, so that production output, P_t matches demand, S_t as closely as is possible.* The caption to Figure 13-6b calls this option *Pattern B*. It is labeled a **chasing policy** because P_t strives to match S_t at all times. Because the demand occurs before the supply can satisfy it, there is a lag in fulfilling the goal. That is why it is said that production chases demand.

   Pattern B (the *chasing policy*) is the solid line in Figure 13-6b. Because P_t cannot exactly match S_t, the actual production line would approach but not fall on the solid line in Figure 13-6b. This kind of situation will be shown later as a combination policy. Meanwhile, the pure chasing policy has as its paramount objective the avoidance of over- and understock inventory costs.

   Production Pattern B strives to chase and match supply with demand—as exactly as possible—for every time period. This goal is represented by $P_t = S_t$. In this situa-

Constant production strategy: The sum of costs associated with a constant workforce must be less than the sum of costs associated with a variable workforce.

Chasing policy: The sum of costs of a variable workforce and underutilized equipment should be less than the sum of costs of reducing overstocks and eliminating backorders.

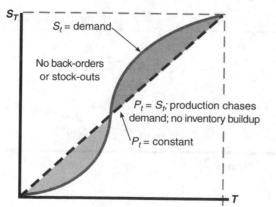

tion, workers are hired, fired, or furloughed in each time period according to the expected demand of the particular time period. Workforce changes are made according to the flexibility of the industry. In some situations, changes are daily. In others, they are weekly, monthly, or even longer.

With perfect forecasts, there can be a perfect match. Perfect forecasts are hard to come by except where there are contracts that specify demand. Even in the case of contracts, it may be difficult to control the workforce size because of shortages caused by illness, weather, and lack of availability of certain skill sets. Also, overstaffing places burdens on the human resources managers who have to deal with personnel needs and the long-term repercussions of asking people to leave without notice.

Fixed-volume, level production shops—as in Pattern A—create a more stable job shop environment than the variable-volume, chasing production policy shops of Pattern B. Greater investments in training can be justified for Pattern A. As a result, the level shop has less start-up and learning waste. It is associated with higher quality products and services. A drawback to Pattern A is that it creates unneeded inventory when supply is greater than demand. It causes out-of-stocks and backorders when supply is less than demand. However, if properly managed, the inventory build-up is used to prevent out-of-stocks and backorders. When inventory build-up beyond a certain point is economically unfeasible, part of the constant workforce is idled.

Such idle time is minimized by the variable-volume job shop of Pattern B. When there is a large amount of demand fluctuation, a variable workforce capability is appealing but there are offsetting costs, which include information systems to keep track of workforce changes. That is the bookkeeping part of the problem. Being able to hire and lay off involves human resources management with a lot of detail. There are unpleasant aspects to layoffs. The use of temporary employees for peak loads and subcontracting, can reduce the need for layoffs.

3. *Find superior combinations of Policies (Patterns A and B).* There are many different variable-volume lines that could connect zero and S_t. Some of these lines are shown in Figure 13-6c. Each is a partial chasing policy and a partial level policy. They are labeled *combination policies* in Figure 13-6c.

The models for AP can provide guidance about minimum cost policies using tangible cost factors. Less tangible factors may have to be included qualitatively. In trying to find the best policy, there may be a cost of spreading management too thin. The systems approach can enable OM to do aggregate planning with costs that reflect human resources management limitations. Companies may find it easier to use mixtures of policies (Patterns A and B) that come closer to being realistic than the pure policies (Patterns A and B).

Combination (C) policies have different patterns for production (partially) chasing demand. What is represented is greater reluctance to react rapidly to match demand. There is more systems inertia.

Each line in Figure 13-6c has different costs. Certain costs disappear when Pattern B is followed instead of Pattern A. At the same time, another set of costs

Workforce size is a variable that is often a function of the volume of business, revenues, and profits. This variability is characteristic of labor-intensive production on the plant floor. It also occurs in the billing and purchasing offices, with R & D, and the sales force.

FIGURE 13-6C Aggregate Planning— Combination Policies (Patterns C)

appears. The cost-mixtures are greater for the lines in Figure 13-6c that deviate further from either of the pure policies. Each curve-solution represents some combination of changing production rates, changing workforce size, varying degrees of overtime utilization, fluctuating inventory levels, and overstocks as well as out-of-stocks.

Combination policies fall between two pure policies. Assume that OM would be happiest with level work conditions because it is never easy to hire and/or let workers go. On the other hand, marketing would be happiest with perfect chasing because it would not produce stock outages. Human resources management is the department that facilitates hiring and downsizing. Therefore, it might be on the same side as OM. Warehouse managers might prefer the marketing point of view because they can achieve better performance measures by avoiding overstocking given limited space. In view of this, combination policies produce the need for negotiations between different parts of the organization.

13-4a Pattern A—Policy: Supply Is Constant

Consider a numerical example of Pattern A. Assume that the workforce is maintained at a constant level (W_t = 38 workers) and that each worker can produce k = 10 units per time period. Then, production will be constant at P_t = 380. This in turn means that inventory will fluctuate as demand sometimes exceeds and sometimes falls below the constant supply of output units.

In Table 13-5, total supply equals total demand (2,280 units) for the 6-month planning horizon.

At the end of the first period, production has fallen short of demand by 40 units. The lack of inventory that requires backordering is indicated by I_t = –40. Backordered work is shown as negative inventory.

The cumulative inventory for month 1 is ΣI_t = –40 units because it is assumed that prior to period 1 there was zero inventory accumulation and no backorders. When cumulative inventory changes signs from minus to plus, it means that backorders have been filled and accumulation of stock has occurred. The details for this example are shown in Table 13-5.

In reality, it is not possible to tell which purchases will be backordered. This is because this inventory is stated in terms of aggregates. Also, some buyers refuse to accept backorders. These orders are known as *fill or kill*. In Table 13-5, all backordered jobs are filled eventually (by the sixth month). The cumulative inventory column shows backorders occurring in four out of six periods, but the value is zero in month 6. That means that all cases of demand greater than supply that have been backordered have been filled. There are no more backorders.

In certain product classes, "fill or kill" is more likely than in others. An airline is not likely to cancel an order for a Boeing 777. Even though Boeing 777s are always backordered—a bankrupt airline has no choice but to cancel. However, an order for the most recent Harry Potter DVD has to be filled. Our children have little patience if a local

TABLE 13-5						
Pattern A—Constant						
Month t	S_t	P_t	I_t	$\sum\limits_{t=1}^{t} I_t$	W_t	$W_t - W_{t-1}$
1	420	380	–40	–40	38	0
2	360	380	+20	–20	38	0
3	390	380	–10	–30	38	0
4	350	380	+30	0	38	0
5	420	380	–40	–40	38	0
6	340	380	+40	0	38	0
Totals	2,280	2,280				

Blockbuster store cannot fill the order. They go across the street or drive 12 miles to find other video stores that can satisfy their immediate need. It is customary to "fill or kill" orders for video and music tapes, CDs, DVDs, and video games that are not available in the first store of choice. Customers are seldom willing to accept backorders for records, tapes, and CDs. The same holds true for cosmetics and gourmet foods. Lipsticks, nail polishes, Brazilian hearts of palm, and real caviar are often fill or kill items. Because they are needed "now," the buyer will travel far and wide to find what is wanted.

Note that in period 2, production, P_t is larger than demand S_t by 20 units. This adds 20 units to inventory, I_t. These units will be shipped to reduce backorders from 40 to 20. The remaining 20 backordered units are shown in row 2 under the cumulative inventory column as –20 units. To be clear, the equation is

$$\sum_{t=1}^{t=2} I_t = -20$$

Summing up, Pattern A has understocks occurring in three of the six months, and it has overproduction in three of the six months. There is good news for this company. At the end of six months, the ups and the downs balance out. Cumulative inventory is measured as zero. It sure looks good to have a constant workforce of 38.

13-4b Pattern B—Policy: Supply Chases Demand

Consider Pattern B, where supply chases demand perfectly. What happens to costs when the workforce level is changed in order to allow production to match demand?

Because $(W_t - W_{t-1})$ will not always equal zero, as in Table 13-5, the production Pattern B ($P_t = S_t$) can be followed by altering the workforce levels. Monthly variation of the workforce is used to match supply and demand. There will be no inventory accumulation if demand can be perfectly predicted so that workforce size can be perfectly adjusted. If perfection is elusive, then production always will be chasing demand, trying to reduce overstocks and decrease backorders.

If perfection is obtainable, then backordering and overstocking costs will not occur. In general, forecasts of demand will deviate from being perfect. Unexpected orders and cancellations are usual. Also, estimates of supply will not match the requirements. Workforce adjustments are difficult to achieve. New workers with specific skills cannot be found. The untrained take time to be brought up to speed.

Running the numbers, again, assume that each worker produces 10 units per time period. Demand in the first period is 420 units and 42 workers have been employed. Perfect forecasts of demand can be made. The results are shown in Table 13-6.

Production in the first period is 420 units, i.e., $P_1 = 420$. Production exactly matches demand, so there is no inventory, i.e., $I_1 = 0$. Cumulative inventory,

$$\sum_{t=1}^{t=1} I_t \text{ also is } 0$$

TABLE 13-6

Pattern B—Chasing

Month t	S_t	P_t	I_t	$\sum_{t=1}^{t} I_t$	W_t	$W_t - W_{t-1}$
1	420	420	0	0	42	0
2	360	360	0	0	36	–6
3	390	390	0	0	39	+3
4	350	350	0	0	35	–4
5	420	420	0	0	42	+7
6	340	340	0	0	34	–8
Totals	2,280	2,280	0	0		–8

No change in workforce size ($\Delta W_t = W_t - W_{t-1}$) is assumed for the first period. Had there been fewer than 42 workers, then backorders would have arisen, and the workforce size in the next period would have been increased to catch up with demand. Whenever a forecast error causes overstocking or backordering, the workforce will be adjusted to catch up and produce zeros in the inventory columns.

In the second period, because the demand is 360, the workforce contracts to 36, which is a reduction of 6. Thus, $\Delta W_t = -6$. Then, the workforce expands to 39 in the third period. The remainder of the record is read from the table in the same way. W_t goes from 35 to 42 to 34. $P_t = S_t$, so there are neither inventories nor stock-outs and, under usual circumstances, all orders are filled with minimum delay. The table portrays production perfectly chasing demand.

The supply chain is value adding continuously and in synchronization with demand. There are no unfilled orders, and there is no inventory sitting around waiting for demand to increase. On the other hand, the costs for changing workforce size can be substantial.

In addition to costs for changing W_t (i.e., related to ΔW_t), there are other costs that include alterations of space requirements and services (such as cafeteria and restrooms) for the workforce. More people need more room and more services. Further, $-\Delta W_t$ causes group morale problems and teamwork failures. These correspond to expenses that are difficult to estimate, but they are there nevertheless.

Contrasting the two cases of A and B, the constant workforce has produced three instances of supply being less than demand. The total shortfall is 90 units. However, backorders never exceed 40, as seen from the cumulative inventory column labeled

$$\sum_{t=1}^{t=6} I_t$$

It should be remembered that cumulative inventory is the measure of actual stock on-hand, which is net stock on-hand.

In the constant workforce case, there is no positive accumulation of inventory. That is by chance because there is nothing to have prevented it from occurring. If the first period had been deleted, there would have been positive inventory to report. Note that for the constant workforce of 38, total demand for 6 periods equals total supply, which is 2,280 units.

The same totals apply to the figures for the chasing policy. In trade for no inventory or backorders, the organization is required to hire 10 workers and lay off 18. The costs of workforce changes need to be contrasted with the savings that result from having no backorders and no inventory accumulation.

Which approach has the lowest expected cost, Pattern A, B, or C? Recall that C-type patterns allow many different combinations of A and B. Thus, it is important to consider configurations that are logical mixtures of Patterns A and B.

13-4c Pattern C_1—Policy: Increase Workforce Size by One

To begin with a simple change, test the workforce level, namely, using the stable workforce size of 38 as a basis:

1. Increase the number of workers from 38 to 39 whenever demand is greater than 380.

2. Decrease the number of workers from 38 to 37 whenever demand is less than 380.

Making unit changes is an entirely sensible way to begin. Results are shown in Table 13-7. The plan *slightly* chases demand when $S_t > P_t$, and thereby reduces backorders. The plan *slightly* reduces overstocks when $S_t < P_t$.

The resulting sum of the cumulative inventory for six periods of this *slightly* chasing policy (C_1) is

$$\sum_{t=1}^{t=6}\sum_{t=1}^{t=6} I_t = 100$$

Month t	S_t	P_t	I_t	$\sum\limits_{t=1}^{t} I_t$	W_t	$W_t - W_{t-1}$
1	420	390	−30	−30	39	+1
2	360	370	+10	−20	37	−2
3	390	390	0	−20	39	+2
4	350	370	+20	0	37	−2
5	420	390	−30	−30	39	+2
6	340	370	+30	0	37	−2
Totals	2,280	2,280				

TABLE 13-7

Pattern C_1— Slightly Chasing

That is the sum of −100 for total backorders and +0 for total stock on-hand.

Next, the sum of workforce changes is

$$\sum_{t=1}^{t=6} \Delta W_t = -1$$

That is composed of +5 for hires and −6 for workforce reductions. There are charges for both types of changes. There are no additional labor charges because the average number of workers for the 6 periods in C_1 is 38.

The comparable figures for Pattern A—the stable workforce policy where $W_t = 38$—are

$$\sum_{t=1}^{t=6}\sum_{t=1}^{t=6} I_t = -130$$

That is the sum of −130 for total backorders and +0 for total stock on-hand. By definition:

$$\sum_{t=1}^{t=6} \Delta W_t = 0$$

That is, 0 for hires and 0 for workforce reductions.

Comparable figures for Pattern B—the chasing policy where no inventory costs occur—are

$$\sum_{t=1}^{t=6}\sum_{t=1}^{t=6} I_t = 0$$

The double sum equals zero, and this number is composed of two parts. There is −0 for total backorders and +0 for total stock on-hand. This result is predictable by the definition of perfect chasing. The next calculation is the sum of workforce changes.

$$\sum_{t=1}^{t=6} \Delta W_t = -8$$

That sum is also composed of two parts. There is +10 for workforce hires and −18 for workforce reductions. These net out to −8.

13-4d The Cost Structure

The costs that apply must be used to decide which is best. Comparing the stable policy A with the slightly chasing policy C_1, there is a reduction of backorders by 30, an increase of 5 for hires, and a decrease of 6 people for workforce reductions.

Say that backorders cost $100 per occurrence, costs for carrying inventory are $25 per unit, hires cost $200 per instance, and reductions cost $300 per event—all per unit time period. Then, for the C_1 policy, the total variable cost, $TVC(C_1)$, is

$$TVC(C_1) = (100 \times 100) + (0 \times 25) + (5 \times 200) + (6 \times 300) = \$12,800$$

Compare this to the total variable costs of the stable workforce of 38 workers. For policy A, the total variable cost, $TVC(A)$, is

$$TVC(A) = (130 \times 100) + (0 \times 25) + (0 \times 200) + (0 \times 300) = \$13,000$$

Preference is for C_1, the *slightly* chasing policy, which has reduced costly backorders at the expense of increased hires and layoffs. The difference is only $200.

Because backorders are driving the preference, it is logical to examine option B, which completely eliminated inventory costs by chasing demand. Total variable cost $TVC(B)$ for the B policy is

$$TVC(B) = (0 \times 100) + (0 \times 25) + (10 \times 200) + (18 \times 300) = \$7,400$$

This is clearly the preferred way to go for the particular costs that have been assumed. Other costs could lead to entirely different conclusions.

Cost trade-off analysis:
Different mixtures of the two pure strategies are feasible. Each blended strategy has a unique total cost, which may be less than the total costs of either pure strategy.

The comparisons are examples of **cost trade-off analysis** using only the variable portions of total cost. The variable portions are those costs that differ between alternative choices. Thus, the total variable costs do not include the costs of the workforce size, W_t, so long as there are no additional wages to be paid. If a policy required hiring a 39th worker, the cost of the individual's wages would have to be included as a variable component.

Another factor to consider is the difference in the costs of increasing the workforce size and of decreasing the workforce size. There is no reason for them to be equivalent. Hiring involves orientation and training. There are many forms of workforce reduction—some are temporary; others are permanent.

Trade-off model: See **Cost trade-off analysis.**

Also, note that when supply (P_t) varies with demand (S_t), workforce adjustment costs could represent overtime costs with a constant size workforce—or a fluctuating workforce size, without the use of overtime. The cost structures must apply to the policies that are followed.

There is a trade-off between workforce adjustment costs and inventory/backorder costs. The **trade-off model** is shown in Figure 13-7, where the *x*-axis runs from smooth or level production at the left to perfect chasing where production matches demand at the right.

Workforce adjustment costs and inventory/backorder costs are added together to create the total cost curve, which has a minimum point. That minimum total cost is associated with the concept of a combination policy, which is not specific. The idea of a 50 percent chasing policy is ambiguous.

Looking at Figure 13-7, imagine that the line describing workforce adjustment costs rises more steeply. Because there are two kinds of workforce adjustment costs, perhaps two

FIGURE 13-7
Trade-Off Model

The positions of the cost lines in this trade-off model determine the point of optimal balance between level production and perfect chasing policy. Using words in place of graphics, the point of minimum cost is a function of workforce adjustment costs and inventory/backorder costs. The minimum total cost point coincides with the optimal degree of chasing.

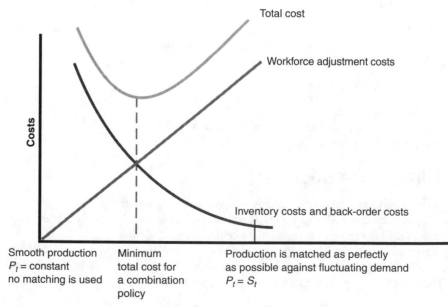

Production Policy

lines should have been used. Because only one line is used in this case, an assumption has been made that the two kinds of costs are equivalent. Possible reasons that the slope of the workforce adjustment cost line has increased could include new government regulations requiring more training and larger severance packages.

When the slope of this line rises more steeply, the effect is to move the minimum cost point of the total cost line (the optimal combination) closer to constant (level) production. If the inventory and backorder cost curve rises, that curve moves upward and to the right. The effect is to move the optimal combination closer to perfect matching of production and demand.

13-5 LINEAR PROGRAMMING (LP) FOR AGGREGATE PLANNING

Figure 13-7 illustrated the way in which total cost reaches a minimum value for some particular production schedule. The goal is to find that **minimum cost assignment schedule.** This is equivalent to identifying the production policy for the minimum cost point on the x-axis of Figure 13-7.

A linear equation can be written for the minimum total cost objective. Also, a set of constraints will be needed to characterize patterns such as those previously described as A, B, and C_1. The advantage of LP for aggregate planning is that computer programs can quickly solve problems with a large number of variables and many constraints. Check out the power of Solver in Microsoft to provide LP solutions.

The nature of **linear programming (LP)** variables and linear programming (LP) constraints now will be explained in terms of symbols, many of which have already been introduced in this chapter. Repetition has its benefits.

S_t = sales in period t (sales demand is forecast on definite orders). If supply < demand, some part of S_t will not be satisfied. LP selects the best demands to fill. Best is defined as achieving the minimum cost solution (and/or the maximum profit solution).

t = the planning horizon that is chosen in terms of *need to plan ahead* and *believability of the forecast*. Time periods can be in days, weeks, months, quarters, or years, depending upon the way that the data are collected and other circumstances of measurement.

Five variables that can be controlled for optimal aggregate planning:

1. W_t = the number of workers at the beginning of each period t. $P_t = kW_t$ – normal production output in period t (k is the output per worker in period t). Ordinarily k is not considered to be a decision variable. However, by selecting different equipment, and by using different skill levels, it is possible to affect productivity. In this case, P_t is derived from W_t and k is considered to be a constant. W_t is the variable that will be used in the LP equation.

2. A_t = additions to the workforce (number of people) at the beginning of period t.

3. R_t = reductions to the workforce (number of people) at the beginning of period t.

4. I_t = inventory (number of units in stock, or out-of-stock) at the beginning of period t.

5. O_t = overtime production (units of output) in period t.

Seven reasonable constraints for each period are

1. $W_t \leq W$, which places limits on the workforce because of space, payroll, and other resource availability.

2. $A_t \leq A$, which places limits on additions to the workforce because of constraints imposed by training facilities and the ability to absorb additional workers.

3. $R_t \leq R$, which places limits on reductions to the workforce because of constraints on ability to process layoffs and company policy regarding the number of layoffs and furloughs that will be permitted in a time period.

Minimum cost assignment schedule: Search for the production schedule that has the minimum total cost along the scale that starts with smooth production and ends with perfect matching of supply and demand.

Linear programming (LP): See Fundamental theorem of linear programming (LP).

4. $W_t = W_{t-1} + A_t - R_t$. This equation describes the size of the workforce at the beginning of each time period t. It is subject to constraints 1, 2, and 3.

5. $I_{min} \leq I_t \leq I_{max}$ places limits on how large or small the inventory held in each period can become. If backorders are allowed, I_{min} can be a negative number. Storage limitations can be the basis for the maximum inventory level at time t.

6. $O_t \leq O$ places a limit on how much overtime is acceptable.

7. $I_t = I_{t-1} + P_t + O_t - S_t = I_{t-1} + kW_t + O_t - S_t$

    This describes the amount of inventory (net stock on-hand, or out-of-stock) at the beginning of each time period t imposed by constraints 5 and 6.

There are five variables and seven constraints for each time period. Say that the time period is months. Then, with a planning horizon of six months there would be 30 variables and 42 constraints. In practice, some of the constraints that have been listed as possibilities would not be exercised. Say that half of them are real constraints. This would result in 30 variables and 21 constraints.

For reasons that are described here, only 21 variables will have values greater than zero. This means that $(30 - 21) = 9$ variables will have zero values. They will not be active variables.

13-5a The Fundamental Theorem of LP

Crucial to understanding LP is the fact that it is a mathematical method consisting of equations that are interdependent. The dependencies are expressed by the **fundamental theorem of linear programming (LP)**. It states that there cannot be more *active variables* than *real constraints*. From the previous paragraph, the assumption has been made that there are 21 real constraints. From the fundamental theorem, there can be only 21 active variables. Twelve of these can be accounted for at the outset.

There are six time periods for the five variables (W_t, A_t, R_t, I_t, and O_t). This results in 30 variables that could be active. Workforce will be positive for all six t. That is six active variables. Inventory levels are likely to be positive for all six t. The result is that 12 active variables have been noted. This means that at least nine uses of overtime, or additions to the workforce, or reductions to the workforce, will be inactive (e.g., set at zero). Inactive variables will not be used.

To obtain a minimum cost LP solution, individual costs must be assigned to the variables, as follows:

c_W = earnings of each worker per time period t
c_A = cost of adding a worker
c_R = cost of reducing the workforce—removing a worker
C_c = cost of carrying a unit for the time period t
c_o = cost of production for an overtime unit

The total cost objective function to be minimized is an all-linear set of equations, as follows:

$$TC = \sum_{t=1}^{t=T} (c_W W_t + c_A A_t + c_R R_t + C_c I_t + c_o O_t)$$

This cost minimization is subject to satisfying the demands, S_t, as described by constraint 7.

The most common objection to use of the LP model is that it has a linear structure for the costs of the objective function and for the constraints. A pioneering aggregate planning model will be briefly explained. It is called **HMMS,** after its creators. HMMS allows nonlinear costs—which require much more work to use. The advantage is that results obtained from a better model of reality are more likely to provide rewards instead of penalties.

Another important factor is the production output represented by k. OM carefully considers how k can be increased by introducing new technology and by improving training methods. This is not part of the LP solution. Note, however, that by increasing k, different solutions will be obtained. Overtime costs can be scaled back, workforce additions can be decreased, and workforce decreases may be possible. The minimum total cost can

---

Fundamental theorem of linear programming (LP): For aggregate planning, supplies and demands will determine the number of different active production assignments that can be made to minimize total costs.

HMMS: Pioneering aggregate-planning model that uses nonlinear costs for its resource constraints.

be reduced considerably by using improved process methods. From the systems perspective, coordination with human resources management for training improvements, and marketing for better product-mix alternatives, can significantly decrease costs.

The solution to the problem requires a great deal of calculation, which only computer programs for LP can handle. It also should be noted that fractional values of some of these variables (i.e., a part of a person to be added to the workforce) may not be feasible if part-time work is not used. When a problem requires integer solutions for the variables, integer programming (IP) software is available. This kind of application makes sense for airline crew scheduling and airline flight schedules.

13-6 TRANSPORTATION MODEL (TM) FOR AGGREGATE PLANNING

The transportation matrix provides a convenient representation of the aggregate-planning problem. It can provide an optimal aggregate solution based on relatively simple assumptions. Computer software can solve these transportation problems using network algorithms[1] or linear programming (LP).

Two versions of transportation matrices are presented. The first one allows no backorders and is easy to solve by hand. The second one permits backorders and their special costs. The second one is laborious to solve by hand if there are more than a few variables and constraints, so computer software is preferred.

Costs that apply to one, or the other, or both versions of the transportation matrix are listed here:

r = normal production labor costs per unit made during the regular work shift
v = overtime or second-shift production costs per unit made
c = inventory carrying costs, per dollar of expenditure over a given time period
b = backorder costs per unit and per time period backordered
I_0 = initial inventory (for the beginning of period $t = 1$)
I_f = final inventory (for the end of period $t = f$)

Table 13-8 presents the first version of the aggregate-planning transportation matrix, which does not allow backorders. Table 13-9 presents the second version of the TM, which permits backorders.

With respect to Table 13-8, demand is shown as the column totals for the first three columns. D_1, D_2, and D_3 are demand levels in the first, second, and third periods.

Final inventory (called I_f) is specified at the bottom of the fourth column. Slack (SL)—which balances supply and demand—is listed at the bottom of the fifth column.

Supply is shown as row totals. The first row is initial inventory (called I_0). Thereafter, rows alternate in presenting production supply for regular time and for overtime, called R_1 and O_1, R_2 and O_2, R_3 and O_3.

The objective is to minimize total cost. Constraints reflect the limited availability of regular and overtime production capacity in hours. As another version of the problem, alternative configurations can be studied where capacity is added or removed by additional hires and/or new equipment technology.

Standard units are required to aggregate different kinds of product where the same resources are used to make diverse models such as small and large cans (aggregated as "cans"), or white, red, and green paint (aggregated as "paint"), or 40, 60, 75, and 100 watt bulbs (aggregated as "bulbs").

The transportation model (TM) is flexible. It does not require a square matrix. Each matrix applies to a specific period of time. Table 13-8 has eight rows and six columns—one of which is a slack column. In this case, a slack column is added instead of a slack row because supply is greater than demand. Thus, $S > D$, so $S - D > 0$ and $S - D = SL$. Then: $S = D + SL$.

On the other hand, the model is linear. This means that unit costs or profits are not able to be changed as a function of volume. Profit saturation and nonlinear cost increases cannot be represented.

TABLE 13-8

Transportation Model for Aggregate Planning—No Backorders Allowed

	| Sales Periods					
	1	2	3	Final Inv.	Slack	Supply
Initial Inv.	0	c	2c	3c	0	I_0
Regular 1	r	r + c	r + 2c	r + 3c	0	R_1
Overtime 1	v	v + c	v + 2c	v + 3c	0	O_1
Regular 2	x	r	r + c	r + 2c	0	R_2
Overtime 2	x	v	v + c	v + 2c	0	O_2
Regular 3	x	x	r	r + c	0	R_3
Overtime 3	x	x	v	v + c	0	O_3
Demand	D_1	D_2	D_3	I_f	SL	Grand Total

Normal transportation methods are used to obtain the minimum cost solution. In this case, however, backorders are prohibited (by the x's in six cells). Each x represents a situation where production units made in the nth period are intended for delivery in the $(n-1)$ period. This is equivalent to making units in February that are intended to satisfy January demands that were backordered. To have the computer program block assignments, backorders are assigned large unit transport costs in the x-marked cells.

Table 13-9 presents the second version of the aggregate planning transportation matrix where backorders are allowed.

This second transportation matrix has new costs, b, which are backorder costs per unit backordered. The new cost is integrated without disruption, and the model can be solved by conventional transportation techniques including computer software using network algorithms or linear programming. Several simple numerical examples are assigned in the Problems Section at the end of this chapter.

Calling the time period months, the transportation matrices in Tables 13-8 and 13-9 cover a planning horizon of one quarter. Note how the carrying costs are zero for the first month. For the second month c is charged per unit carried in that month. For the third month, $2c$ is charged because inventory has been carried two months. Backorder costs are like carrying costs. They grow with each additional month that a unit is backordered. Slack costs are all zero.

13-6a Network and LP Solutions

The AP problem in Table 13-8 has unique characteristics because no backorders are allowed. It can be solved by assigning as many units as possible to the lowest cost cells in each column. Start the process with column 1. When the supply in a row is used up, go to the next lowest cost in the column and assign as many units as possible in that row. The constraints that must be met are the row and column totals. More units than row and column totals allow cannot be assigned to the lowest cost cells.

When column 1 allocations equal the column 1 total, move to column 2. Proceed in the same way, making sure not to assign more units to lowest cost cells than the row and column totals can support. The lowest cost assignments in column 2 may be blocked by

TABLE 13-9

Transportation Model for Aggregate Planning— Backorders Allowed

	Sales Periods			Final Inv.	Slack	Supply
	1	2	3			
Initial Inv.	0	c	$2c$	$3c$	0	I_0
Regular 1	r	$r+c$	$r+2c$	$r+3c$	0	R_1
Overtime 1	v	$v+c$	$v+2c$	$v+3c$	0	O_1
Regular 2	$r+b$	r	$r+c$	$r+2c$	0	R_2
Overtime 2	$v+b$	v	$v+c$	$v+2c$	0	O_2
Regular 3	$r+2b$	$r+b$	r	$r+c$	0	R_3
Overtime 3	$v+2b$	$v+b$	v	$v+c$	0	O_3
Demand	D_1	D_2	D_3	$I_f = 200$	SL	Grand Total

assignments already made in column 1. These blocked assignments cannot be violated. Continue until all columns have been assigned. Solutions obtained in this way are optimal.

It is necessary to understand the equations for solving transportation problems by using an LP model in order to input data correctly for the software. The constraining equations or supply inequalities (which are also called *in-equations*) are

$$\sum_{j=1}^{M} x_{ij} \leq S_i$$

where i = rows (supply); $i = 1, 2, \ldots, N$; and where j = columns (demand); $j = 1, 2, \ldots, M$. This applies to one row at a time.

The demand constraint is

$$\sum_{i=1}^{N} x_{ij} \leq D_j$$

where i = rows (supply); $i = 1, 2, \ldots, N$; and where j = columns (demand); $j = 1, 2, \ldots, M$. This applies to one column at a time.

The grand total is the sum of all active cell assignments and is the total number of units of supply or demand, whichever is larger. The larger value includes active slack values.

$$\sum_i^N \sum_j^M x_{ij} = \text{Grand Total}$$

The objective function to be minimized is

$$TC = \sum_i^N \sum_j^M c_{ij} x_{ij}$$

where TC = total cost of all active x_{ij} assignments.

Data requirements include row totals for all S_i, column totals for all D_j, the number of rows, N, the number of columns, M, and the costs c_{ij} for all i and j. LP software has built-in methods for finding the first feasible solution, which is the starting point for the iterative improvement methodology. In addition, most software permits **sensitivity analysis,** which allows investigation of the effect of altering supply capacities, demand levels, and costs on a "what if" basis.

Sensitivity analysis: Allows investigation of the effect of altering supply capacities, demand requirement, costs of carrying, backordering, etc.

13-7 NONLINEAR COST MODEL FOR AGGREGATE PLANNING (AP)

The linear limitations of LP and the transportation model (TP) are so often cited that it is important to explain what a nonlinear structure might look like. A well-known nonlinear method, called HMMS after its four developers, Holt, Modigliani, Muth, and Simon, was developed at PPG's paint factory.[2] The HMMS model addresses four separate issues.

1. What are nonlinear costs and what nonlinear costs apply to AP?

2. How complex is the HMMS model?

3. How much difference will it make?

4. In practice, how much is it used?

A linear cost equation is $y = cx$. A quadratic, or second order, cost equation is $y = cx^2$. The quadratic cost equation is one form of nonlinear cost equation. With linear costs, when x doubles, the cost y doubles. For example, y goes from c to $2c$ or from $2c$ to $4c$. With nonlinear costs, when x doubles, cost y is squared. For example, y goes from c to $4c$ or from $4c$ to $16c$.

HMMS uses both linear and quadratic cost equations to approximate the actual cost system of the PPG job shop. The approximations are shown as grey dashed lines in Figure

FIGURE 13-8
Cost Functions—Used for the HMMS Aggregate Planning Model

From Charles C. Holt, Franco Modigliani, and Herbert A. Simon. "A Linear Decision Rule for Production and Employment Scheduling." *Management Science*, vol. 2, no. 1 (October 1955). Permission required and granted.

Regular payroll cost = $C_1 W_t$

Workforce W (Man Months)

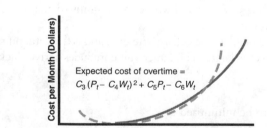

Cost per Month (dollars)

Cost of hiring and layoffs = $C_2 (W_t - W_{t-1})^2$

Workers Laid Off   0   Workers Hired

Monthly Changes in Size of Workforce, $W_t - W_{t-1}$

Expected cost of overtime = $C_3 (P_t - C_4 W_t)^2 + C_5 P_t - C_6 W_t$

Production Rate P_t (Units of Product/Month)

Cost per Month (dollars)

Expected inventory, back-order, and set-up costs = $C_7 [I - (C_8 + C_9 S_t)]^2$
I = Net inventory = inventory - back orders
S_t = Order rate (units of product whose shipment was ordered during the month)

Net Inventory I (Units of Product)

$C_8 + C_9 S_t$

13-8. The only linear cost line among these approximations is *payroll costs*. The solid black lines are generic assumptions that are frequently made about the "true" character of these specific cost functions.

Overtime costs increase in a nonlinear fashion as the production rate increases. The question is how rapid is that increase? The quadratic approximating cost function for overtime increases faster than the curve that was initially assumed. The specific rate of increase for overtime costs must be studied for the specific application as the production rate increases.

Hiring and firing costs were previously discussed. In Figure 13-8, the comparison is being made between the quadratic approximating cost and the linear assumption that is frequently used. Slopes of the linear estimates are different with the discontinuity occurring at the zero point. The quadratic approximation gets better as the number of people being hired and/or fired increases. Distortions around the zero point may not matter too much because the costs are small in that neighborhood.

The *inventory costs* curve takes into account not only stock on-hand and backorders, but also the setup costs that are associated with changing production from one product to another. The approximations are acceptable until the inventory on-hand, or backordered, is large. Good management can keep the actual costs experienced within the range of approximation (and before the costs escalate significantly).

The dashed grey lines in Figure 13-8 are based on the HMMS equations with specific values set for the cost coefficients. These coefficients were supplied by PPG managers to provide the best fit for each product line in the PPG job shop. Thus, payroll is linear and described by $(C_1 W_t)$.

The bifurcated costs of hiring and laying off are captured by one quadratic cost function $C_2 (W_t - W_{t-1})^2$ instead of two lines with different slopes. Only one cost coefficient, namely, C_2, is used to describe the required shape of the curve.

Similar descriptions apply to the other costs. The HMMS model requires four cost coefficients for the overtime payroll. These are $C_3, C_4 \ C_5, C_6$. Further discussion about costs and demand follow.

To evaluate the complexity of the HMMS model, a good starting point is the total cost equation.

Minimize TC $= \sum_{t=1}^{t=T} C_t$

T is the end period of the planning horizon, and C_t in the two equations is now spelled out.

$$C_t = C_1 W_t + C_2 (\Delta W_t)^2 + C_3 (P_t - C_4 W_t)^2 + C_5 P_t - C_6 W_t + C_7 (\sum I_t - C_8 - C_9 S_t)^2$$

Next is the critical constraint requirement for the rational balancing of inventory over consecutive periods:

$$\sum_{t=1}^{t=t^*} I_{t-1} + P_t - S_t = \sum_{t=1}^{t=t^*} I_t.$$

Cumulative inventory from period to period equals inventory at the end of the previous period $(t - 1)$ plus production added to inventory minus shipments from inventory, during the period t. This equality applies for all values of t, called t^*.

The costs, forecast, and variables, as shown in the equation, are identified as follows:

Costs

C_1 = costs related to payroll (i.e., size of the workforce); as C_1 increases, the slope of the payroll line rises.

C_2 = hiring and layoff costs; workforce changes cause exponential increases in cost; C_2 is not exponential.

C_3, C_4, C_5, C_6 = four components of overtime costs; increases in C_4 and C_6 slow the rise in OT costs.

C_7, C_8, C_9 = three different kinds of inventory costs; increases in C_8 and C_9 slow the inventory cost rise.

ΣC_t = total costs over t periods $(t = 1, 2, \ldots T)$

Given by forecast

S_t = demand in units for period t; increases in S_t will reduce the net inventory costs.

Variables

ΣI_t = on-hand inventory minus backorders—end of period t
P_t = aggregate unit production rate—period t
W_t = workforce size—beginning of period t

13-7a Methodology for HMMS

The method for obtaining the optimal solution is detailed in the HMMS text. See Notes at the end of this chapter. The HMMS procedure uses the calculus of partial derivatives, which surpasses the level of math that is expected for this text. Optimum values of W_t, P_t, and I_t must be obtained for each time period, but the computational work is significantly greater than when this is done using LP.

HMMS is complex. It is costly to use. Solving the system of equations is mathematically arduous. Using the computer helps computation greatly. However, finding the correct quadratic cost functions is a large and tedious project in itself. If the cost equations are not accurate, but approximate, LP provides a better alternative.

How much difference will the use of HMMS make? There is no hard data to go on, but using LP properly allows good linear approximations of nonlinear functions. To illustrate, note how the LP model treats workforce additions (hiring) and reductions (layoffs) separately. The HMMS approximation, in this case, is less accurate. Also, there are additional techniques that can be used with LP to further the cause of approximating nonlinear cost functions.

Addressing the final question that was raised earlier, no organizations are known to be users of the HMMS model. This is probably because it is more work than it is worth—especially bearing in mind that LP and the transportation model can be used. However, the HMMS model provides important insight into the proper use of the alternative models.

13-7b Benchmarking the TM, LP, and HMMS Models for AP

The HMMS model stresses the need to get correct cost functions. It provides a basis for management to put costs under a microscope. The accounting department will not have a way to shed light on the real cost structure. Therefore, the discussion will entail a plan to obtain the actual costs experienced by the production department.

HMMS also offers a benchmark for comparison of models. Because it is not linear, and the other models are linear, management must apprise the consequences of making the linearity assumption. It is believed that the linear hypothesis is often quite acceptable. When is it not acceptable? That question has significant importance because LP and TP are often used by management to schedule production in the job shop.

On the other hand, if distortions from the linearity assumption are acceptable, then for ease of use the TM gets first place. It costs much less to use TP than HMMS. In this regard, LP gets a strong second place while HMMS is a distant third.

One immediate benefit of the transportation methodology is that data can be entered in an intuitive way. The rows are supply and the columns are demand. Shortfalls are readily addressed by the slack row or column. LP is more mathematical. The LP formulation of the TP is not an immediate transformation for a manager who is unaccustomed to equations and in-equations.

As a result, even though the HMMS wins first place for its more accurate depiction of the cost structure, LP may be preferred because the software to solve even large LP problems is available with Solver on the Excel spreadsheet. Where AP is used regularly, LINDO and other LP software are at hand with low cost and high reliability. See http://www.lindo.com.

In conclusion, it is useful for operations managers to suggest to aggregate planners that they examine all cost functions for linearity. When significant curvature characterizes a cost curve, the LP model should be designed—as much as possible—to take that into account. LP can be written to represent nonlinear cost functions, under certain circumstances.

SUMMARY

Aggregate planning (AP), an internal production management function, matches classes of jobs with the supportive resources needed to produce each of them. Its relationship to business planning and production scheduling is discussed. The methods for aggregation are explored. Then, three aggregate planning policies are developed and compared. These are level production, supply chasing sales, and combinations. Linear programming (LP) is introduced as a means of solving AP problems. The LP model is an effective means of achieving optimal aggregate plans; however, the linear cost structure may be a limitation.

Next, the transportation model (TM) is introduced for AP. It has the same linear cost constraints as LP. The transportation model for

aggregate planning (backorders not allowed) can be solved by simple network rules. With backorders allowed, the TM can be solved as an LP model. Then, the insightful nonlinear HMMS model is introduced and its second order equations, which can describe costs more accurately, are explained. The three AP models are benchmarked against each other.

Two Spotlight feature boxes conclude this chapter. These boxes illustrate real applications of the material in the chapter. See Spotlight 13-1: Changing the Way We Pay—ATMs and Smart Cards and Spotlight 13-2: Trading Stability for Mobility.

KEY TERMS

Aggregate planning (AP)	HMMS	Sensitivity analysis
Chasing policy	Linear programming (LP)	Sequencing
Constant production strategy	Loading	Standard units
Cost trade-off analysis	Minimum cost assignment schedule	Trade-off model
Fundamental theorem of linear programming (LP)	Planning horizon	
	Production planning	

REVIEW QUESTIONS

1. Why is aggregate planning used? What does it do?

2. What is meant by aggregation of units?

3. Explain standard units of work.

4. Explain the use of backordering for goods.

5. Give an example of how backordering can be used for services.

6. Explain the significance of "fill or kill" and give some examples.

7. Describe the system's nature of aggregate planning from the point of view of classes of resources and product-mix families.

8. Explain why aggregate planning follows strategic planning.

9. Explain the statement that aggregate planning starts a chain reaction in the supply chain of suppliers-producer-customers.

10. Discuss the importance of forecasting for AP.

11. Explain the planning horizon and the updating interval.

12. It has been stated that "For the average job shop product, the best planning interval would range from 3 to 6 months." Why might this statement provide reasonable rule of thumb?

13. Why do forecasts for aggregate planning have an advantage over forecasts for individual (disaggregated) jobs?

14. How can the effects of seasonal demands be taken into account for aggregate planning? Explain.

15. In some job shop industries, a smooth production rate is the preferred choice. Explain what this means.

16. In some job shop industries, the workforce size is altered to chase the expected demands. Explain what this means.

17. Compare smooth or level aggregate production policies with chasing policies. Explain when each is likely to be preferred.

18. At one time, the canning industry was totally dependent on harvest dates. As a result, major workforce alterations occurred sporadically. After careful study, steps were taken to smooth the demand patterns. What measures might have helped?

19. Explain the meaning of this question: How should P_t, W_t, and I_t be varied so as to optimize the systems performance?

20. What is a combination aggregate policy and why is it called partially chasing?

21. Explain how the trade-off model for workforce adjustment costs and inventory costs yields an optimal aggregate planning policy.

22. What is meant by a slightly chasing policy?

23. Describe the use of linear programming for AP.

24. What does the fundamental theorem of linear programming state? How does this theorem provide important guidance?

PROBLEMS SECTION

1. Seven jobs will be in the shop next week. The demand in units for each job (called d_j) and the production rates of the standard operator in pieces per standard operator hour for each type of job (called PR_j) are given as follows:

Job	A	B	C	D	E	F	G
d_j	600	1,000	500	50	2,000	20	800
PR_j	60	20	25	10	40	2	40

What production capacity in standard operator hours is required to complete all of these jobs?

2. Six service calls are on hand for next week. The number of steps required for each has been determined and is listed as d_j. The supervisor is listed as the standard operator, and his or her output rates in steps per standard operator hour for each type of job are listed as PR_j.

Job	A	B	C	D	E	F
d_j	500	400	200	150	2,000	48
PR_j	100	20	25	75	400	12

What workforce capacity in standard operator hours is required to complete all the service calls?

3. It has been estimated that annual demand for five types of soup that are made by The Big Soup Company are as follows:

Soup	A	B	C	D	E
d_j	900	630	240	1800	1,200

Also, there are three plants located in the United States. The most productive plant has been chosen as the standard plant. Its output is listed in standard plant output per day.

PR_j	6	7	2	10	25

The other two plants have indexes of 0.9 and 0.7. There are 250 working days in the year, and all numbers are given in thousands of cases. Is it likely that the three plants can handle the annual demand?

4. Using the information in Problem 3, assume that the two other plants have indexes of 0.8 and 0.7. Is it likely that the three plants can handle the annual demand?

5. Complete Table 13-10 for the 6-month period shown. What kind of aggregate-planning policy is this?

6. Compare the results obtained by completing Table 13-10 in Problem 5 with the results obtained from Table 13-5 in the text. Describe the similarities and differences of the problems and the results.

7. Using the information in Problem 5, what would be the effect of adding another person to the workforce? Specifically, this means increasing the number of workers from 38 to 39. Is this a sensible move?

8. Using Table 13-5 in the text, what would be the effect of adding another person to the workforce? Specifically, this means increasing the number of workers from 38 to 39. Is this a sensible move?

9. Using the information in Table 13-10 in Problem 5, calculate the total variable costs for the 6-month period. Backorders cost $100, and carrying inventory costs $25 per unit per time period. Hires cost $200 per person added, and layoffs cost $300 per person. The cost of an additional person working is $2,000 per month. Fractional payroll amounts can be calculated and used as well. In addition to stating the total variable costs, show the components that make up this value.

10. Using the conditions stated in Problem 7, determine the total variable cost. Compare this total variable cost with that derived in Problem 9. Present your recommendations concerning adding one person to the workforce.

11. Using the conditions stated in Problem 8, determine the total variable cost. Compare this total variable cost with that derived in the text for Table 13-5. Present your recommendations concerning the addition of one more person to the workforce.

12. Complete Table 13-11. What kind of aggregate-planning policy is this? Be as specific as possible in the description of this AP.

13. Write the linear programming (LP) equations for aggregate planning using $k = 500$ and the demand forecast of {17,000, 21,000, 17,500, 19,500, 18,000, 21,000} for the first six months of the year. What additional data is needed to solve the LP aggregate-planning problem?

14. There is sufficient data in Table 13-12 to solve this aggregate-planning transportation model. Assume that carrying costs per unit, c, are stated as dollars per month. Note: Because no backorders are allowed, this particular TM

TABLE 13-10	T	S_t	P_t	I_t	ΣI_t	W_t	$W_t - W_{t-1}$
An Alternative Workforce Pattern	1	340	380			38	0
	2	420	380			38	0
	3	350	380			38	0
	4	390	380			38	0
	5	360	380			38	0
	6	420	380			38	0

T	S_t	P_t	I_t	ΣI_t	W_t	$W_t - W_{t-1}$
1	340	380			38	
2	420	390			39	
3	350	360			36	
4	390	370			37	
5	360	360			36	
6	420	400			40	

TABLE 13-11

An Alternative Workforce Pattern

can be solved directly. Starting inventory, $I_0 = 50$, and final inventory, $I_f = 200$.

15. For the aggregate-planning TM presented in Problem 14, assume that carrying costs per month rise from $1.00 to $1.50 and overtime costs decrease from $3.00 to $2.50 per unit. Specify the solution and comment on the following question: How sensitive is the solution to these changes in costs?

16. Table 13-13 is equivalent to Table 13-12 in Problem 14. It uses the same data. However, in this case, the aggregate-planning transportation matrix *allows backorders*. Start with the result obtained for Problem 14 and see whether allowing backorders will change the result.
What is the answer? (Note that cost $b = \$1/$unit.)

17. Refer to Figure 13-8, which presents three kinds of nonlinear (second order) costs and one kind of linear cost function used by the HMMS–AP model. Make a table of (or plot on graph paper) the regular payroll cost per month for $C_1 = \$100$ per day. Let the workforce range between 35 and 45 workers.

18. Refer to Figure 13-8, which presents three kinds of nonlinear (second order) costs and one kind of linear cost function

used by the HMMS–AP model. Make a table of (or draw on graph paper) the costs of hiring and laying off per month where $C_2 = \$200$ per change. The workforce starts at 35 workers and grows to 45 workers.

19. Refer to Figure 13-8, which presents three kinds of nonlinear (second order) costs used by the HMMS–AP model. Make a table or plot on graph paper the expected cost of overtime where the production rate follows Pattern A but overtime is used to match demand. The costs are $C_3 = \$50/$unit and $C_5 = \$20/$unit, C_4 and $C_6 = \$10/$unit. Remember the relationship between P_t and W_t.

20. Refer to Figure 13-8, which presents three kinds of nonlinear (second order) costs used by the HMMS–AP model. Make a table or plot on graph paper the expected sum of inventory carrying costs, backorder costs, and setup costs where $[(C_8) + (C_9S)] = 40/$unit when $I = 50$. For this case, treat the sum costs $(C_8 + C_9S)$ as a constant. Also, $C_7 = \$30/$unit. Let I range from -50 to 150 units.

TABLE 13-12

Transportation Model for Aggregate Planning—No Backorders Allowed

	Sales Periods					
	1	2	3	Final Inv.	Slack	Supply
Initial Inv.	0	c	$2c$	$3c$	0	I_0
Regular 1	r	$r + c$	$r + 2c$	$r + 3c$	0	$R_1 = 100$
Overtime 1	v	$v + c$	$v + 2c$	$v + 3c$	0	$O_1 = 200$
Regular 2	x	r	$r + c$	$r + 2c$	0	$R_2 = 300$
Overtime 2	x	v	$v + c$	$v + 2c$	0	$O_2 = 200$
Regular 3	x	x	r	$r + c$	0	$R_3 = 100$
Overtime 3	x	x	v	$v + c$	0	$O_3 = 50$
Demand	$D_1 = 200$	$D_2 = 300$	$D_3 = 200$	$I_t = 200$	SL	Grand Total

$c = \$1/$unit per month; $r = $ regular production cost/unit $= \$2$; $v = $ overtime cost/unit $= \$3$

TABLE 13-13

Transportation Model for Aggregate Planning— Backorders Allowed

	Sales Periods					
	1	2	3	Final Inv.	Slack	Supply
Initial Inv.	0	c	$2c$	$3c$	0	$I_0 = 50$
Regular 1	r	$r+c$	$r+2c$	$r+3c$	0	$R_1 = 100$
Overtime 1	v	$v+c$	$v+2c$	$v+3c$	0	$O_1 = 200$
Regular 2	$r+b$	r	$r+c$	$r+2c$	0	$R_2 = 300$
Overtime 2	$v+b$	v	$v+c$	$v+2c$	0	$O_2 = 200$
Regular 3	$r+2b$	$r+b$	r	$r+c$	0	$R_3 = 100$
Overtime 3	$v+2b$	$v+b$	v	$v+c$	0	$O_3 = 50$
Demand	$D_1 = 200$	$D_2 = 300$	$D_3 = 200$	$I_f = 200$	SL	Grand Total

END-OF-CHAPTER QUESTIONS

1. A production and operations management class has turned to Section 13-1 of Chapter 13. The students discover that the title of that section is "What Is Aggregate Planning (AP)?" Initially, most students do not have a clue as to how to answer that question. However, after reading, discussing, and thinking about the material in this section, these students should be able to answer the question and explain when AP is used and what function it serves. Points a. to e. cover the subject, but one item is incorrect to permit the student to differentiate between right and wrong. Which letter marks the wrong statement?

    a. Aggregate planning follows strategic planning. Strategic planning determines the product-mix and resource availabilities. AP determines the production plan.

    b. The driver of AP is forecasted customer demand. When some orders are on hand at the beginning of the planning horizon, there is less probability of forecasting error.

    c. Because the application is the job shop and forecasts are being made for items that take different amounts of work and time, a separate forecast is made for each item.

    d. To be effective, the forecast interval has to provide sufficient lead time to allow the resource mix to be changed. In other words, the planning horizon has to be long enough to permit satisfaction of forecasted demand.

    e. The planning horizon might be six months, which is the shortest period of time that will allow actions to be taken in response to the forecast. Corrections of the forecasts could be done every three months. However, the corrections would apply to the 6-month planning horizon. For example, at the end of the third month a projection would be made for the end of the ninth month.

2. An aggregate-planning problem is no surprise to the Omicron Corporation. OC's job shop is based on converting orders (on hand and expected for the next week) into standard hours. The shop has enough production capacity to allow a 1-week planning horizon, and materials can be obtained within days. There are four departments that can do the same kind of general-purpose work; however, the newest department D(1) is twice as fast as the oldest department D(4). All of the departments are shown in the table where D(x) is the department number. The production manager has been running an aggregate-planning workshop for new employees. The list of statements in a. through e. are correct except for one of the points. Identify the flawed statement.

D(x)	SDH Index	SDH/Week	AH/week
1	1.00	54.0	54.0
2	0.80	64.0	80.0
3	0.60	20.0	33.3
4	0.50	18.0	36.0
Totals		156.0	203.3

    a. A standard department hour (SDH) index has been derived for each department relative to D(1), which is designated as the standard department (index of 1.00).

    b. Department D(1) is the standard department against which the other indexes are created. If any of the other departments work faster on some jobs than D(1), and slower on other jobs, then the concept of the standard department is even more applicable to such otherwise difficult situations.

    c. Actual hours (AH) per week are the real amounts of time that each department has available in the next week. For example, department D(2) is prepared to work two 40-hour shifts yielding 80 hours.

    d. Department D(2) works at only 80 percent of the rate that the standard department D(1) regularly achieves. Therefore, multiplying the index of 0.80 by the actual hours available yields 0.80 x 80 = 64 standard department hours.

    e. There is a total of 203.3 actual hours available from the four departments, but the method of aggregate planning requires use of the total of 156 standard department hours.

3. The Omicron Corporation has five jobs scheduled for next week. They are named *A*, *B*, *C*, *D*, and *E* (in row 1). The table shows how many units of each job are ordered (in row 2). The table then shows the production rate of the standard department on each job (row 3). Row 4 shows demand in units converted into demand in standard departmental hours. The production manager is very pleased with the results of the training program to date. Extending the pop quiz makes sense. What item listed in a. through e. is off-balance?

Job	A	B	C	D	E	Totals
Units ordered	300	210	240	1800	400	2,950
D(1) production rate	6/hr.	7/hr.	6/hr.	30/hr.	25/hr.	
Demand in SDH	50 hrs	30 hrs	40 hrs	60 hrs	16 hrs	196 SDH

a. Dividing the units ordered (for the week ahead) by the production rate of the standard department D(1) converts demand for jobs *A* through *E* from units into standard department hours (SDH).

b. The aggregation of entirely different order sizes and unit work requirements has homogenized *A*, *B*, *C*, *D*, and *E* into a common dimension of SDH.

c. From the table in problem 2, there are 156 standard department hours available for the coming week. Orders on-hand require 196 SDH. There is a shortfall of 40 SDH.

d. Because there is a shortfall of SDH, the problem is changed from aggregate scheduling to capacity adjustment to requirements.

e. Because there is a shortfall of SDH, the significance is that some order will not be completed. For example, if job *C* is not done, then standard hours of supply equals standard hours of demand.

4. Based on the data in Problems 2 and 3, and the conclusions drawn, it is not clear which job or jobs should be backordered in order to match supply and demand. The production manager has given the company trainees a matrix of production rates. These data, which are not in standard hours, were derived directly from the tables in Problems 2 and 3. The manager also prepared a list of suggestions concerning how to proceed.

   The trainees have been asked to study the list of suggestions, a. through e., concerning how to resolve the problem of too much demand. They are asked to consider using the good ideas and rejecting the one bad one that exists in the list. Identify the bad suggestion.

a. Derive the costs, revenues, or profits that count. If possible, go for the profits per unit because maximizing them is our goal and minimizing costs is a secondary goal. Once the profits per unit are obtained, convert them to profits per standard hour.

b. The suggestion in a. seems right, but if it cannot be accomplished quickly enough to deal with the situation for next week; find a heuristic that might help.

Matrix of Production Rates (units per hour)						
	D(1)	D(2)	D(3)	D(4)	Demand (units)	Demand (SDH)
A	6	4.8	3.6	3	300	50
B	7	5.6	4.2	3.5	210	30
C	6	4.8	3.6	3	240	40
D	30	24	18	15	1,800	60
E	25	20	15	12.5	400	16
AH	54	80	33.3	36	Totals	196
SDH	54	64	20	18	156	
Index	1.0	0.8	0.6	0.5	Difference	40

c. One heuristic that has been suggested is to look for the smallest number in the matrix of production rates and backorder that job. Here, there is a tie for lowest productivity for job *A* (value 3) and for job *C* (value 3).

d. Only part of job *A* must be backordered because it requires 50 SDH and only 40 SDH are needed to balance supply and demand. That fact may please marketing because the *A* customer will receive part of the order. All of *C* must be backordered. Probably, both *B* and *E* are poor candidates. If either is backordered, another job must still be chosen. *B* has only 30 SDH and *E* has only 16 SDH.

e. A solution to the problem is announced by the management science department. It has used linear programming to optimize profits. According to this solution, 40 SDH have been assigned to the dummy and that means backordered. The customer will receive a partial shipment of 60 units instead of the 300 units in the original order. Note that it was not coincidence that Job *A* with low productivity in D(4) was chosen for backordering. However, that fact played a part.

Final LP Solution in Standard Department Hours						
	D(1)	D(2)	D(3)	D(4)	Dummy	Demand
A				10	40	50
B	22			8		30
C	32	8				40
D		40	20			60
E		16				16
Total	54	64	20	18	40	196
Index	1.0	0.8	0.6	0.5		

5. In aggregate planning, information is essential for planning and forecasting at level one. The same can be said about information for decision making at levels two and three where aggregate units have the tangible form of being real jobs in the shop. An aspect of aggregate planning (level one) that is often overlooked is the advantage of forecasting for aggregations as compared to forecasting for individual components of the aggregation. Four of the following five statements concerning this subject are correct and one is not. Which is the incorrect statement?

a. Aggregate forecasts have less variability (uncertainty) than the combined variability of the forecasts for the individual components in the aggregation.

b. The variability of a forecast is related to the spread around the expected value (mean value) of the distribution. When a statistical distribution is postulated as a forecast, the mean value and the standard deviation (σ) are stated. Plus or minus one standard deviation ($\pm\sigma$) is related to the range that encompasses about 68 percent of the area of a normal distribution. If the range is $\pm 2\sigma$ standard deviations, then the area covers about 95 percent of the distribution. Two σ means that the forecast will lie within that range 95 percent of the time. This discussion is intended to explain what is meant by the variability of a forecast.

c. If n sales forecasts are made, one for each floor in a Sears store, then the variability of the n sales forecasts relates to the uncertainty regarding the exact amount of sales on each floor. Taken floor by floor, uncertainties add up so that a forecast of the total store sales would have a large range that would be roughly proportional to $n\sigma$.

d. On the other hand, aggregate the floors so that a single forecast is made for the store. This will have a significantly smaller range that will be approximated by $\sigma\sqrt{n}$.

e. This effect of reducing variability of forecasts through aggregation would not apply to forecasting sales for the year, as compared to adding together forecasts for individual months of the year.

6. The table shows the changes in inventory levels that occur over six time periods when a constant workforce is used. The policy of constant workforce was suggested to Alpha Corporation by their consultants because workforce alterations are costly to this technology-oriented company. The production team has come up with a list of considerations a. through e. The vice president in charge of materials management has faulted one of the points as being wrong. Which one is the incorrect statement?

		Constant Size Workforce				
T	**S(t)**	**P(t)**	**I(t)**	**ΣI_t**	**W(t)**	**ΔW(t)**
1	420	380	−40	−40	38	0
2	360	380	+20	−20	38	0
3	390	380	−10	−30	38	0
4	350	380	+30	0	38	0
5	420	380	−40	−40	38	0
6	340	380	+40	0	38	0
Total	2,280	2,280				

Note: $\Delta W(t) = W(t) - W(t-1)$; $P(t) = 10 \, W(t)$

a. Per unit time period, the cost of overstock is $10 per unit and the cost of being out of stock is $20 per unit, all per unit time period; the cost of the constant workforce policy is $2,600 over six time periods.

b. The cost of the workforce change should be examined. To do this, measure the effects of making an *incremental change*. Reduce the workforce in the second period by one person. Then, to satisfy demand, increase the workforce to 39 in period three and return the workforce size to 38 in the fourth period. The result is

	Incremental Change to the Constant Size Workforce					
T	**S(t)**	**P(t)**	**I(t)**	**ΣI_t**	**W(t)**	**ΔW(t)**
1	420	380	−40	−40	38	0
2	360	370	+10	−30	37	−1
3	390	390	0	−30	39	+1
4	350	380	+30	0	38	−1
5	420	380	−40	−40	38	0
6	340	380	+40	0	38	0
Total	2,280	2,280				

Note: $\Delta W(t) = W(t) - W(t-1)$; $P(t) = 10 \, W(t)$

Because the cost of overstock is $10 per unit and the cost of being out of stock is $20 per unit, the cost of inventory adjustments is now $2,800 for the six time periods. In addition, the cost of workforce adjustment is 2 times the cost of reducing size (say $150), plus the cost of one increase (say $250). The total of $3,200 is larger than the cost ($2,600) of the constant workforce policy.

c. The cost of matching production and demand can be calculated readily given that this policy is shown in Table 13.6 in the text. There are no inventory adjustment costs, and the workforce adjustment costs are ($150)(18) + ($250)(10) = $5,200. The chasing strategy costs twice as much as the constant workforce policy.

d. The preference of Alpha Corporation for the constant workforce size is not a surprise given the fact that workers can produce only 10 units per day.

e. It is unlikely, with these particular costs, that the optimal aggregate-scheduling solution will shift from the constant workforce to a solution that blends inventory adjustments with workforce alterations.

7. Linear programming can be used for aggregate scheduling. Some facts about this method are listed in points a. through e. Purposefully, one is incorrect and it is requested that the wrong one be identified.

   a. The objective function is to find the minimum cost aggregate schedule. This is equivalent to determining which production policy has the lowest total cost.

   b. Variables that can be controlled are familiar to aggregate planners. They are $W(t)$, $P(t) = kW(t)$. Changes in workforce size are $A(t)$ for additions and $R(t)$ for reductions. There are also inventory adjustments where $I(t)$ is the inventory at the beginning of period t.

   c. If overtime is used during period t, there is a variable, $O(t)$.

   d. Data inputs are $S(t)$, which are sales in period t. These must be known with relative certainty beforehand. Otherwise the LP will solve for fictitious conditions.

   e. Reasonable constraints must be written for $W(t)$, $A(t)$, $R(t)$, $O(t)$, and $I(t)$. LP must have constraints. In fact, the fundamental theorem of linear programming states that the number of active work assignments in the workforce schedule cannot exceed the number of real constraints.

8. The transportation model is a popular choice for aggregate planning for a number of reasons. Some of these reasons are listed in points a. through e. However, one explanation is off the mark. Which one is that?

   a. Transportation models are less mathematical and easier to understand and use than LP equations, which form an alternate solution method. In other words, these are two roads to the same place.

   b. Transportation models are useful in many applications of which aggregate scheduling is only one. The obvious use is to minimize the cost of transporting goods between origins and destinations. It is beneficial for management to be comfortable with the transportation model because of its broad application base.

   c. A disadvantage of the transportation model is that it requires a "square" matrix, which means that there must be the same number of rows as columns. If the rows are supplies and the columns are demands, then this constraint means that there must be the same number of supply rows as demand columns.

   d. The transportation model is a linear model, which means that the cost per unit is multiplied by the number of units scheduled to be made in a cell. This is not different from linear programming.

   e. The HMMS aggregate-scheduling model permits cost per unit to increase or decrease as more units are scheduled to be made in a cell. The great benefit of nonlinearity is that many "real" costs are not linear. However, the drawback is that the system of equations is large and the work effort is demanding. For most cases that are not academic, managers prefer to get a good enough solution without a major investment in problem-solving.

9. A transportation model for aggregate planning (TAP) has been created by AviationParts Suppliers, Inc. (APS). It covers two sales periods of one month each. The demand for period 1 is called D(1) and similar treatment for D(2). The model is named TAP-NOBO—because *no backorders* are

allowed. The X costs in the matrix are assumed to be so large that no assigned units of production will occur there. TAP-NOBO is being used as a training exercise for its job shop production schedule team. Their first task is to become familiar with the elements of the model and to understand how it works. A list of facts about TAP-NOBO has been circulated to the team members. They have been asked to separate true from false statements. In the list of a. to e. there is one false observation about TAP-NOBO. Which one is it?

Transportation Model for AP with Costs in Cells					
	1	2	INV(F)	Slack	Supply
INV(0)	0	c	2c	0	INV(0)
PR(1)	r	r+c	r+2c	0	REG(1)
PO(1)	v	v+c	v+2c	0	OVT(1)
PR(2)	X	r	r+c	0	REG(2)
PO(2)	X	v	v+c	0	OVT(2)
Demand	D(1)	D(2)	D(FINV)	D(SL)	Total

   a. The final inventory of period 1 is the initial inventory of period 2. Symbolically, the final inventory, called INV(F)—from the prior period, is the initial inventory, called INV(0), of the next period. The reason for setting a stock level at final inventory is that the job shop is expected to be able to fill certain kinds of orders on demand. Not all items are like that, so final inventory for some types of items is zero. APS should not be out of stock on items regularly (though sporadically) demanded by loyal customers. Without final inventory, there would be backorders. Customers would have to wait for the next production run in either regular time during the first period—called PR(1), or in overtime during the first period—which is called PO(1). The amount of stock that could be produced in regular time during the first period is called REG(1) in the matrix. The amount of stock that can be produced using overtime is called OVT(1) in the matrix. The same statements apply to REG(2) and OVT(2).

   b. If all or part of the initial inventory INV(0) is shipped to the customer during the first period to satisfy at least part of the demand D(1), no carrying charge is levied. However, if all or part of INV(0) is kept in stock to be shipped during the second demand period—called D(2), then a carrying cost of c dollars per unit is charged to APS for items shipped. *Customers are not charged.* The model charges APS, thereby increasing its total costs, which the company is trying to minimize. Similar considerations apply to the other costs that are in the matrix.

   c. For items made using regular production in the *first period*, there is a variable cost per unit of r dollars. Items made using regular production in the first period that are *not shipped until the second period* carry a charge to TAP of r + c dollars.

   d. For items made using overtime production in the *first period*, there is a variable cost per unit of v dollars. For items made using overtime production in the *first period* that are *not shipped until the second period,* there is a charge to TAP of $v + c$ dollars. Final inventory is charged for an additional carrying cost, e.g., $r + 2c$ and $v + 2c$.

e. There is a charge of X dollars per unit backordered. If an item produced in the second production period PR(2) is shipped to satisfy a first period order, then the backorder charge of X must be included as part of the total cost solution for the model. It is logical that for some industries X is not prohibitively large. If there is enough production capacity, fill the unsatisfied demand.

10. AviationParts Suppliers, Inc. (APS) has supplied data for use of the TAP-NOBO model. Conclusions about optimum schedules, which minimize total costs, are made in this phase of the training program. Team members have been asked to analyze the matrix of costs, production capacities, and market demands. A list of conclusions (a. to e.) has been published. There is one false conclusion in that list. Which one is it? As a reminder, the model called TAP-NOBO does not allow backorders.

Transportation Model for AP with Costs in Cells					
	1	2	INV(F)	Slack	Supply
INV(0)	0	$2	$4	0	10 units
PR(1)	$5	$7	$9	0	20 units
PO(1)	%8	$10	$11	0	15 units
PR(2)	X	$5	$7	0	25 units
PO(2)	X	$8	$10	0	15 units
Demand	35 units	30 units)	15 units	5 units	85 units

a. As a starting point, the team set up an initial feasible solution by simply making row and column entries starting at the top left and moving down toward the right (which is called the Northwest Corner method). This is shown in the matrix label *units assigned.* Next to that matrix is another matrix, which shows costs of assignments.

Units Assigned				
10				10
20				20
5	10			15
	20	5		25
		10	5	15
35	30	15	5	85

Costs of Assignments				
$0				
100				
40	100			
	100	35		
		100	0	
$140	$200	$135	0	$475

b. This solution satisfies demands and uses all production capacities except five units of overtime production in the second period. Those five units are assigned to the dummy market because supply is greater than demand. The total cost of this schedule is $475.

c. The question arises—is there a better solution? (lower total cost). There are methods, including linear programming and transportation network analysis, for determining, unequivocally, the optimal solution. These methods are not available at this time, but this is a small problem. There is a logical way of using cut and try to solve the problem.

d. Using the trial and error method, with some heuristics to help, four iterations were required to reach the solution shown in the matrix. The saving is $15, which is a little more than 3 percent.

Units Assigned				
10				10
20				20
5		5	5	15
	25			25
	5	10		15
35	30	15	5	85

Costs of Assignments				
$0				
100				
40		55	0	
	125			
	40	100		
$140	$165	$155	0	$460

e. The fact that only 3 percent was saved after so much analysis may indicate that the method is not robust and will cost APS more money than it is worth.

ADDITIONAL READINGS

[Aggregate-planning models were fully developed by 1970. Therefore, a few citations are early, going back to the basics. What is new is the software that can be used to solve large AP problems. Some of these are cited here. In addition, more recent references with present-day perspectives about mathematical programming are given.]

Attaran, M. *MSIS: Management Science Information Systems.* New York: Wiley, 1992.

Attaran, M. *OMIS: Operations Management Information Systems.* New York: Wiley, 1992.

Bowman, E. H. "Production Scheduling by the Transportation Method of Linear Programming." *Operations Research*, vol. 4, no. 1 (February 1956).

Excel Solver for LP solutions

Holt, C. C., F. Modigliani, J. F. Muth, and H. A. Simon. *Planning Production Inventories and Work Force.* Englewood Cliffs, NJ: Prentice-Hall, Inc., 1960.

Holt, C. C., F. Modigliani, and H.A. Simon. "A Linear Decision Rule for Production and Employment Scheduling." *Management Science*, vol. 2, no. 1 (October 1955).

Interfaces. "Special Issue: The Practice of Mathematical Programming." (15 articles covering various aspects of linear and mathematical programming), vol. 20, no. 4 (July–August 1990).

Lasdon, L., and A. Waren. "Gino: General Interactive Optimizer." (software), and J. Liebman, L. Lasdon, A. Waren, and L. Schrage. *Modeling and Optimization with GINO.* Danvers, MA: boyd & fraser publishing co, 1986.

Nemhauser G. L., and L. A. Wolsey. *Integer and Combinatorial Optimization.* New York: Wiley,1988.

Plane, Donald R. *Management Science: A Spreadsheet Approach.* Danvers, MA: The Scientific Press Series, Boyd & Fraser Publishing Co., 1994. (Solvers apply to LP spreadsheets).

Plane, Donald R. *Management Science: A Spreadsheet Approach for Windows.* Danvers, MA: The Scientific Press Series, Boyd & Fraser Publishing Co., 1995. (Solvers apply to LP spreadsheets).

Schrage, L. Lindo: *An Optimization Modeling System*, 4e. (text and software) Danvers, MA: Boyd & Fraser Publishing Co., 1991.

Vollmann, T. E., W. L. Berry, and D. Clay Whybark. *Manufacturing Planning and Control Systems*, 3e. Homewood, IL: Irwin, 1992.

Wallace, Thomas F., and Michael H. Kremzar. *ERP: Making It Happen.* 3e. John Wiley & Sons: New York, July 2001.

What's Best! The Spreadsheet Solver with Users' Guide. boyd & fraser publishing co, 1995. Quattro Pro, Version 6 for Windows, 1995.

What's Best! Version 2.0 for DOS. boyd & fraser publishing co, 1993.

NOTES

1. For archival purposes, one of the first citations was E. H. Bowman. "Production Scheduling by the Transportation Method of Linear Programming." *Operations Research*, vol. 4, no. 1 (February 1956): 100–103.

2. C. C. Holt, F. Modigliani, J.F. Muth, and H.A. Simon. *Planning Production Inventories and Work Force.* Englewood Cliffs, NJ: Prentice-Hall, Inc., 1960. This is also cited for archival purposes.

SPOTLIGHT 13-1
Changing the Way We Pay—ATMs and Smart Cards

A major revolution in banking operations began in the 1970s with the advent of the automated teller machine (ATM). The traditional customer-to-teller relationship was replaced by customer-to-machine interface. Although customers primarily use ATMs for basic banking transactions, such as cash withdrawals and verification of account balances, this was still a trust transaction. It took time for many people to feel secure in the loss of person-to-person contact. A growing number of bank customers have demonstrated willingness to pay for the convenience of automated banking because an automated relationship permits access on a 24/7 basis.

Banks view automated operations as opportunities to obtain significant savings in time and labor costs while extending banking hours. Banks obtain income directly from ATM usage (including surcharge) fees that they do not obtain with tellers. At the same time, the banking industry is searching for ways to expand the use of ATMs so as to generate new sources of revenues. For example, on-screen advertising is being tested, as is ATM use by customers for in-store payments for purchases. Additional revenue opportunities include airline passengers who are choosing to buy their tickets at (ATM) kiosks in the airports. Experiments with kiosks located in downtown areas can generate traffic for multiple purposes including deposits, payments, tickets for airlines and shows, and cash withdrawals.

Gas station customers have become comfortable making credit and debit card payments at credit card ATMs that can ask the customer "Do you want a carwash?" Wal-Mart, Home Depot, Target, King Soopers, etc., are developing customer self-service systems for adding up the bill, bagging, paying, and checking out. Other sources of ATM income such as coupon use, recognition of supermarket loyalty cards, phone cards, Mobile Top-Up (using mobile phones with ATMs to make payments—such as adding to balances on prepaid cards), toll booth payments including automated charging via RFID (radio frequency identification), etc., are on the horizon, or already in use somewhere. Over 7 million people use the Mobil/Exxon SpeedPass, which is an RFID tag that McDonald's is testing at some of its quick-service restaurants.

Most traditional ATMs are freestanding. Recently the most popular ATMs are through-the-wall models that can be fitted for either drive-up or walk-up kiosks. Outdoor units are now made that can withstand extreme weather conditions. Maintenance and repair costs are outsourced. Even transaction costs may be outsourced as well.

In Malaysia, topping-up a smart travel card (such as ez-link) involves a service charge of about 3 percent. In Singapore, ez-link is a contactless smart card (CSC) that has replaced the magnetic farecard with impressive operational results. "Twenty people can now board the bus in one minute using the ez-link card, as compared to 12 if they were to pay cash and 15 if they were to use the magnetic farecard." This "improves boarding time for buses by as much as 50 percent." The increased speed in fareloading

for rail is as much as 60 percent. The ez-link card uses an antenna and an IC chip for wireless radio communication.

Smart card (RFID) technology interacting with ATMs is changing one of the most accepted features of hundreds of years of history. Money may not disappear but it is undergoing major metamorphosis based on electronic payment systems. Wireless transactions allow secure identification because the smart cards transmit a significant amount of information using seamless communications between buyers and sellers.

In Britain, smart cards support dual currencies, i.e., the euro and the pound sterling. Also, new systems provide standards that allow the smart chip to have the same interoperability as the magnetic strip. Europay, MasterCard, and Visa have jointly defined an international standard for smart card payment systems that they have named *EMV* for the sponsors' names. The EMV card fosters secure transactions and ensures international interoperability.

The new card service can be used to shop on the web by means of an electronic purse, which is an instrument that facilitates payments between merchants and their customers. There is support for the notion that the electronic purse may soon replace currency in many routine transactions.

Level Four Software, Ltd. (a U.K company with its head office in Dunfermline, Scotland) has been globalizing ATM use. The opportunities for geographic expansion are great because the euro is common currency across most of Europe (the eurozone). Level Four's ATM Channel Development Suite can develop, test, and rapidly deploy *new content* across a broad network of cash machines. Their ATM Development Suite comprises ATM Developer (designs, configures, and tests new ATM content from desktop PC), ATM Simulator (views and tests ATM downloads from a PC, as if using a real ATM), and ATM Channel Architect (adds interactive functionality to existing ATMs). EMV Fast Track for ATM Developer enables smart card testing directly from desktop PCs.

From the Level Four website (http://www.levelfour.com/channelarchitect.htm), "Pressure is mounting from within banks to increase revenue from their ATM networks. Banks are reluctant to move away from their cash and dash philosophy." However, this reluctance is dissipating as technology enables our monetary transaction system to change.

Sources:
For Speedpass: http://www.speedpass.com/home.jsp.
For a global view of the ATM business, visit the industry association of ATM users: http://www.atmia.com.
For ez-link in Singapore, see http://www.ezlink.com.sg.
For EMV card, see http://international.visa.com/fb/downloads. For electronic purse information, click on "Joint Specifications for Common Electronic Purse Cards."
For electronic purse, also see the top of page 5 in the report written by John Wenninger and David Laster (April 1995): http://www.newyorkfed.org/research/publication_annuals/por95.pdf.

SPOTLIGHT 13-2
Trading Stability for Mobility

According to extensive and ongoing research from 1993 to 2003 by RainmakerThinking, Inc., a consulting firm in New Haven that studies young workers, there has been a profound "generational shift" in the American workplace, a revolution that has had worldwide effects. Bruce Tulgan, founder of RainmakerThinking, Inc., has focused his 10-year study on the employer–employee relationship. Between 1993 and 2003, he and his firm have studied trends that were first noticed in the early 1990s and were dismissed at the time as short-term aberrations. Bruce Tulgan's study points out the fallacy of that belief. Instead, globalization of business and technology, with its high-risk business environment, erratic markets, and unpredictable need for resources, has shaped new necessities for employers. The study states, "To remain viable, employers have been forced to adopt extremely flexible and efficient hiring practices. In turn, employees have adjusted by adopting more aggressive attitudes, expectations, and behaviors."

There is a sense of free agency among young workers who expect to create lifetime careers not with one or two companies, but as independent contractors, selling their services on a project basis to many employers. Each job change means a new negotiation, not only for pay but also for control of the working environment, balance between work and private life, and training for the next job. Free agents quickly realize that survival depends on keeping their skills current. Heather Neely, a consultant at RainmakerThinking, says, "They want to learn constantly because once they stop learning, they stop being viable." According to Tulgan, "Free agency has swept across the entire workforce. Skilled workers of all ages are trading stability for mobility."

The new work preferences are most highly developed in the 30-something workers who have never known a stable workplace and grew up mainly as self-reliant, latchkey children. Mr. Tulgan says that Generation Xers (born 1965–1977) are accustomed to facing problems on their own and have confidence in their ability to fend for themselves. If these young workers seem to be self-centered in their approach, it is prompted by a workplace without job security. "These workers choose employers based on benefits, rewards, and career opportunities. They are all *me* related, rather than where the company will be in 10 to 15 years," said a recruiter.

Peter Cappelli, author of *The New Deal at Work: Managing the Market-Driven Workforce* and professor of management at the Wharton School, has studied Generation X and their younger counterparts, Generation Y (born 1978–1986). In his opinion, both groups believe there is no reward for loyalty and are not anxious to make long-term commitments. If they are seen as disloyal and unwilling to contribute, the reality is that they are adapting to a workplace in which "corporations broke the old arrangement unilaterally. They've seen what's gone on with their parents' generation, and a lack of trust in the corporation is a perfectly rational response to that."

The current economy is putting the concept of free agency to the test. Unemployment is higher among younger workers than in the general population. Jeff Taylor, chairman and founder of the Internet bulletin board Monster.com, said that "of the college class of 2003, 93 percent are still looking for full-time employment (in late October)." They also seem to be sending out mixed messages according to Monster.com statistics. Although leery of company loyalty, many long for a stable and comfortable work environment.

Complicating life for employers is Generation Xers' attitude that everything is open for negotiation. Jeff Chambers, vice president of human resources at SAS, a software company in Cary, North Carolina, says, "They know they are mobile; they know they have opportunities." Recruiters have commented that these workers are accustomed to negotiating with their parents and bring this behavior into the office. Instead of accepting company policy, they will say, "Let's talk about making an exception" or "Let's change the policies." One healthcare recruiter said, "These people think outside of the box." There are pros and cons to such independence for operations management careers.

A frequent point of negotiation is the work–life balance. "No matter how bad the economy gets, these workers won't work in an environment they don't like," said Ann A. Fishman, president of Generational Targeted Marketing, a research company in New Orleans. They are willing to give up salaries to have quality of life in the workplace."

The trends are neither sudden nor exclusive to generational factors. The September 19, 1994, cover of *Fortune* magazine proclaimed, "The End of the Job: No longer the best way to organize work, the traditional job is becoming a social artifact. Its decline creates unfamiliar risks—and rich opportunities." Traditional jobs are disappearing because of technology changes, integrated information systems, a teamwork mind-set, and global diversity. Such issues interact with the generational factors.

Managing younger workers can be challenging. Short attention spans, cell phone conversations, instant messaging, or downloading music while engaged in job-related tasks can drive a boss crazy. Independence and the belief that one should be given special projects rather than dues-paying jobs can be annoying to an employer as well. All this falls heavily on the immediate supervisors of young workers, requiring more time and skill.

One employer said, "They are willing to take on tasks they have no knowledge about and they fearlessly march ahead." RainmakerThinking has a stronger statement. "Welcome to the real new economy: where employers must be ruthless to survive and individuals must be very aggressive to succeed."

Time will tell how well these young free agents and their managers will be able to negotiate a successful journey.

Sources:
Http://www.RainmakerThinking.com. Download execsumm.doc: "Executive Summary: Key Findings of Our Ten Year Workplace Study." (1993–2003), Bridges, William. "The End of the Job." *Fortune* (September 19,1994): 62–74; Connelly, Julie. "Youthful Attitudes, Sobering Realities." (October 28, 2003): E1; Coupland, Douglas. *Generation X: Tales for an Accelerated Culture*. New York: St. Martin's Press, October 1992.

Inventory Management

Chapter Outline

This section explains how to manage inventories of materials that have continuous demands typical of flow shop production. They also are materials that are independent of high-variety job shop end items. The economic order quantity model (called *EOQ*) for purchasing items and for flow shop replenishment of production line materials is developed. Then the economic lot size model (called *ELS*) is designed for intermittent flow shop production. Using these concepts, perpetual and periodic inventory systems are explained, including analysis of when each is preferred. The quantity discount model is a by-product of the EOQ model. It provides further insights for inventory managers.

After reading this chapter, you should be able to:

- Explain what inventory management entails.
- Describe the difference between static and dynamic inventory models.
- Discuss demand distribution effects on inventory situations.
- Discuss lead-time effects on inventory situations.
- Describe all costs that are relevant to inventory models.
- Differentiate inventory costs by process types.
- Explain order point policies (OPP) and when they are used.
- Discuss the use of economic order quantity (EOQ) models for determining the optimal order size for batch delivery.
- Discuss the use of economic lot size (ELS) models for determining the optimal production run for continuous delivery.
- Explain the operation of the perpetual inventory model and explain why it is the most widely-used inventory control system.
- Explain the operation of the periodic inventory model and describe the special circumstances that make its use desirable.

THE SYSTEMS VIEWPOINT

Inventory management encompasses the widest spectrum of activities related to materials. The activities include when and how much to make or purchase. Timing replenishments and decisions about storage are systems issues as well. Materials are used by everyone in the organization. That encourages the systems viewpoint. The purpose of having these materials is to create and distribute the finished products or services to customers. Suppliers are an integral part of the system. The materials can play a direct role as part of the product or an indirect role such as documentation in the office or food for the spirit in the cafeteria. This chapter focuses on an important aspect of the total inventory required by companies. That aspect is to focus on items

When business is slow, management cuts back on inventory. Note the empty areas in this warehouse. That may mean that some customers are going to be told that they will have to wait for delivery of the products they have ordered. Alternatively, inventory carrying costs are charged for inventory that is not turning over and moving out of the warehouse. Determining optimal inventory policies is another P/OM job.

Inventory: Stock on-hand for every practical reason that materials are needed to run an organization.

Lead time (LT): Interval between order placement and order receipt (including recognized need and write up).

that are used continuously and consistently for flow shop operations over long periods of time. Continuous need indicates such inventory is crucial to the strategic plans of the company. The penalty for ignoring the systems point of view ranges from substantial inefficiencies to costly chaos.

STRATEGIC THINKING

Without the systems perspective, everyone, everywhere will be ordering what they need as they need it. Lack of coordination diminishes buying power and loses the knowledge-based benefits of the centralized system. Strategic thinking is required to optimize the production plans of suppliers and producers to best meet the needs of their customers throughout the supply chain. In that way the lowest costs and best deliveries can be achieved for mutual benefit. The information system of a multinational company with a centralized inventory management system has to keep track globally of where everything is, where and when it will be needed, when to order it, and where to store it. It is an enormous system to manage. The strategic thinking that went into designing any such system must be robust and not casual. The need for change is always there when things do not work out as planned. This is revisiting the initial strategies.

14-1 TYPES OF INVENTORY SITUATIONS

Inventory is those stocks or items used to support production (raw materials and work in process items), supporting activities (maintenance, repair, and operating supplies), and customer service (finished goods and spare parts).[1] [This definition, taken from the *APICS Dictionary*, is just part of the definition that is written there. The rest is more technical and requires understanding issues that will be discussed in this chapter—which is devoted to in-depth explanation of inventory. The American Production and Inventory Control Society (APICS) is a professional society that has played an influential role in the inventory management area.]

Who manages inventory? APICS has established the fact that the management of inventory is a major P/OM responsibility. How to manage inventory is dependent on the type of inventory that is involved. Most types of inventory situations are best handled by well-designed computer systems that utilize as much centralization of record keeping and order placement as is feasible. The manifold advantages of the systems perspective with centralized buying includes the fact that larger quantities provide stronger supplier relationships, bigger discounts, a more informed choice of suppliers, and less chance for mistakes.

Each of the seven classes of inventory situations described here requires its own type of management even though they can all be centralized or decentralized according to the dispersion of use for producers, suppliers, and customers.

1. Order repetition—static versus dynamic situations.
2. Make or buy decisions—outside or self-supplier.
3. Demand distribution—certainty, risk, and uncertainty.
4. Stability of demand distribution—fixed or varying.
5. Demand continuity—smoothly continuous or sporadic and occurring as lumpy demand; independent.
6. Lead-time distributions—fixed or varying. **Lead time (LT)** is the interval between order placement and order receipt (including recognized need and write up).
7. Dependent or independent demand—when components are dependent on one or more end items, the information system must be able to calculate linked demands.

14-1a Static Versus Dynamic Inventory Models

To explain order repetition, **static inventory models** have no repetition. They portray "one-shot" ordering situations, whereas **dynamic inventory models** place orders repetitively over long periods of time. A few examples underscore the practical nature of this distinction between one order only, or a repetitive stream of orders for the same item placed over time. The introduction to this chapter noted that dynamic models apply to flow shop production. It was also pointed out that this was the primary focus of this chapter.

The pure static case also is called a one-period model even though under some circumstances a corrective "second shot" may be allowed. The "Christmas tree problem" is a good illustration of the static situation. The owner of a tree nursery that sells Christmas trees locally said that she placed her orders with a Canadian tree farm north of Montreal back in July. Reasoning that it would be a good year—because people were feeling more prosperous than the prior year—she had bought the maximum number of trees that her organization could truck and accommodate.

Unfortunately, the two weeks before Christmas were unusually rainy. This discouraged people from buying trees for the holiday. In the last week before Christmas, the owner had posted sale signs slashing prices. She felt that helped but nevertheless, 25 percent of the trees remained unsold on Christmas eve. Five percent of them were live trees that could be saved, but 20 percent would have to be scrapped.

The seller's problem: how many trees to order in July for next December? Most of the sales take place a few days before Christmas. There is no time to take corrective action. What is to be done if too few trees are stocked? Driving up to Canada to replenish supplies is impractical. Also, there may not be any trees left there to sell. If sales are unexpectedly strong, buying locally will cost too much.

If too many trees are stocked, the best alternative is to advertise discounts hoping to get anyone who was going to buy a tree to buy it from the overstocked dealer. The dealer never really knows whether the order size was over or under, or just right, until Christmas day.

Other static examples include the storekeeper who has to decide how many *Wall Street Journal* newspapers to buy for each day. Only one decision can be made to buy *n* newspapers. In its purest form, there is no opportunity to correct that decision based on later information. Another example is the problem of the hot dog vendor at the ballpark.

Consider the department store buyer who places an order in July for toys to be sold at Christmas time. If the toy is a dud, there is severe overstock. If the toy is hot, there will not be enough stock to meet demand. Both types of situations occur regularly. Another example is the spare-parts order for the complex machine. When placed with the original order, the parts are relatively inexpensive. When required later, because of unanticipated failure, the costs are exorbitant. This spare-parts model is a static decision problem.

In the case of overestimated demand, salvage value is sometimes available. For example, a department store that overbuys on toys, shipped from abroad in time for the holiday season, may be able to sell those toys at a discount after the selling season is finished.

Dynamic situations require different considerations because the demand for such items is constant. Orders are placed repetitively over time. The problem becomes one of adjusting inventory levels to balance the various costs so that total variable costs are minimized. Variable, in this case, means these costs change with order size.

Dynamic models apply to inventories that are used for flow shops, intermittent flow shops, batch work that occurs fairly regularly, and supplies that are used for ongoing support systems—no matter what work configurations are typical of the process. The models developed in this chapter address dynamic situations. Service systems use many kinds of supplies with dynamic demand patterns (as in hospitals, hotels, restaurants, theme parks, airlines, and educational institutions).

Static inventory models: In the static situation, how much to order is a one-shot decision.

Dynamic inventory models: Places orders repetitively over a long period of time.

14-1b Make or Buy Decisions—Outside or Self-Supplier

Inventory is either purchased externally or made internally. The decision about which way to go is dictated by many factors. Cost and quality are among the most important considerations. The choice is called the **make or buy decision.** Make is self-supply; buy is outsourced. One reason for self-supply is that profit paid to the supplier can be saved by being your own supplier. This requires being as efficient as the best of the suppliers (or nearly so). If the volume that the self-supplier produces is significantly lower than the volumes produced by the leading suppliers, it is doubtful that self-supply will be as efficient and, therefore, able to be justified.

Costs can be compared using breakeven analysis. Making the product has significant fixed costs—much larger than the buy option. The variable costs have to be low enough to offset the fixed costs of the investment. With a new process, it is reasonable to assume that variable costs will start high and gradually decrease. They may never decrease enough to warrant choosing the make option on a strictly cost basis.

A car company that has never made windshield glass faces an awesome task if it decides to learn how to do it. An enormous amount of experience is required. During the education period, which can last a long time, costs will be excessive and quality will be erratic. Vertical integration could be used, which entails buying a windshield producer. Vertical integration means buying companies able to provide components that are otherwise purchased from suppliers. The other option is to buy from an expert supplier.

Learning about new process technology—to be up to par or better—is another reason for reaching the decision to make the product rather than to buy it. Eventually, cost and quality advantages are expected to make the buy decision worthwhile. By learning, the company may be better able to deal with suppliers.

14-1c Type of Demand Distribution—Certainty, Risk, and Uncertainty

Decision problems that have certain outcomes do not have a probability distribution. Signing a contract to supply a given number of units converts demand from a risk to a certainty. Locating a supplier down the block reduces delivery time uncertainty. Generally, there is a cost for certainty. Because contracts reduce the producer's risk, the buyer expects the price will reflect this fact. The supplier that locates across the street from the buyer expects compensation for being at that location.

Sometimes certainty is a reasonable assumption. This only works when the degree of variability will not affect the solution. Then, certainty is assumed for convenience and it does not violate the spirit of the model. Linear programming methods and transportation models make this assumption. Lead time for delivery is often treated in this way. Say that two weeks is the average for a specific case. The variability around the average will determine if two weeks can be used as if it were certain. It is important that users of inventory models know when the certainty assumptions are allowable. When lead time variability could cause a stock-out, it cannot be treated as constant.

Buffer stock is stock carried to prevent outages when demand exceeds expectations. Basic methods of inventory dealing with order point policy (OPP) make assumptions about the demand distribution that get translated into buffer-stock levels. The OPP models on which Chapter 14 focuses are based on order point policies. Explanations will be detailed and differences with other inventory models will be highlighted in Section 14-4.

Uncertainty means that there is no good forecast for the probabilities of demand and/or lead-time distributions. When uncertainty exists, the probabilities for various levels of demand occurring are speculative. However, when there is a known risk, some planning can be done. Delivery of critical materials from the port city of Kobe in Japan always was totally reliable until the January 18, 1995, earthquake caused serious delays. Some companies factor such possibilities into their planning and can react quickly.[2] Another example is the 2003 strike in Venezuela, which led to an increase in the price of oil from

$23 to $33 per barrel.[3] There is a finite probability for various events and catastrophes, so having a team ready to assess the situation and find solutions may make a difference.

Order cancellations may be a less severe disaster, but they are usually costly enough to make planning for the event worthwhile. Many production departments have exposure to the risk that an order in process will be cancelled. Contingency planning for cancellations is better production management than reacting to cancellations after the fact.

When forecasting is difficult or impossible, systems are developed to search for advance warning. They are tuned in to whomever might have information about orders. Every effort is made to find the key players who originate the orders and to keep them in the communication loop at all times. Other factors that might trigger orders also are tracked. Efforts are made to gain some control over the uncertain occurrences.

14-1d Stability of Demand Distribution— Fixed or Varying

Uncertainty about setting the right capacity for supply includes the possibility that the demand distribution is changing over time. This could be caused by a stable shift factor such as seasonality. On the other hand, the drivers of change could also be unknown. In the latter case, the instability of causal factors is generally acknowledged to reflect high risk.

If it is known how demand is changing, then the risk levels may be controllable because forecasts of some merit are possible. OPP methods are applicable to predictable demand distributions. The best of these is stable demand but forecasts can be modified if it is known how the distributions are changing. Otherwise, the system is searching in the dark. Other methods than OPP should be used to manage these situations. Material requirements planning (MRP) is one of the most favored alternatives when the demand distribution is unstable.

14-1e Demand Continuity—Smoothly Continuous or Lumpy

Most of the earlier remarks also apply to demand continuity. OPP needs demand continuity that can be described as persistence of the stable demand pattern over a relatively long time period. MRP as an alternative inventory methodology can deal with the lack of smoothly continuous demand. It should be noted that assuming smooth and continuous demand is akin to converting a known risk situation into one of certainty. The assumption is usually valid and can be tested by simulating different patterns that are more or less smooth and continuous and measuring the extra costs incurred for assuming perfect smoothness when, in fact, it is good but not perfect. Such testing is most readily done with computer simulation programs. It is called **sensitivity analysis** whether it is done by hand or computer.

Sensitivity analysis: Allows diagnostic analysis of the effects of changing inventory costs.

14-1f Lead-Time (LT) Distributions—Fixed or Varying

Lead time is the interval between order placement and receipt (order need recognition and write up times are included). Variability of the lead time will be a factor in setting the size of the buffer (safety) stock. As lead times get longer, inventory systems become more sensitive to problems that can arise in the supply chain. One of the main reasons is that with long lead times, correction of errors takes longer. The more critical the materials are for production, the worse this situation becomes. For materials that are not critical, the assumption of fixed lead times does not do too much damage. When materials are critical, inventory planning had best take into account forecasts for the lead-time distribution. In that event, lead-time distributions will assign additional units to buffer stocks. Another name for buffer stock is safety stock because these units are held to provide protection against variability in demand and (where applicable) lead times. Simulation testing for sensitivity is advised for this situation as well as the one covered in section 14-1e.

14-1g Independent or Dependent Demand

Chapter 14 focuses on independent-demand systems. This means that orders can be placed for nondependent items without considering what demand is forecast for the end products of which they are part. For example, labels for a specific kind of jam are dependent on the demand for that particular kind of jam. Beach plum jam is highly seasonal because of the nature of that crop. This part does not meet the criteria for stable, continuous demand that characterizes OPP models. Alternatives to OPP should be used when dependent demand systems are involved. This is applicable for components and subassemblies that are used as parts of one or more finished products that have sporadic demand. The dependency is greatest when both the timing and the quantity for end-product demands is not predictable.

14-2 COSTS OF INVENTORY

The core of inventory analysis lies in finding and measuring relevant costs. Six main kinds of costs are discussed and then, in a seventh category, a few others are mentioned.

The six costs that will be discussed are:

1. Costs of ordering
2. Costs of setups and changeovers
3. Costs of carrying inventory
4. Costs of discounts
5. Out-of-stock costs
6. Costs of running the inventory system

14-2a Costs of Ordering

The best way to determine the cost of an order is to do a systems study of the elements that go into making up and placing an order. The elements are then given costs related to materials and labor used, space required, and equipment charges. It is easy to say how to do the cost analysis, but difficult to get the correct cost allocations. Assume that the purchasing department can process 100 orders per day but things are slow and so it processes only 50 orders per day. Does that mean that the cost of an order is twice as great when things are slow? It does mean that. If things stay slow, redesigning the purchasing department makes sense.

What is needed is the determination of the variable costs of ordering. How long does it take and what skill levels are involved? What should an order cost? The fixed costs of ordering have to be separated from the variable costs. Fixed costs are not changed by the order size or frequency of ordering, so they are not included in the inventory policy model. They are included in the cost of the purchasing department.

It is possible to evaluate the fixed costs to determine if purchasing is carrying too much capacity. Activity-based costing can help to ascertain an optimal size for the order department. If union regulations allow, purchasing people can do other things when they are not occupied with purchasing. This converts fixed costs to variable costs.

With variable costs defined, the systems study of the ordering process continues. It consists of writing up the purchase requisition form, making phone calls in connection with specifications, and ordering, faxing, or mailing purchase orders to the supplier. All costs that increase as a function of the number of purchase requisitions and the size of the orders qualify for inclusion.

Finally, a specific example helps to illustrate how the ordering cost relates to under-capacity of service orders. Assume that the order department now processes 100 orders per week. A new inventory policy requires that 150 purchase requisitions be processed in a week. It is agreed that the ordering department must be enlarged. The increase in labor costs, equipment, and overhead is considered to be an addition to variable costs. Thus, the ordering cost is determined on top of a base-ordering system.

14-2b Costs of Setups and Changeovers

When self-supply is being used, the ordering cost is replaced by the cost of setting up the equipment to do the run. This requires cleaning up from the prior job, which also is called *taking down*. The entire process is known as *changeover*, and the costs can be considerable.

A number of parts may have to be made before the setup is complete. The cost of learning is involved and defectives play a role. When acquiring equipment, changeover times and costs can be as important to consider as output rates. Flexible manufacturing systems (FMS) are notable for their ability to provide fast changeovers, but the expense of the equipment makes the costs of the changeovers high.

14-2c Costs of Carrying Inventory

Good inventory policy maintains the minimum necessary stock on-hand. When demand slackens, companies cut back further on their inventory. They do this because of the belief that the minimum necessary level is going down.

Also, inventory is a form of investment. Capital is tied up in materials and goods. If the capital were free, alternative uses might be found for it. The alternatives include spending for R & D, new product and/or process development, advertising, promotion, and going global. Some firms even put the money into financial instruments, the stock market, or the savings bank.

Expanded capacity and diversification are typical opportunities that, when ignored, incur the cost of not doing that much better with the investment funds. By holding inventory, the company foregoes investing its capital in these alternative ways. Such opportunity costs account for a large part of the costs of carrying inventory.

Inventory carrying costs are variable costs that depend upon the average number of units stocked ($Q/2$), the cost per unit (c), and the carrying cost interest rate that is applicable (C_c). These costs vary with Q, which is the number of units per order.

Inventory carrying costs also include the expense of storing inventory. As was the case for the ordering department, costs should be measured from a fixed base. The key is to find the variable cost component that is associated with storage.

These are the costs over which P/OM can exercise control using inventory policies. Thus, if a company has shelf space for 1,000 units, but can get a discount if it purchases at least 2,000 units, then to get this discount it must expand storage capacity. It can buy or rent additional space.

There are options for ordering large quantities to obtain discounts without requiring expanded storage capacity. One of these is *vendor releasing*, whereby the supplier agrees to deliver small increments of the larger order over time. It will be mentioned again in connection with inventory deliveries for the flow shop.

Another method for reducing storage space requirements is the use of *cooperative storage*. Commonly used supplies are ordered at discount in large quantities, stored in cooperative warehouses, and dispensed to participating hospitals, in the same metropolitan area, on an as-needed basis. Airlines share the storage costs and investment-based carrying costs of commonly used parts such as jet engines. Cooperative sharing reduces storage costs and increases the availability of expensive components that require large dollar expenditures.

Items carried in stock are subject to the costs of pilferage, obsolescence, and deterioration. These costs represent real losses in the value of inventory. Pilferage, which is petty theft, is characteristic of small items such as tools. Department stores suffer from stolen merchandise. Hotels lose ashtrays and towels; pencils and stamps disappear in offices.

Obsolescence may be the most important component of carrying cost because it happens so often and so fast. Obsolescence occurs quite suddenly because a competitor introduces technological change. Also, it can be the kind of loss that is associated with style goods, toys, and Christmas trees. Out-of-season and out-of-style items can lose value and must be sold at a special reduced rate. The determination of how much inventory to carry will be affected by the nature of the inventories and the way in which units lose value over time.

Deterioration affects the carrying cost of a broad range of products. Industrial products that deteriorate with advancing age include adhesives, chemicals, textiles, and rubber. Weather deteriorates iron and wood. Rubber gaskets in pumps can fail. Food is date stamped but even without that documentation the owners of restaurants are keenly aware of the effects of sour milk and stale bread.

Companies put spoilage retardants in foods, but increasingly customers avoid additives. Adding ingredients to prevent spoilage increases material and production costs while decreasing the carrying cost for product deterioration. The net market effect must be factored in as well. Spoiled milk and stale bread are quickly perceived, but customers can avoid buying products before they spoil by noting freshness dating information as required for milk and bread. Whatever cannot be sold because of real or dated deterioration is added to the carrying cost. Some drugs like aspirin are dated. Although drugs are vulnerable to spoilage, many people use them anyway because though ineffective they do not taste bad.

Some products that are not required to use freshness dating are testing its effect on their market share. Consumer advocacy groups are suggesting regulations that automobile tires be dated because there is age deterioration in tire materials. Freshness dating not only increases the carrying cost component, but it also increases demands on operations to make and deliver product as much before the freshness date as possible. Delays in getting dated products to market will decrease productivity and increase carrying costs. It remains to be seen for various product categories that do not currently show elapsed time, whether freshness dating has enough consumer appeal to compensate for the added production and inventory costs.

An additional component of carrying cost includes both taxes and insurance. If insurance rates and taxes are determined on a per unit basis, then the amount of inventory that is stocked will determine directly the insurance and tax components of the carrying costs.

Determination of Carrying Cost

Table 14-1 is furnished as a guide. Numbers have been provided that are similar to the carrying cost computations of most companies in the United States. Each situation is different, so the accountants and operating managers must assess those costs that apply to their particular situation.

14-2d Costs of Discounts

Accepting discounts by buying at least a certain amount of material involves extra costs that may make taking the discount unprofitable. An appropriate inventory cost analysis must be used (and is furnished in a later section of this chapter) to determine whether a discount that is offered should be taken. The extra costs for taking the discount are compared to the savings obtained from the discount. Extra expenses include additional carrying costs. Part of these carrying costs is incurred for additional storage space. Table 14-1 can be consulted for other variable cost components associated with holding extra inventory.

14-2e Out-of-Stock Costs

When the firm cannot fill an order, there is often some penalty to be paid. Perhaps the customer goes elsewhere, but will return for the next purchase. Then the penalty is only the value of the order that is lost. If the customer is irritated by the out-of-stock situation

Category	High	Medium	Low	TABLE 14-1
Loss due to inability to invest funds in profit-making ventures, including loss of interest	15.00	9.00	6.00	**Historically High, Medium, and Low Estimated Carrying Costs**
Obsolescence	3.00	1.00	0.00	**(C_c) for Components**
Deterioration	3.00	1.00	0.50	**of C_c as a Percent of the**
Transportation, handling, and distribution	2.00	1.00		**Product's Cost per Year**
Taxes	0.25	0.10	0.05	
Storage cost	0.25	0.10	0.05	
Insurance	0.25	0.10	0.05	
Miscellaneous	0.25	0.10	0.05	
Theft	6.00	0.10	0.05	
C_c Totals	**30.00 %**	**12.50 %**	**6.75%**	

and finds a new supplier, the customer may be lost forever. The loss of goodwill must be translated into a cost that is equivalent to the termination of the revenue generation of that customer. The specific cost is how much lower the *lifetime value* of that customer becomes.

If the buyer is willing to wait to have the order filled, the company creates a backorder. This calls for filling the order as soon as capacity is available or materials arrive. Backorder costs include the penalties of alienated customers. To avoid this penalty, some mail-order companies prefer to fill customers' orders with a more expensive substitute instead of creating a backorder. The outage cost is related to the decrease in profit margin. However, the goodwill generated by the gesture is an intangible addition to long-term profit. Depending on the system that is used (i.e., backordering, substitutions, fill or kill, and so on), various costs of being out of stock will occur. The lost-goodwill cost is most difficult to evaluate.

Organizations that are not close to their customers frequently ignore lost goodwill. This may occur because the firm does not know how to measure goodwill but it is often the case that the firm does not recognize goodwill. Many bureaucracies are identified as neglecting customer satisfaction inadvertently because they neglect the happiness of their employees who in turn deal with the customers. Disgruntled employees do not make happy customers.

14-2f Costs of Running the Inventory System

Processing costs that are associated with running the inventory system are referred to here as *systemic costs*. This category of costs is usually a function of the size of the inventory that is carried and the importance of knowing the correct stock levels up-to-the-minute. Costs are related to the number of terminals accessing the computer and people that are operating the inventory system. Operating costs also include the amount of systems assistance and programming that is needed. There are training costs. The amount of time that the system operates (round-the-clock) and the number of locations that are networked into the centralized data system (round-the-world) will have to be factored into this cost.

Systems involving many stock-keeping units (SKUs) are dependent upon having an organized information system. There are different SKU part numbers for each model type, as well as for each size and color. Part numbers for SKUs often identify the specific suppliers and where the inventory is stored. When there are frequent online transactions with many SKUs, the amount of detail is great and the systems are expensive to operate.

It makes sense to focus on the SKUs for materials and items that are critical for production. Also, it makes sense to pay special attention to items that have high dollar volume (called A-type) because they can waste the most money if handled badly. If the A-category of the ABC inventory system is large and if there are many critical items to manage, then keeping all the information up-to-date is both important and costly.

The status of work in process (WIP) can be monitored by means of *bar codes* and *optical readers*. Often, this technology and/or RFID (radio frequency identification) are combined with the concept of a paperless factory. There are significant advantages but the systems problems are formidable. Design and equipment choices interact with decisions about what kind of inventory system to use.

14-2g Other Costs

The six costs discussed here are generally among the most relevant ones in determining inventory policy. However, other costs can play a part in specific cases. The costs of delay in processing orders can take on great significance when a heart transplant is involved. Not quite as dramatic, every manufacturer recognizes the costs of delay when lengthy setups are required. Service organizations are sensitive to the costs of delay. Organizations set goals for the maximum time that can be allowed to elapse before answering a ringing phone.

The costs of production interruptions have previously been related to the critical nature of inventory items. Salvage costs can play important roles, as can the costs required for expediting orders. The costs of spoilage for food might be better handled as separate costs instead of as a part of the carrying cost related to obsolescence. The costs of central warehousing as compared to dispersed warehousing can be crucial. In various circumstances, one or more of these costs can dominate the inventory policy evaluation. A strong systems study will look outside the typical boundaries of inventory costs to spot those factors that are influencing the cost/benefit system.

14-3 DIFFERENTIATION OF INVENTORY COSTS BY PROCESS TYPE

Significantly different inventory costs characterize each type of work configuration. These cost differences play an important part in OM planning and in the selection of the best process types to achieve strategic objectives.

14-3a Flow Shop

With the serialized production of the flow shop, the cost of ordering is low. This is because orders for the same items are placed with regularity. Uncertainty and variability are very costly, and they are minimized for flow shop inventory.

The carrying cost of inventory reflects industry profitability. The reason for this relationship is that the carrying cost rate Cc is larger where reinvestments in the process or in marketing and distribution can bring excellent returns on investment. Out-of-stock costs tend to be severe. The line may have to shut down or run at some fraction of total capacity. For this reason, large buffer stocks are usually held in the inventory, in spite of the fact that carrying costs are high. Because of the large quantities of similar materials, purchases can qualify for discounts.

On the other hand, many companies—striving to be lean producers (low waste)—have made efforts to move toward just-in-time (JIT) deliveries of required materials. The goal is to count on trusted relations with few suppliers. The reliability of the supplier is viewed *as if* the supplier were part of the company being supplied. Serialized processes lend themselves to being well balanced and having synchronized flows of materials. Maintaining the balance is dependent upon the actual reliability of the supplier.

There is a loophole for JIT enthusiasts who want discounts. A large amount of material can be purchased at one time to be delivered in small quantities—JIT. This agreement is called **vendor releasing.** It is not available from all suppliers. Buyers must negotiate with suppliers to achieve it.

Vendor releasing: Supplier agrees to deliver small portions of the larger order on a specified schedule.

14-3b Job Shop

The cost of ordering is often high for the job shop. There are many jobs and a great variety of materials used in small quantities. The right vendors have to be located for new work. Quantities are too small to build trust relations with a few suppliers. Vendors may not value the business and take liberties including not delivering when bigger and better opportunities come their way.

It is difficult to get engineering and R & D's attention to develop new materials and components because the order sizes are too small. Carrying costs will tend to be lower than those of the flow shop to the degree that the job shop is less profitable. Overordering to provide protection against defectives leaves an increasing accumulation of small amounts of materials that are difficult to sell as salvage. This increases the costs of obsolescence.

14-3c Projects

Ordering costs for projects are likely to be high. Bidding, which is expensive, is often used. Project managers may have to buy from a variety of vendors with whom they have had little experience. Projects are unique and project purchasing is often not repeated.

For small items that are essentially one-shot, minimum effort is made to bring efficiency and control to the purchasing function. Carrying costs are relatively unimportant, because the inventory is quickly used up. Time minimization drives project management.

The importance of being on time with the project has led to the development of critical path methods. The computer-based critical path calculation facilitates project planning and reporting of project status. These reports to OM permit a great deal of control over out-of-stock items. Though such project-control methods are costly, they are warranted by the high out-of-stock costs. Critical path helps to minimize (or entirely eliminate) the number of outages to which the high out-of-stock costs can be applied.

Inventory management of projects is a unique reflection of costs related to work configurations. Missing the special inventory requirements of projects can be costly.

14-3d Flexible Process Systems (FPS) Including FMS

Flexible manufacturing systems (FMSs) have low ordering costs. This is because there is considerable homogeneity of materials used for products by processes. The variety of materials used more nearly matches the flow shop than the job shop. Flexible process systems (FPSs) have high carrying cost rates because of the large capital investment and the profitability of the technology when it is properly managed.

Out-of-stock costs are less significant than for the flow shop because FMSs run small batches. Other products can be made while waiting for delivery of out-of-stock materials. FMS lot sizes are small, allowing air delivery. Obsolescence of small amounts of inventory are less likely than for the job shop because materials controls are monitored by computers that run the show.

The FPS situation is a cross between flow shop and job shop characteristics. However, these processes have additional unique advantages that are directly attributable to the flexibility of FPS technology. FPS permits better cost control than is available for more traditional work configurations.

14-4 ORDER POINT POLICIES (OPP)

Order point policies (OPP) define the stock level at which an order will be placed. In other words, as withdrawals decrease the number of units on hand, a particular stock level is reached. That number of units, called the **reorder point (RP),** triggers an order for more stock to be placed with the appropriate supplier. These OPP models specify the number of units to order. The time between orders varies depending on the order quantity and the rate at which demand depletes the stock on-hand. So the order size is fixed and the interval between orders varies. This discussion is about one type of order point system called the **perpetual inventory system.** It continuously records inventory withdrawals. Most often it is used online and in real time.

Order point policies (OPP): Define the stock level at which a new order will be placed.

Reorder point (RP): Triggers an order for more stock.

Perpetual inventory system: The interval between orders is variable and the order quantity is fixed.

<table>
<tr><td>TABLE 14-2

Conditions for OPP</td><td colspan="2"></td></tr>
</table>

Continuity Requirement	Model Type
Static order	One-shot, single period
Dynamic orders	OPP
Continuous smooth demand	OPP
Sporadic demand in clusters	MRP

Demand Dependency Requirement	Model Type
Independent	OPP
Components dependent on end item	MRP

Periodic inventory system: The interval between orders is fixed and the order quantity is variable.

Next, another type of order point policy will be described. It is called a **periodic inventory system.** On consecutive specific dates separated by the same amount of time, the item's record is called up and an order is placed for a variable number of units. The order size is determined by the amount of stock on-hand when the record is read. It is the date that triggers the review and the order being placed. Therefore, in this case, the interval between orders is fixed while the ordered amount varies. The order amount is a function of the rate at which demand occurred in the period between reviews of the item's records.

This type of OPP has become outmoded in many companies because powerful computer systems enable the perpetual inventory system to be used. The perpetual system has advantages that will be explained. Nevertheless, the periodic system will be described for two reasons. *First*, it is used to order certain items together from the same supplier. This may be done by small- and medium-sized organizations to obtain carload freight rates because they do not have sufficient volume to fill a freight car with one item. They may also want to deliver a number of different items to retailers on a (say) once-a-week basis. Having a truck run to fulfill requirements of the perpetual inventory system could be far too costly. *Second*, some more advanced inventory models mix the use of the perpetual and the periodic systems with the result that costs are further reduced. Therefore, it is useful to understand the mechanism of the periodic model.

Economic order quantity (EOQ): How many units to order when purchasing items for batch delivery; needed to support flow shop production.

Economic lot size (ELS): How many units to make in a production run; designed for the intermittent flow shop.

Models such as the two mentioned here are based on the concepts and mathematical structure of an **economic order quantity (EOQ)**—the fixed amount to order, or an **economic lot size (ELS)**—the fixed amount to produce. An engineer named Harris in 1913 first developed the EOQ concept. Then ideas behind OPP inventory management have been expanded in many ways to give OM a powerful set of order point inventory models, but Harris' basic structure remains the same.

There is an alternative approach to OPP inventory models. It is called *materials requirements planning (MRP)* and is mentioned and contrasted with OPP. At this moment, the only point to make is that MRP is used when the assumptions about order continuity and consistency of demand that are required by EOQ and ELS are not met. Table 14-2 indicates when OPP models apply.

The most important of the requirements for EOQ and ELS (which are OPP models) are consistency of independent demand over time with relatively smooth and regular withdrawal patterns of units from stock. MRP works for sporadic dependent demand by using information systems control of messy demand patterns. MRP requires the information processing capacity of computers. It did not appear until the 1960s. When OPP is online, dealing with the perpetual inventory management of large numbers of SKUs, computers also are required.

14-5 ECONOMIC ORDER QUANTITY (EOQ) MODELS—BATCH DELIVERY

EOQ models, also called *square root models*, form the basis of most order point policies. They can be related to Japanese inventory methods, which stress small lot production and just-in-time (JIT) deliveries. EOQ calls for JIT when there is:

1. Extreme reduction of the cost of ordering
2. Extreme reduction of the cost of setting up jobs
3. Very high costs of carrying inventory

The Japanese inventory methods also emphasize supplier relationships to accomplish goals that are not directly represented by the inventory models—namely, high product quality, communication of impending problems, short lead times, and delivery reliability. These have all been converted into international methods for dealing with inventory.

How do the costs defined in Sections 14-2 and 14-3 operate in an inventory system where deliveries of purchased supplies are made at regular intervals? The quantities will be delivered in batches of Q units (the order quantity). Also, it is assumed that the production system uses up the inventory at a *constant rate* and that there is *no variability* in this rate or in the delivery intervals. Because of these assumptions, all units that are ordered will be consumed in a fixed period. There will be no salvage costs for excess units, and no stock-outages. Later on, variability in the rate of inventory usage and in the lead-time replenishment interval will be included.

The proposed conditions apply to many P/OM inventory systems. They are applicable to FPS and the flow shop, which receive materials in batches that can be small and delivered just-in-time. They also are relevant for the job shop, or the project or the intermittent flow shop, where the question arises: Should the entire inventory needed to meet demand be purchased at one time, or in several lots, over time?

Although it is assumed that consumption occurs at a uniform, continuous rate, it is seldom a serious problem if the conditions are not exactly met. The objective is to balance the time stream of opposing costs so that an optimal inventory procedure can be designed.

Figure 14-1 shows the relationship of the order quantity, Q, with carrying costs having the linear form aQ, which is called Line A. Figure 14-1 also shows the order cost curve having the nonlinear form b/Q, which is called Line B. Note that a and b are generic constants that will be defined for both EOQ and ELS.

As the number of units (Q) purchased per order increases, the carrying costs rise. This is Line A. As the number of units per order increases, the number of orders placed per year will decrease lowering the ordering costs as shown in Line B.

If the demand (D) for a particular item amounts to 1,000 units per year, all of the units could be ordered at one time. $Q = 1,000$ and only one order would be placed per year. The 1,000 units gradually decrease to zero from the beginning to the end of the year so that the average annual stock would be 500 units. Two orders per year cuts the average annual number of units in half to 250.

$$\overline{Q} = \text{Average inventory with smooth withdrawal} = \frac{Q}{2}$$

Figure 14-2 illustrates the continuous withdrawal pattern that is a critical OPP assumption.

Ordering Quantity Q

FIGURE 14-1
Variable Carrying Cost Line (A) and Variable Ordering Cost Curve (B)

FIGURE 14-2
Constant Withdrawal Order Policies for Q = 1,000 and Q = 500 units; Demand (D) = 1,000 units/year

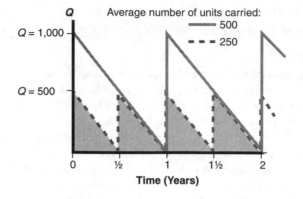

Figure 14-2 shows withdrawal patterns for two different order size policies both of which satisfy demand of $D = 1,000$ units per year. The first policy places a single order of $Q = 1,000$ units once a year. Then, the average inventory is: $\overline{Q} = 500$ units.

The second policy places two orders a year so $Q = 500$ and $\overline{Q} = 250$ units. Note that demand per year (D) divided by the number of units per order (Q) equals the number of orders per year (n).

$$\frac{D}{Q} = n \;\; or \;\; D = nQ$$

The progression is evident: as Q is halved, n is doubled. Figure 14-3 illustrates two additional continuous withdrawal patterns for OPP where the order frequency is increasing.

When $Q = 250$, $\overline{Q} = 125$ units, $n = 4$ orders/year.
When $Q = 125$, $\overline{Q} = 62.5$ units, $n = 8$ orders/year.

Although the ordering cost (related to n) is doubling, the carrying cost is being cut in half because the average inventory ($\overline{Q}$) is cut in half.

14-5a Total Variable Cost

Total variable cost is the sum of the ordering cost and the carrying cost. Thus:

$TVC = CC + OC$ where:

TVC = total variable cost; CC = carrying cost; and OC = ordering cost. The reason that TVC is used instead of TC is that only costs that change (are variable) with different order sizes are included.

The goal is to write the total variable cost equation and then minimize it with respect to the order size Q.

Figure 14-4 shows TVC as the sum of the two cost factors (CC and OC) previously shown in Figure 14-1. The curve that is TVC results from the sum of the carrying cost (Line A) and the ordering cost (Line B).

FIGURE 14-3
Constant Withdrawal for Order Policies Q = 250 and Q = 125; Demand (D) = 1,000 Units/Year

FIGURE 14-4
Total Variable Cost:
TVC = Σ (Carrying Costs + Ordering Costs) in Dollars/Year as a Function of Q

Minimum total variable cost (min TVC) is associated with an order quantity $Q = Q_o$, where Q_o is referred to as Q (*optimal*). Some components of the equation are already familiar.

1. The average number of units carried in stock is $Q/2$, where Q is the number of units purchased/ordered.

2. The average dollar inventory carried is $cQ/2$, where c is the per unit cost of the item.

3. The total variable carrying cost per year is ($cQ/2$), where C_c is the carrying cost rate, previously defined. This is the first term of the total variable cost equation written earlier.

4. The number of orders placed per year is D/Q, where D is the total demand per year.

5. The total variable ordering cost per year is $(D/Q)C_r$, where C_r is the cost per order. This is the other term of the total variable cost equation, TVC.

6. The time interval most often used is a year. This is consistent with the stability of the flow shop and the conceptualization of carrying cost rates and interest rates per year. Adjustments can always be made if needed. For example, if interest rates are volatile a 6-month period may be more accurate. It is essential that all time periods in the equation be the same.

Using math symbols, the total variable cost TVC is described as follows:

$$TVC = (cQ/2)C_c + (D/Q)C_r$$

This equation appears within Figure 14-4 where the costs are shown individually and summed.

The minimum value of TVC can be obtained by trial and error methods. Finding the minimum can be done visually using Figure 14-4. There is no need to use trial and error because the *minimum total variable cost always occurs at the* crosspoint *of Lines A and B*. This statement applies to all equations of the form $y = aQ + b/Q$, which is the structure of the TVC equation shown here and in Figure 14-4.

The minimum total variable cost also can be derived by taking the derivative of y, setting that derivative equal to zero, and solving for the optimal value of Q (i.e., Q_o) as follows:

$$\frac{dy}{dQ} = a - \frac{b}{Q^2} = 0 \text{ or } Q_o^2 = \frac{b}{a} \text{ and } Q_o = \sqrt{\frac{b}{a}}$$

By showing it in this way with just a, b, y, and Q, there are far fewer letters and the structure can be readily seen. This representation assumes that calculus has been studied. If that is not so, there is the graphical approach to derive the position of the minimum value of TVC (see Figure 14-4). There is also the method of setting the two terms of the equation equal to each other.

The general equation (in y) can now be applied to the derivation of optimal order quantity, Q_o, substituting TVC for y.

$$\frac{d(TVC)}{dQ} = \left(\frac{c}{2}\right)C_c - \left(\frac{D}{Q^2}\right)C_r = 0$$

Solving:

$$Q_o^2 = 2DC_r/cC_c \text{ and } Q_o = \sqrt{\frac{2DC_r}{cC_c}}$$

The same result is obtained by setting the two terms of the equation equal to each other. They are equal at the crosspoint. Thus, set $(cQ/2)C_c + (D/Q)C_r$ and solve for Q to obtain the economic order quantity (Q_o). The result is the same as Q_o, as shown earlier.

This square root inventory model is basic. It is the foundation equation for all inventory modeling of the OPP type and applies to flow shops, job shops, flexible processing, and projects. Note that human intuition tends to extrapolate linearly and does not empathize with square root relationships.

If one of the variables under the square root is doubled, what happens to Q_o?

As a specific illustration, if demand (D) in the numerator is increased to $2D$, it is not instinctive that Q_o should increase by $\sqrt{2} = 1.41421356$.

When risk exists in the system because of demand or lead-time variability, a version of the EOQ model can be built in which buffer stock is added to Q_o. Other alterations of the basic model permit discount policies to be examined to ascertain whether the company should take or refuse a discount. When inventory is self-supplied instead of purchased from an external vendor, the model can be converted to indicate optimal run size. This variant is called the *economic lot size (ELS) model*. In all of these cases, which will be addressed shortly, the foundation is the square root model.

14-5b An Application of EOQ

Assume that the carrying cost rate is 6 percent per year. This is quite low, which indicates that the prevailing interest rates on money are in the low category. According to Table 14-1, 6.75 percent would be an average figure for carrying cost rates in a low interest period. Therefore, 6 percent is a conservative estimate in a low interest era.

$C_c = 0.06$ per year or 6 percent per year
$c = \$0.005$ per unit (this is price paid for a unit of a bulk item—1,000 units cost \$5.00; i.e., items such as nails, napkins, and noodles)
$D = 3,000$ units per month = 36,000 units per year
$C_r = \$2$ cost per order

The total annual variable cost equation is

$$TVC = (0.005)(Q/2)(0.06) + (36,000/Q)(2) = 0.00015Q + 72,000/Q$$

$$Q_o = \sqrt{\frac{(2)(36,000)(2)}{(0.005)(0.06)}} = \sqrt{(480)(10)^6} = 21,909$$

This indicates that 21,909 units should be ordered at one time. This number could be rounded off to 22,000 without disturbing anything. To find the number of orders per year, divide demand by order size.

$n_o = D/Q_o = 36,000/21,909 = 1.643$ orders per year, or per 12 months
$t_o = Q_o/D = 21,909/3,000 = 7.3$ months between orders

$t = 1/n$ is introduced for the first time. It is the period of time in months that elapses between placing successive orders.

t could be calculated in years, or in other time periods. It is shown in months between orders, which is most frequently used. $D = 3,000$ units per month has been used.

Accordingly, n in months is calculated:

n_o (*annual*) $/12 = n_o$ (*monthly*) or $1.643/12 = 0.13692$ orders per month

Assume that the current ordering policy is to order 3,000 units every month to exactly match demand and approximate a just-in-time ordering policy. Call this a *demand matching policy*. How does the demand matching policy $TVC_{3,000}$ compare with the optimal policy, $TVC_{21,909}$?

$TVC_{3,000}$ $= 0.00015(3000) + 72,000/(3000)$
$= \$0.450 + \$24.00 = \$24.45$
$TVC_{21,909} = 0.00015(21,909) + 72,000/(21,909)$
$= \$3.286 + \$3.286 = \$3.286(2) = \$6.57$

The optimal policy always has equal carrying and ordering costs. In this case, they are both \$3.286. The optimal TVC saves a considerable amount, namely, $\$24.45 - 6.57 = \$17.88$. If the same kind of savings can be made on many other purchased items, total savings can be substantial.

Optimal TVC is 270 percent lower than the *demand matching policy*. This is because Q for demand matching is small, which associates it with the steeply rising (left-of optimal Q) portion of the total variable cost curve in Figure 14-4.

It should be noted that the total cost curve is steep only when the optimal ordering quantity, Q_o is small. Otherwise, there is room for the total cost curve to spread out on both sides of the minimal value.

The TVC curve flattens out as the order quantity gets larger, and from the sentence before, the TVC curve is flatter when the minimum point occurs at a large order quantity value. For the flatter curves, there is less cost difference between the minimum cost at Q_o and the costs associated with small changes ($\in$) in the order quantity. Measured from low values of Q_o, such small changes as $Q_o \pm \in$ produce large cost changes, especially $Q_o - \in$. Examples of both low and high cost sensitivity are illustrated in the Problems Section at the end of this chapter.

The application of the systems point of view leads to questions: Where should the 7.3 months' supply of these bulk items be stored? Will these bulk items age and deteriorate, or become obsolescent? Why is it that *matching demand* does not provide the just-in-time cost benefits that are so popular?

Small sums are involved. It may well be that the use of EOQ is not worth the bother. For this particular item, the annual expense is $36,000(0.005) = \$180.00$ a year. This is a C-type item in the ABC categories. The savings for going optimal are tremendous on a per unit basis but trivial from the systems point of view.

Now, the questions can be addressed. Where should the 7.3 months' supply of the bulk items be stored? The answer depends on the size, weight, and volume of the items to be stored. Thousands of paper clips can be placed in a very small space, and they require minimum care. If bulky items are likely to age, deteriorate, or become obsolescent, the cost of storage may be so great as to warrant ordering less. Logically, answers depend on the kind of items with respect to size and care. Some items are more vulnerable than others, and the carrying cost calculation should reflect this fact. Paper clips and pencils will be taken home. That adds to the cost of the remaining pencils. Cherries will deteriorate. Computer chips will become obsolete. Inventory management must be logical.

Why is it that matching demand with monthly orders does not provide the just-in-time benefits that are indicated in the popular press? The answer is twofold. The carrying cost, as reflected by the combination of cost per unit and carrying cost rate, cC_c is too low to rule out stock on-hand. In the example, the cost of half a cent per unit, and a 0.06 rate for carrying stock, together are so small that JIT is not called upon as a needed strategy. The *combination* of low unit cost and low carrying cost rate make matching demand with supply unnecessarily costly. On the other hand, low ordering and setup costs, large unit costs, and high carrying costs are foundations for JIT.

FIGURE 14-5
Contrasting Batch and Continuous Delivery Systems (A) portrays delivery in batches and (B) portrays continuous delivery.

Instead of EOQ batch delivery at fixed intervals, a serialized process that can deliver product (or services) on a continuous basis now will be explored. It will be seen that batch production is one extreme of this more general model of production. At the other extreme is continuous production that keeps on running. In between are run lengths determined by the same factors that drive the EOQ model.

14-6 ECONOMIC LOT SIZE (ELS) MODELS

Explaining the ELS model is best accomplished by comparing it with the EOQ model. ELS models provide continuous delivery of product (say, hourly or daily) instead of delivery in batches (say, every three days or once a week). The two options are pictured in Figure 14-5, where a batch delivery of 18 units is made every third day (called A). Continuous delivery of two units every day (called B) is the other option.

Generally, batch delivery is the result of batch manufacture where work is done in stages within the job shop. This is shown in Table 14-3, where 6 units are delivered every 3 days. Batches of work are completed in 3 stages. No units can be delivered until the entire batch is completed on days 3, 6, and 9.

The other possibility is that work is continuous using a flow shop process, and deliveries are made on a relatively continuous basis as shown in Table 14-4. The important distinction to be made is that the output of 6 units shown in Table 14-3 is only available at the end of day 3, whereas 2 units are available at the end of each and every day in Table 14-4.

The (almost) continuous output in Figure 14-5, case B, and in Table 14-4] could be delivered in daily batches of two. Some flow shops can deliver a finished product as frequently as every minute while in others it might be every hour. The producer might decide to deliver the continuously produced product in batches that resemble Figure 14-5, case A, and Table 14-3. Various reasons account for the producer storing continuous output for batch delivery. Among these reasons might be a JIT agreement between buyer and supplier. This JIT agreement could be based on lack of storage space at the buyer's site, and delivery economics where less than fully-filled shipping containers, trucks, or railroad cars are too costly a way to ship product.

Day	Number of Units	Stage of Completion
1	6 units started	Six units are one-third finished.
2		Six units are two-thirds finished.
3		Six units are completed and delivered.
4	6 units started	Six units are one-third finished.
5		Six units are two-thirds finished.
6		Six units are completed and delivered.
7	6 units started	Six units are one-third finished.
8		Six units are two-thirds finished.
9		Six units are completed and delivered.
Total	**18 units finished**	**18 units delivered in 9 days**

TABLE 14-3

Batch Production

Some of these points hold true whether the units are delivered by an outside supplier or produced internally. Production delivery systems are often designed to permit delivery of units only when they are called for by the user. This is called a "pull" system as contrasted to a "push" system. The pull system of production does not allow deliveries to be made to a workstation until that workstation calls for a unit or units of supplies. Some pull systems permit a batch size of no more than one unit to be delivered.

14-6a The Intermittent Flow Shop (IFS) Model

When a flow shop does not have sufficient demand to warrant running it continuously, it can be converted with new setups and changeovers to run other products. It is an intermittent flow shop where run time is called *online* and nonrun time is called *off-line*.

Figure 14-6 pictures the way that an IFS functions for one product. It shows the length of time of the production run [(t_1) goes from 0 to the 400th day]. The time that the system is free to run other kinds of units is shown by the negative sloping line [(t_2) goes from the 400th to the 500th day]. At the 500th day, production of the original product is resumed. The horizontal dashed line at 200 units is labeled *average number of units carried in stock*. This average value is determined by the production rate, the run time, and the demand rate. In the figure, there is another horizontal dashed line at 400 units. It is labeled *maximum storage required*. The size of the storage facility that is required to accommodate units at their stock-level peak is of practical importance. Peak storage quantity occurs just as the production system goes off-line for the original product and switches to another product.

Day	Number of Units	Stage of Completion
1	2 units started	Two units are finished and delivered.
2	2 units started	Two units are finished and delivered.
3	2 units started	Two units are finished and delivered.
4	2 units started	Two units are finished and delivered.
5	2 units started	Two units are finished and delivered.
6	2 units started	Two units are finished and delivered.
7	2 units started	Two units are finished and delivered.
8	2 units started	Two units are finished and delivered.
9	2 units started	Two units are finished and delivered.
Total	**18 units finished**	**18 units delivered in 9 days**

TABLE 14-4

Continuous Production

FIGURE 14-6
The Operation of the Economic Lot Size (ELS) Model for Intermittent Flow Shop Planning

FIGURE 14-6
The Operation of the Economic Lot Size (ELS) Model for Intermittent Flow Shop Planning

Note that Figure 14-6 shows the production rate. The production rate line has a greater slope than the unit accumulation rate line (positive slope between 0 and 400). This is because the net rate of addition to stock on-hand must account for the daily withdrawals from inventories that are being made.

The ELS model portrays intermittent production with continuous deliveries. The stock level continuously increases until the apex is reached, which sets the maximum storage requirement. Then, stock on-hand begins to decrease because production for the item is off-line. Eventually, stock on-hand (SOH) reaches zero (or some protected level of stock—if buffer units are held for service safety reasons).

Next comes the math formulation of the economic lot size (ELS) model. This model gets its name from the fact that the production run quantity is called a *lot*. The model will be used to determine the optimal production lot size, which translates into run time as a function of the production output rate. The model also can be used to study the effect of varying the production rate.

First, read the caption of Figure 14-7. Then, it may be evident that if the production output rate per unit time (p) is increased, then the positive slope of the line rising to the apex increases. In other words, the left side of the SOH triangle rises faster. Also, the production rate dashed line (in Figure 14-6) rises faster.

This means that run time could be shortened leaving longer free times on the production line for other products. Furthermore, note that as the slope of the left side of the SOH triangle increases—rising faster—this triangle looks more and more like the right triangles that characterize EOQ batch models (see Figures 14-2 and 14-3).

Figure 14-7 shows the ELS triangle divided into two right triangles called A and B. The upward slope of the left side of the A triangle represents the net rate of accumulation of the stock on-hand. It is the production rate per day (p) minus the demand rate per day (d), which is labeled ($p - d$). That rate of net accumulation lasts for a time interval labeled t_1.

FIGURE 14-7
The ELS triangle is divided into two right triangles called *A* and *B*: A shows stock accumulation at the rate of ($p - d$), and B reflects continuous deliveries at the rate of (d) units per time period.

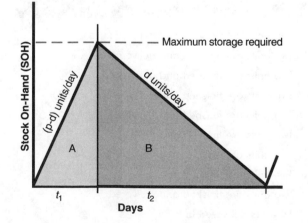

The downward slope of the right side of the B triangle represents the demand per day (d). There is no production going on during that interval called t_2. Although other production activities are going on, their graphs are not displayed. Each of them would have an A-type triangle to represent net accumulation of the particular item that is sharing the production line with the item in Figure 14-7.

The ELS model's ability to determine optimal production run size seems of primary interest to suppliers and producers. The EOQ model's calculation of the optimal order quantity would seem to be of primary interest to buyers and customers. The systems perspective refutes this concept of limited self-interest. The ability of suppliers and producers to obtain minimum cost solutions via adequate production runs operates to the advantage of buyers and customers. The benefits of lower costs and satisfactory delivery times create new markets and get passed on to the customers. The buyer's EOQ solution and the supplier's ELS solution should be complementary and congruent.

The ELS model can provide continuous JIT-type delivery with intermittent production. The discontinuity in production is behind the scenes. This characterizes flexible production systems and intermittent flow shops designed to run one item, and then change over to run another item, using the same or similar equipment, the same workstations, and the same workers. The ELS solution is increasingly encountered with flexible NC, CNC, and other computer-controlled equipment. Because of the ability to change over more rapidly and at lower cost than manually, the economic lot size can be reduced.

The ELS model can run the gamut from the continuous production of the flow shop to short production runs. When the supplier delivers the economic order quantity to the buyer, the production of the required batch can be thought of as being instantaneous. The ELS math model developed here shows the broad range of these properties.

The cost of preparing to produce a product or to provide a service (run the lot) includes setup costs, C_S. Setup costs are producers' costs for preparing the process to do the job. Setup costs are generally significantly larger than order costs that are experienced when buying from suppliers. However, when dealing with FPS (flexible process systems) the setups are pre-engineered. The costs are not repetitive. The ability to achieve rapid setups at low costs, C_S, is the result of large original investments in design and engineering prior to building the equipment.

Setup costs are composed of two main parts:

1. Cost of labor that is required to prepare the facility for the new production run

2. Cost of lost production created by the facility's downtime while being prepared for the new job

Optimal run size is derived in a manner similar to the derivation of the economic order quantity. Many of the variables are the same. Two new variables include p and d, previously mentioned.

Thus:

p = production rate in units per day
d = demand rate in units per day

The total variable cost equation is

$$TVC = \left(\frac{cQ}{2}\right)\left(\frac{p-d}{p}\right)C_c + \left(\frac{D}{Q}\right)C_S$$

where

$$\left(\frac{p-d}{p}\right)\left(\frac{Q}{2}\right) = \text{the average number of units carried in the inventory}$$

As with the EOQ model, the minimum total cost can be derived by taking the derivative of TVC for ELS, setting it equal to zero, and solving for the optimal value, Q_o, as follows:

$$\frac{d(TVC)}{dQ} = \left(\frac{c}{2}\right)\left(\frac{p-d}{p}\right)C_c - \left(\frac{D}{Q^2}\right)C_S = 0$$

$$Q_o^2 = \left(\frac{2DC_S}{cC_c}\right)\left(\frac{p}{p-d}\right) \text{ and } Q_o = \sqrt{\left(\frac{2DC_S}{cC_c}\right)\frac{p}{p-d}}$$

Alternatively, setting the two terms of the ELS equation for TVC equal to each other produces the same result because minimum TVC occurs at the Q_o value where the two lines in Figure 14-4 cross.

Production run size is $Q_o = pt_1$ (where t_1 = run time or online time). Solve for t_1 as shown in Equation 14-1:

$$t_1 = \frac{Q_o}{p} \tag{Equation 14-1}$$

Total time t is required for each complete cycle; thus, $t = t_1 + t_2$ where t_2 is the off-line time. Because the run size (Q_o) must satisfy demand for the entire period t, it follows that: $Q_o = dt$. Then:

$$t = \frac{Q_o}{d} \tag{Equation 14-2}$$

Subtracting Equation 14-1 from Equation 14-2 yields the off-line time:

$$t_2 = t - t_1 = \frac{Q_o}{d} - \frac{Q_o}{p} = Q_o\left(\frac{p-d}{pd}\right)$$

Figure 14-6 provides graphic meaning to the online (t_1) and off-line (t_2) intervals that have been described for the fundamental relationships of ELS.

14-6b An Application of ELS

Units of different colors are to be made on new equipment using an intermittent flow shop that runs 250 days per year. Different colors are run successively on the same line. Production capacity for all units run on the same line is 1,800 units per day. Blue has the largest market share.

Data for blue have been assembled as follows:

Yearly demand for blue = D = 200,000 units per year; and $D = 250d$
Daily demand for blue = d = 800 units per day = $D/250$
Daily production of blue = p = 1800 units per day
Setup cost for blue = C_s = \$20 per setup
Carrying cost rate = C_c = 0.15 of the unit cost per year
Cost of blue = c = \$0.06 per unit

Calculating the optimal lot size:

$$Q_o = \sqrt{\frac{(2)(200,000)(20)(1800)}{(0.06)(0.15)(1000)}} = \sqrt{\frac{(144)(10)^8}{(9)}} = \frac{(12)(10)^4}{3}$$

$$= 40,000 \text{ units}$$

Production run time (t_1) for blue is

$$t_1 = \frac{Q_o}{p} = \frac{40,000}{1,800} = 22.22 \text{ days}$$

Cycle period (t) is determined:

$$t = t_1 + t_2 = \frac{Q_o}{d} = \frac{40,000}{800} = 50 \text{ days}$$

Off-line period between runs is

$$t_2 = Q_o\left(\frac{p-d}{pd}\right) = 40{,}000\left(\frac{1000}{800 \times 1800}\right) = 27.78 \text{ days}$$

This means that 22 days (rounding) are required for the blue run and $50 - 22 = 28$ days (rounding) are available for other colors. The problem of *fitting mixed-model systems* on the same production line is seldom easy. An approach that is used is to start with the individual product optimal assignments. Then modify them with the "cut and try" method. More sophisticated mathematical models also can be used.

When can all of the items of a mixed-model set achieve optimal runs that minimize each of their TVCs? The answer is when there is enough extra capacity so that none of the items (say, colors) are constrained. When demand levels overtax the existing capacity of a mixed-model flow line, it is rare that each item of a mixed-model set can have an optimal run.

For this example, blue is optimal when it has control of 44 percent of the flow shop time. Note: $22.22/50 = 0.44$. If red and green split the remaining time equally, each would have about 28 percent of the available time.

Imagine what would happen if blue, red, and yellow had very similar characteristics. How could all three items be run on the same system? The only way that they can all be run is by cutting down on the run sizes. This means that each of the items will have TVCs that are suboptimal. Thus, overall costs for the system will be minimized but each item would have lower costs if there were no resource constraints. The best that can be done is to achieve the systems' optimal, which is less than the sum of the individual item optimals.

14-6c From EOQ Through ELS to Continuous Production

The ELS equation for optimal run size:

$$Q_o = \sqrt{\left(\frac{2DC_S}{cC_c}\right)\left(\frac{p}{p-d}\right)}$$

lends itself to analysis of extremes. First, if d is almost equal to p, then $(p-d)$ approaches zero. This means that Q_o becomes very large.

$$Q_o \to \infty \text{ as } (p-d) \to 0$$

Numbers grow infinitely large as the denominator of a fraction approaches zero. The conclusion is that if the demand rate is as great as the production rate, then the process should be run continuously. There is no inventory buildup. The slope of the line in Figure 14-8 is near zero. The stock on-hand runs almost flat against the time axis.

On the other hand, if p is much greater than d, i.e., $(p >>> d)$, then

$$Q_o = \sqrt{\frac{2DC_S}{cC_c}}$$

FIGURE 14-8
The ELS model indicates almost continuous production should be used as $(p - d)$ approaches zero.

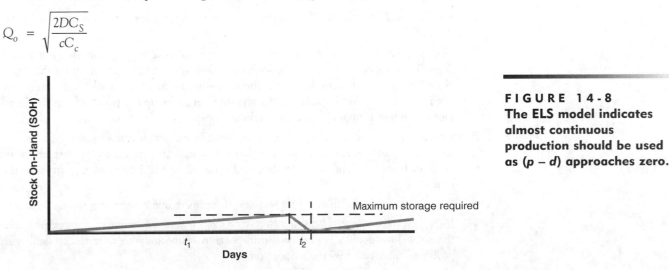

FIGURE 14-9
Lead Time Determines the Reorder Point for Both EOQ and ELS Models
Legend: Lead time = *LT*;
Reorder Point = Q_{RP}

This approaches the EOQ model with setup cost, C_s, instead of order cost, C_r. Stock on-hand rises perpendicularly, as in Figures 14-2 and 14-3, or almost perpendicularly, as in Figure 14-7. This producer can supply the entire order quantity, Q_o, as a batch, on demand, but with a lead time because other jobs are competing for the same equipment. Although this order is internal, this is similar to ordering from outside suppliers.

Between the two extremes for p and d described earlier, many online and off-line combinations of production levels are feasible.

14-6d Lead-Time Determination

Lead time (LT) is the interval that elapses between the recognition that an order should be placed and the delivery of that order. For both EOQ and ELS models, required lead times can be identified by studying the respective graphs. Graphs for EOQ and ELS are shown in Figure 14-9.

First, note how the diminishing stock level reaches a threshold called Q_{RP} on both diagrams. Q_{RP} stands for the stock level of the reorder point. That threshold triggers the order for replenishment. The level of stock that is at the reorder point, *RP*, is based on having enough stock on-hand to meet orders until the replenishment supply arrives. The interval between reordering and receiving that order, with units ready for use, is called the lead time (LT). Figure 14-9 shows the graphical relationship between Q_{RP} and *LT*.

Consider eight components of lead time (LT) for the EOQ case.

1. *The amount of time that is needed for recognition of the fact that it is time to reorder.* If the reorder point is monitored continuously, then this period is as close to zero time as the system permits. If the stock level is read at intervals, then the average interval for noting that the reorder point has been reached is part of the LT interval.

2. *The interval for doing whatever clerical work is needed to prepare the order.* This includes determining how much to order and from whom to order. It might even include preparing for bidding. If multiple suppliers are to be used, this also includes determining how to divide the order.

3. *Mail or telephone intervals for communicating with the supplier (or suppliers) and placing the order.*

4. *How long will it take for the supplier's organization to react to the placement of an order?* This necessitates communication with everyone who participates in filling the order. How long does it take to find out if the requested items are in stock? If the items are not in stock, how long will it take for the supplier to set up the process to make them? How long will it take to produce, pack, and ship?

5. *Delivery time includes loading, transit, and unloading times.* If transshipment is needed, the period must be extended to take that into account. This period begins when the product leaves the supplier's control and ends when the buyer takes control of the items.

6. *Processing of delivered items by the receiving department and determining storage locations.*

7. *Inspection to be sure that items match specifications is generally required.* Checking quantity as well as quality is part of the inspection. Time may be required to deal with problems uncovered by the inspection.

8. *Record-keeping computer time is needed to enter items in the warehouse stock records.* It also is needed to transport the items to the warehouse and to store them properly.

All eight of these lead-time components add together to form the total lead time. Determination of good lead-time estimates requires awareness of all relevant systems factors. Put another way, proper lead-time determination requires a systems study that traces out all contributing factors including the averages and variances of these factors. A similar set of steps applies to using ELS for production run schedules.

14-6e Expediting to Control Lead Time

Expediting is part of the OM function. It is used to control and improve lead times in the plant, in the office, and with outside suppliers and shippers. Expediting is the process of keeping track of the state of an order. It includes reminding and following up with anyone who could be delaying order processing.

Expediters are accountable for making certain that due dates are met. Often, there are many dates and places to be tracked. For example, the Association of American Railroads (AAR) uses data tags (radio transponders called automatic equipment identification—AEI) to provide car location messages (CLM). Transport Canada (TC) uses integrated AEI/OCR (optical character recognition). Both systems provide standardized location information about all railroad boxcars. This is the first step—knowing where things are geographically. Tracking orders in a supplier's factory permits knowledge about the degree of completion of the order.

Expediters also are trained to prevent and remedy problems. Delays are addressed as to causes and corrections. Using information systems to track and evaluate situations, the expediters know how to take action and when to use special capabilities (such as using FedEx) to speed things up.

There is specific contingency training required in the use of equipment such as radio frequency identification (rfid) systems and techniques to take effective action. Such expediting techniques are frequently used in project management where slippage along time lines is considered to carry very high monetary penalties.

14-6f Lead-Time Variability

Lead times are usually variable. There are delays of varying length in each of the eight lead-time components listed earlier. When variance is significant, estimates must be made of the degree of variability.

Appropriate steps should be taken to include the effects of variability in the analyses. Expediting can be considered management's attention to decrease delays (Latin, 15th Century; *expeditus*). It is also the effort to decrease variability. Expediting deals with the causes of variability and attempts to keep those causes under control so that due dates can be met. Expediters strive to keep management and suppliers informed about slippage (due dates that will not be met). Expediting is delay control for lead times, but it also applies to project activities. In addition, expediting is also information dissemination so that all participants are aware of what is happening.

Although lead times are usually variable, they are often treated as if they were fixed, single values. There are two reasons for this:

1. The amount of variability is considered to be small and relatively negligible.
2. It is complex to assume variable demand and variable LT simultaneously.

Then, to take variable lead time into account in a quick and easy way, the idea of increasing protection against stock-outs is used. This is accomplished by assuming a larger (worse case) average than the actual average for the LT. To illustrate, if lead time is known to average 10 days, and it is also known to range ± 2 days almost all of the time, then an estimate of 12 days for LT might be tried out. Extra inventory would be carried to buffer the two days that LT might slip.

How this affects stock levels will now be shown, as the *perpetual inventory system* uses extra stock protection against surges in demand and delays in delivery.

Imagine that the inventory stored in cardboard boxes behind the forklift truck is freshness dated. That procedure has marketing advantages, but the inventory costs are higher. A computerized tracking system can help to control the costs of obsolete and out-of-date stock.

14-7 PERPETUAL INVENTORY SYSTEMS

Perpetual inventory systems continuously record inventory received from suppliers and withdrawn by employees. Most perpetual inventory systems are used online, in real time with some demand variability. The EOQ and ELS models discussed so far do not include demand variability. In many practical situations, this assumption is unrealistic. With modifications, the EOQ and ELS models can deal with demand variability.

Variability of demand arises from variations in order sizes. Variability is passed along the supply chain, affecting everyone. Customers are the primary cause of demand variability. There are other causes of demand variability as well. These include stock on-hand replacement to make up for items lost as a result of warehouse fires, employee pilferage, and the discovery that items in stock cannot be shipped because they are defective.

Consider what occurs when a machine setting changes, creating a large number of rejects that cannot be reworked. Production must run larger numbers of items to compensate for the scrap. More materials must be withdrawn from inventory to be used by the process. The supplier furnished the usual number of units per order that was based on the estimate of the expected demand (D). Because demand is larger than expected, the reorder point Q_{RP} will be reached sooner.

The perspective that will be used to explain how the EOQ model can be modified to protect the buyer will assume batch delivery of the quantity:

$$Q_o = \sqrt{\frac{2DC_r}{cC_c}}$$

The same conditions apply. The processes must be ongoing with item demand being relatively constant over time. It is evident that such modeling does not apply to job shops with small orders because they lack continuity of demand.

The focus now is on items that are stocked regularly, where the demand can vary. The buyer orders the economic order quantity, but has on hand some buffer stock (which is sometimes called *reserve stock* or *safety stock*). The buffer stock is extra stock so that when demand is heavier than expected, orders can still be filled.

An option is to design a perpetual inventory system. It is perpetual because it is an online system, tracking the stock on-hand (SOH) at each transaction of withdrawal or stock entry. To design the system, it will be useful to answer the following questions:

1. How many buffer stock units should be carried?

    The answer involves balancing the added carrying costs for extra stock against the costs of running out of stock. As one cost goes up, the other comes down.

2. When should an order be placed for the buffer stock?

    The buffer stock should be created as soon as it is determined that it is beneficial to have it. It does not have to be replenished when it has been drawn on to avoid stock-outs because the use of buffer stock is expected to average out at zero. The only times that this will not apply will be if the demand system is changing over time or is unstable.

3. How often should an order be placed for buffer stock?

    Once, and then whenever the buffer-stock level needs to be updated.

4. How many units should be ordered to meet expected demand?

    Use the same economic order quantity, Q_o.

5. How often and when should the orders be placed for units to meet the demand?

    An order is placed whenever the reorder point, Q_{RP}, is reached.

6. How does this perpetual system work?

    Withdrawal quantities are entered in the computer each time one or more units are taken out of stock. These quantities are subtracted from the previous stock-level balance to determine the new balance quantity of stock on-hand.

Global package delivery systems have logistic problems to overcome. It is inevitable that they will become low cost, fast, and efficient. Global information delivery systems are already in widespread use.

FIGURE 14-10
Determination of the Reorder Point Q_{RP}

14-7a Reorder Point and Buffer Stock Calculations

The reorder point quantity is designated for each item and is entered in the computer program. When the reorder point has been reached, the program recognizes this fact and an order is placed for the economic order quantity, Q_o.

The stock level of the reorder point (Q_{RP}) is equal to the expected demand in the lead-time period called $\overline{D}_{LT}$, plus the buffer (or safety) stock (BS) quantity. Thus:

$$Q_{RP} = \overline{D}_{LT} + BS \qquad \text{(Equation 14-3)}$$

Figure 14-10 shows the *distribution of demand in the lead-time period*. It also provides a physical interpretation of the components of Equation 14-3.

There are two parts to the construction of the reorder point. The first part is the left-hand side of the bell-shaped curve shown in Figure 14-10. The second part of the construction is the right-hand side of Figure 14-10 that is labeled "Buffer Stock."

The left-hand section of the reorder point goes from zero (at the left side of the diagram) to the mean of the lead-time distribution, which is $\overline{D}_{LT}$.

The right-hand side of bell-shaped curve is divided into two parts. There is the section called *buffer stock (BS)*. It starts at $\overline{D}_{LT}$ and, moving to the right, spans a distance $+k_\alpha \sigma_{LT}$, which, in words is "*k standard deviations of the lead-time distribution*." Thus, adding $+ k_\alpha \sigma_{LT}$, which equals buffer stock, to the mean of the lead-time distribution, $\overline{D}_{LT}$, defines the reorder point, Q_{RP}. The second part of the right-hand side is the tail of the lead-time distribution, which is the probability (α) of going out of stock when the reorder point is set at Q_{RP}.

The reorder point is fully specified by Equation 14-4, where the value of $+k_\alpha$ in $+k_\alpha \sigma_{LT}$ represents a probability design decision regarding stock-out frequencies.

$$Q_{RP} = \overline{D}_{LT} + (BS = +k_\alpha \sigma_{LT}) \qquad \text{(Equation 14-4)}$$

The tail of the distribution (labeled probability (α)) at the right-hand side of Figure 14-10 is carefully chosen. When it is a large tail area, then there will be many stock-outs. If a stock-out represents a life and death situation (e.g., no Type-A blood for critical surgery) or a difficult economic problem (e.g., no spare jet engine) then the probability of going out of stock may have been set too high. This is an economic balancing situation in which the cost of going out of stock versus the cost of carrying more inventory.

Outages happen whenever actual demand in the lead-time period exceeds $\overline{D}_{LT} + k_\alpha \sigma_{LT}$. The probability represented by the tail area determines how often that happens. The value of α is proportional to the area in the tail of the lead-time distribution (labeled probability (α) in Figure 4-10).

The likelihood of an outage occurring can be decreased by increasing the value of k. When $k = 1$, there is about a 16 percent probability of an outage happening during a lead-time period. When $k = 1.645$, there is a 5 percent probability of an outage happening during a lead-time period. When $k = 2$, the number decreases to 2.3 percent and when $k = 3$, the tail area is small at 0.13 percent.

When the tail area is small, then the buffer stock is large and the likelihood of going out of stock is small. The large buffer stock means that the *carrying cost of stock is high to make sure that the actual cost of stock-outages is small.* When the tail area is large, then the amount of buffer stock that is being carried is small and the carrying cost is small but the outage penalties are going to have to be paid more often.

The best way to determine the lead-time distribution is by observation. First, take as large a number of past lead times as the computer records make available and calculate the average lead time (say it is 10 days). Then, again by observation, record the demand over successive 10-day intervals. Plot the distribution and determine the standard deviation.

If the successive 10-day periods are independently distributed, as they usually are, the lead-time distribution obtained by observation will be a reasonable approximation. This assumes the same supplier and delivery system over the sample period. If a change has occurred, then the new lead-time parameters will have to be estimated some other way.

Enough intervals should be collected in the sample to provide a smooth, nearly normal shape for the lead-time distribution when it is plotted. If the distribution appears bimodal or skewed, further statistical investigation is needed. It is best to state the average lead time in small periods of time, such as days, to expedite creating the lead-time distribution.

14-7b Imputing Stock-Outage Costs

Buffer stock is designed to prevent some percent of out-of-stock situations. The size of the alpha tail of the distribution in Figure 14-10 indicates the level of protection being sought. The buffer-stock level that is chosen is based on balancing the costs of stock-outs with those of carrying costs. Thus:

Carrying cost $(BS) = cC_c(k_\alpha \sigma_{LT})$ (Equation 14-5)

and this is derived from the variables and parameters shown here:

c = cost of the unit in dollars/unit
C_c = the carrying cost *rate* as a percent per dollar per year
cC_c = carrying cost in dollars per unit per year
$k_\alpha \sigma_{LT}$ = number of units carried in the buffer stock; k_α has been chosen to limit the probability (α) that demand in the lead time will exceed $k_\alpha \sigma_{LT}$
$cC_c(k_\alpha \sigma_{LT})$ = carrying cost in dollars per year for buffer stock designed to offer an (α) level of protection

The cost of stock-outages relates to their frequency. As k_α gets larger, the frequency of stock-outages decreases. Say that the tail of the distribution with k_α = 1.645 provides protection against demand levels exceeding buffer stock 95 percent of the time. That means that five out of 100 lead-time intervals (or one out of 20 LTs) will experience a stock-outage so

$\alpha = 0.05$

The number of lead-time intervals is the same as the number of orders placed. Say that n = 5 orders are placed per year. Then, an outage is expected once every four years. Stated in an alternative way, it is expected that four years will elapse between stock-outs. Finally, assume that the carrying cost per year for buffer stock is $2,500 obtained by using Equation 14-5. In four years, this sums to a value of $10,000 without discounting.

The value of k_α chosen has an *imputed stock-out cost* of $10,000. Imputed means attributed in the sense that an action attributes value. It is now up to management to decide whether that implied cost seems sensible and is acceptable. In many instances, it is very difficult to determine stock-out costs directly. The direct measure requires finding all of the consequences of the stock-out and then measuring the impact of those consequences. Therefore, the use of imputation of costs provides an appealing alternative. If the imputed cost is accepted, then:

Outage costs $(BS) = $10,000

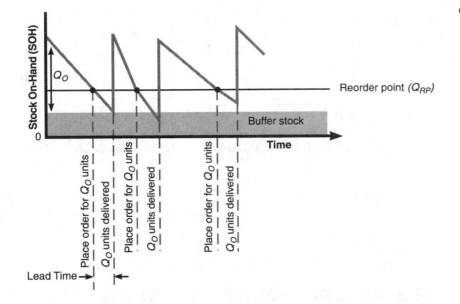

FIGURE 14-11
A Perpetual Inventory System—SOH Computed with Each Withdrawal

14-7c Operating the Perpetual Inventory System

The fastest route to understanding how the perpetual inventory system works is by studying the graphic representation of it. Figure 14-11 illustrates the two parts that have been put together. The EOQ model sits on top of the buffer-stock part.

Follow the stock on-hand line as it forms an irregular sawtooth pattern. When demand becomes greater, the line moves down faster, and when the demand rate decreases, the line moves down more slowly. In other words, when the slope of the line becomes steeper, the reorder point (Q_{RP}) is reached more quickly.

Next, note that the interval between orders is variable depending on whether the demand has been faster or slower than the average rate. When the demand is consistently at the average rate the spacing between orders will be constant and unchanging at:

$$t_o = \frac{Q_o}{D}$$

Note in Figure 14-11, the first of the replenishment cycles stops right at the buffer-stock line. At that point, SOH is zero and no buffer stock is withdrawn. Demand dips into the buffer stock region only for the second replenishment cycle. In other words, buffer stock is called upon once in three replenishment cycles. That buffer stock is the first to be replaced when the next order filled is received and the units are put in stock.

The third of the three replenishment cycles shows an order arriving when the stock level is above the buffer-stock level. If the demand distribution is stable over time, then the buffer-stock level will average out to the planned number of units for buffer stock.

14-7d Two-Bin Perpetual Inventory Control System

The two-bin system is a smart way of continuously monitoring the order point. It is a simple self-operating perpetual inventory system. Figure 14-12 shows the two bins with familiar labels.

Two bins are marked 1 and 2. The optimal order size of Q_o units has been delivered. First, Bin 1 is filled to the reorder-point level. The remaining units from the delivery are put into Bin 2. The bottom of Bin 2 is labeled the reorder point because it is equivalent to the level of the reorder point in Bin 1. Once the reorder point is reached in Bin 1, then Bin 2 filling begins. Spending a few minutes with Figure 14-12 will make clear the construction of the reorder points in Bins 1 and 2.

Withdrawals are made from Bin 2 first. When Bin 2 is depleted, an order is placed for the EOQ, and further units are taken from Bin 1. Each time Bin 2 is emptied, a new order is placed—it is equivalent to reaching the reorder point.

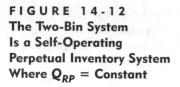

FIGURE 14-12
The Two-Bin System Is a Self-Operating Perpetual Inventory System Where Q_{RP} = Constant

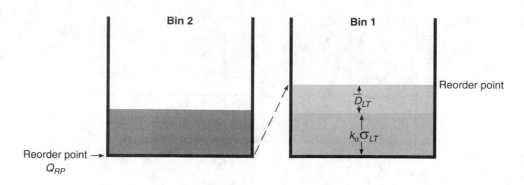

The two-bin system is not feasible for many kinds of items. When applicable, much clerical work is eliminated. This two-bin system is well suited to small items like nuts, bolts, and fasteners. These are things that are too small and too numerous to make withdrawal entries for each transaction. The same reasoning applies to recording withdrawals of liquids, for which the two-bin system approach is ideal.

14-8   PERIODIC INVENTORY SYSTEMS

Periodic inventory systems were more popular than perpetual inventory systems before inventory information was digitized and put online. Periodic inventory systems are based on regular fixed review periods that were ideally suited for manual entries.

Computers outmoded periodic systems based on the convenience of fixed review times. Nevertheless, there are reasons why periodic systems operated by computers continue to be used. These include requirements of suppliers concerning when they will accept orders, requirements of shippers about when they will schedule deliveries, and the need to combine orders to obtain volumes sufficient for shipment discounts. Some organizations have central warehouses that will only accept orders from their regional distributors once a week on a specific day. Also, some industries prefer the regularity of the periodic method, which can be linked to changeover intervals for production processes and other regularities.

Periodic inventory systems also should be understood because advanced inventory models (called *Ss policies*) combine the ordering rules of perpetual and periodic order systems to obtain lower total costs. These can be encountered in big inventory systems installations such as the Armed Forces use.

The optimal interval is based on the familiar square root relationship:

$$t_o = \frac{Q_o}{D} = D\sqrt{\frac{2DC_r}{cC_c}} = \sqrt{\frac{2C_r}{DcC_c}}$$

High-cost items and large carrying costs increase the desirability of short review periods. High ordering costs and large setup costs call for long review periods.

To use the periodic model, first fix the review interval. At each review, determine SOH by adding total receipts and subtracting total withdrawals. An order is placed for a variable quantity contrasting with the perpetual inventory model where it was a fixed quantity at variable intervals.

Figure 14-13 illustrates the way that the periodic order system functions. Note the upper line marked M. Summing the order quantity Q and the stock on-hand, including the buffer stock, sets the value of M. Thus:

$$M = Q + SOH \qquad \text{(Equation 14-6)}$$

As seen in Figure 14-13, SOH includes the expected demand in the lead-time period and the buffer stock. This is:

$$SOH = \overline{D}_{LT} + BS \qquad \text{(Equation 14-7)}$$

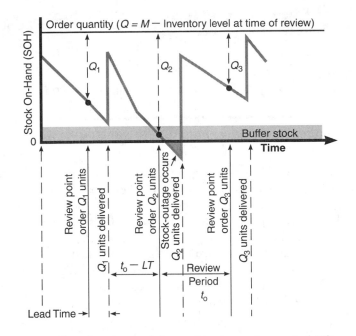

Observe that the order quantity Q is the expected demand in the review period. The review period is also called t_o, and it is so-labeled in Figure 14-13. Functionally, the review period is the fixed interval between successive reviews by the inventory managers. Using this information, Equation 14-6 is rewritten based on Equation 14-7. It becomes Equation 14-8, as follows:

$$M = \overline{D}_{t_o} + \overline{D}_{LT} + BS = \overline{D}_{(LT+t_o)} + BS \qquad \text{(Equation 14-8)}$$

The size of the buffer stock for the periodic review system must include protection against unexpectedly great demand—in a review period plus one lead-time interval. Thus:

$$BS = k_\alpha \sigma_{(LT+t_o)} \qquad \text{(Equation 14-9)}$$

M is calculated as shown in Equation 14-10.

$$M = \overline{D}_{t_o} + \overline{D}_{LT} + k_\alpha \sigma_{(LT+t_o)} = \overline{D}_{(LT + t_o)} + k_a \sigma_{(LT+t_o)} \qquad \text{(Equation 14-10)}$$

Periodic buffer stock is calculated using the distribution of $(LT + t_o)$ because after an order is placed, variations in demand can be experienced during the period t_o. Then a review occurs and an order is placed. Demand variations can continue during LT. Therefore, exposure to variable demand before a correction can be made is over a review period and a lead time. This requires extra stock for protection, and that is a major drawback of the periodic model.

The operation of the periodic model is to determine the review dates. Calculate SOH and order an amount Q_o.

$M - SOH = Q_o$. Thus:

$$M - (\overline{D}_{LT} + k_\alpha \sigma_{(LT+t_o)}) = Q_o \qquad \text{(Equation 14-11)}$$

It is worth noting that $[\overline{D}_{LT} + k_\alpha \sigma_{(LT+t_o)}]$ in $M - [(\overline{D}_{LT} + k_\alpha \sigma_{(LT+t_o)}] = Q_o$ in Equation 14-11 is the same type of formula as used for the reorder point (Q_{RP}) of the perpetual inventory model. Therefore, $M - Q_o = Q_{RP}$. However, the notable difference in buffer stock is not to be overlooked.

Thus: BS (periodic) > BS (perpetual); and in formula: $k_\alpha \sigma_{(LT+t_o)} > k_\alpha \sigma_{(LT)}$

14-9 QUANTITY DISCOUNT MODEL

Accept a quantity discount only when it lowers the total costs. Therefore, to determine when the discounted order quantity should replace the optimal undiscounted order

Quantity (Q units)	Cost per Unit	Total Cost
Q = zero up to Q_1	c	TC(c)
Q = Q_1 up to Q_2	c′	TC(c′)
Q = Q_2 and greater	c″	TC(c″)

TABLE 14-5

Discount Schedule with 3 Price Breaks

(There can be any number of price breaks.)

quantity Q_o, it is necessary to derive the total cost curves. Note that it is necessary to compare total costs instead of total variable costs because for discount analysis the cost of goods purchased must play a significant role in the decision to accept or reject a discount. Lowering the price paid for goods is the purpose of taking the discount but the true criterion must be total costs.

The discounting situation is directly reflected by the schedule shown in Table 14-5.

Total cost is TC using TVC, as previously defined, plus dollar demand (cD, c′D, and c″D) for undiscounted and then discounted costs. To simplify the discussion, only two price breaks will be used.

$$TC(c) = TVC(c) + cD = (cQ/2)C_c + (D/Q)C_r + cD \ (0 \le Q < Q_1)$$
$$TC(c') = TVC(c') + c'D = (c'Q/2)C_c + (D/Q)C_r + c'D \ (Q \ge Q_1)$$

These two total cost curves are drawn in Figure 14-14.

The quantity discount model involves more than one total cost equation but only one line segment is applicable in each cost break's range, i.e., c, c′, and c″. The discontinuities of the curves are shown in Figures 14-14.

Each curve includes its own respective dollar volume. That is cD for the first curve and c′D for the second curve. The top curve, TC(c′) is based on an undiscounted cost c. The bottom curve, TC(c′) is applicable when a discount is available, but it is only applicable at and above the quantity needed to obtain the discount.

Let $Q \ge Q_1$ be the specified quantity required to obtain the discount. Q_j is called the discount quantity break point. If Q_j is Q_1 in Figure 14-14, then the discount must be taken because the TC at b′ is lower than the TC at a. Point a is the minimum TC *without* the discount. In fact, the order quantity should be increased from Q_1 to Q_b, which is the order quantity at point b. Point b is the minimum total cost that can be obtained in the discount region. It is the *lowest* cost that can be acquired.

The top TC curve applies across the range $0 \le Q \le Q_1$. The bottom curve range is $Q \ge Q_1$. Figure 14-14 *magnifies the discontinuity* of the two cost curves, which indicates the principle involved. The top curve is valid left of the vertical line at Q_1 and the bottom curve is valid at and to the right of it. The cost of point b is lower than that of point b′.

In Figure 14-14 where Q_j is specified as being at Q_2, then point b″ provides a lower cost than point a. Therefore, take this discount at break point Q_2. Point a is the minimum total cost without the discount. Point b″ is the lowest total cost that is available in the discount region. Since it is the chosen point, the discount is taken.

Now refer to Figure 14-14 again. If the discount break point $Q_j = Q_3$, then the intersected cost point is e, which is a greater cost than a. Therefore, the order quantity that is related to point a should be used. However, if Q associated with cost point d had been the break point, then there is a tie between the order amounts associated with cost points a and d. When a tie exists, qualitative factors become even more important. No matter what the curves indicate about taking or passing up a discount, qualitative factors must be used to scrutinize the decision.

With a tie, the issue of choosing the larger order size may reflect fear of a delivery disruption. Choosing a smaller order size may indicate an intuition that in the future prices will fall significantly. Similar thinking should always come into play when qualitative factors impinge on making a good decision.

FIGURE 14-14
Quantity Discount Model:
Total Cost Curves
(Break Point, Q_1)

INTERACTIVE FIGURE

Figure 14-14 illustrates a specific discounting situation where Q_o is the minimum point of the discounted total cost curve. The discount should be taken with a larger order quantity b than the minimum amount b' needed to obtain the discount. Point b delivers the minimum $TC(c')$ for the entire range of choices. Still, qualitative factors might apply that lead to the decision to select b'.

Figure 14-14 provides another discounting situation where Q_2 is the break point quantity at the cost b''. This is the lowest cost that can be obtained so the discount should be taken at that quantity. Note how the two TC curves are each applicable only in their own regions.

As part of this analysis based on Figure 14-14, assume that you are instructed to ignore Q_2, and asked to compare strategies that yield costs a and d. From the *total cost point of view*, the inventory planning team would be indifferent about either buying the small amount at point a or buying the large amount at point d. Both have the same total costs, but d has a much smaller cost per unit than a. This could be a major reason for preferring d.

As has been noted, a variety of additional factors can be considered, such as: could there be a change in the material being used; is there a possibility of a strike; can the purchase of a large quantity make it difficult for others to buy it; can the purchase of a large quantity influence the price? These notions might favor point *d*. On the other hand, does this item spoil easily; does it require a large amount of storage space; does it experience obsolescence? These notions are more likely to favor purchasing the smaller quantity associated with point *a*.

The reasoning process that has been applied, and the curves that have been drawn, can be extended to any number of price breaks for quantity discounts. What is recommended is to draw the total cost curves, mark the price break ranges, and examine where the minimum cost points fall. A purely mathematical approach can be computer programmed for rapid decision making when faced with many discount offerings.

SUMMARY

This chapter addresses "independent demand" inventory management. It explains order point policy (OPP) models in terms of demand continuity. The costs of inventory are treated. These include costs of ordering, setups and changeovers, carrying inventory, discounts, stock-outages, and running the inventory system. Process types differentiate inventory costs.

Then, economic order quantity models (EOQ) are developed for batch delivery. The total variable cost equations are set up and solved. Economic lot size models (ELS) for continuous delivery of product are contrasted to EOQ models. The ELS are applied to intermittent flow shops (IFS). There is discussion of lead-time structure, uncertainty, and variability.

Next, the perpetual inventory system with its reorder point and buffer-stock calculations is detailed. This includes operation of the two-bin perpetual inventory control system. The periodic inventory system is explained including why this system is being outmoded by computer capabilities—yet it still is needed in certain situations. The chapter ends with an explanation of how quantity discount models work.

Two Spotlight feature boxes conclude this chapter. These boxes illustrate real applications of the material in the chapter. See Spotlight 14-1: Split the Difference and Spotlight 14-2: E-Shopping—(B2C) and P/OM.

KEY TERMS

Buffer stock
Dynamic inventory models
Economic lot size (ELS)
Economic order quantity (EOQ)
Inventory

Lead time (LT)
Make or buy decision
Order point policies (OPP)
Periodic inventory system
Perpetual inventory system

Reorder point (RP)
Sensitivity analysis
Static inventory models
Vendor releasing

REVIEW QUESTIONS

1. It has been stated that, as a rule of thumb, "the best inventory is no inventory." Discuss this heuristic.

2. For a toothpaste manufacturer, how is the decision made concerning how many caps should be ordered? Could it be a different number than the number of tubes that are ordered at one time?

3. How often should an order size be updated?

4. What method should be used to determine the order quantity for a raw material that is used continuously within a flow shop?

5. What method should be used to determine the order quantity for a raw material that is used continuously within an intermittent flow shop?

6. Who are the people that are responsible for placing orders?

7. Electronic data interchange (EDI) makes communication between connected supply chain participants immediate. How does the use of EDI reduce the order quantity?

8. Using the information in Problem 7, how does the use of EDI reduce the buffer stock?

9. A manufacturer of costume jewelry has a sales force that uses handheld computers with modems. Salespeople take stock at each retail establishment and then call the factory with stock-level data. How does this procedure affect the manufacturing schedule of the company? Explain your answer in terms of ELS models.

10. Benetton is a well-known manufacturer and retailer of clothing all over the world. The Benetton factories are tied in with retailers so that demand information is relatively immediate and complete concerning what is selling and what is not. How does this information affect lot-size planning?

11. Salespeople use handheld telecommunications devices to communicate inventory status to the warehouse in a major toy company. Why is this system needed and what does it affect?

12. What is carrying cost composed of and what is the range of values that will be found for it?

13. What is the logic for a buyer accepting a discount?

14. What is the logic for a seller offering a discount?

15. Why is there an ordering cost and of what is it composed?

16. What is the difference between an ordering cost and a setup cost?

17. When is it likely that an ordering cost will be larger than a setup cost?

18. When is it likely that a setup cost will be larger than an ordering cost?

19. Relate the number of orders placed and the order quantity.

20. Why are order point policies (OPP) called by that name?

21. Why are total variable cost equations written for OPP models instead of total cost equations?

22. When discounts are being considered, total cost equations must be used instead of total variable cost equations. Why is this so?

23. Differentiate between EOQ and ELS models.

24. When is lead-time variability a problem and what can be done about it?

25. How can lead-time variability be modeled?

26. What is a two-bin system? When is it applicable?

27. Describe a perpetual inventory system.

28. When is a perpetual inventory system preferred?

29. Describe a periodic inventory system.

30. When is a periodic inventory system preferred?

31. How can a quantity discount model be used by a buyer and supplier to negotiate a price break point schedule that benefits both of them?

32. Why is it that multiple price break points for many discount levels can be examined in the same fashion as one price break point for a single discount?

33. Is the two-bin inventory system perpetual or periodic?

34. Assume that a new IFS has been set up to make a baby stroller. The ELS analysis is completed and the run size and run time are determined. Discuss what to do with the time, t_2, when the process is not running the product.

35. Distinguish between inventory problems under certainty, risk, and uncertainty.

PROBLEMS SECTION

1. Water testing at the Croton reservoir requires a chemical reagent that costs $500 per gallon. Use is constant at 1/3 gallon per week. Carrying cost rate is considered to be 12 percent per year, and the cost of an order is $125.
   What is the optimal order quantity for the reagent?

2. Continuing with the information about the Croton reservoir given in Problem 1, the city could make this reagent at the rate of 1/8 gallon per day, at a cost of $300 per gallon. The setup cost is $150. Use a 7-day week.
   Compare using the EOQ and the ELS systems. What course of action do you recommend?

3. Water testing at the Delaware reservoir requires a chemical reagent that costs $400 per gallon. Use is constant at 1/3 gallon per week. Carrying cost rate is considered to be 10 percent per year, and the cost of an order is $100.
   What is the optimal order quantity for the reagent?

4. Continuing with the information about the Delaware reservoir given in Problem 3, the town could make this reagent at the rate of 1/4 gallon per day, at a cost of $500 per gallon. The setup cost is $125. Use a 7-day week.
   Compare using the EOQ and the ELS systems. What course of action do you recommend?

5. The Drug Store carries Deodorant R, which has an expected demand of 15,000 jars per year (or 60 jars per day with 250 days per year). Lead time from the distributor is three days. It has been determined that demand in any 3-day period exceeds 200 jars only once out of every 100 3-day periods. This outage level (of 1 in 100 LT periods) is considered acceptable by P/OM and their marketing colleagues. The economic order quantity has been derived as 2,820 jars. Set up the perpetual inventory system.

6. Use the information given in Problem 5, plus the fact that it has been determined that demand in any 50-day period exceeds 4,000 jars only once out of every 100 50-day periods. This outage level (of 1 in 100 LT periods) is considered acceptable by the P/OM and their marketing colleagues. Set up the periodic inventory system.

7. Compare the results derived in Problems 5 and 6. What do you recommend doing? Explain how you have taken into account all of the important differentiating characteristics of perpetual and periodic inventory systems.

8. Consider the recommendation made in Problem 5, taking into account the fact that The Drug Store must combine orders for Deodorant R with other items in order to have sufficient volume to qualify for the distributor's shipping without charge. With this constraint, what are your recommendations?

9. The information required to solve an EOQ inventory problem is as follows:

$c = \$10$ per unit, $C_c = 16$ percent per year, $D = 5,000$ units per year, and $C_r = \$10$ per order

What is the optimal order quantity?

10. Using the information in Problem 9, instead of buying from a supplier the decision is to make the item in the company's factory. The new equipment is able to produce $p = 30$ units per day. Costs are changed to $c = \$6$ per unit and $C_s = \$150$ per setup. What is the optimal run size?

11. Using the information in Problems 9 and 10, which is better: make or buy?

12. Using the information in Problems 9, 10, and 11, what factors that are not in the equations might shift the decision?

13. The following quantity discount schedule has been offered for the situation described in Problem 9.

$c = 10$ $Q =$ up to 300
$c' = 9$ $Q = 300$ to 499
$c'' = 8$ $Q = 500$ and up

Should either of these discounts be accepted?

14. The quantity discount schedule offered in Problem 13 prompted a competitor to offer the following discount schedule:

$c = 10$ $Q =$ up to 250
$c' = 9$ $Q = 251$ to 599
$c'' = 7$ $Q = 600$ and up

Should any of these discounts be accepted?

15. Compare the answers to Problems 13 and 14 and discuss these results, making appropriate recommendations.

16. Murphy's is famous for their coffee blend. The company buys and roasts the beans and then packs the coffee in foil bags. It buys the beans periodically in quantities of 120,000 pounds and assumes this to be the optimal order quantity. This year it has been paying $2.40 per pound on a fairly constant basis.

The company ships 1,200,000 1-pound bags of its blended coffee per year to its distributors. This is equivalent to shipping 24,000 1-pound foil bags in each of 50 weeks of the year. This can be considered to be constant and continuous demand over time.

What carrying cost in percent per year is implied (or imputed) by this policy if an order costs $100 on the average? Discuss the results.

Use:

$$Q_o = \sqrt{\frac{2DC_r}{cC_c}}$$

17. Using the information in Problem 16, suggest a better ordering policy.

18. What production run lengths are individually optimal for each item in the following table?

Item i	Annual D_i	Setup C_{S_i}	Unit Cost c_i	p_i (per day)
1	200	100	6	10
2	400	50	10	12
3	600	20	15	14
4	800	80	9	20

D_i is demand per year; $p_i =$ production run size,
$C_c = 0.24$ per year, and $D_i = 250d_i$ for changing daily demand into yearly demand.

19. Using the information in Problem 18, can all of these items be scheduled to run on the same equipment? Discuss.

20. Using the data in Problem 18, employ cut and try methods to determine a reasonable set of production run lengths so that all items can be scheduled to run consecutively on the same equipment. Compare these results with the individual optimal values obtained in Problem 18.

21. The manager of the greeting card production department has been buying two rolls of acetate at a time. They cost $200 each. Card production requires 10 rolls per year. Ordering cost is estimated to be $4 per order. What carrying cost rate is imputed? Is it reasonable?

22. Using the information in Problem 21, if the cost of rolls of acetate increases to $250 each, what happens to the imputed carrying cost rate? Is this reasonable?

23. Refer to Figure 14-4 in the text and the example upon which it was based. To illustrate the flatness of the total cost curve when Q_o is large, determine the TVC for $Q = 20,000$. Recall that the optimal value presented in the text and related to Figure 14-4 was $6.57 associated with $Q_o = 21,909$ units. These are calculated as follows:

$TVC_{21,909} = 0.00015(21,909) + 72,000/(21,909)$
$= \$3.286 + \$3.286 = \$3.286(2) = \$6.57$

Determine the percent increase in TVC and decrease in Q. Discuss your findings.

24. Using the information in Problem 23, calculate TVC for $Q = 25,000$. What percent increase has occurred in TVC? Calculate the percent increase in Q from the optimal value of $Q_o = 21,909$ units. Does this back up the statement: "The total variable cost curve flattens out as Q_o gets larger. There is less difference between the minimum cost at Q_o and the costs associated with small changes ($\in$) in Q_o such as $Q_o \pm \in$." Note: This requires analysis of the cost effects of making small changes around the point $Q = 25,000$ as compared to the cost effects of small changes around $Q_o = 21,909$.

25. Masters of Travel, Inc. (MTI) gives customers who have purchased travel arrangements a soft canvas shoulder-strap bag. Bags Limited, the company that furnishes these bags to MTI, has suggested that if the order quantity is doubled, it would discount the cost per bag by 20 percent. At present, MTI buys 600 bags imprinted with MTI at a time for $1.50 per bag. This represents a 2-month supply.

Should the discount be taken?

26. Using the information in Problem 25, a competitor to Bags Limited has made the following offer:

Number of Shoulder Bags	Price
600	at $1.45 each
800	at $1.35 each
1,000	at $1.25 each

What should MTI do?

END-OF-CHAPTER QUESTIONS

1. There are many different types of inventory models. When starting an application, the first thing to do is recognize the category of inventory problem so that the appropriate model can be examined and fitted to the specific situation. One of the great benefits of inventory models is that students can practice using them. Savings obtained by those practicing model building are theoretical. However, the effort is worthwhile and begins to build confidence that a real application could make significant savings for actual companies. Having read Chapter 14, the first steps to take relate to being able to discuss the types of inventory models in an informed way. Read the list of salient points (a. through e.) about various types of inventory situations. Identify the one point that is not suitable for the inventory taxonomy (classification system).

   a. Inventory systems are classified by whether their demand distributions are linked to their lead-time distributions. For example, if the lead time required for delivery is long, then the demand will be great. This is one of the reasons that companies often tell their customers that repair will take a longer time than is really needed.

   b. Dynamic inventory models deal with a repetitive stream of orders as compared to static inventory models, which have little or no repetition. As an example of repetitive demand, Tropicana must have cartons (month after month) to fill with orange juice. In contrast, the hot dog vendor puts in one order for the number of hot dogs that he or she thinks can be sold at the final game of the World Series.

   c. At one time, Ford Motor Company made all of its own windshield glass. In the make or buy decision at that time upstream vertical integration seemed to be justified by many factors, including cost and control. Ford no longer makes its own windshield glass because the analysis years later showed different results. Make or buy stock decisions must be reviewed over time because internal and external factors change.

   d. Inventory problems can be categorized by different kinds of risk distributions. Linear programming assumes that demand and lead times are known with certainty. Other types of inventory models such as the perpetual and periodic kind assume demands (and lead times) are distributed according to well-known, well-behaved distributions such as the normal or Poisson distributions. Inventory models that must cope with uncertainty of demand (and lead time) are rare but not unknown. New products may have uncertain demands, which lead to strategic decisions to begin with a "safe" or conservative inventory policy. Then, as more information becomes available, the investments in capacity and stock are increased. Simulation is often used to analyze worst-case scenarios and "what if" situations when uncertainty prevails. Uncertainty can take the form of unstable demand and lead-time distributions that change in erratic ways.

   e. Demand continuity will affect the kind of inventory model that applies. OPP models are applicable when there is continuity of demand. MRP models are used when the demand is sporadic, but not one-time. Table 14.2 shows the conditions for OPP and for MRP in terms of continuity and dependence.

2. Costs are the crucial measurable elements of every inventory model. There are other factors, but if the costs have not been included, and measured correctly, then the inventory situation cannot be resolved. Choose the statement of a. through e. that is not part of proper inventory methodology.

   a. The best way to get the cost of an order is to do a systems study of the steps and procedures that are used by the organization to place an order. It is essential to determine if the same procedures are always followed and if not, when do the variants apply? Divide the fixed costs per year by the number of orders placed per year. Variable costs are added to the applicable fixed costs to obtain the total costs. However, before announcing the cost of an order, in a proper systems study, work simplification is applied. The "best" methods for placing orders should be the basis of the cost of an order. The cost of an order, C_r, is in the numerator of the economic order quantity (EOQ) equation. Therefore, the order quantity, Q, changes with the square root of C_r. When the cost of an order doubles (100 percent increase), the order size increases 41 percent.

   b. Costs of designing, setting up, and running inventory systems must be balanced against the lost benefit of not using them. Also, high systemic costs of computerized perpetual inventory systems frequently lead managers to prefer periodic inventory systems using workbooks.

   c. The setup cost, C_S, is used with the economic lot size model (ELS). It is measured by dividing the fixed costs per year by the number of setups used per year. Variable costs are added to the applicable fixed costs to obtain the total costs. The "best" methods for setups should be determined. Often, there is a lot of opportunity for improvement because traditional ideas about setups have changed as a result of different attitudes and new technology. The setup cost, C_S, is in the numerator of the ELS equation. The run lot size, Q, changes with the square root of C_S. When the setup cost doubles (100 percent increase), the run size increases 41 percent.

   d. The total cost of carrying inventory, cC_C, is composed of the carrying cost rate, C_C, and the per unit cost, c. The carrying cost rate is composed of lost opportunities to use funds in other ways plus charges for storage, taxes, obsolescence, deterioration, pilferage, and insurance. If carrying cost rates are set high, the effect is to decrease the value of Q by the square root of the increase in C_C (which is in the denominator of the EOQ and ELS equations). Carrying cost rates are low when interest rates are low and opportunities for the use of money are limited.

e. Out-of-stock costs are dependent on the expectations of the market. For "fill or kill" systems with high volume items (like lipstick), the cost can be significant if lead time to restock is long. The problem is not the single lipstick sale that is lost. The loss of customer loyalty as a result of sustained out-of-stocks is really damaging. Another aspect often found with catalogue sales is the use of upgraded substitutions. The cost of the upgrade is often smaller to the mail order firm than the cost of disgruntled customers. Markets that accept backorders tend to include large ticket items like airplanes and subway cars. Repairs and home improvements are deferred to later dates. Out-of-stock costs are built into setting levels of safety stock where a balance is struck between carrying additional buffer stock and outage penalties.

3. Delta Corporation has an inventory managers' training program. One exercise is to show how the total cost curve for the economic order quantity (EOQ) is derived for one item in one department. A simple numerical example has been created to avoid computational complexity while driving home important concepts. The data are furnished in the table marked *Data for EOQ Computation*. In addition, Delta has set the demand for the item at $D = 12$ units per month and the cost is $c = \$2,000$ per unit. Identify the incorrect statement made in points a. through e.

Data for EOQ Computation

Q	aQ	b/Q	TVC
1	10	24	34
2	20	12	
3	30	8	
4	40	6	

Legend: Q = units per order; $a = \dfrac{cC_c}{2}$; $b = DC_r$; TVC = total variable cost per month; D = demand per month; c = cost per unit; C_c = carrying cost rate per month; C_r = cost of an order ; the EOC equation:

$$Q_o = \sqrt{\frac{2DC_r}{cC_c}}$$

a. The table indicates that the order size can vary from 1 to 4, as shown in the left-hand column of the table.

b. Coefficient $b = 24$. This information is directly available from row 1, where $Q = 1$ and $b/Q = 24$. Because $b = DC_r$ or $24 = 12C_r$, the cost of an order is $2.00.

c. Coefficient $a = 10$. This information is directly available from row 1, where $Q = 1$ and $aQ = 10$. Because

$a = \dfrac{cC_c}{2}$, or $10 = 2000\dfrac{C_c}{2}$, the carrying cost rate per

month is 0.01.

d. Filling out the total cost column (4) requires summing columns 2 and 3. The minimum total cost occurs when Q is equal to 3 units per order.

e. The part of total cost (*TC*) that reflects variable carrying cost increases linearly as order quantity, Q, increases. The other part of the total cost is called the *variable ordering cost*. It declines geometrically as Q increases. There will be a minimum total cost point in the table but it may not be the same as the actual minimum total cost.

4. Delta Corporation is pleased with the training results. The decision is made to continue the training program for inventory managers by extending the analyses of Problem 3. All of the data are the same. Statements made in points a. through e. include one incorrect observation. Please identify which one is incorrect.

a. The table called *Data for EOQ Computation* presents enough information to plot a total cost curve. When the curve is drawn, there is evidence of a minimum total cost point in the neighborhood of $Q = 2$. Neighborhood means that the minimum could occur where Q is greater than 1 and less than 3. Drawing the curve is useful. Graphs provide different kinds of information such as the rate of change of *TC* with Q.

b. To find out the exact value of Q_o (called *Q-optimal*) is impossible, but the approximate value of the optimal order quantity can be derived.

c. The EOQ equation (shown in Problem 3) indicates the optimal value is the square root of 2.4, which is 1.549. That may be a difficult number to order unless there is a scale transformation (such as all numbers should be multiplied by one thousand).

d. Because the table has Q values of only integer numbers, the square root derivation is essential to understand the situation. Delta has never explained what kinds of units are involved in this inventory problem. If the units are gallons, it is possible to order one and a half gallons to come close the minimum total cost associated with the optimal order quantity, Q_o. It is more likely that it would be thousands of gallons because of the high price.

e. The total cost associated with the optimal order quantity, Q_o, is

$$TC_o = \frac{b}{Q_o} + aQ_o = 15.49 + 15.49 = 30.99 = 31.$$

5. Some general concepts have been learned by the Delta Corporation teams. Management has created a list of points to consider. There is one item that should be corrected before the list is sent to the participants. Which item in a. to e. must be corrected?

a. The EOQ equation is a good example of a trade-off model in which, as the controlling (independent) variable increases, the dependent variable increases for one function and decreases for another function. In this case, the carrying cost, $CC = aQ$ increases linearly with the order quantity. The ordering cost, $OC = b/Q$ decreases geometrically with increasing order quantity.

the square root solution $\left(\sqrt{b/a}\right)$ is the result of finding the minimum point on the total cost curve.

b. It would appear from the graph that the minimum point on the total cost curve occurs at the same location as the crosspoint of the two curves. This is a graphical illusion if they are close, which occurs as a coincidence.

c. Lacking good estimates of the four factors that produce the total cost curve, managers will give their best guess. A guess that is likely to produce an underestimate of Q is less desirable than a guess that is likely to produce an overestimate of Q. The reason is that the total cost curve is much steeper as it gets near to the y-axis. This is called the "under- and overestimation effect."

d. The (optimal) number of orders placed (n_o) when the optimal order quantity is Q_o is determined by $n_o = D/Q_o$. Using the data from problem 3, $n_o = 6/(1.549) = 3.87$, or rounding at 4 orders per month. Alternatively, multiplying 3.87 by 12 months, there are 46.5 orders per year. This is equivalent to $52/46.5 = 1.12$ orders per week.

e. The EOQ model is a major component of both the perpetual and periodic inventory models. However, there is no indicator in the EOQ model as to when to order. That is the function of the perpetual and periodic inventory models where lead time (LT) plays an important role.

6. Delta Corporation's managers' inventory training program has been successful. The decision was made to expand it to include economic lot size modeling (ELS). The same type of exercise that was used to show how the total cost curve is derived for the economic order quantity (EOQ) model is going to be used for ELS modeling. As before, the total cost will be derived for one item in one department. Another numerical example has been created for the ELS situation. It is intended to avoid computational complexity while driving home important concepts. The data are furnished in the table marked *Data for ELS Computation*. Delta has set the demand for this item at $D = 20,000$ units per year and the cost per unit is $c = \$6.00$. Note in the legend under the table that demand per day, $d = 80$ units. Production capacity is $p = 150$ units per day. One of the statements in the list prepared for the trainees (which goes from a. to e.) is incorrect. Identify the incorrect statement.

Data for ELS Computation

Q	aQ	b/Q	TC
500	84	800	884
1,000	168	400	
1,500	252	266.67	
2,000	336	200	

Legend: Q = units made per production run (called the *lot size*);
$a = \dfrac{cC_c}{2}\left(\dfrac{p-d}{p}\right)$; $b = DC_s$; TC = total cost per year; TC is the sum of

columns 2 and 3; D = demand in units per 250 day work year; d = demand in units per day based on $D = 250d$ so $d = 20,000/250 = 80$ units per day; p = production per day = 150 units; $c = \$6.00$, which is the cost to make a unit (includes all relevant factors); C_c = carrying cost rate per year; C_s = setup cost (changeover); the ELS equation for run size is :

$$Q_o = \sqrt{\dfrac{2DC_r}{cC_c}}\sqrt{\dfrac{p-d}{p}}\; ; n = \text{number of orders per year;}$$

$t(1)$ = length of run time in days; $t(2)$ length of wait between runs;
$t = t(1) + t(2)$ = production cycle of run and off-line.

a. The table indicates that the number of units that can be made per run (per lot) can vary from 500 to 2,000, as shown in the left-hand column of the table. Although the table is set up for 500 unit increments, additional rows could be added (say, by 100 unit increments).

b. Coefficient $b = 400,000$, obtained from row 2, where $Q = 1,000$ and $b/Q = 400$. Because $b = DC_s$, it follows that setup cost, $C_s = \dfrac{b}{D} = 20.0$.

c. Coefficient $a = 0.168$, obtained directly from row 2 where $Q = 1,000$ and $aQ = 168$. Solving

$$a = \dfrac{cC_c}{2}\left(\dfrac{p-d}{p}\right) \text{ for } C_c = \dfrac{2a}{c}\left(\dfrac{P}{p-d}\right) =$$

$$\dfrac{2(0.168)}{6}\left(\dfrac{150}{150-80}\right) = 0.12.$$

The carrying cost rate per year is 0.12.

d. Filling out the total cost column (4) requires summing columns 2 and 3. The minimum total cost ($TC = \$518.67$ or $\$519$) occurs when Q is equal to 1,500 units per order.

e. Total cost (TC) increases by a larger increment ($\$49.33$) as Q moves from 1,500 to 2,000 units than when Q decreases by 500 units. Moving from 1,500 to 1,000 units increases TC by $\$17.33$.

7. The table in Problem 6 was built with Q increments of 500 units—ranging from 500 to 2,000. A better minimum exists than associated with $Q = 1,500$ units (as found in Problem 6) but it must be found by analysis. Also, an expanded table has been presented to the Delta team. They have been asked to provide the run time, off-line time, cycle time, and the number of runs per year. Delta team is presented with options a. through e. Which one of these is incorrect?

a. Minimum total cost occurs when Q equals a lot size of 1,543.03. The total cost at that point is $\$518.46$. The two components of this minimum total variable cost (TVC) change in opposite directions as Q changes. The costs of these two are $\$159.23$ for the carry cost factor and $\$359.23$ for the setup cost factor.

b. In the *Solutions for ELS Computation* table, it is apparent that $Q = 1,500$ is near the minimum total cost because the two components (aQ and b/Q) are almost equal. They are equal when at $Q_o = 1543.03$. Another row has been added to the table to show the $Q_o = 1543.03$ solution.

Solutions for ELS Computation

Q	aQ	b/Q	TC	$t(1)$ days	$t(2)$ days	t days	n
500	84	800	884	3.33	2.92	6.25	40
1,000	168	400	568	6.67	5.83	12.50	20
1,500	252	266.67	518.67	10.00	8.75	18.75	13.3
1,543.03	259.23	259.23	518.46	10.29	9.00	19.29	12.96
2,000	336	200	536	13.33	11.67	25.00	10

c. Running the selected lot size (Q) takes a given number of days that are linearly related to the quantity. The optimal run time is 10.29 days with 9 days between runs. The full cycle is 19.29 days. For the 250 working days per year, that means there will be 12.96, or 13 runs per year. See the number of orders, n.

d. If there is a reason to run smaller lot sizes (such as a lack of storage space), that may mean that a cost was not included, or incorrectly estimated. The best candidates for these complaints are the carrying cost and the setup cost. In the case of the carrying cost, perhaps it should have been larger to include extra costs of finding storage space. In the case of the setup cost, perhaps a method has been invented to reduce it, and thereby justify smaller Q-values.

e. The solutions table shows how run time, off-line time, and cycle time are related to the run size and to the number of production runs. With relatively small lot sizes of 500, the number of runs is 40, which is almost weekly. There are limits to reduction of the run size, and 500 units is likely to be very close to that limit.

8. Perpetual inventory models are a powerful means of controlling cost-benefit trade-offs of inventory policies. Instead of doing complex numerical analyses, Delta trainers decided that the first step would be to acquaint all trainees with the fundamental concepts of perpetual methods. In that regard, a list of propositions (a. through e.) was submitted to the team members with the understanding that everyone would read each point carefully to absorb its message. As a team member, please determine which statement is not correct.

a. Most perpetual inventory systems are online. As items are withdrawn from stock, the stock level is reduced immediately. The new stock level is compared to the reorder point, which is equal to the expected demand in the lead-time period. This procedure is applied to all items of the ABC curve.

b. The EOQ model is a fundamental part of the perpetual inventory model. The other fundamental part is the buffer (or safety) stock. Determination of the buffer stock is based on balancing carrying cost against outage costs.

c. Buffer stock is carried like an insurance policy. When needed, because demand (a random variable around a stable mean) is excessive, buffer stock is called upon to fill orders and take care of needs. After the rush on the buffer stock is over, these units are replaced. In effect, it is an extra load of stock, not intended to meet regular demand, which is a prevailing extra carrying cost expense.

d. How much buffer stock to carry is determined by the tail of the distribution of demand in the lead-time period. Perpetual inventory models are favored because the buffer stock need only protect against excessive demand after the reorder point is reached. That is when the replenishment lead time begins.

e. The larger the buffer stock, the further out on the tail of the lead-time distribution is the protection level. When the tail is very small because the buffer stock is large, the probability of ever going out of stock is statistically quite small. A big buffer stock raises the level of the reorder point, which is the sum of the buffer stock and the demand in the lead-time period.

9. Periodic inventory models are an absolute necessity under certain distribution constraints. Periodic systems appeal to many people because of their time-line consistency. Delta trainers concluded that the next step would be to acquaint all trainees with the fundamental concepts of periodic methods. To do that, a list of propositions (a. to g.) was submitted to team members with the understanding that everyone would read each point carefully to absorb its message. As a team member, please determine which statement is not correct.

a. Perpetual and periodic models have pros and cons. One might wish to be able to put perpetual and periodic inventory models together to take advantage of the best of both. That has been done in certain high-investment inventory environments (such as stocks of the U.S. Navy) where the combination models have been studied. (*This statement has been certified to be correct by Delta.*)

b. Most periodic inventory systems are online. If the manager decides to "open the books" early on an item scheduled to be reviewed later, the system will provide all of the information needed to place an order.

c. The reorder point of the perpetual inventory model is a stock level, whereas, for the periodic model it is a point in time, i.e., the reorder point time. The optimal time period equation is $t_o = \sqrt{\dfrac{2C_r}{DcC_c}}$.

d. Buffer stock required by the periodic model is larger than for the perpetual model to yield the same statistical level of protection against stock-outs. The reason is that the periodic model has to carry buffer stock for the expected demand in the lead time period (LT) plus one complete replenishment period (t_o).

e. The amount to reorder is the difference between stock on-hand at the reorder time and the M-level, which is the expected demand in the reorder period plus the lead time plus the buffer stock. The equation is $M = \overline{D}_{t_o} + \overline{D}_{LT} + BS$.

f. Buffer stock to protect the inventory system from going out of stock is determined by the selected tail of the distribution of demand in the lead-time period plus demand in the reorder period. The equation shows how the measure of demand variability (sigma:σ) includes both lead time and reorder period. $BS = k_\alpha \sigma_{LT+t_o}$. When alpha ($\alpha$) is small, k is large, so the probability of going out of stock is low.

g. A primary use of the periodic inventory model is to match the periodicity of the demand or delivery systems. For an example of delivery system requirements, the Frito-Lay truck delivers potato chips to retailers on Route 66 twice a week, on Mondays and Thursdays. For an example of demand system requirements, the manager of the theater has announced that delivery of theater supplies must be made on Saturday evening only.

10. Delta often takes advantage of discounts offered by suppliers. Training inventory managers to recognize when discounts are viable is an important part of the program. On the other side of the coin, Delta produces products that it offers with discounts to its customers. Therefore, the company is interested in taking the inventory discount recognition skills and teaching them to its marketing department pricing managers. The idea is that if you know when to take a discount, you should know when to offer a discount. One SKU is chosen for which discounts have been offered but never taken. Delta buys the economic order quantity for that SKU at the current time.

Data are in the table. The managers have asked the trainee team whether they should accept the vendor's offer to drop the price by 12.5 percent if the company will increase the purchased amount by 36 percent. The discussion about this matter is found in points a. through e., one of which is incorrect. Identify the wrong point.

Demand/yr. (D)	200	Q (opt.)	220.48	cD	$800
Order cost	175	aQ	158.75	TC	$1,117.49
Unit cost (c)	$4.00	b/Q	158.75		
Carrying rate	36%/yr.	TVC	317.49		

a. The 36 percent increase in Q changes the order quantity from optimal to nonoptimal for both the current price and the proposed price.

b. The 12.5 percent decrease in price takes it from $4.00 per unit to $3.50. At the lower price, the optimal order quantity is 236 units. This will work out nicely with the new order quantity that the vendor proposes Delta buy in the future.

c. The total cost of the current buying strategy is shown in the table as $1,117.49. This includes the two kinds of variable costs and the undiscounted cost per unit times the yearly demand.

d. The vendor's recommended buying strategy with the discount has a total cost of $1,005.67. This is a real saving of $111.82, $100 of which is directly attributable to the 50 cent reduction per unit.

e. What is bothersome is the size of the order quantities, with and without the discount. At present, Delta is buying in each order 10 percent more units than the annual item demand. If it is assumed that storage, obsolescence, deterioration, pilferage, etc., are not costly, there still is the capital tied up as inventory. With the discounted policy, Delta is buying in each order 50 percent more units than the annual item demand. The savings reported of $111.82 might not be enough to compensate Delta for pursuing the discounted policy.

ADDITIONAL READINGS

Ellram, Lisa M., and Laura M. Birou. *Purchasing for Bottom Line Impact*, vol. 4. National Association of Purchasing Management (NAPM). Homewood, IL: Irwin, 1995.

Fogarty, D. W., and T. R. Hoffmann. *Production and Inventory Management*. Cincinnati, OH: South-Western Publishing Co., 1983.

Hickman, Thomas K., and William M. Hickman. *Global Purchasing: How to Buy Goods and Services in Foreign Markets*. Business One Irwin/APICS Series in Production Management, Homewood, IL, 1992.

Hyer, Nancy, and Urban Wemmerlov. *Competing Through Cellular Manufacturing*. (Winner of the 2003 Shingo Prize). Productivity Press, 2002.

Killen Kenneth H., and John W. Kamauff. *Managing Purchasing*, vol. 2. National Association of Purchasing Management (NAPM). Homewood, IL: Irwin, 1994.

Leenders, Michiel R., and Anna E. Flynn. *Value-Driven Purchasing*, vol. 1. National Association of Purchasing Management (NAPM). Homewood, IL: Irwin, 1994.

Peterson, R., and E. A. Silver. *Decision Systems for Inventory Management and Production Planning*, 2e. New York: Wiley, 1984.

Plane, Donald R. *Management Science: A Spreadsheet Approach*. Danvers, MA: boyd & fraser publishing co, 1994.

Raedels, Alan R. *Value-Focused Supply Management*, vol. 3. National Association of Purchasing Management (NAPM). Homewood, IL: Irwin, 1994.

Ragsdale, Cliff T. *Spreadsheet Modeling & Decision Analysis: A Practical Introduction to Management Science*, 4e. Cincinnati: Thomson, South-Western Learning, 2004.

Tersine, R. J. *Principles of Inventory and Materials Management*, 3e. New York: Elsevier-North Holland Publishing, 1987.

Vollmann, T. E., W. L. Berry, and D. C. Whybark. *Manufacturing Planning and Control Systems*, 3e. Homewood, IL: Irwin, 1992.

NOTES

1. J. F. Cox, J. H. Blackstone, Jr., and M. S. Spencer, eds. *APICS Dictionary*, 7th ed. APICS Educational and Research Foundation Publishers, 1992.

2. "Sea-Land Beats the Odds in Kobe, Company Is Ready to Resume Shipping," *The New York Times*, (February 4, 1995).

3. "Venezuela's Chávez Asked Brazil's President Lula da Silva to Send Oil Technicians to Break a Month-Old General Strike," *The Wall Street Journal* (January 3, 2003).

SPOTLIGHT 14-1
Split the Difference

Digital Dealmakers

Computers are being used in more and more everyday transactions. Software developed by a company called *SplitTheDifference* relies on algorithms in settling claims between doctors and insurers. It calculates what a doctor might accept in exchange for faster payment. The software has been used in 20,000 negotiations over the past 18 months.

Many other innovations are based on advances in mathematics that enable computers to imitate human behavior and in some cases replace it. Negotiation software may someday be used to settle credit card bills, car loans, and other financial questions. Computers have the capacity to consider millions of offers and counteroffers in seconds.

The possibility of crossing the subtlety of human intellect with a processor's power continues to be a scientific holy grail. Steve White, senior manager in the I.B.M. autonomic computing group, is quoted as saying, "The big difference between humans and machines is that humans are really smart but slow, while machines are stupid but fast. Machines don't make mistakes either. What happens in negotiations is both sides have their own interests. No one ever gets what he wants." He concludes, "So what we are concentrating on is getting computers to talk to each other."

Instead of considering price alone, computers can weigh the relative merits of variables, including quantity, delivery time, and technical specifications. They now can incorporate into the negotiations factors that people may not have considered. The trick is to find a niche where the humans involved will not feel "fleeced" or feel that they are giving too much away to the other side. Effective software must give some control over the process to both sides.

Most companies are a long way from digital dealing because much of their data is on paper or in human memory. Aside from the money and time needed, managers are wary about turning over job functions or decision-making authority to a machine, a hurdle that must be overcome before negotiation software achieves broad acceptance. Robert Hall, a professor of economics at Stanford University and the author of *Digital Dealing: How E-Markets Are Transforming the Economy* (Norton, 2002), is quoted as saying, "There was a huge amount of belief in automated negotiations, but it has turned into a long slog. We're still living in a fax world."

Ariba, a leader in negotiation software, has had success with manufacturers. Ariba's negotiating tool gathers information about a company's inventory, production schedules, and prices, among other things. It uses the information to field inquiries from potential buyers of its products. Bidders who use the software can specify their tolerance for such variables as return rates, reliability, and other factors, which are assigned numerical rankings. By blending quantitative and qualitative information, the software enables users to determine the total cost of a purchase before negotiations begin. Steve Markle, a product manager for Ariba's Spend Management Solutions group, says, "Defining the parameters of the negotiations is as important as the negotiations."

SplitTheDifference found an opportunity to help insurers and doctors haggle over payments that are too small to be handled economically by conventional methods. Roy Ophir, the company's president, said that the software will only work if both insurers and doctors agree to use it. Behavioral patterns emerge from SplitTheDifference's business. Only 2 percent of the insurers' offers are accepted immediately because doctors routinely think they can get a better result without giving anything away in return. Three-quarters of the negotiations end after the second offer, suggesting that doctors have no time or motivation to haggle endlessly. A visit to the SplitTheDifference website will give the reader up-to-the-minute information about DealEngine, version 1.5, and how it works. It explains the difference between DealEngine versus Auctions.

Fujitsu Laboratories of America has produced dealmaking software of their own. Dave Marvit, who has a neuroscience background, and a team of researchers have worked for two years on a software program that can run through millions of potential scenarios in seconds. The software tries to narrow differences between groups that initially disagree. Marvit's group hopes that it will appeal to companies that swap foodstuffs, computer chips, and other commodities. The software is easy to use. "We can run millions of prices and have 1,000 or more negotiations that ask, 'How about this, how about that,'" said Marvit. Negotiators can select preferences for categories like quantity, delivery time, shipping and handling costs, unit prices, and reliability. Buyers can specify one priority, like the lowest price, or specify several categories at once. They might continue asking for a 1 percent discount until the price stops falling.

Marvit predicts that the ease and low cost of running the software will prompt more participants to trade online. In seconds, they will be able to calculate the cost of choosing blue over red or any number of other variables. He says, "It's the opposite of a zero-sum game," where, if one person wins, the other loses.

With digital dealmakers, everyone gets a fair deal.

Source: Belson, Ken. "Digital Dealmakers Meet in the Middle: Software That Can Hasten a Handshake Is Increasingly Part of the Bargain." *The New York Times* (September 11, 2003). http://www.splitThe Difference.com

SPOTLIGHT 14-2
E-Shopping

(B2C) and P/OM

Since the advent of the web, many Internet retailers have not obtained satisfactory financial results. During the same period, leading in-store retailers have been relatively profitable using traditional modes for selling and delivering goods to customers. Studies indicate that operations management methodology could have improved the profitability of Internet consumer-based businesses (called *B2C*).

An illustration is Webvan.com, which began in 1998 and declared bankruptcy in 2001. Webvan remains the biggest e-tailing dollar failure that occurred. Applying in-store retailing standards, Webvan's inability to reach breakeven within a reasonable period of time would not have been tolerated. Yet, the high fixed and variable costs of Webvan's operations might have been controlled if P/OM had been party to top management decisions.

Accomplished operations managers would have seen clearly that the volume of business required to recover fixed costs was not going to be attained within an acceptable planning horizon. When invited to the table, P/OM sits as a watchdog over matters such as these. P/OM is responsible for the cost of goods sold, which consists of materials and labor. It is traditionally accountable for quality, productivity, delivery, and costs.

One can speculate about what blinded Webvan's highly talented executive team. A fair guess is that if venture capitalists do not demand a payback period, neither does management. The impact of operations on the bottom line was overlooked because venture capitalists of that era aggressively pursued capacity growth rates rather than demand volume and commensurate profits. Journalists of that period of time supported the proposition that the Internet was bringing about a technological revolution in business methods. Profits were not the issue.

Uncertainty existed in 1999 about the survival of traditional retailers. In-store retail was labeled pejoratively the "old economy." Internet retailing, labeled the "new economy," was accompanied by astonishing price earnings ratios for dot.com stock prices. In this environment, management concentrated on raising increasing amounts of money—to buy more technology to take control of markets that did not yet exist.

Around March 2000, the "new economy" bubble burst. On Tuesday, July 10, 2001, *The New York Times* front-page headline read, "An Ambitious Internet Grocer Is Out of Both Cash and Ideas." The article stated that Internet-grocer Webvan had spent $1.2 billion of investors' money before declaring bankruptcy. Suddenly, opinions about Internet retailers were as negative as they had previously been positive. Business media now described dot.coms as a transient phenomenon that would never replace traditional modes of selling goods. The Internet business model for retail dot.coms was said to be inherently flawed.

The *flawed-Internet* surmise was as baseless as the *invincible-Internet* proposition. Both opinions were formed without benefit of operations management knowledge and a systems point of view. Gradually, after the bubble burst, recognition grew that ignorance was the culprit, not the Internet. Ideas began to surface about how defects in the business model could be corrected.

Here is how some of Webvan's problems might have been avoided. The firm should not have rushed to invest in technology aimed at serving markets not-yet-existent. Capacity planning needed to be synchronized with revenue growth. Webvan should have preserved cash rather than spending prematurely to erect barriers against competitive entry. The burn rate (of investor cash) was excessive needing controls.

Webvan's problems may have stemmed from erroneous forecasts of market growth timing. This produced an extraordinarily high breakeven point. Perhaps, in the time of Webvan, venture capitalists considered breakeven concepts to be anachronistic. Webvan set up distribution centers across more geography than it could handle over a short time. Its product line was overly ambitious. Probably, its most significant error was to believe that customers would never desire alternative shopping opportunities once their home delivery system was in place.

Another element contributing to failure was that Webvan's managers had no previous experience with the grocery business and supermarket operations. Webvan's managerial expertise was technology and not inventory. The logistics of the supply chain (requiring P/OM expertise) were out of kilter. Carrying costs were too high. Low inventory turns produced aging merchandise. Webvan's technologists were an asset, but team experience with groceries was essential for mastery of supermarket competitions.

As 2001 began, Webvan's market strategy and budget were not creating enough demand to match the warehouse capacities that had been created. It was clear that the cost of switching customers from conventional, in-store shopping to Internet shopping was much higher than had been imagined.

Amazon.com provides a striking contrast. Amazon's management slowed company expansion when the breakeven point increased relative to actual demand. Warehouse costs were slashed and operations were honed to stark efficiency. Marketing took aim at increasing volumes. For example, shipping became free for orders above $25. Partnerships were formed with Target, Circuit City, Toy-R-Us, Borders, and other firms to increase the base and spread the risk. These partnerships provided customers with combinations of online and in-store buying, as well as in-store pick-ups and returns.

Tesco.com and Sainsbury.com in the United Kingdom exemplify successful applications of mixed-mode shopping by established supermarkets. Visit their webpages to illuminate the degree of interchangeability of online and in-store activities. In the United States, Peapod (wholly owned subsidiary of Royal Ahold) partners with Stop & Shop and Giant Food. On its webpages, Peapod describes its commitment to the mixed-mode "clicks and bricks." Webvan might be around today if it had forsaken its pure-Internet strategy.

Sources:

Starr, Martin K. "Application of P/OM to E-Business: B2C E-Shopping." *International Journal of Operations & Production Management*, vol. 23, no. 1 (2003): 105–124.
Http://www.j-sainsbury.com/ecommerce.
Http://www.tesco.com.
Http://www.peapod.com.

Material Requirements Planning (MRP)

Chapter Outline

This section explains how to manage inventories of materials that have sporadic demands. Often their use is dependent on one or more job shop end-items, which necessitates good organization of information. The appropriate information system facilitates material requirements planning, which is known as MRP. The methods, strengths, and weaknesses of MRP are evaluated. The chapter also examines capacity requirements planning, known as CRP, and distribution requirements planning, known as DRP.

After reading this chapter, you should be able to:

- Explain the difference between dependent and independent demand systems.
- Distinguish between the foundations and fundamentals of OPP and MRP.
- Describe when MRP is preferred to the OPP approach for materials planning.
- Explain the importance of the master production schedule (MPS).
- Discuss the role of the bill of material and describe different forms that are used for the BOM.
- Detail the data inputs and information outputs of material requirements planning (MRP).
- Talk about lot sizing methods used for ordering with MRP.

- Describe capacity requirements planning (CRP).
- Explain distribution requirements planning (DRP = DRP1) and relate it to replenishing inventory at the branch warehouses.
- Explain distribution resource planning (DRP = DRP2) and relate it to planning for the key resources of the supply chain.
- Discuss how information systems using coding connect parts from more than one product into a cohesive planning whole.
- Distinguish between two extensions of basic MRP, namely, closed-loop MRP and MRP II.

THE SYSTEMS VIEWPOINT

Material requirements planning (MRP) is inherently a systems approach to the management of the entire supply chain. The method addresses a broad range of P/OM situations for inventory planning using information systems to connect parts from many products in an overall plan of action. MRP employs detail about customers, suppliers, and producer's capabilities to provide guidance for actions of when to order and how much to order, among other things. Time-dependent factors are an integral part of the analysis and solution development.

Systems that require MRP include interdependencies between final assembly products (parents) and parts (components that include subassemblies). In other words, the same part occurs in various products and so when planning production runs, over time the different demand patterns for the parts (or components) in each product must be linked to determine the overall demand for the part. Good systems

Material requirements planning (MRP): An information system that organizes all factors that determine production-scheduling decisions and all support functions including vendors.

analysis is essential for achieving the goals of having *what* is needed, *when* needed, and *where* needed.

STRATEGIC THINKING

The ultimate systems plan is manufacturing resource planning (MRP II), which links OM production planning with marketing goals, financial policies, accounting procedures, R & D plans, human resources management constraints, and so on. Put in an alternative context, MRP II is responsive to the strategic business plan of the company. Thus, new product introductions are most likely to be successful if the total organization is communicating and coordinated. The organization as a whole can mobilize to handle serious problems as they arise, such as large numbers of defectives and major equipment failures.

In line with the need for strategic thinking, reactions to predicaments may include adding physical space and production capacity as well as coproducing, which means subcontracting work to firms having the requisite capabilities. The production budget will have to be changed. From both the strategic and the systems point of view, MRP, in its various forms, helps to achieve functionally-coordinated organizations. By noting the degree of information completeness regarding all functions, it is possible to ascertain at what level of coordination the firm is functioning. MRP II operates at the highest level of coordination. That is very demanding and difficult to achieve. It is a goal worth striving for because it provides one of the most powerful platforms for finding best solutions to the dynamics of change.

15-1   THE BACKGROUND FOR MRP

There always has been a need for a method to deal with the great complexity of inventory control for job shops that have many interdependent parts. The method had to be able to organize all of the data on stock-keeping units (SKUs). It had to keep track of stock levels, and order timing, while coordinating process scheduling with delivery dates for customers. The challenge of organizing all of this information continued to grow with the increasing size of markets, product line variety, and production capabilities.

The first book on MRP, written by Joseph Orlicky, was published in 1975. In the preface to this book, Orlicky states that the development and installation of computer-based MRP systems began in 1960—over 36 years ago.[1] Also, he points out that, "the number of MRP systems used in American industry gradually grew to about 150 in 1971, when the growth curve began a steep rise as a result of the 'MRP Crusade,' a national program of publicity and education sponsored by the American Production and Inventory Control Society (APICS)." Today, there are tens of thousands of companies using various kinds of MRPs, and they are located all over the world.

MRP could not work in a practical way without the powerful computer capabilities that were emerging by the 1970s. The need to be able to manage the massive amount of information required for ordering and scheduling in large job shops became pressing. The ability to meet that need grew even faster.

MRP has drawn broad national attention and support as computer power has become increasingly available at significantly lower prices. It continues to be true that the pros and cons of specific MRP software must be discussed separately from the principles that drive the methodology. In-house programming as well as many software packages are alternatives that need to be evaluated according to circumstances.

15-2   DEPENDENT DEMAND SYSTEMS CHARACTERIZE MRP

MRP applies to a dissimilar class of problems than order point policy (OPP) models, which are used under distinctly different circumstances. OPP models (which are represented by EOQ and FLS) are powerful as long as the assumptions for their applicability hold true. MRP is used when the following OPP assumptions do not hold.

OPP Assumptions

1. Demand is independent. This is true of end products like cars and VCRs whose demand is driven by the marketplace. In contrast, the demand for the raw materials, subassemblies, and components used in the automobiles and VCRs are dependent on the number and types of cars and VCRs that are made. **End products,** which also are called *parent products,* are considered to have independent demand systems.

2. Demand for the item has to be regular and relatively continuous over time for order point models and policies to be applicable. If demand for an end-item is sporadic, so that stock on-hand for components that the end-item uses might sit around waiting for unknown periods of time, then that item does not fit the mode for an OPP application. When this is not the case, so that the inventory gets used up and needs to be reordered on a repetitive basis, the OPP conditions exist.

End products: Also called *parent products*. End-product demand can be sporadic. MRP is the information system that details what must be done to produce the required number of end products. The BOM lists parts and components.

MRP Assumptions

MRP should be used for inventory management of any items that do not satisfy both of the two OPP assumptions. Alternatively, MRP is used when the following two points apply.

1. Demand is dependent because it will organize and control bringing together the kit of interdependent parts and subassemblies to make up the end product. The more complex the dependencies, the more critical is the use of MRP.

2. Demand for the item is sporadic and lumpy. This can occur for end products that have demand patterns that are not smooth and regular. However, quite often sporadic and lumpy conditions occur for parts that are dependent on end products that have regular and smooth demands. The various reasons why this is true include the fact that the part appears in several end products.

Sometimes the part is used by different end products that are produced simultaneously on parallel lines. In other circumstances, the common part is used in different end products that are scheduled to be made at widely separated times. Part demands can change according to which special options of the parent product are being produced.

To illustrate this last point, say that VCRs with different options (one model has two heads—H2, and the other model has four heads—H4) are run on the same line. The line switches from one model to the other on alternating weeks. The demand is fairly constant for VCRs so that 200 are made every day. Note how the demand for the 2-head components and the 4-head components changes on a weekly basis. Every other week there is no need to have stock on-hand for both the H2 and the H4.

Table 15-1 illustrates the sporadic character of the dependent demands for H2 and H4. Although VCR production is smooth and continuous, the demands for components H2 and H4 are discontinuous—fluctuating between needing 1,000 units one week and none the next week.

Dependencies are seldom as regular as in Table 15-1 because the components are used in different end products, each of which has its own demand pattern. Most are only relatively continuous and not as stable as the VCR pattern shown here.

The comparison with regard to stock on-hand for independent and dependent demand systems is shown in Figure 15-1. When reorder point models are used to control stock on-hand for linked parts, parent demand systems often produce inventory swings that lead to overstocks and out-of-stocks. This occurs because the information about the products and the parts are not properly merged. The result is that the inventory levels are mismanaged. Lump withdrawals of parts to supply their parent products create demand surges, which overpower the steady demand pattern required for reorder point models.

	Week 1					2					3.....
Day	1	2	3	4	5	1	2	3	4	5	1
VCRs	200	200	200	200	200	200	200	200	200	200	200...
H2	200	200	200	200	200						200...
H4						200	200	200	200	200	

Week 1	Need 1,000 H2s		Need 0 H2s
Week 2	Need 0 H4s		Need 1,000 H4s
Week 3	Need 1,000 H2s		Need 0 H2s
Week 4	(the pattern continues)		(the pattern continues)

TABLE 15-1

Demand for End-Product VCRs Is Smooth While Demand for Components H2 and H4 Pulses

MRP reflects the systems viewpoint by connecting the parent products and the dependent parts. This linkage is made by managing the combined information concerning dependent demands, SOH, deliveries, and lead times.

15-2a Forecasting Considerations

Reorder point models require that demand distributions exist for their forecasting requirements. When such reliable, long-term forecasts are not feasible, MRP is indicated. This accounts for a broad range of P/OM situations that require MRP because they have irregular demands—and do not have stable distributions.

Even though MRP demands are sporadic and lumpy, they can be predicted as discrete order events when there is advance knowledge about probable order placements. Predictions about the demand for parts are often based on forecasts for the end product. This is the result of dependent demand. The distinction that is being made is between predictions that are generated by customer notification of intentions to buy (use MRP), as compared to forecasts based on demand distributions that exist in a steady state over time (use OPP).

Actual customer orders (CO) on-hand provide relatively solid information about future demands. However, cancellations of orders are not uncommon, so risk factors still play a part in the determination of future events. Often, there are many customers with a variety of types of products (associated with the job shop). This creates numerous interdependencies and sources of change long after order entry for the customer's order. Change also can take place after orders are placed with suppliers for the parts needed to make the end products.

Ollie Wight wrote in 1970, " . . . the number of pages written on independent demand-type inventory systems outnumbers the pages written on material requirements planning by well over 100 to 1. The number of items in inventory that can best be controlled by material requirements planning outnumbers those that can be controlled effectively by order point in about the same ratio."[2] The ratio of papers written for OPP as compared to MRP is now closer to 50/50, but the number of items in inventory that fit MRP instead of OPP is not much changed.

FIGURE 15-1
Stock On-Hand Patterns

15-3 THE MASTER PRODUCTION SCHEDULE (MPS)

The **master production schedule (MPS)** is one of three inputs to the MRP information system. The other two are the bill of material (BOM), which describes what constitutes the end product, and inventory stock-level reports.

Aggregate production planning determines the resource capability and capacity to produce generic product in standard hours or in some other generalized dimension. For example, the aggregate plan might specify the number of gallons of paint to be made in January. The master production schedule converts this number into a time-phased plan, which indicates exactly when each type and color of paint and size of can should be made, and how much of it should be made.

Table 15-2 shows the planning only for January. Similar plans will be made by the MPS for February, March, and all succeeding months.

The basis for the assignments of MPS—quantity to be made of specific models at chosen times—are customer orders and forecasts of orders to come that are considered highly probable. The MPS makes the assignments in response to sales department commitments, which are called **order promising.**

Order promising is defined as "The process of making a delivery commitment, i.e., answering the question, 'When can you ship?' For make-to-order products, this usually involves a check of uncommitted material and availability of capacity. *Syn.* customer order promising, order dating."[3]

Figure 15-2 relates order promising to the time line that characterizes all production scheduling. It shows that the drivers (or inputs) of the MRP system are the customers' orders for parent products, which have been scheduled by the master production schedule (MPS). These are drawn above the parent product process timeline.

Figure 15-2 also shows that the MRP system determines what parts are used by the parent product (Parts 1 through *m*). It indicates when they are required by the process. It physically represents the lead times (LT) between placing orders and receiving them. MRP assignments are shown below the parent product process time line.

Total or cumulative lead time (LT) is defined by APICS as follows: "In a logistics context, the time between recognition of the need for an order and the receipt of goods. Individual components of lead time can include order preparation time, queue time, move or transportation time, and receiving and inspection time. *Syn.* total lead time."[4]

The cumulative lead time for a parent product is found by looking at the longest lead-time path to obtain all of the parts that go into it as the end-item. To assemble A in Figure 15-3 requires ordering B one week before the assembly operation is to begin. Part C must be ordered two weeks before assembly is to begin on part A. Parts D and E are necessary components for part C. Part D has $LT = 2$ and part E has $LT = 4$. The longest path results from A + C + E and that has $LT = 6$, and it dominates cumulative lead time.

Master production schedule (MPS): Converts aggregate plans into a time-phased plan that indicates exactly when each SKU should be made and how much should be run; responsive to customer orders on hand and forecasts.

Order promising: Sales department commitments for delivery; answers the question "When can you ship?"

Total or cumulative lead time (LT): Time between recognition of the need for an order and the acknowledged, genuine receipt of goods.

Week	WGF	WHGF	WGO	RGGL	RHGF	WPGL	YGF	SUM
1	10	10	10					30
2	10		10	15	5			40
3			20			10		30
4			10			10	10	30
SUM	20	10	50	15	5	20	10	130

January Master Production Schedule
Paint Code (Color, Size, Type)
(Table entries are in 000)

TABLE 15-2

Converting the Aggregate Planning Schedule into the Master Production Schedule for January—130,000 gallons Are Required

Legend for paint codes: First letter in sequence is color: W = white, R = red, Y = yellow. Second code place is size: G = gallon, HG = half gallon, P = pint. Third code place is type: F = flat, O = outdoor, GL = glossy. Five letters are possible, as in WHGGL.

FIGURE 15-2
The Time-Phased
MPS Function

Note relationship to later use of the terms: Place order = planned-order release; receive order = planned-order receipt. Examples of parent products include mobile phones, VCRs, DVDs, digital cameras, laptops, bicycles, autos, farm equipment, and industrial machines.

However, if part E is a *standard* item, which means it is stocked, then E should not be considered when calculating total lead time. If D is a *special* item, which means there is no stock on-hand for D, then the lead time $LT = A + C + D = 4$ dominates the cumulative lead time. If both D and E are standard items, then $LT = A + C = 2$ has a longer path than $LT = A + B = 1$. As a final consideration, if C is a standard item, the longest lead-time path is $LT = A + B = 1$.

15-3a Total Manufacturing Planning and Control System (MPCS)

The manufacturing planning procedure started with resource evaluation and forecasting at the aggregate scheduling stages of manufacturing planning. Based on an authorized production plan, it moved to master production scheduling (MPS), which reacts to specific customer order expectations and orders on hand. Once the MPS is accepted and authorized, the planning process proceeds to details of scheduling that are the province of the material requirements planning (MRP) system.

These steps are flowcharted in Figure 15-4. The system called the *total manufacturing planning and control system (MPCS)* captures what takes place in job shops all over the world.

The MPS stage needs to be documented. In Figure 15-5, an MPS chart is shown that is created for every parent product. It represents the middle step—MPS—in the total MPCS shown in Figure 15-4. This MPS chart goes nine weeks into the future with parent-product requirements scheduled for weeks 2, 5, and 9. The MPS must project gross requirements far enough ahead to permit actions to be taken that are needed for the success of parent-product production.

Weeks are the intervals, or time buckets, most often used. However, other periods can be required. Some organizations use short- and long-term master production schedules where the short-term schedules are in days or weeks and the long-term schedules are in months or quarters. The time buckets used reflect the rapidity of changes to schedule, lead-time lengths, and how far ahead it is possible to forecast.

The MPS chart in Table 15-3 has 20 units of parent product to be made in the second week ahead from *now*. If it takes 4 weeks (total lead time, $LT = 4$) to order parts that

FIGURE 15-3
Cumulative Lead-Time Tree

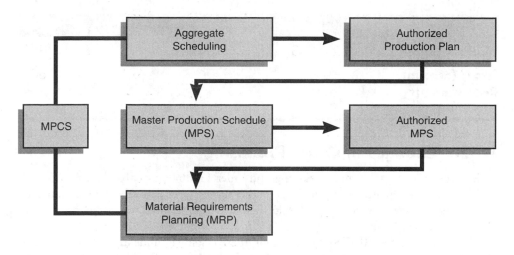

FIGURE 15-4
The Total Manufacturing Planning and Control System (MPCS)

are needed for the parent product, then the order should have been placed already. Note that this chart is updated each week.

The gross amount required moves from the *nth week ahead* to the *n* – 1 week ahead of *now*. Thus, the second week from now at one time appeared as week 5. When it was in the week 5 position, the parts were ordered during week 1. Therefore, it is expected that the necessary order for parts already has been placed for the present *week 2 ahead* gross requirements of 20.

In Table 15-3, there are 45 units required for the *present week 5 ahead*. The planned order should be released now, in week 1. There are 60 units required for the *present week 9 ahead*. Perhaps there should be a planned-order release *in week 5 ahead* for these 60 units. However, the ordering policy, which will be discussed shortly, may determine that the order for week 5 ahead (which is released in week 1) should cover some (or all) of the week 9 ahead requirements. There is a point to be made, namely, the master production schedule is required to have a planning horizon as long as the longest cumulative lead-time function.

15-3b MPS: Inputs and Outputs

Master production schedulers set down the make-build schedule for specific parent products. Their scheduling function moves beyond the generic units of time and money that were the limitations of aggregate scheduling. They deal with real-time and specific SKUs. The master production schedules are partially driven by the sales forecast, which is one of the usual inputs to the production plan. It also is driven by actual orders on hand. It takes into account priorities for orders based on urgency and customer importance. Master production schedulers always seek to make the best use of actual capacity and resources. These considerations are brought together in Figure 15-5.

FIGURE 15-5
Inputs and Outputs of MPS

<table>
<tr><td rowspan="2">**TABLE 15-3**

MPS Chart for *Specific* Parent Product</td><td>Weeks Ahead</td><td>1</td><td>2</td><td>3</td><td>4</td><td>5</td><td>6</td><td>7</td><td>8</td><td>9</td></tr>
<tr><td>Gross (amount) Requirements</td><td></td><td>20</td><td></td><td></td><td>45</td><td></td><td></td><td></td><td>60</td></tr>
</table>

15-3c Changes in Order Promising

Order promising by sales and marketing and order fulfillment goals of production are matched and coordinated by the MPS. If marketing promises dates that production cannot deliver, changes are required either in the due dates promised to customers or in the production schedules for the plant.

In a **make-to-stock (MTS) environment,** there is some latitude in what is scheduled. Also, there may be sufficient inventory in stock to help fulfill order promising. The emphasis is on having sufficient stock on-hand to provide excellent service with minimum delivery times. The MRP emphasis is on finished product, which is usually smaller in number than the number of components that make up the finished product. This is typical of automobiles, homeowners' tools, and VCRs.

In a **make-to-order (MTO) inventory environment,** there is no finished goods inventory to call upon. End-items are produced to customers' orders. Consequently, greater dependency exists between sales, which promises delivery, and OM, which has to produce what is to be delivered. Customers expect finished goods to be delivered on time. This characterizes small- and medium-sized job shops—often called *machine shops*—that work from blueprints and do not have product lines. Carpenters and plumbers live in an MTO environment. On a larger scale, auto replacement part manufacturers including windshield glass have a significant percent of their business as MTO.

The **assemble-to-order (ATO) environment** is one where end items are built from subassemblies. Master production schedules ensure that these subassemblies are available to meet demand within promised due dates. Often the number of components is smaller than the number of finished products, and master production schedules operate at the components or subassembly level. This means that parts and subassemblies are scheduled instead of parent products. In this case, the MPS is only secondarily concerned with parent end products and primarily with making the parts to complete the subassemblies. The master production schedule is focused on the subassemblies much like the modular BOM concentrates on options (see Section 15-4). The heavy equipment industry uses assemble-to-order.

15-3d The Bill of Material (BOM)

The bill of material (BOM) for a dinner party is the cook's shopping list. Job shop production managers used the BOM long before MRP was developed. Now, well past 2003, MRP is widely used. MRP cannot be used without the BOM. The social dinner party was fun but McDonald's and Burger King have a more serious view about the materials required for the manufactured food service business. The bill of material for an automobile is so extensive that it has to be subdivided into subassemblies of components.

The APICS definition is quite complete. A **bill of material (BOM)** is "a listing of all of the subassemblies, intermediates, parts, and raw materials that go into a parent assembly showing the quantity of each required to make an assembly. It is used in conjunction with the master production schedule to determine the items for which purchase requisitions and production orders must be released. There is a variety of display formats for bills of materials, including the single-level bill of material, indented bill of material, modular (planning) bill of material, transient bill of material, matrix bill of material, and costed bill of material. It may also be called the 'formula,' 'recipe,' 'ingredients list,' in certain industries."[5]

Make-to-stock (MTS) environment: There is latitude in what to make and the quantities to produce because various items have finished goods inventories; marketing can (to some extent) meet customers' demands by selling what is in stock.

Make-to-order (MTO) inventory environment: There is no finished goods inventory to meet demand.

Assemble-to-order (ATO) environment: Setting where end items are built from subassemblies.

Bill of material (BOM): Lists all of the subassemblies, parts, and raw materials that go into a parent assembly showing the quantities required.

FIGURE 15-6
Single-Level BOM
Parent product with parts
one level down. The number
of parts needed for the level
above are shown in parentheses.

FIGURE 15-7
Multi-Level BOM
Parent product with parts at all
levels down. This is often called
a product-structure tree, where
the number of parts needed for
the level above are shown in
parentheses.

BOMs include every material that goes into or onto a product. It can also be applied to every material that is needed to deliver a service. This is epitomized by "meals on wheels." In manufacturing, the materials may be screws, nails, rivets, glue, paint, and packaging. Figures 15-6, 15-7, and 15-8, and Table 15-4 display a number of the commonly used BOMs. Each of the different kinds of bills of materials mentioned in the APICS definition captures some important aspects of the MRP process. BOMs are the starting point for actual use of MRP, and the varieties are consequently instructive.

The multilevel BOM (as a tree or in the indented form) is essential for MRP purposes because it captures everything that must be ordered to complete the parent product. The APICS definition is precise, namely "a display of all the components directly or indirectly used in a parent, together with the quantity required of each component. If a component is a subassembly, blend, intermediate, etc., all of its components will also be exhibited and all of their components, down to purchased parts and materials."[6]

FIGURE 15-8
**Multi-Level BOM with More
Detailed Coded Information**

VCR Alpha		**Level 0**	**VCR Beta**		**Level 0**
X(2)		1	G(2)		1
	P(2)	2		P(2)	2
	Q(1)	2		B(1)	2
Y(1)		1	Y(1)		1
	R(1)	2		R(1)	2
	S(4)	2		S(4)	2
	T(2)	2		T(2)	2
Z(1)		1	V(1)		1
	M(1)	2		C(1)	2
	N(1)	2		D(1)	2
B(1)		1	B(1)		1 (Code 2)
	Q(2)	2		E(2)	2 (Code 3)

TABLE 15-4

Multi-Level Indented BOM

Parent product and parts are carried at levels (0, 1, 2, and 3) for two VCR models (the alpha and the beta) as shown here. The number of parts needed for the level above are indicated in parentheses.
(See Figure 15-12 for the VCR-beta product structure and note that because B(1) is low-level coded at level 2, E(2) is at the third level. Low-level coding will be explained shortly.)

Modular BOMs are organized so that product options can serve in place of single-product parents. This BOM is associated with products that can be assembled in many different ways. Thus, assemble-to-order is common with computers that can be configured in many ways using different boards and drives. It also is characteristic of automobile assembly with different packages of features. The options are fewer than the end products, which can combine options in many different ways. Thus, by using options, fewer bills of materials are required to control the ordering and inventories.

The matrix BOM is a special chart constructed by analyzing the BOMs of a family of similar products. It arranges parts in columns and parent products in rows. This is useful where the objective is to make the greatest number of products with the minimum number of parts. This matrix characterizes what is called the *modular product design objective.*

Cost BOMs show complete parent-part hierarchical product structures with the latest costs per part appended. The costs must be regularly updated to prevent incorrect and misleading information. The cost BOMs are useful for purchasing decisions when alternative suppliers are being considered. They also are an important means of determining the costs of parts including raw materials, subassemblies, and components.

Transient or phantom BOMs are used for subassemblies that are not kept in stock. It will be noted here that phantoms are assigned zero lead times and lot-for-lot order quantities (concepts that will be explained later). This permits the MRP system to bypass the subassemblies and go directly to their components.

15-3e Explosion of Parts

The multilevel product structure was called an *explosion* by Orlicky who wrote, "In executing the explosion, the task is to identify the components of a given parent item and to ascertain the location (address) of their inventory records in computer storage so that they may be retrieved and processed."[7]

15-4 OPERATION OF THE MRP

Inventory record files (IRF):
Stock on-hand levels; suppliers' prices and delivery lead times must be current.

The **inventory record files (IRF)** are the third major input to the MRP computer system. The inputs are shown in Figure 15-9 along with the outputs from the MRP system that are about to be discussed.

Stock on-hand levels need to be up-to-date. So should all ordering information, including the suppliers' lead times. The roles of the MPS and the BOM have been discussed already. It is noted that preparation of the MPS involves knowledge of the BOMs as well as the inventory and supplier information.

Input—Drives Plans
- Master Production Schedule (MPS)
- Bill of Materials (BOM) Product Tree
- Inventory Records File (IRF) Stock On-Hand Information
- Inventory Transactions Updating
- Supplier Information Lead Times

MRP System

Output—Drives Actions
- Planned-Order Timetable and Orders Released

Other Outputs
- Changes to Prior Planned Order Releases
- Exception and Performance Reports

FIGURE 15-9
The Inputs and Outputs of the MRP System

15-4a   Coding and Low-Level Coding

When various parent items have had their parts explosion accomplished, **coding** provides a means of identifying the fact that some parts belong to more than one parent. In Table 15-4, note that the indented BOMs of the alpha and beta VCR models share Y(1) sub-assemblies at level one. All components of Y(1) are similarly shared at the next level down. These are R(1), S(4), and T(2). Further, P(2) is used by both models at the second level. The SKU numbers can include coding such as Y(1) and P(2).

When the master production schedule calls for various amounts of alpha and beta VCRs, the MRP must combine the demands of commonly shared parts. For the specific example that is being discussed here (Table 15-4), the MRP program must be able to recognize that one alpha VCR and one beta VCR call for 2Y(1)s, 2R(1)s, 8 S(4)s, 4 T(2)s, and 4 P(2)s. Increased demand for parts shared in common will affect the order quantities in different ways, depending upon the method used to determine order lot sizes.

Coding techniques capture other relevant information about parts, such as data about suppliers, storage locations, and what substitutes exist. Coding of part names is the foundation for an effective information system to link the components and the parents together. It also is the best means of identifying families of parts that can be made with minimal setup changes. Such part-family-oriented processes are the subject that is identified by the name "group technology."

Part numbers should not be chosen randomly. There is so much useful information that can be instantly gleaned from carefully coded part numbers. It is best to code part numbers so that they reflect the level of the part and the product parents of the part. Additionally, as suggested earlier, codes show who are current suppliers of the part, who might be future suppliers of the part, alternative locations for storage, and the type of materials of which the part is made.

The method called **low-level coding** is commonly used to organize order quantity calculations for parts with combined demands. Top-level parents, such as the VCR models, are called the level zero. Parts and components that are one level down are coded level one. Those two levels down are coded level two, etc. This coding scheme shows how distant parts are (in their linkage) from their parent products.

"Once low-level codes are established, MRP record processing proceeds from one level code to the next, starting at level code 0. This ensures all gross requirements have been passed down to a part before its MRP record is processed. The result is planning of component parts coordinated with the needs of all higher-level part numbers. Within a level, the MRP record processing is typically done in part number sequence."[8]

Coding: Provides a means of identifying the fact that some parts are required by more than one parent.

Low-level coding: Organizes order quantity calculations for parts with combined (multilevel) demands; the lowest position of a part determines where the calculation of gross cumulative requirements is made.

FIGURE 15-10
**Product-Structure Tree
for a Hall Coat Rack
with Unfulfilled Low-Level
Coding Requirement**

Low-level coding uses the principle that the lowest position of a part should determine where that part is located for computer scanning. Part B of VCR beta appears as B(1) at both the first and second levels of the multilevel indented BOM in Table 15-4. The MRP software counts down from the level zero to determine order quantities and when to release the orders for parts. Thus, for the beta VCR, it will carry B(1) at level one down to level two where it will combine it with the level two B(1). (This is shown in Figure 15-12.)

Figure 15-10 shows the product structure for a hall coat rack tree where a G part appears at both levels one and two. Figure 15-11 redraws to accommodate the low-level coding requirement. The graphics aside, low-level coding is simply an organizing rule for computing materials requirements.

Exception codes are used to identify important items. This is equivalent to adding on to the part number an exception code indicator to reflect the fact that checks should be made for the accuracy of the data and the status of the part. Ten percent of all items might receive such special coding; this depends on the importance of the customer, the difficulty of the job, or the fact that MRP cannot schedule completion of a level zero product because something has gone awry.

15-5 MRP BASIC CALCULATIONS AND CONCEPTS

Gross requirements GR_t for end-items for week t are required by MRP and stated by the MPS. Inventory information is on file for the prior week's stock on-hand (SOH_{t-1}). There may be some open orders that will be received at the beginning of week t, and these are called scheduled receipts, SR_t.

Projected stock on-hand at time $t = SOH_{t-1} + SR_t$.

FIGURE 15-11
**Product-Structure Tree
for a Hall Coat Rack
with Low-Level Coding
Requirement Fulfilled**

The gross requirements less the projected stock on-hand, at time t, are called the *net requirements*, NR_t, thus:

$$NR_t = GR_t - (SOH_{t-1} + SR_t)$$

The process of determining net requirements is called *netting*. Based on net requirements and order policies, planned-order receipt times and planned-order release times can be determined, as explained here.

If projected stock on-hand is larger than the gross requirements:

$$(SOH_{t-1} + SR_t) > GR_t$$

then, there would be stock on-hand at the end of period t. Thus:

$$SOH_t = SOH_{t-1} + SR_t - GR_t > 0$$

Net requirements would be zero in the previous equation because there was more stock on-hand than gross requirements. However, if

$$GR_t > (SOH_{t-1} + SR_t)$$

then, $NR_t > 0$, and an order must be placed early enough so that with the lead time, delivery can be made at the beginning of period t. This order is called a *planned-order receipt*, PR_t.

In the following equation, $PR_t = 0$ when projected stock on-hand is greater than gross requirements.

$$SOH_t = SOH_{t-1} + SR_t + PR_t - GR_t$$

When there is a shortfall, the size of PR_t must be decided. When **lot-for-lot** ordering is used, this means that the planned-order receipt is equal to the net requirements.

> **Lot-for-lot ordering:** Planned-order receipt will equal the required amounts at each point in time.

$$PR_t = NR_t \text{ with lot-for-lot ordering}$$

If other methods are used for ordering, then the order size can exceed net requirements, and the planned-order receipt, PR_t will be greater than the net requirements.

To keep the charts simple in the examples that follow, scheduled receipts are set to zero. Therefore, projected stock on-hand is the same as SOH_{t-1}.

15-6 MRP IN ACTION

The easiest way to understand MRP is to simulate the action. Here are some scenarios that provide the best explanation of the workings of MRP.

First, create the MPS for the alpha and beta models. Use rough-cut capacity planning (RCCP) to make certain there is enough capacity to produce Table 15-5 specifications. Rough-cut means approximate rather than precise.

Second, develop the product structure for both alpha and beta models, as in Figure 15-12.

Note that because of low-level coding B(1) is at level two placing E(2) at level three. See also the indented BOM in Table 15-4.

Scenario 1
Lot-for-Lot Ordering with No Parts Sharing Parents—Level One

MRP methods will be used to determine order timing for part Z in the alpha model of the VCR. Note that Z(1) occurs only in the alpha model, and at level one. There is one unit per VCR. Lead time (LT) = 2 weeks, which means that LTs for both M(1) and N(1) are less than two weeks. There must be time for the Z component to be assembled after receiving the parts M and N.

The initial SOH = 80. Lot sizing follows a lot-for-lot policy. This means that both the planned-order receipt and the planned-order release exactly match the net requirements number of units. See Table 15-6.

TABLE 15-5	Week										
Net requirements		1	2	3	4	5	6	7	8	9	10
Alpha model		-	60	-	-	-	80	-	-	40	-
Beta model		-	-	50	-	-	20	-	-	-	60

Master VCR Schedule—Alpha and Beta Models

The conclusion is to have an order release (place the order) for 60 units of Z in week 4 for receipt in week 6. Also, order 40 units of Z in week 7 for receipt in week 9. There are two orders, and once the initial stock on-hand is used up, there are no carrying costs. This is due to the fact that lot sizing is done on a lot-by-lot basis. The short lead time makes this feasible.

Scenario 2
Lot-for-Lot Ordering with No Parts Sharing Parents—Level Two

Part N(1) is dependent on part Z(1). One N and one M are needed to make one Z. The use of MRP methods will determine order timing for part N in level two of the alpha model of the VCR. Lead time is one week, and SOH is 40 units. See Table 15-7.

Forty units of stock are carried for three weeks. Two orders are placed. One order is in week 3 and the other order is in week 6. Planned receipt is in weeks 4 and 7.

Scenario 3
Lot-for-Lot Ordering with No Parts Sharing Parents—Level Two

Part M(1) is dependent on part Z(1). The difference between the scenarios for N (shown earlier) and M (now) is that part M has no SOH (SOH = 0 units). Again, MRP methods

FIGURE 15-12
Product-Structure Trees for VCRs, Alpha and Beta

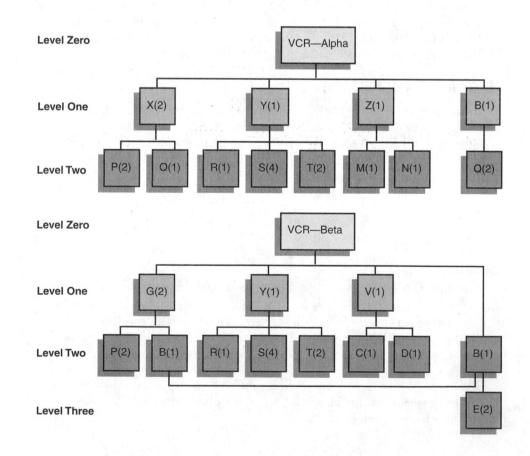

	End Week									
	1	2	3	4	5	6	7	8	9	10
Gross requirements	-	60	-	-	-	80	-	-	40	-
Stock on-hand (SOH)	80	20	20	20	20	-	-	-	-	-
Net requirements	-	-	-	-	-	60	-	-	40	-
Planned-order receipt	-	-	-	-	-	60	-	-	40	-
Planned-order release	-	-	-	60	-	-	40	-	-	-

TABLE 15-6

MRP Plan for VCR Alpha—Z(1)

will be used to determine order timing for part M in level two of the alpha model of the VCR. LT is one week as it was for part N. See Table 15-8.

There is no stock carried. Two orders are placed in weeks 3 and 6 with planned receipt in week 4 and week 7. Table 15-9 summarizes the first three scenarios, which are related in the VCR hierarchy.

Having stock on-hand for Z(1) deferred the need for an order until week 4. Thereafter, the lot-for-lot ordering policy took over. On the other hand, the fact that N(1) had some stock on-hand did not defer an order. It just made it a smaller one. The pattern of dependency is evident in that M and N need to be ordered in weeks 3 and 6 to satisfy Z's need for stock in weeks 4 and 7.

The next, and final, scenario assumes that an economic order quantity Q_o has been determined to set the order size. Note it is used because it minimizes the sum of ordering and carrying costs. Also, it is not the basis for a continuous (dynamic) ordering system with a reorder point.

Scenario 4
Economic Order Quantity for a Part That Shares Parents

Y(1) subassemblies occur in both the alpha and the beta model. Therefore, the demands in the MPS are combined. There is one unit used whichever model is made. $LT = 1$ week, which means that R(1), S(4), and T(2) all have lead times that are one week or less.

The initial SOH = 80. Lot sizing is done using the economic order quantity (EOQ) model. The optimal lot size has been determined to be $Q_o = 90$ units. See Table 15-10.

Y(1) total demand (combines demand for both the alpha and beta models) drives the planned-order releases and receipts. There are three orders, and 230 units are carried over the 7-week period. This 7-week period (which stretches from the end of week 3 to the end of week 10) starts once the initial (SOH) inventory of 80 units is used up.

The average number of units that are carried is equal to 230/7 = 32.86, or 33. For the 10-week period, it is the same (330/10 = 33). Also, there will be 90 − 50 = 40 units carried during week 11.

Note: The supplement to this chapter compares the total costs of all scenarios. That comparison is necessary for the operations manager to make a choice between alternatives.

	End Week									
	1	2	3	4	5	6	7	8	9	10
Gross requirements	-	-	-	60	-	-	40	-	-	-
Stock on-hand (SOH)	40	40	40	-	-	-	-	-	-	-
Net requirements	-	-	-	20	-	-	40	-	-	-
Planned-order receipt	-	-	-	20	-	-	40	-	-	-
Planned-order release	-	-	20	-	-	40	-	-	-	-

TABLE 15-7

MRP Plan for VCR Alpha—N(1)

TABLE 15-8

**MRP Plan for VCR
Alpha—M(1)**

	End Week									
	1	2	3	4	5	6	7	8	9	10
Gross requirements	-	-	-	60	-	-	40	-	-	-
Stock on-hand (SOH)	-	-	-	-	-	-	-	-	-	-
Net requirements	-	-	-	60	-	-	40	-	-	-
Planned-order receipt	-	-	-	60	-	-	40	-	-	-
Planned-order release	-	-	60	-	-	40	-	-	-	-

15-7 LOT SIZING

Lot-for-lot sizing is among the simplest ordering methods, but it places more orders than other methods that order less frequently in larger quantities. Lot-for-lot is as close an approximation to just-in-time as it makes sense to get with an MRP model. However, if there are setups required, then the costs associated with lot-for-lot are likely to be too high, and alternative methods that order less frequently will prevail.

The cost of this policy can be obtained by multiplying the number of orders that are made using lot-for-lot by the cost of an order or setup. As revealed by the simulations (scenarios), with lot-for-lot sizing and no order cancellations, the amount of inventory carried would be zero. MRP systems are not immune to last-minute changes that result in stranding inventory that was earmarked for make-to-order. When orders are canceled, there is stock left, and this might have to be carried for quite awhile.

Grouping periods require summing the demands to cover various fixed periods of time, the length of which is selected based on the concept of an optimal period t_o as shown here. The period also can reflect accounting conveniences and policies of the supplier concerning how often it is able to deliver.

The idea is to decrease the number of orders. If a 4-week fixed period is chosen, 13 orders will be placed per year. It is not difficult to keep track of average inventory carried and to put a cost on carrying stock. If this cost is close to the cost of an order, or setup, multiplied by 13, then a good balance has been established. This approach, called the *part-period model* using an economic part-period criterion, is examined in the supplement to this chapter.

Economic order quantity is calculated for items using the traditional OPP method:

$$Q_o = \sqrt{\frac{2DC_r}{cC_c}}$$

The annual demand, D, can be estimated. The cost per unit, c, is known. The carrying cost, C_c, and the ordering cost, C_r, both must be estimated. The economic order quantity sets the order size. The equivalent to the reorder point is that positive net requirements signal the need to place an order. It is expected that the number of such orders placed will average out to be $n_o = D/Q_o$, and the average interval between orders will be $t_o = 1/n_o$, as calculated here:

TABLE 15-9

**Summary of
MRP Orders Placed**

		End Week									
SOH	Name	1	2	3	4	5	6	7	8	9	10
0	VCR	-	60	-	-	-	80	-	-	40	-
80	Z(1)	-	-	-	60	-	-	40	-	-	-
40	N(1)	-	-	20	-	-	40	-	-	-	-
0	M(1)	-	-	60	-	-	40	-	-	-	-

	End Week									
	1	2	3	4	5	6	7	8	9	10
Gross requirements	-	60	50	-	-	100	-	-	40	60
Stock on-hand (SOH)	80	20	-	60	60	-	50	50	10	-
Net requirements	-	-	30	-	-	40	-	-	-	50
Planned-order receipt	-	-	90	-	-	90	-	-	-	90
Planned-order release	-	90	-	-	90	-	-	-	90	-

TABLE 15-10

MRP Plan for VCR Alpha and Beta—Y(1)

$$t_o = \sqrt{\frac{2C_r}{cDC_c}}$$

The sensible approach for important items is to compare the costs obtained by using the various methods. The methods that have been discussed for economic part period balancing (ppb) are only able to approximate the optimal. It should be pointed out that over a long planning horizon the dynamic programming approach based on the Wagner-Whitin algorithm comes closest to minimizing the total costs, which are the sum of the carrying and ordering costs. Computing time, which has been a stumbling block to implementation of this model for large inventory systems, has been gradually reduced to a practical level.[9] This is for two reasons: better computing algorithms and faster computers.

15-8   UPDATING

There are two approaches for updating the MRP files and records. The first of these is called *regeneration MRP* and the second is called *net change MRP*. APICS definitions should be used as a standard for the field. They are precise and concise.

"**regeneration MRP**—An MRP processing approach where the master production schedule is totally reexploded down through all bills of material, to maintain valid priorities. New requirements and planned orders are completely recalculated or 'regenerated' at that time. *Ant.* net change MRP, requirements alteration."[10]

"**net change MRP**—An approach in which the material requirements plan is continually retained in the computer. Whenever a change is needed in requirements, open order inventory status, or bill of material, a partial explosion and netting is made for only those parts affected by the change."[11]

The MRP records are usually regenerated once a week. However, the variation that exists in practice can be traced to the degree to which change affects the system and how frequently it occurs. Because net change systems respond to transactions and only calculate the effects of that transaction, it is a simpler system requiring less time. Net change systems can be programmed to be activated by exception reports. This allows the system to react quickly to problems that arise.

It is not common practice to rely upon the net change system for all transactions over time. There are too many runs required for small and local effects. The many runs can lead to accumulation of errors instead of corrections. The systems for correction may not have received the same amount of thought and attention as the regeneration program. Consequently, it is often the case that net change is reserved for exceptions and regeneration is used on a regular basis.

15-9   CAPACITY REQUIREMENTS PLANNING (CRP)

Capacity requirements planning (CRP) is an extension of MRP. Sometimes it is necessary to readjust capacity when the MRP system delivers a plan that is not feasible because of capacity limitations.

Regeneration MRP: Thorough, time-demanding method of updating the MRP information system; master production schedule is totally reexploded down through all bills of material.

Net change MRP: Fast and economical method of updating the MRP information system; a partial explosion and netting is made for only those parts affected by the change.

Capacity requirements planning (CRP): Readjust capacity when the MRP system delivers a plan that is not feasible because of capacity limitations.

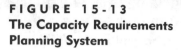

FIGURE 15-13
The Capacity Requirements Planning System

Capacity requirements planning (CRP) is "the function of establishing, measuring, and adjusting limits or levels of capacity . . . (it) is the process of determining how much labor and machine resources are required to accomplish the tasks of production. Open shop orders and planned orders in the MRP system are input to CRP, which 'translates' these orders into hours of work by work center by time period. *Syn.* capacity planning."[12]

There is the short-range picture of shifting capacities and the long-range view of commitments to strategic alterations. CRP addresses the former, which can be called "the more immediate problems." The latter, which is treated in Section 15-13, is called *manufacturing resource planning*, or *MRP II*.

CRP is generally applied to short-term modifications for capacity problems that are encountered as a result of infeasible MRP plans. Specifically, capacity changes can be affected by using overtime, longer and extra shifts, renting more space, and hiring part-time workers. Subcontracting often is used when backlogs arise.

Bottlenecks can be removed by methods studies. Changes can be made in the way that purchasing functions. Priorities can be altered, and sales can be asked to emphasize certain products and not take orders for others. For the most part, these are considered to be stopgap measures that can be employed until the problems are solved in a more permanent fashion.

Figure 15-13 illustrates the way in which capacity requirements planning (CRP) is used to modify the MPS and the MRP system when supply called *resource availabilities* (RA)—and demand called *material requirements (MR)*—do not match.

The fact that CRP operates at a higher level than MRP is an important first step in realizing potentials for the organization. Thus, capacity planning permits consideration of alternative sources of product. What is being made can be shifted to what will be bought, and vice versa. Nevertheless, as will be noted when MRP II is discussed, CRP looks outside the boundaries of MRP on a relatively short-term basis.

Rough-cut capacity planning (RCCP): Used to check that there is sufficient capacity to produce what is needed.

15-9a Rough-Cut Capacity Planning (RCCP)

Rough-cut capacity planning (RCCP) uses approximation to determine whether there is sufficient capacity to accomplish objectives. It serves as a precursor of the CRP process.

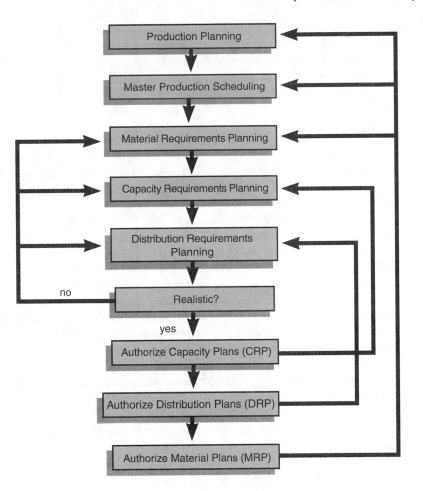

FIGURE 15-14
Closed-Loop MRP

RCCP occurs when the aggregate plan is being transformed into the master production schedule. In order to authorize the MPS (as shown in Figure 15-4), it is essential to check that there is enough capacity to do the job that the MPS describes.

RCCP is used to be certain that realistic objectives are being transmitted to the MRP process. If there is insufficient capacity to produce the MPS, then steps are taken to bring in additional key resources and/or to use subcontracting and/or coprocessing.

Bills of resources (BOR) are used to accomplish these objectives. The **bill of resources (BOR)** is a listing of the key resources needed to make one unit of the selected items (or family of items as in group technology). Resource requirements are identified with a lead-time offset to show the impact of the requirements on resource availability with respect to the time line. RCCP makes use of BOR to determine the expected capacity requirements of the MPS. The BOR also is called the *product load profile* or the *bill of capacity.*

Capacity requirements planning is post-MRP planning. However, capacity planning is going on before this stage in the form of rough-cut capacity planning. It is used to disaggregate the aggregate schedule in order to develop the master production schedule. It also should be noted that the MPS is the basis for the manufacturing budget. If there is not enough production capacity to fulfill orders promised, capacity has to be changed. This will alter the manufacturing budget.

> **Bill of resources (BOR):** Lists the key resources needed to make a unit of various selected SKUs.

15-10 DISTRIBUTION RESOURCE PLANNING (DRP)

When the acronym DRP is used, it refers to *distribution resource planning,* which is akin to MRP II (described later). DRP is the essence of supply chain management. A total systems point of view prevails. The basic distribution system is extended to consider not only how to keep the warehouse supplied but, also, how to configure the key resources of the

Distribution resource planning (DRP2): Operates as an extension of distribution requirements planning (DRP1) by addressing what additional resources are needed in the distribution system.

distribution supply chain including the manufacturing supply. **Distribution resource planning** is referred to as **DRP2** in the following discussion.

Distribution resources can be modified once the underlying *distribution requirements planning* system (defined below) is charted and understood. Note that the distribution requirements planning system is akin to MRP. The acronym DRP is sometimes used to label this extension to MRP. For clarity, distribution requirements planning can be called *DRP1* and defined as follows:

"(1) The function of determining the needs to replenish inventory at branch warehouses. A time-phased order point approach is used where the planned orders at the branch warehouse level are 'exploded' via MRP logic to become gross requirements on the supplying source. In the case of multilevel distribution networks, this explosion process can continue down through the various levels of regional warehouses, master warehouse, factory warehouse, etc., and become input to the master production schedule. Demand on the supplying source(s) is recognized as dependent, and standard MRP logic applies.

"(2) More generally, replenishment inventory calculations may be based on other planning approaches such as 'period order quantities' or 'replace exactly what was used' rather than being limited to solely the time-phased order point approach."[13]

The analogy of DRP1 to MRP is evident. Material requirements connect the supply chain participants. Lead-time dependencies exist as factories feed central warehouses and these, in turn, supply regional warehouses. It will be noted that shipping quantities are much like lot sizing. Lot-for-lot replacement is a potential strategy.

DRP2 is a higher order planning system than the distribution requirements planning system because it also plans for resource availability such as storage space in warehouses, trucking capacity, railroad boxcar availabilities, distribution workforce commitments and training, and cash flow needed to keep the distribution system moving. Thus, DRP2 operates as an extension of **distribution requirements planning (DRP1)** by addressing what resources are needed in the distribution system.

Distribution requirements planning (DRP1): Time-phased order point approach is used to "explode" planned orders at the branch warehouse level via MRP logic.

15-11 WEAKNESSES OF MRP

MRP is vulnerable to variability in lead times. The parent product cannot be made if any one of the items on the lower levels is not delivered on time for the scheduled production runs. This raises the point that a sensible policy might require some safety stock.

MRP is supposed to do away with the need for safety stock. However, OM must evaluate the risk of delayed supplier deliveries and take adequate protective measures. This is done by increasing the lead time by an amount that should cover delivery contingencies. Such "safety time" translates into added stock being carried.

The fact that a production or delivery problem at any level in the hierarchy can shut down the system cannot be treated as an MRP weakness. Whether MRP is used or not, the lack of materials will result in stopping the process. MRP helps to keep problems from arising by documenting the time-phasing for all parts that are needed. Follow-up calls can be made to ascertain the status of orders. Other forms of expediting can be used when slippage seems to be occurring. The weakness of MRP, in this regard, is that it does not automatically check status of orders and expedite them. That remains an organizational matter related to how information is used. Expediting should be treated as an integral part of the MRP organization.

There are problems evaluating MRP software. Many kinds of MRP software are available off-the-shelf. Some companies buy these and then modify them to suit their own particular systems' needs. Large firms often build their own systems. Failures with MRP can often be traced to having chosen software that was not well-suited to the applications.

MRPs are information systems that are vulnerable to data errors. Data entry must be checked carefully for original records, and then for updates. Errors can creep into net-change systems that are difficult to detect. Many organizations have so many parts that it is difficult to be sure that all changes are recorded. Engineering design changes occur so frequently in some companies that it is hard to keep up with them. With MRP, the system for keeping up with changes had better be as good as the MRP system.

One of the worst problems that MRP faces is last-minute changes in orders. It is inevitable that the size of orders will be altered, and that cancellations will occur. To illustrate, assume that the order for 90 Y(1) subassemblies has been placed in week 2 for scenario 4. A week later, sales cancels the beta model VCR run of 50 units. It is possible that no more betas will be made. There is a frantic effort to cancel the 90 Y(1) subassemblies to no avail. Fortunately, the Y(1) subassemblies also are used in the alpha model. The dependent nature of shared parts adds to the complexity of resolving errors and to the severity of potential problems.

15-12 CLOSED-LOOP MRP

Closed-loop MRP is "A system built around material requirements planning that includes the additional planning functions of sales and operations (production planning, master production scheduling, and capacity requirements planning). Once this planning phase is complete and the plans have been accepted as realistic and attainable, the execution functions come into play. These include the manufacturing control functions of input–output (capacity) measurement, detailed scheduling and dispatching, as well as anticipated delay reports from both the plant and suppliers, supplier scheduling, etc. The term **closed-loop MRP** implies that not only is each of these elements included in the overall system, but also that feedback is provided by the execution functions so that the planning can be kept valid at all times."[14]

> **Closed-loop MRP:** Feedback prevails at many levels, and over time, for planning and replanning scheduling, capacity requirements, and sales strategies.

The closed-loop MRP has material requirements planning as one of its steps. It is replete with feedback loops that permit planning and replanning. It extends the MRP concept to include capacity requirements planning, shop scheduling, and supplier scheduling. The first step in the planning hierarchy is production planning, which indicates that master production scheduling is based on more than open orders and sales forecasts.

The essence of the closed-loop MRP systems approach is represented by Figure 15-14. Some diagrams of closed-loop MRPs do not include distribution requirements planning, but good systems thinking endorses its inclusion. MRP becomes more powerful with the additions of closed-loop MRP.

Closed-loop MRP becomes the more powerful MRP II with the addition of business resource planning as discussed in Section 15-13.

15-13 STRENGTHS OF MRP II (MANUFACTURING RESOURCE PLANNING)

MRP II entails total manufacturing resource planning as part of the strategic business plan. Thus, minor capacity adjustments can be made on a short-term basis (CRP); however, longer-term and broader systems perspectives should prevail. For example, marketing considerations raise the possibility of changing the master production schedule to allow for the introduction of new products and the alteration of the company's product mix.

> **MRP II:** Systems plan for operating effectively at the plant level; links P/OM and production planning with marketing goals, financial policies, R & D plans, accounting procedures, and human resource management goals.

Financial planning can access and control what is being done and determine what will be done in the future. Accounting is linked directly to the MRP II cost systems so that accounts payable, accounts receivable, and cash flow are online with production. R & D's agenda is linked to long-term plans for the company and the architecture of its MRP II.

Technology is constantly changing. MRP II encourages and supports reevaluation of the way that work is being done. It permits assessment of the product mix and the input–output processes that are being used.

Competitive shifts in strategy produce forces to alter what is being done. This can be brought up for consideration by any of the systems players—finance, marketing, R & D, HRM, OM, and purchasing. Concretely, MRP II puts business planning into a box hierarchically above that of production planning.

Compare Figures 15-14 and 15-15. The business planning box is not present in Figure 15-14, which depicts closed-loop MRP. The diagram for "closed-loop planning" starts with production planning. In contrast, in Figure 15-15 there is a *feedback loop* connecting

FIGURE 15-15
MRP II

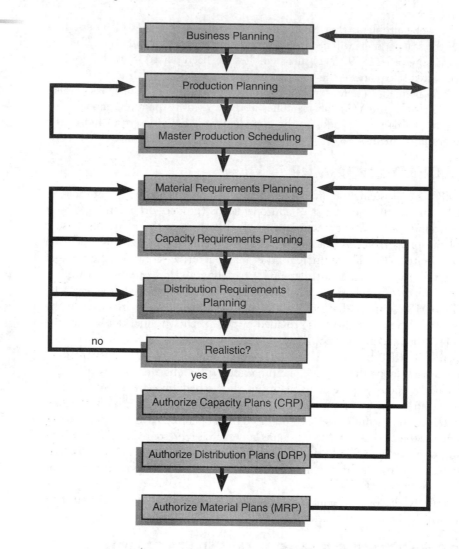

the business planning function with the production planning function. The hierarchical stature of "business planning" for all functions elevates MRP II into the highest levels of strategic thinking.

Because strategic business plans drive the MRP II system, this allows consideration of the effect of buying new machines, changing computer equipment, building new plants, altering the product mix, and modifying advertising and promotion campaigns, among others. Based on systems thinking, changes to any part of the planning process shown in Figure 15-14 should be in line with strategic business plans as developed in Figure 15-15.

Toward this end, note that there is another feedback loop for MRP II from master production scheduling to production planning. This permits coordination of plans and actions to assure achievement of the best plan for manufacturing resources and, thereby, materials requirements. The long-range viewpoint in search of optimal configurations is the essence of MRP II.

Ollie Wight said, " . . . the theme of MRP II (is) managing all of the resources of a manufacturing company more productively." In his book,[15] he then proceeds to develop eight chapters, as follows:

Chapter 8—"The CEO's Role in MRP II"

Chapter 9—"MRP II in Marketing"

Chapter 10—"MRP II in Manufacturing"

Chapter 11—"MRP II in Purchasing"

Chapter 12—"MRP II in Finance"

Chapter 13—"MRP II in Engineering"

Chapter 14—"DRP: Distribution Resource Planning"

Chapter 15—"MRP II in Data Processing Systems"

The scope of MRP II is fully revealed by the intent of this founder of the MRP II system. Each of the eight chapters represents considerations that affect what will be made and what will be ordered. The titles reveal the broad systems scope and appeal of MRP II.

MRP II is the foundation for **Enterprise Resource Planning (ERP).** Transformation of MRP II to ERP in its most far-reaching form is accomplished by converting the Business Planning box at the top of Figure 15-15 into an Enterprise-Wide Planning box. Following the path in Figure 15-15 produces an integrated marketing-production strategy which is intended to combine resources of the company in an optimal fashion. Many firms find that small steps toward the long-run goal of integrating all departments and functions, as well as suppliers, is the wisest course of action. Reported experiences of ERP providers such as SAP, Oracle, and PeopleSoft, indicate how difficult it is to achieve a seamless information system that properly amalgamates POM, finance, marketing, and human resources, etc., into a single-minded management entity.

> **Enterprise Resource Planning (ERP):** Company-wide integration of the information system for seamless planning across all functions.

SUMMARY

Chapter 15 presents the means for appreciating the utility of material requirements planning—widely referred to as MRP. Demands for components and subassemblies that are dependent on the demands for the end-items to which they belong characterize MRP. The first major tool of MRP is the master production schedule (MPS), which fits within the framework of the total manufacturing planning and control sys-tem (MPCS). Differences between make-to-stock (MTS), make-to-order (MTO), and assemble-to-order (ATO) are described. Converting gross requirements into net requirements is explained.

A major component of the information system is the bill of material (BOM), which leads to a product-structure tree reflecting the explosion of parts. Coding and low-level coding are detailed for operating the MRP system. Lot-sizing scenarios are described.

Updating the system is discussed. Then higher orders of MRP systems are presented. These are CRP (capacity requirements planning), DRP [distribution resource planning (DRP2), which is a higher order planning system than the distribution requirements planning system (DRP1) because it also plans for resource availability], closed-loop MRP, and finally, MRP II which is manufacturing resource planning. Although ERP is the logical extension of MRP II, it is as much marketing and financial planning as it is POM planning. Therefore, an in-depth study of ERP is inappropriate for this text.

Two Spotlight feature boxes conclude this chapter. These boxes illustrate real applications of the material in the chapter. See Spotlight 15-1: Innovation—Everyone Has Something to Say About It and Spotlight 15-2: Are Our Ports Safe?

KEY TERMS

Assemble-to-order (ATO) environment
Bill of material (BOM)
Bill of resources (BOR)
Capacity requirements planning (CRP)
Closed-loop MRP
Coding
Distribution requirements planning (DRP1)
Distribution resource planning (DRP2)

End products
Enterprise Resource Planning (ERP)
Inventory record files (IRF)
Lot-for-lot ordering
Low-level coding
Make-to-order (MTO) inventory environment
Make-to-stock (MTS) environment

Master production schedule (MPS)
Material requirements planning (MRP)
MRP II
Net change MRP
Order promising
Regeneration MRP
Rough-cut capacity planning (RCCP)
Total or cumulative lead time (LT)

REVIEW QUESTIONS

1. How does inventory planning differ for the flow shop and the job shop?

2. Explain how MRP relates to the job shop and the flow shop.

3. What is meant by time-phased requirements planning for MRP?

4. What is the difference between updating by "regeneration" and updating by the "net change" method for MRP? Discuss the pros and cons of each method.

5. Explain net requirement, planned-order receipt, and planned-order release. When are they equal and when are they not equal?

6. What is CRP?

7. What is DRP? How does it relate it to distribution requirements planning?

8. Distinguish between MRP, closed-loop MRP, and MRP II.

9. What characterizes dependent demand systems?

10. How do forecasting considerations apply to MRP?

11. Explain the master production schedule (MPS).

12. What is meant by the total manufacturing planning and control system (MPCS)?

13. Explain the bill of material (BOM). How does it relate to the product-structure tree?

14. What purpose is served by the explosion of parts?

15. How does coding and low-level coding impact order policies?

16. What is lot sizing?

17. What are some of the different methods that are used for lot sizing? Describe those that you know.

18. What is the difference between gross and net requirements?

19 Describe the make-to-stock (MTS) environment.

20. Explain the make-to-order (MTO) inventory environment.

21. Explain the assemble-to-order (ATO) inventory environment.

22. How is rough-cut capacity planning (RCCP) used?

23. Explain bills of resources (BOR).

24. What is ERP?

PROBLEMS SECTION

1. The master schedule for end product P is as follows:

Week	Gross Requirements
1	400
2	200
3	200
4	300
5	500
6	100
7	600
8	400

Stock on-hand for p_1, a component of P, is 700. Develop the planned-order release schedule for p_1, assuming a lot-for-lot sizing policy and lead time LT = two weeks.

2. Use the information in Problem 1 to address the following issue: SOH of 700 units is always maintained because there is unreliability of delivery. How does the lot-for-lot sizing policy deal with this issue?

3. With further reference to Problem 1, the cost of a unit of p_1 is \$12. The carrying cost rate is 0.25 percent per week (0.0025). The setup cost to produce p_1 is \$48. Demand per year can be estimated from the table in Problem 1. Use the economic order quantity (EOQ) to set the order size whenever an order is triggered by positive net requirements. Describe the performance of this system.

4. Using the information in Problem 3, what is the expected interval between orders?

5. The master schedule for parent product M is as follows:

Week	Gross Requirements
1	3,400
2	4,200
3	5,200
4	6,300
5	7,500
6	3,100
7	4,600
8	5,400
9	6,600
10	7,800

The policy is to carry no stock on-hand for m_1, which is a subassembly of M. Develop the planned-order release schedule for m_1, assuming a lot-for-lot sizing policy and lead time LT = one week.

6. Use the information in Problem 5 to address the following issue: The MRP manager wants to try 2-period ordering. She requests that you compare your lot-for-lot plan with the 2-period plan. Also, she asks, "Would it help to have some SOH?" Make the comparison and answer the question.

7. With further reference to Problem 5, the cost of a unit of m_1 is $1. The carrying cost rate is 24 percent per year. The ordering cost for m_1 is $25. Demand per year can be estimated from the table in Problem 5. Use the economic order quantity (EOQ) to set the order size whenever an order is triggered by positive net requirements. Describe the performance of this system.

8. Using the information in Problem 7, what is the expected interval between orders?

9. Develop the lot-for-lot ordering scenario for VCR-alpha part Q, using Table 15-5 in the text and the product-structure tree in Figure 15-12. Note: Q appears more than once in the product-structure tree. Also, observe the number of units of Q that are required for each unit of X and for each unit of B. The lead times for both X and B are zero because they can be assembled immediately. The lead time for Q is one week. Part Q has no other parents or end-items than VCR-alpha.

In addition to providing the quantitative ordering instructions, evaluate the performance of the ordering system. Hint: Include in the planned-order release chart levels 0, 1, and 2.

10. Develop the lot-for-lot ordering scenario for VCR-alpha part Q, using Table 15-5 in the text and the product-structure tree given by Figure 15-12. As in Problem 9, note that Q appears more than once in the product-structure tree. Also, observe the number of units of Q that are required for each unit of X and for each unit of B. The lead times for both X and B are one week to assemble. The lead time for Q is one week. Part Q has no other parents or end-items than VCR-alpha.

In addition to providing the quantitative ordering instructions, evaluate the performance of the ordering system. Hint: Include in the chart for planned-order release, levels 0, 1, and 2.

11. Develop the lot-for-lot ordering scenario for VCR-beta part B using Table 15-5 in the text and the product-structure tree given in Figure 15-12. Note that B appears more than once and on different levels of the product-structure tree. Also, observe that only one unit of B is required in both cases. The lead time for G is zero and the lead time for B is two weeks. Assume that part B has no other parents or end-items.

Provide quantitative ordering instructions and an evaluation of the behavior of the ordering system. Hint: Include in the chart for planned-order release levels 0, 1, and 2.

12. Develop the lot-for-lot ordering scenario for VCR-beta part B using Table 15-5 in the text and the product-structure tree given in Figure 15-12. Note that B appears more than once and on different levels of the product-structure tree. Also, observe that only one unit of B is required in both cases. The lead time for both G and B is one week. Assume that part B has no other parents or end-items.

Provide quantitative ordering instructions and an evaluation of the behavior of the ordering system. Hint: Include in the chart for planned-order release levels 0, 1, and 2.

13. Determine what happens to Y(1) subassemblies if 50 VCR-beta units ordered for week 3 are canceled. Use Table 15-5 and Table 15-10. Note that Y(1) subassemblies are used in both alpha and beta end-items.

14. What is the maximum cumulative lead time for parent assembly A where subassemblies B, C, D, and E are all special items with lead times as marked? The usage quantities shown in parentheses are all one-for-one, meaning one B and one C subassembly are required for A, and one D and one E are required for C.

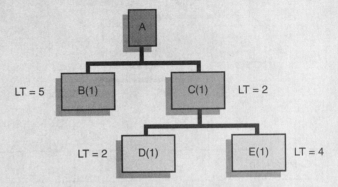

15. Using the graphics and information in Problem 14, what is the maximum cumulative lead time for parent assembly A if subassembly E is a standard item and there is SOH?
Note: Subassemblies B, C, and D are all special items.

16. Using the graphics and information in Problem 14, what is the maximum cumulative lead time for parent assembly A where subassembly B is a standard item with SOH? All other components are special.

17. The product structure BOM shown here does not account for low-level coding. Redraw this graphic so that it is consistent with low-level coding.

18. Using the graphic in Problem 17, what is the maximum cumulative lead time for parent assembly A where subassemblies B, C, D, and E are all special items with lead times as marked? The usage quantities are shown in parentheses.

19. Using the graphic in Problem 17, what is the maximum cumulative lead time for parent assembly A where subassembly C is a standard item for which there is ample SOH. Subassemblies B, D, and E are all special items. The usage quantities are shown in parentheses.

20. To which subassembly in the following BOM does the planned-order release chart apply?

Weeks Ahead	1	2	3	4	5	6	7	8	9
Gross (Amount) Requirements: A		20			45				60
Planned Order Release Date	20			45				60	

21. Complete the planned-order release chart below (marked *work sheet*) so that it applies to subassembly C, which requires two-for-one as shown in the following BOM.

Work Sheet Weeks ahead	1	2	3	4	5	6	7	8	9
Gross (amount) requirements: A		20			45	45			60
Planned-order release: C(2)									

22. Using the graphic in Problem 21, complete the following planned-order release chart below (marked *work sheet*) so that it applies to component D.

Work Sheet Weeks ahead	1	2	3	4	5	6	7	8	9
Gross (amount) requirements: A			25	35	40		20		60
Planned-order release: C(2)									
Planned-order release: D(1)									

END-OF-CHAPTER QUESTIONS

1. MRP *evolutionized* the field of inventory management. There were major quantitative developments in the inventory modeling field for order point policies during the late 1940s and early 1950s. Much research led to important extensions of methodology along the same line from 1950–1970. However, starting in the 1960s, and accelerating throughout the 1970s, MRP began to capture the imagination of inventory managers throughout the world. P/OM needs to be able to explain the differences between MRP and OPP to business students and executives alike. Toward that end, points a. to e. have been developed to provide a lexicon of ideas about these two branches of inventory theory and application. Identify the one point that is not suitable for the comparison of inventory systems.

a. As much as 80 percent of manufactured goods is made in batches. Almost 100 percent of office operations conform to job shop methods. With the exception of quick-service restaurants, service functions vary between custom work and small batch production. Inventory systems for dealing with job shops and batched outputs are MRP-oriented.

b. To explain why OPP inventory systems were the major focus of early research in inventory modeling requires understanding that analytic work in the 1940s and 1950s was influenced and paid for by military organizations. Military needs for *materiel* are both substantial and continuous over time. The logistics of supplying the army, navy and air force are like the requirements of a flow shop production system. OPP is able to provide answers to such continuous demand systems.

c. One of the main assumptions of OPP is that demand is driven by the marketplace, whereas a main assumption of MRP is that demand is driven by the number of end units to be made. OPP systems require a continuous and regular supply of units each and every day. MRP systems are designed to handle sporadic and irregular demand patterns.

d. MRP part demands are dependent on the number of parent products scheduled to be made. However, if an MRP part is used by more than one parent-SKU it is given a different part number and treated independently. Thus, production of the parent is not held up.

e. The reason that demand for a parent product can be smooth while demand for components of that parent product are lumpy or pulsed is that different models of the parent product use different parts. For just this reason, Henry Ford always wanted to make only black Model T automobiles. That is, because it is less expensive to deal with smooth demand than with irregular demand.

2. Material requirements planning operates as an intelligent information system. Understanding MRP inputs and MRP outputs is the first step to understanding what has to be done to make the system work. Choose the one statement (a. through e.) not appropriate to MRP as a proper inventory model.

a. Input: Inventory information about stock on-hand levels, certified suppliers, prices, supplier lead times, problems, and complaints are part of the inventory record file (IRF). When a change occurs in these files, the information should be updated.

b. Input: Bills of material with specifications of what goes into the makeup of the product. Information on product-structure trees includes part numbers, required number of each part, and level coding, including low-level capture. A part specification might be six screws, designated by B[6] at level 3.

c. Input: Planned-order timetable with all indicated order release information. Definition of order release is that full specification of the vendor and the item is documented. Items are listed by SKU and each SKU shows the number of units ordered. This has been released to the vendor with confirmation requested.

d. Input: The master production schedule (MPS) takes into account customer orders on-hand as well as forecasts for the parent products. The master production schedule takes into account the demand for capacity and allocates the capacity delivered by the aggregate planning model for the planning horizon that applied. The MPS makes the best use of the available resources for the actual market demands.

e. Output: Changes to earlier planned-order releases that may be needed because orders are canceled or due dates are changed. Also, performance reports are prepared and delivered including any exceptions that may have occurred.

3. A strong interaction exists between marketing and P/OM in a variety of business functions. One of the most apparent cases occurs when MRP receives its basic plan of action from the master production schedule (MPS). Choose the one statement (a. through e.) that does not appropriately describe the relationship between marketing and P/OM.

a. Order promising dates for delivery of items to customers is done by sales. Order fulfillment is done by P/OM using master production scheduling. If promise dates and fulfillment dates do not match, production has to accept what marketing says.

b. Establishing a make-to-stock environment may require adding capacity so that P/OM can build up inventories to provide a buffer against periods of heightened demand.

c. Having the best possible forecasts helps both marketing and P/OM to plan to deliver product as promised to important customers. It also helps marketing avoid making promises that cannot be fulfilled. Finally, it establishes a basis for assigning priorities to customers. The prioritizing methods could include keeping promises to customers who generate the most revenue. Many alternatives exist. One of the favorites is to increase priority customers who have been most delayed.

d. Especially in a make-to-order environment, there is no inventory for sales to call upon for a customer. There is a lead time for production to make the promised items, which includes finishing the jobs that are being worked on. Priorities may be needed to establish who goes first in a queue of orders. Make-to-order is a tougher situation than make-to-stock and sell-from-stock.

e. Assemble-to-order environments pose different managerial problems than make-to-order ones. If the components and subassemblies are sourced from outside, led by reasonable forecasts, the right materials can be on hand in time for assembly. MRP systems provide lead-time guidance. Because there is less value-adding going on, the ability of production to react to new orders is enhanced as compared to fabrication from scratch. Nevertheless, there are problems that require that marketing and P/OM coordinate promises made and delivery schedules.

4. Interpreting a multilevel indented bill of material chart is necessary for inventory trainees working for MRP certification. The chart is accompanied by a list of points about BOM graphics, charts, and tables. Which one of these points is in error?

Multilevel Indented BOM for CNB Corporation								
1	2	3	4	5	6	7	8	9
		Level	Code				Level	Code
CNBR		0			CNBD		0	
X(2)		1			G(2)		1	
	P(2)	2				P(2)	2	
	Q(1)	2				B(1)	2	
Y(1)		1			Y(1)		1	
	R(1)	2				R(1)	2	
	S(4)	2				S(4)	2	
	T(2)	2				T(2)	2	
Z(1)		1			V(1)		1	
	M(1)	2				C(1)	2	
	N(1)	2				D(1)	2	
B(1)		1			B(1)		1	2
	Q(2)	2				Q(2)	2	3

(Figures within parentheses are the number of units required.)

a. The chart called *Multilevel Indented BOM for CNB Corporation* presents subassemblies in columns 1 and 6, and parts in columns 2 and 7, for the newest computer notebooks of the CNB company. Two models are in production: the regular (CNBR) and the deluxe (CNBD). Alternative representation is available using structured trees instead of this tabular arrangement. In either case, the parent products CNBD and CNBR are at the top with level 0 designation. Level is shown in columns 3 and 8. The indented chart has four columns for each model. The two columns (4 and 9) marked *code* represent low-level coding for parts that require that designation.

b. There are four major subassemblies in each model. Two of them are shared by each notebook, viz., Y(1) and B(1). The demand levels for the shared subassemblies in each model will be added together by the MRP system. The same applies to the total demand for the shared parts that go into each of the subassemblies. MRP is able to cull out and integrate hundreds of shared parts, e.g., common nuts, bolts, and rivets.

c. Both notebook models draw on a set of shared parts. These are P, Q, R, S, and T. The number of units required for each model is the same except in the case of Q. One part Q is required for each subassembly X, and this only applies the CNBR. Two Xs are required for each CNBR, so two part Qs will be needed at level 2.

d. Levels for both models begin at zero. Subassemblies at level 1 proceed to parts at level. Two exceptions occur for model CNBD. In the first, low-level coding of 2 is required for the B subassembly. This is because B units are part of G subassemblies. MRP captures demand for B units at the lowest level and combines all demand for B,

above that point. B also is a subassembly of the regular model. MRP will capture the demand for B in this usage as it searches for common part numbers across all models.

e. The second low-level code exception applies to the two units of Q in model CNBD. These Q are parts joining with subassembly B. Because B is low-level coded at two, Q must be low-level coded at 3. In this case, low-level coding requirements have moved B and Q each one level lower for the deluxe model. The effect on lead time is to delay the order by an additional time period. For example, order these parts one week earlier to allow the MRP system the extra time to move down the hierarchy to capture total demand for B and Q.

5. MRP has a basic structure that can be represented by mathematical equations. Not everyone enjoys the algebra, but it is essential to be able to recognize that these equations are the means by which MRP logic is translated from records into actions. There is one item that should be corrected before this list is shared with trainees from the company's inventory training program. Which item in a. to e. must be corrected?

a. For each parent or end-item, subassembly, part, etc., gross requirements (GR_t) are the total number of units demanded for week t. Inventory information is on file for the prior week's stock on-hand (SOH_{t-1}). Open orders that will be received at the beginning of week t are called: (SR_t). Then, projected stock on-hand at time t is $\hat{SOH}_t = SOH_{t-1} + SR_t$.

b. Gross requirements less projected stock on-hand at time t is called *net requirements*. Thus, $NR_t = GR_t - \hat{SOH}_t = GR_t - SOH_{t-1} - SR_t$. The process of determining net requirements is called *netting*.

c. Based on net requirements and ordering policies, the planned-order receipt times and planned-order release times are determined. If $\hat{SOH}_t > GR_t$, there would be stock on-hand at the end of period t. Thus, $\hat{SOH}_t = SOH_{t-1} + SR_t - GR_t > 0$. Net requirement would be zero because there is more stock on-hand than gross requirements. This means that gross requirements can be met out of inventory.

d. If gross requirements are greater than projected stock on-hand, then an order must be placed for the net requirements. In equations: $GR_t > \hat{SOH}_t$, then, $NR_t = 0$.

e. When an order is needed, it must be placed early enough so that delivery can be made in time. Lead time specifies what "early enough" means. Working backwards from planned-order receipt date, subtract lead time to determine planned-order release date. Planned-order receipt (PR_t) is zero when projected stock on-hand is greater than gross requirements. When projected stock on-hand is less than gross requirements, the size of PR_t must be determined: $\hat{SOH}_t = SOH_{t-1} + SR_t + PR_t - GR_t$. If lot-for-lot ordering is used, then planned-order receipt exactly equals the net requirements. Thus, $PR_t = NR_t$.

6. MRP has a basic structure that can be represented in tabular form. Although mathematical equations are responsible for triggering actions that are indicated by the table, it is feasible to operate the table manually. The MRP inventory trainees are taught to read the tables and to interpret what is taking place. They are being tested with a list of statements about the MRP tables. There is one item that should be corrected before this list is published and distributed. Which item in a. to e. must be corrected?

    a. The table shows stock on-hand for Q at the beginning and end of period 1 is 100 units. Because Q(2) is the indicated usage, the number of end-items that can be made is 50 units of either CNBR or CNBD (or combinations).

    b. Period 2 has gross requirements of 80 units. Satisfying this demand reduces the stock on-hand to 20 units and that SOH will continue through period 4.

Part Q										
End week	1	2	3	4	5	6	7	8	9	10
Gross requirements		80			100	100			70	
Stock on-hand	100	20	20	20	100					
Net requirements					80	100			70	
Planned-order receipt					180				70	
Planned-order release			180					70		

Legend: Stock on-hand at the start of $t = 1$ is 100 units; lead time is two weeks; 2 units of Q are need for each end item, i.e., Q(2); Q demand is accumulated from NBCR and NBCD; the lot sizing policy is lot-for-lot except where net requirements are greater than zero for two consecutive weeks, in which case, combine the two weeks net requirements.

    c. The gross requirements of 100 units in period 5 draw down the SOH = 20 units to zero units. GR_5 triggered NR_5 of 80 units, and these in turn required a planned-order receipt of 80 units. That led to a planned-order release of 80 units in period 3 because the LT = 2 weeks. The table is not correct and needs to be redrawn to show that planned order release in period 3 is 80 units.

    d. The fact that planned-order release is 180 units in period 3 stems from the rule in the legend that lot-for-lot sizing would be bypassed if net requirements are greater than zero for two consecutive weeks. That occurred for NR_5 and NR_6. As a result, the planned-order release is 180 units in week 3 for planned-order receipt of 180 units in week 5.

    e. In week 5, GR_5 = 100; SOH contributes 20; 180 units received; 80 used for gross requirements; leaving 100 units as new SOH.

7. Another type of MRP table puts together a summary of the ordering status of end products, subassemblies, and parts. Because of interactions between parts and dependencies between parents, this table requires understanding and patience on the part of the user. An example of the format

has been created for use by the inventory manager training program. The summary table is a reporting form rather than a calculation sheet for updating information. The table reports on the number of units expected to be delivered (planned-order receipts) over an 8-week period. It is important to confirm that the units required will be on hand to meet the gross requirements, which are shown in the parent row of the table. Students understand that to fulfill planned-order receipts, planned-order releases have been activated with the appropriate lead times. Inventory trainees are taught to read the tables and to interpret situations. Trainees are being tested with a list of statements about the MRP summary table. There is one item that should be corrected before this list is published and distributed. Which item in a. to e. must be corrected?

MRP Summary—Schedule of Planned-Order Receipts									
	End Week	1	2	3	4	5	6	7	8
SOH	SKU Name								
10	Parent – CNBD		80			100			70
80	Subassembly—G(2)		60			200			140
00	Part P(2)	120			400			280	
30	Part B(1)	30			200			140	
00	Subassembly—B (1)		70			100			70
25	Part Q(2)	115			200			140	

Legend: Parent gross requirements are 80 in week 2, 100 in week 5, and 70 in week 8; lead time is one week to obtain parts P, B, and Q, and assemble them into subassemblies. Figures in parentheses indicate the number of units required for assembly.

    a. Left-hand column of the table shows stock on-hand for parent, subassemblies G(2) and B(1), and parts that go into subassemblies. Two G(2) and one B(1) are needed to assemble each parent unit by the due dates. The parent-CNBD has 10 units of SOH. Therefore, only 70 units will be needed in week 2.

    b. Part B is both a subassembly of the parent-CNBD, and a part of the G(2) subassembly. SOH for part B is shown as 30 units. The error being looked for in the table is that SOH for the subassembly is shown as zero. This should be corrected by showing 30 units of SOH for both the subassembly and for the part.

    c. SOH for subassembly G(2) is 80. Because two units of G are required for each parent unit, and 70 parent units are required in week 2, then, 140 units of G are needed. 80 units can be drawn from stock. Then, 60 units have planned-order receipt in week 2.

    d. To make 60 units of G, 120 units of part P(2) are needed (two Ps for one G). No SOH exists for P. Therefore, a planned-order receipt is required for P in week 1.

    e. If there was no SOH for Part B(1), 60 units would be required. However, part B has 30 units of SOH. The net requirement for Part B(1) is 30 units.

8. The analysis of the MRP summary table in Problem 7 has not been completed. Inventory trainees are assigned a new list of statements concerning the information in that table. One item should be corrected before this list is finalized and placed in the trainee's binders. Which item in a. to e. must be corrected?

a. SOH for subassembly B(1) is zero. The SOH for part B(1) has been assigned to the subassembly G(2). Then, 70 units of B(1) are required in week 2 because one unit of B (the subassembly) is required for each parent unit, and 70 parent units are required in week 2.

b. To make 70 units of B(1), a planned-order receipt of 115 units will be required in week 1 for part Q(2). Because two Q parts are required for each subassembly, B(1), there are 140 units to be supplied. SOH for part Q is 25 units. Therefore, $140 - 25 = 115$ units.

c. The remainder of the schedule functions on a lot-for-lot basis. Thus, week 5 gross requirement for the parent-CNBD is 100 units. There is no stock on-hand for any of the parts or subassemblies. This leads to speculation about ordering policy. Might it have been better to order larger quantities of parts (and subassemblies) in the period of weeks 1 and 2?

d. If larger quantities had been ordered of parts and subassemblies in weeks 1 and 2, there would have been additional carrying costs. The week before the start of this MRP summary table showed significant amounts of SOH. This means that larger than lot-for-lot orders had been policy before weeks 1 through 8.

e. There is a lot of volatility in the gross requirements stated for CNBD. If the other model had been included in the MRP summary table, it might have smoothed demand for commonly shared parts and subassemblies. In fact, Bs, Ps, and Qs are known to be common with model CNBR. These should have been included in the MRP analysis. Unless, some unknown other factor has intervened, there is a possible error in the MRP system because shared parts have not been represented.

9. A series of statements has been prepared to describe various aspects of MRP. These cover a number of issues that the well-rounded inventory manager should be able to discuss with comfort. Statements a. through f. are circulating within the company, and one of them is not correct. Which is the flawed statement?

a. If there are significant setup costs, lot-for-lot sizing is not going to deliver a minimum cost method of order sizing. Multiply the number of lot-for-lot orders in a given time period by the setup cost (or the order cost). That gives the inventory cost because there are no carrying costs with lot-for-lot. Carrying some inventory during that same period can reduce the number of setups, which might offset some of the setup costs. Cut and try to get an equitable balance between the number of orders and the carrying costs.

b. MRP is not immune to last-minute changes that strand inventory developed on a make-to-order basis. Stranded inventory units can be carried for long periods of time, or sold as salvage, or destroyed. Real-life scenarios may favor ordering policies that are closer to lot-for-lot because they reduce exposure to the costs of stranded units.

c. The part-period model uses an economic part-period criterion based on annual demand (D) and economic

reorder intervals (t_o) which are the inverse of the economic number of orders, $t_o = \dfrac{1}{n_o} = \sqrt{\dfrac{2C_r}{cDC_c}}$.

The other symbols are familiar from the EOQ model. Part-period balancing divides the year by t_o (say $t_o = 4$ weeks), which means there will be 13 orders. The average inventory carried during the 4 weeks is calculated and compared to the cost of an order. If the inventory carrying cost is greater than the ordering cost, increase the number of orders. Continuing in this way, a nonoptimal heuristic-type solution is obtained.

d. The economic part-period is an attempt to achieve a minimum total cost policy for planned-order release size. Lot-for-lot is one extreme where no carrying charges are incurred. More than lot-for-lot order size results in carrying costs. The minimum total cost policy occurs when setup or ordering costs are equal to carrying costs. The estimate of economic part-period is an effort to achieve this state.

$$\text{Economic Part-Period} = \frac{\text{Total Setup Costs}}{\text{Unit Carrying Cost per Period}}$$

e. Calculations of all kinds must be checked frequently because conditions change. The two most-used methods of updating MRP data sets are regeneration MRP and net change MRP. Regeneration is more time-consuming and can introduce new errors as the total data system undergoes revision.

f. There is a short-range picture of shifting capacities and the long-range view of commitments to strategic alterations. Capacity requirements planning (CRP) addresses the former, which are "the more immediate problems." MRP II is the approach used for the longer-range, strategic solutions to capacity imbalance.

10. The series of statements about MRP that began with Problem 9 has been continued by the training staff because they have been well-received as discussion points. The idea has prevailed that an inventory manager should not be viewed as a specialist but as a generalist with a systems perspective that encompasses business strategy. The discussion statements a. through e. are designed to raise issues about the evolution of MRP to higher and higher decision and control levels within the enterprise. There is a flawed statement. Which one is it?

a. Although rough-cut capacity planning (RCCP) uses approximation to determine if there is sufficient capacity to accomplish objectives, it is viewed by management as a strategic heuristic.

b. Distribution resource planning (DRP) provides a strategic view of supply chain management. It is very much akin to MRP II, but the emphasis is on logistics rather than on manufacturing. The distinction is useful because distribution requirements planning is more like MRP. Thus, distribution resource planning is an extension of distribution requirements planning. It addresses what additional resources are needed in the distribution system.

c. One of the major weaknesses of MRP systems is the vulnerability to variability in lead time. The MRP report states that parent-CNBD can be made but the delivery trucks with part Q have not arrived. The MRP schedule can be searched to find alternative options for the facilities. However, operating under uncertainty is not one of MRP's strong points.

d. Closed-loop MRP operates at a cut below strategic planning. It is able to include all elements that bear on scheduling decisions *as they are currently structured* in the system. Strategy contemplates restructuring opportunities, whereas closed-loop MRP includes executive functions for the overall system with feedback fully operative. It is a strong managerial MRP system.

e. MRP II was the precursor of ERP. In many ways, MRP II provided a better structure than ERP because it centered on the production operations of the firm. ERP has a loftier vantage point, but it also may be too far removed for dealing effectively with issues "where the rubber meets the road."

ADDITIONAL READINGS

AGRA Software. *FastMan* (MRP software). (613-596-3344). Ottawa, Ontario, Canada, 1993.

Baker, K. R. "Requirements Planning," in S. C. Graves, A. H. G. Rinnooy Khan, and P. Zipkin (eds.). *Logistics of Production and Inventory.* Amsterdam: North-Holland Publishing Company, 1993.

Berry, William, Thomas E. Vollman, and D. Clay Whybark. *Master Production Scheduling: Principles and Practice.* Washington, DC: American Production and Inventory Control Society, 1979.

Buzacott, J. A., and J. G. Shanthikumar. "Safety Stock Versus Safety Time in MRP Controlled Production Systems." *Management Science,* vol. 40, no. 12 (December 1994): 1678–1689.

Cox, James F., John H. Blackstone, Michael S. Spencer. *APICS Dictionary,* 7th ed., APICS Educational and Research Foundation, 1992.

GBMS.NET White Paper—Manufacturing by Geneva Systems, Inc. September 2003. http://www.knowledgestorm.com. At the search window enter the keyword MRP to find this white paper.

Heady, R. B., and Z. Zhu. "An Improved Implementation of the Wagner-Whitin Algorithm." *Production and Operations Management Journal,* vol. 3, no. 1 (Winter 1994).

Martin, Andre. *Distribution Resource Planning.* Williston, VT: Owl Publications, Inc., 1982.

Orlicky, Joseph. *Material Requirements Planning.* New York: McGraw-Hill, 1975.

Stern, Joel M., and John S. Shiely (with Irwin Ross). *The EVA Challenge: Implementing Value Added Change in an Organization.* New York: John Wiley & Sons, February 2001. (Chapter 6 extends EVA to the Shop Floor.)

Vollman, Thomas E., William L. Berry, and D. Clay Whybark. *Manufacturing Planning and Control Systems,* 3e. Homewood, IL: Irwin, 1992.

Wight, Oliver W. *The Executive's Guide to Successful MRP II.* Williston, VT: Owl Publications, Inc., 1981.

Wight, Oliver W. *MRP II, Unlocking America's Productivity Potential.* Boston: CBI Publishing Co., 1982.

Young, S. David, and Stephen F. O'Byrne. *EVA and Value-Based Management: A Practical Guide to Implementation,* 1e. New York: McGraw-Hill Trade, November 2000. (MRP in this text is market risk premium, however, economic value-adding is highly related o the goals of MRP II.)

NOTES

1. Joseph Orlicky. *Material Requirements Planning.* New York: McGraw-Hill, 1975, p. ix.

2. Oliver W. Wight. "Designing and Implementing a Material Requirements Planning System." *Proceedings of the 13th International Conference of APICS, 1970.* The quote appears in Joseph Orlicky. *Material Requirements Planning.* New York: McGraw-Hill, 1975, p. 1.

3. Jon F. Cox, John H. Blackstone, and Michael S. Spencer. *APICS Dictionary,* 7th ed. APICS Educational and Research Foundation, 1992.

4. Ibid.

5. Ibid.

6. Ibid.

7. Orlicky op. cit., p. 56.

8. Thomas E. Vollman, William L. Berry and D. Clay Whybark. *Manufacturing Planning and Control Systems,* 3e. Homewood, IL: 1992, p. 34.

9. R. B. Heady and Z. Zhu. "An Improved Implementation of the Wagner-Whitin Algorithm." *Production and Operations Management Journal,* vol. 3, no. 1 (Winter 1994) 55–63.

10. *APICS Dictionary,* 7th ed., 1992.

11. Ibid.

12. Ibid.

13. Ibid.

14. Ibid.

15. Oliver W. Wight. *MRP II: Unlocking America's Productivity Potential.* Boston: CBI Publishing Co., 1982.

SPOTLIGHT 15-1
Innovation—Everyone Has Something to Say About It

Innovations deliver improvements. Opinions differ about what constitutes improvement. Mapping a path to innovation starts with a fork in the road. The question is whether to innovate or defend the status quo. Both require strong commitments and dedicated work. Military concepts of defense or offense are surrogates for the business analogy. Static defenses (like the Maginot line) can be outflanked by innovators.

If the choice selected is to change things, then the scope of innovation is the next decision point. The Japanese kaizen concept is one of continuous incremental improvement. Kaizen has had a significant effect on American manufacturers and service providers. Continuous improvements are likely to be minor changes accomplished slowly.

Major changes occur when radical innovations are adopted to reengineering (REE) processes that seem flawed beyond redemption. "Extreme" innovation has had its share of failures as well as successes. To go for the gold, one starts with a clean slate. Old baggage is discarded. Such start-ups for manufacturing are called *greenfield plants*. Saturn's plant in Spring Hill, Tennessee, is a good example of success.

The pros and cons of REE have been argued. The reward for using radical surgery with an existing system can be high, but the failure penalty is severe. Reengineering is essential if the existing system is unacceptable and cannot be fixed by kaizen.

Alternatively, continuous improvement is rejected when it further institutionalizes a failed product or process. That is like continuous improvement of the slide rule or the buggy whip. On the other hand, continuous improvement is desirable when "good is getting better." Auto safety may require both approaches. In the near term, improve on crash results. In the long term, build cars that drive themselves on smart highways with total safety. An overriding rule is "Don't do better what shouldn't be done at all."

Continuous improvement works with what is familiar. Reengineering seeks to make the strange familiar. Synectics attempts to change the ground rules *making the familiar strange* and *making the strange familiar*.

Course corrections make sense when you know where you are going. They are not helpful when you are deciding where you want to go. The firm's probabilities of success are significantly lower for radical innovations than for course corrections. The most radical level of innovation is associated with disruptive changes in technology.

Disruptive technologies create radical, discontinuous changes in market structure. For example, refrigerators replaced iceboxes swiftly. A more current example would be nonconventional fuel systems to power cars. Many companies support separate research and development efforts within the organizational structure to work on disruptive technologies such as low-fat foods and e-books. The reason for separation is that disruptive technologies threaten existing technologies and can create hostile internal competition. When there is a split message in the organization, it is best to separate the radical innovators from the status quo group.

There remains the question about whether innovation is always a good thing. Bill Moran as vice president of market research for Lever Brothers found that among large companies, the 70:30 rule applied. This means that 7 out of 10 new products do not achieve breakeven. Don't count on the 30 percent to make a fortune either. ABC curves describe the disproportionately large contributions of the critical few. On average, 10 percent of new product launches account for 90 percent of additional revenues.

Is innovation worth the effort? A good business model can help to answer the question. Two major factors are (1) how much does it cost on average to develop new ideas and launch an innovation; (2) how much return does the average successful innovation generate?

In consumer package goods, the payoff for one successful new product launch out of 10 tries may provide sufficient reward to compensate for the costs of developing and launching 9 failures. When the odds slip to 1 in 20, the innovation program is unlikely to pay off. Meanwhile, efforts can be made to cut costs, raise margins, and improve probabilities of winning.

The costs and risks of managing innovations in different ways are discussed by Andrew and Sirkin. They identify three different organizational approaches to innovation.

1. Self-manage all aspects of the total system.
2. Create one or more alliances with logical partners.
3. License the innovation with companies better suited to market successfully.

The first approach has high costs, significant risks, and large payoffs when successful. Second, alliances provide equitable benefits to all parties when there is too much risk and/or not enough knowledge to go it alone (global corporate alliances). Third, minimal investor requirements of licensing make this approach a safe haven (with low payoffs) when marketing and manufacturing competencies are not sufficient.

Buckminster Fuller has the final say: "There is nothing in a caterpillar that tells you it's going to be a butterfly."

Sources:
Andrew, James P., and Harold L. Sirkin. "Innovating for Cash." *Harvard Business Review* (September 2003): 76–83; Hammer, Michael, and James A. Champy. *Reengineering the Corporation: A Manifesto for Business.* New York: Harper Business, May 1994;. Mauzy, Jeff, and Richard Harriman. *Creativity, Inc.: Building an Inventive Organization.* Cambridge, MA: Harvard Business School Press, April 2003; Starr, Martin K. *Global Corporate Alliances and the Competitive Edge.* Westport, CT: Quorum Books, 1991, pp.135–160.
Http://www.maginot-line.com/index.htm.
Http://www.synecticsworld.com.

SPOTLIGHT 15-2
Are Our Ports Safe?

A Conversation with Bruce Richardson, Senior Vice President, AMR Research

In a post–911 world, the topic is safety and security of the port system, which links the global supply chain. The current port system is equivalent to thousands of unlocked doorways all over the world from which anything can be sent or received. Regulation of what comes in, what goes out, and what is moving about the shipping lanes is now related to a new initiative called *Operation Safe Commerce.*

Bruce Richardson is an AMR Research expert on supply chain management, including safe commerce. AMR is an independent research firm with its main office in Boston, with European headquarters in London, United Kingdom. The company's primary focus is on the enterprise software market.

Are our ports safe?
Seven million containers are shipped into the United States every year. About 2 percent of these containers are inspected. That is equivalent to only 384 containers inspected per day. There are not enough inspectors to sample a larger number and, even if there were, 100 percent inspection is not the right answer. A different approach is essential.

What new steps are being taken to improve security at U.S. ports?
The U.S. government initiative for assuring that cargo entering the country will be safe is called Operation Safe Commerce. Its procedures entail complete disclosure to U.S. customs about specific details of all goods that are being unloaded. The details include exact specifications for what is in the containers, precise information about where these goods originated, and identification of every person who came in contact with the cargo during loading and in transit. Operation Safe Commerce requires rapid retrieval of relevant information at the point of entry to permit immediate interdiction, or further investigation. With the current system, even if some of the information is recorded, it is buried in multipage paper documents. It could be in nine or ten languages. Quick retrieval is impossible.

Does new technology play an important role in Operation Safe Commerce?
It is vital to emphasize the critical role of new technology. Safe Commerce requires a smart computer tracking system working hand-in-glove with RFID (radio frequency identification). That tagging system can track shipments on a global scale. The back-end systems will be dealing with enormous quantities of information generated by millions of shipments and transshipments each year. That information needs to be archived because it will be vital to determine cargo movement patterns over years. Appropriate data management methods and technologies will be used.

Will there be benefits to businesses resulting from firms complying with the regulations of Operation Safe Commerce?
Everyone benefits from compliance. Nobody wants a nuclear weapon to be smuggled into the United States under sacks of coffee beans. Emulating Operation Safe Commerce will permit other countries to secure their ports as well. Just as with ISO 9000 and ISO 14000, companies doing global business need

to comply with regulatory requirements in other countries. For example, in Europe, environmental regulations require documentation that Tier 5 suppliers used hazardous chemicals to manufacture imported parts. This type of information will be required for Operation Safe Commerce, and it is already available through coordination and sharing of information sources.

Are there any other benefits?
Improvement of the supply chain as a result of increased visibility means that bottlenecks can be identified. Rapid correction of delays and interruptions will be facilitated by the online information system. Operation Safe Commerce will even enable producers to pinpoint the source of defective products as well as where damage occurs en route. Online awareness about the condition of the supply chain has long been the holy grail of supply chain managers. The new methods provide a significant improvement in the efficiency of the entire supply chain starting with production outputs through shipping logistics to warehouse arrival, receipt, and storage.

What are the keys to starting the Operation Safe Commerce program?
The first thing to realize is that security for transported cargo is not just a good idea waiting to happen. It is here. As a good analogy of how easy it is to miss the message, a lot of people saw the Sarbanes-Oxley Act coming but did not start the ball rolling until late in the game. That makes compliance very costly. Rushing project completions is messy and expensive. It is the antithesis of good project management.

How are companies implementing Operation Safe Commerce?
Successful implementation of Operation Safe Commerce requires an executive-level champion. Distribution center and warehouse managers are not accustomed to such roles. There is a need for a chief of supply chain security (CSS) who understands how to work with both the U.S. and foreign customs organizations. That CSS must also be comfortable with port managers, transportation contractors, and the network of parties that are participants in supply chain logistics. Considering the situation, it also makes sense to partner with individuals and companies that have (or can develop) solid experience in the emerging technologies and business processes required to move materials securely and safely around the world. This is not something that you want to try learning from your mistakes.

What is happening in other countries?
China had $326 billion in exports in 2002, which is 22 percent greater than in 2001. Belgium, along with China in the top 10 world exporters, grew 12 percent in the same time frame. These statistics exemplify the growth in shipping that is taking place worldwide. Companies must expand their IT global reach and achieve just-in-time delivery to be successful. Intensified problems of security make it imperative to know what is in the pipeline and where it is located. Developments in technology and business processes are making it possible to do just that.

Sources:
Richardson, Bruce. senior vice president of AMR Research, Inc. See also http://www.amrresearch.com.
The World Trade Organization at http://www.wto.org.

Supplement 15

Part-Period, Lot-Sizing Policy

The lot-for-lot policy—without errors, cancellations, or changes in order size—exactly matches orders to requirements. Therefore, there would be no carrying cost and many orders. If placing orders is expensive, because a new setup is required in each case, then there would be a preference for fewer orders and some carrying costs. Consequently, a lot-sizing policy that is worthy of consideration is one that balances setup costs with carrying costs.

Ordering more than lot-for-lot results in parts being carried over periods of time. This statement is the basis for the part-period lot-sizing policy. It is an attempt to achieve the minimum total cost policy, which occurs when setup, or ordering, costs are equal to carrying costs. An estimate can be made of the economic part-period. Thus:

$$\text{Economic Part-Period} = \frac{\text{Total Setup Costs}}{\text{Unit Carrying Cost per Period}}$$

The dimensions of this measure are unit months, or whatever time period the carrying costs embody.

Assume that the following costs have been estimated: The unit cost of the part is $10, the carrying cost rate is 1.00 percent per month, and the unit carrying cost for one month is then $10(0.01) = $0.10. The setup cost to produce this component is $15.

$$\text{Economic Part-Period} = \frac{\text{Total Setup Costs}}{\text{Unit Carrying Cost per Period}}$$

$$= \frac{\$15.00}{0.10} = 150 \text{ Unit Months}$$

Next, calculate the number of unit months (part-periods) of each possible ordering policy.

Table 15-11 lists monthly net requirements. These are summed in the column titled "Cumulative Lot Size." Thus, if the order is to produce enough for the first month only, then the lot size will be 20 units. If the order is to produce enough for the first 4 months, then the lot size will be 150 units, etc. The carrying cost per unit calculations are shown here.

The carrying cost is determined for each policy. If the policy is to produce or order enough for only the first month, then there are no carrying costs:

20 units carried for 0 months = 0 part-periods or unit months

Producing or ordering for 2 months entails no carrying charges for the first 20 units. They will be used for production in month 1. There are carrying costs of $4 per unit for the second month. Thus:

20 units × $10/unit × (0.01) × 0 months carried = $0
40 units × $10/unit x (0.01) × 1 month carried = $4
Total units ordered for 2 months = 60 units

					TABLE 15-11

TABLE 15-11

Data Required for Part-Period Lot Sizing

Month	Net Requirements	Cumulative Lot Size	Months Carried	Carrying Cost/Unit	Policy Is: Order for Months Numbered
1	20	20	0	$ 0	1
2	40	60	1	$ 4	1+2
3	60	120	2	$16	1+2+3
4	30	150	3	$25	1+2+3+4

Part-periods = (40 × 1) = 40 unit months
Total cost = $4

Producing or ordering 120 units for the first 3 months requires:

0 units × $10/unit × (0.01) × 0 months carried = $0
40 units × $10/unit × (0.01) × 1 month carried = $4
60 units × $10/unit × (0.01) × 2 months carried = $12
Total units ordered for 3 months = 120 units
Part-periods = (40 × 1) + (60 × 2) = 160 unit months
Total cost = $16

This ordering policy for the first 3 months comes close to matching the prior determination of the economic part-period, which was 150 unit months. It is necessary to see whether the next ordering policy for the first 4 months can come as close.

To determine the carrying cost of producing 150 units for 4 months' requirements, simply add the 3-month total to the carrying cost of the fourth month's net requirements.

30 units x $10/unit × (0.01) × 3 months carried = $9
Carried forward from 3-month lot-size policy = $16
Total units ordered for 4 months = 150 units
Part-periods = (40 × 1) + (60 × 2) + (30 × 3) = 250 part-periods
Total cost = $25

The 3-month ordering policy is indicated in two related ways. First, its economic part-period policy is closest (150 versus 160). Second, the setup cost of $15 is closest to the carrying-cost charges of $16 for a lot size of 3 months' requirements. That meets the criterion of balancing these two opposing costs. Consequently, produce or order 120 units.

The deviation between the economic part-period measure and the chosen order size will vary as a function of the actual net requirements, as shown in Table 15-11.

Problems for Supplement 15

1. Determine the production or order quantity for Table 15-11 when the setup, or ordering, cost is $24.
2. Assume that the following costs have been estimated: The per unit cost of the part is $50, the carrying-cost rate is 2 percent per month, and the setup cost to produce this part is $75. What is the economic part-period?
3. Using the information in Problem 2, calculate the number of unit months (part-periods) of each possible ordering policy for the following table.

Month	Net Requirements	Cumulative Lot Size	Months Carried	Carrying Cost/Unit	Policy Is: Order for Months Numbered
1	30		0		1
2	50		1		1+2
3	20		2		1+2+3
4	40		3		1+2+3+4
5	30		4		1+2+3+4+5
6	25		5		1+2+3+4+5+6

Then, determine the production or order quantity to be used.

4. When the order is placed in Problem 3, start the calculations again from that point. Derive the next order quantity and continue in this way until the data are used up.
5. Use the part-period lot-sizing method for the data in Problem 1 of the "general" Problems Section.

Production Scheduling

Chapter Outline

This section introduces production scheduling of the loading function and the sequencing function for the job shop. *Loading* consists of assigning jobs that are on hand to departments or work centers. It applies to both services and manufacturing. Load charting is detailed and three loading methods are explained. These are based on the assignment method, the transportation method, and a particular heuristic method. *Sequencing* is the next logical procedure because it completes the assignment by specifying the *order* in which jobs are to be done. Various sequencing policies are described.

After reading this chapter, you should be able to:

- Explain why production scheduling must be done by every organization whether it manufactures or provides services.
- Discuss the application of loading to the job shop (often called *job shop loading* or *shop loading*).
- Draw a Gantt load chart and explain its information display.
- Describe how to resolve the loading problem where teams compete for permanent assignment to the best facilities.
- Explain why "best assignments" require the systems approach.
- Relate best-loading assignments to opportunity costs in terms of lowest cost, greatest profit, or fastest completion time.
- Detail the strengths and weaknesses of the assignment model.

- Describe how the transportation model resolves the "no splitting" problem of the assignment model.
- Detail strengths and weaknesses of the transportation model.
- Describe the role of sequencing and how to apply sequencing rules for one facility and for more than one facility.
- Explain the purpose of priority sequencing rules and the means for using them.
- Describe the critical ratio and other priority rules for sequencing.
- Explain how finite scheduling and the OPT concept take bottlenecks into account.
- Explain queue control and synchronized manufacturing.
- Discuss changing the capacity of bottlenecks.

THE SYSTEMS VIEWPOINT

Department scheduling decisions rarely achieve optimal assignments for every job at every facility. Best assignments can seldom be made on a one-by-one basis. Instead, the problem must be looked at as a whole. As an analogy, NASA found that if every component of a space vehicle is optimized with respect to its function and only its function, the "bird will not fly." Instead, the vehicle must be designed together as a coordinated system of components. The same applies to scheduling for the job shop.

The assignment of work and its timing need to be orchestrated. Bottlenecks need to be taken into account, and the goal of synchronized manufacturing requires coordination of the entire job shop with respect to the mix of jobs that is being orchestrated.

The systems approach is called for so that the total set of assignments is optimized. The system's total costs are minimized or the total profits are maximized. Total quality (the sum of individual item qualities) and total productivity (the sum of individual item productivities) are maximized. This means that each and every item is not at maximum quality and productivity. The nature of the goal is to select assignments that—although less than best individually—result in the overall system's best.

STRATEGIC THINKING

Production scheduling is always a system's problem because jobs, people, and teams compete with each other for best facilities. Jobs (as surrogates for customers) also compete with each other concerning which gets done first. Facilities contend with each other for jobs. Departments that do similar work compete with each other for preferred work. Orders placed with suppliers are tied to priorities with respect to jobs and customers—so suppliers' orders also rival each other in terms of importance and how they are treated.

Strategic planning is required to design the facilities, staff the departments, select suppliers, and design the product mix—for the expected blend of job shop orders. In contrast, the flow shop has a specific set of items to be made in volume on dedicated facilities. The flow shop system is predesigned to optimize through synchronization the production schedule.

With the job shop, the company must achieve systems optimization to rationalize the various preferences in a way that is not self-defeating. When the systems point of view prevails, the solutions are company-wide optimizations even though people and facilities experience suboptimal assignments. Over time, the facilities need to be altered in such a way as to minimize the degree of suboptimization. That requires strategic thinking.

16-1 PRODUCTION SCHEDULING: OVERVIEW

> **Production scheduling:** Consists of loading and sequencing; used to deal with the difficulty of optimizing detailed complex arrays of data for all possible schedules.

The final step of **production scheduling** assigns actual jobs to designated facilities with unambiguous stipulations that they be completed at specific times. The steps in scheduling will be reviewed here, moving from generic resource planning to actual assignments at workstations.

1. *Aggregate scheduling* developed resource plans based on forecasts of orders in generic units such as standard hours.

2. Later, with actual orders on hand or with reasonable predictions about orders, the *master production schedule (MPS)* assigned jobs to time slots to permit orders to be placed for required materials using *material requirements planning (MRP)*. These time period assignments are so well defined that they are referred to as *time buckets*.

3. The next step in production scheduling is to load facilities, which means taking the actual orders and assigning them to designated facilities. **Loading** answers the question: Which department is going to do what work? **Sequencing** answers the question: What is the order in which the work will be done?

> **Loading:** Which jobs are to be assigned to which teams or facilities.
>
> **Sequencing:** Job order can make a big difference in the flow time, which is the length of time it takes to process a sequence of n jobs.

To summarize, the third step in production scheduling does both loading and sequencing. Loading assumes that the material requirement analysis has been done and that orders have been properly placed for required materials and for needed parts and subassemblies. It further assumes that the parts will be on hand, as planned. A problem in supplier shipments will delay scheduling production of the affected order.

Specifically, loading assigns the work to divisions, departments, work centers, load centers, stations, and people. Whatever names are used in a given organization, orders are assigned to those who will be responsible for performing the work. Loading releases jobs to facilities.

At this point, sequencing will be explained so that the entire process of production scheduling will be clear to the reader. Sequencing models and methods follow the discussion of loading models and methods. Sequencing involves **shop floor control,** which consists of communicating the status of orders and the productivity of workstations. Sequencing assigns priorities that determine the order with which work will be done. Say that Jobs x, y, and z have been assigned to workstation 1 (loading). Jobs x, y, and z are in a queue (waiting line). Sequencing rules determine which job should be first in line, which second, etc. The objective function can be to minimize system's costs, or to minimize total system's time, or (if margin data are available) to maximize total system's profit.

16-2 LOADING

Loading, also called *shop loading*, is required to assign specific jobs or teams to specific facilities. Loading is needed for machine shops, hospitals, and offices. Although loading assigns work to facilities, it does not specify the order in which jobs should be done at the facility. Sequencing methods (described later) determine the order of work at the facility.

16-2a Plan to Load Real Jobs—Not Forecasts

Aggregate scheduling used standard hours based on forecasts to determine what resources should be assembled over the planning horizon. Loading takes place in the job shop when the real orders are on hand. If the aggregate scheduling job was done well, then the appropriate kinds and amounts of resources are available for loading. The master production schedule also made resource assignments that could be modified if capacity was not adequate. Planning actual shop assignments is a regular, repetitive managerial responsibility. Releasing the jobs, as per assignment, is another.

Each facility carries a backlog of work, which is its "load"—hardly a case of perfect just-in-time in which no waiting occurs. The backlog is generally much larger than the work in process, which can be seen on the shop floor. This is because work not assigned yet is waiting, but not visible. A major objective of loading is to spread the load so that waiting is minimized, flow is smooth and rapid, and congestion is avoided.

These objectives are constrained by the fact that not all workstations can do all kinds of jobs. Even though the job shop uses general-purpose equipment, some workstations and people are better suited for specific jobs than are others. Some stations cannot do jobs that others can do. Some are faster than others and tend to be overloaded. The scheduling objective is to smooth the load with balanced work assignments at stations.

16-3 GANTT LOAD CHARTS

The use of Gantt charts for loading dates to the early 1900s when Henry L. Gantt (1861–1919) developed them as a formal means for assigning jobs to facilities and charting job progress. **Gantt charts** provide a graphic system that is easy to follow by visualizing the progress of jobs and the load on departments. Often these two purposes are combined on one chart. Too much job waiting (overloading), facilities not working at full utilization (underloading), or load imbalances between stations (some busy, others idle) could be seen immediately by someone familiar with these charts.

Gantt charts deal with the system's realities of loading for production scheduling. These are issues such as which jobs have not started that should have started, how much progress toward completion has been made, which departments are overloaded, and which ones are underloaded.

The ideal situation is creative customization (of load scheduling charts) that meets the needs of the process managers and the sales department. Proper charts reflect the interests of customers and the impact of suppliers. Figure 16-1 illustrates the Gantt load chart and the discussion that follows explains it.

FIGURE 16-1
Gantt Load Chart
This is a traditional Gantt load chart. The legend used to explain lines, bars and other chart marks is given in the next section.

The Gantt load chart in Figure 16-1 has a time scale running along the top. The rows represent resources: people, machines, stations, departments, or whatever facilities will be required to do the job. The time scale is labeled in either dated calendar time or with general intervals ahead, such as weeks.

The left-hand side of the chart is the start time. Depending on the time scale, a specific date can be used, or it can be called *time zero*. Bars and lines, running from left to right, convey various kinds of information designed to help the department schedule its production needs.

16-3a Gantt Chart Legend

- For each facility, and week, there is a box that contains a horizontal line and two bars under that line. The lines and bars for each week are divided into 10 units of time. For all four weeks, there are 40 units of time.

- The single horizontal line is the workload percent by the week. All lines start at the left. Moving to the right represents higher percentages of utilization. If the line runs from one side of the box to the other side, then that facility is 100 percent loaded for the week.

- Sequencing decisions have been reached with respect to weekly assignments as per the master production schedule. Orders have been placed with suppliers. Lead times have been calculated so that materials will be received in time to permit production to begin the job in that week. The order in which jobs will be done within each week has not yet been determined. Note: If the time buckets are monthly, then all times are monthly to be consistent.

- The jobs column describes all of the jobs that are waiting at that facility. To the right of the job name is the number of units to be made for that order. The load consists of on-time jobs and backlogged jobs. Work is on time when it is scheduled for production so that delivery can be made on or before the promised **due date.** Work is backlogged when it is going to be late. This is shown by an asterisk in the units column. An additional column can be added to the Gantt load chart to explain the causes and extent of delays.

- The top bar is the cumulative workload at the current time.

- The bottom bar (dark gray) is the cumulative workload at the beginning of the prior week.

Due date: Order promising shows up as a due date on the production schedule.

The cumulative load at each facility is presented in two ways. First, there is the load that exists at the beginning of the current week. Second, there is the load that existed at the beginning of the prior week. Comparing these can be useful to determine where and when the load is increasing, decreasing, or staying the same. This helps the scheduler to assign load where it can be best processed.

Which departments are underutilized *can be seen at a glance*. That is one of the primary purposes of the Gantt chart, which makes no pretense at being a method for optimizing assignments. In management science terms, *Gantt graphics facilitate heuristic methods*—which rely on "rules of thumb" and sound generalizations developed from experience. OM decisions must often be made with fast data scans ("eyeballing") that rely on the assistance of charts such as the Gantt load chart.

The charts can deliver additional information as well. They can show that certain departments have reserved time for preventive maintenance. This would be indicated by blocking off time along the horizontal line. Facility 1 has blocked 10 percent of its time in week 1 with a small box to indicate preventive maintenance.

The charts can show that particular jobs cannot be split up. This is shown by a + sign in the jobs column. Running one job in two departments would mean two setups, which can take too much time, cost a lot, and adversely impact quality control. Two different setups cannot have the same statistical fingerprints. For some jobs, this lack of homogeneity can be a serious problem. Good Gantt charting prevents split assignments that impair productivity and quality.

When jobs cannot be split, for the economic and quality reasons mentioned earlier, they must wait until there is sufficient time available in appropriate departments. Note that facility 2 has 10 percent idle time in the second week. If it does not require scheduled maintenance, this time could be used for process improvement, training, and cross-training exercises.

When meeting due dates is a problem, it is useful to add cumulative backlog of jobs to the Gantt chart. As with total load, the cumulative backlog data should be shown for the current week and the prior week. This information will indicate whether the backlog is increasing, decreasing, or staying about the same. Note: At facility 1, load has increased from 22/40 to 24/40. At facility 2, load has decreased from 35/40 to 31/40. However, it could be that backlog has decreased at the first facility and increased at the second one. Thus, when due date problems are a concern, the Gantt chart should reflect that fact.

As an illustration, the load scenario for facility 1 with due date considerations might be as follows:

Week Number	Load Level Percent of Capacity	Cumulative Load: Current	Cumulative Load: Prior	Cumulative Backlog: Current	Cumulative Backlog: Prior
1	90	9/10	10/10	3/10	2/10
2	70	16/20	15/20	5/20	4/20
3	50	21/30	19/30	6/30	6/30
4	30	24/40	22/40	6/40	7/40

The load at facility 1 by week 4 has increased from 22/40 to 24/40. Due date problems (backlog) have diminished, going from 7/40 to 6/40. Accompanying notes can indicate which backlog situations are considered to be the most serious.

Studying load charts can reveal whether there is a long-term capacity problem. It highlights bottlenecks and problem areas. When work that is scheduled is not completed on time, either the scheduler underestimated the time required for completion, or there is a process problem to be determined.

Constant matching of estimated and actual times improves the database for estimation, monitors process productivity, and reflects on the knowledge and skill of the schedulers. It is important to strive for the load being equally distributed among facilities. Overloaded departments suffer morale problems, especially when they see other departments that have idle capacity. Long-term solutions may be needed to provide capacity balance.

This kind of information must be fed back to the MRP departments and the master production schedulers. Often, the original scheduling concepts were applicable but the character of the jobs changed. Shifting job requirements can lead to an imbalance in load among departments. The changes can favor different materials, machines, and skills. The variability of the order mix is a factor in planning capacity and taking corrective actions during aggregate scheduling. Variability in the loading mix is a difficult problem because the time for resource planning is long past.

Without knowing what the jobs are and the capabilities of the departments, it is not possible to evaluate how good a scheduling job has been done—both in the current week and in the weeks ahead. In a company where management knows its processes and its people, everyone in the organization should be aware of the schedule. Teamwork is the key to successfully adjusting to variability.

Employing the systems perspective, anyone who has some special knowledge that affects quality and/or productivity should feel empowered to communicate with those doing the scheduling. Inputs from various suppliers regarding schedules can be useful. Open lines to learn about customer needs may be essential and lead to schedule revisions.

16-4 THE ASSIGNMENT METHOD FOR LOADING

Assignment method: A decision model for matching n resources with n resource users.

The **assignment method** provides production scheduling with a decision model for matching jobs with facilities in an optimal way. Such loading of facilities determined by this model are subject to a variety of conditions.

The first scheduling question is always which facility, person, or department is best-suited to do the job. That raises another question: If the best-suited facility is occupied, or for any other reason unavailable, what facility is next best?

Using systems thinking, it becomes clear that these questions beg the issue, which is: What set of assignments will produce the overall best schedule? "Best" can be defined in many ways, including highest output quality, greatest productivity, lowest cost, fastest completion, or greatest profit. Best assignments (on a pair-by-pair basis) are unlikely to add up to optimal systems-wide solutions. The assignment problem must be visualized as a collection of paired assignments that interact as a whole.

The assignment model provides solutions when jobs compete for facilities where it is uneconomic to split the job. No splitting means that whichever facility, person, or team gets the job does the whole job. Usually this is because split job setup costs are prohibitive and/or quality control at two facilities is not manageable.

There may be tooling or equipment for only one location. Many factory jobs cannot be worked on at two locations simultaneously. Project assignments are generally of this singular-assignment type.

It is uncommon for department-loading decisions to achieve optimal assignments for every job at every facility. Therefore, it is the set of assignments that is to be optimized. The concessions—which make some assignments that are less than the best—should result in an overall systems best.

Opportunity costs: Costs of not making the best possible assignments of a set of resources to a set of resource users.

The assignment model is based on **opportunity costs,** which are the costs of not making the best possible assignments of jobs to facilities and vice versa. The reason that the best possible assignments cannot be made for every job is that jobs compete with each other for available time on those facilities for which they are best-suited. Thus, consider Table 16-1, which shows the cost per part for jobs 1, 2, and 3 at facilities A, B, and C.

Jobs 1 and 2 have their lowest cost per part when made at facility B. They are in direct competition with each other for the use of this facility. Job 3 has the lowest cost per

TABLE 16-1		**Facilities**		
		A	B	C
Cost per Part for Jobs at Facilities	1	0.10	0.09	0.12
Jobs 2		0.08	0.07	0.09
	3	0.15	0.18	0.20

TABLE 16-2

Job Opportunity Costs—Row Subtraction

		Facilities		
		A	**B**	**C**
	1	0.01	0	0.03
Jobs	2	0.01	0	0.02
	3	0	0.03	0.05

part when assigned to facility A. It is not competing with any other job for that facility. However, this assignment cannot be made until the conflict between jobs 1 and 2 has been resolved. The reason is that whichever job is not assigned to facility B might be better assigned to facility A than job 3.

All the numbers in the matrix are interrelated. This is a systems problem. Assignments should not be made on an individual basis. The assignment model develops comparisons of penalties (opportunity costs) for making an assignment other than the best possible one. To make the necessary comparisons, subtract the smallest number in each row from all other numbers in that row. This yields Table 16-2, which is a matrix of the opportunity costs for not assigning each job to the best possible facility for that job. There is a zero in each job row.

All of the zeros in Table 16-2 are best possible job assignments. Because of the conflict between jobs 1 and 2 at facility B, the solution is stymied. Also, there is an assumption that the orders are of the same size. Otherwise, the matrix should represent total costs, not costs per unit as in Table 16-1. This means that the assignment problem would start with a matrix of total costs.

16-4a Column Subtraction—Best Job at a Specific Facility

Column subtraction yields the opportunity costs at a given facility for assigning jobs that are not the best jobs. These are facility opportunity costs. Using Table 16-1, subtract the smallest number in each column from all other numbers in that column. The opportunity costs of each facility with respect to jobs are shown in Table 16-3. There is a zero in each column.

Job 2 has all zero opportunity costs in its row. It is the preferred job at each facility. The facilities are in competition with each other for job 2. Therefore, thus far, there is no feasible assignment.

16-4b Row Subtraction—Best Facility for a Specific Job

The next step is to subtract the smallest number in each row of Table 16-3 from all other numbers in that row. The instruction is applicable only for rows 1 and 3 because row 2 has all zeros in it. Row subtraction provides the combined opportunity cost matrix in Table 16-4. It represents the penalty for each job being assigned to less than the best facility—and for each facility being assigned to less than the best job. Table 16-4 presents the total opportunity cost matrix.

TABLE 16-3

Facility Opportunity Costs—Column Subtraction

		Facilities		
		A	**B**	**C**
	1	0.02	0.02	0.03
Jobs	2	0	0	0
	3	0.07	0.11	0.11

TABLE 16-4	Facilities		
Column Subtraction First, Row Second Yields Total Opportunity Cost Matrix	**A**	**B**	**C**
Jobs 1	0	0*	0.01
2	0	0	0*
3	0*	0.04	0.04

(* = zeros chosen for assignment of jobs to facilities)

Table 16-4 states that all jobs can be assigned to facility A with zero opportunity cost. If this were acceptable (assuming that there was other work to be done at facilities B and C), then a sequencing problem exists at facility A. That is, which job goes first, which goes second, and which goes third?

All jobs being assigned to facility A is not an acceptable option for this problem. Given that a job must be assigned to each facility without splitting, there is a feasible set of zero opportunity cost assignments. They are shown in the cells of Table 16-4 as asterisks on zeros, with the footnoted statement (* = zeros chosen for assignment of jobs to facilities).

The logic of this assignment starts with the fact that there is only one zero in column C and that is row 2. So, job 2 must be assigned to facility C. There is only one zero in row 3. Job 3 must be assigned to facility A. That forces the assignment of job 1 to facility B.

Note that Table 16-2 was derived by using row subtraction first. This yielded the opportunity costs of each job being assigned to less than the best facility. Using Table 16-2, apply column subtraction to derive the results of Table 16-5.

The same set of assignments as in Table 16-4 results. Although the final matrices are not identical, it is equally correct to use either row or column subtraction first. However, sometimes it turns out to be easier to use one first instead of the other to reduce the matrix to an assignable set of zeroes. There is no way of prejudging which will be easier beforehand. Also, other complications can be encountered. To deal with them requires understanding all opportunity cost relationships of the cells of the assignment model or being able to use appropriate "assignment method" software.

It should be noted that if profit maximization is the goal, and the matrix in Table 16-1 is profit data, then all profit numbers should be subtracted from a number larger than any one of them. To illustrate, if the profit per part, given by the matrix in Table 16-1, is subtracted from $1.00, the result is shown in Table 16-6.

Use the assignment method to minimize profit opportunity costs. The solution can be obtained by using row subtraction first—followed by column. The assignment remains A3, B1, C2. It will be noted that if column subtraction is used first—followed by row subtraction—then an impasse occurs because all of column 1 and all of row 3 have zeros. There is a method for creating a new zero at the lowest value entry that remains. That change is compensated for by adding an opportunity cost to all existing zeros (twice at the intersection of the row and column of zeros). Then, row and column subtraction procedures previously described will continue until a final assignment solution is found.

TABLE 16-5	Facilities		
Row Subtraction First and Then Column Subtraction Yields Total Opportunity Cost Matrix	**A**	**B**	**C**
Jobs 1	0.01	0*	0.01
2	0.01	0	0*
3	0*	0.03	0.03

(* = zeros chosen for assignment of jobs to facilities)

TABLE 16-6

Profits per Part

		Facilities		
		A	**B**	**C**
	1	0.90	0.91	0.88
Jobs	2	0.92	0.93	0.91
	3	0.85	0.82	0.80

The definition of profit opportunity cost is the cost of assigning a job to a facility that does not result in having the best possible profit. In Table 16-6, the assignment of job 2 to facility B results in the largest amount of missed profit, viz., 93 cents. When the matrix of costs in Table 16-6 is minimized, the total amount of missed profit is minimized.

Using the assignment method demonstrates the importance of opportunity costs for loading. The weakness (or strength, when it applies) of the assignment model is that only one job or team can be assigned to each department, facility, or machine at a time. No splitting of assignments is permitted. This condition accurately describes the permanent post of managers to stores, pilots to planes, and chefs to restaurants (i.e., splitting a row assignment between two columns). Also, two pilots cannot be assigned to one plane (i.e., splitting a column assignment between two rows).

16-5 THE TRANSPORTATION METHOD FOR SHOP LOADING

Under certain circumstances, a weakness of the assignment method was that no splits are allowed. When split assignments are allowed, the transportation method can be used. The transportation model embodies the transportation method, which permits assigning more than one job to a machine or team. In Table 16-7, machine 1 is assigned three jobs called A1, B1, and C1. Loading involves matching supply of available machine time, $S(i)$ with demand of jobs for machine time $D(j)$.

Another type of split prohibited by the assignment method is that no job can be divided with that method. In Table 16-7, job C has been split into three parts: C1, C2, and C3.

Although the transportation method overcomes assignment method difficulties, it has certain restrictive assumptions of its own. Split assignments are easy to make, but when demand in units, [called $D(j)$] is loaded against supply in machine hours, [called $S(i)$] the amounts of supply and demand must be put into common terms. A convenient common terminology is to express supply and demand in standard hours.

To create standard hours *it is necessary to assume that strict proportionality exists between the productivity rates of the machines*. To review this concept (developed when explaining aggregate scheduling), note that in Table 16-8, machine 1 is half as fast as machine 2—which has arbitrarily been chosen to be the standard machine (SM). Similarly, M3 is 0.8 as fast as the SM.

TABLE 16-7

Split Assignments of Two Kinds with the Transportation Model Used for Job Shop Loading

Jobs Are Columns (*j*)		Job A	Job B	Job C	Supply S(*i*) Actual Hours
	M1	A1	B1	C1	S(1)= 36
Machines Are	**M2**			C2	S(2) = 54
Rows (*i*)	**M3**			C3	S(3) = 80
Demand D(*j*)		D(A)	D(B)	D(C)	

TABLE 16-8	Machine (*i*)	SMH Index	Relative Productivity
Relative Productivity and the Equivalent SMH Index (for each machine *i*) SMH = standard machine hours	M1	0.5	Half as fast as the SM
	M2 (SM)	1.0	Standard machine
	M3	0.8	80% as fast as the SM

The restrictive assumption is that the SMH index for each machine *applies to all jobs.* It is called the *presumption of productive proportionality.* Thus, M2 is fastest—*for all of the jobs*—by the same amount, in comparison with the other machines. M1 is half as fast as M2 *for all jobs.* The equation for the SMH index is derived in more general terms, as follows:

$$\text{SMH Index of } M(ij) = \frac{\text{production output of } M(ij)}{\text{production output of } M(SMj)} \quad \text{(for all } j \text{ jobs)}$$

For each machine, when the SMH index is multiplied by the actual machine hours available per week, the standard machine hours (SMH) available per week are obtained. Table 16-9 provides the actual machine hours that are available per week converted by means of the SMH index into standard machine hours available per week. Table 16-9 concludes that total SMH = 136 per week. Note that a week was chosen as a convenient period. It could have been a day or a month.

The fact that there are 170 actual machine hours available per week has significance after the resolution of the standard hour problem. The transportation model is solved using the 136 standard hours that are available per week.

Table 16-10 provides production output rates (in pieces/hour) for each machine for every job. The entries in the matrix are labeled *PR(i, j)* where *i* = machine and *j* = job, which is consistent with the notation throughout this section. The production rate of the standard machine for the *j*th job is *PR(SM, j)*. See the second row (machine M2) in Table 16-10.

Now, turning to Table 16-11, demands are initially stated as the *number of units ordered per job.* These can vary greatly because there are many different types of orders. For example, simple, small gears may be needed in large numbers whereas complex, large gears are expensive to make and have low demand. Orders, such as these can put loads on the facilities for various lengths of time. An order for 300 C-type units would take 10 hours on the standard machine, M2. It would take 20 hours on M1.

Demand quantities for goods or services of type *j*, called *D(j)*, must be turned into standard hours to match the amount of supply available from machines of type I, called *S(i)*. Standard hours are also essential to balance out the production differences between making simple and complex products.

To accomplish the transformation of all dimensions to standard hours, start by dividing the number of units demanded for job *x* by the production rate of the standard machine for job *x*. This yields demand in standard hours *D'(j)* instead of demand in units *D(j)*. The equations for units of demand into standard hours of demand are shown on the left side of Table 16-11.

TABLE 16-9	Machine	SMH Index	Actual Hours/Week	SMH per Week
Department Time Converted into SMH	1	0.5	36	18
	2 (SM)	1.0	54	54
	3	0.8	80	64
	Total:	Total actual hours/Week = 170 hours		Total SMH/Week = 136 SM hours

	Jobs	A	B	C	SM Index
	M1	3	3.5	15	0.5
Machines	M2	6	7	30	1.0 (SM)
	M3	4.8	5.6	24	0.8

TABLE 16-10

**Production Rates *PR(i, j)*
in Pieces per Hour for
Machines *i* and Jobs *j***

On the right side of Table 16-11 is the numerical calculation of units demanded divided by the production rates of the standard machine (SM) for each job. This produces numerical values of demand in standard hours. For example, 300 units of A when divided by 6 units per standard hour yields 50 standard hours.

Now, both supply and demand have been converted to the common terms of standard machine hours (SMH). There are only 136 standard machine hours available per week and 140 hours demanded to complete the orders. Therefore, 140 – 136 = 4 standard machine hours of demand will not be satisfied this week. Specifically, supply is less than demand. A backorder will be created if allowed.

A dummy machine is created to pick up the slack. It is called MD (for machine dummy). By definition, MD has zero output for all jobs. Some part of whichever job is assigned to the dummy will not be done. The balanced supply and demand system with all numbers in standard hours including the output rates per standard hour in the upper right-hand corners of each assignment cell is given in Table 16-12.

As with the assignment method, profit can be used instead of cost with the transportation model. Profit per piece, π_j, is calculated for each job j. When π_j is multiplied by the product output rates $PR(i,j)$, the result is $\Pi_{ij} = \pi_j PR(i,j)$, which is profit per standard hour for each machine i. This formulation assumes that costs per piece are the same on all machines. If not, it would be necessary to use $\pi_{i,j}$ for each cell.

Specifically, when that assumption is incorrect, the revenue r_{ij} less the cost c_{ij} is multiplied by the product output rates $PR(i,j)$ for each cell in the matrix. Thus, where π_{ij} = profit per piece for each cell i,j, and Π_{ij} = profit per standard hour for each cell i,j:

$$\Pi_{ij} = \pi_{ij} PR(i,j) = (r_{ij} - c_{ij}) PR(i,j) \qquad \text{(Equation 16-1)}$$

Often, the revenue is simply r_j because it is a function of the job and not the machine. However, if quality differences occur as a result of the machine used, which affects price charged, then Equation 16-1 should be used. Often, costs are unique, i.e., c_{ij}, and Equation 16-1 applies.

When the profit per piece is independent of the machine used, as shown in Table 16-13, then the optimal load assignments are as indicated by the numbers in the matrix that sum to match the supply capabilities and the demand requirements. Note that the product output rates per standard hour have been multiplied by profit per piece to reflect the profit per standard hour. These are shown in the small boxes in the upper right-hand corner of each assignment cell.

Calculation	Actual Units	Standard Hours of Demand
D(j) ÷ PR(SM, j) = D' (j)		
D(A) ÷ PR(SM,A) = D' (A)	300 A units ÷ 6 =	50 standard hours
D(B) ÷ PR(SM,B) = D' (B)	210 B units ÷ 7 =	30 standard hours
D(C) ÷ PR(SM,C) = D' (C)	1800 C units ÷ 30 =	60 standard hours
Total standard hours of demand = 140		

TABLE 16-11

**Convert Job Demands
from Units to Standard
Hours**

TABLE 16-12

Transportation Model

The bold numbers for supply and demand are in standard hours. The internal matrix values in the small boxes in the upper right-hand corner of each assignment cell are output/standard hour; internal numbers in the second row for M2 are the outputs of the standard machine with index = 1. The internal matrix values apply to each job on a specific machine.

	Job A	Job B	Job C	Supply S(i)
M1	3	3.5	15	**18**
M2	6	7	30	**54**
M3	4.8	5.6	24	**64**
MD	0	0	0	**4**
Demand D(j)	**50**	**30**	**60**	**140**

The goal is to find the loading arrangement that uses the resources available to maximize total profit. The optimal loading schedule is shown in Table 16-13 in standard machine hours with the

Maximum total profit $(\Sigma_i \, \Sigma_j \, \Pi_{ij}) = (18 \times 6) + (54 \times 15) + (32 \times 9.6) + (26 \times 5.6) + (6 \times 12) + (4 \times 0) = \$1,442.80$

There are four rows and three columns which means that $M + N - 1 = 6$ assignments should be made for the transportation model. The requisite six are in place. The optimal has been found for this example using the standard techniques employed to solve the transportation model. Software is readily available to solve transportation problems involving many variables. It also can be solved as a linear programming problem.

The solution in terms of standard hours must now be converted back into actual machine hours and actual job units. Divide the standard hour assignments by the SMH index for each machine. This is shown in Table 16-14.

* *For Job A: The load is established by consulting Tables 16-13 and 16-14:*

  18 SMH ÷ SMH index of 1/2 equals 36 actual hours assigned on machine 1 for job A. This yields 36 × 3 = 108 units of A.
  32 SMH ÷ SMH index of 0.8 equals 40 actual hours assigned on machine 3 for job A. This yields 40 × 4.8 = 192 units of A.
  Total 108 + 192 = 300 units as required for job A.

TABLE 16-13

Transportation Model: Matrix Adjusted for Profits, $\pi_{i,j}$

Profit per Piece	$2.00	$1.00	$0.50	
	Job A	Job B	Job C	Supply S(i)
M1	18 | 6	3.5	7.5	18
M2	12	7	54 | 15	54
M3	32 | 9.6	26 | 5.6	6 | 12	64
MD	0	4 | 0	0	4
Demand D(j)	50	30	60	140

	Job A		Job B		Job C		Supply S(i)
M1	36	3		3.5		15	36
M2		6		7	54	30	54
M3	40	4.8	32.5	5.6	7.5	24	80
MD		0	4	0		0	4
Demand Filled	300		182		1800		
Shortages	0		28		0		
Demand D(j)	300		210		1800		

TABLE 16-14

**Transportation Model:
Actual Assignments**

- *For Job B: The load is established by consulting Tables 16-13 and 16-14:*
  26 SMH ÷ SMH index of 0.8 equals 32.5 actual hours assigned on machine 3 for job B. This yields 32.5 × 5.6 = 182 units of B.
  4 SMH are assigned to the dummy machine MD so job B will be partially completed. There is a shortage of (210 − 182) = 28 units for job B.

- *For Job C: The load is established by consulting Tables 16-13 and 16-14:*
  54 SMH ÷ SMH index of 1.0 equals 54 actual hours assigned on machine 2 for job C. This yields 54 × 30 = 1,620 units of C.
  6 SMH ÷ SMH index of 0.8 equals 7.5 actual hours assigned on machine 3 for job C. This yields 7.5 × 24 = 180 units of C.
  Total = 1620 + 180 = 1800 units as required for job C.

The transportation model has been solved for total profit maximization. It is as simple to use costs and solve for total cost minimization. Total time minimization, productivity maximization, and other goals can be chosen as well.

A criterion that must be satisfied for using the transportation approach to shop loading is that reasonable proportionality exists between machine output rates. When the SMH index does not apply, a heuristic modification of the transportation method can be tried. If one machine is especially efficient for job A and another machine is best for job B, the heuristic could make those assignments more profitable, or less costly. In other words, some assignments would be made a priori based on clear advantages. As another alternative, the loading problem can be dealt with by linear programming. It does not have the constraint of proportionality.

16-6 SEQUENCING OPERATIONS

Loading assigns work to facilities without regard to the *order* in which the jobs will be done. Sequencing establishes the order for doing the jobs at each facility. Sequencing reflects job priorities according to the way that jobs are arranged in the queues. There are different costs associated with the various orderings of jobs. Proper loading should precede the sequencing of operations.

Loading and sequencing in a typical job shop are done over and over again. Each time, doing it the right way provides a small savings. This has been demonstrated for loading where doing it the right way can provide better profit or lower costs. The accumulation of small benefits over highly repetitive environments can add up to a substantial cost savings or profit accumulation.

Good sequencing provides less waiting time, decreased delivery delays, and better due date performance. There are costs associated with waiting and delays. Total savings from regularly doing it the right way the first time can accumulate to substantial sums. Rescheduling can be significantly more costly. When there are many jobs and facilities, sequencing rules have considerable economic importance.

16-6a First-In, First-Out (FIFO) Sequence Rule

The most natural ordering for doing work is in the order that the jobs are received. That means that the first jobs into the shop get worked on first. This is called **FIFO** for "first-in, first-out." Supermarkets like to use FIFO for their late-dated products (do not use after 04/04/04). There is a cost advantage in getting older products to be purchased first.

LIFO which is "last-in, first-out" frequently causes spoiled milk problems. That is because the first-in with the earliest date is waiting until all of the later-date items are shipped. If there is no age-spoilage problem then, as its advocates point out, LIFO can save warehouse handling costs. LIFO items are more readily accessible. So, where the product date does not matter; and where you have to move a lot of things away to gain access to the first one in, LIFO may save money.

FIFO is an appealing sequencing policy because it seems to be the fairest rule to follow. Sometimes—to emphasize the fair treatment sense—it is called "first-come, first-serve" (FCFS). Customers can get angry when someone seems to jump to the head of the line. The cost of angry customers is not to be trivialized.

However, by at least one measure that will be discussed in this section, FIFO is unfair because it penalizes the average customer. The penalty is extra waiting time for the setup and processing time of the average order. This means that on-average regular customers will wait longer—even though FIFO satisfies first-come, first-serve.

Customers who regularly submit orders with short setup and processing times will benefit if the job shop does not employ the FIFO rule, but uses instead a shortest processing time (SPT) priority rule. Customers who regularly submit long orders may be discriminated against by the shortest processing rule. If so, compensatory steps can be taken at the discretion of those doing the sequencing. Note Section 16-9 on modified SPT rules.

16-7 GANTT LAYOUT CHARTS

It is useful to visualize the conversion of loading information to sequencing decisions. Loading, in this case, means that each department has a list of assigned jobs. The Gantt layout chart arranges the list in order of processing, i.e., an optimal sequence.

Gantt, the master chart maker, developed the Gantt layout chart to show sequence assignments. Also called a **sequencing chart,** it reserves specific times on the various facilities for the actual jobs that have been assigned. It appears in a number of different forms depending upon the sequencing applications. In any of its forms, it accomplishes specific job assignments, and this is called **layout.**

Figure 16-2 shows how the Gantt layout chart assigns the specific jobs to the particular facilities, over some given period of time.

Past sequences of work can be monitored, concurrently, to discover the state of completion of those jobs that were scheduled to be run in prior time periods. Although Gantt layout charts provide work-schedule control, they offer little help in determining the best-work sequences.

The chart shows the job schedule at each facility and the state of completion of all jobs. The current date is shown by the arrow and its associated vertical line on the chart. Thereby, the chart is divided into time past, present, and future.

It is easy to see which jobs have been finished and which should have been finished but are not. It is simple to look ahead to observe which jobs are coming up and in what order. Thus, the difference between loading and sequencing is that sequencing specifies the precise timing of assignments. Thereby, it allows customers to be notified of delivery dates.

Once an assignment is made it blocks other assignments from being made. Because sequencing charts are revised regularly, assigned time can be unblocked if it appears to

FIFO: The first jobs into the shop get worked on first.

LIFO: The "last-in, first out" rule for providing service.

Sequencing chart: See **Layout chart.**

Layout: Converts loading to specific sequencing of jobs at a facility.

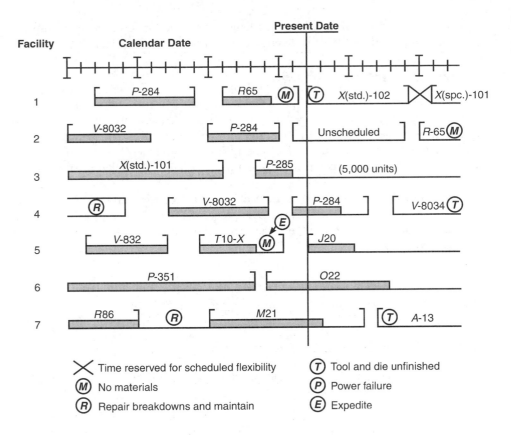

Facility   **Calendar Date**   **Present Date**

X   Time reserved for scheduled flexibility

(M)   No materials

(R)   Repair breakdowns and maintain

(T)   Tool and die unfinished

(P)   Power failure

(E)   Expedite

FIGURE 16-2
The Gantt Layout Chart (A Reserved Time-Planning System)
Status: (1) job P-284 at Facility 4 (F4) is ahead 2 days; (2) job J20 (F5) is ahead 3.0 days; (3) job O22 is ahead 6.0 days; (4) job M21 is ahead 1.1 days; (5) job R-65 (FI) is 2 days short of completion and 2.5 days late waiting for M (materials); (6) job P-285 is 1.5 days late with 5,000 units; (7) job T10-X is 1.5 days short and about 3.5 days late (M) and (E); (8) facility 2 is unscheduled for 7 more days.

permit a better schedule. A correct amount of time is allowed between jobs to account for machine maintenance, to absorb divergences from estimates, and to allow for setups and takedowns.

Frequently, additional symbols are attached to Gantt charts to indicate why a job has not been completed and which jobs are being expedited. Some of these symbols are shown in Figure 16-2. A lot of useful information can be conveyed by means of succinct short-hand notations. Each organization develops its own conventions. Consultants learn a great deal about a company by studying its Gantt charts.

The Gantt layout chart is continually updated. Jobs must be rescheduled because things happen. Machines break down and customers start screaming when priorities change. A good chart must be easy to alter for contingencies such as tool breakage, materials that do not arrive as scheduled, and customers suddenly canceling deliveries because of special circumstances. Sequencing flexibility is easier to accept when the updating of charts (redrawing them) is supported by software. However, there are commercial products that permit some flexibility using on-the-wall Gantt charting.

Jobs are indicated by i, and the symbol n is used to refer to the number of jobs ($i = 1, 2, \ldots, n$) that are waiting to be sequenced through a facility. In the typical job shop, n varies a great deal over time. Also, it is necessary to specify the number of facilities, m, through which the jobs must pass. The character of the sequencing problem is often specified as the n by m problem and represented by $n \times m$.

It is necessary to know how much time every job (i) will spend at each facility. For a given facility, this time is called t_i for the ith job. It is usual for t_i to include job setup time and the work processing or operations times. (From here on, the combination of setup and operations times will be referred to as processing time, t_i.) This does not include waiting time, W_i. The waiting time is nonproductive, as everyone knows who sits in the dentist's waiting room, or waits for the help line to answer.

The degree to which varying patterns of demand requiring different kinds of machines occur in the job shop cannot be underestimated. When a set of jobs follows a fixed ordering, the conditions exist for an intermittent flow shop. Knowledge of technological orderings is required for job shop sequencing. The sizes of orders, the number of alternative facilities for doing each job, the length of production runs, the setup costs and times, among other things, are the determinants of what type of job shop systems exist.

16-7a Evaluation Criteria

Many criteria exist for evaluating production schedule sequencing. To determine how good a production sequence is, evaluation measures called *total flow time* and *mean flow time* are used. These are defined in the following way.

Total flow time: Cumulative time required to complete a group of jobs.

Mean flow time: Average amount of time required to complete each job in a group of n jobs that have been sequenced at a facility.

Total flow time is the cumulative time required to complete a group of jobs. It is composed of the sum of the complete-to-ship times (including waiting time) for each job in the group.

Mean flow time is the average amount of time required to complete each job in the group. It is the average of the wait-to-start and processing times for every job in the group.

The equation for total flow time is the sum of the completion times, C_i for all i jobs that are in the queue:

$$\sum_{i=1}^{i=n} C_i$$

The equation for mean flow time is total flow time divided by n:

$$\sum_{i=1}^{i=n} C_i/n$$

To sequence a group of jobs at a specific facility, define for each job i a waiting time W_i, and a processing time, t_i. These sum to C_i.

$$C_i = W_i + t_i$$

If job $i = 1$ begins at time zero, then its waiting time is zero and its C_i is its processing time, t_i. Thus:

$$C_1 = W_1 + t_1 = 0 + t_1 = t_1$$

Beginning at time zero is the same as saying that the *release time*, called r_i, equals zero. This might be the start of a day or a week, etc.

Table 16-15 is constructed for three jobs A, B, and C, which were received in that order. They are to be processed in that order under the FIFO criterion. This means that job A has a release time, $r_A = 0$.

$\sum_i C_i$ = the total flow time. It is 25. Mean flow time with $n = 3$ is 8.333 as follows:

$$\sum_i \frac{C_i}{n} = \frac{25}{3} = 8\frac{1}{3}$$

Part of flow time and mean flow time is job waiting time, W_i. The goal is to make the total waiting time as small as possible on the assumption that all customers want to have their orders filled as quickly as possible. Therefore, if mean flow time is minimized, this is equivalent to minimizing the mean waiting time because the processing times t_i are fixed by the nature of the jobs to be done.

TABLE 16-15				
Three Jobs to Be Sequenced				
FIFO	**Job$_i$**	**W$_i$**	**t$_i$**	**C$_i$**
1 (first)	A	00	05	05
2	B	05	03	08
3 (last)	C	08	04	12
Sum		13	12	25

If the average completion time $\Sigma_i \frac{C_i}{n}$ is as small as possible, the average customer's order is delayed the minimum necessary time. This can be a primary objective in determining rational sequence priorities.

Figure 16-3 shows the three jobs (A, B, and C) that have been sequenced to be processed in the order of arrival which is the FIFO criterion.

The x-axis is elapsed time. The y-axis shows the sequence used, which is A first, B second, C last. It is the same information given in Table 16-15. Because A goes first, it starts at the top-left. B is the next step down and to the right. C is the final step down and to the right. The steps are all of unit value down, because all jobs are considered to be of equal importance. In Section 16-8, dealing with priority-modified job sequences, the step-down size will be greater for important jobs.

Along the x-axis, job A is completed after 5 minutes. Jobs B and C have to wait that 5-minute period. Then job B is done in 3 minutes while job C waits 3 minutes more for a total of 8 minutes. Next job C is completed at 12 minutes. The completion times of 5, 8, and 12 are added together to obtain total flow time for the group of three jobs.

Other measures used in evaluating the performance of order processing sequences include promised delivery dates. Define d_i as the due date of a job. Then, $L_i = C_i - d_i$ is a measure of lateness of job i when $d_i < C_i$. To minimize average lateness, minimize mean flow time, assuming that promised dates are reasonably determined.

Facility idleness also may play a critical role in sequence determination. However, sequencing models become increasingly difficult to handle with optimizing models, as the number of facilities through which jobs must pass becomes large. Because jobs take different times at each facility, the best sequence at one location may not be best at another.

In sequencing, the degree of data complexity is large. Consequently, heuristics have been developed to cope with the high levels of detail involved in making repetitive sequencing decisions required by many job shops.

16-8 THE SPT RULE FOR *n* JOBS AND *m* = 1 FACILITY ($n \times m = n \times 1$)

The common objective of job-facility sequencing—to minimize mean flow time—is usually equivalent to minimizing average job waiting times, as follows:

$$\min \frac{\Sigma_i^n C_i}{n} = \min \frac{\Sigma_i^n (W_i + t_i)}{n} = \min \frac{\Sigma_i^n W_i}{n}$$

A simple rule achieves this objective. Namely, if a set of n jobs in one facility's queue ($m = 1$) are arranged so that the operations having the shortest processing times (SPT) are done first, then mean flow time and mean waiting time will both be minimized. Sequencing jobs according to their shortest processing times is called the **SPT rule.**

Using the shortest processing time rule (SPT) to sequence Table 16-15 for jobs A, B, and C results in the following decrease in total flow time.

SPT rule: Jobs are rank-ordered by their processing times, t. The job with the smallest t goes first. The job with the next-smallest t goes second, and so forth.

SPT	Job$_i$	W$_i$	t$_i$	C$_i$
1 (first)	B	00	03	03
2	C	03	04	07
3 (last)	A	07	05	12
Sum		10	12	22

$\Sigma_i C_i$ = the total flow time = 22. Mean flow time with $n = 3$ is 7.333 as follows:

$$\Sigma_i \frac{C_i}{n} = \frac{22}{3} = 7\frac{1}{3}$$

There is 12 percent reduction in total and mean flow times.

For further contrast, note the effect of sequencing by longest processing time, called *LPT*.

LPT	Job$_i$	W$_i$	t$_i$	C$_i$
1 (first)	A	00	05	05
2	C	05	04	09
3 (last)	B	09	03	12
Sum		14	12	26

$\Sigma_i C_i$ = the total flow time = 26. Mean flow time with $n = 3$ is 8.667 as follows:

$$\Sigma_i \frac{C_i}{n} = \frac{26}{3} = 8\frac{2}{3}$$

With respect to the SPT result, there is an increase of 18 percent in the total flow time.

Figure 16-4 provides a larger example of SPT, where six jobs have been rank-ordered by their shortest processing times. Thus:

$$t_4 < t_5 < t_2 < t_6 < t_3 < t_1$$

There are $n = 6$ jobs and $m = 1$ facility, as shown in Table 16-16.

$\Sigma_i C_i$ = the total flow time = 165. Mean flow time with $n = 6$ is 27.5 as follows:

$$\Sigma_i \frac{C_i}{n} = \frac{165}{6} = 27\frac{3}{6}$$

FIGURE 16-4
Six Jobs Ordered by Shortest Processing Times (SPT)

SPT	Job_i	W_i	t_i	C_i
1 (first)	4	00	05	05
2	5	05	07	12
3	2	12	08	20
4	6	20	10	30
5	3	30	12	42
6 (last)	1	42	14	56
Sum		109	56	165

TABLE 16-16

Total Waiting Time and Flow Time with SPT

Note that the curve in Figure 16-4 has its convex (curving outward) surface down. This minimizes the area of waiting time, which lies under the curve. This observation is important because it relates the physical character of the graphic approach to the conceptual ideas of minimizing the waiting time of jobs.

In Figure 16-5 the same jobs shown in Figure 16-4 and Table 16-16 are processed according to the rule of customer perceived fairness, which is first-in, first-out (FIFO).

In terms of processing times, FIFO is often a random sequence—without regard to SPT. This is true when any length job is as likely to enter the shop first as any other. Take a ticket and wait your turn, so these orders are processed according to the FIFO rule. Neither the area under the curve nor the mean flow time is minimized. Table 16-17 presents the FIFO waiting times, processing times, and flow time calculations.

$\Sigma_i C_i$ = the total flow time = 211. Mean flow time with $n = 6$ is 35.1667, as follows:

$$\Sigma_i \frac{C_i}{n} = \frac{211}{6} = 35\frac{1}{6}$$

This is an increase in mean and total flow times of 27.88 percent, which is a significant deterioration of customer service.

The waiting time areas under the curves in Figures 16-4 and 16-5 can be determined by multiplying each job's processing time t_i by the number of jobs waiting for that job to finish, and summing them all.

In each figure, there are columns of blocks that represent the number of jobs waiting plus being processed. Each job carries its stack of waiting jobs, except the last one. When the stack size is multiplied by the processing times, the result is total job time spent in the system. It is equal to flow time.

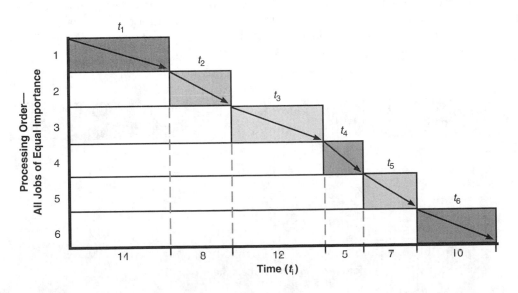

FIGURE 16-5
Jobs Are Processed by FIFO

TABLE 16-17

**Six Jobs to Be Sequenced
with FIFO**

FIFO	Job_i	W_i	t_i	C_i
1 (first)	1	00	14	14
2	2	14	08	22
3	3	22	12	34
4	4	34	05	39
5	5	39	07	46
6 (last)	6	46	10	56
Sum		155	56	211

Table 16-18 shows the computations for Figure 16-4, which is based on the SPT rule.

This is the identical value obtained for waiting time in Table 16-16. Note how the larger values of t_i are multiplied by the smaller values of the number of jobs waiting. That is the SPT effect. If jobs working and waiting had been used, then the stacks would start with 6 jobs waiting and working. Continuing in this way, the number 165 would have been derived for total waiting and working time in the system.

Comparing the results of this stack analysis with that applicable to Figure 16-5 where FIFO sequencing was used, Table 16-19 is obtained.

This is the same value that was obtained earlier in Table 16-17 for total waiting time. Continuing in this way, the number 211 would have been derived for total waiting and working time in the system. In this case, the largest value of t_i happens to be multiplied by the largest value of the number of jobs waiting. FIFO is not a logical sequence if the goal is to minimize waiting time or total time spent in the system.

Sequencing jobs by the SPT rule can help to minimize average delivery lateness, L_i, and maximize fulfillment of delivery promises. It cannot overcome delivery promising that is physically unrealizable. The beneficial effects of SPT follow from the fact that wasted time, W_i, is minimized under that rule.

Note: Because total processing time, $\Sigma_i^n t_i$, is fixed, when flow time, $\Sigma_i^n C_i$, is minimized so is waiting time, and average lateness, L_i.

16-9 PRIORITY-MODIFIED SPT RULES: JOB IMPORTANCE

The SPT rule may need to be modified to take into account the fact that some jobs are more *important* than others. Factors such as a customer's long-term importance, or not wanting to be faulted for failing to keep the promised due date, or needing to avoid lateness (and other issues related to setting special priorities) can be taken care of by dividing each job's time t_i by the relative importance of that job, w_i.

TABLE 16-18

**Total Job Waiting Time
Spent in the System
with SPT**

Job ID	t_i	Multiplied by	Number of Jobs Waiting	=	Job Waiting Time in the System
4	05	X	5	=	25
5	07	X	4	=	28
2	08	X	3	=	24
6	10	X	2	=	20
3	12	X	1	=	12
1	14	X	0	=	00
Total	56		Total waiting time in the system	=	109

TABLE 16-19

Total Job Waiting Time Spent in the System with FIFO

Job ID	t_i	Multiplied by	Number of Jobs Waiting	=	Job Waiting Time in the System
1	14	X	5	=	70
2	08	X	4	=	32
3	12	X	3	=	36
4	05	X	2	=	10
5	07	X	1	=	07
6	10	X	0	=	00
Total	56		Total waiting time in the system	=	155

Thus, *priority ratios* = $\dfrac{t_i}{w_i}$ are rank ordered. The job having the smallest value of $\dfrac{t_i}{w_i}$ is placed first. The job having the next smallest value of $\dfrac{t_i}{w_i}$ is placed second, and so on.

An important job will have a large value of w_i resulting in a small number $\dfrac{t_i}{w_i}$. This will place the job earlier in the priority-modified SPT sequence than would otherwise have been the case. Importance may be assigned a number from 1 to 10 depending on the potential lifetime value of the customer, the profitability or margin contribution of each job, the probability of making an occasional customer into a long-term loyal one, or responding to who yells the loudest.

Alternative interpretations of w_i include lateness such that $\dfrac{t_i}{w_i}$ is the ratio used for SPT. A job that is not late carries an $L_i = 1$. Another system is to let w_i equal the number of days that the job has been waiting to be processed.

16-9a Critical Ratio for Due Dates

As another variant, due date, d_i, is the number of days remaining before promised delivery. A sequencing rule—called *critical ratio*—rank orders the ratios $\dfrac{d_i}{t_i}$. Jobs are sequenced according to the SPT rule applied to these ratios. The smallest ratio is first in line, etc. The first in line will have some combination of least time available until due date divided by longest processing times that obstruct on-time delivery.

Figure 16-6 illustrates the modified SPT rule for priority ratios of $\dfrac{t_i}{w_i}$ but it applies as well to $\dfrac{d_i}{t_i}$.

$$\frac{t_3}{w_3} \leq \frac{t_2}{w_2} \leq \cdots \leq \frac{t_4}{w_4}$$

Time (t_i)

FIGURE 16-6
Jobs Sequenced in the Order of the Smallest Ratios of Weighted Processing Time

The importance weight, w_i, alters the height of the blocks, which is the step size, and thereby the slope of the arrows. Previously, in Figures 16-4 and 16-5, the w_i were all equal to one. Now, the most vertical arrow (which has the largest slope) will belong to the job with the smallest ratio t_i/w_i. The same reasoning applies to the critical ratios.

As shown in Figure 16-6, the ratio of t_3/w_3 is smallest. Therefore, job 3 with processing time t_3 is placed first in the sequence. This ratio rule assures a smooth (convex) function that will minimize the area under the curve.

By using a ratio, the production scheduler who is doing the sequencing gains greater control over the factors. Processing time is an important sequencing factor, but other factors can drive priorities as well.

16-10 SEQUENCING WITH MORE THAN ONE FACILITY ($m > 1$)

The SPT character of the sequencing problem is easy to understand with n jobs and 1 facility. The optimal sequence through the single facility can be calculated. There are $n! = (n)(n-1)(n-2)...(1)$ ways to sequence n jobs through *one* facility.

The complexity of finding the minimum flow-time sequence becomes increasingly difficult as a larger number of facilities is considered. When there are n jobs with $m = 2$ facilities, the method for finding the minimum waiting-time sequence is still fast and concise.

With the $n \times 3$ problem, the optimal sequence cannot always be derived. There are certain conditions that must be met. When m is 4 or greater, heuristic methods must be used to find a satisfactory sequence. Optimization methods cannot be used to minimize flow time. The number of sequencing combinations $(n!)^m$ grows large quickly. Thus, when $n = 5$ and $m = 4$, ... $(n!)^m$ is larger than 200 million.

The SPT concept still applies when jobs must pass through two facilities in a given technological ordering. For example, (say) facility 1 (F1) drills the part. This is followed by facility 2 (F2), which de-burrs the part after the drilling. The technological ordering is set by the process. It is not possible to reverse that order.

Technological ordering also applies to services. In the health care situation, an HMO clinic schedules 5 people for diagnosis to be followed by treatment. Table 16-20 presents the data (in minutes).

S.M. Johnson's algorithm derives the minimum completion times for all "no passing" cases.[1] "No passing" means that the order of processing jobs through the first facility must be preserved for all subsequent facilities.

To use the modified SPT sequencing rule for Table 16-20 where F1 must be done first, select the job (in this case, person) with the shortest processing time in either the F1 or the F2 columns. If this minimum value is in the F2 column, place that person last in sequence (here in fifth place). If the minimum is in the F1 column, put that person in first place. Specifics for this example are that person b requires 2 minutes in the F2 column and will, therefore, be treated last. The next step is to remove person b from the data set and then continue in the same way. In other words, cross out row 2. This removes "b" from the matrix.

Select the smallest number remaining in the matrix. If it is in the F2 column, assign that person to the last place—if it is available—or the next to last place if not. If the smallest number remaining is in column F1, that person is given first place—or next to first place if first place is taken.

TABLE 16-20	Job (Person)	F1 (Diagnosis)	F2 (Treatment)
HMO Sequencing Problem—Time in Minutes	a	6	3
	b	8	2
	c	7	5
	d	3	9
	e	5	4

FIGURE 16-7
Gantt Sequencing Chart for *n* × 2 Problem

Resolve ties by randomly selecting either position for assignment unless some other factors exist for preferring one arrangement or the other. For the previous example, person b goes last, person d goes first, person a goes next to last, person e is treated next to next to last, and person c fills the remaining slot. Note that the smallest number after 2 was 3. Person a has 3 in F2 and person d has 3 in F1. This creates a nonconflicting tie because d goes first and a goes next to last.

The minimum total completion time is 31, as shown by the Gantt chart in Figure 16-7. There is idle time at F2 of 5 minutes. There is no idle time for F1.

16-11   FINITE SCHEDULING OF BOTTLENECKS— OPT CONCEPT

Bottlenecks are well described by their name. The narrowing of the bottle's neck constricts the flow of output. In terms that are more germane to production, the slowest machine sets the pace of the process flow. When the pace of a person or machine is exceeded by the demand for his, her, or its time, waiting lines begin to grow.

Everyone has experienced the feeling of keeping people waiting because other assignments must be completed first. People who are bottlenecks in their organizations (often because of the design of the system and through no fault of their own) are placed under stress. Workstations that are bottlenecks create tension. Job shops always have one or more bottlenecks. These change according to the product mix in the shop.

16-11a   Flow Shops and Continuous Processes Do Not Have Bottlenecks

Properly designed flow shops and continuous processes, such as a refinery, have no bottlenecks. They are designed to eliminate all bottlenecks by preengineering. Their process flows are fully balanced. In the flow shop, machines are timed to supply each other at just the right rate. When people and machines interact at workstations, a paced conveyor belt carries the work between stations. The timing of the conveyor (how fast it moves between stations and how long it stays at the station) is the drumbeat of the processing system.

Bottlenecks are caused by the mismatching of process rates that the flow shop purposefully, and often at great expense, eliminates. The mismatch is not the result of bad management. It occurs because of the mixture of orders that are received and in process for a particular shop configuration. If the job mixture changes, the shop configuration can be altered but it takes time.

However, because bottlenecks are a fact of life for the job shop, it is worth learning to control where and when they occur. This makes bottleneck control an expected and routine part of job shop management. It turns attention to the causes of scheduling problems instead of dealing with the symptoms, which are inability to fill orders on time.

16-11b   Queue Control (OPT, TOC, and Other Approaches)

Multiple bottlenecks usually exist within any process. When processes are being altered from hour to hour, as is the case with batch work, the potential for clogging the pipeline

> **Bottlenecks:** Slowest machine in the line sets the pace of the process.

is large. The damaging effects of queues multiply as the number and length of the waiting lines grow. Orders get misplaced and materials are lost. The chaos level crescendos. The need for queue control is increasingly apparent. Studying the queuing situation at the bottlenecks results in improved production scheduling.

To reduce the wastefulness of queues, the OPT[2] (optimum production technique, also known as optimized production technology) system recommends feeding the bottleneck. This is equivalent to saying that all prior operations should be able to supply the bottleneck with what it needs, when it needs it. Having identified the bottlenecks removes part of the problem. Seeing that they are kept working removes another part of the problem. Finally, when the bottleneck-capacity constraints are unacceptable, they can usually be removed. Then, other bottlenecks emerge.

The creator of **OPT** was Dr. Eliyahu M. Goldratt (see Spotlight 16-2.) After his initial efforts, he and others began to call the approach the **Theory of Constraints** (TOC). The ideas remained the same and the literature that was developed for OPT applied to TOC as well.

The bottleneck's processing rate is called (in OPT and TOC terms) the drum because it sets the production rate for all of the upstream and downstream activities. For synthetic processes (which assemble items), work begins upstream at the tributaries and flows downstream to the trunk encountering various bottlenecks along the way. This is called the V *process* because work moves in the direction of the V-point flowing from upstream to downstream.

Upstream activities (which occur prior to the bottleneck) should be slowed down or stopped to synchronize with the drum. In the stream analogy, if dams cannot slow the flow, then flooding occurs. Levees must be built to contain the backed up waters. Similarly, work in process backs up and needs a place to stay. Containment of excess work to which value is not being added is simply less desirable than slowing the flow to the bottleneck. Flow control can result in smaller lot sizes being made more often.

This is called *finite scheduling* and it follows two important rules of OPT and TOC. These are that the transfer batch may be smaller than the process batch, which provides greater flexibility and less cost. Also, the process batch should be variable and not fixed. Relatively small transfer batches can be used effectively to provide inventory buffers for the bottleneck (drum). The span of protection (called the *time buffer*) is varied to protect the plant against disruptions. For example, the time buffer can be increased from four to five days when there is greater risk of not being able to supply the bottleneck.

Downstream activities cannot expect to receive more work than the fully utilized bottleneck can deliver. The bottleneck sets the course for the rest of the process—that is, until the next bottleneck is encountered—as the work flow moves downstream. In process terms, excess capacity located downstream from the bottleneck may be wasted investment in capacity. If the bottleneck rate is increased, it may not be wasted investment.

16-11c Synchronized Manufacturing

Synchronization requires control of the timing of flows. This includes how much is made at one time and transferred to the next station. Transfer amounts and storage amounts are determined by control mechanisms that can be viewed as valves or gates that can be opened and closed by pulling on ropes to control the flow of materials to the bottlenecks and to the operations that follow the bottleneck. The ropes are like communication links that synchronize the flow rates throughout the system. The controlled flow rates establish the time buffers.

Figure 16-8 illustrates the *drum-buffer-rope* concept, which is the queue-control mechanism designed by OPT and TOC. Queue (flow) control over time and space between stations is essential. It is why these methods are described as being synchronized production-scheduling methodology. The flows are units of work. The methods are said to apply to **finite scheduling,** which means that production is scheduled in batches of finite size for a variety of jobs in the shop—which might coincide with lot-for-lot scheduling.

OPT: Developed to deal rationally with bottleneck-based finite production scheduling. OPT controls queues by supplying the bottleneck with sufficient batches of work.

Theory of Constraints: A mind-set for determining the core problems in production scheduling, project management, and other P/OM activities. Optimizing production scheduling in isolation from other business variables usually does not lead to higher productivity.

Synchronization: Flow shops are predesigned to have perfect synchronization of workstations. Job shops require major efforts to synchronize manufacturing.

Finite scheduling: Controlling the flow of work so that lot sizes and frequency of setups result in minimum total costs.

FIGURE 16-8
The Drum-Buffer-Rope
Model of Finite Scheduling

Variability can disrupt the smooth flow of product. Consequently, it is necessary to provide bottlenecks with assurance that their suppliers will increase production when there are signs that one or more of the bottlenecks could be idled. When any one of the bottlenecks is idled, the existing system is not producing to its maximum.

OPT and TOC use time buffers. Time buffers are different from stock buffers. The latter specify the number of units of stock that should be kept in reserve whereas the former specify the amount of time that the bottleneck can keep working if any of its suppliers are shut off. Time reserves are maintained by means of the communication links that the managers of finite scheduling call *ropes* (see the timing ropes in Figure 16-8).

The bottleneck-feeder stations are aware of the need to monitor and allow for statistical variation in the process. The OPT and TOC time buffers are maintained by regulating the outputs of all feeder stations in line with the status of each time buffer. Being constantly in communication with each other assures that the bottleneck and its feeder systems are integrated. The rope is similar to a ship's telegraph, which can signal the desired speeds of the engine. In this case, it signals the production output rate that is required to prevent idling the bottleneck facilities.

This is symbolically represented in Figure 16-8, which shows shifting bottlenecks for two different order mixes. Order mix I consists of five jobs and order mix II consists of five different jobs. There are time buffers before three bottleneck operations in each case. Also, there are time buffers before the three batch assembly operations. Notice how this job shop is in communication with its bottleneck-constraint system. As the order mix changes, the system shifts bottlenecks (new drums alter timing), it calculates new time buffers, and communication exercises control of upstream production (new ropes).

Raw materials

A   6 units per hour

B   4 units per hour

Operations   C   5 units per hour

D   5 units per hour

E   6 units per hour

Assembly   5 units per hour

Orders   Ship 160 units

FIGURE 16-9
Bottleneck Is Operation B

16-11d Changing the Capacity of the Bottleneck

It is sensible to consider the effect of increasing the capacity of every bottleneck facility. Sometimes by using new technology or more people, a greater volume of work can be done. This may result in shifting the bottleneck to another part of the process. Flow rates can be studied, as in Figure 16-9, to permit bottleneck analysis of specific situations.

Flow is from upstream (A) to downstream (E and assembly to shipping). Bottleneck B (the drum) has a processing or throughput rate of four units per hour. It constrains the system's output rate to four units per hour. The order is for 200 units, so if there are 40 work hours per week, then 160 units will be made in the week. That leaves 40 more units to be made, which requires 10 more hours.

Operation A is instructed to feed the bottleneck, and the time buffer is set to provide an hour of protection in the event that operation A breaks down. B needs four units every hour, which means that between A and B there should be a reserve of four units. This is equivalent to A's working 2/3 of an hour. However, the first two hours A will work at full speed to create the necessary time buffer.

Thereafter, if B works faster and draws down on the hour of buffer stock, A can work longer than the usual 40 minutes to make up the difference. It will be noted that C, D, and "Assembly" all can work at five units per hour. E can produce six units per hour. None of them will be able to work faster than B. The bottleneck B sets the pace.

Complex flow patterns are more difficult to analyze than this simple example, but the basic idea is the same.

1. *Locate the bottleneck.* This is called prospecting for bottlenecks. It involves developing detailed flow-process charts for all important orders in the shop and measuring or estimating the processing rates. Every operation must be included and associated with its processing rate.

2. *Determine appropriate time buffers for the bottlenecks.* Then control the transfer lot sizes and the frequency of delivery from all upstream operations (in this case only operation A needs to be controlled).

3. *Is it feasible to increase the throughput rate of the bottleneck?* Analyze the costs and benefits of increasing the throughput rate (capacity) of the bottleneck. The bottleneck will shift to another place of constraint. Will the new bottleneck be preferred to the prior one? Is the shift acceptable?

With regard to 3., if the use of new technology, costing $100,000, could increase operation B's output to five units per hour, B, C, D, and "Assembly" all become bottlenecks. A time buffer must now be built up between the many bottlenecks so that B can feed C, C can feed D, and so on. It is really easier to have only one bottleneck to tend. Consequently, working overtime with the existing bottleneck might be a better solution.

To evaluate the change in bottleneck configuration, the system can now produce 160 units per week. The additional 40 units (8 × 5) per week times 50 weeks per year yields 2,000 extra units per year. Assume that each of these 2,000 units can bring a $50 profit. The investment in bottleneck reconfiguration will pay for itself in one year. Thus:

V = investment to increase production by X; where X = extra production per year; and π = profit per unit

Then, alter the bottleneck when:

$$\frac{V}{\pi X} \leq n$$

where *n* is the chosen payback period.

For these numbers, $\frac{\$100,000}{\$50(2000)}$ = 1 year payback period. This is likely to be an acceptable investment in bottleneck repair.

SUMMARY

Production scheduling is the culminating series of steps that determines *when* orders are to be worked on and *by whom*. The function goes back to the earliest days of systematic production and assignment of service jobs to work crews. The Gantt load chart was developed at that time, and it is still used. Loading decisions concern which jobs are to be assigned to which teams or facilities. Jobs on-hand are relatively risk free to schedule. Jobs that are on the books as forecasts are problematic. Depending upon the real situation, they may not be scheduled because there is too high a risk of cancellation.

Chapter 16 explains that the assignment method for loading jobs at facilities is powerful but limited to a very real class of situation where job splitting is not permitted. Assignment models can maximize profits or minimize costs. Then, the transportation method is developed for shop loading. It permits job splitting and multiple job assignments at one facility. The drawback of the transportation model is the requirement to use standard units and the presumption of productive proportionality.

Loading is nonspecific to job order, so it is always followed by sequencing. There is strong methodology to determine the best order for job processing. Which job goes first, second, and so on? Service system managers often require first-come, first-serve so that their customers do not get upset. The same applies to production deliveries. Customer systems are criticized when the "fairness criterion" [first-in, first-out; (FIFO)] is violated. Nevertheless, the alternative of processing orders so that shortest processing times (SPT) go first provides benefits to everyone *except* those who regularly have orders that take a long time to process.

Gantt layout charts are used to organize sequencing assignments. The sequencing situation depends on the number of jobs (n) and the number of machines (m) that are available to work on the jobs. Solution methods differ according to the number of facilities (machines, m). In general, the problem size is given by $n \times m$ In Chapter 16, SPT rules are developed for $n \times 1$ and $n \times 2$. The SPT rule can be modified to reflect various forms of priorities including job and customer importance, due date, and lateness.

Chapter 16 concludes with a discussion about identifying bottlenecks and using the optimized production technology (OPT) concepts (also known as the Theory of Constraints—TOC) to deal with bottlenecks. OPT and TOC approach bottlenecks using finite scheduling based on the drum-buffer-rope method for synchronized manufacturing. Bottlenecks set the pace of production. Bottlenecks are protected from being idled by statistical variability using time-based stock buffers. The rest of the system is synchronized to match the input–output performance of the bottleneck.

Two Spotlight feature boxes conclude this chapter. These boxes illustrate real applications of the material in the chapter. See Spotlight 16-1: The Pursuit of Clean Air and Spotlight 16-2: The Fallacy of Pursuing Local Optimums.

KEY TERMS

Assignment method	LIFO	Sequencing chart
Bottlenecks	Loading	Shop floor control
Due date	Mean flow time	SPT rule
FIFO	Opportunity costs	Synchronization
Finite scheduling	OPT	Theory of Constraints
Gantt charts	Production scheduling	Total flow time
Layout	Sequencing	

REVIEW QUESTIONS

1. The Gantt load chart can be used to determine whether the "load" is equally distributed among facilities. To whom is balanced loading important?

2. Explain the statement: "Load real jobs, not forecasts."

3. Opportunity costs are instrumental for loading models and decisions. Are these real costs? Explain.

4. What is the assignment method of loading? What special conditions apply?

5. Distinguish between the maximization model for the assignment problem and the minimization model. Explain the differences.

6. What is the transportation method of loading? What special conditions apply?

7. Distinguish between the conditions necessary for using the assignment model and the transportation model.

8. How do Gantt load charts differ from Gantt layout charts?

9. When does FIFO make sense as a sequencing rule?

10. When does LIFO make sense as a sequencing rule?

11. When should SPT be used?

12. What are priority-modified SPT rules? Give some examples and explain when they should be used.

13. Explain the use of critical ratios for due dates.

14. What is the significance that sequencing charts are convex (curving downward) when the sequencing rule is SPT?

15. What is the significance that sequencing charts are not generally convex (curving downward) when the sequencing rule is FIFO?

16. What is the $n \times 1$ sequencing problem?

17. What is the $n \times m$ sequencing problem?

18. What is the $n \times 2$ sequencing problem? How can it be resolved?

19. What are time buffers?

20. Explain the meaning of drum-buffer-rope for scheduling.

21. What is meant by synchronized manufacturing?

22. Why is OPT called the scheduling theory of constraints?

23. Why is finite scheduling concerned with bottlenecks?

24. Discuss the reasons that job shops and not flow shops are associated with the problem of bottlenecks.

25. When does it pay to remove a bottleneck? What is entailed?

26. Explain why the removal of a bottleneck creates a new one.

27. Describe what is meant by "feed the bottleneck."

PROBLEMS SECTION

1. The matrix of *total costs per day* for jobs 1, 2, and 3—if assigned at facilities A, B, and C of the Rivet and Nail Factory—is

		Facilities		
		A	B	C
	1	$1,000	$ 900	$1,200
Jobs	2	800	700	900
	3	1,500	1,800	2,000

What relatively permanent assignments will minimize total costs per day?

2. The matrix of *costs per part* for jobs 4, 5, and 6—if assigned at facilities A, B, and C of the Rivet and Nail Factory—is

		Facilities		
		A	B	C
	4	$0.10	$ 0.19	$0.12
Jobs	5	0.16	0.14	0.18
	6	0.30	0.36	0.40

The jobs are all of the same size (5,000) and duration. What relatively permanent assignments will minimize total costs?

3. The matrix of costs per part for jobs 7, 8, and 9 if assigned at facilities A, B, and C of the Rivet and Nail Factory is described by the matrix:

		Facilities		
		A	B	C
	7	$0.10	0.09	$0.12
Jobs	8	0.08	0.07	0.09
	9	0.30	0.36	0.40

The jobs are all of the same size (5,000 units) and duration. What relatively permanent assignments will minimize total costs?

4. The executive offices for five vice presidents of an airline are on the tenth floor of the airline's building. The decision is made to assign the offices in such a way as to maximize total satisfaction. Each VP is asked to rank his or her preferences for the available offices. One is

the most preferred location and five is the least preferred. The data are as follows:

Office	VP1	VP2	VP3	VP4	VP5
O1	1	1	2	3	2
O2	5	3	1	2	3
O3	4	2	5	1	1
O4	3	5	4	3	4
O5	2	4	3	5	5

a. What is the best assignment plan from the company's viewpoint?

b. How does this problem relate to production schedules?

c. How does this problem relate to service scheduling?

5. Use the assignment model to achieve an optimal shop-loading arrangement for an intermittent flow shop. Jobs are 1–5 and the facilities are A–E. The per unit profits are given in the following matrix. Relatively continuous production can be expected for each assignment over the next quarter.

Jobs	A	B	C	D	E
1	19	17	15	15	13
2	12	30	18	18	15
3	13	21	29	19	21
4	49	56	53	55	43
5	33	41	39	39	40

6. For the data in Problem 5, a new facility F has become available that can only work on jobs 1, 2, or 3, with unit profits of 14, 11, and 12, respectively.

a. Should one of the current facilities be replaced with F?

b. What information is lacking that could help make the recommendations more definitive?

7. The following matrix has productivity per standard machine hour [PR(i,j)] filled into each box within a machine-job cell. The revenue per piece is givn by column and the cost per piece is given by row.

Revenue per Piece		$2.00	$1.00	$0.50	
Cost per Piece		Job A	Job B	Job C	Supply S(i)
$0.20	M1	3	3.5	15	
$0.10	M2	6	7	30	
$0.30	M3	4.8	5.6	24	
$0.00	MD	0	0	0	
Demand D(j)					

Revenue per Piece		$2.00	$1.00	$0.50	
Cost per Piece		Job A	Job B	Job C	Supply S(i)
$0.20	M1		12	6	18
$0.10	M2			54	54
$0.30	M3	50	14		64
$0.00	MD		4		4
Demand D(j)		50	30	60	140

Determine the profit per standard hour values that should be used. Draw up some blank matrices (without the corner entries) so that these results can be entered, and used for later calculations. These numbers can be filled into the empty boxes within each machine-job cell in the matrix and used for Problem 8.

8. The following matrix has the supply of available standard machine hours in the right-hand column. It has demand in standard hours in the bottom row. Fill in the Northwest Corner (NWC) assignments. This means starting at the upper left-hand box and entering as many units as the row or column sums allow. Then, move to the east or to the south, depending upon whether it is the row or column sum that still needs to be satisfied. Continue in this way until the NWC assignment is complete.

Revenue per Piece		$2.00	$1.00	$0.50	
Cost per Piece		Job A	Job B	Job C	Supply S(i)
$0.20	M1				18
$0.10	M2				54
$0.30	M3				64
$0.00	MD				4
Demand D(j)		50	30	60	140

What is the total profit associated with the NWC assignment?

9. The following matrix has been derived after a number of shifts from the NWC assignment aimed at improving profit.

What is the total profit associated with the "improved" assignment? By how much has it improved the solution obtained with the NWC assignment?

10. Convert the solution obtained for Problem 8—the NWC solution—into actual assignment hours and units.

11. Convert the solution obtained for Problem 9—the improved solution—into actual assignment hours and units. Can you tell if this is the optimal solution?

12. The Door Knob Company has four orders on hand, and each must be processed in the sequential order:

First: Department A—press shop
Second: Department B—plating and finishing

The following table lists the number of days required for each job in each department. For example, job IV requires one day in the press shop and one day in the finishing department.

	Job I	Job II	Job III	Job IV
Department A	8	6	5	1
Department B	8	3	4	1

Assume that no other work is being done by the departments and that "no passing" of jobs is allowed.

Use a Gantt sequencing chart (see Figure 16-7) to show the best-work schedule. (Best-work schedule means minimum time to finish all four jobs.)

13. Using the information in Problem 12, find the best sequence for each department separately.

14. How do the solutions obtained for Problems 12 and 13 compare?

15. The Market Research Store has four orders on hand, and each must be processed in the sequential order:

First: Department A—computer analysis
Second: Department B—report writing and printing

The following table lists the number of days required by each job in each department. For example, job IV requires two days during computer analysis and one day in report writing and printing.

	Job I	Job II	Job III	Job IV
Department A	3	6	5	2
Department B	8	3	4	1

Assume that no other work is being done by the departments and that "no passing" of jobs is allowed.

Use a Gantt sequencing chart to show the best-work schedule. (Best-work schedule means minimum time to finish all four jobs.)

16. Using the information in Problem 15, find the best sequence for each department separately.

17. How do the solutions obtained for Problems 15 and 16 compare?

18. Examine the sequences for the following $n \times 1$ system. There are six jobs with processing times t_i. As these jobs arrived they were named in alphabetical order (A, B, C,...,F).

Job i	t_i	Job i	t_i
A	5	D	9
B	4	E	12
C	6	F	8

What is the SPT sequence? Derive the SPT solution. What are the total and mean flow times for that sequence?

19. Using the information in Problem 18, derive the LPT (longest processing time) solution. What is the LPT sequence? What are the total and mean flow times for that sequence? Compare the SPT and the LPT solutions.

20. Using the information in Problem 18, derive the first-come, first-serve (or FIFO) effect. What is the FIFO sequence? What are the total and mean flow times for that sequence? Compare SPT and FIFO.

21. For Problem 18, what effect does the information that jobs A, B, and C are half as important as jobs D, E, and F have on the sequence solution?

22. For the following $n \times 1$ problem, use a priority-modified SPT rule where the priority is based upon reducing lateness L_i. Work times t_i and lateness are given in the following table for jobs A, B, ... F.

I	t_i	L_i	i	t_i	L_i
A	5	1	D	9	3
B	4	2	E	12	1
C	6	1	F	8	1

What is the optimal sequence and what are its total and mean flow times? Compare the answer with the one obtained for Problem 18.

23. For the following $n \times 1$ problem, use a priority-modified SPT rule where the priority is based upon the critical ratio using due dates d_i and work times t_i as given in the following table.

i	t_i	d_i	i	t_i	d_i
A	5	10	D	9	18
B	4	16	E	12	36
C	6	18	F	8	25

What is the optimal sequence and what are its total and mean flow times? Compare the answer with the one obtained for Problem 18.

24. For the following $n \times 1$ problem, use a priority-modified SPT rule, where the priority is based on the additional information about customer importance called w_i (given in the following table).

i	t_i	w_i	i	t_i	w_i
A	5	6	D	9	3
B	4	5	E	12	2
C	6	4	F	8	1

The more important the customer, the larger the value of w_i.

What is the optimal sequence and what are its total and mean flow times?

25. The problem faced by Information Search, Inc. (ISI) has the processing times shown here:

Jobs (A–E)	A	B	C	D	E
1. Look up references	4	8	9	4	6
2. Write report	3	2	5	7	4

What is the optimal sequence and what are its total and mean flow times?

26. Workstation B is the bottleneck (see Figure 16-9). B has a throughput rate of four units per hour, which constrains the system's output rate to 160 units per week. An order has been received for 240 units, which led to the decision to buy an automatic feeder machine. This machine can raise B's output rate to six units per hour.

What output rate will be achieved? How long will it take to fill the order?

27. Using the information in Problem 26 and in Figure 16-9, what time buffers should be set for workstation A? Are there any other time buffers to be set?

28. Combine the information in Problem 26 with the fact that the feeder machine will cost $25,000. The profit per unit for extra units will be $2.00. Do you agree with the decision to buy the new machine? Explain your response.

29. Combine the information in Problem 26 with the fact that for $50,000 all of the units can be connected with a paced-conveyor belt and run at six units per hour. Will this investment pay off? Discuss the problem of feeding multiple bottlenecks.

END-OF-CHAPTER QUESTIONS

1. Production scheduling must be done by any organization that does work. Familiar to manufacturing, it is equally necessary for service functions. In some instances, it might be called by other names. P/OM is responsible for knowing how, when, and what to schedule. City Hall has come to realize that many municipal functions would profit from understanding production scheduling. A consultant has been hired from the private sector, and she has prepared a test for the city managers. It consists of five statements (a. to e.), one of which is wrong. Assume the role of a city manager and take this test. Which statement about production scheduling is wrong?

   a. The police department writes an average of 500 tickets per day. The variability is very high. On certain days, it is twice that number and on other days it is half as much. The resources required to be scheduled include the ticket writers, the ticket processors, the court requirements, the collection functions, etc. Production scheduling is involved with all of these activities.

   b. Sanitation is a production function. Fortunately, the pickups are already scheduled, as are the drop-offs at the disposal dump. This area does not require additional attention.

   c. Every election seems to be treated as a new project when in fact elections are repeats of batch production operations separated by a year for local elections, two years for state and federal elections, and four years for presidential elections. It is recommended that elections be studied as candidates for production scheduling.

   d. Tax collection by the city is very inefficient whereas the state is very fast and makes few errors. The state production schedulers need to sit down with the city folks. That is a beginning.

   e. The fire department faces uncertain demand. Sometimes there are no calls or simple ones that take a few minutes to correct. At other times, there are requests for help with big fires that can take a long time to subdue. Production scheduling can help a great deal once it has access to the real data.

2. Gantt load charts are 100 years old, but they are still used because they work well. Five statements have been prepared for the City Hall management team about load charting. Most of the managers say that they have been using load charts to obtain reasonable (not quite optimal) capacity utilization in the systems for which they are responsible. Comfort is expressed with these graphic methods. Choose the one statement (a. through f.) not appropriate to load charts.

   a. Proper charts reflect the interests of customers and the impact of suppliers. For example, with respect to security at City Hall, "which jobs have not started that should have begun?" Alternatively, "what progress toward completion has been made?" If the answer is "The security system at City Hall will be installed as soon as possible, but protocols have not yet been created, nor tested," these statements make it quite evident that layout charts have not been drawn. Gantt project charts are in order before the layout charts can be drawn. (*This statement has been accepted as being true by the mayor.*)

   b. Layout charts can show either calendar time or general time units along the *x*-axis. For each department, there is a line indicating workload percent by the week (or day, etc.). In each time bucket, lines start at the left and move to the right, representing a percent of the range. A solid line that spans the box indicates 100 percent load.

   c. Jobs are listed for each department in a separate box at the right of the chart. The number of units to be completed for each job may be shown. The order in which jobs will be done has not yet been determined.

   d. It is helpful to show the cumulative load for each department (facility). It is helpful to see the load for the current week and the prior week. Which departments are falling behind and which are catching up?

   e. Work that has been promised, where the due date is past, is labeled "backlogged." An asterisk can be used to highlight the situation. Backlogged jobs are given top priority. They will be the first ones to be assigned to the department as soon as the current jobs are completed.

   f. The load chart reveals at a glance which departments are underutilized. That is a primary purpose. Gantt load chart users make no pretense that the method will enable optimization of schedules. The load chart graphics facilitate heuristic methods for reaching better generalizations with fast data scans. "Eyeballing" is a key use of the load charts.

3. The assignment method for loading facilities is useful in actual application and also conceptually because of its reliance on opportunity costs with no splitting allowed. An example has been built around the assignment of office spaces (A, B, C) to managers (1, 2, 3) at City Hall. Each manager has stated his or her preference for each office based on a scale of one to ten with one (lowest cost) being best. Which statement a. through e. is wrong?

		Offices		
		A	B	C
	1	9	5	2
Managers	2	8	3	5
	3	8	7	3

   a. No splitting means that each manager must have only one office. Thus, manager 1 cannot be assigned to offices A and B, even part of the time. Also, office A cannot be shared by managers 1 and 2.

   b. Opportunity costs are the costs of managers not having their preferences satisfied. Then, there would be zero total opportunity cost and maximum total satisfaction if the assignments C1, B2, and C3 could be granted. That is impossible because the rule is no-splitting and no-sharing. As a benchmark, the total preference value if each manager got his or her first choice would be 11. This results from summing the smallest cell value for each manager.

	D(1)	D(2)	D(3)	Supply
P(1)	40			40 hrs.
P(2)	5	35		40 hrs.
P(3)		30	10	40 hrs.
P(D)			40	40 hrs.
Demand	45 hrs.	65 hrs.	50 hrs.	160 hrs.

c. If row subtraction is used first, there are no zero opportunity costs (zoc) in column A. B2 is an uncontested zoc. There is a conflict in column C between C1 and C3, both of which have zoc.

d. To resolve the assignment conflicts, column subtraction is used next. It results in an unambiguous set of assignments, namely, A3, B2, and C1. These have a total preference value of 13. There is no assignment that can be made that will have a lower total preference cost.

e. If column subtraction is used first, the assignment solution appears without conflict. There are zeros at A3, B2, and C1. This is the same solution that occurred when row subtraction was used first and followed by column subtraction.

4. City Hall realizes that there is a great deal more learning available from the simple three by three assignment problem set forth in Problem 3. The example is now continued with some different assumptions about the preferences. In this case, each manager has stated his or her preference for each office based on a scale of one to ten with ten (highest revenue) being best. Which statement a. through e. is wrong?

	Offices		
	A	B	C
1	9	5	2
Managers 2	8	3	5
3	8	7	3

a. The objective function has been reversed so that the largest numbers represent the managers' greatest preferences. Then, row subtraction produces a total stalemate with all zeros in column 1.

b. If the matrix derived in a. (which is a matrix of opportunity costs) is followed by column subtraction, the result is an unambiguous solution. A1 is uncontested in the first row. B3 is uncontested in the second column. That eliminates the other zeros except for C2.

c. The assignment from operations in b. has total satisfaction value of $9 + 7 + 5 = 21$, which is the maximum that can be obtained with these data.

d. If every number in the matrix is multiplied by k, the solution will change. A new set of analyses is required.

e. If every number in the matrix has an added value of k, the solution will not change. A new set of analyses is not required.

5. The transportation method is a more powerful alternative than the assignment method for shop loading. City Hospital has always done its manpower planning (a generic name that has not been replaced by peoplepower planning) by cut and try on a large whiteboard. They have been persuaded to try using the transportation method in one of its load planning formats. The resulting example illustrates how the method works, although real problems are significantly larger in size and use more realistic numbers. The list of observations (a. to e.) about the method contains one erroneous statement. Identify the flawed statement.

a. D(1), D(2), and D(3) are departments of City Hospital. D(1) requires 45 hours per week of medical assistance. D(2) requires 65 hours and D(3) requires 50 hours. There are three medical assistants that can be assigned to these departments. They are called P(1), P(2), and P(3). Each has 40 hours of time available per week. The problem is to find the best manpower plan.

b. The transportation matrix shows an initial feasible solution obtained by using the Northwest Corner allocation method. The next matrix has the costs of assigning P(1) to D(1), P(1) to D(2), P(2) to D(1), etc. The costs are purposely single digit to make the illustration simple to follow.

	D(1)	D(2)	D(3)	Supply
P(1)	$5/hr.	$6/hr.	$7/hr.	40 hrs.
P(2)	$6/hr.	$7/hr.	$8/hr.	40 hrs.
P(3)	$7/hr.	$6/hr.	$6/hr.	40 hrs.
P(D)	$0/hr.	$0/hr.	$0/hr.	40 hrs.
Demand	45 hrs.	65 hrs.	50 hrs.	160 hrs.

c. There are more hours demanded than are available. Consequently, a dummy assistant P(D) is created. Whichever department the dummy is assigned to will have a labor shortage. The dummy is given costs of $0 per hour for all departments because it will not be paid. The dummy is indifferent as to which department it is assigned.

d. There is still not enough information to use the transportation model. What is missing is the preference of the assistants for the various departments.

e. The cost of the first feasible assignment solution is $[40(5) + 5(6) + 35(7) + 30(6) + 10(5) + 40(0)] = \$705$. It places the dummy entirely in D(3), which requires 50 hours of work. D(3) does get 10 hours of work from P(3). The assistant P(3) splits his or her time spending 30 hours in department D(2). Note how the transportation model employs splitting a worker's time between departments and how departments share more than one worker.

6. City Hospital is not about to settle for manpower assignments that just happened by dint of a method called Northwest Corner. Hospital schedulers now wish to show how they can manipulate the matrix to provide an optimum (minimum total cost) solution. What are the next steps? A list has been prepared with statements a. to e. and one of these statements is wrong. Which statement is in error?

a. Each cell in the Northwest Corner solution matrix that does *not contain* an assignment is analyzed to determine if costs would increase or decrease if one unit was assigned to that cell in lieu of the current assignment.

b. Put one unit into cell P(1), D(2). Take one unit out of P(1), D(1). Put one unit into P(2), D(1). Take one unit out of P(2), D(2). Shifting that one unit results in $12 of added costs and $12 of subtracted costs. It is a tie, which means that an alternative solution will exist with the same cost. Then, using the same technique, evaluate cell P(D), D(2). The result is that a savings of $1 per unit moved to that cell is available.

c. The maximum number of units that can be moved to cell P(D), D(2) is 40 units. That move should lower the total cost by 40($1) = $40. The discussion ensued as to whether $40 is worth the trouble because it is a savings of 4.3 percent at best.

d. The final assignment solution is shown in the matrix. It has a total cost of $675. One of the managers got very enthusiastic about the transportation method for manpower planning. He stated that it could be used for City Hospital's Call-A-Medic business unit, which is a call center run by the hospital. Call centers are very labor intensive, yet they have major technology interfaces. The discussion touched on call centers, widely used by public utilities (power providers), airline and train reservation systems, and technology purveyors such as Dell, Nextel, and D-link.

Final Assignment Solution				
	D(1)	D(2)	D(3)	Supply
P(1)	40			40 hrs.
P(2)	5	35		40 hrs.
P(3)			40	40 hrs.
P(D)		30	10	40 hrs.
Demand	45 hrs.	65 hrs.	50 hrs.	160 hrs.

e. The transportation model cannot be solved by hand with cut and try when it is of large size. Manpower planning for City Hospital involves hundreds of nurses being assigned to dozens of departments. Linear programming will solve problems of such size (once the data inputs are well organized) with remarkable speed. It will permit sensitivity analyses to be run regarding other factors that drive the manpower loading problem for the hospital.

7. If the loading situation applies to manufacturing with jobs assigned to machines (or work areas such as the foundry, press shop, plating, and assembly), then the transportation model requires transforming job units into standard hours. Hospital schedulers are convinced that this applies to their Hematology Department, where jobs are measured in units that require different amounts of time. Hematology testing facilities take different amounts of time to complete each of the different types of jobs. Hospital schedulers have prepared a list of six statements that relate to the classical facility loading problem. Which single statement in the list (a. to f.) is in error?

a. There are n different kinds of hematology jobs to be done. Each one can be done by the m lab teams, which have different levels of technology at their disposal and various amounts of training.

b. The head of the lab has stated that it is reasonable to assume that proportionality exists between the productivity rates of the m teams. The fastest team has been selected as the standard team. The way that the other teams relate to the standard team is shown in the table.

Simple Example of Shop Loading for Three Teams in the Hematology Department

Team (*i*)	Standard Team Index	Relative Productivity	Actual Hours/ Week	Standard Team Hours/Week
T(S)	1.0	Standard team	54 (Saturday with 9-hour shifts)	54
T(1)	0.8	80% as fast as T(S)	80 (double shift)	64
T(2)	0.5	Half as fast as T(S)	36 (department maintenance)	18
Totals			170 total hours	136 total hours

c. The actual hours that each team has available is converted to standard team hours by multiplying the index times the actual hours. This is shown in the table.

d. Three jobs (A = 300 units, B = 210 units, and C = 1800 units) are waiting to be done by the Hematology Department. They have not yet been assigned to teams for shop loading. Jobs A, B, and C have to be converted to standard team hours. This is done by dividing actual job units by the productivity of the standard team. This is shown as part of the transportation matrix in the following table.

Matrix of Productive Output for Each Team on Each Job				
	Job A	Job B	Job C	Supply in Std. Hrs.
T(S)	6 units/hr.	7 units/hr.	30 units/ hr.	54 std. hrs.
T(1)	0.8(6) = 4.8	0.8(7) = 5.6	0.8(30) = 24	64 std. hrs.
T(2)	0.5(6) = 3.0	0.5(7) = 3.5	0.5(30) = 15	18 std. hrs.
T(D) = Dummy team	0.0(6) = 0	0.0(7) = 0	0.0(30) = 0	4 std. hrs.
Demand in std. hrs.	300/6 = 50	210/7 = 30	1800/30 = 60	Total = 140 std. hrs.

e. The transportation method can now be used to find the maximum total productive output solution. This best shop loading is not restricted to no-splitting of jobs. Jobs assigned to the dummy team will not be done. Four standard hours will not be done at one of the jobs.

f. This problem cannot be done by linear programming because it is a maximization problem with constraints. LP can only deal with minimization problems with constraints. The nature of the constraints is related to the field of hematology.

8. Once the loading problem has been resolved, City Hospital schedulers know that the detailed aspects of assignment ordering must be made. Which nurses will be assigned morning shifts in each department? Who will follow in the afternoons and evenings? Sequences of who follows whom must be established in each department to satisfy the manpower scheduling requirements. Loading decisions did not determine shift assignments. Loading assigned people to departments without their shift designations. City Hospital schedulers decided to use the X-ray Department and sequence the work assigned to it. The list was prepared with relevant points a. through e. Unfortunately, one point on that list is incorrect. Which point is that?

a. Three jobs are in the X-ray Department queue. All that is known about them is the order in which they arrived for processing (A, B, C) and how long they each will take to accomplish. That is the operation times, t_i.

Sequencing Table (LPT)

Arrival Order	Job (i)	W_i Minutes	t_i Minutes	C_i Minutes
First	A	0	17	17
Second	B	17	12	29
Third	C	29	9	38
Total		46 minutes	38 minutes	84 minutes

b. The table shows that by chance the first job to arrive is the longest one. The second is the next longest, and the third is the shortest. Sequencing experts know that this arrangement, which is called longest processing time (LPT), will lead to the longest total wait time (and the highest average wait time) for the set of $n = 3$ jobs. Managers prefer to use FIFO (first-in, first-out) when possible because it seems fair to their customers.

c. The table shows that when the processing order is LPT, the total waiting time is 46 minutes. Processing time is 38 minutes, and that will not change no matter in what order the jobs will be done. The total completion time is 84 minutes which is the sum:

$$\sum_{i=1}^{i=n} C_i = \sum_{i=1}^{i=n} (W_i + t_i)$$

d. A familiar objective in sequencing is to minimize mean flow time which is

$$\sum_{i=1}^{i=n} C_i / n = \sum_{i=1}^{i=n} (W_i + t_i)/n$$

e. The specific value of mean flow time in this case is 21 minutes.

9. Shortest processing time (SPT) will minimize the average waiting time for all jobs. This raises questions about the fairness of FIFO if it penalizes the average job on the waiting line. That was the case in Problem 8 because the FIFO order happened to be the longest processing time (LPT). In general, if random arrivals are serviced with the FIFO rule, then the result will seldom be optimal and will generally fall between the SPT optimal and the LPT worse case. The City Hospital schedulers wanted to demonstrate the truth of this point to all department heads in the hospital. They have drawn up a table based on SPT for the X-ray Department. The new table retained the LPT totals so that a comparison could be made between LPT and SPT. Based on the new table, a list was prepared with relevant points a. through e. One point on that list is incorrect. Which point is that?

a. The same three jobs are in the X-ray Department queue. The schedulers decided to ignore the FIFO rule because A arrived before B, which arrived before C. The first column is now processing order and not arrival order. In this case, the last to arrive, C, is the first to receive processing.

Sequencing Table (LPT)

Processing Order	Job (i)	W_i Minutes	t_i Minutes	C_i Minutes
First	C	0	9	9
Second	B	9	12	21
Third	A	21	17	38
Total Flow-Time-LPT		46 minutes	38 minutes	84 minutes
Total Flow-Time-SPT		30 minutes	38 minutes	68 minutes
Percent improved		34.8%	No change	19%

b. Sequencing experts know that shortest processing time (SPT) will lead to minimum total waiting time (and the lowest average wait time) for the set of $n = 3$ jobs.

c. The table shows that when the processing order is SPT, the total waiting time is 30 minutes. Processing time is 38 minutes. The total completion time is 68 minutes which is the sum:

$$\sum_{i=1}^{i=n} C_i = \sum_{i=1}^{i=n} (W_i + t_i)$$

d. The mean flow time is 68/3 = 22.67 minutes, as shown in the equation.

$$\sum_{i=1}^{i=n} C_i / n = \sum_{i=1}^{i=n} (W_i + t_i) / n$$

$$= (30 + 38) / 3 = 22.67$$

e. The improvement must be viewed in terms of the frequency with which a small but significant saving is obtained. There is a reduction in waiting time of almost 20 percent as a result of using SPT as compared to the worst case LPT situation. The benchmark is extreme because FIFO will seldom produce an LPT ordering.

10. The SPT rule is a benefit to the average customer. However, it penalizes customers with long jobs. In the X-ray Department, there are jobs that take extensive periods of time to prepare. These jobs may constantly be passed over in favor of the short jobs. To avoid problems of this sort, City Hospital's schedulers have decided to use critical ratio procedures (for due dates) and priorities based on cumulative delays to modify SPT rules. The intention is to cover a number of issues that a well-trained production schedule manager should be comfortable discussing. The list of points a. to e. have been sent around the company for observations and comments. One of them is not correct. Which is the flawed statement?

    a. Optimal sequencing can be found when there is one facility ($m = 1$) and any number of jobs (n) to be processed through that facility. When more than one facility exists for processing jobs, i.e., $m > 1$, the problem is too complex. There are no optimal solutions. Simulation must be used with heuristics.

    b. Priority-modified SPT rules can take into account the fact that some jobs are more important to the company than others. This is done by dividing each job's processing time, t_i, by the relative importance of the job, w_i. Thus, t_i/w_i, are rank ordered. The job with the smallest ratio, t_i/w_i, is placed first. Continue in the same way with the next smallest ratios. Important jobs have the smallest modified SPT value.

    c. Alternative interpretations of w_i include lateness, L_i. If a job is not late, $L_i = 1$. Otherwise, the ratios, t_i/L_i, put late jobs at the top of the processing order.

    d. Another system lets w_i equal the number of days that the job has been waiting to be processed. As delay mounts up, the ratio, t_i/w_i, rises quickly to the top of the list.

    e. A sequencing rule that is called the critical ratio rank orders d_i/t_i where d_i is the number of days remaining before the promised delivery.

ADDITIONAL READINGS

Conway, Richard W., William L. Maxwell, and Louis W. Miller. *Theory of Scheduling*. Mineola, NY: Dover Publications (a classic, reissued in paperback), June 2003.

Conway, Richard W. "Priority Dispatching and Job Lateness in a Job Shop." *Journal of Industrial Engineering*, vol. 16, no. 4 (July 1965).

Digital Equipment Corporation. *Factory Scheduler*. Licensed to the Mitron Corp. of Beaverton, Oregon (503-690-8350), 1994.

Goldratt, Eliyahu M. *The Haystack Syndrome*. Great Barrington, MA: North River Press, Inc., 1990.

Goldratt, Eliyahu M. *The Theory of Constraints Journals*, volumes 1–6, Great Barrington, MA: North River Press, Inc., 1990.

Goldratt, Eliyahu M. *It's Not Luck*. Great Barrington, MA: North River Press, Inc., 1994.

Goldratt, Eliyahu M., and Jeff Cox. *The Goal: A Process of Ongoing Improvement*, 2nd Revised Edition. Great Barrington, MA: North River Press, 1992.

Goldratt, Eliyahu M., and Robert E. Fox. *The Race*. Great Barrington, MA: North River Press, 1986.

Plenert, Gerhard, and Bill Kirchmier, *Finite Capacity Scheduling: Management, Selection, and Implementation*. New York: John Wiley & Sons, January 2000.

Red Pepper Software. *ResponseAgents (Optimizing Production Scheduler)*. San Mateo, CA, (415-960-4095), 1994.

Umble M. Michael, and M.L. Srikanth. *Synchronous Manufacturing: Principles for World Class Excellence*. Cincinnati, OH: South-Western Publishing Co., 1990.

NOTES

1. S.M. Johnson. "Optimal Two- and Three-Stage Production Schedules with Set-up Times Included." *Naval Research Logistics Quarterly*, vol. 1, no. 1 (March 1954): 61–68. This article laid the foundation for later work in sequencing theory. It is historically of interest.

2. Eliyahu Goldratt and R. Fox. *The Race*. North River Press, 1986. The OPT system was developed by Eliyahu Goldratt as a commercial product for best scheduling practice. Also visit http://www.goldratt.com for 2003 up-to-date information about AGI and TOC, including its project management (critical chain) developments. The AGI is the Goldratt Institute.

SPOTLIGHT 16-1
The Pursuit of Clean Air

In 1955, the federal government under President Dwight D. Eisenhower decided to deal with air pollution on a national level. The Air Pollution Control Act of 1955 was the first federal legislation of its kind, following pollution-reduction efforts from state and local governments. The federal act identified air pollution as an environmental hazard and assigned to Congress the right to control this growing problem. However, this act did little to prevent air pollution.

Eight years later, the Clean Air Act of 1963 under President John F. Kennedy set emissions standards for stationary sources. Power plants and steel mills were regulated, but the act did not take into account mobile sources of pollution. Under President Lyndon Johnson (1963–1968), the 1965, 1966, 1967, and 1969 (Nixon) amendments authorized governmental departments to set standards for auto emissions and to set air quality standards.

Nixon, in his State of the Union Address in January 1970, said that the American people had entered a "historic period when, by conscious choice, [we] transform our land into what we want it to become." He signed the National Environmental Policy Act, creating a new Council on Environmental Quality. The environmental movement was underway. April 22, 1970, marked the first Earth Day. On July 9, Nixon called for the creation of the Environmental Protection Agency.

That July, Nixon signed the Clean Air Act of 1970, which some compared to President John F. Kennedy's 1961 challenge to put a man on the moon before the end of the decade. The 1970 act presented an extreme challenge, ensuring that all Americans would have air that is safe to breathe within a time frame that initially seemed impossible. It also mandated removal of toxic lead in gasoline. The goal was a 90 percent reduction in automobile emissions from pre–1968 levels. The deadline was the end of 1974, when new model cars for 1975 would be on the market.

An extraordinary crash program of research and development followed. Engineers knew that factories would have to be ready to produce emission controls before the deadline for a mass market. To most engineers, it looked hopeless. However, one man had been working on gasoline emission problems since the end of World War II.

That man was Eugene Houdry. He would have welcomed the Clean Air Act, but he had died eight years earlier. As an engineer, he developed catalytic cracking in the 1920s and 1930s. Houdry's process provided a large part of the aviation fuel needed for the Allied victory in World War II. He was convinced that unburned hydrocarbons from automobile exhaust gases caused lung cancer, and he thought he had a solution.

In 1948, Houdry founded Oxy-Catalyst in Wayne, Pennsylvania, to develop catalyst systems that would oxidize and convert unburned hydrocarbons into harmless byproducts of carbon dioxide and water. By 1959, his catalytic mufflers fit into the exhaust system of automobiles. He is quoted as saying, "Put them on all cars and watch the lung cancer curve dip." His catalytic muffler was awarded a patent in 1962, the same year he died at the age of 70.

At that time, drivers were accustomed to using leaded gas in their cars to achieve higher octane and to prevent engine knocking. However, leaded gasoline limits the effectiveness of catalytic converters. Converters use a combination of catalysts (platinum, aluminum oxide, and palladium) spread out over a honeycomb structure through which exhaust gases must flow to turn harmful gases into harmless H_2O and CO_2. Emissions from leaded gasoline coated the catalysts with lead, making it necessary to replace converters about every 12,000 miles at a cost of approximately $150. That was not considered acceptable to the American public.

By 1969, smog over California freeways was so bad that the state created its own standards. The Engelhard Company in New Jersey was working on a project to reduce carbon monoxide emissions from forklifts in mines and warehouses. Carl Keith of Engelhard (who knew Eugene Houdry's work) began experimenting with unleaded gasoline. Spurred on by the Clean Air Act of 1970, which specified converter effectiveness for at least 50,000 miles, scientists from Corning Glass Works also joined the search for a device that would clean a car's exhaust gases.

Each impossible challenge was met. The government raised standards again and again, and this remarkable handful of company scientists and engineers kept meeting them. The resulting catalytic converter has been called one of the greatest environmental achievements of the twentieth century.

The Clean Air Act of 1990 strengthened and improved existing regulations in many areas: air quality standards, motor vehicle emissions and alternative fuels, toxic air pollutants, acid rain, and stratospheric ozone depletion. The Eurozone has even more stringent regulations than the United States.

China has imposed the most rigorous standards of any country based on a brilliant strategy. As reported by *The New York Times* (November 18, 2003), China's tough rules are intended to pressure auto companies and dealers to introduce hybrids and other clean alternative technologies with the express purpose of minimizing China's dependence on foreign oil.

Toyota's redesigned gasoline/electric hybrid (Prius) delivers 55 to 60 miles per gallon. Toyota scheduled output of 36,000 Priuses for 2004. Honda is selling the Civic Hybrid. GM is planning to mass market hybrid Saturn VUEs in 2005. Ford and DaimlerChrysler have similar timetables.

The large Chinese population with millions of hybrid cars would support flow shop production volumes. With P/OM knowledge, costs would be cut while increasing quality and productivity. A new world market may not be far away that significantly reduces global dependence on petroleum products.

Sources:
Palucka, Tim. "Doing the Impossible." *Invention & Technology* (Winter 2004): 22–31; http://www.cleanairtrust.org/cleanairact. html.
"Legislation: A Look at U.S. Air Pollution Laws and their Amendments"; http://www.a,metsoc.org/sloan/cleanair/cleanairlegisl. html.
"Automakers Show New Alternative Fuel Vehicles at Long Beach Expo." AP Wire (November 16, 2003).

SPOTLIGHT 16-2
The Fallacy of Pursuing Local Optimums

An Interview with Dr. Eliyahu M. Goldratt, Author of The Goal and The Race

 Dr. Eliyahu M. Goldratt, renowned worldwide for developing new production control and management philosophies and systems, challenges companies to "break outside of the box" of conventional practices in their ongoing efforts to achieve business goals. In his early work, Goldratt developed the concept and technology for bottleneck-based finite scheduling. From this he concluded that optimizing production scheduling in isolation from other business variables usually does not lead to higher productivity or achievement of company goals. As his work evolved, he called his ideas the Theory of Constraints (TOC).

Based on systematic thinking processes, TOC studies the cause and effect relationships between dependent aspects of a given problem or project. It provides an overall framework for determining (1) what not to change (not everything is broken); (2) how change (what are the simple, practical solutions); and (3) how to implement change (overcoming the inherent resistance to change). TOC enables the determination of core problems, construction of detailed solutions, and devising of implementation plans. TOC has major applications in production, project management, distribution, finance, marketing and sales, and management strategy but can be used as well to solve any problems that arise in life.

Dr. Goldratt brings his finite scheduling theory and TOC framework to life in his books *The Goal: Excellence in Manufacturing* and its sequel, *It's Not Luck*. He wrote these two business textbooks as novels, "to give the content in a way people can absorb it," he said. The books give students and practitioners of business a "real-life" context for applying Goldratt's ideas for achieving business excellence. (He does not accept credit for inventing this creative genre, however, attributing inspiration to novelist/ philosopher Ayn Rand.) Goldratt has written several traditional texts as well, including *The Haystack Syndrome, The Race,* and *The Theory of Constraints.* In *The Haystack Syndrome,* Goldratt presents evidence that "cost accounting is public enemy number one of productivity." In *It's Not Luck,* he asserts that balance sheets are "nothing more than the liquidation value of the company . . . and should not be used to judge an ongoing operation."

Application of Goldratt's theories have proven that "the core problem right now in most of the industry is a lack of a systems approach." This core problem is referred to throughout his work as "striving to run the whole system based on local optimums." Goldratt teaches that one area of a business may need to sacrifice its own local optimums for the greater good of the entire system. Goldratt sees an eagerness among the business community to embrace systems thinking, but finds major resistance to this approach in academia. He believes that academics who do not present a systems perspective are "sending graduates into the market totally unprepared." Goldratt's theories have met with widespread acceptance, as evidenced through sales of over two million copies of *The Goal*—with no advertising expense incurred! When he's not consulting with managers of the world's largest corporations, Goldratt lives in Israel.

Sources: A conversation with Dr. Eliyahu M. Goldratt and correspondence, August 1, 2003.

Cycle-Time Management

Chapter 17 explains what cycle-time management is and why it has become so important to both manufacturing and service organizations. When operations produce a stream of outputs *repetitively over time*, it is necessary to determine how long the process takes from start to finish. That is a benchmark against which further improvement is measured. It is of paramount importance to analyze the process to find out if any moments can be shaved from that cycle time. Line-balancing for cycle-time control is one kind of effort to smooth the availability of resources along the path of production so that no slowdown occurs. Waiting is waste in the cycle time. These ideas apply to intermittent and continuous flow shops. Differences are drawn between deterministic, stochastic, and heuristic line-balancing situations. The management of cycle time is shown to be an important aspect of time-based management (TBM). Waiting line or queuing models are introduced in this context of balanced work flows when arrivals and servicing times are random variables. The Chapter 17 supplement provides simulation of queuing models.

After reading this chapter, you should be able to:

- Explain the nature of cycle-time management.
- Illustrate the relationship between the line-balancing of serialized production systems and cycle-time management.
- Explain why line-balancing is important.
- Detail the different kinds of line-balancing situations that exist with respect to labor-intensive and technology-oriented workstations.
- Describe the difference between deterministic, stochastic, and heuristic line-balancing situations.
- Explain what needs to be done to balance a production line.
- Relate cycle-time management to time-based management (TBM) and distinguish between tactical and strategic TBM.
- Draw a precedence diagram and calculate output rates for different numbers of stations.

- Describe perfect balance, measure balance delay and line efficiency, and explain why they are useful measures.
- Demonstrate a heuristic line-balancing algorithm and explain why the use of computer software is desirable.
- Relate stochastic line-balancing and queuing models.
- Explain why all service systems can be viewed as queuing systems that must be balanced to satisfy customer expectations.
- Demonstrate how single-channel queuing models can be used to estimate average length of waiting lines and waiting times.
- Describe the role of suppliers in cycle-time management.
- Discuss the advantages and conversion of push-production systems to pull-production systems.

THE SYSTEMS VIEWPOINT

Cycle time provides a measure of the output rates of different parts of the system. For the system as a whole, it is a common denominator that interrelates the timing of activities and flows of materials. Timing is as important to the performance of repetitive production systems as it is to the performance of a symphony orchestra. Cycle time is related to the interval that work stays at each workstation, and to the rate at which items are finished and ship out of the production line. The big systems perspective connects customers' demand rates and suppliers' delivery rates with management's control over production output cycle time. Cycle-time management will reflect decisions about how much to make to ship and how much to make to stock under normal and peak demand conditions. The systems view requires inclusion of the cycle times of internal functions that support the production process, such as production scheduling for components and subassemblies, materials inspection, maintenance, and billing for accounts receivable. The systems viewpoint requires inclusion of cycle times related to delivery of materials and distribution along the supply chain.

STRATEGIC THINKING

When plans are being formulated concerning how to convert money into productive resources, product and service strategies are the focus of attention. The concept of using flow shops to achieve volumes of output that have substantial cost savings is part of that strategy. The signature of a flow shop is its cycle time. There is a theoretical cycle time and a realistic cycle time. Competitive advantage is gained by firms that can decrease the cycle time of an established process. The higher level of margin that results can be used to support marketing, design even better process cycle times, decrease the price of the product line, and to create new products. When cycle-time management is applied to various work configurations, it is feasible to determine which comes closest to satisfying the strategic plans, which can include flow shops that are relatively permanent or the shorter durations of intermittent flow shops (IFS) producing large batches of work. Strategic thinking should include time-based and cycle-time management, as well as just-in-time management for interdependent functions. Synchronization and orchestration are strategic issues of cycle-time management.

17-1 CYCLE-TIME MANAGEMENT

Cycle time is defined as the interval of time that elapses between successive units of finished product coming off the production line.

17-1a Automobiles: Cycle Times

If a completed Subaru comes off the production line in Lafayette, Indiana, every 1.5 minutes, then one and one half minutes would be the cycle time for that assembly line. Using these figures, every hour 40 cars (60/1.5 = 40) would be driven off the end of the line. Output per day would be 720 cars using two 9-hour shifts per day. With two 9-hour shifts per day for 26 days per month, 18,720 cars would be produced per month and 224,640 cars per year. (In this example, each regular shift is 8 hours with 1 hour overtime—and 1 overtime weekend might be worked per month.)

In addition, *if* there are 300 workstations, then to make a car would take 450 minutes, or 7.5 hours, from start to finish. Perhaps 900 employees are on the line and supporting the 300 workstations. Numerical estimates, such as those shown here, help to model the cost of making an automobile. They assist, as well, in establishing rough benchmarks and refining those benchmarks. Additionally, standards need to be set with production methods put in place to achieve the standards and then improve upon them.

From the definition given here, cycle time must be the length of time that a unit spends at each stop point along the (conveyor belted) production line. This means that if

> **Cycle time:** The interval, C, that elapses between successive units of finished work coming off the production line.

the process can be altered so that work in process spends less time at each workstation, then the interval between successive units of finished goods coming off the line can be shortened, resulting in an increased production output rate.

Rewriting the first paragraph in Section 17-1a, "if a completed Subaru comes off the production line in Lafayette, Indiana, every 1.0 minutes, then one minute would be the cycle time for that assembly line. Using these figures, every hour 60 cars (60/1.0 = 60) would be driven off the end of the line. Output per day would be 1,080 cars using two 9-hour shifts per day. With two 9-hour shifts per day for 26 days per month, 28,080 cars would be produced per month and 336,960 per year. In addition, if there are 300 work-stations, then to make a car would take 300 minutes, or 5.0 hours, from start to finish." These numbers are not meant to describe actual Subaru production. However, they are meant to provoke discussion about how cycle time relates to the production output.

When cycle time went from 1.5 minutes to 1.0 minute, this was a reduction of cycle time by 33 percent. That led to a 50 percent increase in the number of cars produced. Productivity increased. The time required to build a car decreased by 33 percent (going from 7.5 hours to 5.0 hours). Cycle-time reductions go right to the bottom line, which is why management is focused on process improvements. It makes good sense to spend money on training and new technology if those expenditures can significantly decrease the cycle time. There is ample evidence that such expenditures can deliver significant improvements in cycle time.

When production rate cycle time is altered up or down, this will change the cycle times for many activities that support the production system. More or less materials may be needed from the automotive suppliers to feed the production line. Fewer or more workers doing their own inspection may be needed to deal with quality and quantity checks. More or fewer auto carriers may be wanted to carry finished autos to retailers and distributors' warehouses. Cycle times of inbound and outbound supplies are interconnected with the fundamentals of the production line. Balanced production systems require understanding cycle timing.

It is not surprising that in recent years, cycle time has become one of the most important OM topics for executives from a broadly diverse set of industries. With pressure on profits, cycle-time improvements can provide financial leverage at the relatively low cost of thinking creatively. Big improvements in output and revenue can be gained at low cost and (often) fairly quickly. Decreasing cycle time by working smarter and not harder has the effect of increasing productivity, decreasing the breakeven point, and increasing the system's effective capacity.

Rolls-Royce provides another example of how improving process design decreases cycle time and raises output. Often, but not always, the extra input costs are minor in comparison to the output gains. The Rolls-Royce manufacturing plant was antiquated and inefficient. Using consultants familiar with Japanese lean methods, they were able to cut the cycle time for making a Rolls-Royce from 50 to 30 days. Although this 40 percent improvement reduced the breakeven point from 2,600 cars in 1992 to 1,300 cars in 1994, the firm did not achieve profitability. Thirty days is still far too long a time to build a car, even a Rolls-Royce. It became evident that a new plant would be needed to alter the situation. They call it a *greenfield* plant, meaning it is start-up from scratch with all new systems. Greenfield plants in the United States include the Saturn plant located in Spring Hill, Tennessee; the Honda plant in Marysville, Ohio; and Toyota plants in Princeton, Indiana, and Georgetown, Kentucky. Greenfield plants generally produce a car a minute.

The improvement just described was not enough to keep the U.K. Rolls-Royce in business. Volkswagen took control of the company, but they used the same plant that had been producing the car for 60 years, viz., the manufacturing facility at Crewe in Cheshire. That did not work out. As pointed out earlier, it can be difficult to cut cycle time significantly without radically changing the factory environment.

BMW then took over Rolls-Royce production from its German rival Volkswagen, which produced its last Rolls in August 2002. BMW built a new Rolls-Royce manufacturing plant for £65 million at Goodwood in West Sussex. The BMW announcement on January 23, 2003, suggests that the company has achieved a breakeven point well below 1,000 cars per year. The plan is to produce 4 cars per day to sell for about £240,000.

A 2-hour cycle time (C = 120 minutes) is still long when compared to U.S. greenfield plant standards of 1 or 2 minutes. However, the Rolls-Royce sells at 10 times the price of an expensive American SUV. C = 120 minutes is significantly better than C = 30 days for the cycle time that Rolls-Royce achieved after major improvement of their manufacturing facility at Crewe in Cheshire.

The NUMMI (Toyota/GM) plant in Freemont, California, is important as the exception that proves the rule. NUMMI took the old (awful) Freemont plant of GM and made it a top-benchmark plant for excellence.

17-1b   Airlines: Cycle Times

To apply cycle time to airline flights, treat each time the *next* plane takes off on the same runway as the *next* finished unit coming off the production line. The interval between takeoffs is the cycle time of the airport for the specific runway. U.S. Airways realized that its cost structure was not competitive (and this was before 9/11). Using good OM practice, they cut the ground time between flights from 45 minutes to 20 minutes. This is equivalent to saying that cycle time was reduced by 25/45 = 55.56 = 56 percent. That would appear to be outstanding but not enough to compensate for the fact that U.S. Airways had too much debt.

From an OM point of view, there is much interest in the fact that cycle time was reduced by 56 percent. This was done by decreasing the number of crew changes, speeding up the check-in procedures, and loading planes with enough food and drinks for several trips. The resulting productivity improvement increased the available seating capacity for the fleet of planes by 3,500 seats per day. There are a number of ways of looking at this improvement. The most direct might be to estimate increased revenues at between $100 and $200 per extra seat yielding a range for additional revenue from $350,000 to $700,000 per day. The conservative yearly estimate is impressive being 365 × $300,000, which is in excess of 10 million dollars.

In fact, much of this estimated revenue would not be realized for a variety of reasons, including the fact that the airlines adhere to their published flight schedules. Less time on the ground and a shorter cycle time might save operating costs and help achieve on-time performance with higher customer satisfaction.

This airline example is particularly useful because it changes perspective. It broadens the applicability of the concept of cycles from the traditional, and entirely correct, notion that cycle time applies to repetitive operations such as an assembly line. In this case, cycle time is appropriate for a set of operations that are linked together as a chain of repetitive activities such as supporting airplane takeoffs.

17-1c   Other Applications of Cycle Times

In setting time standards, there are short and long cycles that comprise the job. Having to go to the storeroom to get materials, such as rolls of tape to seal boxes, may have to be done once every 1,000 boxes sealed. Nevertheless, it is a legitimate cycle that deserves to be studied and that can be improved. Perhaps getting two rolls of tape at a time, or one double roll, would decrease the frequency of work interruption. That change might lower the cost of the job and increase the productivity of the worker.

Industrial engineers are trained to question the methods being employed to perform a task. How far does Joe have to walk to obtain a role of tape? Can storage be moved closer, decreasing the distance? Value analysis raises the question "Is there some better material to use than tape?" Can a glue gun improve the seal and reduce the cost of this operation? Cycle-time improvements often result from worker suggestions.

Cycles exist in the repetitive intervals between placing an order and receiving supplies. Inspection cycles exist between receiving and accepting materials for use on the production line. Just-in-time (JIT) systems can make deliveries faster by providing automatic (computerized) procedures for recognizing that stock levels need replenishment. Bigger trucks require fewer trips but lengthen cycle times. Conversely, smaller trucks have shorter cycle times with less materials being stocked more often. The frequency of deliveries and the stock that is carried as a result are most often viewed as inventory management problems. The decision to use just-in-time deliveries alters the production cycle of suppliers as well as their shipping schedules.

Cycle time is of critical importance to the designers of theme park rides. Disney and Universal design rides to maximize throughput rates. Disney's Tower of Terror has two elevators working side by side doing the double (now triple) drop in the dark that is the core experience. "Guests," however, are only aware of the elevator that they occupy.

Because guests do not enjoy waiting time, FastPass was created by Disney. FastPass allows guests to make reservations on particular rides to avoid waiting on long lines. It is not a far cry to consider the New York City subway as much a ride as the Hulk coaster at Universal's Islands of Adventure or Kraken at Sea World in Orlando. In New York City, the Metropolitan Transit Authority (MTA) is totally aware of cycle time to load and unload the crowded subways at Times Square. In office buildings, the elevator is designed to pick up and drop off crowds of people with different patterns in accord with the time of day. Cycle times are at center stage, influencing productivity, cost, and quality.

17-2   TIME-BASED MANAGEMENT AND SYNCHRONIZATION OF FLOWS

Cycle-time management is one facet of **time-based management (TBM).** It is the aspect of TBM that applies to running a better production process for a flow shop. Better means balanced (as will become evident from materials ahead). Better also can mean a shorter cycle time. This was explained for autos, airlines, and other applications.

Cycle time-based management is generally regarded to be tactical in scope, given that the system has been designed, built, and it is up-and-running. It needs controlling. The reason that it is tactical is that it entails management of the existing production process. To further clarify, tactics are applied to military situations with respect to "small scale" actions serving a larger purpose. Tactical vision is usually applied to situations with limited and/or immediate ends in view.

In contrast to tactical steps and procedures, there are strategic plans and decisions that precede tactical activities. For example, when alternative process designs are under consideration, the decisions about which way to go are strategic ones. The best strategic decisions are made with an understanding of the tactics that will be used under that strategic umbrella. Using retail business as an illustration, strategies relate to where to locate, how big a store, and what to sell. Tactics might be where to advertise, how to price products, when to have sales, how to display merchandise, and what the sale force should say.

Cycle times include how long it takes to make a sale, intervals required for checking out and paying, time to restock the shelves, replenishment intervals, coupon expiration dating, and other details that make that business function. TBM is at work determining the optimal timing through synchronization of the factors. Don't advertise until there is sufficient stock on-hand. Have enough cash register operators so customers are not upset waiting. That is what is meant by tactical aspects of TBM.

The concept of continuous process improvement, instead of reengineering (or radical change), often, but not always, applies to cycle-time reduction. For instance, BMW's success in cutting cycle time for Rolls-Royce required literal interpretation of the greenfield concept. It was necessary to start the new building on a vacant lot. When talking about reengineering, it means starting from scratch. On the other hand, continuous improvement is associated with the idea that "practice makes perfect." The old tried and true recipe prevails but it must be tweaked because the critic wrote a review in *The New York Times,* and he said that rosemary should be added to the broth. In that vein, reengineering restaurants is very difficult in the same location.

Location experts need to think about this. Certain locations are said to be "cursed." For example, every restaurant that opens at a certain location fails. Could it be that the first restaurant at that location failed and thereby put a *blight* on every subsequent restaurant at that location? Customers do not associate a trip to that location for a "good meal"

Time-based management (TBM): Managers' concerns about time lines, schedules, deliveries, and project completions; goals are to be fast-moving, rapid-responders, high velocity without quality losses.

as supportable. A bookstore at the same location might be a big success. Greenfield gives a boost to reengineering the entire system to conform to a clearer strategy.

Another facet of TBM that is increasingly important to operations management is project management. Project management has a different interpretation of cycle time than the flow shop. Often, projects deal with developing a new product or process as quickly as possible. Such developments are considered strategic because they represent a major change in resource usage and company policy. Managing a project would apply to the way in which BMW handled the project of building, installing, and starting up its new production process for Rolls-Royce.

Tactical timing goals must synchronize cycles of all participants. The flows of materials used on the line must get to where they are needed on time. Shipping schedules of finished goods must be synchronized so that inventory pileups do not occur on the shipping docks. When the cycle times of parts of processes are reduced in one place, other places in the process must be adjusted so that balance is maintained and the flows are synchronized. This aspect of cycle-time management is inherent in proper control of the supply chain.

The management of the broad range of activities that can be defined as cycles puts the spotlight on the timing. Substantial reduction of intervals between successive outputs from the production line can usually be obtained by rethinking the way that things are done. Cycle-time management and quality management have a lot of similarities. The reduction of cycle time and the reduction of defectives can result from being clever about process design. Conversely, poor processes result from a lack of teamwork and a shortage of team members' suggestions. Thus, as it is said that some part of quality improvement is free, some part of cycle-time improvement also is free.

In building confidence that one can improve cycle times, the place to start is with line-balancing serialized work configurations. This includes intermittent flow shops. There is often reluctance to spend as freely on line-balancing temporary flow shops as compared to permanent ones. Line-balancing is the main cycle-management technique in both cases—whether the system of supporting machines, conveyors, and training are for dedicated or temporary production purposes.

17-3 LINE-BALANCING METHODS

Line-balancing (LB): Effort to divide total work content into equal (or nearly equal) balanced parts for assignment at each of n workstations. Bad design loads stations unevenly.

Line-balancing (LB) is the effort to *nearly equalize* the output rate capabilities of successive workstations on the production line. LB also is the effort to reduce and match excess idle time at the workstations. Line-balancing has to take into consideration constraints that include the order in which work can be done and the impossibility of splitting some operations between different stations. The overriding objective of LB is to achieve a balance of production resources that can deliver the right amount of production to satisfy demand requirements with minimum waste of resources.

This goal can be directly translated into supply chain terms. LB synchronizes material flows by properly assigning required resources. These include people, production equipment, storage space, and transportation facilities. When production equipment is part of a dedicated flow shop (as in automobile assembly), engineers provide perfect line balance for such mechanized manufacturing systems.

Unlike the engineering of dedicated flow shops, the use of LB for intermittent flow shops (IFS) is common when batch sizes are large enough to warrant a temporary serial form of production. A manufacturer of baby strollers runs different models on the same production line for varying times according to demand. Each model has unique characteristics that change the line-balance requirements. A manufacturer of electric switch boxes makes most models on a job shop basis in batches. When an order is received for batch sizes that tie up machines for more than two days, an intermittent flow shop set up is used. The Market Research Store uses IFS processing only when a report has more than five regions and/or three products being compared. The intermittent flow shop is the process of choice for growth firms and product situations where short life cycles characterize the market. They are so prevalent that line-balancing for cycle management is a necessity for competitive capability.

With IFS, people often are an important part of the production system. The participation of people at the workstations in manufacturing, service systems, and along the supply chain, increases the variability of output rates. The effect of worker variability is particularly important for cycle management using line-balancing of service systems. Variability of service systems is noticeable in both the arrival rate of people and work for servicing, and in the rates at which services are administered.

People and work wait in line, which is inefficient. Then, at other times, the service system is idle, which is inefficient. These aspects of line-balancing will be covered in Section 17-5 on stochastic line-balancing, which is another way of saying line-balancing systems that have random arrivals and/or service times.

Serialized processes are comprised of operations that are repetitive and sequential. They are linked together—usually by a conveyor that moves the pieces and then stops—so that work can be done at each station. Line-balancing requires assigning operations $(i = 1, 2, ..., k)$ to workstations $(j = 1, 2, ..., n)$ so that all of the workstations are about equally busy (previously described as *nearly equalized*). This terminology of line-balancing can be applied to supply chain and service systems.

Some workstation activities are labor intensive. Others are highly mechanized. The spectrum is constantly moving closer to automation. Glasstech's Automotive In-Line Windshield Forming and Annealing System is entirely mechanized. People pollution is the bane of *clean rooms* for semiconductor manufacturing. Yet, people are needed in clean rooms, and windshield manufacturing provides labor servicing and supporting robot equipment. The nursing profession delivers hands-on assistance, which patients require. The social ethic would have it no other way. Although the trend is technologically driven toward increasing automation in volume manufacturing systems, for most service systems it remains labor intensive.

Volume production of semiconductors reflects a unique combination of labor and technology in manufacturing. The production process takes place in a clean room. Workers in full containment garb are part of the process. The slightest bit of dirt on computer chips ruins circuitry. Clean-room technology constantly filters away the smallest particles. Workers interact with machines at workstations within this special environment.

Automotive-assembly line-balancing reflects a broad range of technology and workers. Installing window glass and upholstery is relatively labor intensive whereas, painting and welding are primarily computer and machine driven. Timing is set for the assembly-line conveyors that travel at rates carefully set by engineering and management design. When there are unions, they participate in agreeing to the rate of the **paced-conveyor** system.

The history of line-balancing deserves attention. In the 1940s at the Louisville, Kentucky, plant of General Electric, which manufactures appliances, a group called *Operations Research and Synthesis (OR & S)* led by Mel Salveson decided to investigate the line-balancing problem. Their studies began a stream of activities that led many researchers to contribute results to the line-balancing literature. By the 1960s, a fine body of work existed in all three classes of line-balancing. The three classes, which are deterministic, heuristic, and stochastic line-balancing, are described here.

Deterministic line-balancing is based on the assumption that each total process takes an exact amount of time, which is known and not variable. The total process is made up of operations. The operations' times when added together constitute the total process or total job time. The operations' times are all fixed. If they were not, then the total process time would not be deterministic.

Heuristic line-balancing methods employ "rules of thumb," common sense, logical thinking, and experience to find near-optimal solutions for large problems. These are problems that involve too many operations to allow enumerating and testing all of the possibilities. The number of possible configurations in line-balancing grows rapidly with operations and stations. Only heuristic methods are economically feasible for many real problems.

Heuristics are used when complexity of size is an issue and the flow shop is temporary. When the flow shop is relatively permanent, as in computer-chip manufacturing and

Paced conveyor: A transporter, usually a belt, moving materials between workstations at a fixed rate of speed station stop-time equals cycle time.

Deterministic line-balancing: Total process time for making the product is exactly the same for every unit of product that is completed. To achieve that goal, all operation times are fixed and never vary.

Heuristic line-balancing methods: So many combinations for assigning work to stations that ordinary mathematical optimization solutions do not apply; various rules of thumb constitute a common sense approach to line-balancing.

automobile assembly, engineering efforts can be justified to design perfectly balanced flow shops. That level of expense is not often acceptable for intermittent flow shops, which have sufficient complexity to require heuristic methods and sufficient volume to pay for the application of the heuristic. Under these circumstances, the line-balancing problem offers one of the best examples of a real need for heuristic methods. Heuristic LB can be used in both deterministic and stochastic line-balancing situations.

Stochastic line-balancing: Occurs when variability exists in the form of statistical distributions of operation and/or transport times.

Stochastic line-balancing exists when the assumption of fixed and deterministic times for operations and total process time is not correct. As previously noted, this might be especially relevant for workstations where labor-intensive operations dominate. It also can be critically important where the variability makes it impossible to complete the work at a station. When the conveyor carries defective work to the next station, it often shuts off production for the rest of the downstream line. Thus, bottlenecks emerge that limit the benefits to be gained from serialized flow shop configurations.

Some assembly lines permit workers to stop the conveyors from moving work further when a serious problem arises at their station. This will be discussed later. Also, it is worth noting that the stochastic line-balancing problem is related to queuing models. These models describe the length of queues and the average waiting times that can occur when lines are not balanced. In effect, the demand for service becomes greater than the supply. Queue length is greater when requests for service occur randomly than when requests are evenly spaced.

If demand volume justifies it, the *high-volume, properly balanced flow shop* is the best work configuration to obtain lowest costs and best quality. A smooth running, conveyor-driven flow shop, with its well-timed stream of product, has low WIP (work in process) levels and enjoys economies of scale. It is a production system that moves just the right amount of material between stations.

Serialized production systems, without conveyors to set the pace, can push uncontrolled amounts of materials from one station to another. Line imbalances get translated into uneven workloads. Stations are not designed to handle inventory overloads. The result of worker overloads is the production of poor quality work as the operators speed up to compensate for the extra materials they must process. Push-type production systems create bottlenecks that cause disruptive backups of costly WIP to form. When stations push materials, there is no consistency in what is being delivered for processing by adjacent stations. On the other hand, pulling product along the line with a goal of being just-in-time is part of proper line-balancing.

17-3a Basic Concepts for Line-Balancing

Step 1 is to detail the process to be balanced. This means listing all of the operations that need to be done to make the product or deliver the service. Detailing requires specifying the order in which all operations are to be done. This includes stating which operations must be done before others can be started. A **precedence diagram,** used to chart the sequence, will be described shortly. Knowledge of the process technology is essential to successfully carry out step 1.

Precedence diagram: Chart all relevant operations indicating which operations must follow others.

It is useful to have a number of people review the list of operations and their sequence. Even great chefs have different recipes for baking the same kind of cake. One recipe might be better than another for different volumes of production. Team responsibility for accepting the list of operations and the order for doing the operations is desirable. That team may be called upon to revise the set of operations and the precedence diagram in order to better balance the line.

This first step is often taken for granted. How the job will be accomplished must be precisely stated. The "devil" is in the details. For making toothpaste, it is not enough to state "mix the slurry for 20 minutes." The details include the mixing rate, the quantity mixed, the way the materials to be mixed are loaded and unloaded, and how and when other materials are added.

Other examples of deciding in detail how each of the operations is to be done include which adhesive will be used and how much at what temperature. How will the adhesive be applied? What software will be used and which version on which computer? Such a set of decisions constitutes the first feasible enumeration of the process. Accepting exactly how the job is to be done is the inception of intelligent line-balancing. There is ample proof that it pays to question every facet of the stated procedure before beginning the next step.

Step 2 requires estimating how long the operations will take. Getting these operation times right is important and will be discussed shortly. Step 3 follows acceptance of the process and estimation of the operation times.

Step 3 is to assign the specific operations to workstations. As a goal, **perfect balance (pb)** is sought. PB can seldom be achieved. It is difficult to design processes in which every station along the production line has the same amount of work to do. With pb there is no idle time at any station—no waste exists. Another way of saying this is that the *sum of the operation times for each station would be the same*, and all available time is completely utilized at each station. A constraint to the achievement of perfect balance arises because workstation assignments cannot violate precedence conditions. Before the bread is baked, the dough must be kneaded.

Having equal sums of operation times at each station is not easily achieved because:

1. *Precedence constraints limit flexibility.* Some operations must be done in specific sequences. Others must be done together at the same station (see Section 17-3f, which discusses zoning constraints). Exact arrangements are detailed, drawn, and analyzed using precedence diagrams. Precedence diagrams are discussed later.

2. *Operation times can be increased and decreased in various ways.* The degree of flexibility is limited by the physical process, management policies and practices, technology, and training. When some operations are speeded up, there is a loss in quality. Other operations cannot be done faster unless an entirely new technology is available to be used.

3. *Human performance is variable.* Individuals and teams shift rates over time. These problems, which are pronounced for the intermittent flow shop, can often be circumvented by the use of technology and proper design of the dedicated flow shop. When the flow shop is dedicated, equipment can be designed to be balanced because the expense will be amortized over high production volumes for a long period of time.

The step 3 goal is to assign operations so that the sums of operation times at all stations are about equal. Thus, starting up the process: Raw materials enter station 1 at 9:00 A.M. Stations 2, 3, and 4 are idle. The start-up routine is always involved in the domino effect of prior adjacent workstations passing along their work in process to the next downstream workstation. Between 9:00 and 9:03 A.M., the raw materials are worked on at station 1. Precise operational details must be specified for station 1 activities.

The materials (now, work in process) move from station 1 to station 2 at 9:03 A.M. Station 2 adds value to the work in process it has received from station 1 by using its set

Perfect balance (pb):
See **Balance delay.**

TABLE 17-1		
Log of 4-Station Start-Up	9:00 A.M.	Station 1 begins working. Station 1 is scheduled to take 2.9 minutes to complete its operations. Idle time at station 1 is 0.1 minute.
	9:03 A.M.	Station 1 repeats its operations. Station 2 begins working. Station 2 is scheduled to take 2.7 minutes to complete its operations. Idle time at station 1 is 0.1 minute and at station 2 is 0.3 minute.
	9:06 A.M.	Stations 1 and 2 repeat their operations. Station 3 begins working. Station 3 is scheduled to take 2.8 minutes to complete its operations. Idle time at station 1 is 0.1 minute, at station 2 it is 0.3 minute, at station 3 it is 0.2 minute.
	9:09 A.M.	Stations 1, 2, and 3 repeat their operations. Station 4 begins working. Station 4 is scheduled to take 3.0 minutes to complete its operations. Idle time at station 1 is 0.1 minute, at station 2 it is 0.3 minute, at station 3 it is 0.2 minute, and it is 0.0 minute at station 4.
	9:12 A.M.	All stations repeat their operations until shutdown.

of operations. Precise operational details must be specified for station 2 activities. At the same time, new raw materials enter station 1, and the description in the previous paragraph applies. Station 1 repeats the same operations every 3 minutes.

At 9:06 A.M., station 3 begins to operate on WIP passed from station 2. Continue in this way until all stations are actively engaged. Every 3 minutes, raw materials enter at station 1, and finished goods leave the final station every 3 minutes. Cycle time is C = 3. Table 17-1 provides the start-up log. Figure 17-1 pictures the situation.

After start-up has been accomplished, each of the $n = 4$ stations have operations that take approximately 3 minutes to perform. This is shown in Figure 17-1. However, this system had to go through start-up where, at first, only station 1 is busy; then stations 1 and 2, and so on. Finally all 4 stations are operating, as shown in Figure 17-1. Because constant (deterministic—not statistical) operation times are assumed at each station, the idle times are also constant at each station.

There has been no allowance made for workers to *rest and delay*. There is little slack (elbow room) at any of the stations and none at station 4. If there are people working at the stations, they have needs. Perhaps some person is available to relieve employees who want to use the rest rooms.

Having developed a way to visualize the operation times at stations and their comparative idle time, the best way to understand the concept of line-balancing is to study a small problem. It is useful to bear in mind that real line-balancing problems are seldom so small.

For an example, The Photo Lab is a mail-order film processor. It has developed a computer-controlled color film process that improves the quality of work while speeding up film developing and printing time. The process designers have created a flow shop that starts with mail receipt of film and money. Each cycle ends with an envelope of photo

FIGURE 17-1
A Graphic Interpretation of Work at *n* = 4 Stations, Where Cycle Time C = 3 Minutes

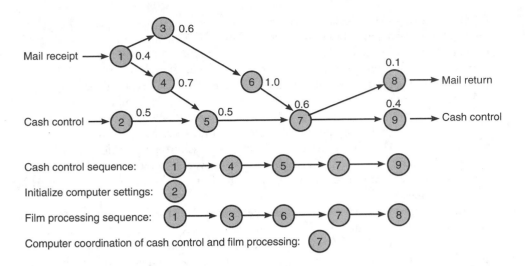

FIGURE 17-2
Precedence Diagram for The Photo Lab

prints and negatives ready for mailing and control of payments for deposit to The Photo Lab's account. At the end of each cycle, the order is completed and shipped.

17-3b The Precedence Diagram of the Serialized, Flow Shop Process

The first version submitted by the process designers to the operations team was changed after detailed discussion of contingencies that might arise. The next version was rejected by the plant manager as being difficult to service. The final process version is shown by the precedence diagram in Figure 17-2. It shows the order of operations. *Precedence diagrams are important graphic displays*, which show what operations *must* be done before others.

This sequence specifies operations that are antecedents and successors. The precedence diagram specifies the progression such that A follows or precedes B. However, the numbers on the nodes do not specify the order in which work must be done. Thus, (1) must precede (3) and (4), but (4) might be done before (3). Similarly, (2) could be done before (1) or vice versa. The lines of the diagram establish the precedence constraints. The diagram shows when precedence must be taken into account and when it does not constrain the system.

The operations that constitute the process are labeled i where $i = 1, 2, ..., k$. For each operation, an operation time, t_i, has been estimated. These times are shown in the precedence diagram of Figure 17-2 and in Table 17-2.

Operation (i)	Operation Time (t_i) in Minutes
1	0.4
2	0.5
3	0.6
4	0.7
5	0.5
6	$1.0 t_{max}$
7	0.6
8	0.1
9	0.4

TABLE 17-2

Operation Times for The Photo Lab

$t_{max} = 1.0$ minute is the longest operation time.

Operation times are estimates because the line has not been set up yet. The actual times can be estimated in various ways. For example, the estimates can be based on simulations that come close to emulating the situation that will hold after the line is running. Having correct estimates is crucial for line-balancing. Therefore, the design will first be balanced; when the system is up and running, the actual line will be rebalanced.

The design of the process, and thereby of the precedence diagram, must be approximately right. Then, the estimates of the operation times will be relatively good ones.

Next, the operations team must estimate how many orders will have to be processed per hour. Say that The Photo Lab currently processes 40 orders (envelopes) per hour, which is 320 orders per 8-hour day or 1,600 orders per week. If more orders than that are received, there will be a waiting line, which will begin to disappear when less than 320 orders are received per day.

With a processing capacity of 320 orders per 8-hour day, if 400 orders are received on a particular day, a waiting line of 80 orders will result. If, on the following day, 260 orders are received, the backlog of 80 will be reduced to 20 orders waiting. These estimates assume that overtime is not used. However, as an alternative to having a waiting line, the process can be run for more than 8 hours per day.

Mail-order film customers do not like to wait but working overtime is costly. Consequently, if the probability that more than 320 orders will be received per day is significant, then the process should be restudied and adjusted. This could arise if the business grows as customers tell their friends about the good service and prices of The Photo Shop. If 320 orders per day is reasonable, then it is sensible to proceed with line-balancing. Perhaps the rate of 40 orders per hour will be attainable under line-balanced conditions.

17-3c Cycle Time and the Number of Stations

Product (completion) output rate O is equal to the time period T divided by the cycle time C. The cycle time has been defined earlier as the time interval that the conveyor stays at each station. It is represented by Equation 17-1.

Cycle Time

T is the time period (e.g., minutes per hour) used to *match* the time dimension of the cycle time (minutes at a workstation) with the time dimension of the output rate (orders per hour).

t_i is the number of minutes required to do the ith operation at the jth station. It will always be true that $t_i \leq C$. To do the entire job (complete the order) requires $\sum_i t_i$. The output to cycle time relationship is:

$$O = T/C \text{ and } C = T/O \qquad \text{(Equation 17-1)}$$

If $O = 40$ orders per hour, and $T = 60$ minutes per hour, the indicated cycle time is $C = 60/40 = 1.5$ minutes per order.

C is the desired cycle time if the demand rate of 40 orders per hour is to be achieved. The process will be designed to have this cycle time as a lower bound. The actual cycle time chosen may be longer to allow for some idle time and to provide workers with an opportunity to rest.

Cycle time, C, in this instance, has been calculated to satisfy demand—with the assumption of perfect balance.

As another example, if daily output (8-hour day) of 300 units was required, then the cycle time would be $480/300 = 1.6$ minutes. In Figure 17-4 with $n = 3$ perfect balance exists, which means that there is no idle time. In contrast, Figure 17-1 has idle time and the line balance is not perfect.

The problem that must next be resolved is the number of workstations (n) to be chosen to deliver the finished units in the required cycle time. The technology of the process will determine how feasible it is to divide operations evenly among the workstations.

Reference to Figure 17-2 and Table 17-2 indicates that the selected output rate of 40 orders per hour may be possible. Every operation time (t_i) is shorter than the cycle time of 1.5 minutes per unit. This includes the longest time of $t_{max} = 1.0$, as shown in Table 17-2. One or more operations can be completed at any of the j stations. For example, $\Sigma_i t_i$ for the specific operations $i = 1, 2,$ and 3 sums to $C = 1.5$ minutes. They could all be done at station 1 without violating precedence constraints.

Number of Stations and Total Work Content

It is a physical reality that the number of stations n must always be an integer. For each integer number of stations, there is an associated cycle time. Consider the product $nC = constant$. As n rises, C decreases.

In this case, the right-hand side constant is the **total work content (TWC)** required to make a completed order (ship a finished unit or, in a service example, complete cleaning the house). TWC is defined in Table 17-3 as 4.8 minutes. Creative ideas about how else to do the job may change that number.

Table 17-3 shows that nine operations (i) must be completed to fill an order for The Photo Lab. The operation times to complete an order range from the shortest activity, which is operation $i = 8$ with a time of $t_i = 0.1$, to the longest operation (identified as t_{max}) for operation $i = 6$.

This sum of operation times $\Sigma_i t_i = 4.8$ minutes is called *total work content* (TWC). The equation relating cycle time (C), the number of workstations (n), and the total work content (TWC) is equal to nc, as follows:

$n*C = \Sigma_i t_i = 4.8$ minutes, and this is perfect balance.

Start with the desired output (O) of 40 completed orders per hour. Next, determine the cycle time to deliver that output. That is, $C = 60/40 = 1.5$ minutes per unit. The total work content is 4.8 minutes.

All of the relevant data are shown in Table 17-3.

When total work content is divided by the desired cycle time, it is possible to derive a noninteger value for n (called $n*$). This case is illustrated by using the data in Table 17-3.

$$n^* = \frac{TWC}{C} = \frac{\Sigma_i t_i}{C} = \frac{4.8}{1.5} = 3.2 \text{ stations}$$

This result of 3.2 stations can be viewed as a minimum (ideal, but infeasible) number of workstations. The actual number of stations n will have to be a larger integer to accommodate all operations in a physically feasible system. Going backwards, TWC cannot be changed unless the job is redesigned. So, the new cycle time for perfect balance is $C = 1.2$ minutes. This is feasible but not necessarily doable because of the assumption of perfect

Operation (i)	Operation Time (t_i) in Minutes
1	0.4
2	0.5
3	0.6
4	0.7
5	0.5
6	1.0 t_{max}
7	0.6
8	0.1
9	0.4
	4.8 = $\Sigma_i t_i$

TABLE 17-3

The Photo Lab's Processing Times

TWC = total work content = $\Sigma_i t_i$ = 4.8 minutes.

balance. The value of C is obtained by dividing the same total work content by the larger integer number of stations, as shown in Equation 17-2.

$$nC = \Sigma_i t_i \text{ and } C = \frac{\Sigma_i t_i}{n} = \frac{4.8}{4} = 1.2 \qquad \text{(Equation 17-2)}$$

Dividing the total work content time (4.8 minutes) by the new integer number of stations determines the number of minutes, C, spent by an order at each station. The cycle time C = 1.2 in Equation 17-2 also is the number of minutes occurring between completion of orders.

Line-balancing divides up the total work content, making assignments of various operations i to each workstation. This has the effect of assigning differing amounts of t_i to the workstations.

Summing up the effects of Equations 17-1 and 17-2, the desired output rate O drives the system. O is used to determine a satisfactory cycle time, C. This first value of cycle time may not be feasible because it leads to a noninteger number of stations. It may not be doable because the assumption of perfect balance is not tenable for the set of operation times. C and $TWC = \Sigma_i t_i$ are used together in Equation 17-2 to determine the number of stations n, working on different operations to fill the orders.

Each order is at a different stage of work in process and completion. The greater the number of stations, the shorter the cycle time. In general, the smaller the cycle time, the larger the output rate. But this will depend on the ability to assign work to stations so as to minimize idle time and approach perfect balance. The various options will be examined, and the most preferred line-balancing architecture will be chosen.

17-3d Cycle-Time Limits

Limits on cycle time can be established. Cycle time can be no less than the longest operation time. It can be no more than total work content time. The alternative statement is also correct and follows the symbols in Equation 17-3, namely, the longest operation time must be equal to or less than the cycle time, and the cycle time must be equal to or less than the total work content.

$$t_{max} \le C \le \Sigma_{i=1}^{i=n} t_i \qquad \text{(Equation 17-3)}$$

In Tables 17-2 and 17-3, the sixth operation has been marked t_{max} because it is the longest operation time. Cycle time must be equal to or longer than t_{max}. If C < 1.0, then the $t_{6 \text{ is max}}$ operation must be completed at more than one station. In this case, $t_6 = 1.0$ would have to be broken into two segments.

It is reasonable to ask if any t_i can be further divided, but especially the long ones. If t_{max} can be divided after the system is set up and running, that should have been done when the process was in the design phase. It *always* is beneficial to have shorter operations that can be assigned to workstations more readily than longer ones. Large t_i are difficult to assign, and they reduce line-balancing flexibility.

Cycle time must be equal to or less than total work content. This follows from using the smallest integer value of $n = 1$ in Equation 17-2, where C = 4.8/n. The Volvo method of production in Sweden assembles an entire car at one station. The cycle time that Volvo uses to assemble the car is that of the total work content. By using parallel "lines," more than one car can be assembled at the same time.

Table 17-4 presents The Photo Lab's chart of all possible cycle times C and hourly output rates O for an integer number of stations $n = 1$ through 9. Note that this chart is based on perfect balance (pb) so for each n, the total idle time is zero. Figure 17-1 does not have pb and pb may not be able to be achieved!

Several points need to be discussed about Table 17-4, Equation 3, and Figure 17-2. Then, references will be made to Figures 17-3, 17-4, and 17-5 because they illustrate related aspects of line-balancing situations.

TABLE 17-4

The Photo Lab's Chart of Possible Cycle Times, C, Also Hourly Output Rates, O = T/C, for Number of Stations, n

n	$C = \sum_i t_i / n$ in Minutes	$O = T/C = 60/C$ Orders/Hour	Total Idle Time in Minutes
1	4.8	12.5	0
2	2.4	25.0	0
3	1.6	37.5	0
4	1.2	50.0	0
*5	0.96	62.5	0
*6	0.80	75.0	0
*7	0.69	87.5	0
*8	0.60	100.0	0
*9	0.53	112.5	0

1. When the number of stations is $n = 5$, or greater, the cycle time C is less than one. This is denoted by asterisks (*) in Table 17-4. Because $t_{(max)} = 1.0$, $n \geq 5$ is not feasible. See Equation 3, which states that C must be equal to or greater than t_{max}, which is 1.0.

2. The desired output $O = 40$ orders completed per hour cannot be achieved directly with less than four stations. $O = 37.5$ with $n = 3$, which is a shortfall. Whereas, $O = 50$ when $n = 4$. If three stations are to be used, some overtime (OT) would be required, but not much, and (OT) might be approved.

3. From Table 17-4, with four stations, the cycle time is 1.2 minutes if perfect balance can be achieved. However, this line cannot be balanced with $C = 1.2$, $n = 4$, and $O = 50$. There is no way to assign the operations to four stations for perfect balance.

4. Note that in Figure 17-3 the cycle time has been enlarged to be 1.5 minutes. Then, the operations can be assigned to the four stations. There is total idle time of 1.2 minutes. Total work content plus idle time ($4.8 + 1.2 = 6.0$) is equal to the maximum capacity to do work which is $nC = 4 \times 1.5 = 6.0$.

5. As will be seen shortly, the measure of line-balance goodness that has been achieved in Figure 17-3 is 20 percent. This is not too bad given the fact that rest and delay is usually allocated about 10 percent. However, station 1 has no idle time whereas stations 2, 3, and 4 average 0.4 minute per 1.5-minute stop. That is an average of 27 percent of the total stop time. This unbalanced allocation of idle times in Figure 17-3 is not acceptable.

6. The nonworking time at each station has been denoted by $x_j = idle\ time$. The sum of idle times is $\sum_{j=1}^{j=4} x_j = 1.2$ minutes. This number is derived in Figure 17-3 at the right-hand side of the chart.

7. If the arrangement in Figure 17-3 can be adjusted so that idle times are more evenly distributed, the situation might be acceptable because a cycle time of $C = 1.5$ produces an output of $O = 40$ completed orders per hour, viz., $O = T/C = 60/1.5 = 40$. That satisfies the stated demand requirement.

FIGURE 17-3
First Line-Balancing Effort for The Photo Lab
$n = 4$; $C = 1.5$ minutes; $O = 40$ orders completed per hour; $x_j = $ idle time at station j

FIGURE 17-4
Second Effort at Line-Balancing for The Photo Lab
$n = 3$; $C = 1.6$ minutes;
$O = 37.5$ orders per hour;
idle time is zero

8. The question now arises: Is there a better arrangement of the operations at the stations that conforms to the requirements of the precedence diagram in Figure 17-2?

9. To begin, note that the arrangement shown in Figure 17-4 is feasible with respect to precedence constraints. In that scenario, cycle time has been increased to 1.6 minutes. There are $n = 3$ stations instead of $n = 4$. Output has decreased to 37.5 orders per hour, which falls short of the required 40, but there is perfect balance, which means there is no idle time. If cycle time is increased by 12.5 percent, that would yield $C = 1.8$ minutes per stop. Output decreases further to $60/1.8 = 33.33$ orders per hour. The one weakness of the scenario is the fact that 9.6 hours instead of 8 hours of production are required per day. Overtime cost has to be applied to 1.6 hours per day. This amounts to an extra 8-hour day per week at overtime.

10. Another possibility is to set up parallel production lines. For example, with perfect balance, two parallel production lines with two stations each would be able to process 50 orders per hour. This is shown in Figure 17-5. It is only practical to have perfect balance if machines and no people work at each station. Assume that people are employed and increase the cycle time by 12.5 percent for rest and delay. This raises the cycle time to $C = 2.7$ minutes. Output decreases from 25 orders per hour at each of the two parallel production lines to 22.22 for a total of 44.44 completed orders per hour. The new arrangement meets the demand of 40 orders per hour and leaves 4.44 orders per hour of excess capacity.

11. Note, for the two stations in parallel production, when $C = 3.0$, $O = 20$ with a total of 40 orders per hour. That is an increase of 25 percent in C, which is excessive for rest and delay. It matches the demand but $n = 1.6$ is infeasible.

12. There is a systems interaction to consider! If it turns out that two parallel lines, each with two stations, lowers production costs while raising the capacity of the process, then OM and marketing could set a reduced price strategy for film processing. This might increase the volume of business and total profit.

13. For cost analysis, the variable costs of production include the number of stations being managed ($c_1 n$), the use of t amount of overtime ($c_2 t$), and the cost of total idle time, $c_3 \sum_{j=1}^{j=n} x_j$. The total cost $TC = c_1 n + c_2 t + c_3 \sum_{j=1}^{j=n} x_j$.

14. It is usually assumed that operation times cannot be shortened, having been chosen as the smallest reasonable components into which the total process or job can be subdivided. This assumption can be relaxed when technological factors permit alternative arrangements. It is important to check out this assumption.

FIGURE 17-5
Perfect Balance with Two Parallel Production Lines
$n = 2$ for each production line;
$C = 2.4$ minutes; $O = 25$ orders
for a total of 50 orders per hour

17-3e Developing Station Layouts

Henceforth, stations will be labeled with Roman numerals to distinguish them from operation numbers. The procedure for developing station layouts is based on the use of precedence diagrams. Place in station I (the first column) all operations that need not follow others. Reference to Figure 17-2 shows that operations (1) and (2) can be placed in station I. See also Figure 17-6.

Then, place in station II operations that must follow those in station I. These are operations (3) and (4). Note that (5) must follow (4) and, therefore, cannot be in the second station (II). Continue to the other station columns in the same way. Thus, in Figure 17-6, The Photo Lab's operations have been placed into the maximum number of stations required by operational sequence, not by operation times.

Sequence is fully specified but column position is not fixed. For example, operation (2) could be done in either station I or II. This first feasible set of five stations is determined by the longest chain of sequenced operations, not in time, but by the number of operations in the chain.

Various orderings exist that can satisfy the precedence requirements. Intracolumn movement is totally free between operations that are mutually independent (not connected by arrows). Thus, at station II, operation (3) could be done before operation (4) or vice versa. This kind of flexibility with respect to the order with which operations are completed at a station is called **permutability of columns.**

Also, operations can be moved sideways from their columns to positions to their right without disturbing the precedence restrictions. Operations (3) and (6) could be done at the third workstation, but (3) must always precede (6). Flexibility to move sideways is called **lateral transferability.**

With this 5-station layout, the cycle time would be set at 1.5 minutes (or more) by the assigned operation times at station III. The total station operation times and idle times are shown in Table 17-5.

There is a great deal of idle time at stations I, IV, and V. Another way of representing this assignment pattern is illustrated in Table 17-6.

Using trial and error methods, efforts should be made to improve upon this line-balancing arrangement. The most promising approach is to turn to heuristic methods for line-balancing, which will be explained in Section 17-4. First, however, this section dealing with concepts of line-balancing is concluded with consideration of perfect and imperfect balance, and a new term, which is **balance delay (d).**

Station	I	II	III	IV	V
Operations	(1), (2)	(3), (4)	(5), (6)	(7)	(8), (9)
Total operation times	0.9	1.3	1.5	0.6	0.5
Idle times	0.6	0.2	0.0	0.9	1.0

TABLE 17-6

The Photo Lab's 5-Station Line-Balanced Layout

Station	i	t_i	Station Sum	Cumulative Sum	Idle Time
I	1	0.4			
	2	0.5	0.9	0.9	0.6
II	3	0.6			
	4	0.7	1.3	2.2	0.2
III	5	0.5			
	6	1.0	1.5	3.7	0.0
IV	7	0.6	0.6	4.3	0.9
V	8	0.1			
	9	0.4	0.5	4.8	1.0
Totals		4.8	4.8		2.7

17-3f Perfect Balance with Zero Balance Delay (*d*)

With cycle time C fixed by design (1.5 minutes for The Photo Lab), the number of stations under perfect balance would be $\Sigma_i t_i \div C = n$, or 4.8/1.5 = 3.2 stations, which is not feasible. The integer number of stations $n = 3$ or $n = 4$ might qualify. Three stations yield a lower production rate. Four stations provide a challenge to make use of excess capacity.

Perfect balance is not a realistic objective for a number of reasons. First, it is difficult to group operations into stations such that the total operation times at all stations are equal. Also, technological factors exist that do not permit operations to be split. Such physical restrictions are referred to as **zoning constraints**.

The system's inefficiency (or imperfect balance) is measured by a quantity *d*, called the *balance delay*. This term refers to the *percent of unproductive time* at the stations. Unproductive time is another name for idle time in a line-balanced system.

$$d = 100 (nC - \Sigma_i t_i) \div nC \qquad \text{(Equation 17-4)}$$

Balance delay *d* equals zero for all cycle times listed in Table 17-4. That is because total capacity (*nC*) is equal to total work content. Equation 5 describes the condition of perfect balance.

$$nC = \Sigma_i t_i \qquad \text{(Equation 17-5)}$$

For The Photo Lab's cycle time of 1.5 minutes, $n = 3.2$ was derived for perfect balance. Even though a noninteger value for the number of stations, $n = 3.2$, is not physically feasible, the calculations with that theoretical *n* demonstrate that $d = 0$.

$$d = 100[(3.2)(1.5) - (4.8)] \div (3.2)(1.5) = 0 \text{ percent}$$

If the integer value of $n = 4$ is used with the cycle time of 1.5 minutes, balance delay would be

$$d = 100 [(4)(1.5) - (4.8)] \div (4)(1.5) = 20 \text{ percent}$$

The illustration in Figure 17-7 aims to show that balance delay is the total idle time of all stations as a percentage of total available working time of all stations. Thus,

$$\sum_{j=1}^{j=n} x_j / nC = (\text{Total Idle Time})/(\text{Total Available Time})$$

Tables 17-5 and 17-6 show the 5-station line-balanced layout for The Photo Lab. Total idle time is 2.7 minutes out of a total work time of $5 \times 1.5 = 7.5$ minutes, which is balance delay, $d = 36$ percent. This degree of balance delay is excessive.

Balance delay is characterized as a systems measure of idle time because it relates total idle time to the total work content of the entire process. For cycle-time management,

Zoning constraints:
Technological factors exist that do not permit operations to be split between workstations.

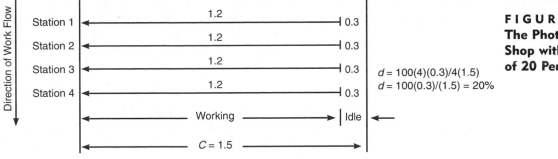

FIGURE 17-7
The Photo Lab's Flow
Shop with Balance Delay
of 20 Percent

the cost of balance delay c_4d may be a better measure than the cost of total idle time $c_3 \sum_{j=1}^{j=n} x_j$ because c_4d describes the percent of processing time that is idle.

17-3g Line Efficiency (Λ)

Line efficiency (Λ) is a related measure used to assess how well the line is balanced. It is

$$\Lambda = \frac{\sum_i t_i}{nC} \text{ where } 0 \leq \Lambda \leq 1$$

Balance delay and line efficiency expressed as a percent (i.e., 100Λ) have a linear relationship with a negative slope as follows:

$d = 100(1 - \Lambda)$. When line efficiency is one, balance delay is zero and both describe the condition of perfect balance. In the example of Tables 17-5 and 17-6, $\Lambda = 0.64$ and $100\Lambda = 64$ percent, whereas $d = 36$ percent.

> **Line efficiency:** Total work content divided by the total capacity to do work.

17-3h Rest and Delay (r & d)

Perfect balance without idle time for rest is expected for a serialized system of interconnected machines, but people require time for rest and delay. Between 10 and 20 percent of station work time normally is added to a perfectly balanced line. If the work at the station is strenuous or fatiguing (e.g., eye strain), then more r & d is added. It is common to call this allowance r & d, but it is in no way related to the R & D of "research and development."

From a systems perspective, cycle-time management has trade-offs to consider between longer cycle times using people and shorter cycle times using technology. Also, with technology it is easier to achieve perfect balance and to maintain greater control over variability. Machines require maintenance and often that can be provided during an off-shift. Also, flexible computer-controlled machines allow using modular product designs, which provides greater market variety while enjoying the benefits of dedicated flow shop technology.

17-4 HEURISTIC LINE-BALANCING

The term *heuristic* has been used by Simon and Newell[1] to describe a common-sense approach to problem solving and decision making. Heuristic models utilize logic derived by observation and introspection. Heuristic approaches replace mathematical optimization efforts when optimization is not sensible or feasible. Heuristic line-balancing uses rules of thumb to set near-equal workloads at successive stations.

Complex formulations of linear programming have been devised to obtain solutions to the line-balancing problem, but in practice they are not acceptable. Heuristic approaches are faster and offer more opportunities for testing alternative solutions. For practicality, they require computer software.

The essence of the heuristic approach is in the application of selective routines that reduce the complexity of a problem. Thus, the assembly line-balancing problem can be treated by simulating the decision-making pattern of managers when faced with this problem. The advantages of this approach are consistency of the decision rules, speed of application, and, by using the computer, the ability to cope with large systems.

The key is to trace out and then embody the thinking process that an intelligent decision maker uses to resolve the line-balancing problem. A few popular heuristics will be described. References will be given to other heuristics with brief descriptions of what they do.

If the product or service output of the flow shop is expected to have a long and stable life cycle, then engineering design will be the preferred method for line-balancing. On the other hand, when the output life cycle is not stable over a long time, shorter-term flow shops (including intermittent flow shops) are needed. These are ideally suited for heuristic resolution.

17-4a Kilbridge and Wester's (K & W) Heuristic

Kilbridge and Wester[2] proposed a heuristic procedure that *assigns a number* to each operation describing how many predecessors it has. This is done using the appropriate precedence diagram. The operations are *rank ordered* according to the number of predecessors each has. Operations with zero predecessors are ranked first in line. They are followed by operations with 1 predecessor, then 2 predecessors, etc.

Then, the *assignments to stations* are made. The first operations assigned to workstations are those with the lowest predecessor numbers. Zero is first, then 1, then 2, etc.

The procedure is illustrated in Tables 17-7 and 17-8, where The Photo Lab is experimenting with the K & W heuristic for an $n = 3$ station design with cycle time $C = 4.8/3 = 1.6$ minutes. The number of predecessors for each operation is obtained using Figure 17-2. The results are listed in Table 17-7.

Operations are assigned to stations in the order of the least number of predecessors. For station I, select operations (2) and (1) in that order because of the following rule for ties. They have a total operation time of 0.9, which leaves 0.7 free time in station I. This follows from $C = 1.6$.

Next, based on tied predecessor numbers, either introduce operation (3) with $t_i = 0.6$ or operation (4) with $t_i = 0.7$ into station I. Following the rule for ties, choose operation (4).

The Rule for Ties

When ties exist, the following rule applies. Choose first the *longest* operation times *that can be used*. Short operations are saved because they are easier to fit into stations later. In this way, upstream stations (with earlier work) are given the least idle time possible. As a result of this rule, in Table 17-8 operation (2) is assigned before (1). Also operation (4) is assigned before operation (3).

TABLE 17-7		
Operation	**Number of Predecessors**	t_i
1	0	0.4
2	0	0.5
3	1	0.6
4	1	0.7
6	2	1.0
5	3	0.5
7	6	0.6
8	7	0.1
9	7	0.4

The Photo Lab Operations Ranked by the Number of Predecessors

Station	I	t_i	Station Sum	Cumulative Sum	Idle Time
I	2	0.5			
	1	0.4			
	4	0.7	1.6	1.6	0
II	3	0.6			
	6	1.0	1.6	3.2	0
III	5	0.5			
	7	0.6			
	9	0.4			
	8	0.1	1.6	4.8	0
Totals		4.8	4.8		0

TABLE 17-8

K & W Heuristic with Cycle Time 1.6 Minutes

Continuing with K & W Assignments

Because operation (4) is assigned to station I, this results in total work time of 1.6 for station I, which is now fully assigned and has no idle time.

Attending to station II, of the remaining nonassigned operations, number (3) has the least number of predecessors (1). It is assigned to station II. Next comes operation (6) with two predecessors. Station II with operations (3) and (6) has a total working time of 1.6. Station II is fully assigned with no idle time.

If operation (6) had required more time than was available at station II, then operation (5) would have been chosen. Operations (7), (8), and (9) could not be used until both operations (5) and (6) are used. That is the information shown in Figure 17-2 about precedent constraints. Operations (7), (8), and (9) will be placed in a station further downstream (later work).

When an operation with the smallest number of predecessors has too long an operation time to be included in the station, the heuristic is programmed to look for the operation with the next smallest number of predecessors that fits the available time at the station and observes precedent constraints. Thus, operations (5), (7), (9), and (8) are assigned at station III, which is fully assigned and has no idle time. Note that operation (9) is assigned before (8) because of the rule concerning ties.

Perfect balance has been achieved using the K & W heuristic. This is shown in Table 17-8. The precedence diagram in Figure 17-8 is subdivided in accordance with Table 17-8 assignments. Three perfectly balanced stations can be used if the technology permits. Assume that people work at the stations. Then, add (say) 0.2 for rest and delay. This adds 12.5 percent to the cycle time. Perfect balance output would be 60/1.6 = 37.5 orders per hour (see Table 17-4). With rest and delay, the output would be further reduced to 60/1.8 = 33 1/3 orders per hour.

At the end of the day, instead of 320 orders being processed, there would be 266 2/3 orders completed. That is 53 1/3 orders shy of expected demand. Dividing 53 1/3 by 33 1/3

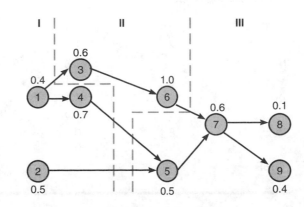

FIGURE 17-8

The Photo Lab's $n = 3$ Assignment Using Kilbridge and Wester's Heuristic with $C = 1.6$ Minutes

yields 1.6 hours of overtime per day (or 8 hours per week) to correct the situation. There are lots of other alternatives including use of the $n = 4$ station line-balance solution.

17-4b Other Heuristics

Helgeson and Birnie's (H & B) heuristic suggested first assigning to stations those operations whose followers have the largest total time. This is the sum of all successors' operations times.[3]

$\sum_i t_i$ i = all followers

H & B called their approach the "ranked positional weight" method.

In Table 17-9 each operation of The Photo Lab example is associated with a weight equal to the sum of all operation times that follow it. Operations are then ranked by descending order of the weight measure.

Check Figure 17-2 to develop the set of weights that appear in Table 17-9. As one example, operations (3), (4), (5), (6), (7), (8), and (9) (not 2) follow operation (1). The sum of these operations' times is 3.9. This is the weight given to operation (1) in Table 17-9.

Similarly, operations (8) and (9) follow operation (7). The sum of their operations' times is 0.5, which is the weight for operation (7) in Table 17-9. One more example uses operation (5), which is followed by (8) and (9) as well as (7). Adding (7)'s time of 0.6 to those of (8) and (9) yields 1.1, which is the weight assigned to operation (5) in Table 17-9.

H & B Assignments

The operations have been assigned to the stations in accordance with the weights. The largest weight is 3.9 for operation (1) and it goes first. Next is operation (3) with a weight of 2.1, and so on. Note that the cycle time of 1.6 minutes was selected to allow comparison with the results of the Kilbridge and Wester heuristic. Four stations are required to use $C = 1.6$ minutes.

Figure 17-9 shows the precedence diagram divided into four station sectors.

Operations are assigned without violating precedence or zoning constraints. When the total time for a station is exceeded, the attempt is made to find an operation further down the list that is feasible. In the case of station I, there are no other downstream operations that are feasible.

The heuristic requires that operations (1) and (3) be included as part of station I. Operations (2), (4), and (6) are the only ones that might then be assigned without violating precedence. The total time for operations (1), (3), and (4) is 1.7 minutes. For (1), (3), and (6), it is two minutes. For (1), (3), and (2), it is 1.5 minutes, and so that was used.

TABLE 17-9

H & B Heuristic with Cycle Time = 1.6 Minutes

Station	Operation in Ranked Order	Station Weight W_t	Station Time t_i	Station Sum	Station Idle Time
I	1	3.9	0.4		
	3	2.1	0.6		
	2	1.6	0.5	1.5	0.1
II	4	1.6	0.7		
	5	1.1	0.5	1.2	0.4
III	6	1.1	1.0		
	7	0.5	00.6	1.6	0.0
IV	8	0	0.1		
	9	0	0.4	0.5	1.1
Totals				4.8	1.6

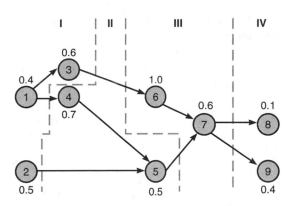

FIGURE 17-9
The Photo Lab Assignment Using Helgeson and Birnie's Heuristic $n = 4$; $C = 1.6$ Minutes

With $n = 3$, the cycle time of 1.6 minutes is fully used up at station III. At station I, the idle time is 0.1, which is close to zero. If stations III and I are not staffed by people but entirely run by machines, then this arrangement might have possibilities. However, station IV is badly underutilized. Perhaps a later inspection or packaging activity could be added to station IV.

The H & B approach does not yield three stations but results in four stations operating under the cycle time of 1.6. Overall, the four stations are unbalanced, and idle time (balance delay) is uneven and high:

$$d = 100(4 \times 1.6 - 4.8)/(4 \times 1.6) = 25 \text{ percent}$$

This same result is obtained by adding up the total idle time in Table 17-9, dividing it by total station time, and making it a percent, i.e., $100[1.6/(4 \times 1.6)] = 25$ percent.

Tonge's Heuristic for Line-Balancing

Tonge's heuristic develops a learning procedure[4] that rewards success and penalizes failure by increasing and decreasing the probability of selecting a heuristic randomly from a catalog of heuristics. Each heuristic assigns operations to stations on its own basis. Those heuristics that require the least number of stations are rewarded. Those that require a greater number of stations are penalized.

Among the set of heuristics employed to establish preference for choosing the next operation to be assigned to a station are

A. Longest operation time, t_i

B. Largest number of immediate followers

C. Random choice of the next operation, i

All assignments are made subject to nonviolations of precedence and zoning constraints.

The choice of heuristic is determined by $p(A)$, $p(B)$, and $p(C)$. These probabilities sum to one. Initially they are all equal, i.e., 1/3. Then, according to the success of the heuristic chosen, the associated probabilities are increased or decreased.

Tonge concludes that this probabilistic approach results in fewer workstations than any single heuristic taken alone—or by random choice of operations.

Arcus' Heuristic for Line-Balancing

Arcus' heuristic[5] sets the pattern for random generation of feasible sequences. All assignments are made subject to not violating any constraints based on precedence, zoning, and feasibility relations. The computer program generates 1,000 line-balance arrangements. The line-balance arrangement chosen is that one out of a 1,000 that requires the minimum number of stations.

On computers in the decade 2010, large problems take a very few minutes to generate thousands of sequences. It is historically interesting to note Arcus' experience in 1966 with a relatively small problem. Arcus reported that the generation of 1,000 sequences for a system of 70 operations on an IBM 7090 required 30 minutes.

It should be noted that for very large problems, the objective of minimizing the number of workstations—with cycle time given—makes good sense. The cycle time is chosen with the output rate in mind.

Also, in spite of its antiquity, E.J. Ignall's article[6] is one of the best summaries of line-balancing approaches.

17-5 STOCHASTIC LINE-BALANCING

Another facet of the line-balancing problem occurs when operation times at the workstations are variable. Most machines have relatively constant operation times; workers do not. Without planning for variability, bottlenecks can arise. Then, a WIP buildup occurs. If a paced conveyor is being used, it may have to be stopped, or other steps must be taken to keep the line moving.

When operation times are randomly distributed over time, they are said to be stochastic. To illustrate, The Photo Lab's operation (6) might vary 95 percent of the time between 0.6 minute and 1.4 minutes with the average time being 1.0 minute. In a system such as shown in Figure 17-7, where the line balance with idle time is nearly perfect, consider the effect if operation (6) shifts from 1.0 to 1.4. The built in leeway is only 0.3, so this production line must stop.

When work at a station can exceed the allotted time, a plan is needed. The alternatives are:

1. Let the unfinished or defective item move on to the next station. Depending on the nature of the problem, successive stations may or may not continue to work on the item.

2. Develop a group of special workers who can shift from station to station to provide extra help as needed.

3. Label this item so it can be removed at the end of the line and reworked then. Stations will not continue to work on items so labeled.

4. Stop the line and correct the problem. This applies not only to the product but also to the part of the process that created the problem.

5. Remove the defective item as soon as it is discovered and let the line move on without it. Downstream stations will have to wait until good items start to reach them again. Take the item to a rework area.

Each plan has a cost that can be determined with analysis. Other plans can be developed that might be more appropriate.

As far as line-balancing is concerned, operation times should be increased to reflect longest times that might be experienced with each operation. The number of standard deviations used will depend on the severity of the penalty that will be paid for having exceeded the cycle time of the paced conveyor. Severe penalties might require more than 3-sigma protection.

The longer operation times used for planning will lead to more stations being required in order to deliver the specified output. The cost for protection against extra long operation times is more stations to manage and increased idle time at those stations. The trade-off analysis must be done with reasonable estimates of the costs to determine what policies to follow.

Generally, methods of statistical process control can be used effectively to control, and sometimes reduce, the variability of the operation times. Programs of total quality management can be started with emphasis on seeking suggestions for improvement from those working on the process.

17-5a Queuing Aspects of Line-Balancing

Queues can form when stochastic behavior characterizes any operation time t_i. The word *stochastic* is commonly used to describe the process that causes a waiting line for service to

Queue

$\lambda = 3$ $\mu = 4$

FIGURE 17-10
A Single-Channel Workstation

form. Say that t_2 and t_4 in Figure 17-6 have variable operation times. This means that operation (5) in station III is sometimes idle while at other times there is a queue made up of different numbers of completed twos (2) and fours (4).

In the same way, assume that t_5 of operation (5) is variable. This affects station IV, and consequently V, with fluctuations of arrivals leading to queues sometimes and idleness at other times. Queuing theory has the ability to describe what happens in such systems.

Queuing theory begins by characterizing arrival rates according to their type of variability. The classic case is random arrivals (Poisson distributed) and random service intervals (exponentially distributed). Although that is frequently a good descriptor, sometimes arrivals are constant (or fall between random and constant). Special cycle-time management is required when variability characterizes operation times.

The paced conveyor is not practical when variability exists for either arrival times or service times. Then, line-balancing is achieved by putting the right amount of service power in place to handle the arrivals. Such balance changes over time as demand cycles from peak loads to normal and below normal loads.

The behavior of **single-channel systems** (e.g., a single workstation) can be described as an input–output system with variable arrivals and variable service times. It is illustrated in Figure 17-10 with an arrival rate λ and a service rate μ. The figure shows that a queue of four has formed in front of the station.

Assume that the workstation has an average output capability of four units per hour ($\mu = 4.0$). μ is the average of a Poisson distribution. The arrival rate of orders averages three per hour ($\lambda = 3.0$). λ is the average of a Poisson distribution.

> **Single-channel systems:** With variable service times and variable arrival rates, a line starts to form when the number of arrivals $n > 1$, during an average service period.

Assumptions for These Queuing Models

The use of this queuing model makes certain specific assumptions. First, the source of arrivals is large enough to be considered infinite. Second, there are unlimited accommodations for a waiting line. Third, service is granted on a first-come, first-served or FIFO basis. Fourth, it already has been stated that this analysis and the equations that follow apply to single-service channels. Fifth, the arrival and service distributions are Poisson. If intervals between arrivals and between services are used (instead of the numbers of events), then both distributions are exponential.

17-5b Single-Channel Equations[7]

$$p = \frac{\lambda}{\mu} = \text{the systems utilization factor}$$

The **systems utilization factor,** for the single channel, is the average number of orders being serviced over time. With a single-channel system, ρ (rho) is the average percent of time that the station is providing service. ρ must be less than one because if it is one or greater, then the system is always occupied and the waiting line will grow indefinitely. Thus: $\rho < 1.0$ is required.

$L = L_q + \rho$ = the average number of orders in the system, which comprises the average number of orders waiting in line (L_q) and the average number of orders being served (ρ).

$$W_q = \frac{L_q}{\lambda} = \text{the average time that an order spends online}$$

L_q was defined as the average number of orders waiting in line. An equation for the L_q of a single-channel station will be given shortly.

> **Systems utilization factor:** Average percent of time that the M-server system is providing service.

$$W = W_q + \frac{1}{\mu} = \text{ the average time that an order spends in the system. It consists of}$$

the average time spent waiting plus the average service time, $1/\mu$.

Figure 17-10 shows the single-channel situation where $\lambda = 3$ and $\mu = 4$. Although the station's output capacity is greater than the demand rate, a waiting line can be expected to develop from time to time. This occurs when either the variable demand becomes greater than the average lambda (λ) and/or the variable service rate falls below the average μ(mu). If both occur simultaneously, the resultant queue can be of formidable size.

Equation 17-6 describes the average number of units in the queue. It is

$$L_q = \frac{\rho^2}{(1 - \rho)} \qquad \text{(Equation 17-6)}$$

where

$$\rho = \frac{\lambda}{\mu} = \frac{3}{4} = 0.75$$

The value of 0.75 or 3/4 is the average number of orders being serviced, and the system's utilization.

For the numerical example, on average 2.25 orders are waiting in queue and 3.00 are in the system:

$$L_q = \frac{9}{4} = 2.25 \text{ orders}$$

and $L = L_q + \rho = 2.25 + 0.75 = 3.00$, which is the average number of orders in the system.

Using Equation 17-6, the equation for L becomes

$$L = L_q + \rho = \frac{(\rho)}{(1 - \rho)}$$

Further, the average time that an order spends in line is

$$W_q = \frac{L_q}{\lambda} = 2.25/3 = 0.75 \text{ hour}$$

And the average time that an order spends in the system is

$$W = W_q + \frac{1}{\mu} = 0.75 + 0.25 = 1.00 \text{ hour}$$

Note that as long as there is a waiting line, the average cycle time between successive completed orders is 0.25 hour or 15 minutes. This means that when there is a waiting line, the station's output rate is four orders per hour. However, output drops to zero when there are no orders in the system. To find out what percent of the time the station is not working, it is useful to determine the probability distribution of system occupancy. Using that distribution some additional insights can be gained.

The probability distribution is denoted by (P_n), where (P_n) equals the probability that the total number of orders in the system is (n). When $n = 0$, there are no orders and the station is idle. When $n = 1$, the station is working but no orders are waiting. When $n = 2$, the station is working (setup times included) and one order is waiting. The pattern continues for $n > 2$.

The values of P_n are derived from Equation 17-7.

$$P_n = (1 - \rho)\rho^n \qquad \text{(Equation 17-7)}$$

Table 17-10 shows the calculations for $\rho = 0.75$.

Figure 17-11 shows the probability distribution for n orders being in the system. The area of the tail of this distribution is the probability (α) that the queue length will exceed $(n - 1)$ for $\rho = 0.75$.

The graph states the probability that the queue will be longer than eight is 0.0563.

This is determined by $\rho(\alpha, n = 9) = \left(1 - \sum_{n=0}^{n=9} P_n \right) = (1 - 0.9437) = 0.0563.$

N	P_n		Probability Density	Cumulative Probability
0	$P_0 = (1 - \rho)$	=	0.2500	0.2500
1	$P_1 = (1 - \rho)\rho$		0.1875	0.4375
2	$P_2 = (1 - \rho)\rho^2$	=	0.1406	0.5781
3	$P_3 = (1 - \rho)\rho^3$	=	0.1055	0.6836
4	*	=	0.0791	0.7627
5	*	=	0.0593	0.8220
6	*	=	0.0445	0.8665
7	*	=	0.0334	0.8999
8	*	=	0.0250	0.9249
9	*	=	0.0188	0.9437
10	*	=	0.0141	0.9578
*	*	=	*	*
*	*	=	*	*
*	*	=	*	*
n	$P_n = (1 - \rho)\rho^n$	etc.	etc.	etc.

TABLE 17-10

Distributions for Single-Channel Queuing Model with Assumptions (above) and $\rho = 0.75$

Work waiting for processing can be expected to be greater than eight more than 5 percent of the time. If only eight units can be stored in front of the station, then at least 5 percent of the time the system will turn away arriving orders and/or shut down. Because this is clearly undesirable, steps should be taken to decrease the probability of exceeding eight units in queue, or to provide more storage space. Storage and waiting problems that can stop production typify cycle-time management for stochastic systems.

Other performance characteristics of this system are apparent from Table 17-10. The station will be idle 25 percent of the time as reflected by $P_0 = 0.25$.

Workstation output is given by Equation 17-8.

Expected output = $(1 - P_0) \mu = (0.75)(4) = 3$ units per hour   (Equation 17-8)

Expected daily output is $3(8) = 24$ units per day. Cycle-time management can take on the task of increasing μ. This might be done by adding an additional station.

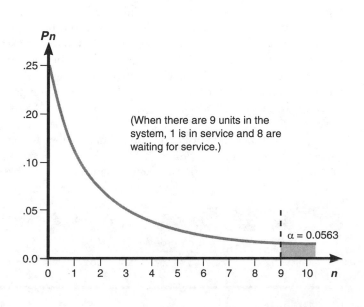

FIGURE 17-11
Probability Density Distribution for $\rho = 0.75$

(When there are 9 units in the system, 1 is in service and 8 are waiting for service.)

$\alpha = 0.0563$

FIGURE 17-12
Multiple-Channel
Workstations Single Queue
(called a Red Carpet)

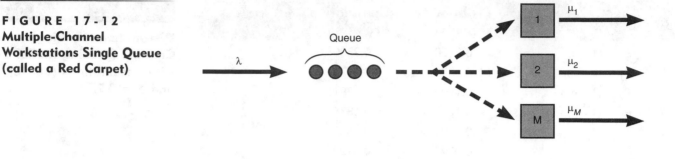

FIGURE 17-12
Multiple-Channel
Workstations Single Queue
(called a Red Carpet)

17-5c Multiple-Channel Equations[8]

Figure 17-12 shows a queue of four orders with arrival rate μ waiting for service by M **multiple-channel stations,** which have service rates of $\mu_1, \mu_2,..., \mu_M$. This kind of waiting system, used by many banks, airline ticket windows, and the post office is called a Red Carpet.

> **Multiple-channel stations:** Effect of multiple channels (stations, servers, systems) is to provide greater systems capacity and to lower the system's utilization.

The system utilization factor when there are M servers is

$$\rho = \frac{\lambda}{M\mu}$$ (Equation 17-9)

To avoid infinite waiting lines $\lambda < M\mu$, which insures that $\rho < 1$ will hold. If the decision is made to use two parallel stations, then M = 2 and

$$\rho = \frac{\lambda}{2\mu} = \frac{3}{8}$$ (Equation 17-10)

when $\lambda = 3$ and $\mu = 4$, as before.

The multiple-channel equations for L, w, etc., are much more complex than for single-channel systems, so only the result is now shown of adding another station. Table 17-11 compares the total number of orders (L) that are in the system—waiting and being serviced. It also compares P_0, which for M = 1 means one station is idle and for M = 2 means both stations are idle.

An additional strategy is available for cycle-time management. If the single-channel workstation can be mechanized so that the service intervals are constant, then L will be reduced by about 35 to 45 percent. Less variability of service times produces significant reductions in waiting lines and in cycle time.

Finally, the kind of system that is being managed can vary greatly. The service units can be part of a job shop. Each station stands alone as an individual, stochastic input–output system providing batch service. When the flow shop configuration is used, then the various service units are interrelated, and the outputs of one system become the inputs to another. This requires careful coordination and matching of the stochastic behaviors of systems that are depending upon each other.

Queues can be comprised of customers' orders waiting for service, WIP waiting for the next machine, airplanes waiting to be cleared to land, or cars waiting at the tollbooth. The waiting line is invisible but present when a busy signal is encountered on the telephone line. Express checkout lanes in supermarkets alter the FIFO priority and would require other models. Parking garages put up the sign "Sorry Full," which turns away arrivals.

Queuing models do not provide optimum solutions for output rates and cycle times. They provide descriptive measures. OM evaluates various designs using these descriptive measurements of queuing criteria. Design changes are made based on test results, and the system is retested. This goes on until a satisfactory production line is obtained.

TABLE 17-11	M = 1	M = 2	Percent Change
Comparison of One and Two Stations with $\lambda = 3$ and $\mu = 4$			
L	3.00 orders	0.85 orders	−72%
P_0	0.25	0.39	+56%

Many different models exist, and most of them have been fully explored in the literature. When the situation does not lend itself to mathematical analysis, then simulation can be used to determine the behavior of the service system (see Chapter 17's Supplement).

17-6   JUST-IN-TIME DELIVERY

In line-balance terminology, each station is a customer for the "supplier" station that precedes it. Just-in-time is a cycle-time management principle that states that delivery to the next station of a specified amount of material is to be made when and *only when that next station is ready* to receive that delivery. Just-in-time (JIT) delivery requires agreement between suppliers and buyers of what, when, where, and how much. It should be noted that JIT puts production at risk in the event that something happens to the supplier or to the supplier's shipper. Thus, risk reduction is achieved by carrying extra stock. This policy is referred to as *just-in-case*.

A **kanban** is any method that calls attention to the fact that the next station wishes to receive a JIT delivery. Kanban is a card used in Japanese manufacturing plants to signal that a delivery will be needed. The word has been adopted all over the world to describe an array of signaling devices that include colorful squares that iindicatea need for supplies when uncovered. Other signals are ping-pong balls dropping through tubes, and lights flashing.

The same concept applies to outside suppliers making deliveries as required by what is needed by the producer. The details require specification of when, where, and how much. Various plants and distributors' warehouses are built with walls that open anywhere along the production line. In this way, supplies can be delivered where they are needed on the production line. Automobile-assembly plants reduce JIT delivery risks by having suppliers located on adjacent land right outside the plant.

Production systems that signal for delivery from upstream stations (including from outside suppliers) are known as **pull-production systems.** They pull materials as they need them to work on. In contrast, production systems that push materials on the downstream stations are regarded as impeding productivity. The smooth flows and balanced cycle times of pull-production systems are gradually replacing the **push-production systems** of earlier production eras.

What accounts for workstations pushing as much WIP as possible onto the next workstation? The motivating factor for such performance is often the accounting system, which records the utilization of workers and equipment and rewards people for using equipment and producing product. The focus is on keeping busy. The result is process bottlenecks and storage space filled with unfinished product, which has carrying costs. Smooth running JIT type pull systems have multiplicative advantages over the management accounting model, which encourages full utilization of all resources and facilities.

Serialized production systems, which are not connected by paced-conveyor belts, must often compensate for variable arrival and service rates. These systems are allowed to work free with kanban serving as the communication link to coordinate the interdependent activities. Such systems are line balanced so that there is the same average amount of work at each station. They also are balanced as much as possible with respect to the amount of variability that characterizes each station.

The previous description also applies to balancing the flows in the supply chain. When strong relationships have been developed with suppliers, the effect of the externality of the supplier to the producer can be minimized. There is rapid communication, trust, and a sense of mutual responsibility. Also, there is less difference between adjacent stations that are entirely within the plant, and adjacent stations that are in two different plants.

There is shared confidence that the quality control system of the supplier will ensure that standards are met or bettered. Deliveries are regular and reliable. Problems at either end are immediately shared. Improvements are suggested by both parties for the other's plants. Suppliers operating in this environment are regarded as part of the buyer's team. The supplier's cycle-time management is the buyer's concern and vice versa.

Another form of cycle-time management that connects suppliers and buyers is *vendor releasing*. This is an agreement that the buyer makes to purchase a quantity that entitles

Kanban: Calls attention to a workstation's need to receive a just-in-time (JIT) delivery.

Pull-production systems: Systems that call for delivery of materials from upstream stations (including outside suppliers) are pulling materials as needed.

Push-production systems: Workstations pushing materials on the downstream stations are impeding productivity. Poor line balance aggravates the situation, causing uneven output.

the buyer to a discount. However, the supplier is in a position to make regular deliveries of parts of the total quantity purchased. To illustrate, six months of supply can be purchased at one time with weekly deliveries of specific amounts that can be changed as per agreement.

Suppliers that offer vendor releasing often can do so because they have other customers, which allows them to produce in larger volumes. By producing either continuously or in substantial economic lot quantities, shipments are permitted directly from the line and only occasionally from stock. Steel and aluminum companies use this delivery cycle-control technique to sell big quantities of product to customers who could not otherwise buy large amounts to earn discounts because they lack storage space.

Volkswagen AG has a plant in the rural town of Resende, Brazil, which is a modular-based consortium. A dozen suppliers coexist within the plant, each contributing their specialized parts to the 1,000 trucks per day that are output. Modularity of design allows a number of different models to be constructed without having to redesign the way that parts from different suppliers (seats, dashboards, chassis) fit together. The production line is well balanced, and the system functions well because of good communications and trust between the parties. VW Resende announced doubling its investment in the plant as of April 1, 2002.[9]

17-7 PUSH- VERSUS PULL-PROCESS DISCIPLINE

As an example of the conversion from a push-production system to a pull-production system, consider the following situation. Say that Joe toasts hamburger buns and Josephine puts the burger between the buns and adds tomatoes, pickles, relish, and sauce. Further, assume that Joe's toaster produces 10 finished crowns and heels per minute while Josephine's production is 6 burgers per minute.

If both work at their top capacities, Joe is pushing 4 extra buns per minute on Josephine; her queue will grow to 240 buns in an hour and to almost 2,000 by the end of the 8-hour shift. Push-production processes are relentless in their overfeeding of the bottleneck process, which in this case is Josephine's operation. To prevent absurd queues from growing, Joe shifts to the french fries department whenever there is no more space left on which to push the finished buns.

Josephine is a student of OM. She has learned about a manufacturing process that uses kanban to signal the need for supplies. From Josephine's point of view, the simplest kanban would be a yellow square on which Joe placed toasted buns whenever the square had no buns on it. The ideal quantity to be called for would be one bun at a time.

To produce this result, Joe's conventional toaster, which delivers all finished goods in a batch, should be replaced with a circular toaster, as shown in Figure 17-13.

Like a Ferris wheel that stops every so often to let passengers depart and new ones embark, the circular toaster deposits a finished bun (crown and heel) and is reloaded to start toasting every 10 seconds. This permits Joe to feed buns to Josephine as they are needed. When the demand drops off, because the peak period is past, Josephine slows

FIGURE 17-13
Serialized Toasting Permits Pull Process

down and makes fewer burgers per minute. Joe must then adjust the bun-loading pattern to feed the bottleneck activity at the rate that it needs to be fed. Josephine has succeeded in pulling buns as needed.

If demand exceeds the capacity of Josephine to make burgers, then a swing person (such as the manager) starts to work alongside Josephine. The setting is turned up on the toaster and its speed of rotation is increased. This effectively increases its throughput rate without jeopardizing quality. The flexibility of the pull system is dependent upon the speed control of the feeding systems.

The pop-up toaster that was formerly used produced a batch of 10 finished buns every minute, and these were delivered en masse to Josephine. Joe thought that he was doing a great job when he really loaded up Josephine's workstation because that is the criterion of high productivity when using a push system. Customers are much happier with the pull one-at-a-time system initiated by Josephine. The buns are fresher. Josephine is happier too because she sets the pace and is not always working to reduce the bun inventory that swamps her workplace.

There is more than ample evidence that pushing output on the next workstation is counterproductive. The pull number does not have to be one. Josephine might have preferred to have two buns delivered to her every time her kanban square was empty.

Pushing production is based on two concepts:

1. The independence of adjacent workstations in the process
2. The objective of having everyone, and every facility, work at maximum capacity

Both points represent nonsystems thinking. Adjacent workstations in any process should be viewed as interdependent. They are connected by material transfer systems, and successive stages of work entail product design dependencies. Workstations always are connected by common systems objectives, which include waste reduction of all kinds including space, WIP, and time.

Hewlett-Packard (HP) has made an exceptional videotape (titled *Stockless Production*) at their Greeley Division in Colorado. It has been used internally to demonstrate to their employees the effectiveness of moving from push- to pull-type production systems.

An intermittent flow shop was set up to make a mock product. The production line consisted of five stations, each with one person doing simple operations to a styrofoam insert that was then put into a cardboard box. The line did not appear to be balanced, but each of the five stations had about the same amount of work to do.

Three different production arrangements were tested. The first pushed six completed units from each station to the next one. The second pulled three units and the third pulled one unit.

The five evaluation measures used were space required, work in process, cycle time, rework quantity, and problem visibility. HP measured cycle time as the interval between start work on a part and its completion. It is shown to be correlated with both work in process and the rework quantity. To determine rework quantity, defective material inserted into the line was detected at the fifth and final station. All work in process queued up between stations was counted to determine how much rework would be required once the problem was spotted.

Table 17-12 shows the results of these push versus pull comparisons.

There is a decrease of 90 percent in cycle time between push 6 and pull 1. The decrease in WIP and rework quantity also is about 90 percent. Space needs are cut in half because WIP is down to four units. Problems can be spotted immediately because the WIP clutter is removed. Everyone who views this tape agrees that the push- versus pull-pilot experiment is impressive. Process visibility had improved so much that the production manager commented that it might be possible to consider automating the line.

JIT processing was a by-product of the switch from push to pull-one production. Cycle-time management is enhanced by this transformation of the process. Line-balancing is a natural outgrowth of the change. No investment was required other than the will to change. There were no costs and the savings are evident and significant. The applicability of this method to real production systems and supply chain functions is immense.

TABLE 17-12		Push 6	Pull 3	Pull 1
Results of the Push Versus Pull Comparison	Space used	2 tables	2 tables	1 table
	Work in progress (WIP)	30 units	12 units	4 units
	Cycle times	3' 17"	1' 40"	0' 19"
	Rework quantity	26 units	10 units	3 units
	Problem visibility	Hidden	Hidden	Visible

SUMMARY

Cycle-time management is the management of the interval between finished goods coming off the production line or the interval between completion of servicing operations. Cycle-time management also is the management of how long work remains at workstations and how much idle time there is at the stations. Line-balancing is used to provide near-equal assignments to all workstations. This prevents some stations from being overloaded while others are idle. Cycle-time management is a form of TBM (time-based management) related to synchronization of material flows including those from suppliers.

The different approaches to line-balancing consist of the deterministic, heuristic, and stochastic models. All require designing the best possible processes using precedence diagrams of serialized flow systems. The general objective is to obtain the desired production output with the minimum number of stations and the least amount of idle time.

Perfect balance, which has zero balance delay, still needs rest time added if people are working on the line. Heuristic models include Kilbridge and Wester's (K & W) line-balancing techniques.

This heuristic approach, as well as others, are discussed. The heuristic models are needed for complex intermittent flow shop systems because the problems are too large for optimization models, and they are too important to ignore the benefits of line-balancing.

Stochastic line-balancing deals with the effects of variability in cycle management. This includes consideration of a variety of queuing models. It should be pointed out that a primary function of queuing models is to facilitate the design of balanced-service systems (requests for service and servicing capabilities) throughout the supply chain. The discussion includes suppliers' participation in effective cycle-time management.

Chapter 17 contains two examples of the conversion of push-production systems to pull-one-unit production systems. The advantages of pull-one unit are detailed. The Chapter 17 supplement deals with simulation of stochastic line-balanced queuing models.

Two spotlight feature boxes conclude this chapter. These boxes illustrate real applications of the material in the chapter. See Spotlight 17-1: Where the Race is Won and Spotlight 17-2: Balanced Scorecards: No Longer Looking through the Rear-View Mirror.

KEY TERMS

Balance delay (d)
Cycle time
Deterministic line-balancing
Heuristic line-balancing methods
Kanban
Lateral transferability
Line-balancing (LB)

Line efficiency
Multiple-channel stations
Paced conveyor
Perfect balance (pb)
Permutability of columns
Precedence diagram
Pull-production systems

Push-production systems
Single-channel systems
Stochastic line-balancing
Systems utilization factor
Time-based management (TBM)
Total work content (TWC)
Zoning constraints

REVIEW QUESTIONS

1. What is cycle-time management?

2. What is line-balancing?

3. How does line-balancing relate to cycle-time management?

4. Do line-balancing and cycle-time management apply to services as well as material products?

5. What is the difference between deterministic and stochastic line-balancing? Can a paced conveyor be used for either one? Explain your answer.

6. Why is it said that heuristic line-balancing is a practical approach to achieving a reasonably good intermittent flow shop? Can a paced conveyor be used for the resulting production line? Explain your answer.

7. Explain why heuristic line-balancing is associated with computer software to run the algorithms.

8. Why is perfect balance often regarded as an unrealistic goal? When is that not the case?

9. Explain permutability of columns.

10. What does lateral transferability mean for line-balancing?

11. What are zoning constraints for line-balancing?

12. Why is it essential to design the best possible process before starting line-balancing?

13. Why is it important to get good estimates for operation times before starting line-balancing?

14. An automated teller machine (ATM) corresponds to a stochastic input–output flow shop system. As such, queuing theory can be used to study the behavior of the system and to provide cycle-time management. Explain.

15. The flow shop is designed to remove stochastic behaviors. Explain this statement and comment on how this objective can be accomplished. When is this objective unrealistic?

16. How do queuing models relate to cycle-time management?

17. For single-channel systems, why is $\lambda > \mu$ a violation?

18. For single-channel systems, why is it necessary to assume that the source population is very large?

19. For single-channel systems, why is it necessary to assume that the storage space can accommodate any number of units?

20. What distinguishes single-channel configurations from multiple-channel configurations?

21. Would the FIFO order of entry make sense for an automated teller machine?

22. For multiple-channel systems, why is $\lambda > M\mu$ a violation?

23. What are the characteristics of Poisson arrivals?

24. What is meant by exponential service times?

25. How can the exponential distribution be stated in terms of the Poisson distribution?

26. Does FIFO hold for supermarket checkout counters?

27. What kind of stochastic situation occurs in a supermarket with n different checkout lanes?

28. What constitutes cycle time in the supermarket checkout situation?

29. What is the supplier's role in cycle-time management?

30. Explain vendor releasing from the point of view of both the buyer and the supplier.

31. When is a push-production system desirable?

32. Explain how to use kanban to convert a push-production system to a pull-one-unit production system.

PROBLEMS SECTION

1. Assume that you are going into business selling replacement tires. Draw a precedence diagram for changing tires. Discuss the way in which this job could be done with a flow shop configuration. Why would a flow shop be preferred? Suggest a possible division of labor that could produce a reasonable line balance.

2. Draw a precedence diagram for the way in which tellers handle withdrawals at the bank. Can this job be accomplished by tellers in flow shop configurations?

3. Line efficiency (Λ) is a measure used to assess line balance. It is

$$\Lambda = \frac{\sum_i t_i}{nC}$$

Determine line efficiency for The Photo Lab where $n = 4$, $C = 1.5$ minutes, and total work content is 4.8.

4. Determine line efficiency (described in Problem 3) and relate it to the balance delay measure shown here.

$$d = 100 \, (nC - \textstyle\sum_i t_i) \div nC$$

for the following conditions: Total work content is 3 hours; there are 180 stations operating with a cycle time of one minute. Compare the results and meanings of d and Λ.

5. For The Photo Lab, what happens if t_{max} can be reduced from 1.0 to 0.7 by improving the technology of the film development step $i = 6$? Refer to Figure 17-2 and Tables 17-2 and 17-3.

6. Using the information in Problem 5, what occurs if t_{max} is reduced from 1.0 to 0.6 by installing two photo developing units in parallel for operation (6)? Develop a table similar to Table 17-4.

7. Use The Photo Lab's precedence diagram in Figure 17-2, but change the operation times in Table 17-2 as follows:

Operation (i)	Operation Time (t_i), Minutes
1	1.4
2	1.5
3	1.6
4	1.7
5	1.5
6	2.0
7	1.6
8	1.1
9	1.4

What productivity rates are possible with perfect balance?

8. Using the information in Problem 7, develop a feasible station layout for $n = 5$. What are the characteristics of this arrangement, i.e., cycle time, productivity, and balance delay?

9. With the information in Problem 7, use Kilbridge & Wester's heuristic line-balancing algorithm. Assume that $n = 4$. What are the characteristics of this arrangement, i.e., cycle time, productivity, and balance delay?

10. Drop operation (9) from The Photo Lab's precedence diagram in Figure 17-2, and alter Table 17-2 as follows:

Operation (i)	Operation Time (t_i), Minutes
1	0.4
2	0.5
3	0.6
4	0.7
5	0.5
6	1.0
7	0.6
8	0.1

What productivity rates are possible with perfect balance?

11. With the information in Problem 10, develop a feasible station layout for $n = 3$. What are the characteristics of this arrangement, i.e., cycle time, productivity, and balance delay?

12. With the information in Problem 10, use Kilbridge & Wester's heuristic line-balancing algorithm. Assume that $n = 4$. What are the characteristics of this arrangement, i.e., cycle time, productivity, and balance delay?

13. Solve The Photo Lab's problem after multiplying all operation times in Table 17-2 by 10. Use the Kilbridge & Wester's heuristic to achieve a productivity level of 20 finished units per 8-hour day.

14. Obtain the solution for Problem 13 using Kilbridge & Wester's heuristic with $n = 4$.
   a. What is the cycle time?
   b. What is the productivity rate?
   c. How much idle time results?

15. Using the information from Problems 13 and 14, do you recommend three or four stations?

16. Using the information from Problems 13, 14, and 15, evaluate working nine hours per day with $n = 3$.

17. Use the information from Problems 13 and 14, plus the fact—just known—that the system can be totally mechanized. Would it be worthwhile to try to speed up certain operations so that an output rate of 40 units per hour is achieved?

18. Use the information from Problem 17. Is it possible to design a balanced flow shop that can deliver hourly output rates of 37.5, 40.0, and 42.5 at the flick of a switch?

19. Figure 17-14 depicts the current line balance used by the Baby's Stroller Company for an intermittent flow shop that makes convertible strollers. These strollers, which can be made into baby car seats, have become increasingly popular. The IFS is now run twice a month for four to five days, and all of the work is done with five stations.
   a. What is the productive output per hour?
   b. What is the balance delay?

20. Viewing the automated teller machine (ATM) as a stochastic, single-channel, input–output system with Poisson arrivals and exponential service times, determine the values of W_q and L_q when $\lambda = 8$ and $\mu = 10$. Note: FIFO holds as well as the other assumptions required for single-channel queuing models.

FIGURE 17-14
Baby's Stroller Line Balance

Station = 1   8
Station = 2   9
Station = 3   7
Station = 4   8
Station = 5   8
$C = 10$ minutes

21. Viewing a vending machine as a stochastic, single-channel, input–output system with Poisson arrivals and exponential service times, determine the values of and W and L for $\lambda = 8$ and $\mu = 10$. Note: FIFO holds as well as the other assumptions required for the single-channel queuing model.

22. View the painting booth in an automobile-assembly plant as a stochastic, single-channel, input–output system with Poisson arrivals and exponential service times. Determine the values of P_0 and P_1, and $P_{n>1}$ for $\lambda = 8$ and $\mu = 10$. Note: FIFO holds as well as the other assumptions required for the single-channel queuing model.

23. For the painting booth described in Problem 22, what kind of in-process (WIP) storage will be needed? Where should it be located?

24. If an assembly line is mechanized with two workstations such that the first station's output rate is three units per minute and the second station's output rate is four units per minute,

what is the output rate of the system—assuming deterministic performance?

25. At The Burger Place, Jane's toaster produces 20 finished crowns and heels per minute while Jim dresses 10 burgers per minute. They have been trained to use push-production methods. When Jane sees that Jim has no more space, she helps out at the drive-through window. What is the waiting line if they both work at rated speed for 15 minutes? How big a storage space does Jim need? How is quality affected?

26. Using the information in Problem 25, convert Jane's operation to a pull-five system. What delivery rate will apply?

27. Using the information in Problems 25 and 26, what kind of a kanban do you recommend for times when demand for burgers drops off to less than 10 per minute? Would it make sense for both Jane and Jim to combine the toast and dress operations and work in parallel? What maximum demand rate could they satisfy?

END-OF-CHAPTER QUESTIONS

1. Cycle-time management is crucial in both manufacturing and services. Understanding the opportunities for competitive advantage can provide major tactical advantages. It is easy to overlook the fact that cycle-time management can lower costs for municipalities (police, fire, sanitation, and hospital services), the post office, tax collectors, etc. To bring this into focus, the local business school has developed a seminar on cycle-time management and has invited the mayor's office, chief of the post office (http://www.USPS.com), bankers, regional industrialists, and hospitality managers to attend at the same time. Before the seminar, a list of points to be covered is circulated among the participants. Calls have been coming in to the seminar leader questioning one of the statements a. to f. Which statement is causing trouble?
   a. Cycle-time management is one facet of time-based management (TBM). This aspect of TBM is tactical in nature. Other aspects of TBM, such as FedEx developed with its Memphis hub for next-day delivery, are strategic. In this regard, consider the following quote from *The Business Journal* (serving the Greater Triad Area, August 7, 2000): "FedEx is the largest single employer in Memphis, with ballpark figures reaching 30,000 people," said Ernest Nichols, Jr., a professor at the University of Memphis, who is also the director of the university's FedEx Center for Cycle Time Research.
   b. The concept of continuous process improvement, instead of reengineering (or radical change), often, but not always, applies to cycle-time reduction. There are many examples of long cycle-times being reduced. For example, call center technology and training have led to shorter wait times for customers; Amazon decreased warehouse cycle times (from order receipt to ship) and thereby obtained significant savings; U.S. Airways improved its cycle times by cutting waiting time on the ground from 45 minutes to 20 minutes. This is a 56 percent reduction in cycle time.
   c. Reengineering (REE) is a strategic initiative. By definition, REE is *once again* starting from scratch. Do it right the first time has to be modified to "do it right the second time around." However, even though short cycle times can often be obtained by redesign, the cost may be too high because the old infrastructure is hard to shed.
   d. First-time start-ups *can* do it right the first time. That has obvious as well as hidden benefits. The obvious advantages are learning from competitors' mistakes and new technology. The hidden start-up advantage over existing competition is no prior infrastructure and few preconceived notions. At the outset, Southwest Airlines (SWA) chose time-based strategic goals that ran counter to industry practice. SWA set goals for achieving fast turnaround from ground to air. Southwest's costs have always been lower than industry benchmarks. Volume of business is well above breakeven.
   e. Nummi in Fremont, California, is a reengineered plant. Originally, it was a General Motors plant that closed for a variety of serious reasons that made it a quality nightmare. Since being reengineered by Toyota, Nummi has become a model plant, receiving the highest ratings in productivity and quality.
   f. Every parcel distribution system has a cycle time that starts with customers sending packages and ends with other customers receiving packages. Delivery of parcels has these dual customers at the input and the output of the transport transformation. It is, however, a production process with no analogies to workstations. Consequently, the concept of line-balancing is not applicable.

2. Continuing along the same line, the faculty seminar leader prepared another set of discussion points regarding cycle-time management and line-balancing. Again, a single statement was introduced that was not correct. Identify the incorrect statement.

a. The intermittent flow shop (IFS) is the work configuration of choice for newly founded firms that are starting up a new product line. After sufficient demand is developed, a permanent flow shop can be put into place. If the new product does not grow demand as expected, investment losses in expensive, serial production technology is avoided.

b. Deterministic line-balancing will not work with the intermittent flow shop. It is intended to be used with dedicated flow shops that employ a lot of technology. The IFS, on the other hand, requires almost all labor. The variability of workers is hard to control, and with several workstations, the amount of idle time will be set by the fastest workers.

c. Deterministic line-balancing calls upon everyone to consider how to make the jobs at the workstations as consistent as possible. For example, a worker holding a part with the left hand while polishing the surface with the right hand will experience fatigue faster than if the part is held by a fixture on the work table. Fatigue increases the variability of the times required to accomplish a task. Fatigue sets in quickly when an employee has to bend down to work. Auto assembly engineers found that raising the entire car by conveyor increased the productivity of workers putting tires on the car.

d. Heuristic line-balancing of an IFS may not be productive unless that IFS has many activities at a large number of stations. The heuristic is used when the complexity of the line is an issue. Most likely, this applies to a dedicated flow shop that employs more labor than technology to maintain a productive output rate.

e. Stochastic line-balancing of an IFS is unlikely to be productive because there is a great deal of analysis and analytic reasoning involved. The IFS is not permanent enough to warrant that kind of approach. On the other hand, if the IFS is used fairly regularly, although not continuously, then these comments should be subjected to scrutiny.

3. A task force of the seminar group prepared a statement about the differences between large companies and small and medium-sized companies. It began by noting that large firms launch new products with big television budgets, as well as magazine and newspaper ad budgets. The TV ads may be coordinated with extensive product sampling to potential consumers' mailboxes. Seminar attendees represented a mixture of large, medium, and small-sized companies as well as nonprofit hospital, educational, and municipal managers. Everyone was interested in the task force conclusions published as a. to f. Which point in particular was cited as being incorrect?

a. Large company rollouts, often on a national scope, are not likely to have production based on an intermittent flow shop. Instead, commitment will be to a dedicated flow shop with proper line balance for a range of volumes.

b. Large firms can commit to a technology-based flow shop whereas a small start-up firm cannot readily do so. One reason for the difference is that large, established firms have experience with the product line. That coupled with extensive market research gives large-firm product managers the confidence to use a "full-scale" (dedicated) flow shop (FS) strategy.

c. For large firms, there are high costs of moving from a "hedge-your-bets" (IFS) strategy to a "full-scale" (FS) strategy. One of these is that large firms have high visibility and keep track of each other's projects. If competitors see a marketing opportunity in a situation that has minimum barriers to entry, they will enter that market. The first company into the market with a dedicated flow shop has erected a significant barrier to entry. A dedicated flow shop provides the "first into the market" with tangible cost and quality advantages.

d. Large firms have sufficient cash to deal with changes in strategies and tactics as they are needed to fine-tune product success. Smaller firms seldom have a cushion to fall back on when changes are required. Therefore, small and medium-sized enterprises (SMEs) prefer to use a hedging strategy.

e. Large firms are not likely to face bankruptcy resulting from a product failure. A smaller-sized business has to husband its resources because permanent flow shops require big investments whereas intermittent flow shops are a hedge investment. SMEs can make mistakes at the IFS level of investment but not at the FS level.

f. Process engineers in large firms can help find alternative uses for flow shop investments that have not been successful. If green speckled detergent does not make it in the market, perhaps red speckled detergent will. The process is the same.

4. Specific elements of line-balancing for cycle-time management are being examined by the seminar group's tax collection and sanitation engineering groups. Which statement in the list from a. to f. is not correct?

a. In line-balancing, step 1 is to detail the process to be balanced. For example, spell out what must be done by the tax collection department. It is essential to list all activities that must be done—start to finish. Documentation is needed. Detail all operations and specify the precise order for doing these activities. Based on these data, the precedence diagram can be drawn to show which activities have to be completed before the next activity can be started.

b. Before going to step 2, it is recommended that a team of colleagues review the list, the sequences, and the precedence constraints. It is better to have tax collectors review tax collection, and sanitation workers review waste management. The reason is that specific process knowledge is essential. Encourage colleagues to add details that may have been missed in the first statement of the process.

c. Step 2 is to estimate how long the various activities will take, bearing in mind that different amounts of resources can be brought to the table. Questions arise such as is it worthwhile buying or leasing a machine? For example, the smallest Pitney Bowes postage machine can process 25 letters per minute. Can the tax collector's office justify renting that technology for the premailing workstation? Would the time to do a job change enough to warrant training? These issues will be addressed again, when changing activity times could help to balance workloads at stations.

d. Step 3 is to assign each of the listed activities to appropriate workstations. The effort is made initially to achieve perfect balance (i.e., $d = 0$, which means there is no idle time at any station). If this is a large-scale problem with many operations, a method for assigning jobs to stations should be chosen. Possible candidates are the heuristic approaches. Software systems are available for accomplishing line-balancing.

e. Step 3 assumes that the number of workstations to use has been determined. The tax office manager has derived four workstations from studying the precedence diagram as follows: B follows A; C follows B; and D follows C. The tax office manager states that four stations will accommodate the precedence constraints. Because the activities are people-oriented, at least four tax office employees will be required to man the workstations.

f. The sanitation engineer has made an effort to determine workstations for the waste management situation. He observes that the collection function normally requires one driver and two truck loaders who move as a team from one workstation to another. The truck is like the conveyor belt. This is an interesting variation of the normal view of the flow shop.

5. The bank manager in the class has taken great interest in cycle-time management. She states that the bank already uses line-balanced flow shop work configurations to process checks. In her opinion, the bank has many other opportunities to create a flow shop for operations that are now being done in batches. Seminar classmates agree that this possibility exists in their firms too and that it deserves attention. The issue of determining the number of workstations for cycle-time management has been raised by many in the class. Faculty of the seminar agree that this area needs attention. They release a new set of statements that deal with this issue. Which one of the statements (a. through e.) is incorrect? The equation for perfect balance (no idle time) will help in addressing Problem 5.
$$nC = \sum_{i=1}^{i=n} t_i$$

a. The determination of how many workstations n to use is based on how much product is needed per time interval. The more workstations used, the shorter the cycle time, C. As the cycle time gets shorter, the output rate goes up. $O = T/C$.

b. The work content for check processing is small. It is reasonable to set the cycle time equal to the work content time and have one person do the entire job. Then, each person functions as a workstation. Many individuals doing check processing would be acting as parallel workstations. This model might work effectively for parking ticket processing.

c. A manufacturing manager in the class describes how his firm (Expensive Shoe Company—ESC) uses the IFS work configuration to fill orders for 90 pairs of very stylish, high-heeled women's shoes. They are expensive and made in limited quantities. They are of top quality with customized hand work. The market is strong. There is a shortage of these shoes and a waiting line for them. The shortage is intentional, being based on limitations of production runs.

d. Assume that each shoe requires an hour of labor, and 80 shoes are to be made in an 8-hour day. Ten shoes per hour is the desired output rate from which the cycle time is derived as 6 minutes per shoe, i.e., $C = T/O = 60/10 = 6$. From the equation $nC = TWC$, or $n6 = 60$ minutes, $n = 10$ workstations.

e. The shoemaker points out that breaking up the job into 10 separate sections will not yield perfect balance, i.e., there will be idle time at some workstations. This fact is not evident from the data, but it is known to the shoe process specialists of this firm. Also, six minutes is too short for an ideal cycle time. A preferable configuration is two parallel production lines of five workstations, each with a cycle time of 12 minutes. It would produce an output rate of five shoes per hour, or 50 pairs of shoes per day.

6. Class representatives of the hotel and hospitality industry are convinced that cycle-time management is applicable to their business. There is no doubt about the fact that theme park designers and managers are totally aware of ride cycle times and throughput rates, which impact on both theoretical and actual hourly ride capacities. The group believes that there are many opportunities to create flow shop type operations that are currently being done in batches. The seminar classmates agree to work together to capitalize on this opportunity, and they have made a list of items for discussion. Which one of the statements (a. through f.) is incorrect?

a. The first item on the agenda is the reduction of work content when 10 workstations are used as compared to one person doing the entire job. Previously, it was stated that one craftsperson required an hour of labor to make a fancy shoe. For the theme park, substitute Cinderella's glass slipper. Assume that with 10 stations, work content is reduced by 25 percent so that each shoe requires only 45 minutes of labor.

b. Cycle time decreases to 4.5 minutes because $10C = 45$ (with perfect balance —pb). Output is equal to $60/4.5 = 13\ 1/3$ shoes per hour. If, as before, 80 shoes are the goal, that will now take 6 hours instead of 8 hours. The 25 percent reduction in work content translates into a comparable work time reduction. Another style of fancy shoe or glass slipper can be made in the remaining two hours per day.

c. Flow shop configurations produce efficiencies, derived from specialization at workstations, with significant payoffs. British economist Adam Smith (1723—1790), in his book, *The Wealth of Nations* (1776), first proposed using the division of labor to produce substantial savings for industrializing countries. Called the *father of modern economics and capitalism*, Smith predicted factories that would benefit from the increasing productivity of specialized labor.

d. Even without productivity gains, flow shops permit delivery of finished product at the end of every cycle. In Problem 5, this meant that a finished shoe could be delivered every 6 minutes. With five workstations, delivery could be made every 12 minutes. With two parallel 5-station flow shops, a complete pair of shoes is ready for delivery every 12 minutes. In Problem 6, with 10 work stations, a finished shoe is available every 4.5 minutes.

e. Assume that 20 percent reduction of total work content is available with four stations. Then, 4C = 48 (assuming pb) and cycle time, C = 12 minutes. That is the same cycle time associated with five stations before benefits from division of labor occurred.

f. As additional workstations are added to the flow configuration, the efficiencies of specialization get better and better. This is because the job is further divided, allowing specialization of ever-smaller fractions of operations.

7. Representatives from the manufacturer of the Expensive Shoe Company (ESC) point out that breaking up the production line into 10 separate work sections will not make sense. They have divided the process into 9 operational steps, many of which can be done together at a single workstation. They are also keenly aware of the desirability of getting close to perfect balance. Bill and Nancy have shown that the actual process being used for one of the most elaborate shoe designs made by the company has total work content of 4 hours and 48 minutes—with their flow shop specialization. Nancy estimates that work content would be 6 1/2 hours without flow shop specialization. Bill tabulated the operations A through J (he skipped I because it looked too much like "one" or "el." He also put into the table the operation times (t_i) and precedence information. The faculty leader of the seminar considered this to be an excellent exercise in line-balancing. He circulated the table with a list of observations, a. to f., one of which is wrong. Which is incorrect?

Operation (i)	Preceded by	t_i (minutes)	No. of Predecessors	Notes
A	Nothing	24	0	
B	Nothing	30	0	
C	A	36	1	
D	A	42	1	
E	B, D	30	3	
F	C	60	2	t_{max}
G	E, F	36	6	
H	G	06	7	
J	G	24	7	
Total	$\sum_{i=1}^{i=n} t_i$	288		

Legend: The entry t_{max} is the longest operation and it is not divisible at this time.
$\sum_{i=1}^{i=n} t_i$ is the total work content.

a. Operation F and the total work content are the upper and lower boundaries on cycle time, C. The situation is described by the equation: $t_{max} \leq C \leq \sum_{i=1}^{i=n} t_i$ and by the numbers, $60 \leq C \leq 288$.

b. A line balance can be found with n = 5, and C = 90 minutes:

Operation (i)	Station Name	t_i (minutes)	Station Sum	Idle Time
A	I	24		
B	I	30	I–54 out of 90 minutes	36 minutes
C	II	36		
D	II	42	II–78 out of 90 minutes	12 minutes
E	III	30		
F	III	60	III–90 out of 90 minutes	Zero
G	IV	36	IV–36 out of 90 minutes	54 minutes
H	V	06		
J	V	24	V–30 out of 90 minutes	60 minutes
Total	Five stations	288 minutes	288 out of 450 minutes	162 minutes

This solution is not looked upon favorably. It was obtained by taking the longest chain of operations in the precedence diagram. That is four links connecting five operations, such as A → D → E → G → J. It has a balance delay measure of d = 36%. That is excessive idle time. The output rate is 2/3 unit per hour or one finished item every 90 minutes.

c. For perfect balance, with the situation described in b., it can be shown that n = 4.

d. A better line balance was obtained by using the Kilbridge and Wester heuristic. The K & W method is based on a number of rules, the first of which is to label each operation with the number of predecessors it has. Operations are assigned to stations in the order of the least number of predecessors. For workstation I, select operations B and A, in that order because of the rule for ties (both have zero number). When a tie exists, select the operation with the longest processing time first, saving short operation times for ease of later fitting.

e. The K & W method yields perfect balance when C = 96 minutes with three stations. The output rate is 0.625 finished items per hour, so 1.6 hours is required for a finished unit to be delivered.

Operation (*i*)	Station Name	t_i (minutes)	Station Sum	Idle Time
B	I	30		
A	I	24		
D	I	42	I–96 out of 96 minutes	Zero
C	II	36		
F	II	60	II–96 out of 96 minutes	Zero
E	III	30		
G	III	36		
J	III	24		
H	III	6	III–96 out of 96 minutes	Zero
Total	Five stations	288 minutes	288 out of 288 minutes	Zero

f. There is a problem, however. No time has been provided for worker R & R (rest and relaxation). If 10 percent is added (say 10 minutes instead of 9.6 minutes), then cycle time becomes 106 minutes. The output rate is 0.566 finished items per hour, so 1.8 hours is required for a finished unit to be delivered. Productivity is negatively affected, but the morale will be sustained.

8. The seminar was demanding. There was a good deal of homework and yet many questions remained unanswered. As a result, it was decided to prepare a list of issues that still needed attention. Which two of the points a. to f. are incorrect?

   a. In Problem 7, there were five stations with a cycle time of 90 minutes, which means that total station time available for work was $5 \times 90 = 450$ minutes. Idle time added up to 162 minutes. Balance delay was derived from the ratio of idle time to total available work time, viz., $162/450 = .36$ or 36 percent.

   b. There are a variety of line-balancing heuristics, including Helgeson and Birnie (H & B). They chose to assign first those operations whose following operations have the least total time.

   c. Queuing aspects of line-balancing are related to stochastic factors such as workers that sometimes are faster and sometimes slower.

   d. Arrival rates at each workstation are not stochastic if a paced conveyor belt is being used to transport work in process, unless the pace is under the control of workers at each of the stations. In the Toyota plant, a worker can stop the line from moving if that becomes necessary. It is interesting to note that although this capability exists, the Toyota lines are seldom down for more than a half minute and even that is very rare.

   e. Service rates at the workstations upstream are viewed as arrival rates at stations that are downstream from them. If arrival rates are distributed around a mean value as a Poisson distribution, it is likely that the service rates of the prior station are exponentially distributed.

9. Josephine and Joe are designing a new quick service restaurant. Their purpose is to take the push out of fast-food production and convert it to a pull system. Joe toasts chicken–tofu burger buns. Josephine puts the chicken–tofu burger between the buns and adds sun-dried tomatoes, gherkins, and barbecue sauce.

   a. Joe's toaster produces 10 finished crowns and heels (of buns) per minute. Josephine's production rate is 6 completed units per minute. Joe is pushing four extra buns per minute on Josephine. Her queue will grow to 240 buns in an hour even though there are no statistical distributions involved.

   b. Assume that Joe's workstation has a variable Poisson output rate with a mean of five buns. Assume that Josephine has a variable service rate of 6 completed chicken–tofu burgers (also Poisson, with 10 seconds on average between completions). Then, the systems utilization factor, (*rho*), $\rho = 0.833$ and the waiting line for Josephine is 6.16.

   c. Serialized production systems that are not connected by paced-conveyor belts must compensate for variable and arrival rates. These systems work well when the arrival rate is controlled by a call for items that is often done using a kanban signal such as a withdrawal card, a light flashing, or a ping-pong ball rolling down a track.

   d. Just-in-time deliveries by a supplier are frequently prearranged where only a change of plans calls for intervention to alter the schedule. Where contract agreements prevail, the method is called *vendor releasing*.

   e. Pull numbers do not have to be one-at-a-time, which epitomizes just-in-time. Several units can be delivered together, which does not require great amounts of storage space and keeps carrying costs on the low side. At the same time, a few-at-a-time is not the same as all-at-once, which is associated with fear of delivery problems termed *just-in-case*.

10. Arrivals, departures, and queues are a fundamental phenomenon in everyday life as well as P/OM. The regularities apply to batch production as well as flow shops. The final seminar of the series dealt with variability of the input–output production system. Some truths about this area of study were set down and circulated for discussion with all members of the seminar. Which one statement on the list is incorrect?

    a. In line-balancing terminology, each workstation is a "customer" for a "supplier." The first station (most upstream in the line) is exposed to the most risk because materials for it come from outside sources. Except in highly engineered flow shops (working like clockwork), variability is always a problem. In batch work environments, materials are moved in lots to the next workstation. Bottlenecks become evident because the work flow stops and takes a place on the waiting line.

    b. When parking garages cannot accept more cars, the sign "Sorry Full" appears. It causes cars to turn away and seek alternative parking spaces. The problem is one of storage. In push-production systems, the inability to store upstream materials moving downstream tends to occur when the work in process is big and bulky. It also occurs when the receiving station experiences slowdowns caused by quality problems, bad materials, equipment breakdowns, and employee difficulties. Storage problems also occur when the supplier speeds up output as a result of new methods and improved materials. Periodic studies are required to rebalance systems subject to change.

c. Pushing production is based on two concepts: (1) the independence of adjacent workstations and (2) the objective of having all resources fully utilized and never idle. The first point is questionable in many systems, but, the second point is always valid.

d. Line efficiency (Λ) is related to balance delay (d). This ratio falls between zero and one. The ratio subtracted from

one could be called *line-balancing inefficiency*. This measure is not related to stochastic line-balancing or queuing, except that if workstation times are variable, then $(1 - \Lambda)$ should be large enough to buffer imbalances.

e. Another way of looking at the trade-offs between skills and technology is the need to have rest and relaxation (also called *rest and delay*) for people to endure repetitive work. With technology, the cost of queues can be avoided; the costs of extra cycle time can be eliminated; variability of quality can be reduced; and sometimes, in addition to improved consistency, other quality standards can be raised.

ADDITIONAL READINGS

Ahmadi, Reza H., and Hernan Wurgaft. "Design for Synchronized Flow Manufacturing." *Management Science*, vol. 40, no. 11 (November 1994): 1469–1483.

Chow, W. M. *Assembly Line Design*. Amsterdam: Marcel Dekker, 1990.

Cooper, R. B. *Introduction to Queueing Theory*, 2e. New York: Elsevier North-Holland Publishing, 1981.

Ghosh, S., and R. Gagnon. "A Comprehensive Literature Review and Analysis of the Design, Balancing and Scheduling of Assembly Systems." *International Journal of Production Research*, vol. 27, no. 4 (1989).

Graves, S. C. "A Review of Production Scheduling." *Operations Research*, vol. 29, no. 4 (July–August 1981).

Gross, D., and C. H. Harris. *Fundamentals of Queuing Theory*, 2e. New York: Wiley, 1985.

Hopp, Wallace J., and Mark L. Spearman. *Factory Physics*, 2e. New York: McGraw-Hill/Irwin, 2004.

Hirano, Hiroyuki. *JIT Implementation Manual: The Complete Guide to Just-In-Time Manufacturing*. Cambridge, MA: Productivity Press, 1990.

Ignall, Edward J. "A Review of Assembly Line Balancing." *Journal of Industrial Engineering*, vol. 16, no. 4 (July–August, 1965).

Japan Management Association (ed.). *Kanban and Just-in-Time at Toyota: Management Begins at the Workplace*. Trans. by D. J. Lu, Cambridge MA: Productivity Press, 1989.

Law, A. M., and W. D. Kelton. *Simulation Modeling and Analysis*. New York: McGraw-Hill, 1982.

Plane, D. R. *Management Science, A Spreadsheet Approach*. Danvers, MA: boyd & fraser publishing co, 1994.

Pritsker, A. A. B., C. E. Sigal, and R. D. J. Hammesfahr. *SLAM II, Network Models for Decision Support*. Pacific Grove, CA: Duxbury Press, 1994.

Ragsdale, C. T. *Spreadsheet Modeling & Decision Analysis*, 4e. Cincinnati, OH: Thomson South-Western, 2004, pp. 668–702.

Vollmann, T. E., W. L. Berry, and D. C. Whybark. *Manufacturing Planning and Control Systems*, 3e. Homewood, IL: Irwin, 1992.

NOTES

1. H. A. Simon and A. Newell. "Heuristic Problem Solving: The Next Advance in Operations Research." *Operations Research*, vol. 6, no. 1 (January–February 1958): 1–10.

2. M. D. Kilbridge and L. Wester. "A Heuristic Model of Assembly Line Balancing." *Journal of Industrial Engineering*, vol. 12, no. 4 (July–August 1961): 292–99.

3. W. B. Helgeson and D. P. Birnie. "Assembly Line Balancing Using the Ranked Positional Weight Technique." *Journal of Industrial Engineering*, vol. XII, no. 6 (November–December 1961): 394–398.

4. Fred M. Tonge. "Assembly Line Balancing Using Probabilistic Combinations of Heuristics." *Management Science*, vol. 11, no. 7 (May 1965): 727–735.

5. A. L. Arcus. "Comsoal: A Computer Method of Sequencing Operations for Assembly Lines." See Elwood S. Buffa, ed. *Readings in Production and Operations Management*. New York: Wiley, 1966, 336–360.

6. E. J. Ignall. "A Review of Assembly Line Balancing." *Journal of Industrial Engineering*, vol. 16, no. 4 (July–August 1965): 244–254.

7. For complete coverage of queuing equations see D. Gross and C.H. Harris. *Fundamentals of Queuing Theory*, 2e. New York: Wiley, 1985.

8. David G. Dannenbring and Martin K. Starr. *Management Science: An Introduction*. New York: McGraw-Hill, 1981, 603–607. See also, D. Gross and C. H. Harris, note 7.

9. *Ward's Auto World*, April 1, 2002.

SPOTLIGHT 17-1
Where the Race is Won

An Interview with Don Stuart, President and CEO, Global Concepts, Inc.

"Demand throughout the supply chain is best managed and satisfied through policies and processes that pull material to the point of use." — Don E. Stuart, President and CEO, Global Concepts, Inc.

"Our pit stops are distribution centers . . . where the race is won. If we can double the speed, we can halve the inventory." Don Stuart's statements epitomize the goals of his company.

After 16 years of serving as AT&T's corporate general manager in Baskin Ridge, New Jersey, and being responsible for supply chain problems, Stuart formed Global Concepts, Inc. (GCI). He had honed cutting-edge precepts for "full-stream" logistics management and reengineering worldwide supply chains, and Global Concepts was the organization that could bring them to clients.

GCI is a privately held company specializing in high-end warehouse and manufacturing management systems. Their suite of logistics tools is designed to reduce supply chain costs on an accelerated basis. Being fast is very important because badly run transportation and warehousing or poor material handling and inventory management not only cost more money than they should, but they also put their companies at risk.

Global's logistics tools are generic until customized for the clients, who are large-scale retailers and manufacturers whose supply chains include not only retail locations, but a complex network of warehouses, service centers, vendors, and often internal manufacturing in order to feed the pipeline to major market segments. Rapid applications have been obtained by assembling a world-class team of logistics experts to research problems and propose solutions providing the best logistics practices. These are embodied in the company's core software product. Instead of having to reinvent the wheel for each client, the company configures its codes to meet specific customer needs. The result, Don Stuart says, is faster implementation and greater returns on investment for the "virtual warehouse" concept.

Global Concepts, Inc., is a logistics solutions company whose product line of software carries interesting names such as Flow Planner, Logistics Engine, and Metrics Advantage. Much of the research and development was done in conjunction with NSF's Industry University Cooperative Research Centers (IUCRC) and the auto parts giant, AutoZone. Home base for Global Concepts is Little Rock, Arkansas, and the company also has operations in Atlanta, Georgia; Birmingham, Alabama; and Oklahoma City.

Don points out that consistency in performance of the supply chain (or the demand chain, as he likes to call it) reduces safety-stock inventory caused by variability. GCI's cost optimization models reduce process variability and operating expenses while improving customer service with less inventory.

Stuart earned a mechanical engineering degree from the University of Arkansas. He has said that, as the years progressed, he accidentally became an expert in logistics. It may have been a coincidence that he was at the right place at the right time, but it was no accident; he knew he was there and he knew what had to be done. AT&T consolidated most of its manufacturing and distribution operations in the early to mid-1990s, prior to the Lucent spin-off, and Stuart had to bring order out of chaos. As an efficiency expert at AT&T, Stuart helped reengineer a business unit, saving the company $800 million in 1995.

Don has served for the last decade as Industry Director at The Logistics Institute (TLI), based at Georgia Tech in Atlanta, and he is Chairman, Industrial Advisory Board, for the NSF's Center for Engineering Logistics and Distribution, which teams experts at the Universities of Arkansas, Oklahoma, Florida, and Louisville. In this capacity, he collaborates on research with Wal-Mart, Tyson's, ConAgra, USPS, UPS, FAA, the U.S. Department of Defense, and transportation agencies, as a partial listing.

Sources: Conversations and correspondence with Don Stuart and his staff, August 1–10, 2003; Wood, Jeffrey. "Global Going National with Software Rollout." *Arkansas Business* (April 21, 2003).

SPOTLIGHT 17-2
Balanced Scorecards: No Longer Looking through the Rear-View Mirror

The landmark book *In Search of Excellence: Lessons from America's Best-Run Companies* started by selecting firms using the 7-S McKinsey Framework, which translates into "comfort slogans" about being close to the customer and keeping things simple, e.g., lean staff and walk-around management. The selection procedure was not based on hard measures except in the finance area, where six numerical scores (including return on equity from 1961 through 1980, compound asset growth for the same set of years, etc.) served as an ultimate screening. Firms that flunked the financial tests were dropped.

Two years later, *Business Week* ran its famous November 5, 1984, "OOPS" cover, which noted that more than one-third of the "excellent 43" firms had fallen on hard times. Examples of chosen companies that had better days before 1980 and then began to encounter serious problems were Atari, Data General, Digital Equipment, Polaroid, Raychem, and Wang Labs. Critics of the original study were quick to point out that the method of selection was flawed. Many of them advocated expanding the scope and range of the metrics that were employed.

The goal of identifying essential attributes of excellent companies is a driving force for reasons that transcend the publishers' motivation to sell books. Managers and students of business make up the market that purchased more than 6 million copies of *In Search of Excellence*. In spite of "OOPS," a follow-up volume, *A Passion for Excellence: The Leadership Difference*, was a resounding success. It also sold millions of copies; both books have been reprinted and are currently available. A more recent winner of that genre is *Good to Great: Why Some Companies Make the Leap . . . and Others Don't*. These books are a delight to read. They are replete with anecdotal material and conclusions that managers take seriously. *Good to Great* is assigned reading in a number of companies. However, these books do not represent scholarly work of academics using scientific methods even though the authors often refer to their studies as research.

If hallmarks of excellence could be identified and made part of a theory of management, then emulation of those characteristics would ensure large profits and long-term survivability. Such a theory is not likely to be achieved in the complex, counterintuitive, economic, and psychological domains that account for business success. That is why the balanced scorecard is an appealing alternative to management fads about the sources and mechanisms for achieving the kind of business excellence that guarantees financial success. The scorecard is tailored to the company's strategies and their execution.

In the early 1990s, Drs. Robert Kaplan (Harvard Business School) and David Norton (president, Balanced Scorecard Collaborative, Inc.) developed a broad-based system of measurement that they called the "balanced scorecard." It was intended to create a strategic management model that could counterbalance the overweight traditionally given to financial measures. This model included marketing and production excellence. It emphasized the systems connections that tie together all relevant elements of business performance. Kaplan and Norton have pointed out that the balanced scorecard (BSC) recognizes that financial measures tell the story of the past.

In an era of rapid, dynamic, technological and sociological shifts, measures are needed to guide every company into the world of its future. The BSC system is composed of four measurable components:

1. The Learning and Growth Perspective (planned transition)
2. The Business Process Perspective (P/OM as part of the family)
3. The Customer Perspective (marketing essentials)
4. The Financial Perspective (using windshields as well as rear-view mirrors)

Each of these elements will be explained in terms of features of the BSC that endear it to P/OM.

Total quality management (TQM) is a basic building block of the BSC. Point 3 requires specifying how we want our customers to see us. In turn, listening to the voice of customers may clarify their satisfaction. A good reference to measurement in this context is the House of Quality

Point 2 necessitates selection of those business processes that are now (or will become) core competencies. Pursuing this vision, how well do strategies function to empower employees to strive for continuous improvements? Quality improvement occurs by means of feedback loops that connect points 1, 2, 3, and 4 in all possible paths from one to another.

Point 1 covers the management of change and transitions. How many successful new products (goods and services) have been created? How can that score be doubled? Process improvement is measurable in terms of better quality, more throughput, and increased product variety (lower setup costs).

Point 4 uses past financial track records to benchmark future achievements. Does the evaluation of plans made in points 1, 2, and 3 promise better financial outcomes in the future? Knowing when to fund programs is an essential part of the financial component.

The BSC is a metric-based information system with continuous feedback. This includes the ability to improve on measurement systems being used. For example, a company evaluating its status with a Baldrige Award committee can reappraise its strengths, weaknesses, opportunities, and threats (SWOT measures).

POM enjoys using the BSC method, and related software, because it brings all parties (marketing, finance, human resources, and accounting) to the same table and occasionally everybody speaks about production issues. After all, the BSC defines "excellence" in terms of many P/OM measurements. For the BSC to work, many more metrics must be developed.

Sources: Http://www.bscol.com. Collins, Jim. *Good to Great: Why Some Companies Make the Leap . . . and Others Don't*. New York: Harper Business, 2001; Kaplan, Robert S., and David P. Norton. "Using the Balanced Scorecard as a Strategic Management System." *Harvard Business Review* (January–February 1996); Peters, Thomas J., and Robert H. Waterman, Jr. *In Search of Excellence: Lessons from America's Best-Run Companies*. New York: Warner Books, 1982; Peters, Thomas J., and Nancy Austin. *A Passion for Excellence: The Leadership Difference*. New York: Warner Books, 1985.

Supplement 17

Simulation of Queuing Models

It has been proposed that a 2-station system such as the one shown in Figure 17-15 be used by the postal system to sort bulk mail.

The output rates of the first and second stations are expected to vary, as shown in Table 17-13.

The average Poisson output rate for station I is 3.4 units per minute and for station II it is 3.6 units per minute. Although II processes at a faster rate than I, a queue will develop, and the storage facility between I and II is needed. The intervals between arrivals and service completions are exponentially distributed.

Station I must stop working when the storage queue gets larger than N. This is a variable that could be changed at a cost if analysis indicates net benefit.

Output rates are converted to intervals between inputs from station I and to service durations at station II by taking the reciprocals. This is column 2 of Table 17-13. Column 3 provides data for the probability density distribution values. Column 4 shows these data converted into cumulative probability distributions values.

Monte Carlo numbers (MCN) are assigned in Table 17-14. They translate the cumulative probability distribution estimates of column 4 in Table 17-13 into number clusters that are like labels for the different output rates and their associated intervals. MCN can be used to generate random sequences of arrivals with different input intervals from station I and service intervals at station II. These generated patterns conform to the respective probability distributions of outputs and inputs at the stations.

By using a random process for selecting numbers, there are 10 chances to pick a Monte Carlo number 00–09, which is associated with an input interval from station I of 0.500 minutes. Similarly, there are 50 chances of picking a MCN 10–59. This is the right proportion of station I input intervals of 0.333 minutes.

An *abbreviated* table of random numbers is used to generate a series of random events. Table 17-15 shows a small set of random numbers produced by computer. The character of the numbers in that table is such that any digit 0 through 9 is as likely to appear as any

FIGURE 17-15
Mail Sorting with Storage of Size N

TABLE 17-13

STATION II—Arrival and Service Rate Distributions

	Output Rate (units/min)	Interval Between Inputs to Station II (minutes)	Probability Distribution Density	Probability Distribution Cumulative
	Column 1	Column 2	Column 3	Column 4
Station I	2	0.500	0.10	0.10
	3	0.333	0.50	0.60
	4	0.250	0.30	0.90
	5	0.200	0.10	1.00
		Service Duration at Station II (minutes)		
Station II	2	0.500	0.10	0.10
	3	0.333	0.30	0.40
	4	0.250	0.50	0.90
	5	0.200	0.10	1.00

TABLE 17-14 **Monte Carlo Number (MCN) Assignments**

Input Interval (min.)	Station I Monte Carlo Numbers	Quantity	Service Interval (min.)	Station II Monte Carlo Numbers	Quantity
0.500	00–09	10	0.500	00-09	10
0.333	10–59	50	0.333	10-39	30
0.250	60–89	30	0.250	40-89	50
0.200	90–99	10	0.200	90-99	10

other. Because each 2-digit MCN is associated with a particular event, the occurrence of all events is similarly random.

Random number tables are useful for instructive purposes, but computer programs are available that generate the numbers as needed for the various algorithms and applications.

A systematic pattern of reading the numbers in the table (i.e., vertically, diagonally, horizontally) must be used so that no bias is introduced in the way that the numbers are selected. Then, reading successive pairs of digits from Table 17-15: The first pair is equivalent to an input interval from station I, and the second pair is equivalent to a service interval at station II.

Note: Successive triplets of digits 000–999 would be used if the probabilities were stated in three places, such that 1.000 would be the sum of those figures. Probabilities expressed to four, five, or more places would be dealing with phenomena that are rare. Then, an important distinction exists between events that can occur (say) one in 10,000 or one in 100,000 times.

Pencil and paper simulations are good for instructional purposes. However, in a real case, the simulation of the 2-station flow shop for sorting bulk mail would be done by computer. The details that are given here reflect the academic approach to encourage understanding of the method.

The simulation consists of choosing successive pairs of random numbers and matching these against the input interval and the service interval Monte Carlo number assignments specified in Table 17-14.

The first pair of random numbers indicates the period of time between the start of the simulation and the first arrival at station II. That interval is 0.5 minutes. The second pair of random numbers specifies how long servicing will take. That service duration is 0.25. Four more random numbers are drawn. The first pair of these random numbers is used to specify the interval until the next arrival at station II. The second pair of these random numbers details the second service time.

TABLE 17-15

Abbreviated Table of Random Numbers

05621	64483	38549	62908	71579	19203	83546	05917	51905
82773	76475	60896	93681	03327	49250	78355	78582	20869
66592	69112	64499	63939	75944	59053	14086	60716	70017
44474	90319	74480	73857	62484	38228	87185	73667	24870
50983	46638	81624	40012	35426	04146	22613	76275	00250
10052	03550	59144	59468	37984	77892	89766	86489	46619
50263	91130	22188	81205	99699	84260	19693	36701	43233

When a sufficient sample is drawn, the behavior of this system can be evaluated. The maximum and average length of the waiting line can be estimated. The bottleneck effect of limited storage between stations can be assessed. The idle time of station II can be estimated, and the overall quality of this stochastic flow shop configuration can be observed to determine whether an acceptable line balance has been achieved.

Cycle-time management will depend on what strategies are available to alter λ and μ. Can station II be faster? Can another station II sorter be added at peak load times? Are there new technologies that might be brought to bear? Perhaps some of the load from station I can be directed to another sorter location.

A left-to-right scan of the top line of the random number table, Table 17-15, shows the following:

05621   64483   38549   62908   71579   19203   83546   05917   51905

The first two pairs of digits are 05 and 62, representing an input arrival interval of 0.500 and a service duration of 0.250. The simulation continues in Table 17-16. This table builds a scenario with the focus on arrival time, completion time, idle time, and queue size.

TABLE 17-16   Eight Steps of the Simulation

Sample Number	Random Numbers		Input Interval	Arrival Time at Station II	Service Duration at Station II	Completion Time at Station II	Idle Time	Queue Size
1	05	62	0.500	0.500	0.250	0.750a	0	0
2	16	44	0.333	0.833a	0.250	1.083	0.083a	0
3	83	38	0.250	1.083	0 333	1.416	0	0
4	54	96	0.333	1.416	0.200	1.616b	0	0
5	29	08	0.333	1.749b	0.500	2.249c,d	0.133b	0
6	71	57c	0.250	1.999c,d	—	—	0	1c
7	91	92f	0.200	2.199d,f	—	—	0	2d
6				2.249d,e	0.250e	2.499d	0	1e
7				2.499f	0.200f	2.699	0	0g
8	03	83	0.500	2.699	0.250	2.949	0	0
*								
*								

Legend:
a—Station II is idle from 0.750 until 0.833 (0.083 minute).
b—Station II is idle from 1.616 until 1.749 (0.133 minute).
c—Station II is busy so arrival number six must wait from 1.999 until 2.249 (0.250 minute).
d—A second unit, arrival number seven, joins the line at 2.199. Assume that there is storage space for it. Otherwise, station I would have to stop at 2.199 and wait until 2.499 before it could begin again. One unit waits from 1.999 until 2.249 (0.250 minute). The other unit waits from 2.199 until 2.249 (0.050 minute).
e—The random number 57 in the sixth sample indicates a service duration of 0.250. So, the sixth arrival begins to be serviced at 2.249.
f—The seventh arrival waits from 2.199 until 2.499 to be serviced. The random number 92 indicates a service duration of 0.200.
g—The line is cleared of waiting units. To this time, station II has been idle a total of 0.216 minute. The waiting line has been occupied by a single unit for 0.200 minute, by two units for 0.050 minute (together 0.100), then by a single unit for 0.250 minute, for a total waiting time of 0.550. There has been no shutdown of station I.

All of the different performance characteristics of the system can be simulated. Complex assumptions can be made that defy mathematical analyses. To illustrate, it has been assumed that the input and service intervals are independently distributed. If this is not so, and they are conditional upon each other, or on prior states, these conditional dependencies can be modeled in a simulation. Math analysis of complex dependencies can be more difficult when discontinuous dependencies account for the systems behavior. With a computer simulation program, is not as difficult to simulate stochastic line-balancing problems involving hundreds of activities.

Problems for Supplement 17

1. Use the following random numbers to simulate the behavior of the 2-station mail-sorting system.

| 10052 | 03550 | 59144 | 59468 | 37984 | 77892 | 89766 | 86489 | 46619 |

2. Use the following random numbers to simulate the behavior of the 2-station mail-sorting system.

| 50263 | 91130 | 22188 | 81205 | 99699 | 84260 | 19693 | 36701 | 43233 |

CASES

Case 17-1

Industry Perspective on Smart Technology— Global Concepts, Inc., at Celestica's Facility in Little Rock

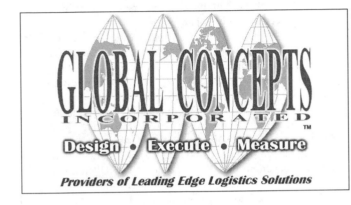

HISTORY OF THE LITTLE ROCK FACILITY

The Celestica plant in Little Rock, Arkansas, was originally AT&T's Repair and Distribution Center. It had supported AT&T Multimedia Group's Global Business Communications Systems (GBCS) business unit. Headquartered in Basking Ridge, New Jersey, GBCS specialized in the design, manufacture, sales, and repair of business telephone systems and other communications equipment.

Before that, the Little Rock facility had been a manufacturing and distribution center for AT&T computers. Then, Little Rock inherited equipment repair operations from a large West Chicago facility in the summer of 1994. A smaller repair and distribution operation in Denver also was consolidated into Little Rock.

AT&T's computer manufacturing facility and warehouse in Little Rock were no longer needed as a result of AT&T's merger with NCR in 1992. That merger created the AT&T Global Information Solutions (GIS) business unit. All computer operations were moved to existing NCR facilities. At that point, AT&T decided to move GBCS repair to the unutilized space in Little Rock. The move afforded advantages such as an available, trained workforce; the lower southern wage rates (as compared to those in West Chicago); and the opportunity to develop a new relationship with the union, which involved establishing the groundwork for a self-directed workforce with worker pay based on performance rewards.

AT&T is no longer in this business. The company has undergone stunning changes since they first moved to Little Rock. Accordingly, the facility has changed hands several times. It went from AT&T to Lucent. Then it became Avaya. In May 2001, the facility was acquired by Celestica, Inc., with headquarters in Toronto, Canada. It is in the top ranks of contract manufacturers in the world. In addition, Celestica also offers supply chain management, product and process design functions, global distribution, and

post-sales repair services. At Little Rock, Celestica specializes in the post-sales returns and repair business. It also offers a variety of additional services as well as third-party distribution for various customers.

COMPANY PROFILE

Celestica, Inc., is a world-class company in the delivery of innovative electronics manufacturing services (EMS). It operates a highly sophisticated global manufacturing network with over 40 operations in Asia, Europe, and the Americas. Celestica also provides a broad range of services to top OEMs (original equipment manufacturers). It is recognized as a leader in quality, technology, and supply chain management; Celestica provides competitive advantage to its customers by improving time-to-market, scalability, and manufacturing efficiency. Celestica provides a range of electronics manufacturing services including design, prototyping, assembly, testing, product assurance, supply chain management, distribution, and after-sales services.

Starting in 2000, Celestica began acquiring assets from numerous companies including Excel Electronics and Lucent Technologies. Little Rock and other U.S. facilities are estimated to account for 50 percent of Celestica's business. Europe and Asia contribute the remainder.

Celestica supplies products and services to over 75 OEMs, including Avaya, Cisco Systems, Dell Computer Corporation, EMC Corporation, Fujitsu, Hewlett-Packard Company, International Business Machines Corporation, Lucent Technologies, Motorola, NEC Corporation, and Sun Microsystems. The products Celestica manufactures can be found in a wide array of end products, including cell phones and pagers, hubs and switches, local area network (LAN) and wide area network (WAN) networking cards, laser printers, mainframe computers, mass storage devices, medical products, modems, multimedia peripherals, private branch exchange (PBX) switches, personal computers, personal digital assistants (PDAs), photonic devices, routers, scalable processors, servers, switching products, token ring products, video broadcasting equipment, wireless base stations, wireless loop systems, and workstations.

For the fiscal year ended December 31, 2002, Celestica's revenue was $8,272 million, down 17 percent compared to fiscal 2001, which had $10,004 million. As the chairman, Eugene V. Polistuk, stated in the 2002 annual report, "It was a difficult year for our customers." In fact, it was the second straight year of broadly-based reductions in corporate spending for information technology and communications infrastructure products. Toward the end of 2003, the economy and Celestica's performance were on the rise. Hoovers lists 40,000 employees of Celestica for 2002 and states that Canadian-based investment firm Onex controls about 85 percent of the company's voting rights. The company's stock trades as "CLS" on the New York Stock Exchange (NYSE).

WAREHOUSE MANAGEMENT SYSTEM (WMS) NEEDS

As business continued to expand at their Little Rock, Arkansas, plant, Celestica recognized the need to pursue a logical warehouse management system (WMS). Their business needs changed because of increases in volume and additional service requirements being offered. Their existing ERP (enterprise resource procurement) warehouse management solution did not meet their needs. It offered breadth across many areas, but not the depth required to meet their growing requirements. Celestica had numerous features that it desired within a WMS system, including

- *Both manufacturing and distribution functionality.* The business expansion extended the distribution needs of their existing repair/rework operation into requirements for additional warehousing/distribution operations.

- *Increased visibility.* Because of the increase in volume, they needed enhanced visibility to manage and monitor both production and distribution.

- *Third-party logistics.* Because they perform distribution for some of their clients, they needed third-party logistics functionality.

- *Incorporating existing systems.* Because certain processes are unique within Celestica, they were looking for a system that could incorporate these processes, including the actual programs into their offering.

- *Focused storage/point-of-use (POU).* Because of the repair/rework activities, they needed a system that would manage these inventories, including automatic replenishment.

- *Short implementation lead time.* Because new business processes were coming online first quarter of 2003, they wanted a WMS that could be installed in 3 months without impacting business.

- *IBM higher support cost.* Their current system was being maintained by IBM, and they needed a system that could greatly reduce these costs.

These features were needed to increase throughput and gain efficiencies while reducing costs to allow the company to compete for additional business.

WAREHOUSE MANAGEMENT SYSTEM RESULTS

Celestica selected Global Concepts (GC) because of its familiarity with the quality and reliability of GC's products and services, and because of Global Concepts' ability to quickly install the WMS without impacting business at costs lower than the competition.

As of 2003, although the system was in the early stages, results suggested that Celestica would be able to increase throughput and significantly improve customer service with increasing volumes while still reducing costs. Additionally, Celestica is considering the installation of Global Concepts WMS at other Celestica facilities, and potentially all of North America.

Project Management

Program Management Organization

Celestica project management presented a special challenge. The project was more challenging because both distribution and repair operations were included in the scope. Also, not only was Global Concepts expected to work closely with Celestica's internal people, but GC was also faced with working with another systems contractor, IBM, whom GC was replacing for WMS. GC accepted this challenge by quickly establishing a team-first environment and listening to concerns from both parties.

Early in the relationship, Global gained the confidence of IBM and Celestica managers in distribution, returns, repair, and systems by providing insights and logistics consulting services that improved operations within the existing systems architecture. A key advantage Global provided was not only systems expertise, but also logistics expertise. GC strives to always allow the processes to drive the system to ensure the best processes for Celestica and not just implement those processes the WMS system will support.

Early meetings involved both managers and operational support personnel from all areas. Great care was taken to carefully understand each organization's needs and areas of concerns. It was very important for Global to conduct high-level meetings with all groups so that each responsible manager could better understand the interaction of the new system with the entire operation. GC's goal and Celestica's desire was to optimize the entire facility and not just improve particular pieces at the expense of other areas. Global's approach involved gaining an in-depth understanding of all the processes and applying logistics expertise to tear down the functional silos. Global was able to accomplish this goal by helping the managers understand the greater good and overall improvements for Celestica.

Program Control

Global assigned a dedicated implementation manager and a lead developer to be the consistent points of contact with those involved in daily operations. These leaders and their team met and/or talked with Celestica on a daily basis to work the operational issues of implementation. Top management was involved as a steering committee and met when the project was in danger of delay due to cross-functional decisions that couldn't be made in a timely manner. The two-pronged approach enabled the operational team to thoroughly understand the issues and to be well prepared to discuss any issues that crossed functional boundaries. This approach kept the quality of the implementation high while also staying on time and on budget. The access to quality information allowed the steering committee to make quick, well-informed decisions that has enabled implementation to proceed at record speed and provide initial functionality for key growth areas in as little as three months.

Risk Management

Because of the aggressive implementation time line, and their past experience with several software application changeouts over the past several years of restructuring that severely impacted operations, Celestica was keenly concerned about how GC would manage the risk. A critical deciding factor was the success of another of GC's customers, AutoZone. Global Concepts employed the same successful techniques used at AutoZone within Celestica. These included:

- Data validation
- Enhanced training
- Phased implementation

Because of Celestica's past WMS experience and Global Concepts' experience with their old system, data validation was easier than usual in a new implementation. Using the three levels of data validation required:

- Reference data analysis
- Optional reference data analysis
- Prescriptive reference data analysis

GC was able to quickly scrub the reference data and correct the few errors that were present. The required reference data analysis checks over 250 different elements to ensure that they have been properly set up within the system. If the analysis finds errors, then it reports the problems in the form of a report for the user to correct. For example, the validation could check to see if a new stock-keeping unit (SKU) has been properly set up within the system. The analysis would ensure that:

- The product has been assigned to a warehouse.
- The product has been assigned to a zone.
- The product has been assigned to a stockroom.
- The product has been assigned to a subzone.
- The product type has been correctly assigned as hazardous or normal.
- The putaway threshold has been enabled.
- The hot SKU threshold has been enabled.

The correct assignment of the sku was important to Celestica because of the 3PL (third-party logistics) work done at the site. If the SKU was not placed in the correct area on setup, then billing would be missed and Celestica would not charge the customer for the item. The analysis also checks to determine if:

- The product has been assigned to a product family and subfamily.
- The product volumetrics have been entered.
- Any alternative names for the SKU like part number or UPC code have been entered.
- The SKU has been assigned to any location.

This tool was used throughout the setup phase or at anytime that changes were made to check for proper configuration settings and correct data. The project managers from both Celestica and Global Concepts used the tool to validate the data and as a management device to quickly and easily determine the status of the project and establish the proper work priorities during the implementation concerning the reference data. The optional reference data analysis and prescriptive reference data analysis are used the same way to check data and settings for configurable processes.

Training was also easier than usual in a new implementation because Celestica's employees were accustomed to using a radio fre-

quency (RF) directed application. Changing to Global's more modern system that incorporated more user-friendly approaches was gladly accepted. Global also spent considerable time training management using ADS (advanced decision support) training to ensure that they understood not only how to use, but also how to manage the WMS system. Because of the many new features and management controls, Global required certification testing for both users and managers.

Even with Celestica's familiarity with an older WMS system, no amount of training can fully prepare a customer for the demands of a new system. Global Concepts phased implementation functionality allowed Celestica to acquire hands-on training in a low stress situation. This was especially important because of the integration of the material handling teams between distribution and repair. In the old environment, Celestica had dedicated material handling groups for raw materials, repair operation, and distribution. Because of the task interleaving capabilities with the logistics engine (LE), it enabled them to merge the group into a single team. The phased implementation allowed the new group to familiarize themselves during this period without the stress of learning in the production environment where mistakes lead to missed orders or the shutdown of repair operations.

Phased implementation also gave GC the ability to test not only the interfaces, but also some custom modules that were added to the system to support Celestica. The ability to test these modules using real data, but without the stress of a production system, enabled GC and Celestica to test faster, more accurately, and without wasting much time developing the data for test scenarios. The phased implementation techniques used at Celestica illustrate Global's ability to control risk. GC was able to limit risk not only within the distribution center (DC) operation, but also to all of the other operations from integrated material movement, to management, from finished goods or raw material receiving, to returns and sorting operation, to repair and manufacturing shops in addition to internal and 3PL operations at the same time.

Change Management

Global Concepts and Celestica were careful not to overlook change management. It was especially critical because not only did it involve internal employees, but it also involved contract employees of IBM. Global Concepts approached the task by quickly forming integrated teams and involving employees at all levels.

Celestica management illustrated their support by participating in meetings and encouraging their employees in staff meetings. Global Concepts' past consulting successes also paved the way for acceptance. Phased implementation also played a critical role because it allowed the employees to learn the system in a low stress, open environment without the pressures of production.

Process Mapping—Obtaining Celestica-Specific Knowledge

The mapping of Celestica's processes was made easier because of the consulting work previously performed. However, due diligence was performed and the processes carefully mapped to ensure a sound understanding at a detailed level. It was approached using the functional operational areas within the facility of:

- Receiving/put-away
- Returns management
- Quality control
- Replenishments
- Picking
- Shipping
- Inventory
- User configuration
- Management/visibility requirements
- IT infrastructure

Each of these areas would be examined in detail, the processes mapped to logistics engine (LE), and the appropriate configurations made within the system to support the processes.

WMS SOFTWARE APPLICATION PROGRAM FUNCTIONALITY

Celestica represents the fact that Global's WMS product, logistics engine (LE), not only functions in a typical DC, but it also functions expertly in a manufacturing, repair, and returns operation. To fully understand the functionality of LE used at Celestica, several terms need to be defined:

- Subzone: Area in the warehouse used to house similar functions; for example, pick locations that will be treated alike.
- Staging/drop zones: Areas in the warehouse where inventory is placed outside of the normal picking areas.
- Vehicle: A conceptual vehicle is created that can perform certain physical functions such as perform put-aways to the overhead rack, and perform conceptual operations such as perform both picking and replenishment activities during the same tour.

• Container: Logistics engine (LE) tracks all inventory, people, and assets within the operation. While inventory is moved around the DC, it must be placed inside a container for tracking purposes. This container could be a pallet, a box, or anything that holds inventory. By scanning the container into an area, all of the contents within the container are automatically moved. This simplifies material movement by reducing the procedure to a single scan of the container rather than each individual item.

In order to make the material flow understandable, Figure 17-16 illustrates the simplified material flow for Celestica. Celestica's requirements mandated that the system handle typical raw material storeroom operations and move materials directly from the dock to POU whether it be quality control, shop floor, or forward areas in the DC.

RECEIVING/PUT-AWAY/QUALITY CONTROL (QC)/RETURNS

Celestica receives pallet, mixed pallet, and small parcel receivals. LE supports all of these methods and provides ASN (advanced ship notice) receiving for qualified vendors. LE also provides a concept called *SKU alias*. SKU alias allows any vendor's UPC or part number to be scanned on the dock and translated to the appropriate SKU number used within Celestica. Because Celestica receives many small complex parts for their telephone repair operation, many of the items pass through a quality control (QC) inspections area before they can be accepted. Celestica has a detailed QC area to certify the purchase order (PO) and perform ad hoc quality inspections on the parts. If the item bypasses QC inspection, personnel could decide to use direct put-away or pallet breakdown receiving.

Direct put-away simply means taking a pallet full of a single item or similar mixed items and, instead of unloading and staging the pallet on the dock, the material is taken directly to the reserve where it will be stored and put away. This eliminates the extra step of staging the pallet on the dock and handling the material an extra time. This feature has saved much time and greatly increased productivity on the receiving dock.

FIGURE 17-16
Simplified Celestica Material Flow

Celestica also has a returns process for broken telephones returned for refurbishment. The process verifies the SKU, collects detailed information, and determines if the phone is capable of being repaired. The process also supports the accounting and disposition associated with a large return and sorting operation. The returns logic determines whether an unrepaired item should be:

- Repaired
- Scrapped
- Transferred
- Salvaged for parts

Global's WMS monitors the sorted materials and makes a timely deplenishment and disposition of these materials as space constraints appear. LE's inbound diagnostics tools help to simplify this process by ensuring quality data and reducing the research performed on many items.

Picking/Replenishments/Shipping

Celestica performs two types of picking: internal picking of items being sent for repair, and external picking for items being sent to customers. Celestica has condition codes for each of the items, but uses forward slots only for external picks because of a lack of space. Celestica performs pallet, case, and broken case picking, and uses both batch and single order picking. LE intermixes cycle counts and opportunity counts into the picking process as part of the task interleaving technique LE provides. This improves efficiencies and accuracies without increasing labor costs.

Celestica sets a minimum and maximum slot quantity for managing its replenishment progress. When a slot reaches the minimum, it sends a replenishment signal to a material handler that automatically fills the slot to the maximum quantity.

LE's replenishment diagnostics help ensure that priorities are properly set to keep efficiencies high. Celestica ships via both less than truckload (LTL) and parcel shipping. Note: as compared with full truck loads (FTL).

Another important feature for Celestica was the ability to function in either a paper or radio frequency (RF) mode. LE provides this functionality for environments where RF access is not feasible and as a backup strategy in the event of an RF failure.

Management Tools

Much like AutoZone, Celestica embraced LE's many management tools. Because their operation was spread across three physically separate areas, managing operations like order picking was challenging. Celestica used GC control tower to provide visibility into the process, making it much easier to manage.

Although Celestica utilizes the management tools, an important feature for them is the ability to perform management overrides. Being a manufacturing and distribution environment operating in three different physical areas, Celestica needed the capability to allow sophisticated users to override the system-directed task under certain circumstances. This pays dividends because in a distributed environment, users can see material moves before the system. This feature allows them to move the

work, and the system is intelligent enough to make the correct assignments.

Distribution/Repair Operations

Celestica performs both distribution and repair within the same operations. The repair operation has several lines utilized for refurbishing phones returned from the field with problems. Like most repair operations, Celestica does not truly know the cause of the malfunction and must diagnose the cause. Because the malfunction of each phone could have a different cause and thus require different parts to refurbish the phones, material management was a problem. Celestica solved their material shortage problems by implementing a real-time point-of-use (POU) storage system at each line to ensure material availability. The POU storage operation is managed by the WMS.

Celestica utilizes a simple two-bin design for their POU. They use material from the first bin; when it is emptied, they scan a bar code label on the bin location and begin using material from the second bin. The bar code scanned automatically creates a replenishment request in the warehouse to send another bin of inventory to the POU. Celestica utilizes vendor package quantities or totes within its POU whenever possible to limit material handling costs, and the bins are sized to hold at least the demand of the line times the replenishment lead time (demand × replenishment LT).

To increase their inventory visibility and flexibility, Celestica treats the first bin as WIP (work in process) inventory and does not attempt to track each individual item used. Even though the second bin is on the floor, LE keeps complete visibility of that inventory and does not assign it to the line until the material is needed. This provides Celestica more inventory flexibility in the event of material shortages, and LE handles all of the transfer and accounting tracking behind the scenes within the system to keep operations simple.

The distribution operation of Celestica is similar to most warehousing operations. They receive, pick, and ship items. Because of the advanced task interleaving and visibility LE provides Celestica, they have been able to combine their material handling staffs. Instead of having people assigned to raw materials, finished goods, and manufacturing like many operations, LE gives them the flexibility to have one large group that floats around the facility and handles all of the material handling tasks. This allows Celestica to reduce the size of the staff without sacrificing any customer service.

Third-Party Logistics (3PL)

Not only does Celestica perform distribution for its own products, but it also performs 3PL services for other companies. To meet their 3PL needs, Celestica required that complex accounting issues be handled within the DC to support their growing third-party–related business. *Even though the material is in the same warehouse, it must be treated as if it were in a separate warehouse.* LE gives Celestica this capability by conceptually creating separate stockrooms even though physically the inventory is in the same area. LE does not allow inventory to be transferred between warehouses, automatically separates the orders, and provides detailed audit trails that are used to calculate the billing for the 3PL customers. LE also initiates cycle counts and opportunity counts to keep inventory accuracy high because customers must know what they have in stock.

Another important feature is the LE's expert system capabilities. Within Celestica's own warehouse and inventory, they have control over their data and its quality. In a 3PL situation, they often do not have quality information. LE has many configuration options that allow Celestica to set parameters that allow the WMS to function without quality data and still achieve many of the efficiencies of good data quality. This feature was lacking in the many systems Celestica evaluated, and it strengthened the results that LE can provide. For example, if the customer has volumetrics, LE can be configured to create a pick tour to fill a pallet and transport to shipping. If volumetrics are not available or inaccurate, LE can be configured to only allow a user to pick a certain number of items before returning to the dock. Although not an optimal situation, it is realty. Many systems cannot handle the lack of data, and they fail. LE can be configured to start slow and then improve as quality data becomes available.

Enhancements

Global Concepts always strives for the processes to drive the system. While mapping Celestica's requirements, there were several unique processes that had to be integrated into the WMS to meet Celestica's needs. Most of these were minor enhancements, but one area called "Receive It" was a unique process that required custom code.

GC worked with Celestica staff to fully understand the process requirements. GC then analyzed the existing solution that was in place. GC was able to utilize much of the code already created by Celestica and incorporate it into LE. GC also took the opportunity to enhance the process to incorporate some advanced features that were not previously possible by combining it with other functional-

ity present within LE. This module now functions as a fully integrated piece of LE.

Interface Software Program

Celestica had relatively complex interface requirements because of the 3PL business and because of the future installation of SAP, a large ERP system. Global Concepts was forced to interface with their existing legacy system and accounting system, MFG-Pro, and any of their large 3PL customers while also supporting the future integration of SAP. Because of the complex requirements, GC used its own internal tool because Celestica required full control over the performance and the ability to create custom exception handling features that could not be found in a commercial product. Figure 17-17 illustrates Celestica's requirements.

Global Concepts used its internal interface software for interface development, management, and control at Celestica. The software performed all of the mapping, file merging and splitting, field translations, and error handling used at AutoZone. It also included the ability to handle multiple inbound interfaces types not used at AutoZone. Because Celestica is involved in the 3PL business, interfaces from these customers were transported directly to LE and requirements driven from them. The outbound reconciliation process was also different because of the accounting requirements for each customer. Even though Celestica has not yet installed their ERP system, Global Concepts created the interfaces to SAP to facilitate its integration when it is installed later this year.

Hardware for Information Systems/Computers and RF Equipment

Celestica runs Global's WMS on a Sun 3500E Enterprise server running the Solaris 9 operating system and using an Oracle 9i database.

FIGURE 17-17
Celestica Information Flow

Global's WMS application has been shown to be able to deliver outstanding performance on what many would consider a low-end hardware solution. Global has been able to fully utilize Celestica's existing 900 MHz network and wide array of LXE RF terminals, allowing Celestica to use almost all existing hardware. Global provides information to a variety of report printers used in production and Zebra bar code label printers at Celestica without changing the source code. Global Concepts WMS is a client server model using the server for most of the computations with access to the database information via the RF and GUI (graphical user interface) clients. The GUI clients were executed from basic Windows machines. Celestica has machines with Windows 98 and XP as well as Windows NT and 2000 running GUI clients.

Installation and Integration

Celestica's system was housed in a climate-controlled room with air conditioning. It had a backup power source in the event of electrical failure. The room had telecommunication access for on-site diagnostics communication as required. Celestica utilizes on-site IBM personnel to maintained the system, including any hardware and/or software upgrades and database backup operations.

To ensure full network convergence, Celestica had its provider, LXE, perform site surveys and frequency spectrum analysis. This ensured solid coverage with no interference, and LXE provided a warranty once they had cleared the site and filed the appropriate permits and licenses on Celestica's behalf. Celestica had security while entering/leaving the DC to ensure only appropriate personnel was allowed.

Celestica utilized an on-site machine to serve as the test system that was physically distinct from their production environment. All data collection and configuration were made to this environment for testing both the software and interfaces.

The plan is to utilize phased implementation. The system will go live over a period of several weeks with a well-planned back-out process if any problems arise. The initial phase will begin in the returns area, with a second phase following closely after on the receiving dock. The last phase involves turning on the rest of logistics engine's standard functionality to support all other DC operations, such as put-away, replenishment, order picking, and shipping. This installation will be completed within the three- to four-month time line.

Testing of Individual Software Program and Entire WMS System

Global Concepts invests a substantial amount of time in testing, at least equivalent to the amount of development time. Developer-level, or unit, testing is accomplished by Global Concepts' development staff, while a second and more complex level of testing is performed by GC support staff. Each test requires a prescribed set of scenarios that vary in complexity and expected outcomes. These scenarios and required data sets are documented prior to execution of the test in order to provide a repeatable set of tests.

Although the majority of software testing is performed by Global staff, both client personnel and IT contract labor are leveraged to maximize the testing effort. Approximately 70 percent of product testing is performed by Global Concepts staff in an internal testing process; the balance of software testing is performed by a combination of IBM contract IT service personnel, Celestica staff, Avaya (a client of Celestica), and Global Concepts. The group testing is to ensure all interface issues are resolved, including data and user interfaces. Some of the participation is simply to supply data and the expected output; other responsibilities are to monitor actual functionality and usability.

The system is so constructed that testing can be accomplished in a modular form. The method of testing for the WMS at Celestica involves:

- Receipt of input data, in the form of internal and customer orders
- Processing a set of returns
- Processing a set of receivals
- Processing a set of internal orders
- Processing a set of customer orders
- Generating and processing replenishments

Each of these has predicted and expected sets of outcomes. The tests scenario results are monitored using real-time inquiries as data is created or modified to determine the correctness and completeness of the outcome. The resulting data, whether output data that would normally be transmitted to the host or production-like updates to inventory, is reviewed and analyzed for correctness and completeness.

Information Systems Security

GC's WMS has several different layers of security at different levels. The system has security for:

- GUI clients
- Database
- Server

The most straightforward security used by Celestica resides within the GUI client called *user admin (administration)*. This utility grants a user privileges based on their login ID and password. For example, a person that only picks items for the WMS may have no need to access the client and requires only limited RF privileges. User admin provides the capability to set access restrictions at the user level. Unlike some other WMS, the configurations are not set for each individual, but rather at a subgroup and group level.

Celestica defined many distinct subgroups that provided access to specific portions of the WMS system. Normally these subgroups revolved around functional operations like receiving, picking, and reporting capabilities for both GUI client and RF access. A group was made up of several distinct subgroups to easily combine features, making it easier to configure and manage access. Individuals were assigned to the various groups. Using this methodology allows changes to be made to the privileges of a picker subgroup, immediately impacting all pickers without changing access for each individual. This is the same way security works within Windows NT.

The next level of security implemented at Celestica revolved around the database. Each user was assigned a distinct database user ID and password that corresponded to their GUI login. As an additional level of security, each user was given database role privileges. Although any use could log into the system, unless the user had the appropriate database role, they were limited to the functions they could perform. For example, two users have database login and passwords. One user might be assigned update privileges to particular tables with the database; another user would only be granted access privileges and would not be capable of making changes. This additional database configuration increases the security within the system, but also increases maintenance if users are commonly added or deleted.

The final level of security revolves around the UNIX login. Celestica chose to have one generic logon for all warehouse users even though GC's WMS could have supported a unique login. This was done to simplify login procedures to a single user ID and password, and to minimize maintenance.

Training

GC's WMS offers six levels of training:

- WMS actual users—training provided to the DC workers. The goal is to teach the user specific procedures within the DC.

- Frontline supervisors—training provided to the floor supervisors. The goal is for supervisors to understand how to use the system to manage the DC and work smarter and not harder.

- Management—training provided to DC and immediate management who do not directly supervise operations, but need to understand and use the information like order tracking, shipping information, etc. The goal is to make the management self-reliant and understand the benefits the system provides to them.

- Support staff—training provided to the personnel responsible for first-line problem solving within the DC. The goal is for this line of users to become the first source of support for the WMS and replace or lessen reliance on GC.

- Super Users—training provided to the personnel responsible for WMS configuration settings and second-line problem solving within the DC. The goal is for this line of users to become the first source of support for the WMS, replace or lessen reliance on GC, and be capable of implementing new sites if required with minimal or no help from GC.

- IT training—there are many levels to this option, from system tester all the way to software engineer capable of making direct modifications to the system. The goal is to teach the user how to maintain and modify the source code.

For every level of training, GC and Celestica utilized a combination of classroom training and hands-on training to provide the needed experience to become proficient in the various aspects of the system. Each of the actual users was taught specific training courses for their particular areas of work. Celestica utilized a trainer concept where GC and Celestica would team teach classes with the goal for Celestica to take over training for all new employees.

For every level of training, certification tests were given. To be deemed proficient, the user needed to obtain a minimum score of 90 percent. The certification tests were multiple choice, with some being strictly questions; others showed actual screen shots of the system and asked them what they should do. The certification is mod-

eled after the computerized testing now being given for the MBA exam. Most of Celestica's tests consisted of between 25 and 50 questions depending upon the functional area and its complexity. Each test question was further classified into functional areas and level of difficulty. After a user took the test, it gave the final score, illustrated the areas where the user was strong or weak, and expressed the difficulty level of questions the user could answer. Celestica could determine what areas were understood, the depth of understanding, and the areas that required additional training even for advanced IT concepts.

Global Concepts utilized the same techniques that were used at AutoZone, including:

- ADS (advanced decision support) training for supervisors and managers

- Super User training

- Support staff

Celestica does not plan to modify LE and will create extension programs utilizing data interfaced from LE instead of changing any code; therefore, only limited IT training was conducted.

Technical Documentation

LE has several levels of documentation that Celestica utilized to support operations:

- Client–GUI online help

- ADS

- Implementation

- Data setup

- Source code documentation

- Certification tests

LE's basic documentation is available online and in both electronic and paper copies. Global Concepts also provided Celestica, and worked with Celestica to create documentation for:

- Contingency/disaster recovery procedures

- Standard system operating procedures

- Backup requirements and frequency

Celestica performs its own hardware maintenance and does not involve Global Concepts directly except for advice.

Operational Support

Global Concepts has contracted with Celestica to provide 24/7 support services to ensure continued proper operation of the WMS. This contract agreement assures Celestica of on-call support and assistance for any system issue at basically any time of day. Global Concepts can respond to such requests for assistance by either going on-site or providing assistance via telephone and remote network login over the Internet.

With the integration of the Celestica-developed returns and receiving modules into the logistics engine product, Celestica users will be reliant on Global Concepts rather than internal support or other contract IT services.

Project Description

The Celestica case study is significant because it illustrates the capabilities of management science models, algorithms, and systems methods. Global Concepts (GC) and its warehouse management system (WMS) are representatives of the advanced analysis methods for both manufacturing and distribution environments. The new methods include tracking material from raw materials using focused storage/point-of-use (POU) concepts to repair operations, and finally to distribution for shipment to customers including some third-party logistics capabilities. Celestica had several custom operations that the WMS was forced to incorporate to support operations at the receiving dock and packing. The results allow Celestica to dramatically improve customer service and reduce cycle times because of the enhanced visibility and tracking the WMS provides.

Questions

1. What logistics issues does this case illustrate?
2. How does a WMS differ from traditional warehouse management?
3. How does Global Concepts' logistics engine improve the operations of the process?
4. In what ways is the Celestica case study significant for the business plans of Global Concepts?
5. Explain why the best system is almost always a hybrid of push and pull production systems? What is the basis for determining the appropriate blend? Note: "Pulling" works best for relatively high production volumes with relatively low variations.
6. How do POU and pulling production affect material handling expense, inventory levels, and customer service?
7. What is the importance of security to both Global Concepts and Celestica?

Transition Management: Preparing for the Future

Part 5 is comprised of Chapters 18, 19, and 20, which focus on various aspects of transition management. Ten issues are highlighted. Two are discussed in Chapter 18, which deals with product development and project management. Chapter 19 explores theories and methods of change that are part and parcel of the P/OM field. Chapter 20 is concerned with environmental issues, problems of ethics, and systems of security. Safety and security have assumed paramount importance in our global view. The World Trade Center became a cataclysmic, mind-changing symbol after the terrorism of September 11, 2001.

Chapter 18, "Product Development and Project Management," encompasses product and/or service development, as well as the congruent process development. The production process must reflect the drivers of product strategy and analysis. Project management is the enabler of the product/process development cycle. Stages and phases of the development process play critical roles. Understanding how to manage projects is essential. Toward that end, critical path methods (CPMs) are explored with attention to cost and timing trade-offs of projects, completion times, and resource leveling.

Chapter 19, "Change Management," explores the pressure to manage change, which has grown consistently greater over the past hundred years. One of the biggest changes in the way business is conducted is related to the use of the Internet for purchasing and selling. E-commerce has had a volatile beginning, but its use perseveres and grows in many ways. This trend will likely accelerate as technology makes itself felt with wireless convenience and voice recognition. Every business is affected. Also, customer relations management (CRM) has become a significant operational expense. Call centers are part of CRM, representing an initial point of customer contact along the product delivery supply chain. CRM operations are best viewed as projects because customer expectations change and competitors offer new incentives (such a free delivery). Project management methods are a way of installing continuous improvement. Reengineering on a greenfield basis is increasingly attractive to speed up change. The most successful companies are those practicing continuous (high velocity) new product development. Chapter 19 focuses on the methods and advantages of organizational ability to engage in continuous new project development.

The title for Chapter 20, "Environmental, Ethical, and Technological Forces," is not a standard title for a text on P/OM. However, the forces for change now have made it a necessity. Operations have major impacts on the environment. By judicious choice of what it does, P/OM can help restore unpolluted ground, rivers, and air. P/OM knows how to assemble the teams that can produce products that can be disassembled so that many parts can be reused. P/OM can choose materials that do not contribute to toxic waste. Design for reutilization is one aspect of P/OM ethical practice. Others include honesty about safety and health. Food and drug materials are issues concerned with ingredients as well as the care and proper treatment (refrigeration) of such products. These are HAACP regulations. Ethics is a systems factor that links P/OM to all of the customers, employees, and suppliers and their interactions with each other. P/OM is often the translator of government regulations including, among other issues, safety of the workplace (OSHA). Ethical benchmarks are changing with worldwide convergence on acceptable environmental standards (ISO 14,000).

Product Development and Project Management

need to change may be driven by forces from *outside* the firm such as competitive actions or customer dissatisfaction. The force may originate *inside* the firm as a result of R & D, creative product development, innovative process management, and other sources of compelling new ideas that will provide competitive advantage. In the decade of the 1990s, forces for change were emerging. In the

decade of 2010, these conditions have accelerated. As a result, projects are not special situations, limited to adventurous firms. Projects are an ongoing way of life for all organizations. Consequently, projects should be supported by permanent organizational systems. Projects are time-based structures for organizing activities to bring about change. To be effective, the organization should be planned proactively—not managed reactively. Without project planning, major transitions will be arbitrary, casual, and less successful.

After reading this chapter, you should be able to:

- Design an effective way of planning new product initiatives.
- Understand the important role of knowledge management (KM).
- Describe the difference between tacit and explicit knowledge in KM.
- Evaluate product development programs.
- Explain the unique work configurations known as projects.
- Classify projects by their various types.
- Describe the life cycle stages of projects. At what stage do ECOs play a part?
- Explain how project managers differ from process managers.
- Discuss project-management leadership and teamwork.
- Explain the basic rules for project management.
- Describe pros and cons of parallel-path project management.
- Describe Gantt project-planning charts.
- Explain the advantages and disadvantages of Gantt project-planning charts.
- Describe how critical-path methods differ from Gantt chart procedures.
- Explain how to use forward-pass calculations to determine the shortest feasible time for project completion.
- Explain how to use backward-pass calculations to determine which project activities are on the critical path.
- Describe what slack means; explain how to derive it.
- Explain when deterministic and probabilistic estimates for activity times apply.
- Show how to use optimistic and pessimistic activity time estimates to obtain a variance measure for activity times.
- Set up a COST/TIME trade-off analysis to determine when to "crash" an activity as compared to doing it in normal time.

- Describe the penalty-reward system that is used for motivating on-time (or better) project completion.
- Discuss the analysis of cost/time trade-offs for crashing projects and explain the relationship of crashing and quality.

- Determine when to use resource leveling to reduce project-completion time.
- Discuss the challenges and opportunities for managing multiple projects.
- Explain why the computer is an essential facility for adequate project management.

THE SYSTEMS VIEWPOINT

Projects have life cycle stages, which means that the project environment is dynamic and changing. It is like a race through an obstacle course where there is planning to "get ready," steps to be taken to "get set," and at the command "go," the race begins. It may take months or years to complete the project, but time to completion is a crucial factor. Many projects are involved with thinking up a new product, building a prototype, testing the concept, evaluating the prototype, and determining what process will be used to make or deliver the product. At this stage, a decision is required to stop, or continue with the same, or changed, design specifications. The project encompasses the product and the process.

What is the stage of the product? **New product development** is entirely different from altering an existing product or process, or both. Project management has different demands placed on it according to the product's life cycle stage. The project to bring out a new product is being raced against the competition. As competitors become faster, the time factor becomes more than an economic issue of how long will it be until return on investment begins. It becomes an issue of whoever is first into the marketplace with a new quality product gains significant competitive advantage. It is known that systems-wide cooperation speeds up project completion while improving the quality of the new product. Companies that do not have the systems viewpoint lack the ability to achieve the level of cooperation necessary to win the race.

New product development:
Stages include concept selection, process specification, pilot plant, market research, and business modeling.

STRATEGIC THINKING

Strategy begins with the planning of new products and processes. Think about the steps that went into the planning for Nissan's new FX45 SUV, a first-time MBA course on security operations; chef Maurice's new menu at Chez M; and Jet Blue's different concept for air travel. The strategy is followed by the tactics of making it happen. Project management, in such cases, requires simultaneous attention to strategic and tactical issues. The product development project system is visionary, but it must also include checking the crucial details. As is often said, "The devil is in the details." Can it be made, will they buy it, how much will they pay, what margin can it deliver, when can it be ready to roll out? Information gathered from every part of the organization as well as suppliers must be analyzed. The tactical details must be congruent with the strategic plans. Until the tactics are thought through, it is not feasible to evaluate the strategies to select the best one to follow. Strategic thinking helps to determine how many projects can be ongoing at the same time.

18-1 DESIGNING NEW PRODUCT-PLANNING INITIATIVES

Products are goods and services that are made and delivered by operations management. New products are required to replace old products that are becoming unprofitable. In addition, new products can help increase the cash flow that sustains a company. New products also provide an opportunity to extend a successful product line, which supports marketing efforts. In short, there are many reasons for a company to be working on line extensions as well as new products that represent different forms of endeavor.

Several rules apply to the new product area. One of these is to choose products that have attributes that are familiar to management because of existing experiences. In other words, try to incorporate what the company is already good at doing, i.e., play to the company's strengths. The following sections on **knowledge management (KM)** relate to methods for systematizing the company's strengths.

Another rule that applies to the new product area is to only offer what customers will want to buy at a price that provides an attractive margin to the seller. Information about what customers will buy that fits the company's capability profile and margin requirements is complex. Essential for success is competent analysis of the complete and appropriate business model.

This requires knowledge of company capabilities and company **core competencies** to be matched with marketing awareness. Correct information gathering is the function of marketing intelligence. Often, this information is available through the market research department. Working closely with operations, market research can help process management improve existing products (changes in taste and appearance, for example). Knowledge about process capabilities interacts with knowledge of the marketplace in helping to fashion new market entries. The systems approach has marketing and operations functioning together. Their combined expertise is a form of knowledge that differs from their individual expertise.

18-1a Knowledge Management Systems

Knowledge management requires having access to an inventory of expertise and skills that can be examined for possible application to a new endeavor. Some call this knowledge directory the yellow pages of in-company expertise. In effect, the company has to document its intellectual capital and special skills. The company has to know *what it knows*, *who has this knowledge*, and *how this knowledge has helped it succeed*. For example, if existing products are successful (at least, in part) because these products embody particular knowledge and understanding of distribution channels, then new market entries might have an advantage if they embody this special expertise.

The same idea works for special capabilities in sales, marketing, operations, engineering (say, in physics, chemistry, or other technical specialties), service, repair, and maintenance. In each case, there may be unique management skills, and/or technical information, in the company's experiential databases. This is the intellectual property of the company gained through its investment in people and their research and experiences. It can exist in people's minds, or on their computers, or stored as paper in files.

Explicit Knowledge

One of the problems of downsizing has been that the HR department may be unaware of the firm's skill and knowledge inventories. There are ample anecdotes about how firms lose critical knowledge when the wrong people accept company severance packages. Too late, the company finds out that only Joe knew how to run a machine that is crucial to complete an important customer's order. Taking an inventory of the firm's skills, experiences, and other explicit forms of special abilities is an essential starting point for a knowledge management system.

Explicit knowledge is the description of what must be done to make things work. Two examples are how to fix a leaky washer on the sink or how to determine the amount of inventory to order from a supplier. The character of **explicit knowledge** is that it allows a successful transfer of "how to" information between the expert and anyone who wants to learn how. Transfer agents can be written words, equations, graphics, icons, spoken words, pictures, and movies.

From a distance learning point of view, explicit information can be studied and used at any time. It is termed *asynchronous information* because the sender and the user do not

Knowledge management (KM): Managing the inventory of knowledge that exists in the company; the ability to find, select, and absorb new knowledge to add to the prior encyclopedic storehouse.

Core competencies: Technical, technological, and production skills possessed by a company interacting with that company's product line.

Explicit knowledge: Form of knowledge that describes what must be done to make things work; can be transferred from teachers to students in words or diagrams.

have to be online together for it to be effective. The asynchronous characteristic of explicit knowledge allows it to be studied as needed. It is in the files and (at least, in theory) recoverable. Intel wrote a white paper, dated August 2002, dealing with information recovery when there are thousands of papers having hundreds of thousands of pages.

The problem of recovering this explicit knowledge is that the database is so large that careful coding is required to use data mining effectively. The paper titled "Information Overload: Inaccessible Data and a Knowledge Management Solution" lays out a systematic approach for discovery and access of the desired explicit information. The web address is http://www.intel.com/ebusiness/it/research/pp023204_sum.htm.

Tacit Knowledge

Knowledge management of complex systems is seldom satisfied by explicit information by itself. There is a great deal of information conveyed by facial expressions such as a raised eyebrow. Body language is often mentioned as a clue to purpose and intentions. There are other clues about what is happening in a system. These can include sights, odors, noises, tastes, tactile memories, temperatures, pressures, and other tacit forms of knowledge.

Distance learning systems have long enjoyed the ease of transferring explicit knowledge via the Internet, by VCR, CD, DVD, written texts, audiotapes, and combinations. However, distance learning systems have long contended with the difficulty (often verging on the impossibility) of transferring **tacit knowledge** over the Internet. It is reassuring to know that in-person, classroom teaching remains the one best way to successfully transfer information of the tacit type of knowledge.

> **Tacit knowledge:** Unstated, implicit, inferred, and unspoken; to access tacit knowledge, consult with people who are seen as being intuitive, instinctive, and perceptive.

Unlike explicit knowledge, tacit knowledge often requires synchronous transmission. This means that the people have to be in the same room, talking face-to-face, to absorb the knowledge. That is the classroom in schools but the meeting room in companies where there is a plan to design new products and services.

Core Competencies

In 1990, Hamal and Prahalad described the benefits of core competencies in their 1990 *Harvard Business Review* article.[1] In the knowledge management arena, these would be described as technical, technological, and production skills possessed by a company. For example, the special expertise that Polaroid had developed for producing instant photography materials focused their competitive efforts on film-makers (Kodak, Fuji) whose product took longer times to develop. At the same time, although Polaroid was the leader in digital cameras, the company misread the future of that product line. Meanwhile, many factors were making the Polaroid process obsolete. See the spotlight box about Polaroid at the end of this chapter.

For many years, Eastman Kodak was the technical and manufacturing leader in photographic films. Eventually, Fuji built its expertise to the point where the rivalry with Kodak was unceasing and intense. Gilette spent a great deal of money on research to maintain its lead in the razor war. Favorite restaurants exist because chefs have "technical" core competencies with their recipes and cooking methods. However, another class of capabilities that is not dependent on the technical and production process expertise is described in the following sections. Instead, it is the result of knowing how to manage a system.

Capabilities Advantages

Two years after the article by Hamal and Prahalad, George Stalk, Philip Evans, and Lawrence E. Shulman distinguished between capabilities and core competencies in their 1992 *Harvard Business Review* article.[2] They identified management expertise as providing competitive advantages. Such expertise can take a variety of forms including smarter procurement, better inventory management, faster new product development, and cross-docking distribution (a la Wal-Mart). Taken together, the core competencies and special capabilities need to be considered when analyzing new product opportunities. W. L. Gore and Company has developed a management style designed to bring a constant stream of

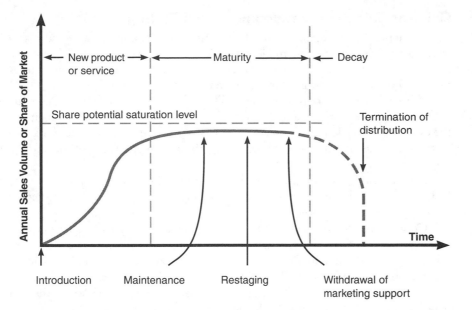

FIGURE 18-1
Stages of Product Development

successful new products into the product line. That is a capability that few organizations (except perhaps W. L. Gore and 3M) can boast about. Because recipes make a great chef, they are the core of favorite restaurant competencies. The other side of the coin would be that ambiance and service are examples of managerial capabilities.

Synergistic Advantages

Synergism is the interaction of elements that when combined produce a total effect that is greater than the sum of the individual elements. Knowledge management strives for combinations of expertise where one plus one is equal to a lot more than two. For example, Wal-Mart's cross-docking combines expertise in the retail business with expertise in purchasing, distribution, and logistics. McDonald's original key to success was the development of its to-go (single-use, all-in-one) packaging. The combination of fast food and the package to carry that food required smart marketing working hand-in-glove with adroit package designers, purchasing, and operations managers.

18-1b Designing New Products

The steps for designing new products all occur before the product Introduction as shown in Figure 18-1. Similiarities also exist between designing new products and redesigning old ones, for maintenance and restaging as shown in Figure 18-1.

The first stage is *concept selection, development,* and *testing.* An example has been chosen that can be worked through to illustrate the steps. It is in the form of a small case about the Sticky Edge Company (SEC).

The Sticky Edge case reflects on the present-day state of the art of stick-on note pads. In general, these pads have a sticky edge of about 0.5 inches in width. SEC is considering developing a new product. It is a new pad with a 1.0-inch sticky edge. A team has been selected and it has found out by talking with the operations manager that (probably) production will be able to reset (quickly and easily) the machinery being used for the standard sticky note. Talks with marketing indicate that a need exists for stronger bonding of notes to paper and cardboard—as well as walls and doors. Marketing is eager to develop a campaign for "industrial strength" stick-on notes, which have been labeled "power notes."

The following list of stages will be discussed in some detail:

1st—Concept selection, development, and testing

2nd—Estimation and business modeling (using spreadsheets)

3rd—Prototype construction and testing

4th—Process specification and pilot plant

Concept Selection, Development, and Testing

The elements that are discussed in the sections on knowledge management play a significant role in *concept selection*. To identify winning concepts (which is the first step in the process of new product development), core competences and special capabilities of the firm need to be examined in terms of market readiness.

Where do good concepts come from? They often originate with the sales force, which is likely to be the first to know that something has changed or needs changing. Perhaps the old product version is no longer the best product available. The sales force is likely to be the first to learn that customers want something different. Competitors often lead the way to change.

Sometimes, change originates with operations. Material prices may have decreased. New technology that is superior to existing technology becomes available. Perhaps competitors are using new materials.

Competitive analysis is always a source of good ideas. Apple Computer provides wonderful examples of product redesign that affects market segments outside of its market sphere. Dell, IBM, Hewlett-Packard, Compaq, Gateway, etc., have copied some of Apple's superior appearance features. The Apple market segment is separated by fundamental differences that make it difficult for non-Apple users to switch. As a result there are good opportunities to imitate Apple in the non-Apple market segment.

Estimation and Business Modeling (Using Spreadsheets)

The note pad with a 1-inch sticky edge is discussed by all project participants in the company—as well as with suppliers. The project team develops estimates for two different quality concepts. All investments and operating costs are based on given specifications of quality. It is not difficult to build the spreadsheet model in Table 18-1. However, the estimates in that table are known to be rough. The spreadsheets are meant to be changed. Better numbers will be used as the new product development team learns more about the project.

Concept 1 has lower quality and price than concept 2. Stickiness for concept 1 will last up to three years. After that, the adhesive will begin to dry up. Concept 2 has a 5-year quality horizon. Table 18-1 presents a draft spreadsheet of the estimates for (a) price per

---

TABLE 18-1

Spreadsheet Summary of the First-Year Business Model for Two Different Concepts

Concept 1						
Price/pack	$10.00	$11.00	$12.00	$13.00	$14.00	$15.00
Demand (000)	200	190	180	165	150	130
Revenue (000)	$2,000.00	$2,090.00	$2,160.00	$2,145.00	$2,100.00	$1,950.00
Cost/pack	$8.00	$8.20	$8.40	$8.65	$8.80	$9.10
Profit (000)	400	532	648	717.75	780	767

Concept 2						
Price/pack	$10.50	$12.00	$12.50	$13.50	$14.50	$15.50
Demand (000)	195	183	170	153	135	114
Revenue (000)	$2,047.50	$2,196.00	$2,125.00	$2,065.50	$1,957.50	$1,767.00
Cost/pack	$8.10	$8.11	$8.12	$8.15	$8.80	$9.00
Profit (000)	468	711.87	744.6	818.55	769.5	741

package of five pads; (b) package demand per year in thousands (Note: Demand falls off as price increases, reflecting estimates of price elasticity that could be geographically sensitive. Production quantities are based on demand expectations.); (c) annual revenue in thousands (the result of multiplication of the two row cells above); (d) cost per package (depreciation is included for the fixed cost component); (e) Annual profit in thousands is calculated on the spreadsheet by subtracting cost per pack from price per pack and then multiplying that quantity by the annual demand.

From Table 18-1, note that concept 1 has highest revenue of $2,160,000 at the $12/package price with demand of 180,000 packs. Concept 2's highest revenue occurs at the $12 price with demand of 183,000 packs. It is $2,196,000, which is $36,000 higher than concept 1's revenue. That is only 1.67 percent higher.

Concept 2 profits are higher for the price range of $10.50 through $13.50. It would have been easier to make comparisons if the two tables for concepts 1 and 2 had used the same price points. For various reasons, real situations are often like this. A similar set of prices could have been developed using interpolation. The highest profit for concept 2 is $818,550 at a price of $13.50 and production of 153,000 packages.

The best profit for concept 1 is $780,000 at a price of $14 with 150,000 packages required from production. No decision will be made at this stage, but prototypes will be manufactured and samples distributed to improve on both sets of tabled estimates.

Prototype Construction and Testing

The decision has been made to create the two kinds of stick-on note pads in the laboratory. If the team had confidence in the estimates of Table 18-1 it might have opted to go straight to the pilot plant that would manufacture the sample quantities on the production floor. Lacking confidence that the market of users will find the 1-inch sticky edge an advantage, the decision is taken to proceed with caution.

Once the prototypes are built, they will be distributed to in-company executives as well as to some other company executives in the neighborhood. Simple market research results will be collected to determine customer satisfaction and to get an idea about how much to charge. The famous POST-IT® Notes were actually tested in this way.

To keep on track, assume that the results thus far are positive. There is interest in the product, and the estimates in Table 18-1 remain unchanged. The next step is important because assumptions about the production system (easy to shift from a 0.5-inch to a 1.0-inch sticky edge) will be tested by the pilot plant manager. Also, the costs per unit become more clear.

Process Specification and Pilot Plant

The operations manager for the 0.5-inch sticky edge process runs into difficulty when trying to convert the edge width to 1.0 inch. An alteration of the machinery would make the conversion easier and less costly. However, the fixed cost for the alteration will add 50 cents to each package of five pads. This is based on a 3-year horizon. The production run (even though under pilot plant conditions) indicates that output rate must be slowed down, which adds 85 cents to each package of five pads. Thus, there is a total increase in the cost per package of $1.35.

Further, the quality envisioned for concept 2 is not feasible for the equipment being used. The product development team agrees to drop the concept 2 version of the product. Concept 1 will be produced on a pilot basis in a lot size of 50,000 units, or 10,000 packages. Results will be collected by market research, and together the management team will make a final decision about this new product.

18-2 EVALUATING THE PRODUCT DEVELOPMENT PROGRAM

Various techniques have been used to test consumer response to the product in the marketplace. Early on it was learned that the price might be too low and a $16.00 price for a package of 5 pads was added. It was noted that demand elasticity took a jump around that

TABLE 18-2	Concept 1						
Spreadsheet Summary of the First-Year Business Model for Concept 1							
Price/pack	$10.00	$11.00	$12.00	$13.00	$14.00	$15.00	$16.00
Demand (000)	180	171	162	148.5	135	117	100
Revenue (000)	$1,800.00	$1,881.00	$1,944.00	$1,930.50	$1,890.00	$1,755.00	$1,600.00
Cost/pack	$9.35	$9.55	$9.75	$10.00	$10.15	$10.45	$11.50
Profit (000)	117	247.95	364.5	445.5	519.75	532.35	450

Building the Golden Gate Bridge in San Francisco was a *major* project. Imagine what it was like to be project manager in charge of creating this magnificent bridge. The construction time line (from January 1933 to April 1937) and bridge statistics can be found at http://www.goldengatebridge.org/research/construction.html. Use the search box to find "seismic retrofit," which is a continuing aspect of the project.

Projects: Time-based endeavors that bring together skills and technology to accomplish goals.

Engineering change orders (ECOs): May appear to be minor alterations in the product design or in the process used, but there are interactions that can lead to severe systems complexities.

price. People liked the increase in sticky area for certain applications. In particular, where there was a fear of loosing the note, an extra-wide edge gave an added sense of security. The fact that notes might not adhere for more than 3 years did not disturb many customers nor did the idea of paying a premium for extra security.

Nevertheless, the team's analysis of Table 18-2 with its revised estimates led to a sense of prudence. Although revenue peaked at the same $12 price, it was down by 10 percent, caused by the 10 percent drop in demand that had surprised market research.

Profit was now maximized at $15, whereas previously, it was at $14. Maximum profit in Table 18-1 was $780,000 as compared to $532,350 in Table 18-2. This quarter of a million dollar decrease is significant. The decline in profitability is 32 percent.

What really bothered the team was the severe drop in profit at $16. Any miscalculation in estimates that would suggest a price increase to fix the problem would not be feasible. Also, there was work going on by the R & D department that would lead to greater stickiness without requiring a larger sticky edge. This led to the suggestion that two varieties be marketed when the new technology was feasible—hold and super-hold—the latter with a premium price. The cost of this alternative would be the same as the current costs. Furthermore, failure of any new entry in this product line could affect the way that customers view other products in the stick-on note product line. The team concluded that caution was the better part of valor.

18-3 DEFINING PROJECTS

Projects are special work configurations designed to accomplish singular or nearly singular goals such as putting on one play, writing new software, creating a mail-order catalog, and constructing a building. Bringing out a new product, building a factory, and developing a new service belong to the same category of unique activities and qualify as projects. Each of these projects consists of a set of goal-oriented activities that end when the goal is achieved. Such undertakings have a finite planning horizon. This is in contrast to the character of batch and flow shop production. Projects have many attributes that are similar to custom work. However, the scale of projects is much greater, involving many participants and resources.

Projects can include some repetitive activities. Building several houses on one land subdivision is a project. Software programming is a project even though use is made of modular components (object-oriented programming). Projects may entail some batch work and even some intermittent flow shop work. However, the project itself integrates activities as it moves toward completion much as each additional chapter is written for a book or floors are added to buildings.

Projects can be classified by degree of simplicity. Many engineering design changes, which result in **engineering change orders (ECOs),** appear to be minor alterations in the product design. However, even simple changes require alterations of the process that can lead to systems complexities. A small design change can destroy the ability of fixtures to hold the parts for all downstream activities. Also ECOs can multiply in number and lead to severe quality problems. These problems are especially noticeable if there is insufficient time to test the interactions of the proposed changes. Having too many ECOs can disrupt the normal business of an organization.

In a well-known business case, a large computer manufacturer fell behind on promised deliveries as a result of trying to correct both errors and steps taken to correct errors. The problem arose in the first place because of the desire to deliver products before they were thoroughly tested. Then, conflicts began to appear when too many ECOs were attempted at the same time.

Projects can be classified by frequency of repetition. Although NASA has launched many shuttle flights, they are not all the same. Challenger blew up on launching (January 28, 1986) because of special conditions. Seventeen years later (February 1, 2003), Columbia burned up during reentry. Again, unique conditions applied. Between these dates, hundreds of successful missions were flown. In space programs, what part can be deemed repetitious; what part is unique and unknown?

Housing developments consist of the same house design being built many times. There are benefits from having repetitive activities within a project. Parts can be purchased with quantity discounts. Training for repetitive activities is justified. The same activity plan (charts) can be used. As the project frequency increases, the project mind-set must remain in place. Plan for contingencies. We are also reminded that object-oriented programming calls upon similar repetitive modules for computer software development.

That mind-set is goal oriented with completion planned for a specific time. If the activities begin to be treated as a repetitive system, then the project orientation has been replaced by one of repetitive scheduling as used by job shops and intermittent flow shops. Note that even though many houses of the same design are being built, there are unique site considerations that must be taken into account. Nevertheless, some builders have produced houses in volume to reduce the costly project factors and replace them with lower manufacturing costs.

Projects can be classified by degree of complexity. Often, the number of issues to consider is very large. Building a new factory is complex. It requires doing a great variety of things that have not been done before. Building another McDonald's may seem at first glance to be highly repetitive. However, the location is different. The officials and their rules are different. Time is different and things change over time (see Countries at http://www.mcdonalds.com).

New product developments are not all the same. Bringing out a new automobile model may seem to be highly repetitive, but there are new elements to deal with every time. The same applies to bringing a new movie to its marketplace. There are lessons learned from prior experiences and then there are the new and different factors to consider. The distinction that is being drawn is between making the last car of a run of 2,000 made that day and the third animated movie brought to a world market by Disney. It may be the same old thing to a few people who are skilled at planning a dinner party. For most people, it remains a daunting project. Although everyone would agree that the dinner party is simpler than launching a shuttle, for many, if not most, it still qualifies as a challenging project.

Projects can be classified by how many entirely new activities are involved. Some projects have few activities that have ever been done before. Examples of such projects might include NASA and the consortium building an international space station together or the construction of a monorail train where the key is the use of entirely new technology.

On a scale of one to ten, where would the construction of the Eurotunnel fall? Called the *Chunnel*, this transportation system under the English Channel connects England to France: Folkestone to Calais in 35 minutes; 4 times an hour; 24 hours a day. Simulation was used a lot to try to understand things that had never been encountered before. Maybe a rating of seven or eight would be appropriate. There was a lot of basic engineering information transferred from other tunnels (see http://www.eurotunnel.com).

18-4   MANAGING PROJECTS

Good project-management methods keep track of what has been done and what still needs to be done. Also, they point to activities that are critical for completion and expedite those activities that seem to be slipping. These points are part of the four project life cycle stages:

1. *Describing the goals* requires developing and specifying the desired project outcomes. (The architect lays out the plans for the building and thereby sets the goals of the project.)

2. *Planning the project* requires specifying the activities that are essential to accomplish the goals. It involves planning the management of the project including the timing of the activities. (The project manager lays out the charts of sequenced activities and estimates how long it will take to do them. The time frame sets in motion the execution of the plan. The builder is usually the project planner.)

3. *Carrying out the project* requires doing the activities as scheduled. (Getting the building permit, ordering the materials, assembling the different kinds of work crews required at the right times, and constructing the building. The builder is usually the project manager.)

4. *Completing the project* can mean disbanding work groups and closing down the project-management team. However, firms that are in the business of project management, such as companies that build refineries, move their crews from project to project. Each project is goal specific and finite. That is the mission of project-management companies as compared to organizations that need to use project management from time to time. The latter cannot avoid the fact that an ECO is a project and needs to be managed as such.

5. *Continuous project teams* is an increasingly attractive option. Companies that are not in the project business might bring out a new product and then disband the project teams when the job is done. As will be discussed later, increasingly organizations opt to maintain continuous project capability.

18-4a   Project Managers as Leaders

Organizations encounter the need for project management whenever they consider introducing a new product or service. Often, they turn to their process managers and appoint them to deal with the project over its lifetime. The kinds of problems encountered in projects are different from those encountered in the job shop and flow shop. Time is money in several ways.

First, until the project is completed there is seldom any return on investment (ROI). Second, when projects are new products, the first into the marketplace with a quality product gets a substantial market advantage. In the same way, when the project is a major process improvement, there may be a cost or quality advantage that also translates into a market differential.

The project manager is constantly trying to reduce the cycle time from inception to completion of the project. This is quite different from the job shop manager who is trying to reduce the cycle time of batches of work waiting to be delivered to customers. It also is different from the intermittent flow shop manager who sets the process-cycle time to deliver the required output to satisfy demand. Although one person can be good at both, a different hat should be worn for each mode.

The project manager is guided by strategic planning, which is tuned to windows of opportunity in the marketplace. This often means putting more resources to work to speed up project completion. Problems arise that slow the project. The costs of such delays can be in the many millions of dollars, whereas the batch shop manager can accept delays that cost much less and are correctable the next time around. Usually, there is no next time around for the project manager.

The ability to manage under pressure and crises is a leadership issue that should be recognized when selecting project managers. Tracy Kidder's description[3] of the enormous stress that was experienced by Tom West's project group when they developed a new computer for Data General (no longer in business) makes memorable reading.

Project managers are accustomed to living with great risk and the threat of large penalties. Their goals are strategic and usually vitally important to top management and the success of the company. Often, their goals are the change-management plans for the company. Thus, the profile of a successful project manager is different from that of job shop and flow shop process managers. Further, project managers often require rapid systems-wide cooperation to resolve their problems quickly. This is a different kind of leadership than that required by process managers who are control-oriented.

18-5 CONTRASTING PROJECTS AND PROCESSES

The major dichotomy of P/OM activities is between α and β:

Change management projects—called (α)—require planning, designing, building, testing, redesigning, and implementing the system. This term refers to the management of change.

Control management processes—called (β)—entail running the system and shielding it from external disturbances. Running the system means controlling inputs, the transformation process, and outputs. Protecting the system involves security and safety.

These are the two main types of P/OM activities. α-type activities are the domain of project managers. β-type activities are the domain of process managers. Organizations such as Bechtel, Computer Science Corporation, EG&G, BE&K, EDS, and IBM devote a lot of their resources to managing projects. They develop managers with expertise in α-type activities. These organizations and their project-management knowledge are often hired by β-type companies that require projects to remain competitive.

18-6 BASIC RULES FOR MANAGING PROJECTS

The following basic rules apply to project management:

1. State project objectives clearly. They should be reduced to the simplest terms and communicated to all team members. There often are many participants in a project, and knowledge about objectives should be shared.

2. It should be made clear to everyone that **change management projects (α)** are a unique work configuration that demands specific capabilities including leadership and teamwork. The contrast should be drawn between (α) and **control management processes (β),** which is the controlled operation of the input–output transformation model.

3. Expertise is required to outline the activities of the project and sequence them correctly. These activities are what must be done to achieve the goals. As a simple example of what happens if the right steps and sequences are not known, when the walls are plastered and painted before the electrical wiring and plumbing are done, the house will have to be unbuilt (going backwards) and then rebuilt to achieve goal completion.

4. Accurate time and cost estimates for all project activities are essential. Slippage from schedule often means real trouble, whereas at other times it can be tolerated because there is sufficient slack. Slack is a time buffer and will be precisely defined in a later section. Project management requires knowing which activities should be monitored and expedited.

5. Duplication of activities, in general, should be eliminated. Under some circumstances, however, parallel-path project activities are warranted, namely:

Change management projects (α): Refers to the management of change, which requires planning, designing, building, testing, redesigning, and implementing the system.

Control management processes (β): Refers to the management of existing systems, which requires operating that system, controlling the inputs, the transformation process, and the outputs.

a. If a major conflict of ideas exists and there is urgency to achieve the objectives, then it is sometimes reasonable to allow two or more groups to work independently on the different approaches. Preplanned evaluation procedures should exist so that as soon as it is possible the program can be trimmed back to a single path.

b. At the inception of a program (during what might be called the exploratory stage), parallel-path research is frequently warranted and can be encouraged. All possible approaches should be considered and evaluated before large commitments of funds have been made.

c. Parallel-path research is warranted when the risk of failure is high, for example, survival is at stake. When the payoff incentive is sufficiently great with respect to the costs of achieving it, then parallel-path activities can be justified for as long a period of time as is deemed necessary to achieve the objectives.

d. When rules 4a, 4b, or 4c are not applicable, the management of parallel-path projects is costly and unnecessary.

6. One systems-oriented person should be responsible for all major decisions. The project manager must be able to lead a team that understands technological, marketing, and production constraints. Multiple project leaders are not feasible.

7. Project-management methods are based on information systems that utilize databases that are updated on a regular basis.
a. Project methods categorize and summarize a body of information that relates to precedence of activities, and their time and cost.
b. Project methods can assess the effects of possible errors in estimates.

18-7 GANTT PROJECT-PLANNING CHARTS

The great chartist, Henry L. Gantt, developed a planning graphic in the early 1900s that is still used in much the same form. Gantt's chart permits a basic project plan to be set down. Then, using trial and error, improvements in project scheduling can be attempted. The Gantt chart does not computerize complex project situations nor does it permit the mathematical analysis of project paths. PERT and CPM methods, which have these capabilities, will be described after Gantt charts are covered.

A Gantt chart is good for small projects and for visualizing the basic structure of any project. Large projects require other techniques where the power of computer-driven project-planning programs can be used. Many computerized, project-planning models are in use.

Figure 18-2 shows successive steps of a Gantt project-planning chart for a manufacturing system. This chart starts with planning, moves through assemblies, and ends with certification. Figure 18-3 shows a chart that describes in general terms the activities required to launch a redesigned automobile. Time lines for both the generic project and the 30-month auto redesign are critical to the Gantt charting method.

Project planners use Gantt charts in two steps. First, set down the necessary activities (*project stages*) to accomplish the project objectives; second, track the status of the project's activities over time. Referring to Figure 18-2, the conventional symbols are bars that show planned start and finish times. The bars are all shaded initially. As work proceeds, a darker shade moves over the lighter one to show the activity's percent completion.

The dashed vertical line is current time. As each day ends, the dashed line moves one unit to the right.

Project stages are listed along the left side of the chart. The planning phase has been completed as scheduled. Materials procurement is behind time. It was supposed to have been completed today. Presumably, the project manager knows what is missing, when it is expected, and what is being affected. Apparently, the materials for fabrication activity 1 arrived because it has been completed on time. The same is true of fabrication activity 2.

Fabrication activity 3 has not been started, and the letter M indicates the problem is material shortage. The delay started six days ago and might seriously compromise the completion time of this project.

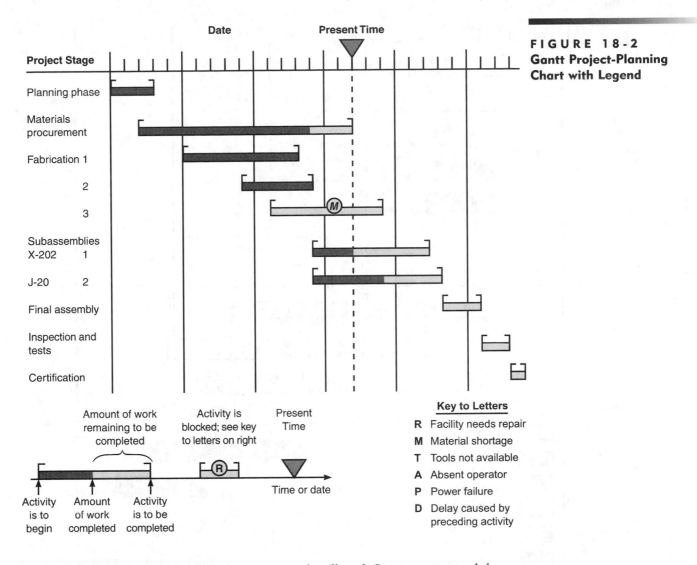

FIGURE 18-2
Gantt Project-Planning Chart with Legend

However, the two subassemblies do not seem to be affected. One is on time and the other is ahead of schedule. Final assembly is scheduled in six days ahead of now. Fabrication activity 3 requires eight days. Unless some way is found to speed it up, the project will be delayed two days. Inspection and certification will be delayed.

The Gantt chart in Figure 18-2 is helpful in tracking a project's progress. The Gantt chart in Figure 18-3 is useful in a different way. It plans a car that requires 30 months from general product specifications and market positioning to public introduction. This is a major reduction in the time traditionally (1950–1980) required from start to finish of an auto. This cycle took four to five years in the 1960s. Detailed attention to how a project is developed will pay off, as a general rule, with significant cycle-time reduction.

Figure 18-3 shows the broad categories of activities that need to be completed to achieve product assembly and launch. Each bar on the chart in Figure 18-3 could be detailed with specific notes and information, as in Figure 18-2. Sometimes, however, too much information obscures the big picture, which relates to the activity bars, their milestones, and project completion.

Technology accounts for the activity structure of the project, i.e., the activities and their sequences. The variables that account for bar length are related to the amount of resources used. Certain activities can be accomplished faster or slower, depending upon the number of people employed, the kinds of facilities that are utilized, and so on. Resource allocations determine time and cost. There are various options. Therefore, for any project there is at least one best sequence to be followed and one best use of resources with respect to cost and time objectives.

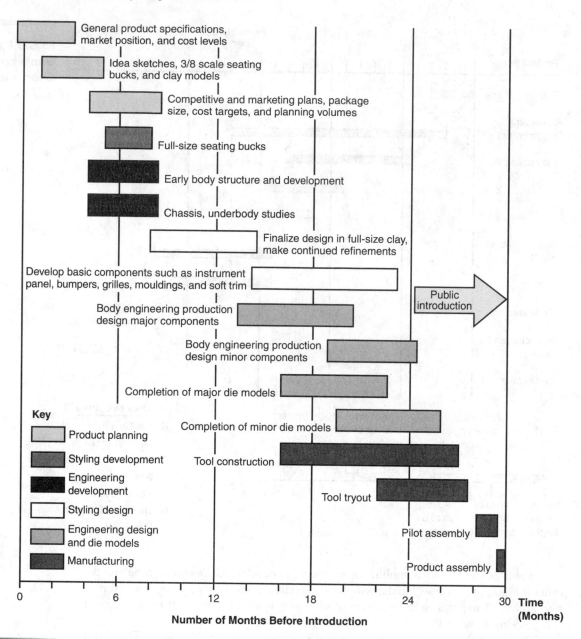

FIGURE 18-3
Gantt Project-Planning Chart for Time Required to Bring a New Car to Market

Critical path methods (CPM): The longest time-path from start to finish of the project; determines completion date of the project.

PERT: Identifies the longest time-path in the project. Emphasis is on estimation as the determinant of project completion time.

Gantt project-planning methods, based on graphical analysis, cannot (1) *lead to optimal resource utilization* or (2) *provide sufficient project-tracking capability* for the complex projects that now are undertaken by large organizations. Because **critical-path methods** (both CPM and PERT) are residents in computers, allowing mathematical calculations, they can achieve (1) and (2). Mathematical methodology is powerful, which justifies careful study of PERT and CPM methods.

18-8 CRITICAL-PATH METHODS

Starting about 1957, two similar approaches to large-scale project planning and tracking were begun at separate locations and for different reasons. These were

PERT—program evaluation review technique—(project network method)

CPM—Critical-path method—(project network method)

PERT was developed by the U.S. Navy Special Projects Office in conjunction with Booz Allen Hamilton for the Polaris submarine launched missile project. This cold war project was considered urgent by the government and time was a critical variable. There were about 100,000 activities divided amongst thousands of suppliers. PERT set up activity networks, ideal for large projects, which could be systematically analyzed by computers.

CPM was a similar method developed by DuPont and Remington Rand, which later became Unisys. It was used to design and coordinate chemical plant operations. Even at the time of development, computers were essential.

Both applications were very successful in reducing project time. Before network methods existed, project slippage was a fact of life. Projects often took 20 percent more time than expected and cost 20 percent more than budget estimates. With PERT and CPM, 20 percent reductions in expected values were experienced. The adoption of the new project methods was immediate within the United States. Many different kinds of software were developed that could be used for very large projects including year-end budget preparation. (See the Additional Readings Section at the end of this chapter.)

PERT and CPM differed only in details. Because *both methods share the notion of a critical path*, this section is called *critical-path methods* for the property of the network and not the name of the program. Further, PERT is the most familiar method to project managers. It was adapted by NASA as NASA-PERT and is required by government agencies for participation in U.S. government projects. Therefore, the discussion refers to the PERT variant of critical-path methods.

18-8a Constructing PERT Networks

Three steps are required to utilize these network models.

1. *Detail all of the activities* that are required to complete the project.

2. *Draw a precedence diagram* for the precise sequencing to be used based on technological feasibility, administrative capabilities, equipment and workforce constraints, and managerial objectives. The rationale for sequential ordering should be documented so that all teammates can share it and the historical record is permanent and explicit.

3. *Estimate the time to perform each task or activity.* The method of estimation for activity times needs to be detailed and related to project quality. For example, more time is required to use double-error checking—to be sure that no project defects occur. Two options are treated with respect to step 3.
   First, *deterministic estimates* for activity times are used.
   Second, *probabilistic estimates* for activity times are used.

Critical path is defined in terms of time. PERT is a time-based method. Time and cost estimates will be related at a later point. For now, time is the crucial parameter. The goal is reduction of planned project completion time—and then, control of project-cycle time to meet the goals of the plan.

18-8b Deterministic Estimates

After the project has been planned, the activities and their sequence are known so the project-precedence diagram can be drawn. Figure 18-4 shows a precedence diagram for a construction project. This diagram spells out what should be done next in the construction of successive floors of a multistory building.

Each activity has a time estimate written on its arrow. That number could have been derived by requesting an engineering estimate. Sometimes it is an average based on historical records of the time required for that activity. Because it is one number, there is no way of inferring variability. Later, two parameters (the average and the variance) for probabilistic estimates will be discussed.

PERT charts are introduced with deterministic estimates to keep the discussion focused on their construction and on the determination of the critical path. Two kinds of charts can be drawn. The first is where activities are represented by circles called *nodes*.

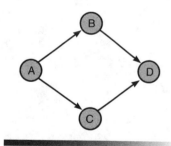

FIGURE 18-4
A Precedence Diagram for Construction of Each Floor of an Office Building

FIGURE 18-5
Activities Are Drawn as Nodes Called "Activities-on-Nodes (AON)"

18-8c Activities Labeled on Nodes (AON)

Networks consist of arrows and nodes. One form of network chart assigns activities to nodes. This is shown in Figure 18-5. Then, the arrows describe the order or precedence of the activities. For example, activity C follows completion of activity A. This is called an activities-on-nodes (AON) network.

Put another way, the AON chart in Figure 18-4 shows that activity A precedes activities B and C. It also states that activity D cannot be done until both B and C are completed. The relationships are summarized in Table 18-3.

There is no ambiguity about these instructions. However, when the activities are drawn on the arrows, there can be confusion about the precedence instructions.

18-8d Activities Labeled on Arrows (AOA)

When the activities are represented as arrows, then the node circles are called *events*. Each node marks either the starting event of one or more activities, or the finishing event of one or more activities, or both. This is shown in the event-oriented, **activities-on-arrows (AOA)** network of Figure 18-6.

This chart is ambiguous because there are two arrows labeled D. One arrow for activity D has to follow the arrow of activity B. The second activity D arrow follows the arrow of activity C. Consideration of the nonambiguous precedence rules in Figure 18-5 reveals

TABLE 18-3		
AON for Figure 18-5		

Activity	Activities That Must *Immediately* Precede
A	None
B	A
C	A
D	Both B and C

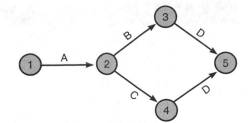

one of several problems that can arise when transferring from **activities on nodes (AON)** to **activities on arrows (AOA).**

This situation cannot be permitted for computational reasons. The computer (using the PERT-network algorithm) cannot distinguish between these two D arrows. The ambiguity is removed by redrawing this network, as shown in Figure 18-7, where a dummy arrow has been added.

The dummy activity in Figure 18-7 is represented by the dashed line inserted between nodes 2 and 3. Dummy activities take zero time to accomplish. This dummy allows activities B and C to join at a single node (4), which precedes activity D. It will not affect time computations along the network paths. However, it allows the computer to keep track of the nodes, as shown in Figure 18-7 and Table 18-4.

Look at Figure 18-6 and note that nodes 3 and 4 are both starting nodes for activity D. Without the dummy, computations would stop. The program cannot resolve this ambiguity. Observe that $t_3 = t_2$ in Figure 18-7.

Note that in Figure 18-7 the dummy activity could as well have preceded activity C instead of activity B. (It is requested that this alternative be drawn in the Problems Section at the end of this chapter.) Also, there is no need for dummy activities when AON is used. However, the computer cannot use the information in the AON diagram because it lacks the start and finish times. AOA supplies the start and finish times and is therefore required for the PERT method. The need to create dummy activities arises only when there is ambiguity about start or finish nodes for an activity—as in Figure 18-6. Dummy activities can be developed by trial and error to address situations of ambiguity with AOA.

The PERT algorithm (rules for calculation) uses the nodes and the activity times to compute four different measures of project timing, (e.g., early start, late finish). Thus, the data in Table 18-4 are the starting point for further computations. This will be explained right after some other network conditions are stated.

Activities-on-nodes (AON): Numbered nodes are the project activities; arrows between nodes show the precedence on activities.

Activities-on-arrows (AOA): Project activities are the connecting arrows. They start with one numbered node and end with the other node.

18-8e Activity Cycles

In planning a project, some activities go through a cycle of steps. For example, a test on a new product design can result in pass or fail. If the product fails the test, then rework is required, and a retest is scheduled for the new rework completion time. Looping back and forth between test, rework, and retest, as shown in Figure 18-8, is not permitted in PERT networks.

The test/redesign cycle shown in Figure 18-8 could occur more than once before the project is completed. Project planners can seldom prespecify the amount of redesign, rework, and testing that will be needed before project completion. Therefore, estimates are made of the likely rework requirements, and the PERT network is drawn in extensive

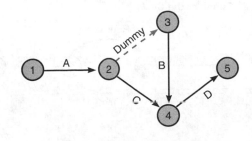

TABLE 18-4

Computer Record of Project Data for Start and Finish Times

Node	Event That Is Tracked	Time	Activity Time
1	Start activity A	t_1	
2	Finish activity A	t_2	$t_A = t_2 - t_1$
	Start activity C	t_2	
	Start dummy activity	t_2	
3	Finish dummy activity	t_3	$t_{dummy} = 0$
	Start activity B	t_3	
4	Finish activity B	t_4	$t_B = t_4 - t_3$
	Finish activity C	t_4	$t_C = t_4 - t_2$
	Start activity D	t_4	
5	Finish activity D	t_5	$t_D = t_5 - t_4$

form as shown in Figure 18-9. This is called an *extensive network* to signify that activities are always moving forward with no arrows allowed to loop backwards. If the estimate is not correct, then the PERT network is redrawn and recalculated. Such updating of PERT networks is normal.

Figure 18-9 presents the project network in extensive form with two test–redesign occurrences followed by product acceptance and release after a third test. Assume that the project planner's best guess was that it was equally likely that one, two, or three redesigns would be needed. The average of two redesigns was used for Figure 18-9. Probabilities can be recalculated as the project proceeds and more information becomes available.

Projects of realistic size have thousands of different activities. Whenever an activity starts or finishes, an event node must be created. The project designer may use few or many activities to represent the same project elements. For effective project design, more activities are better than few because that allows greater activity control. However, activities should not be divided when they are interdependent and indivisible.

18-9 CRITICAL-PATH COMPUTATIONS

Figure 18-10 depicts a project network with three main branches called A, B, and C. The PERT network is drawn for computer use with activities on the arcs.

The project network cannot be used as drawn here. There are two arrows labeled A_2. They were both drawn to show that neither A_3 nor B_2 could begin until A_2 was finished. Figure 18-11 corrects the situation by constructing a dummy activity.

In this reality-based project example, the activities A_1, A_2, and A_3 might be marketing activities needed to launch the new product. Branch B might be production process activities B_1 and B_2. Branch C might be activities C_1, C_2, and C_3, used to develop distribution channels. The branches move ahead together, which is considered good practice. It will help to decrease time to market. The PERT information system has no way of showing that team members are in communication with each other. It can show that teams are monitoring progress.

FIGURE 18-8
PERT Networks Do Not Permit Looping Backwards

Consider the Cycle

All activities are labeled with an activity time t (in days). In addition to the dummy constraint, which insures that A_2 will be completed before either A_3 or B_2 can start, it should be noted that A_3, B_2, and C_3 must be completed before product launch can occur at the last node.

There are four unique paths leading to the launch node.

FIGURE 18-9
PERT Networks Must Be Drawn in Extensive Form; This Figure Indicates That Redesign is Expected to Occur Twice

(Marketing)	Top path: A_1, A_2, A_3
(Marketing and production)	Mixed path: A_1, A_2, dummy, B_2
(Production)	Middle path: B_1, B_2
(Distribution)	Bottom path: C_1, C_2, C_3

18-9a Forward Pass

Every event node in the PERT network will be identified with the following 4-part scorecard. That scorecard shows earliest and latest starts and finishes. Activity time t accompanies the scorecard.

ES	EF
LS	LF

ES = earliest start; dependent on preceding activities
EF = earliest finish; dependent on ES and activity time
EF = ES + t t = activity time

LS = latest start, without delaying project
LF = latest finish, without delaying project
LS = LF – t t = activity time

The node scorecards are now explained in terms of Figure 18-12, which starts scoring ES, the earliest start, and EF, the earliest finish, for the first nodes along each path. For every arrow, the left-hand node is its start time and the right hand node is its finish time.

The earliest start for each beginning node is zero, which is therefore entered in the upper left-hand box of the scorecard. Next, note that the earliest finish EF is equal to ES plus the activity time (t) along the arrow that connects two nodes. Adding $t = 23$, the activity time for A_1 to zero yields 23, which is entered into the upper right-hand box of the scorecard. Doing the same for branches B and C produces pairs of numbers (ES, EF) of (0, 16) and (0, 25) respectively.

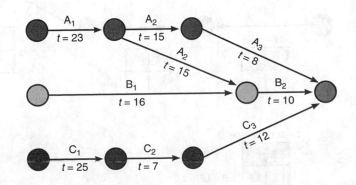

FIGURE 18-10
Basic Pert Chart with an Infeasible Network; There Are Two Arcs Labeled A_2; Dummy Activity Is Needed

FIGURE 18-11
Basic PERT Chart with Activities Named on Arrows and Time Estimates Given

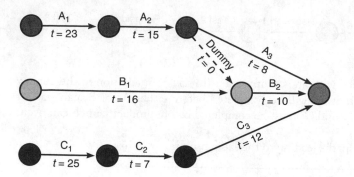

Figure 18-13 completes the calculations for the top two boxes (ES, EF) of every node. The value of EF for each preceding node becomes the value of ES in the next node. In other words, the earliest finish for C_1 becomes earliest start for C_2.

For activity A_2, ES is 23, $t = 15$, and so EF is 38, which is entered in the upper right-hand scorecard for A_2. The same operation is performed for A_3. Carry the previous EF to the new ES. Add the activity time and the entry pair is (38, 46). This is consistent for the dummy activity, which carries forward the same EF of 38 for earliest finish time of A_2 and puts that number into ES for the dummy. Then, 38 plus the dummy's activity time of zero makes EF for the dummy equal to 38 (unchanged).

Skip the B-path for a moment because a second scoring rule applies there. Instead, calculate the values for the C-path. For C_2, (32 = 25 + 7). For C_3, (44 = 32 + 12). The top two boxes of all scorecards have been completed except for the B-path.

When two arrows converge at a single node, which occurs at the start node for B_2 (which is also the finish node for the dummy and for the B_1 arrow), always carry forward to the next earliest start (ES) the largest prior value of earliest finish (EF). Figure 18-14 focuses on just this one part of the network.

FIGURE 18-12
PERT Chart with Initial Calculations for Earliest Finish (EF)

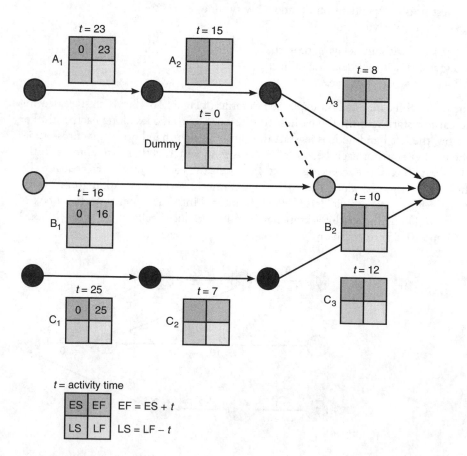

t = activity time

| ES | EF | EF = ES + t |
| LS | LF | LS = LF – t |

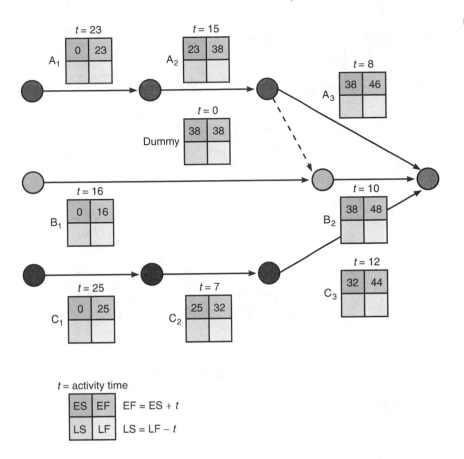

FIGURE 18-13
PERT Chart with All Calculations Completed for Earliest Finish (EF)

Figure 18-14 shows EF circled for both the dummy and B_1. The circled EF is 38 for the dummy. The circled EF is 16 for B_1. The largest value of the two is 38 and so that is entered as ES for B_2.

The **forward pass rule** for arrows converging at a node: *When two or more arrows converge at a single node, choose the largest value of EF among the converging arrows for the ES value of the next activity.* All further accumulation proceeds with this larger number, because it is the earliest possible starting time for the next event in the network. It is the earliest possible starting time for all successive events thereafter. That is why ES = *earliest start, dependent upon preceding activities.*

Forward pass rule: Enables the project managers to determine how long it will take to complete the project; a necessary precursor to use of the backward pass rule.

FIGURE 18-14
When Multiple Arrows Converge at a Node as They Do Here (Dummy and B_1), Then the Largest Value for Earliest Finish (EF) Is Carried Forward; It Is 38

FIGURE 18-15
PERT Chart with Completed Forward Pass; The Earliest Finish (EF) Possible Is the Largest Number AT THE LAST NODE

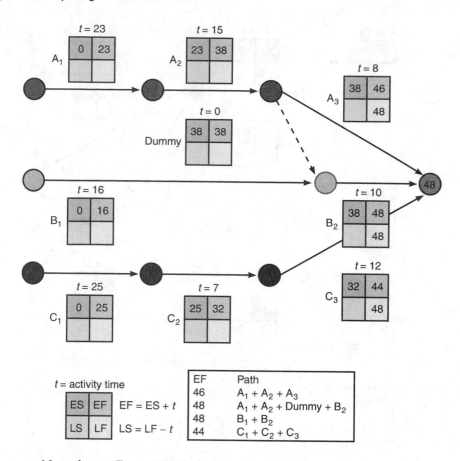

Note that in Figure 18-15, three arrows converge on the last node of the network. The forward passing rule for arrows converging on a node applies here in a different way.

The arrows converging on the last node are A_3, B_2, and C_3. Their EF values are 46, 48, and 44, respectively. There is no next node to carry them to and therefore the largest one specifies the earliest finish time for the project. That number is 48 for the example in Figure 18-15, and it is entered on the final node. It has now been determined that this project requires 48 days for completion.

The procedure just followed is called the *forward pass* through the project network to determine the earliest start and earliest finish times at all nodes. The largest value of the earliest finish (EF) at the last node also is the latest finish time possible for the last node. Thus, EF = 48 days = LF, and 48 is entered for the latest finish (LF) in the bottom right-hand box of the scorecard *for all three arrows* converging at the last node in Figure 18-15. If LF is chosen to be later than 48 days, it would delay the project.

This largest value of EF and LF at the last node in the network is the project-completion time, assuming that nothing unexpected occurs. It also is a measure of the maximum cumulative time of any path through the network, i.e., the longest time sequence of consecutive linked activities through the network.

Although shorter paths exist (for example, all C-branch activities can be completed in 25 + 7 + 12 = 44 days), the longest path dominates all plans concerned with project completion. If this example was the PERT chart for building a new home, don't try to get the certificate of occupancy before 48 days. As an alternative example, failure results if advertising occurs before the new product is on the supermarket shelves. The project team advised marketing to assume 48 *working* days if there are no penalties for being late.

18-9b Backward Pass to Get the Critical Path

Now to determine the activities that constitute the critical path, start with the final node of the last activity and move backwards. For example, which of the four unique paths that were previously listed accounts for the longest time sequence of 48 days? That path is

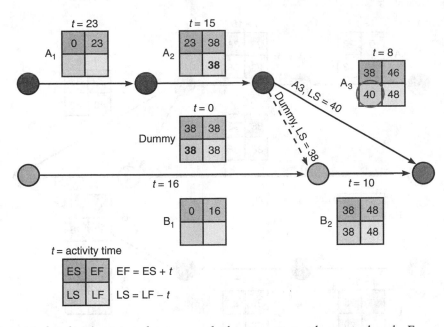

FIGURE 18-16
When Multiple Arrows Radiate from a Node— (See DUMMY and A_3) Then, on the Backward Pass the Smallest Value for the Latest Start (LS) Is Carried Back. This Is the Value of 38 Instead of 40. Note circled values.

called the *critical path*. There is *at least one* path that constitutes the critical path. For a small project network, it is easy to find out which path (or paths) of activities is responsible for the final EF and LF. With real project complexity, the PERT computations (forward and then backward) cannot be done without a computer. The backward-pass part of the algorithm is as follows.

Start with the largest value of latest finish. In the example, this is LF = 48. Move backwards through the network, subtracting activity times in accordance with LS = LF − t. The latest start time (LS) of the $(n + 1)$ node becomes the latest finish time (LF) of the prior nth node. LF is the bottom right-hand box of the scorecard. LS is the bottom left-hand box of the scorecard. Thus, for activity B_2, $(38 = 48 − 10)$.

Note the B_2 scorecard in Figure 18-16. It shows that LF was entered as 48 and $t = 10$ was subtracted yielding LS = 38. This becomes LF for the DUMMY. In Figure 18-16, two arrows emanate from the finish node of activity A_2. These arrows come out of the node, moving from start to finish. This means that in going backwards, these two arrows converge on that same node.

There is a backwards convergence rule that is similar and opposite to the forward convergence rule. It is opposite because it carries back the smallest value of LS. The **backward pass rule** for multiple arrows eminating from a single node: *When two or more arrows meet at a single node, choose the smallest value of LS among the converging arrows for the LF value of the preceding activity's arrow.* All further accumulation proceeds with this smaller number, which is the latest possible finishing time for the preceding activity without delaying the project.

In Figure 18-16, the calculation for the dummy's latest start (LS = LF − t) is $(38 = 38 − 0)$. LS for A_3 is 48 minus 8 equals 40. Because 38 is smaller than 40, 38 becomes LF for A_2. See the circles in Figure 18-16 and the bold faced 38 for LF of A_2.

Figure 18-17 shows all node scorecards filled in with latest starts. The backward pass has been completed. Table 18-5 shows all these results as well as those for EF.

Table 18-6 tabulates the results for latest start (LS) and latest finish (LF) for all three branches of the project network. This includes results previously calculated on the backward pass. In addition, to put all relevant information together in one place, Table 18-6 includes the data for earliest finish (EF) and earliest start (ES) for all three branches of the network.

The results in Table 18-6 are used in three ways. First, they are used to calculate **slack,** which is allowable slippage. Slack, by definition, can be wasted without changing project-completion time. Note how the previously discussed C-branch takes 44 days to complete whereas the critical path takes 48 days. There is slack of four days along branch C. Second, Table 18-6 can be used to identify the critical path, which is the path of zero slack. Third, Table 18-6 allows identification of where slack resides.

Backward pass rule: Enables the critical path to be identified; also permits the determination of slack.

Slack: Translates to allowable slippage in an activity's schedule along a slack path; the amount of time that it is safe to be late in delivering a completed activity. Safe means no addition to project completion time.

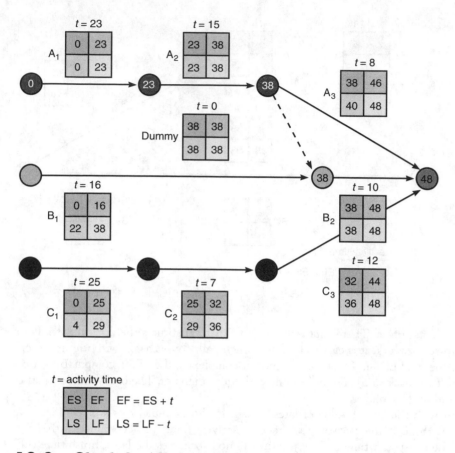

18-9c Slack Is Allowable Slippage

Table 18-6 calculates slack in two ways. Slack = LS – ES = LF – EF. Note that both subtractions produce the same result for each activity. Also, the column marked CP has an X in it if that activity is on the critical path. It will be noted that the X entry coincides with 0 slack values.

The slack of an activity describes the amount of time (here in days) that can be viewed as a safety buffer for slippage. The project manager has to view small amounts of slack and zero slack as the activities that demand constant attention because slippage

TABLE 18-5	Activity	LS = LF – t	EF = ES + t
Latest Start (LS) from Latest Finish (LF) for All Activities and from Figure 18-15 Earliest Finish (EF) and Earliest Start (ES)	A_3	40 = 48 – 08	46 = 38 + 08
	A_2	23 = 38 – 15	38 = 23 + 15
	A_1	00 = 23 – 23	23 = 00 + 23
	B_2	38 = 48 – 10	48 = 38 + 10
	B_1	22 = 38 – 16	16 = 00 + 16
	C_3	36 = 48 – 12	44 = 32 + 12
	C_2	29 = 36 – 07	32 = 25 + 07
	C_1	04 = 29 – 25	25 = 00 + 25
	DUMMY	38 = 38 – 00	38 = 38 + 00

Activity	LS	ES	Slack	LF	EF	CP
A_1	0	0	0	23	23	X
A_2	23	23	0	38	38	X
A_3	40	38	2	48	46	
B_1	22	0	22	38	16	
B_2	38	38	0	48	48	X
C_1	4	0	4	29	25	
C_2	29	25	4	36	32	
C_3	36	32	4	48	44	
DUMMY	38	38	0	38	38	X

there results in project delay. Shortly, it will be shown that reallocation of resources can affect slack, which puts discretionary powers for what is critical, and what is not, in the hands of project planners.

Note the activities with zero slack follow the path A_1 + A_2 + DUMMY + B_2. *This is the critical path.* It is the set of activities that define the shortest time in which the project can be completed without slippage. Figure 18-18 shows the critical path with darker lines than the rest of the network.

In Figure 18-18, where slack exists, the amount is indicated. The C-path has slack = 4 for all three C activities. If C_1 starts four days late, all the slack is used up for C_2 and C_3. Contiguous slack along a path is shared slack.

If activity A_3 is delayed two days, it becomes part of the critical path. Activity B_1 has 22 days of slack. That is a great deal of slack for a project with a critical path of 48. B_1 can be delayed in starting or take much longer to be done than expected. The project manager might think about transferring some people from B_1 to one of the critical activities to relieve the stress. That tactic is called *resource leveling* and it will be discussed later.

Using the 3-branch example of marketing, production, and distribution brings up the question of Best Practice. Because production has 22 days of slack at B_1, it might seem acceptable for OM not to get involved in the project immediately. However, that is no longer acceptable practice. Instead, production should get involved with marketing issues to help expedite work along the critical path and to share insights and systems perspectives. From a systems point of view, note how the dummy activity shows an important systems linkage between A_2 and B_2. Production has the opportunity to work on marketing issues, and then marketing has a little leeway to work on production issues. This is termed *concurrent project management.*

The slack situation is represented by Figure 18-19 in a concise way where both B and C's slack is allowed to be used up. Then, both paths of the project become critical. Only activity A_3 can be allowed to slip without increasing project-completion time. This illustrates how more than one project path can be critical. Management is hard pressed to handle projects that have a large percent of critical activities.

Knowing which activities have slack is important. It is probably wasteful to expedite activities A_3, B_1, C_1, C_2, and C_3. It is likely to be useful to expedite along the critical path. Note that such information about slack and the critical path are not available using the Gantt chart.

FIGURE 18-18
Critical Path and Slack
Are Shown

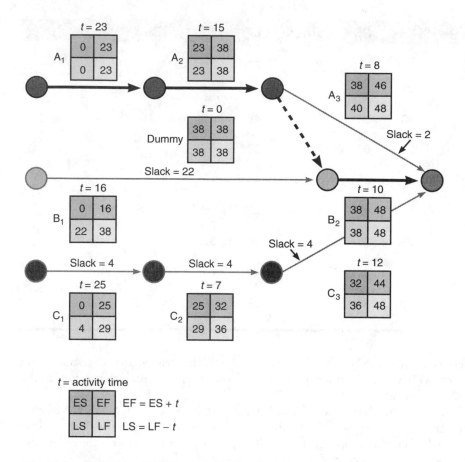

t = activity time

ES	EF
LS	LF

$EF = ES + t$

$LS = LF - t$

18-10 ESTIMATES OF TIME AND COST

Project management requires good estimates of time to manage the critical path and use slack resources in a proper fashion. Delivery of the finished project must be on time. As will be explained shortly, there can be penalties for being late.

As for cost estimates, when project bidding is used, underestimating the cost of a job results in lower bids with higher probabilities of the bid being accepted. The actual higher cost of the job reduces profit. A good estimator increases the organization's revenues by not overestimating costs, which produces bids that are too high, resulting in lower probabilities of winning the bid.

Management relies upon its ability to estimate before hard data are available. Organizations that deal in projects track the estimating capabilities of their employees by maintaining historical records of their estimation errors. The following equation can be maintained for all project managers who make estimates.

Estimate – Actual result = Error

Using this equation to collect data, it is possible to evaluate estimators in terms of

1. How close their *average error* is to zero

2. How dispersed (*variability*) are their errors

3. Whether their errors tend to be overestimates or underestimates (*error bias*)

FIGURE 18-19
When B and C Are Delayed
in Starting as Shown, Then
3 Paths Become Critical

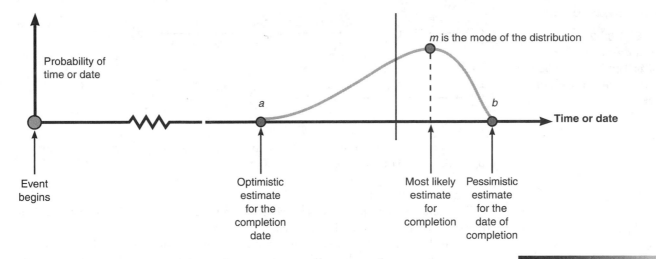

Basically, there are three different methods for obtaining estimates:

First, is a person's opinion derived from their experiences.

Second, is the pooling of several individuals' opinions derived from their experiences. Many different pooling techniques are available, the most obvious being to use the average value.

Third, several parameters of estimation are requested from an individual, and these are combined by a computing formula (called *multiparameter estimation*). As in the second method, the pooling of several persons' opinions can be achieved.

For PERT, the prevalent estimation procedure is either the first or the third method. The U.S. Navy helped to develop multiparameter estimation, which uses the beta (three parameter) distribution. The PERT system requires three different estimates of time for each activity. These are

1. An *optimistic* estimate, called a

2. A *pessimistic* estimate, called b

3. A *most likely* estimate, called m

The three estimates are combined to give an expected (mean) elapsed time, called .

$$t_e = \frac{1}{6}(a + b) + \frac{2}{3}(m)$$

If a single number is given as an estimate, it is the mode value, m. The computing formula adds variance information by providing a range between shortest likely and longest likely times. A possible distribution for these three elapsed time estimates is shown in Figure 18-20.

The three values a, b, and m are used to estimate the mean of a unimodal beta distribution. For the unimodal beta distribution, if a and b are equally spaced above and below m, then $m = t_e$. That is

$$t_e = \frac{1}{6}[(a = m - x) + (b = m + x)] + \frac{4}{6}(m) = m$$

When a and b are not symmetric around m, the mean, t_e, is moved in the direction of the greatest interval.

A beta estimate of the variance (σ^2) associated with the mean value t_e is given by:

$$\sigma^2 = \left[\frac{1}{6}(b - a)\right]^2$$

This method of estimating the variance is appealing because a single estimate of variance without historical data is difficult to make and hard to believe. Beta provides a logical basis for estimating the range.

FIGURE 18-20
A Possible Distribution for Activity Time Estimates Using the Beta Distribution

FIGURE 18-21
**The Variance of the Path
Is Equal to the Sum of the
Variances of the Individual
Activities**

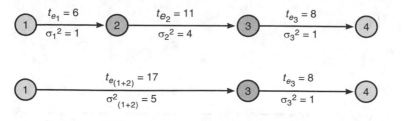

The sum of the means of successive activities is the mean of the path. Thus, for the top (marketing) path:

$$t_{(A_1 + A_2 + A_3)} = t_{A_1} + t_{A_2} + t_{A_3}$$

The same kind of equation can be written for all the other paths. The sum of the variances of successive activities is the variance of the path.

Figure 18-21 illustrates how the mean and the *variance* are combined by summation.

The rule concerning the sum of activity variances requires that the activities should be independent in this regard. This means that if one activity is late it will not affect any other activity's time. Then the following equation describes the variance of the top (marketing) path:

$$\sigma^2_{(A_1 + A_2 + A_3)} = \sigma^2_{A_1} + \sigma^2_{A_2} + \sigma^2_{A_3}$$

The variance of the *critical path* (mixed-marketing and production) is

$$\sigma^2_{(A_1 + A_2 + \text{Dummy} + B_2)} = \sigma^2_{A_1} + \sigma^2_{A_2} + \sigma^2_{\text{Dummy}} + \sigma^2_{B_2}$$

The variance of the production path is

$$\sigma^2_{(B_1 + B_2)} = \sigma^2_{B_1} + \sigma^2_{B_2}$$

The variance of the bottom distribution path is

$$\sigma^2_{(C_1 + C_2 + C_3)} = \sigma^2_{C_1} + \sigma^2_{C_2} + \sigma^2_{C_3}$$

Note that the paths share activities, so that the *variances of the paths* are not independent. This is not a problem as long as the *variances of the activities* do not affect other activities.

When the variance of a noncritical path (based on t_e) is larger than the variance along the critical path, it is possible that the noncritical path will become critical. This means that the original critical path switches to the new one. Simulations can be run using the mean and variance information to determine the percent of time that each path becomes critical. Top attention should be paid to the paths that become critical most often.

18-11 DISTRIBUTION OF PROJECT COMPLETION TIMES

When activity times vary, project-completion time varies. Assume that off the critical path there is enough slack to make variances along the critical path the main point of interest. An analysis of the variation of critical-path time provides risk estimates of major interest to project managers who promise to deliver the finished project at a specific time. There are penalties for being late.

Figure 18-22 shows the mean and the variance (in parentheses) for each activity.

The variances are summed proceeding along the critical path. At the final node that signals project completion, the mean of the critical path (48) is shown with the estimated variance (16).

Figure 18-22 is based on a normal distribution. It illustrates a probability of 0.95 that the actual completion time will fall within the range of 40 to 56 days. The left tail of the distribution reflects the 0.25 probability of an early completion of the project. The right tail of the distribution reflects the 0.25 probability of being late in completing the project. The figure illustrates that the mean of 48 days $\pm 1.96\sigma$ ranges from 40.16 days to 55.84 days.

FIGURE 18-22
Distribution of Project-Completion Times Around the Expected Time of 48 Days. The Probability is 0.05 That Actual Completion Time Will Not Fall Within the Range of 40 to 56 Days.

Each tail contains the probabilities of an event occurring approximately 25 out of 1,000 times. The right-hand tail contains long completion dates (above 55.84 days). The left-hand tail contains short completion dates (below 40.16 days). Also, it is interesting to note that the probability is 50 percent that the actual project-completion time will exceed 48 days or, conversely, be less than 48 days.

To summarize, there is a 95 percent probability that the actual completion date will fall within the range of 48 days ±1.96σ. Because σ = 4, 1.96σ = 7.84, and 48 + 7.84 = 55.84, and 48 – 7.84 = 40.16, providing the means to discuss penalties for being late and rewards for being early. This range can be used to specify an earliest and latest project completion date for contract negotiations.[4] For readers' convenience, a table is provided in Note 4 at the end of Chapter 18 that shows useful ranges for different values of k in $k\sigma$.

18-11a The Effect of Estimated Variance

The analysis of project-completion times can be extended to reflect the effect of variance on all of the paths in any project network.

Path		Expected Completion Time	Total Variance	95% Range (1.96σ)
1	A_1, A_2, A_3	46 days	16	38.16—53.84
2*	A_1, A_2, Dummy, B_2	48 days*	16*	40.16—55.84*
3	B_1, B_2	26 days	15	18.40—33.59
4	C_1, C_2, C_3	44 days	35	32.40—55.60

* Path 2 is the critical path.

The variance of path 4 is so large that the upper limit of 55.60 is almost the same as the upper limit of the critical path (55.84). If the activities along the critical path remain as expected, but the path 4 activities require excessive times, then completion will be dominated by a new critical path, C_1, C_2, and C_3, which could take as much as 55.6 days. This can occur within the 95 percent probability range. Path 4 is near-critical with 44 days (versus 48 days), and its variance is twice that of path 2.

This means that careful managerial attention should be paid to the distribution activities of path 4. These Path 4 activities can shift to critical. They can dominate the situation and cause the targeted completion date of the project to be missed.

18-11b Why Is Completion Time So Important?

There are three dimensions for assessing projects. These are completion time, total cost, and quality of results. All three are important, but it is often the case that the targeted date for finishing the project is the first factor considered.

This is not surprising. Certain products have marketing "windows of opportunity." Textbooks must be available in time for adoption, toys must be ready for Christmas, and roses need to bloom for Valentine's Day. Projects to launch planetary probes have specific windows defined by such factors as closeness to Earth, position of the Sun, and so forth. Seasonal factors produce a window for the Alaska pipeline and for new TV shows.

Even when the window concept does not apply, "as soon as possible" frequently does. Projects usually involve large investments that do not start paying off until the project is completed. When viewing project costs against when return on investment (ROI) begins, managers have come to prefer spending more of the project investment in the present rather than in the future. Spending *now* to decrease completion time makes sense if a positive cash flow (or other benefits, such as hospital beds) can be obtained as soon as possible.

In bidding situations, project-completion time is a major determinant for winning the award. Frequently, contract terms include stiff penalties for failing to bring the project in on time.

18-11c Progress Reports and Schedule Control

At all stages of the project, the manager will ask for progress reports. Each activity, especially those with suppliers, should report status on a regular, predetermined basis. Usually, daily computer printouts indicate activities that are ahead, those that are behind, and by how much. Shifts in the critical path are reported. New slack values appear and are constantly monitored. Continually updated, the network reflects project progress and problems.

Teamwork requires that progress reports be shared by all. When problems arise, there is mutual concern. Shared efforts can be made to move resources from one part of the network to another to keep schedule. The topic of allocating resources is relevant at the beginning design stage of the project. It also applies continuously during the project's lifetime when redesign is referred to as *reallocation of resources*.

One aspect of reallocation is *resource leveling*. Before resource leveling could be addressed, it was necessary that the PERT method be thoroughly understood. It is then reasonable to address trade-offs between time and cost, which will be done after resource leveling is discussed.

18-12 REDESIGNING PROJECTS

There are methods for designing projects so that resources can be used in the best way. Redesign can result in improving the performance of projects such as shortening the critical path, getting closer to target-completion time, and meeting the budget. Stringent project quality goals have to be set, monitored, and met. Steps to improve project-completion dates should not be permitted to damage project quality and/or project quality control.

18-12a Resource Leveling

Resource leveling: Where slack exists, there is potential for resource trade-offs that can reduce nonvalue-adding time while decreasing the time required for completion of the project.

Resource leveling is an important concept for project design. The fundamental idea of **resource leveling** is to switch extra resources from places where they are not essential to places where they could be used immediately. Alternatively, resource leveling aims to balance resource assignments across activities over time. It also provides some control for time-based management (TBM) of project life cycles and facilitates shortening the critical path. It is a method for improving the speed of project achievements and for being able to implement rapid-attainment project management.

The *beginning game* is thoughtful and deliberate. The design of many projects is such that they start slowly while many ideas are being considered. There is much slack in activities that are off the critical path as reports are written and approvals are sought. There seems no need for urgency. The critical path is itself stretched out by bureaucratic organization of the project.

The *end game* has everything coming to a head very quickly. The end game has a time deadline that begins to appear to be looming. Then, it is decided that time must be made up. There is a surge in spending to speed up the project. Often, in the rush, mistakes are made and damage control uses up time that was meant for thoughtful and deliberate means to bring the project to a successful conclusion. It is well-known to project managers that this type of pattern is not desirable. Unless caught by circumstances, present-day project management avoids this damaging scenario.

In search of shorter project cycles, the newer approach to projects uses a multifunctional team with rapid communication to secure approvals. The cash-flow pattern is far more balanced from start to finish. Resources are assigned along all paths so that the critical path can be shortened and slack imbalances can be corrected before the beginning, or early on in the project's time line.

Resource leveling seeks to move people from overstaffed activities to those that are understaffed. It attempts to reallocate money from where there is overspending to where there is underspending. These efforts at leveling must make sense in technological and process terms. Similarly, the project manager would prefer smooth demand for cash instead of sporadic cash outflows. If, among a set of simultaneous activities, a few are receiving the greatest percentage of project expenditures, it often is desirable to level these allocations. Once the decision is made to use resource leveling, trade-off techniques can be designed to address the specific objectives.

A project that experiences fluctuating calls on its resources is hard to manage. If a large workforce is required for some project intervals and not for others, then an effort should be made to redesign activities so as to level the workforce requirements over time. It is costly and disruptive to make large changes in the project group size. Facilities are built or rented for specific occupancy levels. Overall, the task of managing a project is impeded by uneven resource-demand patterns.

The existence of slack is an important basis for resource leveling. To illustrate, three people have been shifted from activity B_1, which has 22 days of slack, to activity A_1 on the critical path of Figure 18-18. The assumption is made that each added person decreases activity time by one day. Similarly, it is assumed that each removed person increases activity time by one day. The assumptions are applied to the two activities, A_1 and B_1. The result is resource leveling, as shown in Figure 18-23.

Several effects are to be noted. The critical path remains unchanged with respect to nodes and activities. However, the length of the critical path has decreased from 48 to 45. Project manager and clients will be pleased. Slack for B_1 has decreased from 22 to 16. Because 22 seemed excessive, no one is likely to object, except the C-branch manager. Shared slack along the C-path has been reduced from 4 to 1. This could lead to some objections because the distribution branch of the project has three activities that are urgent (with near-zero slack).

If management is not up to handling the situation, a smaller resource shift could be tried (as suggested in the Problems Section at the end of Chapter 18). Other options should be analyzed. A starting point is the shift of three workers. Try shifting one more worker and then, one less.

Resource leveling can apply to resources other than the workforce, including materials, technology and equipment, suppliers, managerial and administrative time, and cash to pay both direct and indirect costs. It is worth pointing out that simple assumptions

FIGURE 18-23
Resource Leveling; Three Employees Shifted from B₁ to A₁ (Compare with Figure 18-18)

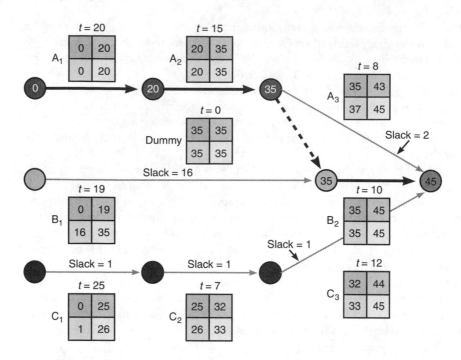

about the effects of trading off resources (such as the one-for-one assumption made earlier about workers and days) need to be replaced with knowledgeable estimates of the effects of resource changes. This begins to be accomplished in the section on COST/TIME trade-offs.

Trading off resources between activities does not have to result in a shorter critical path. Instead, better project quality might sometimes be achieved by moving resources from the critical path to slack paths, which would increase the length of time required to complete the project. Another possible advantage is that there would be fewer critical activities to manage. Sometimes it is possible to utilize resources for expediting and control to improve the variance along the critical path. Doing this does not change the target date, but reduces the risk of deviating from the target date and stabilizes the project.

The previous discussion of resource leveling assumes that the amount of resources is held constant. It is only the allocation of resources that is altered. Another option is to *withdraw resources* or to *add new resources*. This approach changes budgetary constraints. Changing the budget is a strategic issue.

The tactical aspect of resource leveling is that it can affect the entire system without changing the budget. All project team members are impacted when resources are shifted, and they should be kept informed of project alterations. Good resource allocation decisions are a P/OM project-management responsibility.

18-13   COST AND TIME TRADE-OFFS

The approach thus far has dealt only with time and is called *PERT/TIME*. Another way to consider changing critical paths and slack time is by means of **trade-offs** of cost and time. It is often possible to reduce the critical-path duration by spending more money. Resource leveling shifts costs among activities but does not add new funds or reduce existing funds. The project manager transfers funds from activities with slack to activities on the critical path.

What must be known is how adding or decreasing the resources employed (and their costs) affects the times required to complete activities. The comparison to be made is between *crash* programs (using peak resource allotments) and *normal* programs with minimum resource utilization.

Assume that the project plan is to run all activities on a crash basis. This means that each activity will be done in the least possible or minimum time. Crash entails additions

Trade-offs: Spend more money on project resources, and finish sooner, or vice versa.

to the project budget. If the alternative objective to minimize cost is used, this will stretch out project time and reduce spending. The relationship of cost and time has received considerable investigation. The objectives of minimum cost and minimum time are negatively correlated, as a general rule. This means that crashing to achieve minimum time has maximum costs. Minimum cost activities have maximum times associated with them. One can dream up exceptions to the rule; however, more resources cost more money. When properly used, more resources should decrease the time required to accomplish a project.

Maximum quality (qualities) attainment is a third objective that project managers take very seriously. As the Challenger and Columbia space shuttle tragedies showed, project-quality goals are not guaranteed. They do not take care of themselves. Project quality is a design, engineering, and OM responsibility. Flawed technology, faulty design standards, poor building techniques, and improper materials can slip past as a result of pressure to do more, faster. Project crashing must be done with great care. It is essential that crash-time spending should be sufficient to avoid mistakes (e.g., cutting corners to meet a deadline).

Cost-cutting with normal-time project procedures can also inflict penalties. Failures in bringing a new product or service to the marketplace often can be traced to the project instead of the product. This is a systems problem requiring extensive coordination between engineering, marketing, distribution, and OM. The project team is accountable.

18-13a PERT/COST/TIME/(and QUALITY)

PERT/COST/TIME begins in the same way as PERT/TIME, i.e., with the precedence-based network of activities. However, in this case, two separate estimates for each activity are derived. These are:

Crash time: A minimum time estimate and its cost

Normal time: A minimum cost estimate and its time

Figure 18-24 shows the relationships between each pair of estimates.

The data for these COST/TIME relationships are presented in Table 18-7 for numerical clarity.

The best way to understand how to use these numbers is to apply them. This is done in Figure 18-25, where activities A, B, C, and D are illustrated in normal-time and crash-time networks.

The network on the left is based on the minimum cost, normal, or max-time estimates for each activity. It is so simple a network that, for ease of explanation, the critical path is determined using only activity times. Earliest finish (EF) is shown in the 2-box scorecard. EF for the upper branch of the network is 17. EF is 22 for the bottom branch, which is the critical path. The shortest completion time for the network is 22.

PERT/COST/TIME: Spend more—finish faster; spend less—finish in normal time.

Crash time: Crashing an activity means spending as much as it takes to achieve *minimum* activity time. Crashing is generally used to decrease the length of the critical path.

Normal time: *Normal* activity time is associated with the minimum necessary spending on project activities because there is no great stress on completing the project as soon as possible.

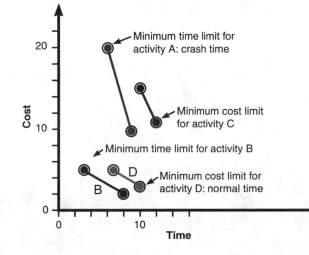

TABLE 18-7				
Data Table for [Normal and Crash Times (t)] and [Normal and Crash Costs (c)]				
Activity	**Normal max t**	**Normal min c**	**Crash min t**	**Crash max c**
A	9	10	6	20
B	8	2	3	5
C	12	11	10	15
D	10	3	7	5

The network on the right is based on the maximum cost, crash-time estimates for each activity. Again, the critical path is determined using only activity times. Earliest finish in the 2-box scorecards is 9 for the upper branch and 17 for the lower branch, which remains the critical path under crash-time conditions.

Table 18-8 sums the costs and times for normal and crash conditions.

If 22 is unacceptable for project completion, then crashing C and D will increase costs from 14 to 20, which is a 43 percent increase. The decrease in time from 22 to 17 is a 23 percent decrease. It should be noted that there may be no advantage in crashing A and B, which in normal time is 17. However, the entire network becomes the critical path if A and B remain at normal time while C and D are crashed. Slack of 5 shared by A and B in the all-normal configuration is removed when only C and D are crashed.

Assume the team goal is for project-completion time to be as close to 20 days as possible. Normal-time project planning misses the mark by +2 days, and the crash program overshoots the objective by −3 days. Accordingly, partial reductions can be made in activity times, requiring partial cost increases. Thus, activity C can be reduced from $t = 12$ to $t = 11$, which will mean that $c = 11$ will increase to $c = 13$. These numbers are obtained by interpolating the figures in Table 18-8 or by using the graphs in Figure 18-24.

Another alternative is to crash specific activities along the normal-time critical path but not all activities on that path. In this case, crash either C or D. In this way, the critical path can be shortened selectively until such time that

1. Another path becomes critical, and then it is selectively reduced, or

2. The modified critical path is acceptable

As a rule of thumb, select first those activities along the critical path where the ratio of cost increases to time reductions is smallest. Thus, select those activities on the critical path where

$$|\Delta Cost| \div |\Delta Time|$$

is smallest. Then the next-to-smallest ratio is used, and so on, until a satisfactory compromise between time and cost is achieved. If the critical path switches, the next alterations are made along the new path.

FIGURE 18-25
Comparing Normal-Time and Crash-Time Networks (Dark lines represent critical paths)

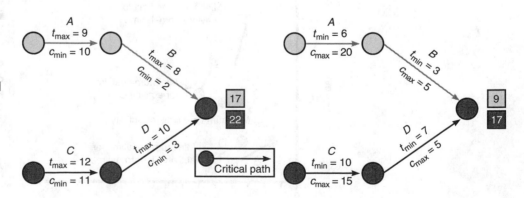

Activity	Normal max t	Normal min c	Crash min t	Crash max c
A	9	10	6	20
B	8	2	3	5
Upper-branch sums	17	12	9	25
C	12	11	10	15
D	10	3	7	5
Lower-branch sums	**22**	**14**	**17**	**20**

TABLE 18-8

Normal- and Crash-Times and Total Times and Total Costs (Bold numbers represent critical paths' calculations)

Using the data in Table 18-8, the smallest measure of the ratios (of the absolute values)

$$|\Delta Cost| \div |\Delta Time|$$

applied only to activities along the critical path is associated with activity D with a ratio equal to 2/3 while C has a ratio of 2. This is shown in Table 18-9.

For activity D, $t_{max} = 10$, $t_{min} = 7$. Using the normal-time critical path of 22, set $t = 8$ instead of 10. This produces the requested critical path of 20. Making that partial change for activity D, when $t = 8$, $c = 4 \ 1/3$. This is derived by using interpolation of Table 18-8 or from the graph of Figure 18-24. The interpolation is done as follows:

$$\frac{c_{max} - c_{min}}{t_{max} - t_{min}} = \frac{2}{3} = \frac{c_D - c_{min}}{t_{max} - t_D} = \frac{c_D - 3}{10 - 8} = \frac{c_D - 3}{2} = \frac{2}{3}$$

whence

$$c_D = \frac{4}{3} + 3 = 4\frac{1}{3}$$

The critical path remains C and D with total project-completion time of 20 and total cost of 15 1/3. The slack for the upper path of A and B is 20 – 17 = 3. Figure 18-26 shows this trade-off solution with an EF 2-box scorecard.

Trade-off models in project planning represent one of the most advanced aspects of P/OM capabilities. Projects are the means by which change is brought about and progress is achieved. Project-management abilities enable changes to be made to the product line, to the organization, and to the environment.

18-14 MULTIPLE PROJECT MANAGEMENT

In an environment that is totally supportive of managed change, project management can take on an organizational dimension that is significant. This is because many people have more than one project assignment. In the chapter on change management, methods are discussed for dealing with many new products and/or process changes. Many firms, in search of improvements, have subscribed to doing a great number of process improvement initiatives. These tend to be going on simultaneously and require competent **multiple project management.**

Multiple project management: Management of multiple projects calls on all of the skills required to manage a very complex project that has many suppliers and workers. Resource leveling can be used effectively between projects.

Activity	Increase (ΔCost)	Decrease (ΔTime)	Ratio
C	+4	–2	2
D	+2	–3	2/3

TABLE 18-9

Smallest $\left|\dfrac{\Delta Cost}{\Delta Time}\right|$ Ratio

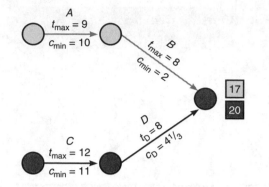

Multiple projects create challenges and opportunities. One of the *challenges* is to compartmentalize the assignments so that time lines are not sacrificed on one project at the expense of another project.

Resource leveling has been described within a single project. In that case, the resources are traded off between branches of the one project. It is not difficult to extend resource leveling so that skills are borrowed and loaned between different projects as needed. As in single project management, the idea is to look for free resources that can be shifted to a borrowing project without damaging the time line and quality of the lending project.

Employees have to be supported in making such shifts. Confusion is an enemy of efficiency that often appears when the juggler is not trained in that skill. For handling multiple projects, software has emerged that can help organize efficient collaboration. As an example, CRN News reported on its webpage on February 4, 2003, that "Groove Networks has updated its collaboration software, adding tighter Outlook and Sharepoint integration. . . ." Microsoft offers its Sharepoint Team Services and Sharepoint Portal Server to expedite collaboration both internal to the firm and with its external partners. See http://crn.channelsupersearch.com/news/crn/39739.asp.

In addition to resource leveling, the cost/time trade-offs that were previously discussed can be analyzed with respect to budget allocations across multiple projects. Using this cost/time technique permits the firm to set reasonable limits on how many projects can be handled at one time. It allows setting time lines for project completions that are consonant with the company's resources. Balancing new product needs and process change improvements against resources available is an essential planning discipline.

Big projects contain subprojects that are often concerned with quite disparate physical and aesthetic characteristics. At a point, the design of the wing and the design of the airplane seats must be related to each other, if in no other way than in terms of a shared weight limit. Communications between the team members working on wings and those working on seats can be optimized by sharing developments in each subproject.

Multiple project management faces challenges and *opportunities*. Among the challenges is the need to be juggling ideas and schedules. Sharing information in an efficient way is an opportunity for coordination, synergy, and serendipity. The coordination of big projects can be enhanced by use of a control room where the walls are display panels showing the progress of various project teams. When the complexity is reduced because there are fewer projects (or a not-that-big project) to deal with, the control room may be more like an automobile dashboard with just a few of the right dials and displays to do the job. Projects that are well understood require less management time.

SUMMARY

Chapter 18 begins with an explanation of new product development, which is a classic example of a crucial project. The chapter emphasizes the relationship between product development and project management. New products are best chosen to benefit from the special skills and experiences that have been significant in the success of other products for the company. The inventory of knowledge is connected to the knowledge management system, which has core competencies and capabilities as its foundation. Management of both explicit and tacit knowledge is discussed with respect to the stages of new product development, which are concept selection, development, and testing. To promote evaluation of the product-development program, estimation and business modeling are used. A spreadsheet model is created to exemplify the power of a proper business model. If the spreadsheet passes muster, the next stages are prototype construction, testing, process specification, and pilot plant operation.

All of this does not happen by chance. Good project management is essential. Chapter 18 explains that projects are sets of activities designed to accomplish goals. These goals, when achieved, terminate the project. Projects constitute a unique OM work configuration. Gantt project-planning charts are introduced and then critical-path methods and PERT are examined. Networks of activities are constructed leading to the determination of critical paths, which are the set of activities that determine project duration being the longest time path from the beginning to the end of the project. Slack is calculated and used for resource leveling aimed at reducing project time.

In pursuit of more rapid completion times, COST/TIME trade-off analysis is employed for critical-path time reduction. Some other details of project management that are covered include differences between deterministic and probabilistic time estimates for activity times, different network-construction methods, activities labeled on nodes (AON), activities labeled on arrows (AOA), forward and backward passes to determine the critical path, and the distribution of project-completion times. The topic of multiple projects is introduced prior to materials ahead that deal with the management of change.

Two Spotlight feature boxes conclude this chapter. These boxes illustrate real applications of the material in the chapter. See Spotlight 18-1: Next-Generation Technology and Spotlight 18-2: Polaroid.

KEY TERMS

Activities-on-arrows (AOA)
Activities-on-nodes (AON)
Backward pass rule
Change management projects (α)
Control management processes (β)
Core competencies
Crash time
Critical path methods (CPM)

Engineering change orders (ECOs)
Explicit knowledge
Forward pass rule
Knowledge management (KM)
Multiple project management
New product development
Normal time
PERT

PERT/COST/TIME
Projects
Resource leveling
Slack
Tacit knowledge
Trade-offs

REVIEW QUESTIONS

1. How does new product development relate to project management?

2. Why is knowledge management a foundation for new product development?

3. What is the difference between explicit and tacit knowledge? Why does it matter?

4. What is the difference between core competencies and management capabilities?

5. How do the differences in question 4 relate to the differences in question 3?

6. How is the spreadsheet-based business model used to evaluate the quality of a new product?

7. What is a pilot plant? What effect does a pilot plant have on new product development and project management?

8. What is unique about project management? Frame your answer in terms of other OM work configurations.

9. Explain the construction and use of Gantt project-planning charts.

10. What are the strengths and weaknesses of Gantt project-planning charts?

11. Classify projects by type and describe project life cycles.

12. Why is the project manager considered a leader?

13. Why is teamwork repeatedly mentioned when discussing good project management?

14. The current air-traffic control system is one of two systems that were funded using the concept of parallel-path project development. Can this dual expenditure be justified?

15. What is PERT's relationship to critical-path methods?

16. What does the forward pass accomplish in critical-path methods?

17. What does the backward pass accomplish in critical-path methods?

18. What is the critical path and how does knowing it help project managers?

19. What is slack and how does knowing it help project managers?

20. What is the difference between deterministic and probabilistic estimates of activity time?

21. Evaluate the strengths and weaknesses of the beta method for obtaining time estimates.

22. What are the strengths and weaknesses of PERT?

23. Explain how resource leveling is done and for what purposes.

24. Describe how COST/TIME trade-off methods can be used given the decision to spend an additional 10 percent on the project.

25. Describe project crashing and contrast it to normal time.

26. What advantages can be gained by, and what are the dangers of, using crashing?

27. What are the challenges and opportunities of managing multiple projects?

PROBLEMS SECTION

1. Set up teams to work together on the construction of a Gantt chart for the project of implementing the introduction of a new product on a national rollout basis. This new product is a shampoo that claims that it stimulates the growth of hair. Market research reports that the new product will obtain more than 50 percent of the market by year's end if the store price of $1.50 is used. The problem that marketing foresees is not having enough product to meet supermarket demands. The suggestion has been made to hold back the demand by charging $10.50 per bottle initially. The price would be reduced gradually as production grows to meet the potential demand.

First, sketch out an approach. Note how working with a team improves the creativity of solutions and the quality of problem solving.

2. Set up teams to work together on the construction of a Gantt chart for the project of implementing the engineering change order (ECO) to replace the faulty motherboard in 500 computers. The steps, setup times (SUT), and times per unit (*t*) are given in minutes. One person is doing the work in batches of 500, i.e., step a is completed on 500 computers before step b is begun.
   a. Remove 4 screws and lift off case: SUT = 60, *t* = 2.
   b. Detach cables: SUT = 70, *t* = 1.
   c. Remove faulty motherboard: SUT = 15, *t* = 0.5.
   d. Replace with new motherboard: SUT = 15, *t* = 0.5.
   e. Attach cables: SUT = 45, *t* = 3.
   f. Put cover on with four screws: SUT = 60, *t* = 4.
   g. Inspection check: plug in and turn on: SUT = 20, *t* = 3.
   h. Mark computers that do not pass test: SUT = 30, *t* = 1.
      First, sketch out an approach. Note how working with a team improves the creativity of solutions and the quality of problem solving.

3. Use the team approach to draw a Gantt project chart (for Problem 2 data) but in this case two people are working at adjacent stations. The second person starts to work on step b as soon as the first person completes step a on 10 computers. Thereafter, let the two people operate in a logical way. Note that the second person has 80 minutes to set up for step b. Setup time for step a is 60 minutes, and 10 units take two minutes each for an additional 20 minutes.

4. Convert the Gantt project-planning chart of steps required to bring a new car to market (Figure 18-3) into an appropriate critical-path PERT-type diagram. Make whatever assumptions you require. Discuss the advantages and disadvantages of each form of representation.

5. Convert Figure 18-27, where activities are labeled on nodes (AON), into an equivalent figure where activities are labeled on arrows (AOA).

6. The Gantt project chart in Figure 18-28 has vertical lines drawn upward from the upper left-hand corner of each activity bar. Where these lines intersect the prior (upper) activity is the "milestone"" that when reached allows that next activity to begin. To illustrate, the activity "order materials" is 13/20 finished when the activity "receive materials" becomes active presumably because materials ordered earlier begin to be received. Note that the position of "Build A" is triggered by a milestone in the "Design" activity. There is no overlap with "Receive Materials." How can this be explained?

7. Using the information in Problem 6, draw a PERT diagram with activities-on-nodes (AON).

8. Using the information in Problems 6 and 7, draw a PERT diagram with activities-on-arrows (AOA).

FIGURE 18-27
Activities-on-Nodes (AON)

FIGURE 18-28
Gantt Project Chart

9. The Delta Company manufactures a full line of cosmetics. A competitor recently developed a new form of hair spray that appears to be successful and potentially damaging to Delta's position in the marketplace. The sales manager has asked the operations manager (OM) what the shortest possible time would be for Delta to reach the marketplace with a new product packed in a redesigned container. The OM has drawn up the following table:

Activity	Initial Event	Terminal Event	Duration (Days)
Design product	1	2	30
Design package	1	3	15
Test market package	3	5	20
Distribute to dealers	5	6	20
Order package materials	3	4	15
Fabricate package	4	5	30
Order materials for product	2	4	3
Test-market product	2	7	25
Fabricate product	4	7	20
Package product	7	5	4

  a. Construct the appropriate PERT diagram.

  b. Apply the estimates of activity duration to the arrows.

10. Using information in Problem 9, make the forward pass to fill out the ES and EF part of the 4-box scorecard. As a reminder: ES = earliest start, EF = earliest finish, LS = latest start, LF = latest finish, and EF = ES + t, LS = LF – t, t = activity time.

ES	EF
LS	LF

What is the shortest feasible completion time for this project?

11. Using the information in Problems 9 and 10, make the backward pass to fill out the LS and LF part of the 4-box scorecard. As a reminder: LS = latest start, LF = latest finish. Identify the activities on the critical path.

12. Use the information in Problems 9, 10, and 11 to determine the slack for each activity. Neither the sales manager nor the OM is satisfied with the way the project is designed. However, the OM insists that because of the pressure of time, the company will be forced to follow this plan. In what ways does this plan violate good practice?

13. Use the information in Problems 9, 10, 11, and 12. The decision is made to form an engineering task force with people from sales, production, distribution, engineering, and R & D. The first recommendation of this team is to use resource leveling in the initial design-product and design-package phases. It is noted that one-for-one applies, which means that if a person is moved from package to product design, the package-design activity time will increase by one day and the product-design activity time will decrease by one day. Up to 10 people can be shifted in this way. Do you recommend doing so?

14. The engineering task force has redesigned the project for the Delta Company as follows:

Activity	Initial Event	Terminal Event	Duration (Days)
Design product	1	2	30
Design package	1	3	15
Test market package	3	2	0
Distribute to dealers	5	6	20
Order package materials	3	4	15
Fabricate package	4	5	30
Order materials for product	2	4	3
Test-market product and package	2	7	25
Fabricate product	4	7	20
Package product	7	5	4

The product and package will be test-marketed together, which has necessitated adding a dummy activity for test-market package.
a. Construct the appropriate PERT diagram.
b. Apply the estimates of activity duration to the arrows.

15. Make the forward pass using the information in Problem 14. Complete the ES and EF boxes (part of the 4-box scorecard). What is the shortest feasible completion time for this project?

16. Make the backward pass using the information in Problems 14 and 15, to fill out the LS and LF part of the 4-box scorecard. Identify the activities on the critical path.

17. Use the information in Problems 14, 15, and 16.
a. Determine the slack for each activity.
b. Evaluate the project design.
c. Compare the results of Problems 9 through 13 with the results for Problems 14 through 17.

18. Entertainment is a service area that has demonstrated growing awareness of the importance of OM for improving productivity and quality. Filmmaking uses OM for various scheduling activities as well as layout on location. Movies and films are costly and complex projects that benefit from the application of critical-path methods.

The PERT network in Figure 18-29 has been developed by the film's producer.

The following table provides crash and normal time, and cost information for the activities required to make the next major box-office winner.

Activity	t_{min}	t_{max}	c_{min}	c_{max}
A	5	9	5	12
B	10	12	4	10
C	3	8	9	15
D	6	7	3	8
E	4	14	12	20
F	5	7	9	12
G	2	3	6	11
H	7	10	2	9
I	3	5	7	9

Find the critical path if all activities follow normal time.

19. Using the information in Problem 18, find the critical path if all activities are crashed.

20. Use the information in Problems 18 and 19 to compare the slack that exists in normal versus crash.

21. Consistent with Problem 20, what are the total costs of normal versus crash?

22. Use the information in Problem 18. Assume that the director wants a target date halfway between the required total project times of crash and normal planning.
a. Use resource leveling with cost and time trade-offs to achieve the objective.
b. How can resource leveling over time and between activities be applied to the project of filming a movie? Treat both the overtime and between activities aspects of shifting resources. Note the degrees of freedom that exist for the time order of scenes.

23. Although dummy arrows are a finer point of PERT construction, they play an important role when needed as in Problem 14 where the engineering task force recommended that test-marketing the product and the package could be done together. When dummies were discussed in Figure 18-7, it was stated that the dummy activity could as well have preceded activity C, instead of activity B. Redraw Figure 18-7 to create this alternative.

24. Three people were shifted from activity B_1, which has 22 days of slack, to activity A_1 on the critical path of Figure 18-18. The assumption was made that each added person decreases activity time t by one day. Similarly, it was assumed that each removed person increases activity time t by one day. The results of this resource leveling were shown in Figure 18-23. Using the same assumptions with respect to the same two activities, A_1 and B_1, shift four people (instead of three) from B_1 to A_1. Discuss the results.

25. Using the information in Problem 24, shift two people from B_1 to A_1. Discuss the results.

26. You are requested to make a model of a PERT network out of string. Use the PERT chart for filmmaking in Figure 18-29. String models of a project network require that the length of the pieces of string be cut to scale. The length of string should be proportional to the time of the activity. The pieces are tied together in conformance with the PERT precedence diagram. When the strings are pulled taut (between the starting node and the final node), the critical path is revealed as the tight part of the string model. The other strings show their degree of slack by drooping. Comment on the applicability of this analog model.

FIGURE 18-29
PERT Chart for Filmmaking

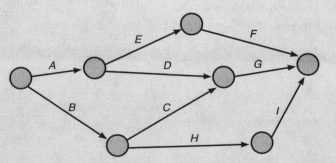

END-OF-CHAPTER QUESTIONS

1. Every book that The Famous Publisher (TFP) brings to market is a project of many activities. There are various people who manage the stages of publication. Selection of the authors and the subject of the book is the beginning of a chain of events that results in bound, printed paper, or a CD, or an Internet text, or all three. TFP's managers recognize that they are dealing with projects all of the time, but they do not employ project management methods. The general manager and the chief editor have assembled their top managers for analysis of this situation. A list of topics has been circulated for the meeting. It contains points a. through f. Which of these points is incorrect?

   a. The publishing business does not have time lines like other projects. This is because authors are like artists. They work when they are inspired and the clock does not keep time as it does for a construction job.

   b. Knowledge management is applicable to the publishing business in several ways. TFP needs to catalog who are the experts in the various activities that make book publishers successful. A directory of these people needs to be created so that issues can be resolved as quickly as possible.

   c. TFP's KM experts can be categorized by the amount of explicit knowledge versus tacit knowledge that their specialization represents. For example, the editors and the production people can set standards for the condition of the manuscript when it is submitted. That way, less editorial and styling work is required. Production schedule methods are entirely explicit.

   d. On the other hand, issues of permissions and royalties for copyright-protected materials may involve negotiations. Similarly, requesting authors to make changes that reviewers suggest might be better handled by people experienced in the tacit knowledge domain of personalities and negotiating techniques.

   e. There are core competencies with respect to manuscript preparation in special page preparation software. There are also managing capabilities for keeping production teams on time and running quality control on the transformed manuscript, which epitomizes the input–output transformation model of P/OM.

   f. Core competencies are particularly important to manuscripts that are transformed into CDs and Internet-available texts. The Internet permits links to be explored by readers, and interactive dialogs can be embedded in the manuscripts.

2. Continuing with The Famous Publisher's quest for structured project management, the chief editor suggests that the assembled group start with the idea that new books should be treated as if they were new products. This means developing new books according to marketing principles rather than waiting for book ideas to be brought to the publisher by agents and authors. A list of applicable concepts (a. through f.) was drawn up and circulated. Identify the single incorrect statement.

   a. Concept selection would read like a publisher's wish list of titles. Perhaps 10 such titles would be developed with a page description of what that title would entail.

   b. Idea development would determine which authors are most suitable and what it would take to enlist their support for the project, i.e., assign writers to books (title by title).

   c. Market research would now be used to test the concepts and the titles. A book failure would be defined by market research results indicating that sales volume would be below the breakeven point.

   d. An interesting issue arises as to whether the publisher would be better off paying the writer by time instead of paying royalties on sales. The business model would make estimates of cost, time, and the risk of failure (defined as an expected sales volume below the breakeven volume). If the expected volume of sales is low, then the royalty payment method is probably preferred. If the expected volume of sales is high, then a single payment to the writer is likely to be chosen.

   e. Authors selected to write specific books may not agree to the chosen method of reimbursement. This is an area for negotiation. The process of selecting authors should take into account the type of payment that is likely and the type of author that has been selected. An issue for discussion is why should TFP accept books that have low expected sales volume? If TFP adopts the new product development (NPD) model used by consumer package goods companies (CPG), then books that have low sales volume estimates (and poor profitability) will be rejected.

   f. NPD for CPG companies includes testing prototypes (such as a new shampoo and its container). The final step in the NPD is the process specification and the pilot plant. Both of these steps still need to be taken by TFP.

3. A large consumer package goods company (CPG) is getting ready to launch its newest bar soap. The marketing–production task force has met with the CEO, and he has raised a series of issues about preparations for the launch. This is the list a. to e. Which statement is incorrect?

   a. There are four project (not product) life cycle stages. The first stage is to fully specify the goals of the project. For example, specify how many cases are to be sold in the first three months of the national rollout. That kind of detail is required.

   b. Stage two is planning all the activities that are required to fulfill the goals. Activities and their time lines need to be comprehensive. For example, explain where and how this much product will be made. Give the pros and cons of using an intermittent flow shop as compared to a dedicated flow shop. Discuss project characteristics including completion time, costs, critical path, slack amounts and with which activity branches slacks exist, opportunities to speed things up, and threats to the plan.

   c. Carrying out project activities comes next. Full reporting is needed of how resources are being utilized. For example, track how many people are working on the various component parts of this project over time. Show the payroll and material expenses on a daily and cumulative basis. Project managers must report on exceptions, missed deadlines, and new threats to successful completion. If expediting is required, explain what is being done.

d. Project-completion reporting can sum up goals exceeded, matched, and not realized. This is for time, money, quality, and competitive responses. Plans for disbanding or for continuing teams with other goals and objectives should be outlined. For example, if there are going to be further NPD for bar soaps, this project team would be ideal for the next assignment.

e. Performance reports on all team members are needed to finalize the project. Grades should be given so that future teams can be drawn from the very best. Top project managers should be given increased process management responsibilities. The best project managers could now be given the production lines for the new bar soap.

4. According to the CPG project manager, there are a number of important guidelines for the effective management of projects. The marketing–production task force responded to the CEO and has now prepared a list of additional facts to consider. They have circulated this list amongst themselves and sent copies to the project manager and to the CEO. Both are complimentary, but the project manager takes issue with one of the team's points a. through e. Which statement is bothering the project manager?

a. Often there are many participants working on some aspect of the same project. For example, there is a team working on packaging the soap so that it stays attractive. Packages on display get shabby from customer handling. Other teams are working on marketing, advertising, and speeding up the production process while maintaining high quality. The key to success is communication so that everyone is reminded about the project goals and is informed about the current status.

b. Duplication of project activities should be eliminated except if major differences of opinion exist about how to do something. Also, parallel-path activities are warranted if there is no opinion about how to achieve some goal or if there is serious risk of failure if the wrong fork in the road is taken.

c. Multiple project managers are better than one alone. Having several people running the show broadens perspective. It shares stress and lets several sets of shoulders carry the burden. Projects are so rich in detail that one person cannot be blamed for everything.

d. Project management is based on well-designed information systems. The system reports regularly on status for each ongoing activity, which includes many supplier activities. Errors in estimates such as how long a given activity would take need to be corrected as soon as the new information is obtained.

e. Gantt project-planning charts are helpful. They provide graphic evidence of project activities, sequences, time status, and problem areas. As soon as the project is defined, a Gantt chart should be created, and it needs to be kept up-to-date. There needs to be one dedicated Gantt charter on the project team.

5. The pizza chain manager in the seminar class has taken great interest in Gantt charts for project planning as well as critical-path methods (CPM) and PERT. Every time a new product is offered, all employees go through a series of training steps related to making the product and serving it to the customers. The ideal way to handle the new product introduction is in the form of a project. The manager realizes that Gantt charts do not optimize resource utilization whereas PERT charts can be used for that purpose. Yet, he feels that there is a special utility derived from Gantt charting that makes it the best way to start a project, even when it is planned to follow Gantt with PERT. The pizza chain manager has written down some points (a. through j.) that seem relevant and has asked his teammates to provide feedback. Team members do this and report two errors. What two points are in error?

a. PERT and CPM are both methods for determining the critical path, which is the *longest time path through the network of precedence-sequenced activities* required for the project. PERT and CPM are so similar that only one or the other needs to be mentioned. The pizza manager prefers PERT because of its use by NASA.

b. The features that differentiate PERT from CPM include their histories and their methods of estimation. First, their histories: PERT was developed by the Special Projects Office of the U.S. Navy with the assist of Booz Allen Hamilton and Lockheed Missile Systems, for the Polaris missile program. CPM was developed by DuPont and Remington Rand (now Unisys) for construction of a chemical plant. Dates of development for both PERT and CPM were about the same—1957–958.

c. One explanation for the nearly simultaneous creation of two critical-path methods was the need to deal effectively with increasingly complex projects. Prior to the mid-1950s, the state of the art in computing was not up to the task.

d. The second distinguishing feature is that PERT has provisions for using the beta distribution for estimation purposes. Beta has three parameters, which take the form of pessimistic, optimistic, and most likely (modal) estimates. The beta distribution is remarkably well-suited to conflate these three disparate points of view.

e. The equations for conflation can be exemplified with a simple numerical illustration. Assume that the pessimist estimates two hours to hang a picture on the wall; the optimist estimates 18 minutes. Records show that (for this class of picture-hanging parameters) most often this activity takes 45 minutes. The estimate of the mean of the distribution (called t_e) is $1/6(120 + 18) + 2/3(45) = 55$ minutes.

f. The variance of the beta distribution is $[1/6(120 - 18)]^2 = 289$, which means that the standard deviation is 17. There is a 68 percent probability that the true value of the time to hang the picture will be between 38 and 75 minutes.

g. The Gantt chart, as well as PERT charts, indicates when project completion will occur. The problem with Gantt charts is that they do not indicate which activities are on the critical path. Guesses could be made, but not if the project has many activities.

h. The reason that project managers (who advocate use of computers for projects) like to start with Gantt charting is that Gantt brings project managers closer to the core of the problem. Gantt provides a hands-on feeling for project planners.

i. Gantt encourages visualization of project activities. This allows better insight about the need for doing activities in a different way than they are currently being done.

j. Milestones trigger the start of next-in-line activities in the sequence of activities that are part of the Gantt project-planning system. PERT charts need to create activities that end before and start after a milestone. There are pros and cons for both types of situations.

6. The managers of Oil Changers, Inc. (OCI) have told the class that their company has been using PERT for customer-based projects. They classify a project as a set of activities bundled together to meet customer demand. For example, a project might be to change and rotate tires or replace a muffler assembly. The managers presented a typical situation to the class members that permits calculations of forward pass, backward pass, critical path, and slack. The precedence diagram can be stated in terms of AON and then converted to AOA by the students. Thus, for AON, A precedes B, which precedes D; also, A precedes C, which precedes D.

The OCI managers point out that every aspect of the problem is simplified if each team member creates the AON graph for these relationships. That way, a visual understanding of the problem develops. Then, an AOA graph can be drawn from the AON graph. After all class members had drawn their graphs, the OCI managers handed out a list of points (a. to e.) concerning important calculations that can be made and problems that project planners can expect to encounter. The faculty leader has noted that there are two erroneous statements. Class members are asked to identify the incorrect statements.

a. When the AON chart is converted to AOA, a problem will be encountered. Namely, two arrows will have been labeled activity D. This situation cannot be permitted. The computer will not be able to distinguish between the two D arrows.

b. Ambiguity can be removed by redrawing the AOA network with a dummy activity that requires zero time. The dummy is inserted between the end of arrow A and the beginning of arrow B. This alters the prior precedence chart to: A precedes dummy, which precedes B, which precedes D; also, A precedes C, which precedes D.

c. With the dummy in place, the forward pass algorithm produces the "earliest" results in the table. The earliest start (ES) and earliest finish (EF) boxes can be completed, but the latest start (LS) and latest finish (LF) cannot be completed until the backward pass is done.

Activities	Earliest Start (ES)	Latest Start (LS)	Slack	Earliest Finish (EF)	Latest Finish (EF)
A	0			5	
Dummy	5			5	
B	5			9	
C	5			12	
D	12			15	

d. It is evident that the project as currently designed will take 12 days. Also, the time required for each activity is evident from the subtraction of EF minus ES. Thus, A = 5 days, dummy = 0 days, B = 4 days, C = 7 days, and D = 3 days.

e. Slack cannot be determined until the sideways pass is complete. Once that is done, it will be possible to specify the critical path. The length of the critical path is already known.

7. Managers from the Expensive Shoe Company (ESC) ask that the exercise started by their classmates from Oil Changers, Inc. (OCI) be continued so that the PERT table can be completed. Everyone agrees that they have enough information to use the precedence diagram for the backward pass. They have continued the practice of creating a list of conclusions (a. to e.) and, as in Problem 6, point out there are two mistakes to be noted. Which points contain the errors?

Activities	Earliest Start (ES)	Latest Start (LS)	Slack	Earliest Finish (EF)	Latest Finish (EF)
A	0	0	0	5	5
Dummy	5	8		5	8
B	5	8	3	9	12
C	5	5	0	12	12
D	12	12	0	15	15

a. The forward pass rule encountered the special situation of two or more arrows converging at a single node. Convergence occurred when the ends of arrows B and C (indicating conclusions of activities B and C) entered the node from which activity D's arrow begins. The rule is to choose the largest value of EF; the choice is between B's EF = 9 and C's EF = 12. The latter becomes D's ES = 12.

b. The backward pass rule encountered the special situation of two or more arrows emanating from a single node. That occurred where the dummy arrow and activity C's arrow begin at the conclusion of activity A. The rule is to choose the smallest value of LS; the choice is between the dummy's LS = 8 and C's LS = 5. The latter becomes A's LF = 5.

c. Slack can only be calculated by subtracting (for each activity) the earliest start time from the latest start time, i.e., LS – ES. Slack is associated with an activity but if a sequence of activities has slack, that is called a *slack path*.

d. The critical path, by definition, has zero slack. It is the longest time path of activities for the project that defines project completion. Any slippage along the critical path will delay the project. Therefore, in this example, the critical path is A→C→D.

e. Activities that are not on the critical path are the dummy and activity B. The dummy always requires zero activity time, so slack is meaningless for that arrow. Slack is simply a computational convenience. However, slack of 5 days that is associated with activity B is meaningful and useful. This will be demonstrated in Problem 8.

8. Everyone in the class is happy to learn how project managers determine critical paths. Organizational awareness about project management is low. When that fact is recognized, then the large body of knowledge about projects can be brought to the table. Understanding how to determine the longest time path of a project becomes a management necessity. But, that raises the issue of how to modify the critical path. Students in this class already know how to calculate the amount of project slack that is available. Now, they need to understand how slack can be used to modify the time length of the critical path. All class members agree to create a list of discussion points about this topic. The faculty leader edits these statements, noting that there is one point that should be changed because it is not true. Which point should be changed?

   a. Slack is often an underutilized resource. This is especially true when conscious project management is not practiced. Those aware of critical paths do not overlook or ignore slack. However, if project managers are happy with the critical path (time of completion), and with the proposed budget, consideration of slack is unnecessary.

   b. The data used in Problem 7 apply to Problem 8. An additional fact is that C's activity time of $t = 7$ days can be changed to $t - 1 = 6$ days by transferring one worker from activity B to activity C. In turn, the activity time for B goes from $t = 4$ days to $t + 1 = 5$ days because B has one less worker. This process is known as resource leveling.

   c. Resource leveling can only take place when there is slack. The resource is moved from the activity with slack to the critical path. The best trade-off rule is to move slack resources to that activity on the critical path that will result in the largest decrease in activity time.

   d. Specifically, transfer workers from slack activities so as to achieve the largest reduction in critical-path time. If all activities on the critical path are shortened by the same amount of time, then there is no special place along the critical path to favor in awarding the extra resources.

   e. If the project is large and has nearly-zero slack activities throughout, then the project is a challenge for management. Managers can only handle (monitor for slippage) a limited number of critical activities at one time. When there is slippage at a critical activity, the manager has immediate responsibilities to expedite (e.g., get suppliers to deliver on time, replace faulty o-rings, etc.). Under these circumstances, it is good project management to bring in new resources so that the entire project is not critical.

9. Students have requested that Problem 9 address issues raised but not treated in Problem 8—for example, the effects on the critical path of moving slack to critical activities. The question has arisen about using resource leveling for multiple projects because it works so successfully on the multiple paths within a single project. Another issue is the question of using mean and variance to account for variability of critical-path measures. A new list of statements is created by the class members. It has five points, a. to e., and two of these points are wrong. Where are these errors?

   a. The one-for-one assumption is: Take a worker away—add a day; add a worker and subtract a day. Using the one-for-one assumption, when a worker from B is moved to C, the

effect is to decrease the length of the critical path from 15 to 14 days without changing the critical path (i.e., A→C→D) and without increasing project costs.

   b. Using the one-for-one assumption, when two workers are moved from activity B to activity C, the effect is to switch the critical path to A→dummy→B→D, which yields a completion interval of 13 days.

   c. Multiple projects are equivalent to independent paths within one project. One launching by NASA typifies this multiplicity of ongoing activities that join at (or near) the end of the project. Independence is the same as saying that nodes are not shared. There is good reason to use resource leveling between multiple projects. Efficient employment of resources benefits the overall organization.

   d. An issue must be faced that is not unlike one that occurs within any single project. Namely, how truly transferable are resources between activities? The one-for-one assumption is more likely to exist for intertwined paths of a single project than for the independent paths of multiple projects. Nevertheless, cross-training for somewhat similar activities can be viewed as an option for project management.

   e. Multiple projects are usually totally independent of each other. Nevertheless, to a limited extent, resource leveling can be used in spite of the independence between projects. Trading resources between activities is possible when the activities are functionally equivalent. For example, a welder on the Brooklyn Bridge can weld as well on the George Washington Bridge. A stone and marble mason could work on the cathedral at Notre Dame de Chartres as well as Notre-Dame Cathedral in Paris.

10. The seminar class was instructed that resource leveling should be used before cost/time trade-offs to control the length of the critical path (completion time) and to employ resources efficiently. The logical sequence is described in points a., b., and c. The procedure for cost/time trade-offs is assigned in point d. Then, in point e. a comparison is made with resource planning. Problem 10 assumes that the data for activity times and the critical path are those obtained in Problem 6, point d., and Problem 7, point d. Those numbers are shown again in the table of Problem 10, point d. The critical path is A→C→D with completion time of 15 days. Using these data, a series of points (a. to e.) was developed and provided to all members of the seminar class. Questions are asked, "Are any of these points incorrect?" "If so, which are not right?"

   a. The logical procedure is to start with "normal time" activity assignments. "Normal time" means that there is no urgency for completion and costs are minimal.

   b. Next, analyze the project network for opportunities to employ slack resources. Slack resources are idle resources. They become value-adding when they are used to reduce the length of the critical path.

   c. Next, use business modeling to determine the benefits of earlier completion times. For example, if the house can be rented a month earlier, then benefit is an extra month's rent. The dollar benefit needs to be compared with the added costs of crashing chosen activities to finish the project earlier.

   d. The crash versus normal table of times (days) and costs is

Activity	Normal Time Maximum t	Normal Time Minimum c	Crash Time Minimum t	Crash Time Maximum c	Ratio $\Delta c \div \Delta t$
A	5	$10,000	3	$22,000	12/2 = 6
B	4	8,000	2	16,000	8/2 = 4
C	7	14,000	4	28,000	14/3 = 4.67
D	5	10,000	3	20,000	10/2 = 5
Dummy	0	0	0	0	0

The decision has been made to allow an addition to the budget of $8,000. The benefits of crashing each activity are measured as the ratio of the increase in cost divided by the decrease in time. Column 6 shows this ratio. The smallest value is best because it provides the biggest reduction in activity time per dollar. Based on these ratio results, crash activity B.

e. The activity times are listed as though they are deterministic. If that is not the case, then it would be advisable to examine the effects of variability (of activity times) on the critical path.

11. Before this seminar class graduates as nearly-certified project managers, the faculty insisted that one more set of exercises be assigned. These are the issues that often get missed during project-management instructions. A series of points (a. to g.) were developed and provided to all members of the seminar class. The question is, "If any of these points are incorrect, which are they?"

a Testing activity results is a familiar part of project management. Sometimes, it turns out that the system fails the test. For example, the pipe leaks, or the meat is still tough. Because of the extensive nature of PERT diagrams, it is not possible to cycle back to an earlier node. Therefore, it is necessary to build test failures, repair, and retesting into the PERT charts initially. A risk-averse strategy is to assume failure and extend the time of the risky activity accordingly.

b. The *failure-repair-retest* sequence may not have affected the critical path. If it seems to be prudent, because failures are common to this activity, two or more of these redo loops can be included in the extensive network form. When the redo loop impacts the critical path, then the critical path should be calculated with and without the *failure-repair-retest* sequence. As soon as the activity passes the test, the safety provision should be dropped out.

c. When an earthquake severely damaged a California freeway, Caltran made a contract with a construction company that penalized that company if completion of the repair took longer than an agreed-upon date. This is not an unusual provision. What was different was a reward for early completion. The reward increased as the completion became earlier. The actual completion date was sooner than anyone had expected.

d. To exemplify the penalty–reward situation, assume that activities A, B, C, and D are associated with a mean time for completion and the variance of the distribution. This is in contrast to the beta distribution, which has optimistic, pessimistic, and most likely estimates that conflate to provide an estimate of the mean.

Activity	Mean Time	Variance
A	5	1
B	4	6
C	7	1
D	3	2
Dummy	0	0

For the path A→C→D, the total mean time is 15 and the total variance is 4. For the path A→dummy→B→D, the total mean time is 12 and the total variance is 9.

Variances are the square of the standard deviation, and these can be summed for well-behaved distributions (e.g., the normal distribution is assumed in this case).

e. The standard deviation of path A→C→D is 2. The range for plus and minus one standard deviation for this path could produce a value as high or higher than 15 + 2. It could produce a value as low or lower than 15 − 2. There is a 32 percent probability that one or the other of these extremes will occur.

f. The standard deviation of path A→dummy→B→D is 3. The range for plus and minus one standard deviation for this path could produce a value as high or higher than 12 + 3. It could produce a value as low or lower than 12 − 3. There is a 32 percent probability that one or the other of these extremes will occur.

g. From points e. and f., there is a reasonable possibility that the current critical path, A→C→D, could take on the value 13, and the other path could become the critical path with a value of 15. When there is variability, it is essential to monitor all paths that could become critical if the dice roll that way.

ADDITIONAL READINGS

Burke, R. *Project Management: Planning and Control*, 2e. New York: Wiley, 1994.

Hartley, J. R. *Concurrent Engineering: Shortening Lead Times, Raising Quality, and Lowering Costs*. Cambridge, MA: Productivity Press, 1992.

Heldman, K. *PMP: Project Management Professional Study Guide*. Alameda, CA: Sybex Publishing, April 2002.

Kerzner, H. *Project Management: A Systems Approach to Planning, Scheduling and Control*, 8e. New York: Wiley, 2003.

Meridith, J. R., and S. J. Mantel. *Project Management: A Managerial Approach*. New York: Wiley, 1995.

Project Management Institute. *A Guide to the Project Management Body of Knowledge*. Philadelphia, PA: PMI, 2000.

Pyron, T., et al. *Using Microsoft Project 2002*. Indianapolis, IN: Que Publishing, September 2000.

Scholtes, P. R., et al. *The Team Handbook*. Joiner Associates (608-238-8134). Madison, WI, 1989.

Shaughnessy, H. *Collaboration Management: New Project and Partnering Techniques*. New York: Wiley, 1994.

Uyttewaal, E. *Dynamic Scheduling with Microsoft Project 2000: The Book By and For Professionals*. New York: International Institute for Learning, Inc., June 2001.

Project Software:

Thousands of options exist. See http://www.project-management-software.org and click on "Project Management."

Many of the options work together with Microsoft Project for Windows, 2002.

Some of the options are web-based including:

Celoxis

FreeTaskManager. As the name implies, this software is free; it is also multiproject software that is web-based.

Pacific Edge

Project.net (includes collaboration software)

Tenrox project tracking - Projeca

VCS

Vertabase Pro

NOTES

1. Gary Hamel and C. K. Prahalad. "The Core Competence of the Corporation." *Harvard Business Review* (May–June 1990).

2. George Stalk, Philip Evans, and Lawrence E. Shulman. "Competing on Capabilities: The New Rules of Corporate Strategy." *Harvard Business Review* (March–April 1992).

3. Tracy Kidder. *The Soul of a New Machine*. Boston, MA: Little, Brown & Co., 1981.

4. This assumes a normal distribution, which would result if a number of beta distributions were added together to form a single distribution for the project as a whole.

Number of Standard Deviations ($k\sigma$) ±from the Mean	Probability That the Actual Time Falls Within the Specified Range
1.00	0.680
1.64	0.900
1.96	0.950
3.00	0.997

SPOTLIGHT 18-1
Next-Generation Technology

A congressional mandate has called for one-third of ground combat vehicles to operate unassisted by 2015. Ashlee Vance, in the October 9, 2003, edition of *The New York Times*, has painted a fascinating picture of a technology that would enable a machine to guide itself at a decent speed across obstacle-laden terrain. The Defense Advanced Research Projects Agency (DARPA), an arm of the Defense Department, has handed out millions of dollars to contractors for new designs for robotic land vehicles, with little to show for it. Because no military contractor has met the challenge, the Defense Department is placing a $1 million dollar bet that Team Phantasm, or perhaps one of the dozens of other teams like it, will produce a robotic machine that can travel a chosen route within a 10-hour time limit. If successful, it would be the vehicle of choice for the U.S. Army and, at the same time, open the gates of opportunity for civilian use undreamed of at this moment.

Teams from universities and small companies, as well as hobbyists, compete in the Grand Challenge for Autonomous Ground Vehicles, a contest that pits the challengers against one another in a race for the 7-figure bounty. Their unmanned vehicles must perform general route selection and navigation as they follow the Challenge route over the rough terrain of the Mojave Desert from Barstow, CA, to Las Vegas. Speed will be the deciding factor, and the time limit is designed to push vehicle speeds far beyond current technologies. The route will cover approximately 250 miles.

Vehicles must sense their environment to perceive terrain features, ground conditions, obstacles, and other Challenge vehicles. The route will consist of a series of waypoints and boundaries that define a corridor within which the vehicles must remain. The corridor width will vary from miles to tens of feet and will guide the vehicles across open terrain, winding trails, and paved roads. The route will be cleared of non-Challenge traffic.

As Ashlee Vance describes it, each vehicle must see, steer, accelerate, brake, and navigate on its own, with guidance only from a series of global positioning system (GPS) coordinates that will be revealed by DARPA two hours before the race. Each team will enter the data into computers on its vehicle and then turn over the vehicle to DARPA.

The vehicles will start with 20 yards between each of them. Each will be governed by an on-off system. They will have to guide themselves from one GPS point to the next, passing around or over ditches, water, rocks, barbed wire, and other vehicles. The only information given to the vehicle owners by DARPA is that obstructions on the route can be overcome or dodged by a commercial 4 x 4 truck. The rules for the race are posted at http://www.darpa.mil/grandchallenge. The machines must average 20 miles an hour over all, while avoiding houses and other buildings.

One relatively low-cost approach has been taken by Warren Williams and Bill Zimmerly, two team members who named themselves Team Phantasm. Williams is a calibrator of electrical instruments and (as a hobby) creates robots for the BattleBots competition where machines fight each other to destruction. Zimmerly is a semiretired programmer and network administrator who likes to write software. Using gear donated by Kawasaki Motors, they are building their all-terrain vehicle with a dome made of bulletproof material that can open up like flower petals, righting itself if it rolls over. Their budget is $50,000.

The Carnegie Mellon group, known as the Red Team, has millions of dollars and a long list of corporate sponsors. William Whittaker, a professor at Carnegie Mellon's Robotic Institute, is a pioneer in building unmanned robots. Some of his work has included building robots to investigate hazardous waste sites and building systems for planetary exploration. More than 30 fellow faculty members and students are working with him to outfit a Hummer with the latest autonomous technology for the Grand Challenge. The school's reputation as a robotics powerhouse is on the line.

The team from California Institute of Technology has a budget of $400,000. They have prepared a 1996 Chevrolet Tahoe, enlisting help from Northrop Grumman, which has won defense contracts in the past for its robotics work. David van Gogh, the project manager for CalTech, is quoted as saying, "DARPA has been funding contractors for awhile, and they want to speed things up. This contest lets people take risks and plays on human nature."

Despite the enthusiasm and competitive spirit, the consensus seems to be that no one will win the race in the foreseeable future. Each team must submit a technical paper that will determine whether it is eligible. So far only a handful of teams have passed this hurdle. Most teams generally wish they had more money, like Team Arctic Tortoise from Alaska. Some hope to start businesses as a result of their work.

The competition will be held approximately every 18 months starting on March 13, 2004, until someone wins, there are no more funds, or there are no contestants. DARPA will retain "right of first access" to the team technology but the groups will retain ownership of their intellectual property. Mr. Whittaker is quoted as saying, "I don't know whether there will be a winner, but there aren't going to be any losers."

Source: Vance, Ashlee. "Robotic Road Trip on a Military Mission." *The New York Times* (October 9, 2003).

SPOTLIGHT 18-2
Polaroid

A Great Technology Company—Perfectly Suited for a World That No Longer Existed

"Over the years, I have learned that every significant invention has several characteristics. It must be startling, unexpected, and must come to a world that is not prepared for it."
—Edwin H. Land

In the fast-paced technological world of digital imaging and smart machines, no one would have believed that Polaroid Corporation, the world leader in instant imaging, would not be able to overcome its rivals (HP, Kodak, Olympus, Canon, and Sony, among others) in the production of digital cameras and related products. Unfortunately, Polaroid ran out of cash and on April 30, 2002, filed a reorganization plan in the bankruptcy court. Why did this happen?

Polaroid's founder, Edwin H. Land (1909–1991), was a prolific inventor from the day he left Harvard at the end of his freshman year in 1926. He conducted research on light polarization and filed for his first patent in 1929 after inventing the first synthetic sheet polarizer. With his scientific and entrepreneurial genius, Land conceived and produced his own products and marketed them for use in sunglasses, glare-free auto headlights, and 3-D stereoscopic photography. Land held over 500 U.S. patents.

One day, the story goes, he was inspired by his 3-year-old daughter, who asked him why she couldn't see a photo he had taken of her right away. It was through his Polaroid Corporation, founded in 1937 in Massachusetts, that Land was immortalized for his invention and marketing of instant photography. The first Polaroid camera was sold to the public in November 1948. Today the word "Polaroid" has three definitions in *Webster's New World Dictionary*: a trademark for transparent material capable of polarizing light; a camera that produces a print within seconds; and the Polaroid (Land) camera.

Land spent his entire adult life experimenting and innovating in the field of optics, from recording systems used by the United States in World War II to developing a theory of human color perception. As a science advisor to Eisenhower during the Cold War, he spearheaded the development of the U-2 spy plane and helped design NASA. His 535 patents stand second only to Thomas Edison. Land was awarded the Medal of Freedom, the highest honor granted to civilians in the United States. In 1980, Edwin Land retired as CEO of Polaroid, having given the world a camera that revolutionized photography. He also left a company culture based on science, patents, and a proud and honorable tradition.

Another revolution was underway in the early 1980s. Polaroid Corporation was aware of the challenge of digital camera technology and had commenced work in this field of innovation before many of its competitors. The company had a great brand, brilliant scientists and engineers, and a large global marketing and distribution system. Polaroid knew what intense competition it would face. Somehow it failed to realize that a radical change in company culture and methods of manufacturing and marketing would be needed. They had been accustomed to long product development cycles and decades-long patent protection.

In a new manufacturing environment where the cost and capabilities of computer chips constantly change (Moore's Law), a different style of management was necessary. Also, Polaroid's core capabilities and skills were in optics and films. They were not in software, storage technologies, and electronic digital signal processing.

In order to enter the digital market, Polaroid had to make large investments. Its first digital offerings did not catch on. Helios, a digital laser-imaging system designed to replace printing of X-rays, was launched in 1993. Several hundred million dollars in investment did not bring the expected return. In 1996, Polaroid launched its first digital camera, the PDC-2000, aiming at professional photographers as customers. It retailed for between $2,995 and $4,995. Other digital cameras from competitors were available for less than $1,000. The company's real effort to enter the consumer market came in late 1997. It was too late. With declining instant-film sales, inability to generate sufficient profits from the digital business, and demands for investment in technology, the company had trapped itself by incurring dramatic losses of revenue.

Switching its strategy, Polaroid focused on becoming a "new products" company in 1998. By year's end, it showed a net loss of $51 million despite its $1.8 billion in net sales.

In 1999, the company switched again, deciding to refocus on its core business and exiting its new-products approach. That year showed a record sale of 9.7 billion instant cameras along with 400,000 digital cameras. Although its revenues were great (Polaroid's net sales were $1.9 billion, its highest on record), its earnings were miniscule. Statements made to investors in October 2000 by Polaroid's chairman and CEO, Gary T. DiCamillo, did not seem to reflect the company's cash drains and increasing competition. In reality, Polaroid's business plan was perfectly suited for a world that no longer existed.

On April 30, 2002, Polaroid was in bankruptcy court. A tidal surge of competition in digital media had broken Polaroid apart, washing away a wonderful company that tried, up to the last moment, to survive. The last press releases give the impression of a great Titanic, unable to either stay or correct its course.

Note: All of Polaroid's assets were sold to OEP Imaging Corp., which was then renamed the Polaroid Corp. on July 31, 2002. The old Polaroid Corp. changed its name to Primary PDC. As such, it operates under the protection of Chapter 11 of the U.S. bankruptcy code to settle claims.

Sources: Http://www.primarypdc.com.
Http://web.mit.edu/invent/iow/land.html.
Http://inventors.about.com/library/inventors/blpolaroid.htm.

Change Management

Change is always occurring in the way that business is conducted. It is noticeable if you pick up a book on P/OM written 20 years ago how little reference is made to certain topics that are in the spotlight these days (e.g., supply chain management and new product development). Another aspect of change is the recognition that certain topics that had much attention paid to them 20 years ago are no longer of major concern and importance (e.g., time and motion study and work simplification). More subtle is the change in the way that some topics are treated. For example, project management has been an important part of P/OM since 1950; however, projects were assumed to be constrained by engineering and subject to immutable laws concerning how long it takes to construct a building or bring out a new car.

Change occurred when management recognized that it could affect completion times, project costs, and quality by reorganizing the way that jobs were done. Concurrent management of project activities can be used now in place of sequential management to speed project completion. Continuous multiple project systems are able to produce a stream of new product developments. Communication among project participants has been amplified by email. Procurement using the Internet has altered project inventories and selection of suppliers. Geographically dispersed teams work round-the-clock using technology that did not exist 20 years ago to communicate about project management, production, and research. Methods for continuous improvement are mixed with reengineering to bring about fundamental changes in the business model.

After reading this chapter, you should be able to:

- Explain why organizations must be able to adapt to change.
- Explain why projects at one time were constrained by engineering assumptions and/or geographic boundaries.
- Explain why projects are no longer constrained by engineering assumptions and/or geographic boundaries.
- Describe how email changes the way in which project participants communicate.
- Discuss the effect email has on project teamwork.
- Describe what special contributions OM can make to change management for adopting new technologies,
and the timing of change. Discuss concurrent engineering in this regard.
- Describe three factors that must exist for change to take place and explain how they combine into a powerful force for change.
- Describe the operations manager as a change agent and—at the same time—as a team player.
- Explain why a vision of what the future can become must be understood by the team players and supported by top management.
- Describe various forms of benchmarking including by process type and self-benchmarking.

- Provide a list of "smart" benchmarks that capture essential OM characteristics of processes.
- Relate benchmarking to both continuous improvement (CI) and reengineering (REE) aspects of change management.
- Describe continuous improvement methods.
- Explain the reengineering and business process redesign.
- Discuss the principles of reengineering.

- Categorize procurement over the Internet as continuous improvement or REE
- Give some examples of companies that live by the principles of continuous reengineering.
- Explain how the Ferris Wheel models continuous multiple project systems.
- Describe the kind of change that the Internet brought to project and process management.

THE SYSTEMS VIEWPOINT

To be successful, change managers must adopt the broadest systems perspective. New forces arise continuously, and in response to them, strategic adaptation must occur. External change must be met by internal adaptation. Change is met by counterchange, and stimulus by response. Teamwork is essential because even small changes ripple through the system, creating new conditions that have to be managed.

The change management team communicates with employees at every level from top to bottom. Strong teams attempt to determine how a change strategy might affect every activity of the organization. Tracing cause and effect is a systems task particularly well-suited to OM talents and abilities. Permission must be granted explicitly and implicitly that allows cutting across all functional boundaries (e.g., marketing).

Five of the most important factors that force change in this area are environmental, ethical, technological, global, and security. The proper response of the organization to challenges and opportunities in each of these areas is to bring change management capabilities into focus. Change management is able to use combinations of continuous, incremental improvement (CI) and reengineering (REE), which reexamines all assumptions and starts from scratch to bring about change. Grading performance does not stop when the manager gets the diploma. All activities of a Stage IV company are constantly being graded and being compared with who is best in class. That comparison is called *benchmarking*.

Benchmarking is the trigger for dissatisfaction when the system being graded falls short of what has been determined to be best-practice achievements. Such dissatisfaction leads to both continuous improvement and REE. Managing change requires implementing modifications that will have the most desirable performance improvement. To benchmark successfully, it is necessary to know what goals are being sought and how they are being measured. The runner's goal of coming in first is frequently supplanted by a higher goal of breaking the record. A profit goal can be similar, with long-term damage resulting. Chosen rates of stable growth may be preferable. Nonprofit goals can be viewed as maximization of the benefit to cost ratio.

STRATEGIC THINKING

Bureaucracies tend to develop strategies dedicated to protecting the status quo. Dissatisfaction with this strategy occurs when the status quo becomes unacceptable, which can occur for many reasons. Social disapproval (concerning environmental impact and ethical factors related to customers, employees, and stockholders) can call for a different strategy. Similarly, failure to compete successfully can be indicated by falling profits, failure to maintain technological leadership, and global miscalculations in markets and/or plant locations. OM must be part of the change (or transition) management team. It can provide a "vision" of what operations and technology might be like in the future. Such vision is derived from benchmarking other companies used as models of excellence.

Strategies are often created by emulation of companies that have been rated excellent. Business periodicals regularly publish information that describes the "best managed" companies. Lists today are gone tomorrow, indicating that what led to past excellence may not continue in the future. *Business Week*'s cover on November 5, 1984, stated, "OOPS! First published two years ago, *In Search of Excellence* quickly became a best-seller . . . . The authors name America's best-run companies—and claimed to have found the reasons for their success. But some of those companies aren't looking so excellent any more." (*In Search of Excellence: Lessons from America's Best Run Companies,* by Tom Peters and Robert Waterman, Jr., Warner Books, November 1982).

19-1 ADAPTATION TO EXTERNAL CHANGES

When **change management** is discussed, what is meant is that managers will reach strategic decisions leading to actions that will help their organizations adapt to significant changes in the competitive realm. Success demands systems thinking and cooperation. Table 19-1 illustrates company adaptation to several types of external changes.

New competitors appear with no old investment burdens. They start without the old designs and obsolete equipment their competitors have. Newcomers can put all of their investments into new technology, deriving improved products from better processes. OM is able to evaluate the competitive advantage.

The old barriers to entry that kept competitors out of a market included:

1. Lack of experience with the technology and a learning curve to become as good as the existing suppliers
2. Difficulty in taking customers away from existing suppliers
3. Large investments to become as good as existing suppliers

These three principles no longer apply. Technology changes continuously and rapidly. It transfers almost immediately. The owner of the latest technology has cost and quality advantages, which the old supplier's customers find irresistible. There are global sources of capital that are constantly searching for best return on investment. Start-up companies have distinct advantages over established companies because experience with the old technology drags down innovative use of the new technology. OM is fully apprised of the technological advantages of start-ups and the importance of timing when upgrading old technology.

Change management: Managing modification of the transformation process, including the inputs and the outputs, is a major challenge and opportunity.

External Changes	Company Adaptation
New technology is available	Company strives to adopt the new technology rapidly
New environmental regulations are created	Company meets or beats the new regulations
Ethical problems receive public attention	Company changes procedures to fulfill or raise new ethical expectations
Company adopts higher ethical and/or environmental standards	Other companies change procedures to meet or raise ethical and/or environmental standards
There are new global competitors and new competitive methods	Company changes to become more effective as a global competitor
Company invents new global initiatives	Other companies respond with new counter-initiatives which increase the intensity of global competitiveness

TABLE 19-1

Change Management

External changes force management to adapt by selecting strategies to manage transition.

New technology forces established companies to find ways to adapt. The transition from old to new technology must be managed. Timing is crucial. Old facilities are modified or closed down. On a global scale, many of the old auto-assembly plants have been closed by DaimlerChrysler, Ford, and GM to keep pace with what new plants can achieve in quality and cost. OM's participation is critical on the technology management team.

New rules and regulations regarding environmental impacts of both processes (smokestack emissions) and products (auto-engine emissions) force change and adaptation. OM is the change manager in charge of meeting pollution controls and recycling requirements.

Customers change in what they expect. Health and safety considerations have forced entire industries (such as food and automobiles) to adapt to new customer levels of needs and wants. Customer-driven changes have occurred in what is considered to be acceptable quality. Raising standards of quality is part of a continuing dynamic that new competitors turn to their advantage. If OM cannot help the company adapt quickly enough, the market falters and the financial system withdraws its support.

Employees change in what they expect. In the first half of the twentieth century, they were told what to do and they did what they were told. After 1950, a desire to participate in planning and decision making became more immediate. Increasingly, P/OM could justify replacing people with technology. Some managers did work that computers could do faster and more accurately. Many causes have led to company downsizing and a sense of alienation. The trust of the company, which was repaid with loyalty, has been damaged.

Suppliers change what they make, how they manufacture, what services they offer, their quality standards, and what they charge. The buyer now goes to the global market. New organizations appear continuously. Start-ups have the new technology advantage, which was discussed earlier in terms of "cost and quality advantages that . . . customers find irresistible." The advantages of dealing with established suppliers certified by OM for their current **capabilities** and likely future improvements must be weighed against the strategy of switching suppliers. OM is needed on that strategy planning team.

Community expectations change, which the company calls home to its plants, warehouses, and offices. Environmental expectations are real. The ethical conduct of the company is important. In the book *The 100 Best Companies to Work for in America*, one of the six rating characteristics is pride in work and company.[1] There can be no pride in working for a company considered lacking in ethics by employees.

Global activity is changing. It is increasing for every one of the preceding factors. Companies are becoming global in activities and mind-set. This forces continuous and substantial change. The communities mentioned earlier can be anywhere in the world. Customers, employees, and suppliers speak many different languages and use a variety of currencies. Rules and regulations change by crossing borders. Although teamwork is essential to manage such change, OM has a major role to play on that team.

19-2 OM'S PART IN CHANGE MANAGEMENT

OM brings special knowledge to the change management team; this knowledge consists of three parts.

1. *Familiarity with technology* and the timing of technological change, which includes technological forecasting and knowing when it is best to adopt a new technology and leave behind an old one. If a new start-up company has a technological advantage, there may be a benefit to not imitating that technology. Instead, by waiting for further technological development the company can "leapfrog the competition." To retain customers during the transition may require price cuts and full disclosure of the intended strategy. There are other scenarios that OM is uniquely suited to suggest and evaluate. Knowledge of timing is complex and critical. The OM advantage stems from experience with the technology of processes.

2. *Understanding the interaction between technology and environmental protection* takes the form of pollution controls for land, air, and water. It applies to processes and products. P/OM contains the body of knowledge that is essential for greening the globe.

Capabilities: Capabilities-based strategies are reflected in smart management of business processes.

Whether the reference is to replenishment in forestry, preventing oil spills, or nuclear contamination, the issues arise from operations and technology, which are both in the comfort zone of P/OM.

3. *Understanding the responsibility for ethical production practices:* A major area of ethics is related to the honest effort to deliver a safe and healthy product to customers. The quality of products is the responsibility of OM. Shipments of cans that might explode or foods that might be tainted often can only be stopped by operations managers. Other managers do not know the specifics of each day's production output.

If adequate standards are not maintained during production, and these problems are ignored, it is likely that deliveries will be made of unsafe food, toys that are dangerous, and cars that should not be driven. The design of the product also plays a part. Design is acknowledged to be a responsibility shared by OM and others. Design for manufacturability (DFM) and design for assembly (DFA) are subject to the conditions of design for safe use by customers and design for nonspoilage during manufacture.

The product must be safe to make. Ethics of the workplace reflect integrity to protect employees from noxious fumes, toxic substances, unsafe machines, nonsanitary facilities, jumbled storage, and combustible materials. The factories and offices can be nice places to work. Care of the environment is free but takes caring from OM.

OM also encounters ethical issues when dealing with suppliers. In many places in the world, incentives to purchase from a particular supplier are not called bribes. There are ample examples of companies using inferior materials to save money. OM can oversee and enforce honest dealings with suppliers, maintain the integrity of government contracts, and end the need for whistle-blowers. It may be impossible to put an exact cost on the damage done to workforce morale when management practice is unethical, but it is too high a cost to pay at any time.

19-3 FACTORS THAT ALLOW ORGANIZATIONAL CHANGE

Having established some of the reasons that OM has a special role in dealing with transitions and change management, it is important to point out that changing strategies for products and processes often require organizational changes. These organizational changes are not readily achieved by a bureaucracy that champions the status quo. There are specific conditions that must be fulfilled for change to occur. Various models describing the conditions for change have been proposed. The Gleicher model described here is an accepted change model. Accordingly, the term includes the description of circumstances for transformation. It is **Gleicher Model (conditions for change).**

Dr. David B. Gleicher's model was used to structure a meeting of the American Assembly aimed at change management. The 3-day conference was convened to discuss reversing the declining competitiveness of the United States.[2] The meeting addressed the issue of increasing the values of each of the three factors that promote change.

The model proposes that the product of three factors (D, V, P) must be greater than C to allow organizational change to take place. C is the total cost of bringing about the planned changes.

Thus: $D \times V \times P > C$

The factors are

1. *Dissatisfaction* with the current situation (D)
2. *Vision* of what the future can become (V)
3. *Practical first steps* to achieve the vision (P)

Note that because the three factors are multiplicative, if one of them is zero, then there can be no change. Further, when all three factors are greater than zero, their product might be greater than the cost (C) of changing the situation. If $D \times V \times P > C$, then change is likely, assuming that no other factors negatively impact the change.

Gleicher model (conditions for change): The product of three factors, D, V, and P, must be greater than the cost of change, C.

Dissatisfaction: Benchmarking is the trigger for dissatisfaction with the status quo.

Vision: Clear and unambiguous view of what the future can become.

Practical first steps: "The devil is in the details" captures the essence of practical first steps; requires articulated goals and believable tactics for realizing initial goals.

Increasing **dissatisfaction** with the current situation is often the result of comparing a company with its competitors. If it is learned from the comparison that "they" can build a car in 20 hours while it takes "us" 40 hours, the seeds for dissatisfaction (D) have been sown. Methodical comparisons called *benchmarks* are developed by the OM benchmarking function, to be discussed shortly.

The cause of dissatisfaction with the current situation (20 versus 40) also provides a vision (here, a productivity target) of what the future can become. Benchmarking usually has the ability to indicate the causes of dissatisfaction (cycle time needs reduction) and targets to shoot for (20 hours per car). **Vision** has various meanings but the one intended here is "something seen otherwise than by ordinary sight." Two words that often accompany this nonordinary sight are "wisdom" and "imagination."

Practical first steps include design studies aimed at using fewer parts and allowing quicker assembly; process improvement studies to replace workers with faster machines for tedious and repetitive work; and work simplification studies to redesign workstations so that teamwork can make the job more productive and less arduous. OM can be expected to be involved in this change management situation from beginning to end.

The American auto industry has changed a great deal. It benchmarked itself against the Japanese auto industry, resulting in high D and clear vision as to where it must go. Various efforts were made to find practical first steps and, over time, good answers were found. Problems still remain. More change management is needed. Industries that have used downsizing extensively have noted that it has the effect of eliminating dissatisfaction. Those that remain are satisfied to still be employed. Downsizing also obscures vision unless it is clearly identified as a means to the vision and not an end in itself.

The kind of vision that is obscured is the need for new product innovations and new state of the art plants. It also is significant that both unions and management in the U.S. auto industry have had different visions, which in systems terms is equivalent to turning competition inward instead of keeping it external. The first practical steps would be to get everyone playing on the same team with a shared set of clearly stated objectives.

The components of the change model can be identified with OM activities in Table 19-2.

There are other routes to be followed, but the activities in Table 19-2 are basic OM contributions to change management. For example, vision is not useful unless it has real support from above.

OM can serve best as a change agent when it is part of a team. Many companies stress teamwork for change management. Concurrent engineering, which is widely used for project management, requires the team-oriented approach. Project management allows OM to provide a practical means for moving toward the realization of a goal.

19-4 OM'S BENCHMARKING ROLE IN CHANGE MANAGEMENT

Systematic comparative measurements made between similar processes (functions, departments, products, services, and so on) are benchmarks. The procedure for making comparative measurements is called *benchmarking*. Comparisons can be made between different industries. IBM, when developing mail and telephone-order services, benchmarked

TABLE 19-2	**Factor OM**	**Activity**
OM Activities for Change-Management Factors	Dissatisfaction (D)	Benchmarking (comparing your performance with Best Practices)
	Vision (V)	Best-Practice estimates derived from benchmarking or by proposing product and process innovations
	Practical first steps (P)	Project management often implementing new technology

that process with Lands' End, which is known to be a leader in mail-order service. Disney is frequently benchmarked for comparisons in customer relations.

Xerox played an important role in bringing serious attention to benchmarking. It remains committed to benchmarking. See http://www.benchnet.com. Click on "benchmarking, past, present and future" and scroll to the bottom of the page. Note: Xerox is ranked fourth after TRW, Bank of America, and American Express.

Xerox has had some difficult times in spite of its commitment to benchmarking. Perhaps, it would have been one of the companies that disappeared by 2003 had it not been for those early benchmarking initiatives. The history of benchmarking starts before 1990, when a Xerox executive sent a group to Japan to determine quality goals. He stated, "This competitive benchmarking resulted in specific performance targets rather than someone's guess or intuitive feel of what needs to be done—which is the real power of the process."[3] The benchmarks were effective. Xerox stated that defects were decreased by 84 percent using the new targets.

It is noteworthy how benchmarks permit global comparisons. Benchmarking is most useful when there is a clear correspondence of processes and their purposes and goals. The accounts payable function of Mazda and Ford led to improvements for the latter. Other processes that could benefit include the productivity of specific production processes. Anheuser-Busch regularly benchmarks all of its plants. Credit-approval, repair and maintenance, accounts receivable, performance appraisal, salary reviews, and so on, are other examples of processes that lend themselves to benchmarking.

Comparisons require at least two parties. Access must be available for the comparison to be made. Companies that would like to benchmark themselves against the competition can only use measures that are available through information in the public domain, such as annual reports, and newspaper and magazine articles. Data from newspapers and magazines must be used with care. Sometimes information is obtained from suppliers that are shared with competitors. There is an ethical question that arises. If competitors share information, there are legal issues about collusion. Benchmarks are sometimes available when there are joint ventures, as was the case with Mazda and Ford.

Benchmarking similar departments in the same organization is a teamwork concept as long as it is used to encourage cooperative improvement and not as a basis for penalizing the lower-grade departments. In the Anheuser-Busch case, it is expected that the newer plants will have higher benchmark grades.

Self-benchmarking over time provides useful insights concerning self-improvement. Individual athletes in every kind of sport track themselves. Coaches use detailed team statistics to guide them in their efforts to design winning teams. Government departments track trade, productivity, unemployment benefits, the velocity of money, and so on.

Benchmarking can only be as good as the relevance of the measures that are used. There are three determinants. First, the measure must be appropriate. Second, measurement must be done properly. Third, the entities being compared must be comparable. Even if all three conditions are met, some benchmarks provide more insight than others. If they capture the competitive factor, they are "smart."

A list of **smart benchmarks** might include the following 10 target variables:

> **Smart benchmarks:** Based on those dimensions that are most valuable for steering tactics and for redirecting strategies.

1. *Cycle time*. The inverse is output rate, so short cycle times are chosen to increase output rates.

2. *Net margins* (after-tax income as a percent of revenue). Detroit's new-found obsession with net margins reflects its quest to improve the way it designs and builds cars and trucks. "It's a good management tool to keep everyone focused on where we need to go," according to Jack Smith, General Motors CEO.[4]

3. *Return on equity*. Increasingly popular among chief financial officers (CFOs).

4. *Inventory turns* per year, measured by net annual sales divided by average inventory level. It is increasingly used in preference to direct measures of profit.

5. *Days of inventory*. 365 divided by inventory turns.

6. *Delivery speed.* How many days, hours, or minutes does it take to deliver? Fast-track deliveries are typically 3 days instead of a month.

7. *Project life cycle intervals.* Rapid completion is often half the customary response time.

8. *Breakeven volume.* Comparison with industry norms and with the organization's BEP over time are both beneficial.

9. *Breakeven time.* Hewlett-Packard developed this measure to indicate how long a period is required for a new product to reach breakeven volume.

10. Other insight-building benchmarks include multidimensional quality mapping, which shows the position of competing products on more than one dimension, team accomplishments, and levels of **core competencies.**

Core competencies:
See **Capabilities.**

Some Best-Practice measures should reflect long-term survival of the enterprise. These measures can relate to environmental concerns, ethics, mastery of global business practices, and grasp of future technological developments.

Benchmarks have been criticized for various reasons. Government measures (such as unemployment, productivity, and the consumer price index) have been changed from time to time, which makes them difficult to track over time. Company measures of resource utilization (machine and people) can be counterproductive. Measures of overhead can be misleading. Quarterly financial report statements are cited as a cause of short-term decisions. End-of-month shipments are used to meet quotas, distorting production schedules and adversely impacting quality.

The systems complexity of benchmarking is exemplified by the U.S. government's monthly publication of flights that are delayed more than 15 minutes. The airlines that come out on top use this data in their marketing campaigns. Delays due to mechanical problems originally were excluded but later were made part of the on-time measure of performance. Various airlines have complained that this causes pressure to defer repairs to keep good grades.

An airline analyst says that a better measure of reliability is the percentage of flight miles canceled, because a canceled trip irks travelers far more than minor delays.[5] Cancellations are measured by the percentage of scheduled miles that are actually flown. Criticism of a cancellation benchmark could be made if airlines failed to cancel flights (because of weather and mechanical problems) in order to maintain good grades. What starts out as a good idea to benchmark airline performance becomes complicated by issues of how these benchmarks are used and possibly abused. The power of benchmarking to influence behavior in unexpected ways must be taken into account.

19-5 CONTINUOUS IMPROVEMENT (CI) FOR CHANGE MANAGEMENT

Continuous improvement (CI):
Uses constant effort to find better ways to produce a product and deliver a service. Scope is local, limited to incremental change, and persistent.

Products, Continuous development: See Continuity and Ferris Wheel model.

Projects, Continuous development: See Continuity and Ferris Wheel model.

Two approaches are used to accomplish planned change. OM is comfortable and involved with both kinds of change. First is **continuous improvement,** which is a constant effort to find better ways to produce the products and deliver the services.[6] This is often local with conversions being done to the existing process. Because it is incremental, gradual, and tactical, OM plays a large role in originating, implementing, and evaluating the results. In this category, both **products, continuous development,** and **projects, continuous development,** are relevant terms.

Within the scope and surveillance of P/OM, a continuous improvement program should be reviewed by the change-management team. Decisions to make simple changes can obscure opportunities for fundamental and sweeping changes associated with reengineering (REE). Adherents to the continuous improvement track have made commitments that place them in opposition to REE. One of the first decisions that change management faces is which track to take—the gradual or the extensive road to change.

The administration of specific improvements can be as simple as a new method for deciding when machine adjustments are to be made. It should not be as complex as the implementation of a new technology. A change of real magnitude deserves a total systems study, which is characteristic of reengineering (examined in the next section).

Because continuous improvement changes are improvements to existing systems, a systems study to question goals and purposes is not undertaken. Benchmarking plays the guiding role in continuous improvement activities. It provides the basis for making course corrections on the journey to excellence. Work simplification, inventory reductions, material replacements, and information system changes are typical of continuous improvement programs.

19-5a Planning Transitions

The prescription for successful continuous improvement changes includes total management involvement for implementation. When Chemical Bank introduced new technology for its stock transfer system, senior management sat down with members of the workforce to provide hands-on training in the new procedures.

A lot of careful thought went into planning the transition. There was recognition of the fact that it is normal to resist change. Therefore, senior managers listened to the employees' problems related to changing. Adjustments could be made when warranted because those that had planned the changeover were on the production line with those that do the work. That also signaled the importance of the changes being made.

When the (change) managers of the Royal Bank of Canada developed an expert system for monitoring risk with sophisticated technology, they stressed the importance of dialogue with members of the workforce. One of their purposes was to prevent employees from feeling threatened by the new technology. They did this by emphasizing employee ownership of the new technology and methods. They accented the need for teamwork to successfully facilitate making the changeover. The implementation team was aware of the need to listen, hear, and make adjustments during the transition period.

19-6 REENGINEERING (REE) FOR CHANGE MANAGEMENT

Reengineering (REE)—also called *business process redesign*—seeks radical improvements over a reasonable period of time. REE is at the opposite pole from continuous improvement. Reengineering (REE) requires total replacement of existing systems with new systems that have been designed from scratch. The "reasonable period of time" requirement is relative to the situation. What is meant by "reasonable period of time"? The answer is: Reengineering is not associated with long-term, theoretical research. Reengineering is associated with short-term, application-oriented research.

Reengineering has disturbed even its adherents because of extreme claims. Hammer and Champy wrote the original book in 1993, which started an REE crusade.[7] In 1995, Champy writes, "on the whole . . . reengineering payoffs appear to have fallen well short of their potential. *Reengineering the Corporation* set big goals: 70 percent decreases in cycle time and 40 percent decreases in costs; 40 percent increases in customer satisfaction, quality and revenue; and 25 percent growth in market share."[8] Studies done by Champy's company, CSC Index, showed that "participants failed to attain these benchmarks by as much as 30 percent."

Such failures would be successes for many companies. In addition, the causes of failures can be traced to doing REE incorrectly. Champy's book strives to right that wrong by elaborating on the requirements for success. These have to do with identifying the core processes of the business (such as new product development for the pharmaceutical business and customer service for a bank). "Identify those key operational processes, reassemble the work that goes into them in line with the core mission of the business."[9] This is operations-management territory, and OM knowledge is a crucial ingredient for success.

One important variant of REE highlights a different purpose using the same methodology. **Breakpoint business process redesign** "focuses on creating strategic-level competitive advantages through breakthroughs in the *core business processes that most affect customers and shareholders*."[10] The idea is to select functions to reengineer that can create market response that is much greater than the resources required to achieve it. Emphasis

Reengineering (REE): Starts from scratch with practical first steps. Radical changes occur when the design process begins with a blank piece of paper.

Breakpoint business process redesign: Strategic-level competitive advantages in the areas of the company's core business processes.

is placed on competency-based competition, which almost always involves OM and logistics-type capabilities.

Time-based management (including rapid-response project life cycle management and fast-delivery cycle times) is one form of special capabilities. Four principles of capabilities-based management are stated by George Stalk, Philip Evans, and Lawrence E. Shulman in their seminal article, "Competing on Capabilities,"[11] as follows:

1. The building blocks of corporate strategy are not products and markets but business processes.

2. Competitive success depends on transforming a company's key processes into strategic capabilities that consistently provide superior value to the customer.

3. Companies create these capabilities by making strategic investments in a support infrastructure that links together and transcends traditional SBUs and functions. (SBUs are strategic business units.)

4. Because capabilities necessarily cross functions, the champion of a capabilities-based strategy is the CEO.

OM is central to a capabilities-based strategy. What is happening is that fundamental axioms of business, which have been followed with great success for 100 years, are no longer valid. Those axioms can be replaced by reengineering business processes. This change-management methodology entails great responsibility for OM. As Booz Allen Hamilton state, "Where once the challenge was to find ways to be more competitive with the products or services you produced, it now lies in figuring out how to produce better products or services with which to compete."[12] The shift is from marketing and sales reliance to the systems approach with project teams composed of OM, marketing and sales, R & D, engineering, and everyone else involved.

General principles of reengineering and redesigning business processes are listed as a sequential set of steps:

1. *Identify special core qualities, competencies, and capabilities* of the company. Some companies have developed unique ability to turn over inventory; others have developed a manufacturing skill in working with special materials. Rare process skills are required for making fine chocolate, and the same applies to automotive windshield glass. A company that will be mentioned shortly has people with special knowledge and a mind-set about hearing-aid technology.

2. *Identify core processes* that deliver the core capabilities described in step 1. Core processes are broad-based. For example, merchandising methods and pricing might be credited with the achievement of fast inventory turnover. Alternatively, electronic data interchange (EDI) linking retail stores, distribution, and delivery systems might be the core process responsible for delivering fast turnovers.

3. *Trace cross-functional transactions* (between OM, marketing, distribution, suppliers, and so on) in detailed systems terms—for the core processes. To illustrate, assume that Fidelity Investments wants to examine how their computer systems are used by customers to make unassisted, discounted stock trades by telephone. OM's backroom operations handle the calls, which would then be related to cash management, marketing activities, accounts receivable, accounts payable, customer services, and so on.

4. *Develop detailed process analyses,* including the activities that are part of cross-functional transactions. The process components are made up of people, machines, and workstations.

5. *Benchmark* cost, time, and quality for each process component. Include such measures as customer satisfaction, cycle times, productivity, and complaints and errors. Some benchmarks will be broad-based and others detailed. Fidelity Investments will probably want to benchmark against Charles Schwab & Co., and vice versa. They might be able to do this on broad measures, such as customer satisfaction derived from market research. Data for operations are not likely to be shared by these competitors. Each can propose target-improvement levels for process components. This is done in the next two steps.

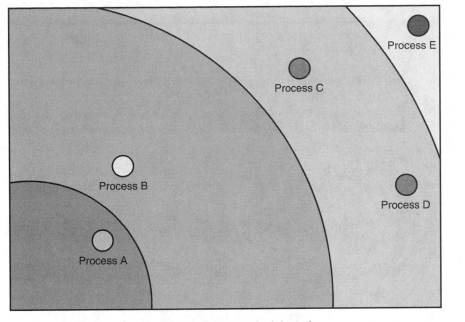

Process Improvement Anticipated

F I G U R E 1 9 - 1
Priorities Using Efficiency Frontiers for Re-engineering Different Processes (Based on Process Role in Delivering Capabilities and Process Improvement Anticipated)

6. *Select processes to be redesigned.* Figure 19-1 (adapted from a Booz Allen Hamilton figure)[13] provides a sensible way to prioritize processes with respect to their impact on the desired capabilities and the degree to which each process can be improved.

19-6a Process Role in Delivering Core Capabilities

Various processes have been listed in step 2 that can deliver the core capabilities. However, the processes do not deliver all core capabilities equally. Process A has the least ability to deliver the core capabilities chosen in step 1 whereas process E has the best ability. Process C is next best and then processes B and D are tied for the third best position. It is important to bear in mind that all five processes have been chosen because they deliver the core capabilities in varying degrees. In other words, the value of the origin of the y-axis is not known.

19-6b Process Improvement

The x-axis reflects the degree to which each process can be improved. This evaluation is based on the information that was developed using steps 4 and 5. Process E promises the greatest improvement, followed by processes D, C, B, and A, in that order.

The arcs shown in Figure 19-1 are called **efficiency frontiers** because they separate the regions with respect to their combined power to deliver improved capabilities. In effect, these frontiers represent combinations of delivery capabilities (DC) and improvements anticipated (IA) that are considered to be equally desirable. In equation form, they might be approximated by arcs of circles:

$$(DC)^2 + (IA)^2 = R^2 \qquad (R \text{ is the circle's radius})$$

Financial analysis uses risk-return efficiency frontiers in much the same way that reengineering employs the DC-IA frontiers. Four regions have been demarcated. Process A is in the worst region. Process E is in the best region and should be chosen for reengineering. Note that efficiency frontiers drawn through rocesses C and D do not provide much differentiation. If it is decided to reengineer two processes, the choice between processes C and D is not clear.

Figure 19-2 provides another way of prioritizing the projects, which clears up the ambiguity for choosing processes C or D.

Efficiency frontiers: Because the chosen process can be improved a great deal, and that will help the performance of the company significantly, it will fall on a high-priority (large radius) efficiency frontier.

Using quadrant differentiation, processes in quadrant I are the most important processes for delivering the capability and have the greatest potential for improvement. That makes them ideal subjects for REE. Quadrant II is high on special capabilities but low on improvement potential. As noted here, this may be because these processes have been already reengineered. Quadrant III is low in delivering the selected capabilities but high in improvement potential. Processes A and B in quadrant IV are not attractive candidates for reengineering.

After reengineering, process E will move from its position in quadrant I to quadrant II, as shown in the bottom box of Figure 19-2. It should be located high up in the left-hand corner, indicating that little opportunity remains for this process to be further improved. Process E continues to play a major role in delivering core capabilities. Successful reengineering will result in a cluster of processes in the upper left-hand corner of the bottom box in Figure 19-2. The potential for process improvement will have been used up, and the company's core capability is as good as it is going to get under the current set of systems conditions, i.e., core assets (capabilities, such as intellectual capital) are being used to the best of the company's ability.

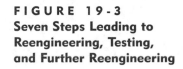
FIGURE 19-3
Seven Steps Leading to
Reengineering, Testing,
and Further Reengineering

7. *Set target levels* for improved performance, such as—cut customer waiting time in half, reduce cycle time by 70 percent, decrease perceived difficulty for customer to order online so that it takes half as long, increase inventory turnovers from 6 to 10, set the maximum number of times that the phone should ring before being answered at 3 rings, and so on. Many of the targets listed in this paragraph are typical CRM (customer relationship management) goals. See http://www.crm-forum.com.

8. *Reengineer the process*.

9. *Test, evaluate, and replan* (stop REE if and when satisfied).

Figure 19-3 is a concise rendering of the reengineering process. Feedback loops are added. They go from step 9 to steps 6, 7, and 8. This is consistent with *Test, evaluate, and replan* (9).

It is necessary to be able to reconsider what processes to redesign (6). It is usual practice to reset the target levels (7) and to continue reengineering the process originally selected (8). To accomplish step 8 (reengineer the process), some additional heuristics (rules of thumb—from A to Z) should be considered. These are not intended to be applied sequentially, and a number of the heuristics overlap.

A. Question the current task structure. For each task ask:
    Why is this done? Why is this done this way?

B. Before deciding to use reengineering, check the benefits of using continuous-improvement methods instead. continuous improvement and REE should not be used simultaneously.

C. When the core processes, goals, and subgoals are understood (steps 1 through 6) and the targets are set (step 7), REE starts with a clean sheet of paper in an effort to achieve the targets. Because benchmarking is an ongoing activity, the processes selected and/or the targets may change.

D. For reengineering, focus on *task design*, not on task execution.

E. Search for radically different approaches. Thinking outside the box is encouraged because almost everything in the box is worn out. Innovative thinking is easier for some people than others. Methods exist for making the strange familiar (familiarization) and the familiar strange (defamiliarization) that are applicable to students in kindergarten.

F. Empower people to consider leading creative projects. (Note: The discussions of Oticon Holding S/A, W. L. Gore & Associates, Inc., and MMM, which follow. These cases provide a small window on what is known about the creative process and organizational catalysts of creativity, such as leadership.)

G. Organize processes around outcomes, not tasks. (If the process to be reengineered is "grant credit," then organize to grant credit and not to do a sequence of tasks such as check on credit history, request credit references, check on credit references, analyze references, analyze income, etc.)

H. Using team collaboration, simultaneously work on as many activities as possible. Strive to avoid sequential activities where one must be finished before another can begin. Experience with **concurrent engineering (CE)** has shown how CE speeds up project completion. When team members work in parallel, individuals can coordinate tasks that are various parts of the job. Another way of stating this is: Delinearize the process for rapid completion with the highest project quality.

> **Concurrent engineering (CE):** Parallel and simultaneous work along many project paths; more resources early in the project's evolution. CE uses a team-oriented framework.

I. When possible, make those who use the output of a process part of the group creating that output.

J. Combine information processing with output-producing work. In other words, quantity and quality data should be recorded and analyzed by the same people that produce the product or service. Thus, someone who does credit accounting should be part of the process for setting credit ratings and granting credit.

K. Employ geographically dispersed resources as though they were centralized (using computer technology).

L. Make decisions where the work is done.

M. Place quality controls with the people who do the work.

N. Capture information only once and as close to its source as possible.

O. Develop detailed process flowcharts for the existing processes and for the proposed new processes. "An indispensable tool in Business Process Re-engineering is process mapping. Competitive realignment . . . requires an extensive understanding of the activities that constitute core business processes and the processes that support them, in terms of their purpose, trigger points, inputs and outputs and constraining influences."[14]

P. Successful reengineering emphasizes balancing process flows—not maximizing production flow rates. Increasing output rates can be accomplished in many ways—after the balanced flow has been achieved.

Q. Stress every employee's right to choose to do what needs to be done—instead of fulfilling a job description.

R. Experiment with alternatives before finalizing new process configurations to avoid suboptimization.

S. Use **pilot studies** of proposed changes. These can be run in parallel to existing processes. Pilot plants are scaled-down models of the factory or service system.

> **Pilot studies:** Small-scale systems used to test feasibility of the process. The assumption is that if the pilot scale works, then the full-scale system will work.

T. Implement REE changes for only part of the system before expanding the application to the entire system. This requires choosing a sample set of items to manufacture in the new way, a sample of accounts payable to be handled in the reengineered fashion, and a sample set of credit applications to be approved or rejected by the new methods. Then, if the experiment is successful, extend implementation to a larger subset and eventually to the entire system. Call this *partial applications*.

U. Have patience! Efforts that do not work out can be learned from and should encourage further creative experimentation.

V.   Institute a continuous reengineering program. This means that steps 6 through 9 in Figure 19-3 should be ongoing.

W.   Continuous benchmarking is a learning process (step 5 and heuristic rule C). Search for new benchmarks and continue to measure existing benchmarks over time. Translate benchmarks into targets.

X.   Select new processes to be redesigned (step 6). Successes and failures are indicators for new REE opportunities.

Y.   Constantly reset the target levels (step 7).

Z.   Successful reengineering often requires reorganization.

19-6c Oticon Holding S/A

In 1991, Lars Kolind, then president of Oticon Holding S/A,[15] reorganized this 89-year-old Danish hearing-aid company. His reengineering of Oticon satisfies the 26 heuristics listed here. Kolind has left Oticon, now, but his out-of-the-box legacy remains. See Chapter 3, Spotlight 3-2.

Oticon Holding S/A is home-based in Hellerup, Denmark. The company was organized by Lars Kolind to reengineer its business processes continuously. Oticon embraced radical redesign using continuous project management without labeling it reengineering.

To compete with Siemens, Philips, and Sony, Kolind (as CEO) freed everyone in the organization to generate and develop new ideas. He called his plan the "disorganization" of Oticon with the goal of achieving the "ultimate flexible organization." Departments and titles disappeared. All activities became projects initiated and pursued by informal groups of motivated individuals. Jobs were reconfigured to be fluid, matching individual abilities and company needs. Project leaders were empowered to find and hire the right people.

All offices were eradicated and replaced with open spaces filled with uniform workstations, each consisting of a desk without drawers and a desktop computer. (In section 20-5, "Readying Operations Management for Future Conditions," the growing use of the "hotel office" concept is described along with that of the "virtual office," see section 20-5e, "Virtual Offices.") Everyone has access to all information with few exceptions. Incoming mail is optically scanned and then shredded. As a constant reminder of the no-paper policy, the remains of the shredded paper plunge into a glass cylinder, which is a centerpiece of the company's cafeteria.

Kolind changed how people communicate in the organization. Informal dialogue is the accepted mode of communication, replacing all memos and other formal documentation, including electronic messages. All Oticon employees think twice before sending email to Kolind. They opt to avoid his deeming them "superfluous" by electronic return. Kolind believes that oral communication is "ten times more powerful, more creative, quicker, and nicer" than memo writing.

Because it has almost entirely done away with paper, Oticon requires employee computer fluency. A computer identical to those in Oticon workstations was offered to every employee for home use in exchange for a commitment to learn to use it.

The staff leaped at the opportunity, forming a "PC Club" to train each other outside of working hours. With computers installed at home, the concept of working hours disappeared. Kolind observed "that everyone works more and they're much more flexible."

Two aspects of this company's continuous reengineering process tell the tale. Traditionally, hearing-aid companies focus on the technology required to make small hearing aids smaller. Oticon generated the vision to be the best in any hearing-aid user-satisfaction survey in the world. A successful Oticon design was a bigger unit for hearing better. Aimed at looking like a modern communications system, it was not pink, but silver-gray like a mobile phone.

Second, Oticon is now the third largest hearing-aid manufacturer in the world. It grew 23 percent in a declining market and increased its gross profits by 25 percent. Price per unit was reduced 20 percent in two years. Startling new designs account for the excellent earnings growth. There are about 100 ongoing projects of various magnitude, which have fine prospects.

This innovative company, which has earned ISO 9001 certification, epitomizes change management. *Industry Week* reports that Oticon is "now observed as a prototype for the company of the future," providing "vital strategies for survival" in a "knowledge-based era." Lars Kolind believes this applies in 2003.

19-7 RAPID COMPLETION OF PROJECTS: TIME-BASED MANAGEMENT (TBM)

Time-based management (TBM): Responsible for fast delivery of goods and services to customers and rapid development of new products.

An area of capability called **time-based management (TBM)** has captured increasing attention because of the success that companies have had using it. TBM elevates time to a position that is equal in importance to cost, quality, and productivity. Time is considered a surrogate for profitability, market share, customers' satisfaction, and so on. Being able to deliver product to customers quickly is one form of TBM. Cutting project duration by a significant amount is another valued form of TBM. Whoever is able to be first into the marketplace with a quality product gains a significant advantage.

The need for speed in project completion has increased as global competitors are empowered by technology. Some are new companies having the advantage of not being encumbered with old plants and old ideas. The time between technological feasibility and new products that embody the new technology has been cut between a third and a half by practitioners of TBM. Technological diffusion concerning the state of the art, and what is feasible, is nearly instantaneous among high-technology players. Many of these companies are home-based in Asia and Europe, and they set up new facilities in North America.

The methods for shortening project life cycle time include PERT analysis with particular emphasis on cutting the critical-path time without jeopardizing quality. Resource management includes resource leveling and COST/TIME trade-offs, which previously have been discussed. Utilization of project funds is often directed toward the goal of minimizing project duration.

The way that the resources are managed has changed considerably as rapid-completion project management has gained adherents because of its clear-cut competitive advantages. The use of more resources at the beginning of the project is encouraged. Project managers used to defer resource utilization until quite late in the project's life cycle.

A main reason for this delay in the early allocation of resources was the compartmentalization of authority, which meant that each group would be left alone to conclude its assignment. Not until approval had been granted for that part of the project would the next stage be authorized to proceed.

Projects, Rapid completion: From scratch, design, build, and produce a car in one year, instead of three years.

Figure 19-4 shows the difference in timing of resource utilization under the time-based project management scenario (new) as compared to the traditional (old) project system. Design for manufacture (DFM) and design for assembly (DFA) are examples of outcomes of using this early resource-allocation orientation of rapid-completion project management. It is useful to note that the appropriate index listing for this subject is **projects, rapid completion.**

It is directed toward preventing the need for later changes by thinking everything through as early as possible. The concept requires many points of view being used in the initial stages of the project. The idea is to dream up (conjecture about) contingencies leading to engineering design changes that could arise and delay the project. The management of resources to achieve early-spending benefits of early project completion is called *concurrent engineering*.

19-7a Concurrent Engineering (CE)

Concurrent engineering (CE) is a time-based management approach that employs more resources earlier in a team-oriented framework than the sequential, compartmentalized project engineering method. The CE approach spends money faster at the start, but it usually reduces project time and improves project quality.

Concurrent engineering is also defined as multifunctional, parallel-path project management. The comparison is made between a football team or a rugby team and a relay

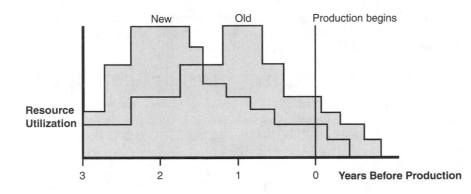

New   Old   Production begins

Resource
Utilization

3   2   1   0   **Years Before Production**

FIGURE 19-4
More Resources Are Allocated to the Project Initially to Prevent Later Changes to Correct Mistakes

race. In rugby, all team players work together to carry the ball down the field. The conventional project management analogy is the relay race, where compartmentalized project groups complete their activities in isolation before handing the baton over to the next group. Every segment runs its own race, i.e., obtains separate approvals that are required before the next one in line is allowed to run.

Figure 19-5 aims to portray the managing team concept for concurrent engineering used to develop a new product (a new production system, etc.). The essential difference with the traditional way is that all channels now communicate with each other from start to finish. The noncompartmentalized structure has to be carefully orchestrated and monitored because there is a tendency to stray back to the old way.

The early use of noncompartmentalized resources has been adopted by many high technology and aerospace companies. In these industries, there is a long history for simultaneous engineering, which put various engineering skills on the same team. Automotive and heavy industry companies also relate to the "simultaneous engineering" approach. The idea is for technical teams to share their knowledge with the focus on joint problem solving.

The terms *parallel planning* and *parallel engineering* are used because they highlight the fact that a multifunctional team is a permanent part of the project-resource plan. This team (or task force) is in many instances multidisciplinary when various branches of science and engineering are called upon to play a part. The team is expected to define the project goals in great detail and depth. The team is responsible for uncovering potential problems and for taking whatever steps are necessary to avoid them. Quality issues are therefore at the top of the task force's agenda. CE requires a culture in which everyone is responsible for quality.[16]

CE is a way of assuring project quality. It strives to achieve team-based, seamless transfers of information. Successful teams have strong leaders who are experimental innovators. Teams often include customers' and suppliers' organizations. Principles of disassembly are used to accelerate learning. Benchmarking is a common practice to provide best-practice standards.

CE methods are known to be used by companies such as AT & T, Boeing, Daimler-Chrysler, Deere & Company, Eastman Kodak, Ford, GE, GM, Hewlett-Packard, Honda of

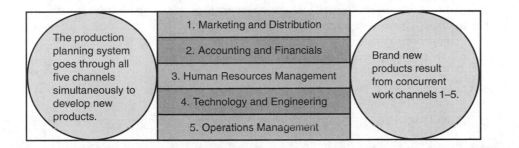

The production planning system goes through all five channels simultaneously to develop new products.

1. Marketing and Distribution
2. Accounting and Financials
3. Human Resources Management
4. Technology and Engineering
5. Operations Management

Brand new products result from concurrent work channels 1–5.

FIGURE 19-5
Continuous, Multifunctional Concurrent-Engineering Team Develops a New Product

America, IBM, Ingersoll-Rand, Komatsu, Nissan, Northrop, Siemens, Toyota, and the U.S. Air Force. This list of 18 organizations represents far less than 1 percent of the companies that are known to use CE for project management.

19-8 CONTINUOUS PROJECT-DEVELOPMENT MODEL

Continuity: Refers to project teams that upon completing a project, or even during the activities of a project, begin another project; benefit of not dissipating project skills and knowledge.

Global competitors have used CE to develop *continuous* project-management systems. **Continuity** refers to project teams that complete one project and then move to another. In this way, project skills are not dissipated when a project is completed. Because product and process improvement is an ongoing effort, the task force often supports the use of continuous improvement.

Continuity in project management also refers to the use of project teams in different parts of the world so that the work can progress as it follows the sun. Teams using distance-learning technologies can transfer information about the status of projects. The media are the Internet, interactive video, etc. Data travels from east to west as team specialists communicate what has been learned and what needs to be done.

Engineers at General Electric–Fanuc (a long-term U.S.–Japan joint venture) design devices used to control factory operations that function around the clock, using a telelink with Japan.[17] Each day's accomplishments are downloaded from GE in the United States to Fanuc in Japan in the afternoon, and uploaded from Japan the next morning. See http://www.gefanuc.com. Global companies are using round-the-clock shifts with CAD/CAM to design and manufacture textiles. Bells and whistles are not really needed. Two-shift project management is a major step ahead of one-shift in cutting project time.

19-8a W. L. Gore & Associates, Inc.

W. L. Gore & Associates[18] has been practicing continuous reengineering long before that term was invented. The company makes Gore-Tex® brand fabric, a synthetic material that is popular for outdoor (and camping) use because of its waterproof and breathable qualities. It is made of an expanded form of polytetrafluoroethylene (PTFE) or Teflon. This company, founded in 1958 by Bill Gore, a former research chemist with DuPont in Newark, Delaware, makes many other electronic, industrial, and medical products with PTFE and Gore-Tex expanded PTFE, including specially-coated guitar strings.

Products have been developed by the 6,600 associates who work for the company. There are no employees—everyone is an associate. Gore uses a "lattice organization," which is intended to connote freedom to move in any direction; to lead, to grow, or to commit to new projects, for example. Many of the associates have developed ideas that have garnered supporters. Leaders arise when their ideas inspire others to follow them. Everyone is encouraged to develop projects leading to new products.

This continuous project-development method has achieved great results. The company has experienced steady growth with 2003 sales reaching $1.3 billion. The company has generated 650 U.S. patents in its 45 years of operation, which is more than 14 domestic patents per year. It has hundreds of different successful products based on its core competencies with PTFE and Gore-Tex expanded PTFE.

There are 45 plants worldwide and, on average, 147 associates per location. This indicates another lattice organization principle, which is to stay under 200 people per plant. Small plants with no authoritarian hierarchy encourage people to communicate with each other in creative ways. Because there are no bosses, sponsors act as advocates for associates in compensation matters. Advice flows freely in all directions because there are no titles and there is no formal organization.

The basic principles of this global company with manufacturing sites located throughout the world can be summed up as fairness, freedom to grow and innovate, self-commitment, and communication. See Innovations Awards 2003. http://greatplacetowork.com/education/innovate/honoree-2003-wlgore.htm.

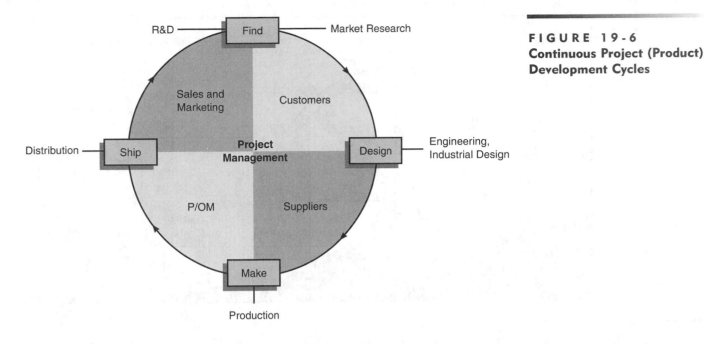

FIGURE 19-6
Continuous Project (Product) Development Cycles

19-8b Ceaseless Reengineering— Project Management Cycles

Oticon and Gore are two companies that provide useful models of ceaseless reengineering driven by means of continuous project development. Both companies have an internal focus that is insistent on pleasing customers. Oticon and Gore avoid hierarchies and grant employees freedom to be creative and to search for better ways to satisfy customers. Both firms are continuously reinventing themselves without needing special names such as reengineering.

Another innovative organization is 3M (MMM—also known as the Minnesota Mining and Manufacturing Co.). 3M has an astounding record of new product development, and the organization supports the same kind of personal creativity that characterizes Oticon and Gore. A useful self-assignment for students who are interested in being champions of innovation within their firms is to research 3M using search engines on the web.

Figure 19-6 is an explanation of how continuous project-management systems function.

The project-management team is multifunctional, which facilitates the coordination of finding, designing, making, and shipping the product. The *find-design-make-ship* cycle must be supported by appropriate functions. All functions participate in each stage, but some of the main effects are as follows: Find and design are best done while everyone "listens to the voice of the customer." Design and make should be coordinated with suppliers. P/OM connects make and ship. Sales and marketing drive shipping. Market research and R & D back up the creative impulses of the project-oriented management. Only a systems attitude (state of mind) can adequately relate all of these cross-functional considerations.

When one project leader finishes the cycle, another can take over the released resources. Alternatively, the same project leader can go through another product-development cycle with the purpose of making new contributions or further improvements. The same model applies to the dynamics of projects starting and finishing. A well-managed project wheel is constantly turning. The number of turns of this wheel measures the revenue-generating energy of the system. Still some failures are bound to occur. When properly viewed, these provide learning experiences that improve the probabilities of future successes.

FIGURE 19-7
The Ferris Wheel Model of Continuous Project (Product) Development

Ferris Wheel model: Provides a model of continuous, new product development, and ceaseless project management.

19-8c Ferris Wheel Model for Continuous New Product Development

Project starts and completions are modeled by occupants getting on and off the Ferris wheel in Figure 19-7. Timing the wheel is management's strategy.

The **Ferris Wheel model** for project management is based on the amusement park ride, which has *n* separate seating compartments. The wheel makes a complete rotation in *T* minutes and stops every *C* minutes to let the riders get off and others get on.

For an interesting history of the Ferris wheel see http://users.vnet.net/schulman/Columbian/ferris.html. If one is in London, a visit to the London Eye[19] will provide an up-to-date view of what a Ferris wheel can be like. See http://www.londoneye.com/default.asp.

To apply the model to projects, let *T* equal an average project's total development time (in days) and let *n* equal the number of projects that are actively being pursued. Then, the average interval between project completions (in days) *C* is given by:

$$C = \frac{T}{n}$$

Say that $T = 730$ days (2 years) and $n = 100$ projects, then, on average, a project is completed every 7.3 days. That is kind of amazing for even a dedicated new product system. Recapping, it takes 2 years on average to complete a new product time line (start-up to release). This company has 100 real projects in process. For most companies, that is an exceptionally heavy load.

$C = 730/100 = 7.3$ days

Also, *O*, the output per year (the number of projects completed per year), is given by:

$O = 365/C = 365/7.3 = 50$ projects completed per year

When the numerator (365 days per year) is divided by *C*, the result is projects completed per year. If the numerator was set at 30 days per month, then $30/7.3 = 4.1$ projects completed per month. Similarly, with 7 days per week, there would be $7.0/7.3 = 0.96$ projects completed per week. That is quite a feat—worthy of being called prodigious project production.

19-8d Probability of Project Success

Not all projects succeed. This is especially the case for new product development projects. The bottom line can be stated in equation form, but it is easier to understand when numbers are used. Say that on average 70 percent of this class of new product projects fail. Although it is a high number, it is likely to be in the right arena. Alternatively, the probability of success is denoted by p_s and

$$p_s = 0.30$$

Then, the number of project successes would be

$$Op_s = 50(0.30) = 15$$

The output in projects completed per year, $O = 50$, was derived in the prior section. Given the probability of success and the expected output, there would be 15 project successes per year. It should now be apparent why the appropriate index term for this subject is **projects, probability of success.**

Projects, Probability of success: p_s is the probability of product success. Given O project completions per year, $p_s O$ is the number of successes.

19-8e Net Profit of Continuous Project Development Program

If each project has an average cost of $100,000 per year, then the average load of $n = 100$ projects has a total cost of $10,000,000 per year.

Assume that average gross margin for each *successful* project is $1,000,000 per year. (Gross margin is sales revenue less manufacturing costs but not including selling, administrative, and development costs.)

The 15 successful projects will generate total gross margin of $15,000,000. Subtracting from this amount the total development costs of $10,000,000 yields a profit of $5,000,000. Even after administrative and sales costs are subtracted, there is substantial profit from engaging in continuous project development.

Note: It more than compensates for the cost of failed projects. Further, the development costs for successful products rapidly diminish, while the revenue stream grows. Also, the pool of successful products increases so that total gross margin continues to climb in successful companies.

Small increases in $p_s = 30$ will improve the net profit figures substantially. The organizational models used by Oticon, W. L. Gore & Associates, and 3M are geared to have high values of p_s. Success means that revenue will be generated that outstrips costs so that net profit results. Otherwise the business model for continuous product development will indicate firm failure.

High values occur when people are motivated to use teamwork to create new revenue-generating ideas, a pattern that is successful only in a nonauthoritarian change-management setting. (It is suggested in the Problems Section at the end of Chapter 19 that a sensitivity analysis be run by varying values of p_s.)

SUMMARY

The need for transition is often apparent, but the managers of the organization are not able to make the necessary changes. Bureaucracy deflects efforts to change. Chapter 19 describes a change model that is comprised of four factors. Using these factors, P/OM can develop systems that encourage change. The approach for determining what to—and how much to—change is related to the method of comparisons using benchmarking. Technology is advancing at an incredible rate, creating new global competitors. The Internet may not have created a new cohort of young millionaires, but it did permanently alter the way that procurement operates along the supply chain. Further, it produced an advantage for the swift. Rapid completion of new products can spell the difference

between net profit or loss. Continuous new product project development provides major competitive advantage. Descriptions of three companies that lead in continuous product development are presented. Also, P/OM has mastery over continuous-improvement methods for gradual change as well as reengineering. P/OM can fix a broken system using reengineering (REE starts with a clean slate) to redesign the system.

Two Spotlight feature boxes conclude this chapter. These boxes illustrate real applications of the materials in the chapter. See Spotlight 19-1: Shouldice Surgery and Spotlight 19-2: Ethics by Regulation.

KEY TERMS

Breakpoint business process redesign
Capabilities
Change management
Concurrent engineering (CE)
Continuity
Continuous improvement (CI)
Core competencies

Dissatisfaction
Efficiency frontiers
Ferris Wheel model
Gleicher model (Conditions for change)
Pilot studies
Practical first steps
Products, Continuous development

Projects, Continuous development
Projects, Probability of success
Projects, Rapid completion
Reengineering (REE)
Smart benchmarks
Time-based management (TBM)
Vision

REVIEW QUESTIONS

1. What is OM's role in change management?

2. What eight factors are forcing the organization to change?

3. How do the four elements of the Gleicher change model work?

4. Use the Gleicher change model to explain why a new CEO might say that another vision statement is not needed.

5. What is the effect of downsizing on change management?

6. Why do schools teach that downsizing is not reengineering?

7. The elevators are kept locked at Oticon in Denmark to encourage meetings on the stairwells. What purposes are served?

8. What are the various kinds of benchmarking that are used?

9. What is continuous benchmarking?

10. How do smart benchmarks differ from other ones? Exemplify.

11. Why should continuous-improvement programs be regularly reviewed by a change management team?

12. It has been said that transition planning and training should include senior management. Explain this and give examples.

13. Provide nine reengineering principles and explain them.

14. What purpose is served by the reengineering heuristics, A through Z. Pick the half you like the most, and explain why.

15. What is the purpose of time-based management (TBM)?

16. How does concurrent engineering relate to project management?

17. Explain the resource-management principle that CE uses.

18. What is the special role of teamwork for CE?

19. Why is it said that computers are essential for project management?

20. What are the usual goals of rapid-completion project management?

21. Why is it pointed out that Oticon Holding S/A and W. L. Gore & Associates, Inc., do not use the term *reengineering* even though both companies are excellent examples of continuous reengineering?

22. What are the benefits of continuous project development?

PROBLEMS SECTION

1. Using the Gleicher model, assume that: $D = 9$, $V = 7$, $P = 1$, and $C = 40$. Will the organization be likely to accept change?

2. In Problem 1, there is a lot of dissatisfaction and a good vision of what the future could be like. There is much resistance to change. C is more than four times larger than D. Practical first steps are unknown ($P = 1$). Then, a consulting firm is hired that recommends a 15 percent workforce reduction. What changes might be expected in the original set of numbers?

3. *Business Week* benchmarks business schools every two years. There has been criticism of the benchmarks used.
a. Develop the lines of the criticism that are deserved.
b. Develop a set of criteria that you believe would permit an accurate comparison of business schools.

4. Make a chart for the benchmarks developed in Problem 3. Then rate your own school on each of the criteria from 1 to 7, where 7 is best. If you have friends attending other business schools, ask them to rate their schools using your benchmark criteria. Compare the ratings and discuss what they mean.

5. Referring to Problem 4, if you want to combine the numbers in some way to get a single number (as *Business Week* does), a scoring model will have to be developed. One possibility is to multiply the following ratings. If there are n ratings for each school, then the index value for school A is
a. $Index_A = R_{1A} \times R_{2A} \times R_{3A} \times \ldots \times R_{nA}$. Use this scoring model and explain your results.
More complex scoring systems weight the ratings before multiplying them. For example:
b. $Index_A = R_{1A}{}^{w_1} \times R_{2A}{}^{w_2} \times R_{3A}{}^{w_3} \times \ldots \times R_{nA}{}^{w_n}$. Use this scoring model and explain your results.
c. Compare the results in a. and b.

6. To improve the school, which factors should be changed first? (Use the information developed for Problems 3, 4, and 5.)

7. For the economic analysis of continuous project development, the probability that a project is successful is $p_s = 0.30$; $T = 730$ days (average total project development time in days); $n = 100$ projects (number of active projects). The average cost of projects is $100,000 per year. Average gross margins of successful projects is $800,000 per year.
a. What is the estimated total gross margin?
b. What percent increase of p_s is required to increase the estimated total gross margin by 50 percent?
c. What percent increase of p_s is required to increase estimated total gross margin by 100 percent?

8. For the economic analysis of continuous project development, $p_s = 0.50$. Also, $T = 500$ days (average total project development time in days); $n = 100$ projects (number of projects actively being pursued); projects have an average cost of $50,000 per year. Successful projects have average gross margins of $100,000 per year.
a. How many successful projects will occur per year?
b. Do you recommend this arrangement?

9. Ferris Wheel, Inc., has generated over 1,200 patents worldwide in its 37 years of operation—better than 32 per year.
a. What is the average interval in days between patents granted?
b. What kind of system could generate this number of projects for products that are unique enough to be awarded patents?

10. Various methods are used by companies to determine their best candidates for significant improvement using process reengineering. Efficiency frontiers (Figure 19-1 in the text) are approximated by the equation $(DC)^2 + (IA)^2 = R^2$ where DC = delivery capabilities; IA = improvements anticipated, and the radius, R, reflects the combined power of the efficiency frontier.
a. Calculate the efficiency frontier values for the following table:

Project	A	B	C	D	E
R^2	4	4	9	9	16
DC	1.414		2.122	3	3
IA		2			

b. Rank order your preference for these projects and explain.

11. Draw the chart indicating the appropriate efficiency frontiers and the points for each project as obtained in the table for Problem 10. Rank order your preference for projects.

12. Construct a quadrant differentiation chart using the data in Problem 10 and the quadrant center point of 2.2. Compare the results with those from the chart in Problem 11.

13. Set up the best possible schedule for project continuity using concurrent-engineering methods. The company and its suppliers have research offices in New York City (0), San Francisco (−3), Tokyo (+14), and London (+5). The number of hours that separates each city are within parentheses. Is there any way of maintaining perfect project continuity?

END-OF-CHAPTER QUESTIONS

1. Change in external business conditions is always occurring. There is a question about whether change is happening more often and if the changes are more extreme. The Famous Publisher (TFP) has taken the classes for project management and has now set up an Adaptability Management Council (AMC) to deal with rapid changes in the textbook publishing field. AMC has issued a list of topics for debate at a meeting next week. The list is being sent to all textbook editors and managers before the meeting. Which points a. to e. are incorrect?

   a. Transitions in the publishing business are taking place but at a speed that allows everyone in the field to evaluate the situation and devise plans for eventualities. For example, e-books were first heralded as replacing paper books, distance learning was proclaimed as the classroom replacement, and the Internet was going to deliver most classroom materials, including textbooks. None of this has happened, yet.

   b. New technology is streaming into place in publishing. Few authors write books with quill in hand. Harry Potter's author, J. K. Rowling, is an exception. The students at Hogwarts School for Witchcraft and Wizardry, not surprisingly, use quills and not computers. On the contrary, the technology of editors, compositors, graphic designers, and printers is changing at a remarkable rate. Yet, the publishing industry has tamed the technology. It has used it to do what it always has done, in somewhat faster and better ways, rather than being changed by it in any fundamental way.

   c. Start-up publishing companies have an opportunity to use technological innovations (such as the Internet) in unique ways that are likely to set new standards for textbook publications. There can be significantly lower text prices, which will provide market entry to companies that have not been able to compete with the Big Guys before.

   d. Price alone will not make the difference. At least part of the education market has a kinked elasticity curve, which means that demand goes up when price is increased. Kinked elasticity is associated with customers that want high quality and use price as proof that they are getting it. Wedding gifts and the best schools need to be priced high to convey this message.

   e. Technology change supports new processes that deliver higher quality products. For example, graphics will be dynamic, quizzes will be interactive, and Internet links will be active connections to the real world. Perhaps most important of all, there can be constant updating of materials. This replaces the traditional 3-year revision cycle for textbooks.

2. Some large, quick-service restaurants (QSR) have been studying the possibilities of using robotic servers as part of the preparation and counter-delivery operations. Advances in robotic technology have made this option reasonable to consider. This purpose is to obtain cost efficiencies, increased service speed, and other quality improvements. A SWOT analysis has been done by one of the major chains. Their task force report has been circulated to top planners, and it has gotten a great deal of response, including identification of faulty conclusions. Which points a. to e. are not correct?

   a. Strengths include being among the first to test the new restaurant concept. Marketing sees the new technology appealing to children. Being first to market is generally a significant advantage. Robots could act as a barrier to entry if their costs are significant. Copycat QSRs might find duplicating the robotic technology of established chains too costly, lacking the advantage of being first with unique appeal. P/OM input to the design of the new server technologies is essential for productivity, maintenance, costs, and quality controls.

   b. Weaknesses caused by ignoring robotics include the likelihood that new firms will enter the business and be first to market with a new customer appeal. A reverse weakness occurs if an ethical problem arises as a result of using the robots for customer service in lieu of the current workforce. Layoffs will be criticized, generating ill will. Any dangers that exist in contact between robots and customers must be fully explored because an accident of any kind will be exploited.

   c. Opportunities exist with respect to health claims. Robots will not carry infectious Hepatitis A, which is a fairly common food handler safety issue. Robots will not get surly if someone criticizes their performance and does not leave a tip. Programmed machines can be used to clean up rest rooms and to maintain strict rules of sanitary food handling.

   d. Threats (*challenges* is a preferred way of viewing this) arise because machines are often associated with environmental pollution. It takes energy to operate a robot, but the amount of energy would probably be far less than a person needs to drive to work. It will be a challenge to establish the benefits to the environment of employing robots, but that case is worth exploring.

   e. The SWOT summary is positive for robots. The task force will likely conclude that several experimental sites should be developed to examine the effects of robots on all of the factors in a. through d. Market research with both parents and their children could provide benchmarks for establishing levels of robotics that would be suitable at the start. This level might be increased over time, and that is another subject for study

3. The American Assembly (in conjunction with Columbia University) held a seminar of several days, in 1988, at Arden House in the Ramapo Mountains of New York to discuss how to get the United States back on track with respect to global competitiveness and world-class productivity. Dr. David Gleicher's model was used to analyze the situation because it explains conditions for achieving organizational transformation. Seminar attendees agreed that the model captured fundamental elements necessary to bring about change. An evaluation of the success of the model was made after the seminar. This evaluation was published and

circulated among the attendees, who agreed with four of the following five points. Which point was considered to be incorrect?

a. Dissatisfaction of business and society with the competitive situation that existed during the 1980s was rampant because customers in the United States were buying products (such as automobiles) made abroad. There was more purchasing by U.S. consumers from foreign companies than vice versa, so there was a trade deficit. That situation has now been rectified because of efforts like the Arden House seminar.

b. Michigan University's Surveys of Consumer Confidence can be a surrogate measure of dissatisfaction (D) in the Gleicher model. The same applies to the Conference Board's Index of Consumer Confidence. A recent time series is tabled here.

Date	Index of Consumer Confidence
February 2003	64.0
April 2003	86.0
June 2003	83.5
July 2003	76.6
Base Year: 1985	100.0

When D decreases markedly, only one of four factors is in place to trigger change.

c. A clear vision (V) of a better state of affairs is another one of four factors that must be in place to permit change to occur. An articulated vision for a company might be measured in terms of an achieved return on investment (or return on equity), an employment level, market shares, margin contributions, and inventory turns.

d. What constitutes practical first steps (P) toward achieving the vision is unique to each situation. It is assumed that practical first steps are congruent with long-term strategies of the organization. They must also be consistent with the short-term, tactical activities that are taking place. Practical first steps are tactics that may not be scrutinized for their short-term benefits because they are stepping-stones toward a goal. However, because they are practical, they can be achieved without risk of long-term damage to the company.

e. The influence of substantial dissatisfaction, multiplied by the strength of an attractive vision of the future, is a compelling force for change. However, until the two change agents are empowered by practical first steps, the combination will not be a viable force for change. Even then, the energy for change must overcome the inertia that is embodied in the cost of change. There is a great cumulative cost incurred when all of the players agree to change their way of life. The force for change, $D \times V \times P$, must overpower the cost of changing, C, i.e., $(D \times V \times P) > C$.

4. A group of managers meets regularly to consider various ways to improve individual member's performance. These managers come from all of the familiar functional areas within a firm. There are about equal numbers from operations, finance, marketing, HRM, accounting, engineering, and R & D. They agree to build a list of *smart* benchmarks. Meeting together, they pare the list to the top five benchmarks to determine whether each function has its own best benchmarks or whether all areas of the business benefit by using the same smart benchmarks. Which benchmark listed in a. through e. is not so smart?

a. *Breakeven volume* is interesting to managers of all functional areas because it is a common goal in any organization to achieve the demand volume at which level loss stops. For example, every employee of a museum profits from knowing how many visitors per month are required to pay for their salaries and all other costs.

b. *Return on investment* is important to financial managers, who use this measure to determine if the capital investments of the company are sufficiently rewarding. *Return on equity* is also used by financial managers to benchmark themselves against other companies with equity financing. *Return on assets* is also used for benchmarking by financial executives. These are all ratios and permit determination of the balance between output and input of investments.

c. *Delivery quality* is a measure of how many units arrive in unsatisfactory condition. This is an important measure of performance for marketing and logistics managers. Poor delivery quality is related to items that are damaged in transit. These must be returned for replacement. The process of replacing damaged items is costly. Some companies do not replace items and instead refund the customer's payment after the item is returned.

d. *Days of inventory* or *inventory turns* are measuring many complex interactive factors. These measures are of primary interest to the P/OM, marketing, and financial managers. In other words, most managers want to know if there is a slowdown in inventory turns. Change management is called for when the inventory begins to accumulate. The first question to answer is why has inventory begun to accumulate? The second question concerns what to do about that.

e. *Cycle time* is a smart benchmark that reflects a complex of factors. Because those factors are primarily production- and operations-oriented, cycle time is considered to be a smart P/OM benchmark. However, a look underneath the cloak reveals that marketing's ability to deliver on time is a function of the cycle time. More study shows that return on assets will be conditioned by cycle time. There are other aspects to cycle time as well, including the ability to finish a project and get to market first.

5. "Dent Free (DF) takes the dings out." The radio jingle is widely known. DF's regional manager has participated in the process management seminar class. He has expressed great interest in applying continuous improvement methods to the operations of the hundreds of stores that the company operates all over the United States, beginning with the Southeast region. The DF manager says continuous improvement is a natural evolution of the long-term commitment of the company to offer better services at lower prices. Another manager in the seminar is in charge of maintenance for the Always-on Power Company (APC). It has recently experienced serious outages. In fact APC was

considered to be at the core of a series of events that led to widespread blackouts in the Midwest and the East Coast in August 2003. In class, the APC manager discussed the fact that power companies have used continuous improvement for many years. That has led to patching networks, which she stated has contributed to serious power failures for companies all over the world. Recently, this was reinforced by an extensive power failure in the London (UK) power grid, which had been the recipient of conscientious continuous improvement. The APC manager went on record as a staunch advocate for total reengineering (REE) based on employing new technology to produce coherent innovative systems rather than patched and "band-aided" systems. The seminar faculty leader saw this difference in approach as an opportunity to examine the pros and cons of continuous improvement versus REE. Accordingly, each manager was asked to create three top reasons for using the system that he or she advocated. There is one error in the continuous improvement list (a., b., and c.) and one error in the REE list (d., e., and f.). Identify the two flaws.

a. Continuous improvement requires a constant effort to find better ways to produce products and deliver services. This is often a local effort where team members will ask for suggestions from a variety of individuals. There is no requirement that all parts of a production line be included in the system under study. It is expected, though, that upstream and downstream neighbors of the process path being improved will be consulted when changes are being considered. That is another way of describing a "local effort."

b. Dent Free is an organization ideally suited to using continuous improvement. This stems from the fact that no DF store is big enough to undertake a major project. However, ideas are readily transferred from one location to another. DF's manager has recommended that a Suggestion Team be created to review ideas and check out the consequences of implementing a continuous improvement proposal on a company-wide basis.

c. The DF manager has recognized that resistance to continuous improvement-type changes is likely to be greater than resistance to the more sweeping changes of a total reengineering (REE). This, he states, is because the backing of management is not as evident in small changes as in large ones. To counter this effect, he has developed a newsletter issued by the general manager that proclaims and supports the continuous improvement list of the month.

d. APC prefers the broad systems approach of REE because patching the energy grid is a stopgap measure. It does not address the fundamental issue of matching energy supply when surges of demand for power occur that are above peak capacity. The production supply of energy can become insufficient if a transformer breaks down or a power line is broken.

e. The energy network must be made smart by employing algorithms that match existing capacity to demand without shutting down power-generating systems. Smart algorithms are required to determine how to measure and ration all existing capacity. The operation of such algorithms requires a variety of technological capabilities to monitor and control the system. The smart power

system that results cannot be put into place by methods of continuous improvement. Neither power plants nor power management systems are constructed by continuous improvement. "Reengineer the power system," says the APC manager. "It is not the same as improving Dent Free."

f. The Dent Free manager disagrees. He states his beliefs as follows: "It is very rare that several of our stores experience peak demand at the same time. That is why power outages have occurred so infrequently. Major blackouts in the Northeastern United States happened in 1959, 1961, 1965, 1977, and in 2003. The record speaks for itself. The intervals between the episodes were 2, 4, 12, and 26 years. Continuous improvement is working. Conservatively, the next expected blackout is 52 years, or 2055."

6. The discussion about when to use continuous improvement or REE that was developed in Problem 5 has captured a great deal of attention. The district manager of Oil Changers, Inc. (OCI) told the class that his firm has been using continuous improvement for years. Recently, a new CEO was hired who decided to employ breakpoint business process redesign. The procedure has just begun, so the result is unknown. The OCI manager asked if anyone else in the class had utilized this system. No one had a similar experience, but there were many issues raised in the ensuing discussion. Points a. through j. have been written down, and at least one of these 10 items is not held to be correct. Identify the incorrect point or points of conjecture.

a. Breakpoint business process redesign (BPR) is a variant of REE, which ignores ordinary returns on improvement investments. Instead, it seeks out exceptional returns stemming from breakthroughs such as developing a new market based on much lower price but higher quality resulting from converting a batch process into a flow shop.

b. Special capabilities in time-based management (for exceptionally fast delivery or rapid development of new products) are additional examples of business process breakthroughs. In this regard, it has been pointed out that the foundation of corporate strategy is neither products nor markets but business processes. Special capabilities support BPR.

c. P/OM can be the portal to process breakthroughs. Working with R & D, engineering and materials management, suppliers, and customers, production and operations managers are on the firing line. They can be stodgy bureaucrats who view change with distaste (no BPR), or risk-taking innovators who embrace the concept of breakthrough design. When human resource managers hire production and operations managers, they are determining the probable direction for future innovation in that organization.

d. Innovations will not be accepted by an organization that fears change. An innovator working for the company has to strive hard to create the factors that support change, i.e., dissatisfaction with the current situation, a vision of what the future can become, practical first steps to move toward goals of the vision, and an ability to demonstrate that the costs of change are less than the benefits of transition.

e. Efficiency frontiers exist with respect to REE and BPR that are similar to those used by finance for risk–reward combinations. Everybody prefers low risk and high return. Most people will accept higher risk levels if, and only if, there is sufficient increase in the potential return on the investment. The same trade-off considerations apply to the changes that might be accomplished by reengineering. When breakthrough results are sought, the risk levels of the project failing to accomplish its objectives can be expected to increase.

f. In a risk–reward hierarchy, continuous improvement projects are least risky and least rewarding. Next in line are the higher risks and larger rewards that are associated with starting from scratch with REE. Maximum risk and commensurate largest rewards are coupled with extraordinary breakthroughs using BPR.

g. It is the OCI manager's opinion that BPR is far too risky for the oil-change business. Customers come to locations expecting fast and traditional procedures to be used to change their oil. Innovations in process are likely to create a feeling of insecurity that the job is being done in the right fashion.

h. The manager of the Always-on Power Company states that for her industry, the time has come to move toward a set of higher-risk, revolutionary (rather than evolutionary) changes to the power grid. Among other considerations, the use of solar panels has been significant in Japan but not the rest of the world. The use of windmills is not new, but they have been faulted because they are so often disabled by lightning. In fact, lightning is another source of power that has been overlooked. She advocates new smart algorithms for monitoring and controlling the flows of powers between sections of the power grid.

i. The Dent Free manager is in favor of choosing projects that have a high probability of success. He believes that his firm benefits most from the clever use by management "improvement patches" and the use of band-aid solutions to keep things going when troubles arise. His experience with "disruptive REE-type projects" is that they cause more trouble than they are worth. He calls everyone's attention to the fact that the U.S. power grid did a great job for 28 years.

j. The Dent Free manager also states that he is in favor of a change-management team to determine if a seemingly small change could possibly lead to an unsuspected big problem somewhere else in the system. He recommends the change-management team to act as a check on continuous improvement systems that are not well-thought-out.

7. The Big-Width Shoe Company (BWSC) manager requests the faculty leader to help the seminar class develop a set of principles for reengineering and for developing breakthrough business process redesigns. The exercise was completed with five principles having been stated. These were handed to the faculty leader, who complimented the class on four out of five, saying that only one of the five was incorrect. Which one of a. through e. is not right?

a. Identify and define the special core qualities, abilities, and competencies of the men and women who work for the company. Also, review the information and experience stored by the company in the form of documents, blueprints, bills of material, special supplier relationships, etc. Similarly, list advantages of the company such as facilities, locations, customers, and suppliers. REE and BPR should focus on these knowledge management strengths.

b. Identify and define the special process capabilities of the firm. Examine every function that the company requires and rate the processes that it uses to fulfill the functions. With respect to each process, it is useful to know if the company is less good than others, as good as others, better than any others, and uniquely superior to others. REE and BPR should focus on any processes that could be converted from less good and as good to uniquely superior to others.

c. Do not get involved with cross-functional transactions because departmental opposition to REE and BPR is the kiss of doom for achieving successful change. A successful strategy is to use P/OM as the core function that needs to be reengineered. When the problem crosses into another functional area, then it is time to sit down with a managerial counterpart to negotiate a reasonable accommodation between parties.

d. Develop detailed process analyses of all activities including cross-functional events. Benchmark cost, time, and quality for each process component. Propose and set target improvement levels for each process component.

e. Select the processes to be redesigned after prioritizing projects with respect to their impact on desired capability goals and the degree to which each process can be improved. Focus on task design and not task execution.

8. Rapid completion of projects is a new frontier that has only begun to be developed. The mind-set of project management in the twentieth century was inspired by engineering estimates of how long it should take to do a job that was based on pre-computer time lines. After 1950, the rapid growth of computer capabilities changed that time line, but project managers stayed with the conventions that they had grown up with because that made them comfortable. This discussion began with an in-house seminar group being held for Bridge-Builders, Ltd. This firm builds refineries, theme park rides, large warehouses, bridges, etc. Management wants to know if their planning horizons are based on old concepts, as described by the faculty leader in terms of pre-computer time lines. The CEO asks, "Are we operating by early twentieth century standards?" A project management team has drawn up a list of seven relevant facts (a. through g.). How much of this list is correct?

a. A project-oriented organization should have concurrent engineering capabilities. That enables it to bring all functional knowledge to bear on the project at the outset. As a result, development speed will be increased significantly. For example, Boeing's 777 was designed completely by computer. This bypassed the wind tunnel experiments that used to take great amounts of time to collect and analyze.

b. A project-oriented organization should have continuity capabilities, which means that it has a variety of projects going on at the same time. This means that efficiencies of redundant information and experience are built into the project system.

c. With continuity, some projects are later stages of earlier ones. Project overlaps are preplanned design features. For example, models 245 and 255 of a Hewlett-Packard calculator were designed at the same time. The 245 was to be released six months before the 255. Both used all the same components except for a different chip. The 255 had a more powerful chip that would replace the less powerful 245 chip when the new model was introduced to the market as an entirely new unit.

d. The continuous project (product) development cycle always starts with sales making a suggestion for a new product based on a competitive product that has come to the attention of marketing. If this new product is still in development, then the information is like an intelligence report, which gives the company additional time to react. It is crucial to get a competitive offering on the shelves as soon as possible so that the "first to market" advantage of the competitor is diluted.

e. The continuous project (product) development cycle can start in many different ways. For example, "finding" can happen in any functional part of the organization. P/OM can develop new process abilities. These can cut production costs, increase quality of the product or service, and decrease time to delivery.

f. R & D is often the source of such changes, as is market research, which discovers things that customers want. There are examples of customers not knowing what they want until they are shown what they can have. Customers may need instructions before they know what is good for themselves.

g. The find–design–make–ship cycle involves almost everyone in the organization. It is vital to understand that a company following this plan moves toward becoming a flow shop for the *production of projects*. Lower costs and shorter times to completion with higher quality achievements are some advantages of flow shops—as compared to batch shops. On the other hand, if projects prosper by being treated as relatively unique situations, then the customized approach of the "artisan" project manager has advantages over attempts to shoehorn projects into a mold that does not properly fit their distinctiveness. Managers of Bridge-Builders, Ltd., are intrigued by statement g. and encourage further discussion in pursuit of agreement, accord, and consensus.

9. The Ferris wheel provides a useful model for those wishing to move their project management methods from the twentieth century to the twenty-first century. The wheel developed by bridge builder George W. Ferris for the 1893 Chicago World's Fair was an answer to the Eiffel Tower built for the Paris Exposition of 1889. There is more historical information in the following URL, but it is worth noting that the wheel was a money-maker. Charging 50 cents for a ride grossed $726,805.50, and that helped with breakeven That amounts to 1,453,611 riders in 36 wooden cars, each one holding up to 60 people. That means there could have been more than 2,000 people on the wheel at any one time. See http://users.vnet.net/schulman/Columbian/ferris.html.

Package Goods Masters (PGM) had a line of shampoos, dentifrices, soaps, and mouthwash products that were regularly renewed with new containers, perfumes, tastes, cleaners, ingredients, and claims. The new product launch process involved teams that carried R & D concepts into market testing. Then pilot plant product was market tested with its packaging. New products with successful tests were released to production and launched with advertising and coupons. PGM ran simulations of continuous project management based on a development time per new product

of 18 months. The objective was to launch a new product every three months. To determine management's understanding of the continuous new product method, a fact sheet from a. through f. was prepared. Which of these facts might be in error?

a. Cycle time (C) for the Ferris wheel is the time between cars stopping for passengers to get on and off. Cycle time (C) for the project "wheel" is the time between new product start-ups. Similarly, it is also the time between successive new product launchings. PGM requested that $C = 3$ months.

b. For the Ferris wheel, the time between complete rotations is T. Cycle time, $C = T/n$. There will be n cars to fill. For PGM, $C = 3$ months and $T = 18$ months. Then, $n = T/C = 18/3 = 6$ projects underway at all times.

c. Management wants to know how many new projects will be started per year. This is equivalent to how many new products will be launched per year. The output will be O and O = (12 months per year) ÷ (C months between launchings) = 12 ÷ 3 = 4 new product launches per year.

d. For the Ferris wheel, O is equivalent to how many cars will be emptied and refilled (say) in an hour. To get Ferris wheel figures, assume that a complete rotation of the Ferris wheel takes $T = 1.5$ hours (90 minutes). With $n = 6$ cars, $C = 90/6 = 15$ minutes between each car stop.

e. Also, O = (60 minutes per hour) ÷ (C minutes between stops) = 60 ÷ 15 = 4 car stops per hour.

f. The strength of the Ferris wheel model is that the amusement park wheel will perform as calculated. The project wheel will also be precisely correct as if it were a well-made timepiece.

10. Package Goods Masters (PGM) has a new product failure ratio of five out of ten. Failure is acknowledged when management cancels introduction or withdraws the item from inventory. There are many factors that define a new product failure. One of these is that gross margin does not reach at least $1 million per year. (Gross margin is sales revenue per year less all manufacturing costs per year.) This PGM requirement is said to be necessary but not sufficient for the definition of success. In other words, if gross margin meets the requirement but market share is not large enough, or if nonmanufacturing costs are too great, that project can be canceled. Average project development costs are $150,000 per year. If these costs grow too large, the project is withdrawn and counts as a failure. Project teams are asked to evaluate the analysis that is presented in points a. through j. The question is asked, Which of these points is incorrect?

a. On average, $T = 18$ months. The plan calls for $n = 6$ new product projects. As a result, $900,000 is tied up in project development investments per year.

b. Project output per year is four. Of these, two projects are deemed successful.

c. Successful projects will generate $2 million of total gross margin per year.

d. Gross profit (total gross margin less total project costs per year) is calculated to be $1.1 million.

e. Management is not thrilled with these performance numbers and has asked for an assessment of the effect of changing n from six to ten projects. They have also asked for new project selection and development methods that can raise the probability of success to 75 percent. The revised results are shown in f. through j.

f. If $T = 18$ months and $n = 10$ new product projects, then $1,500,000 is tied up in project development investments per year.

g. Project output per year is now 6.67. Of these, five projects are deemed successful.

h. Successful projects will generate $5 million of total gross margin per year.

i. Gross profit (total gross margin less total project costs per year) is calculated to be $3.5 million per year. This is more than three times the profit previously obtained.

j. Management is very pleased with this result and intends to announce that continuous project management will be adopted by PGM.

ADDITIONAL READINGS

Beckhard, R., and R. Harris. *Organizational Transitions*. Reading, MA: Addison-Wesley, 1987.

Biztech Network provides interesting readings pro and con business process reengineering at http://www.brint.com/BPR.htm. There are also articles dealing with benchmarking.

Carr, D. K., K. S. Dougherty, H. J. Johansson, R. A. King, and D. E. Moran. *Breakpoint: Business Process Redesign*. Arlington, VA: Coopers & Lybrand Series, 1992.

Champy, James. *Re-engineering Management: The Mandate for New Leadership*. New York: Harper Business, 1995.

Hammer, Michael. *Beyond Re-Engineering*. New York: Harper Collins, 1995.

Hammer, Michael. "Forward to Basics." *Fast Company* (November 2002) (insights with a radical flavor). See http://www.hammerandco.com. Click on the article in the lower right-hand margin.

Hammer, Michael, and James Champy. *Re-Engineering the Corporation*. New York: Harper Business, 1993.

Imai, Masaaki. *Kaizen: The Key to Japan's Competitive Success*. New York: Random House Business Division, 1986.

Johansson, Henry J., Patrick McHugh, A. John Pendlebury, and William A. Wheeler III. *Business Process Re-Engineering: Breakpoint Strategies for Market Dominance*. New York: Wiley, 1993.

McGrath, Michael E. *Product Strategy for High-Technology Companies: How to Achieve Growth, Competitive Advantage, and Increased Profits*. Burr Ridge, IL: Irwin Professional Publishing, 1995.

Miller, Jeffrey G., Arnoud De Meyer, and Jinichiro Nakane. *Benchmarking Global Manufacturing: Understanding International Suppliers, Customers, and Competitors*. The Irwin/Apics Series in Production Management, Burr Ridge, IL: Irwin, 1992.

Puchek, Vladimir, Noel Tichy, and Carole K. Barnett (eds.). *Globalizing Management: Creating and Leading the Competitive Organization*. New York: Wiley, 1993.

Stalk, G., P. Evans, and L. E. Shulman. "Competing on Capabilities: The New Rules of Corporate Strategy." *Harvard Business Review* (March–April 1992).

Tabor, Richard. *Global Quality: A Synthesis of the World's Best Management Methods*. Burr Ridge, IL: Irwin, 1993.

NOTES

1. R. Levering and M. Moskowitz. *The 100 Best Companies to Work for in America*, rev. ed. A Plume Book. New York: Penguin Group, 1994.

2. "Running Out of Time: Reversing America's Declining Competitiveness." Conference held at Arden House, Harriman, New York, November 19–22, 1987. For details, see M. K. Starr (ed.). *Global Competitiveness: Getting the U.S. Back on Track*. 74th American Assembly, Norton, New York, 1988.

3. C. J. McNair and K. H. J. Leibfried. *Benchmarking: A Tool for Continuous Improvement*. Harper Business, 1992, p. 20.

4. *USA Today* (March 1, 1995): 4B.

5. The quote from Julius Maldutis at Salomon Brothers is reported in *The New York Times*, March 7, 1995, in an article by Adam Bryant, p. C5.

6. Continuous improvement also is called *kaizen*. See Masaaki Imai. *Kaizen: The Key to Japan's Competitive Success*. New York: Random House, 1986.

7. Michael Hammer and James Champy. *Re-Engineering the Corporation*. New York: Harper Business, 1993.

8. James Champy. *Re-Engineering Management: The Mandate for New Leadership*. New York: Harper Business, 1995, p. 3.

9. Ibid, p. 112.

10. D. K. Carr, K. S. Dougherty, H. J. Johansson, R. A. King, and D. E. Moran. *Breakpoint: Business Process Redesign*. Coopers & Lybrand Series. Arlington, VA, 1992, p. v.

11. G. Stalk, P. Evans, and L. E. Shulman. "Competing on Capabilities: The New Rules of Corporate Strategy." *Harvard Business Review* (March–April 1992): 57–69.

12. Booz Allen Hamilton. "Understanding the New Environment." *Business Process Redesign: An Owner's Guide*. OPER 401, 13M, 1993, p. 4.

13. Ibid, p. 14.

14. Henry J. Johansson, Patrick McHugh, A. John Pendlebury, and William A. Wheeler III. *Business Process Re-Engineering: Breakpoint Strategies for Market Dominance*. New York: Wiley, 1993, p. 209.

15. Information about Oticon has been derived directly from conversations with employees of the firm and an article by Polly LaBarre. "The Dis-Organization of Oticon." *Industry Week* (July 18, 1994): 23–28. Oticon, Inc., the U.S. daughter company of the Danish parent, manufactures and repairs in Somerset, New Jersey. It is not paperless but shares many of the innovations developed in Denmark. Among its creative products and programs are its services for children that include the Oticon 4 Kids Club and brightly colored hearing instrument decorations.

16. J. R. Hartley. *Concurrent Engineering: Shortening Lead Times, Raising Quality, and Lowering Costs*. Cambridge, MA: Productivity Press, 1992, p. 19.

17. C. R. Morris. "The Coming Global Boom." *The Atlantic* (October 1989): 56.

18. The information on W.L. Gore & Associates was derived by speaking directly with individuals who work for the firm and from the write-up of this company appearing in *The 100 Best Companies to Work for in America* by Robert Levering and Milton Moskowitz, rev. ed. A Plume Book. New York: Penguin Group, 1994. Also see http://www.gore.com.

19. London Eye is run by The Tussaud's Group with partners British Airways and Marks Barfield Architects as of 2004.

20. If payments start at the beginning of the period, the first payment would be one dollar. In other words, the first period payment will be equal to 1.00 in Table 19-3. All other payment amounts will be dropped to the $(n + 1)$ row.

21. For example, "Table of Present Values of an Annuity." R. S. Burington. *Handbook of Mathematical Tables and Formulas*, 5e. New York: McGraw-Hill, 1973. (Current reprint available.)

SPOTLIGHT 19-1
Shouldice Surgery

The Focused Factory in Healthcare is Epitomized by Shouldice

Dr. Edward Earle Shouldice, a major in the Canadian army during World War II, discovered that many young men were denied enlistment because of untreated hernias. Because of world crisis (1940), doctors and hospital resources were scarce, especially for surgical repair of hernias, which were nonemergency procedures that took approximately 3 weeks of hospitalization.

Shouldice took on the challenge. He operated on 70 of these men, contributing his services at no cost and using an innovative method that hastened their recovery. His patients were delighted with the success, and news of the surgery spread the word about the Shouldice method of treatment. After the war, hundreds of patients contacted Dr. Shouldice to request surgery. Because of a scarcity of hospital beds, Shouldice opened his own hospital in Toronto, Canada.

In 1945, with a cook, secretary, and nurse, he was repairing two hernias per day in a single operating room. In 1953, he purchased a large country estate in Thornhill, Ontario, and converted it to the current facility, which sits on 20 acres of landscaped grounds including a putting green. The hospital is an 89-bed facility with 5 operating theaters and a team of 10 surgeons that serves a worldwide clientele. Visitors are likely to pass groups of patients who stroll about in lounging robes because they have had their hernias repaired on the previous day. Shouldice uniquely combines a nonhospital ambience with 55 years of accumulated experience with hernias.

Shouldice surgical teams perform only hernia operations. They have repaired more than 270,000 hernias with a greater than 99 percent success rate. The average chance of hernia recurrence after a Shouldice repair is less than 1 percent, compared to the North American average of over 10 percent. These performance measures explain why Shouldice is often referred to as a model for benchmarking. Harvard professor Regina Herzlinger selected the Shouldice model in her book, *Market Driven Health Care*.

Patients receive local anesthesia, contributing to the exceptional safety of the operation. A sedative (sleeping pill) is provided the night before surgery. The average operation takes 45 minutes. A Shouldice patient's postoperative recovery begins as he or she walks out of the operating room. The following morning there is an exercise program with fellow patients. Confidence builds quickly in the hernia repair. Comparing notes and discussing concerns with other patients is an excellent way to dispel anxieties. The average hospital stay is 3 days. Patients return to work in an average of 8 days after their hernia repair.

Shouldice Hospital performs 32 operations per day on average, 242 days per year. This results in about 7,600 happy people per year. The hospital surgeons do not work on weekends. Because these doctors have exclusively devoted all their time and resources to the practice of hernia surgery, they have developed a valuable sixth sense in the recognition and handling of all the problems that surround hernia pathology.

A hernia is the protrusion of an organ through a weakness in the abdominal wall. This weakness can be congenital, acquired (from heavy lifting), or created following abdominal operations. Hernias do not go away—they only get bigger. Women get hernias, too. (Every week there is an average of 10 women at Shouldice for surgery.) There are no stereotypes for hernias. At Shouldice, patients have ranged from 4 months to 100 years of age.

To understand the method of repair, one must know that the muscles of the groin portion of the abdominal wall have 3 distinct layers. The Shouldice method repairs each layer in turn by overlapping its margins as the edges of a coat overlap when buttoned. The end result reinforces the muscular wall of the abdomen. No foreign bodies such as synthetic screens or meshes are used, except in extreme cases where there is tissue damage. The Shouldice method is called pure tissue repair.

Claims by other institutions that they use the "Shouldice technique" or the "Canadian method" do not take into account that the "formula," though not a secret, extends beyond surgery to the total care package. Operating rooms are designed for efficient flow shop surgery, and participants are practiced in synchronized activities. The teams are aware of anomalies and prepared for contingencies in a way that is the hallmark of focused factories, which were first introduced to the P/OM field by Wick Skinner in 1974. Focused factories comprise specialized groupings (cells) of core competencies. They concentrate on practice to perfection of one clearly defined process. Specialization occurs as a result of high volumes of similar work.

In 1947, a few patients suggested an annual reunion, which has now grown to an average of 1,000 patients who gather annually to renew friendships. The event includes dinner, entertainment, camaraderie, and a medical checkup. Following up on all patients every year after they leave is an integral part of Shouldice research efforts.

This is a rare instance of medical care matching best practices in production. Shouldice Hospital provides business students with the chance to learn the considerable benefits occurring with reorganization of traditional thinking. Working in such an environment empowers everyone to continue this practice. The Shouldice site on the Internet is a marvel in conveying information to potential candidates for surgery. The site will soon have a simplified web-based method of completing medical questionnaires so that a surgeon can review the information and the Shouldice staff can arrange a booking date in a timely manner. They will also send, on request, an 18-minute video, "Understanding Hernias."

Courtesy of Shouldice Hospital, November 24, 2003.

Sources: Http://www.shouldice.com. Herzlinger, Regina. *Market Driven Health Care*. Boston, MA: Addison Wesley, 1999; Skinner, C. Wickham. "The Focused Factory." *Harvard Business Review* (May 1974): 113–121.

SPOTLIGHT 19-2
Ethics by Regulation

Enron and the Sarbanes-Oxley Act of 2002

Mark Twain once said, "Always do right. This will gratify some and astonish the rest." If he were here to comment on the technology and telecommunications boom of the 1990s, Twain would have been the first to point out the delusional expectations that governed behavior of top executives and investors in corporate America. It was irrational to believe that stock prices could rise indefinitely, along with profits, salaries, and ROI. Goldman Sachs, swept up by euphoria, took Internet grocer Webvan public, investing over $100 million of its own money in Webvan before it failed.

The delusional expectations of that era were based on the commonly held conviction that a sea change in economic fundamentals had occurred. Enron Corporation's attempt to hide mounting losses by placing its stock in secret partnerships would have been illogical if the company feared that its stock value would drop significantly.

Created through the merger of two midsize natural-gas pipeline companies in the late 1980s, Enron reinvented itself as an energy trading giant in the 1990s. At one point in 2000, its value approached $100 billion, with its natural-gas pipeline business representing less than 10 percent of the company's imputed worth. Unfortunately for employees and shareholders, Enron's other businesses (power plants, risk management, trading commodities, etc.) ate up cash at an astounding rate with no honest prospect of turning a profit.

The difficulty of separating the delusional from the dishonest has given prosecutors a hard time in even the most obvious cases of fraud. It provides a challenge for ethicists and social historians to explain what actually happened when the bubble burst.

Information is one of the most vital, strategic assets any organization possesses. When record-keeping practices of U.S. corporations, professional service firms, or other business entities come under suspicion, trust in the corporate system is damaged. Examples of corporate unethical behavior include shredding documents to obstruct justice by Enron, falsification of financial statements by WorldCom, and the criminal trial of Arthur Andersen for destruction of audit records. The Andersen trial led to the sudden and dramatic demise of one of America's best-known professional service firms. It shows the significance of record-keeping issues and the necessity for systematic compliance with record retention policies and procedures.

In November 2001, the SEC issued a subpoena to Arthur Andersen requesting records related to public accounting work it performed for Enron. In January 2002, Andersen officials disclosed that the company had destroyed a number of records related to Enron audits. The officials said that the records were destroyed before receiving the subpoena. If shown to be true, this was in conformity with company policy, which permitted the destruction of nonessential records relating to specific audits, without criminal intent.

Federal prosecutors alleged that Andersen destroyed the audit records after the SEC investigation had begun and that Andersen officials were fully aware that they would be asked to produce records. It is illegal to destroy records relevant to pending or ongoing litigation. Many leading clients of Arthur Andersen withdrew their business from that firm after criminal charges were disclosed. Arthur Andersen drastically reduced its workforce and sold several of its operations to competitors before going out of business. Strong

reaction from public officials, legislators, regulatory authorities, shareholders, and law enforcement agencies (because of the Andersen case and other high-profile incidents) led to the Sarbanes-Oxley (SOX) Act of 2002. It is widely viewed as the most important corporate reform legislation since the Securities and Exchange Act of 1934. Signed into law on July 20, 2002, SOX specifies requirements and penalties that address corporate accountability issues raised by the Andersen case, WorldCom, Tyco, etc. The SOX Act applies to all U.S. public companies and public accounting firms, including those that perform audit work for foreign subsidiaries of U.S. companies. All public company CEOs and CFOs must personally certify that periodic financial disclosures accurately reflect the company's financial condition and fully comply with applicable securities laws.

The SOX Act criminalizes destroying or tampering with corporate accounting records. It created a new federal crime: the destruction, mutilation, or alteration of corporate records with the intent to impede or influence a government investigation or other official proceeding including the simple contemplation of such an event. Violations by executives and employees are punishable by fines of up to $5 million and up to 20 years in prison.

Noncompliance with specified minimum retention periods for accountants' work papers, correspondence, and other records that contain analyses, opinions, conclusions, financial data, or other information about corporate audits can result in large fines and prison sentences of up to 10 years. The act creates a Public Company Accounting Oversight Board (PCAOB) with broad authority to subpoena records produced by public accounting firms and their clients. See http://www.pcaobus.org.

In the wake of the Sarbanes-Oxley Act, there may be unexpected company benefits. Forced into extreme makeovers, companies might be willing to install more effective processes and procedures as well as documentation and testing. Improving and consolidating hardware and applications could simplify operations and cut costs.

PROJECTED LONG-TERM TENDENCIES

In—More accounting jobs and privately-held companies, operational transparency and simplification, enforcement bureaucracy

Out—Going public without careful consideration, ready access to capital markets, aggressive risk-taking by large companies, creative experimentation, and innovative globalization

On January 15, 2003, the Securities and Exchange Commission adopted a rule requiring companies to disclose whether they have a code of ethics for their CEO, CFO, and senior accounting personnel. It may never be known whether ethics by regulation can produce better company policies. Clearly, however, ethics founded on integrity and principled business practices build trust and sustainability in organizations.

Sources: Knee, Jonathan A. *New York Times Book Review* (October 26, 2003); McLean, Bethany, and Peter Elkind. *The Smartest Guys in the Room: The Amazing Rise and Scandalous Fall of Enron.* New York: Portfolio, 2003; http://www.sec.gov/news/press/2003-89a.htm. http://www.arma.org.

Supplement 19

Net Present Value Model (NPV) Applied to Make or Buy Decisions

Assume that the investment to make the product is $1,000,000 and the operating costs for making the product are $500,000 per year. The alternative is to buy the product from a supplier for $750,000 per year. The same volume is assumed in each case.

THE MAKE OR BUY MODEL

How do these plans compare? The simplest analysis is based on the fact that the make plan saves $250,000 per year. In 4 years, the savings will pay for the $1,000,000 investment. Is that soon enough?

The answer will depend on the product life cycle and the expected life of the investment. If it is more than the breakeven time of four years, then making the product can have cost savings as well as process-learning advantages. There also may be a quality benefit because the self-supplier is closer to the customer than the external supplier.

Disadvantages include complexity. There is only so much management time available. Risk always is a factor. In spite of the prediction that the mature phase of the life cycle extends beyond four years, there always is room for error and a potential loss of some part of a $1 million investment.

There are those who insist that the make or buy model should discount the cash flows. To do so, an estimate for the interest value of money is required. For example, 6 percent per year might be the amount that could be obtained by investing a given sum of money in bank certificates. The estimate of this interest rate will vary depending upon the size of the company, its growth potential, capital requirements, and going interest rates. Successful organizations can earn higher returns simply by plowing back all available cash into their production output.

The 6 percent rate will be used for the illustration, recognizing that it is not easy, but necessary, to determine the appropriate rate of interest. What is the net present value of $750,000 per year for the cost payment stream as a function of the time period employed? The same question applies to $500,000. A time period of five years will be used.

The formula for discounting cash flow (DCF) to obtain net present value (NPV) is

$$NPV = \sum_{n=1}^{n=n'} CF_j \left(\frac{1}{1+i} \right)^n$$

where

NPV = net present value
Option j = 1: CF_1 = $750,000 is the annual cash flow for purchasing the product, or
Option j = 2: CF_2 = $500,000 is the annual cash flow for operating costs to make the product.
$CF_j(n)$ = when cash flow differs for each period (n)
i = interest rate, 6 percent per year
n = the year number $(n = 0, 1, 2,...n')$
n' = the planning horizon, five years in this case

$$\sum_{n=1}^{n=n'} \left(\frac{1}{1+i} \right)^n = \left(\frac{1}{1+0.06} \right)^1 + \left(\frac{1}{1+0.06} \right)^2 + ... + \left(\frac{1}{1+0.06} \right)^{n'}$$

This equation for NPV assumes that the costs of making and purchasing are delayed until the end of the period.[20] Thus, each dollar paid out at the end of the first year would have earned 6 percent interest and consequently costs less than a full dollar. At year end, the account would show a balance of $1.06. The bill that has to be paid is $1.00. The actual cost would be $1.00 − 0.06 = $0.94. That is why deferring payment to year end decreases the cost.

The calculation for the end of the first year is

$$\left(\frac{1}{1+0.06}\right)^1 = 0.943$$

Table 19-3 shows how present value changes as a function of time periods. Tabled values, available for different interest rates and time periods, make present value analysis easy.[21] Also, calculators and computers are programmed to provide these figures.

The 4-year savings derived from *making* in preference to *buying*—with discounting—is $(2,598,750 - 1,732,500 = 866,250)$ and the 5-year savings is $(3,159,000 - 2,106,000 = 1,053,000)$.

Thus, with discounting almost five years of savings are required to pay for the investment in the equipment to make the product. Because of the risky nature of the decision, the discounting procedure adds a more conservative note than the nondiscounting method, but it still is fine-tuning an estimate that is rough in any case.

Given the decision to make the product, the paramount issue for P/OM is how to configure the system and how to run it. The approach to use is how to do the job better than the suppliers would have done it. If possible, gain an advantage from being a start-up with respect to newer technology and materials. An experimental and creative point of view is encouraged instead of the more typical "this is how it has always been done" attitude of specialists. Ultimately, the design must be determined and the conservative point of view that emphasizes reliability takes over.

			Buying		Making	
n	x	y	750,000	750,000	500,000	500,000
1	0.943	0.943	707,250	707,250	471,500	471,500
2	0.890	1.833	667,500	1,374,750	445,000	916,500
3	0.840	2.673	630,000	2,004,750	420,000	1,336,500
4	0.792	3.465	594,000	2,598,750	396,000	1,732,500
5	0.747	4.212	560,250	3,159,000	373,500	2,106,000

where:

$$x = \left(\frac{1}{1+i}\right)^n, \text{ and } y = \sum_n \left(\frac{1}{1+i}\right)^n, \text{ etc.}$$

TABLE 19-3

Present Values for Make or Buy Example (for $i = 0.06$; $CF_1 = 750,000$ and $CF_2 = 500,000$)

CASES

Case 19-1

Industry Perspective on the Environment— The Saturn Project—Saturn Corporation

This case study is written in two parts.

The first part depicts details of the development of Saturn from its inception in June 1982 until May 1994. One item has been edited in the original story and that relates to the use of the lost foam casting process, which has been replaced by traditional casting methods. Discussion of the lost foam process has been removed from the first part of the Saturn case.

The second part of the case is the chronological history of the Saturn Corporation as maintained in the archives of the company.

PART 1

In June 1982, General Motors (GM) assigned its Advanced Product and Design Team to answer the question, "Can GM build a world-class-quality small car in the United States that can compete successfully with the imports?"

This effort grew into what GM called the Saturn Project. The team used a "clean-sheet" (greenfield) approach—unbound by traditional thinking and industry practices—to set up the small car project. This approach afforded the opportunity to design the manufacturing process in parallel with the product and to adopt lean production philosophies and techniques. The Saturn Project's challenge in designing the process, product, and manufacturing facility was to eliminate the $2,000 per unit cost advantage that Japanese automakers held over U.S. manufacturers.

With the Saturn Project underway, another GM group gathered to study ways to improve management-labor relations. This "Group of 99," composed of GM managers and staff personnel from 17 GM divisions and United Auto Workers (UAW) members from 140 regions, revealed the willingness of these two factions to work together as partners to accomplish business objectives. In 1985, the Saturn Project merged with the Group of 99 to become the Saturn Corporation. With a $5 billion commitment, GM established Saturn as a wholly owned subsidiary. A "Gang of Six" was appointed, which included a president and vice presidents for planning, engineering, manufacturing, sales, and finance.

The newly assembled group immediately separated into research teams to study intricate aspects of what Saturn could be. During a 2-month period, members of the new team visited 49 GM plants and 60 benchmark companies worldwide to gather ideas in preparation for setting up the new system. According to Jay Wetzel, vice president for engineering, "We had the benefit of being able to start everything new, where other (GM) platforms had to work off their heritage and their existing facilities. We had the opportunity to take some risks in high technology that other units of General Motors may not have pursued."[1]

GM planned to export successful processes and operations developed at Saturn to improve efficiency and competitiveness at all of its manufacturing facilities. Cost objectives and special union-management relations were achieved. By the year 2000, many aspects of the Saturn system had become established practice at other GM companies.[2]

In July 1985, the selection of Spring Hill, Tennessee, as the site for the new manufacturing facility was finalized. Five years later, the first Saturn rolled off the assembly line. Saturn manufactured its one-millionth car in early summer 1995. In October 1999, 2.2 million Saturns had rolled off the production line. The company sold 250,000 units of its 1999 models and had brought out new designs for year 2000, including a popular 3-door version. Saturn's share of the total U.S. new-car market has been about 3 percent and limited by its production capacity. The strategy is to increase capacity and the share numbers with an expanded product line, but not at the expense of the company's mission and philosophy.

In defining Saturn's mission and philosophy, team members established Saturn's commitment to protect and preserve the environment Saturn's founders designed and built the mile-long, 4.5-million-square-foot manufacturing facility in Spring Hill around this commitment to protect the environment and to maintain the aesthetic value of the land.

THE SATURN SYSTEM

The Spring Hill plant is a "fully integrated" auto factory. This means all major parts for Saturn's coupes, sedans, and wagons are manufactured at one facility. The integrated nature of the plant facilitates interaction between business units and perpetuates quality-mindedness and information exchange throughout the system.

Saturn manufactures approximately 1,150 cars per day. In a 20-hour day of two 10-hour shifts, that's roughly one car per minute. In 1995, the average price of a Saturn was $14,950; Saturn team members know that the company loses about $14,950 every minute the production line is down. As of spring 1995, approximately 8,000 team members work at the Spring Hill facility.

The three major "business units" at Saturn are Powertrain (engine and transmission), Body Systems, and Vehicle Systems (general assembly and interior systems). Components manufactured in Powertrain, Body Systems, and Vehicle Systems are conveyed overhead into the Vehicle Systems assembly area. Figure 19-8 illustrates the basic layout of the Saturn manufacturing and assembly complex. Following is a brief summary of the production activities within the business units.

Powertrain

Die cast operations: Molten metal casting of parts including transmission cases, transmission parts, and engine covers.

FIGURE 19-8
The Overall M&A Complex

Transmission assembly: Manual and automatic transmissions built on the same line. Flexibility to build up to 75 percent of either transmission to meet market demand.

Engine machining line: Flexible machining allows for one machining line instead of the traditional two.

Final engine assembly: Assembles both high-performance and standard engines on the same line.

Body Systems

Steel body (or spaceframe) components: Rolled steel is cut to size on large transfer presses. These presses allow for a finished part to be manufactured using one press instead of the traditional five or six. Quick die changes are an integral part of Saturn's stamping plans. Saturn team members have achieved die changes of less than 10 minutes.

Body panels: Utilizing three different types of polymer pellets, composite panels are prepared in a 24-hour-a-day injection molding operation.

Body fabrication: Welding of the various components of the spaceframe, including the body side, motor compartment, rear compartment, and floor pan. The central point in body fabrication is the body framing and respot welding line.

Paint: Various components for Saturn vehicles are run through a phosphate and ELPO system, which applies the rust-resistant undercoating, a robotic and manual sealer process, and a base coat/clear coat paint system. A completely automated panel storage and retrieval system has the capacity to store up to 900 complete sets of exterior panels.

Vehicle Systems

Skillet application: A unique ergonomic means of moving spaceframes and associates along the assembly line that emulates a stationary workstation. Associates step on the moving wooden skillet platform, move with the car to perform work, and then step off when they're finished.

Cockpit operation: All components are installed and tested for electrical functionality prior to installation in vehicle. Cockpit installation is traditionally a cumbersome procedure involving technicians getting down on their backs to do the necessary wiring on the instrument panel. At Saturn the cockpit is built outside the car so people don't have to assume the awkward positions.

Trim installation: Employing the skillet system, all interior and exterior trim is installed.

Towveyor operation: Conveyor that tows the completed Powertrain and then installs it in spaceframe.

Exterior (body) panels scissor lift: Scissor lifts used to elevate car for ease of panel installation by team members.

Interior systems: Injection molding and trim fabrication for interior.

Quality and Teamwork

Quality is paramount to success in the small car market. Meeting and exceeding customer requirements and expectations on a consistent basis is one of Saturn's key strategies for success. Quality at Saturn starts at the shop-floor level with the teams (Saturn refers to teams on the shop floor as *work units*). Teams are responsible for day-to-day car building and for constant product-quality monitoring. All Saturn employees are called *team members.* Everyone at Saturn is associated with a team. All shop-floor UAW members are on a team. Each business unit (Powertrain, Vehicle Systems, and Body Systems) has about 217 work units (or teams) for a total of 651. Business units are divided into modules, which are subdivided into teams (or work units). (As an example, the Door Finesse team is in the "Front-end" module of the Vehicle Systems business unit.) Each team has from 8 to 15 members.

Within each team, one person is responsible for gathering and analyzing information on quality issues. This person shares all quality information with team members. Module quality advisors look at outgoing (or between team) quality. The advisors provide a communication bridge between the teams so each team knows what its internal customers upstream and downstream in the process require to make a quality, world-class vehicle. A series of Quality Councils, composed of team members and management, meet on a periodic basis to set quality goals and provide general direction in terms of quality elements.

When problems arise, the team identifies the cause. The team may solicit help from engineering and operations (whose work areas also are located in the factory) in deciding what actions to take to solve the problem. A total quality action team (TQAT) may be formed to work on a specific problem. Saturn team members are not told by management how to perform work or solve problems. They are made aware of what needs to be done and then the teams decide how to proceed. This includes who performs the jobs and whether a job is best done by a robot or a person. All decisions are made by consensus with the goal of promoting quality.

Quality is considered from the very beginning of a project in ascertaining what Saturn's target customers are looking for in a vehicle. Other quality inputs are obtained through warranty information and outside surveys done by organizations such as J.D. Power and Associates, which generates customer and dealer satisfaction comparisons. In 1999, Saturn ranked second (#2) in J.D. Power's Dealer Attitude Study. It was the only domestic nameplate within the top 10. There is a clear relationship between satisfied customers, profitability, and happy dealers.[3] All customer-related quality information gathered is analyzed and formatted to be understood by the teams. This helps team members understand what piece of the information they can affect to improve the product from the customer's perspective. In other words, customer feedback in this format is the means through which product quality is improved at Saturn. The Saturn homepage is replete with information about the company and its product lines. Go to http://www.saturn.com.

Saturn's Environmental Initiatives

Saturn upheld its commitment to protect and preserve the environment in designing and constructing the Spring Hill production and assembly facility. The commitment continues in an effort Saturn calls "Designs for the Environment" that involves managing environmental issues throughout the product life cycle, from design through postconsumer disposal of Saturn automobiles and parts. Bill Miller, manager, Environmental Affairs, Manufacturing/Central Services, said it has been Saturn's experience that "with very few exceptions, things that are environmentally correct are also things that make sense from an economic standpoint. . . . If you think about it, pollution is nothing more than inefficiency in a process. The more efficient you make the process, the more environmentally correct it's going to be, and the more money you are going to make."

Impact of Facility on Physical Environment and Community

Saturn's approach in building in Spring Hill focused on how the facility would impact the residents' quality of life. Spring Hill residents were concerned that the plant would change the rural nature of the landscape. Saturn succeeded in maintaining the rural countryside. About half of the 2,450 acres it owns are devoted to a working farm. To further preserve the landscape, Saturn used the same fencing materials as local farmers and painted the factory colors that blend in with the sky.

The company moved 6 million tons of dirt and rocks to build the factories. Rock from an on-site quarry was used to make the aggregate for the concrete used in construction. This eliminated having to truck hundreds of thousands of loads of materials to the site. The excavation site for the plant was 20 feet below ground

level, and the dirt removed was used to sculpt hills to hide the plant from the road. The Saturn plant is barely detectable from the Saturn Parkway, which links the facility to I-65 in Tennessee.

Finally, Saturn moved the trees from the excavation site rather than using the usual method of bulldozing and burning them. The company determined that it was not only more environmentally sensitive to save the trees, but more cost-effective as well. The uprooted trees were put in a nursery until they were used in landscaping around the office complex a few years later. On-site ponds were constructed to control storm water, provide water for fire protection, and provide areas for wildlife.

Impact of Manufacturing Process on the Environment

Saturn took various initiatives to protect the environment from pollution caused by the automobile manufacturing process. Saturn uses environmentally sound processes in painting and engine casting. Further environmental initiatives include designating loading docks for hazardous wastes, avoidance of underground tanks, and conducting stream surveys to measure water quality. Saturn reprocessed or recycled more than 40,000 tons of waste in 1994.

The Painting Process.

One of the major environmental hazards associated with auto manufacture is painting the cars. Saturn was the first car manufacturer to use water-based rather than solvent-based paints. Water-based paints cause only 1/3 to 1/5 of the emissions of solvent-based paints during the painting process. Painting is done in a clean-room environment in paint spray booths where robots spray paint the car. Paint that misses the car flows into a water river under the paint spray booth. The water is taken into a large central room where the paint is separated from the water. (This is a challenge, because water-based paint is water soluble.) Chemicals that electrically charge the paint differently from the water are added to the mix so the paint will float. The paint is then skimmed off and run through a vacuum filter to get the remaining water out. The resulting nontoxic sludge is shipped to a landfill.

Airborne paint contaminates are captured in a carbon adsorption system. This system was developed to comply with the Clean Air Act of 1990 and to keep Saturn in compliance with future air standards (such as ISO 14000), which Miller predicts will become increasingly stringent. The $21 million carbon adsorption system is a series of stainless steel ducts and carbon beds. The system was installed by helicopter on the paint shop roof. The carbon adsorption system works like a carbon filter in an aquarium system by trapping pollution in the carbon. Then pollutants (volatile organic compounds in this case) are removed from five 85-foot-long carbon beds with hot air. The air stream is directed through a thermal oxidizer (or incinerator) and then burned. This process destroys more than 99 percent of the remaining pollutants.

Hazardous Waste Loading Docks.

In studying other GM manufacturing plants, Saturn found that loading docks are one of the major sites of chemical spills. Loading docks slope down toward the base of the building and typically, at the lowest point, have drains that go to the storm water system.

Because of Saturn's extensive use of just-in-time delivery, the possibilities for spillage increased. To prevent contamination in the event of a spill, each business unit building at Saturn has a loading dock designated for hazardous materials. The drains at the low points of these docks lead to blind sumps, so if spills occur, the materials are contained.

Above-Ground Tanks.

Tanks containing fluids used at an assembly plant, such as gasoline and windshield washer fluid, typically are contained in underground tanks. Saturn chose to locate all of its tanks above-ground. The tanks are surrounded by containment materials to prevent leakage.

Stream Surveys.

For assurance that the water supply is not being contaminated, Saturn tests the water in local streams about every other year. The company also participates regularly with the U.S. Geological Survey of water conditions. According to Miller, the water quality of the streams is better now than before the Saturn plant began operations.

Recycling of Scrap Material.

All scrap materials resulting from the manufacturing process are recycled, including metal, plastic, casting sand, wood, corrugated paper, and office paper. As an example, as far back as December 1994, Saturn began a full-scale program for collecting bumpers. New bumpers are exchanged for damaged bumpers through the supply chain, from Saturn plant to Saturn retailer to body shop. There is also a comprehensive end-of-life-of-vehicle management program.

Impact of Product on the Environment

Recyclability of Car Parts.

Recyclability of the plastic parts in a Saturn was considered in the design stage of the product life cycle—in anticipation of the post-consumer disposal stage. The exterior of a Saturn contains three different types of polymers, each of which is recyclable. Fascias (or bumpers) are made of a dent-resistant polymer that won't mark up in low-impact collisions. Fender and quarter panels are made of a nylon alloy, which provides good bump resistance. The doors are made of a polycarbonate that can bounce back upon impact.

Saturn has instituted a recycling program wherein retailers return damaged plastic parts to Spring Hill. Retailers load damaged plastic car parts on Saturn trucks that have just delivered service parts, for the return trip to the factory. In a cross-division cooperation with General Motors Research and Packard Electric Division, Saturn has developed systems for reprocessing all painted thermoplastic body panel and fascia materials on the vehicle. The doors, rocker covers, and decklids are reprocessed into Saturn rocker supports. Fascias are reprocessed into Saturn wheel liners. After being reprocessed into plastic pellets, fenders and quarter panels are used

in bearing retainers at GM Saginaw Steering Division. (Saturn is working on a process to strip paint from parts using CO_2 pellets. This will allow the company to recycle plastic parts back to their original use.)

Sustainable Development

Saturn has demonstrated that achievement of a quality product and a commitment to protecting and preserving the environment are not mutually exclusive. The company chose to be proactive from an environmental standpoint with regard to customers, the legislative arena, and in order to be competitive globally. Saturn's environmental commitment can be summed up by the term *sustainable development*, which is popular in environmental discussions today. Bill Miller says that although the term is still developing, it essentially means "doing things right today to make sure that future generations have it at least as good as it is right now. A lot of what we've done, and are doing, here at Saturn fits right into that. . . ."[4]

PART 2

What follows is the chronological history of the Saturn Corporation starting in 1994 as maintained in the archives of the company.

Important Dates in Saturn History

Saturn Corporation was formed as a wholly-owned subsidiary of General Motors in January 1985. The Saturn concept began in 1982 as a response to increasing import competition and a traditional, adversarial relationship between union and management. The two would ultimately form a partnership to study and implement an innovative way to develop and market U.S.-manufactured small cars. Together, this partnership created a distinct and clear mission, supported by a philosophy and set of shared values. Saturn's mission, philosophy, and values are all directed toward recapturing new customers and achieving world-class levels of quality and customer enthusiasm.

The 7-million-square-foot manufacturing and assembly site in Spring Hill, Tennessee, originally produced the Saturn S-Series. In 1999, Saturn added a second vehicle line, the midsize L-Series sedan and wagon, which are built in Wilmington, Delaware. A third vehicle, the VUE sport utility vehicle, began production in Spring Hill in 2001, and the all new Saturn ION sedan and quad coupe replaced the Saturn S-Series in 2002.

As a greenfield site, the auto plant balances people and technology with an advanced focus on ergonomics and environmental stewardship.

During the last 15 years, Saturn has reshaped the way automakers build and sell cars. How the Saturn vision became reality is a unique story, and these are the significant events in Saturn's continuing development.

January 1994	Saturn announces that it realized an operating profit (before taxes and interest) for calendar year 1993. Operating profits had been reported for the months of May through December, with the exception of July.
January 5, 1994	"The Saturn Homecoming" event is announced. Saturn owners will be invited to Spring Hill on June 24–25, 1994, to tour the birthplace of their cars, meet team members and other owners, and enjoy a wide variety of family events.
March 2, 1994	The "Saturn Mobility Program" is announced. This program reimburses up to $1,000 for the installation and cost of adaptive equipment for physically challenged owners.
May 1994	Saturn produces its 700,000th car.
June 1, 1994	Saturn goes online with an interactive marketing program on the Prodigy computer service. Prodigy subscribers are able to access information on Saturn products, request full-line brochures, and locate their nearest Saturn retailer. The service also includes an electronic bulletin board that allows Saturn owners, prospects, and team members to talk to one another.
June 24–25, 1994	44,000 Saturn owners and their families attend the Saturn Homecoming in Spring Hill. Throughout this weekend and summer, Saturn retailers also held regional homecoming events attracting over 130,000 customers. In all, 1 of every 6 Saturn customers participated in the homecoming.
July 1994	Saturn's 300th retail facility opens.
August 1994	Saturn introduces its 1995 models.
October 1994	Saturn produces its 800,000th car.
October 1, 1994	Saturn's rating of 95 percent North American content is placed on the customer information label of all vehicles, as required by the American Automotive Labeling Act.
October 4, 1994	In an effort to enhance its competitiveness throughout the small car market, GM's North American operations announces the formation of the Small Car Group, formalizing a strategic relationship between Saturn and the Lansing Automotive Division. Skip LeFauve is named executive in charge of the new group, while retaining his position as Saturn president.
January 4, 1995	Saturn announces record sales were established in 11 of 12 sales months during 1994. In addition, total 1994 calendar year sales was 286,003 vehicles; this represented a 25 percent increase over the 1993 calendar year.
February 1995	Saturn produces its 900,000th car.
April 13, 1995	The Saturn Used Car Process is announced at the New York International Auto Show. Saturn brings its popular new-car selling ideas to the used-car business. Each Saturn certified used car must pass a stringent 150-point inspection and is reconditioned prior to resale. Saturn certified used cars also come with a 3-day moneyback/30-day trade-in guarantee and limited warranty.
June 1, 1995	Saturn's one-millionth vehicle (a dark green 1995 SC2 coupe) is produced at the Spring Hill, Tennessee, manufacturing and assembly complex.
August 8, 1995	Donald W. Hudler is appointed president of Saturn Corporation, replacing Richard G. "Skip" LeFauve, who assumes the newly-created position of chairman of Saturn Corporation. Hudler had been Saturn's VP of Sales, Service, and Marketing.
January 4, 1996	General Motors announces at the Greater Los Angeles Auto Show that it will produce the EV1 electric vehicle. M also reveals that the car will be distributed and marketed by Saturn beginning in the fall of 1996. Initial availability will be in the Los Angeles, San Diego, Phoenix, and Tucson markets.
August 6, 1996	GM, Saturn, and the UAW announce that Saturn will build a new generation vehicle at the Wilmington, Delaware, facility. The project, known as Project Innovate, will be a larger vehicle in the Saturn line. Prior to Saturn production, the facility will start building the Chevrolet Malibu during the 1997 model year and produce it into the 1999 model year.
October 15, 1996	Saturn announces that the GM-badged EV1 electric will be offered only through a lease program, with a capitalized lease cost of $33,995 (prior to any federal, state, or local credits or incentives). In addition, the launch date of December 5, 1996, is revealed.
November 14, 1996	GM chairman Jack Smith and Lansing Craft Centre plant manager Maureen Midgley drive an EV1 electric vehicle onto a transporter, signifying the first shipment of the GM-badged cars to Saturn retailers in Southern California and Arizona.

November 20, 1996	Saturn announces it will start selling right-hand-drive cars at 14 outlets in Japan beginning in April 1997. It was also announced that the total number of nine retailer agreements had been signed to date.
November 22, 1996	Saturn's right-hand-drive SL2 sedan, SW2 wagon, and SC2 coupe models make their public debut at the Osaka Import Automobile Show in Osaka, Japan.
December 5, 1996	The first GM EV1 electric vehicles are delivered to customers through Saturn's 24 retailers serving Southern California and Arizona.
January 17, 1997	A blue SC2 becomes the 1.5-millionth Saturn vehicle produced at its Spring Hill, Tennessee, facility.
March 6, 1997	Saturn announces that it will begin sales of right-hand-drive models (SL2, SW2, and SC2) in Japan on April 5, 1997. Pricing will be comparable with competitors and, like its U.S. philosophy, will use a no-haggle/no-hassle sales strategy.
March 15, 1997	A black-gold SC2 coupe is the first Saturn right-hand-drive vehicle to be unloaded at the Port of Toyohashi, Japan. A total of 220 Saturn sedans, wagons, and coupes were carried aboard the cargo ship *Turandot*.
April 1, 1997	Saturn president Donald W. Hudler assumes the additional duty of chairman of Saturn Corporation. Skip LeFauve, Saturn's first chairman, becomes GM's senior VP for Global Leadership Development and Global Human Resource Processes.
April 5, 1997	Saturn begins its first day of sales in Japan through eight retailers.
October 10, 1997	Saturn announces adjustment of the manufacturer's suggested retail prices (MSRPs) on 1998 SL1 and SL2 sedans, and makes them retroactive to the start of sale of the 1998 model year.
November 21, 1997	First day of availability and first delivery of GM EV1 electric vehicles in Sacramento, California. This represents the fifth market area overall for the vehicle, and the first in Northern California.
March 11, 1998	By a margin of 2-to-1, Saturn team members of UAW Local 1853 in Tennessee voted to continue working under the current memorandum of agreement, thus recognizing and supporting the basic principles of the Saturn's unique labor/management partnership.
March 31, 1998	First day of availability and deliveries of the GM EV1 electric vehicles in the San Francisco Bay area. This represents the sixth market area for the vehicle, and the second in Northern California.
August 24, 1998	Saturn debuts a right-hand-drive (RHD) version of its wagon intended to exceed the expectations of rural U.S. postal carriers. The 1999 SWP wagon uses the basic RHD configuration developed for Saturn–Japan products.
October 1998	Cumulative deliveries of the GM EV1 electric vehicle surpass the 500 mark. This milestone was accomplished after 22 months on the market even though the vehicle was only available for lease in California and Arizona.
October 30, 1998	Saturn unveils its 1999 3-door coupes at the New England International Auto Show in Boston. The driver's side rear access door will become a standard feature on all SC1 and SC2 models beginning in early November 1998.
November 4, 1998	Production of the "world's first" 3-door coupe rolls off the Spring Hill assembly line.
November 10, 1998	The second stage of Saturn's unique retail experience, Retail Environmental Design (RED) 2, begins rollout. The initiative enhances retail facility design and appearance to support Saturn's warm, friendly, and helpful brand image.
December 7, 1998	Saturn announces two new mid-size Saturns will join its product lineup in 1999 when the all-new L-Series sedan and wagon debut at Saturn retailers in the United States and Canada. The LS and LW will compete with midsize imports such as Toyota Camry and Honda Accord.
December 14, 1998	Building on its record of retail innovation, Saturn forms Saturn Retail Enterprises (SRE), an independent retail operating company. Based in Charlotte, North Carolina, the new organization will own and operate Saturn retail facilities. Saturn also announced that Donald W. Hudler will be the CEO of Saturn Retail Enterprises upon retirement January 1, 1999, as Saturn chairman and president. Replacing Hudler as president and chairman of Saturn will be Cynthia Trudell, who also was elected a GM vice president. Trudell was president of IBC Vehicles, a wholly-owned GM operation in Luton, England, which produces the Frontera 4wd vehicle.

December 22, 1998	The Saturn SL sedan earns the maximum 5-star ratings for both driver and passenger protection in frontal collision tests conducted by the National Highway Traffic Safety Association (NHTSA). The SL is the first light passenger car to earn double 5-star ratings in NHTSA's New Car Assessment Program.
January 2, 1999	Saturn's two-millionth vehicle (a red 1999 3-door SC2 coupe) is produced at the Spring Hill, Tennessee, manufacturing and assembly complex.
February 11, 1999	A second Saturn Homecoming is announced. Saturn owners will be invited to Spring Hill on July 30–31, 1999, to meet team members and other owners while enjoying entertainment and a variety of family events. Saturn retailers around the country also will plan special homecoming events.
March 31, 1999	The Saturn L-Series sedan and wagon are unveiled to the media at the 1999 New York Auto Show.
July 8, 1999	The 2000 Saturn L-Series sedan and wagon are previewed to Saturn owners and guests at hundreds of Saturn retail locations across the country.
July 30–31, 1999	60,000 Saturn owners and their families attend the second Saturn Homecoming in Spring Hill, Tennessee. Throughout the weekend and summer, Saturn retailers also held regional homecoming events attracting over 150,000 customers.
August 2, 1999	The redesigned Saturn S-Series coupe and sedan go on sale at Saturn retailers across North America.
April 25, 2000	GM's $1.5 billion capital investment in Saturn announced. Saturn's plan includes the potential for four new products over the next 4 years. Saturn announces a series of strategic moves to aggressively grow the brand. • GM approved Saturn's sport utility vehicle (SUV), which will go into production at Saturn's Spring Hill, Tennessee, facility in late 2001. • GM will make a $1 billion capital investment in Saturn's Spring Hill manufacturing facility through 2002. • Saturn's SUV and next generation small cars will include GM's new global 4-cylinder engine. Spring Hill was awarded GM's third production module for this engine, including strategic machining and assembly. • One of Saturn's undisclosed future models will include a high-tech V6 engine from GM's recent agreement with Honda.
May 15, 2000	Saturn announces new airbag technology, head curtain airbags, to be available as an option in September.
July 10, 2000	Saturn donates 48 cars to automotive service education programs across the country.
August 8, 2000	Spring Hill breaks ground for Powertrain L850 building, which will product the global Ecotec engine.
August 29, 2000	The AA press, a giant metal stamping machine, arrives in Spring Hill from Japan.
October 6, 2000	Saturn unveils the 2002 Saturn VUE sports utility vehicle at the South Florida International Auto Show in Miami.
February 16, 2001	Saturn donates 23 more cars to automotive service education programs.
April 18, 2001	Annette Clayton appointed as president of Saturn Corporation.
June 27, 2001	Saturn debuts "Lightship" as cornerstone of promotional plan for VUE.
August 8, 2001	Saturn repeats number-one rating in the J.D. Power Sales Satisfaction Index.
November 16, 2001	Saturn sponsors MADD safety campaign.
February 1, 2002	Saturn transitions to new ad agency—San Francisco–based Goodby, Silverstein and Partners.
February 8, 2002	Saturn VUE wins Best Small SUV award in the 20th Annual Driver's Choice Awards run by *Motorweek/PBS*'s television show.
April 26, 2002	New ION quad coupe unveiled at the New York Auto Show.
June 1, 2002	Production of Ecotec engine for VUE and ION begins in Spring Hill.
June 15, 2002	Saturn receives award from Good Sam Club as "most RV friendly dinghy vehicle."
July 10, 2002	Saturn ranks number one in 2002 J.D. Power Customer Service Index Study—the first nonluxury brand to earn the top spot since 1986.
July 2002	Saturn introduces mid-cycle enhancement of L-Series, giving the car a more upscale appearance.

August 15, 2002	Saturn ranks highest in 2002 J.D. Power Sales Satisfaction Index for the third consecutive year.
August 29, 2002	After producing more than 2.7 million small sedans, coupes, and wagons, Saturn Spring Hill produces last Saturn S-Series, and introduces the all-new Saturn ION Sedan.
September 8, 2002	Saturn Spring Hill awarded most valuable pollution prevention award by National Pollution Prevention Roundtable.
October 28, 2002	The National Committee for Employer Support of the Guard and Reserve presents Saturn with award for going above and beyond legal requirements for granting leave for military duty.
November, 2002	Second consecutive year Saturn sponsors MADD safety campaign.
January 6, 2003	Saturn announces plans to offer GM hybrid powertrain on Saturn VUE.
February 2, 2003	GM announces 2005 mid-van contender for Saturn.
April 8, 2003	Saturn introduces the performance vehicle line—the Saturn VUE Red Line and the ION Quad Coupe Red Line.
April 2003	Saturn ION quad coupe begins arriving at Saturn retailers.
June 18, 2003	Saturn transmission operations were cited as the most improved transmission plant in productivity on the 2003 "Harbour Report."

Questions

1. Discuss the "systems thinking" that went in to planning and building the Saturn facility and products.
2. Do you think simultaneous engineering was employed in designing the plant and products? Why or why not?
3. What was the importance and symbolism of the Group of 99 and Gang of Six to the "clean-sheet approach"? Discuss.
4. Explain how the Saturn Project in effect reengineered the automobile manufacture process.
5. If each business unit has 217 work units, and each work unit has 8 to 15 members, how many Saturn employees are "associated with" teams rather than "members of" teams? What kinds of functions do you think these Saturn employees perform?
6. How is quality ensured at Saturn? Discuss the role of quality councils and the TQAT.
7. Why does it make more sense economically for manufacturers to use processes that minimize pollution?
8. How does Saturn fit in the community? Discuss the company's concern for the environment.
9. Discuss the ways in which Saturn has demonstrated that achieving a quality product and environmental sensitivity are not mutually exclusive.
10. The product line of Saturn expanded significantly during 2003 and 2004. What are these product line extensions and how do they affect the position of Saturn in the global automotive marketplace?
11. Average automobile customer loyalty "hovers around 44 percent." What is the loyalty of Saturn owners? Explain the difference. (See last reference).
12. What is the unique character of the union-management relationship at Spring Hill, Tennessee?

Notes

1. Charles J. Murray. "Engineer on a Mission." *Design News*, Engineering Quality Award issue (1994).
2. Conversations with John J. Resslar, manager of the Design of the Environment at the World Wide Facilities of the General Motors Corporation. "It's all about managing life cycles," he said on March 16, 2000. Subsequent discussions in October 2003 with Professor Resslar, Ms. Jennifer Graham, and Ms. Susan Holmgren have led to major updatings of the original Saturn materials.
3. Susan Holmgren. "Saturn Again Places Second Behind Lexus in the J.D. Power Study." *Saturn Newsline* (January 6, 2000).
4. Gary S. Vasilash. "The Environment at Saturn." *Production* (April 1994).

References

Michael Bennett. "The Saturn Corporation: New Management-Union Partnership at the Factory of the Future." *Looking Ahead*, vol. xiii, no. 4 (April 1992). (Published by the National Planning Association, Washington, DC.)
Richard G. LeFauve and Arnoldo C. Hax. "Managerial and Technological Innovations at Saturn Corporation." *MIT Management* (Spring 1992).
Jack O'Toole and Jim Lewandowski. "Forming the Future: The Marriage of People and Technology at Saturn." Presentation at Stanford University Industrial Engineering and Engineering Management, March 29, 1990.
Saul A. Rubinstein and Thomas A. Kochan. *Learning from Saturn.* Ithaca, NY: Cornell University Press, February 2001.
Raymond Sarafin. "The Saturn Story." *Advertising Age* (November 16, 1992).
Gary S. Vasilash. "The Environment at Saturn." *Production* (April 1994).
James P. Womack. "The Lean Difference: An International Productivity Comparison and the Implications for U.S. Industry." *Looking Ahead*, vol. xiii, no. 4 (April 1992). (Published by the National Planning Association, Washington, DC.)
James P. Womack, Daniel T. Jones, and Daniel Roos. "The Machine That Changed the World: The Story of Lean Production." *Harper Perennial* (1991).
Numerous Saturn Corporation documents, including "Important Dates in Saturn History," "Saturn Fact Sheet—Sales and Marketing Highlights," "Quality Information for Students," and news release on "Saturn's Environmental Initiatives," June 24, 1994.
Go to http://www.saturnfans.com for what is called "Saturnalia." This is the Saturn owners' fan club that has announcements such as, "Saturn set a land speed record at the Bonneville Salt Flats with a 212.684 MPH run on October 17, 2003."
Go to http://www.saturnfans.com and click on "Saturn Books and Repair Manuals." at the Barnes & Noble Bookstore, click on "Saturn Books." Note that part of the answer to Case Question 11 is found in the discussion of Vickie Lenz. *The Saturn Difference: Creating Customers Loyalty in Your Company.* Hoboken, NJ: John Wiley & Sons, February 1999.

Source: Printed with permission of the Saturn Corporation.

Environmental, Ethical, and Technological Forces

Chapter Outline

hapter 20 deals with environmental restrictions that affect organizations and considers ethical issues from both legal and psychological perspectives. Then, Chapter 20 considers the impact of 9/11/01 on safety and security for customers, employees, suppliers, citizens, and bystanders. This last category brings to mind questions about crisis management and contingency planning. These subjects are treated together under the security umbrella. In the OM profession, Chapter 20's topics are at the forefront of research and attention. These topics pose difficult but exciting places to be working.

After reading this chapter, you should be able to:

- Describe the special capabilities and core competencies that P/OM offers that can support greening the environment, i.e., how P/OM contributes to greening the environment.
- Discuss limitations on P/OM contributions to greening the environment.
- Explain how maintenance affects the environment.
- Describe how OSHA, CDC, FDA, and other governmental organizations relate to environment and to ethics.
- Describe the four parts of design for disassembly (DFD)
- Explain applications of design for disassembly (DFD) and its role in environmental protection.
- Explain water-jetting and why this technology might be important for environmental protection.
- Explain recycling concrete and why this technology is protective of the environment.
- Explain how P/OM can maintain or change ethical standards (nationally and internationally).
- Relate ethics and quality integrity.

- Relate quality integrity and the Hazard Analysis and Critical Control Point (HACCP) system.
- Describe the workings of the Hazard Analysis and Critical Control Point (HACCP) system.
- Describe the application of food and drug testing by the Food and Drug Administration.
- Explain what it means to ready the organization for future technology (e.g., vision-able robots).
- Describe P/OM's role in doing business on a global scale. Draw on ISO 14000 and the SME Enterprise Wheel.
- Explain the consequences of using ISO 14000/14001. What are its limitations?
- Explain how P/OM relates to safety and security for customers and employees.
- Discuss P/OM's role in crisis management.
- Explain how contingency planning relates to crisis management.

THE SYSTEMS VIEWPOINT

The second kind of change force is from the outside. It is not the result of "our" strategic planning, but it could be the result of "someone else" creating a new competitive situation. The Twin Tower catastrophe (9/11/01) led to a chain of consequences for the airlines that had to be dealt with in a systems fashion. New airlines like Jet Blue had an easier time than giant bureaucracies like United and American. The big picture has to be grasped right away. Waiting for a series of pieces to fit together as with a jigsaw puzzle is too little too late. *Once the systems picture is understood*, then creative strategic thinking is the only way to survive. Survival always precedes winning. Crisis management with contingency planning is a preview method that attempts preparations for hurricanes, earthquakes, senseless acts of terrorism, war, incompetence, and crime. There are sound reasons to invest in an operations management point of view.

STRATEGIC THINKING

The business organization works with two kinds of change forces. There are those that arise inside the firm in response to the desire to advance the cause. Continuous product development is an example of the company striving to become better, bigger, and richer. This occurs when a Stage III company seeks to become a Stage IV company. *Good to Great: Why Some Companies Make the Leap . . . and Others Don't* (Jim Collins, Harper Business, 2001) is a book that epitomizes the urge to excel. The title of Chapter 1 of Collins' book provides insight by itself. It is "Good Is the Enemy of Great." To transform an organization so that it achieves constancy of superior achievement requires, at the outset, sound strategic planning to bring about change. If times are considered to be good, it is difficult to risk going from "good to worse."

Old polyurethane foam from automotive seating can be ground, reprocessed, and then molded again into new seat cushions. P/OM strives to find ways to reuse materials because in most well-thought-out cases, reusing is both good for the environment and is cost-saving for the company.

Reuse: A reusable part can quickly be returned to inventory. Reusable plastics, glass, paper, and metal may require more value-adding than a nut, bolt, or gear that can be reused with just cleanup.

Ethics: Ethical standards must be established in multicultural environments that satisfy the various participants.

20-1 ADAPTING TO EXTERNAL FORCES

Unanticipated external forces imposed from outside allow only a reactive mode. A way around that is to imagine what could possibly happen and then prepare a response. This is called *contingency planning*. For example, without warning a law is passed that reduces smokestack emissions. Using contingency planning, the company would have pre-thought the possibility and documented a strategy to deal with the situation. Contingency plans permit managers to anticipate a range of happenings and even to prepare proactive responses in the event that one of them occurs. It should be noted that companies like Toyota have successfully developed elaborate contingency plans for handling problems arising on the plant floor.

Historical records indicate that environmental standards will continue to increase in scope and rigor. The environmental effects of operations (e.g., pollution control and take-back laws for material reuse) will be impacted by society with increasing frequency and severity. Pre-thinking creative **reuse** of recycled parts can lower costs, improve products, and meet new stringent laws about the percent reuse of a car's components that are current in parts of Europe—and coming to North America. Technology is making some major shifts occur. Gas-guzzling engines will disappear as research for replacement technology is funded.

Laws passed to achieve environmental goals can take many forms such as prohibition on cutting trees, drilling for oil, and limits on effluents. **Ethics** of operational constraints have become another factor of growing concern to P/OM. Ethical issues, like environmental issues, take the form of external forces of limitation and constraint. However, there are examples of such constraints surprising the constrained by producing great profits rather than excessive costs. In other words, the consequences of unexpected ethical issues can be positive as well as negative. Ethics do not have to be external forces. For example, Chick-Fil-A® is a remarkably successful quick-service restaurant (QSR) that closes on Sundays. Take a look at http://www.chick-fil-A.com. Click on "History" at the bottom and then on "why we are closed on Sundays." Researching at http://www.QSR-magazine.com can reveal how successful Chick-Fil-A® is in the QSR business.

There is also a lot of uncertainty about what is ethical in a diverse and disparate multination cultural milieu. This necessitates understanding how disparate cultures view work, gifts and bribes, pay, holidays, unions, syndicates, the Internet, and contracts (to chose a few of many issues). It also highlights the communication problems when customers, suppliers, and fabricators speak different languages. There has been deep interest in the ethics of the food industry's commitment to provide healthful food and drugs. Chapter 20 looks into some of the operational aspects of this commitment.

Readying the organization for technology developments is an operations management responsibility. For example, if health care is going to employ hospital robots for various orderly and even nursing functions, the training requirements are part of the P/OM job. Technology issues get tentacles into every aspect of this chapter. Examples are presented of the reuse of materials (recycling) and a cleaning method (water-jetting) that reduces pollutants. Technology interacts with safety and security in many ways that can be cited and many more ways that are unfolding.

Chapter 20 examines the consequences of external events that have occurred recently. For example, the terrorist destruction of the World Trade Center in New York City on September 11, 2001, has altered more than the budget for safety and security. It has changed the methods, processes, and procedures that are associated with the management of security operations.

Airlines' operations are an obvious illustration. Among the many operational issues that need to be considered: What items get on board as cargo? Which people get on board as passengers (or, Who gets to take their shoes off before boarding the plane)? The issues continue once on board the plane. What are the rules for passengers waiting to use bathrooms? Are cockpit doors locked and unbreachable? Are there marshals on board? What technology is used to monitor the situation?

The four factors that underlie adapting to external forces will continue to be the environment, ethics, new technology, and doing business in the global community. These factors cross over and interact. For example, new environmental laws in Germany change the cost structure of cars in Japan. U.S. decisions to prohibit oil drilling in Alaska change the research agenda for car engines in Detroit, Tokyo, and Seoul.

Ethic laws that prohibit giving bribes (which are called *gifts*, in some countries) can lead to a change in the method of doing business. For example, aircraft firms have share-based arrangements with parts manufacturers in the countries where there will be product purchase support, and that is not considered unethical at this time. Technological development of computers brought the end of the world for Kueffel and Esser. Global methods (like Japanese car manufacturing) changed the way that cars were designed and made by GM, DaimlerChrysler, and Ford. The advanced method is more productive, less costly, less polluting, and more recyclable.

20-2 GREENING THE ENVIRONMENT: MAINTENANCE

Environmental upgrading is called **greening the environment**. P/OM has capabilities for both protecting and upgrading the environment. Without P/OM's awareness and technical knowledge, the environment can be degraded irreversibly. With increasing ecological damage, proactive steps to repair the situation fall on OM shoulders. Using technology and good management, and driven by a sense of what is ethically correct, OM can help limit, if not prevent, ecological harm. Often, it can do more than that by cleaning up messes (say in lakes and rivers) that were brought about by forces long gone and even natural (not man-made) disasters.

Following are some examples of initiatives that can be taken to prevent environmental damage. Some of these methods are cost-effective as well.

> **Greening the environment:**
> Greening is meant to connote that efforts are successful to achieve sustainable land and water resources.

20-2a Water-Jetting Maintenance

Water-jetting exemplifies a technology that has now been developed to a point where it can replace toxic maintenance methods that are used to remove paints and other coatings. It is also used for cutting shapes with water and abrasives. The *Thomas Register* (2003) lists more than 20 companies that provide marine hull treatment and about 100 other companies for other applications. This method of **water-jetting** has been used to strip paint from planes before repainting them.

A journal article dated April 2002[1] makes the relevance of the process evident, "Most large ocean-going vessels, whether they be crude oil tankers, bulk cargo ships, military, Coast Guard, or chemical tankers, generally have hull plating that is made up of steel which is protected by layers of anti-corrosive (usually epoxy) and anti-fouling coatings. Over time such coatings succumb to failure modes . . . . These coating systems must be renewed. . . . Historically, traditional surface preparation and coating renewal work has been a low tech, labor and time intensive, environmentally challenging endeavor."

The traditional method is to blast the coatings with abrasive grit. There are six major problems with that process. These are (1) large volumes of potentially toxic airborne particulate (lead and chromate laden dust); (2) machinery failures caused by the dust and grit; (3) reduced visibility in dry docks; (4) inability of other trades to work in the vicinity of blasting; (5) massive labor-intensive cleanup effort after blasting and prior to painting; (6) waste collection and disposal. Old methods have a lot of disadvantages that need to be reconsidered because technology has changed. New tech methods do not suffer problems 1 through 6.

Significant technological advances in water-jetting equipment design have provided shipyards, owners, and operators a means of achieving high-production hull treatment in addition to selective coating removal down to individual layers of paint for large marine structures.

Advanced Systems Technologies, Inc., based in Huntsville, Alabama, is an example of a company that has been doing water-jet surface removal for a long time. The Lydia Frenzel Conference Center provides newsletters and white papers on various cleaning applications at http://www.lydiafrenzel.com.

These companies design ultra-high pressure systems (20,000–55,000 psi), which can remove paint and asbestos as well as heavy metals. A number of these companies market surface cleaning services using open-cycle "men on guns" or various semiautomatic systems. A survey of companies listed by *Thomas Register* (2003) indicates that 40,000 psi seems to have become a standard pressure.

Men on guns is the labor-intensive application of this technology. Precision robotic controls have been used for de-painting and de-coating large military vehicles such as aircraft and ships. A mainstay product in widespread commercial use removes corrosion and tenacious thermal barrier coatings such as plasma-sprayed ceramics and felt metals from jet engines and other industrial equipment components.

Water-jetting is a cost-effective and environmentally sound alternative approach to many conventional coating removal methods such as chemical stripping, incineration, machining, and abrasive blasting. The conventional technique for removing paint from aircraft skin is by applying methylene chloride, a toxic solvent that requires that workers use protective latex clothing and special breathing apparatus. Aircraft engine parts are dipped in toxic chemical baths, whereas high-pressure water-jet technology uses only water to achieve effective cleaning and de-coating.

Special computer-designed water-jet end-effectors and nozzles coupled to a 6-axis manipulator mounted on a 21-foot arm, attached to a 2-axis, 30-foot rotating vertical column and transported on a wire-guided AGV (automated guided vehicle), comprise the world's largest mobile robot. The depth of the de-coating can be regulated precisely, allowing paint to be stripped one layer at a time. Particles are captured when the water is filtered during recycling by a closed-loop water reclamation system.

The water-jet system has many potential applications. It has been researched as a method for cleaning airport runways. It can be a replacement technology for machine cut-

Water-jetting: High water pressure technology that replaces toxic maintenance methods used to remove paints and coatings. Also, cuts shapes with water and abrasives.

ting tools, concrete cutters, and shoe leather and carpet cutting. It has been suggested for radioactive waste removal and as a coal mining method. An experimental application is surgical removal of basal cell carcinomas. New industries that are emerging, based on water-jet technology, owe their start-up to NASA technology.

20-2b Water Supply Maintenance

It is an OM responsibility to choose the best maintenance functions. Maintenance decisions are often flawed because of a preference for what is familiar. There is a strong tendency to believe that what was done in the past was carefully chosen as best. In fact, once procedures are installed, it takes a point of view (such as value analysis) to recheck for new materials and methods. Although it is sensible to test the old way against the new, it is not always done. Maintenance seems an old fashioned function in a society that uses things up and then throws them away. It should be viewed as being on the cutting edge of materials and methods.

Water maintenance is a good example. Treatment of pools with chlorine is standard in the United States. There are some adventurous users of alternatives such as bromine and the combination of ozone with chlorine or bromine. Distillation and various forms of filtration are used for drinking water. NASA developed a silver iodide system for drinking water that has been adopted by some European municipalities for pool and spa maintenance. Individual users of this new technology also can be found in the United States.

When comparing systems, what should matter is not that maintenance prefers the "tried and true" but the comparative qualities of the results and the costs incurred. There is some evidence that silver iodide is a strong contender for Best Practice. Still, it is not surprising that most pool maintenance follows traditional chlorine treatment plans. Research on cost/benefits of alternative water treatments is ongoing.

Reference to the AWWA webpage indicates the breadth of issues that relate to water maintenance. (See http://www.awwa.org.) The Benchmarking Clearinghouse covers outstanding practices for water and wastewater utilities of all sizes. It provides 22 key performance indicators and support for sections, which are the states and regional groupings of states. The association has created the Self-Assessment and Peer Review Forum (SA/PRF) in addition to the quality program for utilities called *QualServe*™. The increasingly important topic of security for water systems is included under education and training as the new vulnerability assessment.

The Association of Metropolitan Sewerage Agencies (AMSA) is organized for purposes of information dissemination as well as lobbying. The sewerage function is another operations management arena that is often overlooked. Note: http://www.amsa-cleanwater.org. AMSA has various vulnerability self-assessment tools (VSAT™) for joint water/wastewater utilities as well as small and medium-sized water utilities. This organization provides many training sessions on the use of VSAT™ software.

In its political activities, AMSA is an enabling organization for the legislation unanimously approved by the U.S. House of Representatives on October 7, 2002. This is The Wastewater Treatment Works Security Act, H.R. 5169, which authorized $200 million in grants to EPA (Environmental Protection Agency) for vulnerability assessments and security enhancements at POTWs (Publicly-Owned Treatment Works).

Maintenance managers may be the most reluctant operations managers to adapt new technologies. Why is this so? Maintenance is what keeps old systems running. For example, the condition of elevators needs to be checked and often breakdowns occur so that both preventive and remedial maintenance seem to be required. Some countries buy used airplanes and buses that are not kept up to par.

The upkeep of old plants is difficult without replacement parts and budget for them. Often, old facilities are installed with maintenance instructions that are ambiguous. Such older facilities abound in third world countries, but there are many of them in the United States as well. Innovative maintenance is tough to support under such circumstances. OSHA (Occupational Safety and Health Administration of the U.S. Department of Labor) has been said to dictate (occasionally) procedures that management would like changed, but alteration of methods is not easy to accomplish. Otherwise, a visit to http://www.osha.gov reveals important contributions made by this government organization to health and safety.

When it is cheapest to use a standard but hazardous method that does the quality job, it is the hazard part that must be evaluated. Every effort needs to be made to investigate the applicability of replacing harmful maintenance methods with new technologies that reduce pollutants. The same reasoning applies to workstation dangers that were overlooked in a different era. Asbestos problems are a good example.

20-3 GREENING THE ENVIRONMENT: DESIGN FOR DISASSEMBLY (DFD)

There are many associations devoted to various aspects of recycling. Some representative ones will be included in this discussion. In the United States, the Vehicle Recycling Partnership (VRP) was formed in 1991 "to promote and conduct research to aid in the development of technology for the recovery, reuse and disposal of materials from retired vehicles. The partnership falls under the United States Council for automotive research or USCAR, an organization set up to facilitate, monitor and promote pre-competitive research and development activities among DaimlerChrysler, Ford and General Motors." At the webpage http://www.uscar.org, click on "Teams" and then click on "VRP," which is in the top list of initiatives.

Every year, there are about 10 million vehicles that are scrapped. In the United States, about 75 percent of the material by weight from the 10 million cars is recycled. As a benchmark, approximately 60 percent of aluminum cans are recycled. The figures for paper are in the neighborhood of 30 percent and 20 percent for glass products. European standards are leading the way for disposability at **end-of-life-of-vehicle (ELV)** and for eliminating **substances of concern (SOC)**, which include lead, mercury, cadmium, and hexavalent chromium. An agreement has been reached to entirely eliminate hexavalent chromium. Ford will do so by July 2005; GM, by model year 2006; and DaimlerChrysler, by January 2007.

The goals of USCAR's VRP are to

- Reduce the total environmental impact of vehicle disposal.

- Increase the efficiency of the disassembly of components and materials to enhance vehicle recyclability.

- Develop material selection and design guidelines.

- Promote socially responsible and economically achievable solutions to vehicle disposal.

In the United Kingdom, BMRA (British Metals Recycling Association) organizes the individual recyclers. BMRA offers a wide array of training courses. In addition, it has an educational program intended to teach consumers about recycling. There is a special effort to reach children at an early age with the message. See http://www.britmetfed.org.uk.

In Canada, the Ontario Automotive Recycling Association (OARA) links hundreds of associations and committees, including The Wisconsin Department of Natural Resources, with its waste management program and its recycling trade associations. OARA has committees working on salvage problems and a collision industry action group (CIAG). To see the linkage and diversity, visit http//www.oara.com. Also see http://www.dnr.state.wi.us/org/caer/cfa/EL/Section/brownfield.html and http://www.dnr.state.wi.us/org/aw/wm/markets/category.html.

20-3a Take-Back Laws

One purpose of many of these organizations is to learn how to design robust take-back functions. The system under study is a reverse supply chain. Materials flow from consumers with end of life (used up, or damaged) products back to the manufacturer who

End-of-life-of-vehicle (ELV):
Eventually close to 100 percent of vehicles, computers, etc., will be returned for recycling and/or disposal by the manufacturers.

Substances of concern (SOC):
Agreement has been reached to entirely remove Cr(VI) by January 2007.

made that product in the first place. The manufacturer is held accountable to do the best possible thing with the returned materials. The government may hold the manufacturer responsible, but the trade associations are often the basis of industry agreements that are intended to head off more legislation about take-backs. The five elements of accomplishment for products in general are

- *Products that can be dismantled quickly and easily.* It is not enough that these materials are easily recycled. If it is difficult to get at those materials, they will go to the "dump." Economical dismantling is essential.

- *Components that can be reused* (sometimes for a second time without any additional operations). At other times, process refurbishing is needed, and it must be economically justifiable.

- *Parts that can be disposed of safely.* When reuse is not possible, then destruction and reduction must lead to safe disposal. The process can include pulverization, making the material liquid, putting it into containers, and burying it in caves thousands of feet below the surface (like depleted uranium). The ultimate question is where can dangerous used-up materials be safely stored? Safely means out of harm's way. No one is happy with the caves under Yucca Mountain, Nevada, as the solution for depleted uranium.

- *Materials that can be recycled.* This brings up a distinction between materials that are reused and materials that are recycled. The recycling process for paper is a good example. All qualifying paper products (the commodity) are mixed together and treated chemically to form a substance that can be transformed into paper. The benefit is that fewer trees are needed to make a given amount of paper. Tire and glass recycling follow the same pattern.

- *Materials that can be reused* (where reuse, in comparison to recycle, is related to the amount of reprocessing required). In recycling paper, there is a good deal of reprocessing. In contrast, a disposable camera is returned by the customer with the film in it for film processing. That camera has parts that can be used again with a minimum amount of reprocessing. Parts such as spool take-ups for the film, and lens components that are undamaged, can be collected from the spent camera and put into the new camera. Perhaps a component like this needs a part replaced or resized for a new model. Initial design can significantly increase the percent of reusable parts.

Ten years ago, *Fortune* magazine stated that the people working in the five bullet point areas discussed earlier "are riding the hottest new production trend in the world: **design for disassembly (DFD)**."[2] It is hotter today. The pressure has been building up for several reasons. One factor that accounts for the growing importance of DFD is the *increasing cost of the disposal of waste*. A second factor is the tough (and getting tougher) European **take-back laws.** They compel manufacturers to take back used product. As a direct result, manufacturers are forced to design cars, telephones, copy machines, and refrigerators that are quick to disassemble and, as much as possible, reusable. BMW set up experimental plants for disassembly with a goal of recycling 95 percent (by weight) of its cars.

The handwriting is on the wall. Review the program of the Conference on European Electronics Take-Back Legislation. It was sponsored by INSEAD and Berkeley, and held at Fontainebleau, France, in October 2002. The program is located at http://www.insead.edu/CMER/events/takebackworkshop/program.htm.

An equally important factor is the cost savings that can be realized. Economic and ecological benefits are so well correlated that in the United States, without take-back laws, Detroit's car makers work with auto-part recyclers to reuse 75 to 80 percent of the weight of American cars. The effort to increase this percent will result in continuous innovations using new materials and principles of assembly–disassembly. The United States is on board with the European Union and with Japan.

DFD innovations are exemplified by the Saturn Corporation (the wholly-owned subsidiary of GM). Saturn developed a new disassembly line that was more energy efficient than the previous method of shredding cars. The new method of recycling had the

Design for disassembly (DFD): DFD innovations can be rewarding in terms of rapid disassembly, reduction in the number of parts required, reuse (rework and remanufacture), and recycle (with safe disposal).

Take-back laws: Governmental rules are being invoked in Europe and in the United States (at a slightly slower rate) to ensure material reuse and/or proper disposal.

capability to recycle 83 percent (by weight) of Saturn cars with a goal of 95 percent within five years.[3]

The design of the car promotes recycling. Thermoplastic side panels for Saturn doors is an industry first. The panels do not dent, which has been an effective advertising selling point. The plastic can be recycled, which pleases environmentalists. Saturn returns damaged accident parts from retailers nationwide using the roundtrip of its repair-parts trucks to Spring Hill, Tennessee, for recycling.

The methods and tools of life cycle management are well thought out at Saturn. The company is a model of corporate commitment to environmental protection. The Saturn initiative spans design and construction of the manufacturing/assembly facility through the entire product life cycle. Saturn describes the cycle as:

Design→Manufacture→Consumer Use→Post-Consumer Disposal

Saturn has a permanent manager of environmental affairs, who coordinates an initiative called *Designs for the Environment.*

OM coordination of design for manufacturing, assembly, and disassembly is paramount in many industry applications: Xerox and Panasonic (copy machines), Kodak and Fuji (cameras), John Deere and Caterpillar (tractors), and IBM and HP (computers). HP recycles 3.5 million pounds of electronic equipment per month. Sony has developed a cooperative take-back program with the state of Minnesota.

German engine manufacturer, Deutz, rebuilds 3,500 engines for tractors each year at their Uebersee Remanufacturing Service Center. The company states it can rebuild an engine in 3 days. See http://www.deutzusa.com/parts/xchange1.html. In the United States, Springfield Remanufacturing Corporation has similarly remarkable rebuild statistics. See http://www.srcreman.com.

Hewlett-Packard Compaq (still called *HP*) continues to be a leader in the DFD area. It rebuilds and recycles every workstation that is returned to the company. HP's manager of product stewardship stated: "In the hierarchy of the three R's of design for the environment, the first two—reduce [the number of product parts] and reuse [the parts]—rank above recycling."

Table 20-1 expands the usual three R categories of design for disassembly into four P/OM objectives.

The Silicon Valley Toxics Coalition is devoted to informing its members about current events for these topics. In a strongly worded announcement at http://www.svtc.org (click on "European E-Waste Laws Enacted" and request article), the SVTC points out that the European Parliament passed two laws on February 18, 2003, that will affect U.S. companies doing business in any country of the European Union. The laws deal with extended producer responsibility. The first, known as WEEE (waste from electronic and electrical equipment) requires free take-back of e-waste by final owners and demands that equipment producers be completely responsible for financing the collection, treatment, recovery, and disposal of all waste.

The second law, known as RoHS (restriction of the use of certain hazardous substances), requires ending the use of lead, mercury, cadmium, and other toxic materials on a timetable that extends over nearly six years. See http://www.svtc.org/cleancc/weee/euweee/directive/weee_article_ens.htm.

Remanufacturing: Disassemble the returned product. Reuse good parts, repair damaged parts, replace unusable parts to make a new product.

TABLE 20-1

Four R Categories as P/OM Objectives of the DFD Initiative

1. Rapid disassembly.
2. Reducing the number of parts needed.
3. Reusing, reworking, and **remanufacturing** parts. If step 3 can only be done *n* times, then after *n*.
4. Recycle the material or dispose of it safely.

It is beneficial to review the effects of some reuse strategies. Eastman Kodak converted its throwaway camera concept to recyclable cameras because environmentalists were disturbed and planning to take action. Internal parts are now reused up to 10 times, and 87 percent of the camera (by weight) is reused or recycled. These products have been reported to be among Kodak's most profitable products.

For Xerox, remanufacturing and recycling of parts was saving approximately $500 million per year. Xerox had a team called *Asset Recycle Management Organization*, which worked exclusively on DFD. There is an interesting webpage at: http://es.epa.gov/tech-info/case/comm/asset-d.html. Xerox, today, may have turned its attention to other matters. Once its financial stability is insured, it may return to the DFD initiative it helped to create.

Design for assembly (DFA) has lowered production costs and is related to DFD. That which is easier to put together, generally is easier to take apart. With thoughtful design, DFA and DFD become symmetrical functions. Bearing this in mind, lowering assembly costs is often a prelude to allowing robotic assembly.

Design for automation (DFAU) raises another level of accomplishment if the same robot can disassemble returned units. Computer PCs are a natural candidate, which is to be kept in mind when reviewing the EU challenges listed earlier with respect to the Silicon Valley Toxics Coalition.

20-3b Reverse Supply Chains

The attention that has been paid to improving supply chain performance has been outstanding. As a result, whether the supply chain is efficient or not, it could be made so if there is organizational buy-in. The supply chain of consumer products (e.g., to supermarkets) is quite efficient. On the other hand, the supply chain of the healthcare industry is highly inefficient. In 1998, the EHCR (Efficient Healthcare Consumer Response) tried to model its supply chain on that of the grocery industry's ECR and failed in the United States.

The Canadian EHCR remains as an organization dedicated to the idea of manufacturers, hospitals, and group buying organizations promoting efficient health care through the use of electronic commerce enabling technologies including bar codes and EDI. There is no evidence that the Canadian EHCR is any more successful than the U.S. initiative, which failed eventually.

The take-back movement has grown stronger for several reasons, including the unexpected monetary gains that companies have experienced once they agree to participate in end-of-life product recovery. The imposition of intelligent end-of-life (EOL) objectives for products may make the difference.

Reverse supply chains manifest themselves in a number of ways. For example, "smart" remanufacturing can lower costs and improve quality. Resource recovery has the potential to reduce the cost of materials. There is also a reduction in the cost of failures, which require repair or replacement. Add the realization that governments will be increasingly holding fabricators responsible for end-of-product life disposal and additional forces emerge for planned reverse logistics.

The average return rate of products is substantial (about 20 percent). The variability is also significant. Working with a mail-order firm provided an estimate for catalog item returns of about 30 percent. Department stores may have less than 8 percent returns. Most of the returns are not brought or sent back because they are defective. A charge of 10 percent or 15 percent for so-called "restocking" has not been well-received by customers. Therefore, a good number of stores consider returns as a cost of doing business. However, it is not evident that many managers know how much returns cost.

Companies do not use process analysis to determine the costs of various strategies for dealing with returned goods. Companies like Home Depot and Costco have return policies that do not require receipts as long as the product is carried by the company. Analyses of what happens to the stream of returned products is not available. However, with

Design for assembly (DFA): Product is designed to be put together efficiently, meaning at minimum cost and with higher quality standards.

Design for automation (DFAU): Robots can decrease assembly costs and bear the brunt of difficult work such as welding and painting with toxic materials. Quality and speed of assembly work increases while the cost goes down.

Reverse supply chains: There is a reverse delivery logistic at end-of-life for both used up and damaged products.

some observation, and logic, it is easy to conjecture that a large percent of returns are put back on the shelves. A small percent of faulty products are returned to vendors for credit. The vendor's process with returned items is more complex.

Information about take-back to vendor remanufacturing is available through strong sources such as the National Center for Remanufacturing & Resource Recovery. It is located at the Rochester Institute of Technology. See http://www.reman.rit.edu. A reasonable estimate for 2002 is that remanufacturing is a $75 billion industry in the United States. When looked at on a worldwide basis, remanufacturing may be three times the amount just stated for the United States.

In Table 20-2, the location of remanufacturing in the reverse supply chain is shown in two parts. There is the traditional outbound system that moves to the customer. But first, the customer must return product to the company. The latter is the non-traditional inbound system. The supply loop is formed when the two parts are taken together. *Supply loop management* is the new term being used to describe managing the forward and reverse loops in a strategic way.

An informative website with respect to end-of-life (EOL) generic product directives and supply loop management is available from Cardone Industries at http://www.cardone.com/English/Club/Corporate/ceo1.asp. Although it is directed to automobile remanufacturing (ELV), the big picture for EOL emerges immediately.

Next, it is useful to delve deeper into the question "What is meant by reverse logistics?" Specifically, the term means the take-back, send-back, and receive-back portion of the supply chain. Reasons for the reverse flow include normal customer returns, government rules to take back and dispose of pollutants, and cost benefits to the company if it can save money by retrieving and reusing materials.

Customers return products for a variety of reasons. There are expected rates of return by industry type. *Abnormal return rates might be symptoms of serious defects* in manufactur-

TABLE 20-2

Supply Loop Management
Forward Supply Chain called Outbound; Reverse Supply Chain called Inbound; Taken Together, Forward and Reverse Are Called the Supply Loop.

Outbound: Suppliers→Manufacture→Ship to Consumers

Inbound: Consumer Returns Product or Company Retrieval Occurs→Inspect Returned Product→Repair, Refurbish, and Relabel→Post-Consumer Disposal

Some Ideas for Efficient Reverse Supply Chains

Step Number	Step Description
1.	Company takes back old parts in the same truck that delivers new product.
1A.	Customers might be persuaded to return used-up products for disposal.
1B.	Analyze trade-in potentials as a reverse supply chain marketing strategy.
1C.	Is there a remarketing strategy for replacement?
2.	Take-backs must be sorted by part types, model, age, condition, etc.
2A.	Evaluation process requires testing and smart decisions to refurbish or dispose.
3.	New, reused, and refurbished parts are put together in an assembly kit.
3A.	Assemble, relabel, and repackage.
4.	Steps 2., 2A., 3., and 3A. are remanufacturing. That process can be optimized.
5.	Remarketing of the refurbished product if not replacement.
6.	Redistribution of the remarketed product starts the outbound supply chain.

ing and delivery. Knowing what the expected return rate should be is important. When this is exceeded, understanding the cause of abnormal returns is critical for quality control. Returns must be inspected to find out what is wrong with the take-backs.

The economics of repair and refurbishment change over time. A refurbished computer from an old era might be an interesting antique, but it might not be suitable as a business machine for data processing and keeping spreadsheet accounts. At one time, repairing old phones (Merlin) by AT&T at Little Rock was cost-beneficial. When phone prices dropped significantly, and wireless phones took a solid share of the telephone set market, the economic benefits of remanufacturing this product shifted. AT&T gave up on this business.

Good original design helps to ensure that remanufacturing is feasible. There are many pressures to use design as the first step toward remanufacturing, not the least of which is the fact that the city dump will not be permitted to serve as the ultimate destination of all defunct products. Thereby, the life expectancy of old products will be extended. It is interesting that this also applies to old people with new body parts.

Transportation is a critical component of both forward and reverse supply chain management. As in the case of Saturn Corporation where the auto-delivery carrier becomes the vehicle for returning used parts, integration can occur between forward and reverse planning. Consider the logistics planning required by the Springfield Remanufacturing Corporation (http://www.srcreman.com), which remakes dozens of engine parts and products for tractors and combines. Their customers are OEMs (original equipment manufacturers) as disparate as Isuzu, Case, Komatsu, John Deere, and Nissan.

20-3c Construction and Demolition (C&D) Reverse Supply Chain

"Publicity-wise, C&D recycling is a poor stepchild to the more famous recovery and reuse of paper, plastics, aluminum cans, etc. …But by weight and volume, C&D recycling is the biggest recycling industry in North America. According to the U.S. Environmental Protection Agency (EPA), 215 million tons per year of municipal solid waste (MSW) is generated in the U.S. C&D, which is made up primarily of concrete, asphalt, wood, gypsum, demolition metals and asphalt shingles, is estimated by industry observers to reach more than 300 million tons annually. It is generated from roadbuilding and highway maintenance, plus from building renovation, demolition and construction."[4]

Recycling of paper, cans, etc., has not been easy to fund because it does not readily turn a profit. On the other hand, C&D is generally a profitable enterprise. **Recycling concrete** and asphalt is important for its sheer volume and the difficulty of disposal without the reuse capability. There are economic advantages as well. The Construction Materials Recycling Association (CMRA) estimates that 105 millions tons of concrete are recycled every year. See the Spotlight feature, Paving in Place, in Chapter 12.

> **Recycling concrete:** Recycling concrete from the old road to the new road is an excellent example of end-of-life (EOL) product recovery.

20-4   ETHICS AND OPERATIONS MANAGEMENT

Greening the plant environment should come naturally to P/OM because health and safety start with workers on the production line. Discussions about methods for establishing workstation safety can be found in the earliest industrial engineering literature. However, the Occupational Safety and Health Administration of the U.S. Department of Labor (see prior reference to OSHA; http://www.osha.gov) has met with a lot of problems to fulfill its mission—basically, to save lives, prevent injuries, and protect the health of America's workers. For the complete mission statement, see the webpage.

20-4a   Ethics: Health and Safety of Employees and Customers

There are many causes of safety lapses and health threats. Ignorance, incompetence, and indifference are some of the culprits. Although these three situations are all bad for responsible production system behavior, they are not directly greed-based. Where greed is a root cause, it is correct to state that ethical failure is immediately responsible. For example, if managers perceive an opportunity to save money by cutting corners, which may affect customers deleteriously, then they have clearly violated ethical standards. Ignorance of the law is no excuse from a legal point of view, but when it comes to ethics, if the managers were ignorant of the ill effects caused by their decisions, then there is a basis for debate. It could be an ethical failing not to be educated and informed about the consequences of ignorance.

It is always a crucial question: What effect do innocent bad decisions and not-so-innocent decisions to cut corners have on the health and well-being of employees and customers? It was bad judgment to have big investments in a company 401(k). The fact is that bad investments in a retirement plan do affect health and welfare of employees. Management has an ethical obligation to show that all possible contingencies were examined in matters related to employee and customer health and safety.

Retirement plans may be the core of ethical study and research in the future because many companies have indicated interest in abrogating their "contracts" with employees after many years of employment. It may be that due diligence and proper performance of management will be required to fulfill employees' expectations regarding pensions. It is likely that if corners have been cut that jeopardize the pensions of employees (already and soon to be) retired, there will be legal recourse.

Starting with Enron and continuing with WorldCom, Tyco, etc., the meltdown of the stock market in the period from 2000 through 2003 was accompanied by a host of ethical horrors. These are not just accounting errors. The operations management area is impacted by improper funding to produce the product and/or service. Deals are made that bypass customers, stockholders, and employees. A few managers make outrageous amounts of money.

20-4b Ethics and the Supply Chain

There are no examples, on record, of where inside trading in stock is done by operations managers. The financial area is not the domain of operations. On the other hand, purchasing agents are not expected to accept substantial presents that are intended to influence the choice of suppliers. Many companies have strict rules that require gift-refusals by buyers. For example, the U.S. government is adamant about the ethical standard of "take no gifts." This strict standard is interesting when compared with the unwritten rules of many non-American companies that believe that gifts are a proper way to start a relationship.

How can policies be so out-of-kilter with each other? When business relations are viewed as a matter of personal trust rather than legal obligations, then gifts are not hard to understand. Friends and families interchange gifts throughout the year as a sign of caring. The family basis for a gift-giving culture does not exist in the United States and many other parts of the world. Therefore, in gift-culture countries, the United States is not considered to be polite, kind, or trustworthy. A dilemma exists in this situation because the legal mind-set is not considered to be ethical in these cultures. The result is a culture split between what is considered ethical and what is felt to be trustworthy.

Inventory managers have been cited for ethical crimes in a variety of circumstances. In one instance, order sizes were triple economic order quantities. Investigation indicated that payoffs were given to executives for large order sizes, but there were no price discounts awarded to the company. The ethical violation is evident, and yet it was argued that in this culture, the salary of managers was expected to be augmented by payoffs. The excess materials were deteriorating as a result of aging. Overbuying created an ethical problem because individuals benefited while the company was damaged. The same would apply if the supply chain was used for personal gain at the expense of product obsolescence and product deterioration. In the example given earlier, the products were rubber and synthetic tires.

In the supply chain, the ethical problems are related to overordering, paying too much, and accepting poor qualities—for personal gain. Ethical issues can take on other forms such as pocketing discounts instead of passing them to the company; making deals with uncertified vendors; eliminating the best bids from consideration; and refusing to consider eligible competitors.

In the international supply chain, there are some additional ethical factors. The supply chain distance can be greater and transit times longer. This is especially true when sea transportation is used. Hewlett-Packard ships printers from the West Coast of the United States to Europe and Asia. Lead times are extensive and pipeline inventory substantial. See the Spotlight on Kevin Howard of Hewlett Packard at the end of this chapter. Lead times must also include delays that are sometimes a function of legal requirements and interpersonal activities including payoffs to customs and to other regulators of the flow of goods across national boundaries. Lead time management often interacts with ethical issues.

There is another gray area related to selling expensive products (like airplanes) without using bribery. "*The Wall Street Journal* reported last week that Airbus was in talks with China for the sale of between 30 and 50 A320 airliners, worth up to US$2.7 billion." The issue of ethics arises when reading on: "Airbus has spent some US$80 million in setting up a training and support center in Beijing, (and) also signed a deal with China on co-producing wing parts for A320 planes" (*China Daily*, August 28, 2001).[5] Bribes are illegal in the many countries, but training investments and coproducing deals are widely used by many companies. Airbus is not alone; Boeing has the same kind of partner-sharing arrangements.

20-4c Ethics and Environment

Enlightened companies take great pains to be ethical in every respect. This begins by management setting examples of doing what is known to be right when confronted with opportunities to gain advantage by using nonethical behaviors. This is why many auto companies in the United States work together at pollution reduction in the external environment.

The same applies to the internal environment, i.e., in the plant. A good example of successful interactions between OSHA, management, unions, and workers is found in counteracting dangers caused by painting autos. Enormous strides have been made by the automobile industry in protecting employees from the harmful fumes and chemicals of the paint. Painting exemplifies systems that pollute both the internal and the external environments.

Saturn was the first car manufacturer to use water-based rather than solvent-based paints. Water-based paints have about one-fourth of the emissions of solvent-based paints. Painting is done in a clean room using paint booths and robots to do the spraying. Extra paint flows into a water river under the paint room, and the paint is later separated from the water using electric charges with special chemicals that cause the paint to float. Workers are not put in harm's way, and the effluent that reaches the ground is not polluted. There are two points to discuss that derive from the Saturn example.

First, a greenfield plant (like Saturn) has the advantage of being able to do things right the first time. Second, an old plant must be redesigned and rebuilt at high costs, including the cost of lost production while changing over from one system to the other. The ethical issues in going from old to new are further complicated by legal differences that arise when new laws are enacted that only apply to new structures. This type of law, called a *grandfather clause*, exempts old businesses from a new government regulation.

It is not unusual that established systems are regulated under different rules than new systems because of point 1, which is that greenfield facilities can embody new technologies and meet new standards within reasonable economic parameters whereas old systems would go bankrupt. Grandfather clauses are the explanation for old nightclubs being responsible for *all* of the tragic fires where hundreds of people are killed or injured (e.g., in Chicago and Providence during 2003). Old clubs have not been held to the same standards as the new ones with respect to building materials, smoke detectors, and sprinkler systems.

Hazard reduction for workers, customers, and communities is a matter of ethics. These ethics are a set of acceptable social standards for proper behavior. In the United States, standards have been moving toward higher ideals of winning on merit in a community sense, in the plant/office, and in the supermarket. Consumer examples include increasingly stringent labeling of food ingredients, cigarette package warnings, expiration dating, tamper-proof drug packaging, seat belts, and front/side airbags. OSHA has been strict in demanding safety in the workplace.

Ethics is not a separate part of business. When ethical precepts are treated as separate, it is not possible to build an ethical infrastructure. Ethics requires the systems point of view because the standards must be known and accepted by everyone who works for the company. It is not possible to conform to an ethical standard if some of the employees think it is all right to cut corners on quality, ship inferior product, overcharge some customers, solicit kickbacks, take bribes, and even steal office supplies. Pilferage can range from minor items to large-scale theft that significantly reduces a company's profitability. No matter how small, the business environment is damaged by a culture that permits theft.

20-4d Ethics and Quality Integrity

When accepted practice is bypassed, it is critical to document the reasons for changing procedures. An acceptable explanation for the change is that there is a better way to do that job. Striving for continuous improvement is to be rewarded. On the other hand, if ignorance, incompetence, and/or indifference are responsible for changing procedures, the ethical response is to require an explanation. Then, when it is clear that the original procedure was best, reset the system and eliminate the causes of the problems.

Were the wrong people hired to do the job? Were the people who were hired fine but their training on the job was not up to par? There are times when motivation is missing. An unmotivated workforce is often the cause of business problems. This explains why downsizing for cost reduction becomes a possible cause of reduced customer loyalty, and that translates into lower market share and reduced revenues. The critics of downsizing refer to it as an ethical breach. Supporters point to the fact that with current circumstances, the firm would be forced into bankruptcy or closing. There is an ethical dilemma as a result. Decisions to downsize have to be decided by competent evaluations of the pros and cons.

If the problem stems from the fact that customers perceive that they are receiving less quality for the price of the product and, thereby, lower value, the question must be raised about the cause of the perception. The size and weight of the product may have been downsized. The taste or effectiveness of the product may have been changed. There is an ethical question about the consistency of quality (and quantity) that customers have come to expect. Changes of this sort are seldom seen as life threatening but they can be when a new ingredient is added to a product that produces allergic reactions in some percent of users. If the ingredient was added to save money, that raises further ethical questions.

Contaminated food is responsible for a great deal of illness and death. Sources of the contamination are traceable to operations associated with preparing and handling that food. The ethical standards are clear. Because they fail quite often, what are the possible explanations? Causes could be managerial ineptness, or incompetence, or managerial ignorance. As stated in a prior section, ignorance of what is required for safe and healthy operations is not an excuse. Therefore an ethical boundary is crossed when an operator does not know how to run a safe plant, or airline. Inebriated pilots are intolerable examples of unethical behavior.

When quality problems arise for customers because of employee self-interest, the worst form of ethical failure has occurred. When bad decisions for company quality turn out to be motivated by self-interested decision makers, the focus of the ethical transgressions becomes a legal matter. For example, there are documented stories about managers who have been stressed by their bosses to ship production units to meet quotas while looking the other way on quality requirements. There are cases in the courts filed by customers claiming personal loss caused by poor quality for tires, auto gas tanks, hot coffee, and bugs in soda. Claims are not proof of quality malfeasance, but each situation must be judged on its own merits.

It is difficult to keep employees' morale high when the company they work for is under siege for asbestos litigation. By end of the first quarter of 2003, the asbestos litigation cost was over $200 billion, and nine defendants had gone out of business.[6] See http://www.kazanlaw.com/Home/asbestosdiseases.html. Some settlements are being reached but the interaction of ethics and asbestos seems to go on and on. For example, in a class-action lawsuit, ABB (facing 220,000 claimants) has agreed to pay the lawyer in the case in addition to the plaintiffs in order to obtain an agreement for an end to legal actions. The suits arise from the boiler work done by the Combustion Engineering division of ABB. *The New York Times* has the headline "A Caldron of Ethics and Asbestos."[7]

Similar reasoning applies to tobacco companies faced with the attorneys general for tobacco-caused illness. The settlement with the states' attorneys general was hundreds of billions of dollars in 1998, and lawsuits by individuals continue. Exxon employees were unhappy about the *Valdez* oil spill in Alaska. That was March 24, 1989. See the turn of events by visiting the Exxon Valdez Oil Spill Trustee Council at http://www.oilspill.state.ak.us.

Although it was not Pan Am's fault, there was a quality integrity problem after the bomb blast destroyed Flight 103 in December 1988 over Lockerbie, Scotland. Travelers on Pan American Airlines did not feel safe. Airline revenues went into a major decline—and ultimately into bankruptcy. All employees lost their jobs. Common stockholders lost every cent of their investments. It has been speculated that a change of name might have helped the airline survive. Would it have been unethical to change the airline's name?

In a variety of cases, there are potential whistle-blowers who do not speak up because the ethics of tattling on fellow managers frequently overrides the ethic of righting a wrong. How often that situation occurs is unknown because the whistle-blowers do not speak up. What is evident is that when whistle-blowers do speak up, management often ignores those warnings.

Enron and Arthur Andersen might still be in business if top management had listened to their whistle-blowers. WorldCom might be healthier if evidence of wrongdoing had not been swept under the rug. In the short term, unethical management may get away with bad practice. In the long run, it is reasonable to believe, unethical management will not prosper. Management, employees, stockholders, and customers lose as company stock values plunge, products are unavailable, and jobs are gone. The unethical are losers.

Ethics, Quality Integrity, and CDC/FDA

For P/OM, one of the most important ethical issues is to deliver safe and healthy products and services. That standard is called **quality integrity**. The definitions of integrity are many, including honesty, veracity, and truthfulness. For business, this may mean producing the product according to standards that have been set by government regulators. It also means not shipping product to customers that deviates from standards. One of the most sensitive areas to monitor for ethical adherence to standards is in foods and drugs. This includes meat and poultry processing plants, food canning operations, egg production, food shops, and restaurants At the same time, the CDC-related Agency for Toxic Substances and Disease Registry (ATSDR) was set up in 1980 by the Comprehensive Environmental Response, Compensation, and Liability Act, which is known as the Superfund. ATSDR prevents exposure to hazardous wastes and deals with environmental spills of hazardous materials.

The U.S. Department of Health and Human Services includes the Food and Drug Administration **(FDA)** and the Centers for Disease Control and Prevention (CDC). The CDC has 8,500 people employed in 12 centers, institutes, and offices (FY2000, from the website http://www.cdc.gov). The centers are used to identify trends and new concerns about diseases (such as botulism). In 2002, the CDC estimated that 76 million people got sick, 325,000 were hospitalized, and between 5,000 and 8,000 people died as a result of

Quality integrity: Ensure delivery of products and services good for the safety and health of customers. P/OM must also provide a secure and accident-free working environment for employees. Such standards are the foundation of quality integrity.

FDA: The FDA monitors quality integrity for food producers, warehouses, distributors, retailers, and restaurants.

CDC: Centers for Disease Control and Prevention, located in Atlanta, Georgia; the lead federal agency for protecting the health and safety of people—at home and abroad. The CDC has responsibilities that are new and not well-defined since the potential of bioterrorism has emerged as a global threat.

Blast off into the cloud brings to mind that HACCP was developed by NASA in its pioneering work in the 1960s to create safe food for the astronauts in the space program. Later it was applied by the FDA as a preventive system of food hazard control in the sale and preparation of fish and other foods to consumers. It is now widely used by P/OM in appropriate applications.

Courtesy: NASA.

Hazard Analysis and Critical Control Point (HACCP) System: System designed to prevent food hazards from arising without being detected. It is a quality control system that detects the presence of defective process management.

---

food-borne illness. The identification of causes is difficult and the estimates are rough. This is a difficult area for estimation because many cases are not reported. Also, a common cause has to be identified if there is an outbreak of illness in an area of the country. CDC estimated that seafood accounted for 4.8 percent of reported cases of food-borne illness (from 1987 to 1994).

The FDA has taken numerous steps to provide consumers with protection against tainted foods and food poisoning. The causes of such illness are associated with the quality integrity of food products from a number of points of view including sources and handling. One of the strongest initiatives is the operation and the application of Hazard Analysis Critical Control Point (HACCP) principles to establish procedures for safe processing and importing of fish and fishery products.

HACCP also monitors unpasteurized fruit juices. In 1998, the U.S. Department of Agriculture established HACCP for meat and poultry processing plants. The FDA intends to extend HACCP "to eventually use it for much of the U.S. food supply." (From the *FDA Backgrounder*, "HACCP: A State-of-the-Art Approach to Food Safety," October 2001) See http://vm.cfsan.fda.gov/~lrd/haccp.html.

Hazard Analysis Critical Control Point (HACCP) System

It is not necessary to restrict discussion of the **Hazard Analysis Critical Control Point (HACCP) System** to the seafood industry, which is comprised of organizations engaged in fishing, aquaculture, fish farming, fish and shellfish processing, and packing. It applies to all foods and drugs and can be extended to hazard analysis for all products and services. How much effort should go into the control of hazards is an ethical issue. The government sets standards that companies can elect to surpass. The FDA's evaluation of the HACCP seafood program for fiscal years 2000/2001 (September 23, 2002) reveals positive improvements with an average compliance of 88 percent. See http://www.cfsan.fda.gov/~comm/seaeval2.html.

Hazard analysis critical control point's application as a preventive system for hazard control was pioneered by the Pillsbury Company in the 1960s to create safe food for the space program. The program was applied successfully and since that time has been consistently extended and developed. It is one of the largest scale quality control programs that can be found in the field of operations management. HACCP is an excellent example of total quality management where inspection and testing are not sufficient by themselves to achieve satisfactory quality.

"HACCP is a science-based system of preventive controls for food safety that commercial food processors develop and operate to identify potential problems and keep them from occurring. The evaluation covers implementation of the HACCP program by about 4100 U.S. seafood processors...this report shows that the seafood HACCP program has increased the margin of safety for American consumers...But this report also identifies segments of the industry that need continued focus and government oversight."[8]

Interactive quality monitoring is needed to assure that food poisoning does not occur at all. The FDA intended to make HACCP mandatory for the seafood industry. Nevertheless, only a small percent of the industry is obliged to take remedial steps to correct problems.

Seven steps for using HACCP's principles are as follows:

1. *Analyze hazards.* These are the causes of food being unsafe for consumption. The key is to identify potential hazards associated with a food and identify measures to control those hazards. Hazards include biological, such as a microbe; chemical, such as a toxin; or physical, such as ground glass or metal fragments. The principal seafood-related hazards that cause food-borne illnesses are bacteria, viruses, and natural toxins.

2. *Identify critical control points in the process.* The CCP are points in a food's production where the potential hazard can be controlled or eliminated. The CCP start with the raw state and go through processing, shipping and point-of-consumption by the consumer. The CCP could be cooking, cooling, chilling, packaging, sanitation procedures, or employee and plant hygiene. The critical control points are identified with respect to the hazards examined in step 1.

3. *Establish preventive measures with critical limits for each control point.* Critical limits are boundaries of safety for each critical control point. They specify thresholds for preventive measures to be taken for temperatures, times, moisture levels, available chlorine, pH, etc. The critical limits can be derived from sources such as regulatory standards and guidelines, experimental studies, literature surveys, and experts. For example, this could include setting a minimum cooking temperature (to ensure the elimination of harmful microbes).

4. *Establish procedures to monitor critical control points.* This is a planned sequence of observations or measurements to assess whether a critical control point is under control and to produce an accurate record for future use in verification. Just like with quality control charts, this system monitors the process at critical prevention points to spot trends indicative of potential trouble, or of real trouble. It is expected that corrective action will be taken to bring the process back into control before a real problem deviation occurs, or to correct a real problem. Also important is the written documentation for use in verification of the HACCP plan. For example, identify how, and by whom, the cooking time and temperature are to be set and monitored.

5. *Establish corrective actions to be taken when monitoring shows that a critical limit has been exceeded.* For example, what should be done if the minimum cooking temperature is not fulfilled? Three things need to be done:
    a. Determine the disposition of food produced during a deviation. Should the food be disposed of and how should that be done safely? Can the food be reprocessed?
    b. Correct the cause of noncompliance to ensure that the critical control point is under control.
    c. Maintain records of food disposal, reprocessing, and the corrective actions for noncompliance.
   Because food poisoning is an unacceptable quality deviation, the disposition of spoiled food becomes an obvious subject to be determined and documented. Spoiled food can be salvaged by the unwary. This is an interesting aspect of the reverse supply chain. HACCP sets down good methods for industry to utilize. What happens to defective product should be decided as part of every quality control system. This is an ethical commitment, too.

6. *Establish procedures to verify that the HACCP system is working properly.* This step includes verification that the critical limits are appropriate and functioning as intended. The step also is used to make sure that all aspects of HACCP are being followed. Finally, it ensures periodic revalidation of the plan to make certain that it is still relevant to raw materials, technology, and all other process factors and conditions. For example, the recording devices for time and temperature must be tested to verify that the cooking unit is working properly.

7. *Establish effective record-keeping systems to document all significant aspects of the HACCP system.* Maintain records of hazards and their control methods. Document monitoring of safety requirements and actions taken to correct potential problems. Basic principles must be backed by sound scientific knowledge. For example, use correct, published microbiological studies on time and temperature factors to control food-borne pathogens. The records show critical control points, critical limits, and all relevant data generated by the process during its operation. [9]

The implications of the HACCP system for assuring the quality of outputs of processing technologies are significant. The essence of the ethics in this case is to employ the system to protect customers and employees. The design of process technology should have as an objective minimum costs for achieving the HACCP objectives. The attention to documentation and methods for updating changes in conditions make HACCP a superior operational system.

All organizations entering the seafood industry and related businesses (as the use of HACCP grows for foods in general) will learn the HACCP regulations in order to be in compliance. This adds another dimension when planning and choosing process technologies. It is design for compliance. The rules must be understandable and compliance must be possible using reasonable technology and training.

Appropriate information technology makes the record-keeping system a boon and not a burden. HACCP is a pragmatic system that has the potential to cure some basic problems. The shellfish industry is being destroyed by the fear of toxic poisoning. People who like to eat raw oysters and clams are giving them up because of misgivings. If HACCP can save the shellfish business, jobs would be saved and consumers' health protected. The rewards are large and the costs are small.

This is an excellent example of the dynamics of ethics. Improvements in ethics are aided and abetted by governmental regulation. Unfortunately, some improvements are inhibited by government bureaucracy.

The HACCP model reflects good management of ethics. It might well be adopted by those who manage new food processes that use genetic materials and biotechnology. Hormones fed to cows to increase milk supplies and irradiation of food products to retard spoilage are two areas of concern. If they are definitely established to be safe, then HACCP can be used to monitor and control the process dosages of biological materials and radiation. For environmental processes, it may be useful to consider the application of the HACCP principles and seven steps to pollution control and hazardous waste disposal management.

For process technologies in general, HACCP has relevance as an application of TQM under governmental regulation. Quality, a primary OM responsibility, always has been regulated, to some degree, by the federal government. Examples are weight, purity, and so on. New rules make change management essential.

Quality has been under constant discussion in the courts (product liability cases, etc). The difference is that HACCP regulates QC methodology whereas, previously, quality was only regulated as an end result. HACCP regulates quality at the process level.

The Occupational Safety and Health Act of 1970 (OSHA) provides precedence for governmental regulation of systems and processes. Inspectors are used to check workplace conformance to safety rules. There have been many complaints about bureaucracy and strenuous efforts have been made to have OSHA function as a positive complement and not antagonistically with business. It is hoped that HACCP regulators can learn from the OSHA experiences.

While OSHA is concerned with the safety of the process, HACCP deals with the quality of outputs from the process. Related to this subject is product liability, which will be increasingly associated with HACCP-type rules. Even at the current time, the courts require documentation of efforts to "design for safety" and the use of QC methodology to assure safety.

From these trends, it is evident that the systems perspective is necessary. It is required to deal with changes that are occurring in the regulatory and legal systems that promote ethical business in the United States and globally. OM has the lead role with HACCP. It must coordinate activities with R & D, process engineering, the legal departments, and the government regulators. The customer must not be lost in a regulatory jungle.

Food and Drug Testing

Food and Drug Administration regulations for testing new drugs are extensive. Running counter to the fast-track project management theme, pharmaceutical product cycles take many years. During that time, P/OM fabricates test materials (in batches) working with R & D and prepares suitable facilities and quality control methods for each stage. Many quality tests and drug effectiveness tests are required. New drugs go through years of laboratory studies followed by three phases of clinical testing with people.[10]

"The Tufts Center for the Study of Drug Development (CSDD) has been tracking drug development costs for 25 years. The newest research on development costs reveals a price tag of $802 million per drug. . . . The average drug takes 12 years and must overcome a very selective process. Tufts research reports that of every 5,000 potential new drugs tested in animals, only five are promising enough to be tested in humans; only one of those five is eventually approved for marketing."[11]

Some consider the FDA to have overly conservative testing standards and requirements. The main pros and cons associated with stringent test specifications, requirements, and standards are captured by the following two points:

- *Undertesting* includes inadequate testing methods and deficient testing technology. Both can lead to disasters. The ethics of approving drugs with insufficient evidence is contrasted with the ethical issue of having a drug that might cure an illness but withholding it from a patient who will die without it.

- *Overtesting* delays the acceptance of effective drugs. The dilemma is that if that drug works, then people are dying unnecessarily.

Two examples are presented for the first point. First, a vaccine was rushed into production to counter a predicted swine flu epidemic. One of the vaccine manufacturers, operating under crash project conditions, made process-technology errors that were not picked up in testing because that would have delayed the vaccination program. The result was that a far larger number of people died from the vaccine than from the swine flu, which never became an epidemic. The coincidence of failures in this case can all be attributed to the axiom that "haste makes waste."

Second, the story about the drug thalidomide reflects the complicated trade-off between the risks and benefits of testing delays. European governments have organizations equivalent to the FDA in the United States. Some of them had approved the use of thalidomide as a tranquilizer after a shorter period of testing with a smaller sample than was permitted in the United States.

The drug was never legally accepted by the FDA for the United States. It turned out that this drug adversely affected the fetus if taken by women in the early months of their pregnancy. European testing had overlooked the early months even though use of tranquilizers was common during that period. Thalidomide children were born with serious deformities, which reinforced the conservative nature of the FDA in the United States.

There are two kinds of potential errors that pose ethical quandaries for OM and the organization. Should undertesting errors be preferred to overtesting errors? Some pharmaceutical and biotechnology firms would like FDA standards to be less stringent. They feel testing costs too much and takes too long. They believe that more funds would be invested in R & D for new drugs if test standards were relaxed. The opposition asserts that people are suffering and dying unnecessarily while the testing is proceeding. They propose delivering test products to those suffering serious illnesses. The counterargument is that shorter test periods mean more profits for the pharmaceutical industry.

The FDA, in recognition of this ethical issue, has speeded up the testing of AIDS drugs and cancer treatments. It has permitted their use for seriously ill patients before approval is granted. Aside from that, many reject the claim that the high cost of testing discourages the development of new drug technologies. They cite the fact that the pharmaceutical industry in the United States has done an excellent job of creating new drugs while making a great deal of money.

OM in the pharmaceutical industry emphasizes quality control as much as, or more than, any other industry. The cost of quality in pharmaceutical production is very high and there is pressure to find ways to cut these costs while increasing quality standards. The subject is an ideal candidate for reengineering. Because the FDA is known to accept change slowly and with great care, the topic of how ethics relates to the policies of change and transition management is totally relevant.

20-5 READYING OPERATIONS MANAGEMENT FOR FUTURE CONDITIONS

Factories and offices of the future will look very different from their present-day counterparts. P/OM will be practiced under different circumstances and in different ways. Today's management has to be prepared for substantial change. Predictions of changes to expect are useful but hardly likely to hit the bull's-eye. The only way to benchmark these expectations is by noting current state and then extrapolating patterns of development. Some directions for change seem to be evident. Benchmarking against fundamental trends produces the following insights.

The September 19, 1994, cover of *Fortune* proclaimed, "The End of the Job: No longer the best way to organize work, the traditional job is becoming a social artifact. Its decline creates unfamiliar risks—and rich opportunities."[12]

In the decade that has gone by since this article was published, traditional jobs continue to disappear as a result of new technology, integrated information systems, a different mind-set that strives for teamwork with much involvement in projects, and the global network of business.

Historic events changed the frozen landscape of superpowers vying with each other until 1990. The Berlin Wall was built August 13, 1961. East Germany opened the wall November 9, 1989, and by the end of 1990 it was torn down. For more detailed information, see http://www.dailysoft.com/berlinwall. Since that time, the development of the Internet fostered the instant and inexpensive communication required for a global community. However, the events of September 11, 2001, triggered a new set of conditions that put safety and security from hidden terrorists at the top of the list for priorities in economic development. That has put a damper on global development. However, the effect is just one of damping, not stopping.

20-5a Mobile Robots

Many repetitive, unpleasant, and dangerous jobs can now be assigned to machines. Fixed machines can do some jobs, but they are limited by the lack of mobility. Robots[13] that move along in-floor guidewires are less constrained, but still restricted compared to people. With better sight, robots play a greater role in factory and office designs. Contributions come from many sources worldwide.

The Purdue Robot Vision Laboratory (part of Purdue University's School of Electrical and Computer Engineering) "performs state-of-the-art research in sensory intelligence for the machines of the future. This laboratory has made pioneering contributions in 3D object recognition, vision-guided navigation for indoor **mobile robots**, task and assembly planning" (http://rvl.www.ecn.purdue.edu/RVL).

The Robot Vision Group at Technische Universität München is part of the Institute for Real-Time Computer Systems (RCS) at the Department of Electrical Engineering and Information Technology. On their website, they list various research projects including Human and Robot Hand-Eye Coordination (http://www.rcs.ei.tum.de/research/rovi).

The Robot Vision Group, which is part of the Intelligent Systems Lab at the School of Engineering, University of Guelph, Ontario, Canada, explores "real-time dynamic visual processes (e.g., tracking, optical flow, binocular vision) . . . for various applications such as elderly or disabled aids, search and rescue robotics, intelligent automobiles, . . . tracking animals (e.g., pigs), traffic surveillance and wearable computing for the disabled" (http://www.eos.uoguelph.ca/webfiles/robotvision).

A significant text, called *Robot Vision*,[14] is used as part of an MIT course on robot design. It was written by Professor Berthold Horn. This text has been described as presenting a solid framework for subjects such as machine vision, binary image processing, and pattern recognition.

Past predictions about robot advances have fallen short of reality. However, it would be a mistake to overlook the true state of affairs, which is that steady advances are being made in improving machine capabilities. Robots can perceive objects in color and in three dimensions with speed and accuracy. With high performance vision, robots can achieve significant mobility and dexterity. This is transforming the fields of manufacturing, logistics, mining, space prospecting, and service operations.

Robots have to be able to see objects in their path in 3D. That allows them to react intelligently to avoid obstacles, find targets, recognize patterns, and provide intelligent human services for the elderly and handicapped. Additionally, they can provide remote virtual reality displays of actual environments that are deadly for people. For example a

Mobile robots: Robots with mobility are especially useful for safety and security. Service robots are being built smaller, smarter, more mobile, and less expensively. Mobile nurse and orderly robots are increasingly used in healthcare services.

robot can go inside volcanic craters, nuclear reactors, the depths of the ocean, airless space, and can defuse a bomb.

20-5b Operational Issues for Safety and Security

Security has become one of the most important OM service concerns. The P/OM responsibility for quality extends to the safety of travelers on planes, buses, and subways. Quality covers the well-being of people at the opera, theater, concert, visiting a theme park, or in the supermarket. Quality covers the well-being of people when they pick up their mail. Other forms of transportation, water and air quality systems, office buildings, and theme parks are undergoing similar alterations of operations to provide customer and citizen safety under potential terrorist attack conditions.

Prior to the World Trade Center attack, industrial security was considered to be a special calling that was not the concern of all managers. Today, security is a general management concern. It is also a field in which operations management should be involved. Entirely new approaches *now* have to confront the problems of industrial insecurity. Much more must be known before there is satisfaction that all systems are as secure as they can be made.

The American Society for Industrial Security (ASIS) would be likely to take exception to the idea that security has only recently emerged as an operational concern. It is the P/OM field that has not been aware of developments in security and not ASIS, which was founded in 1955. ASIS International has 33,000 members in 208 chapters worldwide.

ASIS is very active in training and education. Courses include assets protection, securing the global workplace, emerging trends in security, and in providing certification programs. The CPP (Certified Protection Professional) program has two types of certification, viz., PCI (professional certified investigator) and PSP (physical security professional). See http://www.asisonline.org.

New P/OM Developments to Enhance Safety and Security

How secure is the mail room? The health threat of anthrax (sent through the mail after September 11) closed major buildings in Washington, DC, and post office facilities. Scientists have determined that the anthrax powder had been made recently (within 2 years). Investigators said that the theory it had been stolen from an old batch in a lab could be dismissed. The threat that the perpetrator could do it again was evident from the dating. See the reference dated June 24, 2002, http://www.smh.com.au/articles/2002/06/23/1023864529925.html. The forensics are good but not sufficient to have identified the culprit. Could Sherlock Holmes have done better without radiocarbon dating?

In companies, someone has to take responsibility for detecting mail room and waiting room dangerous packages. United States Postal Service (USPS) states, "The mail center is a major gateway into any business or government agency." USPS provides a *Mail Center Security Handbook* and a quick reference guide for *Best Practices for Mail Center Security*. See http://www.usps.com/news/2001/press/pr01_1022gsa.htm.

One option to be encouraged and developed is the use of smart robots designed specifically to help deal with threats of these kinds. Technological innovation post September 11, 2001, is highlighting issues of security. The expectation is that some useful breakthroughs will occur. There are a number of promising areas for forensic technological systems.

These include DNA identification, fingerprint data-mining, retinal identification, and face and body-shape identification. Pre-911 privacy protection has changed to allowing identification as a requirement for entrance to systems that are vulnerable to those who would do them harm. There will continue to be many debates concerning individual rights to privacy and secrecy as well as societal rights to protect citizens. Technology may make the issue moot by being able to identify those who do not belong at a particular place without publishing their personal data.

Operations management always benefits from transparency. Secrecy in operations is not about to become a contentious issue. There is no benefit in hiding sources of pollution or machines that are unsafe. There are no advocates for protecting the source of contamination of a food production process.

One security focus that has dominated the press and the mind-set of people is air safety. Air marshals are on many planes. In addition, vision systems are being installed by some airlines. "Jet Blue Airlines has installed them in its planes so the pilot can watch the passengers." In Times Square, there are over 200 surveillance cameras. In Washington, DC, when the police chief was asked how many cameras he can hook into, he replied, "It's . . .practically unlimited."[15] Surveillance cameras are ubiquitous in stores, ATM machines, and national monuments. In England, there are over two million cameras that were installed to counter IRA terrorism. There are various estimates ranging between 300 and 500 for the number of times a day that the average Londoner is recorded on film.

The utility of cameras is questionable until they are part of a data-mining system that can compare items to sort out potential dangers. For example, Tampa police used face recognition surveillance at Super Bowl XXXV (January 28, 2001). Cameras scanned faces in the audience and compared them with the facial phenotypes of people known to pose problems. There were no reports of any "hits."

This technology is rudimentary, but taxonomies are developing along various lines. Johns Hopkins School of Medicine—CCDD lists eight craniofacial dimensions to observe. These are listed on the webpage of the Center for Craniofacial Development and Disorders at http://www.hopkinsmedicine.org/craniofacial/Physician/GrowthChartsFace-Measure.cfm.

Security before emplaning is provided by the TSA (Transportation Security Administration). This safety assurance service operation is run by the U.S. government. It combines human and technology-based inspections with guidelines for continuous improvement. Who will be responsible for benchmarking this quality control system? Methods of operations management combined with research on technology and methodology that could improve security is required. For example, computer simulations of scenarios of security breaches could help determine the effectiveness of various strategies in lowering probabilities of foiling the culprits.

Following the Columbine High School massacre (April 20, 1999) there has been dedicated interest and deep concern about preparations for problem management in schools. The Crisis Prevention Institute (CPI) provides training for administrators, teachers, and instructional aides in the "management of disruptive, assaultive, and out-of-control behavior in a school setting." This P/OM service area is gaining attention. CPI's webpage heading is "School-Community Partnerships: Building a safer, healthier and brighter future for our children"(http://kcsos.kern.org/schcom/stories/storyReader$70).

Since 9/11, corporate security officers (CSOs) have been appointed in many major companies. These corporate security officers are on the constant lookout for booby traps, loaded guns, and opportunities for mischief, malfeasance, and mayhem. At the same time, security in many locations, such as theme parks and theaters, is capable of providing cardiopulmonary resuscitation (CPR) and first aid while awaiting EMS (emergency medical services). EMS is an operations management service application that requires P/OM capabilities. Note the process flow diagram at the Seattle–King County Regional EMS System webpage at http://www.metrokc.gov/health/ems/taskforce/execsummary.htm.

Dogs have been used for drug-sniffing and more recently for bomb material sniffing. There are machines that are also capable of sniffing bomb materials. It is hoped that, eventually, mobile robots will have even greater effectiveness. There is also the development of very small robots related to basic microbiological nanotechnology. See the websites http://www.nano.org.uk/courses.htm and http://www.robotbooks.com/molecular-robots.htm.

The Columbia shuttle accident that occurred in January 2003 is an event likely to promote the use of robots for space exploration. There has always been pressure to move more manned space exploration toward robotic sojourns. The drones that filled the sky over Afghanistan and then over Iraq are another example of robots replacing old methods of warfare. It is worrisome that drones are available to all sides in a conflict. Increasingly, aerial robots are being perfected to have incredible mobility and vision.

Robot-controlled cars are likely to have far fewer accidents. As will be discussed shortly, robots in the healthcare field can serve a remarkable number of functions. The point that is being made is that major changes are on the horizon for business as computers have been given sensory capabilities. They can see, smell, hear, and feel. They can measure temperatures and pressures. Then, in addition, computers have been given mobility. They can move and communicate without wires over large distances with a non-mobile database at home. Computers can lift, push, and grasp, so they can do work as robots on the line. They have the remarkable capability of changing settings in nanoseconds to do a different job. When they are properly engineered and programmed, robots can repeal the law of changeovers (re set-ups).

20-5c Crisis Management of Operations

Ensuring safety and security have become a normal part of everyday life. However, when an event occurs that is an act of nature (like a powerful earthquake or hurricane), a crisis occurs. Contingency planning for such situations can be very helpful. However, often there are surprises about the size or strength and the location of the epicenter, as well as the path of the storm. If all possible scenarios could have been anticipated, preparations for dealing with each of them might have been available. Crisis management is most effective when the assumption of worst cases is made. The biggest storm ever experienced, going through the most populated area in the region, is a good beginning (*The Perfect Storm*, Sebastian Junger, St. Helens, OR: Perennial Press,1999.).

Crisis events could be the result of a failure of technology. All the phones are out because a cable has been cut. This happened in New York City in the 1900s. What happens if the IT system is down because a giant power failure has occurred? The company that has done contingency planning knows what to do in such a situation. The response to great stress is not likely to be inexpensive, but the cost of incurring the losses due to the crisis are far greater.

Crises of the two types described here are manageable because they are imaginable. To some extent, the scenarios of what will happen when nature erupts and technology fails can be defined. The steps for dealing with them can be logical. What must be understood is that terrorist attacks are not illogical, but they are diabolical. Movie scriptwriters know how to dream up the diabolical. Original credits for the World Trade Center destruction does not go to the terrorists who copied the story from Hollywood movie scripts.

When one seeks protection from home burglars, the best advice can be obtained from a home burglar turned consultant. When the nation seeks protection from terror, it is probably best to go to the source of most of the deadly ideas...Hollywood scriptwriters and the science fiction authors.

The issue of importance, according to *Contingency Planning & Management* magazine (January–February 2003), is business continuity planning (BCP). How much downtime can a business survive? How much backup, replication, and redundancy can the firm afford? Disaster recovery is another way of stating the problem. See http://www.disaster-recoveryworld.com and http://www.contingencyplanning.com.

ISO 17799 for Operational Security

The International Organization for Standardization is a thriving community of academics, politicians, and practitioners. See their front page on the web: http://www.iso.org/iso/en/ISOOnline.frontpage.

Information about their code of practice for information security is found at http://www.iso.org/iso/en/CombinedQueryResult.CombinedQueryResult?queryString=ISO+17 799.

Also found on the web is the explanation of ISO 17799: http://www.iso17799software.com/what.htm. This is from a company that provides software and an ISO 17799 Toolkit. There is a slide presentation that notes that ISO 17799 allows "facilitation of trading in a trusted environment." This slide presentation can be seen at http://www.iso17799software.com/presentation/sld001.htm.

The information and security-based ISO standard is briefly explained here. Books can be purchased in English only about this detailed security standard from the ISO. The 10 major sections of ISO 17799 are

1. Business continuity planning—to counteract interruptions due to major failures or disasters.

2. System access control—to control access to information and prevent unauthorized access to that information and ensuring security when using mobile telenetworking facilities.

3. System development and maintenance—to ensure security is built into operational systems.

4. Physical and environmental security—to prevent unauthorized access, damage, and interference.

5. Compliance—to avoid breaches of criminal and civil law, and to ensure compliance with security.

6. Personnel security—to reduce risks of human error, theft, fraud, or misuse of facilities.

7. Security organization—to manage information security within the company.

8. Computer and operations management—to prevent damage to assets and interruptions to business activities.

9. Asset classification and control—to maintain appropriate protection of corporate assets and to ensure that information assets receive an appropriate level of protection.

10. Security policy—to provide management direction and support for information security.

There have been many discussions about protecting privacy on computers that are connected to the Internet. Intrusion detection of web perversions including (1) stealing intellectual property, (2) e-shop lifting (by altering information), (3) hijacking information (taking over a website), and (4) defacing and disabling a website. Companies are turning to vulnerability assessments. As in quality of manufactured goods and providing services, fixing a mistake costs much more than preventing it from happening.

On the other hand, the Tokyo Conference of ISO had as its objective to recognize that "The development of the Information Society must be based on platforms of internationally interoperable technical standards, accessible for all." This is the Tokyo Declaration adopted at the Asia–Pacific Regional Conference for the World Summit on the Information Society (WSIS), held in Tokyo, Japan, on January 13–15, 2003. See http://www.iso.org/iso/en/commcentre/events/2003/wsis.html.

The conflict between secure and private Internet connections and open platforms will be a challenge for those in operations of information systems over the next decade. Probable solutions will derive from the ability of technology to keep private that which is entrusted while sharing that which is of mutual benefit.

20-5d Service Robots

Industrial and manufacturing robots are a multibillion-dollar industry worldwide, whereas the service robot industry is at an earlier stage of development. There are few commercially viable service robots on the market today. Those that do exist provide real services and should not be confused with consumer "toys, pets, and gadgetry." Entertainment robots sell more for their "wow" factor than for their ability to perform useful tasks. Nevertheless, the entertainment robots can begin to provide services later on. For example the entertainment robot that Sony named AIBO can be seen at http://www.us.aibo.com.

AIBO means *companion* in Japanese and is an acronym for Artificial Intelligence roBOt. There is an advanced model that has a wireless card, and it can pick up and send email. AIBO is one of many robots listed in the robot directory at http://psychology.about.com/library/bl/blrobo_all.htm. However, this so-called "complete list" is not nearly complete because many organizations and academic institutions are working on various aspects of robotic behavior with the purpose of learning how to provide services that sometimes includes mobility, dexterity, voice recognition, and voice response.

The book *Service Robots*[16] by Gernot Schmierer and Rolf Dieter Schraft explores specific robots that provide service functions, including refueling, cleaning, surveillance, firefighting, sorting, cooking, marketing, nursing care, and space exploration. Note the previous section where robots were used for paint removal and cleaning by water-jetting. Also, no list is complete that does not include a robotic system that provides information about flight arrivals and departures for all the major airlines—as though the caller is speaking with a charming operator.

Other robotic issues are related to cyborgs and autonomous robots. Cyborgs are combinations of human beings and robots that result from implants such as pacemakers and hearing aids. A text that explores the autonomous (self-willed robots that improve their own design) is *Robo Sapiens: Evolution of New Species*.[17] This book has been praised for its great photographs, and it has great reviewers' quotes from Sir Arthur C. Clarke, author of *2001: A Space Odyssey* ("mind-stretching, frightening") and Ray Kurzweil, author of *The Age of Spiritual Machines: When Computers Exceed Human Intelligence* ("inevitable merger of human and machine").

The actual state of affairs is that there is a great deal of interest, both academic and practical, but there are only a few significant service robots that are commercially available. Joseph Engelberger, the "father of robots" and a pioneer in both industrial and service robots in the United States, has continued to believe that the situation will change significantly. The Joseph F. Engelberger Robotics Award Fact Sheet is available on the website of the Robotic Industries Association (RIA) (http://www.robotics.org/public/articles/index.cfm?cat=296). Eighty-five awards have been given through 2002.

The majority of the awards are given for factory automation. However, vision and mobility capabilities are being further developed and, eventually, they can translate into service provider capabilities. In 2002, North American manufacturing firms ordered 10,573 robot units valued at $811 million in revenue from North American suppliers. The Department of Computer Sciences at the University of Tubingen in Germany has been developing mobile service robots (called *Colin* and *Robin*). The webpage describes the requirements of such mobile service systems (http://www-ra.informatik.uni-tuebingen.de/forschung/service/welcome_e.html).

People need no longer be exposed to hazardous working conditions. Such problems are being addressed by the Association for Robotics in Hazardous Environments (RHE)—created in 1994 by RIA, which was founded in 1974 by the Society for Manufacturing Engineers located in Ann Arbor, Michigan. As effective substitutes for people operating in hazardous environments, robots require excellent vision and mobility. RHE issues are available in a variety of ways. Since 1998, it has been accessible through the hub listed here. Note: A hub is not a website. It is a portal to thousands of websites. After clicking on the portal address, enter—RHE—in the search box—and click "search" (http://www. Trhubnet.com).

Service Robots for Health Care

Pyxis HelpMate® SP, a mobile service courier robot from Cardinal Health, moves around healthcare facilities without tracks or guide wires delivering medications, meals, lab specimens, and more wherever needed. Pyxis HelpMate SP is shown in Figure 20-1.

People working in hospitals are more comfortable when they give names to their robots. That is why in Durham, NC, Pyxis HelpMate SP is called TOBOR. The 400-pound robot has a safe in its midsection for medicines and bags of intravenous fluids labeled with the name and bar code of the intended patients.

Pyxis HelpMate SP works around the clock, costing the hospital less than $5 an hour to lease. "Whenever a new patient is admitted to the Veterans Affairs Medical Center, ... a four-foot eight-inch talking robot rolls up to the nurses' station nearest to the patient's

**FIGURE 20-1
HelpMate SP is Stepping Ahead of the Doctors in a Hospital Corridor**

(Photo courtesy of Cardinal Health, Inc.)

**FIGURE 20-2
Homerus is a Non-mobile
Centralized Pharmacy
Automated Dispensing
System**

(Photo is courtesy of Cardinal Health, Inc.)

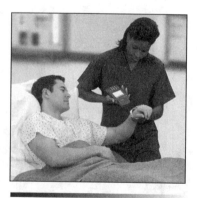

**FIGURE 20-3
Pyxis Veri5™ is a Handheld
Bar Code Scanner**

(Photo is courtesy of Cardinal
Health, Inc.)

room, bringing doses of whatever drugs the doctor ordered. TOBOR, the robot, is a delivery 'droid' that glides along the corridors day and night ferrying medicines from the hospital's central pharmacy to its wards."[18]

Pyxis HelpMate SP's computer brain plots its routes to over 30 possible destinations within the Veterans Affairs Medical Center. Pyxis HelpMate SP employs sonar, infrared sensors and communicates via RF Ethernet. It avoids people and obstacles and proclaims to patients and visitors in the elevator or corridor, "I am about to move; please stand clear."

Cardinal Health has placed more than 100 of its Pyxis HelpMate SP robots in U.S. hospitals. Pyxis HelpMate SP provides hospitals with an economical way to better service the nursing units, allowing nurses more time for patient care. Pyxis HelpMate SP is reliable with no history of absenteeism, and it is as content with night shifts as day shifts. Also, Pyxis HelpMate SP is bi-lingual with English and Spanish.

Pyxis Homerus® is an integrated centralized pharmacy with automated dispensing systems that offer a broad range of capabilities. It is a robot that retrieves pharmaceuticals from its own storage system. It packages the medicines in appropriate doses with information bar code controls for accuracy. Homerus combines iPak™, a unit-dose barcode packaging system, and iStar, a medication storage and retrieval system, to take automated filling of patient cassettes to a new level of cost effectiveness. See Figure 20-2.

Pyxis Homerus has the computer database and the bar coding system to bring high accuracy to the delivery of medicines, assuming that the doctors prescriptions are correct. It helps eliminate medication errors delivered to patients by pharmacy or nursing. Pyxis Veri5™ is a medical management system that helps eliminate sources of error in the supply chain between the pharmacy and the patient. Pyxis Veri5 is a handheld bar code scanner (Figure 20-3) that provides an automated double check of the "5Rs". See Box 20-1 for a discussion of the "5Rs".

Pyxis HelpMate SP, Pyxis Homerus and Pyxis Veri5 bring a level of quality control to the nurse-patient healthcare interaction that typifies advances from new technologies. Robots, scanners and computers verify the patient's "5Rs". P/OM is greatly assisted by this technology and methodology.

Pyxis HelpMate SP can be compared to its cousins in the industrial robot sector, which are trackless industrial AGVSs (automated guided vehicle systems). Both require extensive navigational abilities. Using walls and ceilings as guides, they access internal maps that confine them to preprogrammed routes. Attention to details is required for success in both applications.

Glimpsing the future, production people will be accustomed to working with mobile service robots (MSRs) that can navigate corridors and carry materials between stations. Mobile service robots will alter service industries, providing rapid set-ups, maintenance, deliveries, repair, and cleaning services. MSRs have a role to play in both developed economies and underdeveloped economies. There are economic and cultural issues about jobs in the service sector that portend shortages in service functions all over the world.

Mobile service robots with vision and speech could transform the service sector much as industrial robots with flexibility in changeovers and multiple set-ups have revolution-

BOX 20-1 *The 5 Rights of Medication (Drug) Administration*	The "5 Rights of Medication (Drug) Administration" are called the "5Rs." It is something that every nursing student learns and abides by throughout their careers of service. A general definition of these "5Rs" is summarized under Nursing Responsibilities Regarding Drugs: 1) Use the RIGHT drug 2) Give to the RIGHT person 3) Give the RIGHT dose 4) Give by the RIGHT route 5) Give at the RIGHT time Nurses must be ready to respond to interactions between drug and patient (i.e., the nurse must be aware of drug reactions and side effects). When a breakdown occurs the consequences range from terrible to tragic.

ized manufacturing. Note that robots are particularly well-suited when second and third shift staffing is a problem. They can change the cost structure of services and the quality delivered by service industries.

Contact between customers and clients is the service interface. Young customer expectations may not be the same as their elders. Even the seniors show signs of shifting. The indications are that customers are learning to deal with robots and preferences are changing. For example, many people prefer to use the kiosks for checking in at the airport to avoid waiting on line for a person. Another example of the swing to using computers and robots rather than clerks—given the choice—are ATMs and online banking with the Internet. Game-playing advocates perceive complex robots as being very "cool." Combine transactional flexibility of ATMs (automated teller machines) with the "potential creativity" of artificial intelligence (AI)[19], the mobility of robots, voice recognition, and response; the result is a plausible revolution for service delivery systems. See the Spotlight feature box in Chapter 13, "Changing the Way We Pay—ATMs and Smart Cards."

20-5e Virtual Offices

Offices become virtual when no space is dedicated to specific individuals. They are like mobile offices and have an equivalency to mobile robots. The trend to what have been called *nonterritorial offices* has been going on for a long time. For example, 10 years back, *The Wall Street Journal* had an article that began "Sales representatives at American Telephone & Telegraph Co.'s Sacramento, California, office lost their desks. They were given laptop computers, cellular telephones and portable printers and told to create 'virtual offices' at home or at their customers' offices."[20] Since that time, AT&T has developed a great deal of experience with telework. They have drawn an important distinction between tactical telework, as an informal or alternative work arrangement, and strategic telework, as a formal component of a firm's business strategy. Most organizations use tactical telework when their people are traveling, or working from home. The strategic approach is a formal commitment to nonassigned office space, roaming desks, and assuming that the office is where the manager's laptop is found.

See the AT&T article "Following the Telework Compass: Lessons from Two Enterprise Transformation Projects" (http://www.att.com/telework/article_library/compass.html).

The varieties of virtual offices include:

1. *Working at home.* This transfers the cost of space from the company to the worker. It is being used to decrease commuting by car. AT&T, IBM, and other organizations are experimenting with this plan in California where increasingly tough regulations are expected to be passed requiring companies to limit the number of employees permitted to travel to a particular work site (to reduce environmental pollution). Note the Valley Metro telecommuting case study of IBM (with specific reference to pollution control in Arizona.[21]
(http://www.valleymetro.maricopa.gov/Rideshare/Telework/ local_studies_ibm.htm).

"Working at home moms" (WAHM) are independent operators and entrepreneurs as contrasted with large companies using telework methods as cost savers and people pleasers. See http://www.wahm.com.

2. *Working from cars, hotels, and customers' offices.* These mobile offices are staffed by mobile workers. The move to mobile offices is associated with functions that require extensive travel to customers' sites. Thus, salespeople, accountants, auditors, consultants, and service team members are logical candidates for mobile-office assignments. The effect is to increase the amount of time that these kinds of professionals spend with their customers, which both parties find rewarding.

3. *Working in nonassigned spaces at the company site.* This is called *hoteling, hotel offices,* and the *check-in-and-out office.* There also is doubling up (or better) the number of people assigned to one office. The method is used by Oticon S/A, in Denmark, American Express, 3 COM, Catalyst 400, and many other companies. Companies have reported increasing the employee-to-desk ratio in a range of from 2-to-1 to 5-to-1. There is also *hot desking,* which allows many employees to share the same desk or computer or phone because the technology recognizes the PIN of that employee and has the right database to use. See http://www.merchantinter.net/telecomunications/telecomunications/features/hotdesking.htm.

    See the list of hoteling and hot desking companies compiled for the United Kingdom at http://www.cix.co.uk/~optima/telework/ListByOrg.htm.

4. *Renting virtual offices* from companies such as Regus, which use their space and facilities to do hoteling around the world. Officescape is another example; see http://www.officescape.com/services.asp. Also, see HQ Global Workplace, which has over 200 business centers in the United States (http://www.hq.com) and eoffice in London (http://www.eoffice.net).

The advantages of virtual offices are increased operational efficiency, agility to adapt to change, and flexibility to increase or decrease space on a seasonal basis and to grow with the business. Upsizing and downsizing are readily accomplished.

At a point in time, the advertising agency TBWA/Chiat/Day reengineered its offices using combinations of the four points shown here, proclaiming satisfaction with the results. IBM's seven regional U.S. markets converted to virtual office configurations. Private offices were replaced by "small team rooms" for use by the mobile executives.[22] Companies that have used virtual offices note that management changes are required to make this major shift in working modes effective and productive. Some companies have slowed the pace of virtualizing, and telecommunication is not always lauded. When virtualizing is used properly, it is reported that "the amount of office space needed for certain types of employees—those who travel a good deal—has declined to 48 square feet a person from 200 square feet."[23]

Technology makes the virtual office possible. Change management methods of P/OM are needed to adopt technologies that make the virtual office work. There is also need to get people to accept the new modus operandi and to have them use the new systems effectively.

20-6 ISO 14000/14001

ISO 14000/14001: ISO 9000 series is acknowledged worldwide as the accepted set of standards for quality management. ISO 14000/14001 sets similar standards for environmental management. The ISO 17799 Toolkit addresses operational security.

Global environmental (and ethical) benchmarks will change the way that business is done worldwide. "Ready for **ISO 14000/14001**? Just when you thought ISO 9000, the certification that shows manufacturers are observing international quality standards, was in place, the International Organization for Standardization in Geneva now aims for environmental management guidelines by 1996."[24]

The ISO 14000/14001 guidelines are now fully developed and being used broadly. See the manuals and training software of AQA Press, for example http://www.aqapress.com. This webpage is dated January 2003. There are many supportive materials available from ISO directly; see http://www.iso.org/iso/en/iso9000-14000/iso14000/iso14000index. html.

"Many organizations have undertaken environmental reviews or audits to assess their environmental performance. On their own, however, these reviews and audits will seldom be sufficient to provide an organization with the assurance that its performance not only meets, but will continue to meet, its policy requirements. To be effective, they need to be conducted within a structured management system, integrated with overall management activity and addressing significant environmental impacts."[25]

The ISO 14000 series is designed to set standards for conformity assessment leading to certification. It is designed to provide organizational structure and management discipline for achieving excellence in environmental performance. ISO 9000 does not deal with specific qualities. The ISO 14000 series does not deal with specific environmental qualities, such as emission levels. Like ISO 9000 standards, the ISO 14000 standards are coordinated by the American National Standards Institute (ANSI) in cooperation with the American Society for Quality Control (ASQC).

ISO 14001 starts with an articulated environmental policy followed by management systems to plan the environmental program. Management must provide for operations and implementation (including training, methods for communication, documentation, and emergency preparedness).

There will also be a provision for checking and taking corrective action. Monitoring and measuring will be detailed so that nonconformance can be prevented, but when it occurs, it is corrected. The methods allow a certified environmental systems audit and review.

Reengineering and continuous improvement can have substantial environmental impacts. Every TQM and JIT program can affect the environment. Companies with ISO 14001 certification will not be forced to select which country's standards it will follow. Often this approach leads to conflicts of standards between countries. ISO has provided unified global standards and certification procedures. Like ISO 9000 series, ISO 14000 has been adopted by all countries.

ISO 14000 is a good way to wind down this chapter because it embodies care for the environment and ethics in an organizational and management context. The idea of a uniform codification prevents an operational nightmare of trying to satisfy the environmental requirements of many different countries.

20-7 VISION OF A FULLY INTEGRATED GLOBAL COMPANY

Readying operations management for future conditions requires understanding new demands of society and new developments in technology. Implementing world-class performance in a dynamically evolving system requires the systems point of view, which brings all-important elements to the table.

Comprehensive vision must be supported by a totally interconnected informing system (communicating information system). A picture of what this infrastructure might look like is shown in Figure 20-4, where it is called the *SME Manufacturing Enterprise Wheel.* A similar wheel of six concentric circles can be drawn for service industries. Differences between the integrating wheel for manufacturing and customer services would be thought out in detail. Creating the service enterprise wheel is a worthwhile project.

Start with the customer (1) who could be located anywhere in the world. Move to people organized for teamwork (2). This organization is designed to share knowledge by using the systems approach (3). The next concentric circle employs the systems approach to relate customer support, product/process factors, and manufacturing (or customer services) (4). The next level (5) connects resources and responsibilities to monitor and guide all decisions that are made at the fourth level. The outer part of the wheel (6) is the rim, which encloses, connects, links, and shares everything in the system. Six is named the manufacturing (or service) infrastructure.

FIGURE 20-4

SME Manufacturing Enterprise Wheel

Copyright „ 1993, Third Edition. Society of Manufacturing Engineers, Dearborn, MI 48121 Reproduction of this CASA/SME Manufacturing Wheel is permitted.

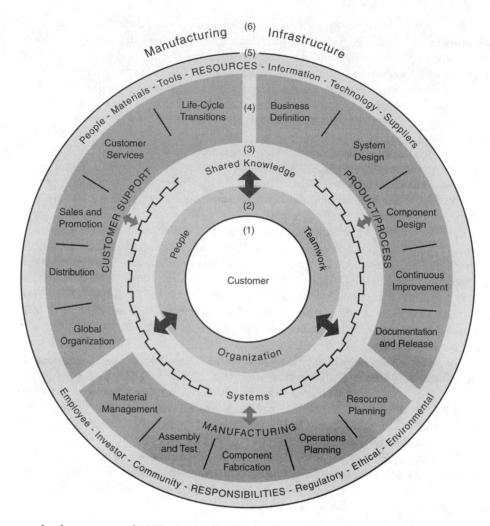

SME wheel: Graphic provides a "vision" of a fully integrated global company; links resources and responsibilities.

In the summer of 1993, CASA/SME (the Computer and Automated Systems Association of the Society of Manufacturing Engineers) announced this new version of the prior enterprise wheel. The old wheel (1985) was called the *CIM Enterprise Wheel.* CIM stood for *computer-integrated manufacturing.* The center of that wheel focused on information systems architecture and databases.

World-class manufacturers organize, integrate, and invest their resources to achieve new levels of customer satisfaction. The new manufacturing enterprise wheel is a recognition of the significant progress to date, and the progress yet to be made, in manufacturing. It serves as an overview of today's Best Practice in total enterprise integration.

This new wheel centers on the customer. It considers "the virtual enterprise," which is the inclusive system of all of the people who are teamed together to achieve company objectives. The new wheel stresses "the need to integrate an understanding of the external environment, including customers, competitors, suppliers, and the global manufacturing infrastructure."[26] The **SME wheel** provides a vision of a fully integrated global company system.

More than 10 years have elapsed since the new SME enterprise wheel was launched. Is it still relevant? CASA/SME presents the LEAD award annually. LEAD stands for Leadership and Excellence in the Application and Development of Integrated Manufacturing. The criteria for the LEAD award, written up in the September 2002 issue of *Manufacturing Engineering,* seem to adhere to the SME Manufacturing Enterprise Wheel. There were three winners: The Institute of Production Engineering at Tampere University of Technology (Tampere, Finland), International Truck Company (Warrenville, Illinois), and Medtronic Corp. (Minneapolis, Minnesota). The emphasis is on integrated manufacturing, and the wheel shows all of the parts that must be tied together.

SUMMARY

Chapter 20 highlights environmental issues that are both threats and opportunities for companies. The weakness of many companies is that environmental regulations and restrictions happen before the firm is prepared to match the rules. It is a strength to be ready for the expectations as they arise so that fines can be avoided and processes to achieve the goals can be developed at a reasonable price. Chapter 20 also focuses on ethical problems. In particular, there are ethical issues when quality is sacrificed to save money. It may not be a grave example, but when a package size is unchanged although the weight of the unseen contents is reduced, there is quality issue. Spoiled food and contaminated water are operational responsibilities. Problems stemming from lack of know-how or indifference are unacceptable.

Examples of environmentally sound OM processes are presented. With care and attention to ecological impacts, companies can save money and improve the environment at the same time. Similar results apply to benefits from being ethical. There is a cost, but the gains are greater. In this regard, quality integrity is an ethical issue. The HACCP program for seafood quality is a model of effective FDA regulation of total quality. Time to test and release new drugs is another issue for debate. Chapter 20 examines the impact of 9/11 on safety, security, crisis management, and contingency planning. All are P/OM responsibilities.

OM is on the team that can prepare the organization for future technology. Trends include smart robots that can move without wires. Technological developments are changing services and manufacturing. The virtual office is possible because of new technology. Learning to use it is a P/OM responsibility.

Three Spotlight feature boxes conclude this chapter. These boxes illustrate real applications of the material in the chapter. See Spotlight 20-1: Good Ethics Makes Business Good, Spotlight 20-2: Securing the Right Decision, and Spotlight 20-3: Saving Time and Money by Postponement.

KEY TERMS

CDC
Design for assembly (DFA)
Design for automation (DFAU)
Design for disassembly (DFD)
End-of-life-of-vehicle (ELV)
Ethics
FDA

Greening the environment
Hazard Analysis and Critical Control Point
   (HACCP) system
ISO 14000/14001
Mobile robots
Quality integrity
Recycling concrete

Remanufacturing
Reuse
Reverse supply chains
SME wheel
Substances of concern (SOC)
Take-back laws
Water-jetting

REVIEW QUESTIONS

1. Would simulated attacks on buildings, reservoirs, theaters, cruise ships, etc., help to evaluate current security procedures? Explain.

2. It is said that operations management is the one functional area closest to Best Practice of ethics. Why would this be so?

3. Operations management is the harshest critic of ethical failures. Why?

4. Describe the history of ethics as practiced by operations, financial, and marketing management.

5. Explain what take-back means. How is take-back changing the way that the supply chain operates?

6. What are the four aspects of DFD? Explain the role of DFD.

7. Why does water-jetting qualify as an OM greening technique?

8. Why is recycling concrete used as an example of OM greening the environment?

9. What five phases are used for environmental evaluations?

10. Explain the lack of quality integrity as an ethical issue.

11. Describe the Hazard Analysis and Critical Control Point (HACCP) system. What are the HACCP objectives? What are the seven recommended steps of HACCP?

12. How does HACCP relate to TQC and TQM?

13. Why is HACCP called a custodian of social ethics?

14. Explain the problems associated with overtesting and undertesting the safety and effectiveness of food and drug products.

15. What is the role of the CDC? How does the FDA relate to CDC?

16. What is the potential impact of healthcare robots?

17. What are the advantages of mobile robots that can move without wires?

18. Explain the impact of the virtual office on operations management decisions.

19. TBWA/Chiat/Day, an advertising agency, used hoteling, American Express uses hot desking. When are these office configurations beneficial? Hoteling is still used, but was a failed experiment at Chiat/Day, see http://www.wired.com/wired/archive/7.02/chiat_pr.html.

20. Relate the virtual office to the "end of the job" concept.

21. How can P/OM help globalize operations?

22. Explain how ISO 14001 can help P/OM support its firm's success in global opportunities.

23. Explain the power of the SME wheel. If time allows, include an explanation of each concentric ring.

PROBLEMS SECTION

1. When office space is reengineered using hoteling, the square feet needed per employee may decrease from 200 to 48.
   a. What is the percent decline in space?
   b. At $12 per square foot per month, what is the saving per employee?
   c. If there are 1,000 employees, what is the total monthly saving?
   d. What business functions are best suited to hoteling?

2. Knowing that you have completed an OM course, the principal of your high school invites you to give a presentation to a high school class about global careers in OM. Show an outline of the presentation.

3. What is hot desking?

4. Benchmark the recycling system that is currently used by your community against the ideal one that you envision. Explain the factors that count and the criteria that you believe would permit an accurate comparison of systems.

5. Benchmark the ethics system that is currently used by your company (or community) against the ideal one that you envision. Explain the factors that count and the criteria that you believe would permit an accurate comparison of systems.

6. Over the years, the 1-pound cans of some coffee manufacturers have remained the same size, but the contents have gone from 16 ounces to 13 ounces and more recently to 10 or 11 ounces. In some cases, the print line that identifies the weight of the contents has gotten noticeably smaller.
   a. Determine the percent decrease from 16 to 13 ounces. If the price of a pound of coffee is $8 and law requires that the same price per ounce be maintained, what would be the price for 13 ounces?
   b. Is there an ethical issue in this case? Can the argument for maintaining package size be justified?

7. Over the years, yogurt containers have remained about the same size but contents by weight have decreased. Can this fact be discerned by the customer? Is there an ethical issue in this case?

8. Set up a flowchart to indicate how the HACCP system could be applied to an upscale fish restaurant. Note the seven steps for HACCP and make certain that all seven are represented on the chart.

9. Develop a scoring model for comparing alternative reverse supply chain systems for:
   a. Paint cans where the paint has been used up and the cans have to be discarded
   b. Old computers that include the monitor, the hard drive, and the printer
   c. Worn tires for automobiles; for 18-wheel trucks
   d. Totaled automobiles (*totaled* means damaged so badly they are sent to the junk yard; however, parts can still be reused)

10. There are claims that teleworking is inefficient. Argue both the pros and cons of this statement.

11. What is the current rate of use of teleworking? Is it likely to increase or decrease in the future?

12. What does teleworking have to do with P/OM?

13. Create the Hazard Analysis and Critical Control Point (HACCP) system using the seven recommended steps for:
    a. A fishing boat
    b. Trucks carrying fish to the distributor
    c. The retailer of fish

14. What is the long-term effect of vision improvements on robots?

15. Detail an operations management plan for opening a quick-service restaurant in:
    a. Japan
    b. The United Kingdom
    c. The United States

16. Research the steps that need to be taken to obtain ISO 14000/14001 for a new branch in Australia.

17. 7-Eleven food stores in Japan have used JIT deliveries to such an extent that the company has been accused of creating road pollution. How would application of ISO 14001 help to sort this problem out?

END-OF-CHAPTER QUESTIONS

1. The IQ (intelligence quotient) test is well-known, widely-used, and considered to be only one possible measure of intelligence. Other measures have emerged, one of which is called the EIQ (emotional intelligence quotient). It was developed by Daniel Goleman and Richard Boyatis, who have developed the EI Consortium. It offers tests of EI competencies. See http://www.eiconsortium.org. The relationship of EI to ethics is apparent from examining the emotional competence framework. There are two parts to this framework in the Goleman system. The first component is personal competence. The second component is social competence. Points a. through e. are related to personal competence. Points a. to e. highlight the ways in which ethical decision making is dependent upon the level of an individual's personal emotional competency. Which one of these points is not consistent with the fundamentals of personal emotional competencies?
   a. Three building blocks of personal competence are self-awareness, self-regulation, and motivation. (This is certified to be a correct answer.)
   b. Self-awareness requires accurate self-assessment. It is unethical for someone to do a job that requires competence that they do not have. If someone flies a plane who is posing as a licensed pilot, that may be no

more unethical than a CEO who does not take proper care of company business.

c. Self-regulation includes self-control, trustworthiness, and taking responsibility for personal performance. It is unethical for a manager to hire a person known to be incompetent to do the job for which they are hired, e.g., nepotism or more.

d. Motivation is the third component of personal competence. It includes the drive for achievement, which can include the desire for power, personal advancement, and increased earnings. Greed is neither condoned nor condemned as an attribute of emotional intelligence, because it is a basic human emotion.

e. Motivation also includes commitment. This permits the individual to align with the goals of the group, and with the organizational objectives.

2. The EIQ (emotional intelligence quotient) test has received an increasing amount of attention. It measures a different kind of intelligence than traditional IQ tests, which do not capture many of the elements of ethical behavior. From Problem 1, the first component of the EIQ is personal competence—how we manage ourselves. The second component is social competence—how we handle relationships. In Problem 2, points a. through e. are related to social competence. The points highlight ways in which ethical decision making is dependent upon the social aspects of an individual's emotional competency. Which of these points is not consistent with the fundamentals of social emotional competencies?

a. Two building blocks of social competence are empathy and social skills. (This is certified to be a correct answer.)

b. Empathy is awareness of others' feelings, needs, and concerns. It leads to a service orientation, which anticipates, recognizes, and thereby permits meeting customers' needs. Ethical issues about customers' needs also include health and safety factors. The same service orientation applies to employees, suppliers, and the communities in which the company operates.

c. An additional factor that relates to the emotional intelligence of an individual in a social system is empathy to help another person bolster his or her abilities. However, issues of competitiveness arise. Situations occur where a person must fend for themselves at the expense of others in the organization. It is not intelligent to give assistance to another person who may be promoted and become the boss.

d. Social skills is the second building block of social competence. There are many components to include. Among these are team capabilities, negotiation skills, change management expertise, and good communication proficiency.

e. Returning to empathy as an ingredient of social competence, emotional intelligence is strongly related to cultivating diversity opportunities.

3. Protecting the environment is an ethical issue that managers of every company must consider. There is a tendency to jump to the conclusion that only large manufacturing companies can impact the environment. Yet, in Japan, 9,700 7-Eleven stores are owned by Ito-Yokado Co., Ltd. 7-Eleven Japan Co., Ltd., was responsive to complaints that too many trucks were making just-in-time deliveries, causing road congestion and pollution. 7-Eleven changed its delivery schedules to remove objections. 7-Eleven was started in 1927 by the Southland Ice Co. of Dallas, Texas. It was named for its hours of doing business. In 2003, 73 percent of the 25, 000 stores around the world (5,800 in North America) are owned by Ito-Yokado Co., Ltd. Assume that a company in the convenience store category (like 7-Eleven) convenes a worldwide meeting of its managers to discuss environmental issues. The agenda has been listed as points a. through e. One of these points is unacceptable to the general manager. Which point is objectionable?

a. Maintenance is a major aspect of environmental protection, i.e., greening the environment.

b. Other major topics that relate to greening the environment include production take-back rules, which require disassembling products and recycling an increasing percent of products. For example, BMW has created an experimental plant with the goal of recycling 95 percent (by weight) of its automobiles.

c. The Green Party is a major advocate of political action to achieve more productive maintenance of facilities. For example, how are roads, bridges, and tunnels maintained? Although Green Parties can be found all over the globe, productive maintenance is their main concern.

d. A serious maintenance problem is related to stripping old paints and coatings from ships, buildings, and airplanes. An important new opportunity for coating and surface removal uses water-jetting technology to replace old surfaces with new protective surfaces.

e. The *Thomas Register* (2003) lists more than 20 companies that provide marine hull treatment. There are many other applications for water-jetting, including gas turbine coatings and airplane surfaces.

4. The ways in which business organizations affect the environment are useful to enumerate. As a result of the conference of convenience store managers, a task force was set up to list some of the impact zones. This list is presented here for approval. There is one point that was rejected by the steering committee of the conference. Which point a. through e. deserves to be reworked?

a. A short list regarding air quality includes smokestacks, delivery trucks, company cars, ships and boats, airplanes exhausts, air-conditioners, air-blowers, windmills, wind vanes and wind turbines http://www.ndseed.org/htmls/past_vanes.htm. In addition to the North Dakota seed URL, see the URL concerning green power purchasing: (http://www.eere.energy.gov/greenpower/home.shtml). Many items on this list not only affect air quality, but they also have significant noise levels.

b. Water is used and altered by industry in various ways. As a coolant and refrigerant, it is employed by trucks, cars, boats, and airplanes. It participates in many chemical processes. Water is treated for purification (pools and drinking water), distillation, and pressure hosing including water-jetting. As another example of multiple impacts, jet ski complaints include their effect on air, water, and noise levels.

c. Waste and sewage are major environmental factors that affect air and water as well as requiring special disposal methods. The Environmental Protection Agency has received $200 million in grants as a result of the Wastewater Treatment Works Security Act, H.R. 5169. The European Union (EU) Land Directive banned disposal of whole tires in July 2003 and "shredded tyres from July, 2006." Bicycle tires are not subject to this ban. See the Landfill Directive published in the official *Journal of the European Communities*, July 16, 1999 (http://www.tyredisposal.co.uk/landfill.asp).

d. Asbestos has not been used as a building material for over 30 years. It is not treated as an environmental problem as a result. The same applies to pesticides like DDT (banned in the United States in 1972) and PCBs (banned in the United States in 1976).

e. Pesticides can affect the water table and impair the safety of drinking water. Oil and gas drilling activities have contaminated water tables in Colorado and New Mexico. Oil and natural gas pipelines have ruptured with greater frequency than one expects. The effects of radiation exposure from high voltage lines, X-rays, high-altitude flying, and (naturally occurring) radon are being scrutinized. The effects of spills at sea (such as the Exxon *Valdez*) and by railroads and trucks have promoted litigation long after the events occurred. Dumping of medical products at sea creates hazards when they are washed ashore.

5. USCAR stands for United States Council for Automotive Research. This organization is sponsored by DaimlerChrysler, Ford, and General Motors. USCAR is the umbrella organization of the three companies, formed in 1992 to strengthen the technology base of the U.S. domestic auto industry. This is accomplished using precompetitive, cooperative research. Using the website http://www.uscar.com, determine which one of the following points, a. through e., is wrong.

a. USCAR and the U.S. Department of Energy have joined an industry/government research initiative that is aimed at freeing the nation's personal transportation system from petroleum dependence and from harmful vehicle emissions.

b. The FreedomCAR partnership was announced January 9, 2002. There is no single strategy to solve the dependence problem. The United States buys 26 percent of the world's oil to satisfy 55 percent of its market requirements. In other words, the United States produces only 45 percent of the petroleum it uses. Supply and demand are out of synchronization and will get worse unless various steps are taken. The current gap between supply and demand is projected to more than double by 2030 if no steps are taken to remedy the situation.

c. Detailed results of R & D are documented. Significant results will be reported at the website http://www.cartech.doe.gov. Clicking on "What's New," the categories are progress reports, materials research, batteries research, fuels research, and an archive.

d. The Vehicle Recycling Partnership (VRP) was formed November 1991. It has P/OM goals to reduce the environmental impact of vehicle disposal. It calls for the efficient disassembly of components and materials to enhance vehicle recyclability.

e. The Institute of Electrical and Electronic Engineers Standards Association is developing the first universal standard for motor vehicle event data recorders (MVDER). This black box is similar to those that monitor airplane crashes. The project is called *IEEE P1616* and it will define what data should be captured. Data will include date, time, location, velocity, heading, number of occupants, and seat belt usage. This will apply to personal autos, trucks, buses, ambulances, fire trucks, and other vehicles. The black box can be used to establish personal blame in court cases.

6. Take-back laws and regulations are predicated on careful and clever preplanned DFD (design for disassembly). Five essential elements have been listed by the managers of Contronics, which provides electronics manufacturing services to OEMs for mobile phones, computers, workstations, and computer peripherals. The tide is changing. More attention is being placed on DFD than on DFA. In fact, the head designer has told a conference group that they are the same thing. He lists the five essentials and throws in a sixth for a ringer. "Keep awake," he tells the audience. "I have included one statement in a. to f. that is not good advice." Which is that statement?

a. Design products without using super-adhesives to hold parts together. The best adhesives are those that hold until instructed otherwise.

b. Create a manual of fastenings and fastening methods. Rank them in terms of how well they hold things together under vibration, heat, etc., and how readily they come apart when that state is required. It may help to examine children's blocks and construction sets.

c. Choose components that can be reused with minimum rework (or, if possible, with no rework). Set the target price for a component that can be used n times at a multiplier of n times the cost that would be paid for that component if it would be used once. For example, be willing to pay $3 for a spool that can be reused three times, if a single-use spool was acceptably priced at $1. (Target price is determined by the amount that the buyer will be willing to pay to the seller. It applies to auctions as well as bids for project awards.)

d. Components that require hazardous-care disposal should be priced at the cost of the component plus the disposal cost per unit. If that is not acceptable, search for an alternative material. If possible, get away from designs that require special care for disposal. Examine new processes as often as possible for recycling and disposal.

e. Use analysis to identify materials that can be moved through the reverse supply chain as inexpensively as possible. The total systems cost is the logistics cost of original transport (to the customer), plus the reverse supply chain take-back logistics cost to return the material to be recycled, plus the costs of recycling that material. (The costs of the entire supply loop are relevant.)

f. Consider the advantages of locating a recycling facility close to the customers' return-of-product access points rather than at the remanufacturing plant. For example, melt down car doors before returning them in the reverse supply loop to the door-making location.

7. Ethics and operations management are inextricably related to each other. Safety, security, and health (SS&H) have gone from being mundane expectations in a time of peace to being seriously threatened prospects in a time of war. Of the five statements a. through e., one is not correct. Which one is incorrect?

   a. The assignment to protect safety, security and health (SS&H) falls squarely on the shoulders of P/OM. Innovative two-way cooperation is required with IT (information technology) to select and monitor variables that capture and preserve the well-being of employees and customers. Companies with products that provide explosive detection systems (EDS) are being rewarded by higher stock market valuations since airports, buildings, and theaters are considering installing this line of products. Visit http://www.mistralgroup.com/SEC_exdetect.asp.

   b. Accidents need to be fully documented and studied for both employees and customers. OSHA (Occupational Safety and Health Administration) of the U.S. Department of Labor establishes protective standards guidelines. OSHA enforces these standards and provides outreach and technical assistance to employers and employees, and charters an advisory committee to identify research opportunities. Visit http://www.osha.gov.

   c. OSHA has a four-pronged comprehensive approach to ergonomics, which is the art and science of designing and arranging physical interfaces with the human body (e.g., chairs) and senses (e.g., dials) for effective, efficient, safe and healthful use by people. For example, OSHA addresses musculoskeletal disorders (MSDs) in the workplace. The four segments of OSHA's strategy for reducing injuries and illnesses are listed in point b.

   d. ISO 14000 provides OSHA guidelines for employees' safety and health. ISO 14001 embodies the security aspects of SS&H by requiring measures to prevent willful acts by employees that are harmful to other employees. OSHA does not include issues related to terrorism in its guidelines.

   e. Innovative technologies are being developed that will bring about major changes in security. In point a., cooperation of P/OM and IT are stressed. An example of this would be the use of perceptrak,™ which utilizes content analysis and behavior recognition software to identify "potentially suspicious people, vehicles, and objects." Visit http://www.cernium.com/products/index.html.

8. Eras have tipping points. Calm and tranquil eras can tip to stormy and violent epochs. The cold war was filled with tension. When it ended, there was conjecture that a calm and peaceful time would begin. In retrospect, it was a mistake to believe that hard times were over when the Berlin War fell. Historian Francis Fukuyama (*The End of History*, Free Press, January 1992) believed that the liberal democratic, capitalistic system had triumphed once and for all. That meant that the U.S. form of government would be unchallenged, hence the end of history. However, new wicked problems that society and management faced after

the end of the Soviet Union were threats from terrorism, ecological–technological disaster potentials, global warming, computer virus assaults, cyberterrorism, and SARS-like plagues. In response, government agencies and international organizations created some operations-oriented steps to deal with the shift in types of threats from the cold war era to the post-9/11 era. Discussion and examples are included in points a. through e. Which one of these statements is not correct?

   a. ISO 17799:2000 is a set of guidelines for the security of information systems. Although this is broadly applicable, it was drawn up to apply to operations. ISO 17799 is intended to minimize the risk of systems failure and to protect the integrity of software and information. Application to e-business systems is evident. ISO 17799:2000 was developed by the same International Organization for Standardization in Geneva, Switzerland, that created ISO 9000.

   b. There are 10 major sections in ISO 17799:2000. These are designed to facilitate trading in a trusted environment. Three of the major sections in ISO 17799:2000 are (1) business continuity planning to counteract interruptions caused by disasters, (2) physical security to prevent unauthorized access, damage, and interference, and (3) personnel security to reduce risks of human error, theft, fraud, or misuse of facilities. Visit http://www.iso17799software.com/what.htm.

   c. ISO 17666:2003 is an ISO guideline for reducing project risks. Although it is designed to apply to space programs, it is also intended to be used by any industry that wishes to minimize project risks. This ISO guideline provides templates to systematically assess, plan, measure, and report risks throughout the development of the projects.

   d. The Department of Homeland Security issues threat-level warnings. Visit: http://www.dhs.gov. Click on "Threat Advisory" in the upper right-hand corner for details on these threat conditions. These advisories apply to municipal services [police, fire, EMS, and TSA (Transportation Security Administration)], but have no bearing on industrial, commercial, or service operations. Visit http://www.emsmagazine.com for timely updates on EMS systems.

   e. Hazardous waste operations and emergency response (HAZWOPER) training is required by OSHA. This is for employees who are designated by their companies to respond to hazardous material emergencies. Organizations that are in compliance with other OSHA safety requirements and trained for HAZWOPER have a great head start in coping with natural disasters (e.g., earthquakes or hurricanes) or willful violence (e.g., terrorism).

9. Some business benefits of ISO 14000 are listed here. They have been provided by the International Organization for Standardization in Geneva, Switzerland, at http://www.iso.org/iso/en/iso9000-14000/tour/benef14k.html. The posted concepts have been interpreted and expanded to fit the interests of P/OM. Four of the five listed points are correct. Which one is in error?

   a. Some managers will do what is necessary to avoid legal penalties for polluting. They will do only what is required to comply with legislation. This is a reactive P/OM strategy based on spending as little as possible to conform. For example, contamination of air and water is kept just below the allowable threshold. There is usually a large opportunity cost for using this strategy.

b. The opportunity cost for not being proactive by keeping contamination levels far below allowable thresholds is related to low community esteem and lack of customer admiration for the company. Regulators may look longer and harder at a company that is known to barely comply with regulations.

c. Additional benefits accrue to companies that consider part of their mission to be reduction of waste products by encouraging reuse, remanufacture, rework, and recycling. There are usually material and energy savings from reuse strategies.

d. The drawback for companies using ISO 14000 is that different rules apply in various parts of the world. If two countries subscribe to ISO 14000, there is less likelihood that each country will demand that its own regulations be followed. Nevertheless, the ISO 14000 in one place may not be acceptable in another.

e. ISO 14000 can help to lower distribution costs. If too many trucks are delivering too few items, causing unacceptable pollution, the company EMS should detect that fact. The EMS will provide faster alert than would be available from environmental activists who break the news.

10. Technology is being developed to counteract high threat levels. Defense and protection requires analysis of threats. Security-technology for EDS (explosive detection systems) is in process. Fingerprint and face identification systems are being improved. See http://www.identix.com for automated biometric identification, mobile, remote, and continuous scan ID platforms. Robot technology provides access that is least life-threatening and invasiveness. Technology is also being developed to improve safety in healthcare systems. In addition to technology, there are many algorithms for improving the quality of life that are on the drawing boards or in test. A list of potential applications of new technology and improved systems has been developed by the P/OM students in a distance-learning class. They have assembled this list and circulated it amongst themselves for verification. Several of the 16 points a. through p. are incorrect. Identify which ones are wrong.

a. Hazard Analysis and Critical Control Point (HACCP) system is an airport security system that is able to detect explosives and gases. It is based on 3-sigma quality control charts. It can automatically send a signal when an out-of-control point is detected.

b. Mobile robots have been used successfully for various kinds of police work including bomb squad operations.

c. HACCP was pioneered by the Pillsbury Company (http://www.pillsbury.com) in the 1960s to create safe food for the space program.

d. Dogs have been successfully used for detecting drugs and explosives.

e. Service robots have been developed (see http://www.pyxis.com) for use in hospitals, which has significantly reduced healthcare errors.

f. Pillsbury, not the Food and Drug Administration (FDA), uses the Doughboy to promote their products.

g. HACCP requires that companies handling spoiled foods develop safe ways to dispose of them. This is called a *food deviation*. HACCP also required that records of food disposal be maintained.

h. Thalidomide unexpectedly caused severely adverse birth defects. This drug (used for morning sickness) never received approval by the U.S. Food and Drug Administration. Many problems arose because it had been approved for use in Europe. See http://www.fda.gov/cder/news/thalidomide.htm.

i. Pyxis Homerus® is an integrated centralized pharmacy with automated dispensing systems. It retrieves pharmaceuticals from its own storage system and packages appropriate doses with information bar codes for accuracy.

j. Pyxis Homerus® addresses the 5Rs as stated in *Nursing Responsibilities Regarding Drugs*. These are entirely operational issues, as follows: Use the right drug, dose, and route, at the right time for the right person.

k. Security has unique problems to address when telecommuting and telework are used either from home base or with hot-desking, hoteling (aka virtual offices). Among the dangers is the transfer of confidential information under insecure conditions. Also, unknown occupants can examine files and computer records. For hot-desking, see http://www.eoffice.net and for hoteling, see http://www.dea.com/Hot.asp.

l. The website http://manufacturing.stanford.edu provides virtual online plant tours that can be used to provide security information.

m. The SME Manufacturing Enterprise Wheel is a total systems approach that centers on the customer. Among the factors that need to be added when the next update of the wheel appears are safety, security, and health issues.

n. IDs can be accurate without being invasive. Fingerprints, facial structure, retina prints, etc., provide reliable information.

o. Robots of many kinds could help to repatriate jobs that are currently going abroad. However, new techno-robots will not bring people-jobs back to the United States. The hourly wage for robots may not please the union leaders.

p. Contingency planning is planning for the possible, not the inevitable, nor only the probable. The possible includes the improbable, and it may be wise to take another look at the impossible. Contingency planning deals with more than forecasts of events to come. It can alter the probabilities of future events.

ADDITIONAL READINGS

Capek, Karel. *Rossum's Universal Robots (R.U.R.)*. 1920. For a list of up-to-date references to R.U.R., see http://www.uwec.edu/Academic/Curric/jerzdg/RUR. Note: The Czech word "robota" means drudgery or servitude; "robotnik" is a serf. *R.U.R.* was first published in English in 1923. It has been performed on stage for many years.

Collins, Jim. *Good to Great*. New York: Harper Collins, October 2001.

Department of Health and Human Services, Food and Drug Administration (FDA). *Proposal to Establish Procedures for the Safe Processing and Importing of Fish and Fishery Products*, 21 CFR Parts 123 and 1240 [Docket Nos. 90N-0199 and 93N-0195]. Also, U.S. FDA Center for Food Safety and Applied Nutrition (CFSAN), Office of Seafood, FDA's Evaluation of the Seafood HACCP Program for Fiscal Years 2000/2001, September 30, 2002.

Greene, Richard Tabor. *Global Quality: A Synthesis of the World's Best Management Methods*. Burr Ridge, IL: Irwin, 1993.

Historical information for the HACCP program. *Federal Register*, vol. 59, no. 19 (January 28, 1994). Companion document: "Fish and Fishery Products Hazards and Controls Guide." *FDA Draft Document*, PB94-140-985.

Horn, Berthold K. P. *Robot Vision*. Cambridge, MA: MIT Press, March 1986. Also, see Chae, H. An, Christopher G. Atkeson,

and John Hollerbach. *Model-Based Control of a Robot Manipulator*. MIT Press, March 2003.

Imai, Masaaki. *Kaizen: The Key to Japan's Competitive Success*. New York: McGraw-Hill/Irwin, November 1986.

Imai, Masaaki. *Gemba Kaizen: A Commonsense, Low-Cost Approach to Management*. New York: McGraw-Hill Trade, March 1997.

McGrath, Michael E. *Product Strategy for High-Technology Companies: How to Achieve Growth, Competitive Advantage, and Increased Profits*. Burr Ridge, IL: Irwin Professional Publishing, 1995.

Menzel Peter, and Faith D'Aluisio. *Robo Sapiens: Evolution of New Species*. MIT Press, September 2000.

Puchek, Vladimir, Noel Tichy, and Carole K. Barnett (eds.). *Globalizing Management: Creating and Leading the Competitive Organization*. New York: Wiley, 1993.

Schmierer, Germot, and Rolf Schraft. *Service Robots*. (German edition, 1996). A. K. Peters, Ltd., July 2000.

Stalk, G., P. Evans, and L. E. Shulman. "Competing on Capabilities: The New Rules of Corporate Strategy." *Harvard Business Review* (March–April 1992).

Summers, David A. *Waterjetting Technology*. London, England: E. F. Spon, Ltd., Division of Chapman & Hall, 1995.

NOTES

1. John Odwazny, Carlos Da Maia, and Gordon Kuljian (figures by Dr. Lydia Frenzel). "Advances in High Production Robotic Water-Jetting for the Marine Industry." *Journal of Protective Linings and Coatings*. (April 2002): 47–56.

2. Gene Bylinsky. "Manufacturing for Reuse." *Fortune* (February 6, 1995).

3. This information was obtained in conversation with John J. Resslar, Champion, Designs for the Environment, Saturn Corporation. Update, March 2000. John J. Resslar is now manager of the Design for the Environment at the World Wide Facilities of the General Motors Corporation.

4. William Turley. *Headline News* at http://www.recyclingtoday.com, March 2, 2003. Also, "9/11 Clean-Up Memories Linger." *C&D News* (October 22, 2002).

5. "Airbus to Deepen Investment, Cooperation in China." *China InfoFlash* (August 2001): 1.

6. "Economic Cancer." *Lawyer News* (September 23, 2002).

7. Alex Berenson. "A Caldron of Ethics and Asbestos." *The New York Times, Business Day* (March 12, 2003): C1, 22.

8. Department of Health and Human Services, Food and Drug Administration. *Proposal to Establish Procedures for the Safe Processing and Importing of Fish and Fishery Products*, 21 CFR Parts 123 and 1240 [Docket Nos. 90N-0199 and 93N-0195]. Also, U.S. FDA Center for Food Safety and Applied Nutrition (CFSAN), Office of Seafood, FDA's Evaluation of the Seafood HAACP Program for Fiscal Years 2000/2001, September 30, 2002.

9. For steps 1–7, many of the phrases are taken directly from the government document cited in Note 6. Modifications occur in "HACCP: A State of the Art Approach to Food Safety." *FDA Backgrounder* (October 2001), and those are also included. At the same time, liberal paraphrasing has been used.

10. J. A. DiMasi. "Cost of Innovation in the Pharmaceutical Industry." *Journal of Health Economics*, Amsterdam, Elsevier Publishing Co., vol. 10, no. 2 (July 1991): 107–142. The breakdown is: Laboratory studies: 3.5 years; 1st Phase—Safety, 1.0 year; 2nd Phase—Testing Effectiveness, 2.0 years; 3rd Phase—Extensive Clinical Testing, 3.0 years; FDA Review, 2.5 years; Total Time: 12.0 years.

11. For 2002 data, see the article by J. A. DiMasi. "The Economics of Pharmaceutical Innovation:Trends in Costs, Risks and Returns." *CPSA 2002 Digest* (October 8, 2002). Proceedings at http://www.milestonedevelopment.com/CPSA/2002.

12. William Bridges. "The End of the Job." *Fortune* (September 19, 1994): 62–74.

13. The word *robot* was derived from the Czech words *robota*, meaning "work" and *robotnick*, meaning "worker," by Karel Capek for his play, "RUR (Rossum's Universal Robots)," written in 1920.

14. Berthold K. P. Horn. *Robot Vision*. MIT Press, March 1986. Also, see Chae, H. An, Christopher G. Atkeson, and John Hollerbach. *Model-Based Control of a Robot Manipulator*. MIT Press, March 2003.

15. CBS News Sunday Morning. "Close Watch." April 21, 2002. http://www.cbsnews.com/stories/2002/04/19/sunday/main506739.shtml.

16. Gernot Schmierer and Rolf Dieter Schraft. *Service Robots*. London, England: A. K. Peters, Ltd., July 2000. This book was first published in German in 1996.

17. Peter Menzel (photography) and Faith D'Aluisio. *Robo Sapiens: Evolution of New Species*. MIT Press, September 1, 2000.

18. Susan Okie. "Robots Make the Rounds to Ease Hospitals' Costs." *The Washington Post* (April 3, 2002).

19. Described in *Computer Models of the Fundamental Mechanisms of Thought*, by Douglas Hofstadter and the Fluid Analogies Research Group, New York: Basic Books, 1995.

20. Mitchell Pacelle. "Vanishing Offices: To Trim Their Costs, Some Companies Cut Space for Employees." *The Wall Street Journal* (June 4, 1993): A1.

21. Also, see the *e-WorkWire Newsletter*, of Valley Metro, Maricopa, Arizona (Winter 2003).

22. Montieth M. Illingworth. "Virtual Managers." *Information Week* (June 13, 1994): 44. For the Virtual Assistant, see *Business Week* (Enterprise), (September 14, 1998).

23. Susan Diesenhouse. "Price Waterhouse Tries Check-In-and-Out Office." *The New York Times* (December 7, 1994).

24. Business Bulletin, *The Wall Street Journal* (March 9, 1995): 1.

25. Quote from International Standards Organization (ISO) working paper *ISO/TC 207/SC 1/N 47 for ISO/CD 14001 Environmental Management Systems—Specification with Guidance for Use*, Geneva, Switzerland, September 2000.

26. Computer and Automated Systems Association of the Society of Manufacturing Engineers (CASA/SME). *The New Manufacturing Enterprise Wheel*, 3e. Publication of CASA/SME, Dearborn, MI, 1993.

SPOTLIGHT 20-1
Good Ethics Makes Business Good

S. Truett Cathy, Chairman of Chick-fil-A®, Inc., Cautions, "Never Overextend Yourself."

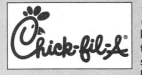

S. Truett Cathy, the founder and chairman of Chick-fil-A, Inc., has earned his success by consistently creating and delivering superior value. The Cathy family has been building restaurants and fast-food franchises that have been winning the loyalty of customers, franchisees, team members, and friends for over half a century. Truett opened his first restaurant in 1946. According to Cathy, anyone can open a restaurant. Keeping it open for many decades is the true test of success. After opening more than 1,000 Chick-fil-A stores in 36 states, with the expectation that the franchisee operators will commit to running their enterprise for at least two decades, Cathy's recent book *Eat Mor Chikin®: Inspire More People. Doing Business the Chick-fil-A Way* will encourage readers to look deeper, go further, and try harder.

The story of S. Truett Cathy, his wife, Jeannette Cathy, their three children, and how they have succeeded in working together to grow a billion-dollar business is an important P/OM story. By the age of eight, young Truett was making money selling Coca-Cola and magazine subscriptions from door to door, overcoming a speech impediment, and learning ways to please his customers. By the age of 12, he had bought a bicycle and was old enough for a paper route. At home, he enjoyed the trial and error of cooking (his mother never used a recipe) and learned how to clean up after himself in the kitchen. Truett used his mother's methods of marinating and cooking chicken when he began to develop his famous Chick-fil-A® Chicken Sandwich, the first gourmet-type product in a fast-food restaurant. He tells people to remember to do things right each and every time, not just sometimes. To quote him, "A person can have a pleasant experience in a restaurant 50 times but be disappointed or treated rudely just once and never come back. It is so important to be consistent in your service as well as the quality of your product."

Truett Cathy learned that it is a "do-it-yourself" world. Keeping his priorities in order is a central commitment. A deeply religious man, Cathy avoids making long-range life plans. He prefers to remain open to unexpected opportunities. He believes that we change ourselves and the world by our response to the unexpected opportunities that come along every day. Most of them are opportunities to give—our time, our love, or our resources. He asks readers: How will you respond today? In all his relationships, Cathy finds joy in giving when he does not expect anything in return. Truett gives much of his time and resources to support and guide young people, who appreciate smiles and hugs as much as popcorn and ice cream. Because his daughter invited him to visit her and her husband in Brazil, he now maintains a Brazilian foster care home for children as part of his WinShape Foundation in the United States, which has also provided more than 17,000 $1,000 scholarships to students who attended more than 2,300 colleges across the country. The foundation also runs summer camps for children.

A caveat from Truett Cathy to seekers of success: "Never overextend yourself." Cathy would rather have 70 restaurants operating efficiently and professionally than 500 restaurants where only one-half are run well. This lesson was learned in the early days when he and his brother Ben were building their business with no money for advertising. "We had to build our restaurant on satisfied customers, one at a time," he writes. He warns against the formula of borrowing as much money as you can, renting a fancy office, and starting out with the image of success. He believes that the most common reason companies fail is their desire to grow faster than they can manage, especially companies that make a public offering and find themselves staring at a pile of money. Truett writes, "All they want to do is to grow. But you have to digest growth as you go. Slight economic downturns can force layoffs of employees to salvage the company. You don't build a good reputation by discharging people, but rather by developing people." He continues, "I want everyone who works at Chick-fil-A to feel secure that we will not resort to layoffs because we are overextended."

The company's record speaks for itself. Chick-fil-A, advertised by a few spelling-challenged cows climbing on billboards, is the second-largest quick-service chicken restaurant in the nation based on sales. It has consistently maintained its 36-year consecutive sales growth. Dan Cathy, one of Truett's sons, said that posting sales gains every year since the first outlet opened in 1967 is a testament to the chain's restaurant operators and "our prudent expansion policy."

Truett Cathy shares business problems with his family as well as important business decisions. Deciding to give employees and their families a chance to be together at least one day a week illustrates the company's profound commitment to family. No Chick-fil-A store is open on Sunday. The Cathy sons [Dan is president and COO and Don (Bubba) is senior vice president] and daughter, Trudy Cathy White, have signed a covenant with their parents, pledging to stay closed on Sundays and keep the company private. Dan says his father has laid out a solid business blueprint he intends to follow closely, adding, "He's been an incredible role model as a business person."

Sources: Cathy, S. Truett. *Eat Mor Chikin®: Inspire More People. Doing Business the Chick-fil-A Way*. Decatur, GA: Looking Glass Books, 2002; Jackson, Jerry W. "Chick-fil-A Inc. Pecks Out Yet Another Profitable Year." *Orlando Sentinel CFB* (January 27–February 2, 2003); Pedicini, Sandra. "Devotion Drives Chick-fil-A Founder." *Orlando Sentinel* (August 10, 2003); http://www.successfactors.org/911/cathy.html.

SPOTLIGHT 20-2
Securing the Right Decision

Humpty Dumpty Might Still Be in One Piece

Considering his fragile state, if Humpty Dumpty had thought through his decision to sit on the wall, he might still be in one piece. The same goes for top executives who fail to consider both the unintended as well as intended consequences of a decision. The first wrong move will topple the others, says crisis management advisor Robin Cohn. That's why she calls these actions "domino decisions."

No matter the industry or problem, a domino decision can impact security. The resulting anger of those negatively affected, including employees, protest groups, and victims, will cause them to act-out in some way, Robin explains. Theft, damaging media leaks, and sabotage are all possible by-products; a company must be ready.

Unfortunately, many executives don't understand that all decisions have ramifications, notes Robin, author of the *PR Crisis Bible* and president of Robin Cohn and Company. She's seen the consequences. With more than 20 years of advising top executives, she has managed such crises as a plane crash, hijackings, government investigations, product boycotts, and corporate scandals.

A domino decision can bring down companies and top executives, Robin warns. Too often, executives look for short-term results without thinking of their impact down the road. For example, what if the auditing firm Arthur Andersen had resigned the Enron account when its internal auditors warned of Enron's illegal accounting practices? Yes, the company would have lost a top client who brought in millions of dollars. Yet, the firm would still be in business.

What if Firestone had recalled its tires when it first saw growing claims of tire separation in 1992? A recall would have been expensive. However, in 2000, a National Highway Traffic Safety Administration investigation and a massive public uproar led to a recall of 6.5 million tires. Firestone's once sterling brand name was irrevocably damaged.

Another pitfall in decision making is not looking at the big picture, Robin explains. For example, a domino decision brought down Don Carty, American Airline's former chairman and CEO. To avoid bankruptcy, American Airlines asked three unions to make painful and costly concessions. At the same time, the company approved retention bonuses and pension payments for top executives. The unions were outraged when they learned of the executive perks and threatened to vote against concessions. The controversy forced the airline to drop its plans to compensate top executives, and Mr. Carty was fired. The unions later approved the concessions.

"This crisis could have been avoided if decision makers had seriously considered the ramifications of granting bonus packages while asking their own employees to make sacrifices," Robin says.

Such is the problem of executive entitlement. Robin warns top executives about acting upon the belief that "some are more equal than others." In addition, many make the false assumption that actions can be kept quiet or won't be noticed. This ivory tower mind-set often skews decisions to benefit top management at the company's expense. Take Enron. The company began facing losses. The top executives realized that telling the truth would be bad for the stock and their own enrichment. Private partnerships were created to get the debt off the balance sheet. Five years later, the domino decision to hide losses wound up costing the now-bankrupt company $1.2 billion in market value.

"While top executives might have control in the executive suite, they don't in the outside world," Robin concludes.

Damaging domino decisions don't only occur in the corporate suite. Robin points to the case of the Augusta National Golf Club when it refused women membership in 2002. This move attracted a great deal of controversy. This domino decision had ramifications that went beyond a golf club's membership rules to ultimately hurt Augusta's economy. The club hosts the prestigious Masters Tournament. Due to the decision, many corporate leaders stayed away, not wanting to be perceived as supporting the club's policy. Sponsors canceled, protesters were outside the gates, and overall attendance fell. Hotels, restaurants and other services were left feeling the pinch during what should have been the biggest money-making event of the year.

It's important to note that not all domino decisions are bad. In some cases, a good decision can contain a crisis and win praise, Robin points out. Johnson & Johnson's provides a famous example. Facing the 1982 scare over Tylenol capsules laced with cyanide, CEO James Burke made the decision to own up to the problem and fix it. That domino decision to act responsibly wound up enhancing both the company's and Mr. Burke's reputation. "Ultimately, the right ethical decision is also the right business decision," Robin emphasizes.

Whether it is product tampering (Tylenol), angry unions (American Airlines), protesters (Masters Tournament), a company going out of business (Arthur Andersen), or accidents from unsafe tires (Firestone), a company needs to have security plans in place for internal and external consequences.

The pressures of a crisis situation can often affect judgment. Yet, that's the time when clear thinking is essential. To avoid a damaging domino decision, Robin recommends the following:

- Think things through. What are you trying to accomplish? Who will be affected? How will this decision be perceived? Do you have all the information? What are the alternatives? What could go wrong?
- Examine what could really happen versus what you would like to have happen.
- Always consider which way the public-opinion wind is blowing.
- Get feedback: Encourage others to play devils' advocates.

Source: Robin Cohn, author of The PR Crisis Bible, is a nationally recognized crisis management advisor who works with executive decision makers to avoid or contain any problem that affects a company's reputation and bottom line.

Robin Cohn and Company
20 W. 64th Street, #11-U
New York, NY 10023 212-874-6108
jnfo@crisiscontrol.com
http://www.crisiscontrol.com

SPOTLIGHT 20-3
Saving Time and Money by Postponement

An Interview With Kevin Howard of Hewlett-Packard

What do Burger King and the Hewlett-Packard Company have in common that earns P/OM accolades for both companies? The answer is postponement to allow customization of a product and its packaging resulting from careful analysis and design.

Burger King prepares its Whopper or burger sandwich and then places it under the cover of a steam table for up to 10 minutes so that it can be finalized to satisfy the customer's request. Other items are stored in a Henny Penny warmer for up to 30 minutes. These work-in-process (WIP), inventoried items enable Burger King to make good on their marketing statement, "Have it your way."

A more complex postponement strategy was begun by the Hewlett-Packard Company (HP) in 1989. HP started manufacturing generic models of ink-jet printers at their Vancouver, Washington factory and in Singapore. These printers were shipped to three distribution centers (DCs) around the world where they were "localized" for their final destination. Localization means adding country-specific power modules and language-specific software and manuals to the boxes at the DC sites. Before 1989, printers were made and packaged in line with forecasts for country and language-specific SKUs.

To better respond to fluctuating demands for specific localized configurations of printers without increasing inventory levels, analyses were done by HP engineers and P/OM consultants from academia. Some of the people who worked on this project were Brent Carter, Manager for Special Projects, Kevin Howard, HP packaging logistics engineer, and Hau Lee, a professor at the Stanford Business School. To avoid forecasting which had sizeable errors of both types (overstocks and out-of-stocks), they studied various systems of postponing fulfillment until actual orders were on-hand.

Kevin Howard's assignment was to determine a way to localize printer shipments This was first accomplished by using a new box design to ship the printers from the manufacturing plants to the distribution centers (DCs). These boxes had a flap that could be opened and the localizing materials inserted at the DC without removing the printers from the pallets. This allowed DCs to localize the units at a point in the distribution process when demand was known which resulted in major savings. However, as Howard said, "It was clear to me we were paying a lot for shipping this empty space in the boxes ... and were spending (for Europe, at that time) almost $400,000 a year on repackaging boxes that had been damaged during distribution overseas."

Considerable product damage resulted from repetitive handling of boxes. Some damage was caused by fork lift trucks as the boxed printers were moved on wood pallets. Who would have guessed that fork lift truck operators would take greater care with printers they could see than with

boxes that made the product invisible? Packaging experts might confirm that large anonymous cardboard boxes are a natural target for lift forks and a place to stand on for stacking. With a visible product, damage rates decreased to near-zero, representing significant savings.

Howard's second improvement was accomplished in the early 1990s. Instead of palletizing half-empty printer boxes, unboxed printers were packed on cavitated foam trays so that more could fit on a wood pallet. Elimination of boxes allowed pallet density to increase from 32 units per pallet to 60 units per pallet. This process permitted shipping more printers. It also decreased product damage because trays could be moved as a unit, which did away with box-by-box handling.

A third improvement replaced heavy wood pallets with plastic (polyethylene) slip sheets that provided flexible platforms for shipping. Special fork lift truck adapters to handle slip sheets and elimination of the wooden pallets allowed HP to get 25 percent more printers in the stack and to reduce transportation, storage, and materials handling costs by 25 percent.

Kevin Howard believed that the use of wood pallets was "a tragic misuse of our natural resources." He said that a significant percent of all hardwood cut down in the U.S. goes into the manufacture of 520 million wood pallets per year—360 million of which are thrown away after one use. The reuse rate in Europe is better because of standardized pallet designs and agreements to re-employ these pallets.

In the 1990s, the high-density polyethylene (HDPE) sheets, which are the thickness of a cardboard cereal box, were made of 100% recycled milk jugs. Also during that period, HP returned the used slip sheets to the manufacturer for recycling. These plastic slip sheets continue to be recycled.

When this study was first undertaken, HP was shipping about 150,000 printers per month. A decade later, that number has grown to more than 3 million per month. Densifying the loads from 32 boxed printers on a pallet to 75 unboxed printers on a slip sheet saved tens of millions of dollars in logistics costs. Adding language-specific accessories and electrical connections at the DC rather than at the factory reduced inventory carrying costs about 20%, saving many millions of dollars annually. Additionally, inventory levels decreased for the supply chain pipeline and for the safety stock required to keep out-of-stocks at a specified service level.

Presently, HP has many plants in many places in the world, but it continues to use postponement of final packaging and country-specific product differentiation. The systems approach, as described above, continues to increase flexibility and reduce unnecessary waste. Contrary to the old maxim, he who hesitates may be consciously avoiding irreversible mistakes by using the postponement method.

Sources: Kevin Howard, "Postponement of packaging and product differentiation for lower logistics costs," invited paper presented to the Council of Logistics Management Conference, Michigan State University, May 1991, and conversations with Kevin Howard, December 2003.

Glossary

A

ABC classification: Materials purchased for use by P/OM processes can be classified by their importance in several ways. For one of these ways, see **Criticality**. The most widely used ABC classification of inventory is by dollar volume, which drives cash flow "in" and "out." ABC classifies inventory items in rank order by dollar volume. Generally, 25 percent of *all* items (SKUs) contribute 75 percent of *total* dollar volume. These are called A-type SKU. That means 75 percent of *all* items (SKU) represent only 25 percent of the *total* dollar volume. These are called B- and C-types, which although labeled the *insignificant many*, for some purposes they are hardly trivial. ABC relationships do bring awareness to materials management of the critical importance of the few. The ABC contribution to production methods is attributed to Del Harder of the Ford Motor Company.

Acceptance sampling: Inspecting acceptability of suppliers' shipments by using sampling of required qualities instead of 100 percent inspection. The sampling plan is a statistical method for estimating the probability of accepting a production batch (many units) by sampling a small number of units from the batch. If a certain number of defectives are found in the sample, the batch will be rejected because of the statistical relationship of defectives in the sample to defectives in the batch. Statistical design of acceptance sampling plans requires knowledge of how these parameters relate to the average percent defectives in the batches.

Acceptance sampling methods: Set the inspection parameters for drawing a sample from a production lot. If the sample fails to pass the test because it has too many defectives, then the entire lot is inspected. Defectives are removed, which is called *detailing*. The result is a defect-free lot. If the sample passes the test, there may be some defectives according to the design of the test. Acceptance sampling assumes that the production process is stable.

Action learning: (1) A training technique that rotates employees through a variety of jobs in pursuit of broader understanding of the company's goals and methods. Action learning is a systems-oriented pedagogical method. For example, marketing managers are assigned to machines on the plant floor, and production managers are asked to collect market research data at local supermarkets. When purchasing is switched to accounting and human resource managers are assigned to purchasing, remarkable insights can develop.
(2) Trading jobs for a period of time allows one to stand in the other's shoes and encourages systems-wide thinking. Action learning spurs team building and has the advantage of role-playing for more than a few minutes. Companies that use action learning are at the training forefront because it seems disruptive to managers who want to maintain the status quo.

Activities-on-arrows (AOA): Also known as activities-on-arcs, the project network is structured with numbered node circles connected by arrows. The project activities are the connecting arrows. They start with one numbered node and end with the other node. Sometimes more than one activity (arrow) converges at a node (use the forward pass rule) or more than one activity (arrow) leaves a node (use the backward pass rule). See **Activities-on-nodes, Backward pass rule**, and **Forward pass rule.**

Activities-on-nodes (AON): The project network is structured with numbered node circles connected by arrows. The numbered nodes are the project activities. Arrows between nodes show the precedence of activities. Project software can be read easily as AON, but forward and backward pass computations require AOA concepts. See **Activities-on-arrows, Backward pass rule**, and **Forward pass rule**.

Activity-based costing (ABC) systems: Replaces traditional, volume-driven cost accounting methods with expenses only for resources actually used by the production system. ABC systems make clear the labor costs that would not have been incurred if the job had not been done. These costs must be incurred when the job is done. Further, ABC makes evident the labor costs that would have occurred whether or not the job is done. These costs are divided into used and unused portions. ABC can be credited with raising awareness about making cost allocations that are representative of the actual labor and materials that an activity uses.

Actual capacity: The realistic maximum amount of storage space or output rate that can be achieved with the existing configuration of resources and the accepted product or service mix plans. Strategic planners know that decisions about capacity are among the most important P/OM activities. In the hierarchy of capacity measurement, volume and volume flow rates trump measures of area and length. Capacity breakeven area relates to the number of tables in a restaurant that are allowed and can be serviced. Linear capacity relates to the number of cars that can travel on a 4-lane highway. Capacity of an elevator or a swimming pool is a volumetric concept. Similarly, the actual capacity of a warehouse might be stated as the number of cubic feet the warehouse holds. The ultimate measure of the production system is its actual throughput capacity—the number of units that the P/OM system can produce and ship. Engineers design systems with theoretical flow specifications that assume everything works perfectly. P/OM deals with the fact that nothing works perfectly all of the time. Actual capacity is the realistic interpretation of the theoretical maximum capacity.

Aggregate planning (AP): The specific purpose of AP is to schedule production for the job shop. When there are a variety of machines and workers with (some) crossover capabilities, it is essential to develop a set of common denominators (e.g., standard hours). Then, resources can be grouped and schedules developed for jobs to be done. Resource utilization (e.g., second shift and/or overtime) affect job completion times. Specifically, different job–machine combinations are transformed into standard hours of supply and demand. Standard hours of supply are measured by the output of a designated standard machine. Aggregate planning converts strategic *company plans* into *production plans*, which lead to the tactical determination of production schedules. See **Standard units**.

Analytic process: A production process that starts with one ingredient. Using appropriate transformation techniques, the process turns a single, basic ingredient into several or (even) many products. For example, cabbage can be transformed into coleslaw, sauerkraut, and the cabbage that goes with corn beef. Also, some single basic ingredients, SBI's, can be taken apart for various uses, e.g., cream and milk. Further, analytic processes can start with a few rather than only one basic ingredient.

Artificial intelligence (AI): Based on copying the nervous system of human beings to develop mechanisms that have the capability of sensing and learning. More broadly, aimed at understanding the nature of intelligence, including the ability to compute, remember, and to make good decisions. The purpose is to engineer systems analogous to neural networks that exhibit such intelligence.

Assemble-to-order (ATO) environment: Setting where end items are built from subassemblies. Master production schedules ensure that the subassemblies are available to meet demand within promised due dates. Fabrication of parts takes place offline. Common to computers and cell phone assembly. Contrast with make-to-stock (MTS) and make-to-order (MTO). Heavy equipment industry prefers to use ATO; however, market realities and competitive actions have created need for inventories of finished goods for many (standard) types of equipment.

Assignable causes: Identifiable causes of process problems that create variability. They are traceable and can be removed. This is in contrast to chance causes. Also called *special causes*, methods of statistical quality control are aimed at identifying and removing them to reduce variability. The aim is for only chance cause variability to remain.

Assignment method: A decision model for matching *n* resources with *n* resource users. Examples of assignment problems are legion: how to assign *n* jobs requiring various skills to *n* workers possessing various skills. Assign managers to stores, boats to slips, horses to starting positions, etc. The method provides the *best* assignment where *best* can be lowest total cost, highest total revenue or profit, and greatest total satisfaction. The square matrix epitomizes the constraint of no splitting of a resource between users and no sharing of several resources by any one user. The method minimizes the sum of the opportunity costs. See **Opportunity cost.**

Average performance: There are various uses for the phrase. One applies to performance evaluation where judgment of the evaluator is that performance is average. A more specific meaning is associated with time studies where many observations are taken by an observer using a stopwatch or by a computer timing operations. Sum *N* numbers and divide by *N* to obtain average performance (or average time), which is then adjusted to obtain productivity standards.

B

Backward pass rule: Also known as the backward convergence rule, it is similar and opposite to the forward pass (or convergence) rule. The backward pass rule: When two or more arrows emanate from a single node, choose the arrow with the smallest value of the latest start time. The backward pass rule enables the critical path to be identified. It also permits the determination of slack. Taken together with the forward pass rule, the fundamental parameters of the project can be calculated. These calculations for the network can be manual, but for projects of realistic size, software is essential to manage the network algorithms and the information system that underlies them. For details of the methods, the text should be consulted. See **Critical path methods (CPM), Forward pass rule,** and **Slack.**

Balance delay (*d*): A percentage measure of idle time across all of the workstations that participate in the complete process cycle. Perfect balance is when $d = 0$. Anything other than perfect balance delay is an assessment of the system's inefficiency. When $d > 0$, imperfect balance prevails. This equation calculates the percent of unproductive time at the total set of flow shop process stations that accounts for the process cycle time, C. $d = 100(nC - \Sigma_i t_i / nC)$ where *n* = number of work stations; C = cycle time; $\Sigma_i t_i$ = total work content, also called *TWC*; and nC = total flow shop workstation time available. Note that $nC - TWC$ = idle time across all workstations. See **Cycle time** and **Line efficiency.**

Baldrige Award: Public Law 100–107 is the Malcolm Baldrige National Quality Improvement Act signed into law on August 20, 1987, by the U.S. Congress. This award for quality management (in the sense of TQM) resulted from the fact that the United States had been sensitized to the high costs of inferior quality by Japanese successes in making automotive products within the United States.

Bar chart: Graphical method that uses bars of different lengths to present numerical and/or statistical data. For example, along the *x*-axis are different types of events such as various spectator sports. The height of the bars might indicate the number of people who attended each type of sport in the prior year. That number is measured along the *y*-axis. Bar charts are considered to be among the easiest graphical representations to understand.

Benchmarking: (1) A method for comparing processes with one that is considered to be the best. The secret is to choose significant dimensions for comparison and then to measure those dimensions in an accurate way. Customer satisfaction is a popular benchmark with many service firms. This dimension is difficult to measure. (2) A systematic method for comparing one process with another. The idea is to use what is learned to improve. Comparing our systems with the "best" can assist the effort to emulate the leaders. It is not easy to identify leaders in similar processes. The secret is to choose significant dimensions for comparison and measure those dimensions in an accurate way. For some, the goal is to get "better than the best."

Best in class: The top choice for the benchmarking standard. It is the candidate to beat. Note the benchmarking reference to "better than the best." It fits the World Series in baseball or the Super Bowl in football.

Best location: Location, location, location . . . what are they talking about? This answer is based on pragmatic (observed) information: A *necessary* but *not sufficient* condition for success in business is to get the right location. The right (or best) location is defined by the function of the facility and the characteristics of its products and services. For example, in the retail business, best locations generate high-contact frequencies with "potential customers." Location is best when it is specially tailored to the particulars of the situation, e.g., close to the market, near suppliers, able to draw on highly-skilled work pools, facilitates joining about 12,000 other maquiladoras (U.S. and others-owned and -operated assembly factories located along the 2,100 mile border that separates Mexico and the United States, employing over 1 million workers). See http://www.uwec.edu/geography/ Ivogeler/w188/border/maquil.htm. A popular alternative: Be in Beijing.

Best practice: A process standard based on identifying those who perform the process in the best way yet known. Benchmarking should set best practice as the standard for comparison.

Bidding: Provides the appearance (and allows the reality) of purchasing decisions that are not influenced by donations or outright gifts. Suppliers meet specifications, including costs and delivery dates, and the buyer chooses the offer that is preferred. Selection includes many factors, including vendor reliability. Quality can suffer from buying on price alone. Government requirements often specify the manner in which bidding is to be conducted, including number of bidders.

Bill of material (BOM): Describes in detail what constitutes the end product. One of three inputs to the MRP information system, viz., MPS, IRF, and BOM. For a dinner party, it is the cook's shopping list. BOM lists all of the subassemblies, parts, and raw materials that go into a parent assembly showing the quantities required. A variety of display formats for BOM exist, including single-level, indented, modular, transient, matrix form, and "costed" bill. It is called the "formula, "recipe," or "list of ingredients" in some industries.

Bill of resources (BOR): Lists the key resources needed to make a unit of a specific SKU or various selected SKUs (or a family of items, as in group technology). Resource requirements are identified with a lead time to show the impact of requirements on resource availability. The BOR is also called the *bill of capacity* and the *product load profile.*

BOM: See **Bill of material (BOM).**

Bottlenecks: Well described by the narrowing of the bottle's neck, which constricts the flow of output. In production terms, the slowest machine in the line sets the pace of the process. When the throughput rate of the bottleneck is exceeded, a waiting line or queue starts to develop.

Breakeven: In casual discussion, breakeven connotes the fact that enough units of product were sold to offset the costs and begin to make a profit. Airlines talk about their load factor, which is the percent of total seats filled. For example, U.K. carrier easy-Jet reported that from 2001 to 2002 their load factor increased from 82.6 percent to 85.9 percent. The breakeven load factor is dependent upon the type of aircraft; its fuel efficiency; other operating costs, including food and crew salaries; length of flight; and ticket prices (including discounts for revenue management). Every system has the goal of operating at volume levels above breakeven.

Breakeven point (BEP): The sales volume point at which total costs exactly equal revenues. Profit is zero. Then, as sales volume increases, profit > 0. Models of breakeven are at the crux of capacity decisions. With overcapacity, it takes patience to grow the business to breakeven and beyond. Undercapacity may mean that the breakeven point cannot be reached until the company expands its capacity. Attention must be paid to the forecast probabilities that supply volumes to meet demand will be above or below the BEP. Decision modeling combines the location of the BEP and the slope of the profit-loss line to permit selection of the optimal process.

Breakpoint business process redesign: Finding strategic-level competitive advantages in the areas of the company's core business processes. Breakthroughs at that level become core competencies of the organization. These innovations will have the greatest impact on the customers and shareholders of the firm. Competency-based competition is almost always related to P/OM. An important variant of reengineering.

Buffer stock: Additional stock carried to prevent outages arising from demand exceeding expectations. The forecast is for the expected stock requirements. Buffer stock (BS) is held in inventory just in case the demand is above the forecast. Also called safety stock, these extra units can also be called upon when lead time for deliveries is greater than had been anticipated. Overall protection against the effects of variability on supply.

Build: Alternatives to "build a new facility" would be either "rent" or "buy." There are many examples of "buy, tear down, and rebuild." This choice is needed when undeveloped land is not available in the right location.

Buy: Make a list of all potential sites and buildings. Then, do a rent or buy (and build) analysis. See **Build** and **Rent.**

C

Capabilities: Capabilities-based strategies are reflected in management of business processes, for example, production scheduling and inventory management. Core competency-based strategies are applied to management of process technologies, for example, large, laminated glass windshields.

Capacity: There are two basic types of capacity. One is storage space and the other is throughput flow rates. Mental capacity is not part of this treatise. Storage capacity is exemplified by "maximum loading" for the school auditorium. That is a measure of how many people are permitted to be seated at one time in a given square area by the fire department. In contrast, warehouse storage space is often volumetric because products can be piled to the roof. The two storage examples differ because of the way that each facility is filled and emptied. Dynamic capacity measures relate to the flow rate of liquid through pipes and product output from the production process. Flow shop throughput rates reflect cycle time, C. For any particular job, C is a function of the number of workstations.

Capacity requirements planning (CRP): (1) This is an extension of MRP. It is necessary to readjust capacity when the MRP system delivers a plan that is not feasible because of capacity limitations. CRP is the process of determining how much labor,

equipment, and facilities resources are needed to fulfill the production schedule. Open shop orders and planned orders in the MRP system are input to CRP, which is the function that establishes, measures, and adjusts levels of capacity.
(2) There are two aspects to CRP. First is strategic. Second is tactical. Chapter 10 is focused on the strategic issues of CRP. These relate to long-term planning for capacity including breakeven points and optimal allocation of resources. Shorter-term tactical issues are related to materials requirements planning (see MRP in Chapter 15).

Capital productivity: A partial accounting for productivity that is due to invested capital. The output divided by the input model prevails in two ways. First is units produced per dollar of capital. Second is dollar value of units produced per dollar of capital. The measures are taken over successive periods of time.

Cause and effect charts: Organize and illustrate what causes quality problems. All factors that impinge on quality are listed in a hierarchy of categories and subcategories. These are conveniently illustrated by the fishbone diagram developed by Ishikawa. The figure is also known by his name. The key to understanding quality achievement is developed by this taxonomical method that identifies classes and subclasses of the variables responsible for variability in the finished product or service.

c-chart: Control chart for multiple numbers of defectives in a single unit. For all control charts, there is an upper-control limit and a lower-control limit around a process average. With c-charts the process average is for the number of defects found per unit. For example, mail order catalogues have printing-run defects that can be counted. Before the presses are set up to do a final run, it is useful to take a pilot-run sample. Using the pilot-run sample, create the c-chart and provide good SQC analysis to see if the process is stable (under control).

CDC: Centers for Disease Control and Prevention, located in Atlanta, Georgia. CDC is an agency of the Department of Health and Human Services of the U.S. government. It is the lead federal agency for protecting the health and safety of people—at home and abroad. CDC provides credible information to enhance health decisions. CDC serves as the national focus for developing and applying disease prevention and control, environmental health, and health promotion and education activities. CDC has responsibilities that are new and not well-defined since the potential of bioterrorism has emerged as a global threat. The operational issues that CDC faces are of substantial interest to P/OM. For the latest health and safety information, consult http://www.cdc.gov.

Centers for Disease Control and Prevention (CDC): See **CDC.**

Certification of suppliers: Process of grading (pass–fail) suppliers to assure conformance to standards set as necessary by P/OM. The factors required include quality assurances, delivery performance, product improvement, cost control, and reliability as a partner.

Chance causes: See **Assignable causes.**

Change management: Managing modification of the transformation process, including the inputs and the outputs, is a major challenge and opportunity in the rapidly changing environment of business. Alterations are required to maintain market status and financial well-being. Change management increases the capabilities and competencies of the firm. See **Capabilities** and **Reengineering.**

Change management projects (α): This term refers to the management of change, which requires planning, designing, building, testing, redesigning, and implementing the system. These are project management responsibilities. It is important to clarify the differences between project management and process management as to purpose and procedures. See **Control management processes (β).**

Changeovers: The steps that need to be taken to prepare equipment and people to do a new job. The term *setup* refers to the start-up of a new job. *Take down* is cleanup and put away from an old job. Taken together they create the chain of events for changeover. Refer to economies of scope and check SMED for fast changeovers.

Chasing policy: This policy, or strategy, of chasing demand is based on a total cost structure that rewards matching market demand. The firm has to be able to produce variable amounts of work so that supply can correspond to demand. Production output increases to match above-average demand. It slows down to match below-average demand. To justify the chasing strategy, the sum of costs of a variable workforce and underutilized equipment should be less than the sum of costs of reducing overstocks and eliminating backorders. The idea of chasing someone is to follow them and to catch up with them. In inventory terms, catching up may not occur. Instead, the chase is continual with the goal of getting as close as possible in matching supply and demand. Rarely will the match be exact. See **Constant production strategy.**

Classification by attributes: Units are classified as accepted or rejected, e.g., it is too heavy for the delivery system.

Classification by variables: Variables like weight can be measured on a continuous scale.

Closed-loop MRP: A system built around MRP that connects the planning functions of sales and operations. Closed-loop signifies that feedback prevails at many levels, and over time, for planning and replanning shop scheduling, supplier scheduling, capacity requirements, and sales strategies. MRP becomes more powerful with the addition of the closed-loop planning adjustment system, as it moves toward MRP II.

Coding: After parent products have had their parts explosion accomplished, coding provides a means of identifying the fact that some parts are required by more than one parent. The MRP must combine the demand of commonly shared parts. Coding captures that and other relevant information about parts, such as certified suppliers, storage locations, and acceptable substitutes. Coding of part names is the foundation for effective information systems linking components and parents together.

Compensating for defectives: More defectives are produced at start-up than later on in the production of a specific batch of units. Because of start-up defectives, to ship the ordered quantity, produce more than the order size. The compensation can be a substantial percentage of the order size if the batch size is small, job setup is complicated, and the worker's learning curve is slow to achieve the standard production rate.

Computer-aided design (CAD): Design done by software that creates drawings for any product or structure that normally requires graphic communication for implementation. CAD also provides test procedures to determine if quality and structural goals can be achieved.

Computer-aided manufacturing (CAM): Manufacturing done by software that is in communication with the CAD programming. CAD communicates the design specifications to the CAM software, which translates the specs into instructions and controls for the production machinery. CAD and CAM work together to determine the feasibility of manufacturing the new design and suggest improved design alternatives.

Computer-aided process planning: The application of computer software to organize and evaluate the performance of a process. This includes scheduling production and determining resource requirements. Factory floor simulations allow alternatives to be tested in pursuit of continual improvement.

Concurrent engineering (CE): Parallel and simultaneous work along many project paths is supported and encouraged. CE employs more resources early in the project's evolution. CE uses a team-oriented framework. Faster completion as compared to the traditional sequential-compartmentalized, engineering method of project management. Not only are there time-based management (TBM) advantages, but there are also quality improvements arising from team contributions made at the start, before commitments are made that lead to irreversible operations. Has been called *simultaneous engineering.*

Conflict resolution: Disputes impair team performance. Until disputes can be resolved by management, interpersonal team problems will damage organizational performance. Conflict resolution, based on empirical studies, has led to the development of methodology that can be used to settle disagreements. Teams reach many decisions that can include wage determinations for members. Before wage determination by teams is used, conflict resolution skills must be developed by management.

Constant production strategy: The workforce is maintained to produce a *constant level of output,* called k. To achieve this, hiring and training are only for replacement, which occurs because employees stop working of their own accord. There is no plan to reduce the workforce. To justify the constant production strategy, the sum of costs associated with a constant workforce must be less than the sum of costs associated with a variable workforce. Spelling this out, the summed costs of carrying inventory when demand is less than k, or of lost orders and backorders when demand is more than k, should be less than the sum of costs of a variable workforce and underutilized equipment. See **Chasing policy.**

Constraints, theory of: The theory of constraints, developed by Eliyahu Goldratt, describes a production scheduling system that optimizes overall performance (throughput) by recognizing constraints and minimizing their deleterious effects. The synchronized production system was called OPT, but theory of constraints is now preferred terminology.

Continuity: Related to continuous project development. Continuity refers to project teams that upon completing a project, or even during the activities of a project, begin another project. Multiple project participation, if configured properly, has the benefit of not dissipating project skills and knowledge. Traditional breakup of the project group at completion can impose penalties associated with the question, "Why reinvent the wheel?" Continuity also refers to the use of project teams in different parts of the world. Project activity progresses as it *follows the sun;* part of the team will always be awake. Transnational companies have customer support systems (24/7) that move around the globe (Southeast Asia to Europe to North America and the Far East).

Continuous improvement (CI): One of two major approaches to accomplish planned change. Continuous improvement uses constant effort to find better ways to produce a product and deliver a service. Emphasizes conversions of existing processes. Scope is local, limited to incremental change, and persistent. Continuous improvement versus reengineering (REE), the other major approach. REE's scope is global, systems-wide, and starts from scratch. Continuous improvemtent is also called *kaizen* because many firms in the United States learned continuous improvement methodology from Japanese practitioners. Visit http://www.kaizen-training.com.

Continuous processes: Produce one product continuously; or may result from the design of analytic process flows that fan out derivative products a part of a continuous stream, e.g., petroleum refineries.

Control chart: Foundation stone graphical method of statistical quality control (SQC). Chart is based on the process average for percent defectives, with upper- and lower-control limits and plotted points of successive sample means. Control limits are distanced from the process average so that the probabilities of sample means exceeding these thresholds are preselected odds (e.g., 0.001, 0.0001) if the process is stable. The distribution from which the sample means are drawn is considered to be normal. At start-up, the control chart is expected to exhibit lack of control, meaning that more sample means exceed the control limits than is statistically warranted. The process is stabilized (brought under control) by removing assignable causes. See **Control limits.**

Control limits: See **Control chart.** Upper-control limits (UCL) and lower-control limits (LCL) are developed in different ways depending upon the type of chart being used. For $\bar{x}$-charts, the distance of the upper and lower limits from the process average $(\bar{\bar{x}})$ are based on the range of the measured variables (R). For p-charts, the distance of the upper and lower limits from the process average $(\bar{p})$ are based on the standard deviation associated with $(\bar{p})$. The value of p is often determined by the definition of "defective" and the use of go/no go gauges. See *p*-chart.

Control management processes (β): This term refers to the management of existing systems, which requires operating that system, controlling the inputs, the transformation process, and the outputs. Management must shield the system from external disturbances that threaten process continuity, as well as employee, customer, and vendor security and safety. The responsibility for process management belongs to P/OM. It is important to clarify the differences between process management and project management as to purpose and procedures. See **Change management projects (α).**

Core competencies: Technical, technological, and production skills possessed by a company interacting with that company's product line. For example, in the 1920s, the Ford Motor Company used sequenced assembly. No other company understood the requirements of that production system, at that time. Wal-Mart uses cross-docking to speed inventory deliveries and minimize inventory costs. No other company understood the requirements of that logistics system at the time of its inception. It is not evident that any other company has mastered the system and can emulate it. See **Capabilities.**

Cost benefit: Comparison of costs and benefits that applies to alternative facility configuration decisions. The comparison is difficult to make when some of the benefits are not readily stated in dollars. Not all costs are in dollars either. There are intangible costs such as foregone preferences based on closeness to family. Cost-benefit analysis can be applied to alternative suppliers, designs of products and processes, and to managers of departments.

Costs of quality: Costs that include (1) costs of preventing defects; (2) costs of appraisal (inspecting for defects and often removing them); and (3) the costs of failures, which can comprise costs stemming from replacement warranties, costs associated with legal actions, and costs resulting from customer dissatisfaction with the company's products.

Cost trade-off analysis: The generic trade-off model balances the improvement in one factor against the deterioration in another as a result of changing a systems variable (such as order size). For aggregate planning, the choice between a constant workforce and varying the workforce (to match demand) is based on comparison of the total costs associated with each strategy. Many different mixtures of the two pure strategies are feasible. Each blended strategy has an associated set of costs and a unique total cost, which may be less than the total costs of either pure strategy. This trade-off model examines all options.

Crash time: Project managers make the comparison between *crash* times for project completion and *normal* times. Crashing an activity means spending as much as it takes to achieve *minimum* activity time. *Normal* activity time is associated with minimum spending. COST/TIME trade-off analysis is used to determine if, when, and with what activities crash time should be used. Crashing is generally used to decrease the length of the critical path. This speeds up completion, but be wary of quality deterioration. It is often wasteful of money to crash all activities. Instead, activities on the critical path are selected to be crashed. The first selected are those activities that provide the largest decrease in project time for the least amount of investment. Crashing should not be equated with rushing, which is associated with making mistakes. Crashing should not endanger the practices of safety-first and error-free performance. See **Critical path methods (CPM)** and **Normal time.**

Criticality: When part behavior causes process or product failure or a marked degradation in performance, that part is considered critical, no matter what its cost. Some items are production-critical. For want of a gasket, a refinery can be shut down. Run-

ning out of a specific bolt can stop an automobile assembly line. The shuttle cannot be launched if a critical part that malfunctions cannot be replaced. It is a judgment call as to which part has A-type criticality. Probably an office running out of paper clips would call that a C-type critical event. To Office Depot, they may be an important B-type in-stock item. However, if failure to supply paper clips causes a good customer to shift permanently to a competitor, being out of stock on paper clips may be an A-type critical failure.

Critical path methods (CPM): Project management models are made up of networks of project activities designed for optimal use of resources and monitored for progress against a specific completion date. The critical path determines completion date. It is especially important to track the critical path, which is the longest time-path from start to finish of the project. The critical path determines completion date of the project. Called by various names including CPM and PERT, these are all network methods that are best analyzed by computer software that keeps track of the abundance of information about schedules and progress. See **PERT, Backward pass rule,** and **Forward pass rule.**

Cross-docking: Wal-Mart pioneered the widespread use of this method to transfer goods from incoming trucks at receiving docks to outgoing trucks at shipping docks. These docks are adjacent. Many warehousing steps are saved, but this logistic method requires excellent communication and information about what is needed and in-charge scheduling. P/OM and IT (information technology) need to coordinate the shipments from suppliers and the demands of the stores. Stock in the trucks is pipeline inventory.

Cross-training: Permits workers to enjoy job rotation between stations of the flow shop and also between areas of specialization in the job shop. Cross-training reduces worker boredom; raises self-esteem; increases flexibility for process changeovers; provides new insights about how to improve the process; and has no downside because workers seem to like it.

Custom shop: The name for the work configuration used for products or services that are made-to-order, and usually one of a kind.

Cybernetics: Study of similarities between human brains and electronic systems. Compares the way that electronic signals are generated by information in the computer system with signals transmitted between adjacent neurons across a boundary called a synapse in the body.

Cyborg: A coined word combining "cyb" from *cybernetics* with "org" from *organism*. A form of technology that assigns people and machines to work jointly to achieve results that neither could obtain by acting alone. Pacemakers are an excellent present-day example. Embedded GPS chips to locate missing persons is around the corner.

Cycles: Repetitive patterns of sequenced values, which generally return to the same starting point. For example, alternating current (AC) follows a sinusoidal curve. Tidal cycles repeat themselves over time with variations in amplitude according to the lunar phase. High and low tides are regular, occurring monthly. This information is published in tide tables to help sailors. Long cycles such as summer high temperatures are annual. Very long economic cycles have been hypothesized. View the 54-year Kondratieff Wave at http://www.angelfire.com/or/truthfinder/index22.html. When cycles appear to exist, forecasting must take them into account in predicting future states.

Cycle time: The interval, C, that elapses between successive units of finished work coming off the production line. For example, if every 2 1/2 minutes a completed automobile leaves the Subaru assembly line in Lafayette, Indiana, then the cycle time for that assembly line is 2.5 minutes. Productive output rate is determined by T/C. For example, if C is in minutes and T is minutes per hour, then, T/C for Subaru is 60/2.5, which equals an output rate of 24 autos per hour. Waiting time is waste in cycle time. Failure of suppliers to deliver materials needed by the flow shop will introduce delays that increase the cycle time. Good cycle-time management is diligent to see that value-adding operations are ongoing. Proper cycle-time management develops a well-balanced process for the total work content assigned to n workstations during the cycle time. See **Time-based management (TBM)**.

D

Data check sheets (DCSs): Spreadsheets can be used to count and record defectives by types and times of occurrence. Organization of the data is aimed at tracking the frequency of events that relate to process qualities. For example, hotels keep track of "room not ready" complaints by time of the year and day of the week. Analysts can apply a variety of techniques to cull information from a well-prepared DCS.

Days of inventory (DOI): Total stock on-hand divided by the average demand per day gives a measure of how long it will be before the stockroom and warehouse are empty. To derive average DOI, divide average total stock on-hand by average demand per day. DOI is directly related to turnover. If the DOI indicates that the stockroom would be empty in 12 days, then the turnover is 365/12 = 30+ days, or once a month, which is 12 times a year. Purchasing times replenishment orders so that the warehouse does not run out of stock every DOI cycle.

Decision model: Elements of decision models are specific and found whenever a decision problem exists. There are strategies, states of nature, probabilities of states of nature (forecasts for these probabilities), expected values for outcomes, and strategies chosen for delivering outcomes in line with goals and objectives. In Chapter 10, breakeven models are extended using decision models as in Supplement 10.

Demand: Units of product (goods and/or services) requested for delivery within a period of time constitute demand. Many descriptions refer to types of demand such as peak, off-peak, and average demand. "Market demand" is not a tautology because "individual, regional, and national demand" exist. "Market demand" is not "actual sales" until the product is shipped and paid for by the customers. Differences between supply and demand create market forces for producers to increase or decrease production. "Variability of demand" costs can be removed or reduced by using contracts but there is a price to be paid for reduction of uncertainty. Effective forecasting reduces the costs of demand variability. Erratic (or capricious) demand patterns are the bane of forecasters.

Deming: Acknowledged as the Father of the Quality Movement in Japan, Dr. W. Edwards Deming became a leader in the American quality revolution after 1980. Deming's Quality Cycle of Plan-Do-Check-Act was adopted by many companies, which sought to improve product quality to levels that had been previously rejected as too costly.

Deming Prize: Prize that has been awarded since 1951 by JUSE (Japanese Union of Scientists and Engineers). Recipients can be organizations from any country, and the award criterion is to have achieved outstanding quality performance. Florida Power and Light won the prize in 1989.

Design for assembly (DFA): (1) The product is designed to be put together efficiently, meaning at minimum cost and with higher quality standards. Conscious DFA is preplanning components as well as final assemblies. This not only lowers production costs and cuts cycle times, but it also allows architectural design of the assembled building blocks. It would be asking for trouble to construct a building in which the floors, walls, and façade assemblies are not rationalized as a system until the construction crew is ready to put the building in place. Another example of the need for DFA is toys that are often purchased in knocked-down format. Parents are on the spot to show their children that they can understand the instructions (manuals are often badly written) to put the toy together. Many toys are not well-designed for assembly. The same applies to furniture assembled by the customer. These examples illustrate that DFA is not

a theoretical subject of interest to manufacturers alone. Also, DFA is related to the design for disassembly.
(2) P/OM acts as liaison between the product designers and the assemblers on the production line. Changes are made in both design specifications and assembly procedures to simplify assembly. Many times the discussion about DFA must bridge the space between assembly and fabrication, which unites DFA with DFM and the designers. This means greater productivity and throughput as well as cost reduction and quality improvement. See **Design for disassembly (DFD)**.

Design for automation (DFAU): Robots can decrease assembly costs and bear the brunt of difficult work such as welding and painting with toxic materials. A component of design for assembly addresses benefits of robot assemblers for precision assembly as well. The quality and speed of assembly work increases while the cost goes down. DFA and DFD are symmetric (congruent) in the planning of put-together and take-apart. Robots are able to disassemble returned units when design for automation (DFAU) has been used. See **Design for assembly (DFA)** and **Design for disassembly (DFD)**.

Design for disassembly (DFD): The stages are design; manufacture and ship; consumer use; and postconsumption disposal. DFD innovations can be rewarding in terms of rapid disassembly, reduction in the number of parts required, reuse (rework and remanufacture), and recycle (with safe disposal when only partial reuse is possible). Advantages accrue in many ways. For example, there is a story about the expensive car that needs four hours to disassemble the door to empty the ashtray. DFD can be a consumer benefit when repair is required. Also, reuse and rework can save a great deal of money. Society benefits when rational design decreases mountains of undesirable waste. See **Greening the environment**.

Design for manufacturing: (1) P/OM must consider the locations chosen for fabrication in the relationship between product designers and production personnel. Plant location can be related to the technology-skills mix employed in fabrication. The degree to which labor-intensive work is employed will also be a function of plant location choices. Some manufacturing facilities will not support technology-based design for manufacturing (DFM). Equipment performance evaluation is also part of the DFM procedure. Productivity of equipment must be related to the volume of work rate required. The inherent variability of the technology must be compatible with designers' tolerances.
(2) P/OM acts as liaison between the product designers and the production personnel who fabricate that part, and related parts, using various manufacturing facilities. Changes are made in both design specifications and fabrication procedures to simplify operations. Many times the discussion about DFM must bridge the space between fabrication and assembly, which unites DFM with DFA and the designers. This results in greater productivity and throughput as well as cost reduction and quality improvement.

Design tolerances: Minimum and maximum dimensions for parts that fit together for proper performance. For example, the door of a car must fit within the door opening in the auto chassis. The fit must be snug. Too tight a fit makes opening the door difficult. With a fit too loose, the door rattles. Noise (and even rain) gets into the car.

Deterministic line-balancing: Line-balancing (LB) is the effort to divide total work content into equal balanced parts (of the cycle time, C) at each of n workstations. Deterministic LB is based on the assumption that the total process time for making the product is exactly the same for every unit of product that is completed. To achieve that goal, all operation times are fixed and never vary. That means that statistical distributions are not applicable to the work times. Line-balancing with fixed operation times is much simpler than if work times are considered to be variable. Deterministic assumptions are valid when machinery is doing all of the work. For example, all of the functions of an automated bottling plant run at the set rate because there is no human participation. Paced conveyors are an effective means of creating deterministic process results.

Dimensions of quality: There are endless numbers of ways to enumerate the dimensions of quality. Six of the eight Garvin dimensions are a good start for tangible qualities, but the intangibles are more difficult to treat. The key point is that no form of quality can be achieved until that form is defined precisely.

Dissatisfaction: Benchmarking is the trigger for dissatisfaction with the status quo. If a benchmark shows that another person, department, or company is better than "we" are, then "us" and "them" resentment takes over. However, dissatisfaction alone will not lead to change efforts using CI or REE. The fact that dissatisfaction (D) is greater than zero is a necessary but not sufficient condition for change as hypothesized by the Gleicher model. See **Gleicher model.**

Distribution requirements planning (DRP1): An extension to MRP, DRP1 relates to replenishing inventory at the branch warehouses. A time-phased order point approach is used to "explode" planned orders at the branch warehouse level via MRP logic. Collectively, they become *gross requirements* for suppliers. In the case of multilevel distribution networks, the explosion process continues down through the various levels of regional warehouses that are coupled to the master warehouse, factory warehouse, etc.

Distribution resource planning (DRP2): Related to MRP II, using broad systems perspective, additional supply chain considerations are extended to warehouses and manufacturing. DRP2 is a higher order planning system than DRP1 because it also plans resource availability such as storage space in the warehouse, trucking capacity, railroad boxcar availabilities, workforce training, etc. DRP2 operates as an extension of distribution requirements planning (DRP1) by addressing what additional resources are needed in the distribution system.

Drift-decay quality phenomenon: Decay of product performance can occur as a result of usage or age. For example, the light output of a bulb diminishes to a point where the lumens are insufficient for reading. We expect less decay from alkaline batteries than from the traditional carbon zinc batteries. The quality issue is how fast is the rate of decay?

Due date: Sales and marketing promise delivery on a specific date (called *order promising*). From the P/OM point of view, the result of order promising shows up as a due date on the production schedule. Missing due dates is not the same as backlogging (postponed delivery at the time of order promising). Missing due dates is broken promises. P/OM schedules try to minimize the number and severity of these occurrences, i.e., how often they occur and how much delay occurs before delivery.

Dynamic inventory models: The inventory models are contrasted with static inventory models. Dynamic models require a continuing stream of inventory decisions whereas static inventory models permit one decision (or at most a few decisions). Places orders repetitively over a long period of time.

E

Economic lot size (ELS): The ELS model focuses on how many units to make in a production run. It is designed for the intermittent flow shop, which applies sequenced operations to various products that can be made on the same production line with changeover costs. This is a smaller investment commitment than required by the continuous flow shop (e.g., auto assembly). ELS also contrasts with the economic order quantity (EOQ) model, which aims at deciding how many units to buy from a supplier at one time. This is a useful distinction that applies to the *make* versus *buy* concept faced by all manufacturers. The make versus buy model can also apply to services that consume supplies. See also **Economic order quantity (EOQ).**

Economic order quantity (EOQ): The EOQ model focuses on how many units to order when purchasing items for batch delivery.

These supplies are intended for relatively continuous use as needed to support flow shop production. Another name for this model is the *optimal order quantity model*. The relatively continuous use of the ordered items is expected to continue over a long planning horizon, and the rate of use does not have to be constant, but it should be fairly stable. See also **Economic lot size (ELS).**

Economies of scale: (1) Reductions in cost per unit that can be obtained by purchasing greater quantities of goods and services. Discounts may be gotten for larger purchase orders, and investments in innovation can be increased. More training, improved methods, and new technology are cost justified.
(2) Reductions in variable costs directly related to increasing volumes of production output. Scale, as used here, refers to production unit volumes.

Economies of scope: Realized when set-up cost reductions allow more frequent changeovers without increasing the cost per unit of output. Smaller lots sizes provide greater variety without increasing inventories. These advantages can stem from creative engineering as well as flexible (computerized) production technology.

Efficiency frontiers: These are trade-off boundaries. For finance, where the technique originated, different amounts of risk and return are plotted as curved lines of equal expected profits. This analogy has been applied to the selection of processes for reengineering. Those processes should have the potential for major improvement. Process improvement that can be anticipated is denoted as IA. That process should also be important to the performance of the company. It should deliver capabilities that are significant to the well-being of the company—called *DC*. Because the chosen process can be improved a great deal, and that will help the performance of the company significantly, it will fall on a high-priority efficiency frontier. In typical management terms, this is often called *the low hanging fruit*.

Elasticity: The term used to describe the strong systems interaction between market demand and price charged. Often referred to as the price–demand elasticity, it is a rate-of-change measure expressing the degree to which demand grows or contracts in response to price decreases or increases, respectively.

ELV: See End-of-life-of-vehicle.

Empirical testing: Testing product design characteristics is well-known in market research. It is also well-known as a check against poor design performance that might be hidden otherwise. For example, after months of use, a lightbulb might shatter at failure. Fatigue testing and simulation can speed up time and frequency of product use to provide information about a product's behavior at a distant time in the future. Empirical means that the testing is not theoretical (on paper) but it is observed as a real event with the actual product. Empirical testing is not in place of theoretical design; it is in addition to gain experiential and pragmatic knowledge. Testing can range from health of foods to safety of airplanes and protection of product from packaging.

End-of-life-of-vehicle (ELV): Standards are being set that become increasingly rigorous for disposability at ELV. Percentages are raised step-wise and eventually close to 100 percent of vehicles, computers, etc., will be returned for recycling and/or disposal by the manufacturers

End products: Also called *parent products* are considered to have independent demand systems. Materials and components that are part of the end product are dependent on end-product demand, which can be sporadic and lumpy. MRP is the information system that details what must be done, including ordering supplies, to produce the required number of end products on schedule. The same parts can appear in various end products, and MRP manages the overlap.

Ends: Final part of the means–end chain where what appears to be an end (goal) is the means (cause) for a higher-level goal. Means and ends are part of the process planning system.

Engineering change orders (ECOs): Projects with many engineering change orders are not simple to handle. These may appear to be minor alterations in the product design or in the process used, but there are interactions that are usually unforeseen that can lead to severe systems complexities.

Enterprise Resource Planning (ERP): Company-wide integration of the information system for seamless planning across all functions.

Ergonomics: The systematic study of how people physically interact with their environment, equipment, facilities, machines, and products. (Ergo is a combining form meaning work, from Gr. érgon.) An alternate name is *human factors.* Because people differ in size and shape by age and lineage, there are significant design questions that must be decided. For example, for AT&T the Henry Dreyfuss designers created one of the first single-unit mouth and ear telephones that could be used by both grownups and children around the world. Although ergonomics starts with physical efficiency, issues of safety and comfort emerge. There are also complex psychological issues related to productivity, job turnover, absenteeism, and accident rates.

Ethics: A set of moral principles determined by culture and society. Business ethics is a subset of societal ethics, which must be congruent with social norms and moral practices. What is moral is a judgment of conformance to standards of "right" behaviors. Each culture has its own norms for what is right. Therefore, ethical standards must be established in multicultural environments that satisfy the various participants. Ethical situations are encountered with respect to such issues as how customers complaints are treated, employee retirement plans are managed, union–management relations are administered, community members cooperate, impacts, environmental evaluations, etc. See **Greening the environment.**

Expediting: Actively following up on orders to make sure that deliveries will be on time. When delays are encountered, expediters are to assess the urgency of the situation and to initiate remedial actions that are in line with the situation. For example, if the supplier's trucking company is on strike, send a company truck to bring the items needed for production.

Experience curve: Rate of decrease in per unit costs is between 20 and 30 percent for each doubling of production output volume. The Boston Consulting Group found this result after collecting relevant data for many thousands of processes. They named this phenomenon the "Experience Curve." Volume is a surrogate for experience, learning, and discounts for higher volumes.

Expert systems: Computerized sequences or strings of intelligent inquiries with answers that are modeled on what "experts" would do to solve specific problems or to accomplish given tasks. Emulating experts takes time but has the advantage of storing more than one expert's method of approach in a software package. Expert systems learn and remember so that the departure of an expert can be an anticipated event without damaging consequences. Expert systems can compare experts' performance and activate the best expert string for a selected problem.

Explicit knowledge: The form of knowledge that describes what must be done to make things work. The character of explicit knowledge is that it can be transferred from teachers to students in words or diagrams. It is unconcealed and evident. For example, explicit knowledge includes how to replace a washer in the faucet or how to change the font of a Word document. Transfer agents can be words, pictures, equations, etc. Tacit (implicit) knowledge, which is the other form, is not transferable by word or picture. For example, how to teach a student to become intuitive may illustrate the difficulties of transferring intangible information. See **Knowledge management** and **Tacit knowledge.**

Extrapolation: The process of moving from observed data (past and present) to the projected values of future points. For example, the best guess for the next (extrapolated) value of the time series 2, 4, and 6 is 8. In this case, the linear trend is projected ahead to the future point not yet known.

Extreme quality achievement: Zero defects is called an extreme goal, but Philip Crosby showed that it is a reasonable goal. This is because the conformance to standards must be as near to perfect as possible if the standards are properly chosen. Six-sigma from Motorola, on the other hand, is extreme by present day quality achievement levels. In this case, the product designers and process engineers must create a production system that can yield no more than 3.4 defectives per million parts. Many companies want to match the Motorola-pioneered standard of six-sigma.

F

Facilities planning: Four main components are geographic location, structure and specific site, equipment choice, and layout. Some of the analysis is quantitative, but a lot of it is qualitative. A major driver is the type of work configuration and process technology that will be used.

FDA: The U. S. Department of Health and Human Services includes the Food and Drug Administration (FDA) and the (CDC). The FDA monitors quality integrity for food producers, warehouses, distributors, retailers, and restaurants. One of the most far-reaching FDA initiatives is HACCP, which began with the fishing industry and has now expanded to poultry and meat-processing plants. For the latest FDA developments, consult http://www.fda.gov. See **Hazard Analysis and Critical Control Point (HACCP) system.**

Ferris Wheel model: The Ferris Wheel stops and fills one of n cars with people (project team starts up). The car travels a complete cycle in time, T. Project cycle time, $C = T/n$. When a car empties, symbolically, a project has been completed. The Ferris Wheel provides a model of continuous, new product development. See **Project, Continuous development.**

FIFO: The most natural sequence for doing work is in the order that the jobs are received. That means that the first jobs into the shop get worked on first. The sequence rule: first-in, first-out is called FIFO. It can be compared to LIFO (last-in, first-out), which is the most comfortable rule on a crowded elevator. LIFO is not the supermarket manager's favorite sequencing rule for dated products, such as bread and dairy. It is the good shopper's rule as they reach behind the milk cartons out in front. People say that FIFO is fair. That is a psychological expectation. People get upset when a late arrival breaks into the waiting line and gets in front of them, or is chosen for service by the system's server. FIFO is seldom the basis for economic systems fairness. See **LIFO** and **SPT rule.**

Finite scheduling: Controlling the flow of work so that lot sizes and frequency of setups result in minimum total costs. The flow of smaller lot sizes being made more often can provide flexibility when capacity constraints prevail that create bottleneck effects. Also, process batch sizes should be variable rather than fixed for additional flexibility. See **TOC** and **OPT.**

Fixed costs (FC): Like rent, they have to be paid whether or not any units are sold. Like an insurance policy, they apply to a specific period of time. FCs are greater for flow shops than for job shops, and greatest for flexible manufacturing systems. Administrative and supervisory charges are treated as fixed costs. Overhead (fixed) costs exist before a single unit of product (goods and/or services) is delivered to customers.

Flexible manufacturing systems (FMS): (1) Machines and computers (called manufacturing cells) that work together and can be programmed to produce a menu of different products. The changeover time to move from one menu item to another is negligible because of the computer-controlled tools and transport devices. This is not limited to manufacture. Flexible process systems (FPS) include flexible service systems (FSS) and flexible office systems (FOS).

(2) Systems designed to produce a variety of outputs at low cost. Computer-controlled changeovers that are fast and inexpensive are engineered into the system. Because the method requires detailed analysis to overcome constraints imposed by each product's manufacturing requirements on the others, flexibility is limited.

Flexible office systems (FOS): See **Flexible manufacturing systems (FMS).** Office processes are in many ways similar to manufacturing with both job shop batch production and flow shop (or intermittent flow shop) work configurations. Computer controlled FOS can be designed to change over from one job to another with negligible setup times.

Flexible process system (FPS): (1) Encompasses flexible manufacturing systems (FMS) as well as flexible information systems. The latter can provide a variety of service functions. At the heart of such flexibility is the design interchangeability of the product line. Computers reconfigure the production system. An example of a flexible production system would be the palette of colors used by the artist to paint different pictures. (2) A generic name for all kinds of computer-controlled robotic and machine systems that can change over to offer a menu of products. See **Flexible manufacturing systems (FMS).**

Flexible service systems (FSS): See **Flexible manufacturing systems (FMS).** In quick-service restaurants, theme parks, the U.S. Post Office, FedEx, and UPS, there are ample examples of flexible service systems.

Floor plan model: Drawings of the plant floor to achieve capacity goals, obtain balanced workloads and minimum operating costs, low levels of work in process and least storage space, and minimum travel distance for people and parts. Sketches and drawings with dollhouse-like cutouts are par for the course.

Flow shops (FS): Serialized work configurations where one unit of work is at various stages of completion at sequential workstations that are located along the line of production.

Food and Drug Administration (FDA): See **FDA.**

Forecasting: The act of describing future events and their probabilities of occurrence. For example, there is a 20 percent probability that it will rain tonight and an 80 percent probability that it will not rain tonight. Predictions are event specific—such as *it will rain this evening so take your umbrella.* There are many forecasting methods including guessing and a host of scientific techniques.

Forecasting momentum: The time series being forecast is observed to follow a course or direction that appears to be the result of an inherent force (momentum). Its movement becomes more predictable as a result of this impetus or momentum. For example, an actor's career is said to lose momentum when successive pictures are failures. Conversely, momentum can accelerate performance as a car racing down a hill has momentum assisted by gravity. However, tipping points can be reached. Suddenly the momentum evaporates. This effect keeps stock market forecasts speculative.

Forward pass rule: Also known as the forward convergence rule, it is similar and opposite to the backward pass (or convergence) rule. The forward pass rule: When two or more arrows converge at a single node, choose the arrow with the largest value of the earliest finish time. The forward pass rule enables the project managers to determine how long it will take to complete the project. It is a necessary precursor to use of the backward pass rule. Taken together with the forward pass rule, the fundamental parameters of the project can be calculated. See **Backward pass rule** and **Critical path methods (CPM).**

Functional field approach: The functional fields are P/OM, marketing, finance, etc. The functional field approach is widely used, and it means that everyone is on their own. Marketing is not responsible for who makes the product, where it is made, how much it costs to make, etc. Marketing does care about consumers' perceptions of product quality. With the functional field approach, operations management is strictly tactical.

Fundamental theorem of linear programming (LP): The LP model uses a set of interdependent equations to express resource constraints that determine the solution of an optimal product mix problem. The fundamental theorem of LP states that there cannot be more active variables (i.e., products actually made) than the number of real constraints. For aggregate planning, supplies and demands (over the planning horizon) will determine the number of different active production assignments that can be made to minimize total costs (within the planning horizon).

G

Gantt charts: Henry L. Gantt invented a number of different charts used by P/OM. One type of chart is known as the Gantt load chart (assign actual jobs to specific departments). A load chart provides a graphic system that makes it easy to visualize how much work has been assigned to each facility. Another type of chart is the Gantt layout chart, which establishes the exact order in which jobs are to be done at each facility. It is simple to observe the progress of jobs, jobs waiting, idle facilities, load imbalances (some departments overloaded, others underutilized). Causes of problems can be noted as well. See **Layout chart.**

General-purpose equipment (GPE): Primarily used in the job shop because it is flexible machinery that can do many different kinds of jobs. For example, a lemon juicer might not be able to get juice from an orange, but a larger juicer could do grapefruit, orange, lemon, and lime.

Gleicher model (Conditions for change): Specifies the *circumstances* that are necessary for an organization to change *what* it is doing (as well as *how, where, when,* and *why*). The model built by Dr. David Gleicher hypothesizes that the product of three factors, *D, V,* and *P,* must be greater than the cost of change, *C.* Thus: $(D \times V \times P) > C$. If any one of these three factors is zero, no change can occur. See **Dissatisfaction, Practical first steps, and Vision.**

Greening the environment: There are many facets to this objective. Maintenance is an area where cleaning involves toxic chemicals and harmful residues. Environmentally-sound maintenance may take the form of emission controls on smokestacks and water-jetting to remove coatings. Production processes may have side effects that have to be cleaned. Greening is also accomplished by design for reuse, recycling, and proper disposal when remanufacturing cannot be used. Greening is meant to connote that efforts are successful to achieve sustainable land and water resources. Vegetation thrives with proper management of the ecosystem. Visit http://www.greeningofindustry.org.

Group technology (GT): Processes that specialize in *families* of similar parts and/or activities. Technology exists that enables a process to make parts of common design in different sizes with no significant changeover costs. Such parts might be screws, bolts, washers, gears, and cams. GT encourages specialization in parts. See also **Modular production (MP).**

Group technology cellular manufacturing systems: An application of flexible manufacturing systems (FMS). When workstations are linked and designed to work together on common sets of projects, they are called cellular manufacturing systems. Families of parts that have many characteristics in common but vary in specific ways are said to reflect group technology. Thus, small-, medium-, and large-size washers are family members if they can be made by a machine with adjustable diameters.

H

Hazard Analysis and Critical Control Point (HACCP) system: HAACP is a system designed to prevent food hazards from arising without being detected. It is a quality control system that detects the presence of defective process management. It also specifies what procedures to follow with food product that is out of control. It is one of the largest scale quality control programs in the field of P/OM. HACCP is an excellent example of total quality management. HACCP provides detailed specifications for monitoring temperatures and controlling process variables that can lead to food contamination. See **FDA.**

Heuristic line-balancing methods: Line-balancing problems are large and unwieldy. There are so many combinations for assigning work to stations that ordinary mathematical optimization solutions do not apply. This complexity has led to proposals for the use of various rules of thumb, which constitute a common sense approach to line-balancing problems. For example, Kilbridge and Wester assign a number to each operation that counts how many predecessors it has. Lowest predecessor numbers are assigned to workstations first. Many rules of thumb exist to handle complications such as ties. Linear programming methods can be used for line-balancing but may not be worth the effort because heuristics are remarkably robust.

Heuristics (rules of thumb): These are methods for discovery, guides for problem-solving, and procedures for experimental learning. One of the most popular is the trial and error technique with feedback to reward steps in the right direction. "Rules-of-thumb heuristics" are based on detailing the procedures followed by successful employees, such as the scheduler who has been using reason, observation, and common sense to provide reinforcement for what works and negative feedback for what fails to work. Evaluation of results produces learning. The reason to use heuristics is that no algorithm has been developed to solve the problem.

Histograms: Relative frequency distributions of categories of events can be informative. Histograms are bar charts that illustrate the relative frequencies of a set of outcomes as a discrete probability distribution. For example, for a specific June in Orlando, Florida, spreadsheet data was recorded for daily daytime maximum temperatures. Histograms were drawn for the relative frequencies of the temperature spectrum. Because there are 30 days in June, each unique reading has a frequency of 1/30 = 0.033. Five June days had max daily temperature of 85 degrees F. The histogram bar for 85 degrees was 0.167 in height.

HMMS: A pioneering aggregate-planning model that uses nonlinear costs for its resource constraints. The acronym is from the first letter of each scientist's last name. Provides better answers but at a cost that limits use to academic understanding.

House of Quality (HOQ): A mapping and tracking system for all relevant quality dimensions for a real product. It has been used by Merrill Lynch to study in detail and depth the quality of their CMA. GE, Xerox, Ford, etc., have used the HOQ in a number of different ways. The HOQ method can be used for extreme quality achievement such as six-sigma.

I

Information systems: Good information systems capture all data relevant to P/OM planning and decision making. That includes raw materials, components on hand, finished goods, work-in-process, available operators, and technology that can be utilized. It includes data about money, materials, people (in-firm and marketplace), equipment, processes, space, energy, competitors, and anything else that counts.

Inspection: Observation of product qualities can be made by eye or with instrumentation. Nonconformance with standards for acceptance results in a reject of the item. Inspection (appraisal) of outputs is one of the three costs of quality that must be balanced against the other two (viz., cost of failure and cost of prevention). 100 percent inspection is often inaccurate as well as costly. The key to recall: Inspectors can reduce defectives shipped but not defectives made.

Intelligent information system: Captures the management issues of *what to buy, when to buy, from whom to buy, how much to buy, how much to pay,* etc. Distinguished from a ledger that notes stock on-hand, shipments expected, sales, and withdrawals.

Interchangeable parts: A manufacturing concept that makes batches of parts (e.g., rifle barrels), any one of which will fit into the assembled products (rifles). The reason that the parts are interchangeable is that each one fits within the design tolerances.

Intermittent flow shop (IFS): Used when demand does not justify establishing a dedicated flow shop. An IFS is run for an interval of time and then shut down until it is required again.

Internal MM system: MM is materials management. The internal MM system controls production materials flowing to and through the process. Controls work in process on the plant floor and finished goods in the warehouse. The external MM system tracks shipments to distributors and retailers. Internal and external systems must be synchronized and coordinated to be effective.

Inventory: Stock on-hand for every practical reason that materials are needed to run an organization. Items can be classified as raw materials, subassemblies, outsourced components, work in process, and finished goods. In addition to repair and maintenance supplies, there are office supplies and gasoline, oil, and tires for the delivery trucks. Inventory is tying up assets at a carrying cost that is justified by the fact that when the item is needed there is a penalty to pay for not having it on hand. To make the decisions there are materials managers known as inventory managers who specialize in inventory management.

Inventory record files (IRF): One of three inputs to the MRP information system, viz., MPS, BOM, and inventory record files (IRF). Stock on-hand levels need to be up to date. Similarly, all ordering information including suppliers' prices and delivery lead times must be current. If the inventory record files are not up to date, the MRP system will produce anomalies that penalize production such as supply shortfalls and cost overruns.

Inventory turns: See **Turnover.**

I/O profit model: The input–output model captures all costs and revenues so profit can be determined. An optimal configuration of the factors can be used to improve the breakeven point and to maximize profit.

IRF: See **Inventory record files (IRF).**

ISO 14000/14001: ISO stands for the International Standardization Organization. It is located in Geneva, Switzerland. The ISO 9000 series is acknowledged worldwide as the accepted set of standards for quality management. ISO 14000/14001 sets similar standards for environmental management. The methodology is the same as with ISO 9000. Both sets of standards explain what management approaches are desirable. Both do not specify details of quality such as permissible percent defectives, or acceptable emission levels. The ISO 14000 series have been widely accepted on a global basis. Such standards for conformity are sorely needed. Disparate environmental standards would make multinational and transnational firms follow different drumbeats all over the world. How bright would the world be, and how many readers of Harry Potter would exist, if every bulb manufacturer used its own socket size? Growing in importance is the ISO 17799 Toolkit. It addresses operational security.

ISO 9000 series: The International Organization for Standardization (ISO, located in Geneva, Switzerland) provides quality certification for 146 national standards bodies of which 94 are full-fledged members of countries. The ISO 9000 series relates to generic management systems standards for quality. These apply to any organization, large or small, and whatever its product—including whether its product is a service. In addition, ISO has set more than 14,000 standards for a vast variety of product attributes, which has untold benefits in removing chaos from global trade. ISO also sets generic management systems standards for environmental conditions under ISO 140000. See http://www.iso.ch.

J

Japanese Industrial Standard Z8101: Standard that dates from 1981. It is the set of Japanese standards equivalent to the EURO/U.S.A.–ISO standards. But, Japanese standards are not precisely ISO-equivalent as can be seen from the following URL. It describes how to get Phillips head screw drivers that properly engage with cross-head screws on R/C helicopters made by HeliProz, Inc. Cross-head screws used by HeliProz are manufactured in Japan. Western screwdrivers do not fit them. This is a good example of the need for true standardization. Matching screwdrivers to screw heads illustrates the requirement for transparency (of) and conformance to standards by cooperating partners in the global economy. See http://www.heliproz.com/jisdrivers.html.

Job evaluation: Evaluation of existing jobs permits job enrichment and improvement, and work simplification. The latter expands viewpoints to permit systems evaluation of sets of interlinked jobs. The traditional view, which is to study the individual job, lacks the scope of systems thinking.

Job shop (JS): Used when there are many varieties of products to process in small quantities. Volume is not sufficient to justify flow shop efficiencies gained from special purpose equipment.

Just-in-case: An inventory delivery principle associated with a play-it-safe production philosophy. Fear of production interruptions leads to safety-stocking of critical parts. This is counter to the lean and agile principle of just-in-time.

Just-in-time: An inventory delivery principle associated with a lean-and-mean company philosophy. Under JIT, suppliers must provide exactly what is needed for production until the next delivery is made. The presence of defective components would stop the system, so total quality assurance is required. The interval between replenishment is kept small, which means that inventory carried is minimized.

K

Kanban: Any method that calls attention to a workstation's need to receive a just-in-time (JIT) delivery. An array of signaling devices for JIT delivery. In Japanese, a card sent to a prior station or upstream supplier that a need exists for a specified amount of product.

Knowledge management (KM): Begins with managing the inventory of knowledge that exists in the company. Knowing where that knowledge resides (the directory) and being able to access it on demand are part of KM. In addition, KM assumes the ability to find, select, and absorb new knowledge to add to the prior encyclopedic storehouse. Knowledge with regard to managing change and controlling the system's behavior is vital. The inventory of explicit and tacit knowledge exists in core competencies and managerial capabilities. See **Core competencies, Explicit knowledge,** and **Tacit knowledge.**

L

Labor productivity: A partial accounting for productivity that is due to the use of human labor to do the job. The output divided by the input model prevails in two ways. First is units produced per dollar of labor. Second is sales dollar value of units produced per dollar of labor. Both measures are taken over successive time periods.

Lateral transferability: Operations are assigned to workstations, which form a sequential chain. When precedence diagrams permit operations to be assigned to earlier or later workstations, there is lateral flexibility. A lateral pass in football is a sideways transfer of the ball. Lateral is parallel to the line of scrimmage or away from the opponent's goal. The reason for the name in line-balancing is that precedence diagrams are drawn from left to right. Switching the workstation position of an operation is a left to right (or vice versa) movement called *lateral transferability*.

Layout: (1) Plan for the arrangement of the working environment of the company's facilities. Where should machines and people be placed in the plant, office, or customer-service center? Where should power outlets be located? Where should the rest rooms be positioned? A variety of methods and criteria can be brought to bear on such questions.

(2) The Gantt layout chart converts loading to specific sequencing of jobs at a facility. Loading is a *list* of jobs, in no particular order, at a facility. The Gantt layout chart arranges the list in order of processing. It does this in an optimal sequence. It is no surprise that the chart is also called a *sequencing chart.* See **Floor plan model.**

Lead time (LT): (1) The interval that elapses between seeing the need for and placing an order and receiving the goods or services. It might even help to call it the period between *need and get.* LT is a crucial parameter for process design. Major improvements can be made by decreasing LT and/or by reducing its variability.

(2) An interval of time between first knowing that there is a need to place an order for stock and when that stock is put in a specific place and logged in as available for use. A simpler definition is that lead time is the interval between order placement and order receipt (including recognized need and write up). As can be seen from the first definition, lead time can be more complex than the simple definition. This is because prior to ordering there can be delays due to a variety of problems. Also, after the delivery to the receiving dock materials can be lost or stored incorrectly, and the computer and/or paperwork to notify users that materials are back in stock must be adequate. There is an expected lead time for any replenishment period and variability that can make delivery sooner or later than expected.

Lean production systems: Processes that have been designed to minimize their inherent wastes—of time, materials, and their surrogates (money). The methods to achieve leanness were developed during the era of new Japanese auto manufacturing (1970–1990). Lean processes do not tolerate unnecessary waiting or redoing (e.g., defectives). That makes lean firms faster in producing and delivering. By 2000, many U.S. auto firms had become lean producers. Other lean industries include computer-assembly and wireless phone manufacturers. Wal-Mart maintains its position as a lean retail and distribution center.

Learning curve: Describes how repeated practice decreases the time required to do a job. Captures the benefit of repetition and experience in quantitative terms for employees doing the same job routinely. Learning curves are based on mathematical models of learning from repetition. The learning function increases actual manufacturing capacity. Learning also alters capacity and quality in service operations; also decreases defectives, which indirectly increases useful output.

Leveling factors: Used in time studies of work to convert average time (average performance) to normal time (or adjusted time). Aimed at deriving useful productivity standards, leveling reduces the output rate of faster than normal workers. It increases the output of slower than normal workers. Leveling factors are assigned by trained time study operators.

Life cycle stages: Facility decisions are a function of the life cycle stages of the items in the product line. The history of the company will explain the mixture of start-ups, mature products, products in restaging, products being retired. For each stage, products require different work configurations and floor layouts for plants. Company size will play a large role in determining optimal layouts for offices. Alternative geographical locations may be desirable for products at different stages.

Lifetime value (LTV) of customers: Customer loyalty relates to the probability of purchasing again and again from the same store (or the same brand). Lifetime value is the stream of revenue spent by each loyal customer over the lifetime of his/her relationship with the store (or brand). When a dissatisfied customer switches to another store (or brand), the stream of revenue switches from the old store to the new one. This is called the lost LTV of a customer and it can be significant. Tens of thousands of dollars are involved when a customer switches from one supermarket to another. LTV for an average customer can be segmented, e.g., average female, 18 to 25 years of age.

LIFO: This is the "last-in, first-out" rule for providing service. It sets the service priority based on arrival time. Imagine that the "take-a-number" machine in the bakery is fixed so that the latest arrival gets the smallest number. As always, the server behind the counter gives preference to holders of smallest numbers. That is the way that LIFO operates. Early arrivers might have to wait a long time for service. In the social ethic, LIFO is not fair. However, to exit from a crowded elevator, LIFO may be essential. See **FIFO** and **SPT rule.**

Line efficiency: Is known as capital lambda (Λ). $\Lambda = \Sigma_i t_i / nC$ where $0 \leq \Lambda \leq 1$. It is the total work content divided by the total capacity to do work. Line efficiency can be expressed as a percent, i.e., 100Λ. The relationship of balance delay and line efficiency is $d = 100(1 - \Lambda)$. See **Balance delay.**

Linear programming (LP): Mathematical modeling technique employed by P/OM to achieve optimal use of resources. Variations include the optimal product-mix problem, production scheduling using overtime, and other capacity-sensitive situations. It is significant that often the optimal product-mix solution does not fully utilize available capacity because the LP algorithm moves toward the selection of higher total profit margin products. See **Slack** and **Fundamental theorem of linear programming (LP).**

Linear regression: A statistical technique for determining the best straight line $y = mx + b$ that can be fitted to a set of data $\{x, y\}$. The best fit is the line that minimizes the sum of squares of the deviations of the points from the line.

Line-balancing (LB): The effort to divide total work content into equal (or nearly equal) balanced parts for assignment at each of n workstations. Operations are done at the workstation during the cycle time, C. Bad design loads stations unevenly. Deterministic LB is based on no variability in operation times; stochastic LB is when variability exists in the form of statistical distributions of operation times. For example, a teller's time to complete a bank transaction could be a withdrawal, or a deposit, or both. There could be one or many checks, or withdrawal slips. Process engineers reduce uncertainty of output rates by using paced conveyors to provide fixed work time at stations.

Loading: Loading decisions concern which jobs are to be assigned to which teams or facilities. Assigning jobs on-hand is relatively risk-free. Assigning jobs that are on the books as forecasts is risky business. They may not be scheduled (loaded) because there is too high a risk of cancellation. *Second* level of aggregate planning is loading. Assign jobs to departments before sequencing jobs within departments. For example, a set of jobs is given to John and a different set to Mary. The order in which they do their jobs must follow loading.

Logistics: Tactics of materials management for buying, storing, and transporting materials of all kinds as required by the company's supply chain. Logistics includes product distribution through the supply chain to the customers. Original use: Branch of military science dealing with the movement, procurement, and maintenance of equipment, facilities, and personnel. Derivation from *loger*, to lodge (finding quarters for soldiers).

Lot-for-lot ordering: The planned-order receipt (materials required to fulfill end product schedule) will equal the required amounts at each point in time. In MRP language, planned-order receipts are to be equal to net requirements. In MRP notation, $PR_t = NR_t$.

Low-level coding: MRP labels the level of parts on the end product's assembly-sequence tree. Low-level coding organizes order quantity calculations for parts with combined (multilevel) demands. Parents at the treetop are labeled level zero. Parts and components one level down are called level one. The next level down is coded level two. This coding scheme shows how distant parts are (in their linkage) from their parent product. MRP record processing starts a level code zero and moves down the tree. This assures that all gross requirements are assigned to a part before its MRP record is processed. Low-level coding uses the principle that the lowest position of a part determines where the calculation of gross cumulative requirements is made. A part appearing in both level one and level three will transfer requirement at level one to level three for calculating total requirements for that part. Low-level coding is a systematic, efficient planning rule for computing material requirements.

M

Machine-operator chart (MOC): Provides a means for visualizing the way in which workers (can) tend machines over time. They encourage visual analysis of the interactions of operators with the equipment they run, set up, take down, changeover, and repair. MOC charts can be used to reduce changeover times.

Make or buy decision: Purchase from outside (outsource) or make it internally (self-supplier) is a complex issue. The decision is cost-oriented but not just cost minimization because there are other factors to consider such as vendor reliability, supplier creativity in improving product, lack of understanding opportunities to innovate, and reliance on outside managers. Factors can change over time, e.g., new technology can be developed that would shift buy to make or vice versa.

Make-to-order (MTO) inventory environment: In this environment, there is no finished goods inventory to meet demand. End items are produced to customers' orders. The sales force pledges delivery dates. The pledges translate into due dates that put the production system under stress to live up to promises. Machine shops, carpenters, and plumbers live in an MTO environment. One of the advantages of holding stock is that it can buffer periods when demand is greater than supply. That benefit is lost in an MTO situation.

Make-to-stock (MTS) environment: There is latitude in what to make and the quantities to produce because various items have finished goods inventories. Production scheduling follows an aggregate plan to minimize total costs or maximize revenues (or profits). Forecasts, in conjunction with priorities and due dates, provide opportunities for optimal solutions. Because forecasts help determine the production schedule, inventory levels can be shared with marketing, which is in a position to adjust forecasts through selling strategies and pricing. Further, marketing can (to some extent) meet customers' demands by selling what is in stock.

Management of technology (MOT): Management of technology is equivalent to managing the transformation process of the P/OM input–output system. MOT requires knowing what technologies exist, their state of development, and when to shift from one format to another. Mastery of technology with regard to productivity, variety, and quality are essential. Optimal timing of adoptions is part of the job description.

Manufacturing: The processes that constitute the transformation function of the I/O model; those processes that produce goods.

Master production schedule (MPS): One of three inputs to the MRP information system, viz., BOM, IRF, and MPS. Converts aggregate plans into a time-phased plan that indicates exactly when each SKU should be made and how much should be run. Responsive to customer orders on hand and forecasts. In MRP terms, the MPS calls for various amounts of parent products to be produced by a given date. Fits in the framework of the total manufacturing planning and control systems (MPCS). Used in conjunction with the BOM, it determines the items for which purchase requisitions and production orders must be released (triggering action). Helps assemble-to-order (ATO) by making sure that subassemblies are available to meet requirements within promised due dates. The MPS has to be updated regularly to incorporate new orders and to reflect other changes in existing conditions. See **Regeneration MRP.**

Material requirements planning (MRP): An information system that organizes all factors that determine production-scheduling decisions and all support functions including vendors. The MRP system includes customers' orders on-hand, forecasts of future requirements, inventory on-hand, and capacity availabilities. Applied to job shops where batch production of a variety of different items is the typical situation. A systems approach to the rational management of the entire supply chain with respect to inventory ordering and stocking. Because batch production is prevalent in the economy, MRP is used more often than its counterpart, order point policy (OPP). However, the economic order quantity (EOQ) model can play a role in determining order size.

Materials management (MM): Organizing and coordinating all management functions that are responsible for every aspect of materials movements, storage, and transformation. Organizational responsibility as a functional area with vice president for materials management being a top management representative. The cost of materials has become an increasingly dominant part of companies' cost structures. Requires management of the entire system of supply and demand, including product transportation through distribution channels.

Materials management information system (MMIS): The MMIS provides online information about stock levels for all materials and parts. This includes stock on order, lead times, supplier data, costs of materials, discount schedules, and transportation modes. All materials and parts include raw materials, components, subassemblies, work in process, and finished goods.

Materials management system (MMS): Triggered by marketplace demands (via forecasts), which deplete stocks that cause inventory managers to place replenishment orders through purchasing agents with suppliers and vendors. Contrasting terms that are consistent with original derivations: from Latin, *venditor*, to sell; from Latin, *supplere*, to fill up.

Mean flow time: Average amount of time required to complete each job in a group of n jobs that have been sequenced at a facility. It is the average of the "wait-to-start" plus processing time for every job in the assigned group. The equation for mean flow time (MFT) is $MFT = \sum_{i=1}^{i=n} C_i / n$.

Mean time between failures (MTBF): A product's expected lifetime of satisfactory utility in normal application is well-described by mean time between failures. Nonfailure (and reliability) is defined by continuity of "satisfactory utility." A competitive benchmark of MTBF is a useful guide when considered in conjunction with customer acceptance of failure.

Methods analysis: Systematic examination of all operations in every process. The objective is to search for better ways to do the jobs that the company requires. Encourages process alternatives by combining steps, eliminating operations, making work easier, and raising product quality and the quality of life for employees.

Minimum cost assignment schedule: This refers to the trade-off model for aggregate planning of the workforce. There is a need to search for the production schedule that has the minimum total cost along the scale that starts with smooth production (at one extreme) and ends with perfect matching of supply and demand (at the other).

Mobile robots: Many repetitive and dangerous jobs can be assigned to machines. Fixed machines have limited abilities; mobile machines are far more useful. Mobile robots require guidance or vision capabilities, both of which are under development. Robots with mobility are especially useful for safety and security. There is growth in the application of robotics for hazardous situations including nuclear energy, bomb squads, toxic gas and fluid spills, etc. Service robots are being built smaller, smarter, more mobile, and less expensively. They can be thought of as point of contact, mobile computers. Mobile nurse and orderly robots are increasingly used in healthcare services.

Models: Attempts to image the real thing can be physical, like an airplane model or a plant layout model. Location decision models use numbers in equations for costs and preferences to maximize company performance.

Modular production (MP): The principle of modularity is to design, develop, and produce the minimum number of parts (or operations) that can be combined in the maximum number of ways to offer the greatest number of different products or services. Both modular production (MP) and group technology (GT) represent a focus on commonality of parts within product groups; for example, various sizes of motors for vacuum cleaners of different powers. Computer memories and speed are another fine example. MP increases realizable capacity of the production system by increasing the process supply capabilities as well as demand volume.

MPS: See **Master production schedule.**

MRP: See **Material requirements planning.**

MRP II: The definitive systems plan for operating effectively at the plant level is manufacturing resource planning (called MRP II). It links P/OM and production planning with marketing goals, financial policies, R & D plans, accounting procedures, and human resource management goals. MRP II is responsive to the strategic business plan of the company, but it does not create or drive that plan as does enterprise resource planning (ERP). The subject of enterprise planning is a top management issue rather than a sole P/OM responsibility. If ERP is the scope of company planning, then MRP II will dovetail with it, because production should be a balanced component of the overall plan.

Multifactor productivity: Measured by the U.S. Labor Department, this is also called *total productivity*. It reflects the joint effects of many factors including labor and capital. It includes the impact of new technology, economies of scale, managerial skills, etc. The measure is obtained by dividing the dollar value of goods and services over time by the total dollar value of all input resources expended over the same time period.

Multiple-channel stations: In queuing systems, if there are more arrivals (n) than servers (M), i.e., n > M, a line develops with n − M waiting for service. If there is one occupied server, (M = 1), the next arrival must wait. If there are two busy servers, (M = 2), no waiting occurs until a third arrival. The effect of multiple channels (stations, servers, systems) is to provide greater systems capacity and to lower the system's utilization, ρ. See **Single-channel systems.**

Multiple decision makers: Quantitative scoring models can work with more than one person's evaluations of locations, suppliers, products, processes, etc. However, it is very unlikely that everyone will agree on all dimensions that are being scored. Averaging the scores of multiple decision makers reduces variability. Extreme highs cancel extreme lows. Alternatively, cluster dimensions on which there is agreement, separating them from the dimensions where there is substantial disagreement. Have the multiple decision makers (MDMs) discuss the disagreements with the goal of ascertaining the basis of differences of opinion and the goal of changing minds. Run sensitivity analyses to determine which extremes alter the selections of the scoring models. Simulations based on the data might prove valuable. The possibilities are numerous; this is still the tip of the iceberg.

Multiple project management: Managers and workers have more than one project assignment in many companies today. A variety of product development and process improvement initiatives are going on at the same time. The management of multiple projects calls on all of the skills required to manage a very complex project that has many suppliers and workers. Information control is critical. The challenges are to share resources, including management, and to compartmentalize assignments so time lines are not sacrificed on one project at the expense of another. Resource leveling can be used effectively. See **Resource leveling.**

N

Net change MRP: A fast and economical method of updating the MRP information system. The MRP files are composed of three components, viz., BOM, IRF, and MPS. If the information system is out of date, then the MRP system will fail. Therefore, updating all three files on a regular basis is crucial. Net change MRP is one of two methods widely used for updating. See **Regeneration MRP** for the other. APICS defines net change MRP: ". . .the materials requirements plan is continually retained in the computer. Whenever a change is needed in requirements, open order inventory status, or bill of material, a partial explosion and netting is made for only those parts affected by the change." Thus, if notified that an alteration has occurred in the situation, changes to the MRP data files are made only for the affected items. APICS is the acronym for the highly regarded American Production and Inventory Control Society.

Net present value (NPV): Method for determining the value of keeping or changing technology. NPV does this by discounting the cost of future expenditures and the value of future savings. A dollar today is worth a dollar. A dollar received or paid out a year from today is less than a dollar by the amount of interest that it would have earned during the year. NPV calculations show the time stream of values for applicable interest rates and planning horizons. See NPV in Supplement 19.

Neural networks: See Artificial Intelligence (AI) and Cybernetics. The neural network model has been applied in a variety of complex situations with success. It is an adaptation of human synaptic neuron networks that provide sight, sound, smell, thinking, and reminiscing. Found to be a good basis for developing artificial intelligence and expert system capabilities.

New product development: Stages include concept selection, idea development, testing concepts, estimation and business modeling, prototype construction and testing, process specification, and pilot plant. The many stages are combinations of information collection based on R & D in the laboratories, market research regarding the opinions of people, and business modeling. If any link in the chain is weak, the system is liable to severe failure. See **Projects.**

Normal time: (1) *Normal* activity time is associated with the minimum necessary spending on project activities because there is no great stress on completing the project as soon as possible. In other words, the project budget reflects the least amount of money that has to be spent to complete the project in (what the project manager deems to be) a reasonable time. COST/TIME trade-off analysis is not required because project managers are satisfied with completion dates. See **Crash time** and **Critical path methods (CPM).**
(2) The output rate of an average worker is the expected production rate of the process. Using normal time, managers can determine how many people to employ to fill demand.

Northwest Corner (NWC) method: Transportation models are solved using linear programming methods. Alternatively, they can be solved using network algorithms that employ the Northwest Corner (NWC) method. Put the largest possible shipment in the upper-left corner and move downward and toward the right as further assignments are made. This network procedure can be speeded toward final solution by rearranging rows and columns following clever heuristics.

O

Olympic perspective: In a chapter dedicated to quality, the Olympic perspective deserves consideration. Problems have surfaced with the administration of the Olympics but not with the credo and goals of this international competition for excellence. Quality is a global concern, and the five rings of the Olympiad represent the union of the continents of the world. Although sporting contests abound, the Olympic ideals are sports interacting with culture and the environment. The Olympic credo is faster, higher, and stronger. It is not fastest, highest, and strongest. The idea of striving to be better is readily translated into dynamic goals of continuous improvement for management. The idea of striving to be better is also focused on ethical issues for the International Olympic Committee (IOC).

OM system: An alternative name for the P/OM system used to make goods or furnish services. OM is more service-oriented than P/OM.

Operating characteristic curves (O.C. curves): Graphics that show what happens to the probability of accepting a lot as the actual percent defective in the lot goes from zero to 100. Each O.C. curve is a unique sampling plan designed to minimize the penalties for making two kinds of errors. Buyer's risk (Type II error) is to accept lots that have too many defectives because samples indicate they are fine. Seller's risk (Type I error) is to have lots rejected by the buyer because the samples indicate they have too many defectives when in fact they are fine.

Operations: The activities that are used to produce (and deliver) goods or furnish (and deliver) services to customers. This term is not always used with the production of goods but is always used with services.

Operations management: Managing activities used to produce (and deliver) goods or furnish (and deliver) services to customers. The implication of this term is that management is professional and effective.

Opportunity costs: These are the costs of choosing options that are less than the best. The analysis of net benefits for each available option requires detailed study of all system elements. Differences between the best net benefit and other option net benefits are opportunity costs. Time needs to be considered as well because short-term net benefits are unlikely to be considered more important than long-term net benefits. Examples of situations that require opportunity cost analysis include selection of the second-best location to get the first-choice facility. The system's best choice has zero opportunity cost. See **Assignment method.**

OPT: (1) Developed by Dr. Eliyahu Goldratt to deal rationally with bottleneck-based finite production scheduling. The acronym stands for optimal production technique (also, optimized production technology). OPT controls queues by supplying the bottleneck with sufficient batches of work so that it operates at close to maximum capacity. Other features relate to the rhythm of the throughput at the bottleneck (called the *drum*).
(2) Original name for a finite production scheduling technique. The lots are of finite size. OPT techniques, developed by Eli Goldratt's company, are now called *Theory of Constraints (TOC)*. Operational production scheduling remains the goal of TOC. The objective is synchronized manufacturing by making assignments so that flows are continuous, stations are balanced, and bottlenecks are fed without queues forming. See **Theory of Constraints** and **TOC.**

Order point policies (OPP): Inventory levels drop as stock is withdrawn for use by the production system. OPP are policies that define the stock level at which a new order will be placed. Lead time is a crucial factor in determining the reorder point (RP). OPP applies to both economic order quantity (EOQ) and economic lot size (ELS) type systems with a fairly stable, continuous pattern of stock withdrawals. See **(EOQ)** and **(ELS).** OPP is used with both perpetual and periodic inventory systems. The order point for the periodic model is the order interval. (See **Perpetual inventory system** and **Periodic inventory system**).

Order promising: Sales department commitments for delivery are the basis for the assignments of the MPS. Quantities of specific models to be made at chosen times result from customer orders and forecasts of orders that are considered highly probable. Order promising is also called order dating, which answers the question "When can you ship?"

P

Paced conveyor: A transporter, usually a belt, moving materials between workstations at a fixed rate of speed (station stop-time equals cycle time). The belt may stop so that workstations can be immobile.

Pareto analysis: Determines the most frequent types of defects and puts them in rank order. Pareto charts graphically depict the frequency of each kind of problem, facilitating identification of frequent defects. The rank order helps assign remedial priorities. For example, complaints to the hotel manager have been put together on a spreadsheet. The most frequent one might not be the most serious one. Therefore, Pareto data have to be reinterpreted for impact on customer dissatisfaction. A Pareto frequency distribution is the best way to begin the analysis of quality problems. Pareto diagrams that use relative frequencies (sum to 100) are often preferred.

Payback period: Justification for new technology may be based on the net present value method. The payback period (PP) is an alternative calculation that requires less math and (some say) is more intuitive. PP is defined as the period of time required for an investment to produce revenues that pay back the debt. For example, a $100 investment that generates $5 per month of revenue will take 20 months (1 year and 8 months) to pay for itself. There is no discounting of the value of money with PP. Also, if the revenue of $5 per month requires $3 for materials and labor, that leaves only $2 per month for cost recovery (CR) based on profit. Fifty months (4 years and 2 months) are needed for total CR.

p-chart: p-charts plot successive sample measures of the percent defective for specific quality attributes. It has upper- and lower-control limits distanced from the process average ($\bar{p}$) so that the probabilities of the sample values of p exceeding the thresholds are preselected odds (e.g., 0.001, 0.0001) if the process is stable. At start-up, the control chart is expected to exhibit lack of control, meaning that more sample values of p exceed the control limits than is statistically warranted. The process is stabilized (brought under control) by removing assignable causes. See **R-chart.**

Perfect balance (pb): See **Balance delay.**

Performance evaluation: Lauded for feedback it provides allowing employees *at all levels* to improve their performance and to provide incentives and rewards for excellence. Criticized for being inaccurate and subjective, there is mistrust on the part of those who are below average. Statisticians note that even in a random process 50 percent of the class must be below average.

Periodic inventory system: Periodic inventory systems use regular, fixed review periods (e.g., weekly or monthly) to review existing inventory levels. On consecutive, specific dates separated by the same amount of time (an interval derived to minimize total costs), each item's record is opened. An order is placed for a variable number of units. Note that for this system, the interval between orders is fixed and the order quantity is variable. The order point for the periodic model is the open-order interval. Before computers were powerful, periodic inventory systems were far more popular than their perpetual cousins. Periodic are still more appealing for certain types of inventory situations, e.g., there is one delivery per week (Thursdays) by our company to Point Barrow, Alaska. See **Order point policies (OPP)** and **Perpetual inventory system.**

Permutability of columns: Flexibility often exists within a workstation concerning the order in which operations will be done. If two operations are assigned to a workstation and either one of them can be done first, the decision about order should be made and adhered to thereafter. Random selection will defeat the advantages of systematic procedures, which often lead later to unexpected improvements in doing the job. For example, at a workstation, either open the jar or get the pickles for the jar could be done first. The manager might express a preference for getting the pickles after opening the jar because the next step is fill the jar with pickles. See **Lateral transferability.**

Perpetual inventory system: Perpetual inventory systems are most often online, real-time, computer-driven systems. They are triggered to action by the stock level dropping to the reorder point (RP). The RP is a function of the expected demand in the lead-time period. When the RP is reached, an order of fixed size (EOQ) is placed with the supplier. Note that for this system, the interval between orders is variable and the order quantity is fixed. Perpetual inventory systems exemplify management by exception (MBE) where stock withdrawals, recorded by computer, are automatically acted upon when the RP level occurs. Management action occurs when special information is received (which is the exception)—say that a design change is about to be made to the part. Then, managers will override the automatic reorder mechanism. The two-bin perpetual inventory system

(before and since computers) is a physical analog that does not require record keeping. See **Economic order quantity, Lead time, Periodic inventory system,** and **Reorder point (RP).**

PERT: Program evaluation review technique is a project network method. Like the critical path methods (CPM), PERT identifies the longest time-path in the project Emphasis is on estimation as the determinant of project completion time. See **Critical path methods (CPM).**

PERT/COST/TIME: This is the trade-off between quick completion and low cost. The theory is spend more—finish faster; spend less—finish in normal time. The PERT project network method is designed to balance the project goals. See **Critical path methods (CPM)** and **PERT.**

Pilot studies: *Scalability* is a term describing how adaptable a process is to changes in demand volume and throughput rates. Pilots are small-scale systems used to test feasibility of the process. The assumption is that if the pilot scale works, then the full-scale system will work. This assumption is not without risk. However, the alternative is so costly that there is willingness to assume that risk. It is much less expensive to build a pilot plant than the full-scale plant. If operations fail with the pilot, the losses are minor in comparison to the alternatives. *Scalability* is a term associated with IT projects where system performance may start to deteriorate as there are more users, larger databases, and increasing complexity of process requirements.

Planning horizon: *First* level of aggregate planning is to determine the appropriate planning horizon for forecasting demand. It *cannot be less than the longest lead time* for production. If the company forecasts 600 units will be required and that will take 3 months of production, then the planning horizon is set so that the 600 units can be delivered on time. Three months is the planning horizon even though all other orders can be filled in one month.

Practical first steps: Many companies have vision statements, and they may have strategies for realizing their visions. Visions are articulated goals, and strategies are specific, but undetailed plans for achieving goals. Tactics are the missing link. Tactics deal with very elementary issues that connect all of the dots. The saying that "the devil is in the details" captures the essence of practical first steps. The initial challenge is to answer the elusive query "what do we do first?" The Gleicher (conditions for) change model requires articulated goals and believable tactics for realizing initial goals. Believability that the plan can work (practical steps) is strongly dependent on documenting exactly what to do at start-up. See **Gleicher model (Conditions for change), Dissatisfaction,** and **Vision.**

Precedence diagram: Goal is to design the best possible processes using precedence diagrams of serialized flow shop systems. Precedence diagrams chart all relevant operations indicating which operations must follow others, e.g., take off before landing. In addition to sequencing data, times for accomplishment of each operation are listed on the precedence diagram. Good engineering develops processes that save steps and allow efficient line-balancing for intermittent flow shops. At Nascar races, changing a tire is done in moments because ordinary process constraints have been bypassed.

Predictive maintenance (PDM): Maintenance based on knowledge of signs and symptoms that something is likely to go awry in the future.

Preventive maintenance (PM): Maintenance performed before failure. Part of total productive maintenance (TPM), it is an option that is the opposite of remedial maintenance (RM), where repairs start after failure. PM works on a regular schedule based on the knowledge of mean time between failures (MTBF). Why wait for the failure to occur? Predictive maintenance (PDM) helps to determine the MTBF.

Principle of modularity: See **Modular production (MP).**

Process: At the core of P/OM. A process is a series of activities or steps required to transform materials and components into intermediates or finished goods. The service delivery process is totally qualified in the same sense.

Process analysis: The detailed study of activities required to make the product or deliver the service. After analysis comes design and redesign.

Process charts: Graphics for doing process analysis. They are also useful for doing process design and redesign.

Process steps: Stages of the process.

Product callbacks: Have costs that include labor and material rework, decreased customer loyalty, and potential litigation losses that stem from events preceding the callback. These are costs of failure that should be compared with costs of detection and correction prior to shipping product, and the costs of prevention of defectives in the first place.

Production: Activities used to create (and deliver) goods or furnish (and deliver) services to customers. This term is not used with services but it is common with the manufacture of goods.

Production management: Managing activities used to produce (and deliver) goods to customers. The implication of this term is that management is professional and effective.

Production planning: The first level is aggregate planning and it is the only level that requires a forecast. See Planning horizon. Production planning at the second level is loading. At level three, it is sequencing. Loading for the factory is often called shop loading. Loading in service organizations is called "manpower" planning.

Production scheduling: Subject of Chapter 16, it consists of loading and sequencing. Because of combinatorial richness (there are so many ways to set up schedules) and the difficulty of optimizing such detailed complex arrays of data, the two steps of loading and sequencing are used. Assignment and transportation models can assist in the loading function. Sequencing algorithms are available for the second part of production scheduling. Production scheduling is always a systems problem because jobs, people, and teams compete with each other for best facilities.

Production standards: Criteria specifying the amount of work (specific units or service times) to be accomplished in a given period of time. These standards are statements of the expected output rates from which the costs of the product can be estimated. Production standards permit supply and demand analysis to determine shortfalls or reassignment of resources.

Productivity standards: Average performance adjusted by an allowance for rest and delay. They are used to calculate expected output rates. Productivity standards allow process managers to determine how many workers will be required to meet demand.

Products, Continuous development: See **Continuity and Ferris Wheel model.**

Projects: (1) Special work configurations designed to accomplish singular (or nearly singular) goals. Time-based endeavors that bring together skills and technology to accomplish goals such as building structures, putting on a play, writing new software, launching new products (including publishing a new book), and organizing activities (industrial, social, military, political) to bring about change.

(2) A unique type of work configuration that is used for start-up purposes with major new undertakings including structures and systems. Project management is responsible for following the planned time line and being within budget.

Project management: Projects are undertakings (usually of considerable complexity) that are unique or relatively unique such as building a factory, launching a spacecraft, staging a play, starting a business, or bringing a new product to market. Project management is managing these non-repetitive activities in a way that is both professional and effective.

Projects, Continuous development: See **Continuity and Ferris Wheel model.**

Projects, Probability of success: p_s is the probability of product success (defined as meeting specific profit goals). Given O project completions per year, p_sO is the number of successes.

Projects, Rapid completion: There is increasing pressure to cut project time significantly. For example, from scratch, design, build, and produce a car in one year, instead of three years. Many factors play a role in achieving this objective, including concurrency and continuity. See **Concurrent engineering and Products, Continuous development.**

Pull-production systems: Production systems that call for delivery of materials from upstream stations (including outside suppliers) are pulling materials as needed. The contrast is with upstream stations pushing finished materials on downstream stations. The advantage of pulling is that materials are delivered just-in-time or nearly so depending upon how many units are called for by a pull signal. The disadvantage of pushing production is that production variability can create overloads on the downstream stations leading to quality problems. Upstream stations may be overproducing. Suppliers are asked to deliver small quantities (almost JIT) rather than full deliveries, which have to be put in storage with both receipt and withdrawal costs. See **Push-production systems.**

Purchasing agents (PAs): With their buying organizations, they buy supplies the company requires. This applies to every aspect of the company's needs, including supplying production and feeding the people who eat in the cafeteria, keeping the rest rooms tidy, and giving oil to the maintenance staff for the forklift trucks. Purchasing is a traditional function that has been evolving in many interesting ways, including the use of extensive online purchasing and auctions to obtain multiple bids. Purchasing agents are one of the best listening devices invented to learn about new materials and what competitors are doing.

Pure number: See **Scoring model.** Quantitative comparison of two options poses problems of combining multiple dimensions. Oft referred to as the problem of adding apples and oranges. In P/OM, it is more likely to be the problem of adding costs and qualities together. Scientists solved that problem long ago by taking ratios of the items to be compared. Scores for each dimension of every option have exponents to reflect their importance, and these are multiplied to obtain a single number. The ratios of the products of the powers yield a pure number because all dimension are canceled.

Push-production systems: Workstations pushing materials on the downstream stations are regarded as impeding productivity. Poor line balance aggravates the situation, causing uneven output. This volatility makes it difficult to trace quality problems and causes work-in-process to pile up in places. Smooth flows and balanced cycle times of pull-production systems are gradually replacing the push-production systems of earlier eras. See **Pull-production systems.**

Put-away: The end step before the next setup, make ready cycle. It is another term for *Take Down* in the *Changeover* cycle.

Q

Quality circles (QCs): Groups with teamwork assignments for quality achievement. Such teams are often part of a quality function deployment (QFD) initiative. Many QCs are associated with CWTQM (company-wide TQM). The deployment of quality concerns throughout the company is assisted by QCs because everyone has an opportunity to belong to one or more circles. All aspects of company activities are fair game for study.

Quality control (QC): Quality achievement is a major P/OM systems responsibility. Quality pervades every aspect of all firms' performance. Therefore, P/OM should be a partner in strategic planning. Control of quality is a tactical function. It remains the engineering prescription when a staff department audits quality. There is precedent for external policing of quality. For example, companies' Best practice does not use a QC department to serve as police enforcers.

Quality function deployment (QFD): A comprehensive program with a complete agenda for extending quality throughout the firm's activities. It includes quality circles and company-wide total quality management. QFD was started in Kobe at Japanese shipyards owned by Mitsubishi. Later, it was employed by Toyota as well as other Japanese and U.S. manufacturers, including Ford Motor. QFD employs Taguchi methods as well as the philosophy and approaches of six-sigma.

Quality integrity: One of the most important ethical issues for P/OM is to ensure delivery of products and services good for the safety and health of customers. P/OM must also provide a secure and accident-free working environment for employees. Such standards are the foundation of quality integrity. Events can be thrust on a company that destroy the feeling of quality integrity. Companies may take extraordinary measures to restore the sense of integrity. For example, in 1982, using crisis management, Johnson & Johnson reacted to Tylenol tampering with effective public relations that saved the day. Perrier water was similarly successful. Corporate social responsibility (CSR) is associated with responses that are open, honest, and swift. Deviant behaviors used by some companies to defraud the community, customers, and employees are the reverse of CSR. However, every case must be judged on its own. Quality integrity is a systems property. See **Ethics.**

R

R-chart: Control limits are applied to the range (R) chart, which usually is a companion to the $\bar{x}$-chart. Together the two charts supply powerful diagnostics for process behavior. Range is measured for each sample of size n by $R = x_{max} - x_{min}$. The mean of the sample measures is $\bar{R}$. It is used to determine the control limits with tabled factors that are a function of n. The limits are distanced the equivalent of $k\sigma$ from the mean so that the probabilities of sample range values exceeding these thresholds are pre-selected odds (e.g., 0.001, 0.0001) if the process is stable. The range chart checks that the spread of the distribution around the mean stays constant. See $\bar{x}$-**chart.**

Recycling concrete: Recycling concrete from the old road to the new road is an excellent example of end-of-life (EOL) product recovery. Environmentalists generally approve of such cradle-to-the-grave recovery and reuse system. However, there has been opposition by local citizens because of on-site noise and odors. See **Remanufacturing, Reuse,** and **Reverse supply chains.**

Reengineering (REE): (1) Given substantial dissatisfaction with things as they are and a vision of what might be, REE starts from scratch with practical first steps. Starting from scratch can be opposed by those in favor of gradual (continuous improvement) changes. There are territorial issues that may lead caretakers of the current system to fight radical changes that occur when the design process begins with a blank piece of paper. This is only one cause of REE failure. Another is to underestimate the complexity of the challenge and the commitment for success.
(2) Starting from scratch to redesign the process. The goal is to make major improvements. Major means dramatic and "revolutionary" rather than "evolutionary." Reengineering is the opposite of continuous incremental changes, which Japanese production experts call "kaizen."
(3) This term is used to signify that the current processes are to be completely redone so that goals can be achieved more effectively. The concept of starting from scratch means that planners are not constrained by prior system elements and structures.

Regeneration MRP: A thorough, time-demanding method of updating the MRP information system. The APICS definition is "... the master production schedule is totally reexploded down through all bills of material, to maintain valid priorities. New requirements and planned orders are completely recalculated or 'regenerated' at that time." See **Net change MRP** for the alternative method to update MRP, and the APICS reference. All three MRP input files (BOM, IRF, and MPS) take part in the recomputation of the entire data set. All MRP records are usually regenerated once a week. More frequent regeneration is used when the penalties for outdated data are severe.

Relative productivity: A measure of comparison between similar processes. These can be comparisons of productivity between two different Budweiser breweries, or between a Budweiser brewery and a competitor's brewery, or between the same breweries over time. In this case, relative productivity is used as a benchmark, and it is critical that the identical measure be used for each unit in the comparison.

Remanufacturing: The list of companies that remanufacture is impressive and always growing. Because of economic advantages, remanufacturing is not a temporary phenomenon. As companies improve their designs of renewable components, remanufacturing becomes more attractive. Continual improvements in materials and technology are also shifting market shares to enhance the value of remanufacturing. Feasible remanufacturing candidates are on the drawing boards. Main advocates include Tom's of Maine, Xerox, Panasonic, Kodak, Fuji, John Deere, Caterpillar, BMW, and Deutz in Germany.

Remedial maintenance (RM): Maintenance after failure.

Rent: Rent, buy, or build are familiar choices for buildings, facilities, land, and equipment. Rent (lease) payments are made regularly by a tenant (lessee) to a landlord (lessor). There is a contract conveying property to another for a specified period in consideration of compensation. These are treated as fixed costs even when there are provisions for terminating the agreement with sufficient notice and payment.

Reorder point (RP): Triggers an order for more stock. This order can be placed automatically with a "trusted" supplier. The will be no managerial intervention unless an instance qualifying for MBE occurs. Then, the special situation will be brought to management's attention for review including choice of supplier. Systems can alert management to slowdowns occurring in withdrawals (interval between RPs is statistically greater than expectation).

Resource leveling: Where slack exists, there is potential for resource trade-offs that can reduce nonvalue-adding time while decreasing the time required for completion of the project. Sometimes the resource is a person reassigned to work with a different team for a day or two. At other times, it is the transfer of equipment or facilities, such as a truck, or a place to store materials. See **Multiple project management** and **Slack.**

Reuse: There are many associations devoted to various aspects of recycling materials. Reuse is one of the recycling categories that is economically attractive because a reusable part can quickly be returned to inventory. Reusable plastics, glass, paper, and metal may require more value-adding than a nut, bolt, or gear that can be reused with just cleanup. In remanufacturing, there are combinations of new parts and reusable, repairable, reworked parts. Pre-planned design decisions for reuse after disassembly can change the economics of the product, including breakeven points, margin, and return on investments. See **Design for disassembly, Recycling concrete, Remanufacturing,** and **Take-back laws.**

Reverse supply chains: Take-back momentum is increasing because end-of-product-life recovery is a social necessity as populations grow larger and life styles produce increasing amounts of disposable material. There is a reverse delivery logistic at end-of-life for both used up and damaged products. Automobile recycling commands so much attention that the acronym ELV is used for end-of-life-of-vehicle. Also on the agenda is disposal of SOC (substance of concern). Increasingly, manufacturers are held responsible for Best Practice with returned materials (intelligent ELV objectives) and for providing the means for return delivery.

Saturn trucks deliver cars to dealers and return with damaged plastic doors and body parts. See **Reuse, Remanufacturing,** and **Take-back laws.**

Robots: See Cyborgs and flexible process systems (FPS). Robots are evolving from mechanical devices that perform complex, repetitive, and often unpleasant, tasks into computer-controlled systems with broad sensory abilities, discernment, and forms of intelligence. Although in its infancy, robotics has transformed manufacturing technology, military and police reconnaissance, and is now beginning to provide service functions. The forces that propel increasing use of robots are miniaturization, artificial intelligence, improved sensory capabilities, and information feedback. "Robot," derived from the Czech word *robota* (compulsory labor) was first used in the play called "RUR" (Rossum's Universal Robots), written by Karel Çapek in 1926. One definition of robots includes the fact that they are made to look like people. Some service robots continue this trend.

Rough-cut capacity planning (RCCP): At the time that the aggregate plan (AP) is being transformed into the master production schedule (MPS), RCCP is used to check that there is sufficient capacity to produce what is needed. The method uses approximation based on the bill of resources (BOR) to determine if actual capacity is adequate to match the expected capacity requirements of the MPS. Capacity requirements planning is post-MRP planning operating at the plant or enterprise level where strategic business decisions will be made about investments in additional capacity. Rough-cut capacity planning is working at the shop floor level doing the disaggregation of the aggregate plan into actual work assignments to meet real demand. RCCP can result in deferral of shipments when capacity is insufficient.

Runs: A run of numbers on any control chart is a succession of values that fall either above or below the mean line. It is like a string of heads or tails, which becomes increasingly unlikely as the streak continues. This makes runs a great telltale that something is awry with the system's behavior because normal performance is a random drawing of heads and of tails. Runs also provide diagnostic information about health of the quality system. Strings below the mean have different process interpretations than above the mean. If runs are accelerating (meaning that distances from the mean are increasing) that connotes momentum in the system's deterioration. More urgency for remedial action is indicated.

S

Scatter diagrams: Figures composed of data points that are thought to be associated with each other, as calories consumed (x) and weight (y). This relationship is not expected to be precisely linear, but a pattern may emerge for particular groups of people such as those who live in a region of the world where fish is the main staple. If data for x and y are related, the relationship is likely to appear upon visual inspection. The same correlation would be difficult for most people to spot in tables of numbers.

Scientific management: The name given to the systematic approach to doing work well, developed by Frederick Winslow Taylor in the late 1800s and early 1900s. Scientific management stressed the fact that there was a best way to do work. In search of the best way, the various factors that made up the job were listed, observed, and analyzed. During the 1930s, practitioners of the approach were called *efficiency experts*. In later years, this work became the province of industrial engineering.

Scoring model: Compares quantitatively alternative options for a broad variety of situations. Various kinds of scoring models serve different purposes. Monetary analyses of costs and revenues for business options are used effectively. Business decisions often cannot rely exclusively on straight dollar comparisons. The same applies to a credit agency scoring the status of an individual's financial soundness. Scoring models using ratios can be employed with mixed dimensions because ratios produce *pure numbers*. Scoring models unify the many tangible and intangible costs and benefits that are relevant in a complex compari-

son. They are a means for organizing and combining personal guesses, somewhat speculative estimates, and hard numbers. Use of sensitivity analysis is recommended for exploring the effects of errors in estimations. See http://www.myfico.com for practical examples of personal credit scoring.

Sensitivity analysis: (1) By using high and low estimates, it is possible to test the sensitivity of a business model (e.g., linear programming, scoring, and transportation models) to a range of conditions. If alternative A is the preferred option under expected (average) conditions, and this remains the case when estimates are at their extreme values, then the decision is stable. However, if shifts occur, then it is important to home in on better estimates to which the solution is sensitive.
(2) Whether conducted by hand, laptop spreadsheet, or full-scale computer software, sensitivity analysis allows diagnostic analysis of the effects of changing inventory costs, including purchase price (get a discount for ordering more); labor, materials, fabrication and assembly costs; carrying costs; ordering costs; setup costs; and market demands. Tests are run in response to managers' "what if" questions. When done systematically, and with innovative ideas, sensitivity analysis improves system performance.

Sequenced assembly: Henry Ford's contribution to the world of production. In 1912, he set up the continuous flow assembly line, and production was never the same again. The key was synchronization and control of the process flows including those flows from vendors to feed the "mass production" line.

Sequencing: (1) The second part of production scheduling, sequencing follows the loading function. Job order can make a big difference in the flow time, which is the length of time it takes to process a sequence of n jobs. Shortest processing time (SPT) will produce the shortest flow time. See **Mean flow time, SPT rule, Total flow time.**
(2) *Third* level of aggregate planning is sequencing. It provides the best ordering for jobs to be done at each department. Best can be defined in a number of different ways. A primary basis for establishing optimal sequence is to minimize the time jobs spend waiting. There are other bases too.

Sequencing chart: See **Layout chart.**

Service: P/OM needs to delineate both the differences and similarities between producing goods and providing services. The service category is complex because it includes every form of work except manufacturing of goods. That means the teaching of students, caring for patients in a healthcare facility, entertaining the guests at a theme park, cleaning the apartment, serving the food, marrying the couple, running the library, providing the concert, making the movie, and going to the theater are all classified as services.

Setup(s): The start of the changeover cycle. It is the common term for engineering process shifts to stop making one item and start making another.

Shop floor control: Consists of tracking and communicating the status of orders in the job shop. It also requires monitoring and reporting on the productivity of workstations. Knowing what is having value-added, and what is waiting, helps to expedite jobs, decrease idle time, and increase value-adding.

Simulation: The imitative representation of the functioning of a system or process by means of the functioning of a surrogate system or process. The methodology of mechanical simulation for testing has been used for many years. For example, the device that turns a doorknob 6,000 times an hour can test the fatigue limits of the latch bolt springs in days instead of having to wait years for failure to occur. In the same empirical fashion, dropping packages permits testing durability. Growing import is placed on the results derived from crashing cars with dummies into walls. The dummies are filled with chips that communicate with computers to reveal forces experienced during crashes on their bodies. Car designers as well as buyers follow these results with interest. Simulations can now be run entirely on computers using math equations to represent special situations such as air turbulence effects on planes and large waves on ship hulls.

Single-channel systems: A single server (M = 1) is providing service. With variable service times and variable arrival rates, a line starts to form when the number of arrivals n > 1, during an average service period. Simple queue equations are available to describe the behavior of the system. Single-channel systems are a special case of multiple-channel systems, for M = 1. See **Multiple-channel stations.**

Single-minute exchange of dies (SMED): An interesting nonfiction story. Taiichi Ohno of Toyota Motor Manufacturing in Japan demanded revolutionary changes of setup times, and he asked Shigeo Shingo to cut setup times for a particular operation from four hours to three minutes. Shingo did even better. He established procedures for setups that take less than a minute. This was a sea-change in P/OM.

Six-sigma: Goals first set by Motorola in 1986. Philip Crosby Associates had preached zero defects long before that time. However, each firm had its own approach. Crosby stated that conformance to specifications is crucial. When choosing specs that are attainable, zero defects are a reasonable goal. Motorola, on the other hand, wanted product design and production processes that could deliver near-zero defects (six-sigma is 3.4 defects per million parts). See Motorola University at http://mu.motorola.com.

SKU: The catalogue of stock-keeping units (SKU) presents every different part carried, sold, or purchased by the company. A unique identification number exists for each of the distinct parts. These ID numbers tell as much as possible about the item: suppliers, materials, sizes, colors, shapes, styles, and family tree (which model in the lineage).

Slack: (1) Free time at a project activity. This translates to allowable slippage in an activity's schedule along a slack path. The slack between activities describes the amount of time that it is safe to be late in delivering a completed activity. Project managers view activity paths with limited amounts of slack as potential problem areas because minor events can change limited slack operations into activities along the critical path.

(2) Unused departmental capacity. The term means that there is room for maneuvering. It is the antonym for tightness and constraint on freedom in the system. In various LP applications, slack can apply to unused materials, people, money, and machine capacities. Linear programming optimizations of profit often occur with some unused capacity. The term is also used for projects to indicate some flexibility in the use of resources to avoid missing deadlines. Resources associated with slack paths can be traded off to critical paths (where deadlines exist) to assure completion on schedule. See **Critical path methods (CPM)** and **Multiple project management.**

Slope: Low breakeven points are preferred to high BEPs. However, the slope of the profit line before and after breakeven determines how fast loss and gain occur when demand falls below or rises above the BEP.

Smart benchmarks: An assessment of company performance can be obtained by comparison with a competitor, another division of the same organization, or with the same department over time. Benchmarking is costly and time-consuming. Therefore, a limited number of dimensions can be measured. Which dimensions are the most important to make the basis of comparison? Smart benchmarks are based on those dimensions that are most valuable for steering tactics and for redirecting strategies. For example, return on equity is increasingly popular with chief financial officers (CFOs), and inventory turns are favored by companies like Wal-Mart and Thomasville Furniture.

SME wheel: This graphic provides a "vision" of a fully integrated global manufacturing company. Links resources and responsibilities within the three sectors of product/process, manufacturing, and customer support. Organizational issues are at the core and participate with people and teamwork to satisfy the requirements of customers. Information and technology are in an outer ring that surrounds the entire complex. Minor effort is needed to recast the wheel for any nonmanufacturing system.

SOC: See **Substances of concern.**

Special-purpose equipment (SPE): Primarily used in the flow shop. It is designed for one-, two-, or three-shift relatively continuous operation. SPE is efficient in repetitive production of the same kind of unit. In automobile assembly, several similar cars can be run through the same line with no major changeovers required to shift models.

SPT rule: Shortest processing time is a powerful heuristic rule for decreasing the time required to complete operations for n jobs. Jobs are rank-ordered in their processing times, t. The job with the smallest t goes first. The job with the next-smallest t goes second, and so forth. The SPT rule can be modified to give priority to jobs that have waited a long time in the queue. Other priority rule modifications of SPT include preference for most profitable, or loyal, customers or for due date compliance. Contrast with FIFO and LIFO.

Standard units: Jobs are converted from pieces of work (order size) into standard hours required to make the pieces and fill the order on a designated machine called the standard machine. This facilitates aggregate planning for the use of production resources and the timing of events to meet expected demands (work schedules).

Static inventory models: There is only one chance to order the right amount of stock. Corrections that are allowed by dynamic inventory models do not operate in the static situation where how much to order is a one-shot decision. There is almost no second-guessing allowed when deciding how many Christmas trees to order for the three sales weeks before December 25. Sometimes the no-repetition rule is bent a bit to allow one corrective action. Thus, a mail order catalogue preparing for the holiday season may place a first order for toys in August. Then, after observing competitors, finishing ongoing market research, and monitoring toy store sales, the decision is made to increase stock on-hand with another order placed in September. See **Dynamic inventory models.**

Static inventory problem: Classical inventory problem with some special characteristics, namely, how much to buy when there is only one purchase occasion allowed. Not usually applicable to flow shop inventories, but necessary for job shops and project management. The company that fabricates toys for Christmas may set up in August with various suppliers, each getting one order. This is also relevant to the static repair problem, where the generator is purchased with a given number of spare parts. The static problem is: Given a parts-failure distribution, how many spare parts should be bought with the generator?

Statistical process control (SPC): This set of statistical methods is part of statistical quality control (SQC). It is the control charting aspect of SQC. See **Statistical quality control (SQC).**

Statistical quality control (SQC): Statistical quality control (SQC) encompasses SPC as well as other statistical methods, including acceptance sampling. Walter Shewhart's work on SQC was published in 1930. It created a taxonomy for control of quality that led to a revolution in quality standards and capabilities throughout the world. His methodology detailed all of the factors that resulted in process variability. Shewhart explained what steps should be taken to reduce variability. He provided charts to stabilize and control a system. His work also pointed to the fact that inherent variability could only be reduced by changing the management of the process and the process itself. See **Control chart** and **Statistical process control (SPC).**

Stochastic line-balancing: Stochastic line-balancing occurs when variability exists in the form of statistical distributions of operation and/or transport times. It is more difficult to balance stochastic production lines because the arrival rates and the service rates at the stations are erratic and unpredictable. Line-balancing has queuing elements at work. Simulation can be useful to test performances of various line-balancing strategies. Simulation is a strong method for analyzing the stochastic line-balancing system. See **Line-balancing.**

Strategic business units: (SBUs) are independent subdivisions of the company. They are considered to be coherent (likely self-contained) profit-making entities for the company. The management of each SBU is expected to describe clear and unambiguous strategic plans for their product lines. Generally, tactical business units are a subsidiary part of the strategic business units, which include products and processes.

Strategy: The big plan. It is directly translated into "do the right thing." Tactics is translated into "do it the right way." Strategy is the term used to describe the comprehensive and overall planning for the organization's future. In the military context, strategy must destroy the enemy capability. In the business context, strategy must be product-oriented and marketing-aware to take the customer and the competition into account. Planning military actions such as where to engage the enemy and under what circumstances is the familiar use of the term *strategy*. Derived from the Greek word *strategía*, meaning "generalship," military strategists are master planners. Their partnership with tacticians is of great importance.

Substances of concern (SOC): These include mercury, lead, cadmium, and hexavalent chromium, Cr(VI). The last chemical in this list was the subject of the Erin Brockovich movie regarding contamination of drinking water with Cr(VI), which is discussed as a suspected carcinogen. See http://www.grac.org/ChromiumWhitePaper.pdf. An agreement has been reached to entirely remove Cr(VI) by Ford (July 2005), GM (August 2006), and DaimlerChrysler (January 2007).

Suggestion system: Depends upon who is speaking: Employee contributions are a great source of ideas for improvement. If no one reads the suggestions, the system is a sham. There is ample evidence that this discrepancy is a function of management's attitude and desire to employ teamwork.

Supply chain: The linkage between raw materials and finished products (goods and services) delivered into the hands of the customers. In fact, the supply chain is the fully-connected input-transformation-output (I/T/O) system. Fabrication is the one form of transformation most commonly associated with supply chains. However, transportation, entertainment, (healthcare) operations, and education are a few others. Transportation in the supply chain is crucial. Storage points occur at many locations because warehousing is essential for supply chain management. A notable point is that materials upstream (starting at the headwaters) have less investment in transformation. The investment in materials increases as they move downstream. The form of materials becomes more specific. The supply chain is replete with information of varying kinds, including the state of materials and the flow of money. The degree of finalization of all transactions (in information theory terms) is measured by its entropy. The state of the products (goods and services) transits from high entropy to low entropy as the products approach the ultimate consumer. The supply chain does not stop at retail distribution if there are any warranties and repair guarantees. What are raw materials to some are finished products to others. Thus, copper used as a raw material in auto production is a finished good from the point of view of the copper mines.

Synchronization: Flow shops are predesigned to have perfect synchronization of workstations. Job shops require major efforts to synchronize manufacturing. Synchronization requires control over the timing of flows. This includes how much is made at one time. Transfer amounts and storage amounts are determined by control rules as derived by finite scheduling methods. See **OPT** and **TOC.**

Synergy: The result of a set of agents producing a greater effect when acting together than the sum of their separate effects when acting alone as individuals. For example, if three forces can each produce a pound of pressure when acting alone, but when acting in concert they produce five pounds of pressure, there is synergy.

Synthetic or **predetermined time standards:** Used to make estimates for jobs that do not yet exist from a subset of common elements. Estimates influence choices in development of new designs. The process is part of design for manufacturing (DFM) and design for assembly (DFA). The time to accomplish units of work are generic (or synthetic) modules such as lift, grasp, and turn. They are also called *predetermined time standards*.

Synthetic process: Production process that starts with many ingredients. Using appropriate transformation techniques, the process combines the various materials, components, subassemblies, etc., into a single, basic product or into several similar products. For example, tires, windshields, upholstery, engines, chassis, etc., go to form the car, which requires thousands of parts.

Systems approach: This is contrasted with the **functional field approach.** The systems approach is the big view that includes everything that might account for what is happening. The systems approach accents connections and interactions between all functions (such as marketing and finance).

Systems utilization factor: λ is the average arrival rate and μ is the average service rate. For single-channel systems, $\rho = \lambda/\mu$. If $\lambda = 3$ and $\mu = 4$, then $\rho = 3/4 = 75$ percent. Rho is the average percent of time that the station is providing service. If that figure is close to 100 percent, then the system is overloaded. By providing M servers, the capacity problem is alleviated. For multiple-channel systems, $\rho = \lambda/M\mu$, which is the average percent of time that the M-server system is providing service. If $M = 3$, $\lambda = 3$, and $\mu = 4$, then, $\rho = 1/4$, which is an underloaded system. See **Single-channel systems.**

Syzygy: The point when maximum tidal pull is exerted because the planets and the moon have lined up to support each other's gravitational forces. Generally, forces exert pulls in different directions and offset or cancel each other. Syzygy comes from the Greek word for "conjunction," and it is also the only word in the English language that has no vowels and three y's. Parenthetically, y takes on vowel-like sounds, as in "duty."

T

20:80 rule: Twenty percent of the total number of problems (complaints) that have been checked off (on the data check sheet) are likely to occur 80 percent of the time. Pareto charts call attention to these high-frequency events. It is often necessary to separate the critical minority of complaints from the inconsequential majority. Call-A-Nurse is constantly faced with sorting out the requests for advice about health problems that are not life threatening (but frequent) from the few that are critical life or death matters requiring immediate hospital emergency room attention. The quality issues in this instance demand great diagnostic abilities being exercised over the phone.

Tacit knowledge: Significant information is transferred by tacit means such as a body language. Tacit knowledge is unstated, implicit, inferred, and unspoken. It is difficult to describe tacit knowledge because it is not evident. Because it is unclear, it is not possible to catalog it or put it into a yellow page–type directory. The only way to access tacit knowledge is to consult with people who are seen as being intuitive, instinctive, and perceptive. Such people are associated with areas of awareness that make them specialists. Project teams often operate at a distance from each other. Distance learning can be crucial to project management, and it is not effective with tacit knowledge. The classroom beats the Internet in transferring tacit knowledge. See **Explicit knowledge** and **Knowledge management.**

Tactics: Detailed procedures required to carry out strategic plans. Derived from the Greek word *taktikós*, meaning "fit for arranging," military tacticians are masters of maneuvering resources subject to strategic battle plans.

Taguchi methods: It is often said that the Western industrialized world uses goalpost standards for quality. This means that as long as the football goes between the two goal posts it counts as a field goal score. Taguchi proposed an optimal quality point and spoke about a loss function to describe deviations from that optimal. The loss is larger as the deviation becomes greater. Using design of experiments, Taguchi advocates designing the product and the process together to deliver the minimal loss value (the closest statistical result to the optimal value). See http://kernow.curtin.edu.au/www/Taguchi/INTRO.HTM or use Google to search for Taguchi methods.

Take-back laws: Governmental rules are being invoked in Europe and in the United States (at a slightly slower rate) to ensure material reuse and/or proper disposal. Laws can force a company to take back discarded and used-up product from customers for recycling and reemployment. However, prethinking creative reuse of recycled parts can lower costs, improve quality, and satisfy new stringent laws about the percent reuse of a product.

Team building: Focus is on removing adversarial attitudes and replacing them with a sense of "family." Trust-building training is enhanced by a common set of goals. Trust spurs cooperative (or team) learning. Special considerations apply to cross-cultural team building.

Team learning: Also called *cooperative learning*; applies to group effort to achieve excellence with a specific process. Team members learn to coordinate with each other to perform activities with speed and precision. Learning how each task impacts on other tasks leads to mutual changes rather than just individual improvements. Focus on the orchestra and not on individual instruments.

Technology: Equipment employed to accomplish the transformation that is basic to the fundamental P/OM input–output model of production. Equipment includes machines, computers, tools, and communication systems. It can include human/machine combinations known as cyborgs.

Technology trap: By default, new technology is often applied to the management of old (legacy) systems. The resulting effect is to gain little improvement and to further institutionalize antiquated systems and procedures. To avoid this trap, systems studies should upgrade the way that work is done in keeping with the capabilities of new technology.

Theory of Constraints: A mind-set for determining the core problems in production scheduling, project management, and other P/OM activities. Recognition of problems leads to construction of detailed solutions, as well as means for implementing them. After OPT, Goldratt's research included additional systems factors and provided a higher level of diagnosis and prescription called Theory of Constraints (TOC). Goldratt found that optimizing production scheduling in isolation from other business variables usually does not lead to higher productivity. Using TOC, the systems viewpoint is broad. It encompasses more restricted specifics of bottleneck-based finite scheduling (called *OPT*). See **OPT.**

Time and motion study: Sampling and recording what workers do to make, finish, or pack a product. Can be used for service operations such as a serving counter at McDonalds, the back room of a bank, tellers' windows, etc. Detailed descriptions of each activity are given, including the observed times. Later study can change the workplace configuration. It can suggest alternative locations for materials as well as different tools and fixtures. Training may be recommended to improve the time required for accomplishments. Videos may be used to provide scenario repetitions for further study by team members.

Time series: A stream of numbers that represents different values over time. They are always presented in time-ordered sequence for one or more specific variables.

Time series analysis: The analysis of a stream of numbers in a time series. For example, the time series could be temperatures taken daily for a month, or barometric pressures observed every hour for a week. The values of the variables change over time because of various factors such as the multitudinous forces that create weather patterns at different times of year. Time series analysis of business variables such as daily sales (demand) and production output (supply) can provide valuable insights even though the underlying causal factors that account for these time series are not shown or explained.

Time study: The study of how long it takes to do specific operations. Unlike work sampling, where the goal is to find out what is being done. In time study, the time required to complete specific jobs is captured. Sometimes computers are able to monitor the system. This is done, for example, for many variables in call centers. It is also standard practice for check-processing activities in the back room of the bank. In other cases, the same stopwatches that are used to time high school sprinters can be used to find out how long it takes to unload a truck or to check out customers in the supermarket.

Time-based management (TBM): An inclusive term for managers' concerns about time lines, schedules, deliveries, and project completions. The goals are to be fast-moving, rapid-responders, high velocity without quality losses. TBM includes schedule control, cycle-time management, and synchronization of production flows. The logistics of delivery and the ability to move rapidly into new markets are major elements of TBM. At the tactical level, it consists of tracking and reporting the status of orders, expediting jobs, decreasing idle time, and increasing value-adding. Elevates time to a variable of equal importance with cost, quality, and productivity. Time is a surrogate for profitability, market share, and customers' satisfaction. Time-based management is responsible for fast delivery of goods and services to customers and rapid development of new products. As such, time is both a strategic variable and a tactical factor. TBM is increasingly important as competitors excel in surpassing customer temporal expectations.

TOC: See Theory of Constraints.

Tolerance limits: The plus and minus parts of tolerance limits (e.g., 6.00 ± 0.05) are like the goalposts described in the entry for Taguchi methods. The normal inspection process accepts products that measure within the upper and lower values of the tolerance limits. Statistical quality control (SQC) charts have equivalent upper and lower control limits. When the set of sequential sample means falls inside those "posts," the process is assumed to be stable. This is the most often used method for SQC.

Tolerance matching: Quality products must have parts that fit together properly. Windows in houses, doors on autos, CD discs in CD players, Philips head screw drivers, and Philips head screws are a few examples. Proper fitting requires careful matching of tolerances. The scenario starts with design of two parts and specification of their tolerance limits. Testing comes next with the parts at their limit extremes. If the fit is too loose or too tight, redesign is used until the fit is "just about right." The process that makes the parts must be able to produce them to tolerance limits. Testing by go/no go gauges (or some equivalent) should create no more defectives than the original plan specifies.

Total costs = TC = FC + TVC: TC are the sum of fixed costs and total variable costs. Breakeven occurs where the total cost line intersects the total revenue line.

Total flow time: The cumulative time required to complete a group of jobs. It is composed of the sum of complete-to-ship times, $C_i = W_i + t_i$. This includes waiting-to-be-done times (W_i) and job processing times (t_i). The equation is: $TFT = TFT = \sum_{i=1}^{i=n} C_i$.

Total or cumulative lead time (LT): The time between recognition of the need for an order and the acknowledged, genuine receipt of goods. Individual components of lead time can include order preparation time, waiting-line time, transport time, computer-processing time (in-stock records of replenishment materials), and inspection time at the receiving docks. The maximum cumulative lead time for a parent product is found by looking at the longest lead-time path to obtain all of the parts that go into it as the end item. Because standard items are in stock, they have zero lead time. Special items which are not in stock participate in the computation of total or maximum lead time.

Total productive maintenance (TPM): The rational blend of maintenance alternatives. It contains both preventive and remedial maintenance (PM and RM).

Total productivity: See **Multifactor productivity.**

Total quality management (TQM): The result of applying systems vision to every aspect of quality in the organization. TQM assumes that what the file clerk is doing impinges on the quality output of the process. Everybody counts, all of the time, so there is a need to integrate the effects of the total supply chain with the product line and the processes used in offices as well as on the plant floor. Note that the consumer plays a crucial role. If the voice of the consumer is not being heard within the House of Quality, then there is a listening problem and quality function deployment is, at best, partial.

Total revenue = $TR = (p)V$: Total revenue is price per unit (p) multiplied by the volume (V) sold (not just made) in a period of time, T. TR applies to the same period of time, T. The emphasis is on the goods and services being sold in the marketplace because revenue creates a positive cash flow for the company only when the goods are paid for with cash and not IOUs There have been S.E.C. problems with companies claiming sales that are still accounts receivable. Total revenue is the sum of positive cash flows from various models (SKUs) made or delivered by the same process. The same summation applies to various services delivered by the same process. The breakeven point occurs where the total revenue line intersects the total cost line.

Total variable costs = $TVC = (vc)V$: The result of multiplying the variable cost per unit (vc) by the number of units or volume (V) produced. These are also known as total direct costs. The total variable cost for 10 units is $10vc$.

Total work content (TWC): What does it take to bake a cake? Every detail must be documented and then drawn up in a precedence diagram, which shows order and time required for each operation. The sum of all operation times required to bake this specific cake is called the total work content. Another baker may do this job in a different way, which would produce a different value of TWC. It is likely to produce a different quality evaluation as well. For the equation form of TWC, see Balance delay.

Trade-off models: These are generic models in which raising the size of (x) brings increasing advantages of one kind (benefit) while creating larger penalties of another kind (costs). The decision maker chooses how much of x to use to balance the benefits and costs. For example, raising the order size will increase the amount of stock on-hand, which lowers the risk of going out of stock. It also decreases the number of orders that must be placed. On the other hand, it raises carrying costs and increases storage space required. Trade-off models are managers' delights because they provide opportunity for discretionary control. See **Cost trade-off analysis.**

Trade-offs: Project managers are constantly required to reach smart cost/time trade-offs. Spend more money on project resources, and finish sooner, or vice versa. See **PERT/TIME/COST** and **Slack.**

Transformation: The big T is one of the most important parts of the P/OM system. It is the transformation process capability to cut metal, polish brass, take temperatures, pack toothpaste cartons, build cars, and so forth. Transformation moves customers from one city to another. The transformation from hurting and damaged to well and repaired results from successful healthcare processes. The transformation from bad to good student is still not obvious. How are great managers fashioned? That too is still not obvious.

Transportation models: Minimize shipping costs or maximize profits where production facility location and market (shipped to) differentials exist. The data for this model include production capacities at different plants, market demand, and shipping costs per mile along each route. For example, plants exist in Dayton, Atlanta, and Denver, and each has different costs of production. Warehouses are in Seattle, Dallas, and Trenton, and the selling price in each market is different. To which warehouses should the plants ship? Solution is available by either linear programming or network methods.

Turnover: It is the objective of supply chain managers to achieve as many inventory turns as possible. Turns are counted by the number of times per year that the warehouse is emptied and refilled. Each turn promises beneficial cash flow. Turns are measured by annual net sales divided by total average stock on-hand. Turnover can also be measured by dividing 365 days by DOI.

V

Value added: Raw materials have value added by the transformation process of P/OM, which makes them into parts that conform to blueprints. Assembly operations add value by combining and fastening parts to form an entity that did not exist previously (e.g., an automobile). Value added is what P/OM processes do that creates profits in the form of revenues greater than costs. When materials sit without value being added, there is a loss to the company. Flow shops are efficient cash generators. They have the advantage of adding value on continuous basis.

Value analysis (VA): (1) Adopted by materials managers since 1940, when the U.S. Navy championed the application of VA. The main ideas are to search for alternative materials as replacements for the current ones with quality gains and cost advantages. Monitor technological developments to avoid missing new materials opportunities not yet recognized. Stress creativity and innovation in the continuing effort to find better materials. Purchasing agents need management support in the value analysis quest.

(2) A systematic investigation of purchased parts decisions. Applied originally to materials, the extension of VA to services is appealing. The primary questions are whether alternatives exist of superior quality and/or lower prices. Within the quality issue is reliability of delivery and the utility of supplier research to improve the product. Value analysis with its cross-boundary queries epitomizes the systems approach. The U.S. Navy developed VA methods.

Variable costs per unit = vc: Variable costs are charges attributable to each unit of product that is made and/or delivered. They are also called *direct costs* because they are paid out only on a per unit basis. Examples are material used and labor employed to make a finished unit of product. The total variable cost for seven units is $7vc$.

Variety: The number of product alternatives (in a given product class) that are made available to the customer. The product has to satisfy a variety of customer types (called *market segments*). Variety of choice is also an important nonfunctional quality dimension. P/OM can help produce variety at a low cost by using smart methods to move from one variation of the product to another. It is known that Jello customers like to switch flavors and colors from time to time. Some processes have minimum changeover costs and times.

V-A-T: This is not your VAT tax. It is the categorization developed by Eli Goldratt's organization, and marketed as OPT, for classifying processes. V-processes are analytic. They start with a single commodity that is then refined to create dozens of by-products. A-processes are synthetic. They start with several inputs that are combined to yield a marketable product. T-processes are combinations of V and A. Bottlenecks are most likely to occur with T-processes because of conflicting patterns with aggregation (assembly through synthesis) and disaggregation (disassembly through analysis).

Vendor releasing: Supplier agrees to deliver small portions of the larger order on a specified schedule. The buyer obtains some of the discount benefits of large volume purchasing. The seller gets the benefits of higher certainty regarding demand for the item being sold. The buyer gets closer to just-in-time delivery with its advantages of lower storage costs, decreased carrying costs, and other benefits.

Vision: Clear and unambiguous view of what the future can become. Vision statements are articulated goals. Some companies have spent a great deal of time developing vision statements, but they lack vision-linked strategies for realizing the goals. Even when formulated strategies exist, tactics can be missing. Tactics include practical first steps for goal achievement. Vision (V) of an improved situation cannot by itself lead to change. If dissatisfaction with the current situation is not great enough, then change will not occur. V > 0 is a necessary but not sufficient condition for change. See **Gleicher model (Conditions for change).**

W

Wage determination: Based on normal time, a reasonable piecework wage can be determined by management. Because learning curve effects enable employees to produce more units after stabilization, the wage is modified so as to provide incentive for maintaining higher productivity. In general, wages are determined by job difficulty, training required, skill level needed, and value to the firm. Comparisons with other companies in the same industry and region can be helpful.

Water-jetting: High water pressure technology that replaces toxic maintenance methods used to remove paints and coatings. Also, cuts shapes with water and abrasives. Historically, traditional surface preparation and coating renewal work has been a low-tech, labor- and time-intensive, environmentally challenging endeavor.

Work centers: Combinations of people, materials, and machines that work together on specific job assignments. Work centers can be moved around on the plant or office floor. The assignment of work centers to specific space locations on the plant or office floor should minimize costs (or times) of transport of materials, work in process, and finished goods. Multistory buildings need 3-dimensional solutions. Facility layout and work center space assignments interact.

Work configuration: Another name for a type of production process. The main categories of work configurations are custom work, job shop or batch work, flow shop and intermittent flow shop, project, and flexible process system including flexible manufacturing system. Continuous flow production systems are highly engineered flow shops.

Work in process (WIP): It exists in the form of incomplete jobs that cannot be shipped or put into finished goods storage. WIP waits for completion of the value-added operations. In the flow shop, jobs move sequentially from workstations upstream to those downstream. At each station, further transformation is taking place and value is being added. In the job shop, batches of work are undergoing (generally) nonsequential transformations. Value added is the P/OM process contribution to raw materials and components. In the job shop, there are noticeable amounts of work that are waiting for additional value added.

Work sampling: Provides information about the percentage of time that various activities are being done during the day. Method is applicable for studying services such as office operations, R & D departments, and hospitality employees without workstations. Work sampling can be used to determine how effective training programs are in getting people to use different methods and mixes of methods to accomplish their goals. It is essential to explain to those observed that the purpose is to make the job being done easier and better.

X

x̄-chart: Basic quality control chart designed for variables measured on a continuous scale such as tire pressure and particle emissions. Samples of size n are taken successively. The derived sample means are numbered to maintain their correct order. Control limits are applied to the x̄-chart as well as its companion R-chart. The limits are distanced the equivalent of $k\sigma$ from the mean so that the probabilities of sample mean values exceeding these thresholds are preselected odds (e.g., 0.001, 0.0001) given that the process is stable. Taken together, the two charts supply powerful diagnostics for aberrant process behavior.

Z

Zed defects (ZD): A policy that requires eliminating any and all causes of defects. It is crucial to realize that a zero or zed defects policy is determined by what is defined to be acceptable quality. In other words, the definition of defects determines what conformance to standards is required. Quality definitions determine defect rates that will be measured. Consider extension of the application of ZD to human systems where malfunctions can lead to serious problems in such instances as surgery, air control, and piloting ships and planes.

Zero breakdowns: An option of TPM. The policy of zero breakdowns requires eliminating any and all malfunctions and failures. Machine breakdowns come to mind but should be extended to encompass other equipment such as computers and communication networks. Redundancies are used by banks, power plants, etc., to back up systems in case of failures.

The next extension of the application of zero breakdowns is to human systems where malfunctions can lead to serious problems in such instances as surgery, air control, and piloting.

Zero defects: The six-sigma discussion starts out with two different approaches to zero or zed defects. It is noteworthy that when zero defects is not the standard, then some level of defects is expected. For example, some number of eggs that are in the display case of the local supermarket are cracked. Most supermarket managers accept that defective rate. Say it is 2 percent. A zero-defect manager knows that certain brands have packages that yield a significantly smaller breakage rate. Also, that manager could inspect incoming eggs to remove those that are already broken when put on display. Clear packages could help staff eliminate broken eggs. That manager may become a zed-defect person.

Zero-error mind-set: An abhorrence of defectives and determination to prevent them from occurring. This attitude is common to Japanese P/OM. It is not common among even the cognoscenti of P/OM in the Western world. "Cognoscenti" is a useful literary word (from Italian) for the people who are knowledgeable. Developing a zero-error mind-set requires culture-changing programs within the country, let alone the firm.

Zoning constraints: Technological factors exist that do not permit operations to be split between workstations. These physical restrictions can relate to the fact that a specific machine or human skill required is available at only one station, or that time is required for a chemical reaction, or a quality check at a single workstation. Although zoning is primarily a physical constraint, there are instances of psychological zoning. Often it is referred to as *territoriality*.

Name Index

Subject Index

Note: Page numbers in italics identify an illustration. An italic *t* next to a page number (e.g., 45*t*) indicates information that appears in a table.

Ancient Saying...

When students are ready, teachers appear.